C000170972

COLLINS FAMILY ENCYCLOPEDIA

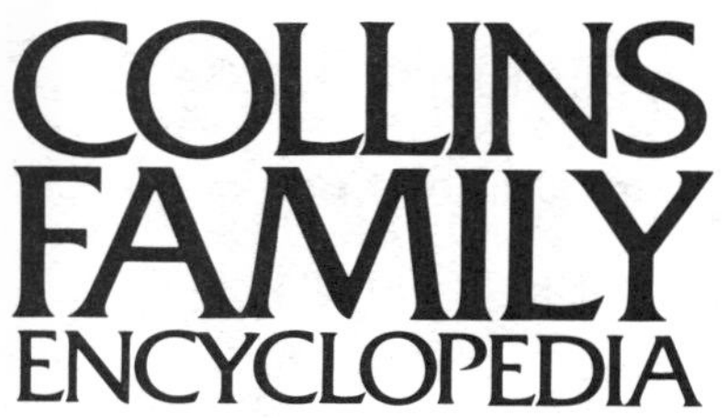

Collins
London and Glasgow

First Published 1981

© **Wm. Collins Sons & Co. Ltd.**

ISBN 0 00 434320 4

Collins Family Encyclopedia
is based on and abridged from
Collins Concise Encyclopedia

Printed in Great Britain by
Wm. Collins Sons & Co. Ltd.

PREFACE

The *Collins Family Encyclopedia* is intended as a compact but comprehensive work of reference for the 1980s, providing both quick answers for the person in a hurry, and also a wealth of interesting knowledge for the more leisurely browser. Over 12,000 entries range over all fields of human activity, from archaeology to space exploration, from Socrates to Stalin, from acupuncture to zoology. The straightforward A to Z listing means that answers can be found quickly and easily, and the clear and concise style is designed so that the basic facts on any subject can be grasped immediately. Over 300 illustrations augment the text, and should, we hope, encourage children as well as adults to 'look and learn'.

The coverage of the *Collins Family Encyclopedia* can, very roughly, be put under various broad headings. Information about the natural world includes plants, animals, geology, astronomy, meteorology, and so on. The *Encyclopedia* is also both a dictionary of biography and a world gazetteer: famous men and women from all times and all walks of life are here, as are all the countries of the world, their main cities and political divisions, their deserts, mountains and rivers. Population figures are based on the latest data; it should be noted that in the case of cities the populations of greater urban areas have been given, where available.

The constantly developing field of science and technology is covered in the discoveries of scientists, and in the numerous entries on substances and theories, inventions, processes and machines. Religion, philosophy and the arts are similarly treated, articles on people and movements being carefully interrelated. World history, with its kings, wars and treaties, is presented in terms of facts rather than opinions, and the world today, with its politicians and parties, new nations and ideological divisions, is viewed from a similarly objective standpoint. Every effort has been made to check all the facts in this book and to ensure that all information is completely up-to-date at the time of going to press.

Finally, I would like to thank my colleague, Clare Crawford, for her invaluable assistance in editing this *Encyclopedia*.

Ian Crofton

ABBREVIATIONS USED IN THE ENCYCLOPEDIA

AD	anno domini
admin.	administration, administrated, administrative
agric.	agricultural, agriculture
alt.	altitude
anc.	ancient
anon.	anonymous
Arab.	Arabic
at. no.	atomic number
at. wt.	atomic weight
Aug.	August
autobiog.	autobiography
auton.	autonomous, autonomy
av.	average
b.	born
BC	before Christ
biog.	biography
bor.	borough
C	central
c	about
cap.	capital
cent.	century
cm	centimetre, centimetres
co.	county, company
co. bor.	county borough
coll.	college
co. town	county town
d.	died
Dec.	December
dept.	department
dist.	district
E	east
eg	for example
Eng.	English
esp.	especially
est.	estimated
estab.	established
etc	and so on
excl.	excludes, excluding
Feb.	February
Finn.	Finnish
fl	flourished
Flem.	Flemish
Fr.	French
ft.	foot, feet
Ger.	German
Gk.	Greek
gm	gram
govt.	government
ha.	hectare, hectares
Heb.	Hebrew
h.e.p.	hydro-electric power
hist.	historical
hr	hour
hq.	headquarters
Hung.	Hungarian
ie	that is
in.	inch, inches
incl.	include, including, included
indust.	industrial, industry
isl.	island
Ital.	Italian
Jan.	January
Jap.	Japanese
jct.	junction
kg	kilogram
km	kilometre, kilometres
kmh	kilometres per hour
L.	Lake
lat.	latitude
lb	pound (unit of weight)
long.	longitude
max.	maximum
mfg.	manufacture, manufacturing
mi	mile, miles
min.	minimum, minute
mm	millimetre
MP	Member of Parliament
mph	miles per hour
Mt.	Mount
Mts.	Mountains
mun. bor.	municipal borough
N	north
Nov.	November
NT	New Testament
Oct.	October
orig.	originally
OT	Old Testament
penin.	peninsula
PM	Prime Minister
Pol.	Polish
pop.	population
Port.	Portuguese
prehist.	prehistoric
prob.	probably
protect.	protectorate
prov.	province
pseud.	pseudonym
pub.	published
R.	River
RC	Roman Catholic
Russ.	Russian
S	south
sec	second
Sept.	September
Span.	Spanish
sq km	square kilometres
sq mi	square miles
St	Saint
St.	Street
str.	strait
Swed.	Swedish
territ.	territory
Turk.	Turkish
TV	television
UK	United Kingdom
UN	United Nations
univ.	university
US	United States
v	against
vol.	volume
WW	World War
W	west
yd	yard, yards

Aachen (Fr. *Aix-la-Chapelle*), city of W West Germany. Pop. 243,000. Indust. centre in coalmining area, railway jct. Thermal baths from Roman times. N cap. of Holy Roman Empire, cathedral (10th cent.) has Charlemagne's tomb. Badly damaged in WWII.

Aalborg, city of NE Jutland, Denmark, on Lim Fjord. Pop. 155,000. Port, shipbuilding; cement; textiles.

Aardvark

aardvark, *Orycteropus afer,* nocturnal burrowing mammal of C and S Africa, order Tubulidentata. Long snout, extensile sticky tongue; diet of ants, termites. Also known as antbear, earth pig.

aardwolf, *Proteles cristatus,* burrowing hyaena-like mammal of Protelidae family, inhabiting scrubland of S Africa. Diet of termites, carrion.

Aargau, canton of N Switzerland. Area 1404 sq km (542 sq mi); cap. Aarau (Helvetic cap., 1789-1803). Crossed by fertile valley of R. Aare. Cereals, fruit. Mineral springs.

Aarhus, city of E Jutland, Denmark, on Kattegat. Pop. 246,000. Port; trade, transport centre; oil refining.

Aaron, in OT, elder brother of Moses and leader with him of Israelites in march into 'promised land'. First high priest of Hebrews.

abacus, calculating device consisting of frame with beads which slide back and forward on parallel wires or in slots. Widely used in Middle East, Orient and Russia.

Abadan, city of SW Iran, on Abadan isl. at head of Persian Gulf. Pop. 296,000. Oil refining and export centre.

Abakan, city of USSR, cap. of Khakass auton. region, SC Siberian RSFSR. Pop. 128,000. Produces textiles, metal products. Founded in 1707 as fortress.

abalone, gastropod mollusc, genus *Haliotis,* found mainly on Californian coast. Shell, resembling human ear, source of mother-of-pearl; flesh commonly eaten. Ormer, *H. tuberculata,* found in Channel Islands.

Abbasids, Arab dynasty of caliphs. Overthrew OMAYYAD dynasty (750) and moved cap. from Damascus to Baghdad. Achieved great fame and splendour under Harun al-Rashid. Destroyed (1258) by Mongols under Hulagu Khan.

abbey, in Christian religion, monastic house in which a community of at least 12 monks or nuns live, ruled by an abbot or abbess. First abbey founded (c 529) by St Benedict at Monte Cassino, Italy.

Abbey Theatre, Dublin home of Irish National Theatre Society, founded during Irish literary revival of early 1900s, by W.B. Yeats, G.W. Russell (A.E.), Lady Gregory. Works by Synge, O'Casey received 1st presentation.

abdication, formal renunciation of high public office or authority, usually by monarch. In UK requires consent of Parliament, most famous example being Edward VIII (1936).

abdomen, in mammals, part of body below the thorax and above the pelvis; separated from thorax by the diaphragm. Contains stomach, intestines, liver, kidneys, *etc.* In insects and crustaceans, hind part of body beyond thorax.

Abdul Hamid II (1842-1918), Ottoman sultan (1876-1909). Dismissed Midhat Pasha whose newly-framed constitution he then suspended (1876). Pursued pro-German policy after Congress of BERLIN. Deposed by Young Turks.

Abel, in OT, second son of Adam and Eve. Killed by his brother CAIN. A shepherd, his offerings were accepted by God when those of Cain (a tiller of the soil) were refused.

Abelard, Peter or **Pierre Abélard** (1079-1142), French scholar. Held universals to exist only in thought but based in particular objects. Applied Aristotelian logic to faith in *Sic et Non.* Charged with heresy (1121). Remembered through their letters for tragic romance with Héloise, provoking his castration by her uncle. Regarded as founder of Univ. of Paris.

Aberdare, urban dist. of Mid Glamorgan, S Wales. Pop. 40,000. Coalmining; cables, electrical goods mfg.

Aberdeen, George Hamilton-Gordon, 4th Earl of (1784-1860), British statesman, PM (1852-5). Helped bring Austria into coalition against Napoleon with Treaty of Töplitz

(1813). Failed to keep Britain out of Crimean War, resigned as PM after censure.

Aberdeenshire, former county of NE Scotland, now in Grampian region. Grampian Mts. in SW. Crops, livestock (esp. beef cattle); fishing, granite quarrying. Has offshore oil indust. Co. town was **Aberdeen,** city and admin. hq. of Grampian region, on R. Dee. Pop. 209,000. Chief Scottish fishing port, tourism, shipbuilding, oil rig service industs. Became royal burgh (1179). Has univ. (colls. 1494, 1593); cathedral (14th cent.). Called 'Granite City'.

aberration, in astronomy, apparent displacement of position of star or other heavenly body, caused by motion of earth. During earth's annual motion about sun, star appears to move in small ellipse. Effect discovered by Bradley (1725), who used it to estimate speed of light.

aberration, in optics, failure of lens or mirror to form perfect image. In spherical aberration, light rays from a point source are focused at different points. In chromatic aberration, edges of images are coloured because refractive index of lens varies for light of different wavelengths.

Aberystwyth, mun. bor. of Dyfed, W Wales. Pop. 11,000. Tourist resort. Has coll. of Univ. of Wales (1872); National Library of Wales (1911).

Abidjan, cap. of Ivory Coast, on Ebrie Lagoon. Pop. 850,000. Admin., commercial centre; railway terminus; exports coffee, cocoa, timber, fruit via outport at Port Bouet; univ.

abolitionists, in US history, advocates of end to Negro slavery. Influenced by British anti-slavery campaign success (1833). Activities culminated in John Brown's abortive raid (1859) on Harpers Ferry. Unyielding attitude of abolitionists helped bring about Civil War.

abominable snowman, *see* YETI.

aborigine, *see* AUSTRALIAN ABORIGINES.

abortion, in medicine, spontaneous or induced expulsion of foetus from the womb before 28th week of pregnancy. Sometimes referred to medically as miscarriage if it occurs after 16th week; this term popularly refers to accidental premature birth at any stage.

Aboukir or **Abukir,** village of N Egypt, on Aboukir Bay. Scene of Nelson's victory (1798) over French fleet in the 'Battle of the Nile'.

Abraham, regarded as father of Jewish nation. In OT received Jehovah's promise of Canaan as land for his descendants. Prob. historical figure, but more important in Bible as archetype of the man of faith. *See* ISAAC.

Abraham, Plains of, *see* QUÉBEC (city).

abrasive, material used for scouring, grinding or polishing. Natural forms incl. corundum, emery and diamond. Artificial forms incl. carborundum (silicon carbide), boron carbide and synthetic diamond.

Abruzzi e Molise, region of SC Italy, in Apennine Mts. Sparsely populated, no large towns. Agric. (livestock, cereals, grapes) in fertile valleys.

Absalom, in OT, King David's favourite son. Instigated revolt against his father. After defeat, was killed by Joab while caught in a tree.

abscess, swollen area in body tissue in which pus collects as a result of infection. Occurs in tooth sockets, inner ear, skin, *etc.* Treated by antibiotics, but may require surgical drainage.

absinthe, green-coloured liqueur flavoured with wormwood, anise and other aromatics; contains from 60% to 80% alcohol. Now banned in most countries because of toxic effect of wormwood on nervous system.

absolute zero, temperature zero point on absolute or Kelvin scale, corresponding to -273.15° C. Theoretically lowest possible temperature, when molecular motion ceases.

absolutism, doctrine or system of govt. under which the ruler has unlimited power. Absolute monarchy *fl* in Europe 16th-18th cent., was defended by HOBBES.

abstract art, non-representational painting and sculpture, relying on form and colour to achieve aesthetic and emotional impact. Abstract art of 20th cent. derives from fauvism and cubism; early exponents incl. Kandinsky (1st abstract work 1910), whose early work emphasizes expressive use of colour, and Mondrian, who developed pure geometric style out of cubism. Brancusi was noted exponent of abstract sculpture.

abstract expressionism, school of American painting which developed after WWII; characterized by emphasis on artist's spontaneous and self-expressive application of paint in creating abstract work. Leading exponents incl. Pollock, Franz Kline and Rothko.

absurd, philosophical term used by CAMUS to describe meaninglessness of human existence in an irrational world. Precondition of much existentialist philosophy and literature as in novels of SARTRE, plays of Beckett, Ionesco. More personally experienced than SCEPTICISM.

Abu Bakr or **Abu Bekr** (573-634), Arab leader. Important early convert to Islam, became devoted follower of Mohammed, who married his daughter. Succeeded Mohammed as 1st caliph (632); expansion of Islam into major world religion began under his rule.

Abu Dhabi, isl. sheikdom of United Arab Emirates, on Persian Gulf. Area *c* 67,300 sq km (26,000 sq mi); pop. 236,000; cap. Abu Dhabi. Has rich oil reserves.

Abu Simbel, village of S Egypt, on R. Nile. Site of 2 temples built *c* 1250 BC by Rameses II, rebuilt in sections 1964-8 above flood waters of Aswan High Dam.

Abydos, ancient city of C Egypt, on R. Nile. Former religious centre, with temples to Osiris; burial place of many kings.

Remains date from 3100-500 BC.

Abyssinia, *see* ETHIOPIA.

acacia, genus of tropical and subtropical trees of Leguminosae family. Pinnate leaves with clusters of yellow or white flowers. Many cultivated as ornamentals; yields gum arabic, dyes, tanning aids, furniture woods. Species incl. cooba, *Acacia salicina,* an Australian wattle.

academy, originally olive grove near Athens where Plato and followers met. Modern academy is learned society promoting arts, sciences, often publicly financed.

Acadia (Fr. *Acadie),* hist. region of E Canada, comprising Nova Scotia, Prince Edward Isl., part of New Brunswick. French founded Port Royal, its chief town, in 1605; ceded to British 1713.

acanthus, genus of perennial herbs of Mediterranean region. White or coloured flowers with deeply cut spiny leaves. Stylized form of leaf used as architectural ornament, esp. on capitals of Corinthian columns, from *c* 5th cent. BC.

Acapulco, winter seaside resort of SW Mexico, on Pacific. Pop. 402,000. Has many hotels, excellent beaches; facilities for deep-sea diving, fishing. Fruit, cotton trading.

acceleration, rate of change of velocity. Gravitational acceleration is acceleration of free-falling body caused by gravitational attraction of Earth. Assumed constant near Earth's surface, equals *c* 981 cm/sec^2. Varies with altitude and longitude.

accelerator, in physics, device used to impart high velocities to charged particles by accelerating them in electric fields. Linear and cyclic are used in nuclear research, esp. investigation of elementary particles of matter. Examples incl. bevatron, betatron, cyclotron, synchrotron.

accentor, sparrow-like Eurasian bird, genus *Prunella.*

accessory, in law, a person who, although absent, helps another to break or escape the law. May be an accessory before (or after) the fact, *ie* one who aids the accused before (or after) the commission of the crime.

accipiter, any of genus *Accipiter* of small hawks with short wings, long tails. Species incl. goshawk, *A. gentilis,* and sparrow hawk, *A. nisus.*

accordion, portable reed organ. Wind is supplied by bellows and is directed to the reeds by keys and buttons, which sound accompanying chords. Invention variously attributed to Buschmann of Berlin (1822), Damien of Vienna (1829) and Bouton of Paris (1852).

accountancy, keeping or inspecting of financial data concerning persons and organizations. Data should incl. specific assets, liabilities, income, expenses, net receipts.

Accra, cap. of Ghana, on Gulf of Guinea. Pop. 738,000. Admin., commercial centre; railway terminus and port, exports cocoa, hardwoods, gold; Univ. of Ghana nearby. Grew round 2 17th cent. forts; cap. of Gold Coast colony from 1876.

accumulator or **secondary cell,** device used to store electricity. Current is passed between 2 plates in a liquid, causing chemical changes by electrolysis. When plates are electrically connected, reverse chemical changes cause current flow.

acetaldehyde (CH_3CHO), colourless liquid, formed by oxidation of ethanol. Used in dye and hypnotic drug mfg. Occurs in body during decomposition of ingested alcohol.

acetic acid (CH_3COOH), organic acid contained in vinegar. Colourless liquid with pungent smell, obtained by destructive distillation of wood or oxidation of acetaldehyde. Its esters incl. cellulose acetate, used to make plastics.

acetone (CH_3COCH_3), inflammable colourless liquid, the simplest KETONE. Obtained commercially from isopropanol. Used as paint and varnish remover and organic solvent.

acetylcholine, organic chemical secreted at ends of nerve fibres; stimulates adjacent nerve cells, thus transmitting impulses through nervous system.

acetylene (C_2H_2), colourless gas, produced by action of water on calcium carbide or from natural gas. Used in welding and organic synthesis; burns with intense flame when mixed with oxygen in oxyacetylene burner.

acetylsalicylic acid, *see* ASPIRIN.

Achaea, admin. dist. of S Greece, in Peloponnese, cap. Patras. Currants, olives; sheep, goats. Cities formed powerful Achaean League 280-146 BC, until conquered by Rome.

Achilles, in Greek legend, warrior and Greek leader in Trojan War. As child, was dipped in R. Styx by his mother, Thetis, to make him invulnerable, but water did not touch heel she held him by. At Troy, killed Hector but was killed by Paris with an arrow which struck his only vulnerable spot, his heel. Hero of Homer's *Iliad.*

Achill Island, Co. Mayo, W Irish Republic. Area 148 sq km (57 sq mi). Mountainous; agric., fishing, tourism. Bridge from mainland.

acid, substance which liberates hydrogen ions in aqueous solution (Arrhenius' theory). Reacts with base to form salts. Strength measured by concentration of hydrogen ions (pH scale); those undergoing complete ionization (*eg* hydrochloric acid) are strong. Most acids corrode metals, turn litmus red and taste sour.

acidosis, condition in which alkalinity of human blood is less than normal. May be caused by failure of lungs to eliminate carbon dioxide, kidney failure, malnutrition, diabetes.

acne, skin disease caused by abnormal activity of sebaceous (grease) glands; common among adolescents and young adults. Characterized by pimples on face, back and chest; alleviated by ultraviolet light (which occurs in sunlight).

Aconcagua, mountain of W Argentina, highest of Andes Mts., close to Chile border and Uspallata Pass. Height 6960 m (22,835 ft).

aconite, *see* MONKSHOOD.

Acorn

acorn, ovoid fruit or nut of OAK. Consists of nut itself in cup-shaped base. Formerly used as food for pigs.

acoustics, branch of physics dealing with propagation and detection of sound.

Acre (Heb. *Acco),* port of N Israel, on Bay of Haifa. Pop. 34,000. Steel, chemical indust. Christian centre during 13th cent. Crusades. Mainly Turkish rule (1517-1918), British (1918-48).

acropolis, elevated fortified citadel of ancient Greek cities. Surviving buildings of Acropolis in Athens incl. Propylaea, PARTHENON, Erectheum and temple of Athena Nike, mostly constructed under Cimon and Pericles in 5th cent. BC.

acrylic paint, emulsion paint used by artists, formed by adding pigment to acrylic resin. Can be applied with water to obtain thin washes or directly in thick impasto, imitating oil paint.

Actaeon, in Greek myth, a hunter. Angered Artemis by watching her bathe. She changed him into a stag and he was torn to pieces by his own hounds.

actinides, name given to group of elements with at. nos. from 89 to 103. Incl. uranium, actinium, thorium and 11 man-made transuranic elements. All radioactive and metallic.

actinium (Ac), radioactive metallic element; at. no. 89, at. wt. 227. Discovered (1899) by Debierne in pitchblende.

action painting, term originally used as synonymous with ABSTRACT EXPRESSIONISM, but has come to imply more extreme examples of painter's spontaneous self-expression, involving apparently random application of paint to canvas. Pollock was leading exponent.

Actium, promontory of NW Greece, opposite modern Préveza. Site of Octavian's naval defeat of Antony and Cleopatra (31 BC).

act of God, in law, unforeseeable, unavoidable accident caused by extraordinary natural event. Injured party cannot normally claim damages.

Acton, John Emerich Edward Dalberg Acton, Baron (1834-1902), English historian. Prominent Liberal and RC, became professor of modern history at Cambridge (1895). Planned *Cambridge Modern History,* wrote many celebrated essays.

Acts of the Apostles, fifth book of NT. Written in Greek *c* AD 60, traditionally ascribed to Luke. Describes growth of early church, incl. missionary journeys of Paul.

actuary, statistician employed by govt. department, insurance company or other business. Calculates possibilities and risks involved in insurance, lotteries, *etc.*

acupuncture, form of medical treatment of ancient Chinese origin. Consists of insertion of needles into determined parts of body to relieve pain and treat disease.

Adam and **Eve,** first man and woman in creation story of OT book, Genesis. Adam was formed from dust; Eve from one of Adam's ribs taken while he slept. *See* EDEN, GARDEN OF.

Adam, Robert (1728-92), Scottish architect. With brother, **James Adam** (1730-94), designed numerous public buildings, houses and interiors, in highly refined style derived from Classical architecture. Works incl. London's Adelphi (now destroyed), Syon House, Osterley Park. Also applied principles to furniture design.

Adams, John (1735-1826), American statesman, president (1797-1801). A Patriot leader, defended Declaration of Independence (1776) as representative at Continental Congress. Served as vice-president (1789-97) under Washington. As president, retained his political integrity despite Federalist-dominated Congress' attempts (*eg* Alien and Sedition Acts) to discredit Jeffersonian Republicans. His son, **John Quincy Adams** (1767-1848), was also president (1825-9). While secretary of state (1817-25), promulgated Monroe Doctrine (1823) on foreign policy in the Americas. A Federalist, elected president by House of Representatives over Jackson after neither candidate had obtained majority of electoral coll. votes.

Adana, city of S Turkey, on R. Seyhan. Pop. 475,000. Trade centre; cotton goods, tobacco. Colonized by Romans; revived under Harun al-Rashid *c* 782.

addax, *Addax nasomaculatus,* large antelope of N Africa, esp. Sahara. Has whitish-grey coat, long spiralling horns.

adder, *Vipera berus,* poisonous European snake; bite painful but rarely fatal. Variable colour pattern, normally zigzag band edged by dark spots. Name also applied to African puff adder and various harmless American snakes.

addiction, compulsive uncontrolled use of habit-forming substances, *eg* alcohol or drugs; marked by physical dependence on drug, tolerance to it, and harmful effects on user and society. Sudden cessation may cause withdrawal symptoms, characterized by acute physical and mental distress.

Addington, Henry, *see* SIDMOUTH.

Addis Ababa, cap. of Ethiopia. Pop. 1,133,000. Admin., communications centre, railway to Djibouti; coffee trade, food processing. Hq. of OAU. Cap. of Ethiopia from 1896; cap. of Italian E Africa 1936-41. Has Imperial palace, 2 univs.

Addison, Joseph (1672-1719), English poet, essayist, moralist, politician. Contributed to *Tatler*, collaborated with STEELE in *Spectator* developing Augustan ideals of culture in masterly prose style.

additive, inclusive term for wide range of chemicals added to substances to produce desired effect, *eg* anti-knock agents in petrol, food preservers, mould inhibitors.

Adelaide, city of SC Australia, on Torrens R., cap. of South Australia. Pop. 900,000. Commercial, indust. centre; exports (via Port Adelaide) wheat, wool, wattle bark, fruit, animal products; univ. Settled (1836) by free immigrants. Museum; Anglican, RC cathedrals.

Adélie Land, region of Antarctica, S of 60°S and between 136° and 142° E. Part of French Southern and Antarctic Territs. Discovered 1840. Site of research station.

Aden, port of SW Southern Yemen, on Gulf of Aden. Pop. 285,000. Free port since 1850; oil refining, salt mfg. British colony from 1839, joined Federation of South Arabia (1959) with British protect. of Emirates of South. Became cap. of independent Southern Yemen (1970).

Aden, Gulf of, arm of W Arabian Sea, between Southern Yemen and Somali Republic.

Adenauer, Konrad (1876-1967), West German statesman, chancellor (1949-63). Twice arrested during Nazi regime. Took part in founding (1945) Christian Democratic Union. Championed W European cooperation esp. through formation (1957) of EEC. Advocated German reunification through free elections and supported De Gaulle's policy of European independence of US.

adenoids, masses of lymphoid tissue in upper part of throat behind the nose. Nasal infection in children resulting from overgrowth sometimes necessitates surgical removal.

Adige (anc. *Athesis*, Ger. *Etsch*), river of N Italy. Flows *c* 360 km (225 mi) from Resia Pass on Austrian border via Trento, Verona, to Adriatic N of R. Po. Irrigation, h.e.p.

Adirondack Mountains, range of NE New York, US; in S extension of Laurentian Plateau. Rise to 1629 m (5344 ft). Many lakes, waterfalls; extensively forested. Tourist resort area.

Adler, Alfred (1870–1937), Austrian psychologist. After studying with Freud, founded own school of individual psychology. Rejected Freud's emphasis on sexual motive in behaviour in favour of drive for power; believed inferiority complex fundamental to personality problems.

administrative law, laws and judicial decisions made by executive under powers given it by legislature of state. In 20th cent., govts. have increased such powers. In UK, ministers of the Crown may make orders, *etc*, amending or overriding statutes. Select Committee on Statutory Instruments acts as watchdog on executive.

admiral, brilliantly coloured butterfly of Nymphalidae family. Species incl. red admiral, *Vanessa atalanta*, common in Europe and North America.

Admiralty, in UK, former govt. dept. for admin. of naval affairs. Absorbed by ministry of defence (1964). Also refers to its hq. (1723-5, with modern additions) in Whitehall.

Admiralty Islands, group of small isls. of SW Pacific, in Bismarck Archipelago, NE of New Guinea. Area *c* 2070 sq km (800 sq mi); pop. *c* 28,000. Chief isl. Manus.

Adonis, in Greek myth, handsome youth disputed by Aphrodite and Persephone. When killed by wild boar, Zeus arranged for him to spend summer above ground with Aphrodite and winter in underworld with Persephone. Hence celebrated as symbolic of yearly cycle of vegetation.

Adowa, *see* ADUWA.

adrenal gland, either of 2 endocrine glands against upper ends of each kidney. Consists of inner part (medulla) which secretes noradrenaline and adrenaline, and outer layer (cortex) which secretes steroid hormones that influence CARBOHYDRATE formation, sexual development, and control salt and water balance in body.

adrenaline, hormone secreted by medulla of adrenal gland. Stimulates heart action and sympathetic nervous system, raises blood pressure and blood sugar level; used to treat asthma.

Adrian IV, orig. Nicholas Breakspear (*c* 1115-59), English churchman. Only English pope (1154-9); defended papal supremacy against opponents, incl. Frederick Barbarossa. Prob. gave Ireland as fief to Henry II of England.

Adrianople, *see* EDIRNE.

Adriatic Sea, arm of Mediterranean Sea between Italy (W) and Yugoslavia, Albania (E). Length *c* 800 km (500 mi); W coast is straight, low-lying; E coast is steep, rocky. Many ports, tourist resorts.

Aduwa or **Adowa,** town of N Ethiopia. Pop. 16,000. Scene of decisive defeat (1896) of Italians by Ethiopians under Menelik II, securing Ethiopian independence.

Adventists, evangelical sects who believe that Second Coming of Christ to Earth is imminent. Largest body is Seventh Day Adventists, formally organized in US in 1863. Observe Saturday as Sabbath.

advocate, in law, person appointed to plead another's cause, esp. in court or court-martial, *ie* English barrister or counsel, Scottish and French advocate, American attorney. Lord advocate of Scotland is senior law-officer of the Crown responsible for criminal prosecutions; retires with govt. by which appointed.

Aegean Sea

Aegean Sea, arm of Mediterranean Sea between Greece and Asia Minor. Linked by Dardanelles with Sea of Marmara and Black Sea. Many isls. incl. Cyclades, Dodecanese, Euboea, Sporades. Ports, tourism.

Aegina (mod. *Aigina),* small isl. of Greece, in Saronic Gulf. Sponge fishing, olives, vines. Ancient commercial centre (struck 1st Greek coins) until pop. expelled by Athens (431 BC).

Aegisthus, in Greek myth, incestuous son of THYESTES and his daughter Pelopia. Killed his uncle ATREUS to allow his father to regain throne. Lover of Clytemnestra, he slew her husband, Agamemnon, on his return from Troy. Killed in revenge by Orestes.

Aeneas, Trojan leader in Homer's *Iliad* and classical legend. Vergil's *Aeneid,* epic poem in 12 books (30–19 BC) develops him into exemplar of Roman virtues and forefather of Rome's founders, using story to celebrate Augustus' empire. After fall of Troy, Aeneas sets out to find new home, is delayed in Carthage by love for DIDO, but eventually reaches Italy to found Alba Longa.

aeolian harp, zither-like instrument made from strings of varying thickness, all tuned to the same note. Placed out of doors, produces series of rising and falling harmonies when the wind blows over it.

Aeolian Islands, *see* LIPARI ISLANDS.

Aeolus, in Greek myth, ruler of the winds which he kept in cave on isl. of Aeolia. Gave Odysseus winds adverse to him tied in leather bag.

aerial or **antenna,** in electronics, a conductor used to transmit or receive radio waves. In transmitter, signal from circuit causes electrons in antenna to oscillate, producing electromagnetic radiation. This radiation induces oscillations

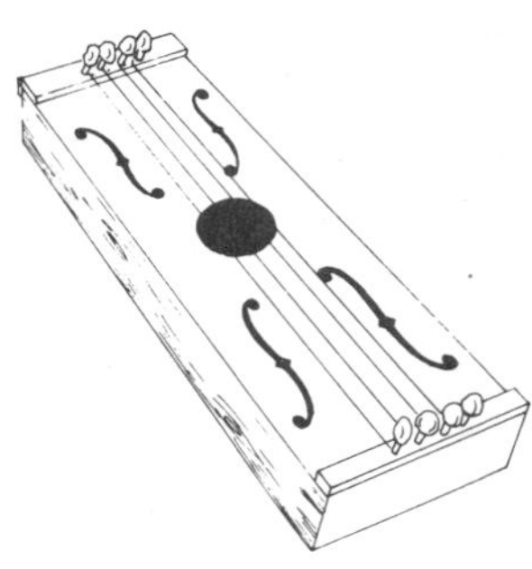

Aeolian harp

in receiving aerial, which are then amplified.

aerodynamics, branch of fluid mechanics dealing with forces (resistance, pressure, *etc*) exerted by air or other gases in motion. Concerned with principles governing flight of aircraft, wind resistance of vehicles, buildings, bridges.

aeroembolism or **bends,** bodily disorder caused by formation of nitrogen bubbles in blood and body tissues following too rapid decrease in atmospheric pressure. Characterized by nausea, pain in muscles, paralysis. Most commonly suffered by deep-sea divers who return to surface too quickly.

aeronautics, science of the design, construction and operation of all heavier-than-air aircraft. *See* AERODYNAMICS, AVIATION.

The first successful aeroplane, built by the Wright brothers

aeroplane [UK] or **airplane** [US], powered heavier-than-air aircraft which derives lift from action of air against (normally) fixed wings and is driven forward by a screw propeller or by JET PROPULSION. Stability is provided by vertical and horizontal tailpieces; control by flaps (ailerons) on trailing edge of wings. Designs range from early biplane (double-winged) types, monoplanes incl. delta-wing shapes, and swing-wing types suitable for supersonic flight. For history, *see* AVIATION.

aerosol dispenser, container in which gas under pressure is used to aerate and dispense liquid through a valve in the form of spray or foam. Used for insecticides, paints, polishes, *etc.*

Aeschylus (525-456 BC), Greek tragic poet. Founded classical Greek TRAGEDY, introducing 2nd actor and thereby dramatic dialogue. Only 7 of *c* 90 plays survive, of which masterpiece is trilogy *Oresteia*. Also wrote *The Persians, Seven against Thebes*.

Aesculapius, *see* ASCLEPIUS.

Aesop (6th cent. BC), semi-legendary fabulist. Body of native Greek fable ascribed to him. Moral conveyed through stories of animals, *eg The Tortoise and the Hare*.

aesthetics, branch of philosophy concerned with nature of art. Plato contended that beauty lay in object itself; Epicurus that it lay in eye of beholder.

Aethelbert, *see* ETHELBERT.

Aethelred the Unready, *see* ETHELRED.

Aetolia, region of WC Greece, N of Gulf of Patras. Part of admin. dist. of Aetolia and Acarnania, cap. Missolonghi. Mainly mountainous. Formed Aetolian League 4th cent. BC against Achaea, Macedonia; defeated by Rome 189 BC.

Afars and the Issas, French Territory of the, *see* DJIBOUTI.

Afghan hound, breed of large hunting dog. Long narrow head, prominent hip bones, silky thick hair. Stands *c* 68 cm/27 in. at shoulder.

Afghanistan, republic of SC Asia. Area 647,500 sq km (250,000 sq mi); pop. 15,108,000; cap. Kabul. Language: Afghan. Religion: Islam. Mainly mountainous, dominated by Hindu Kush; agric., stock rearing in river valleys and plains. Dry continental climate, cold in winter, hot in summer. Modern Afghanistan estab. in 18th cent; kingdom created 1926. Republic proclaimed after military coup (1973). Instability led to occupation by Soviet troops (1979).

Africa, second largest continent of the world. Area *c* 30,262,000 sq km (11,684,000 sq mi); pop. *c* 400,000,000. Bounded by Mediterranean (N), Red Sea (NE), Indian Ocean (SE, S), Atlantic (W); incl. Madagascar, Cape Verde, Ascension, St Helena isls. Largely ancient plateau; Great Rift Valley in E; mountain ranges incl. Atlas, Ethiopian Highlands, Ruwenzori, Drakensberg; highest point Mt. Kilimanjaro (5892 m/19,340 ft). Main rivers Congo, Limpopo, Niger, Nile, Zambezi; main lakes Albert, Chad, Nyasa, Victoria. Has vast inland deserts, incl. Sahara, Libyan, Kalahari; extensive tropical savannah; jungle, rain forests along equator. Widespread subsistence agric., export crops incl. cocoa, groundnuts, cotton, hardwoods. Mineral resources incl. gold, diamonds, copper, petroleum, iron ore. Earliest prehist. man may have lived in E Africa; advanced civilization developed in Egypt before 3000 BC. N coast colonized by Romans after fall of Carthage (146 BC); Arabs introduced Islam from 7th cent. European exploration began 15th cent., led to extensive colonization in 19th cent. by UK, France, Germany, Italy, Belgium; most colonies became independent in mid-20th cent.

Afrikaans, language of West Germanic group of Indo-European family. Developed from Dutch of 17th cent. Boer settlers in S Africa. Contains many Hottentot, Bantu, English loan-words.

Agadir, town of SW Morocco, on Atlantic Ocean. Pop. 189,000. Port for fertile agric. dist., exports fruit, vegetables; fishing. Visit by German gunboat *Panther* (1911) caused diplomatic crisis with France. Devastated by earthquake (1960).

Aga Khan, hereditary title of the head of the Ismaili Moslem sect.

Agamemnon, legendary leader of Greek forces in Trojan War; king of Mycenae. On his return from Troy, was murdered by his wife, Clytemnestra, and her lover, Aegisthus.

agaric, any fungus of Agaricaceae family, esp. of genus *Agaricus*. Blade-shaped gills on underside of the cap. Incl. common edible field mushroom, *A. campestris*.

agate, hard, semi-precious gemstone. Chalcedonic variety of silica, formed mainly of fine-grained quartz. Has bands of 2 or more colours.

agave, genus of plants native to tropical America and SW US of family Amaryllidaceae. Spirituous liquor (mescal) distilled from agave sap. Some cultivated for their fibre, *eg* sisal.

aggression, in social psychology, form of behaviour characterized by unprovoked attacks or acts of self-defence. In psychoanalysis, used in special sense by Adler as the manifestation of the 'will to power' over others. In international law, important concept with, as yet, no satisfactory general definition, but used for certain specific acts, *eg* invasion, by one state against another.

Agincourt (mod. *Azincourt*), village of N France. Scene of victory (1415) of Henry V of England over French during Hundred Years War.

agnosticism, maintenance of position that the human mind cannot know anything beyond material phenomena. Term coined by T.H. Huxley (1869).

agouti, rabbit-sized rodent, genus *Dasyprocta*, of forests of Central and South America. Tailless, short-haired; destructive of sugar cane.

Agra, city of Uttar Pradesh, NC India, on R. Jumna. Pop. 592,000. Founded 1566, Mogul cap. until 1658; hist. buildings incl. Taj Mahal and Akbar's fort.

Agricola, Gnaius Julius (*c* AD 37-93), Roman general. Elected consul in 77. Became governor in Britain (*c* 78-*c* 85) and extended Roman rule into Scotland.

agriculture, science and art of farming, incl. the cultivation of soil, production of crops and raising of livestock. Use of chemical fertilizers, herbicides and insecticides, fast-ripening and disease-resistant crops with high yields, specialized animal breeding, advanced mechanization leading to large-scale production, have revolutionized modern agriculture.

Agrigento (anc. *Agrigentum*), town of S Sicily, Italy. Pop. 49,000. Formerly called Girgenti. Harbour at Porto Empedocle; sulphur trade. Founded *c* 580 BC by Greek colonists; taken by Romans 210 BC. Many Greek, Roman remains.

agrimony, plant of genus *Agrimonia* of rose family. Aromatic pinnate leaves with small yellow flowers. Grows wild in N temperate regions and cultivated in herb gardens.

Agrippa, Marcus Vipsanius (*c* 63-12 BC), Roman general. Adviser of Augustus, helped in defeat (31 BC) of Antony at Actium.

Agulhas, Cape, headland of W Cape Prov., South Africa. Most S point of Africa. Danger to shipping; lighthouse.

Ahab (d. *c* 853 BC), Israelite king (*c* 874-*c* 853 BC). In OT, provoked Hebrew prophet, Elijah, by allowing his wife, Jezebel, to encourage worship of Baal. Politically, consolidated empire; Syrian wars ended with his death in battle.

Ahaggar or **Hoggar Mountains,** highland region of S Algeria, in WC Sahara. Rises to Mt. Tahat (3000 m/9850 ft).

Ahmedabad, cap. of Gujarat state, W India. Pop. 1,742,000. Cotton textiles. Cultural and religious centre.

Ahwaz, city of SW Iran, cap. of Khuzistan prov., on R. Karun. Pop. 329,000. Railway jct.; petrochemical indust.

Aidan, St (d. 651), Irish missionary. Estab. monastery on Lindisfarne. Christianized Northumbria.

Aintab, *see* GAZIANTEP.

Ainu, hairy, European-like aboriginal inhabitants of Japan. Language unrelated to any known linguistic stock. Driven to N islands, fewer than 17,000 remain, supporting themselves by hunting and fishing.

aircraft, any machine designed to travel through the air, whether heavier or lighter than air, incl. AEROPLANE, AIRSHIP, AUTOGIRO, BALLOON, HELICOPTER, glider.

aircraft carrier, type of warship with extensive flat deck space on which aircraft can take off and land. Developed at end of WWI; in WWII overtook BATTLESHIP in strategic importance.

Airedale, breed of dog, largest of terrier group. Wiry black and tan coat; stands 58 cm/23 in. at shoulder.

air plant, *see* EPIPHYTE.

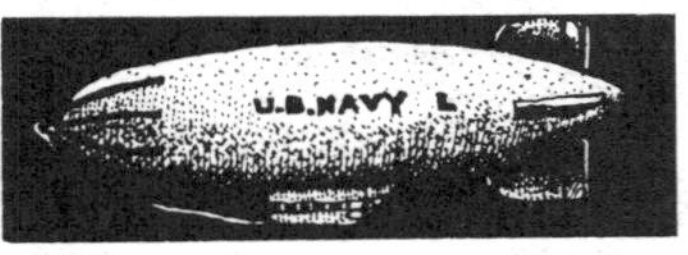

Nonrigid airship of World War II

airship or **dirigible,** any self-propelled aircraft that is lighter than air and can be steered. Usually a large gas-filled container with attached means of propulsion and steering, and suspended compartment for passengers or freight. German Zeppelin type with rigid gas-carrying hull used for bombing in WWI. After WWI, British and American types used for passenger-carrying, until destruction by fire of several incl. British R101 (1930), German *Hindenburg* (1937). Non-rigid types (blimps) using non-flammable helium rather than hydrogen continue in use.

Aisne, river of N France. Flows *c* 240 km (150 mi) from Argonne via Soissons to R. Oise near Compiègne. Scene of heavy fighting in WWI.

Aix-en-Provence, town of Provence, SE France. Pop. 111,000. Commercial centre, agric. market. Roman *Aquae Sextiae,* founded 123 BC near thermal springs. Cap. and cultural centre of Provence in Middle Ages. Univ. (1409), town hall, cathedral. Birthplace of Cézanne.

Aix-la-Chapelle, *see* AACHEN.

Aix-la-Chapelle, Treaty of, settlement (1668) ending French invasion of Spanish Netherlands (War of Devolution). France retained most conquests in Flanders. Also name of treaty (1748) concluding War of AUSTRIAN SUCCESSION (1740-8). Chief result was ceding of Silesia to Prussia. Pragmatic Sanction upheld, confirming Maria Theresa's right to inherit Habsburg possessions from her father Charles VI.

Ajaccio, town of W Corsica, France, on Gulf of Ajaccio. Pop. 45,000. Port, resort, fishing. Birthplace of Napoleon.

Ajanta, village of Maharashtra state, SC India. Buddhist cave temples dating from *c* 200 BC-AD 700 nearby.

Ajax, legendary Greek hero of Trojan War, second only to Achilles in bravery. Killed himself when beaten by Odysseus in contest for Achilles' armour.

Akbar, orig. Jalal ed-Din Mohammed (1542-1605), Mogul emperor of India (1556-1605). Grandson of BABER. Expanded territ. by conquest of Afghanistan and all N India. Introduced admin. reforms and promoted religious tolerance.

Akhenaton, *see* IKHNATON.

Aksum or **Axum,** ancient town of N Ethiopia. Pop. 10,000. Coffee trade. Cap. of Aksumite empire 1st-8th cent.; religious centre, Ark of the Covenant reputedly brought here by descendant of Solomon.

Alabama, state of SE US. Area 133,667 sq km (51,609 sq mi); pop. 3,665,000; cap. Montgomery; chief city Birmingham. Plateau in N; plain in S (cotton, corn production) stretches to Gulf of Mexico. Drained by Alabama, Tombigbee rivers. Coal mining, quarrying, iron and steel, petroleum industs. Spanish exploration in 16th cent.; French settlement 1702; ceded by French to British 1765. Seat of Confederate govt. 1861-5. Admitted to Union as 22nd state (1819).

alabaster, fine-grained, translucent variety of gypsum. Light-coloured or white, often streaked. Softer than marble, often used for statues, ornaments.

Alain-Fournier, pseud. of Henri Alban Fournier (1886-1914), French author. Reputation based on novel, nostalgic fantasy *Le Grand Meaulnes*, in English *The Lost Domain* (1913). Killed in WWI.

Alamein, El, village of N Egypt, W of Alexandria. Scene of decisive defeat (1942) of Germans under Rommel by British under Montgomery; prevented Axis occupation of Egypt.

Alamo, *see* SAN ANTONIO.

Alanbrooke, Alan Francis Brooke, 1st Viscount (1883-1963), British general. Commander-in-chief of British Home Forces (1940-1), he was chief of Imperial General Staff (1941-6).

Aland Islands *(Ahvenanmaa)*, archipelago of SW Finland, at mouth of Gulf of Bothnia. Area 1505 sq km (581 sq mi); main town Mariehamn. Fishing; barley, flax growing. Incl. *c* 6000 isls., 80 inhabited. Held by Finland from WWI. Pop. Swedish-speaking.

Alaric I (*c* 370-410), Visigothic king. Served with Visigothic troops of Roman emperor Theodosius I; proclaimed their leader in 395. Invaded and plundered Greece (395–6). Invaded Italy (401, 408); sacked Rome 410.

Alaska, state of US, in NW North America. Area 1,518,776 sq km (586,400 sq mi); pop. 382,000; cap. Juneau; largest town Anchorage. Arctic Ocean in N, Pacific in S. Polar climate in N; tundra region drained by Yukon R.; S volcanic ranges stretch W to Aleutian Isls. Scattered Eskimo pop. Fish, fur, timber, minerals are main resources. Important oil strike in late 1960s. Of strategic importance; has D.E.W. line radar system. Settled by Russians in 18th cent.; bought by US 1867. Gold strikes 1899, 1902. Admitted to Union as 49th state (1959).

Alaska Range, mountain system of SC Alaska, US. Incl. North America's highest peak, Mt. McKinley (6194 m/20,320 ft).

Alba, Fernando, Duque de, *see* ALVA.

Alba Longa, ancient city of C Italy, near Castel Gandolfo. Founded 12th cent. BC, reputed birthplace of Romulus and Remus. Destroyed 7th cent. BC by Rome.

Albania *(Shqipnija)*, republic of SE Europe, on Adriatic. Area *c* 28,500 sq km (11,000 sq mi); pop. 2,608,000; cap. Tirana. Language: Albanian. Religions: Islam, Eastern Orthodox. Mainly mountainous; lower marshy but fertile areas near coast. Cereals, tobacco, olives; slow indust. development. Turkish until 1912; Italian occupation in WWII, communist govt. estab. 1946 under Hoxha.

Albany, cap. of New York state, US; on Hudson R. Pop. 798,000. Port and shipping centre; printing and publishing, varied mfg. industs. One of oldest US cities. Dutch settlement estab. 1614; English control 1664; became cap. 1797.

albatross, large sea bird of genus *Diomedea*, found in S hemisphere. Long narrow wings, hooked beak; excels in sustained flight. Largest species is wandering albatross, *D. exulans*.

Albee, Edward Franklin (1928-), American playwright. Known for one-act absurdist plays, incl. *The Zoo Story* (1958), and first full length play *Who's Afraid of Virginia Woolf?* (1962).

Albert I (1875-1934), Belgian king (1909-34). Sponsored resistance to German invasion during WWI. Initiated social reforms in Belgium and Belgian Congo. Killed in climbing accident.

Alberta, Prairie prov. of W Canada. Area 661,188 sq km (255,285 sq mi); pop. 2,009,000; cap. Edmonton; other major city Calgary. Scenic Rocky Mts. in W; mainly forested in N; agric. plains (wheat, cattle) in S. Drained N by Peace, Athabaska rivers. Leading oil, coal producer; large natural gas reserves. Ceded by Hudson's Bay Co. to Canada 1869; became prov. 1905.

Albert Nyanza or **Lake Albert,** lake between W Uganda and NE Zaïre. Area 5345 sq km (2064 sq mi); part of Great Rift Valley. Fed by Victoria Nile, Semliki rivers; drained by Albert Nile. Discovered 1864, named after Prince Consort.

Albert [Francis Charles Augustus Emmanuel] of Saxe-Coburg-Gotha, Prince (1819-61), German prince, consort of Queen Victoria of Britain. Promoted arts and scientific developments, notably Great Exhibition of 1851.

Albigensians, religious group of S France, *fl* 12th-13th cent. Regarded as heretics, adopted Manichaean doctrine of duality of good and evil, held that Jesus lived only in semblance. Movement killed by Albigensian Crusade proclaimed by Pope Innocent III (1208), and by Inquisition.

albinism, condition in humans, animals and plants, characterized by deficiency of pigmentation. In humans, manifested by white skin, white hair and pink eyes; inherited as a recessive genetic character.

albumin or **albumen,** in biochemistry, one of group of water-soluble proteins occurring in animal and vegetable fluids and tissues. Found in blood, milk, muscles, egg-white (albumen).

Albuquerque, health resort of C New Mexico, US; on Rio Grande. Pop. 385,000; state's largest city. Railway jct.; railway engineering, food processing. Founded 1706.

Alcatraz, rocky isl. of W California, US; in San Francisco Bay. Military prison from 1859; federal prison 1933-63, now closed.

alcázar, fortress or palace built by the Moors in Spain. Best known are those in Seville and Toledo.

alchemy, early form of chemistry, with philosophical and magical associations. Came to Europe through Islamic science, which used methods and traditions of Egyptians, Babylonians, and philosopy of Greeks. Best known for attempts to make gold from base metals.

Alcibiades (*c* 450-404 BC), Athenian

statesman. Helped form alliance of Argos, Mantinea and Athens against Sparta; defeated at Mantinea (418). Led Sicilian expedition of 415; accused of sacrilegious mutilation of statues of Hermes in Athens before embarkation, fled to Sparta. Returned to Athens (411), won several battles before naval defeat at Notium (407). Murdered in Phrygia.

Alcock, Sir John William (1892-1919), English aviator. With **Sir Arthur Whitten Brown** (1886-1948), made 1st Atlantic crossing in an aeroplane (1919).

alcohol, organic compound obtained from HYDROCARBON by replacement of 1 or more hydrogen atoms with hydroxyl (-OH) radicals. Name applies esp. to ETHANOL (ethyl alcohol). Other alcohols incl. METHANOL, GLYCOL, GLYCEROL.

alcoholism, pathological condition caused by excessive consumption of ethyl alcohol. Chronic form leads to vitamin deficiency, gastritis, cirrhosis of liver, brain damage. May be treated by drugs, psychotherapy or by organizations such as Alcoholics Anonymous.

Alcott, Louisa May (1832-88), American author. Semi-autobiog. novels, *eg Little Women* (1868-9), are now children's classics.

Aldabra, small atoll group in Indian Ocean, NW of Madagascar. Formerly part of British Indian Ocean Territ., now admin. by Seychelles. Noted for rare plants and animals, esp. giant land tortoises.

aldehyde, organic compound of form RCHO where R is an ALKYL or ARYL group. Examples incl. benzaldehyde, C_6H_5CHO, used in perfume and dye mfg., ACETALDEHYDE and FORMALDEHYDE.

alder, deciduous shrub or tree of genus *Alnus* of cool temperate regions. Toothed leaves and cone-like fruit. Wood is water resistant; used for pumps, millwheels, bridges, *etc.* Bark yields brownish dye.

Alderney, northernmost of Channel Islands, UK. Area 8 sq km (3 sq mi). Main town St Anne. Cattle rearing, potato growing.

Aldershot, mun. bor. of Hampshire, S England. Pop. 33,000. Has large military training centre, estab. 1854.

Aleppo (Arab. *Haleb),* city of NW Syria. Pop. 843,000. Trade in wool; produces silk and cotton goods. Once a centre of caravan trade with East, taken by Turks (1517) and held until WWI.

Aleutian Islands, chain of *c* 150 isls. in Bering Sea, between USSR and Alaska, US; extension of Aleutian Range. Pop. *c* 8000. Incl. Unimak, Unalaska, Andreanof Isls. Mainly mountainous with several volcanoes. Small groups of Russo-Eskimo fishers and fur trappers.

Alexander III, orig. Orlando Bandinelli (d. 1181), Italian churchman, pope (1159-81). Opposed by 3 successive anti-popes, forced to seek refuge in France 1162-5; supported by Lombard League in contest with Frederick Barbarossa, who was defeated at Legnano (1176). Supported Becket against Henry II of England. Summoned Third Lateran Council (1179), which estab. rules for future papal elections.

Black alder

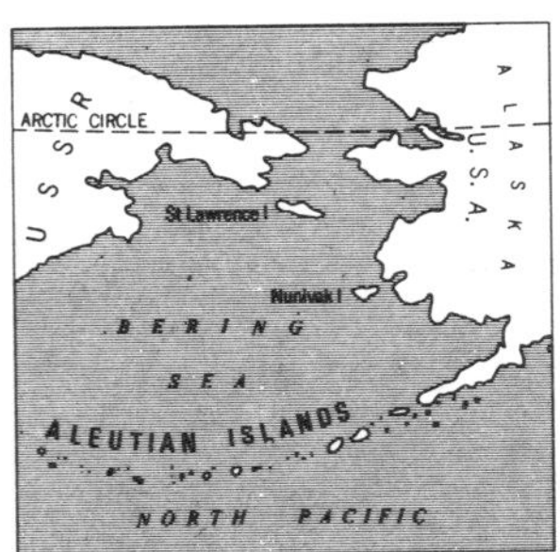

Aleutian Islands

Alexander VI, orig. Rodrigo Lanzol y Borja (1431-1503), Spanish-Italian churchman, pope (1492-1503). Elected pope by bribery, his papacy was notorious for political intrigue and favouritism shown to his illegitimate children (incl. Cesare and Lucrezia Borgia).

Alexander I (1777-1825), tsar of Russia (1801-25). Succeeded his father, Paul I, at whose murder he prob. connived. Early attempts at domestic reform failed. Joined alliance against Napoleon in 1805; series of defeats resulted in peace with Treaty of Tilsit (1807). Successfully countered Napoleon's invasion of Russia (1812);

attended Congress of Vienna (1814-15) to map out political settlement of Europe. Fearing liberalism, promoted Holy Alliance with Austria, Prussia to retain European status quo.

Alexander II (1818-81), tsar of Russia (1855-81). Son of Nicholas I, initiated reform programme that incl. Edict of Emancipation (1861), freeing serfs; failure of changes resulted in increasing terrorism. Adopted expansionist foreign policy in Asia. Assassinated by anarchist.

Alexander III (1845-94), tsar of Russia (1881-94). Son of Alexander II, he took measures, particularly by increasing police powers, to crush liberalism, enforce persecution of Jews and minorities. Advocated peace in foreign policy.

Alexander [III] the Great (356-323 BC), Macedonian king. Son of Philip II of Macedon, succeeded father in 336. After subduing an uprising in Thebes, began conquest of Persian Empire (334). Gained control of most of Asia Minor, defeating Darius III at Issus (333). Occupied Egypt, where he founded Alexandria. Returning to Mesopotamia, destroyed Persian army at Gaugamela on Tigris (331). Pushed on into Bactria and India, reaching Punjab by 326. Army refused to go beyond R. Hyphasis and Alexander returned to Susa (324). Attempted to fuse Greek and Asian cultures by marrying his officers to Asian wives (he married Bactrian princess Roxana). Died of fever in Babylon.

Alexander I (*c* 1078-1124), king of Scotland (1107-1124). Son of Malcolm III; succeeded brother Edgar to throne. Crushed Celtic rebellion, continued anglicization policy; built many abbeys *eg* Scone, Inchcolm. Succeeded by brother David.

Alexander II (1198-1249), king of Scotland (1214-1249). Supported English barons against King John. Invaded England twice, but disputes settled by marriage to Henry III's sister.

Alexander III (1241-86), king of Scotland (1249-86). Victory over Haakon IV of Norway at Largs (1263) led to acquisition of Western Isles and Isle of Man.

Alexander, Harold Rupert Leofric George, Earl Alexander of Tunis (1891-1969), British field marshal. In WWII, directed retreats from Dunkirk (1940) and Burma (1942); led invasion of Italy through Sicily, becoming Allied commander-in-chief of Mediterranean forces. Governor-general of Canada (1946-52).

Alexander Archipelago, group of *c* 1000 isls. off SE Alaska, US; part of Alaska Panhandle. Consists of summits of submerged mountain system; densely forested. Pop. mainly Indian.

Alexander Nevski, St (1220-63), Russian national hero. Grand duke of Vladimir-Suzdal, acquired name Nevski after defeating Swedes on the Neva (1240). Victorious over Livonian Knights near L. Peipus (1242).

Alexandria *(El Iskandarîya),* city of N Egypt, between L. Mareotis and Mediterranean Sea. Pop. 2,320,000. Major port, railway jct., air terminal; exports cotton; cotton industs. Founded 332 BC by Alexander the Great, partly on former Pharos isl. Ancient Jewish, Greek, Arab cultural and educational centre (libraries, univ.); Roman prov. cap. Declined after taken by Arabs (7th cent.); revived 19th cent. when joined to Nile by canal. Remains of ancient city incl. Pompey's Pillar, ruins at Pharos, catacombs.

alfalfa or **lucerne,** *Medicago sativa,* European leguminous forage plant. Trifoliate leaves, purple clover-like flowers. Naturalized in most temperate regions and used extensively in US for fodder, pasture and as a cover crop.

Alfred the Great (849-99), king of Wessex (871-99). Most of reign spent fighting Danish invaders. Retreat to Somerset (878) gave rise to legend of Alfred and the cakes. Later routed Danes at Ethandun, enabling him to bring in reforms, legal code based on strong centralized monarchy. Created navy. Great interest in culture led to revival of clerical learning, estab. of Old English prose. Translated many Latin works, inspired others. ANGLO-SAXON CHRONICLE begun at his command.

algae, chlorophyll-containing plants of division Thallophyta. Found in fresh and salt water. Range from unicellular forms, usually microscopic, to multicellular forms up to 30 m/100 ft in length. Incl. pond scum, seaweeds.

Algarve, coastal region and prov. of S. Portugal, cap. Faro. Tourism; fruit, fishing. Last Moorish stronghold in Portugal, reconquered 1249.

algebra, branch of mathematics which generalizes operations of ordinary arithmetic by allowing letters or other symbols to stand for unknown quantities. Modern abstract algebra develops axiomatically systems that arise in many branches of mathematics; incl. ring theory and group theory.

Algeciras, town of Andalusia, S Spain, on Algeciras Bay. Pop. 82,000. Port; fishing, tourism. Founded 711 by Moors; new town built 1760. Scene of European powers' conference (1906) on Morocco.

Algeria, republic of N Africa. Area 2,388,000 sq km (922,000 sq mi); pop. 18,515,000; cap. Algiers. Languages: Arabic, French. Religion: Islam. Sahara in S; coastal plain, Atlas Mts. in N. Cereals, dates, wine production; fishing; mineral resources incl. major oil, natural gas fields. Incl. ancient region of Numidia. Arabs introduced Islam in 7th cent.; stronghold of Barbary pirates 16th-18th cent.; occupied by French from 1830. Violent campaign fought by FLN in 1950s, led to independence (1962) after referendum.

Algiers (Arab. *Al-jezair,* Fr. *Alger),* cap. of Algeria, on Bay of Algiers. Pop. 1,503,000. Major port, exports wine, fruit; admin., commercial centre, univ. (1879). Founded 10th cent.; base for Barbary pirates 16th-18th cent. Taken by French (1830). Badly damaged during independence conflict. Has 16th cent. fortress.

Algonquin or **Algonkin,** North American Indian tribe. Among first tribes to make alliance with French settlers (early 17th cent.). Dispersed by Iroquois, remnants in Québec, Ontario.

algorithm, in mathematics, systematic procedure for solution of a problem in a finite number of steps. Computers may be programmed to use algorithms to solve complicated equations quickly.

Alhambra, fortified palace of Moorish rulers of Granada, Spain. Built largely in 14th cent., its interior is richly decorated in Islamic style.

Ali (*c* 600-61), 4th caliph (656-61). Married Fatima, daughter of Mohammed. His rule was opposed by Muawiya, who became caliph on abdication of Ali's son, Hasan. Murdered by fanatics. Shiite-Sunnite division in Islam began after his reign.

Ali, Muhammad, orig. Cassius Marcellus Clay (1942-), American boxer. Won world heavyweight title (1964). Licence to box withdrawn (1967-70). Regained title with defeat of George Foreman (1974). Lost title to Leon Spinks (1978) but regained it same year. Lost to Larry Holmes (1980).

Alicante, city of SE Spain, on Mediterranean Sea, cap. of Alicante prov. Pop. 213,000. Port, exports wine, fruit, tobacco; tourist resort. Castle on hilltop site fortified from Greek times.

Alice Springs, town of SC Northern Territ., Australia, on Todd R. Pop. 11,000. Railway to Adelaide; centre for surrounding cattle raising, mining industs.; tourism. Founded (1889) as Stuart; cap. (1926-31) of former Central Australia.

alien, in law, resident of a country who owes political allegiance to another country. Subject to laws limiting entry to countries, conditions of residence.

alienation, in social sciences, term used to refer to estrangement of part or whole of personality from experience. Used as important concept by Marx for effects of economic production and class system on workers ('alienated labour').

alimentary canal, in mammals, tubular passage from mouth to anus, concerned with intake of food, its digestion and disposal of residual waste products. Incl. pharynx, oesophagus, stomach, intestines, rectum.

alimony, in law, allowance ordered by court to be paid by husband to separated or divorced wife.

aliphatic compounds, organic compounds containing only straight or branched open chains of carbon atoms, as opposed to closed rings of carbon atoms in AROMATIC compounds. Incl. paraffins, olefines, fatty acids.

alkali, soluble hydroxide of a metal, esp. an alkali metal. Term also applies to any strong BASE. Alkalis neutralize acids and turn litmus blue. Used in manufacture of soap, paper, glass.

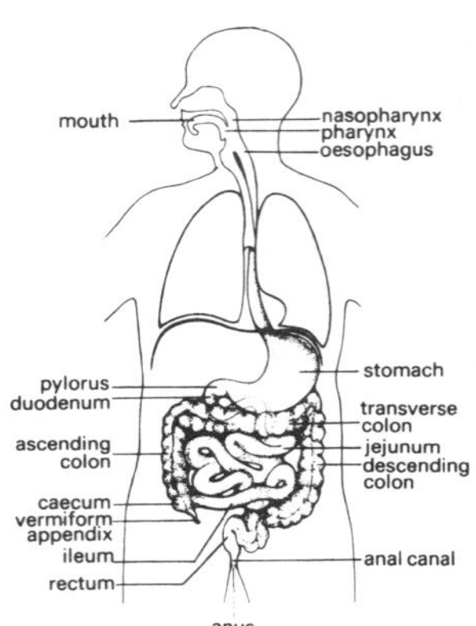

Alimentary canal

alkali metals, the univalent metallic elements lithium, sodium, potassium, rubidium and caesium.

alkaloid, any of group of organic bases containing nitrogen, often of plant origin and having medicinal or poisonous effects. Examples are morphine, quinine, caffeine.

alkyl group, in chemistry, univalent hydrocarbon RADICAL of form C_nH_{2n+1}.

Allah, Arabic name for God used by Moslems and Arabic-speaking Christians.

Allahabad, city of Uttar Pradesh, NC India, near confluence of Jumna and Ganges. Pop. 491,000. Hindu pilgrimage centre.

Allegheny Mountains, W range of Appalachian system, NE US. Extend from N Pennsylvania to Virginia; rise to 1480 m (*c* 4860 ft) at highest point. Rich coal, iron ore deposits.

allegory, narrative or description in which characters, objects, incidents, form extended metaphor for system of religious, political or social ideas. Very strong in medieval Europe, more recent examples range from Bunyan's *Pilgrim's Progress* to Orwell's *Animal Farm*.

Allen, Ethan (1738-89), American Revolutionary leader. Organized Vermont militia, known as Green Mountain Boys; seized by British during attempt to invade Canada.

Allen, Bog of, peat bog of EC Irish Republic, between rivers Shannon and Liffey. Peat used to fuel power stations.

Allenby, Edmund Henry Hynman, 1st Viscount Allenby of Megiddo (1861-1936), British field marshal. Commander of British Expeditionary Force (1917-19), invaded Palestine and decisively defeated

Turks at Megiddo (1918). High commissioner for Egypt (1919-25).

Allende, Salvador (1909-73), Chilean statesman. Elected president (1970), becoming 1st Marxist head of govt. in South America. Withdrawal of financial credit by West followed agrarian reforms and nationalizing foreign investments. Subversion by CIA and US indust. fuelled domestic discontent. Allende died in military coup.

allergy, hypersensitivity to usually harmless specific substance, *eg* pollen, hair, various foods, or physical conditions (heat and cold). Believed to be caused by antibodies which cause local tissue inflammation by release of histamine while providing little immune protection. Allergic disorders incl. skin rashes, asthma, hay fever.

Allier, river of C France. Flows *c* 435 km (270 mi) from Cévennes via fertile Limagne to R. Loire near Nevers.

alligator, large aquatic reptile of crocodile family; 2 species: *Alligator mississippiensis* of S US, and smaller *A. sinensis* of Yangtze valley, China. Leather greatly valued, leading to diminution of species; now protected in US.

allium, genus of bulbous plants of lily family. Strong-smelling leaves; umbellate white, yellow or red flowers. Found in Europe, N Africa, Asia, North America. Species incl. onion, garlic, chives, leek, shallot.

allotropy, property that certain chemical elements have of existing in 2 or more forms, with different crystalline structures and physical properties. Carbon, sulphur and phosphorus exhibit allotropy.

alloy, metallic substance composed of 2 or more metals or of metallic and non-metallic elements. May be a compound, mixture or solid solution. Common alloys are brass (copper, zinc) and steel (iron, carbon).

All Saints' Day, in RC and Anglican churches, feast day (1 Nov.) instituted by Pope Gregory IV in honour of all saints, known and unknown. One of principal feasts in RC calendar.

All Souls' Day, in RC calendar, feast day (2 Nov.) on which church prays for faithful still suffering in purgatory.

allspice, berry of allspice tree, *Pimenta officinalis,* of myrtle family. Yields pungent aromatic spice.

alluvium, sand, silt or gravel transported and deposited by running water. Provides excellent crop-growing conditions on river flood plains or in delta areas, *eg* Nile, Ganges rivers.

Alma-Ata, city of USSR, cap. of Kazakh SSR. Pop. 914,000. Cultural and indust. centre; machinery, textile mfg. Formerly called Verny.

Almería, city of S Spain, on Gulf of Almería, cap. of Almería prov. Pop. 126,000. Port, exports minerals, fruit (esp. grapes). *Fl* under Moors (8th-15th cent.) as naval base. Medieval castle, cathedral.

almond, *Prunus amygdalus,* tree of warm temperate regions, native to W Asia. Fruit has nut-like edible stone or kernel which yields oil. Sweet almonds used in cooking and confectionery. Bitter almonds used in manufacture of flavouring extracts, cosmetics, medicine.

Alpaca

alpaca, *Lama pacos,* domesticated South American mammal, related to llama. Bred for its fleecy brown or black wool.

alphabet, any system of characters used to record a language in which there is (theoretically) a one-to-one relationship between each character and sound. Developed by Phoenicians (*c* 1400 BC) possibly from signs derived from Egyptian hieroglyphic writing. Transmitted from NW Semites to Greece (first recorded *c* 8th cent. BC), used in ancient Rome. Forms basis of alphabets in W European and several recently written African and Asian languages. Cyrillic alphabet, also developed from Greek, used in Russian. Hebrew and Arabic alphabets are also still in use.

Alpha Centauri, brightest star of constellation Centaurus, visible in S hemisphere. Has 3 components, incl. Proxima Centauri, nearest star to Earth beyond Sun (4.3 light years away).

alpha particle, positively charged helium nucleus, consisting of 2 neutrons and 2 protons, emitted during spontaneous decay of nucleus of certain radioactive elements, *eg* uranium 238. Relatively low penetrating power.

alpine rose, any of various European and Asiatic alpine RHODODENDRONS.

Alps, mountain system of SC Europe. Extend from Franco-Italian border through Switzerland, Germany, Austria to Yugoslavia. Many glaciers, valleys, snow-capped peaks. C Alps incl. Mont Blanc (highest), Monte Rosa, Matterhorn, Jungfrau. Crossed by many passes incl. Brenner, Great St Bernard, Mont Cenis, Simplon. Dairying, timber, h.e.p., tourism esp. winter sports.

Alsace (Ger. *Elsass),* region of NE France, between Vosges Mts. and R. Rhine. Main towns Colmar, Mulhouse, Strasbourg. Agric. in Rhine plain, vineyards on Vosges foothills, potash mining. Long disputed by France and Germany. Annexed by France in 17th cent.; incorporated, with part of Lorraine, into Germany (1871) as imperial territ. of Alsace-Lorraine. Restored to France after WWI.

alsatian or **German shepherd,** sheepdog of wolf-like appearance, used in police work and as guide dog for blind. Stands *c* 63 cm/25 in. at shoulder.

Altai, mountain system of USSR (S Siberia), W Mongolia and N China. Reaches 4506 m (14,783 ft) at Belukha. Rich mineral deposits incl. lead, zinc, silver.

Altamira, cave site of Santander prov., N Spain. Cave contains drawings of animals made in late Magdalenian period; discovered 1879.

Altdorfer, Albrecht (*c* 1480-1538), German painter. First European to stress romantic use of landscape.

alternating current (AC), electric current that periodically reverses its direction of flow, changing continuously to reach a maximum in one direction, then in the other. Used extensively because of ease of changing voltage; transmitted at high voltages to minimize energy loss.

alternation of generations, in biology, occurrence of generations of an organism in alternate order, one of which reproduces sexually, the other asexually. Phenomenon exhibited by many coelenterates, which alternate between sedentary asexual polyps and free-swimming sexual medusae (jellyfish).

Althing, legislature of Iceland. Oldest European assembly, convened 930. Dissolved 1800-74 during period of direct rule by Denmark.

altimeter, device used to measure altitude. Types in use incl. aneroid barometer. Absolute altimeter, used by aircraft, works by reflecting radio signals from Earth's surface.

alto, in singing, term used for highest male voice; also lowest female voice. In instruments of similar range, usually pitched between soprano and tenor.

alum, hydrated double sulphate of potassium and aluminium, used as mordant in dyeing and fireproofing agent.

alumina or **aluminium oxide** (Al_2O_3), chemical compound occurring naturally in clay, and as main component of bauxite. Also found in almost pure form as corundum.

aluminium or **aluminum** (Al), silvery metallic element; at. no. 13, at. wt. 26.98. Ductile and malleable; good conductor of heat and electricity. Obtained commercially by electrolysis of bauxite and cryolite. Used pure or alloyed where lightness is required, *eg* in aircraft or cooking utensils.

Alva, Fernando Alvarez de Toledo, Duque de (1508-82), Spanish general, administrator. Commanded armies of Charles V, Philip II. As regent (1567-73) in Netherlands for Philip II, instituted 'Court of Blood' (Alva boasted of *c* 18,000 executed) to crush rebellion against Spanish tyranny. Conquered Portugal (1580).

alyssum, genus of plants of Cruciferae or mustard family. Greyish leaves, small yellow or white flowers. Native to Eurasia.

AM (amplitude modulation), *see* MODULATION.

amalgam, alloy containing mercury. Gold and silver amalgams occur naturally; tin, copper and other amalgams are man-made. Used in dentistry, mirror mfg.

amanita, genus of widely distributed fungi. Most species have russet cap with white markings and are poisonous.

amaranth, any of genus *Amaranthus* of plants of worldwide distribution. Garden species cultivated for colourful foliage and showy flowers.

Amarna, Tel-el-, *see* TEL-EL-AMARNA.

amaryllis, genus of bulbous plants native to S Africa. Several white, purple or pink flowers on single stem.

Amati, family of Italian violin makers in Cremona in 16th and 17th cents.

Amazon, river of South America; main stream of largest river system in world. Formed in N Peru by confluence of Marañón, Ucayali; flows E 6280 km (*c* 3900 mi) across Brazil to the Atlantic. Main tributaries incl. Negro in N, Tocantins, Xingu, Tapajos in C Brazil. Tropical jungle along banks; major source of rubber during late 19th cent.; inhabited by primitive Indian tribes. Recent economic development in region.

Amazons, in Greek legend, nation of female warriors living around Euxine Sea (Black Sea). As 9th labour Heracles was required to obtain girdle of Amazon queen, Hippolyte. She was captured by Theseus, and bore him Hippolytus.

amber, yellow, often transparent fossil resin, derived from now extinct conifers. In highly polished form, used since prehist. times for beads, amulets, *etc.*

ambergris, waxy substance secreted from intestine of sperm whale, found floating in tropical seas. Physiological significance undecided. Used as perfume fixative.

Ambrose, St (*c* 340-97), one of fathers of Roman church. Elected bishop of Milan (374), denounced Arianism, encouraged use of hymns in worship (Ambrosian chant).

ambrosia and **nectar,** in Greek myth, the food and drink of the gods, giving immortality and eternal youth.

Amenhotep III (*fl* 14th cent. BC), Egyptian pharaoh (*c* 1410-1372 BC). Ruled during an age of great splendour, his empire at peace. Built great monuments at Thebes, incl. temples at Luxor and Karnak. Succeeded by IKHNATON.

America, *see* NORTH AMERICA, CENTRAL AMERICA, SOUTH AMERICA.

American Federation of Labor and Congress of Industrial Organizations

(AFL-CIO), federation of auton. labour unions in US. Estab. by merger (1955).

American football, eleven-a-side team game played with oval leather ball. Developed from English rugby in 1870s into major college sport. Professional form was organized into leagues in 1920.

American Indians, pre-European inhabitants of the Americas. Central and South American cultures incl. MAYA, TOLTEC, AZTEC, INCA, Chibcha, some of which reached high cultural level; all fell during Spanish conquest. North American Indian tribes driven back by westward expansion into Indian Territories. Some 400,000 remain in US and Canada. Extremely diverse culture, but divides loosely into NW coast, Plains, Plateau, E woodlands, Northern, and SW groupp. Most tribes were relatively settled farmers, food gatherers or hunters but the advent of the horse in late 17th cent. revolutionized Plains culture; led to nomadic hunting of buffalo from horseback with bow and arrow, and the last serious resistance to white hegemony. Although largely assimilated into Western culture, 20th cent. has seen movement towards preserving Indian culture throughout Americas.

American Revolution (1775-83), uprising resulting in independence from Britain of Thirteen Colonies of North America. By mid-18th cent., colonists had begun demands for limited self-govt.; Stamp Act (1765) caused colonial opposition to 'taxation without representation'. Further resentment after Townshend Acts (1767), levying duty on British manufactured goods, resulted in Boston Massacre (1770) and BOSTON TEA PARTY (1773). Parliament subsequently passed Intolerable Acts (1774); representatives of colonies listed grievances at Continental Congress of 1774. Conflict began (April, 1775) at Lexington. Washington appointed to lead Continental Army; Declaration of Independence adopted July, 1776. Badly prepared volunteer forces of colonists defeated in Québec campaign (1775-6); fighting inconclusive until British defeat (Oct. 1777) at Saratoga, followed by hard winter for colonial army at Valley Forge. French gave rebels crucial aid and British were pushed N from Carolinas (1780-1), leading to Cornwallis' surrender (Oct. 1781) and conclusion of hostilities. Treaty of Paris (1783) formally recognized independence of US. Conflict also known as American War of Independence.

American Samoa, *see* SAMOA.

americium (Am), man-made radioactive element, at. no. 95, mass no. of most stable isotope 243. Silvery-white metal, discovered (1944) by bombarding plutonium with neutrons.

Amerindians, term applied to AMERICAN INDIANS, particularly those of South America.

amethyst, semi-precious gemstone, a variety of quartz. Violet or purple in colour.

Amharic, official language of Ethiopia, belonging to SW Semitic branch of Afro-Asiatic family.

amides, organic compounds obtained by replacing hydrogen atoms of ammonia, NH_3, by organic acid radicals, *eg* acetamide, CH_3CONH_2.

Amiens, city of N France, on R. Somme, cap. of Somme dept. Pop. 153,000. Agric. market; textile centre from 16th cent. Cap. of Picardy until 1790. Cathedral (13th cent.).

Amiens, Treaty of (1802), settlement between Britain, France, Spain and Batavian Republic in which Britain returned most of its gains from French Revolutionary Wars; France agreed to evacuate Naples.

Amin, Idi (1925-), Ugandan political leader. Seized power in 1971 military coup. Nationalized UK-owned firms. Expelled Uganda Asians and ruthlessly suppressed opponents. Overthrown 1979.

amines, compounds obtained by replacing hydrogen atoms of ammonia, NH_3, by organic radicals. Divided into primary, secondary or tertiary amines according to whether 1, 2 or 3 hydrogen atoms are replaced.

amino acids, organic compounds in which carboxyl (COOH) and amino (NH_2) groups are linked to central carbon atom. Essential to living tissue as they link to form proteins; 22 occur in animal proteins. In man, 8 cannot be synthesized and must be incl. in diet.

Amirante Islands, dependency of the Seychelles in Indian Ocean. Pop. *c* 100. Exports copra.

Amis, Kingsley (1922-), English writer. One of ANGRY YOUNG MEN. Works incl. satirical novel *Lucky Jim* (1954) attacking academic establishment.

Amman, cap. of Jordan. Pop. 672,000. Commercial, indust. centre. Textile mfg.; noted marble quarries nearby. As Rabbath Ammon, cap. of Ammonites; named Philadelphia in 3rd cent. BC. Great pop. increase after Israeli wars (1949).

ammeter, instrument used for measuring strength of electric current in ampères.

ammonia (NH_3), pungent-smelling highly soluble gas. Forms weak base ammonium hydroxide NH_4OH when dissolved in water. Produced from atmospheric nitrogen by Haber process. Used in manufacture of explosives and fertilizers and as refrigerant.

ammoniac or **gum ammoniac,** gum resin prepared from milky exudation from stem of plant, *Dorema ammoniacum,* native to Iran, India, Siberia. Used in perfumes, manufacture of porcelain cements and in medicine as an expectorant.

ammonite, coiled fossil mollusc of class Cephalopoda. Has elaborately chambered shell. Common in Mesozoic era, extinct by end of Cretaceous period.

amnesia, temporary or prolonged loss of memory. Suppression of memory may be caused by neurosis; permanent loss may result from head injuries.

amoeba, microscopic one-celled animal of class Rhizopoda. Consists of naked mass of protoplasm. Moves and feeds in water by action of pseudopodia (false feet); reproduces by fission.

Amon, in ancient Egyptian pantheon, creator of universe. Represented as ram or man with ram's head. Identified with Greek Zeus and Roman Jupiter.

Amos, prophetic book of OT, written by shepherd Amos *c* 750 BC. Attacks hypocritical worship, social injustice. Made up of 3 parts, God's judgment on Gentiles and Israel; sermons on fate of Israel; visions of destruction. Final promise of redemption is prob. by later writer.

Ampère, André Marie (1775-1836), French physicist. Extended Oersted's findings on interaction of electricity and magnetism; showed that electric currents exert forces on one another. Formulated Ampère's law on strength of magnetic field induced by current flowing in conductor.

ampère or **amp,** SI unit of electric current; defined as current in pair of infinitely long, infinitely thin, parallel wires that produces force of 2×10^{-7} newtons per metre of length.

amphetamine, colourless liquid, used in form of sulphate to stimulate central nervous system. Used to overcome depression, aid slimming by suppression of appetite. Addiction can cause heart damage and mental disturbance.

Amphibia (amphibians), class of cold-blooded vertebrates comprising frogs, salamanders and legless, worm-like caecilians. Larva is aquatic, breathing through gills; undergoes rapid metamorphosis to terrestrial lung-breathing adult.

amphitheatre, circular or oval theatre with an open space surrounded by rising rows of seats. Earliest dates from 1st cent. BC; used by Romans for staging gladiatorial contests. Examples incl. ruined Colosseum in Rome.

Amphitrite, in Greek myth, one of the NEREIDS. Wife of Poseidon, by whom she was mother of Triton.

amplitude, in physics, the maximum departure from equilibrium of an oscillatory phenomenon, *eg* alternating current or swinging pendulum.

Amritsar, city of Punjab state, N India. Pop. 408,000. Carpet mfg.; trade in cotton, skins. Sikh religious centre, site of Golden Temple. Scene of 1919 nationalist massacre by British.

Amsterdam, cap. of Netherlands, at confluence of Ij and Amstel rivers. Pop. 965,000. Major port, indust. centre (shipbuilding, chemicals, diamond cutting and polishing). Built on piles, with radial and concentric canal system, many bridges. Canal links to North Sea, Rhine delta. Chartered *c* 1300, Hanseatic trade centre; at cultural, commercial height in 17th cent. Taken by French 1795; cap. from 1815 (admin. sits at The Hague). German occupation in WWII. Churches (13th, 15th cent.), Rijksmuseum, van Gogh museum, univs. (1632, 1882).

Amu Darya (anc. *Oxus),* river of C Asia. Length *c* 2500 km (1550 mi). Rises in Pamir Mts., flows W along Afghanistan-USSR border and NW through Turkmen SSR and Uzbek SSR to enter Aral Sea by long delta.

Amundsen, Roald (1872-1928), Norwegian explorer. First to reach South Pole (1911), 35 days ahead of R. F. Scott. First to navigate Northwest Passage (1903-6). Flew over North Pole (1926) with Umberto Nobile, whom he tried to rescue from polar air crash (1928); died in search.

Amundsen Sea, part of S Pacific Ocean, E of Ross Sea, extending into Ellsworth Highlands, Antarctica.

Amur (*Heilung-kiang*), river of NE Asia. Length *c* 2900 km (1800 mi). Flows SE forming much of Soviet-Chinese (Manchuria) border before turning NE to Tartar Str. Navigable, ice-free May-Oct.

amylase, enzyme which helps convert starch into sugar. Found in saliva, pancreatic juices and in some plants.

Anabaptists, originally pejorative name for various Protestant sects which deny validity of infant baptism. Applied historically to German followers of Thomas Münzer (d. 1525), who preached separation of church and state, and were persecuted as heretics.

anaconda, *Eunectes murinus,* semi-aquatic constrictor snake of boa family from tropical South America. Olive green with black spots; reaches lengths of 7.5 m/25 ft.

anaemia, disease resulting from reduction in number, or in haemoglobin content, of red blood cells. Caused by loss of blood by bleeding, excessive destruction of red cells, iron deficiency, *etc.* Characterized by paleness, weakness, breathlessness.

anaesthetics, drugs which produce loss of sensation, either in restricted area (local anaesthetic) or whole body (general anaesthetic). General anaesthetics in use incl. ether, cyclopropane, sodium pentothal, nitrous oxide. Local anaesthetic acts on peripheral nerve endings in region of application; drugs used incl. procaine and novocaine. Early experimenters in use of anaesthetics incl. C. W. Long (ether, 1842) and J. Y. Simpson (chloroform, 1847).

analgesic, drug used to relieve pain. Those used incl. derivatives of salicylic acid (*eg* aspirin), and opium (*eg* phenacetin).

analog computer, *see* COMPUTER.

analysis, in chemistry, decomposition of a substance into its elements or constituent parts to determine either their nature (qualitative analysis) or proportion (quantitive analysis).

analytical or **coordinate geometry,** branch of geometry in which position is defined by reference to coordinate axes and curves described by algebraic equations.

anarchism, in politics, theory that all forms of authority interfere with individual freedom and that state should be replaced by freely-associating communities. Early principles outlined by Zeno of Citium; modern anarchist theories developed by William GODWIN, PROUDHON and BAKUNIN, who introduced terrorism as strategic means of resisting organized govt. Theories influenced syndicalists, esp. in Spanish Civil War.

Anastasia (b. 1901), Russian princess. Daughter of Nicholas II, believed assassinated with rest of royal family (1918) after Russian Revolution. Several women, notably Anna Anderson, have since claimed her identity without conclusive proof.

Anatolia, *see* ASIA MINOR.

anatomy, branch of science concerned with structure of plants and animals, and with their dissection. Pioneers in its study incl. Galen, whose findings dominated medical thought until 16th cent., and Vesalius, who founded modern descriptive anatomy.

Anaxagoras (*c* 500-*c* 428 BC), Greek philosopher. Developed dualistic theory of universe composed of particles arranged by an omnipresent intelligence *(nous)*. Also studied astronomy, correctly explaining eclipses.

Anaximander (*c* 611-547 BC), Greek philosopher. Held that world consists of primary matter *(apeiron)* which is eternal and indestructible. Invented sundial, map.

ancestor worship, religious practices based on belief that souls of the dead continue to be involved with their living descendants.

Anchises, in Greek myth, member of royal house of Troy, father of Aeneas, by Aphrodite. Carried from burning remains of Troy by Aeneas, whom he accompanied on his voyages.

Anchorage, town of SC Alaska, US; at head of Cook Inlet. Pop. 161,000; state's largest, most important town. Transport jct.; fishing, oil, mining centre. Military bases estab. in WWII. Badly damaged by earthquake (1964).

anchovy, small herring-like marine fish of Engraulidae family. *Engraulis encrasicholus,* found in Mediterranean, used as food.

Ancona, city of the Marches, EC Italy, on the Adriatic Sea; cap. of Ancona prov. Pop. 108,000. Port, shipbuilding, sugar refining. Founded 4th cent. BC by Greeks from Syracuse; *fl* under Romans (triumphal arch erected AD 115 to Trajan). Romanesque cathedral.

Andalusia *(Andalucía),* region and former prov. of S Spain. Incl. Sierra Morena (N), Guadalquivir basin (C), Sierra Nevada (S). Irrigated agric., fruit growing, bull breeding; rich mineral resources, fishing, tourism. Settled 11th cent. BC by Phoenicians; *fl* under Moorish rule (8th-15th cent.) esp. at Córdoba, Granada, Seville.

Andaman and Nicobar Islands, union territ. of India, in SE Bay of Bengal. Area: Andaman Isls. 6500 sq km (2500 sq mi); Nicobar Isls. 1830 sq km (700 sq mi). Pop. 115,000; cap. Port Blair (pop. 26,000). Timber, copra exports.

Andersen, Hans Christian (1805-75), Danish author. His 168 fairy tales (pub. 1835-72), incl. 'The Ugly Duckling', 'The Emperor's New Clothes', 'The Red Shoes', children's classics combining symbolic significance with humour and whimsy.

Andes, major mountain system of South America, extending N-S 8000 km (5000 mi) from Venezuela to Cape Horn. Rises to highest point at Aconcagua (6960 m/22,835 ft) on Chile-Argentina border. Forms volcanic plateau in Bolivia, narrow ranges in Ecuador, Colombia. Peruvian Andes was centre of ancient Inca civilizations. Indian pop. in high basins; important deposits of copper, silver, tin. Region subject to earthquakes.

Andhra Pradesh, state of SE India. Area 275,000 sq km (106,000 sq mi); pop. 44,000,000; cap. Hyderabad. Largely plains; mountains (Eastern Ghats) in E. Rice, sugar cane grown. Formed in 1956.

Andorra

Andorra, republic of SW Europe, in E Pyrenees. Area 495 sq km (191 sq mi); pop. 30,000; cap. Andorra la Vella. Language: Catalan. Religion: RC. Under nominal Franco-Spanish suzerainty. Many high peaks, up to *c* 3050 m (10,000 ft). Pasture (cattle, sheep), tobacco, fruit; tourism.

Andrew, St (*fl* 1st cent. AD), fisherman, one of Twelve Disciples of Jesus. Traditionally, missionary to Gentiles, crucified on X-shaped cross. Patron saint of Russia, Scotland. Feast day 30 Nov.

Andrewes, Lancelot (1555-1626), English churchman, scholar. Bishop of Chichester (1605), Ely (1609), Winchester (1619). Opposed Puritanism; helped translate Authorized (King James) Version of Bible.

androgen, name given to any male sex hormone which gives rise to secondary sexual characteristics. Natural androgens are steroids produced in testes and adrenal cortex.

Andromache, in Greek myth, wife of Hector of Troy. At fall of Troy Greeks killed her child and she became slave of Neoptolemus, son of Achilles. Later married Helenus, brother of Hector.

Andromeda, in Greek myth, daughter of Cepheus by Cassiopeia. Rescued from sea monster by Perseus, who subsequently married her. Andromeda, Cassiopeia, Cepheus were placed among the stars at their death.

Andromeda Galaxy, spiral galaxy in constellation Andromeda, *c* 2 million light years away; visible to naked eye as dim patch of light.

Andros, Aegean isl. of Greece, northernmost of Cyclades. Area 375 sq km (145 sq mi); main town Andros.

anemone, genus of plants of buttercup family, widely distributed in temperate and subarctic regions. Cultivated garden varieties have showy variously coloured flowers, *eg* European pasqueflower *A. pulsatilla*.

aneroid barometer, instrument for measuring atmospheric pressure. Consists of partially evacuated metal container, thin lid displaced by changes in atmospheric pressure, thus causing a pointer to move.

aneurism or **aneurysm,** abnormal bulge of weakened wall of an artery; caused by syphilis, atheroma, injury, high blood pressure. Bulge may burst, resulting in serious internal bleeding; treatment by surgery.

angel, in theology, immortal being. According to traditions of Judaism, Christianity and Islam, intermediate between God and man. Classified into 3 choirs: (1) seraphim, cherubim, thrones; (2) dominions, virtues, powers; (3) principalities, archangels, angels. Angels of hell are followers of Satan.

Angel Falls, waterfall of SE Venezuela, on Caroní tributary. Prob. highest waterfall in world. Height 979 m (3212 ft).

angelfish, brightly-coloured fish of Chaetodontidae family. Spiny headed, with laterally-compressed body; inhabits tropical reefs.

angelica or **archangel,** plant of genus *Angelica,* esp. *A. archangelica.* Cultivated in Europe for aromatic odour and root stalks which are candied and eaten, and for roots and seeds yielding oil used in perfume and liqueurs.

Angelico, Fra, orig. Guido di Pietro (1387-1455), Italian painter, Dominican friar. Work is characterized by simple direct style, and purity of line and colour. Painted frescoes *c* 1440 in convent of San Marco, Florence, and in chapel of Pope Nicholas V in Vatican.

Angers (anc. *Juliomagus),* city of W France, on R. Maine, cap. of Maine-et-Loire dept. Pop. 181,000. Wine, glass, textiles; largest French slate quarries nearby. Hist. cap. of Anjou from 9th cent. Castle, cathedral (both 13th cent.).

Angevin, noble family of medieval Europe. Descended from Fulk the Red, 1st count of Anjou, France, whence the name. Comprised 2 main lines: 1) rulers of parts of France (from 9th cent.), Jerusalem (1131-86), PLANTAGENET kings of England (from 1154); 2) branch of CAPETIANS, incl. rulers of parts of France (from 1246), kings of Naples and Sicily (from 1266), Hungary (from 1308), Poland (from 1370).

angina pectoris, disease characterized by sudden attacks of chest pain extending down left arm. Caused by obstruction of coronary arteries, resulting in lack of oxygen to heart muscles.

angiosperm, any plant of class Angiospermae, incl. all the flowering plants, characterized by having the seeds enclosed in an ovary. Opposed to GYMNOSPERM.

Angkor, ruins in W Kampuchea. Incl. Angkor Thom, ancient cap. of Indo-Chinese Khmer empire, and Angkor Wat temple.

anglerfish, any of Lophiidae family of bottom-dwelling marine fish. Worm-like filament growing from head lures prey to its mouth.

Angles, Teutonic people originally inhabiting what is now Schleswig-Holstein (S Denmark, N Germany). Settled in late 5th cent. in E, N and C England in area of later kingdoms of East Anglia, Northumbria and Mercia.

Anglesey, isl. of Gwynedd, NW Wales, separated from mainland by Menai Strait. Area 705 sq km (272 sq mi); main town Holyhead. Agric., *eg* livestock rearing. Tourist industs.

Anglican Communion, informal organization of the Church of England and derived churches with closely related faith and forms, incl. Church of Ireland, Episcopal Church of Scotland, Protestant Episcopal Church in US. Representatives meet every 10 years at Lambeth Conference with archbishop of Canterbury presiding. *See* ENGLAND, CHURCH OF.

angling, sport of fishing with rod and line. Freshwater fish sought by anglers incl. salmon, trout, bass and pike; saltwater varieties prized incl. tuna, marlin and swordfish.

Anglo-Catholicism, *see* OXFORD MOVEMENT.

Anglo-Saxon Chronicle, annals of English history, begun under Alfred the Great *c* 891, written in Old English. Simultaneous compilation at 7 different places gives varied picture of English history, incl. Danish invasions, clerical corruption, stories. Peterborough Chronicle continues to 1154.

Anglo-Saxon language, *see* ENGLISH.

Anglo-Saxon literature, written works in Old English. Poetry unrhymed, suited to narrative, not lyric. Heroic epic BEOWULF, *Battle of Maldon, etc,* reveal Germanic pagan heritage and oral tradition, although recorded in Christian era. Elegaic verse incl. *Deor, The Wanderer.* Literary prose begun in reign of ALFRED with translations from Latin and the ANGLO-SAXON CHRONICLE.

Anglo-Saxons, Teutonic peoples who settled in England in 5th-6th cent. Incl. ANGLES,

SAXONS and JUTES. Term also used generally for non-Celtic inhabitants of British Isles before Norman Conquest; recent use for Anglo-American society, its values and attitudes.

Angola, formerly Portuguese West Africa, republic of WC Africa. Area (incl. CABINDA) 1,246,600 sq km (481,300 sq mi); pop. 6,732,000; cap. Luanda. Languages: Bantu, Portuguese. Religions: animist, Christian. Narrow coastal strip, interior tableland; main river Cunene. Livestock, fishing; exports coffee, diamonds, oil. Colonized 16th cent. by Portuguese, centre for slave trade until 19th cent. Civil uprisings in 1960s ruthlessly suppressed. Independent 1975; war between competing liberation groups ended in victory (1976) for Marxist forces.

Angora, *see* ANKARA.

angostura bark, bitter aromatic bark of 2 South American trees, *Galipea officinalis* and *G. cusparia*. Used in medicine and in preparation of liqueurs and bitters.

Angoulême, town of W France, on R. Charente, cap. of Charente dept. Pop. 98,000. Road and rail jct., wine, paper mfg. Seat of counts of Angoumois from 9th cent. Cathedral (12th cent.).

Angry Young Men, applied to several British authors of 1950s, incl. John Osborne, Kingsley Amis. Work characterized by resentment of establishment.

Angström, Anders Jons (1814-74), Swedish physicist. Pioneer in spectroscopy, he investigated solar spectrum, and discovered hydrogen in Sun. Unit of measurement of wavelength of light named after him (1 angstrom = 10^{-10} m).

Anguilla, isl. of E West Indies, in Leeward Isls. Area 91 sq km (35 sq mi); pop. 6500. Exports cotton, salt. Former British colony with ST KITTS, Nevis; associate state of St Kitts-Nevis-Anguilla; nationalist unrest led to landing of British troops (1969).

Angus, former county of E Scotland, now in Tayside region. Co. town was Forfar. Grampian Mts. in N; Sidlaw Hills in S; fertile Strathmore in C. Barley, potato growing; livestock rearing. Known as Forfarshire until 1928.

anhydride, in chemistry, non-metallic oxide or organic compound (*eg* sulphur trioxide) which reacts with water to form an acid; or metallic oxide (*eg* calcium oxide) which reacts with water to form a base.

aniline ($C_6H_5NH_2$), colourless oily liquid, obtained from coal tar or by reduction of nitrobenzene. Used in manufacture of dyes, plastics and drugs.

animal, any member of animal kingdom, as opposed to plant kingdom. Distinction between plants and animals is largely based on means of feeding; most plants manufacture food from inorganic substances, whereas animals must eat food containing necessary proteins. Animals are also usually capable of independent movement and have nervous systems. Some unicellular organisms, *eg Euglena*, possess chlorophyll but have certain animal characteristics. Animals are classified into *c* 20 phyla ranging from unicellular Protozoa to Chordata, which incl. all vertebrates. *See* CLASSIFICATION.

animism, in primitive religion, belief that material objects and natural phenomena contain a spiritual force which governs their existence. In philosophy, doctrine that the essential force of life is irreducible to the mechanistic laws of natural science.

anise, *Pimpinella anisum*, herbaceous plant of Mediterranean regions. Small white or yellow flowers. Its seed (aniseed) is used medicinally to expel intestinal gas and in cookery for its liquorice-like flavour.

Anjou, hist. region of NW France, cap. Angers. Drained by R. Loire. County from 9th cent., finally annexed (1481) to French crown by Louis XI. Plantagenet rulers of England descended from counts of Anjou.

Ankara, cap. of Turkey, in C Anatolia; formerly Angora. Pop. 1,701,000. Commercial centre; trade in mohair from Angora goats; leather goods, textile mfg. Cap. of Roman province of Galatia in 1st cent AD; has ruined marble temple. Replaced Constantinople (1923) as Turkish cap.

Annaba, city of NE Algeria, on Mediterranean Sea. Pop. 313,000. Formerly called Bône. Port, exports phosphates, iron ore; iron, chemical industs. Important city of ancient Numidia, Roman *Hippo Regius*. Episcopal see of St Augustine 396-430.

Annam, hist. kingdom and French protect. of SE Asia. Dominated by Annam Highlands. Part of VIETNAM after 1954.

Annapolis, cap. of Maryland, US; near mouth of Severn R. Pop. 30,000. In fruit-and vegetable-growing region. Became colonial cap. 1694; US cap. 1783-4. Mainly residential with many hist. buildings; has US Naval Academy.

Annapurna, mountain range in Nepalese Himalayas. Has 2 high peaks: Annapurna I, height 8078 m (26,502 ft), and Annapurna II, height 7938 m (26,041 ft).

Anne (1665-1714), queen of England, Scotland and Ireland (1702-14). Daughter of James II, last Stuart monarch. Act of Union (1707) made her 1st queen of Great Britain and Ireland. Reign dominated by War of Spanish Succession (1701-14), in which British forces were commanded by MARLBOROUGH, a leading favourite. Succeeded by George I under Act of Settlement (1701), none of her children having survived her.

annealing, process by which materials, esp. metals, are relieved of strains, rendering them less brittle. Involves application of heat and slow controlled cooling.

Anne Boleyn, *see* BOLEYN, ANNE.

Annecy, town of SE France, on L. Annecy, cap. of Haute-Savoie dept. Pop. 101,000. Resort, textiles, paper mfg.

Annelida (annelids), phylum of worms, incl. earthworms, leeches and aquatic worms, *eg* ragworm, lugworm. Body made of jointed segments.

Anne of Austria (1601-66), queen of France, daughter of Philip III of Spain. Wife of Louis XIII, acted as regent (1643-61) for son Louis XIV. Regency dominated by MAZARIN, whom she may have married secretly.

Anne of Cleves (1515-57), English queen, fourth wife of Henry VIII. Marriage (1540), arranged by Thomas Cromwell to build alliance with Germany, nullified 6 months later.

annual, plant which germinates, flowers, seeds and dies within 1 year, *eg* zinnia. Biennial completes life cycle in 2 years, flowering in 2nd year. Many crop vegetables are biennials which are harvested after 1 year when they have produced a food store but have not yet run to flower, *eg* cabbage, carrot. Perennial has life cycle of more than 2 years, *eg* tulip.

Annunciation, Feast of the, or **Lady Day,** holy day (25 March) commemorating announcement to the Virgin Mary, by angel Gabriel, that she was to be the mother of Jesus.

anoa, *Anoa depressicornus,* smallest member of buffalo family, found in Celebes. Stands *c* 1 m/40 in. high at shoulder; horns almost straight.

anode, *see* ELECTRODE.

anomie or **anomy,** individual's lack of ethical values, rules, resulting from personal disorganization or from inability to find solution to contradictory norms in society (*see* DURKHEIM). Also applied to social structure without norms.

Anouilh, Jean (1910-), French dramatist. Plays revolve on problem of purity *v* worldly maturity, *eg Antigone* (1942), *L'Alouette* (1953) on Joan of Arc, *Becket* (1959) on Becket's relationship with Henry II.

Anschluss (Ger.,=joining), term referring to German annexation of Austria (1938). Policy developed by Hitler and advocated in Austria by National Socialists although contravening peace treaties of 1919.

Anselm, St (*c* 1033-1109), Italian churchman, theologian, archbishop of Canterbury (1093-1109). Denied right to appoint bishops claimed by William II, Henry I of England. Exiled; reconciled in compromise agreed by pope. First to incorporate Aristotelian logic into theology, promulgated ontological proof of God's existence.

Anshan, city of Liaoning prov., NE China. Pop. 1,050,000. Metallurgical centre; major iron and steel plant, chemicals mfg.

ant, insect of Formicidae family, comprising thousands of widely-distributed species. Lives mainly in underground colonies with various castes maintaining division of social activities, *eg* cultivating fungi, 'milking' aphids, guarding colony. Most ants wingless sterile workers; adult males winged and short-lived. Fertile females (queens) shed wings and start colonies after nuptial flight.

Antakya or **Antioch,** town of S Turkey, on R. Orontes. Pop. 58,000. Founded *c* 300 BC, became important commercial city under Romans and early centre of Christianity. Changed hands often; fell to Crusaders (1098) and Mamelukes (1268). Declined in importance; attached to Syria after 1919, restored to Turkey in 1939.

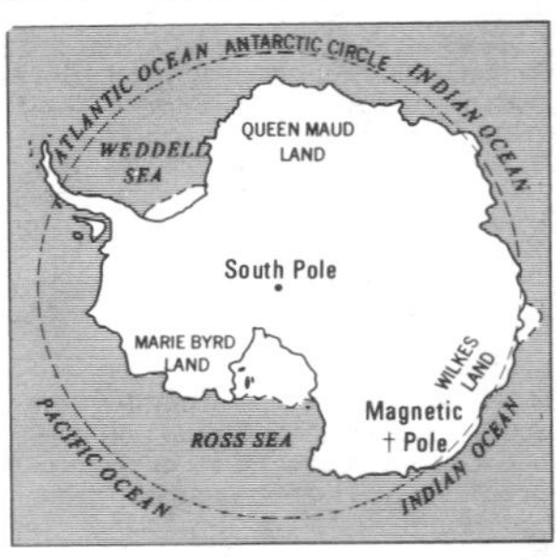

Antarctica

Antarctica, continent surrounding South Pole, completely covered by ice shelf. Area *c* 13,000,000 sq km (5,000,000 sq mi). Comprises 2 geologically distinct regions, E and W Antarctica, joined by immensely thick ice cap. Ellsworth Highlands rise to 5140 m (16,860 ft) at Vinson Massif, highest point on continent. Early explorations made by Bellingshausen (1819-21), Weddell (1823), Ross (1841-2); Amundsen reached South Pole first (1911), month before Scott; Byrd first flew over Pole (1929). Area S of 60°S reserved for international scientific research. *See* AUSTRALIAN ANTARTIC TERRITORY, BRITISH ANTARTIC TERRITORY, NORWEGIAN ANTARCTIC TERRITORY, ROSS DEPENDENCY, ADÉLIE LAND. Chile, Argentina, USSR and US also maintain bases. Unassigned area incl. Ellsworth Highlands, Marie Byrd Land, Bellingshausen and Amundsen seas.

Antbear

antbear or **giant anteater,** *Myrmecophaga jubata,* South American mammal, order Edentata. Shaggy grey coat, long snout; diet of ants, termites.

anteater, one of several mammals, *eg* pangolin, echidna, antbear, characterized by long snout, sticky tongue and ant diet.

antelope, hoofed ruminant of Bovidae family, found mainly in Africa. Species incl. bushbuck, bongo; largest is giant eland. Horns hollow and unbranched.

antenna, *see* AERIAL.

antennae, in zoology, flexible jointed appendages on heads of most arthropods. Function mainly sensory (touch, smell), but used by some crustaceans for swimming or attachment.

Anthony, St or **Anthony of Egypt** (*c* 251-*c* 356), Egyptian ascetic. Traditionally, founder of 1st Christian monastery. His temptation in the desert was popular subject of religious art.

anthracite, hard, shiny black variety of COAL. Has high carbon content, burns with smokeless flame and has good heat-producing capacity; widely used as domestic fuel. Dates mainly from Carboniferous period.

anthrax, infectious disease of cattle, sheep, *etc*; can be transmitted to man as localized inflammation of skin producing pustules, or as fulminating pneumonia. Caused by *Bacillus anthracis*; treated by penicillin and other antibiotics.

anthropology, scientific study of man and his societies. Developed in early 19th cent. Deals with evolution, distribution, social organization, cultural relationships. Distinguished from sociology in its tendency to concentrate on data from non-literate peoples, and historical emphasis.

Antibes, town of SE France, on Côte d'Azur. Pop. 56,000. Port, resort, flower-growing centre; perfume, chocolate mfg. Greek colony founded 4th cent. BC. Roman remains.

antibiotic, chemical substance, produced by bacteria, moulds, fungi, *etc*, which in dilute solution has capacity of inhibiting growth of or destroying bacteria or other micro-organisms. First observed and named was penicillin (by Alexander Fleming, 1928); those used to treat infectious diseases incl. streptomycin, aureomycin, chloromycetin.

antibody, protein produced in vertebrate cells to counteract presence in body of specific antigens (enzyme, toxin) associated with invading bacteria or viruses. By combining chemically with antigens, antibodies form defence mechanism against disease-producing organisms and provide immunity to later attacks.

Anti-Comintern Pact, agreement between Germany and Japan (1936). Stated policy of opposition to international communism. Enlarged (1941) to incl. most AXIS countries.

Anti-Corn Law League, *see* CORN LAWS.

anticyclone, area of relatively high atmospheric pressure, normally creating dry, cloudless conditions, warm in summer, cold in winter. Air moves spirally outwards to areas of lower pressure; deflection by Earth's rotation causes clockwise wind circulation in N hemisphere, anti-clockwise in S hemisphere.

antifreeze, substance of low freezing point added to a liquid to depress its freezing point. Ethylene glycol is used in cooling systems of water-cooled engines.

Antigone, in Greek myth, daughter of OEDIPUS and Jocasta; sister of Polynices and Eteocles. Accompanied her father in exile to Colonus, returned to Thebes after his death. Despite prohibition of Creon, she performed funerary rites over Polynices. As punishment, buried alive in rock tomb where she committed suicide.

Antigua, isl. of E West Indies, in Leeward Isls. Area 280 sq km (108 sq mi); pop. 74,000; cap. St John's (pop. 24,000). Sugar cane, cotton growing; exports sugar, molasses, rum. Has important tourist industs. Discovered by Columbus (1493). Settled by British in 17th cent.; became associate state (1967) with dependencies Barbuda, Redonda.

antihistamine, name given to drugs which neutralize effects of histamine in human body. Used in treatment of allergies.

Anti-Lebanon, mountain range on Syria-Lebanon border. Highest point Mt. Hermon 2814 m (9232 ft). Once noted for timber, now barren.

Antilles, isl. group of Caribbean, incl. all West Indies except Bahamas. Greater Antilles consist of Cuba, Jamaica, Hispaniola, Puerto Rico. Lesser Antilles consist of Leeward and Windward Isls., Netherlands Antilles.

anti-matter, hypothetical matter composed of ANTI-PARTICLES. Ordinary matter and anti-matter brought in contact should annihilate each other, liberating radiation energy. Thus anti-matter cannot exist long in our universe.

antimony (Sb), brittle silver-grey semi-metallic element; at. no. 51, at. wt. 121.75. Occurs as oxide or as stibnite Sb_2S_3. Produced by roasting ore and reducing oxide with iron. Used in making alloys, and in medicine.

antinomianism, in Christian theology, doctrine that faith alone, not obedience to moral law, is necessary for salvation. Heresy prevalent in Middle Ages; upheld by Anabaptists.

Antioch, *see* ANTAKYA.

Antiochus [III] the Great (d. 187 BC), Syrian king (223-187 BC). Reconquered much of earlier Seleucid empire. Invaded Greece but was defeated by Romans at Thermopylae (191). Following him into Asia Minor, Romans destroyed his army at Magnesia (190).

anti-particles, particles analogous to ELEMENTARY PARTICLES of matter but having opposite charge and magnetic moment. Brought into contact, an elementary particle and its anti-particle annihilate each other, producing radiation and other elementary particles. Anti-particle of electron is POSITRON.

antipodes, places diametrically opposite in location on the globe, *ie* separated by 180° of longitude and by the Equator. Term commonly used in UK to refer to Australia or New Zealand.

antipope, pope set up by a group within RC

church against the one chosen by church laws and whose election has subsequently been declared uncanonical. *See* SCHISM, GREAT.

anti-Semitism, antipathy towards Jews. Manifested from Roman times to 19th cent. through persecution and restriction (*see* GHETTO). Religious cause stressed until 19th cent., subsequently practised for political, social or economic gains, reaching its height in Nazi Germany. Hitler instigated extermination of *c* 6 million Jews (1939-45). In E Europe, esp. USSR, Poland, Jews have suffered restrictive laws, recurrent violence, POGROMS.

antiseptic, chemical used to curb growth of or destroy micro-organisms, usually on living tissue, and thus to prevent infection. LISTER introduced use in surgery following Pasteur's research. Modern development is technique of asepsis, *ie* production of germ-free conditions for surgery.

Antisthenes (*c* 444-*c* 370 BC), Greek philosopher. Sophist in early life, but subsequently disciple of Socrates. Founded school of CYNICS at Athens.

antitoxin, antibody formed in body to neutralize poisons (toxins) released into bloodstream by bacteria. Can be given by injection for short-term effect against toxins, *eg* those of diphtheria and tetanus.

Antofagasta, port of N Chile, on Pacific coast. Pop. 160,000. Nitrates, copper exports. Its occupation by Chileans initiated war (1879-84) with Bolivia, which ceded territ. to Chile. Has artificial harbour; railway link with Bolivia.

Antonine Wall, Roman wall, C Scotland. Length 60 km (37 mi), extending from R. Forth to R. Clyde: built 142 AD, marked Empire's northern frontiers. Abandoned *c* 185.

Antoninus Pius (AD 86-161), Roman emperor (138-161). Adopted by Hadrian as his successor in 138. Encouraged art, science and building during peaceful reign. Built Antonine Wall.

Antony, Mark or **Marcus Antonius** (*c* 83-30 BC), Roman soldier, political leader. Served with Caesar in Gaul, taking his side during civil war. After Caesar's assassination (44), aroused the mob to expel conspirators from Rome. After conflict with Octavian, joined him and Lepidus in 2nd Triumvirate, which ruled the empire for 5 years. He and Octavian defeated Brutus and Cassius at Philippi (42). While in Asia Minor, fell in love with Cleopatra. Deprived of power by senate, was defeated by Octavian at Actium (31). Joined Cleopatra in Egypt, where he killed himself.

Antrim, former county of NE Ireland, co. town was Belfast. Low basalt plateau; scenic valleys ('Glens of Antrim'); Giant's Causeway on N coast. Main industs., agric., fishing, linen mfg., shipbuilding. **Antrim,** town on Lough Neagh. Pop. 2000. Has 10th cent. round tower.

Antwerp (Flem. *Antwerpen,* Fr. *Anvers),* city of N Belgium, cap. of Antwerp prov. Pop. 662,000. Port and commercial centre on R. Scheldt. Sugar, oil refining; shipbuilding, textiles; diamond trade. Gothic cathedral (1352). Trade centre of 16th cent. Europe, declined after sack by Spaniards (1576), closure of Scheldt (1648-1795). Prosperity regained from 19th cent. Damaged in both WWs.

Anubis, in ancient Egyptian pantheon, god who led the dead to judgment. Depicted with head of a jackal.

anus, in mammals, posterior opening of alimentary canal, through which waste is excreted.

anxiety, in psychology, reaction ranging from uneasiness to complete panic when individual is faced with real or apparent threat. Classified normal and neurotic.

Anzio (anc. *Antium),* town of WC Italy, on Tyrrhenian Sea. Pop. 16,000. Fishing port. Birthplace of Caligula, Nero. Scene of Allied landings (1944).

aorta, main artery of body, conveying blood from left ventricle of the heart to all parts of body except the lungs.

Aosta, town of NW Italy, in the Alps, on R. Dora Baltea. Cap. of Valle d'Aosta prov. Pop. 39,000. Tourist centre; metals, chemicals. Roman ruins, medieval cathedral.

aoudad or **Barbary sheep,** *Ammotragus lervia,* wild N African sheep with large curved horns. Resembles goat; highly adaptable to climatic extremes.

Apache

Apache, North American Indian tribe. Warlike hunters of SW. Successfully resisted advance of Spanish colonization but inter-tribal warfare reduced numbers. Some 80,000 still live in reservations, mainly in Arizona.

apartheid, racial segregation on grounds of colour, practised in South Africa from 1948. In Afrikaans, word means 'apartness'; policy aimed at achieving separate development of races, effectively restricting residence, movements, occupations of non-whites.

ape, any of Pongidae family of Old World tailless monkeys, particularly those most closely related to man (gibbon, orangutan, gorilla and chimpanzee).

Apennines, mountain range of Italy. Extends *c* 1300 km (800 mi) from Maritime Alps to Calabria and Sicily. Livestock, agric. on lower slopes; marble quarries. Formerly widely forested. Highest peak Monte Corno (2913 m/9560 ft), C Italy. Earthquakes, esp. in S; volcanoes, incl. Vesuvius.

aphelion, point furthest from Sun in orbit of planet about Sun. Opposite is perihelion.

aphid or **plant louse,** small soft-bodied insect of Aphididae family. Causes much damage to plants by sucking sap and carrying virus disease. Common greenfly, pest of roses, is an aphid.

Aphrodite, in Greek myth, goddess of love, beauty, fertility. Daughter of Zeus and Dione, or sprung from sea into which a severed member of Uranus had been thrown. Unfaithful wife of Hephaestus, being variously connected with Ares, Dionysus, Hermes, Poseidon and the mortals Anchises, Adonis. Had power of granting beauty and charm. Identified by Romans with Venus.

apocalypse, form of prophetic writing common in ancient Hebrew and Christian literature. Depicts end of the world in visions of triumph of good over evil. NT book of REVELATION is often known as the Apocalypse.

Apocrypha, Jewish writings of *c* 300 BC - *c* AD 100 not incl. in the canon of sacred scripture by the Council of Jamnia (AD 90) and now excluded by most Protestant churches. Consists of 14 books included in SEPTUAGINT and VULGATE.

apogee, point farthest from Earth in orbit of Moon or satellite about Earth. Opposite is perigee.

Apollinaire, Guillaume, orig. Wilhelm Apollinaris de Kostrowitski (1880-1918), French poet, b. Rome. His art criticism established CUBISM as a movement, which influenced poetry *Alcools* (1913), *Calligrammes* (1918).

Apollo or **Phoebus Apollo,** in Greek myth, son of Zeus and Leto, born with his sister Artemis at Delos. God of social and intellectual attributes of Greek civilization, *eg* prophecy, healing, purification, music, archery. Represented as ideal of youthful beauty. Cult centred at Delphi where oracular utterances were given by his priestess, Pythia.

Apollonius Rhodius (*c* 295 BC - after 247 BC), Alexandrian scholar, poet. Wrote epic *Argonautica* about Jason and the Golden Fleece.

Apollo programme, *see* SPACE EXPLORATION.

apologetics, the branch of theology which deals with the formal defence of a religious belief. Major Christian apologists incl. Augustine, Aquinas, Pascal, Karl Barth. Since 19th cent., principal attacks on belief have come from psychology, Darwinism, historical criticism of Gospels.

apoplexy or **stroke,** sudden paralysis with total or partial loss of consciousness and sensation, possible loss of speech, and other after-effects of varying severity. Caused by bleeding from arteries in brain, thrombosis or embolism.

apostle, name given to TWELVE DISCIPLES of Jesus (sometimes excluding Judas Iscariot), and also to other early missionaries of Christian church, *eg* St Paul, St Barnabas.

Apostles' Creed, *see* CREED.

apostolic succession, doctrine that the religious authority and mission conferred by Jesus on St Peter has come down through an unbroken succession of bishops. Basis of religious authority in RC, Eastern Orthodox and Anglican churches.

Appalachian Mountains, system of E North America. Extend 2570 km (*c* 1600 mi) from Québec (Canada) to C Alabama. Incl. White, Green, Catskill, Allegheny, Blue Ridge, Black Mts. Mt. Mitchell is highest point (2037 m/6684 ft). Rich in mineral resources, esp. coal.

appeasement, policy of acceding to demands of hostile power in attempt to maintain peace. Used by British, French towards AXIS powers in late 1930s; culminated in MUNICH PACT.

appendix or **vermiform appendix,** in man, outgrowth of large intestine in lower right abdomen. No known function. Infection may result in appendicitis which usually necessitates removal of appendix.

Appian Way (anc. *Via Appia*), ancient road of Italy, begun 312 BC, extending *c* 560 km (350 mi) from Rome to Brindisi.

apple, any tree of genus *Malus* of rose family. The common apple *M. sylvestris* has hard, round, red, yellow or green edible fruit. Economically important esp. in North America, Europe and Australia. Several thousand varieties.

apple of discord, in Greek myth, golden apple inscribed 'for the fairest' thrown among guests at wedding of Peleus and Thetis by Eris. Claimed by Athena, Hera and Aphrodite, and awarded by PARIS to Aphrodite who in return helped him kidnap Helen, thus starting the Trojan War.

Appleton, Sir Edward Victor (1892-1965), English physicist. Investigated reflection of radio waves by ionized particles in upper atmosphere; located Kennelly-Heaviside layer and discovered Appleton layers above this. Awarded Nobel Prize for Physics (1947).

Appomattox Courthouse, building near Appomattox, S Virginia, US. Scene of Confederate General Lee's surrender to Union on 9 April, 1865, marking end of Civil War.

apricot, *Prunus armeniaca,* tree with downy, orange-coloured edible fruit. Native to Far East, introduced into Europe and US.

a priori, in logic, term denoting that which comes before experience, as opposed to *a posteriori* denoting that which comes after experience. Hence formal logic is *a priori* while empirical data is *a posteriori.*

apse, vaulted semicircular or polygonal projection at sanctuary end of church.

Apulia *(Puglia),* region of SE Italy. Hilly in C, plains in N and S; cereals, olives, vines, almonds. Prone to drought. Part of medieval Norman kingdom of Sicily.

Aqaba, Gulf of, thin arm of NE Red Sea. Jordan's only sea outlet. Blockade by Egypt in 1967 war failed on Israeli capture of Sinai Penin.

aquamarine, semi-precious gemstone, a variety of beryl. Transparent, blue or blue-green in colour; used in jewellery.

Aquarius, *see* ZODIAC.

aquatint, method of etching by tone rather than line, giving effect similar to water colour or wash drawing. Transparent tones are obtained by biting printing plate with acid through porous ground.

aqueduct, artificial channel constructed for conducting water. Name often applies to bridge built in series of arches to carry water across a river or valley.

aquilegia, genus of herbs of buttercup family. Species incl. COLUMBINE.

Aquinas, Thomas, *see* THOMAS AQUINAS, ST.

Aquitaine, region of SW France. Fertile plain drained by R. Garonne; main cities Bordeaux, Toulouse. Cereals, vineyards, fruit and vegetable growing. Roman prov. from 56 BC; powerful medieval duchy (name corrupted to *Guienne*) under English rule from 1152; retaken by France (1451).

Arabia

Arabia, penin. of SW Asia, between Red Sea and Persian Gulf. Mainly desert inhabited by pastoral nomads; rich oil deposits in E. Tribes united (6th cent.) by Mohammed who founded Islamic religion. Under control of OTTOMAN Turks until 1918, Saudi Arabia emerged as dominant country of region after 1925.

Arabian Nights, also known as *The Thousand and One Nights,* series of stories in Arabic, linked by story of Scheherazade, who keeps her husband in suspense by telling him stories over 1001 nights, thus escaping death, fate of all his previous wives. Incl. tales of Ali Baba, Sinbad and Aladdin. Only partly Arab in origin, the collection draws on all leading Eastern cultures.

Arabian Sea, part of NW Indian Ocean; lies between Arabia and India.

Arabic, SW Semitic language of Afro-Asiatic family. Spoken in most of N Africa, Sudan, Arabian peninsula, Lebanon, Syria and Iraq.

Arabic numerals, number signs 0 1 2 3 4 5 6 7 8 9; of Hindu origin, they were introduced into Europe by translation of Arabic texts during Middle Ages.

Arab-Israeli wars, series of conflicts, culminating on 4 occasions in outright war between Israel and Arab countries over existence in Palestine of independent Jewish state of Israel. Its proclamation (1948) led to immediate invasion by neighbouring Arab states; ended (1949) by UN armistice. Resulted in increased territ. for Israel, Egypt and Jordan. Egyptian seizure (1956) of Suez Canal precipitated Sinai campaign in which Israel succeeded in occupying Gaza Strip and most of Sinai; Israel gave these up on agreeing to UN cease-fire (Nov. 1956). Third war broke out in June, 1967, after Egypt blockaded Gulf of Aqaba to Israeli shipping. Israel extended frontiers to control W R. Jordan, E bank of Suez Canal, Sinai and Jordanian sector of Jerusalem. Fourth war (Yom Kippur war), Oct. 1973, involved Israeli crossing of Suez Canal after early Egyptian successes, as well as repulse of Syria at Golan Heights. UN supervised ceasefire following intervention by KISSINGER. Israel withdrew from Egyptian side of Suez Canal and after 1979 treaty also from Sinai.

Arab League, organization of Arab states formed (1945) to promote cooperation, esp. in defence and economic affairs; attempted joint Arab action against existence of state of Israel. Original members were Egypt, Syria, Lebanon, Jordan, Iraq, Saudi Arabia, Yemen; 11 more subsequently joined. Collective security agreement came into force 1952; failures in 1960s, esp. 1967 war, resulted in decline in League's importance as unifying force in Arab world.

Arabs, name given to large group of Arabic-speaking people in W Asia and N Africa bound by common tradition, Islamic religion and Arabic language. Main Arab countries are Egypt, Saudi Arabia, Iraq, Lebanon, Syria, Sudan, Libya, Tunisia and Algeria. Divided into settled Arabs and Bedouin nomad herdsmen.

Arachne, in Greek myth, Lydian girl who challenged Athena to contest in weaving. Depicted love of the gods, thus angering Athena who destroyed the work. Hanged herself and was turned into spider by Athena.

Arachnida (arachnids), class of arthropods incl. spiders, scorpions, mites, ticks, king crabs. Mainly terrestrial, but king crab is aquatic. Characterized by 2 body sections and 6 pairs of appendages, 4 being locomotory.

Arafat, Yasser, (1929-). Palestinian resistance leader. Head (since 1968) of more moderate resistance groups, Palestine National Liberation Movement (Al Fatah) and Palestine Liberation Organization.

Arafura Sea, extension of W Pacific Ocean, between Australia and New Guinea. Linked to Coral Sea by Torres Str.

Aragon, Louis (1897-), French writer. After early associations with DADA, wrote surrealist novel *Le Paysan de Paris* (1926). Became Communist; later works incl. poetry, *eg Le Crève-Coeur* (1941) inspired by participation in Resistance.

Aragón, region and former prov. of NE Spain. Incl. Pyrenees foothills, Ebro valley, part of C plateau; arid, sparsely pop. Main towns Saragossa, Huesca. Sheep rearing, irrigated agric., mineral deposits. Independent kingdom from 1035; united with Catalonia 1137, with Castile 1479 by marriage of Ferdinand and Isabella.

Aral Sea, inland sea of USSR, on Kazakh-Uzbek SSR border; 4th largest lake in world. Area *c* 67,000 sq km (26,000 sq mi). Slightly saline; no outlet. Fished for carp, perch.

Aramaic, language of Syria belonging to NW Semitic branch of Afro-Asiatic family. Now dead, widely spoken in centuries before and after Christ. Superseded by Arabic.

Aran Islands, small, rocky isl. group of Co. Galway, W Irish Republic, in Galway Bay. Largest is Inishmore. Fishing.

Ararat, Mount *(Agri Dagi),* mountain of NE Turkey, near border with Iran and Soviet Armenia. Height 5156 m (16,916 ft), traditional resting place of Noah's Ark.

Arbroath, town of Tayside region, E Scotland. Pop. 23,000. Formerly Aberbrothock. Fishing indust. (famous for smoked haddock); tourist resort; cloth mfg. Has 12th-cent. abbey; scene of Robert I's Declaration of Independence (1320).

arbutus, genus of trees or shrubs of the heath family with dark-green leaves, clusters of pinkish flowers and strawberry-like berries. Widely grown as ornamental.

arc, electric, luminous and intensely hot discharge produced when current flows through a gap between 2 electrodes; characterized by high current and low voltage. Carbon arcs used as sources of very bright light; heating effect utilized in electric arc furnace.

Arcadia, admin. dist. of S Greece, in C Peloponnese. Mainly mountainous. Isolated; pastoral farming from ancient times.

arch, curved structure, *eg* of bricks or stone blocks, which supports weight of material over an open space. Keystone (inserted in centre of arch) pushes stress outwards. Types used incl. pointed arch, characteristic of Gothic buildings, and semicircular arch, employed by Romans and revived in Renaissance.

Archaean era, *see* PRECAMBRIAN.

archaeology, the study of human past by systematic examination and tabulation of excavated relics. Little interest was shown in ancient remains until Renaissance. Systematic classification dates from concept of THREE AGE SYSTEM, introduced in 1818. Scientific contributions to modern archaeology incl. radioactive dating methods.

archaeopteryx, earliest known fossil bird (Jurassic period), probably descended from dinosaur. Feathers on tail and wings; possession of teeth and claws on wings indicates reptilian origin. Flightless.

Archangel *(Arkhangelsk),* city of USSR, port of NW European RSFSR; at mouth of N R. Dvina. Pop. 385,000. Port icebound much of year, kept open by icebreakers; exports timber. Sawmilling and fishery centre. Founded 1553 with estab. of Muscovy Co.; only Russian seaport until St Petersburg founded (1703).

archangel, chief ANGEL. Best known are Michael, Gabriel, Raphael.

archbishop, high dignitary in episcopal churches. The archbishops of Canterbury and York are principal dignitaries of Church of England.

archerfish, *Toxotes jaculator,* freshwater fish of East Indies. Captures insect prey by spitting jets of water at them.

archery, art of shooting with bow and arrow, formerly practised in hunting and warfare, today solely a sport. Origins prob. reach back over 50,000 years; bow-making techniques were improved in Near East from *c* 2500 BC. Decisive in battles in Middle Ages (Crécy, Agincourt) until introduction of gunpowder.

Archimedes (*c* 287-212 BC), Greek mathematician, physicist, inventor. Created science of hydrostatics and worked out the principle of the lever. Determined areas under curves and volumes of solids by methods akin to calculus; obtained accurate approximation for π. Enunciated Archimedes' principle - upward thrust exerted on body immersed in fluid equals weight of fluid displaced.

archipelago, group or chain of islands. Ancient name for Aegean Sea and formerly used for any sea with many isls.

architecture, art of designing and constructing buildings, ideally aiming for maximum beauty and utility. Styles are influenced by climate, materials and techniques available, social and cultural settings. In 20th cent. techniques such as steel frame and reinforced concrete have revolutionized architecture.

arctic fox, *Alopex lagopus,* small fox of

Arctic region. Valued for slate-grey fur which turns white in winter.

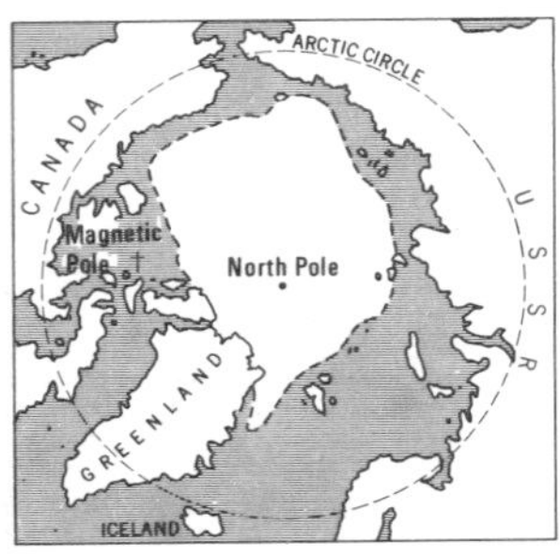

Arctic

Arctic Ocean, ocean surrounding North Pole, lying entirely above Arctic Circle (66½°N). Area *c* 14,300,000 sq km (5,500,000 sq mi). Connected to Atlantic by Greenland Sea, to Pacific by Bering Strait. Largely covered by ice, which breaks into drifting pack-ice in summer.

Ardennes, plateau of SE Belgium, NE France, Luxembourg. Extensive woodland, some agric. Battlefield in both WWs.

Ares, in Greek myth, son of Zeus and Hera; god of war. Loved by Aphrodite. Appears as instigator of violence or as tempestuous lover. Identified by Romans with Mars.

Argentina

Argentina, federal republic of S South America, on Atlantic. Area 2,776,889 sq km (1,072,157 sq mi); pop. 26,393,000; cap. Buenos Aires. Language: Spanish. Religion: RC. W boundary formed by Andes; cotton growing in Chaco plain (N); pop. and wealth in Pampas (beef, wheat produce); arid Patagonia plateau in S (sheep rearing, oil); indust. concentrated in Buenos Aires. Spanish colonization in 16th cent.; independence struggle led by San Martín (achieved 1816); republic estab. 1852. Ruled by successive dictatorships in 20th cent., esp. Perón (1946-55, 1973-4).

argon (Ar), inert gaseous element; at. no. 18, at. wt. 39.95. Found in air (0.9%); obtained by distillation of liquid air. Used to fill electric lamps, fluorescent tubes and as inert atmosphere for welding. Discovered (1894) by Rayleigh, Ramsay.

argonaut or **paper nautilus,** marine cephalopod mollusc, genus *Argonauta*, related to octopus. Female builds itself thin translucent shell to incubate eggs.

Argonauts, in Greek myth, band of heroes led by JASON, sent to bring GOLDEN FLEECE from king of Colchis to Greece. Sailed in ship *Argo* suffering many trials on outward and homeward journey, *eg* the clashing rocks, Scylla and Charybdis.

Argonne, hilly woodland of NE France, in Champagne and Lorraine. Strategic WWI battleground.

Argos, ancient city of S Greece, in NE Peloponnese. Pop. 20,000. Occupied from Bronze Age; 'Diomed' of Homer's *Iliad*. Centre of Argolis, dominated Peloponnese from 7th cent. BC; taken by Sparta *c* 494 BC, by Rome 146 BC. Heraeum temple nearby.

Argyll, Archibald Campbell, 8th Earl of (1607-61), Scottish nobleman. Led Covenanting forces against royalists in Civil War. After execution of Charles I, supported Charles II who had agreed to introduce Presbyterianism to England. Submitted to Cromwell (1652); beheaded after Restoration. His son, **Archibald Campbell, 9th Earl of Argyll** (1629-85), was beheaded for aiding Monmouth's rebellion. **John Campbell, 2nd Duke of Argyll and Duke of Greenwich** (1678-1743), was general responsible for quelling Jacobite rebellion of 1715.

Argyllshire, former county of W Scotland, now in Strathclyde region. Incl. some of Inner Hebrides; co. town was Inveraray. Mountainous; indented coast. Sheep, forestry, fishing, distilling, tourism.

aria, in music, composition for voice, esp. solo with orchestral accompaniment. A feature of operas, cantatas, oratorios since 1600.

Ariadne, in Greek myth, daughter of King Minos and Pasiphaë, who gave THESEUS the skein of thread by which he found his way out of the labyrinth after slaying the Minotaur. Fled with Theseus, but deserted by him on Naxos, was found by Dionysus who married her.

Arianism, *see* ARIUS.

Aries, *see* ZODIAC.

Ariosto, Ludovico (1474-1533), Italian poet. Famous for epic poem *Orlando Furioso* (1532) on Roland, sometimes called greatest Renaissance poem. Also wrote lyrics, satires, dramas.

Aristarchus of Samos (3rd cent. BC), Greek astronomer. Reputed to be 1st to hold theory that Earth revolves about Sun.

aristocracy, in political theory, term used for govt. by elite, usually hereditary, designated as best equipped to rule. Usage has widened to denote class from which governing elite is drawn, or those who by birth or wealth occupy privileged position.

Aristophanes (*c* 450–*c* 385 BC), Greek comic poet. Although not innovative, plays are greatest of Greek comedies, mixing political, social and literary satire, vigorous rather than savage. Only 11 plays extant, incl. *The Clouds, The Wasps, The Birds, Lysistrata,* and *The Frogs.*

Aristotle (384-322 BC), Greek philosopher. Pupil of Plato, tutor of Alexander the Great. Established the methods of Western philosophy in *eg, Analytics, Metaphysics, Ethics, Politics, Poetics.* Believed in Divine Being, but unlike Plato did not posit separate world of ideal essences. Held that happiness, goodness in man come from use of reason, *ie* fulfilment of intended function. Enlightened monarchy with aristocracy was his political ideal.

arithmetic, branch of mathematics dealing with real numbers, their addition, subtraction, multiplication, and division. Term also applies to study of whole numbers (integers), esp. prime numbers.

Arius (*c* 256-336), Libyan theologian. Advanced theory (Arianism) that Christ was not co-equal or co-eternal with God, thus renouncing Trinity. Condemned as heretic at 1st Council of Nicaea (325). Arianism persisted in N Africa and Spain until 6th cent.

Arizona, state of SW US. Area 295,024 sq km (113,909 sq mi); pop. 2,270,000; cap. Phoenix; other major city Tucson. Forested Colorado Plateau in C (incl. Grand Canyon), desert in S. Agric. irrigated by several dams (*eg* Roosevelt, Coolidge); fruit, vegetables, wheat, beef, cotton farming. Copper, silver mining. Largest Indian pop. in US (many reservations). First explored in 16th cent. by Spanish; purchased by US (1848). Admitted to Union as 48th state (1912).

ark, in OT, *see* NOAH.

Arkansas, state of SC US. Area 137,539 sq km (53,104 sq mi); pop. 2,109,000; cap. Little Rock; other major cities Fort Smith, Hot Springs. Ozark Mts. in NW; Mississippi R. forms E border; crossed by White, Arkansas, Ouachita rivers. Agric. incl. cotton, soya bean growing, livestock farming; important bauxite mines. Part of French Louisiana Purchase (1803). Admitted to Union as state (1836).

Arkansas, river of C US. Rises in Rocky Mts. of C Colorado. Flows SE 2330 km (*c* 1450 mi) through Kansas, Oklahoma, Arkansas to Mississippi. Chief tributary Canadian R.

Arkwright, Sir Richard (1732–92), English inventor. Developed mechanical spinning process (patent, 1769) which provided basis for mass-production in cotton indust.

Arles, town of Provence, SE France, on Rhône delta. Pop. 50,000. Agric. market, wines, silk mfg. Important Roman, Gaulish centre; archbishopric from 4th cent. Cap. of kingdom of Arles (933-1378). Roman remains incl. arena, theatre; has cathedral (11th cent.).

arm, in man, upper limb of body, extending from shoulder to wrist. Skeleton is formed by humerus in upper arm, radius and ulna in forearm.

Armada, Spanish, fleet of 130 ships sent (1588) by Philip II of Spain to carry invasion force against England. Attacked by English fleet under Howard and Drake off Plymouth, and later broken up by fire ships off Calais. Suffered heavy losses through storm damage while escaping via Scotland and W coast of Ireland; less than half of fleet reached Spain.

armadillo, burrowing mammal of Dasypodidae family found from S US to South America. Body armour-plated with bony discs; rolls up into ball when threatened.

Armageddon, in Bible, esp. Book of Revelation, scene of last, decisive battle between forces of good and evil, to be fought before the Day of Judgment.

Armagh, former county of S Northern Ireland. Low-lying in N; hilly in S. Agric.; cattle rearing; linen mfg. Co. town was **Armagh.** Pop. 12,000. Ecclesiastical cap. of Ireland from 5th cent. Has Protestant, RC cathedrals.

Armagnac, former French province in Gascony, cap. Auch. Noted for brandy.

Armenia, hist. region and former kingdom, now divided between Turkey, Iran and USSR. Mainly plateau, incl. Mt. Ararat and sources of Tigris and Euphrates. Embraced Christianity (303); changed hands repeatedly, with Russia taking what is now Armenian SSR from Persia in 19th cent. Turkish attempts to suppress Armenian nationalism led to massacres (1894-1915).

Armenian Soviet Socialist Republic, constituent republic of SW USSR, bounded on S and W by Iran and Turkey. Area 29,800 sq km (11,500 sq mi); pop. 3,031,000. Cap. Yerevan. Mainly mountainous with high plateaux; produces cotton, tobacco, wine; minerals incl. copper, molybdenum, zinc. Region seized by Russia from Persia (1828); incorporated by USSR (1920).

Arminius, Jacobus, orig. Jacob Harmensen (1560-1609), Dutch reformed theologian. Opposed Calvinist teaching of absolute predestination. Teachings formulated (1622) by Simon Episcopus became known as Arminianism.

armistice, truce before signing of peace treaty; temporary stopping of hostilities by mutual agreement. Armistice Day (11 Nov.) anniversary of WWI armistice (1918), commemorated by National Day of Remembrance (UK), Veterans Day (US).

Armstrong, Louis ('Satchmo') (1900-71), American jazz trumpeter, band leader, singer. First musician to develop a solo style in jazz, he created stunning improvisations that defined the role of the soloist.

army, organized body of men, trained and armed for military combat on land. Professional standing army developed with growth of Roman Empire. In feudal Europe, military service was obligatory among knights and yeomanry. System declined with increased use of mercenaries. CONSCRIPTION was introduced during French Revolutionary Wars. During peacetime, modern army often made up of enlisted volunteers.

army ant or **driver ant,** nomadic ant, esp. of genus *Eciton* found in South American tropics. Travels in long columns, devouring animals in its path.

Arnhem, city of EC Netherlands, on R. Rhine, cap. of Gelderland prov. Pop. 284,000. Railway jct., engineering, textiles. Scene of defeat (1944) of British airborne assault.

Arnhem Land, aboriginal reserve of NE Northern Territ., Australia. Pop. *c* 4000; white settlement confined to mission stations. Mainly swamp and grassland; monsoon climate. Bauxite development at Gove.

Arno, river of NC Italy. Flows 240 km (150 mi) from Apennines via Florence, Pisa to Ligurian Sea. Fertile, scenic valley.

Arnold, Benedict (1741-1801), American general. Held commands during American Revolution, but plotted to betray West Point garrison. Discovered but escaped and later fought for British.

Arnold, Thomas (1795-1842), English educator. As headmaster of Rugby (1827-42), he reformed English public school system, creating modern pattern. Also a classical scholar, historian. His son, **Matthew Arnold** (1822-88), was a poet and critic. Held that poetry should be 'criticism of life', saw culture as the only means to save society from Victorian materialism. Poems incl. 'The Scholar Gypsy' (1853).

aromatic compounds, in chemistry, organic compounds derived from benzene. Many such compounds, esp. those discovered first, have recognizable odours.

Arquebus

arquebus or **harquebus,** small-calibre gun operated by matchlock, precursor of the musket. Prominent in 16th cent. Italian wars.

Arran, isl. of Strathclyde region, W Scotland. Area 430 sq km (166 sq mi); pop. 4000; main town Brodick. Tourism, hill-walking.

Arras, town of N France, on canalized R. Scarpe, cap. of Pas-de-Calais dept. Pop. 54,000. Agric. market, engineering. Medieval tapestry indust. Hist. cap. of Artois, under Spanish rule 1493-1640.

arrest, seizure and taking into custody of person by authority of law. In civil law, can only take place on issue of court order. Arrest may be made with or without warrant when a crime is thought to have been committed.

arrowhead, any aquatic perennial of genus *Sagittaria* of water plantain family. Arrow-shaped leaves, small, white, cup-like flowers.

arsenic (As), chemical element; at. no. 33, at. wt. 74.92. Exists in 3 allotropic forms, commonest being grey crystalline arsenic. Occurs as realgar (As_2S_3), white arsenic (AS_2O_3) and arsenopyrite (FeAsS). Its extremely poisonous compounds used in weed and insect killers, also medicinally.

art, visual, branch of human activity, divided into PAINTING, SCULPTURE and ARCHITECTURE. Individual articles in this encyclopedia on styles of painting incl.: MANNERISM, IMPRESSIONISM, FAUVISM, CUBISM, POP and OP ART, FUTURISM, ABSTRACT EXPRESSIONISM, POST-IMPRESSIONISM, ABSTRACT ART. For various articles on architectural styles *see*: BAROQUE, ROCOCO, ROMANESQUE, NORMAN ARCHITECTURE, GOTHIC, EARLY ENGLISH, PERPENDICULAR, DECORATED STYLE, NEO-CLASSICISM, GOTHIC REVIVAL.

art deco, decorative style of late 1920s and 1930s, deriving its name from Exposition Internationale des Arts Décoratifs et Industriels Modernes (1925) in Paris. Characterized by geometric design, bright metallic surfaces.

Artemis, in Greek myth, daughter of Zeus and Leto; sister of Apollo. Virgin goddess of hunting, wildlife, chastity, childbirth. Associated with the moon. Identified by Romans with Diana.

artemisia, genus of perennial herbs of Compositae family. Native to temperate and arctic regions. Scented foliage and small rayless flowers. Species incl. wormwood, mugwort, sagebrush, tarragon.

arteriosclerosis, hardening and thickening of walls of the arteries. Usually caused by deposition of fatty material, *eg* cholesterol, in linings of arteries. Frequently occurs in old age.

artery, any vessel carrying blood from heart to body tissues. Arteries have thick walls, lined with elastic fibres and muscles to withstand blood pressure.

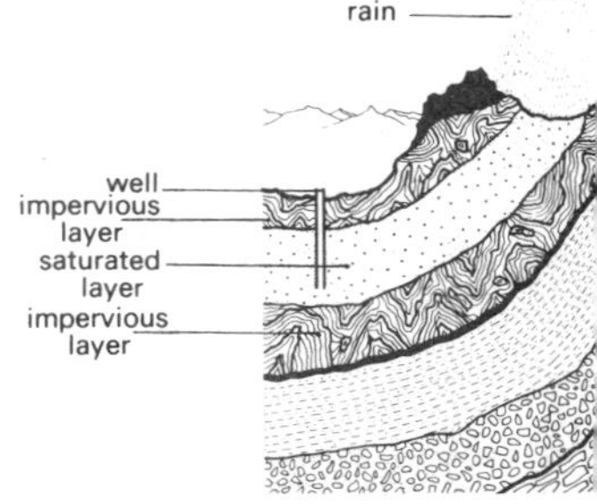

Artesian well

artesian well, drilled well which relies on

hydrostatic pressure to force water to surface. Pressure created within fold of rock which comprises water-bearing layer sandwiched between impermeable strata.

arthritis, inflammation of joints. Rheumatoid arthritis, most severely crippling form, is characterized by inflammation of connective tissue around joints, esp. those of wrist and hand; often leads to deformity of joints. Cause unknown. Osteoarthritis is degeneration of joints, with loss of cartilage lining and growth of bone. Occurs mainly in elderly people, esp. in joints of leg and spine.

Arthropoda (arthropods), largest phylum of animal kingdom, incl. arachnids, crustaceans, insects, centipedes, millipedes. Segmented body, horny outer skeleton, primitive brain; various jointed appendages serve as limbs, gills or jaws.

Arthur, *see* ARTHURIAN LEGEND.

Arthurian legend, mass of interrelated stories prob. drawn from Celtic legend centring on King Arthur and his court. Arthur first mentioned in Celtic literature, *c* 600, as leader of Britons. GEOFFREY OF MONMOUTH's *Historia* (*c* 1135) portrayed Arthur as conqueror of W Europe. Wace's *Roman de Brut* (*c* 1155) introduced Round Table. CHRÉTIEN DE TROYES (12th cent.) wrote 5 romances dealing with Arthur's knights. First treatment of Tristram and Isolde story was by 13th-cent. German poet Gottfried von Strassburg. After 1225 literary tradition continued only in England, with anon. *Sir Gawain and the Green Knight* (*c* 1370) and MALORY's *Morte d'Arthur*. Full story makes Arthur illegitimate son of King Uther Pendragon, who demonstrates royal blood by removing sword from stone. Later receives invincible sword Excalibur from Lady in the Lake, and estab. court at Camelot, marrying Guinevere and gathering around his Round Table best knights of Christendom. Decline begins with Holy Grail quest (dispersing knights), with Sir Lancelot's love for Guinevere, and ends with Sir Mordred (Arthur's son) fatally wounding Arthur. He is taken to Avalon, whence he will return in time of national peril. Other figures incl. Sir Galahad and Sir Percival, pure heroes of Holy Grail quest; Sir Gawain, Arthur's nephew; Merlin, magician and adviser to Arthur; Morgan le Fay, Arthur's half-sister and enchantress.

artichoke, name for 2 different garden vegetables of Compositae family. *Cynara scolymus*, native to Africa, is French or globe artichoke. Jerusalem artichoke, *Helianthus tuberosus*, is perennial sunflower with tuberous roots used as vegetable or livestock feed.

artificial insemination, method of introducing semen from male into female artificially to facilitate fertilization. Widely used in propagation of animals, esp. livestock. Sometimes used in humans when normal fertilization impossible.

artificial kidney, mechanical device which substitutes for lost kidneys. Blood is led from arteries by cellophane tube and waste products removed by DIALYSIS.

artificial respiration, restoration or maintenance of breathing by manual or mechanical means. Mechanical devices used incl. IRON LUNG. Mouth-to-mouth method involves forcing breath into patient's mouth, while holding his nostrils shut.

artillery, originally any form of armament involving discharge of a projectile, incl. bow, catapult. Now any type of heavy firearm fired from carriage or platform.

art nouveau, term used to describe style of decorative art, at its height in Europe and North America *c* 1890-1910. Characterized by flat curvilinear designs based on natural forms. Applied in architecture and interior design (by Horta, van de Velde, Mackintosh), jewellery, book illustration (by Beardsley), glassware (by Louis Tiffany).

Artois, region and former prov. of N France, cap. Arras. Mainly agric., incl. part of Franco-Belgian coalfield. Disputed by France and the Habsburgs, finally taken by France 1640. Scene of many battles in WWI.

Aryan, Sanskrit word used for peoples speaking Indo-European languages. The Aryans originally spread (from *c* 2000 BC) throughout Mesopotamia from S Russia and Turkestan. Term used, with little scientific basis, in Nazi ideology to designate Indo-European race.

aryl group, in chemistry, organic RADICAL or group of atoms derived from aromatic compounds, *eg* phenyl radical C_6H_5.

asbestos, silicate mineral with fibrous structure. Common forms are chrysotile (type of SERPENTINE), crocidolite; often found as veins in other rock. Resistant to fire and acid, fibres may be pressed into plasterboard, woven into ropes, clothing, pipe insulation, *etc.* Major sources in Canada, South Africa, Rhodesia.

Ascension, isl. in S Atlantic, NW of St Helena. Area 88 sq km (34 sq mi). Site of American satellite tracking station. Dependency of St Helena since 1922.

Ascension, Christian festival, celebrating the bodily ascent of Jesus into heaven on the 40th day after Resurrection.

asceticism, doctrine that man can reach a higher spiritual state by rigorous self-discipline and self-denial. Has been common in the major monotheistic religions, also Hinduism, Buddhism and among the CYNICS. May involve prolonged fasting, self-mutilation, flagellation.

Asclepius, mythical Greek physician, son of Apollo. Learned art of medicine from CHIRON. Killed by Zeus for raising Hippolytus from the dead. Worshipped as god of healing, esp. at Epidaurus. Serpent was sacred to him. Known as Aesculapius by Romans.

ascorbic acid or **vitamin C,** crystalline water-soluble solid, occurring in fruit and vegetables. Necessary in diet of humans and guinea pigs to form fibres of connective tissue (absence causes scurvy). Identified 1932. Held to be effective in counteracting colds.

Ascot, village of Berkshire, S England. Has famous racecourse at Ascot Heath estab. 1711.

asdic, *see* SONAR.

ash, any tree of genus *Fraxinus.* Pinnate leaves, winged fruit, tough elastic wood. Source of valuable timber.

Ashanti, admin. region of S Ghana. Hilly and forested, produces cocoa, hardwoods; noted for gold working. Hist. stronghold of Ashanti tribe, cap. Kumasi; wars against British in 19th cent. led to annexation by Gold Coast colony (1901), break-up of Ashanti confederation. Region of Ghana from 1957.

Ashcroft, Dame Edith Margaret Emily ('Peggy') (1907-), English actress. Notable in Shakespearian roles and as Margaret in *Dear Brutus,* Miss Madrigal in *The Chalk Garden.*

Ashes, the, mythical cricket trophy said to be held by the winning team of test series between England and Australia. Name derives from mock obituary of English cricket written in *Sporting Times* (1882), stating that 'the body will be cremated and the ashes taken to Australia'.

Ashkhabad, town of USSR, cap. of Turkmen SSR; near Iran border. Pop. 315,000. Textile mfg. Founded 1881, almost destroyed by earthquake in 1948.

Ashtart, *see* ASTARTE.

Ashton, Sir Frederick William Mallandaine (1906-), British choreographer, dancer, b. Ecuador. Founder choreographer to the Royal Ballet, director (1963-70). Ballets incl. *Façade, Enigma Variations, Tales of Beatrix Potter* (film, 1971).

Ash Wednesday, first day of Christian LENT, seventh Wednesday before Easter. Name derived from custom of rubbing ashes on the forehead as sign of penitence.

Asia, largest and most populous continent of the world. Bounded by Pacific (E), Arctic (N), Indian (S) oceans; stretches from Ural Mts. (USSR) and Asia Minor in W to Bering Str., Japan and Indonesia in E. Area *c* 43,300,000 sq km (16,700,000 sq mi). Pop. *c* 2,250,000,000. Mountain ranges incl. Himalayas, whose peaks; *eg* MT. EVEREST, are highest in world. Major rivers Yenisei, Ob in Siberia; Yangtze, Mekong, Amur (S, SE); Indus, Ganges (S), Tigris, Euphrates (SW), centres of earliest known civilizations. Cold Siberian tundra merges in S with coniferous forestland; wooded steppes merge into desert regions of W China. In SE are fertile monsoon coastlands and river valleys of China, Japan, India, Indonesia and Indo-China, all densely populated and supported by rice crops. Vast oil reserves in SW desert regions (Arabia) now exploited; mineral resources in Siberia being developed.

Asia Minor or **Anatolia,** penin. of W Asia, between Black Sea, Mediterranean and Aegean; comprises Asiatic Turkey. High plateau crossed by Taurus Mts. in S; dry interior with many salt lakes. Scene of ancient cultures and numerous invasions; fell to Ottoman Turks 13th-15th cent.

Asmara, city of N Ethiopia, cap. of Eritrea prov. on plateau. Pop. 364,000. Trade centre in agric. region; textiles, ceramics mfg.; univ. (1958). Railway link to Massawa. Cap. of Italian colony of Eritrea from 1890 until taken in 1941 by British.

asp, one of several species of small poisonous snakes incl. *Vipera aspis* of S Europe, and Egyptian cobra.

asparagus, *Asparagus officinalis,* perennial garden vegetable native to Eurasia, cultivated in Britain, US. Tender shoots considered delicacy. Decorative species incl. *A. plumosus.*

aspen, any of several species of poplars with flattened leaves. Incl. *Populus tremula* of Europe. Soft wood of some species is source of pulp.

asphalt, brown or black tar-like substance composed of various hydrocarbons. Occurs in asphalt lakes; obtained as residue of petroleum distillation. Used in road making and water-proofing.

asphodel, hardy stemless plant of genera *Asphodelus* and *Asphodeline* of lily family, native to Eurasia. Has showy flower spikes.

aspidistra, genus of Asiatic herbs of lily family. Has stiff, glossy, evergreen leaves, dark inconspicuous flowers near ground. Cultivated as house plant.

aspirin or **acetylsalicylic acid,** white crystalline solid used to reduce fever and relieve pain. Dangerous in excessive doses as it may cause bleeding in stomach.

Asquith, Herbert Henry, 1st Earl of Oxford and Asquith (1852-1928), British statesman, PM (1908-16). Headed Liberal govt. which introduced national insurance scheme after depri·ing Lords of veto power in 1911 PARLIAMENT ACT. Attempt to estab. Irish Home Rule failed. Resigned in favour of Lloyd George following WWI reverses.

Asiatic wild ass

ass, small horse-like mammal, genus *Equus,* found wild in semi-desert areas of Africa and Asia. Noted for endurance; domesticated varieties, incl. donkey, used as pack animals. Mule is offspring of jackass with horse mare, hinny offspring of she-ass with horse stallion; both sterile.

Assad, Hafiz al-(1928-), Syrian political leader and soldier. Became president (1971), led Syria into 1973 war with Israel.

Sent troops to establish ceasefire in Lebanese civil war (1976).

Assam, state of NE India. Area *c* 77,700 sq km (30,000 sq mi); pop. 14,952,000; cap. Shillong. Almost enclosed by mountains; pop. concentrated in fertile river valleys, *eg* Brahmaputra. Heavy rainfall; produces timber, tea, rice. Incl. Northeast Frontier Agency union territ.

Assassins, members of a secret sect in Islam, founded *c* 1090 in Persia. Distinguished by total obedience to their leader, supposedly while under the influence of hashish. Regarded murder as sacred duty to eliminate enemies, incl. Crusaders. Purged by Mongols (from 1256).

Assent, Royal, in UK law, formal consent given by sovereign to bill after its passage through Parliament, condition of its becoming an act of Parliament. Last refused by Queen Anne (1702).

Assiniboine, river of Canada. Rises in E Saskatchewan, flows SE 950 km (590 mi) into Manitoba to join Red R. at Winnipeg.

Assisi, town of Umbria, C Italy. Pop. 25,000. Religious, tourist centre, overlooking Spoleto valley. Birthplace of St Francis; churches (frescoed by Cimabue, Giotto) built (13th cent.) over his tomb.

assizes, in England, court sessions held periodically by judges of High Court in regions to try civil and criminal cases. Assize towns grouped in 7 circuits, with 2 judges travelling each circuit.

Association football or **soccer,** eleven-a-side team game played with round leather ball. Follows rules set down by Football Association in London (1863). Played worldwide, esp. on professional basis in Europe and South America. First professionals in England (1880s), League estab. 1888. International competition is controlled by FIFA (founded 1904) which organizes World Cup every 4 years (first held 1930).

Assuan, *see* ASWAN.

Assyria, ancient empire of SW Asia, centred on Ashur on upper R. Tigris. *Fl* 9th-7th cents. BC when it gained ascendancy in Middle East esp. under Sargon II and Sennacherib. Conquered Egypt 671 BC under Esarhaddon and reached height of its power under Assurbanipal. Empire declined rapidly and cap. Nineveh was destroyed 612 BC by Medes and Babylonians.

Astaire, Fred, pseud. of Frederick Austerlitz (1899-), American dancer, singer, film actor. Known for films, esp. with Ginger Rogers, expressing 1930s' elegance, wit, *eg* *Top Hat* (1935), *Swing Time* (1936).

Astarte or **Ashtart,** Semitic goddess of fertility and love. Associated with planet Venus. Identified with Babylonian Ishtar, Ashtoreth of Bible and Greek Aphrodite.

astatine (At), radioactive element of halogen group; at. no. 85, mass no. of most stable isotope 210. Half-life 8.3 hrs. First prepared 1940 by bombarding bismuth with alpha particles.

aster, large genus of perennial plants of Compositae family. Purplish, blue, pink or white daisy-like flowers. Most garden varieties derived from North American autumn-blooming species. Cultivated as Michaelmas daisies in Europe.

asteroid or **planetoid,** minor planet of Solar System. Over 1600 recognized, most of which lie in belt between Mars and Jupiter. Largest and 1st discovered (1801) is Ceres, diameter 686 km (427 mi).

asthma, chronic disorder characterized by difficulty in breathing. Results from spasm of muscles in bronchial tubes and is accompanied by accumulation of mucus. Often caused by allergy or emotional stress.

Asti, town of Piedmont, NW Italy, cap. of Asti prov. Pop. 76,000. Distilleries; famous for sparkling wines (Asti Spumante).

astigmatism, irregularity in curvature of lens (incl. eye lens); results in inability to bring whole of an image into focus and consequential distortion. Use of cylindrical lens corrects astigmatism of eye.

Astor, Nancy Witcher, Viscountess, née Langhorne (1879-1964), British politician, b. US. Was 1st woman to sit in House of Commons (1919-45). Famous political hostess, influenced govt. policy through 'Cliveden set', Conservative group who met at her Cliveden house parties.

Astrakhan, city of USSR, SE European RSFSR; on Volga Delta. Pop. 458,000. Centre of river transport; shipbuilding, fish processing (esp. caviare). Cap. of Tartar khanate, taken by Ivan the Terrible 1556.

astringent, drug used to contract body tissue and check bleeding, mucus secretion, *etc.* Examples incl. aluminium salts, tannin, silver nitrate.

astrolabe, ancient and medieval scientific instrument used to measure altitude of heavenly bodies. Consisted of graduated metal disc with pivoted sighting arm.

astrology, form of divination based on theory that all events on Earth are determined by movements of heavenly bodies. Basis of ancient astronomy, from which it diverged after Copernicus. Individual's fate predicted by use of horoscope, map of heavens at time of birth, drawing on chart of ZODIAC.

astronomy, scientific study of nature, position and motion of heavenly bodies. Of ancient origin, *fl* under Greeks; their findings, summarized by Ptolemy, were displaced by Copernican theory in 16th cent. Newton's laws of motion and gravitation provided basis for later study. Branches incl. astrophysics, cosmology, radio and X-ray astronomy.

astrophysics, branch of astronomy dealing with physical properties of heavenly bodies and also their origin and evolution.

Asturias, region and former kingdom of NW Spain, hist. cap. Oviedo. Cantabrian Mts. in S; hilly woodland, pasture. Coalmining from Roman times, metal industs.; cattle raising, apple orchards. Christian stronghold during Moorish conquest; kingdom joined with León (866), later with Castile. Principality 1388-1931.

Asunción, cap. of Paraguay, port on Paraguay R. Pop. 565,000. Major commercial, transport centre; food processing, textile mfg. Founded *c* 1536. Centre of Spanish colonization in S of continent.

Aswan or **Assuan** (anc. *Syene*), city of S Egypt, just below First Cataract of the Nile. Pop. 259,000. Trade, tourist centre; chemicals indust.; syenite quarries. Nearby are Aswan Dam (completed 1902); Aswan High Dam (completed 1970), 111 m (365 ft) high, 4.8 km (3 mi) wide, has created L. Nasser, reservoir (area *c* 5180 sq km/2000 sq mi) providing irrigation, h.e.p. for Egypt and Sudan.

Atacama Desert, arid region of N Chile-S Peru, between Andes and Pacific coast. Alt. 610 m (*c* 2000 ft). Has rich nitrate, copper, iron ore deposits.

Atahualpa (d. 1533), last Inca ruler of Peru. Seized whole empire after defeating half-brother Huáscar. Captured (1532) by Spanish conquistador Pizarro, who had him killed.

Atalanta, in Greek myth, huntress famed for speed and skill. Ran race with suitors on condition that she would marry first man to outstrip her; the others would be killed. Hippomenes, or Melanion, won race by dropping 3 golden apples which Atalanta stopped to pick up.

Ataturk, Kemal, orig. Mustafa Kemal Pasha (1881-1938), Turkish military and political leader. Participated in Young Turks revolt (1908). Estab. rival govt. in Asia Minor (1919) against Allied-controlled Constantinople regime after Turkey's collapse in WWI. Repulsed Greek invasion from Anatolia (1919-22); re-estab. Turkish sovereignty over occupied territs. First president of Turkey (1923-38), ruled as dictator. Introduced Westernizing reform programme.

Athabaska, river of NC Alberta, Canada. Rises in Rocky Mts., flows NE 1230 km (765 mi) to **Lake Athabaska** (on N Alberta-Saskatchewan border); area 8100 sq km (*c* 3120 sq mi). Rich oil-bearing sands along lower course of river.

Athanasian Creed, statement of Christian belief maintaining belief in the Trinity, as opposed to Arianism (*see* ARIUS). Formerly attributed to Athanasius, now believed to date from 6th cent.

Athanasius, St (*c* 296-373), Egyptian theologian, patriarch of Alexandria. Maintained consubstantiality of Jesus with God, opposing ARIUS at 1st Council of Nicaea (325).

atheism, denial of existence of God or gods. Occurs in ancient times, *eg* in Socrates' attack on religious orthodoxy of Athens; again in 19th cent. with belief in an inherent conflict between science and religion. *See* AGNOSTICISM.

Athelstan (*c* 895-939), king of England (924-39). Consolidated and built upon work of his grandfather, Alfred; defeated union of Scots, Danes and Welsh at Brunanburh (937).

Athena or **Pallas Athena,** in Greek myth, patron goddess of Athens, personification of wisdom, patron of intellectual and practical skills. Represented as warlike virgin goddess, having sprung fully-armed from the head of Zeus. PARTHENON erected to her on Acropolis. Identified by Romans with Minerva.

Athens *(Athínai)*, cap. of Greece, on Plain of Attica. Pop. 2,101,000. Admin., indust., cultural centre; univ.; Greek Orthodox archbishopric. Foremost Greek city state from 5th cent. BC, esp. under Pericles. Won Persian Wars, but defeated by Sparta (404 BC); decline followed defeat by Philip of Macedon (338 BC); sacked by Rome (86 BC). Fell to Turks 1458, rebuilt as cap. of independent Greece (1834). Buildings incl. Acropolis, Parthenon. Now forms one city with **Piraeus,** largest Greek port. Exports wine, olive oil. Built *c* 450 BC.

atherosclerosis, type of arteriosclerosis associated with deposits of fatty material, usually cholesterol, in lining of arteries. Factors linked to its cause incl. eating of animal fat, tobacco smoking, lack of exercise.

athlete's foot, *see* RINGWORM.

athletics, physical games and contests, divided into field (throwing, jumping, vaulting) and track (running) events. History can be traced as far as Greek games of 13th cent. BC. Modern athletics date from 19th cent.

Athos or **Akti,** penin. of NE Greece, easternmost part of Chalcidice penin., Macedonia. Rises to Mt. Athos (*Hagion Oros:* 'Holy Mountain'), 2032 m (6670 ft) high; incl. 20 Basilian monasteries (founded 10th cent.), created an autonomous state 1927.

Atlanta, cap. of Georgia, US. Pop. 1,790,000. Transport and commercial centre; textiles, steel products. Founded 1837 as Terminus, renamed 1843. City burned by W. T. Sherman during Civil War.

Atlantic Cable, submarine telegraph cable linking Britain and US. Successfully laid (1866) through efforts of Cyrus Field (1819-92). Telephone cable link between UK and Canada completed 1961.

Atlantic Charter, programme drawn up (Aug. 1941) by Churchill (Britain) and F.D. Roosevelt (US), stating general aims for post-WWII peace. Goals incl. in UN declaration (1942).

Atlantic City, resort of SE New Jersey, US; on Absecon Beach (sand bar). Pop. 188,000. Has board walks, luxury hotels, auditorium; holds political conventions.

Atlantic Ocean, world's 2nd largest ocean. Area 82,362,000 sq km (*c* 31,800,000 sq mi). Extends from Arctic to Antarctic, between Americas and Europe and Africa. Greatest depth at Milwaukee Deep (8530 m/28,000 ft) just N of Puerto Rico. Chief ocean currents Equatorials and subsidiaries: Gulf Stream and Labrador in N, Brazil and Guinea in S.

Atlantis, legendary large island in western sea. Plato describes it as a Utopia, destroyed by earthquake. Solon identified it with Santorin in Cyclades isls., which erupted *c* 1500 BC causing destruction of Minoan civilization by fire and tidal wave.

Atlas, in Greek myth, a Titan, son of Iapetus and Clymene. For his part in Titans' revolt against Olympians, condemned to hold up sky. Identified with Atlas Mts. in N Africa.

Atlas Mountains, system of NW Africa. Extend *c* 2400 km (1500 mi) from SW Morocco to N Tunisia. Incl. Tell Atlas, Saharan Atlas (Algeria); High Atlas (Morocco) rise to 4163 m/13,664 ft at Djebel Toubkal. Resources incl. phosphates, coal, oil, iron ore.

atmosphere, combination of gases surrounding a celestial body. For Earth, it consists mainly of nitrogen (78%), oxygen (21%). Extends up to *c* 950 km (600 mi), becomes rarer with distance from Earth's surface, 99% of mass of atmosphere being within 80 km (50 mi). Layers, in ascending order, are TROPOSPHERE, STRATOSPHERE, mesosphere, thermosphere, exosphere. Atmosphere forms protective shield; absorbs and scatters harmful radiation, causes solid matter to burn up. Also *see* IONOSPHERE

atoll, form of CORAL REEF. Circular or horseshoe-shaped, encloses a lagoon.

atom, in chemistry, smallest particle of an element which can take part in chemical reaction. Atom consists of positively charged nucleus, where its mass is concentrated, surrounded by orbiting electrons; nucleus is composed of protons and neutrons, the number of protons equal to number of electrons. *See* ELEMENT.

atomic bomb, weapon deriving explosive force from nuclear fission. Detonated by rapidly bringing together 2 subcritical masses of fissile material (*eg* uranium 235 or plutonium 239), with total mass exceeding critical mass. Ensuing chain reaction releases nuclear energy, yielding intense heat and shock waves, gamma and neutron radiation. Developed during WWII and first used on Hiroshima.

atomic clock, extremely accurate clock utilizing vibrations of atoms and molecules. Originally ammonia and caesium used; now hydrogen maser gives accuracy of *c* 1 part in 10^{13}.

atomic energy, *see* NUCLEAR ENERGY.

atomic mass unit or **amu,** unit of mass, 1/12 of mass of most abundant isotope of carbon (mass no. 12). Equals *c* 1.66×10^{-27} kg.

atomic number, number of protons in atomic nucleus of an element.

atomic theory, study of structure of fundamental components of matter. Early contributors incl. DEMOCRITUS (5th cent. BC) who held that matter is composed of minute indivisible particles (atoms) in motion. Modern theory began with John DALTON (1808) who held that elements are made of identical atoms, whose physical and chemical properties are different from those of atoms of other elements. A theory of internal structure of atoms was formulated by RUTHERFORD and improved by BOHR, who used quantum theory to describe electron orbits about central nucleus. Most recent theories rely on probabilistic methods of WAVE MECHANICS.

atomic weight, average mass of atom of specified isotopic composition of an element, measured in atomic mass units. Usually natural isotopic composition taken.

atonality, in music, absence of a key or tonal centre. Much of modern 'classical' music has moved away from definite tonal centres. Developed in work of Ives, Schoenberg, Webern, Bartók.

atonement, in Christian theology, the effect of Jesus' sufferings and death in bringing about the reconciliation of man to God.

Atonement, Day of (Heb. *Yom Kippur*), most important Jewish holy day on 10th day of 7th month, Tishri (late Sept. or Oct). Day of prayer for forgiveness.

Atreus, in Greek myth, king of Mycenae; father of Agamemnon and Menelaus. To avenge treachery of his brother, THYESTES, he killed Thyestes' sons and served their flesh to him at a banquet. Killed by AEGISTHUS.

atrium, in anatomy, either of two upper chambers on each side of heart. Left atrium receives oxygenated blood from lungs; right atrium receives venous blood from rest of body.

Attica *(Attiki),* admin. dist. of EC Greece, cap. Athens. Cereals, olive oil, wine. In legend, ancient state formed by Theseus; dominated by Athens from 5th cent. BC.

Attila (*c* 406-53), king of the Huns (434–53). Ruled over most of area between the Rhine and Caspian. Forced Rome to pay tribute and invaded Gaul when tributes ceased. Defeated at Châlons (451). Later invaded Italy but withdrew N after abandoning plan to capture Rome (452).

Attis, in Phrygian pantheon, god of vegetation. After death, caused by self-castration, spirit passed into pine tree; violets grew from his blood, symbolizing rebirth of plant life. Spring festival celebrated death and resurrection.

Attlee, Clement Richard Attlee, 1st Earl (1883-1967), British statesman, PM (1945-51). Rose to Labour Party leadership (1935), after serving in 1924 and 1929 Labour govts. Deputy leader in Churchill's wartime coalition cabinet (1942-5). His own admin. inaugurated nationalization of major industs., created National Health Service; concluded Palestinian mandate and granted independence to India. After 1951 election loss, led opposition until retirement (1955).

attorney, in law, person empowered to act as agent for or in behalf of another, esp. a lawyer. *See* ADVOCATE.

aubergine, deep purple fruit of eggplant, *Solanum melongena,* native to India. Cultivated widely esp. in Mediterranean region.

aubretia, genus of plant of Cruciferae

family. Showy purplish flowers, often cultivated in rock gardens. Native to Middle East.

Auch, town of SW France, on R. Gers, cap. of Gers dept. Pop. 24,000. Agric. market, wine, brandy. Major city (*Auscorum*) of Roman Gaul; cap. of Armagnac from 10th cent., of Gascony from 17th cent. Cathedral (15th cent.).

Auckland, city of N North Isl., New Zealand, on isthmus between 2 harbours. Pop. 746,000. Major port for overseas trade; exports dairy produce, fruit, timber. Shipbuilding, engineering industs.; food processing. Univ. (1882). Former cap. of New Zealand (1840-65).

Auden, W[ystan] H[ugh] (1907-73), English poet. Led left-wing literary movement in 1930s. Plays with Isherwood incl. *The Ascent of F.6* (1937). *Collected Poetry* (1945) contains best-known verse. Also wrote opera libretti (incl. text for Stravinsky's *The Rake's Progress*). Settled in US 1939.

Audubon, John James (*c* 1785-1851), American naturalist, artist. Published (1827) *Birds of America* featuring his colour paintings. National Audubon Society (1886) studies and protects birds of US and Canada.

Augsburg, city of S West Germany, on R. Lech. Pop. 246,000. Railway jct., textile centre. Roman colony founded 14 BC by Augustus. Important commercial centre 15th-16th cent.

Augsburg, Peace of, settlement (1555) of problems created within Holy Roman Empire by Reformation. Estab. principle that choice between Lutheranism and Catholicism was to be made by individual princes.

Augsburg Confession, official statement of Lutheran beliefs. Presented to Charles V at Diet of Augsburg (1530).

Augurs or **Augures,** college of officials in ancient Rome who interpreted signs *(auspicia)* of divine approval or disapproval in natural phenomena, *eg* eclipse, meteors, flight or feeding of birds.

Augusta, cap. of Maine, US; on Kennebec R. Pop. 23,000. Trading post estab. 1628. Mfg. industs. developed with damming of river (1837).

Augustine, St (354-430), Numidian churchman, theologian. Brought up as Christian, but not baptized until 387 after period of great doubt recorded in spiritual autobiog. *Confessions*. Bishop of Hippo in N Africa (396-430), defended Christianity against heretical beliefs incl. Manichaeism, Pelagianism. Other works incl. *City of God*.

Augustine of Canterbury, St (d. *c* 605), Roman Benedictine missionary, 1st archbishop of Canterbury. Sent (596) by Pope Gregory I to England, and introduced Roman doctrines, calendar into England.

Augustinians, religious orders in RC church which live according to Rule of St Augustine of Hippo. First organized in 11th cent.

Augustus, full name Gaius Julius Caesar Octavianus (63 BC–AD 14), 1st Roman emperor. Adopted as son and heir by Julius Caesar. On Caesar's death, entered into ruling coalition (2nd Triumvirate) with Lepidus and ANTONY. Subsequent conflict with Antony and Cleopatra culminated in his victory at Actium (31 BC), leaving him master of Rome. Assumed leadership (28 BC), given title Augustus. Rule marked by prosperity, flourishing of the arts.

auk, diving bird of Alcidae family of N hemisphere, with webbed feet, short wings. Flightless great auk, *Pinguinus impennis,* was largest species; became extinct in mid-19th cent. through hunting.

Auld Alliance, long-standing alliance between Scotland and France against common enemy, England, from 12th to 16th cent.

Aurangzeb (1618-1707), Mogul emperor of India (1658-1707). Seized throne by imprisoning father, Shah Jehan. Extended empire through military conquests. Fanatical supporter of Islam, destroyed Hindu temples and antagonized Sikhs.

Aurelian, full name Lucius Domitius Aurelianus (*c* 212-75), Roman emperor (270–5). Successful military leader, acclaimed emperor by his troops. Secured Danube and Rhine frontiers against barbarians and defeated ZENOBIA of Palmyra; recaptured Gaul.

Aurelius, Marcus, *see* MARCUS AURELIUS ANTONINUS.

Aurora, in Roman religion, goddess of dawn, identified with Greek Eos.

aurora, coloured light phenomenon visible at night in near-polar regions. Aurora borealis (northern lights) seen in N hemisphere, aurora australis in S. Believed to be caused by collisions of air molecules and charged particles from Sun, deflected towards poles by Earth's magnetic field.

Auschwitz, *see* OŚWIECIM.

Austen, Jane (1775-1817), English novelist. Works deal with middle-class provincial society, but her ironically witty analysis of character and moral problems is profound and universal. *Emma* (1816) and *Pride and Prejudice* (1813) are most popular, but *Sense and Sensibility* (1811), *Mansfield Park* (1814), *Northanger Abbey* and *Persuasion* (both pub. 1818) all show the same skilful construction.

Austerlitz *(Slavkov),* town of SC Czechoslovakia. Pop. 5000. Scene of battle (1805) in which French under Napoleon defeated combined Austro-Russian force.

Austin, cap. of Texas, US; on Colorado R. Pop. 446,000. In irrigated agric. region; food processing industs. Estab. as cap. 1839. Has Univ. of Texas (1883).

Australasia, term referring normally to Australia, New Zealand, New Guinea and adjacent isls. May also refer to all Oceania.

Australia, smallest continent, between Indian Ocean (W) and Pacific Ocean (E). Forms, with Tasmania, Commonwealth of Australia. Area 7,690,000 sq km (2,970,000 sq mi); pop. 14,249,000; cap. Canberra. Language: English. Religions: Anglican, RC. Comprises 6 states: New South Wales, Queensland, South Australia, Tasmania, Victoria, Western Australia; also Capital Territ., Northern Territ. Narrow coastal lowlands, except for Nullarbor Plain in S; Great Dividing Range in E; vast arid tableland in W. Climate varies from tropical monsoon in N to temperate in S. Isolation led to distinct flora and fauna *eg* giant eucalyptus, marsupials. Agric. incl. sheep rearing, wheat and fruit growing; minerals incl. gold, lead, copper, zinc, uranium, bauxite, oil, iron, coal; industs. incl. iron and steel, chemicals. E coast claimed (1770) for Britain by Cook. Originally used as penal settlement; pop. increased greatly after gold discoveries *c* 1850. Separate colonies federated 1901 to form Commonwealth.

Australian aborigine

Australian aborigines, ethnic group of Australian mainland (mainly N and NE). Nomadic hunters, they have primitive material culture but complex social system with totemic worship. Weapons incl. boomerang. Est. pop. is 70,000 mostly on reservations.

Australian Alps, mountain range of SE New South Wales and NE Victoria, Australia. Incl. Snowy Mts.; highest peak Mt. Kosciusko. Winter sports area.

Australian Antarctic Territory, all isls. and mainland S of 60°S and between 45° and 160°E (with exception of Adélie Land); comprises almost half of Antarctica. Incl. Enderby, MacRobertson, Princess Elizabeth, Wilhelm II, Queen Mary, Wilkes, George V lands and parts of Victoria Land.

Australian Capital Territory (ACT), territ. of SE Australia, enclave within New South Wales. Area, incl. Jervis Bay port, 2432 sq km (939 sq mi); pop. 198,000; cap. Canberra. Mainly grassy or forested upland; drained by Molonglo R. ACT created 1911 to incl. site of new federal cap.

Australian rules football, eighteen-a-side team game played with an oval ball. Dates from 1858, rules being revised in 1866. Derived from soccer, rugby and Gaelic football.

Australopithecus, extinct genus of hominid family from which modern man may have evolved. Tool-making form *A. boisei* (formerly known as *Zinjanthropus*), *c* 1.8 million years old, was discovered (1959) by Leakey in OLDUVAI GORGE.

Austria

Austria *(Österreich),* republic of C Europe. Area 83,851 sq km (32,375 sq mi); pop. 7,508,000; cap. Vienna. Language: German. Religion: RC. Mainly mountainous, fertile Danube plain in NE. Agric. (cereals, cattle, pigs), timber, coal, iron ore, h.e.p. Indust. centres Vienna, Graz, Linz. Ruled by Habsburgs 1282-1918, centre of Holy Roman Empire; incorporated Hungary, expanded with Partitions of Poland (18th cent.). Became Austrian empire (1804); unrest in Hungary led to dual monarchy (1867), collapsed 1918. Forcibly made part of Nazi Germany 1938-45; occupied by Allies 1945-55.

Austrian Succession, War of the (1740-8), European conflict precipitated by Maria Theresa's succession to Habsburg lands, by PRAGMATIC SANCTION, challenged by Bavarian elector (later Emperor Charles VII). Frederick II of Prussia, by claiming and invading Silesia, started war; withdrew (1745) after obtaining most of Silesia. Bavaria withdrew from war after death of Charles VII (1745) when it was overrun by Austrians. War concluded by Treaty of AIX-LA-CHAPELLE.

Austro-Hungarian Monarchy or **Dual Monarchy,** reorganized form of Habsburg empire, estab. (1867) to placate Hungarian nationalist aspirations. Hungary given control of internal affairs, union of crowns of Hungary and Austria maintained. Dissolved 1918.

Austro-Prussian War, conflict (June-Aug. 1866), between Prussia, supported by Italy, and Austria, allied with several German states. Prussia won quick victory over German states and defeated Austrians at Sadowa. Peace of Prague resulted in Austria ceding Venetia to Italy; Prussia annexed Frankfurt, Hanover and Hesse-Kassel. War provided 2nd stage in estab. of German Empire in 1871. Also known as Seven Weeks War.

Authorized Version, English translation of the Bible, pub. in 1611 with the authorization of King James I (also called King James Bible). Prepared by committee of Protestant scholars under direction of Lancelot Andrewes.

autism, psychosis, esp. of children, characterized by withdrawal from contact with other humans and disregard for external reality.

auto da fé (Port.,=act of faith), ceremonial burning of heretics in public. In widest use during Inquisition in Spain and Portugal; last known use in Mexico (1815). Also refers to trial and sentencing of alleged heretics by Inquisition.

autogiro or **gyroplane,** aircraft that moves forward by means of a powered propeller and is supported in air mainly by a revolving horizontal aerofoil turned by air pressure and not motor power. Used for its ability to make short take-offs and landings.

automation, in industry, automatic control of processes by self-regulating machinery. Such machinery makes use of part of its output effect to modify and correct input (feedback), using *eg* electronic sensing devices.

automobile or **motor car,** self-propelling passenger vehicle usually powered by INTERNAL COMBUSTION ENGINE. Wheels driven via GEARBOX. Developed in Germany by Karl Benz (*c* 1885), Gottlieb Daimler, and in US by Henry Ford.

autonomy, in politics, freedom of region or colony to act without external constraint, specifically referring to limited self-determination; often granted as prelude to complete independence, *eg* UK granted extensive internal legislative powers to Canada, Australia before their independence.

autumn crocus, *see* MEADOW SAFFRON.

Auvergne, region and former prov. of C France, in Massif Central, cap. Clermont-Ferrand. Cereals, livestock, cheese mfg.; mineral springs. Mainly mountainous. Hist. part of Aquitaine, part of France from 1527.

Avalon, in Celtic myth, isle of blest or paradise, sometimes identified with Glastonbury (Somerset). *See* ARTHURIAN LEGEND.

Avebury, village in Wiltshire, England, SW of Swindon. Site of Neolithic stone circle, older and larger than that at Stonehenge. Many stones removed in earlier times for building material.

Ave Maria (Lat.,=hail, Mary), prayer to Virgin Mary, fixed in present form by Pope Pius V (16th cent.).

aviation, operation of heavier-than-air aircraft. History of aviation highlighted by Wright brothers' 1st flight in heavier-than-air craft (US, 1903); Louis Blériot's flight across English Channel (1909); Alcock and Brown's transatlantic flight (1919); Charles Lindbergh's solo Atlantic crossing (1932). First transatlantic passenger service begun by Pan American Airways (1939). Years following WWII saw development of jet propulsion and supersonic flight.

Avicenna, Arabic name Ibn Sina (980-1037), Persian philosopher, physician. Estab. classification of sciences used in medieval schools of Europe. Known for his *Canon of Medicine*.

Avignon, town of Provence, S France, on R. Rhône. Cap. of Vaucluse dept. Pop. 154,000. Wine trade, silk mfg., tourist centre. Papal see during 'Babylonian Captivity' (1309-77), remained under papal control until 1791. Town walls, papal palace (both 14th cent.); ruins of 12th cent. bridge.

Avila, town of C Spain, on R. Adaja, cap. of Avila prov. Pop. 31,000. Tourist and religious centre. Cathedral, town walls (both 11th cent.). Birthplace of St Teresa.

avocado or **avocado pear,** tropical American tree, *Persea americana*. Yields pulpy, green or purple, pear-shaped edible fruit.

avocet, long-legged wading bird related to snipe, genus *Recurvirostra,* with worldwide distribution. Feeds by sweeping upward-curving bill through water.

Avogadro, Amadeo, Conte di Quaregna (1776-1856), Italian physicist. Formulated Avogadro's hypothesis, that equal volumes of gases at same temperature and pressure contain equal numbers of molecules, thus explaining Gay-Lussac's law of combining volumes.

avoirdupois, systems of weights used in UK: 16 drams = 1 ounce, 16 ounces = 1 pound, 28 pounds = 1 quarter, 4 quarters = 1 hundredweight, 20 hundredweights = 1 ton. In US, hundredweight = 100 pounds, ton = 2000 pounds.

Avon, Anthony Eden, 1st. Earl of, *see* EDEN, ANTHONY.

Avon, county of SW England, on Bristol Channel. Area 1337 sq km (516 sq mi); pop. 922,000; admin., hq. Bristol. Created 1974, incl. parts of Gloucestershire, Wiltshire, Somerset.

Avon, several rivers of UK. **1,** flows 154 km (96 mi) from Northamptonshire via Stratford into R. Severn at Tewkesbury. **2,** flows 120 km (75 mi) from Gloucestershire via Bath, Bristol into Bristol Channel at Avonmouth. Also name of other rivers in Scotland, Wales.

Axis, coalition of states (1936-45), active in WWII. Grew out of German-Italian alliance (1936); joined by Japan in Berlin Pact of 1940. Later incl. Hungary, Romania, Bulgaria, Slovakia, Croatia. Also *see* ANTI-COMINTERN PACT.

Axolotl

axolotl, aquatic larval salamander, genus *Ambystoma,* of SW US and Mexico. Does not develop into terrestrial adult amphibian, but can breed.

Axum, *see* AKSUM.

Ayer, Sir A[lfred] J[ules] (1910-), English philosopher. Brought LOGICAL POSITIVISM to attention of English readership in *Language, Truth and Logic* (1936). Other works incl. *The Foundations of Empirical Knowledge* (1940), *The Problem of Knowledge* (1956).

Ayesha (*c* 611-678), favourite wife of Mohammed. Helped father, Abu Bakr, succeed to caliphate on Mohammed's death. Fomented revolt against ALI, 4th caliph.

Aylesbury, mun. bor. of C England, co. town of Buckinghamshire. Pop. 41,000. Main indust. food processing.

Ayrshire, former county of SW Scotland, now in Strathclyde region. Hills in SE. Dairying (Ayrshire cattle) potato growing; coalmining industs. Co. town was **Ayr,** royal burgh on R. Ayr. Pop. 48,000. Small port, resort; textile, engineering industs.

azalea, widely distributed genus of shrubs or trees, now usually considered a subgenus of genus *Rhododendron.* Deciduous leaves and funnel-shaped flowers of various colours. Many varieties cultivated.

Azerbaijan Soviet Socialist Republic, constituent republic of SW USSR; on Iran border. Area *c* 86,600 sq km (33,400 sq mi); pop. 6,028,000; cap. Baku. Crossed by Caucasus Mts. in N; C plain watered by R. Kura and tributaries. Produces cotton, wheat; major oil deposits in Apsheron penin., centred on Baku. Territ. ceded to Russia in 19th cent. by Persia, incorporated by USSR (1920).

azimuth, in astronomy, arc of horizon between its N or S point and vertical circle passing through zenith and centre of heavenly body.

Azores *(Açores),* archipelago of N Atlantic, admin. dist. of Portugal *c* 1450 km (900 mi) W of Lisbon. Area 2300 sq km (888 sq mi); largest isl. São Miguel, has chief town Ponta Delgada. Volcanic, rises to 2315 m (7600 ft). Fruit, vegetables grown; winter resort. Settled by Portuguese mid-15th cent.

Azov, Sea of (Latin *Palus Maeotis),* N arm of Black Sea, to which it is connected by Kerch str. Area *c* 37,700 sq km (14,500 sq mi). Shallow, with many sandbanks and low salinity; receives R. Don near town of Azov. Important fisheries.

Aztec, American Indian people of C Mexico. Ruling group at time of Spanish conquest (16th cent.). Noted for highly sophisticated civilization, centred on cap. Tenochtitlán on site of modern Mexico City.

B

Baal, fertility god of N Semites, worship spread to Carthage and Egypt; name later applied to gods of particular towns. BEL of OT.

Baal-Schem-Tov, orig. Israel ben Eliezer (1700-60), Russian Jewish teacher. Founded HASIDISM movement.

Babel, Tower of, in OT, structure erected by Noah's descendants in Babylonia. Symbol of pride of city-dwellers who sought to rebel against God by building a tower to heaven. Thwarted by God's confusing their language so that they could not understand each other.

Baber or **Babar,** title given to Zahir ed-Din Mohammed (*c* 1482-1530), Indian emperor, founder of Mogul dynasty. Conquered most of N India (1526), invading from Afghanistan.

Babirusa

babirusa, *Babirussa babirussa,* wild pig of Celebes. Has backward-curving tusks; inhabits marshy forest.

baboon, large short-tailed monkey, genus *Papio,* found mainly in Africa. Fierce, with dog-like teeth and snout; lives in large social groups.

Babylon, ancient city of Babylonia, on N bank of Euphrates. Its ruins are in C Iraq, S of Baghdad. Important under Hammurabi (*c* 1750 BC) who made it cap. of Babylonia. Destroyed *c* 689 BC by Assyrians, rebuilt and achieved great splendour under Nebuchadnezzar. Its Hanging Gardens were one of the Seven Wonders of the World.

Babylonia, ancient empire of S Mesopotamia. Grew to power in 18th cent. BC under Hammurabi. Conquered and ruled by the Kassites until *c* 1150. Recovered under Assyrian rule, which it later overthrew with capture of Nineveh (612). Under Nebuchadnezzar, empire was extended over Mesopotamia, Egypt, Palestine. Absorbed into Persian empire after Cyrus' conquest (539 BC).

Babylonian Captivity, in history of Israel, period from fall of Jerusalem to Babylonians (586 BC) until creation of new Jewish state (538 BC) in Palestine. Many Jews were removed to Babylonia at this time. Term also applied to period in Middle Ages when papacy moved from Rome to Avignon, France. Began (1309) under Clement V, ended (1377) under Gregory XI.

Bacchanalia, ancient Roman festivals in honour of Bacchus, god of wine. Excesses caused them to be banned by the Senate (186 BC).

Bacchus, Roman name for Greek god DIONYSUS.

Bach, Johann Sebastian (1685-1750), German composer. Music director in several royal courts, supreme organist of his time. Bach's music came when the adoption of equal temperament made great harmonic movement possible; combined this with immense contrapuntal skill to produce some of the most assured music ever composed. His work consists mainly of keyboard works, pieces for instruments and orchestra, and religious music. Works incl. *Mass in B minor, St John Passion, The Well-tempered Clavier, Brandenburg Concertos.* His son, **Carl Philipp Emanuel Bach** (1714-88), was also a composer. Compositions characteristic of mid-18th cent., in reaction against his father's polyphonic style. His half-brother, **Johann Christian Bach** (1735-82), lived in London from 1762, where he enjoyed royal patronage. Wrote operas, symphonies, piano concertos.

backgammon, game played on a special board by two people. Each has 15 pieces which are moved according to the throw of dice. Played by Greeks and Romans and still common in countries of E Mediterranean; enjoyed popularity in West in mid-20th cent.

Bacon, Francis (1910-), British painter, b. Dublin. Works emphasize repulsiveness and horror of human condition. Incl. *Velázquez' Innocent X.*

Bacon, Francis, Baron Verulam (1561-1626), English philosopher, statesman. In *The Advancement of Learning* (1605), *Novum Organum* (1620), developed INDUCTIVE METHOD as replacement for deduction from Aristotelian authority. Also known for *Essays* (1597-1625) on religious, ethical matters. Lord Chancellor (1618); removed from office (1621) for corruption.

Bacon, Roger (*c* 1215-*c* 1292), English friar, scholar, scientist. Believed scientific experiment and learning necessary complement to faith. Credited with discovery of gunpowder; worked in optics.

bacteria, large group of usually one-celled micro-organisms, found in soil, water, plants and animals. Considered plant-like, they lack chlorophyll and multiply rapidly by simple fission. 3 typical shapes: rod-shaped (*bacillus*), spherical (*coccus*) and spiral (*spirillum*). Many are active in fermentation, promotion of decay of dead organic material and NITROGEN FIXATION. Pathogenic (parasitic) bacteria, 'germs', produce wide range of plant and animal diseases.

Bactrian camel, *see* CAMEL.

Badajoz, city of W Spain, on R. Guadiana, cap. of Badajoz prov. Pop. 103,000. Food processing, border trade centre. Former seat of Moorish emirate. Moorish citadel, 13th cent. cathedral.

Baden, region of SW West Germany. Former state, from 1952 part of Baden-Württemberg. Incl. picturesque Black Forest and part of Jura; vineyards, minerals, tourism.

Baden-Baden, town of SW West Germany, in Black Forest. Pop. 40,000. Tourism; thermal springs in use from Roman times.

Baden-Powell, Robert Stephenson Smyth, 1st Baron Baden-Powell of Gilwell (1857-1941), British army officer. Defended Mafeking (1899-1900) during Boer War. Founded BOY SCOUTS.

badger, *Meles meles,* nocturnal burrowing carnivore of Europe and N Asia, with black and white striped head. Diet of rodents, insects.

badminton, game played by volleying a light shuttle, either of feathers or nylon, over a net using gut-strung rackets. Played by 2 or 4 persons. Rules were drawn up in 1870s.

Baekeland, Lee Hendrik (1863-1944), American chemist, b. Belgium. Developed photographic paper using Velox process. Synthesized bakelite, a phenol-formaldehyde resin used for electrical insulation.

Baffin, William (*c* 1584-1622), English explorer. Piloted 2 unsuccessful expeditions (1615-16) to find Northwest Passage.

Baffin Island, largest and most E island in Canadian Arctic; in SE Franklin Dist., Northwest Territs. Area 476,068 sq km (*c* 183,810 sq mi). Eskimo pop.; whaling, fur trapping. Separated from Greenland by Baffin Bay, connected by Davis Str. to Atlantic.

Bagehot, Walter (1826-77), English economist, social and literary critic. Author of classic interpretation of govt., *The English Constitution* (1867).

Baghdad, cap. of Iraq; on R. Tigris. Pop. 2,970,000. Road, rail, air route jct.; produces textiles and cement. Founded 763, *fl* under caliph Harun al-Rashid as centre of commerce and learning. Declined after sack by Mongols (1258). Became cap. of independent Iraq (1921).

bagpipe, musical wind instrument consisting

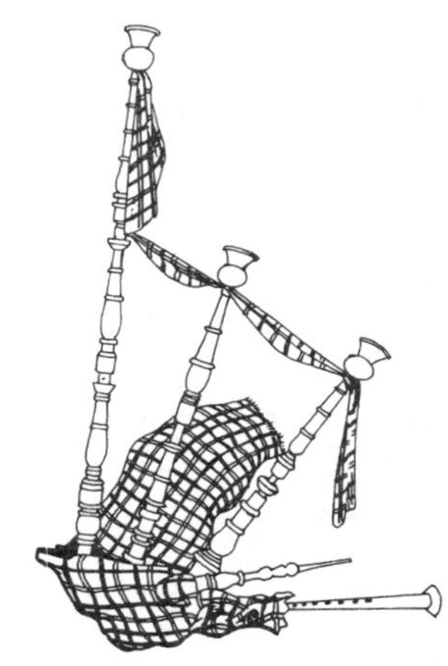

Scottish bagpipe

of bag inflated either by bellows or by player's breath blown through pipe; bag is squeezed by arm to force air out into several reed pipes. Chanter pipe has finger holes to produce melody; drones produce continuous bass notes. Of ancient Asiatic origin, bagpipes were introduced to Europe by Romans. Bagpipe playing as art form is esp. developed in Scotland and Ireland.

Baguio, summer cap. of Philippines, mountain resort in NC Luzon isl. Pop. 85,000. Gold mining centre.

Bahaism, religion founded in 19th cent. by Baha Ullah (1817-92), Persian religious leader. Bahaists believe in the unity of all religions, universal education, equality of the sexes and world peace.

Bahamas, coral isl. state of *c* 700 isls. in N West Indies; member of British Commonwealth. Incl. Andros (largest), New Providence, SAN SALVADOR. Area 11,404 sq km (4403 sq mi); pop. 225,000; cap. Nassau. Subsistence agric.; some timber, fish, salt, exports. Important tourist industs. Settled by English in 17th cent.; crown colony until independence in 1973.

Bahia, *see* SALVADOR, Brazil.

Bahrain or **Bahrein,** isl. group of E Arabia, in Persian Gulf. Area *c* 595 sq km (230 sq mi); pop. 345,000; cap. Manama. Important oil reserves; dates grown. Sheikdom under British protection until 1971; allied with United Arab Emirates.

Baikal, Lake, freshwater lake of USSR, SC Siberian RSFSR. Area *c* 31,500 sq km (12,200 sq mi). World's deepest lake, reaching depth of 1742 m (5714 ft).

Baird, John Logie (1888-1946), Scottish inventor. Pioneer of television, gave 1st transmission demonstration (1926) using mechanical scanning disc. Demonstrated colour television 1939.

Baja California (Lower California), narrow penin. of NW Mexico, between Gulf of California and Pacific. Mainly mountainous, arid climate; vegetation and pop. concentrated in irrigated region near US border.

bakelite, *see* BAEKELAND.

Baker, Sir Samuel White (1821-93), English explorer. Explored Nile and tributaries from 1861. First European to reach Albert Nyanza (1864).

Bakst, Léon, orig. Lev Nikolayevich Rosenberg (1868-1924), Russian painter. Gained international reputation for stage and costume design while working with Diaghilev's Ballets Russes.

Baku, city of USSR, cap. of Azerbaijan SSR; on Caspian Sea. Pop. 1,550,000. Centre of oil producing area of Apsheron penin.

Bakunin, Mikhail Aleksandrovich (1814-76), Russian anarchist. An aristocrat, active in Revolution of 1848; eventually exiled in Siberia but escaped 1861. Expelled (1872) from First INTERNATIONAL for opposition to Marxists. Believed in complete freedom, with violence as revolutionary means.

Balakirev, Mili Alekseyevich (1837-1910), Russian composer. Leader of nationalist Russian school of music; founded group of composers called 'the Five'.

Balaklava, suburb of Sevastopol, USSR, Ukrainian SSR; on Crimean penin. Scene of charge of Light Brigade on 25 Oct. 1854 during battle of Crimean War.

balalaika, Russian guitar, usually with three strings, fretted fingerboard and triangular body.

balance of payments, statement of account of a country comprising record of all public and private transactions between that country and all other countries. Takes into account all gifts, foreign aid, loans, interest on debts, payments for goods and received payments for exports, shipping and commercial services abroad, interest on overseas investments.

balance of power, policy of preventing one nation from gaining sufficient power to threaten security of other nations. Formulated by Metternich at Congress of Vienna (1815), served as basis for 19th cent. foreign policy of European nations. Again underlay post-WWII relations between US and USSR.

Balanchine, George, orig. Georgi Melitonovich Balanchivadze (1904-), American choreographer, dancer, teacher, b. Russia. Co-director with Diaghilev of Ballets Russes in Paris (1924-8). Directed New York City Ballet from 1948. Known for choreography of Stravinsky's music.

Balboa, Vasco Nuñez de (*c* 1475-1519), Spanish conquistador. Joined in conquest of Darién; crossed isthmus (1513), becoming first to reach Pacific. Beheaded for treason.

bald eagle, *Haliaeetus leucocephalus,* North American bird of prey. Black, with white head, neck and tail. Feeds on dead fish, rodents. National emblem of US.

Balder, in Norse myth, son of Odin, god of light, peace, virtue, wisdom. Killed by the trickery of Loki after attempt by his mother to make him invulnerable.

Baldwin, James (1924-), American author. Best known for first novel, *Go Tell it on the Mountain* (1953), but essays on Negro problems incl. equally important *Notes of a Native Son* (1955).

Baldwin, Stanley Baldwin, 1st Earl (1867-1947), British statesman, PM (1923-4, 1924-9, 1935-7). Leader of Conservative Party (1923-37). First term ended on protectionist tariff issue; later instrumental in ending General Strike (1926). Rise of fascism in Europe and constitutional crisis over Edward VIII's abdication marked 3rd term.

Bâle, *see* BASLE.

Balearic Islands

Balearic Islands *(Islas Baleares),* archipelago of W Mediterranean Sea, forming Baleares prov. of Spain. Area 5012 sq km (1935 sq mi); cap. Palma. Incl. Majorca, Minorca, Iviza, Formentera. Tourism, agric., fishing. Inhabited from prehist. times; under Moorish rule 10th cent.-1235; united with Aragón 1349.

Balfour, Arthur James Balfour, 1st Earl of (1848-1930), British statesman, PM (1902-5). His Conservative govt. resigned after cabinet split over Joseph Chamberlain's proposals for tariff reform (1905); party heavily defeated in 1906 election. As foreign secretary, drew up BALFOUR DECLARATION (1917).

Balfour Declaration (1917), assurance of British protection for Jewish settlement of Palestine. Drawn up by foreign secretary Balfour and contained in letter to Rothschild of British Zionist Federation.

Bali, isl. of Indonesia, just off E Java. Area *c* 5700 sq km (2200 sq mi); pop. 2,250,000. Mountainous, with fertile soil and good climate; produces rice, copra, coffee. Balinese are Hindus.

Balkan Peninsula, SE Europe. Extends S from rivers Danube, Sava. Comprises Albania, Bulgaria, Greece, European Turkey, Yugoslavia. Includes Balkan Mts. (Bulg. *Stara Planina*), range of C Bulgaria. Rise to 2372 m (7785 ft).

Balkan Wars (1912-13), two short wars for possession of Ottoman Empire's European territ. Serbo-Bulgarian alliance (1912) led to First War (Oct.), in which Turkey lost most European possessions. Austria, Hungary and Italy, at a meeting of Great Powers in London, created (1913) an independent Albania, thwarting ambitions of Serbia, which then demanded greater share of Macedonia from Bulgaria. Latter attacked Serbia (June, 1913), only to be attacked by Romania, Greece and Turkey. Second Balkan War ended with Treaty of Bucharest (Aug. 1913), in which Bulgaria lost territ. to all its enemies. Serbian territ. ambitions contributed to outbreak of WWI.

Balkhash, Lake, shallow lake of USSR, in SE Kazakh SSR. Area *c* 18,200 sq km (7000 sq mi). E part saline; W part, fed chiefly by R. Ili, fresh; no outlet.

Ball, John (d. 1381), English priest. Expounded Wycliffe's doctrines; excommunicated (1376) and imprisoned. Released by rebels, became a leader of PEASANTS' REVOLT (1381); caught and executed.

ballad, orig. (medieval British) narrative song in short stanzas, often with refrain, usually of popular origin, and orally transmitted, though sometimes composed by minstrels for noble audience.

ballade, poetic form set to music, *fl* 13th and 14th cent. in Provence and Italy. Composers, esp. Chopin and Brahms, used term for dramatic piano pieces.

Ballance, John (1839-93), New Zealand politician, b. Ireland, premier (1891-3). His Liberal govt. introduced widespread constitutional and social reforms.

Ballarat, city of S Victoria, Australia. Pop. 58,000. Railway Australia. indust. centre; trade in wool, wheat, fruit. Mining town from 1851 gold rush; scene of EUREKA STOCKADE miners' revolt (1854).

ballet, dramatic entertainment combining music, dance, mime, spectacle. Ballet as known today descends from court festivities of French, Italian Renaissance. Developed by French, esp. at Louis XIV's court where Lully and Molière created *comédies-ballets,* combination of dance and speech. The 5 classical foot positions were adopted in 18th cent., classical white dress and *en pointe* style in 19th cent. In 20th cent., rigid traditions attacked by Isadora Duncan and Diaghilev's Ballets Russes.

Balliol, or **de Baliol, John** (1249-1315), king of Scotland (1292-6). Disputed succession with Robert the Bruce. Edward I of England invited to arbitrate; Balliol chosen, but had to swear fealty. Later revolted; was captured by Edward, who then annexed Scotland.

balloon, non-powered aircraft obtaining lift from bag filled with lighter-than-air gas or hot air. Montgolfier brothers credited with invention (hot-air type, 1783). Hydrogen type first flown (1783) by J. Charles. Used for military observation since Napoleonic Wars. Now used for meteorological research, normally filled with helium for its non-flammability.

balm or **bee balm,** *Melissa officinalis,* many branched lemon-scented perennial of thyme family with white, lipped flowers.

balsa or **corkwood,** *Ochroma lagopus,* tree of Central and South America and West Indies. Strong, light wood used in model-making.

balsam, several trees, shrubs and plants of family Balsaminaceae which yield aromatic balsam.

Baltic Sea

Baltic Sea (Ger. *Ostsee*), sea of N Europe. Bordered by Denmark, Germany, Finland, Poland, Sweden, USSR. Linked to North Sea by Oresund, Great and Little Belt, Kiel Canal. Shallow; small tides. Hist. area of Hanseatic trade. Intensive fishing.

Baltic States, hist. name for countries on E shores of Baltic Sea, incl. Livonia, Estonia, Latvia, Lithuania (all now in USSR).

Baltimore, port of N Maryland, US; on Chesapeake Bay inlet. Pop. 2,148,000. Has natural harbour; exports coal and grain. Commercial, indust., railway centre; shipbuilding, steel indust., oil refining. Built 1729, with growth based on shipbuilding. Johns Hopkins Univ. (1876).

Baluchistan, region of SW Pakistan bounded by Iran, Afghanistan and Arabian Sea. Arid and mountainous; inhabited by Baluchis, Pathans. N controlled by British after Afghan wars of 19th cent.

Balzac, Honoré de (1799-1850), French novelist. Best known for *La Comédie humaine,* extensive series of novels incl. *Eugénie Grandet* (1833), *Père Goriot* (1834), which attempted to represent contemporary French society by creating a complete, detailed fictional world.

Bamako, cap. of Mali, on R. Niger. Pop. 400,000. Admin., commercial centre; river port, railway to Dakar. Former cap. of French Sudan.

bamboo or **cane,** semitropical or tropical grasses of the genera *Bambusa, Arundinaria, Phyllostachys.* Rapidly growing clump plant propagated by spreading underground roots. Some attain 35 m/120 ft. *Bambusa arundinacea,* hard, durable, with hollow stems, is used in buildings, furniture, utensils, paper making. Young bamboo shoots of some species are edible.

Banaba, *see* KIRIBATI.

banana, *Musa sapientum,* large perennial Asian plant, now widely cultivated in tropical regions of W hemisphere. Simple leaves, clustered flowers with edible fruits growing in large pendent bunches. Rich in carbohydrates.

band, a group of musicians, usually smaller than an orchestra. A brass band consists principally of brass instruments; a percussion or rhythm band mainly of percussion instruments. Bands are also named by the kind of music they play, *eg* dance band, military band. A 'big band' is large dance band consisting of sections of saxophones, trombones and trumpets overlying a rhythm section.

Banda, Hastings Kamuzu (1902-), Malawi statesman. Campaigned against Federation of Rhodesia and Nyasaland; imprisoned 1959-60. Became PM (1963), and president (1966) after Nyasaland had become republic as Malawi.

Bandaranaike, Sirimavo (1916-), Sri Lankan politician, PM (1960-5, 1970-77). First woman PM, she entered politics following her husband Solomon Bandaranaike's assassination (1959) while PM.

bandicoot, nocturnal Australasian marsupial of Peramelidae family, comprising *c* 20 species. Rat-like, with pointed muzzle.

Bandung, city of W Java, Indonesia. Pop. 1,202,000. Textile, rubber product mfg. Resort in beautiful surroundings. Scene of first conference of Afro-Asian countries, when neutrality between E and W was proclaimed.

Banff, resort town of SW Alberta, Canada. Pop. 4000. Nearby is Banff National Park; area 6641 sq km (2564 sq mi). Scenic lakes, glaciers, hot springs.

Banffshire, former county of NE Scotland, now in Grampian region. Cairngorm Mts. in S, fertile coastal plain in N. Cattle, fishing, distilling. Co. town was **Banff,** royal burgh (chartered 1163) on Moray Firth. Pop. 8000. Resort.

Bangalore, city of S India, cap. and railway jct. of Karnataka state. Pop. 1,654,000. Textile indust., electrical apparatus, machinery mfg. Tata Institute of Science (1911). Founded 16th cent.

Bangkok (*Krung Thep*), cap. of Thailand, port near mouth of R. Chao Phraya. Pop. 4,702,000. Exports teak, rice, rubber; rice milling, oil refining. Became cap. 1782; royal temple (1785) has famous image of Buddha.

Bangladesh, republic of SC Asia, at N end of Bay of Bengal. Area *c* 143,000 sq km (55,200 sq mi); pop. 84,655,000; cap. Dacca. Language: Bengali. Religion: Islam. Consists mainly of deltas of Ganges, Brahmaputra and Meghna rivers; densely populated. Agric. economy based on rice, tea and esp. jute. Subject to flooding and cyclones. Was East PAKISTAN from 1947 until civil war led to independence (1971).

Bangladesh

Bangor, port of E Northern Ireland, on Belfast Lough. Pop. 35,000. Tourist resort; former shipbuilding indust. Has ruins of 6th-cent. abbey.

Bangor, city of Gwynedd, NW Wales, on Menai Strait. Pop. 15,000. Tourist resort. Has Univ. of Wales coll. (1893); 16th cent. cathedral.

Bangui, cap. of Central African Republic, on R. Ubangi. Pop. 187,000. Port and trade centre, textile indust. Univ. (1970). Founded 1889.

Banjermasin or **Bandjarmasin,** cap. of Kalimantan prov. (Borneo), Indonesia. Pop. 282,000. Port near mouth of R. Barito. Exports oil, rubber.

banjo, stringed musical instrument with a circular parchment resonator and open back. Of African origin but developed in US, where it was brought by black slaves.

Banjul, cap. of Gambia, at mouth of R. Gambia. Pop. 48,000. Admin., commercial centre; port, exports groundnuts, hides. Founded 1816, known as Bathurst until 1973.

banking, conduct of financial transactions through institutions primarily devoted to accepting deposits and making loans. Practised in classical times; large-scale banking in Middle Ages dominated by Italian families. Modern banking developed during 18th-19th cent. in W Europe and US.

Bank of England, central bank of Britain, founded (1694) as commercial bank. Bank Charter Act (1844) estab. present system. Responsible for issue of bank notes, funding of national debts, *etc.* Nationalized 1946.

bank rate or **minimum lending rate,** minimum rate at which Bank of England makes loans to commercial banks and other prime borrowers. As other lending rates are closely related to bank rate, high rate restricts borrowing and lending, low rate encourages expansion of credit. Thus used as instrument of monetary control.

Banks, Sir Joseph (1743-1820), English naturalist. Accompanied Cook in expedition around the world (1768-71), accumulating remarkable plant collection. Leading figure in development of Kew Gardens.

banksia or **bottle brush,** genus of evergreen trees and shrubs of Protraceae family named after Sir Joseph Banks. Widely distributed in S hemisphere, esp. Australia.

Banks Island, SW Franklin Dist., Northwest Territs., Canada. Area 67,340 sq km (*c* 26,000 sq mi). First explored 1851.

Bannister, Sir Roger Gilbert (1929-), English physician. First man to run the mile in under 4 min. (Oxford, 1954). Best time was 3 min. 58.8 sec.

Bannockburn, town of Central region, C Scotland. Site of battle (1314) in which Robert the Bruce's victory over Edward II of England secured Scottish independence.

Banting, Sir Frederick Grant (1891-1941), Canadian physician. With C.H. Best, isolated (1921) insulin from pancreas; later purified it for use in treating human diabetes. Shared Nobel Prize for Physiology and Medicine (1923).

Bantry Bay, inlet of SW Irish Republic, 40 km (25 mi) long. Anchorage; oil storage. Scene of attempted French landing (1796). At head is port, Bantry (pop. 2000).

Bantu, African ethnic and linguistic group, *c* 70 million. Stretch from Equator south, except for extreme SW Africa. Physically diverse, classified mainly on language. Highly developed pre-European conquest; developed protective confederations in 19th cent., incl. ZULU and Basuto. Name, meaning 'the people', commonly used in South Africa for all native people.

banyan, E Indian fig tree, *Ficus benghalensis.* Branches send out aerial roots which reach ground to form new trunks, creating large sheltered area. Sacred among Hindus.

baobab or **boojum,** *Adansonia digitata,* large tree native to Africa, India. Broad trunk adaptable to storage of water. Yields edible fruit (monkey bread). Bark used in making paper, cloth, rope. Leaves used medicinally.

baptism, in most Christian churches, sacrament admitting a person into Christianity. Involves ritual purification with water and invocation of grace of God to free the soul from sin.

Baptists, Christian denomination holding that BAPTISM should be given only to believers after confession of faith, and by immersion in water rather than by sprinkling. First English Baptist congregation formed (*c* 1608) in Amsterdam under John Smyth.

Barabbas, in NT, prisoner chosen by the mob, in accordance with Passover custom, to be released by Pilate in place of Jesus.

Barbados, low-lying isl. state, in British Commonwealth. Most E of West Indies. Area 430 sq km (166 sq mi); pop. 250,000; cap. Bridgetown. Has fertile agric. soil; sugar cane growing; molasses, rum mfg. Winter tourist resort. Claimed by English 1605; independence 1966.

barbary ape, *Macaca sylvana* tailless monkey of N Africa, S Spain and Gibraltar. Only monkey native to Europe.

Barbary Coast, coast of N Africa from Morocco to Libya. Named after Berbers, the chief inhabitants. Notorious for piracy on European shipping (16th-19th cent.), ended by French capture of Algiers (1830). Name also applied to waterfront dist. of San Francisco, US, after 1849 gold rush.

Barbary sheep, *see* AOUDAD.

barbastelle, *Barbastella barbastellus,* common European bat, with almost black fur. Roosts in large colonies.

barbel, freshwater fish of carp family, genus *Barbus,* found in Asia, Africa, Europe. Thread-like growths (barbels) hanging from jaws act as organs of touch.

barberry, any deciduous shrub of genus *Berberis.* Spiny leaves, sour red berries, yellow flowers. Ornamental species, often used in hedges.

Barbirolli, Sir John (1899-1970), British conductor. In 1936 succeeded Toscanini as conductor of the New York Philharmonic Orchestra; best known as the conductor of the Hallé Orchestra (Manchester) from 1943 to 1968.

barbiturates, group of drugs derived from barbituric acid, used to promote sleep and as sedatives. Overuse may lead to addiction.

Barbizon School, group of French landscape painters who made their centre at Barbizon in Forest of Fontainebleau in 1840s. Members incl. Millet, Daubigny.

Barbuda, *see* ANTIGUA.

Barcelona, city of Catalonia, NE Spain, on Mediterranean Sea. Cap. of Barcelona prov. Pop. 1,810,000. Major port; indust., commercial centre; univ. (1430). Founded by Carthaginians; taken (801) by Charlemagne, independent countship from 9th cent. *Fl* after union (1137) of Aragón and Catalonia. Catalan cultural centre, focus of radical movements. Seat of govt. (1938-9) in Civil War. Cathedral (13th cent.), palaces.

Barebone, Praise-God (*c* 1596-1679), English nonconformist lay preacher. Member of provisional assembly (Barebone's Parliament) nominated by Cromwell (1653) after dissolution of Rump Parliament.

Barents or **Barentz, Willem** (d. 1597), Dutch explorer. Made 3 unsuccessful attempts to find Northeast Passage, reached Spitsbergen and Novaya Zemlya.

Barents Sea, extension of Arctic Ocean, lying N of Norway and bounded in part by Franz Josef Land and Novaya Zemlya. Ice-free ports, *eg* Murmansk, and fisheries in S.

Thames sprit-sail barge

barge, large boat, usually flat-bottomed, used for transportation on sheltered waters. Common on Nile in ancient Egypt. Modern barges towed by tugs or self-propelled.

Bari, cap. of Apulia (Puglia). SE Italy, on Adriatic Sea. Pop. 387,000. Major port; oil refining, textiles; univ. (1924). Roman colony *(Barium)*; taken (1071) by Normans, embarkation point for medieval Crusades. Cathedral (12th cent.), basilica with relics of St Nicholas.

barite, barytes or **heavy spar** ($BaSO_4$), heavy, white or colourless mineral. Consists of orthorhombic-shaped crystals; occurs in massive or granular forms. Uses incl. paint pigment, medical radiology.

baritone, in singing, high bass voice, midway between bass and tenor.

barium (Ba), silvery metallic element; at. no. 56, at. wt. 137.34. Occurs as BARITE and as carbonate; prepared industrially by reduction of barium oxide. Compounds used in glass, paint and fireworks; sulphate taken internally to help obtain X-ray pictures of digestive tract.

bark, outer covering of the stems and roots of trees and woody plants. Consists of 2 layers; the inner of living flexible cork-like material, the outer a dead inflexible shell. Many barks have economic uses *eg* as in hemp, flax, jute or as flavourings, *eg* cinnamon, or drugs, *eg* quinine, cocaine.

Barking, bor. of NE Greater London, England. Pop. 151,000. Has large power station. Motor vehicles indust. Created 1965 from Barking, Dagenham.

barley, genus *Hordeum* of grass family, probably originating in Asia Minor. Cultivated since prehistoric times. Most common cultivated form is *H. vulgare*. Unbranched stems rise in clumps and bearded seed heads extend from the grains. Used to make malt and in cooking.

barnacle, sedentary crustacean of subclass Cirripedia, found on rocks, piers and boat hulls. In some species, *eg* acorn barnacle, body enclosed in limy plates. Other naked varieties parasitic on marine invertebrates.

barnacle goose, *Branta leucopsis,* European goose with black and white plumage. Eaten on fast days in Middle Ages, as it was believed to be fish, hatching from barnacle.

Barnard, Christiaan Neethling (1922-), South African surgeon. Performed 1st human heart transplant operation (Cape Town, Dec. 1967).

Barnardo, Thomas John (1845-1905), British social reformer, b. Ireland. Known for founding 'Dr Barnardo's Homes', refuges for destitute children.

Barnet, bor. of W Greater London, England. Pop. 290,000. Created 1965 from parts of Middlesex, Hertfordshire. Scene of Yorkist victory (1471).

barn owl, long-legged pale owl of Tytonidae family with worldwide distribution, esp. *Tyto alba.* Lives in farm buildings; hunts mainly by sound.

Barnsley, town and admin hq. of South Yorkshire met. co., N England, on R. Dearne. Pop. 222,000. Coalmining; engineering, textiles industs.

Barnum, Phineas T[aylor] (1810-91), American showman. Exploited public taste for sensational, *eg* exhibiting midget Tom Thumb. Estab. circus 'The Greatest Show on Earth' (1871).

barometer, instrument used to measure atmospheric pressure. Comprises mercury-filled tube closed at upper end and held inverted in mercury-filled vessel. Height of mercury in tube gives atmospheric pressure. *See* also ANEROID BAROMETER.

Barons' War (1263-7), in English history, war between Henry III and his barons, led by de MONTFORT. Henry's defeat at Lewes (1265) led to summoning of Great Parliament. De Montfort was defeated and killed at Evesham (1265).

Baroque, in art and architecture, style characterized by much dramatic ornamentation and use of curved lines. Flourished from *c* 1580-1730; main exponent was Bernini. In music, refers to style prevalent *c* 1600–*c* 1750.

Barra, isl. of Outer HEBRIDES, W Scotland. Chief town Castlebay.

barracuda, voracious tropical fish of Sphyraenidae family. Great barracuda, *Sphyraena barracuda,* is largest, *c* 1.8 m/6 ft long.

Barranquilla, port of N Colombia, near mouth of Magdalena R. Pop. 692,000. Sugar refining, textile, chemical mfg.

barrel organ, mechanical organ in which a barrel armed with pins rotates and trips levers that admit air to organ pipes, to produce a single piece of music. Barrel is usually turned by hand.

Barrett Browning, Elizabeth, *see* BROWNING, ROBERT.

Barrie, Sir J[ames] M[atthew] (1860-1937), Scottish author. Plays incl. classic nostalgic fantasy *Peter Pan* (1904), also *The Admirable Crichton* (1902), *Dear Brutus* (1917). Wrote novels *eg The Little Minister*

(1891), *Sentimental Tommy* (1896).

barrister, in England, qualified member of legal profession who presents and pleads cases in courts. In higher courts has exclusive right to appear on behalf of litigant, but (with few exceptions) can do so only on solicitor's instructions. To qualify, student must join one of four INNS OF COURT; becomes 'junior', then King's (or Queen's) Counsel. *See* ADVOCATE.

barrow, in archaeology, mound erected over burial place. European barrows, dating from Neolithic times, are usually long or round. Building of barrows for burial of important people lasted into Saxon and Viking times.

Barrow, town of Alaska, US, on Barrow Point on the Arctic Ocean. Most northerly town of US. Pop. 2500. World's largest Eskimo settlement. Oilfield at Prudhoe Bay.

Barrow-in-Furness, bor. in Furness area of Cumbria, NW England. Pop. 64,000. Iron and steel mfg., shipbuilding, engineering industs.

Barry, Sir Charles (1795-1860), English architect. With Pugin, designed Houses of Parliament at Westminster (1840-6).

Barry, mun. bor. and port of S Glamorgan, S Wales, on Bristol Channel. Pop. 42,000. Exports coal, steel.

Barrymore, Lionel (1878-1954), American stage and film actor. Film roles incl. Rasputin in *Rasputin and the Empress* (1932). His sister, **Ethel Barrymore** (1879-1959), was a leading American stage actress, and played many 'character' parts in films. Their brother, **John Barrymore** (1882-1942), also acted on stage and in film. Known for 'profile' as young matinée idol, then romantic star of 1920s.

Barth, Karl (1886-1968), Swiss Protestant theologian. Believed authority of God is revealed in Jesus and biblical study is superior to philosophy. Early opponent of Nazism.

Bartók, Béla (1881-1945), Hungarian composer, pianist. Collected folk music, which influenced much of his work; compositions subsequently became more dissonant. His 6 string quartets greatly extended quartet medium; other works incl. *Concerto for Orchestra*, opera *Bluebeard's Castle*.

Bartolommeo [del Fattorino], Fra (1475-1517), Italian painter of Florentine school. Worked with Raphael in development of high Renaissance style. Works incl. *Pietà* (Florence).

Barton, Sir Edmund (1849-1920), Australian statesman, PM (1901-3). Leader of movement for federation of Australian colonies, became 1st PM with independence.

baryon, in physics, one of class of elementary particles, comprising protons, neutrons, and HYPERONS. All experience STRONG NUCLEAR INTERACTION and obey Fermi-Dirac statistics, *ie* are FERMIONS.

barytes, *see* BARITE.

basalt, fine-grained igneous rock, occurring abundantly in volcanic lava. Usually black or dull grey in colour. Basalt flows underlie sediments beneath all oceans, and form many land masses.

base, in chemistry, substance which yields hydroxyl (OH) ions if dissolved in water. Reacts with acids to form salt and water. Inorganic bases obtained by adding water to metal oxide; strength depends on degree of ionization. More generally, base defined as substance that accepts protons (thus amines are organic bases).

baseball, nine-a-side team game played with bat and ball, mainly in US. First organized team was New York Knickerbockers (1845); 1st professional team Cincinnati Red Stockings (1869). Major League baseball is played by 26 teams divided between National and American Leagues. Leading teams from the 2 leagues meet annually in World Series to determine champion.

Basel, *see* BASLE.

Bashkir, auton. republic of E European RSFSR, USSR. Area *c* 144,000 sq km (55,000 sq mi); pop. 3,848,000; cap. Ufa. Plateau and mountainous area in S Urals; extensively forested. Forms E part of Volga-Ural oilfields, connected by pipeline to refineries at Omsk. Natural gas, coal, metal ores.

Basic English, acronym for British American Scientific International Commercial English. Artificial international language, formulated by C.K. Ogden and I.A. Richards (*c* 1928). Its vocabulary of 850 common English words is capable of expressing most concepts.

basil, several aromatic, perennial herbs or shrubs of Labiatae (mint) family, native to Asia. Leaves are used in cookery.

Basildon, urban dist. of Essex, SE England. Pop. 138,000. Engineering, printing industs. Designated new town (1955) incorporating 4 Essex bors.

basilica, large Roman building used as public meeting place; usually rectangular with an interior colonnade and aisles on each side. With advent of Christianity, many were converted into churches.

basketball, five-a-side team ball game. Devised 1891 by James Naismith at Springfield, Mass., US. Extremely popular sport in US colleges; professional National Basketball Association was formed 1949.

basking shark, *Cetorhinus maximus*, large shark, reaching length of 9.7 m/35 ft; common to N Atlantic. Harmless, feeds on plankton.

Basle (Fr. *Bâle*, Ger. *Basel*), city of NW Switzerland, on R. Rhine. Pop. 369,000. Commercial, indust. centre at head of Rhine navigation; railway jct. Roman *Basilia*; joined Swiss Confederation 1501. Oldest Swiss univ. (1460).

Basque Provinces (Basque *Euzkadi*), region of NE Spain, incl. Alava, Guipúzcoa, Vizcaya provs. Name sometimes incl. Basque areas of Navarre, Gascony (France). Chief cities Bilbao, San Sebastian, Guernica (hist. seat of Basque parliaments). Iron, lead, zinc mining, engineering, fishing. Basques are an ancient people of obscure origin; unique language, distinctive customs. Settled here 9th cent., estab. kingdom of Navarre; later lost independence to Castile. Autonomous Basque govt. in Civil War defeated (1937) after Guernica bombed. Basque nationalism remains source of unrest, despite granting of limited autonomy (1979).

Basra (Arab. *Al Basrah),* city of SE Iraq. Pop. 371,000. Port on Shatt-al-Arab. Oil refining. Exports petroleum products, dates.

bass, in singing, the lowest adult male voice. Also applied to instruments of similar range.

bass, marine and freshwater fish, incl. sea bass (Serranidae) and sunfish (Centrarchidae) families, found in North America, Europe.

basset, breed of short-legged long-eared hound, used in hunting. Stands *c* 36 cm/14 in. at shoulder.

bassoon, orchestral woodwind instrument of oboe family. Wooden or metal tube is bent back on itself, double reed being brought within reach of player's mouth by curved metal tube. Contrabassoon is lower in pitch.

Bass Strait, channel between Tasmania and mainland Australia; greatest width *c* 240 km (150 mi). Has major oil, natural gas deposits.

Bastia, town of NE Corsica, France, on Tyrrhenian Sea. Pop. 50,000. Port, exports wine, fish, timber; cigarette mfg.; tourist centre.

Bastille, former state prison in Paris. Stormed as 1st act of French Revolution by Parisian mob (1789) and razed to ground. Anniversary of destruction, 14 July, is national holiday.

Basutoland, *see* LESOTHO.

Greater horseshoe bat

bat, noctural mammal of order Chiroptera, found in tropical and temperate regions. Only true flying mammal, elongated fingers are joined by membranous wing. Some tropical species are fruit-eating; most others insectivorous, locating prey and navigating by echo sounding. Blood-sucking varieties, *eg* vampire bat, in South America. Gregarious, living in groups in caves, *etc*; sleeps upside down suspended by claws.

Batavia, *see* DJAKARTA.

Bates, H[erbert] E[rnest] (1905-74), English author. Known for novels of rural life, incl. *My Uncle Silas* (1939), *The Darling Buds of May* (1958). Also wrote short-stories of service life under pseud. 'Flying Officer X'.

Bath, city of Avon, SW England, on R. Avon. Pop. 84,000. Roman *Aquae Sulis* built *c* AD 50 on site of thermal springs. Medieval wool indust. Fashionable 18th cent. spa. Famous for Georgian architecture of Nash, Wood.

batholith or **bathylith,** mass of intrusive igneous rock. Usually granite, forms substructure to many mountain or upland regions. Steep-sided, descends to unknown depths.

Bathsheba, in OT, wife of Uriah the Hittite. David sent Uriah to death in battle and then married her. She bore him Solomon.

Bathurst, *see* BANJUL.

bathyscaphe, *see* SUBMERSIBLE.

bathysphere, *see* SUBMERSIBLE.

batik, Indonesian method of applying coloured designs to cloth. Parts not to be dyed are coated with wax which can be removed after immersion of cloth in dye.

Batista [y Zaldívar], Fulgencio (1901-73), Cuban political leader. Military coup (1933) brought him to power; became president 1940. Exiled to US (1945), reinstated after leading 2nd coup (1952). Overthrown (1959) by CASTRO.

Baton Rouge, cap. of Louisiana, US; port and indust. town on Mississippi R. Pop. 412,000. Cotton, sugar exports; oil refining. Fort estab. by French (1719). Became cap. 1849.

Battersea, part of Wandsworth bor., S London, England, on S bank of R. Thames. Has power station, amusement park, famous dogs' home.

battery, group of cells used as source of electric power. Common dry battery usually consists of Leclanché cells.

battleship, large, armoured warship equipped with heavy guns. Evolved from ironclad warship of 19th cent., built of steel by 1870s. Britain's *Dreadnought* (1906) introduced the 'all-big-gun' class of warship. Extensively used during WWI, became obsolete in WWII with development of aerial divebombing.

Baudelaire, Charles Pierre (1821-67), French poet, important SYMBOLIST. His single collection *Les Fleurs du Mal* (1857) attempts through imagery to evoke the mystery of life and temper morality with aesthetics. Also translated his great influence, Poe.

Baudouin (1930-), king of Belgium (1951-). Son of Leopold III, on whose abdication he became king.

Bauhaus, school of design, architecture and craftsmanship, founded (1919) by Walter Gropius in Weimar, Germany; aimed at union of creative arts and technology of modern mass-production. Moved to Dessau, then to Berlin; closed by the Nazis (1933). Its ideas and teaching influenced both art and industrial design.

bauxite, clay-like mineral deposit, a mixture

of hydrated aluminium oxides. Colour varies from white to reddish-brown. Chief source of aluminium and its compounds; major deposits in France, USSR, West Indies.

Bavaria *(Bayern),* state of SE West Germany. Area 70,531 sq km (27,232 sq mi); cap. Munich. Uplands, plains, valleys; principal rivers Danube, Main. Agric., forestry, tourism. Indust. centred in Munich, Nuremberg, Augsburg. Duchy then kingdom, under Wittelsbach dynasty 1180-1918. Hist. separatist region, joined Federal Republic 1949.

Bayern, *see* BAVARIA.

Bayeux Tapestry, piece of embroidery depicting invasion of England by William the Conqueror (1066). Length *c* 70 m/230 ft; prob. made in 11th cent. Preserved in Bayeux Museum, France.

Bay of Pigs, inlet of S Cuba. Scene of unsuccessful invasion by Cuban exiles backed by US forces in attempt to overthrow Castro regime (1961).

Bayreuth, town of EC West Germany. Pop. 65,000. Textiles, metals, pottery mfg. Home of Wagner, who designed the opera house (built 1876); annual Wagner festival.

bay tree or **bay laurel,** *see* LAUREL.

BBC, *see* BRITISH BROADCASTING CORPORATION.

BCG vaccination, preventive vaccination against tuberculosis, usually administered to children at *c* 13 yrs. Initials stand for bacillus of Calmette and Guérin.

beagle, small hound with short legs and drooping ears, developed in England to hunt hares. Stands *c* 33 cm/13 in. at shoulder.

Beaker People, people of early Bronze Age, arrived in Britain *c* 2000-1800 BC, bringing first metal weapons and tools. Prob. built part of stone circles at Avebury and Stonehenge.

bean, edible seed of several plants of Leguminosae family. Inexpensive source of protein. Species incl. runner bean, soya bean, haricot bean.

bear, large mammal of Ursidae family of Europe, Asia, America. Shaggy fur, short tail; walks flat on soles of feet. Solitary, sleeps through winter in cold climates. Eats little flesh, diet mainly vegetable. Varieties incl. BROWN, BLACK, GRIZZLY, HONEY, KODIAK, POLAR bears.

Bear, Great and Little, *see* URSA MAJOR and URSA MINOR.

bearded lizard, *Amphibolurus barbatus,* agamid lizard of Australia. Inflates beard-like membrane of scales around throat when aroused.

Beardsley, Aubrey Vincent (1872-98), English artist, illustrator. Produced highly stylized, often grotesque, black and white drawings.

Beatitudes, in NT, eight blessings given by Jesus at the opening of the Sermon on the Mount.

Beatles, the, British rock musicians, one of most successful groups ever. Comprised John Lennon (1940-80), Paul McCartney (1942-), George Harrison (1943-) and Ringo Starr, orig. Richard Starkey (1940-). Gained worldwide following in the 1960s. Disbanded *c* 1970, subsequently active individually.

Beaton or **Bethune, David** (1494-1546), Scottish churchman, cardinal-archbishop of St Andrews. Attempted to assume regency for Mary Queen of Scots. As chancellor (1543), opposed Henry VIII's plans for subjugation of Scotland. His persecution of Protestants led to burning of George Wishart. Murdered in revenge.

Beatrix (1938-), queen of Netherlands (1980-). Succeeded on mother Juliana's abdication.

Beatty, David Beatty, 1st Earl (1871-1936), British admiral. Led squadron in defeat of German navy at Jutland (1916).

Beaufort Scale, measure of wind velocity; varies from 0 for calm to 12 for hurricane force. Devised in 1805 by Sir Francis Beaufort.

Beaufort Sea, part of Arctic Ocean, bounded by Banks Isl. (N Canada) in E and N, Alaska in S.

Beaumarchais, assumed name of Pierre Augustin Caron (1732-99), French dramatist. Best known for comedies *The Barber of Seville* (1775), *The Marriage of Figaro* (1784).

Beaumont, Francis (1584-1616), English dramatist. Wrote mainly in collaboration with FLETCHER.

Beaune, town of Burgundy, E France. Pop. 17,000. Agric. market, centre of Burgundy wine trade.

Beauvais, town of N France, cap. of Oise dept. Pop. 49,000. Agric. market. Centre of Gobelins tapestry indust. until WWII. Cathedral (1227).

Beauvoir, Simone de (1908-), French novelist, essayist, member of EXISTENTIALIST movement. Works incl. *The Mandarins* (1954), fictionalized account of Sartre circle, *The Second Sex* (1949) analysing position of women in society.

beaver, large rodent of Europe and North America, genus *Castor.* Amphibious; webbed hind feet and broad flattened tail. Colonial, lives in 'lodges' in river banks; constructs dams in rivers, streams. Numbers depleted by fur hunters.

Beaverbrook, William Maxwell Aitken, 1st Baron (1879-1964), British statesman, newspaper owner, b. Canada. Bought *Daily Express, Evening Standard,* founded *Sunday Express.* Advocate of imperialism; later organized munitions production while in Churchill's war cabinet (1940-5).

Bechuanaland, *see* BOTSWANA.

Becket, Thomas á, *see* THOMAS À BECKET, ST.

Beckett, Samuel (1906-), Irish author, settled in France 1932; works in English and French. Best known for tragi-comedy *Waiting for Godot* (1954). Also wrote novels *eg Murphy* (1938), *Molloy* (1951). Nobel Prize for Literature (1969).

Becquerel, Antoine Henri (1852-1908), French physicist. Discovered radioactivity

(1896) when he observed clouding of photographic film by uranium salt. Shared Nobel Prize for Physics (1903) with the Curies.

bedbug, small parasitic insect of Cimicidae family with flattened wingless body. Infests beds, walls, feeding on warm blood of mammals, birds.

Bede or **Baeda** (*c* 673-735), English historian, theologian. Known as the Venerable Bede, spent life as Benedictine monk. Best known for *Ecclesiastical History of the English Nation*.

Bedfordshire, county of SC England. Area 1234 sq km (476 sq mi); pop. 495,000. Wheat growing, market gardening; indust. centre Luton. Admin., hq. **Bedford,** mun. bor. on R. Ouse. Pop. 73,000. Agric. equipment mfg., light industs.

Bedouin, nomadic ARABS of Saudi Arabia, Syria, Jordan, Iraq, N Africa. Dependent on camel, sheep breeding. Land divided into tribal orbits under a sheik.

bedstraw, any plant of genus *Galium*. Square stem, stalkless whorled leaves, small white or coloured flowers.

bee, four-winged hairy insect of worldwide distribution, order Hymenoptera. Bees are social or solitary. Solitary bees nest in soil or hollow stems. Social bees, incl. bumble bee, cuckoo bee, honey bee, live in colonies, usually operating caste system of queen, workers (infertile females) and male drones. Agents of flower pollination when seeking nectar.

beech, large, widespread family of trees incl. the beeches, oaks and chestnuts, but esp. genus *Fagus* with smooth, grey bark, hard wood, pale green leaves and edible 3-corned nuts. Wood is used in furniture and building.

Beecham, Sir Thomas (1879-1961), English conductor. Founded London Philharmonic Orchestra (1932) and Royal Philharmonic Orchestra (1947). Popularized works of Richard Strauss, Delius.

bee-eater, small brightly-coloured bird of Meropidae family, found in tropical and sub-tropical areas of Old World. Feeds on bees, other insects.

beer, alcoholic beverage made by brewing aqueous extract of cereals, esp. malted barley, with hops. Malted barley is crushed and mixed with warm water, which allows enzymes present in malt to convert its starch into sugar. Solution obtained (wort) is boiled with hops, which provide flavouring. Liquid is cooled, mixed with yeast and allowed to ferment. Quantity of malt and water, as well as length of fermenting, determine alcoholic content (usually from 3% to 6%).

Beerbohm, Sir [Henry] Max[imilian] (1872-1956), English writer, caricaturist. Known for witty theatre criticism, only novel *Zuleika Dobson* (1911) fantasy set in Oxford.

Beersheba, commercial town of SC Israel. Pop. 84,000. Trade centre for tribes of Negev desert. Pottery, glass mfg. Hist. associated with Abraham, Elijah.

beet, several varieties of biennial plants of genus *Beta* with edible leaves, thick fleshy white or red roots, widely cultivated as food crop. The sugar beet, *B. vulgaris,* native to Europe and grown in North America, provides *c* 30% of world's sugar. The garden beet or beetroot has red-veined leaves, edible root. Variety *cicla* is cultivated for leaves, known as beet spinach or Swiss chard.

Beethoven, Ludwig van (1770-1827), German composer, pianist. In early life, had some teaching from Mozart, Haydn; concert debut 1795. One of most original and influential composers, bridged Classical and Romantic eras in creating music of great emotional impact and formal qualities. Suffered increasing deafness from 1801 onwards. Among best-known works are orchestral, choral, chamber works and piano sonatas, *eg* Third (*Eroica*), Fifth, Sixth (*Pastoral*) and Ninth (*Choral*) symphonies, as well as *Moonlight Sonata, Mass in D,* string quartets and opera *Fidelio*.

Hercules beetle of South America

beetle, any insect of order Coleoptera (comprising *c* 250,000 species). Biting mouthparts; horny forewings cover membranous hind wings and protect body. Undergoes complete METAMORPHOSIS.

Begin, Menachem (1913-), Israeli political leader, b. Russia. Premier (1977-). Leader of *Likud* party. Signed peace treaty with Egypt 1979. Nobel Peace Prize (1978).

begonia, genus of succulent herbs with ornamental leaves and clustered red, pink or white flowers. Native of tropics. Many cultivated varieties.

Behan, Brendan (1923-64), Irish playwright. Known for black comedies, *The Quare Fellow* (1956), *The Hostage* (1959). Autobiog. *Borstal Boy* (1958) describes his formative years in IRA.

behaviourism, in psychology, doctrine that valid data consists only of the observable and measurable in individual's responses, not valuing subjective or introspective accounts.

Beida, town of NE Libya in Cyrenaica. Pop. 32,000. Govt. offices, univ. Built from 1961, designated as future national cap.

Beira, town of SC Mozambique, on Mozambique Channel. Pop. 50,000. Port, exports copper, tobacco, tea; large transit trade, rail links with Malawi, Zimbabwe, Zambia.

Beirut, cap. of Lebanon. Pop. 702,000. Port on Mediterranean. Trade centre since Phoenician times. Focus of foreign education; 4 univs. Financial centre; food processing. Became cap. of Lebanon under

French mandate (1920). Badly damaged in civil war in late 1970s.

Bel, in OT, prob. refers to Babylonian god Marduk, and BAAL of Phoenicians.

Belém, seaport of NE Brazil, cap. of Pará state, on Pará R. Pop. 772,000. Exports nuts, timber, jute. Centre of early 20th cent. rubber export boom.

Belfast, cap. and port of Northern Ireland, on Belfast Lough. Pop. 362,000. Admin., commercial centre. Shipbuilding; linen, tobacco mfg. Has Queen's Univ. (1845). Severely damaged by bombs and fires in religious conflict from 1969.

Belfort, town of E France, cap. of Territ. of Belfort dept. Pop. 56,000. Commands Belfort Gap between Vosges and Jura. Cotton mills, metal working. Successfully resisted Prussian siege (1870-1); remained French when Alsace ceded (1871) to Germany.

Belgae, tribes of mixed Celtic-Germanic origin, described by Julius Caesar. Occupied parts of Belgium and NE France, whence they spread to S England *c* 100 BC. Introduced coinage, potter's wheel, improved standards of agric. in England.

Belgian Congo, *see* ZAÏRE.

Belgium (Fr. *Belgique,* Flem. *België*), kingdom of NW Europe. Area 30,510 sq km (11,780 sq mi); pop. 9,840,000; cap. Brussels. Languages: Flemish (N), Walloon French (S). Religion: RC. Main rivers Meuse, Scheldt. Sandy area in N (Flanders), fertile plain in C; forested plateau in SE (Ardennes). Intensive agric. (cereals, flax, livestock). Extensive trade along North Sea coast and canal network. Heavy indust. (metals, textiles) on SC coalfield. Divided into independent duchies, counties in Middle Ages. Ruled by Burgundy, Habsburgs, Spain, France, Netherlands; independent monarchy from 1830. Colonized Congo (*see* ZAÏRE). German occupation in both WWs.

Belgrade (*Beograd*), cap. of Yugoslavia and of Serbia, at confluence of Danube and Sava. Pop. 775,000. River port, railway jct.; commercial, indust. centre, esp. textiles, chemicals, electrical goods; univ. (1863). Fortified (3rd cent. BC) by Celts. Held by Turks 1521-1867; became cap. of Serbia 1882, of Yugoslavia 1918. Has Turkish citadel.

Belisarius (*c* 505-65), Byzantine general. Served under Justinian I. Defeated Vandals in Africa (534). Fought against Goths in Italy, capturing Ravenna (540). Thwarted Bulgarian attack on Constantinople (559).

Belize, British crown colony of Central America, on Caribbean. Area 22,965 sq km (8867 sq mi); pop. 153,000; cap. Belmopan. Mainly flat with dense forests (valuable timber exports); Maya Mts. in interior. Tropical climate. Sugar cane, citrus fruit growing. English settlement (17th cent.) disputed by Spanish; colony estab. 1884; name changed from British Honduras (1973). Independence due 1981. Former cap. **Belize,** port at mouth of Belize R. Pop. 39,000. Timber exports; fish packing.

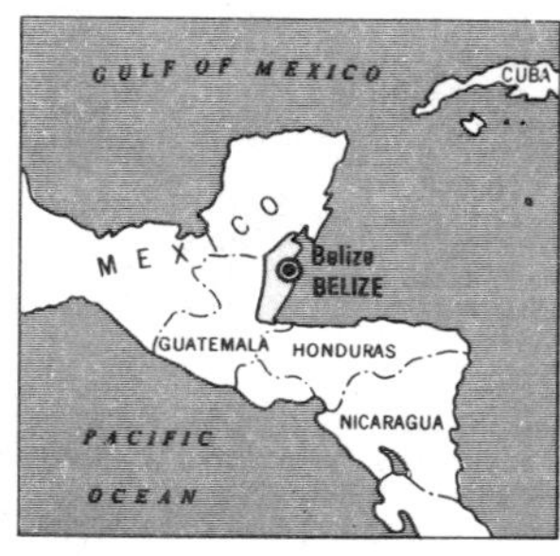

Belize

Bell, Alexander Graham (1847-1922), American scientist, inventor, b. Scotland. Gave 1st successful transmission of sound by telephone (1876). Patented device (1876) and organized Bell Telephone Co. (1877).

bell, (1) orchestral percussion instrument made of long tubes of brass, struck with mallet; (2) hollow cup-like vessel, usually made of metal, which rings when struck by an internal clapper or external hammer. Bells are often hung in sets and can be played by mechanical means to produce tunes (*see* CARILLON) or by groups of ringers who go through permutations of the diatonic scale, called change-ringing.

belladonna, *see* NIGHTSHADE.

Bellerophon, in Greek myth, hero who slew the CHIMAERA with help of winged horse, Pegasus. Angered Zeus by attempting to fly to heaven on Pegasus. Was thrown to earth and crippled or killed.

bellflower, *see* CAMPANULA.

Bellingshausen Sea, part of S Pacific Ocean, W of British Antarctic Territ. Named after leader of Russian expedition (1819-21).

Bellini, Jacopo (*c* 1400-70), Italian painter. Few of his paintings survive, but his 2 surviving sketchbooks were used by his 2 sons and Mantegna. **Gentile Bellini** (*c* 1429-1507) was prominent portraitist and painter of processions and ceremonies. Worked at court in Constantinople (1479-81). **Giovanni Bellini** (*c* 1430-1516) taught Giorgione and Titian. Works, characterized by lyrical handling of landscape.

Bellini, Vincenzo (1801-35), Italian composer. Known for lyrical operas *Norma* and *La sonnambula.*

Belloc, [Joseph] Hilaire [Pierre] (1870-1953), English writer, b. France. Known for collections of gruesome humorous verse, *eg Cautionary Tales* (1908). Also wrote novels, historical biog.

Bellow, Saul (1915-), American novelist, b. Canada. Works incl. *The Adventures of*

Augie March (1953), *Herzog* (1964). Nobel Prize for Literature (1976).

bell-ringing, *see* BELL.

Belmopan, cap. of Belize since 1973. Founded 1970. Pop. 5000.

Belo Horizonte, city of E Brazil, cap. of Minas Gerais state. Pop. 1,557,000. Centre of mining area (iron, manganese); agric. centre (cotton, cattle); steel indust., textile mfg., diamond cutting. Brazil's 1st planned city, built at end of 19th cent.

Belorussia, *see* BYELORUSSIAN SOVIET SOCIALIST REPUBLIC.

Belsen, village of NE West Germany, in Lower Saxony. Site of concentration camp under Nazi regime.

Belshazzar, in OT, son of Nebuchadnezzar, last king of Babylon. During debauched feast, writing appeared on wall which Daniel saw as ill omen. That night Cyrus captured Babylon.

Beltane, *see* MAY DAY.

beluga or **white whale,** *Delphinapterus leucas,* whale of Arctic seas, *c* 4.6 m/15 ft long.

Benares, *see* VARANASI.

Benbecula, isl. of Outer HEBRIDES.

Ben Bella, Ahmed (1919-), Algerian political leader. Joined Algerian nationalist movements, founder (1954) of FLN in Cairo. Twice arrested by the French, returned to become premier (1962). Elected president (1963), ousted in coup (1965).

bends, *see* AEROEMBOLISM.

Benedict XV, orig. Giacomo della Chiesa (1854-1922), Italian churchman, pope (1914-22). Maintained strict Vatican neutrality in WWI, concentrated on relief of war suffering.

Benedictines, RC monastic order, estab. by St Benedict (*c* 480–*c* 547) at Monte Cassino (*c* 529). Stressing communal living and physical labour, they also did much to preserve learning in early Middle Ages. Notable Benedictines were St Gregory the Great and St Augustine of Canterbury.

Benelux, economic union of Belgium, Netherlands, Luxembourg. Estab. (1958) after customs union ratified in 1948.

Beneš, Eduard (1884-1948), Czech statesman, president (1935-8, 1945-8). Exiled during WWII, headed provisional govt. in London, re-elected president after Czech liberation. Resigned after Communist coup of 1948.

Bengal, region of NE India and Bangladesh in Ganges-Brahmaputra delta. Under British control following victory at Plassey (1757). Divided (1947) into largely Hindu West Bengal and Moslem East Bengal (now in BANGLADESH). **Bay of Bengal** is arm of Indian Ocean between E India and Burma.

Benghazi or **Bengasi,** city of NE Libya, in Cyrenaica on Gulf of Sidra. Pop. 282,000. Port, admin. centre, railway jct. Founded by Greeks. Centre of Italian colonization from 1911 until taken by British in WWII. Cap. of Cyrenaica prov. 1951-63; joint cap. (with Tripoli) of Libya 1951-72.

Ben-Gurion, David (1886-1973), Israeli statesman, b. Poland. Leader of Mapai party, 1st premier (1948-53) of Israel; returned for 2nd term (1955-63). Broke away from Mapai (1965).

Benin or **Dahomey,** republic of W Africa. Area 112,700 sq km (43,500 sq mi); pop. 3,377,000; cap. Porto Novo. Official language: French. Religions: native, RC. Mainly subsistence agric.; exports coffee, cotton, palm oil. Native kingdom 17th-19th cent. with cap. at Abomey, promoted slave trade. Colonized (1892-3) by French; territ. of French West Africa from 1899. Independent from 1960, has had unstable govt.

Benin, city of S Nigeria. Pop. 136,000. Centre of rubber, palm and timber producing area. *Fl* 14th-17th cents. as cap. of Benin kingdom; famous for iron, ivory, bronze carvings. Taken (1898) by Britain.

Bennett, [Enoch] Arnold (1867-1931), English author. Known for realistic novels set in industrial Staffordshire, *eg Anna of the Five Towns* (1902).

Ben Nevis, *see* NEVIS, BEN.

Bentham, Jeremy (1748-1832), English philosopher. Trained in law, early exponent of UTILITARIANISM in *Introduction to the Principles of Morals and Legislation* (1789); taught that govt. should consider 'the greatest good for the greatest number'. Founded (1824) *Westminster Review* with James Mill.

Benue, river of N Cameroon and E Nigeria. Flows *c* 1450 km (900 mi) W from Adamawa Highlands to R. Niger at Lokoja.

Early Benz automobile

Benz, Karl (1844-1929), German engineer. Credited with building 1st automobile with internal combustion engine (*c* 1885). In 1926 his company merged as Daimler-Benz.

benzene (C_6H_6), colourless liquid hydrocarbon; found in coal tar and produced from petroleum by cracking. Structure as hexagonal ring of 6 carbon atoms, linked by alternate double and single bonds, with hydrogen atom joined to each carbon atom, described by Kekulé. Used as solvent and as starting point of numerous aromatic compounds.

Beograd, *see* BELGRADE.

Beowulf, Old English epic. Composed 8th cent., tells story derived from folk tale and

Scandinavian history. In first part, young Beowulf rescues Danish court from water monster Grendel and Grendel's mother. In second part, after long and honourable life, Beowulf is called on to defend country from dragon, does so but dies and is given hero's funeral.

Berbers, Hamitic peoples of N Africa, of unknown origin. Previously Christian they became Moslem by 10th cent. under Arab domination. Apart from the TUAREG they are now settled agriculturists with local industries, *eg* metalwork, pottery, weaving.

Berchtesgaden, town of SE West Germany, in Bavarian Alps. Pop. 5000. Tourism, salt mining, woodcarving. Site of Hitler's mountain retreat.

Berg, Alban (1885-1935), Austrian composer. Disciple of Schoenberg; developed 12-note technique to greater heights of expression than his master. Works incl. 2 operas, *Wozzeck* and *Lulu,* violin concerto and *Lyric Suite* for string quartet.

Bergamo, city of Lombardy, N Italy, cap. of Bergamo prov. Pop. 127,000. Engineering, textiles. Incl. old walled hilltop town, with 12th-cent. cathedral, Renaissance chapel.

bergamot, several plants incl. species of *Monarda,* native to North America, with oval leaves aromatic when crushed. Bergamot also designates a type of pear-shaped orange, *Citrus bergamia,* rind of which yields an oil used in perfumery.

Bergen, city of SW Norway. Pop. 213,000. Port, fishing, shipbuilding, tourism. Founded 1070, *fl* in Middle Ages, member of Hanseatic League. Rebuilt after fire (1916); German naval base in WWII, severely damaged.

Bergman, [Ernst] Ingmar (1918-), Swedish writer-director. Known for expressionist films with themes of alienation of individual from God, problems of personal relationships. Films incl. *The Seventh Seal* (1956), *Persona* (1966).

Bergman, Ingrid (1917-), Swedish actress. Best known for films made after move to Hollywood (1938), incl. *Casablanca* (1943).

Bergson, Henri (1859-1941), French philosopher. Anti-rationalist, believed in direct intuition as basis of knowledge. Saw evolution as opposition of life-force to intransigence of matter. Nobel Prize for Literature (1927).

Beria, Lavrenti Pavlovich (1899-1953), Soviet political leader. Powerful head of Russian secret police (1938-53); tried and executed during post-Stalin power struggle.

beriberi, deficiency disease caused by lack of vitamin B_1 (thiamin) in diet. Characterized by neuritis, swelling of body, *etc.* Occurs mostly in Far East where diet is largely of polished rice.

Bering, Vitus Jonassen (1681-1741), Danish explorer. Employed by Peter I to explore N Siberia; proved that Asia and America not connected. Died on Bering Isl.

Bering Sea, extension of N Pacific, between E Siberia and Alaska. Navigable only in summer. Explored by Bering *c* 1728. Bering Strait connects it to Arctic Ocean.

Berkeley, Busby, orig. William Berkeley Enos (1895-1976), American song-and-dance director. Known for spectacular, kaleidoscopic sequences in 1930s films, incl. *Dames* (1934).

Berkeley, George (1685-1753), Irish bishop and philosopher. Leading anti-materialist, saw the existence of perceived world as dependent on act of the perceiver. Major work, *Treatise concerning the Principles of Human Knowledge* (1710).

Berkeley, Sir Lennox (1903-), English composer. Has written works in traditional forms, esp. for human voice. Compositions incl. chamber music, operas, symphonies.

Berkeley, residential town of W California, US; on E San Francisco Bay. Pop. 117,000. Mfg. industs. Has most famous part of Univ. of California (1873).

·**berkelium** (Bk), transuranic element of actinide series; at. no. 97, mass no. of most stable isotope 247. First prepared 1949 by bombarding americium with alpha particles.

Berkshire, county of SC England. Area 1255 sq km (484 sq mi); pop. 673,000; admin., hq. Reading. In Thames basin; rich agric. incl. dairying, pigs, wheat, oats. Chalk downs cross C.

Berlin, Irving, orig. Israel Baline (1888-), American composer, b. Russia. Popular songs and musicals incl. 'White Christmas', *Annie Get Your Gun.*

Berlin, city of NE Germany, on R. Spree, divided into East and West Berlin. East Berlin (pop. 1,101,000) is cap. of East Germany; West Berlin (pop. 1,951,000) is West German enclave, connected to west by specified land routes and air 'corridors'. Indust. and mfg. centre. City was cap. of Prussia, then of United Germany 1871-1945. Severely damaged in WWII, military occupation divided city after 1945. Soviet blockade of W sectors (1948-9), relieved by airlift, erection of Berlin wall (1961).

Berlin, Congress of (1878), called to review terms imposed on Turkey by Russia at end of RUSSO-TURKISH WARS; chaired by Bismarck, incl. Disraeli, Andrassy. Revised boundary between Greece and Turkey, placed Bosnia and Hercegovina under Austro-Hungary; Serbia, Montenegro, Romania recognized as independent.

Berlinguer, Enrico (1922-), Italian politician. Secretary of Communist party from 1972, his attempts to redefine party role within Western democracy ('EURO-COMMUNISM') resulted in electoral gains.

Berlioz, [Louis] Hector (1803-69), French composer. Wrote many large-scale works, often with a literary basis, in which he made innovations in orchestration. Works incl. *Symphonie fantastique, Romeo et Juliet,* opera *The Trojans.*

Bermuda, coral isl. group of *c* 300 isls. in NC Atlantic. British crown colony, Bermuda largest isl. Area 52 sq km (20 sq mi); pop. 58,000; cap. Hamilton. Indust. based on year-round US tourism. Discovered by

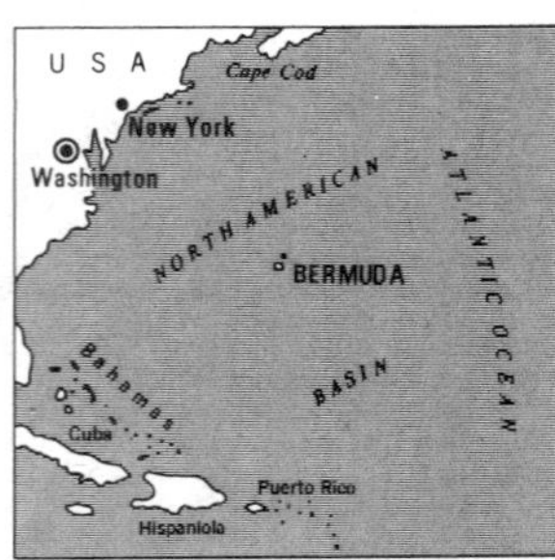

Bermuda

Spanish (1515); settled by English (1609).

Bern (Fr. *Berne*), cap. of Switzerland and Bern canton, on R. Aare. Pop. 284,000. Knitwear, chocolate mfg.; printing, publishing. Hq. of Universal Postal Union; univ. (1834). Founded 1191, medieval town remains. Cap. from 1848.

Bernadette, St, orig. Marie Bernarde Soubirous (1844-79), French visionary. As a girl claimed to see visions of Virgin Mary at Lourdes, now a centre of RC pilgrimage. Canonized in 1933.

Bernadotte, Jean Baptiste Jules, *see* CHARLES XIV.

Bernard, Claude (1813-78), French physiologist. Considered founder of experimental medicine, his numerous investigations incl. work on chemistry of digestion and functions of pancreas.

Bernard of Clairvaux, St, (1090-1153), French churchman, scholar. Founded Cistercian monastery of Clairvaux (1115). Influential in contemporary politics, securing recognition for Pope Innocent II. Mystical in theology, opposed rationalism of Abelard, Arnold of Brescia. Inspired 2nd Crusade (1146).

Bern Convention, *see* COPYRIGHT.

Bernese Oberland, Swiss mountain group, incl. Eiger, Mönch, Jungfrau. Interlaken and Grindelwald are main resorts.

Bernhardt, Sarah, pseud. of Rosine Bernard (1844-1923), French actress. Best-known roles incl. Phèdre, Hamlet.

Bernini, Giovanni Lorenzo (1598-1680), Italian sculptor, architect. Greatest practitioner of Italian Baroque style. Appointed architect to St Peter's (1629), he created colonnades and piazza in front of the church. Works incl. *Ecstasy of St Theresa* (1645-52).

Bernoulli, Jacob or **Jacques** (1654-1705), Swiss mathematician. Developed Leibnitz's calculus; estab. principles of probability theory; discovered Bernoulli numbers. His brother **Johann Bernoulli** (1667-1748), was a pioneer of calculus of variations. His son, **Daniel Bernoulli** (1700-82), worked on fluid motion (Bernoulli's principle), kinetic theory of gases and probability theory.

Bernstein, Leonard (1918-), American pianist, composer, conductor. Music makes fresh use of American idioms, esp. musicals *On the Town, West Side Story*. Works also incl. religious music.

Berwick-on-Tweed, mun. bor. of Northumberland, NE England, at mouth of Tweed. Pop. 11,000. Salmon fishing. Long disputed by Scotland, became neutral territ. 1551; incorporated 1885.

Berwickshire, former county of SE Scotland, now in Borders region. Lammermuir Hills in N (sheep); Merse lowland in S (cereal growing). Co. town was Duns.

beryl, very hard mineral, silicate of beryllium and aluminium. Comprises hexagonal crystals which may be extremely large. Gem forms are EMERALD, AQUAMARINE.

beryllium (Be), hard corrosion-resisting metallic element; at. no. 4, at. wt. 9.01. Occurs as BERYL; obtained by electrolysis of fused salts. Used for making light alloys and in windows for X-ray tubes.

Berzelius, Jöns Jakob, Baron (1779-1848), Swedish chemist. Gave composition of numerous compounds and compiled table of atomic weights. Discovered selenium, thorium, cerium. Introduced modern chemical symbols and formulae.

Besançon, city of E France, on R. Doubs, cap. of Doubs dept. Pop. 124,000. Textiles univ. (1691). Hist. cap. of Franche-Comté. Roman arch, 12th cent. cathedral, palace.

Besant, Annie, née Wood (1847-1933), English theosophist, social reformer. Tried, but acquitted, for immorality after pub. birth control pamphlet (1877). Disciple of Helena BLAVATSKY; went to India, where she helped further nationalist cause. President of Theosophical Society (1907-33), wrote much on THEOSOPHY.

Bessarabia, hist. region of Moldavian SSR and W Ukrainian SSR. Disputed by Russia and Turkey; ceded to Russia (1812). Declared itself independent (1918) and joined in union with Romania; recovered by USSR in WWII.

Bessel, Friedrich Wilhelm (1784-1846), German astronomer. In 1838, was 1st to determine accurately parallax of a star (61 Cygni), thus finding its distance from Earth. Compiled star catalogue and introduced Bessel's function in mathematics.

Bessemer, Sir Henry (1813-98), English industrialist, inventor. Developed (*c* 1856) Bessemer process in mfg. of steel in which impurities are removed by oxidation when air is blown through molten pig iron.

beta particle, electron or positron emitted by radioactive nucleus. Electron emitted when neutron spontaneously decays into proton, an anti-neutrino being produced as well. Penetration power *c* 100 times that of alpha particle.

betatron, cyclic accelerator used to obtain high energy beam of electrons by accelerating them in rapidly increasing magnetic field.

Betelgeuse, red supergiant star in constellation Orion. Of variable brightness, due to pulsation; *c* 260 light years away.

betel palm, *Areca catechu,* palm native to SE Asia. Source of betel nut, an astringent, orange, nut-like fruit, widely chewed in E for its stimulant effect.

Bethlehem (Arab. *Beit-Lahm*), town of W Jordan. Pop. 24,000. Considered birthplace of Jesus.

Betjeman, Sir John (1906-), English poet and architectural authority. Known for light, witty verse. Works on architecture reflect love of Victoriana. Poet laureate (1972).

Bevan, Aneurin (1897-1960), British politician. As minister of health (1945-51), inaugurated nationalized health service. Resigned over social services cuts, became leader of the left within Labour Party; later, advocated nuclear disarmament.

bevatron, cyclic accelerator used to accelerate protons and other particles up to 6 GeV. Used at Univ. of California (Berkeley) to discover anti-proton.

Beveridge, William Henry (1879-1963), British economist, b. India. Prepared govt. report proposing social security system (1942), planned spending for full employment (1944).

Beverley, mun. bor. of Humberside, N England. Pop. 17,000. Former co. town of East Riding of Yorkshire. Has 13th cent. minster.

Beverly Hills, town of S California, US; suburb of Los Angeles. Pop. 33,000. Home of Hollywood film stars.

Bevin, Ernest (1881-1951), British politician and labour leader. Instrumental in union merger creating Transport and General Workers' Union. Minister of labour in wartime cabinet (1940-5); foreign secretary (1945-51), worked for closer ties with US through anti-Soviet policy.

Bexley, bor. of SE Greater London, England. Pop. 214,000. Created 1965 from several Kent towns.

Bhagavad-Gita (Sanskrit, = song of the blessed one), philosophical dialogue contained in the Mahabharata epic. Incl. much of basis of Hindu thought and philosophy.

Bharat, ancient Hindi name for India, now used officially.

Bhopal, cap. of Madhya Pradesh, C India. Pop. 298,000. Textile mfg. Cap. of former princely state of Bhopal. Had women leaders (19th cent.).

Bhutan, kingdom of SC Asia. Area *c* 47,000 sq km (18,000 sq mi); pop. 1,240,000; cap. Thimbu. Language: Tibetan variant. Religion: Mahayana Buddhism. In E Himalayas, bordered by India, Tibet. Parts of S annexed by British in 19th cent; British, then Indian protect.

Bhutto, Zulfikar Ali (1928-79), Pakistani political leader. Succeeded to presidency (1971) on overthrow of Yahya Khan. PM (1973-77), effected reconciliation with independent Bangladesh. Re-elected 1977, but deposed by military coup; executed for murder of political opponent.

Biafra, *see* NIGERIA.

Bialystok, city of NE Poland, cap. of Bialystok prov. Pop. 198,000. Railway jct.; textile mfg., machinery. Founded 14th cent.; under Russian rule 1807-1919.

Biarritz, town of SW France, on Bay of Biscay. Pop. 30,000. Developed in 19th cent. from fishing village into fashionable resort.

Bible, sacred book of Christianity. The canon, or standard list, of books making up OLD TESTAMENT is accepted by most churches and is also sacred book of Judaism. The APOCRYPHA, some books of which are accepted by the Eastern Orthodox church, is recognized by the RC church apart from 2 books of Esdras and the Prayer of Manasses. The canon of 27 books of NEW TESTAMENT is same for all Christian churches. Bible was 1st book to be printed by GUTENBERG, in Latin (*see* VULGATE). Translators into English incl. WYCLIFFE, TYNDALE; AUTHORIZED VERSION most famous translation. RC scholars pub. DOUAY version.

bicycle, light, two-wheeled vehicle driven by pedals. First bicycle (with treadles and driving rods) built (1840) in Scotland by Kirkpatrick MacMillan. The 'boneshaker' with rotary cranks built (*c* 1865) in Paris. Subsequently, light spoked wheels with rubber tyres introduced. Pennyfarthing had large, driven front wheel (up to 163 cm/64 in. diameter) giving higher gear ratio, with rear wheel as small as 30 cm (12 in.). Safety bicycle with equal-sized wheels and sprocket-chain drive first manufactured by James Starley (*c* 1885) in Coventry. Developments incl. freewheeling rear hub, variable ratio gears.

Biddle, John (1615-62), English religious leader, founder of UNITARIANISM.

Biedermeier style, name given to German style of furniture and decoration of period 1818-48. Resembled French Empire style, but simpler.

biennial, *see* ANNUAL.

big-bang theory, in cosmology, hypothesis that universe evolved from highly dense concentration of matter which underwent enormous explosion *c* 10,000 million years ago. This accounts for expansion of universe observed by HUBBLE. Its plausibility increased with observation in 1960s of uniform background radiation emanating from outer space. Opposed by STEADY-STATE THEORY.

bighorn or **Rocky Mountain sheep,** large wild sheep of NW North America, incl. *Ovis canadensis.* Male has heavy curling horns, female small upright horns.

Bihar, state of NE India. Area 174,000 sq km (67,000 sq mi); pop. 56,332,000; cap. Patna. N fertile plain crossed by Ganges; rice grown. Important producer of coal, iron ore. Buddhist centre.

Bikini Atoll, in Marshall Isls., C Pacific

Biedermeier cabinet

Ocean. Pop. removed prior to US atomic bomb tests (1946-58).

Bilbao, city of N Spain, at mouth of R. Nervión, cap. of Vizcaya prov. Pop. 458,000. Port, exports wine, iron ore; shipbuilding, iron and steel indust. Seat of Basque autonomous govt. (1936-7) in Civil War.

bilberry, blaeberry or **whortleberry,** *Vaccinium myrtillus,* small shrub native to N Europe and Britain. Has small, globular, bluish-black, edible fruit. Similar species are cultivated in US (*see* BLUEBERRY).

bile, bitter yellow-brown fluid secreted by the liver. Found in gall bladder, from which it is discharged into duodenum to aid digestion, esp. of fats. Colour results from carrying waste products of haemoglobin destruction.

bilharzia or **schistosomiasis,** disease caused by infestation of veins by flukes of genus *Schistosoma.* Larvae in water penetrate skin and adult worms settle in urinary bladder. Eggs cause inflammation of tissue, leading to degeneration of bladder, liver, *etc.*

billiards, game played with cue and 3 balls (1 white cue ball, 1 red and 1 white object ball) on oblong cloth-covered slate table, edges of which are cushioned. Scoring is by pocketing object or cue ball, or by cannons (striking the 2 object balls successively with cue ball). Played in England and France from 16th cent.

bimetallic strip, strip of 2 different metals bonded together in such a way that strip buckles when heated (as metals expand at different rates). Used in thermostats.

bimetallism, use of two metals (usually gold and silver) as monetary standard with fixed values in relation to each other. Both metals circulate as legal tender. Term does not apply to systems where other metals (*eg* copper, nickel) are used as token coinage.

binary number system, representation of integers using only digits 0 and 1 to powers of 2. Thus the number 2 is represented by $1 \times 2^1 + 0 \times 2^0 = 10$, and 23 by $1 \times 2^4 + 0 \times 2^3 + 1 \times 2^2 + 1 \times 2^1 + 1 \times 2^0 = 10111$. Used in computing as 0 and 1 can be represented electrically as *off* and *on.*

binary star, star consisting of 2 components, revolving about common centre of gravity under effect of mutual gravitation. Very common; *c* 50% of stars in our galaxy are binaries.

binding energy, in physics, energy required to decompose atomic nucleus into constituent protons and neutrons. Binding energy of neutron is energy required to remove neutron from nucleus.

bindweed, widely distributed family of plants with long climbing stems, of genera *Convolvulus* and *Calystegia.*

binocular, optical instrument for viewing distant objects. Consists of 2 telescopes (binoculars) mounted so that a separate image enters each of viewer's eyes giving greater perception of depth than single image. Normally uses prisms to reduce length.

binomial theorem, in mathematics, theorem giving expansion of powers of $x + y$ in terms of powers of x and y.

biochemistry, chemistry of living things. Two main branches: determination of structure of organic compounds present in living organisms, *eg* plant pigments, vitamins, proteins; elucidation of chemical means by which substances are utilized or made in living organisms.

Bioko Island, isl. of Equatorial Guinea, in Gulf of Guinea. Area 2020 sq km (780 sq mi); cap Rey Malabo. Of volcanic origin, rises to 3007 m (9870 ft). Hot, wet climate; produces cocoa. Formerly called Fernando Po, Macías Nguema Biyoga.

biological warfare, the use of living organisms or their toxic products to induce death or incapacity in humans and animals and damage to plant crops etc. Use condemned by Geneva Convention (1925).

biology, science and study of living things, comprising BOTANY and ZOOLOGY. Study of form and structure of an organism is morphology; of the functions, physiology; of reproduction and early growth, embryology; of fossil remains, palaeontology. For division of plants and animals into series according to similarities and relationships, *see* CLASSIFICATION.

bionics, in biology, the study of certain functions, esp. those relating to the brain, that are applicable to the development of electronic equipment, such as computer hardware, designed to operate in a similar manner.

biosphere, that part of the Earth's crust and atmosphere which contains living organisms.

birch, family of deciduous trees comprising ALDERS and birches, genus *Betula.* Latter is hardy, with papery white bark; yields hard wood.

bird, any of class Aves of warm-blooded, egg-laying, feathered vertebrates, with forelimbs modified into wings; *c* 8700 living species. Believed to have evolved from reptiles; *see* ARCHAEOPTERYX.

bird of paradise, bird of Paradisaeidae family of New Guinea and adjacent isls. Males brightly coloured with elongated tail feathers, brilliant ruffs.

Birkenhead, Frederick Edwin Smith, 1st Earl of (1872-1930), British politician. Led Conservative opposition to Irish Home Rule, later prosecuted CASEMENT as attorney general (1915-19). Served as lord chancellor (1919-22).

Birkenhead, co. bor. of Merseyside met. county, NW England, on Wirral penin. Pop. 135,000. Port on R. Mersey, docks opened 1847. Has tunnel link with Liverpool.

Birmingham, city of West Midlands met. county, WC England. Pop. 1,041,000; 2nd largest British city. Transport centre; metal working, esp. vehicles, firearms. Main expansion during Indust. Revolution. Has 2 univs.

Birmingham, city of NC Alabama, US; at S end of Appalachian Mts. Pop. 791,000; state's largest city. Iron and steel centre; cement, textile, chemical mfg. Railway jct. Founded 1871.

Birobidzhan or **Birobijan,** town of USSR, Khabarovsk territ., RSFSR. Pop. 56,000. Sawmilling, clothing mfg. Cap. of Birobidzhan Jewish auton. region, formed 1928 as centre for Soviet Jews. Mainly agric., with mining and forestry.

birth control, *see* CONTRACEPTION.

Biscay, Bay of, inlet of N Atlantic Ocean, lying between Ushant Isl., NW France, and Cape Ortegal, NW Spain. Noted for strong currents, heavy seas.

Bismarck, Otto Eduard Leopold, Fürst von (1815-98), German statesman, chief minister of Prussia (1862-90), architect of German Empire. War with Denmark (1864) resulted in acquisition of Schleswig; friction over Holstein led to Austro-Prussian War (1866), in which Prussian leadership in Germany was consolidated. Provoked French into Franco-Prussian War (1870-1), in which Prussia annexed Alsace-Lorraine. With formation (1871) of German Empire, he became its 1st chancellor. Ruled autocratically (known as 'iron chancellor'), controlling domestic and foreign policies. Engaged in struggle (*Kulturkampf*) between state and Catholic church, but, as with his opposition to socialism, it eventually failed. Resented by William II; dismissed 1890.

Bismarck, cap. of North Dakota, US; railway jct. on Missouri R. Pop. 35,000. Agric. market (esp. spring wheat). Cap. from 1883.

Bismarck Archipelago, volcanic isl. group in SW Pacific; part of Papua New Guinea. Area *c* 49,700 sq km (19,200 sq mi). Incl. New Britain, New Ireland, Admiralty Isls.

bismuth (Bi), metallic element; at. no. 83, at. wt. 208.98. Occurs as metal or as oxide

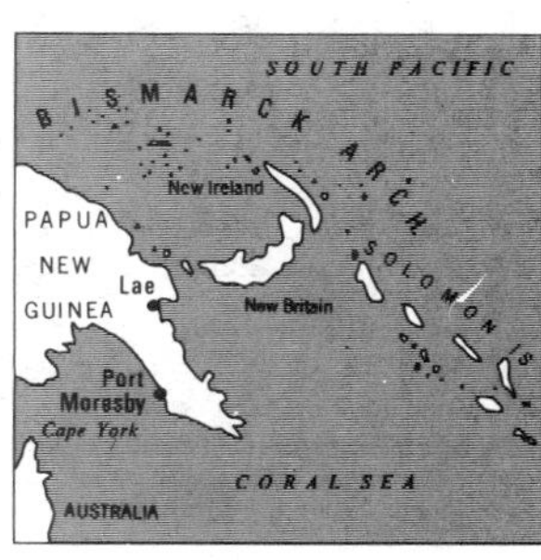

Bismarck Archipelago

Bi_2O_3; obtained by reducing oxide with carbon. Used in metal castings and making alloys of low melting point; compounds used in medicine.

bison, hoofed mammal of cattle family with shaggy mane, short horns, humped back. American bison or buffalo, *Bison bison,* once numerous on Great Plains; now protected after over-hunting. European bison or WISENT very rare.

Bissau (Port. *Bissão*), cap. of Guinea-Bissau, on Geba estuary. Pop. 109,000. Admin. centre; port, exports hardwoods, copra, palm oil. Cap. of Portuguese Guinea from 1942.

bittern, wading bird of heron family, genus *Botaurus,* with speckled plumage, long pointed bill. Male emits booming call.

bittersweet, *see* NIGHTSHADE.

bitumen, name given to various mixtures of hydrocarbons, esp. solid or tarry mixtures obtained as residues on distilling coal tar, petroleum, *etc.*

Bivalvia (bivalves), aquatic molluscs of class Lamellibranchiata. Shell formed from 2 hinged halves. Incl. oysters, mussels, clams.

Bizet, Georges, orig. Alexandre César Léopold Bizet (1838-75), French composer. Best known for opera *Carmen.*

Black, Joseph (1728-99), Scottish physician and chemist, b. France. Showed that carbon dioxide is produced when calcium carbonate is heated and investigated its properties. Investigated specific and latent heat.

Black-and-Tans, nickname of irregular force in UK, enlisted for service in Ireland as auxiliaries to Royal Irish Constabulary during disturbances of 1919-22. Name arose from khaki colour of uniform worn with black accessories of Royal Irish Constabulary.

black bear, *Ursus americanus,* most widespread and numerous North American bear, smaller than brown bear. Lives in forests; diet of roots, berries. Himalayan black bear, *Selenarctos thibetanus,* forest-dwelling bear found from Persia to Himalayas.

Blackbeard, *see* TEACH, EDWARD.

blackberry or **bramble,** *Rubus fructicosus,* low, rambling shrub with white flowers and black fruit. Edible berries.

blackbird, one of various thrush-like birds, males black with yellow beak, females brown. Common European variety is *Turdus merula.*

black body, in physics, ideal surface or body which absorbs completely all radiation falling on it. Must also be perfect emitter of radiation, total depending only on absolute temperature. Planck's attempts to explain spectral distribution of black body radiation led to quantum theory.

black bryony, *Tamus communis,* only European species of yam family. It has small greenish flowers followed by green then red poisonous berries.

blackbuck, *Antilope cervicapra,* long-horned antelope of W India. Male black above, white on belly. Female fawn and white.

Blackburn, town of Lancashire, NW England. Pop. 102,000. Cotton weaving, textile machinery, chemicals, paint mfg.

Black Country, indust. area of WC England, centred in S Staffordshire. Formerly affected by smoke and soot from foundries, factories, *etc.*

Black Death, outbreak of plague which affected Europe *c* 1346-9. Catastrophic effect on pop., killing over ⅓ of inhabitants of many areas.

black earth or **chernozem,** fertile black or dark brown soil. Consists of modified form of LOESS, rich in HUMUS. High nutrient content, good structure make it very suitable for agric., as in *eg* USSR, NC North America.

Blackett, Baron Patrick Maynard Stuart (1897-1974), English physicist. Used cloud chamber to photograph nuclear disintegration (1925). Awarded Nobel Prize for Physics (1948) for this work and for subsequent improvements of Wilson cloud chamber.

Blackfoot, North American Indian tribes. Settled in 19th cent. on upper Missouri and N Saskatchewan rivers and W to Rocky Mts. Plains buffalo hunters, noted for hostility to settlers and complex ritual. A few remain on reservations in Alberta, Montana.

Black Forest (*Schwarzwald*), wooded mountain region of SW West Germany. Highest peak is Feldberg (*c* 1490 m/4900 ft). Tourism, forestry. Source of Danube, Neckar rivers.

black-headed gull, *see* GULL.

Black Hills, mountains of NC US, in SW South Dakota, and NE Wyoming. Rise to 2207 m (7242 ft). Forestry, tourism, mineral resources (esp. gold). Gold rush in 1873. Famous sculptures of 4 US presidents at Mt. Rushmore.

black hole, hypothetical state of sufficiently massive star that undergoes gravitational collapse within a certain radius. Region of space around black hole is so distorted that light cannot escape from black hole and so it can never be observed. Certain X-ray stars are believed to be binary companions of black holes.

Black Hole of Calcutta, name given to small room in which British garrison of Calcutta were imprisoned overnight (1756) after successful attack by nawab of Bengal. Most prisoners died of suffocation.

blackjack, *see* VINGT-ET-UN.

Blackpool, town of Lancashire, NW England. Pop. 151,000. Leading English coastal resort; has famous tower (158 m/520 ft), illuminations.

black power, economic and political power sought by American blacks in struggle for civil rights. Incl. variety of specific movements. Arose as reaction to limited success of non-violent civil rights movement in 1950s and 60s.

Black Prince, *see* EDWARD THE BLACK PRINCE.

black rat, *Rattus rattus,* common rat of Middle Ages in Europe, largely displaced by brown rat. Carried plague from Asia.

Black Sea (anc. *Pontus Euxinus*), inland sea of SE Europe, bounded by USSR, Turkey, Bulgaria, Romania. Area *c* 414,000 sq km (160,000 sq mi). Linked to Sea of Azov (NE) by Kerch Str.; to Aegean (SW) by Dardanelles. Almost tideless; marine life in upper levels only.

blackshirts, members of fascist organization. Refers specifically to militant units of Italian Fascist party (estab. 1919). Term also refers to Hitler's elite bodyguard (*Schutzstaffel* or SS).

black swan, *Cygnus atratus,* only swan native to Australia, unique to that country.

blackthorn or **sloe,** *Prunus spinosa,* European deciduous spiny shrub of rose family. Short spikes of small, white flowers are followed by small, astringent fruits (sloes or sloe plums) which are used to flavour sloe gin.

black widow, black venomous spider of tropics and subtropics, genus *Latrodectus.* Female, much larger than male, often eats it after mating. Bite of female intensely painful, rarely fatal.

bladder, *see* GALL BLADDER and URINARY BLADDER.

bladderwort, plant of genus *Utricularia* of Eurasia and N America, esp. *U. vulgaris,* water bladderwort with finely-divided leaves and small bladders. These capture minute water animals and digest them.

blaeberry, *see* BILBERRY.

Blake, Robert (*c* 1599-1657), English admiral. Defeated Prince Rupert's fleet (1650), Tromp and Dutch navy (1653). Estab. English sea power in the Mediterranean (1654) with victory at Tunis. Captured Spanish treasure fleet (1657). Helped organize Commonwealth's navy.

Blake, William (1757-1827), English poet, engraver, artist. Translated Biblical symbolism into his own mythology, in

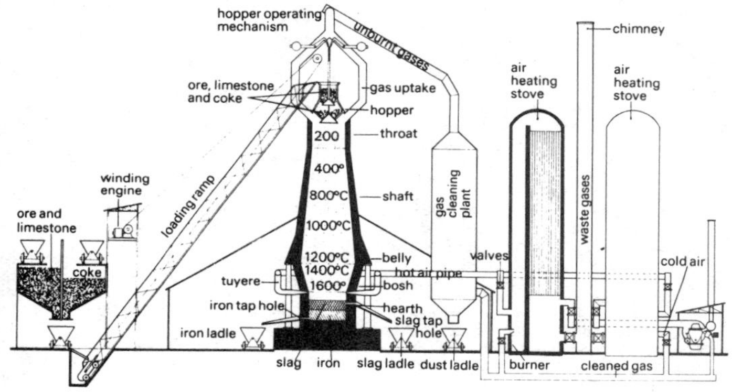

Blast furnace

works incl. *Songs of Innocence* (1789), *Songs of Experience* (1794), and long, complex 'prophetic books', *eg The Marriage of Heaven and Hell* (1793). Precursor of Romanticism in belief in imagination, individual liberty, simplicity. Illustrated own work.

Blanc, Louis (1811-82), French political leader. A socialist, he advocated system of cooperative workshops. Member of provisional govt. of 1848.

Blanc, Mont, *see* MONT BLANC.

Blanchard, Jean Pierre or **François** (1753-1809), French balloonist. With John Jeffries, made 1st crossing by air (1785) of English Channel in a balloon.

blank verse, unrhymed verse; in English usually of iambic pentameters. Used in dramatic and epic poetry from Shakespeare and Milton to present.

Blantyre, city of S Malawi, in Shiré Highlands. Pop. 229,000. Commercial, indust. centre on Mozambique-L. Malawi railway. Founded (1876) as mission by Livingstone, named after his birthplace. Joined to nearby Limbe in 1956.

Blarney, village of Co. Cork, S Irish Republic. Castle (15th cent.) contains Blarney Stone, kissing of which reputedly gives one persuasive speech ('blarney').

blast furnace, tower-like furnace used to smelt metals, esp. iron, from their ores. Mixture of ore, coke and limestone is placed in furnace and heated by a blast of air introduced from below. Molten metal separates from slag produced and both are drained off from bottom of furnace.

Blaue Reiter, Der, name given to group of expressionist painters, incl. Marc, Kandinsky, Macke and Klee, working in Munich 1911-14.

Blavatsky, Helena Petrovna, née Hahn (1831-91), Russian theosophist. Founded Theosophical Society in New York (1875). Her *Isis Unveiled* (1887) is the textbook of THEOSOPHY.

bleaching, decolorization of coloured matter by chemicals. Common bleaches incl. sodium hypochlorite solution (NaOCl), which acts by oxidation, and sulphur dioxide (SO_2), which acts by reduction.

bleeding heart, any plant of genus *Dicentra* with fern-like leaves and drooping clusters of pink, heart-shaped flowers.

Blenheim (*Blindheim*), village of SC West Germany. Scene of defeat (1704) of French by Prince Eugène and Marlborough in War of Spanish Succession.

Blériot, Louis (1872-1936), French aviator, inventor. Designed monoplane in which he made (1909) 1st English Channel crossing in heavier-than-air machine.

Bligh, William (1754-1817), British admiral. Remembered for mutiny (1789) on his ship, *Bounty*, while on an expedition in Pacific.

blight, general term for many diseases of plants esp. those caused by fungi of family Erysiphaceae which are seen as a white dust on leaves of plant. Also refers to attack by bacteria or insects, *eg* greenfly.

blimp, *see* AIRSHIP.

blindness, partial or complete loss of sight. Often results from degenerative diseases associated with ageing; other causes incl. glaucoma, cataracts, *etc*.

blindworm, *see* SLOW-WORM.

Bliss, Sir Arthur (1891-1975), British composer. Master of the Queen's Musick (1953-75). His music, vigorous and romantic, incl. *Colour Symphony*, ballet *Miracle in the Gorbals*.

blister beetle, soft-bodied beetle of Meloidae family, often of bright metallic colouring. Some varieties harmful to crops. Cantharides, a blistering agent, formerly extracted from wings of Spanish fly, a S European species.

Blitzkrieg (Ger., = lightning war), form of

large-scale surprise attack involving motorized forces with air support. Developed by Germans in WWII.

Bloemfontein, judicial cap. of South Africa and cap. of Orange Free State. Pop. 180,000. Commercial, transport, educational centre; univ. (1855). Founded 1846.

Blois, town of Orléanais, NC France, on R. Loire. Cap. of Loir-et-Cher dept. Pop. 45,000. Wine and brandy trade. Château (13th cent.) was residence of counts of Blois, and later of French kings.

Blondin, Charles, pseud. of Jean François Gravelet (1824-97), French tightrope walker. Famous for crossing of Niagara Falls on rope at height of *c* 50 m (160 ft).

blood, principal fluid of circulatory system in higher vertebrates. Carries oxygen and cell-building material to body tissues and disposes of carbon dioxide and other wastes. Composed of plasma (55%) and cells (45%). Red blood cells (erythrocytes) contain haemoglobin which combines with oxygen in lungs and thus enables oxygen to circulate to tissues. White blood cells (leucocytes) destroy bacteria and form antibodies to neutralize poisons. Smaller blood platelets (thrombocytes) help initiate blood clotting.

blood groups, classification of human blood into groups according to compatibility of red cells of one group with plasma of another. Incompatibility results in agglutination (clumping) of cells which must be avoided in transfusions. Four main groups, A, AB, B and O, used in system devised by Karl Landsteiner (1900).

bloodhound, large black and tan dog, with drooping ears, wrinkled forehead, keen sense of smell. Stands *c* 69 cm/27 in. at shoulder.

blood poisoning, name given to 3 conditions: toxaemia, presence in bloodstream of toxin produced by pathogenic bacteria; septicaemia, spread of bacteria through bloodstream; cellulitis, spread of bacteria from a wound to nearby tissue.

blood pressure, pressure exerted by blood on walls of arteries. Varies with heartbeat between *c* 120 mm/4.72 in. of mercury (systolic pressure) and 80 mm/3.15 in. (diastolic pressure); increases with age. Obesity, arteriosclerosis cause high blood pressure.

bloodstone or **heliotrope,** semi-precious gemstone, a variety of chalcedony. Mostly dark green, speckled with red jasper.

blood transfusion, transfer of blood from one mammal to another of same species. BLOOD GROUPS of donor and patient must be determined to avoid destroying transferred red cells.

blood vessels, in higher vertebrates, system of vessels through which blood circulation takes place. They comprise: arteries, carrying blood away from heart; veins, carrying blood towards heart; capillaries, minute vessels which form subdivisions of arteries and then form first small veins. Exchange of material between blood and tissue occurs through thin walls of capillaries.

Bloody Assizes, *see* JEFFREYS, GEORGE.

Bloomsbury group, name given to group of English writers, artists, intellectuals who met in Bloomsbury district of London from 1906. Incl. Virginia and Leonard Woolf, Lytton Strachey, E.M. Forster, Duncan Grant, Keynes, Bertrand Russell. 'Bloomsbury' values represented an elitist sensitivity to art and friendship.

blowfly, two-winged fly of Calliphoridae family, commonly called bluebottle. Maggots develop in and feed on living tissue or decaying matter.

Blücher, Gebhard Leberecht von (1742-1819), Prussian field marshal. Contributed to Allied victories against Napoleon at Leipzig (1813), Waterloo (1815).

Bluebeard, villain of traditional tale; prob. based on murderer, Gilles de Rais. Many versions of tale incl. Maeterlinck's *Ariane et Barbe-bleue* (1901) and operas by Offenbach, Bartók.

bluebell, plant of many species, esp. of genera *Campanula* and *Mertensia,* bearing blue, drooping, bell-shaped flowers. *See* SQUILL.

blueberry, several plants of genus *Vaccinium,* esp. the high-bush blueberry, *V. corymbosum,* a profusely-branched North American shrub with sweet, edible berry.

bluebird, small North American songbird of thrush family, genus *Sialia.* Male has blue plumage, red breast.

bluebottle fly, blue-coloured BLOWFLY.

blue collar, grouping of workers in semi-skilled or unskilled occupations, usually manual labour. Term derived from traditional colour of workshirts. *See* WHITE COLLAR.

bluegrass, several grasses of the genus *Poa,* important in lawns and pastures. Known as meadow grass in Britain.

blue-green algae, any of the division Cyanophyta of microscopic ALGAE that contain a blue pigment which masks the green chlorophyll. Widely distributed in unicellular or colonial bodies on moist soil, rocks and trees and in fresh or salt water. Help maintain soil fertility by fixing atmospheric nitrogen and preventing erosion.

Blue Nile, *see* NILE.

blues, fundamental form of American vocal music, deriving from Negro work songs, and usually melancholy and reflective in mood. Its melodic inflections (blue notes) have influenced much of today's popular music.

blue tit or **tom tit,** *Parus caeruleus,* European titmouse with yellow underparts and blue cap.

blue whale, *Balaenoptera musculus,* whalebone whale of worldwide distribution, now rare from over-fishing. Plankton diet. Largest known mammal, reaching length of 30 m/100 ft.

Blum, Léon (1872-1950), French statesman. Headed 1st POPULAR FRONT govt. (1936-7), instituted sweeping labour reforms. Arrested (1940) by Vichy govt., imprisoned by Germans (1942-5). Again premier 1946-7.

boa, large tropical constrictor snake of Boidae family. Best known is boa constrictor, *Constrictor constrictor,* of Central and South America.

Boadicea, *see* BOUDICCA.

boar, strictly, male pig. Wild boar, *Sus scrofa,* of Europe, N Africa, Asia, probably forerunner of domestic pig; coarse hair and enlarged canine tusk.

bobcat or **wildcat,** *Felix rufa,* small lynx of North America, with reddish-brown coat. Nocturnal hunter. Also called bay lynx.

bobsleighing, winter sport in which two or four persons descend course of icy, steeply-banked twisting inclines aboard a bobsled, an open, steel-bordered vehicle with sledge-like runners.

Boccaccio, Giovanni (1313-75), Italian poet, b. France. Friendship with PETRARCH influenced him greatly. Best known for bawdy secular classic *Decameron.*

Bodensee, *see* CONSTANCE, LAKE.

Bodleian Library, Oxford Univ., England, library famous for collection of rare books and manuscripts. Named after Sir Thomas Bodley, who restored it in late 16th cent. after original library (estab. 15th cent.) destroyed. Receives copy of every book pub. in UK under Copyright Act (1911).

Boeotia (*Voiotía*), region of EC Greece. Ancient cap. Thebes, led Boeotian League 6th cent. BC. Modern admin. dist., cap. Levadia.

Boer War or **South African War** (1899-1902), conflict between Britain and Transvaal Republic-Orange Free State alliance; result of protracted dispute between British and Boers over British territ. ambitions. Aggravated by discovery of gold (1886). Immediate cause was Britain's refusal to withdraw troops from Transvaal following Jameson Raid (1895). British forces were besieged at Ladysmith, Kimberley and Mafeking by superior Boer army. After arrival of heavy reinforcements under Roberts and Kitchener, British relieved Mafeking, invaded Transvaal and occupied Pretoria by July, 1900. Boers adopted guerrilla tactics, led by Botha and Smuts, but were forced to submit (1902). Peace signed May, 1902, in Treaty of Vereeniging.

Boethius, Anicius Manlius Severinus (*c* 480-*c* 525), Roman philosopher. Minister under Emperor Theodoric; wrote *The Consolation of Philosophy* while awaiting execution for treason.

Bogart, Humphrey [De Forest] (1899-1957), American film actor. Famous in tough, cynical roles of 1940s, esp. as private eye in *The Maltese Falcon* (1941), *The Big Sleep* (1946), and as Rick in *Casablanca* (1942). Later films incl. *The African Queen* (1952).

Bogotá, cap. of Colombia, in E Andean valley; alt. 2610 m (*c* 8560 ft). Pop. 2,855,000. Cultural, financial centre; textile, chemical mfg.; tobacco, food products. Founded by Spanish (1538) on Chibcha Indian site; cap. from time of Colombian independence. Has Univ. (1572), OAS hq.

Bohemia (*Cechy*), region and former prov. of W Czechoslovakia. Mainly plateau; chief rivers Elbe, Moldau. Agric. (cereals, fruit); minerals (esp. uranium); spas. Indust. centred in Prague, Plzeň (beer). Hist. kingdom; Czech from 1918.

Bohr, Niels Henrik David (1885-1962), Danish physicist. Used quantum theory to explain hydrogen atom spectrum, postulating that electron moves in restricted orbits about atomic nucleus. Theory superseded by wave mechanics. Awarded Nobel Prize for Physics (1922).

boil, in medicine, inflamed nodule around root of a hair or in a sweat gland. Often caused by infection with *Staphylococcus aureus.* Can be treated by antibiotics.

Boise, cap. of Idaho, on Boise R. Pop. 75,000; state's largest city. Trade, transport centre. Grew after 1863 gold rush; became agric. centre after building of Arrowrock Dam (1911-15).

Bokhara, *see* BUKHARA.

boletus, genus of fleshy fungi, with thick stems and caps, often brightly coloured. Widely distributed; several species are poisonous but the cèpe, *Boletus edulis,* is edible.

Boleyn, Anne (*c* 1507-36), English queen, 2nd wife of Henry VIII. Mother of Elizabeth I; she was executed for alleged adultery.

Bolingbroke, Henry St John, Viscount (1678-1751), English Tory politician. Opposed George I's accession, was impeached and fled to France. Helped plan Jacobite uprising of 1715. Pardoned (1723).

Bolívar, Simón (1783-1830), South American revolutionary, b. Caracas; called the 'Liberator'. Rose to leadership during revolution against Spain (1810). After victory at Boyacá (1819), elected president of Greater Columbia. After meeting with SAN MARTÍN at Guayaquil, helped liberate Ecuador (1822), Peru (1824), created Bolivia. Resigned from presidency (1830).

Bolivia, landlocked republic of C South America. Area 1,098,580 sq km (424,162 sq mi); pop. 5,137,000; cap. Sucre; admin. cap. La Paz. Languages: Spanish, Quechua, Aymará, Guaraní. Religion: RC. Andes and tableland (incl. L. Titicaca) in W; tropical rain forests in NE, Chaco plain in SE. Important tin, silver, copper mines (esp. at Potosí) are main source of wealth. Native Indians (Inca ruled) overrun by Spanish (16th cent.); gained independence under Sucre (1824). Wars with Chile, Brazil, Paraguay reduced territ.

Böll, Heinrich (1917-), German author. Works critical of modern society incl. *Letter to a Young Catholic* (1958), novels *eg Billiards at Nine-thirty* (1959). Nobel Prize for Literature (1972).

boll weevil, *Anthonomus grandis,* grey weevil which lays eggs in cotton bolls;

larvae feed on cotton fibres. Major pest of S US, Mexico.

Bologna, city of Emilia-Romagna, N Italy, cap. of Bologna prov. Pop. 481,000. Engineering, printing, foodstuffs. Roman *Bononia,* on Aemilian Way. Leading medieval centre of learning, with law school, univ. (1200); scholars incl. Dante, Petrarch. Under papal rule from 1560, united with Sardinia 1860. Many medieval buildings.

Bolshevism, Russian revolutionary movement which seized power (Oct. 1917). Movement originated at Russian Social Democratic Congress (1903) in London, when radical wing led by LENIN prevailed in dispute over strategy and split from moderates (Mensheviks) headed by PLEKHANOV. Bolsheviks became Russian Communist party (1918), Mensheviks losing all support by 1921.

Bolton, bor. of Greater Manchester met. county, NW England. Pop. 260,000. Cotton spinning, woollens, textile machinery mfg.

Bolzano (Ger. *Bozen*), city of Trentino-Alto Adige, NE Italy, on R. Isarco. Cap. of Bolzano prov. Pop. 107,000. Tourist centre on route to Brenner Pass; textiles, engineering. Passed to Italy from Austria (1919).

Bombay, cap. of Maharashtra state, W India, on Arabian Sea. Pop. of greater city 5,971,000. Indust. centre, major port; exports cotton, cotton goods. Under Portuguese control (1534), ceded to Charles II of England; passed to East India Co. Has extensive university (1857).

Bonaparte, Corsican family, of which NAPOLEON I was a member. Among his siblings were: **Joseph Bonaparte** (1768-1844), king of Naples (1806-8) and of Spain (1808-13), forced to abdicate; **Lucien Bonaparte** (1775-1840), contributor to Napoleon's success in coup d'état of 18 Brumaire (1799); **Louis Bonaparte** (1778-1846), king of Holland (1806-10), removed by Napoleon for defying anti-English Continental System; **Caroline Bonaparte** (1782-1839), wife of French marshal MURAT and queen of Naples (1808-15); **Jérôme Bonaparte** (1784-1860), king of Westphalia (1807-13).

Bonar Law, Andrew, *see* LAW, ANDREW BONAR.

Bonaventure, St, orig. Giovanni di Fidanza (1221-74), Italian philosopher. Attempted to reconcile Aristotelian philosophy with Christianity but placed emphasis on the mystical.

bonds, *see* SHARES.

Bône, *see* ANNABA.

bone, hard tissue which forms skeleton in vertebrates. Consists of cells held in a matrix of protein fibres and inorganic salts (mainly calcium phosphate). Cells are connected by network of blood vessels and nerves (Haversian canals). Blood-forming marrow is contained in cavities of long bones.

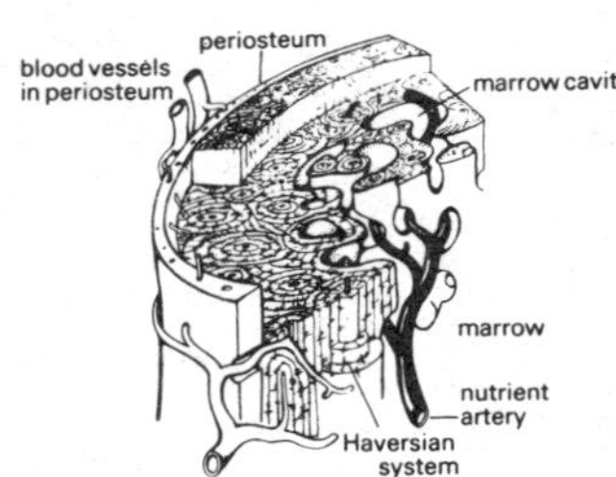

Section of long bone

bongo, *Boocerus eurycerus,* large spiral-horned antelope of equatorial African forests.

Bongo

Bonhoeffer, Dietrich (1906-45), German Lutheran theologian. Led Church's resistance to Nazism; headed secret theological school (1935-40). Hanged by Nazis.

Boniface, St, orig. Winfrid (*c* 675-*c* 754) English Benedictine monk, missionary in Germany. Created archbishop of Mainz (745). Killed by pagans in Friesland.

Bonington, Richard Parkes (1802-28) English painter. Known for landscapes in water colour and historical scenes.

Bonin Islands (*Ogasawara-gunto*), volcanic isl. group of Japan, in Pacific *c* 960 km (600 mi) S of Tokyo. Japanese military base in WWII; occupied by US (1945-1968).

Bonn (anc. *Castra Bonnensia*), cap. of West Germany, on R. Rhine. Pop. 285,000. Admin. centre; publishing, pharmaceuticals, furniture, univ. (1784). Became cap. 1949; has Bundeshaus (Parliament building). Birthplace of Beethoven.

Bonnard, Pierre (1867-1947), French painter. His early work was characterized by decorative colour and simplified flat form. Later work often depicts intimate domestic interiors and landscapes, using heavier paint.

bonsai, art of dwarfing trees in small containers by pruning roots and branches. Technique, first practised in Japan, predates 13th cent. Specimens can be 300-400 years old.

booby, large tropical seabird of Sulidae family, related to gannet. Dives underwater to catch fish.

boojum tree, *see* BAOBAB.

bookkeeping, systematic recording of money transactions. In double entry bookkeeping, assets are recorded in one column with liabilities in another.

Book of Changes, *see* I CHING.

Boole, George (1815-64), English mathematician, logician. Known for *An Investigation of the Laws of Thought* (1854), in which logic is treated symbolically, using operations akin to those of algebra. Ideas influenced subsequent work in mathematical philosophy and are important in computer technology.

Boone, Daniel (1734-1820), American frontiersman. Explored and settled Kentucky in 1770s. His adventures became part of American folklore.

Booth, John Wilkes (1838-65), American actor. Confederate sympathizer, shot President Lincoln in Ford's Theatre, Washington; killed 2 weeks later.

Booth, William (1829-1912), English evangelist preacher. Developed Salvation Army (1878) from missionary work among poor in London.

Boothia, low-lying penin. of S Franklin Dist., Northwest Territs., Canada. Area 32,331 sq km (12,483 sq mi). Most N part of mainland; has magnetic N pole.

Bootle, town of Merseyside met. county, NW England. Pop. 74,000. Seaport on R. Mersey; extensive timber trade.

borage, any of Boraginaceae family of hairy herbs, shrubs and trees of Asia and Europe, esp. Mediterranean region.

borax or **sodium tetraborate** ($Na_2B_4O_7.10H_2O$), crystalline salt, found naturally as tincal. Used in borax bead test to detect the presence of certain metals, as antiseptic and in glass mfg.

Bordeaux, city of SW France, on R. Garonne, cap. of Gironde dept. Pop. 591,000. Port, centre of Bordeaux wine trade; univ. (1441). Hist. cap. of Aquitaine and Guienne, under English rule (1154-1453). Has attractive 18th cent. architecture.

Borders, region of SE Scotland. Area 4670 sq km (1803 sq mi); pop. 101,000; admin. hq. Newtown St Boswells. Created 1975, incl. former Berwickshire, Peeblesshire, Selkirkshire, Roxburghshire.

bore, tidal wave found in many river estuaries. Caused by inrush of water, opposed by river current, into progressively narrower and shallower channel. Occurs in *eg* Seine, Severn, Hooghly, Bay of Fundy.

Borges, Jorge Luis (1899-), Argentinian author. Known for personal form of semi-fictional essay 'Ficcione' reflecting interest in philosophical subjects, collected in translated *Labyrinths* (1962).

Borgia, Cesare (1476-1507), Italian political leader. Son of Rodrigo y Borja (later Pope Alexander VI), who made him a cardinal at age of 17. Resigned after murder (1498) of brother at which he prob. connived. Schemed with the French to capture cities of Romagna and estab. his own principality. Fell ill (1503), then lost power as Julius II forced him to restore possessions to papacy. Died fighting for king of Navarre. His sister, **Lucrezia Borgia** (1480–1519), was alleged to be involved in her brother's intrigues. Married Alfonso d'Este (1501) who became duke of Ferrara; made court centre of artistic and intellectual life.

boric or **boracic acid** (H_3BO_3), crystalline soluble solid, with weak acid properties. Used in eyewash and in making enamels.

Boris Godunov, *see* GODUNOV, BORIS.

Bormann, Martin (1900-45?), German political leader. One of Hitler's chief associates, gained prominence in Nazi party, esp. after 1941. Disappeared at end of WWII, long sought for war crimes. Declared dead (1973) by West German govt.

Born, Max (1882-1970), British physicist, b. Germany. Shared Nobel Prize for Physics (1954) for work on statistical interpretation of wave functions, which helped describe electron behaviour.

Borneo, largest isl. of Malay Archipelago. Area *c* 743,000 sq km (287,000 sq mi). Largely dense jungles and mountains; interior sparsely populated by Dyaks. Important oilfields; rubber and copra exports. Divided into 4 sections: Indonesian Kalimantan, former British colonies of Sabah and Sarawak (now part of Malaysia), and British protect. of Brunei.

Bornholm, isl. of Denmark, in Baltic Sea off S Sweden. Area 588 sq km (227 sq mi); main town Rönne. Mainly hilly; tourism, agric., fishing. Danish since 1660.

Borodin, Aleksandr Porfirevich (1833-87), Russian composer. Member of Russian nationalist group of composers 'the Five'. Works incl. 2 symphonies, opera *Prince Igor,* from which came 'Polovtsian Dances', 3 string quartets. Was also professor of chemistry.

Borodino, Battle of, fought (Sept. 1812) during Napoleonic Wars, at Borodino, near Moscow. Russian forces under Kutuzov engaged Napoleon's army in defence of Moscow. French entered Moscow one week later.

boron (B), non-metallic element, existing as brown amorphous powder or dark crystals; at. no. 5, at. wt. 10.81. Occurs in borax and boric acid. Steel alloy used as moderator in nuclear reactors. Borazon (BN), prepared at high temperature and pressure, used in indust. grinding; harder than diamond and more resistant to heat.

borzoi, long-haired Russian wolfhound. Silky whitish coat, narrow head. Stands *c* 76 cm/30 in. at shoulder.

Bosch, Carl (1874-1940), German chemist.

Adapted HABER process to indust. production. Invented Bosch process for large scale production of hydrogen. Shared Nobel Prize for Chemistry (1931).

Bosch, Hieronymus (*c* 1450-1516), Flemish painter. Famous for his fantastic allegorical and religious scenes, painted in minute detail and bright colour; depicted grotesque half animal, half human creatures and strange plants.

Bosnia and Hercegovina, auton. republic of WC Yugoslavia. Area 51,115 sq km (19,735 sq mi); cap. Sarajevo. Mountainous, mainly within Dinaric Alps; main river Sava. Agric. (cereals, fruit, tobacco) in valleys. Bosnia annexed Hercegovina (14th cent.), fell to Turks 1463; ceded to Austria-Hungary 1878; focus of pre-WWI conflict with Serbia, Russia. Part of Yugoslavia from 1918.

boson, in physics, elementary particle, *eg* photon and certain mesons, that does not obey Pauli exclusion principle.

Bosporus or **Bosphorus,** narrow str. separating European and Asiatic Turkey; 32 km (20 mi) long, links Black Sea with Sea of Marmara. One of its inlets, the Golden Horn, forms harbour of Istanbul. Of great strategic importance, controlled by Turks since 1452.

Bossuet, Jacques Bénigne (1627-1704), French churchman, noted orator. Attacked Protestantism, quietism (esp. that of FÉNELON) and the Jesuits.

Boston, cap. of Massachusetts, US; on Massachusetts Bay. Pop. 3,553,000. Atlantic seaport; financial, trade, cultural, education centre. Machinery, textiles, publishing indust. Settled by Puritans 1630. Focus of pre-Revolution activity (Boston Massacre 1770; Boston Tea Party 1773; Bunker Hill 1775); Lexington and Concord battles fought nearby (1776); Boston anti-slavery movement (1831). Indust. growth with 19th cent. shipping. Has many hist. buildings.

Boston Tea Party, pre-American Revolution incident (1773) caused by British govt.'s retention of tea tax after repeal of Townshend Acts imposing duty on specified goods. Group of angry Boston citizens, disguised as Indians, threw tea from ships into harbour.

Boston terrier, small dog, bred in US from bulldog and bull terrier. Brindled or black coat. Stands *c* 41 cm/16 in. at shoulder.

Boswell, James (1740-95), Scottish author. Known for masterly biog. of friend Dr Samuel Johnson (1791). Also wrote many miscellaneous articles, *eg Private Papers*, discovered in 20th cent.

Bosworth Field, scene of last battle of Wars of Roses (1485) in which Richard III was defeated and killed by forces of Henry of Richmond, later Henry VII. Near Market Bosworth, Leicestershire.

botany, branch of BIOLOGY, science that deals with plants, their life, structure, growth and classification. Systematic plant CLASSIFICATION begun by Aristotle and his pupil Theophrastus, and improved upon by Linnaeus. Studies of plant anatomy, embryology and reproduction made by 18th cent.

Botany Bay, inlet of Tasman Sea, E New South Wales, Australia. Site of landing (1770) by Cook and Banks. Now surrounded by Sydney suburbs; oil refinery, airport on shores.

Botha, Louis (1862-1919), South African soldier and statesman. Commanded Boers in war with Britain (1899-1902). Premier of Transvaal (1907-10), 1st PM of Union of South Africa (1910-19). During WWI, conquered German South West Africa.

Botha, Pieter (1916-), South African political leader. Defence minister (1965-); succeeded Vorster as PM (1978-), while holding onto former post.

Bothnia, Gulf of, N arm of Baltic Sea between Sweden (W) and Finland (E). Aland Isls. at mouth. Ice-bound in winter.

Bothwell, James Hepburn, 4th Earl of (*c* 1536-78), Scottish nobleman, 3rd husband of Mary Queen of Scots. Mary's confidant after murder of RIZZIO (1566), responsible for assassination (1567) of DARNLEY. After abducting and marrying Mary, he was forced by Scottish nobles to flee to Denmark.

bo tree, name given by Buddhists to *Ficus religiosa*, the sacred fig tree under which Buddha was enlightened.

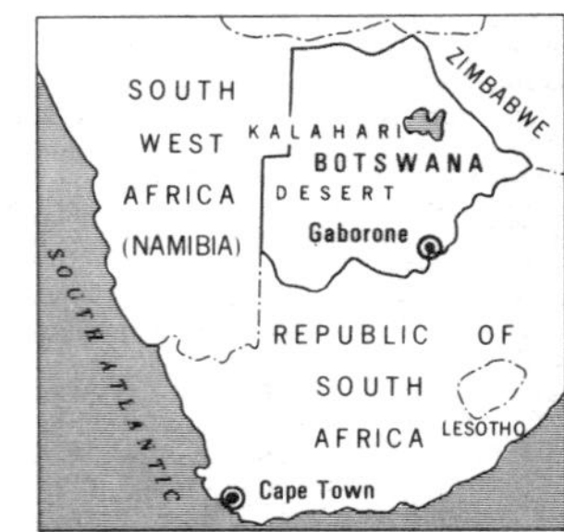

Botswana

Botswana, republic of S Africa; formerly Bechuanaland. Area 600,000 sq km (231,000 sq mi); pop. 726,000; cap. Gaborone. Languages: Tswana, English. Religions: native, Christian. Mainly dry plateau, Okavango Swamp in N, Kalahari Desert in S; nomadic pastoralism, exports cattle, hides. Main food crops maize, millet. Created Bechuanaland Protect. 1885; independent as Botswana from 1966; member of British Commonwealth.

Botticelli, Sandro, orig. Alessandro dei Filipepi (*c* 1445-1510), Italian painter. One of the leading Florentine painters of the Renaissance, his work is noted for delicacy, expressive line and its slight archaism. Most famous works are *Primavera* and *Birth of Venus*.

bottlenosed dolphin, *Tursiops truncatus,* Atlantic cetacean, with short snout. Larger than common dolphin, *c* 3.6 m/12 ft long. Sociable, responsive to human contact; has been much studied.

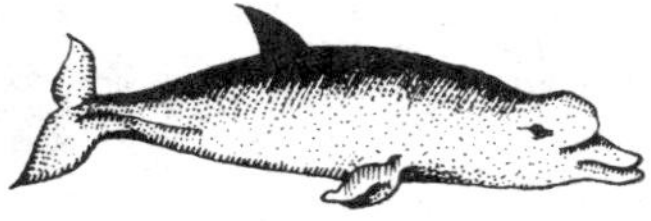

Bottlenosed whale

bottlenosed whale, *Hyperoodon rostratus,* N Atlantic beaked whale, related to sperm whale; *c* 6.4 m/21 ft long.

botulism, rare type of food poisoning caused by toxin produced by bacterium *Clostridium botulinum,* sometimes found in improperly preserved or canned food. Characterized by muscular paralysis; often fatal.

Boucher, François (1703-70), French painter. His work is considered the embodiment of French 18th cent. rococo taste. Director of Gobelins tapestry factory from 1755.

Boudicca or **Boadicea** (d. AD 62), British queen of Iceni in East Anglia. Led revolt (61) against Romans following brutal annexation of her dead husband's territ. Burned Colchester and London. Her army was defeated by Paulinus; she took poison.

Boudin, Eugène Louis (1824-98), French painter. Painted numerous coastal and harbour scenes, noted for their luminous skies. Advocate of painting directly from nature.

Bougainville, Louis Antoine de (1729-1811), French navigator. Circumnavigated globe 1767-9, after which he wrote *Description d'un voyage autour du monde.*

Bougainville, largest of Solomon Isls., SW Pacific; part of Papua New Guinea. Area *c* 10,050 sq km (3880 sq mi). Mountainous, rises to *c* 2590 m (8500 ft) at Mt. Balbi, an active volcano.

bougainvillea, small genus of ornamental, tropical American evergreen vines with brilliant red or purple flowers.

Boulanger, Georges Ernest Jean Marie (1837-91), French general. War minister (1886-7); gained great popular support as leader of Boulangist movement. Suspected of dictatorial ambitions, fled to Belgium and London (1889). He committed suicide.

boulder clay or **till,** unstratified mixture of clay, sand, gravel and boulders, transported and deposited by retreating glacier. Type of DRIFT.

Boulez, Pierre (1925-), French composer. Extended 12-note technique of Schoenberg to fixed organization of all musical elements. Also a noted conductor.

Boulogne (-sur-Mer), town of Picardy, N France, on English Channel. Pop. 50,000. Port, ferry services to Dover and Folkestone (England); fishing indust.

Boult, Sir Adrian Cedric (1889-), British conductor. Formed BBC Symphony Orchestra in 1930 and was its principal conductor until 1949; moved to London Philharmonic Orchestra until 1957. Championed music of Holst, Vaughan Williams, Elgar.

Boumedienne, Houari (*c* 1932-1978), Algerian political leader. Overthrew Ben Bella (1965), became chief of state as head of revolutionary council.

bouncing Bet, *see* SOAPWORT.

Bounty, naval ship, *see* BLIGH, WILLIAM.

Bourbon, royal house of Europe. Ruled France, Spain, Two Sicilies and Parma. **Antoine de Bourbon** (1518-62) became king of Navarre; his son became Henry IV, 1st Bourbon king of France, whose descendants reigned until 1830 (except 1792-1814). Line of Bourbon-Spain started in 1700 with accession of grandson of Louis XIV, Philip V of Spain. Bourbon-Sicily came from Spanish house, founded (1759) by Ferdinand I of the Two Sicilies, ending with Francis II in 1861. Bourbon-Parma (1748-1860) was founded by younger son of Philip V of Spain.

bourgeoisie, the mercantile class of any country. Prominent from end of medieval period, when they successfully opposed feudal nobility. In Marxist theory, class which, since end of Middle Ages, rose to power, overcoming nobles, monarchs, to reach exclusive political sway in modern state.

Bourges, town of C France, cap. of Cher dept. Pop. 74,000. Route centre, armaments mfg. Hist. cap. of Berry. Cathedral (13th cent.).

Bourguiba, Habib ben Ali (1903-), Tunisian political leader. Led struggle for independence from France, involved in peace negotiations (1954). Elected premier (1956), then president (1959).

Bournemouth, town of Dorset, S England (formerly in Hampshire). Pop. 146,000. Resort on Poole Bay; has many hotels, convalescent homes.

Bouvet Island, isl. in S Atlantic, *c* 2900 km (1800 mi) SSW of Cape Town. Discovered 1739, Norwegian dependency since 1930.

Bovidae, family of even-toed UNGULATES, order Artiodactyla, incl. cattle, sheep, goats, antelopes.

bow, *see* ARCHERY.

Bowdler, Thomas (1754-1825), English physician, editor. Expurgated literary texts, esp. those of Shakespeare, of anything 'which cannot with propriety be read aloud in a family'; hence to 'bowdlerize'.

bowerbird, small bird of Australia, New Guinea, family Ptilonorhynchidae. Male builds bower, decorated with feathers, shells, to attract female.

bowhead, *Balaena mysticetus,* large-mouthed arctic whale which has become rare through overfishing. Now a protected species.

bowling, tenpin, indoor game played by rolling a ball at 10 wooden 'pins'. Game consists of 10 frames, a player being allowed to bowl twice if necessary in a frame. Modernized form of game believed to have been originally introduced into America by Dutch settlers in 17th cent.

bowls or **lawn bowling,** outdoor game dating at least from 13th cent. in England. Played on green, divided into 6 rinks. Opponents alternately roll balls close to small white ball (jack) and attempt to dislodge those previously rolled.

box, evergreen shrub of genus *Buxus* of Europe and N Asia. Common variety, *B. sempervirens,* is slow growing and used for clipped hedges.

boxer, short-coated dog of German origin. Fawn or brindle coloured, with protruding jaw. Stands *c* 58 cm/23 in. high at shoulder.

Boxer Rebellion (1898-1900), uprising in China by the Boxers, secret society dedicated to removal of foreign influence. Encouraged by dowager empress Tzu Hsi. Revolt crushed by joint European, Japanese, American forces.

boxing, sport of fighting with the fists. Boxing with soft leather coverings on fists was incl. in ancient Olympic games. Bare fisted boxing revived in 18th cent. England in form of prize fighting. Rules for boxing with gloves were devised *c* 1867 under patronage of Marquess of Queensberry.

Boyd Orr, John Boyd Orr, 1st Baron (1880-1971), Scottish biologist. First director-general (1945-8) of UN Food and Agriculture Organization. Awarded Nobel Peace Prize (1949) for contributions to study of nutrition and world food problems.

Boyle, Robert (1627-91), Irish scientist. Enunciated Boyle's law, that volume of a gas kept at constant temperature is inversely proportional to its pressure, following experiments with air. Forwarded atomic view of matter, and distinguished between elements and compounds.

Boyne, river of NE Irish Republic, flows 130 km (80 mi) from Bog of Allen via Kildare, Meath to Irish Sea near Drogheda. Scene of battle (1690) in which William III of England defeated Jacobites under James II.

Boy Scouts, non-military, non-political international organization of boys over 12 years old. Estab. (1908) in UK by Baden-Powell; association incorporated by royal charter (1912), and spread worldwide. Parallel organization for girls is Girl Guides (1922).

Brabant, area of Belgium and Netherlands. Former prov. of Low Countries, duchy from 12th cent. Prosperous medieval wool, textiles trade centred in Antwerp, Brussels, Louvain. Ruled from 15th cent. by Habsburgs. Divided 1830; Brabant, Antwerp are Belgian provs., North Brabant is Dutch prov.

Brachiopoda (brachiopods), phylum of marine invertebrates, often called lampshells. Brachiopod has bivalve shell enclosing soft body. Fossil species of Palaeozoic, Mesozoic eras are common; *c* 250 living species, *c* 30,000 extinct.

bracken or **brake,** several species of FERN, esp. European and American *Pteridium aquilinum,* with coarse, sharp stem and branched spreading fronds. In some places a pernicious weed. Roots once used in tanning and the fronds in thatching.

Bradford, city of West Yorkshire met. county, N England. Pop. 463,000. Woollens, worsteds, textiles, engineering industs. Church (15th cent.) now cathedral.

Bradley, Andrew Cecil (1851-1935), English literary critic. Best known for *Shakespearean Tragedy* (1904) stressing an understanding of Shakespeare's characters as a key to the plays. His brother, **Francis Herbert Bradley** (1846-1924), was English philosopher. Opposed logical empiricism by differentiating between the psychological event and formal meaning in thought.

Bradman, Sir Donald George (1908-), Australian cricketer. A prolific run scorer, he played for Australia (1928-48), captain from 1936.

Bragg, Sir William Henry (1862-1942), English physicist. Researched into penetrating power of alpha particles. Shared Nobel Prize for Physics (1915) with his son, **Sir William Lawrence Bragg** (1890-1971), for working out theory of X-ray diffraction and using it to determine X-ray wavelengths and crystal structure.

Brahe, Tycho (1546-1601), Danish astronomer. Improved astronomical instruments, thus obtaining positions of heavenly bodies with unprecedented accuracy.

Brahma, in Hinduism, supreme and eternal spirit of the universe. Personified as creator in divine triad (*see* also VISHNU, SIVA).

Brahman or **Brahmin,** in Hinduism, member of priestly (highest) Hindu CASTE. Only Brahmans may interpret the sacred Vedic texts.

Brahmaputra, river of NE India, *c* 2900 km (1800 mi) long. Rises in Himalayas of SW Tibet as Tsangpo, flows through fertile Assam valley; merges with Ganges in Bangladesh.

Brahms, Johannes (1833-97), German composer, pianist. Settled in Vienna (1863). Despite romantic inclinations, he worked in classical forms. Works incl. 4 symphonies, a Requiem, piano and violin concertos, choral and orchestral compositions, and chamber music.

Braille, Louis (*c* 1809-52), French inventor. Blind from the age of three, he devised (1829) the system of raised point writing and printing named after him, enabling the blind to read and write.

brain, in vertebrates, that part of central nervous system enclosed in skull. Divided into 3 main sections: hindbrain, midbrain and forebrain. Hindbrain contains brain stem, extending from spinal cord; anterior to this is cerebellum, which coordinates muscular movements. Midbrain contains control network for senses of sight and

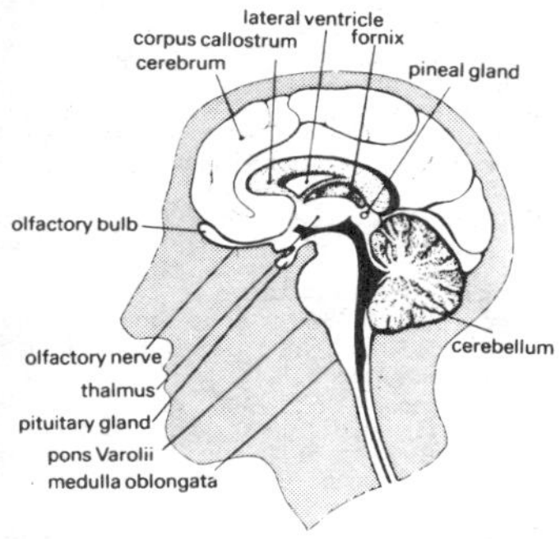

Section of the brain

hearing. Forebrain contains: thalamus, which receives and distributes incoming sensations and perceives sensation of pain; hypothalamus, which regulates body temperature, heart beat, metabolic rate, *etc*; relatively huge cerebrum, divided into 2 hemispheres with 4 paired lobes. Cerebrum controls sensations of vision, hearing, touch, *etc*, and higher mental processes.

brake, *see* BRACKEN.

Bramante, Donato (1444-1514), Italian architect. Major architect of high Renaissance; engaged by Julius II to rebuild St Peter's, Rome (1503).

bramble, *see* BLACKBERRY.

Branchiopoda, subclass of primitive aquatic crustaceans, with many pairs of flattened, leaf-like limbs. Well-known example is daphnia or waterflea.

Brancusi, Constantin (1876-1957), Romanian sculptor. Pioneer of abstract sculpture; his work, in wood, stone and highly-polished metal, is noted for its simplification of natural forms.

Brandenburg, town of C East Germany, on R. Havel. Pop. 90,000. Agric. machinery, textiles. Cathedral, town hall (both 14th cent.). Cap. of former Brandenburg prov. of Prussia.

Brando, Marlon (1924-), American stage and film actor. First known for 'primitive male' roles, as in play *A Streetcar Named Desire* (1947), film *On the Waterfront* (1954). Later developed range in films with *The Godfather* (1972), *Last Tango in Paris* (1973).

Brandt, Willy, orig. Herbert Ernst Karl Frahm (1913-), German statesman. Active in Norwegian resistance during WWII. Mayor of West Berlin (1957-66) until joined coalition govt. First Social Democrat chancellor (1969-74). Awarded Nobel Peace Prize (1971) for policies of seeking to improve relations with E European countries.

brandy, name for alcoholic spirit distilled from any wine. Best-known grape wine brandy is cognac, made from white grapes in Charente (France). Kirsch is distilled from fermented cherry juice, and slivovitz, of E Europe, from plums.

brant goose, *see* BRENT GOOSE.

Braque, Georges (1882-1963), French painter. Early work was in fauve style. Collaborated with Picasso in development of cubism until 1914; originated use of collage in his paintings. Later work incl. still lifes and landscapes in less abstract style.

Brasília, cap. of Brazil, in C federal dist. Pop. 763,000. Built as cap. with intention of stimulating growth in undeveloped interior; inaugurated 1960. Univ. (1960).

brass, name applied to various alloys of zinc and copper; sometimes containing other metal components. Ductile, resists corrosion.

brassica, *see* CABBAGE; TURNIP.

brass instruments, instruments in which sound is produced by vibration of the lips within a mouthpiece, *eg* FRENCH HORN; TROMBONE; TRUMPET; TUBA.

Bratislava (Ger. *Pressburg*), city of S Czechoslovakia, on R. Danube. Pop. 350,000. River port; agric. market, oil refinery (pipeline from Ukraine 1962). Cap. of Hungary 1541-1784 and Slovakia 1918-45. Gothic cathedral, town hall (13th cent.).

Braunschweig, *see* BRUNSWICK.

Brazil

Brazil (*Brasil*), republic of E South America. Area 8,511,965 sq km (3,286,470 sq mi); pop. 115,397,000; cap. Brasilia; major cities Rio de Janeiro (former cap.); São Paulo. Language: Portuguese. Religion: RC. Covers nearly ½ of South American continent. Has extensive Atlantic coastline; mainly agric. esp. coffee, cotton, sugar cane growing. Tropical forested Amazon basin produces rubber. Mato Grosso plateau in undeveloped interior (mineral resources *eg* iron ore, manganese). Drained by Amazon (W), Paraná-Paraguay (S), São Francisco river systems. Indust. concentrated in São Paulo, Minas Gerais regions (esp. cotton, steel, chemicals, engineering). Portuguese settlement began in 16th cent.; pop. gradually mixed. Independence gained (1822); republic estab. 1889. Govt. instability of 20th cent. broken by Vargas' dictatorship (1930-45).

brazilnut, edible seeds of tree *Bertholletia excelsa,* of nettle family, native to Brazil. Large woody fruits contain *c* 20 three-sided edible oily nuts.

Brazzaville, cap. of the Congo, on Stanley Pool of R. Congo, opposite Kinshasa (Zaïre). Pop. 290,000. Admin., commercial centre. River port; trade in wood, rubber, minerals from interior to coast. Founded (1880).

bread, food baked from kneaded dough made from flour, water and yeast (used as raising agent). Unleavened bread contains no raising agent. Wheat flour is generally used, but rye is sometimes employed. White bread is made from grain from which husk has been removed.

breadfruit, large, round, pulpy fruit of Malayan tree, *Artocarpus altilis,* found throughout S Pacific and tropical America. When baked the fruit can be used as bread substitute.

Breakspear, Nicholas, *see* ADRIAN IV.

bream, *Abramis brama,* European freshwater food fish of carp family. Protruding mouth used for feeding on bottom.

breast, in human female, either of 2 milk-secreting (mammary) glands. Develops with onset of puberty. Towards end of pregnancy, hormones from pituitary gland stimulate secretion of milk. Corresponding male glands are undeveloped.

breccia, rock composed of small angular fragments, bound together in matrix of cementing material. Normally formed close to origin of constituent fragments, unlike CONGLOMERATE. Examples incl. cemented scree deposits.

Brecht, [Eugen Friedrich] Bertolt (1898-1956), German dramatist. Early work expressionist; best known for Marxist dramas, *eg The Threepenny Opera* (1928) with music by Weill, *Mother Courage and Her Children* (1939), *The Caucasian Chalk Circle* (1945).

Breconshire or **Brecknockshire,** former county of SC Wales, now in Powys. Mountainous in S, incl. Brecon Beacons (National Park). Coalmining; agric. **Brecon** or **Brecknock,** mun. bor. and admin. hq. of Powys. Pop. 6000. Has cathedral (1923) formerly Priory Church.

breeder reactor, nuclear reactor which, in addition to creating atomic energy, produces more nuclear fuel by neutron bombardment of suitable radioactive elements, *eg* uranium 238.

breeding, attempt to improve genetic strains of plants and animals by careful selection of parent stock. Cattle are bred to improve meat or milk yield; cereals are bred to be more disease resistant and give larger and more rapid yields.

Bremen, city of N West Germany, on R. Weser, cap. of Bremen state. Pop. 568,000. Major port; indust., commercial centre. Hanseatic League member from 1358; has medieval cathedral, town hall. Badly damaged in WWII.

Bremerhaven, city of N West Germany, at mouth of R. Weser. Pop. 142,000. Outport for Bremen; major fishing, ferry port. Founded 1827.

Brenner Pass (Ital. *Passo Brennero*), on Austro-Italian border. Height 1370 m (4500 ft); road (1772), railway (1867) connect Innsbruck with Bolzano.

Brent, bor. of W Greater London, England. Pop. 255,000. Created 1965 from Wembley, Willesden mun. bors.

brent goose or **brant goose,** *Branta bernicla,* small, dark goose with black head. Breeds in Arctic, winters along Atlantic coasts of North America and Europe.

Brescia, city of Lombardy, N Italy, cap. of Brescia prov. Pop. 215,000. Indust. centre; iron, munitions, textiles. Roman *Brixia,* has temple of Vespasian (AD 73); medieval cathedrals.

Breslau, *see* WROCLAW.

Brest, city of Brittany, NW France, on Atlantic Ocean. Pop. 154,000. Port, fishing; major French naval base.

Brest-Litovsk, Treaty of, peace treaty in WWI, signed (1918) by Soviet Russia and Central powers at Brest in USSR, after 1917 armistice. Russia recognized independence of Ukraine and Georgia, confirmed independence of Finland, gave up Poland, Baltic states and part of Byelorussia to Germany and Austro-Hungary; also made some concessions to Turkey. Terms renounced at end of WWI.

Breton, André (1896-1966), French author. Involved in DADA, later founded SURREALISM in 3 manifestoes (1924-42).

Breton, language, *see* CELTIC.

brewing, *see* BEER.

Brezhnev, Leonid Ilyich (1906-), Soviet political leader. President (1960-4) until he succeeded Khrushchev as first secretary of Communist party's Central Committee. Policies incl. DETENTE with US, growing estrangement from China, extension of Soviet influence in developing countries. Supported invasion (1968) of Czechoslovakia. Formally acknowledged as head of state after changes to Soviet constitution (1977).

Briand, Aristide (1862-1932), French statesman. Began as Socialist, heading several govts. (1909-29). Foreign minister (1925-32), helped conclude Locarno (1925) and Kellogg-Briand (1928) pacts, aimed at maintaining European peace. Shared Nobel Peace Prize (1926) with Stresemann.

briar, sweetbriar or **eglantine,** *Rosa eglanteria,* European species of bush rose. Hooked white or pink single flowers, scarlet fruit (hips) which are rich in vitamin C.

bridge, card game for four players derived from WHIST. Most popular form is contract bridge, invented (1925). Rules governing

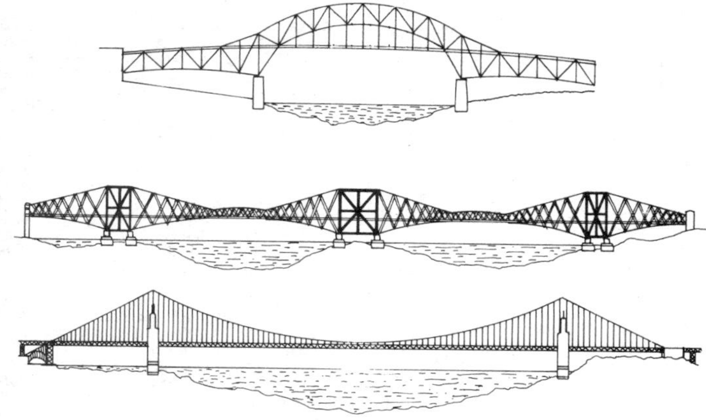

Steel arch, cantilever and suspension bridges

tournament play determined by Portland Club, London, European Bridge League, and American Contract Bridge League.

bridge, structure to carry road, railway or canal over gap or barrier. Most common types are cantilever, suspension and arch bridges. Some of world's best-known bridges incl. Forth Railway Bridge, Scotland (cantilever); Brooklyn Bridge, New York (suspension); Sydney Harbour Bridge, Australia (steel arch); Golden Gate Bridge, San Francisco (suspension).

Bridgeport, town of SW Connecticut, US; on Long Isl. Sound. Pop. 397,000. Munitions mfg., engineering, plastics indust. First settled as fishing community (1639).

Bridges, Robert Seymour (1844-1930), English poet. Works incl. *Shorter Poems* (1890), *The Testament of Beauty* (1929). Poet laureate (1913).

Bridget, St (*c* 453-*c* 523), Irish abbess. Regarded as founder of 1st women's religious community in Ireland at Kildare. Also called Brigid, Bride.

Bridgetown, cap. and seaport of Barbados, on Carlisle Bay. Pop. 97,000. Popular tourist resort. Exports sugar, rum, molasses.

Bridie, James, pseud. of Osborne Henry Mavor (1888-1951), Scottish playwright. Plays incl. *The Anatomist* (1931) on Burke and Hare.

Brie, region of N France, E of Paris. Cereals, cattle rearing; noted for dairy produce, esp. cheese. Early medieval county, cap. Meaux.

Brigantes, early people of N England. Under queen Cartimandua became client-state of Rome, but defeated in AD 71 by Agricola. Unsuccessful revolt (155) led to estab. of many more Roman forts and settlements.

Bright, John (1811-89), British politician. Noted orator, joined by COBDEN in leading Anti-Corn Law League, advocating free trade; Corn Laws repealed (1846). Championed middle classes on basis of laisser-faire doctrines.

Brighton, co. bor. of East Sussex, S England. Pop. 158,000. Seaside resort, popular since Royal Pavilion built 1817 by Prince Regent (George IV). Univ. of Sussex (1959) is nearby.

brill, *Scophthalmus rhombus,* European marine flatfish of turbot family. Valued as food.

Brindisi, town of Apulia, SE Italy, on Adriatic Sea, cap. of Brindisi prov. Pop. 85,000. Port; petrochemicals, engineering. As Roman *Brundisium* was naval station, terminus of Appian Way. Medieval castle, cathedral.

Brisbane, city of E Australia, cap. of Queensland; on Brisbane R. Pop. 958,000. Admin., commercial centre; port, exports wool, wheat, fruit, minerals. Founded (1824) as penal colony; first free settlers came 1838; state cap. from 1859. Univ. of Queensland (1909).

bristletail, primitive, wingless insect with long antennae. Divided into 2 orders: 1) Diplura, eyeless with 2 long tail filaments; 2) Thysanura, with compound eye, body scales. Species incl. SILVERFISH.

Bristol, city of Avon, SW England, on R. Avon. Pop. 412,000. Seaport, food processing, aircraft mfg., tobacco indust. Medieval wool trade; 17th-18th cent. slave trade. Univ. (1909).

Bristol Channel, inlet of Atlantic between SW England and Wales, *c* 136 km (85 mi) long. Chief river is Severn; extreme tidal range.

Britain, Battle of, German air offensive (Aug.-Oct. 1940), intended to destroy British defences prior to invasion. Luftwaffe lost 1733 aircraft and abandoned tactic in mid-Oct., though night raids continued.

British Antarctic Territory, all isls. and mainland S of 60° S and between 20° and 80° W. Area *c* 388,500 sq km (150,000 sq mi). Incl. Graham Land, parts of Coats Land and Weddell Sea, South Shetland and South Orkney Isls.

British Broadcasting Corporation, administrative body for UK radio and TV broadcasts. Estab. by royal charter (1927) it is controlled by a board of governors appointed by the crown and responsible to Parliament. Revenue comes from sale of TV licences and publications.

British Columbia, coastal prov. of W Canada; incl. Vancouver, Queen Charlotte Isls. Area 948,600 sq km (366,255 sq mi); pop. 2,567,000; cap. Victoria; major city Vancouver. Mainly mountainous. Coast Mts. rise to Rockies in interior; main rivers Fraser, Columbia; h.e.p. Major timber indust; dairy, fruit, mixed farming; fisheries; copper, lead, zinc mining; aluminium smelting. Acquired by Hudson's Bay Co. (1821), became prov. 1871; linked with E by railway (1885).

British Commonwealth of Nations, *see* COMMONWEALTH, BRITISH.

British Guiana, *see* GUYANA.

British Honduras, *see* BELIZE.

British Indian Ocean Territory, colony formed (1965) from Chagos archipelago, Des Roches, Farquhar and Aldabra isls. Pop. 2000. Last 3 isls. part of Seychelles from 1976.

British Isles, archipelago of NW Europe in Atlantic Ocean, comprising GREAT BRITAIN, IRELAND. Incl. Hebrides, Orkneys, Shetland, Isle of Man, Isle of Wight, Scilly Isles, Channel Isls.

British Library, national UK library, created 1973. Formerly the library and reading room of the British Museum. Under the Copyright Act (1957) a copy of every book published in the UK must be delivered to the Library.

British Museum, national museum in London, founded (1753) on basis of Sir Hans Sloane's collection; opened to public 1759. Collection incl. coins and stamps, books and manuscripts, *eg* Lindisfarne Gospels, Egyptian antiquities, *eg* Rosetta Stone, classical sculpture, *eg* Elgin Marbles.

British North America Act (1867), constitution of Canada, passed by British Parliament, embodying plans for federal govt. agreed at Québec Conference (1864). Provided for division of provincial (enumerated) and federal (residual) legislative powers; safeguarded independence of courts and special language and educational status for Québec prov. Also allowed for admission of further provs.

British Standards Institution (BSI), originally Engineering Standards Committee, formed by various engineering bodies (1901, granted charter 1929) who voluntarily prepared and pub. agreed mfg. standards for their products. The BSI now covers over 60 major industs. in UK.

Brittany (*Bretagne*), region of NW France, occupying penin. between English Channel and Bay of Biscay; hist. cap. Rennes. Rocky coast, natural harbours (*eg* Brest), interior largely moorland. Agric., esp. fruit, vegetables; fishing, tourism. Ancient *Armorica*; settled by Celts from Britain *c* 500 AD. Medieval duchy, incorporated (1532) into France. Breton language still spoken in rural areas, distinctive customs retained.

Britten, [Edward] Benjamin (1913-76), English composer. Highly personal composer, worked in traditional idioms and forms, principally opera and vocal music. Works incl. operas *Peter Grimes* and *Billy Budd*, oratorio *A War Requiem*.

Brno (Ger. *Brünn*), city of C Czechoslovakia. Pop. 363,000. Commercial and indust. centre, esp. textiles, engineering. Besieged by Swedish (1645). Cap. of Moravia (1938-45).

broadcasting, public transmission of sound and images by radio and television. Sound broadcasting began *c* 1920 in US, 1921 in UK, 1st public TV service begun by British Broadcasting Corporation (1936). Developments since incl. use of high frequencies (VHF) to increase available radio space, and colour TV.

Broads, The, *see* NORFOLK.

Broadway, street of New York City. Passes through theatre district, hence synonymous with American commercial theatre.

broccoli, *Brassica oleracea,* plant related to the cauliflower but bearing tender shoots with greenish buds cooked as vegetable. Native to S Europe and cultivated widely in N temperate zones.

broch, circular dry-stone tower, up to 15 m (50 ft) high, found mostly in N and NW Scotland. Used as fortified homestead in early Christian times.

Brocken, mountain of East Germany highest of Harz Mts. (1142 m/3747 ft) Traditional meeting place of witches on Witches' Sabbath (May 1).

Brocken spectre, natural phenomenon named after highest of Harz Mts., in which greatly enlarged shadow of observer is projected onto bank of cloud or mist below him. May be accompanied by 'glory' circular rainbow bands seen round shadow, caused by diffraction.

Broglie, Louis Victor, Prince de (1892-) French physicist. Awarded Nobel Prize for Physics (1929) for theory of wave nature of electron, starting point of wave mechanics

Broken Hill, city of W New South Wales, Australia. Pop. 30,000. Silver, lead, zinc, gold mining; market town for large pastoral area.

Bromberg, *see* BYDGOSZCZ.

bromine (Br), reddish-brown volatile liquid element of halogen family; at. no. 35, at. wt. 79.91. Vapour has choking, irritating smell. Occurs in salts found in sea water and mineral deposits. Used in organic synthesis; compounds used in photography (silver bromide) and formerly in medicine.

Bromley, bor. of SE Greater London, England. Pop. 292,000. Created 1965 from Bromley, Beckenham mun. bors., 4 NW Kent towns incl. Orpington.

bronchitis, inflammation of air-passages (bronchial tubes) in lungs. Acute form may be caused by viral or bacterial infection. Chronic form, characterized by regular coughing with mucus, may be caused by smoking, air pollution, fog.

Brontë sisters, three English novelists. Produced some of most famous fiction of early 19th cent. **Charlotte Brontë,** pseud. Currer Bell (1816-55), wrote semi-autobiog. works incl. *Jane Eyre* (1847), *Villette* (1853), *The Professor* (1857). **Emily Jane Brontë,** pseud. Ellis Bell (1818-48), wrote single novel, masterpiece *Wuthering Heights* (1847), imaginative verse. **Anne Brontë,** pseud. Acton Bell (1820-49), known for *The Tenant of Wildfell Hall* (1848), also collaborated with sisters in poetry and juvenilia. Their works show effect on powerful imaginations of wild surroundings and intense isolated family life.

Brontosaurus

brontosaurus, extinct semi-aquatic herbivorous dinosaur, genus *Apatosaurus.* Over 21.3 m/70 ft long, with long neck and tail, it weighed *c* 30 tons. Bones have been found in Jurassic strata of US.

Bronx, *see* NEW YORK CITY.

bronze, alloy consisting mainly of copper and tin; may contain zinc and aluminium. Used to make medals, bells, *etc;* phosphor bronze used in springs, aluminium bronze in bearings.

Bronze Age, archaeological period characterized by use of bronze weapons and tools. Dates from before 3500 BC in Middle East, is associated with beginning of recorded history. Placed between Stone and Iron Ages.

Bronzino, Angelo, real name di Cosimo Allori (1503-72), Italian painter. Noted for his portraits in mannerist style; his sitters were rendered in unemotional, elegant manner. Works incl. *Venus, Cupid, Time and Folly.*

Brooke, Alan Francis, *see* ALANBROOKE.

Brooke, Rupert Chawner (1887-1915), English poet. Known for romantic, patriotic verse, esp. 'Grantchester' and *1914 and Other Poems* (1915). Died of septicaemia on Dardanelles expedition.

Brooklyn, *see* NEW YORK CITY.

broom, shrubs of 3 related genera *Cytisus, Genista, Spartium* of Leguminosae family, with yellow, white or purple flowers.

Brouwer, Adriaen (*c* 1605-38), Flemish painter. Known for genre scenes of peasant life, often set in taverns; later work was usually monochromatic.

Brown, Sir Arthur Whitten, *see* ALCOCK, SIR JOHN WILLIAM.

Brown, Ford Madox (1821-93), English painter, b. France. Associated with the Pre-Raphaelites, and profoundly influenced by them. Works incl. *Work* and *The Last of England.*

Brown, John (1800-59), American abolitionist. Belief in need for armed intervention to free slaves led to his capture of govt. arsenal at Harpers Ferry, West Virginia (1859). It was retaken and Brown was hanged.

Brown, Lancelot ('Capability') (1716-83), English landscape gardener. Laid out gardens at Chatsworth, Blenheim, *etc,* in informal style.

brown algae, any of the division Phaeophyta of large ALGAE that contain a brown pigment which masks the green chlorophyll. Often have air bladders and a gelatinous surface. Mainly marine group abundant in colder latitudes.

brown bear, *Ursus arctos,* omnivorous bear of Europe, Asia, North America. Variations in size of species, with Kodiak bear of Alaska largest; also incl. GRIZZLY BEAR. Rare in Europe, now protected.

Brownian motion, unceasing random movement of small particles suspended in fluid. Described by Scottish botanist Robert Brown (1827). Caused by bombardment of particles by continuously moving fluid molecules; theoretical explanation given by Einstein (1905).

Browning, Robert (1812-89), English poet. Known for long poem, *The Ring and the Book* (1868-9), earlier poetry 'Pippa Passes', 'My Last Duchess'. Work notable for metric innovation, dramatic monologue allowing shifting viewpoint. His wife, **Elizabeth Barrett Browning** (1806-61), was also a poet, known for *Sonnets from the Portuguese* (1850), addressed to husband. Known for their love affair, overcoming her jealous father and her own invalidism.

brown rat, *Rattus norvegicus,* large rodent of Muridae family. Of Asian origin, reached Europe, US in 18th cent. Destruction of foodstuffs, spread of disease make it major pest.

brownshirts (*Sturmabteilung* or SA),

paramilitary force (storm troops) of Nazi party, founded in 1922. Wore brown uniform, distinct from black of the *Schutzstaffel* (SS).

Bruce, Robert, *see* ROBERT THE BRUCE.

brucellosis, *see* UNDULANT FEVER.

Bruch, Max (1838-1920), German composer. Best known for violin concertos.

Brücke, Die ('the bridge'), group of German expressionist painters, incl. Kirchner, Schmidt-Rottluff and Heckel, founded in Dresden (1905). Work, characterized by vivid symbolic colour, distortion. Disbanded 1913.

Bruckner, Anton (1824-96), Austrian composer. Influenced by Wagner in producing grandiose works, albeit principally for orchestra in classic forms. Major compositions incl. 9 symphonies, several masses and *Te Deum*.

Brueghel or **Bruegel,** family of Flemish painters. **Pieter Bruegel** (*c* 1525-69) was noted for his painting of landscape, peasant village scenes, allegories, and religious subjects. His son, **Pieter Brueghel** (1564-1638), known as 'Hell Brueghel' copied many of his father's works. Another son, **Jan Brueghel** (1568-1625), known as 'Velvet Brueghel', painted landscapes and still life.

Brugge (Fr. *Bruges*), town of NW Belgium, cap. of West Flanders prov. Pop. 119,000. Agric. market, lace mfg.; ship canal to Zeebrugge. Prosperous medieval wool trade, Hanseatic centre. Cloth Hall, belfry (13th cent.) with carillon.

bruise, bleeding into injured skin following a blow, *etc.* Discoloration results when red blood pigment loses its oxygen and later breaks down into bile pigments.

Brumaire, second month of French Revolutionary Calendar (officially operating 1793-1805). Coup of 18 Brumaire (9-10 Nov. 1799) overthrew DIRECTORY and created consulate under Napoleon.

Brummell, George Bryan ('Beau') (1778-1840), English dandy. Close associate of the Prince Regent (later George IV), he became recognized arbiter of fashionable dress in Regency period. Died in squalor following quarrel with the prince.

Brunei, sultanate of N Borneo. Area *c* 5760 sq km (2200 sq mi); pop. 201,000. Cap. and main seaport, Bandar Seri Begawan (formerly Brunei), pop. 37,000. Rubber, fruit grown; rich oil deposits. Became British protect. 1888. Independence due 1983.

Brunel Isambard Kingdom, (1806–59), an authority on rail traction, steam navigation and civil engineering, was responsible for building of much of Great Western Railway. Designed steamships *Great Western* (1838), *Great Eastern* (1858).

Brunelleschi, Filippo (1377-1446), Italian architect. Pioneer in scientific study of perspective and the creation of controlled space, based on mathematical proportion. Most famous for design of dome of Florence cathedral (1420).

Brunei

Brunhild, Brynhild or **Brünnhilde,** i Germanic myth, great female warrior. I NIBELUNGENLIED defeated by SIEGFRIED, an causes his death. In *Volsungsaga*, is chie of Valkyries, loved by Sigurd, whom sh kills for infidelity, then commits suicide Story adapted by Wagner in *Ring of th Nibelung*.

Bruno, Giordano (1548-1600), Italian philo sopher. Rejected dogma on grounds tha knowledge is infinite and final truth canno be established. Formulated monadi theory of universe. Influenced Spinoza Leibnitz. A Dominican, burned as heretic.

Brunswick (*Braunschweig*), city of NE Wes Germany, on R. Oker. Pop. 267,000. Foo processing, machinery, publishing indust Formerly cap. of duchy of Brunswic (1635-1918) and state (1918-46). Hanseati League member from 13th cent. Ha medieval cathedral, town hall, fountain.

Brussels (Fr. *Bruxelles*), cap. of Belgium, o R. Senne. Pop. 1,042,000. Commercia indust. centre (textiles, esp. lace); railwa jct. Gothic cathedral, Grand' Place, tow hall (15th cent.), Atomium (1958); uni (1834). Hq. of EEC, NATO. Cap. of Brabar from 15th cent., of Belgium fro independence (1830).

Brussels sprouts, *Brassica olerace gemmifera*, vegetable of CABBAGE famil Small edible heads are borne on stem.

Brutus, Marcus Junius (*c* 85-42 BC), Roma political leader. Sided with Pompey again Caesar in civil war; pardoned after batt of Pharsala. Joined Cassius in assassinatio of Caesar (44), but had to flee Macedonia. Defeated by Antony an Octavian at Philippi (42); committe suicide.

bryony, any of a genus, *Bryonia*, of perenni vines of the gourd family with large flesh roots and greenish flowers. *See also* BLAC BRYONY.

Bryophyta, small phylum of plant kingdo comprising mosses and liverworts. Wide distributed on moist soil and rock Reproduction is normally by spores.

bubble chamber, vessel filled wi superheated transparent liquid used study nature and motion of charged atomic particles. Passage of particle through liquid causes string of bubbles to appear, which are then photographed.

Buber, Martin (1878-1965), Austrian philosopher. Exponent of religious existentialism; influenced by Kierkegaard and HASIDISM. Works, esp. *I and Thou* (1923), explore the individual's personal dialogue with God. Settled in Jerusalem (1938).

Buchan, John, 1st Baron Tweedsmuir (1875-1940), British author, statesman, b. Scotland. Best known for adventure novels, esp. *The Thirty Nine Steps* (1915). Governor general of Canada (1935-40).

Bucharest (*Bucureşti*), cap. of Romania, on R. Dambrovita. Pop. 1,934,000. Cultural, commercial, indust. centre. Cathedral (17th cent.), former royal palace, univ. (1864). Cap. of Walachia from 1698; of Romania from 1861.

Buchenwald, village of SW East Germany, near Weimar. Site of Nazi concentration camp in WWII.

Büchner, Georg (1813-37), German dramatist. Wrote 2 stark, realistic tragedies, *Danton's Death* (1835), *Woyzeck* (pub. 1879).

Buck, Pearl S[ydenstricker] (1892-1973), American novelist. Wrote novels based on experiences in China, *eg* trilogy *The House of Earth* (1935). Nobel Prize for Literature (1938).

Buckingham, George Villiers, 1st Duke of (1592-1628), English courtier. Royal favourite under James I, arranged Charles I's marriage to Henrietta Maria of France. Expeditions against France during Charles' reign met with little success. Assassinated. His son, **George Villiers, 2nd Duke of Buckingham** (1628-87), was powerful courtier under Charles II. Member of CABAL ministry.

Buckingham Palace, official London residence of British sovereigns since Queen Victoria's reign. Built (1703) for the dukes of Buckingham; bought as private residence by George III. Reconstructed (1825-36) by John Nash.

Buckinghamshire, county of SC England. Area 1882 sq km (726 sq mi); pop. 525,000; admin. hq. Aylesbury. Chiltern Hills in S; fertile valley in N. Cereals, fruit, vegetable growing, livestock rearing. **Buckingham,** mun. bor. on R. Ouse. Pop. 5000. Market town, dairy produce.

buckthorn, family of deciduous and evergreen trees and shrubs, Rhamnaceae, native to Europe and N Asia. Some species have thorny branches. Fruit has purgative properties and yields dye, Chinese green.

buckwheat, any of several plants of genus *Fagopyrum,* grown for their black tetrahedral grains from which a dark nutritious flour can be made.

Budapest, cap. of Hungary, on R. Danube. Pop. 2,082,000. Admin., commercial centre; heavy industs.; food processing, agric. market. Formed from union of Buda and Pest (1872). Roman *Aquincum*; 13th cent. church, univ. (1635), 19th cent. basilica. Damaged during Russian siege (1945) and in revolution (1956).

Buddha (Sanskrit, = the enlightened one), title given to Siddhartha Gautama (*c* 563-483 BC), Indian ascetic, founder of BUDDHISM. Renounced luxury for asceticism following prophetic vision and after 6 years' contemplation found perfect enlightenment under sacred bo tree in Buddh Gaya, thus becoming the Buddha. Life then devoted to teaching of path to enlightenment.

Buddhism, religion of followers of BUDDHA, widespread in SE Asia, China and Japan; originally related to Hinduism, it was in part reaction against its formalism. The 'four noble truths' are: life is sorrow; origin of sorrow is desire; sorrow ceases when desire ceases; desire is ended by following the 'noble eightfold path'. That path comprises: right belief, right resolve, right speech, right conduct, right occupation, right effort, right contemplation, right meditation. Final goal is Nirvana, the annihilation of all desires and passions and cessation of rebirth. *See* MAHAYANA and ZEN BUDDHISM.

budgerigar, *Melopsittacus undulatus,* Australian parakeet, with many domestic varieties. In wild, green with yellow head. Colour variations produced by selective breeding. Lives in nomadic flocks; diet of seed, grain. Popular pet and excellent mimic, introduced to Europe in 1840s.

budget, govt. statement for estimated revenue and expenditure for forthcoming year. In UK, presented by chancellor of the exchequer to Commons, sitting as Committee of Ways and Means.

Budweis, *see* CESKÉ BUDEJOVICE.

Buenaventura, seaport of W Colombia, on Pacific. Pop. 136,000. Coffee, hides, sugar, platinum and gold exports. Founded *c* 1540, grew with building of railway to Cali (1914).

Buenos Aires, cap. of Argentina, on W Río de la Plata estuary. Pop. 8,436,000. Country's chief port, indust., commercial centre. Beef, wheat, wool exports. Settled permanently 1580; became cap. 1880. Prospered with development of Pampas in 19th cent. Has cathedral, univ. (1827).

Buffalo, city of W New York, US; on L. Erie and Niagara R. Pop. 1,327,000. Major Great Lakes port and transport jct. serving Middle West. Grain, iron, coal shipping; iron and steel, chemical mfg., flour milling.

buffalo, any of various large forms of cattle. Species incl. Cape buffalo, and Indian WATER BUFFALO. Name also popularly applied to American bison.

Buffalo Bill, *see* CODY, WILLIAM FREDERICK.

Buffet, Bernard (1928-), French painter. Known for his austere portrayal of figures, religious scenes and city life; work characterized by cold tonality and prominent black lines.

Bug or **Western Bug,** river of E Europe. Rises in NW Ukrainian SSR, flows *c* 800 km (500 mi) NW into Poland to join R. Vistula below Warsaw. Forms part of Poland-USSR frontier. **Southern Bug** flows *c* 850 km (530 mi) SE through Ukrainian SSR into Black Sea.

bug, any insect of suborder Heteroptera of order Hemiptera. Sucking mouthparts; front wings half membranous, half thickened. Wingless varieties also exist. Term also popularly applied to any insect or insect-like animal.

Buganda, *see* UGANDA.

bugle, any plant of genus *Ajuga*. Perennial, with numerous running stems and spikes of white, pink or blue flowers.

bugle, valveless form of trumpet which produces only notes of the harmonic series; all bugle calls are confined to these notes.

building society, financial organization that accepts savings from the public to be placed in share accounts on which dividends are paid and from which mortgage loans on homes are made. Orig. directly controlled building of houses. First estab. Birmingham, England (1781).

Bujumbura, cap. of Burundi, on L. Tanganyika. Pop. 157,000. Admin. centre; port, exports coffee, cotton, hides. Estab. as German military post (1889). Formerly called Usumbura, was cap. of Ruanda-Urundi.

Bukavu, city of E Zaïre, on L. Kivu, cap. of Kivu prov. Formerly called Costermansville. Pop. 182,000. Port, commercial centre; coffee, pharmaceuticals indust.

Bukhara or **Bokhara,** town of USSR, S Uzbek SSR. Pop. 185,000. Centre of cotton producing area; once famous for carpets. Centre of Islamic learning under Arab rule in 8th cent. Cap. of emirate of Bukhara until 1920.

Bukharin, Nikolai Ivanovich (1888-1938), Soviet political leader. Leading Bolshevik theorist after Lenin's death, advocated gradualist policies on collectivizing agric. Executed in Stalinist party purges.

Bukovina, region of NE Romania and SW USSR (Ukraine), in Carpathian foothills. Main town Chernovtsy. Ceded by Turkey to Austria (1775); Romanian from 1918, N part to USSR (1940).

Bulawayo, city of SW Zimbabwe. Pop. 339,000. Indust., commercial centre, agric. market, railway engineering. Founded 1893.

bulb, underground storage and reproductive structure of certain plants. Formed by swelling of leaf bases, constructing sheath round embryo flower. Distinct from corm which is formed by swelling of stem, as in crocus; rhizome which is an elongated underground swelling of stem, as in iris; and tuber which is a swollen underground branch, as in potato, or root as in dahlia.

Bulganin, Nikolai Aleksandrovich (1895-1975), Russian military and political leader. Helped plan 1941 defence of Moscow against German invasion. Armed forces minister (1947-9), premier (1953-8), succeeded by KHRUSHCHEV.

Bulgaria, republic of SE Europe, on Balka Penin. Area 110,899 sq km (42,818 sq mi pop. 8,814,000; cap. Sofia. Language Bulgarian, Turkish. Religions: Easter Orthodox, Islam. Balkan Mts. run E-W across C, Rhodope Mts. in SW. Lowland i N (Danube basin), SE; Black Sea in I Continental climate; cereals, tobacc wine, attar of roses. Coal, oil industs. de veloping. Invaded 7th cent. AD by Bulga from Russia; Turkish rule (1395-187 ended by Russia; independent monarch (1908). Lost territ. in Balkan Wa (1912-13), WWs. Communist govt. esta (1946).

Bulge, Battle of the, popular name for la German offensive (in the Ardennes) WWII on Western Front (Dec. 1944-Ja 1945).

Bull, John, *see* JOHN BULL.

bull, papal pronouncement, more solem than a brief or encyclical, traditional sealed with lead. Famous bulls inc *Exsurge Domine* (1520) against Luthe *Pastor aeternus* (1871) on pap infallibility, *De Humanae Vitae* (1968) c birth control. Also used to proclai canonization of a saint.

bulldog, breed of dog once used in bu baiting. Square-jawed, with powerful gri Stands between 33-38 cm/13-15 in. shoulder.

bullfighting, national spectacle of Spa (where it is known as *corrida de toros* also popular in S France and Lat America. Matador, aided by banderiller and picadors, makes passes with cape ar manoeuvres bull to tire it for the kill.

bullfinch, *Pyrrhula pyrrhula,* bird of finc family found in woodlands of Europ North America, Asia. Male has pink breas black wings.

bullfrog, *Rana catesbeiana,* largest Nor American frog, up to 20 cm/8 in. lon Catches prey (mice, frogs, insects) wi tongue. Male emits deep croak as mati call.

bullhead, any of several marine ar freshwater fish of Cottidae family, found N hemisphere. European bullhead miller's thumb, *Cottus gobio,* is main nocturnal river species.

Bull Moose Party, *see* PROGRESSIVE PARTY.

Bull Run, stream of N Virginia, US. Scene 2 Confederate victories during Civil W (1861, 1862).

bulrush, several species of perennial sed of genus *Scirpus,* growing in wet land water. Slender, round or triangular ster tipped with brown spikelets of minu flowers.

bumble bee, social bee of worldwi distribution, usually of genus *Bomb* Yellow and black hairy body, rounder th honey bee. Also called humble bee.

Bunker Hill, Battle of (June, 1775), American Revolution, conflict in whi British victory failed to break colonis siege of Boston. Actually fought on near Breed's Hill (Charleston, Mass.).

Bunsen, Robert Wilhelm (1811-99), German scientist. Pioneered spectrum analysis, thus discovering elements caesium and rubidium. Contributions to chemical apparatus incl. Bunsen burner and zinc-carbon battery.

bunting, any of various small, brightly-coloured birds of Emberizidae family. Species incl. YELLOWHAMMER, SNOW BUNTING.

Buñuel, Luis (1900-), Spanish film writer-director. First known for surrealist films (using Dali's sets), incl. *Un Chien andalou* (1928); later films mock bourgeois and religious hypocrisy, *eg Viridiana* (1961).

Bunyan, John (1628-88), English author and preacher. Known for classic religious allegory *The Pilgrim's Progress* (1678) which exerted great influence on English prose. Imprisoned (1660-72) for unlicensed preaching.

Burbage, Richard (*c* 1567-1619), English actor-manager. First to play many major parts in plays of Shakespeare, Jonson, Fletcher. Estab. Globe Theatre at Southwark, London.

burbot, *Lota lota,* freshwater fish of cod family, widely distributed in Europe, Asia, North America. Barbels on nose and chin; broad, flat head. Sometimes called ling.

burdock, *Arctium lappa,* tall spreading large-leaved perennial plant native to Europe, found in North America. Purple flower heads are surrounded by hooked bristles which dry to form burrs. An essence made from plant is used in a soft drink and formerly in medicine.

bureaucracy, literally 'rule by officials', used in sociology to describe a form of administrative organization, typified, according to WEBER, by rational decision-making, impersonal social relations, routinization of tasks, and centralized authority.

Burgess, Anthony, pseud. of John Burgess Wilson (1917-), English novelist, critic. Best known for novels criticizing modern society, *eg A Clockwork Orange* (1962).

Burgh, Hubert de (d. 1243), English statesman. Chamberlain to King John, became chief justiciar (1215) until charged with treason (1231). Later pardoned, restored to earldom of Kent.

Burghley, William Cecil, 1st Baron (1520-98), English statesman. Chief adviser as member of privy council to Elizabeth I, instrumental in consolidation of Protestantism and in execution of Mary Queen of Scots (1587).

burglary, in law, breaking and entering any building with intent to commit a felony. 'Breaking' is not limited to forcible entry, but can incl. entry by use of threat, fraud, *etc.*

Burgos, city of N Spain, cap. of Burgos prov. Pop. 136,000. Textiles, leather goods; tourism. Founded 9th cent., cap. of Castile until 11th cent. Franco's cap. during Civil War (1936-9). Famous Gothic cathedral (1221) contains tomb of El Cid.

Burgoyne, John (1722-92), British army officer, playwright. During American Revolution led poorly trained troops in invasion from Canada, was forced to surrender at Saratoga (1777).

Burgundy (*Bourgogne*), region of E France, hist. cap. Dijon. Famous for wines (esp. in Chablis, Côte d'Or). Medieval duchy, at cultural and commercial height in 14th-15th cent.; ruled most of NE France, Low Countries. Passed to France (1477).

Burke, Edmund (1729-97), British statesman, writer, b. Ireland. Prominent Whig orator, pamphleteer, wrote *Thoughts on the Present Discontents* (1770), attacking George III's influence in politics, and advocated emancipation for American colonies. Instigated impeachment and trial (1787-94) of HASTINGS. Broke with party (1791) over French Revolution, which he denounced.

Burke, Robert O'Hara (1820-61), Irish soldier, policeman, explorer. With W.J. Wills, crossed Australia from Melbourne to Gulf of Carpentaria as leader of Victorian expedition (1860-1). Both died of starvation on return journey.

Burke, William (1792-1829), Irish murderer. Notorious for killing, with fellow-Irishman William Hare, at least 15 people to sell bodies to Edinburgh anatomist. Burke was hanged on Hare's evidence.

Burma, Union of, republic of SE Asia. Area *c* 678,000 sq km (262,000 sq mi); pop. 32,205,000; cap. Rangoon. Official language: Burmese. Religion: Buddhism. Agric. concentrated around Irrawaddy valley; major rice growing area separated from India and Bangladesh by mountain ranges. Exports incl. teak, petroleum, rubies. Annexed by Britain in 19th cent.; became prov. of India (1885-1937); independent republic (1948).

Burmese cat, breed of short-haired domesticated cats. Originally brown, now blue and cream varieties bred.

Burne-Jones, Sir Edward Coley (1833-98), English painter. Associated with Pre-Raphaelites. Known for his paintings of medieval subjects, which have a dream-like romantic quality.

burning bush, *Euonymus attropurpureas,* North American tree widely cultivated as ornamental for its brightly coloured autumn foliage.

burning bush, in OT, bush out of which voice of God spoke to Moses on Mt. Horab (Exodus 3: 2), assuring Moses of deliverance of Israel from Egypt. Emblem of Presbyterian church in remembrance of its early persecution.

Burnley, town of Lancashire, NW England. Pop. 76,000. In coalmining area; cotton weaving, textiles; machinery mfg.

Burns, John (1858-1943), British labour leader. Helped lead London dock strike (1889) for higher wages. Socialist advocate, served as Independent Labour MP (1892-1918).

Burns, Robert (1759-96), Scottish poet. Gained fame with *Poems, Chiefly in the Scottish Dialect* (1786). Best known works incl. 'Tam o'Shanter', 'The Jolly Beggars', 'Holy Willie's Prayer', 'To a mouse', reflect background as tenant-farmer's son but encompass witty anti-clericalism, political radicalism.

Burroughs, Edgar Rice (1875-1950). Created Tarzan in *Tarzan of the Apes* (1914). Also wrote science fiction.

Burroughs, William (1914-), American novelist. Works incl. *Junkie* (1953), *The Naked Lunch* (1959), using experimental forms to convey a world at mercy of technology, drugs.

Bursa, city of NW Turkey. Pop 346,000. Agric. trade; textile, carpet mfg. Cap. of Ottoman Turks (1326-1402), until sacked by Tamerlane. Has mosques and tombs of early sultans.

Burton, Sir Richard Francis (1821-90), English explorer, writer. Visited Mecca and Medina (1853) in Moslem disguise. Attempted, with J.H. Speke, to find source of Nile; reached L. Tanganyika (1858). Later explored W Africa, Brazil. Wrote accounts of travels, translated *Arabian Nights* (1885-8).

Burundi

Burundi, republic of EC Africa. Area 27,800 sq km (10,750 sq mi); pop. 4,256,000; cap. Bujumbura. Languages: Bantu, French. Religions: native, Christian. Mainly high broken plateau; L. Tanganyika in SW. Cattle rearing, tin mining, exports coffee. Formerly a kingdom, part of German East Africa from 1899, of Belgian colony of Ruanda-Urundi after WWI. UN Trust territ. from 1946; independent 1962, became republic 1966. Has traditional rivalry between Tutsi and Hutu.

bushbaby, small arboreal mammal of tropical Africa, genus *Galago*. Nocturnal, with large eyes, bushy tail; capable of great leaps. Mainly insectivorous.

bushmaster, *Lachesis muta*, large poisonous snake of pit viper family, found in Central and South America. Unlike other pit vipers, lays eggs. Reaches lengths of 3.7 m/12 ft.

Bushmen, remnants of aboriginal race of S Africa, now confined to C and N Kalahari Desert. Nomadic hunters living in groups of 50-100. Noted for cave paintings.

bushrangers, Australian robbers of 19th cent. Originally escaped convicts living in bush, raiding settlements. Later, gold discoveries led to incentive for organized gangs raiding highways, banks.

bustard, any of Otididae family of Old World birds, related to crane. Ground-living, can run quickly. Large size makes flight difficult.

butane (C_4H_{10}), gaseous hydrocarbon of paraffin series. Obtained from natural gas and petroleum. Used as fuel, stored under pressure.

Bute, John Stuart, 3rd Earl of (1713-92), British statesman, PM (1761-3). George III's chief exponent of Tory policies against Whig supremacy. Resigned after unpopular treaty ending Seven Years War (1763).

Buteshire, former county of W Scotland, now in Strathclyde region. Incl. isls. in Firth of Clyde (Bute, Arran, Great and Little Cumbrae). Agric., tourism. Isl. of **Bute** (area 145 sq km/ 56 sq mi) has the former co. town, Rothesay.

Butler, James, *see* ORMONDE.

Butler, R[ichard] A[usten], Baron Butler of Saffron Walden (1902-), British politician. Minister of education (1941-5), sponsored 1944 Education Act. In Conservative govts. (1951-64), he was chancellor of the exchequer (1951-5), foreign secretary (1963-4).

Butler, Samuel (1612-80), English poet. Known for *Hudibras*, mock-epic satirizing Puritan cant and hyprocrisy.

Butler, Samuel (1835-1902), English author. Known for autobiog. novel, *The Way of all Flesh* (1903), condemning his Victorian upbringing; *Erewhon* (1872) satirizing received opinions.

butter-and-eggs, *see* TOADFLAX.

buttercup, herbs of Ranunculaceae family with alternate leaves and glossy yellow flowers. Native to cooler regions of N hemisphere. Pernicious weed.

butterfly, insect of group comprising, with moths, order Lepidoptera. Scales on body, wings (2 pairs, often brightly coloured). Uses proboscis to suck nectar. Four stage life cycle: egg, larva, pupa, adult. Larva is caterpillar, usually herbivorous. Mainly diurnal.

Buxtehude, Dietrich (1637-1707), Danish composer, organist. Organist at Lübeck from 1668. Organ compositions influenced Bach.

buzzard, any of numerous heavily-built hawks, esp. genus *Buteo*, with short broad wings, soaring flight.

Byblos, chief city of Phoenicia in 2nd millennium BC. Trade centre with Egypt as early as 2800 BC.

Bydgoszcz (Ger. *Bromberg*), city of NC Poland, on R. Brda and Bydgoszcz canal, cap. of Bydgoszcz prov. Pop. 327,000. River port, railway jct.; textile mfg., machinery. Founded 14th cent.; under Prussian rule 1772-1919.

Byelorussian or **Belorussian Soviet Socialist Republic,** constituent republic of W USSR. Area *c* 208,000 sq km (80,000 sq mi); pop. 9,559,000; cap. Minsk. Mainly low-lying, with Pripet Marshes in S; large areas forested. Peat major source of power. Region disputed by Poland, Russia until it passed to Russia (1795); joined USSR 1922. Area greatly increased by acquisitions from Poland in 1945. Has seat in UN. Also called White Russia.

Byng, John (1704-57), British admiral. Failure to relieve Minorca (1756) from French siege resulted in his court martial and execution.

Byrd, Richard Evelyn (1888-1957), American explorer, aviator. Made 1st flight to North Pole (1926), to South Pole (1929). Led 5 US expeditions to Antarctica 1928–56.

Byrd, William (*c* 1543-1623), English composer. Composed both Anglican and RC music, incl. motets and 3 Masses. Also wrote string and keyboard music, madrigals. A master of polyphony, regarded as one of foremost early English composers.

Byron, Lord George Gordon Noel, 6th Baron Byron of Rochdale (1788-1824), English poet. Best known for *Childe Harold's Pilgrimage* (1812-18), *Don Juan* (1819-24). Regarded as embodiment of Romanticism, left England (1816) for Italy. Died at Missolonghi while aiding Greek fight for independence.

Byzantine art, style of art blending Oriental and Hellenistic traditions, *fl* in (Christian) Byzantine Empire from 5th cent. In architecture, substituted circular church building for straight lines of Roman basilica. Mosaics and painting marked by use of rich colours (esp. gold), stylized figures, geometrical designs.

Byzantine Empire, former empire of SE Europe and Asia Minor. Named after Byzantium, rebuilt as cap. and renamed Constantinople (AD 330) after Constantine I. Territ. incl. (at various times) Asia Minor, Balkan Penin. incl. Macedonia, Thrace, Greece, Illyria. Main language Greek; main religion Orthodox Christianity. State estab. as direct successor to Roman Empire; suffered barbarian invasions 4th-6th cents. *Fl* as centre of art, architecture, education, law, esp. under JUSTINIAN I. Involved in political schism with West (800), religious schism (1054); suffered Turkish, Norman attacks in 11th cent. Fourth Crusade diverted to sack Constantinople (1204). Empire partially recovered under Palaeologus family; finally fell (1453) to Turks.

Byzantium, ancient city on shores of Bosporus, on one of 7 hills of modern ISTANBUL.

C

cabal, term for secret group of policy-makers, originating from Charles II of England's advisers. Name from initials of members - Clifford, Arlington, Buckingham, Ashley and Lauderdale.

cabala, cabbala or **kabbala,** occult religious philosophy developed by certain Jewish rabbis in Middle Ages. Adherents believed that every letter and number in Scripture was part of a significant mystical system, accessible only to the initiate. Became basis of letter and number formulae of medieval magic.

Cabbage

cabbage, *Brassica oleracea capitata,* leafy vegetable of mustard family from which cauliflower, broccoli, kohlrabi, Brussels sprouts and KALE are derived. Native to E Europe, it has been cultivated for more than 4000 years. Varieties are green, white or red, with various leaf forms.

cabbage white butterfly, *Pieris brassicae,* insect whose larvae feed on cabbage, other plants.

cabbala, *see* CABALA.

Cabinda, exclave of Angola, W Africa. Area 7250 sq km (2800 sq mi); pop. 51,000; main town Cabinda. Exports coffee, hardwoods, oil. Separated from Angola (1886) when mouth of R. Congo ceded to Belgian Congo (now Zaïre).

cabinet, in govt., group of advisers responsible to head of state, who themselves usually head executive depts. of govt. Evolved out of English PRIVY COUNCIL to become a body of ministers selected by prime minister from major party in House of Commons. Cabinet is responsible for executing govt. policy, and is answerable to Parliament. Also, it coordinates activities of state's depts. Members of US cabinet not drawn from either house of Congress.

Cabot, John, English form of Giovanni Caboto (*c* 1450-98), Italian navigator, explorer. Led English expedition (1497) in search of W sea route to Orient. Landed in E Canada, laying basis for English claims to North America. His son, **Sebastian Cabot** (*c* 1485-1557), explored Río de la Plata region (1526-30) for Spain; later entered service of Henry VIII. Founded 'Merchant Adventurers' which estab. trade with Russia.

cacao, *see* COCOA.

cactus, plant of family Cactaceae comprising several hundred species mainly native to tropical regions of North and South America. Most species adapt to drought by storing water in fleshy stem.

caddis fly, any insect of Trichoptera order with hairy wings and body, very reduced mouth-parts. Nocturnal, resembles moth. Larvae aquatic.

Cade, Jack (d. 1450), English rebel. Leader of Kentish uprising (1450) against Henry VI. Rebels defeated royal force and occupied London, but were pardoned and dispersed. Cade was hunted down and killed.

Cadíz, city of SW Spain, on Bay of Cadíz, cap. of Cadíz prov. Pop. 142,000. Port, exports wine, fruit; shipyards, naval base. Founded *c* 1100 BC by Phoenicians; held 8th-13th cent. by Moors; *fl* in colonial era (16th-18th cent.), centre of New World trade. Has 2 cathedrals (13th, 18th cent.).

cadmium (Cd), soft silvery-white metallic element; at. no. 48, at. wt. 112.4. Occurs in zinc ores and as greenockite (yellow sulphide); obtained during production of zinc. Used in alloys, accumulators and as moderator in nuclear reactors; compounds used as pigments in paint.

Caecilia, *see* GYMNOPHONIA.

Caen, city of Normandy, N France, on R. Orne. Cap. of Calvados dept. Pop. 183,000. Port; agric. market, textiles (esp. lace), mfg. Important medieval centre; has three 11th cent. churches. Much destruction, incl. univ. (1432), during WWII.

Caernarvonshire, former county of NW Wales, now in Gwynedd. Mountainous except for Lleyn Penin. in SW; incl. SNOWDON. Sheep farming, slate quarries, tourism. **Caernarfon,** mun. bor. and admin. hq. of Gwynedd, on Menai Strait. Pop. 9000. Port, tourist resort. Castle (13th cent.)

Caerphilly, urban dist. of S Glamorgan, S Wales. Pop. 41,000. Coalmining; cheese mfg. Has largest Welsh castle (13th cent.).

Caesar, [Gaius] Julius (*c* 102-44 BC), Roman soldier, statesman. Governor of Further Spain (61), estab. military reputation. Formed 1st Triumvirate with Crassus and Pompey on return to Rome (60). Appointed ruler of Gaul, greatly enlarged the empire by subjugating the Gauls (58-51). Struggle for power with Pompey and the senate culminated in civil war (49) when Caesar's armies crossed the Rubicon into Italy. Routed Pompey at Pharsala (48) and pursued him into Egypt; there he met Cleopatra, by whom he had a son. Created dictator for 10 years (46), began to restore order to empire. Appointed dictator for life (44), he was assassinated by group of former supporters under Brutus, Cassius. Wrote *Gallic Wars, Civil War*.

Caesarean section, surgical operation for delivery of baby by cutting through mother's abdominal wall and front of uterus. In legend, Julius Caesar was said to have been born this way.

caesium or **cesium** (Cs), soft metallic element, at. no. 55, at. wt. 132.91. Highly reactive; ignites in air and combines vigorously with water to form powerful alkali. Used in photoelectric cells. Discovered (1860) by Bunsen and Kirchhoff.

caffeine, alkaloid drug present in coffee, tea, *etc*; stimulates heart and increases alertness when subject is tired.

Cage, John (1912-), American composer. Known for experimental, controversial works, esp. those using random elements, *eg Music of Changes,* electronic and silent music. Created 1st 'happening' (Black Mountain Coll. in 1952).

Cagliari, town of S Sardinia, Italy, on Gulf of Cagliari. Cap. of Cagliari prov. Pop. 242,000. Port, exports salt, metal ores, fish; univ. (1626). Carthaginian city, taken (238 BC) by Romans. Held by Pisa 11th-14th cent. Roman remains incl. amphitheatre; 2 Pisan towers.

Cagney, James (1899-), American film actor. Known for mannered playing in gangster roles, esp. in *The Public Enemy* (1931), *The Roaring Twenties* (1939).

Caicos Islands, *see* TURKS AND CAICOS.

caiman, reptile of alligator family of Central and South America. Species incl. black caiman, *Melanosuchus niger*, can reach length of 4.6m/15ft.

Cain, in OT, elder son of Adam and Eve. Killed his brother ABEL in jealousy when Abel's offerings were accepted by God. Condemned to wander the earth.

Cainozoic era, *see* CENOZOIC.

Cairngorms, mountain range of NE Scotland, in GRAMPIANS. Highest point Ben Macdhui (1309 m/ 4296 ft). Has nature reserve; tourist industs., incl. climbing, winter sports (esp. at Aviemore).

cairn terrier, small shaggy dog of Scottish origin. Bred to chase vermin from burrows. Stands 25 cm/10 in. high at shoulder.

Cairo *(El Qâhira),* cap. of Egypt, at head of Nile delta. Pop. 5,921,000, largest city in Africa. Admin., commercial, indust. centre; cement, textile mfg., brewing. Site of Roman *Babylon;* Old Cairo *(El Fustât)* founded 7th cent., New Cairo founded 969. Ruled by Ottoman Turks 1517-1798. Hist. Islamic religious, educational centre, has *c* 200 mosques, El Azhar Univ. (972), Saladin's citadel (12th cent.), many museums. Pyramids of Gîza nearby.

Caithness, former county of N Scotland, now in Highland region. Has infertile moorland and hills. Sheep farming, crofting, fishing. Co. town was Wick.

Calabria, region of SW Italy, penin. between Tyrrhenian, Ionian seas. Main town Reggio, cap. Catanzaro. Underdeveloped region, mainly mountainous, partly forested. Vines, fruits, olives; h.e.p. in La Sila mountains. Ancient *Bruttium*; part of medieval Norman kingdom of Sicily, of kingdom of Naples from 1822.

Calais, town of Nord, N France, on English Channel. Pop. 100,000. Port, fishing, ferry service to Dover (England). Under English rule (1347-1558) following long siege by Edward III.

calcite ($CaCO_3$), mineral form of calcium carbonate. Consists of hexagonal crystals; white, often slightly coloured by impurities. Forms incl. chalk, limestone, marble. Used in building, cement and fertilizer mfg.

calcium (Ca), soft white metallic element; at. no. 20, at. wt. 40.08. Occurs as carbonate (limestone, marble, chalk) and sulphate (gypsum). Obtained by electrolysis of fused calcium chloride. Essential constituent of living organisms, found in bones and teeth.

calculator, electronic, numerical calculating device employing a microprocessor incorporated into a single chip of semiconducting material. Series of keys are used to enter numbers or commands into the calculator; results of calculations usually appear on electronic display panel. More advanced calculators possess keys for special mathematical functions, have memories and can be programmed.

calculus, branch of mathematical analysis dealing with continuously varying functions and their rates of change. Concerned with such problems as drawing tangents, calculating velocity, determining area and volume, *etc*. Divided into DIFFERENTIAL and INTEGRAL CALCULUS.

Calcutta, cap. of West Bengal, E India. Pop. 7,031,000. Major port, exports raw materials; indust. centre, jute milling, textiles. Founded *c* 1690 by East India Co.; scene of 'Black Hole' massacre of British garrison (1756). Cap. of India 1833-1912. Univ. (1857).

Calder, Alexander (1898-1976), American sculptor. Invented the mobile, form of kinetic sculpture. His static sculpture uses simple shapes of flat metal welded together.

Calderón [de la Barca], Pedro (1600-81), Spanish playwright. Known for classic of Spanish theatre, *Life is a Dream* (*c* 1636). Also wrote many classical comedies, religious plays.

Caledonia, Roman name (from 1st cent. AD) for Britain N of Antonine Wall. Now used poetically for whole of Scotland.

Caledonian Canal, waterway of N Scotland built by Thomas Telford (1847). Length 97 km (60 mi), connects Loch Linnhe with

Moray Firth via lochs Lochy, Oich and Ness.

calendar, systematic division of year into months and days. Ancient Chinese and Egyptian calendars based on phases of moon with adjustments to fit solar year. Julius Caesar introduced Julian calendar (45 BC), dividing year into 365 days and inserting additional day every 4th year. Inaccurate by 10 days in 1582 when Pope Gregory XIII ordered readjustment, not adopted by Britain until 1752.

Calgary, city of S Alberta, Canada; on Bow R., in foothills of Rockies. Pop. 470,000. Railway jct.; oil refining, meat packing, flour milling. Founded 1883. Has annual Calgary Stampede.

Cali, city of SW Colombia, in W Andean valley. Pop. 990,000. Indust., agric. centre; sugar refining, textiles, footwear, soap mfg. Founded 1536; grew after railway to Buenaventura built (1914).

calico, form of plain weave cotton cloth, originating in Calicut, India. Imported into England in 17th cent., it was produced there in large quantities in 18th cent.

Calicut, *see* KOZHIKODE.

California, state of W US. Area 411,000 sq km (158,690 sq mi); pop. 21,520,000; cap. Sacramento; chief cities Los Angeles, San Francisco, San Diego. Most populous state in US. Bounded by Pacific in W, Sierra Nevada in E, Coast Range shelters fertile Central Valley. Varied climate. Irrigation widely used for agric.; fruit, cotton, vegetables, wine, cattle and dairy produce. Fisheries, aerospace, silicon chip, defence industs; fuel minerals esp. oil. Spanish settled in 18th cent.; republic estab. after Mexican War (1846); ceded to US (1848); gold rush (1849) resulted in great pop. increase. Admitted to Union as 31st state (1850).

California, Gulf of, narrow arm of Pacific, separating Baja California from W Mexico. Fishing, pearl diving.

californium (Cf), transuranic element; at. no. 98, mass no. of most stable isotope 251. First prepared (1950) at Univ. of California by bombarding curium with alpha particles.

Caligula, real name Gaius Caesar Germanicus (AD 12-41), Roman emperor (37-41). Ruled tyrannically after an illness which is believed to have left him insane. Said to have made his horse a consul. Assassinated.

caliph, name given to successors of Mohammed who assumed leadership of Islam. First caliph was ABU BAKR. Dispute over right of descendants of ALI to succeed to caliphate led to split between SHIITES and SUNNITES. Muawiya estab. Omayyad dynasty in Damascus; it was destroyed by Shiites (750), who set up Abbasid dynasty in Baghdad. Title later assumed by sultans of Turkey.

Callaghan, [Leonard] James (1912-), British statesman, PM (1976-9). Posts in Labour govt. incl. chancellor of the exchequer (1964-7), foreign secretary (1974-6). Succeeded Wilson as PM. Term marked by efforts to combat high inflation. Resigned as leader of Labour Party (1980).

Callao, major seaport of W Peru. Pop. 297,000. Pacific depot for Lima, handling most of Peru's imports. Fish processing, agric. related industs. Founded 1537; occupied by Chile (1881-3). Destroyed by earthquake (1746).

Callas, Maria, née Calogeropoulou (1923-77), American soprano. Born in New York of Greek parents, trained in Athens. Became internationally renowned opera singer in 1950s. Famous roles in *Tosca, Norma, Aïda.*

calligraphy, art of fine writing. Practised by Chinese from 5th cent. BC, it was regarded as equal to painting; also important in Japanese art from 7th cent. AD. In Islamic art, decoration of Koran represents highly refined development of calligraphy.

calorie, unit of heat energy; defined as quantity of heat required to raise temperature of 1 gram of water by 1° C. Equals 4.1855 joules. With capital initial letter, Calorie = 1000 calories.

Calvary (Lat., *calvaria* = skull; translation of Aramaic *golgotha*), scene of Jesus' crucifixion outside walls of Jerusalem.

Calvin, John (1509-64), French theologian, Reformation leader. Converted to Protestantism (*c* 1533); systematized Protestant theology in *Institutes of the Christian Religion* (1536), rejecting papal authority. Estab. theocratic republic in Geneva as centre of CALVINISM.

Calvinism, Protestant doctrine formulated by CALVIN. Distinguished from Lutheranism by doctrine of PREDESTINATION, salvation for the elect. Other tenets incl. justification by faith alone, subservience of state to church. Adopted by Huguenots in France, spread to Scotland through teachings of John Knox and influenced Puritans in England and New England. Associated with PRESBYTERIANISM.

Calypso, in Greek myth, nymph, daughter of Atlas. In Homer's *Odyssey* she entertained ODYSSEUS for 7 years when he was shipwrecked on Ogygia.

calypso, humorous song, often extemporized on topical or amatory theme, sung to traditional Caribbean melody and accompaniment.

Camargue, The, region of Rhône delta, S France. Mainly marsh, lagoons in S. Fishing, marine salt indust.; horse and bull rearing, some agric. (incl. rice) on reclaimed land. Frequented by many species of wild bird. Nature reserve.

Cambodia, *see* KAMPUCHEA.

Cambrai, town of Nord, NE France, on R. Escaut (Scheldt). Pop. 40,000. Hist. textile centre, gave name to cambric. Scene of formation of League of Cambrai (1508) against Venice. Under Spanish rule 1595-1677.

Cambrian Mountains, mountain system of Wales. Runs N-S, incl. highest peak SNOWDON, Cader Idris, Plynlimmon.

Cambrian period, first geological period of Palaeozoic era; began *c* 570 million years ago, lasted *c* 70 million years. Extensive seas. Typified by trilobites, graptolites, brachiopods; some algae, lichens. Also *see* GEOLOGICAL TABLE.

Cambridge, city of E Massachusetts, US; near Boston on Charles R. Pop. 100,000. Has Harvard (oldest US univ., 1780) and Radcliffe Univs., Massachusetts Institute of Technology. Industs. incl. scientific instruments, printing and publishing. First settled 1630.

Cambridgeshire, county of E England. Area 3409 sq km (1316 sq mi); pop. 570,000. Incl. Isle of Ely. Fertile fens, artificial drainage; cereals, sugar beet, fruit, vegetable growing. Admin. hq. **Cambridge,** city on R. Cam. Pop. 102,000. Univ. (1209) has 23 residential colls. (oldest Peterhouse, 1284). Medieval trading centre. Electronics indust.

Camden, bor. of NW Greater London, England. Pop. 192,000. Created 1965 from Hampstead, Holborn, St Pancras met. bors.

Arabian camel

camel, mammal of Camelidae family, related to llama, order Artiodactyla. Arabian camel or dromedary, *Camelus dromedarius,* has 1 hump; Bactrian camel, *Camelus bactrianus,* of C Asian deserts, has 2 humps, shaggy coat. Fat stored in humps helps desert survival. Used as pack animal and for riding.

camellia, genus of flowering evergreen shrubs and small trees of Theaceae family, native to Asia. Cultivated in warm climates and greenhouses. Most important economically is tea plant, *Camellia chinensis,* from India and China.

Camelot, *see* ARTHURIAN LEGEND.

Camembert, village of Normandy, N France. Gave name to a cheese, first made here in 18th cent.

cameo, carving in relief on hard or precious stones or on shells. Agate and sardonyx are used so that raised design can be cut in a lighter layer than background. Cameos, esp. portrait heads, were highly developed in ancient Greek and Roman eras. Revived in late 18th cent.

camera, light-proof container with lens that focuses optical image to be recorded on light-sensitive film. Developments incl. adjustable focus lens to allow objects at various distances to be recorded sharply, variable aperture settings (*f* stop) to control amount of light entering camera, high-speed shutters to photograph moving objects and linked light meters to control these variables automatically. The motion picture camera takes a series of photographs (usually 24 per sec) which when projected at same rate gives impression of movement.

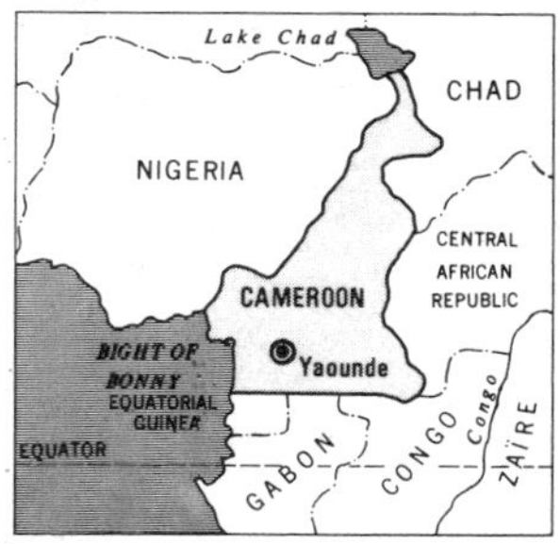

Cameroon

Cameroon (Fr. *Cameroun),* republic of WC Africa, on Bight of Biafra. Area 474,000 sq km (183,000 sq mi); pop. 8,058,000; cap. Yaoundé. Languages: French, English. Religions: Christianity, Islam, animist. Savannah in N; tropical forest in W; elsewhere mainly plateau. Produces cocoa, coffee, bananas, groundnuts; bauxite mining. Formerly German (Kamerun); taken by Allies in WWI. Divided (1919) into British, French Cameroons; both UN Trust Territs. from 1946. French Cameroons independent from 1960; S part of British Cameroons joined to form federal republic (1961); N part joined Nigeria.

Cameroon, Mount, volcano of W Cameroon. Highest peak of W Africa, reaches 4067 m/13,350 ft.

Camões or **Camoens, Luis Vaz de** (*c* 1524-80), Portuguese poet. Best known for epic *The Lusiads* (1572) celebrating Portuguese history and exploits of Vasco da Gama.

camomile or **chamomile,** any plant of genera *Anthemis* or *Matricaria* of aster family. Common European species, *A. nobilis,* is used for the astringent and bitter camomile tea.

Campania, region of S Italy, main town Naples. Largely fertile, produces hemp, fruit, tobacco; mountainous interior. Many coastal resorts. Roman region much smaller, incl. sites of Pompeii, Herculaneum.

campanile, in architecture, Italian bell-tower usually built separately from main building, *eg* church or town hall.

campanula, genus of plants of bellflower family with bell-shaped flowers. Found in temperate parts of N hemisphere and widely cultivated.

Campbell, Scottish noble family, *see* ARGYLL.

Campbell, Sir Malcolm (1885-1949), British motor racing enthusiast. Broke world speed record on land (1935) in *Bluebird* car and on water (1939) in boat of same name. His son, **Donald Malcolm Campbell** (1921-67), broke world water record in turbo-jet hydroplane and land record (both 1964). Died in attempt on water record.

Campbell, Mrs Patrick, née Beatrice Stella Tanner (1865-1940), English actress, friend of Wilde, Shaw. Known for role of Eliza Doolittle in Shaw's *Pygmalion*.

Campbell-Bannerman, Sir Henry (1836-1908), British statesman, PM (1905-8). Liberal leader, his admin. was marked by self-govt. for South African colonies and growth of conflict between Commons and Lords.

Camperdown *(Kamperduin)*, village of North Holland prov., NW Netherlands. Naval battle fought offshore (1797) in which British defeated Dutch.

camphor, volatile, crystalline substance with strong, characteristic odour, derived from wood of camphor laurel, *Cinnamomun camphora*. Used to protect fabrics from moths, in manufacturing cellulose plastics, and in medicine as an irritant and stimulant.

Campion, Edmund (*c* 1540-81), English Jesuit martyr. Favourite of Elizabeth I before his conversion to Catholicism. Became Jesuit missionary (1580), preached with effect until captured; executed for treason.

Campion, Thomas (1567-1620), English poet, musician. Best known for songs for the lute.

campion, various flowering plants of genera *Lychnis* and *Silene* of the pink family.

Camus, Albert (1913-60), French writer, b. Algeria. In essay *Le Mythe de Sisyphe* (1942), outlined theory of ABSURD which permeates novels, *eg L'Etranger* (1942), *La Peste* (1947). Member of SARTRE circle but broke away. Awarded Nobel Prize for Literature (1957).

Canaan, OT name for region W of R. Jordan. The 'promised land' occupied by Israelites after Exodus from Egypt. Subsequently known as Palestine.

Canada, federal country of N North America, independent member of British Commonwealth. Area 9,976,128 sq km (3,851,787 sq mi); pop. 23,499,000; cap. Ottawa; major cities Montréal, Toronto. Languages: English, French. Religions: Protestant, RC. Stretches from Pacific to Atlantic, from Arctic to the Great Lakes; extreme climate. Comprises 10 provs. as well as Yukon and Northwest Territs. Rocky Mts. divide coastal British Columbia (timber, wood pulp, h.e.p.) and agric. Prairies (wheat); Ontario, Québec (major concentrations of pop. and indust.); Maritimes, Newfoundland (fisheries); C Laurentian Plateau (copper, nickel, oil). Explored 1534 by Cartiér, settled by French in 17th cent.; competing claims to sovereignty resolved by British victory at Québec (1759). Independence (1867) uniting Upper (Ontario) and Lower (Québec) Canada with Nova Scotia, New Brunswick; subsequently enlarged by W expansion with development of Canadian Pacific Railway.

canal, artificial waterway used for transportation, drainage and irrigation. Transportation canals may be provided with locks so that level of water can be changed to raise or lower boats. Extensive network built in Britain in 18th cent. Usefulness superseded by development of railways.

Canaletto, properly Antonio Canale (1697-1768), Italian painter. Specialized in topographically accurate views of Venice.

canary, *Serinus canarius*, small singing finch of Canary Islands, Azores. Grey or green in wild; yellow varieties bred in captivity.

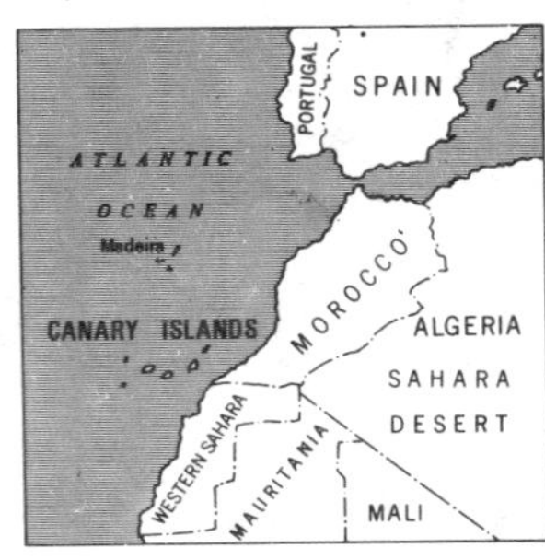

Canary Islands

Canary Islands, isl. group of Atlantic Ocean off NW Africa, comprising 2 provs. o Spain. Isls. incl. Grand Canary, Lanzarote Tenerife. Area 7270 sq km (2807 sq mi) main towns Las Palmas, Santa Cruz de Tenerife. Volcanic, rise to *c* 3700 m (12,10 ft). Banana, tobacco growing, fishing tourism. Spanish from 1476.

canasta, card game, a variation of rummy for two to six players, using a double deck of cards. Originated in Montevideo (1949).

Canaveral, Cape, E Florida, US. Missile testing centre, launch point of satellites spacecraft. Known as Cape Kennedy 1963-73.

Canberra, cap. of Australia, in Australian Capital Territory, on Molonglo R. Pop 215,000. Admin. centre; national library univ. (1929). Founded 1913, replace Melbourne as cap. 1927.

ancer, *see* ZODIAC.

ancer, group of diseases resulting from disorder of cell growth. Cancer cells grow without control or need, locally at first, but later they may spread to other parts of body via lymph vessels or veins. Causes incl. chemical agents, *eg* dyes and hydrocarbons, cigarette smoke, radiation, viruses, hereditary factors. Treatments incl. X-rays and radioactive sources, hormones, surgery and chemotherapy.

ancer, Tropic of, parallel of latitude 23½°N of Equator. Marks most N position at which Sun appears vertically overhead at noon. At this line, Sun shines directly overhead at June solstice.

andela (cd), SI unit of luminous intensity, equivalent to 1/60 of intensity of 1 sq cm of blackbody radiator at temperature of solidification of platinum (2046°K).

andia, *see* IRÁKLION.

andle, mass of tallow or wax surrounding a wick, used as source of light when burned. Known since Roman times, candles, usually of tallow, became widespread in Europe during Middle Ages. Modern candles are usually machine-moulded from paraffin wax.

andytuft, annual or perennial herb of cabbage family, native to S and W Europe.

ane, *see* BAMBOO; RATTAN; SUGAR CANE.

anidae, the dog family. Carnivorous mammals, incl. wolf, fox, jackal, dog.

anna or **Indian shot,** genus of plants of Cannaceae family, native to tropical America and Asia. Many varieties cultivated for striking foliage and brilliant flowers.

annabis, *see* HEMP.

annae *(modern Canna),* town of Apulia, S Italy. Scene of Hannibal's victory (216 BC) over Romans.

annes, town of Provence, SE France, on Côte d'Azur. Pop. 68,000. Resort, casinos; fruit and flower growing, perfume mfg. Annual international film festival.

annibalism, practice in certain societies of eating human flesh. Has occurred among many peoples at many times. Normally associated with the ritual attempt to transfer properties of victim to other members of group.

anning, George (1770-1827), British statesman, PM (1827). Tory foreign secretary (1807-9), planned capture of Danish fleet (1807). Supported Spanish American and Greek independence movements after succeeding CASTLEREAGH as foreign secretary (1822). Advocated free trade and Catholic Emancipation.

anning, process of preserving cooked food by sealing it in airtight containers, afterwards subjected to heat. Method was invented in early 19th cent.

annon, a smooth-bore piece of artillery, used until the 19th cent., firing shot of 24-47 lb (11-21 kg). The term also now refers to large machine guns carried by fighter aircraft.

anoe, narrow, light boat ending in a point at each end. Usually propelled by paddles but sail or motor may be used. Important in the culture of several primitive peoples. *See* CANOEING, KAYAK.

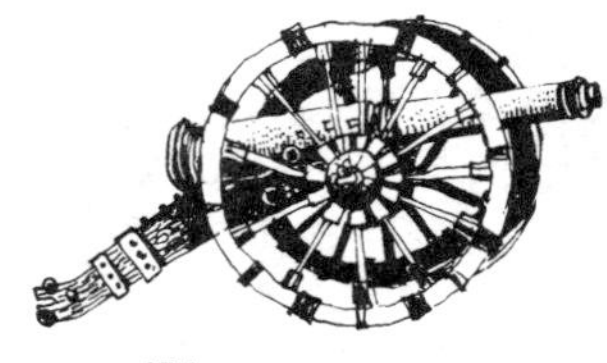

17th-century cannon

canoeing, sport of propelling a canoe through water. Divided into various activities: slalom, down river or wild-water racing, long distance and sprint racing. Popularized in later 19th cent.

canon, musical form in which a melody is repeated note for note so that it overlaps itself. A catch or round is a simple vocal canon.

canonization, process by which RC church gives official sanction to veneration of dead person as a saint. Formal canonization dates from 1634. Case for canonization consists of proof of 4 miracles and evidence of an exemplary life.

canon law, body of laws governing the ecclesiastical affairs of a Christian church. In RC church, systematized in *Codex juris canonici* (1918). In Church of England, based on canons pub. in 1604 and subsequently revised. Only clergy are bound by it, unless laws are authorized by Parliament or declared old custom.

Cantabrian Mountains, range of N Spain, extending *c* 480 km (300 mi) E-W parallel to Bay of Biscay coast. Rise to 2648 m (8687 ft) at Peña Cerredo. Rich in coal and iron. Source of R. Ebro.

cantaloupe, *see* MELON.

cantata, sacred or secular piece of music of several movements for chorus and orchestra, usually with vocal soloists; similar to oratorio but shorter.

Canterbury, city of Kent, SE England, on R. Stour. Pop. 33,000. Roman *Durovernum;* hist. cap. of Saxon Kent. Abbey founded 597 by St Augustine who was 1st archbishop. Seat of Anglican primate. Pilgrimage centre since Becket's murder in cathedral (1170). King's School (*c* 600, refounded 1541). University of Kent (1965).

Canterbury, region of EC South Isl., New Zealand. Area 36,000 sq km (13,900 sq mi); pop. 398,000; chief city Christchurch. Extends from Pacific coast (E) to Southern Alps foothills (W). Sheep, dairy farming on Canterbury Plains; tourism, h.e.p. in mountains.

cantilever, in architecture, horizontal beam supported at one end only and carrying a load at free end or evenly distributed along exposed portion. Used in bridge building for large spans, *eg* Forth Railway Bridge, Scotland.

Canton, China, *see* KWANGCHOW.

Canton and Enderbury Islands, in Phoenix Isls., C Pacific Ocean. Jointly admin. from 1939 by US, UK; US renounced claim in 1979 treaty with KIRIBATI. Originally source of guano for US, also export copra.

Cantonese, *see* CHINESE.

Canute or **Cnut** or **Knut [II] the Great** (*c* 955-1035), king of England, Denmark and Norway. Invaded England 1015, sole ruler from 1016; estab. more efficient admin., codified law. King of Denmark from 1018, of Norway after invasion in 1028.

canvas, strong unbleached fabric made from flax, hemp etc. Used for sails, tents and as surface in oil-painting.

canyon, deep, narrow gorge, often with steep sides. Usually formed in arid areas by rivers cutting into soft rock, low rainfall preventing erosion of canyon walls. Grand Canyon, US, is largest in world.

capacitor, device for storing electric charge, usually consisting of 2 or more conducting plates separated by insulating material (dielectric). Used in electrical devices, *eg* radios. Formerly called condenser.

Cape Breton, isl. of Canada, forms E part of Nova Scotia. Area 10,282 sq km (*c* 3970 sq mi). Rugged terrain, fishing, lumbering, coal mining, steel production. French colony 1713-58; joined with Nova Scotia 1820.

Cape Horn, *see* HORN, CAPE.

Cape hunting dog, *Lycaon pictus,* wild dog of S and E Africa. Hunts in packs.

Cape of Good Hope, *see* GOOD HOPE, CAPE OF.

Cape [of Good Hope] Province, prov. (largest) of SW South Africa. Area 720,000 sq km (278,000 sq mi); pop. 4,235,000; cap. Cape Town. Plateau, drained by R. Orange. Produces cereals, tobacco, fruit, vines; diamond (Kimberley), copper (Okiep) mining. Settled from 1652 by Dutch at Table Bay, by Huguenots (1689). Annexed 1806 by Britain; became prov. of Union of South Africa (1910).

caper, any plant of genus *Capparis,* esp. a prickly, trailing Mediterranean bush, *C. spinosa,* tiny green flower buds of which are pickled.

capercaillie or **capercailzie,** *Tetrao urogallus,* large grouse-like bird of N Europe. Grey-coloured; found in coniferous forests.

Capet, Hugh, *see* CAPETIANS.

Capetians, dynasty of French kings, named after Hugh Capet (*c* 938-96), 1st Capetian ruler. Direct descendants of his ruled 987-1328, last was Charles IV. Throne then passed to House of Valois.

Cape Town or **Capetown,** legislative cap. of South Africa and cap. of Cape Prov. Pop. 1,096,000. Port on Table Bay, at foot of Table Mt. Admin., commercial centre, univ. (1918). Founded (1652) by Dutch; cap. of Cape Colony until 1910. Oldest South African white settlement.

Cape Verde Islands, country of EC Atlantic. Area 4040 sq km (1560 sq mi); pop. 314,00 cap. Praia. Incl. 10 isls. of volcanic origi Stock raising, fishing; exports coffee, frui Colonized 15th cent. by Portugues Independent 1975, retains links wit Guinea-Bissau.

Cape York Peninsula, penin. of Queensland, Australia, between Coral Se and Gulf of Carpentaria. Northernmo point of Australian mainland. Aborigin reserves; cattle ranching, bauxite minin First part of Australia sighted b Europeans (Jansz, 1606).

capillaries, *see* BLOOD VESSELS.

capillary action, force resulting fro adhesion, cohesion and surface tension liquids which are in contact with solid Accounts for water rising in capillary tub because adhesive force between glass an water exceeds cohesive force betwee water molecules.

capital, in architecture, the top part of column, pilaster or pier, which transmi the weight of the superstructure to th supporting column.

capital, in economics, originally interes bearing money; now all means production and distribution, *eg* land, plan transport, raw materials, potential yielding income.

capitalism, economic system in whic means of production and distribution a privately owned and operated for prof Importance dates from Industri Revolution, characterized by fr competition, later by large corporatio and varying degrees of govt. regulatic often as technocratic state capitalism (s CORPORATE STATE). As term, capitalis developed by Marx in historical analys (DIALECTICAL MATERIALISM) as stage evolution of society.

capital punishment, legally sanction taking of life as punishment for crim Once recognized penalty for sacrilege a offences against property, in 20th ce usually reserved for treason, murd Abolished in UK in 1965.

Capone, Al[fonso] (1899-1947), Americ gangster, b. Italy. Notorious for leadersh of crime syndicate in Chicago during pro bition era of 1920s.

Cappadocia, mountainous region of As Minor, in C Turkey. Independent kingdo in 3rd cent. BC, with cap. at Maza became Roman prov. in AD 17.

Capri, isl. of S Italy, in Bay of Naples. Area sq km (4 sq mi). Tourist centre w famous Blue Grotto. Site of ruined villas emperors Augustus, Tiberius.

Capricorn, *see* ZODIAC.

Capricorn, Tropic of, parallel of latitu $23\frac{1}{2}$°S of Equator. Marks most S position which Sun appears vertically overhead noon. At this line, Sun shines direc overhead at December solstice.

capuchin, commonest monkey of Cent and South America, genus *Cebus,* incl. c species. Hair said to resemble mon cowl.

capybara, *Hydrochoerus hydrochoeris,* largest rodent, up to 1.2 m/4 ft long, resembling giant guinea pig. Lives in groups, good swimmer; found on river banks of South America.

car, *see* AUTOMOBILE.

Caracas, cap. of Venezuela, linked to Caribbean port La Guaira. Pop. 2,576,000; alt. 945 m (*c* 3100 ft). Oil refining, textile mfg. Founded 1567. Cap. from 1829.

Caractacus or **Caradoc** (*fl* AD 50), British chieftain. Led resistance against Romans (43-51). Captured and taken to Rome, where his life was spared by Claudius.

carat, unit describing quantity of gold in an alloy: 1 carat is 24th part of pure gold, thus 15 carat gold contains 15 parts gold and 9 parts alloy.

Caravaggio, Michelangelo Amerighi da (1573-1610), Italian painter. Famous for his revolutionary use of light and shade, and rejection of idealization. Had great influence on subsequent artists.

Caraway

caraway, white-flowered biennial herb, *Carum carvi,* of parsley family with spicy, strong-smelling seeds which are used as flavouring.

carbide, compound of an element, usually metal, with carbon. Incl. calcium carbide (CaC_2), used to make acetylene, and silicon carbide or Carborundum (SiC_2), used as abrasive.

carbohydrate, organic compound of carbon, hydrogen and oxygen with general formula C_x $(H_2O)_y$, incl. sugars, starches and cellulose. Formed in green plants by PHOTOSYNTHESIS; starch essential to human diet, providing energy during its oxidation.

carbolic acid, *see* PHENOLS.

carbon (C), non-metallic element; at. no. 6, at. wt. 12.01. Exists in 3 allotropic forms: crystalline diamond, graphite, and amorphous carbon (charcoal, lampblack, coke). Numerous compounds subject of organic chemistry. Used in electrodes; activated charcoal, specially treated to remove hydrocarbons, absorbs gases.

Carbonari ('charcoal burners'), Italian political secret society. Aimed at expulsion of foreign rulers and estab. of democracy. Active in uprisings (1820, 1831), later merged with Young Italy movement of MAZZINI.

carbon dioxide (CO_2), colourless gas, found in atmosphere; formed by combustion of carbon or heating carbonates. Dissolves in water to form weak unstable carbonic acid. Exhaled by animals and absorbed by plants, which convert it into carbohydrates and oxygen by photosynthesis. Used in production of mineral water, in fire extinguishers; solid carbon dioxide known as 'dry ice' used as refrigerant.

carbon fibre, material composed of extremely fine filaments of pure carbon bonded together. Great strength-to-weight ratio and heat resistance; valuable in reinforcing components of jet engines.

Carboniferous period, fifth geological period of Palaeozoic era; began *c* 345 million years ago, lasted *c* 65 million years. Divided into Lower Carboniferous, or Mississippian, and Upper Carboniferous, or Pennsylvanian. Many crinoids, brachiopods; increasing amphibians, fish, insects, 1st reptiles. Club mosses, horsetails led to development of vast COAL seams. Also *see* GEOLOGICAL TABLE.

carbon monoxide (CO), colourless inflammable gas, formed by incomplete combustion of carbonaceous fuels. Extremely poisonous, as it combines with haemoglobin of blood, making this unavailable to carry oxygen. Occurs in exhaust fumes of petrol engines, coal gas.

Carborundum, *see* CARBIDE.

carboxylic acid, organic acid containing 1 or more carboxyl (COOH) groups, *eg* formic acid.

carbuncle, inflammation of tissue beneath the skin, of same kind as a BOIL, but larger and with several heads through which pus is discharged.

Carcassonne, town of Languedoc, S France, on R. Aude. Cap. of Aude dept. Pop. 46,000. Tourist centre, wine trade. Divided by R. Aude into ancient hilltop 'Cité' (castle, cathedral, town walls) and 'Ville Basse' (founded 1247).

Carchemish, ancient city of S Turkey, on Euphrates near Syrian border. Centre of neo-Hittite culture *c* 1000 BC; scene of victory of Nebuchadnezzar II over Necho II (605 BC) which ended Egyptian power in Asia.

cardamom or **cardamon,** spice from seed capsules of E Indian plant, *Elettaria cardamomum,* used in curries and pickling.

Cardiff, cap. city and port of Wales, city and admin. hq. of South Glamorgan, admin. hq. of Mid Glamorgan. Near Bristol Channel on R. Taff. Pop. 278,000. Major coal, iron, steel exports. Admin., commercial centre; has coll. of Univ. of Wales. Site of Roman station; 11th cent. castle.

Cardigan, James Thomas Brudenell, 7th

Earl of (1797-1868), British army officer. Led the disastrous charge of the Light Brigade at Balaklava (1854) in the Crimean War. The woollen garment called a cardigan is named after him.

Cardiganshire, former county of W Wales, now in Dyfed. Main town Aberystwyth. Plateau in E (livestock rearing), lowland along coast (oats, barley growing). Co. town was **Cardigan,** mun. bor. on R. Teifi. Pop. 4000. Agric. market.

Carib, South American Indians of separate Carib language family, formerly inhabiting Lesser Antilles. Named by Columbus, noted for their ferocity (a corruption of Carib gives English word 'cannibal'); also expert navigators. Some 500 pure-blooded Caribs remain on Dominica.

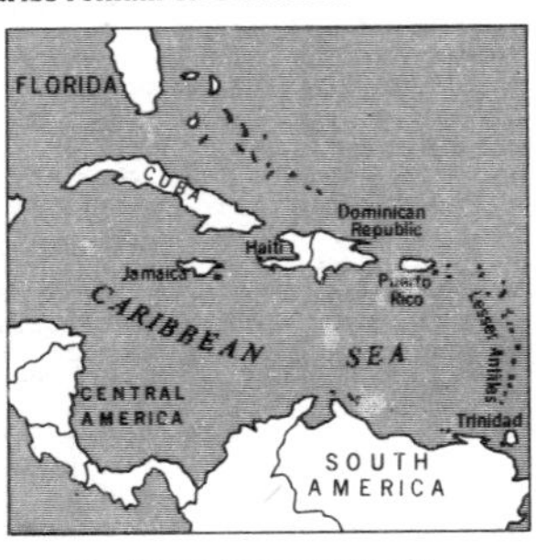

Caribbean Sea and Islands

Caribbean, sea of W Atlantic Ocean, bounded by Venezuela, Colombia, Central America. Area 1,942,500 sq km (*c* 750,000 sq mi). Linked with Gulf of Mexico by Yucatán Channel. Has many isls. *eg* West Indies, Greater and Lesser Antilles. Named after Carib Indians who once inhabited coastal areas.

caribou, large North American deer, resembling reindeer, genus *Rangifer*. Native of Arctic and subarctic. Both sexes have antlers.

carillon, set of bells worked by keyboard and pedals, or automatically. The world's largest carillon, at Cincinnati, Ohio, contains 83 bells in a tower 91m (300 ft) high. Originated in Low Countries, *c* 16th cent.

Carinthia *(Kärnten)*, prov. of S Austria. Area 9531 sq km (3680 sq mi); cap. Klagenfurt. Mountainous, incl. GROSSGLOCKNER, many lakes. Timber, mining. Incorporated into Austria 14th cent.

Carl XVI Gustaf (1946-), king of Sweden (1973-). Succeeded grandfather Gustavus VI.

Carlisle, city and admin. hq. of Cumbria, N England, on R. Eden. Pop. 99,000. Railway jct., textile mfg. Roman *Luguvallum;* hist. strategic site in border wars; has castle (1092), cathedral (12th cent.).

Carlists, supporters of descendants of Don Carlos de Bourbon (1788-1855), 2nd son of Charles IV of Spain, as pretenders to Spanish throne. Defeated in civil war (1833-9) by forces of Isabella II, and failed in uprisings (1860, 1869, 1872). Also lost civil war of 1873-6 despite gains in Basque provs., Catalonia. Supported fascists under FRANCO in Spanish Civil War (1936-9).

Carlow, county of Leinster prov., SE Irish Republic. Area 896 sq km (346 sq mi); pop. 39,000. Mountains in SE. Agric., dairying, livestock. Co. town **Carlow,** pop. 9000. Market town. RC cathedral (19th cent.).

Carlyle, Thomas (1795-1881), Scottish writer. Translated Goethe, Schiller. Distrust of democracy, belief in divinely-informed hero expressed in *French Revolution* (1837), *On Heroes, Hero-Worship* (1841). Also wrote biog. *Frederick the Great* (1858-65). *Sartor Resartus* (1833-4) is spiritual autobiog.

Carmarthenshire, former county of S Wales, now in Dyfed. Mountainous in NE (livestock rearing), agric. in lowlands. Coalmining, metal industs. centred on Llanelli in SE. **Carmarthen,** mun. bor. and admin. hq. of Dyfed, on R. Towy. Pop. 13,000. Dairy centre, on site of Roman town *Maridunum*.

Carmel, Mount, mountain of NW Israel, rising 546 m (1792 ft) from Haifa. Associated in Bible with prophet Elijah. Carmelite order was founded here in 12th cent.

Carmelites, in RC church, mendicant friars and nuns of the order of Our Lady of Mt Carmel. Founded as order of hermits in Palestine *c* 1150. Stress contemplative aspects of religious life and have incl several mystics, *eg* ST THERESA OF AVILA, St John of the Cross. Known as White Friars.

Carnac, town of Brittany, NW France, on Quiberon Bay. Pop. 4000. Site of *c* 3000 menhirs (standing stones) arranged in rows, among which are ancient burial chambers.

Carnarvon, *see* CAERNARVONSHIRE.

carnation, *Dianthus caryophyllus,* perennial herbaceous plant with many cultivated varieties.

Carnegie, Andrew (1835-1919), American industrialist, b. Scotland. Estab. steel business based in Pittsburgh which produced by 1900 one quarter of total US steel. Sold out (1901) to US Steel Corporation and devoted his fortune to funding of libraries, univs.

Carnivora (carnivores), order of flesh eating mammals with large canine teeth. Terrestrial group, Fissipedia, incl. dog, cat otter, bear, lion. Marine group, Pinnipedia incl. seal, walrus.

carob, leguminous tree, *Ceratonia siliqua,* of E Mediterranean, bearing leathery brown pods with sweet pulp which are sometimes used as fodder.

Carol II (1893-1953), king of Romania (1930-40). Renounced right to succession (1925), but deposed son Michael (1930) and took throne. Overthrown (1940).

carol, song of annual religious festivals, esp

Christmas. Some of the tunes originate in folk song while others are borrowed from secular music or specially composed.

Caroline Islands, archipelago of W Pacific Ocean. Area 900 sq km (350 sq mi); chief isls. PALAU, Ponape, Truk, Yap. Main crops copra, sugar cane, tapioca; also produce bauxite, phosphate, guano. Discovered 1526 by Spain, bought (1899) by Germany. Occupied by Japanese from WWI; part of US Trust Territ. of the Pacific Isls. from 1947. In 1978 joined Marshall Isls. to form Federated States of MICRONESIA.

Caroline of Brunswick (1768-1821), German princess, consort of George IV of England. Married (1795) prince of Wales, but they were separated (1796). She refused to renounce her rights at his accession; George's subsequent divorce proceedings were abandoned.

Carolingians, dynasty of Frankish rulers, succeeding Merovingians (751) through Pepin the Short. His son, Charlemagne, crowned Western emperor (800); empire split by Treaty of Verdun (843) among his grandsons who founded dynasties ruling Germany until 911 and France until 987. Succeeded by Capetians.

carp, freshwater fish of Cyprinidae family, esp. *Cyprinus carpio,* of worldwide distribution. May be cultivated as food fish. Goldfish is domestic variety of golden carp.

Carpathians, mountain range of EC Europe, curving from Czechoslovakia through SW Ukraine to Romania. Rise to 2662 m (8737 ft) in Tatra Mts. (Czechoslovakia). Forests; minerals; tourism.

Carpentaria, Gulf of, shallow inlet of Arafura Sea, N Australia, between Arnhem Land and Cape York Penin.

carpet or **rug,** thick fabric, usually of wool, used as a floor covering, *etc.* Carpet making reached a high point of artistry in Turkey, Persia and C Asia in 16th cent. European production dates from 17th cent. at such centres as the Savonnerie in Paris. In England, Axminster, Wilton and Kidderminster were important centres. Power loom introduced 1841 made mass-production possible.

carpetbagger, American political term popularized in post-Civil War period. Referred to speculators and entrepreneurs who started business in devastated Southern states with no more than they could carry in a carpetbag.

Carrantuohill, mountain of Co. Kerry, SW Irish Republic. Highest in Ireland (1040 m/3414 ft).

Carrara, town of Tuscany, NC Italy. Pop. 68,000. Centre of Italian marble indust. Has medieval cathedral.

carriage, non-self-propelling wheeled vehicle, used esp. for carrying passengers; strictly refers to 4-wheel types. Covered horse-or mule-drawn carriage dates from *c* 15th cent. Public stagecoach much used in 17th and 18th cent. Hansom cab (2-wheel) plying for hire introduced in London (1834). Other 2-wheeled carriages incl. stanhope, tilbury, gig, sulky, dog-cart. Private 4-wheeled carriages widely used in 19th cent. incl. brougham, landau, victoria. Open 4-wheeled carriages incl. phaeton, wagonette, brake.

Brougham carriage

carrion crow, *see* CROW.

Carroll, Lewis, pseud. of Charles Lutwidge Dodgson (1832-98), English writer, mathematician. Known for classics of inverted logic, ostensibly for children, *eg Alice's Adventures in Wonderland* (1865), *Through the Looking-glass* (1872). Also wrote nonsense verse incl. *The Hunting of the Snark* (1876).

carrot, *Daucus carota,* widely distributed biennial plant of parsley family, with fleshy, orange-coloured edible roots. Derived from Queen Anne's lace or wild carrot.

Carson, Edward Henry Carson, Baron (1854-1935), Irish politician. Opposed Irish Home Rule and rallied Ulster in support of British govt. during WWI, serving in wartime cabinets. Denounced creation (1921) of independent Irish Free State.

Carson City, cap. of Nevada, US; near California border. Pop. 15,000. Grew in late 19th cent. after nearby silver strike. Resort town. Named after Kit Carson, (1809-68), American frontiersman and Indian fighter.

Cartagena, seaport of N Colombia, on Caribbean. Pop. 355,000. Has canal link to Magdalena R. Oil pipeline terminus; exports agric. produce. Founded (1533) by Spanish, it was frequently sacked and invaded.

Cartagena, city of Murcia, SE Spain, on Mediterranean Sea. Pop. 147,000. Port, exports iron and lead; metallurgical centre, naval base. Founded *c* 225 BC by Hasdrubal; major port under Romans. *Fl* 16th-18th cent. with New World trade.

cartel, in economics, association of manufacturers or traders to fix prices, sales quotas or to divide markets. Shares many characteristics of MONOPOLY.

Carter, Howard (1873-1939), English archaeologist. Working with Lord Carnarvon in Valley of Kings in Egypt, discovered (1922) tomb of Tutankhamen.

Carter, James Earl ('Jimmy') (1924-), American statesman, Democratic president (1977-81). Upheld human rights abroad. Helped bring Israel and Egypt to peace table.

Carthage, ancient city of N Africa, near modern Tunis. Founded 9th cent. BC by Phoenicians; estab. colonies in Sardinia, Sicily, Spain. Trade rivalry with Rome led to PUNIC WARS, city finally destroyed 146 BC. New colony founded 44 BC by Romans; Vandal cap. from AD 439. Totally destroyed (698) by Arabs.

Carthusians, order of monks in RC church. Most austere, silent order, each member living in individual cell. Founded (1084) by St Bruno (*c* 1030-1101) at Chartreuse, France.

Cartier, Jacques (1491-1557), French navigator, explorer. In search of Northwest Passage, made 2 voyages (1534, 1535-6) exploring E Canada, Gulf of St Lawrence. Reached St Lawrence R.; proclaimed French sovereignty.

Cartier-Bresson, Henri (1908-), French photographer. Known for extreme naturalism, as well as news photographs of important international events.

cartilage or **gristle,** tough whitish tissue which forms part of skeletal systems. Lines moving surfaces of joints and forms external ear, nose, *etc.* Skeletons of embryos are largely formed of cartilage, which gradually turns to bone.

cartography, the art and science of map making, now generally applied to all stages from field survey to finished map. Ancient Babylonians produced earliest known map (*c* 2500 BC); Greeks estab. principles of cartography little altered until 17th cent. First world atlas produced by Mercator (1569). Modern cartography founded by Delisle and d'Anville; 1st systematic national survey pub. 1756 in France, followed 1801 by British Ordnance Survey.

Cartwright, Edmund (1743-1823), English inventor. Inventor the powerloom (1785) and wool-combing machines.

Caruso, Enrico (1873-1921), Italian operatic tenor. Achieved fame in Europe and America. One of 1st singers to exploit gramophone recording successfully.

caryatid, in Greek architecture, supporting column in form of draped female figure. Famous examples found on porch of Erechtheum, Athens.

Casablanca (Arab. *Dar-al-Baida*), city of N Morocco, on Atlantic Ocean. Pop. 1,753,000. Indust., commercial centre; major port, exports phosphates, manganese. Founded 16th cent. by Portuguese on site of ancient *Anfa.*

Casals, Pablo or **Pau** (1876-1973), Spanish cellist, conductor. Renowned for interpretation of Bach's cello pieces, he raised status of cello as a solo instrument.

Casanova de Seingalt, Giovanni Giacomo (1725-98), Italian adventurer, writer. Known for *Mémoires* (1826-38) which recount his fluctuating affairs, both financial and sexual, on travels across Europe.

Cascade Range, N extension of mountain system of W US; from California through Oregon, Washington to S British Columbia (Canada). Mt. Rainier in Washington is highest point (4392 m/14,410 ft).

Caryatid from Erechtheum, Athens

casein, main protein of milk, precipitated by addition of acid or rennet. Chief constituent of cheese; used to make plastics, adhesives.

Casement, Sir Roger David (1864-1916), Irish nationalist. Served in British consular service in Belgian Congo and Peru. Attempted to gain German aid for Irish rebellion (1916), returning to Ireland in German submarine. Captured and hanged for treason.

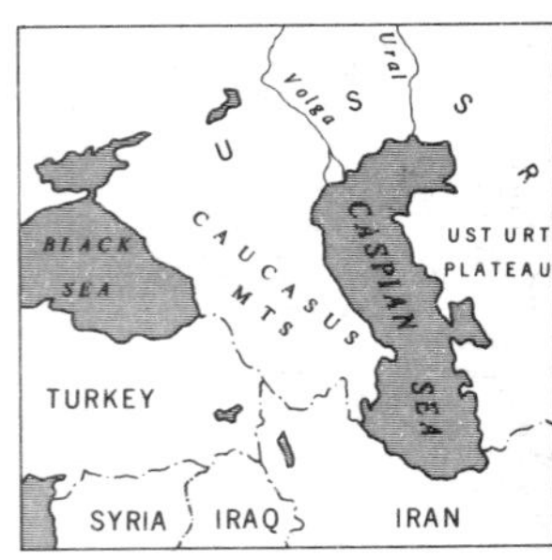

Caspian Sea

Caspian Sea, salt lake between Europe and Asia, world's largest inland sea. Area *c* 373,000 sq km (144,000 sq mi). Almost entirely in USSR, part of S shore in Iran. Receives R. Volga and R. Ural, no outlet. 27m (90 ft) below sea level, its level decreases by evaporation. Sturgeon fisheries.

Cassandra, in Greek legend, daughter of King Priam of Troy. Prophetess of Apollo who caused her prophecies never to be believed. After fall of Troy, captive of Agamemnon; killed with him by his wife Clytemnestra.

cassava or **manioc,** any of several tropical American plants of genus *Manihot* of the spurge family, having edible starchy roots used to make tapioca.

Cassel, *see* KASSEL.

cassia, the bark of a tree, *Cinnamomum cassia,* of the laurel family, native to SE Asia. Used as a cinnamon substitute. Also a genus, *Cassia,* of herbs, shrubs and trees of Leguminosae family, common in tropical countries. The cathartic drug senna is prepared from the leaves of *C. acutifolia* and *C. angustifolia.*

Cassino, town of Latium, C Italy, at foot of Monte Cassino. Pop. 19,000. Monastery on summit founded 529 by St Benedict; used as stronghold by Germans (1944), destroyed by Allied bombing. Restored 1964.

Cassius [Longinus], Gaius (d. 42 BC), Roman soldier. Pardoned by Caesar after supporting Pompey in civil war (48 BC). He became a leading figure in the conspiracy to assassinate Caesar (44 BC). With Brutus, he was defeated by Mark Antony at Philippi, where he committed suicide.

Cassowary

cassowary, *Casuarius casuarius,* large flightless bird of N Australia, New Guinea, with brightly coloured neck and head, capped by bony crest; related to emu.

castanets, percussion instrument consisting of a pair of shell-shaped wooden blocks joined by a piece of string; held between thumb and fingers and clicked rapidly together. A pair is usually held in each hand. Much used in Spain.

caste, in Hindu population of India, exclusive social grouping. Classified by Brahmans (*c* AD 200) into 4 divisions with Untouchables below these; now *c* 3000 castes. Traditionally, no member of any caste may marry outside it; rules may also regulate occupation and diet. Discrimination by caste made illegal (1947).

Castiglione, Baldassare, Conte (1478-1529), Italian author. Wrote *Libro del Cortegiano* (1528; English *The Courtier,* 1561), lively collection of dialogues on Renaissance courtly morals and manners.

Castile *(Castilla),* region and former kingdom of C Spain. Largely arid plateau, drained by Douro, Tagus rivers; divided by mountains into Old (N) and New (S) Castile. Limited agric. incl. cereals, fruit, sheep; mining. Independent from 10th cent.; led fight against Moors. United with León (1230), Aragón (1479) to found Spain. Language became standard Spanish.

castle, fortified dwelling characteristic of medieval times. Principal features of Norman castle were: rectangular donjon or keep, which served as living quarters; inner bailey (courtyard) surrounding the keep and separated from outer bailey by a wall; outer walls of masonry, from which round towers (bastions) projected; moats, crossed by drawbridges, which protected outer walls.

Castlereagh, Robert Stewart, 2nd Viscount (1769-1822), British statesman, b. Ireland. As Irish secretary crushed French-backed revolt (1795). Secretary of war during Napoleonic wars, helped plan Peninsular campaign. Fought duel with George CANNING after alleged political betrayal, resigned 1803. Foreign secretary (1812-22), helped organize 'Concert of Europe' opposing Napoleon. Favoured moderate settlement at Congress of VIENNA (1814-15), maintenance of conservative interests in Europe. Committed suicide.

Castor and Pollux, *see* DIOSCURI.

castor oil, extracted from seeds of Palma Christi shrub, *Ricinus communis,* native to subtropical regions, but widely cultivated as ornamental. The oil is used medicinally as a quick-acting laxative; also used in paint and varnish indust.

castration, removal of sex glands (testicles) of male animal. Results in sterility and curbing of secondary sex characteristics when practised on children. Used to improve meat quality and decrease aggressiveness of farm animals.

Castro [Ruz], Fidel (1927-), Cuban revolutionary and political leader, premier (1959-). Organized Cuban revolutionary forces while in Mexico and returned to lead successful guerrilla campaign (1956-9), which overthrew BATISTA. Proclaimed (1961) allegiance to Communist bloc; supported revolutionary movements in Latin America. Collectivized agriculture, expropriated industs.

casuistry, originally, branch of ethics which deals with delicate moral questions by applying general principles. Term also refers to arguing away of ambiguous acts with hair-splitting subtleties.

cat, any animal of Felidae family, incl. lion, leopard, tiger. Carnivorous, with sharp claws used for climbing trees, holding prey. Numerous varieties of domestic cat, *Felis catus,* probably derived from African wildcat, *F. lybica.*

catacombs, early Christian subterranean cemeteries arranged in vaults and galleries; those in Rome date mainly from 3rd and early 4th cents. and cover *c* 600 acres. Also served as places of refuge during Christian persecutions; later became shrines of pilgrimage. Others were in Naples, Syracuse, Paris, *etc.*

Catalan, Romance language of Italic branch of Indo-European family. Spoken in Catalonia, Valencia, Balearic Islands, Roussillon region of SE France, and is Andorran official language.

catalepsy, unconscious fit, resulting in temporary loss of feeling and rigidity of muscles. May occur in epilepsy, schizophrenia, hysteria.

Catalonia *(Cataluña),* region of NE Spain, hist. cap. Barcelona. Hilly, drained by R. Ebro. Almond, fruit growing, wine mfg.; metal, textile industs. based on h.e.p. Frankish county from 9th cent.; united with Aragón (12th cent.), with Castile (15th cent.). Autonomous govts. (1932-4, 1936-9, 1977-) reflect hist. strong Catalan nationalism.

catalyst, any substance which speeds up or slows down rate of chemical reaction, but is itself unchanged at end of reaction. Plays important role in indust. preparation of ammonia, sulphuric acid, *etc.* Platinum, nickel, manganese dioxide are catalysts.

Catania, city of E Sicily, Italy, on Gulf of Catania. Cap. of Catania prov. Pop. 402,000. Port, shipbuilding, sulphur refining, food processing; univ. (1434). Founded 8th cent. BC by Greek colonists. Often damaged by eruptions of Mt. Etna.

cataract, in medicine, disease of eye in which lens becomes opaque, causing partial or total blindness. Commonly results from ageing; treated by surgery.

catarrh, term for inflammation of mucous membrane, esp. of nose, causing a discharge of mucus. Rhinitis now describes such inflammation of nose.

catastrophe theory, mathematical theory that uses topology to describe ways in which a dynamic system can pass through a point of instability *eg* the point at which water being heated turns into steam. Applications in many subjects, incl. economics, sociology, biology.

catastrophism, in geology, theory that features of Earth's crust change by means of isolated catastrophes. Rejects theory of evolution implicit in UNIFORMITARIANISM. Now generally discarded.

catchment area, area in which all water drains into a particular river, lake or reservoir. Separated from adjacent catchment area by high land forming a WATERSHED.

caterpillar, worm-like, segmented, larva of butterfly or moth. Usually herbivorous, has strong jaws. Moults skin *c* 5 times to allow growth. Pupates in cocoon spun from silk thread.

catfish, any of a large group of scaleless freshwater and marine fish, abundant in New World. Whisker-like sensory barbels around mouth.

Cathars, generic name for adherents of dualistic heresies in medieval Europe, esp. ALBIGENSIANS.

Catherine [II] the Great (1729-96), tsarina of Russia (1762-96), b. Germany. Married (1744) the future Peter III, whom she had deposed by conspiracy headed by the Orlovs shortly after his accession. Reforming zeal unfulfilled after peasant rebellion (1773-5) and French Revolution. Her reign was marked by territ. expansion at expense of Poland, ascendancy in Near East after wars (1768-74, 1787-92) with Turkey and annexation of Crimea. A monarch of the Enlightenment, encouraged development of Russian literature. Lovers incl. Orlov, Potemkin.

Catherine de' Medici, *see* MEDICI.

Catherine of Aragon (1485-1536), queen of England, 1st wife of Henry VIII; mother of Mary I. Daughter of Ferdinand and Isabella of Spain. Discontent with their marriage and lack of a male heir led Henry to seek annulment on grounds of illegality. Pope's refusal led to English Reformation.

Catherine of Braganza (1638-1705), Portuguese princess, consort of Charles II of England.

Catherine of Siena, St (1347-80), Italian Dominican nun, mystic. After vision of united Church, convinced Pope Gregory XI to leave Avignon for Rome. Teachings contained in *A Treatise on Divine Providence.*

Catherine of Valois (1401-37), French princess, consort of Henry V of England. Gave birth to Henry VI (1421). Secret marriage to Owen Tudor after Henry V's death (1422) provided basis for subsequent Tudor claims to English throne.

cathode, *see* ELECTRODE.

cathode rays, stream of electrons emitted from cathode when electrical discharge takes place in tube containing gas at very low pressure.

cathode ray tube, vacuum tube in which cathode rays are directed by electric fields to strike fluorescent screen and produce illuminated traces, visible outside tube. Used in oscilloscopes and television picture tubes.

Catholic Emancipation, name given to series of acts passed in Britain (1780-1829) which relieved British RCs from the legal and civil disabilities accumulated since time of Henry VIII, *eg* restrictions on land inheritance, debarment from forces, judiciary, univs.

Catiline, (Lucius Sergius Catilina) (*c* 108-62 BC), Roman politician. Twice failed to be elected consul (66, 63); after his 2nd failure when defeated by Cicero, formed scheme to take power by force. Conspiracy exposed by Cicero in 4 orations; Catiline killed in subsequent battle.

catmint or **catnip,** *Nepeta cataria,* plant of mint family, with downy leaves, spikes of bluish flowers. Native to Britain and Europe.

Cato, Marcus Porcius or **Cato the Elder** (234-149 BC), Roman statesman. Appointed censor (184), tried to restrict entry to senate to those he considered worthy. Opposed introduction of Greek culture in favour of ancient Roman simplicity. Campaigned for the destruction of Carthage. Wrote *De Re Rustica,* treatise on agric.

Cato Street conspiracy, *see* THISTLEWOOD, ARTHUR.

Catskill Mountains, range of E New York, US; part of Appalachian Mts. Rise to 1231 m (4040 ft). Area provides water for New York City. Popular tourist area.

cattail or **reed mace,** any of genus *Typha* of tall marsh plants with reed-like leaves and long, brown, fuzzy, cylindrical flower spikes. Used in making baskets and matting.

cattle, ruminant mammals of genus *Bos.* In particular domestic cattle, *Bos taurus,* used for dairy products, meat, hides. Milk breeds incl. Ayrshire (brown and white), Friesian and Holstein (black and white), Guernsey (fawn and white), Jersey. Meat producers incl. Aberdeen Angus (black), Hereford (red with white face). Normandy and short-horn are dual purpose.

Catullus, Gaius Valerius (*c* 84-*c* 54 BC), Roman poet. Works incl. love poems, satires, epigrams. Personal approach, intense feeling and colloquial style make him major influence on European literature.

Caucasus, mountain system of SW USSR, between Black and Caspian seas. Highest peak is Mt. Elbrus (5631 m/18,481 ft).

cauliflower, variety of cabbage, *Brassica oleracea botrytis.* Has a dense white mass of fleshy flower stalks which form edible head. Introduced from Cyprus in 16th cent.

Cavafy, Constantinos (1863-1933), Greek poet, b. Egypt. Works incl. ironic narrative poems on Greek past, homosexual love lyrics.

Cavaliers, in English Civil War (1642-8), supporters of Charles I in his struggle with Parliament's forces (Roundheads).

cavalry, mounted soldiers, important from classical times down to the 18th cent. because of their speed and mobility. Declined during the 19th cent. but were still used for reconnaissance and skirmishing in the early part of WWI. Now all UK cavalry regiments are armoured units except for the Household Cavalry, retained for ceremonial purposes.

Cavan, county of Ulster prov., NC Irish Republic. Area 1891 sq km (730 sq mi); pop. 58,000. Hilly moorland, largely infertile; many lakes. Some agric., livestock; distilling. Co. town **Cavan,** pop. 3000. Ruined abbey; modern RC cathedral.

cave, natural chamber or cavity in Earth's crust. Sea-caves formed by wave action or by abrasion due to pebbles, boulders, *etc* being hurled against cliff. Inland caves usually found in limestone areas, formed by running water dissolving rock.

Cavell, Edith (1865-1915), English nurse. Matron of nurses' training institute in Brussels. Shot by the Germans for helping Allied soldiers to escape over Dutch frontier in WWI.

Cavendish, Henry (1731-1810), English scientist, b. France. Investigated properties of hydrogen ('inflammable air') and carbon dioxide. Researched into composition of water and air. Measured density of Earth.

cave paintings, *see* ALTAMIRA; LASCAUX.

caviare, salted eggs of sturgeon prepared, mainly in USSR and Iran, as a table delicacy.

Cavour, Camillo Benso, Conte di (1810-61), Italian statesman. Premier of Sardinia (1852-9, 1860-1), secured French alliance which brought Sardinia's union with Lombardy after war with Austria (1859). Sponsored Garibaldi's campaign leading to unification (*Risorgimento*) of Italy under VICTOR EMMANUEL II.

Cawnpore, *see* KANPUR.

Caxton, William (*c* 1422-91), first English printer. Learned printing trade in Cologne and then printed in Bruges (1475) his own translation of *Recuyell of the Historyes of Troye,* 1st book pub. in English. Returned to England to set up press in Westminster, where he printed 1st dated book in England, *Dictes or Sayengis of the Philosophres* (1477).

Cayenne, cap. of French Guiana, Atlantic port on isl. at mouth of Cayenne R. Pop. 25,000. Original source of Cayenne pepper. Exports rum, gold. Had penal settlement 1854-1938.

cayenne, very hot red pepper made from dried pods of several species of *Capsicum,* native to South America.

Cayman Islands, coral group of West Indies, NW of Jamaica. Area 260 sq km (100 sq mi); pop. 12,000. cap. Georgetown. Comprise Grand Cayman, Little Cayman, Cayman Brac. Famous for turtles; turtle products, shark skin exports. Admin. by Jamaica until 1962; British colony.

CBI, *see* CONFEDERATION OF BRITISH INDUSTRY.

Ceauşescu, Nicolae (1918-), Romanian political leader, president (1974-). Succeeded Gheorghiu-Dej as Communist Party general secretary (1965), continued policy of independence within Soviet bloc.

Cebu, isl. of Philippines. Area *c* 4400 sq km (1700 sq mi). Grows corn, sugar cane, peanuts; coal and copper mined. **Cebu** is chief town and port; pop. 419,000.

Cecil, Robert, *see* SALISBURY, ROBERT CECIL, 1ST EARL OF.

Cecil, William, *see* BURGHLEY, WILLIAM CECIL, 1ST BARON.

cedar, coniferous tree of genus *Cedrus* of pine family, with short needle leaves arranged in close spiral on spine-like branches. Has durable wood with characteristic fragrance. Species incl. notable cedar of Lebanon, *C. libani.*

celandine, name of 2 unrelated plants. Lesser celandine, *Ranunculus ficaria,* of buttercup family is small herb with heart-shaped leaves and yellow flowers. Greater celandine, *Chelidonium majus,* of poppy family is erect, branched herb with divided leaves and yellow flowers.

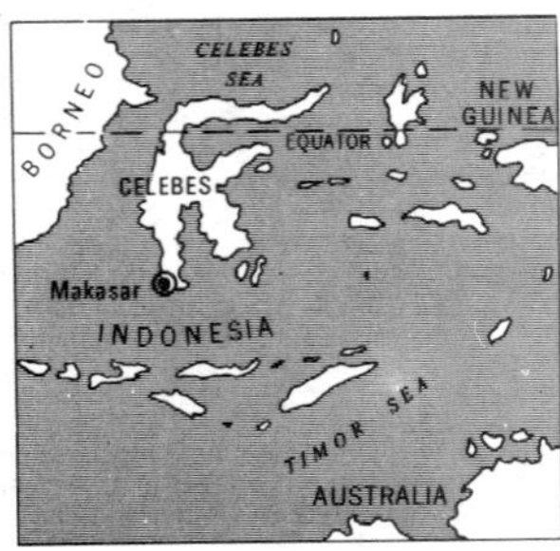

Celebes

Celebes or **Sulawesi,** isl. of Indonesia. Area *c* 186,000 sq km (72,000 sq mi); pop. *c* 9,000,000. Irregular shape comprises 4 penins; largely mountainous with forests. Exports coffee, timber, copra, spices. Under Dutch control by 1670.

celery, *Apium graveolens,* biennial plant of parsley family, native to Europe and America. Blanched stem used in salads and as vegetable, dried leaves as flavouring.

celesta, or **celeste,** orchestral keyboard instrument invented (1886) by Auguste Mustel in Paris. Hammers strike steel bars attached to wooden resonators.

cell, fundamental unit of living matter. Consists of mass of protoplasm bounded by a membrane and, in case of plants, additional rigid cell wall. Usually contains central NUCLEUS surrounded by cytoplasm, in which enzyme systems which control cell's metabolism are situated. Plant cells also contain chloroplasts in which photosynthesis takes place. Cells reproduce themselves by various methods of division. *See* MEIOSIS and MITOSIS.

cell, voltaic, device for producing electric current by chemical action. Two main types: primary cell and secondary cell or ACCUMULATOR. Primary cell usually irreversible in action. Variety of Leclanché cell, in which electrodes are carbon and zinc and electrolyte is ammonium chloride, used in common dry cell.

Cellini, Benvenuto (1500-71), Florentine sculptor, goldsmith. Famous works incl. gold salt-cellar and bronze statue *Perseus.* Best known for *Autobiography* giving vivid

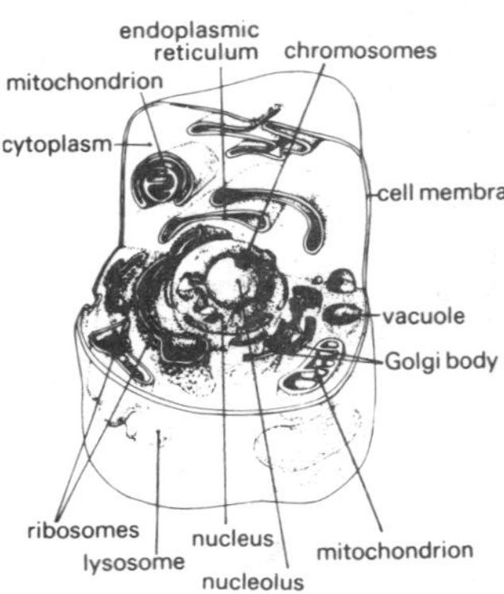

Animal cell

picture of artistic life in Rome an Florence.

cello or **violoncello,** low-pitched member o violin family. Developed in 17th cent., i gradually replaced bass viol as bass line i orchestras and chamber groups, and a solo instrument.

cellulose, chief constituent of cell walls o fibres of all plant tissue. Indigestible b humans, digestible by many animals, e cattle. White polymeric carbohydrate, in soluble in water. Nearly pure in the fibre o cotton, linen, hemp. Basis of nitrocellulose celluloid, collodion and guncotton. Used i manufacture of rayon, plastics, explosives.

Celsius, Anders (1701-44), Swedish invento astronomer. Devised (1742) Celsius o centigrade TEMPERATURE scale.

Celtic, branch of Indo-European languag family. Spoken throughout Europe befor Roman conquest, now exists as subgroups: Brythonic (Breton, Welsh, an extinct Cornish); Goidelic or Gaelic (Iris Gaelic, Scottish Gaelic and extinct Manx Continental, 3rd subgroup, now extinct.

Celtic Sea, area of NE Atlantic between S coast of Ireland, Pembrokeshire coas Cornwall, W coast of Brittany.

Celts, ancient people who inhabited W and Europe. Associated with La Tène cultur (beginning in 5th cent. BC), which sa development of iron working an characteristic linear art. Invaded N Italy i early 4th cent. BC and later reache Greece and Asia Minor. Romans gaine control of their territs. in Italy by 222 B and most of their territ. in France an Belgium during Gallic Wars (58-51 BC.) I British Isles restricted to Scotland, Wale Cornwall, Ireland by Germanic invasion following Roman withdrawal.

cement, material which bonds together surfaces. Portland cement made by mixin powdered limestone and clay and heatin product; mixed with water and sand make mortar, or with sand, gravel and water to make concrete.

Cenozoic or **Cainozoic era,** fourth and most recent geological era, incl. time from end of Mesozoic era to present day. Began *c* 65 million years ago. Comprises Tertiary and Quaternary periods. Alpine, Himalayan mountain building; extensive glaciation; formation of deserts. Typified by evolution of modern flora and fauna; dominance of mammals, emergence of *Homo sapiens*. Also *see* GEOLOGICAL TABLE.

censorship, system in which circulation of writings, presentation of plays, films, TV programmes, works of art, *etc*, may in whole or part be prohibited. In UK, films are voluntarily submitted to British Board of Film Censors, sale of publications may be banned under Obscene Publications Act (1857). Censorship is feature of totalitarian states.

census, official, usually periodic, count of population and recording of economic status, age, sex, *etc*. Estab. in ancient times amongst Jews, Romans for tax purposes. Census of England and Scotland first took place in 1801, has been done every 10 years since.

centaur, in Greek myth, one of race of beings with upper body of human, lower of horse. Represented as tending to riotous living and wine. *See* CHIRON.

centigrade temperature, *see* TEMPERATURE.

centipede, any carnivorous many-legged arthropod of class Chilopoda. Flat segmented body with poison claws on first segment; *c* 35 pairs of legs. Widely distributed; largest species *c* 30 cm/12 in. long.

CENTO, *see* CENTRAL TREATY ORGANIZATION.

Central, region of C Scotland. Area 2621 sq km (1012 sq mi); pop. 272,000; admin. hq. Stirling. Created 1975, incl. former Stirlingshire, Clackmannanshire, SW Perthshire.

Central African Republic

Central African Republic, republic of C Africa. Area 623,000 sq km (241,000 sq mi); pop. 2,370,000; cap. Bangui. Languages: Sangho, French. Religions: animist, Christian. Largely savannah-covered plateau, tropical forest in S; drained by Ubangi, Shari rivers. Cotton, coffee growing; diamond, uranium mining. Formerly Ubangi-Shari territ. of French Equatorial Africa, independent from 1960. Member of French Community. Proclaimed empire (1976) by President Bokassa who made himself emperor. Overthown (1979).

Central America, isthmus connecting North and South America, comprising Guatemala, Costa Rica, Nicaragua, Honduras, Belize, El Salvador, Panama, and some Mexican states. Area 584,000 sq km (*c* 230,000 sq mi). Has many volcanic mountains, coastal plains; tropical climate. Subject to earthquakes. Bananas, coffee, cotton produce. Panama Canal links Caribbean, Pacific. Had ancient Maya civilizations. Region comprised Central American Federation (1825-38).

Central Committee of the Communist Party, in USSR, executive, possessing real power over Supreme Soviet legislative structure. Its members elected from Party Congress, who, in turn, elect Politburo and Secretariat.

Central Intelligence Agency (CIA), independent executive bureau of govt. of US estab. by National Security Act (1947) as centre for all foreign intelligence operations. Allen Dulles, director (1953-61), strengthened CIA and emboldened tactics. Scandal broke (1974) with discovery that CIA had been massively involved in illegal domestic espionage. Senate Intelligence Committee found (1975) CIA, from 1950s, had policy to assassinate foreign leaders, disrupt foreign govts.

Central Treaty Organization (CENTO), defensive military alliance, formed 1955 by Iraq (withdrew 1958), Iran, Turkey, Pakistan and UK on basis of Baghdad Pact; US interests represented. Disbanded 1979.

centre of gravity, in physics, point on body where its weight can be considered as concentrated. Centre of mass defined similarly. These correspond in constant gravitational field.

centrifugation, means of separating solid, whose particles are too fine to be filtered, from a liquid. Liquid spun at high velocity so that centrifugal force moves denser material, *eg* suspended solids, to sides of tube containing liquid. Ultracentrifuge, working at greater speeds, used to determine particle size and molecular weights in polymers.

Cephalonia *(Kefallinía),* isl. of Greece, largest of Ionian Isls. Area 925 sq km (357 sq mi); main town Argostolion. Mountainous; fruit, wine.

Cephalopoda (cephalopods), class of molluscs, incl. squid, octopus, cuttlefish, with prehensile tentacles around mouth. Usually no shell (*see* ARGONAUT). Numerous fossil species.

Ceram, isl. of Indonesia, in S Moluccas. Area *c* 17,000 sq km (6600 sq mi). Mountainous with dense forests in interior; produces copra, sago.

ceramics, art and science of making POTTERY.

Cerberus, in Greek myth, three-headed dog which guarded passage to and from the underworld (Hades). Last labour of Heracles was to capture him.

cereal, variety of annuals of grass family cultivated for edible fruit, known as grain. Cereal crops cover *c* ½ world's arable land, chief in order of acreage being wheat, rice, millet, sorghum, maize, barley, oats, rye. Some cereals fermented to make alcohol.

Ceres, Roman fertility goddess of the earth and growing corn, identified with Greek goddess DEMETER.

cerium (Ce), soft metallic element of lanthanide group; at. no. 58, at. wt. 140.12. Alloyed with iron, used in lighter flints. Compounds used to make gas mantles.

Cervantes [Saavedra], Miguel de (1547-1616), Spanish novelist. Known for satire of chivalric romance, *Don Quixote* (1605-15), influential in development of novel. Also wrote pastoral romances, many plays.

cervix, *see* UTERUS.

Ceské Budejovice (Ger. *Budweis*), town of SW Czechoslovakia, on R. Moldau. Pop. 78,000. Beer mfg.; timber, graphite industs. Noted for Baroque architecture.

Cestoda (cestodes), class of ribbon-like flatworms without gut or mouth. Body divided into numerous segments. Parasitic in intestinal canals of vertebrates. Species incl. TAPEWORM.

Cetacea (cetaceans), order of aquatic fish-like mammals. No hind limbs; front limbs modified into flippers. Divided into toothed whales, *eg* dolphin, porpoise, sperm whale, and toothless whales, *eg* blue whale.

Cetewayo (*c* 1836-84), Zulu chieftain. Led determined resistance to British advances into his territ. until defeated (1879) at Ulundi.

Ceuta, Spanish enclave in NW Morocco. Area 18 sq km (7 sq mi); pop. 88,000. Free port and military post. Spanish from 1580, now part of Cádiz prov.

Cévennes, mountain range of S France, SE of Massif Central. Runs SW-NE for *c* 240 km (150 mi), highest peak Mont Mézenc (1754 m/ 5755 ft). Source of many rivers, incl. Loire, Allier, Lot. Largely barren limestone. Sheep rearing.

Ceylon, *see* SRI LANKA.

Cézanne, Paul (1839-1906), French painter. Encouraged by Pissarro, he abandoned a violent romantic style for impressionist landscape technique. Later work was distinguished from impressionism by emphasis on structural analysis and use of tone and colour to express form. His attempts to reduce forms to their geometric equivalents influenced cubism.

c.g.s. system of units, system of physical units based on centimetre, gram and second. Superseded by SI units for scientific works.

Chaco or **Gran Chaco,** large lowland plain of C South America, stretching from S Bolivia through Paraguay to N Argentina. Sparse pop.; unexploited resources. Bolivia and Paraguay warred for regional control (1932-5).

Chad

Chad, republic of NC Africa. Area 1,284,000 sq km (495,000 sq mi); pop. 4,309,000; cap. Ndjamena. Official language: French. Religions: animist, Christian, Islam. Savannah in S; desert, Tibesti Mts. in N. Main river Shari, flows into L. Chad in SW. Cotton, peanut growing in S; nomadic pastoralism in N. Crossed by trans-Saharan caravan routes. Former territ. of French Equatorial Africa, independent from 1960. Member of French Community.

Chad, Lake, lake of NC Africa. Mainly in SW Chad, partly in NE Nigeria, SE Niger, NW Cameroon. Area varies with season, up to *c* 26,000 sq km (10,000 sq mi); fed by R. Shari, no outlets. Now much smaller than when discovered (1823).

Chadwick, Sir James (1891-1974), English physicist. Discovered neutron during bombardment of beryllium by alpha particles (1932); awarded Nobel Prize for Physics (1935).

chaffinch, *Fringilla coelebs,* finch common in European woodlands. Male has pinkish breast, white bars on brown wings.

Chagall, Marc (1889-), Russian painter. His imaginative, richly coloured art is based on reminiscences of Russian-Jewish village life; has designed stained glass and murals. Fantasies influenced surrealists. Lived mainly in France from 1910.

Chagos Archipelago, isl. group in C Indian Ocean, NE of Mauritius; part of British Indian Ocean Territ. Exports copra.

Chain, Sir Ernst Boris (1906-79). British biochemist, b. Germany. Shared Nobel Prize for Physiology and Medicine (1945) with Fleming and Florey for initiating work on penicillin.

chain reaction, in physics, self-sustaining nuclear reaction of FISSION type. Occurs when neutrons emitted from uranium 235 cause fission of further uranium nuclei. Basis of atomic bomb and nuclear reactors.

chalcedony, variety of silica, consisting mainly of extremely fine quartz crystals. Occurs in many different forms, some semi-precious, *eg* agate, bloodstone, chrysoprase, onyx.

Chalcidice *(Khalkidikí),* penin. of NE Greece, on Aegean Sea; modern admin. dist., cap. Polygyros. Incl. ATHOS. Wheat, olives, wine; magnesite mining. Colonized 7th cent. BC from Chalcis (whence name).

Chalcis *(Khalkis),* town of E Greece, cap. of Euboea admin. dist. Pop. 24,000. Port, agric. trade. Active colonizer (*eg* Chalcidice, Sicily) from 8th cent. BC.

Chaldaeans, Semitic people who inhabited S Babylonia from *c* 1000 BC. Empire flourished under Nebuchadnezzar II but fell to Cyrus the Great (539 BC).

Chaliapin, Feodor Ivanovich (1873-1938), Russian bass singer. Famous as Boris Godunov in Mussorgsky's opera. Also known for his recitals.

chalk, soft, fine-grained limestone, white in colour. Consists mainly of calcareous skeletal material, laid down in Cretaceous period. Used to make putty, plaster, quicklime, cement.

Chalon-sur-Saône, town of Burgundy, EC France, on R. Saône and Canal du Centre. Pop. 53,000. River port, wine and grain trade. Cap. of kingdom of Burgundy in 6th cent.

Chamberlain, Joseph (1836-1914), British politician. Reform mayor of Birmingham (1873-6). Resigned (1886) from Gladstone's cabinet over Irish Home Rule policy, leading Liberal Unionist revolt. Colonial secretary (1893-1903), his imperial expansionist policies helped precipitate Boer War. Championed imperial preference tariffs, resigned 1903; this split coalition with Conservatives, leading to 1906 election defeat. His son, **Sir [Joseph] Austen Chamberlain** (1863-1937), was Conservative chancellor of exchequer (1903-6, 1919-21). Helped negotiate Irish settlement (1921). Foreign secretary (1924-9), instrumental in signing of LOCARNO PACT (1925) guaranteeing German borders; awarded Nobel Peace Prize (1925). His half-brother, **[Arthur] Neville Chamberlain** (1869-1940), was PM (1937-40). Chancellor of exchequer before succeeding Baldwin at head of National govt. Used 'appeasement' policy in attempting to limit Hitler in E Europe, signing MUNICH PACT (1938) over Czechoslovakia. Led Britain into WWII, resigning (1940) after German invasion of Norway.

chamber music, music for performance by a small number of singers or players, *eg* a string quartet. Originally intended for performance in a private house but now mainly to be heard in smaller concert halls.

Chambéry, town of SE France, cap. of Savoie dept. Pop. 54,000. Tourist centre; vermouth, silk mfg. Hist. cap. of Savoy. Cathedral (14th cent.).

chameleon, any of Chamaeleontidae family of lizard-like Old World reptiles. Long prehensile tail, eyes capable of independent movement. Extends tongue to catch insects. Undergoes colour change to match surroundings.

chamois, *Rupicapra rupicapra,* ruminant mammal intermediate between antelope and goat. Agile jumper, found in mountains of Europe and SW Asia. Name also applied to leather of animal.

Chamonix, town of Savoy, E France, in Chamonix valley. Pop. 8000. Alpine resort, base for ascent of mountains in Mont Blanc region.

Champagne, region and former prov. of NE France, cap. Troyes. Divided into 3 by parallel ridges; dairying in E, sheep rearing in C, champagne in W (esp. around Rheims, Epernay). Main rivers Aisne, Marne, Seine. Powerful medieval county. Incorporated into France (1314). Battleground in many wars.

champagne, sparkling white wine produced around Rheims and Epernay in Champagne district of France. Sparkling quality is obtained by adding cane sugar to wine which has been bottled following initial fermentation; this induces a secondary fermentation in the bottle.

Champlain, Samuel de (1567-1635), French explorer. Made several voyages to E Canada and NE US; sailed up St Lawrence R. (1603), founded Port Royal (1605) and led 1st colonists to Québec (1608). Initiated fur trade; laid basis for French claims in North America.

chancel, part of E end of church around altar, reserved for clergy and choir. Often separated by railings or screen from main body of church.

Chandigarh, joint cap. of Punjab and Haryana states, N India. Pop. 219,000. Built in 1950s to designs by Le Corbusier.

Chandler, Raymond (1888-1959), American detective story writer. Created cynical private detective, Philip Marlowe. Crime novels incl. *The Big Sleep* (1939), *Farewell, My Lovely* (1940).

Changchun, cap. of Kirin prov., NE China. Pop. 1,200,000. Railway jct.; major motor vehicle production centre, esp. trucks, tractors; film studios. Cap. of Manchukuo under Japanese (1934-45).

Changkiakow *(Kalgan),* city of Hopeh prov., N China. Pop. 1,000,000. Trade centre, food processing. Military centre in Manchu dynasty, on caravan route between Peking and Ulan Bator.

Channel Islands (Fr. *Iles Normandes),* UK isl. group in S English Channel. Area 194 sq km (75 sq mi); pop. 130,000. Main isls. Jersey, Guernsey, Alderney, Sark; main town St Helier (Jersey). Separate laws, taxes; languages incl. English, French, Norman dialects. Market gardening, dairying, tourism. Isls. English from Norman Conquest (1066). German occupation (1940-5).

chansons de geste, medieval French epic poems (late 11th-early 14th cent.) Best known and oldest is *Chanson de Roland* (*c* 1098-1100). *See* ROLAND.

chant, a vocal melody usually sung as part of a ritual, often religious and often unaccompanied. The melody is usually sung in unison. PLAINSONG is a medieval religious chant from which Western art music grew.

Chantilly, town of Picardy, N France. Pop. 10,000. Horse racing centre; popular resort. Former lace mfg. centre. Hist. château.

Chaos, in Greek myth, disordered void from which sprang GAEA, mother of all things earthly and divine.

Chaplin, Sir Charles Spencer ('Charlie') (1889-1977), British film actor, producer, director. Famous for creation of tramp-like clown figure, with baggy pants, toothbrush moustache, distinctive walk.

Chapman, George (*c* 1560-1634), English poet, dramatist, translator. Best known for sophisticated verse translation *The Whole Works of Homer* (1616) which inspired Keats's sonnet.

char, food fish of salmon family, genus *Salvelinus*, inhabiting deep cold lakes.

charcoal, *see* CARBON.

Chardin, Jean Baptiste Siméon (1699-1779), French painter. Noted for his still lifes and genre scenes of simple domestic interiors, devoid of sentimentality.

Charente, river of WC France. Flows *c* 355 km (220 mi) from Haute-Vienne dept. via Angoulême to Bay of Biscay opposite Oléron Isl. Region of cattle raising, cognac production.

charge, electric, fundamental attribute of elementary particles of matter. By convention, electron carries 1 negative unit of electric charge, proton 1 positive unit; matter containing excess of electrons is negatively charged, *etc.* Like charges repel each other, unlike charges attract each other. Measured in coulombs.

Egyptian chariot of c 1500 BC

chariot, earliest form of horse-drawn vehicle, with 2 wheels and waist-high guard at front of car. Originated in Mesopotamia *c* 3000-2000 BC; widely used in ancient world for war, passenger-carrying and races.

Charlemagne or **Charles I** (742–814), king of the Franks (771-814), emperor of the West Romans (800-14). Son of Pepin the Short. Sole ruler of Franks on death of brother Carloman (771). In support of pope, defeated Lombards and became their king (774). Led campaign against Moors of NE Spain (778); subjugated Saxons (772-804), forced their conversion to Christianity. Crowned emperor by Leo III, whose papal ambitions he had supported; created strong empire by estab. marches, efficient admin. His court at Aachen (Fr. *Aix-la-Chapelle*) became centre of learning. Life became centre of medieval cycle of romance and legend, notably in the *Chanson de Roland*.

Charles [II] the Bald (823-77), king of West Franks (843-77), Holy Roman emperor (875-7). With brother, Louis the German, defeated Lothair I at Fontenoy (841); became West Frankish king by Treaty of Verdun (843). Succeeded Louis II as emperor (875).

Charles V (1500-58), Holy Roman emperor (1519-58), king of Spain as Charles I (1516-56). Son of Philip I of Castile, became greatest Habsburg and most powerful ruler in Europe. Wars against France during 1520s ended in consolidation of influence over papacy. Promoted Catholic reform with Council of Trent (1545). Enlarged Spanish empire in Americas, conquering Mexico and Peru. After 1530, increasingly delegated powers in Germany to his brother, later Ferdinand I. Fierce opponent of Protestantism, broke power of Reformation princes in Germany (1547), but later signed Peace of Augsburg (1555) allowing choice of religion to be made by individual princes. Retired to monastery (1556).

Charles I (1600-49), king of England, Scotland and Ireland (1625-49). Succeeding father James I, offended public by Catholic marriage. Struggle with Puritan-dominated Parliament led to Petition of Right (1628) asserting Parliament's supremacy. Charles ruled repressively without Parliament (1629-40) until Scottish wars forced him to recall it. Long Parliament of 1640 had STRAFFORD beheaded and ended arbitrary taxation and Star Chamber courts. Defeated in ensuing CIVIL WAR (1642-6), captured 1646. Tried by Puritan-controlled court, convicted of treason and beheaded.

Charles II (1630-85), king of England, Scotland and Ireland (1660-85). Fled to France (1646), crowned king in Scotland (1651) after father Charles I's death; escaped again when defeated by Cromwell. Restored as king (1660), aided by CLARENDON, his chief minister. CABAL ministry replaced Clarendon in 1667. Charles entered 2 Dutch wars to assert commercial supremacy. Secretly allied with France (1670), promising to restore Catholicism. Forced to approve TEST ACT (1673), directed against Catholics; later blocked Exclusion Act (1681) against his brother James by dissolving Parliament, after which he ruled absolutely. No legitimate heirs, succeeded by brother. Important features of reign incl. development of political parties, advances in trade and sea power, territ. expansion and growth of Parliament's power.

Charles [VI] the Well Beloved (1368-1422), king of France (1380-1422). Under power of regent until 1388; insane after 1392. Rival factions fought for power, leading to civil war between houses of Orléans (Armagnacs) and Burgundy. Invasion and victory of Henry V of England at Agincourt (1415) led to Treaty of Troyes (1420) recognizing Henry as Charles's successor.

Charles VII (1403-61), king of France (1422-61). Excluded from succession by father Charles VI, ruled from Bourges until Joan of Arc raised siege of Orléans and had him crowned at Rheims (1429). During reign, English expelled from all France except Calais, ending Hundred Years War.

Charles X (1757-1836), king of France (1824-30). Led ultra-royalist group before following his brother, Louis XVIII, to throne. Abdicated after liberal-inspired July Revolution. Died in exile.

Charles [Gustavus] X (1622-60), king of Sweden (1654-60). Invaded Poland (1655). Wars with Denmark (1658-60) resulted in territ. expansion into Danish lands in Sweden.

Charles XII (1682-1718), king of Sweden (1697-1718). Challenged by alliance of Denmark, Poland and Russia, routed Danes and defeated Peter the Great at Narva (1700), crushed Poland. Campaign in Russia (1708-9) ended in defeat at Poltava; fled to Turkey. Invaded Norway (1716), killed during siege of Fredrikssten.

Charles XIV (1763-1844), king of Sweden and Norway (1818-44). Born in France as Jean Baptiste Jules Bernadotte, became one of Napoleon's marshals. Adopted (1810) as heir to Swedish throne by Charles XIII, for whom he ruled. Joined alliance against Napoleon; secured union of Sweden and Norway (1814) before ascending throne. Founder of present dynasty.

Charles [Philip Arthur George], Prince of Wales (1948-), heir to British throne. Son of Elizabeth II and Prince Philip. Married Lady Diana Spencer 1981.

Charles, Jacques Alexandre César (1746-1823), French physicist. Evolved Charles' law: at constant pressure volume of gas is directly proportional to its absolute temperature. Made 1st successful ascent in hydrogen balloon.

Charles Albert (1798-1849), king of Sardinia (1831-49). Avoided revolution by granting constitution (1848). Warred with Austria in Italy; defeated at Novara, abdicated in favour of his son, Victor Emmanuel II.

Charles Martel (*c* 688-741), Frankish ruler. Grandfather of Charlemagne. United Merovingian kingdoms. Thwarted Moslem invasion of Europe with victory at Poitiers (732).

Charles the Bold (1433-77), last duke of Burgundy (1467-77). Son of Philip the Good, father of Mary of Burgundy. Confirmed opponent of Louis XI of France. Aimed to restore Lotharingian kingdom; killed while fighting Swiss after he had annexed Lorraine.

Charleston, port of S South Carolina, US; on Atlantic inlet. Pop. 371,000. Naval depot; timber, fruit, cotton exports. Settled by English (1670). Civil War opened with Confederates firing on Fort Sumter (1861); besieged by Union forces (1863-5). Has famous botanical gardens.

Charleston, cap. of West Virginia, US; on Kanawha R. Pop. 256,000. Rail, trade and indust. centre. Oil refining; chemical, glass mfg. Expanded around Fort Lee; became permanent state cap. 1885.

charlock, *Brassica arvenis,* plant of mustard family with yellow flowers, seedpods. Pernicious weed in Britain.

Charlotte, city of SC North Carolina, US. Pop. 593,000; state's largest city. Transport jct.; cotton, textiles, chemical mfg.

Charlottetown, seaport of Canada; cap. of Prince Edward Isl., on S coast. Pop. 19,000. Exports dairy produce, potatoes. Settled 1768; scene of Canadian confederate conference (1864). Univ (1855).

charm, in nuclear physics, supposed fundamental attribute of elementary particles, manifested by non-zero charm quantum number. First predicted theoretically, its status was enhanced by discovery (1974) of the psi (J) particle, believed to be composed of a new type of charmed QUARK and corresponding anti-quark.

Charon, in Greek myth, boatman of R. Styx who ferried souls of the dead to underworld (Hades). A coin was placed in the mouth of the dead to pay for this service.

Chartism, movement in Britain for social and political reform, estab. 1838. Roots lay in decline in working class conditions during economic depression of 1830s. Principles contained in 'People's Charter', submitted to Parliament: universal manhood suffrage, equal election dists., vote by ballot, annual parliaments, abolition of property qualification for MPs, payment of MPs. Petition's rejection followed by riots; movement declined in 1840s, esp. after 1848. Brought about some reforms.

Chartres, town of N France, on R. Eure, cap. of Eure-et-Loir dept. Pop. 37,000. Market town; tourist and pilgrimage centre. Medieval county, duchy from 1528. Famous Gothic cathedral (12th-13th cent.) with stained-glass windows.

Charybdis, *see* SCYLLA.

chat, insectivorous bird of thrush family, esp. of genera *Cercomela* and *Saxicola.* Whinchat and stonechat are species.

château, term originally denoting a French medieval castle. With development of castles into places of residence rather than defence in 15th and 16th cents., name came to describe large country houses and estates.

Chateaubriand, François René, Vicomte de (1768-1848), French author, diplomat. Forerunner of French romanticism through egoism, impassioned prose, interest in the exotic. Works incl. novel *Atala* (1801), autobiog. *Mémoires d'Outre-tombe* (1848-50).

Chatham, 1st Earl of, *see* PITT, WILLIAM.

Chatham, mun. bor of Kent, SE England. Pop. 57,000. Naval base, estab. by Henry VIII.

Chattanooga, town of SE Tennessee, US; on Tennessee R. Pop. 392,000. Timber products, machinery mfg. Centre of Tennessee Valley Authority irrigation and h.e.p. schemes. Scene of several battles (1863) during Civil War.

Chatterton, Thomas (1752-70), English poet. Known for 'forgeries' of poetry by imaginary 15th cent. priest, Thomas Rowley. Work has considerable imaginative, poetic power. His suicide made him a hero of later Romantics.

Chaucer, Geoffrey (*c* 1340-1400), English poet. Member of king's household. First important poems derived from French works, in content or style, *eg Romaunt of the Rose* (*c* 1370). After visiting Italy influenced by Dante and Boccaccio, whose *Filostrato* he used for *Troilus and Criseyde* (*c* 1385-6). Best known for unfinished cycle *Canterbury Tales* (*c* 1387), collection of 23 tales narrated by pilgrims en route from London to Canterbury. Works preeminent in estab. of modern English as literary language.

checkers, *see* DRAUGHTS.

Cheddar, village of N Somerset, England. Famous for cheeses. Scenic Cheddar Gorge is nearby.

cheese, food made from curds of soured milk. Numerous varieties of cheese are usually divided into hard cheeses, *eg* Cheddar, Edam and Gouda, and soft cheeses, *eg* Brie and Camembert. Various micro-organisms introduced into cheese produce characteristic flavours, *eg* those of Stilton.

Cheetah

cheetah, *Acinonyx jubatus,* dog-like cat of grasslands and semi-deserts of Africa, SW Asia. Small head, long legs, black-spotted tawny coat. Fastest of all land mammals, reaching speeds of 112 km/70 mph.

Chekhov, Anton Pavlovich (1860-1904), Russian dramatist and short story writer. Known for plays of great psychological insight, *eg The Seagull* (1896), *Uncle Vanya* (1899), *Three Sisters* (1901), *The Cherry Orchard* (1904).

Chekiang, maritime prov. of E China. Area *c* 103,600 sq km (40,000 sq mi); pop. 31,000,000; cap. Hangchow. Contains fertile Yangtze delta (rice). Mountainous, densely populated. Rice, tea, wheat, cotton grown.

Chelmsford, admin. hq. of Essex, SE England. Pop. 58,000. Light industs. Church (1424, rebuilt 19th cent.) now cathedral.

Chelsea, *see* KENSINGTON AND CHELSEA.

Cheltenham, town of Gloucestershire, W England. Pop. 70,000. Spa from 18th cent.; has famous racecourse.

chemical warfare, the use of POISON GAS or liquids as a weapon, started by the ancient Greeks with sulphur fumes. Prohibited by the Hague Declaration (1899) but employed with deadly effect on the Western Front in WWI, using chlorine, phosgene and mustard gas. Again outlawed at the Washington Conference (1922) it was not used in WWII.

chemistry, science concerned with composition of substances and their reactions with one another. Usually divided into organic, inorganic and physical chemistry. Organic chemistry deals with compounds of carbon, excluding metal carbonates and oxides and sulphides of carbon. Inorganic chemistry deals with elements and their compounds, excluding organic carbon compounds. Physical chemistry is application of physical measurements and laws to chemical systems and their changes.

Chemnitz, *see* KARL-MARX-STADT.

Chengchow, cap. of Honan prov., EC China. Pop. 1,050,000. Rail jct.; textile centre; meat packing, fertilizer mfg.

Chengtu, cap. of Szechwan prov., SC China. Pop. 1,250,000. Port on R. Min. Textile, paper mfg. Cultural, commercial centre; 2 univs. Ancient cap. of Shu Han dynasty 3rd cent.

Cheops, *see* KHUFU.

Chequers, Tudor mansion in Buckinghamshire, England. Official country residence of UK prime minister.

Cherbourg, town of Normandy, N France, on N coast of Cotentin penin. Pop. 40,000. Transatlantic port; major fortified naval base from 17th cent.

Cherenkov, Pavel Alekseyich (1904-), Soviet physicist. Discovered Cherenkov effect when high energy charged particles move through medium at velocity exceeding that of light in the medium; used in detection of subatomic particles. Shared Nobel Prize for Physics (1958).

Cherokee, North American Indian tribe. Largest in SE US. Settled farmers with advanced culture. Frequently fought Iroquois and were valuable allies of British against the French. Estab. (1827) Cherokee Nation with govt. modelled on that of white settlers. Became US citizens (1906), now mainly in North Carolina and Oklahoma.

cherry, tree of genus *Prunus* of rose family. Smooth stone enclosed in fleshy, usually edible fruit. Native to Asia Minor. Most varieties are derived from sweet-cherry, *P. avium.*

Cherubini, [Maria] Luigi (1760-1824), Italian composer. Lived in Paris from 1788. Best known for opera *The Water-carrier*

(French title *Les deux journées*). Also wrote church music.

chervil, *Anthriscus cerefolium,* annual herb of parsley family with sweet, aromatic leaves used for flavouring in cookery. Native to Russia.

Chesapeake Bay, largest Atlantic inlet of US; separates E Maryland and part of Virginia from mainland. Length 320 km (*c* 200 mi). Important oyster, crab fisheries.

Cheshire, county of NW England. Area 2322 sq km (896 sq mi); pop. 920,000; admin. hq. Chester. Wirral penin. in NW; low-lying, drained by Mersey, Dee. Dairying, esp. cheese; shipbuilding; salt, chemical industs.

chess, game for 2 players, each with 16 pieces, played on a board divided into 64 squares, alternately black and white. Pieces are moved according to conventional rules. Prob. originated in India, later spreading to Persia and Middle East. Popular in W Europe by 13th cent.

chest, *see* THORAX.

Chester, city and admin. hq. of Cheshire, NW England, on R. Dee. Pop. 63,000. Railway jct.; metal goods mfg. Roman *Devana Castra;* medieval walls intact. Cathedral dates from Norman times; has 16th-17th cent. timbered houses.

Chesterfield, Philip Dormer Stanhope, 4th Earl of (1694-1773), English statesman, man of letters. Remembered for *Letters to His Son* (pub. 1774).

Chesterton, G[ilbert] K[eith] (1874-1936), English author. Known for novels of ideas, *eg The Man Who Was Thursday* (1908); 'Father Brown' detective stories. Also wrote literary criticism, RC apologia.

chestnut, tree of genus *Castanea* of beech family found in N temperate regions. Species incl. edible sweet or Spanish chestnut, *C. sativa.* Fruit is burr-like, containing 2-3 nuts. Wood is strong and durable. *See* HORSE CHESTNUT.

Chevalier, Maurice (1888-1972), French film actor, singer. Achieved fame in Paris revues of 1920s, became international film star in 1930s.

Cheviot Hills, range on Scotland-England border, rising to 815 m (2676 ft) on The Cheviot. Sheep rearing (Cheviot breed).

chevrotain or **mouse deer,** mammal of Tragulidae family of forests of Asia, Africa. Resembles deer, but has no antlers. Smallest of ruminants, reaches heights of 30 cm/1 ft.

chewing gum, *see* CHICLE.

Cheyenne, North American Indian tribe. Originally farmers on Cheyenne R., became nomadic buffalo hunters after introduction of horse (*c* 1760). Colorado gold discovery (1858) forced Cheyenne into reservation where govt. neglect provoked raids by the Indians, who were then massacred by US army at Sand Creek (1864). Now mainly in Montana.

Cheyenne, cap. of Wyoming, US; in extreme S of state. Pop. 41,000. Transport jct., commercial centre in cattle rearing region. Territ. cap. 1869.

Chiang Ch'ing, *see* GANG OF FOUR.

Chiang Kai-shek (1887-1975), Chinese military and political leader. Emerged as head of revolutionary Kuomintang in 1920s, leading expedition (1926-8) in N resulting in overthrow of Peking govt. Leader (1928-48), ruled with extensive power. Fought local warlords and, with Communists, resisted Japanese invasions; later driven from mainland (1949) in civil war with Communists. After 1950, challenged Communists from Taiwan-based Nationalist govt.

Chianti, Monti, small mountain range of Tuscany, C Italy, W of R. Arno. Grapes for Chianti wine grown on slopes.

Chicago, port of NE Illinois, US; on SW shore of L. Michigan. Transport and indust. hub of US Middle West. Pop. 7,658,000. Shipping, railway centre; important grain market; large meatpacking indust., machinery mfg. Growth began after completion of Erie Canal. Became a city (1837); devastated by fire (1871). Univ. (1892).

Chichester, Sir Francis (1901-72), English yachtsman, aviator. Made 1st E-W solo flight across Tasman Sea (1931). Best known for sailing around world single-handed in *Gipsy Moth IV* (1966-7).

Chichester, city and admin. hq. of West Sussex, SE England, Pop. 21,000. Agric. market. Roman remains incl. amphitheatre; has church (11th cent.).

chicken, *see* FOWL.

chickenpox, infectious virus disease, usually of young children. Characterized by eruption of small spots which later become blisters. Incubation period of 2 to 3 weeks.

chickpea, bushy annual plant, *Cicer arietinum,* of Leguminosae family. Cultivated in India for edible seeds contained in pods.

chickweed, low annual or perennial herb of genus *Stellaria* of pink family, native to temperate regions. Small, white flowers.

chicle, gum-like substance derived from latex of tropical American trees, esp. sapodilla, *Achras sapota,* of Yucatán and Guatemala. Introduced into US as rubber substitute and basis of chewing gum.

chicory, *Cichorium intybus,* European annual plant, also grown in US. Leaves used in salads; root ground and roasted as coffee substitute. *See* ENDIVE.

chiffchaff, *Phylloscopus collybita,* European bird of warbler family. Olive-green and brown; distinctive song, giving rise to name.

chiffon, sheer lightweight fabric made of silk, rayon or cotton.

Chihli, *see* HOPEH and POHAI, GULF OF.

Chihuahua, town of N Mexico, cap. of Chihuahua state. Pop. 366,000. On C plateau in cattle-raising, mining region; textile mfg., smelting indust.

chihuahua, small dog, originating in Mexico. Large pointed ears; stands 13 cm/5 in. high at shoulder.

chilblain, painful inflammation of skin of hands and feet, caused by contraction of blood vessels in response to cold.

Chile

Chile, republic of W South America. Area 756,945 sq km (292,256 sq mi); pop. 10,857,000; cap. Santiago. Language: Spanish. Religion: RC. Comprises narrow coastal strip W of Andes extending S to Tierra del Fuego, with outlying Easter, Juan Fernández isls. Important mining in Atacama Desert region (copper, nitrates, iron ore). Agric. in SC valleys (sheep, cattle rearing). Conquered by Spanish in 16th cent.; Indian resistance until 19th cent. Independence gained under San Martín (1818); gained N region in war with Bolivia, Peru (1879-84). First South American country to elect Marxist govt. (1970); fell in military coup (1973).

chili, *see* PEPPER.

Chiltern Hills, SC England. Chalk range *c* 88 km (55 mi) long, running SW-NE through Oxfordshire, Buckinghamshire, Hertfordshire.

Chimaera, in Greek myth, fire-breathing monster with lion's head, goat's body, dragon's tail. Killed by Bellerophon.

chimes, set of bells, usually sounded as a signal, *eg* of the hour. The chimes heard in an orchestra consist of a set of tubular bells which are struck with hammer.

chimpanzee, *Pan troglodytes,* ape of African tropical forests. Black hair, naked face; diet of fruit, small animals. Walks on all fours. Most intelligent ape, can use simple tools. Stands *c* 1.5 m/5 ft tall.

China, People's Republic of, state of E Asia. Area *c* 9,561,000 sq km (3,691,500 sq mi); pop. 975,230,000; cap. Peking, largest city Shanghai. Official language: Peking Chinese; religions: Confucianism, Buddhism, Taoism. Comprises 21 provs., 5 auton. regions. Mountainous in N (Manchuria) and W (TIBET), descends to fertile valleys, plains in E. Chief rivers incl. Hwang Ho, Yangtze. Climate extreme in N, subtropical in S. Agric. economy, esp. rice, wheat; textile mfg. Great mineral potential, coal mining. China ruled by succession of imperial dynasties until 1912.

China

Chiang Kai-shek's rule (1928-49) ended by estab. of Communist govt. under Mao Tse-tung. Joined UN 1971.

china clay or **kaolin,** fine, whitish clay. Consists mainly of kaolinite (hydrous aluminium silicate). Used in pottery, paper, rubber mfg., medicine. Major sources in US, France, England.

China Sea, *see* EAST CHINA SEA, SOUTH CHINA SEA.

chinchilla, small squirrel-like rodent of Chinchillidae family found in South American Andes. Bred on farms in North America, Europe for its valuable fur.

Chinese, chief language group of Sino-Tibetan family. Has largest number of speakers in world. Official language of China is Mandarin, from N China, on which is based new 'national tongue', *Kno-yu,* renamed by Communists *p'u t'ung hua.* Other forms incl. Wu, Fukienese, Cantonese, Hakka. All variants share literary language *wenyen,* which is very different from vernaculars, and *paihua,* vernacular adopted by Communist regime for all writing.

Chinese lantern or **winter cherry,** *Physalis alkekengi,* plant of nightshade family of Eurasian origin. Bears fruit in inflated orange calyx which is dried to form floral decoration.

Chinghai, *see* TSINGHAI.

Chios *(Khíos),* isl. of Greece, in Aegean Sea off Turkey. Area 870 sq km (336 sq mi). Wine, figs, mastic. Main town, **Chios,** is a port; pop. 24,000. Ancient Ionian city state. Traditional birthplace of Homer.

chip, small slice of semi-conducting material, *eg* germanium or esp. silicon, used in transistors and INTEGRATED CIRCUITS. *See* SILICON CHIP.

chipmunk, burrowing North American, Asian rodent of squirrel family. Common chipmunk of E North America, *Tamias striatus,* has cheek pouches, striped markings on head, back. Diet of nuts, berries.

Chippendale, Thomas (1718-79), English cabinet maker. Pub. *The Gentleman and*

Cabinet Maker's Director (1754), important book of furniture designs, primarily in the rococo style, but sometimes inspired by contemporary taste for Gothic or Chinese style.

Chirico, Giorgio de (1888-1978), Italian painter, b. Greece. Precursor of surrealism, his early work conveys mood of mystery and unease.

Chiron, in Greek myth, wisest and kindliest of the CENTAURS. Skilled in medicine, prophecy, taught Asclepius, Achilles, Jason.

chiropractic, system of medical treatment based on theory that disease is caused by interference to normal nerve function, which can be restored by manipulation, esp. of backbone. Originated by D. D. Palmer (1895).

Chittagong, cap. of Chittagong division, SE Bangladesh. Pop. 890,000. Major seaport on R. Karnaphuli. Exports jute, tea. Oil refinery, iron and steel works.

chivalry, system of organization and code of personal conduct pertaining to medieval knighthood. Reached zenith at time of Crusades (12th–13th cents.). In ideal form involved knightly class in strict observance of qualities of loyalty, piety, valour, honour; also emphasized nobility of womanhood. Battlefields and tournaments served as arenas for displaying these virtues. Mixture of military and Christian ideals, seen most clearly in formation of military-religious orders, *eg* Knights Templars, Knights Hospitallers. Large body of literature grew around chivalric ideals, *eg* CHANSONS DE GESTE, epic poems of the TROUBADOURS. Also *see* ARTHURIAN LEGEND.

chives, *Allium schoenoprasum,* perennial plant of onion family. Tubular leaves used in salads and as flavouring.

chlorine (Cl), greenish-yellow gaseous element; at. no. 17, at. wt. 35.45. Occurs in sodium chloride (common salt) in sea water and rocks; obtained by electrolysis of brine. Used in manufacture of hydrochloric acid, bleaches, and much organic synthesis; also used to purify water.

chloroform ($CHCl_3$), volatile liquid with sweet smell. Produced by action of chlorine on methane. Used as industrial solvent and formerly as anaesthetic.

chlorophyll, complex pigment existing only in plants which make their own food by PHOTOSYNTHESIS, *ie* autotrophs. Molecule similar to blood pigment, haemoglobin. Chlorophyll is green, but colour may be masked by other pigments. Absent from all heterotrophs, *eg* fungi, animals.

chocolate, *see* COCOA.

choir, trained body of singers. A full choir is divided into 4 ranges of voices (sopranos, altos, tenors and basses) and each group normally sings a separate line from the others.

cholera, acute infectious disease caused by bacterium *Vibrio cholerae*; contracted from food or water contaminated by human faeces. Characterized by severe diarrhoea, muscular cramps, dehydration. Controlled by proper sanitation.

cholesterol, white fatty alcohol of STEROID group, found in body tissue, blood and bile. Assists in synthesis of vitamin D and various hormones. Excessive deposits of cholesterol on inside of arteries are associated with arteriosclerosis and coronary heart disease.

Cholon, *see* HO CHI MINH CITY.

Chomsky, [Avram] Noam (1928-), American linguist. Posited 'deep structure' (possibly common for all languages) from which innumerable syntactic combinations may be generated using transformational rules resulting in 'surface structure' (different for each language). Later wrote political commentaries.

Chopin, Frédéric François (1810-49), Polish composer, pianist. Lived in France from 1831. A leader of the Romantic movement, Chopin composed almost entirely for piano. Expanded harmonic concepts in his mazurkas, ballades, nocturnes, études, *etc.* Lived with George Sand from 1838 to 1847.

chorale, hymn of Protestant church, usually written in 4 parts for choir but generally sung in unison by congregation. Tunes often used in German Baroque music as themes for larger choral works.

chord, in music, any group of notes that are heard at the same time, but usually 3 or more. The formation of chords is studied in HARMONY.

Chordata (chordates), phylum of animals possessing a NOTOCHORD at any stage of development. Incl. vertebrates, hemichordates, tunicates.

Chou, Chinese imperial dynasty (*c* 1000-249 BC). Period marked by great expansion of realm and mediocrity of emperors; by end of dynasty, China had broken up into semi-independent states. Many advances in agriculture, use of metals, literature, education, and industry.

Chou En-lai (1898-1976), Chinese political leader, premier (1949-76). Helped found (1922) Chinese Communist Party. Cooperated with Chiang Kai-shek against Japanese invasions, but fought against him (1930) after split with Kuomintang. Participated in LONG MARCH (1934-5). First premier and also foreign minister (1949-58), remaining in power despite ideological differences with Chairman Mao Tse-tung.

chough, mainly European bird of crow family, genus *Pyrrhocorax,* with black plumage and red feet.

chow chow, breed of dog developed in China. Thick brown or black coat, black tongue. Stands 50 cm/20 in. high at shoulder.

Chrétien de Troyes or **Chrestien de Troyes** (*fl* 1170), French poet. Wrote verse romances, 1st treatments of ARTHURIAN LEGEND, using elements of legend, Christian thought, code of courtly love.

Christ, *see* JESUS CHRIST.

Christchurch, city of E South Isl., New

Zealand, on Canterbury Plains. Pop. 297,000. Outport at Lyttelton exports wool, meat, dairy produce; food processing. Founded 1850 as church settlement. Has Anglican cathedral, univ. (1873).

Christian X (1870-1947), king of Denmark (1912-47). Figurehead of national resistance during German occupation of WWII.

Christian Democrat parties, *see* CONSERVATISM.

Christiania, *see* OSLO.

Christianity, religion of those who believe that Jesus is the realization of the Messiah prophesied in OT and who base their faith on his life and teachings, as recorded in the NT and on Jewish myth and history of OT. Early Church tended to be highly organizational and this tendency, coupled with geographic spread of Christianity, soon resulted in variety of churches (*eg* RC, Eastern Orthodox, Coptic). Subsequent reformed churches (*see* REFORMATION) were reaction against what was felt to be formalism and authoritarianism of traditional RC church.

Christian Science, religion founded by Mary Baker EDDY and practised by the Church of Christ, Scientist. Adherents believe that evil and disease can only be overcome by the individual's awareness of spiritual truth in his own mind.

Christie, Agatha Mary Clarissa, Dame, (1891-1976), English author. Known for *c* 50 works of detective fiction, *eg The Murder of Roger Ackroyd* (1926), and plays, esp. *The Mousetrap* (1952). Created private detective Hercule Poirot.

Christina (1626-89), queen of Sweden (1632-54). Patronized arts and scholars, but ruled extravagantly. Refused to marry, abdicated (1654) in favour of cousin Charles X. Settled in Rome, became a Catholic; failed in attempts to regain throne.

Christmas, in Christian calendar, celebration (on 25 Dec.) of the birth of Jesus Christ. Not widely celebrated until Middle Ages, although its near coincidence with the winter solstice links it with many ancient festivals.

Christmas Island, territ. of Australia, in Indian Ocean S of Sunda Trench. Area 142 sq km (55 sq mi); pop. 3500. Large phosphate deposits. British from 1888; admin. from Singapore after 1900; transferred to Australia 1958.

Christmas Island, one of Line Isls., C Pacific Ocean, part of Kiribati. Area 577 sq km (223 sq mi); largest atoll in the Pacific. Produces copra. Sovereignty disputed by US.

Christmas rose, *see* HELLEBORE.

Christopher, St (Gk., =Christ bearer), possibly a Christian martyr of Asia Minor (3rd cent.). Legendary carrier of infant Jesus over a river, sins of the world borne by Jesus making burden almost impossible. Patron saint of travellers, often represented on medallions.

chromatography, method of analysis or separation of chemical mixtures by allowing solution of mixture to flow through column of adsorbent material. Components are adsorbed in different layers, appearing as distinct bands or spots.

chromium (Cr), hard white metallic element; at. no. 24, at. wt. 51.996. Occurs as chrome iron ore (chromite); obtained by reducing oxide with aluminium. Used in manufacture of stainless steel and as protective coating on steel.

chromosome, microscopic thread-like structure found in nucleus of living cells. Consists of linear arrangement of genes which control hereditary characteristics of organism; DNA is basic constituent. Body cells in each species contain same number of chromosomes, usually occurring in pairs. There are normally 46 in human cells.

chromosphere, *see* SUN.

Chronicles 1 and **2,** in OT, books detailing history of David, thus paralleling and supplementing Kings 1 and 2. Incl. detailed descriptions of worship in the Temple.

chronometer, highly accurate clock, used esp. at sea to determine longitude. First successful marine chronometer constructed by John Harrison (1761).

chrysanthemum, genus of annual or perennial herbs of daisy family. Native to Orient, but widely cultivated. Late blooming red, yellow, or white flowers.

chub, fish of carp family. Species incl. *Leuciscus cephalus,* European freshwater fish.

Chungking, city of Szechwan prov., SC China on jct. of Yangtze-Chialing rivers. Pop 3,500,000. Major commercial, indust. centre; shipyards; produces steel, motor vehicles, textiles. Cap. of China during Sino-Japanese War (1937). Former treaty port, opened 1891.

Churchill, John, *see* MARLBOROUGH.

Churchill, Lord Randolph Henry Spencer (1849-95), British statesman. Drafted Conservative policy for increased democracy, but resigned (1886) as chancellor of the exchequer over high military expenditure. His son, **Sir Winston Leonard Spencer Churchill** (1874-1965), was PM (1940-5, 1951-5). Journalist and soldier before election to Parliament (1900), he headed Admiralty ministry (1911-15) until failure of Dardanelles campaign in WWI discredited him. Served in Lloyd George's govt. (1917-21), Conservative chancellor of the exchequer (1924-9). Regained influence by opposing 'appeasement' policies towards Germany and replaced Neville Chamberlain at head of wartime coalition govt. Became symbol of British resistance during WWII; attended series of international conferences (Yalta, Potsdam, *etc*) to oversee settlement of the War. After 1945 leader of the Opposition until returned to power in 1951; retired 1955. Written works incl. *The Second World War* (6 vols., 1948-53), for which he was awarded Nobel Prize for Literature (1953).

Churchill: 1, river of WC Canada. Rises in

NW Saskatchewan, flows E 1600 km (1000 mi) through Manitoba to Hudson Bay. Main tributary, Beaver R. H.e.p. at Island Falls. **2,** river of S Labrador, E Canada. Flows 970 km (*c* 600 mi) from Grand Falls to L. Melville; Churchill Falls is site of one of world's largest h.e.p. plants. Formerly called Hamilton R.

Church of England, *see* ENGLAND, CHURCH OF.

Church of Scotland, *see* SCOTLAND, CHURCH OF.

Chu Teh (*c* 1886-1976), Chinese military and political leader. With Mao Tse-tung led the Long March (1934-5). Commanded Chinese Communist forces during WWII and ensuing civil war. Appointed deputy chairman of People's Republic 1949. Denounced during 1967 'cultural revolution'.

Chuvash, auton. republic of EC RSFSR, USSR; in middle Volga valley. Area *c* 18,300 sq km (7070 sq mi); pop. 1,293,000; cap. Cheboksary. Wooded steppeland; main occupations agric. and forestry; notable woodworking.

CIA, *see* CENTRAL INTELLIGENCE AGENCY.

cicada, any 4-winged insect of Cicadidae family of warm areas. Eggs laid in holes bored in twigs or plant stems. Males make loud noise by vibrating tymbal organ.

Cicero, Marcus Tullius (106-43 BC), Roman orator, statesman. Appointed consul (63) in opposition to CATILINE. Exposed Catiline's conspiracy to seize power by force in 4 famous orations. Sided with Pompey during civil war; pardoned by Caesar. Attacked Antony in 2 *Philippics*; on reconciliation of Octavian and Antony he was executed on orders of Antony. Famous for series of letters, giving picture of Roman life. Philosophical and rhetorical works are masterpieces of Latin prose.

Cid, El, *see* DÍAZ DE VIVAR, RODRIGO.

cider, fermented apple juice containing from 4% to 7% alcohol. Major areas of production are Normandy and Brittany in France, Norfolk and SW of England.

cigar, compact roll of tobacco leaves for smoking. Indians of West Indies and parts of South America smoked cured tobacco leaves in pre-Columbian times; cigar smoking was introduced into Europe in late 16th cent. Cigars have been machine-made since *c* 1900 but finest cigars, are hand-made.

cigarette, roll of finely cut tobacco wrapped in thin paper. Popular tobaccos are those grown in Virginia, Georgia, the Carolinas in US, and in Turkey, Syria and Greece. Cigarette smoking has grown enormously in popularity in 20th cent. but its links with lung cancer, bronchitis, heart disease have led to anti-smoking campaigns.

Cilicia, region of Asia Minor, in SE Turkey between Taurus Mts. and Mediterranean.

Cimabue, Giovanni, orig. Cenni di Pepo (*c* 1240-*c* 1302), Italian painter. Regarded as founder of modern painting. Forms link between Byzantine style and more realistic style of early Renaissance. Works incl. frescoes, mosaics.

cinchona, genus of tropical South American trees from the bark of which quinine and related medicinal alkaloids are obtained. Widely cultivated in Asia and East Indies.

Cincinnati, city of SW Ohio, US; on Ohio R. Pop. 1,626,000. Transport jct., commercial centre. Industs. incl. machine tools, chemical mfg., meat packing. Founded 1788; focus of shipping in 19th cent.

Cincinnatus, Lucius Quinctius (*fl* 5th cent. BC), Roman soldier. Appointed dictator (458 BC) he defeated the Aequi, then resumed life as a farmer 16 days later.

cinema, art and business of making films. Nineteenth cent. developments in camera, film, projectors resulted in public screening by 1896. Film-making in US at first estab. in New York, with Hollywood becoming centre after 1913. Films were silent, accompanied by piano or organ, until *The Jazz Singer* (1927) introduced dialogue. Colour perfected with Technicolor (1932). Genres of Hollywood's 'golden age' (1930s and 1940s) incl. westerns, musicals, detective thrillers. Post-war developments incl. Italian social realism (late 1940s), *nouvelle vague* (France, late 1950s).

cineraria, ornamental blooming plants of genus *Senecio*. Varieties incl. popular garden plant, dusty miller, and greenhouse *S. cruentus*.

cinnabar (HgS), mercury ore mineral. Heavy, red or brown in colour; consists of mercuric sulphide.

cinnamon, sweet spice from dried inner bark of E Indian evergreen tree, *Cinnamomum zeylanicum*, used in cookery and medicine.

Creeping cinquefoil

cinquefoil, plant of genus *Potentilla* of rose family, with yellow or white flowers and fruit like small, dry strawberry. Most species are perennial herbs from N temperate and subarctic regions.

Cinque Ports, originally ports of Hastings, Romney, Hythe, Dover, Sandwich, S England. From 11th cent. given extensive Crown privileges for supplying warships. Winchelsea, Rye, others added later.

circulation (blood), *see* BLOOD VESSELS; HEART; LUNGS.

Cirencester, urban dist. of Gloucestershire, W England. Pop. 13,000. Agric. market. Roman *Corinium,* remains incl. amphitheatre. Has ruined 12th-cent. abbey.

cirrhosis, degenerative disease of liver, marked by excessive formation of fibrous scar tissue. Often caused by chronic alcoholism or malnutrition.

cirrus cloud, *see* CLOUD.

Cistercians, in RC church, monks of order founded (1098) by St Robert of Molesme and St Stephen Harding. Derived from Benedictine order, stressed asceticism. Influential in introducing new agric. techniques in Europe. *See* TRAPPISTS.

citric acid, soluble crystalline organic acid, found in lemons, oranges, *etc.* Obtained by fermentation of glucose. Used in flavouring effervescent drinks.

citrus, genus of evergreen trees and shrubs of family Rutaceae, native to Asia. Bear oranges, lemons, limes, citron, grapefruit, *etc.*

Ciudad Real, town of C Spain, cap. of Ciudad Real prov. Pop. 42,000. Agric. market, textile mfg., brandy distilling. Founded 13th cent.; Gothic cathedral.

African civet

civet, small cat-like carnivore of Viverridae family of Africa, SE Asia. Possesses scent producing glands, secretion used in perfume mfg.

civil disobedience, non-violent opposition to law or govt. policy by refusing to comply with it, usually on the grounds of conscience. Advocated by M.L. King while leading black civil rights movement in US (1950s, 1960s). More extreme form of opposition pursued by GANDHI in Indian struggle for independence.

civil engineering, branch of ENGINEERING dealing with planning, designing and construction of *eg* bridges, harbours, tunnels. Also incl. alteration of landscape to suit particular needs.

civil law, body of codified law governing individual's private rights, distinct from public and CRIMINAL LAW. Based on Roman law, esp. as laid down in *Corpus juris civilis* and revived 11th-12th cent. Adopted by continental Europe, Latin America, some Asian states. Most English-speaking countries have COMMON LAW.

civil rights, rights guaranteed to individual by law. Universal Declaration of Human Rights, passed (1948) by UN, incl. list of basic civil rights which should be available to all people in world. In US, set out in 13th, 14th, 15th and 19th Amendments to Constitution. Extended by acts of Congress to give minority groups, esp. blacks, equal rights. Four acts passed 1866-75, further three in 1957, 1960, 1964, latter three as result of civil rights movement's opposition to racial discrimination. Voting Rights Act (1965), originally aimed at protection of blacks' voting rights, extended to foreign-language minorities (1975). Feminists have since taken advantage of 1964 Civil Rights Act's provisions on employment, *etc.* In UK, Race Relations Acts (1965, 1968) set up Race Relations Board, to which cases of discrimination made illegal by acts can be referred. Equal Pay Act (1970), Sex Discrimination Act (1975) gave women rights in employment, education, services.

civil service, body of those employed by central govt. other than those in armed forces, judiciary. In UK entry has been by examination since 1855.

Civil War, in English history, conflict (1642-6, 1648) between supporters of Charles I (Royalists or Cavaliers) and of Parliament (Roundheads). Struggle was culmination of Parliament's attempt to limit king's powers, *eg* by PETITION OF RIGHT (1628); central to dispute was Charles' belief in divine right to rule as opposed to Parliament's legislative rights, esp. over taxation. King was supported by majority of nobles, Catholics, and Anglicans, and Parliament by merchants, gentry, Puritan movement and initially by Scottish Presbyterians. Parliamentary forces, organized (1644-5) into New Model Army, gained decisive victories at Marston Moor (1644), Naseby (1645) under CROMWELL and Fairfax. First phase of war ended with king's surrender to Scots (1646). Second phase, following king's escape and Scottish intervention on his side, ended with Cromwell's victory at Preston (1648).

Civil War, in US history, conflict (1861-5) between Union (Northern states) and Confederacy (Southern states). Causes incl. disagreement over prohibition of slavery in W territs. (*see* KANSAS-NEBRASKA BILL), also issue of states' rights. Southern states seceded from Union (1860-1), during which time LINCOLN was elected president; fighting started with Confederates firing on Fort Sumter (April, 1861). Early Southern successes, esp. under R.E. LEE, reversed in Gettysburg campaign (June-July, 1863). Gradual Union military ascendancy under U.S. GRANT culminated in retreat of Southern troops towards Richmond and Sherman's advance into Georgia (May-Sept. 1864). Lee eventually surrendered at Appomattox Courthouse (April, 1865). Union victory marred by assassination of Lincoln, whose EMANCIPATION PROCLAM-

ATION (1862) abolishing slavery was upheld; seceding states were readmitted to Union under RECONSTRUCTION.

Civitavecchia, town of Latium, WC Italy, on Tyrrhenian Sea. Pop. 38,000. Port of Rome from 1st cent. AD; fishing, cement. Citadel designed by Michelangelo.

Clackmannanshire, former county of Scotland, now in Central region. Ochil Hills in N; plain of R. Forth in S. Coalmining, brewing, distilling. Co. town was **Clackmannan,** pop. 2000.

clam, one of various bivalve molluscs, living in sand or mud. Round clam, *Venus mercenaria,* of NW Atlantic coast, common edible species.

clan, form of social group whose members trace descent from common ancestor. Term originally used in Scottish Highlands but extended to similar groups elsewhere. The clan includes several families but traces descent through one line only and is exogamous.

Clare or **Clara, St** (*c* 1193-1253), Italian nun. Disciple of St Francis of Assisi, founded order of Franciscan nuns, 'Poor Clares'.

Clare, John (1793-1864), English poet. Known for *Poems Descriptive of Rural Life and Scenery* (1820), *The Shepherd's Calendar* (1827) on changing countryside, vanishing customs. Went insane in middle age, died in asylum.

Clare, county of Munster prov., W Irish Republic. Area 3188 sq km (1231 sq mi); pop. 85,000; co. town Ennis. Hilly in E, N; rugged coast. Many bogs, lakes; low-lying, fertile along Shannon estuary. Agric., salmon fishing; prehist. remains.

Clarendon, Edward Hyde, 1st Earl of (1609-74), English statesman. After death of Charles I, became Charles II's chief adviser in exile. Appointed lord chancellor at Restoration (1660), favoured religious toleration; later, however, enforced Clarendon Code (1661-5), statutes strengthening Church of England. Lived in exile after dismissal (1667). Wrote *History of the Rebellion.*

clarinet, single-reed woodwind instrument with cylindrical bore, invented late 17th cent. Usually pitched in B flat and A. Occasionally used as a solo instrument.

Clark, Jim (1937-68), Scottish racing driver. Twice world champion (1963, 1965). Died in crash at Hockenheim circuit.

Clark, Kenneth Mackenzie Clark, Lord (1903-), British art historian. His writings incl. *Leonardo da Vinci* (1939), *Landscape into Art* (1949), and *Civilisation* (1970), based on popular lecture series for television.

class, social, *see* SOCIAL CLASS.

Classicism, in the arts, adherence to qualities regarded as characteristic of ancient Greece, Rome, incl. rationality, restraint, formal precision. *See* ROMANTICISM.

classification, in biology, systematic grouping of animals and plants into categories according to structural similarities and evolutionary relationships. Broadest division is into 2 kingdoms, Plantae (plants) and Animalia (animals); 3rd kingdom, Protista, consisting of all protozoans, algae, fungi and bacteria, is sometimes used. Kingdoms are divided into 6 taxa: phylum (equivalent in botany is division), class, order, family, genus, species (from most to least inclusive). Species is smallest unit of classification, usually defined as those animals or plants capable of interbreeding only among themselves. Closely related species are grouped into same genus. Binomial (two-part) Latinized nomenclature used in international scientific descriptions of animals employs genus name, whose initial letter is capitalized, followed by species (specific) name, uncapitalized. Man belongs to species *Homo sapiens,* genus *Homo,* family Hominidae, order Primates, class Mammalia, phylum Chordata.

Claude Lorraine, pseud. of Claude Gellée (1600-82), French painter. Famous for his poetic treatment of landscape, depicting mythical seaports and country around Rome.

Claudius I (10 BC-AD 54), Roman emperor (AD 41-54). Nephew of Tiberius, succeeded Caligula as emperor through support of Praetorian guard. Reign marked by territ. expansion; made Britain a province (43). Poisoned, prob. at instigation of wife Agrippina, who persuaded him to accept her own son Nero as his heir.

Clausius, Rudolf Julius Emanuel (1822-88), German mathematician, physicist. Developed concept of entropy and introduced 2nd law of THERMODYNAMICS. Contributed to kinetic theory of gases.

Claverhouse, John Graham of, *see* DUNDEE, 1ST VISCOUNT.

clavichord, small keyboard instrument, developed in 15th cent. Small tangents (blades) of brass, activated by keys, press against strings, simultaneously sounding them and stopping them.

Clay, Cassius, *see* ALI, MUHAMMAD.

clay, fine-grained earth, consisting mainly of hydrous aluminium silicate. Sticky and plastic when wet, hardens when dry or fired. Used for making bricks, tiles, pottery, drainage pipes.

Cleanthes (*c* 300-220 BC), Greek philosopher. *See* STOICISM.

cleft palate, congenital defect caused by failure of 2 halves of palate to unite; often associated with divided or hare lip. Repair may be effected by surgery carried out in infancy.

cleg, *see* HORSEFLY.

clematis, genus of perennial plants and woody vines of the buttercup family usually with brightly coloured flowers.

Clemenceau, Georges (1841-1929), French statesman, premier (1906-9, 1917-20). Headed coalition govt. that helped secure victory in WWI. Opposed President Wilson in post-war settlement at Versailles (1919); resigned amidst criticism for his moderate stand towards Germany.

Clement VII, orig. Giulio de' Medici (1478-1534), Italian churchman, pope (1523-34). Supported Francis I of France against Emperor Charles V, who besieged Rome (1527) and imprisoned him. Refused to sanction Henry VIII's divorce from Catherine of Aragon.

Cleopatra (69-30 BC), Egyptian queen. At age of 17, became joint ruler with brother, Ptolemy XII. Deprived of power, she was reinstated with aid of Julius Caesar, by whom she bore a son in Rome. Returned to Egypt after Caesar's death, later to become mistress of Mark Antony. Their union was opposed by Octavian, who destroyed their fleet at Actium (31 BC). They retired into Egypt and both committed suicide.

Cleopatra's Needles, popular name for 2 ancient Egyptian obelisks in red granite, originally erected at Heliopolis (*c* 1475 BC). Later removed to Alexandria (*c* 14 BC), one was presented to Britain (1878), the other to America (1880); they stand on Thames Embankment, London, and in Central Park, New York.

Clermont-Ferrand, city of SC France, in Massif Central, cap. of Puy-de-Dôme dept. Pop. 225,000. Rubber mfg. centre, metal goods; univ. (1808). Hist. cap. of Auvergne; scene of church council (1095) leading to the Crusades. Gothic cathedral (13th cent.).

Cleveland, [Stephen] Grover (1837-1908), American statesman, Democratic president (1885-9, 1893-7).

Cleveland, county of NE England. Area 583 sq km (225 sq mi); pop. 568,000; admin. hq. Middlesbrough. Centred on R. Tees. Iron, steel mfg.; heavy indust. Created 1974 incl. parts of N Yorkshire, Durham.

Cleveland, port of NE Ohio, US; on L. Erie at mouth of Cuyahoga R. Pop. 2,902,000; state's largest city. Majoı iron ore shipping centre; steel mfg., oil refining, chemicals mfg. First settled 1796.

climate, average meteorological conditions of a place or region, taken over a period of years. Dependent on many factors, *eg* latitude, nearness to sea. Studied as climatology.

Clive, Robert, Baron Clive of Plassey (1725-74), British soldier, administrator. In military service of East India Co., won series of victories, notably at Arcot (1751), Calcutta, Plassey (1757). Consolidated British power in India, ousting French. As governor of Bengal promoted reform. On return to England (1767), charged with accepting bribes; acquitted but committed suicide.

closed shop, organization hiring only labour union members as employees, either throughout or for particular jobs. Subject of indust. and political conflict in US and UK.

cloud, mass of water droplets or ice crystals suspended in the atmosphere. Formed by condensation of water vapour, normally at considerable height. The 3 primary cloud types are *cirrus, cumulus, stratus.* International classification now identifies 10 basic forms, distinguished by height. High clouds (over *c* 6100 m/20,000 ft) incl. *cirrus, cirrostratus, cirrocumulus.* Intermediate clouds (*c* 2000 m/6500 ft to *c* 6100 m/20,000 ft) incl. *altocumulus, altostratus.* Low clouds (below *c* 2000 m/6500 ft) incl. *stratus, nimbostratus, stratocumulus.* Clouds growing vertically upwards incl. *cumulus, cumulonimbus.* Certain clouds are associated with particular weather conditions, *eg nimbostratus* with continuous rain or snow, *cumulus* with fair weather, *cumulonimbus* with thunderstorms.

cloud chamber, in physics, enclosed chamber containing supersaturated vapour used to detect paths of charged particles. Particle produces ions as it passes through chamber; path seen as row of droplets formed by condensation of liquid on these ions.

clouded leopard, *Neofelis nebulosa,* nocturnal carnivore of cat family of SE Asian forests. Arboreal, with long heavy tail.

clove, pungent dried flower bud of evergreen shrub, *Eugenia caryophyllata,* of myrtle family, native to East Indies. Used whole for pickling and flavouring, ground for confectionery; oil used medicinally.

clover, any plant of genus *Trifolium* of Leguminosae family. Low-growing trifoliate plant with small flowers in dense heads. Widespread in temperate regions. Used as forage crop and to allow NITROGEN FIXATION in soil.

Clovis I (*c* 466-511), Frankish king (481-511). Son of Childeric I; founded Merovingian monarchy in Gaul and SW Germany. Converted to Christianity (496), estab. court at Paris; thus laid foundations of Charlemagne's empire and modern France.

club foot, hereditary deformity of the foot, in which the sole is turned inwards and the heel drawn up. May be cured by manipulation or surgery.

Cluj (Hung. *Kolozsvár),* city of WC Romania. Pop. 262,000. Commercial, indust. centre of Transylvania. Prob. dates from Roman times. Gothic church (14th cent.); seat of 4 bishoprics.

Cluny, town of Burgundy, E France. Pop. 4000. Grew around large Benedictine abbey (founded 910) which became major religious and cultural centre in Middle Ages.

Clwyd, county of NE Wales. Area 2425 sq km (936 sq mi); pop. 382,000; admin. hq. Mold. Created 1974, incl. former Denbighshire, Flintshire.

Clyde, river of W Scotland. Flows 170 km (105 mi) from S Lanarkshire via fruit-growing and heavy indust. areas (Glasgow, Clydebank) to Firth of Clyde. Has shipbuilding industs., ports, tourist resorts.

Clydebank, town of Strathclyde region, W Scotland, on R. Clyde. Pop. 48,000. Shipyards.

Clytemnestra, in Greek myth, daughter of Leda and Tyndareus. Unfaithful wife of Agamemnon, whom she murdered on his return from Troy; lover of Aegisthus. Mother by Agamemnon of Orestes, Electra and Iphigenia. Killed with Aegisthus when Orestes avenged his father's death.

coal, dark brown or black combustible mineral. Occurs in bands or seams in sedimentary rock. Formed over millions of years by heating and compaction of partly decayed vegetable matter; various stages, in order of increasing carbon content, are peat, lignite, bituminous coal, anthracite. Coals occur from Devonian period on, with max. in Carboniferous. Used as fuel, also in production of coke, coal gas, plastics. Major sources in US, UK, France, Australia, China, USSR.

coal gas, gas made by destructive distillation of coal. Main constituents are hydrogen (50%), methane (30%). Used for heating, illumination, being replaced in UK by natural gas. Poisonous, as it contains carbon monoxide.

coal tar, thick black liquid obtained by destructive distillation of coal. Distillation and purification yield such compounds as xylene, toluene, benzene, phenol. Pitch remains as a residue.

coastguard, govt. organization employed to defend nation's coasts, aid vessels in distress, prevent smuggling, *etc.* In UK was estab. after Napoleonic Wars to prevent smuggling, but now concerned mainly with lifesaving.

Coast Mountains, range of W British Columbia, Canada. Run parallel to Pacific Coast for 1610 km (1000 mi). Rise to highest point at Mt. Waddington 4042 m (13,260 ft).

Coati

coati, any of genus *Nasua* of arboreal mammals, related to raccoon, found in Central and South America. Long snout; omnivorous.

cobalt (Co), hard silvery-white metallic element; at. no. 27, at. wt. 58.93. Occurs combined with arsenic and sulphur; obtained by reducing oxide with carbon or aluminium. Used in alloys; radioactive cobalt 60 used to treat cancer. Compounds used in pigments (esp. blue).

Cobbett, William (1762-1835), English political journalist. Campaigned for social, economic reform in his *Weekly Political Register* (1802-35). Best known for *Rural Rides* (1830) describing conditions in the country.

Cobden, Richard (1804-65), British politician. With John Bright, leader of Anti-Corn Law League; fought for repeal of Corn Laws, achieved (1846) under Peel.

Coblenz, *see* KOBLENZ.

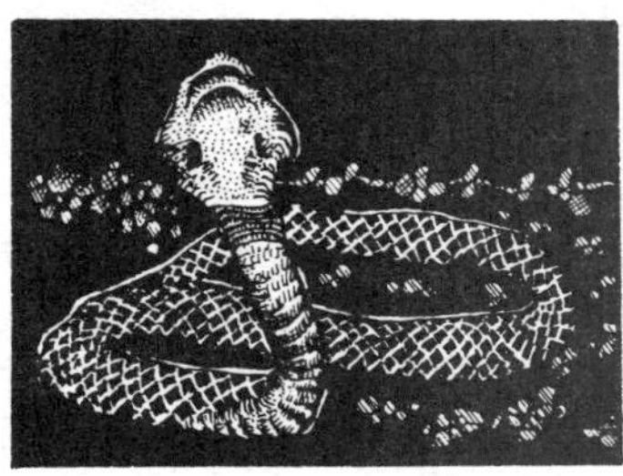

Indian cobra

cobra, highly venomous snake of Elapidae family, found in Africa and Asia. Opens hood of skin around neck when angered. Largest species is king cobra, *Naja hannah,* reaching 5.5 m/18 ft.

coca, tropical South American shrub, *Erythroxylon coca,* dried leaves of which are the source of cocaine.

cocaine, white crystalline alkaloid obtained from leaves of coca plant. Formerly used as local anaesthetic, it is a habit-forming drug, causing temporary elation and hallucinations.

Cochin, seaport of Kerala state, SW India, on Arabian Sea. Pop. 438,000. Exports coconut products. Chief port of former princely state of Cochin. Earliest European settlement in India (1503) following visit of Vasco da Gama.

Cochin China, former French colony of SE Asia. Contained within VIETNAM after 1954.

cockatoo, easily domesticated crested parrot of Australia, New Guinea, Philippines. Plumage mainly white, edged with yellow or pink.

cockchafer, *Melolontha melolontha,* European species of beetle with black head, thorax and reddish-brown wing cases.

Cockcroft, Sir John Douglas, (1897-1967), British physicist. With E.T.S. Walton first to split nucleus of the atom (1932). Shared Nobel prize for physics (1951). Director of UKAEA research establishment, Harwell (1946-58).

Cockerell, Sir Christopher, *see* HOVERCRAFT.

cock-fighting, sport of setting trained cocks, usually bearing metal spurs, to fight against each other. Can be traced back as far as 12th cent. in England. Banned in Britain and America in mid-19th cent. Still popular in parts of Asia and Latin America.

cockle, one of group of edible bivalve molluscs, genus *Cardium.* Body enclosed by 2 heart-shaped ribbed shells with scalloped edges.

cockroach, any insect of suborder Blattaria, found worldwide, esp. in tropics. Flat, brownish body, long antennae; emits unpleasant odour. Omnivorous, pest of foodstores. *Blatta orientalis* is cosmopolitan domestic species.

cocoa or **cacao,** *Theobroma cacao,* spreading tree of Sterculia family, found in forests of South America. Grows to av. height of 10 m/30 ft and has large, round fruits each containing 20-40 seeds or beans (cacao). These when roasted and powdered (cocoa) are used in chocolate and as a beverage.

coconut, *Cocos nucifera,* tropical tree bearing large, brown, hard-shelled fruit. Edible white kernel (copra) and 'milk' used in confectionery. Yields oil used in soap; husk provides fibre for matting; leaves used as roof covering.

Cocos or **Keeling Islands,** group of 27 small coral isls., S of Sumatra; under Australian admin. since 1955. Area 13 sq km (5 sq mi); pop. 600. Discovered (1609) by Captain Keeling of East India Co. Exports copra.

Cocteau, Jean (1889-1963), French author, artist, film director. Avant-garde works deal with theme of poet as defier of destiny, risking destruction. Known for ballets for Diaghilev; novels, *eg Les Enfants terribles* (1929, film 1950); plays, *eg La Machine infernale* (1934); films, *eg Orphée* (1950); autobiog., poetry.

Cod, Cape, narrow sandy penin. of SE Massachusetts, US. Famous holiday resort, fishing area. Pilgrim Fathers landed here (1620).

cod, food fish of Gadidae family of N Atlantic, N Pacific. Atlantic cod, *Gadus morhua,* found esp. off coasts of Newfoundland and Iceland, commercially important. Cod-liver oil source of vitamins A, D.

codeine, alkaloid drug derived from opium and similar to morphine. Used medicinally to relieve pain and suppress coughs.

Cody, William Frederick (1846-1917), American showman. Known as 'Buffalo Bill'. Worked as frontier scout. After 1883 toured US, Europe with his 'Wild West Show'.

coeducation, system of education in which students of both sexes are instructed together. Early examples in Scotland and American colonies (17th cent.). Elsewhere, widespread coeducation, esp. in univs. and colleges, did not come until early 20th cent.

Coelacanthidae (coelacanths), order of primitive marine fish, known from fossils of Devonian period. Believed to be ancestors of land animals. Living specimen of genus *Latimeria* discovered (1938) off E Africa; other species found since then.

Coelenterata (coelenterates), phylum of aquatic, mainly marine, animals. Life cycle generally involves alternation between asexual sedentary polyp and free-swimming sexual medusa (jellyfish).

coffee, *Coffea arabica,* evergreen shrub native to Arabia, grown extensively in Brazil, Africa and Asia. Seeds roasted and ground to make beverage. Unknown in Europe until 17th cent.

Coggan, [Frederick] Donald (1909-), English churchman, archbishop of Canterbury (1974-80).

Cognac, town of W France, on R. Charente. Pop. 23,000. Produces famous brandy.

cognac, *see* BRANDY.

Coimbra, city of C Portugal. Pop. 46,000. Wine, grain market. Univ. (1537), 2 cathedrals. Flourished from Roman times; cap. of Portugal 1139-1260.

coins, *see* NUMISMATICS.

Coke, Sir Edward (1552-1634), English jurist, statesman. Championed Parliament, common law, principles of personal liberty against James I's assertion of royal prerogative. Leader of parliamentary opposition from 1620, under Charles I drew up Petition of Right (1628). Wrote *Institutes,* a legal classic.

Coke, Thomas William, Earl of Leicester of Holkham (1754-1842), English agriculturist. Remembered for systematic improvement of methods of arable farming and of breeding livestock.

coke, residue from destructive distillation of coal; contains *c* 80% carbon. Used as smokeless fuel and in preparation of metals from their ores in blast furnaces.

cola or **kola,** *Cola acuminata,* tree of W tropical Africa, West Indies and Brazil. Nuts yield caffeine and extract used in flavouring soft drinks.

Colbert, Jean Baptiste (1619-83), French statesman. Chief adviser to Louis XIV after 1661, leading exponent of mercantilist policies to develop nation's wealth. Protected indust. with subsidies and tariffs, price regulation. Had road and canal network built, encouraged trade and colonization, increased naval power.

Colchester, town of Essex, SE England, on R. Colne. Pop. 76,000. Market town; has Univ. of Essex (1961). Ancient British cap., Roman *Camulodunum,* part of town wall remains; has Norman castle.

cold, common, acute inflammation of mucous membranes of nose and throat; believed to be caused by any of *c* 50 different viruses. Most common human ailment. Lack of immunity to common cold prob. caused by new strains of virus developing from earlier ones.

Cold War, economic and political rivalry between nations, without actual military conflict. Popularly used for post-WWII struggle between Communist nations and West.

cole, *see* KALE.

Coleoptera, *see* BEETLE.

Coleridge, Samuel Taylor (1772-1834), English poet, critic. Estab. English Romanticism in publication, with Wordsworth, of *Lyrical Ballads* (1798) incl. 'The Rime of the Ancient Mariner'. Other works incl. 'Kubla Khan' (1816), philosophical, critical reflections in *Biographia Literaria* (1817).

Colet, John (*c* 1467-1519), English humanist. Noted for his exegesis of Pauline theology at Oxford (1497-1504). Dean of St Paul's (1505); refounded and endowed St Paul's School (1509).

Colette, [Sidonie Gabrielle] (1873-1954), French novelist. Known for analytical studies of women, *eg* 'Claudine' series (1900-3) of semi-autobiog. novels written with 1st husband, and for *Chéri* (1920), *Gigi* (1945).

Coll, isl. of Inner HEBRIDES.

collage, art form in which bits of paper, cloth or other objects are stuck to a canvas or other surface. Much used by cubists, and by Matisse in later works.

collar bone or **clavicle,** part of shoulder extending from shoulder blade (scapula) to breastbone (sternum).

collective bargaining, in indust. relations, term for negotiations between employer and employees' representatives, usually labour union, to agree pay, conditions of work, union rights.

collective farming, agric. cooperative movement. In USSR, Stalin instituted (1929) *kolkhoz* method in which land, farm equipment were pooled and profits shared among members. Although almost all Soviet agric. was collectivized by 1938, state farms, paying the workers, were later introduced. Chinese cooperatives place greater emphasis on communal living and encourage participation of indust. workers. Israeli kibbutzim also place great emphasis on communal living.

college, institution of higher education. Generally, smaller in size and spread of curriculum than UNIVERSITY; several colleges may constitute university. Earliest were in Paris (12th cent.), preceding famous centres of learning at Oxford and Cambridge univs. Industrial Revolution led to need for scientific and technical training (technical colleges); late 19th cent. brought colleges of education.

collie, breed of long-haired sheepdog, developed in Scotland. Long narrow head; stands 56-66 cm/22-26 in. at shoulder. Kelpie is Australian sheepdog developed from collie or dingo-collie cross.

Collingwood, Cuthbert Collingwood, Baron (1750–1810), British admiral. Distinguished himself at St Vincent (1797) and took command at Trafalgar (1805) after Nelson's death.

Collins, Michael (1890-1922), Irish Sinn Fein leader. Organized guerrilla warfare against British. With Arthur Griffith, estab. (1921) Irish Free State. Briefly (1922) head of state and army, before he was assassinated.

Collins, [William] Wilkie (1824-89), English novelist, associate of Dickens. Known for thrillers *The Woman in White* (1860), *The Moonstone* (1868), latter regarded as 1st English detective novel.

colloid, solid, liquid or gaseous substance made up of very small insoluble particles that remain in suspension in solid, liquid or gas medium of different matter. Examples incl. solutions of starch and albumen. Suspension of colloidal particles in gas is called an aerosol, *eg* fog and smoke.

Colmar (Ger. *kolmar*), town of Alsace, E France, cap. of Haut-Rhin dept. Pop. 63,000. Major textile mfg. centre, wine trade. Free imperial city from 1226, annexed by France (1681). Many medieval buildings.

colobus monkey, genus of slender African monkeys, usually with long black and white fur, and no thumbs. Treetop dwelling; diet of leaves, fruit.

Cologne *(Köln)*, city of NW West Germany, on R. Rhine. Pop. 981,000. River port, railway jct.; indust., banking centre; univ. (1388). Perfume mfg., incl. 'eau-de-Cologne'. Roman *Colonia Agrippinensis*; powerful medieval archbishopric, Hanseatic League member from 1201. Gothic cathedral (begun 1248). Badly damaged in WWII.

Colombia, republic of NW South America. Area 1,138,900 sq km (439,700 sq mi); pop. 25,645,000; cap. Bogotá. Language: Spanish. Religion: RC. Has Pacific and Caribbean coasts; Andes in W; tropical forests, grasslands in E; uninhabited lowland in interior. Chief rivers are Cauca, Magdalena. Coffee, bananas are chief crops; important mineral resources incl. platinum, oil. Spanish colony from 16th cent. Independence gained under Bolívar in 1819; known as New Granada until 1863. Panama seceded in 1903; civil war 1949-53.

Colombo, cap. and chief port of Sri Lanka. Pop. 607,000. Commercial centre; exports rubber, tea. Univ. (1870). Under Dutch control in 17th cent., ceded to British (1796). Site of Colombo Plan conference (1950), on Commonwealth-US aid to S and SE Asia.

colon, the large INTESTINE.

Colorado, state of WC US. Area 270,000 sq km (104,247 sq mi); pop. 2,583,000; cap. Denver. Mainly in Rocky Mts., mean alt. 2070 m (*c* 6800 ft), plains in E. Has sources of Rio Grande, Arkansas, Colorado rivers. Agric. incl. potato, sugar beet, alfalfa, wheat growing, stock raising. Coal, uranium, molybdenum mining. Part of Louisiana Purchase of 1803; had gold, silver strikes in 19th cent. Admitted to Union as 38th state (1876).

Colorado, two rivers of SW US, **1,** rises in Rocky Mts., N Colorado, flows SW 2334 km (1450 mi) through Utah, Arizona (Grand Canyon). Forms much of Californian border. Continues into Mexico to Gulf of California. Provides h.e.p. and irrigation from numerous dams, *eg* Hoover. **2,** rises in NW Texas, flows SE 1439 km (894 mi) to Gulf of Mexico. Also has several dams.

Colorado beetle or **potato beetle,** *Leptinotarsa decemlineata,* leaf-eating beetle originally of W North America, now found wherever potatoes cultivated. Yellow, with black stripes. Serious pest of potatoes, other garden vegetables.

Colorado Springs, town of C Colorado, US; at foot of Pikes Peak. Pop. 287,000. Health and holiday resort. Has US Airforce Academy.

Colosseum or **Coliseum,** largest amphitheatre of ancient Rome, built *c* AD 75-80. A 4-storied oval building, it held *c* 45,000 people on tiers around the arena. Still largely extant.

Colossians, Epistle to the, NT book, traditionally attributed to St Paul while in prison at Rome (*c* AD 62). Warns the church at Colossae of dangers of false teaching, asserts pre-eminence of Christ.

Colossus of Rhodes, bronze statue of sun god, Helios, which stood in Rhodes harbour. Built by Chares *c* 292-280 BC, it was *c* 30 m (100 ft) high. One of seven wonders of the ancient world, it was destroyed by an earthquake (224 BC).

colour, sensation resulting from stimulation of retina of the eye by light of certain wavelengths. Any colour can be produced by combining beams of primary colours, red, green and blue. Pigmented objects produce colour by absorbing certain wavelengths and reflecting others; primary pigment colours are red, yellow and blue.

colour blindness, inability to distinguish between certain colours, esp. red and green. Red-green form is a sex-linked character, being transmitted from women to their sons; thus it is much more common in men. *See* SEX CHROMOSOME.

Colt .45 army revolver (1873)

Colt, Samuel (1814-62), American inventor. Patented the revolving-breech pistol (1836) and set up a large arms factory at Hartford, Conn.

coltsfoot, *Tussilago farfara,* plant of daisy family. Common weed of N temperate regions. Large heart-shaped leaves, hairy, scaly stalk, yellow spring flower.

Columba or **Columcille, St** (*c* 521-97), Irish missionary. Estab. Celtic monasteries in Ireland at Derry, Durrow, Kells. Set up monastery on Iona (563) as centre for the conversion of N Scotland. Made extensive and successful missionary journeys among the Picts.

Columbia, cap. of South Carolina, US; on Congaree R. Pop. 365,000. Cultural, education centre. Agric. industs. esp. cotton, textile mills. Founded as cap. 1786.

Columbia, river of W US and Canada. Rises in Rocky Mts. (SE British Columbia). Flows 1950 km (*c* 1210 mi) to US border; then SW through Washington, which lower course separates from Oregon, before reaching Pacific. Snake R. is chief tributary. Supplies irrigation for surrounding agric. regions from Grand Coulee, Bonneville dams. Source of h.e.p.

Columbia, District of, *see* DISTRICT OF COLUMBIA.

columbine, plant of genus *Aquilegia* of buttercup family, incl. *c* 70 species found in temperate regions.

columbium, *see* NIOBIUM.

Columbus, Christopher, English form of Cristoforo Colombo (1451-1506), Italian navigator. Engaged for many years in Portuguese sea trade; sailed westward (1492) for Ferdinand and Isabella of Spain in *Santa María, Niña,* and *Pinta,* landing on Watling Isl. in Bahamas. On 3 subsequent voyages reached Leeward Isls., Puerto Rico, Cuba, Jamaica, Hispaniola, and American mainland from Orinoco to Panama, believed by him to be East Indies.

Columbus, cap. of Ohio, US; on Scioto R. Pop. 1,069,000. Indust. and transport centre; produces aircraft, car parts, mining machinery. Founded as state cap. 1812.

column, in architecture, slender upright structure generally consisting of cylindrical or polygonal shaft, with base and capital; used as a support or ornamental member in a building. Greeks perfected design of columns in temples, *eg* Parthenon. *See* ORDERS OF ARCHITECTURE.

Colwyn Bay, town of Clwyd, N Wales. Pop. 26,000. Seaside resort.

coma, state of complete and prolonged unconsciousness from which patient cannot be aroused. Caused by brain disturbance, *eg* injury, poisoning, lack of oxygen.

Comanche, North American Indian tribe. Separated from SHOSHONE and settled (*c* 1680) in S Texas and W Oklahoma. Nomadic plains warriors, fiercely opposed to white man. Greatly reduced by war and disease to *c* 1500 (1904), when confined to Oklahoma reserve.

Combination Acts (1799, 1800), in UK, laws outlawing trade unions. Unions went underground until laws were repealed 1824.

COMECON, *see* COUNCIL FOR MUTUAL ECONOMIC ASSISTANCE.

Comédie-Française, French national theatre in Paris estab. 1680 from a company of Molière's actors.

comedy, originally drama or narrative with happy ending and non-tragic theme (*eg* Dante's *Divine Comedy),* now usually given humorous treatment. In England, tradition goes back through Latin writers, *eg* Plautus, to Greek dramas of Aristophanes, Menander. In France, Molière combined *commedia dell'arte* with classical influence in Comedy of Manners, which developed in England into Restoration comedy (Congreve), and later into satirical character comedies of Goldsmith, Sheridan, Wilde; 20th-cent. social comedies written by G.B. Shaw, Noël Coward.

comet, heavenly body moving under influence of Sun. Consists of bright nucleus, surrounded by hazy gaseous mass (coma). When passing near Sun, tail of gaseous material may be formed, pointing away from Sun. Generally follows elongated elliptical orbit, returning at calculable intervals, *eg* Halley's comet.

Comintern (Communist International), also known as Third International, association of world Communist parties estab. by Lenin (1919). Leading members incl. Zinoviev, Trotsky, Radek, Bukharin. Founded to give leadership to more extreme elements of world socialist movements, dominated by Russian Communists. Anti-Comintern Pact formed (1936) by Germany and Japan. Dissolved 1943.

commedia dell'arte, Italian dramatic genre dating from 16th cent. Travelling actors improvised on stock characters (Harlequin, Scaramouche, *etc*). Conventions influenced Shakespeare, Jonson, Molière, de Vega, Goldoni, later developed into pantomime.

commerce, the buying and selling of goods, esp. on large scale, *eg* between countries. Carried on in ancient times around Mediterranean by Egyptians, Sumerians, Phoenicians. Crusades stimulated European trading aspirations, trade superiority eventually passing to cities of N Italy. Exploitation of New World by Spain gave her brief hegemony. The 17th, 18th cents. were marked by rivalry between Dutch, British and (later) French. Industrial Revolution gave Britain superiority in 19th cent. Recent developments incl. European Economic Community and growing trade between Communist and capitalist blocs. *See* MERCANTILISM, FREE TRADE.

commodity, in economics, term for anything which is limited in supply and thus has a value in exchange.

common law, law of nation based on custom, usage, and legal precedent. Distinct from but complementary to statute law. Important in England where it became estab. in 13th cent., influenced English-speaking countries.

Common Market, European, *see* EUROPEAN COMMUNITIES.

Commons, House of, *see* HOUSE OF COMMONS.

Commonwealth, govt. of England under Cromwell and Parliament (1649-60); *see also* PROTECTORATE.

Commonwealth, British, free association of UK and ex-colonies. Evolved from dominions, estab. as autonomous by Statute of WESTMINSTER (1931) after Imperial Conference (1926). Commonwealth Relations Office estab. 1947, with which Colonial Office was merged (1966). Member states incl. Canada, Australia, New Zealand, India, many African, Asian, Caribbean states. South Africa withdrew (1961), Pakistan (1972). Territs. dependent on UK incl. Hong Kong, Gibraltar, Bermuda.

Communion, Holy, *see* EUCHARIST.

Communism, Mount, highest peak of USSR, in Pamir Mts., Tadzhik SSR; height 7495 m (24,590 ft).

Communism, modern, international movement advocating revolutionary overthrow of capitalism (*see* MARXISM), arising out of Marx and Engels' *Communist Manifesto* (1848). Guided by principles of communal ownership of means of production, everyone receiving according to his need and working according to his capacity. Marxian Communism spread through founding of First INTERNATIONAL and rise of Social Democratic parties in Europe. Radical form taken (1903) in Russia when Bolsheviks, under Lenin, urged immediate violent revolution to overthrow CAPITALISM and estab. world socialist state. Bolsheviks triumphed in RUSSIAN REVOLUTION (1917). Stalin consolidated Communist power in USSR during 1930s. Soviet victory in WWII brought addition of E European satellites to Communist bloc. Links with China after estab. of Communist state (1949) under Mao Tse-tung; in early 1960s China's accusations of Soviet conciliation with West brought rift. Western powers involved in conflicts in attempts to contain spread of Communism, esp. Korea (1950-3), Vietnam (1965-73).

communism, social or economic system or theory in which property (esp. means of production) is held in common by all members of society, not by individuals. As theory of govt. and social reform, communism can be attributed to Plato who in *Republic* outlined society with communal property. In England, forms of communism manifested in Sir Thomas More's *Utopia* and the DIGGERS. Recent attempts based upon principles of communism incl. Israeli *kibbutzim*, 'drop-out' settlements in US. Movement tends toward agric. based communities, although modern COMMUNISM developed as reaction to capitalist exploitation following Industrial Revolution.

Communist Manifesto, *see* MARX, KARL.

Communist Party, a political organization based on principles of Communism, as developed by Marx and Engels; modified by Lenin, Stalin and others, dedicated to estab. state socialism. In USSR developed from Bolshevik-Menshevik split (1903), gained power during Russian Revolution (1917). Later centralized, wielding real power through CENTRAL COMMITTEE. In China founded 1921, developed under Mao Tse-tung; protracted struggle with Kuomintang, interrupted by WWII, ended with Communist triumph and estab. of People's Republic (1949). In Americas, Communist Party govts. incl. that under Castro in Cuba and short-lived one under Allende in Chile. Communist parties in West have attempted to gain power through electoral process (EUROCOMMUNISM) and trade union activities.

Como, town of Lombardy, N Italy, at S end of L. Como. Cap. of Como prov. Pop. 99,000. Tourist resort. Famous in Middle Ages for craftsmen (silk, *etc*). Marble cathedral, Gothic town hall.

Comoro Islands, republic in Indian Ocean, at N end of Mozambique Channel; comprise group of volcanic isls. Area 2170 sq km (838 sq mi); pop. 320,000; cap. Moroni. Language: French. Religions: Islam, Christianity. Produce vanilla, copra, cocoa, coffee. Formerly French overseas territ., became independent 1975.

company, limited, in UK, organization, public or private, and legally registered, formed to carry out activities (usually on profit basis). Each partner is liable under 1855 Limited Liabilities Act for only the amount of his investment. Act brought British practice in line with that of Continent. In US, corporations are functionally and legally similar.

compass, name given to 2 instruments: mathematical compass is used to draw circles and measure distance; magnetic compass is used to determine direction by allowing magnetic needle to swing on a pivot towards N Magnetic Pole.

competition, in economics, term for the degree to which the market can be influenced by buyers and sellers. Perfect competition is a theoretical model, in which many producers with no control over price produce goods which are sold to competing buyers. In fact, market limited by industrial cooperation, patents, *etc*. *See* MONOPOLY, SUPPLY AND DEMAND.

Compiègne, town of Ile-de-France, N France, on R. Oise. Pop. 33,000. Armistice of 1918 and French surrender of 1940 both signed in nearby forest.

complex, in psychology, idea or group of ideas arising in the mind as result of highly emotional experience, and repressed partly or wholly, as result of conflict with other ideas accepted by individual. Most famous example is Oedipus complex.

complex number, in mathematics, number expressed as formal sum $a + bi$, where a and b are real numbers and i is square root of -1. Complex numbers form an extension of real number system in which all polynomials have roots.

Compositae, largest and most highly advanced family of flowering plants. Characterized by flower heads composed of dense clusters of small flowers surrounded by a ring of small leaves, *eg* daisy, thistle, artichoke, chrysanthemum.

comprehensive education, system of state-financed education combining various types of SECONDARY SCHOOL, drawing pupils of all abilities from surrounding catchment area. *See* GRAMMAR SCHOOL.

Compton-Burnett, Dame Ivy (1892-1969), English novelist. Known for stylized, formal dialogue novels, *eg Elders and Betters* (1944), *Mother and Son* (1955).

computer, device which, by means of stored instructions and information, performs large numbers of calculations at great speed or may be used to compile, correlate and select data (data processing). Two types; digital, which processes information in numerical form, usually in BINARY SYSTEM, and analog, which represents information in terms of quantities (*eg* current or voltage) rather than by digital counting. Sequence of calculations controlled by program, *ie* series of precisely defined instructions fed into machine. Specialized programming 'languages' evolved to describe operations which machine will carry out. Early examples incl. calculating machines designed by Babbage (1834).

Comte, [Isidore] Auguste [Marie François Xavier] (1798-1857), French philosopher. Disciple of Saint-Simon. Founder of POSITIVISM. Delineated 3 stages (theological, metaphysical, positive) in all fields of knowledge; rejected metaphysics in favour of modern science.

Conakry or **Konakry,** cap. of Guinea, on Tombo Isl. Pop. 526,000. Admin., commercial centre; railway terminus and deepwater port, exports alumina, iron ore, bananas.

Conan Doyle, *see* DOYLE, SIR ARTHUR CONAN.

concentration camp, institution for detention of elements of population deemed dangerous by regime. Term first applied to British examples in Boer War. Used esp. by Germans during WWII against 'undesirables', *eg* Jews, Poles; notorious examples incl. Buchenwald, Dachau, Oswiecim.

Concepción, town of SC Chile, near mouth of Bío-Bío R. Pop. 513,000. Textile, leather, glass mfg. Export centre through port of Talcahuano. Major coalfields nearby. Founded 1550. Has suffered many earthquakes.

concertina, a form of accordion in which both sets of fingers operate buttons or studs while squeezing and expanding the bellows. Invented in 1829.

concerto, music for one or more soloists and orchestra, usually in 3 movements or sections. A *concerto grosso* features a group of instrumentalists with orchestra. A concerto for orchestra is a display piece to demonstrate virtuosity of the entire orchestra.

conch, marine mollusc, with spiral one-piece shell. Species incl. *Strombus gigas* of West Indies. Shell used as simple trumpet.

Concord, *see* BOSTON, Massachusetts.

Concord, cap. of New Hampshire, US; on Merrimack R. Pop. 30,000. Granite quarrying nearby; printing indust. Settled *c* 1725.

Concorde, first supersonic (Mach 2.2, 2160 kmph/1200 mph) passenger aircraft developed jointly by France and UK. Maiden flight, Toulouse (March, 1969). Services inaugurated (1976).

concrete, building material made of sand and gravel, bonded with cement; dries to form hard stone-like substance. May be strengthened by introducing steel rods (reinforced concrete). Used by Romans for construction of roads and buildings.

Modern concrete dates from discovery of portland cement in early 19th cent.

Condé, Louis [I] de Bourbon, Prince de (1530-69), French nobleman. Huguenot leader, led Protestant forces in religious wars of 1560s. Army defeated by Catholic forces, killed at Jarnac. His great-grandson, **Louis [II] de Bourbon, Prince de Condé** (1621-86), known as the 'Great Condé', won major battles during Thirty Years War. Led FRONDE uprising, defeated in battle of the Dunes by Turenne (1658). Pardoned by Louis XIV, later fought successfully for him against the Dutch.

condenser, in chemistry, device for condensing vapour into liquid, consisting of glass tubes cooled by air or water.

condenser, in electricity, *see* CAPACITOR.

condor, New World vulture, inhabiting high mountain regions. Black plumage with white markings on wings, neck. Two species: nearly extinct Californian condor, *Gymnogyps californianus,* and Andean condor, *Vultur gryphus* (wingspan *c* 3 m/10 ft).

conduction, thermal, transfer of heat from hotter parts of a medium to colder parts by passage of energy from particle to particle. In metals, heat flow is largely due to motion of energetic free electrons towards colder regions.

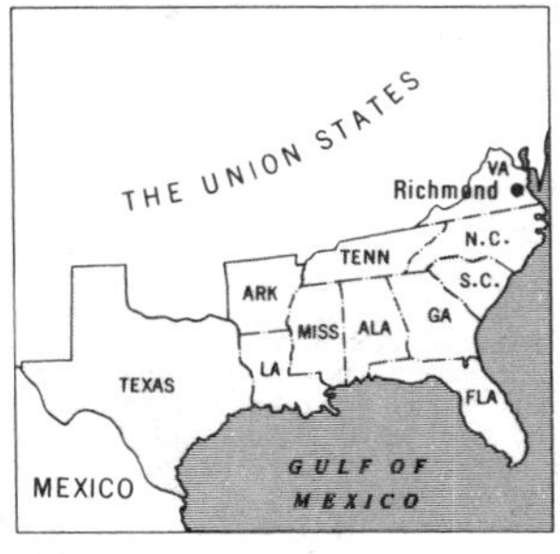

Confederacy

Confederacy or **Confederate States of America** (1861-5), govt. estab. by Southern states of US which seceded from Union. After election of Lincoln as president, 7 states left Union (early 1861) followed by 4 more after Lincoln's declaration of war. Jefferson Davis was elected president. For subsequent history, *see* CIVIL WAR (US).

Confederation of British Industry (CBI), organization representing the interests of British employers, particularly on economic questions. Founded 1965.

Confederation of the Rhine, *see* RHINE, CONFEDERATION OF THE.

confession, in RC, Orthodox and High Anglican churches, disclosure of sin to priest to obtain absolution. *See* PENANCE.

Confucius, latinized form of K'ung Fu-tzu (*c* 551-*c* 479 BC), Chinese philosopher and social reformer. Advocate of ethical system founded on absolute justice and moderation with the aim of stabilizing society. Teachings became basis of Confucianism, developed as state religion with adherence to traditional values.

conger eel, any of Congridae family of scaleless saltwater eels. Long dorsal fin, sharp teeth, powerful jaws. European conger, *Conger conger,* reaches length of 2.1 m/7 ft.

conglomerate, in geology, rock composed of rounded fragments, bound together by cementing material. Normally formed of transported pebbles, unlike breccia. Examples incl. single pebble type, mixed pebble type, and glacial conglomerates.

Congo, People's Republic of, republic of WC Africa. Area 342,000 sq km (132,000 sq mi); pop. 1,459,000; cap. Brazzaville. Languages: Bantu, French. Religions: animist, Christian. Mainly tropical forest, exports hardwoods, sugar, tobacco, coffee; main food crops cassava, yams. Lead, potash mining; aluminium indust. Coast explored 15th cent. by Portuguese, interior 19th cent. by de Brazza. Base of French trading (17th-19th cent.). Territ. (Middle Congo) of French Equatorial Africa from 1910; independent 1960. Member of French Community.

Congo, Republic of, *see* ZAÏRE.

Congo or **Zaïre,** river of WC Africa, 2nd longest (*c* 4800 km/3000 mi) in Africa. Rises in SE Zaïre, called R. Lualaba until reaching Stanley Falls; middle course curves SW, forming part of Zaïre-Congo border, widening at Stanley Pool. Enters Atlantic by wide estuary, forms part of Zaïre-Angola border. Navigable for ocean-going vessels to Matadi. Mouth discovered (1482), explored by Livingstone (1871); 1st descent made by Stanley (1874-7).

Congregationalism, faith and form of organization of a Protestant denomination in which each member church is self-governing. Based on belief that each congregation has Christ alone at its head. First appeared in 16th cent. England as revolt against state control of Established church; principles formulated by Robert Browne (*c* 1550-1633).

Congress of the United States, legislature of US federal govt., as distinct from executive and judiciary, estab. (1789) by Article I of Constitution. Comprises an upper house (SENATE) and a lower house (HOUSE OF REPRESENTATIVES).

Congress of Vienna, *ee* VIENNA, CONGRESS OF.

Congress Party (Indian), *see* INDIAN NATIONAL CONGRESS.

Congreve, William (1670-1729), English playwright. Known for Restoration comedies, esp. *Love for Love* (1695), *The Way of the World* (1700).

conic sections, in geometry, curves produced by intersection of a plane with a right circular cone. Consist of ellipse, circle, parabola, hyperbola and degenerate cases of these. Much studied by ancient Greek geometers.

conifer, class of woody perennials comprising 6 families, *c* 500 species. Mainly evergreen trees bearing cones. Trees cultivated for timber, pulp, resin and turpentine. Incl. PINE, cypress, yew, sequoia.

Coniston Water, lake of Cumbria, NW England. In Lake Dist. at foot of Old Man of Coniston. Length 8 km (5 mi). Scene of Campbells' water speed records (1939, 1959).

conjunctivitis, inflammation of membrane covering inside of eyelids and front of eye. Caused by infection with viruses or bacteria; usually treated by antibiotics.

Connacht or **Connaught,** prov. of W Irish Republic and ancient kingdom. Area 17,122 sq km (6611 sq mi); pop. 418,000. Comprises cos. Galway, Leitrim, Mayo, Roscommon, Sligo.

Connecticut, New England state of US. Area 12,973 sq km (5009 sq mi); pop. 3,117,000; cap. Hartford. Mainly lowland with indented coastline; divided by Connecticut R. Agric. incl. tobacco growing, dairy, poultry farming. Granite, sandstone quarrying. Mfg. industs. incl. machinery, tools, firearms, textiles, clocks and watches; defence industs. First settled by Dutch, later by Puritans from Massachusetts in 17th cent. One of original 13 colonies of US.

Connemara, region of Co. Galway, W Irish Republic. Lakes, mountains. Tourism.

Connolly, James (1870-1916), Irish nationalist. A Socialist, he supported labour movements in US and Ireland. Captured and shot helping to lead 1916 Easter Rebellion.

Conquistador (Span.,=conqueror), name given Spanish leaders in conquest of Americas, *eg* Cortés, Pizarro. Suppressed and exploited Indian pop. in search for gold and silver. Expeditions estab. Spanish empire.

Conrad, Joseph, orig. Teodor Józef Konrad Nalecz Korzeniowski (1857-1924), English novelist, b. Poland. Works, often set at sea, concerned with man's ability to cope with testing situations, *eg Lord Jim* (1900), *Typhoon* (1903), *Victory* (1915). Short stories, *eg* 'Heart of Darkness' (1902), often contain his most intense work.

conscientious objector, a term first used in WWI for those who objected to combatant service for moral or religious reasons. They were given legal status in UK by the Military Service Act (1916) and in WWII the Military Training Act (1939) prescribed alternative forms of service.

conscription, compulsory enrolment of citizens for military purposes. Recorded in Greece and Rome, it was first used in modern times by Napoleon in 1798. Most states have invoked it at some time.

conservation laws, in physics, laws stating that total value of some quantity does not change during physical processes, *eg* total electrical charge of a system remains constant. Laws of conservation of mass and of energy have been combined into single mass-energy law following Einstein's demonstration of equivalence of mass and energy.

conservatism, tendency to preserve and to oppose changes in estab. institutions or practices. In politics, manifested in parties advocating policies founded on belief in free enterprise, distrust of state intervention, and conservation in particular of sovereign and religious institutions. In UK, **Conservative Party** replaced TORY Party after Reform Bill of 1832. Survived splits in 1846 and 1905, became champion of propertied democracy and imperialism. Shared major party status with Liberals until 1922, after which alternated with Labour Party in govt. Prominent figures incl. Peel, Disraeli, the Chamberlains, Baldwin, Churchill. In European democracies, conservative policies often promoted by Christian Democrat parties.

Constable, John (1776-1837), English painter. With Turner, leading English landscape painter of 19th cent.; his direct observations of nature, capturing effects of changing light, influenced French Romantic painters. Works incl. *The Hay Wain* and *View on the Stour.*

Constance *(Konstanz),* town of S West Germany, on R. Rhine at exit from L. Constance. Pop. 61,000. Port; produces textiles, chemicals. Held by Austria 1548-1805. Hist. buildings incl. minster (11th cent.), Dominican monastery. Scene of Council of Constance (1414-18) where Hus was condemned.

Constance, Lake (Ger. *Bodensee),* on Swiss-Austro-German border. Rhine enters at SE, leaves NW. Area 531 sq km (205 sq mi). Tourism, fishing. Ancient lake dwellings.

Constanta, city of SE Romania, on Black Sea. Pop. 257,000. Resort; main Romanian port, exports grain, timber, petroleum. Founded by Greeks; rebuilt by Emperor Constantine 4th cent. Ceded by Turkey to Romania (1878).

Constantine [I] the Great (*c* 288-337), Roman emperor (306-37). Proclaimed emperor by troops in Britain on death of his father Constantius (306). Defeated rival Maxentius (312) in battle before which he is said to have had vision of Christ's cross. Legally recognized Christianity in empire with Edict of Milan (313). Gained control of E part of empire by 324 with defeat of rival Licinius. Consolidated and rebuilt empire; moved capital to Constantinople on Bosporus (330). Became a Christian 337.

Constantine II (1940-), king of Greece (1964-8). Went into exile after military junta took power (1967). Monarchy abolished by junta (1973); decision confirmed by popular vote (1974) after overthrow of junta.

Constantine (anc. *Cirta),* city of NE Algeria. Pop. 350,000. Grain, leather, wool trade. Ancient cap. of Numidia; destroyed AD 311, rebuilt AD 313 by Constantine I.

Constantinople, *see* ISTANBUL.
constellation, in astronomy, name given to groups of stars. In N hemisphere, names largely mythological, *eg* Orion; in S hemisphere (mapped 16th -18th cent.) named after animals or scientific equipment, *eg* Telescopium. Greeks recognized 48 constellations; now 88 are recognized.
constitution, whole system of govt. of a country. In wide sense, applied to both laws and customs which estab. and regulate govt.; more narrowly, to selection of these which are codified in document. Most nations have written constitutions, UK being notable exception.
constructivism, artistic movement in Russia during years 1917-22, characterized by abstract and geometric design, massive structural form and use of modern materials. Principal exponents were brothers Antoine Pevsner and Naum Gabo.
consul, title of two chief magistrates of ancient Rome. Most powerful office of republic, controlling army, treasury, civil affairs. Became nominal under empire. Term also used (1799-1804) for one of three highest officials of French republic; Napoleon Bonaparte was first consul.
consumption, *see* TUBERCULOSIS.
continent, large continuous land mass on Earth's surface. Seven usually distinguished: Africa, Antarctica, Australasia, North America, South America, Europe and Asia (sometimes taken as one, *ie* Eurasia). Upper level of Earth's crust, forming continents, consists of SIAL; lower level, underlying continents and ocean floors, of SIMA. Prob. formed at time crust first solidified, each continent has Precambrian shield at centre. Over ⅔ area of continents lies in N hemisphere.
Continental Congress (1774-89), legislature of Thirteen Colonies of America. First Congress sent petition of grievances to king, abolished trade with Britain. Second issued Declaration of Independence (4 July, 1776), created Continental Army, conducted American Revolution. Estab. Articles of Confederation, governed under them until Constitution adopted (1789).
continental drift, theoretical process by which continents on Earth's surface have changed their position through time. Alfred Wegener suggested (1912) that in Palaeozoic era all land masses were joined as 1 continent (called 'Pangaea'), later splitting into 2 ('Laurasia' and 'Gondwanaland') which slowly split and drifted into present positions. Also *see* SIAL, SIMA, PLATE TECTONICS.
continental shelf, submarine ledge bordering most continents. Covered by shallow water, usually less than *c* 180m/600 ft deep. May show continental features, *eg* cliffs, river valleys. Commercially important, *eg* most fishing grounds, petroleum found there.
Continental System, policy devised (1806) by Napoleon I to curtail British power by economic boycott and unify European states under his rule. All trade with Britain forbidden. Its failure was result of British naval superiority.
contrabassoon, *see* BASSOON.
contraception or **birth control** or **family planning,** prevention of conception. Methods used incl. sterilization, abstinence during certain phases of female ovulation, (rhythm method), hormone preparations (the 'Pill'), prevention of sperm entry into uterus, or intra-uterine devices. Modern movements for birth control began in 19th cent. following predictions of overpopulation by Malthus. Widely opposed on religious grounds, (*eg* by RC church) and in certain underpopulated countries; it has greatly reduced birth rate in many countries.
contralto, in singing, lowest female voice, also called ALTO.
convection, transference of heat in liquids or gases by actual motion of fluid. Fluid in contact with heat source expands, becoming less dense; it rises and its place is taken by colder, denser fluid. Resulting circulation of fluid is called convection current.
convolvulus, *see* BINDWEED.
cony, name given to mammals of order Hyracoidea, incl. damans, dassies and hyraxes.
Cook, James (1728-79), English naval officer, explorer. Commanded *Endeavour* on scientific expeditions to S Pacific (1768-71), mainly to observe transit of planet Venus; reached Tahiti, explored coasts of New Zealand and E Australia, claiming latter for UK. Landed at Botany Bay (1770). On 2nd voyage (1772-5) crossed Antarctic Circle, explored S Pacific, discovering Norfolk Isl. (1774). On 3rd voyage (1777-9) failed to find passage to Atlantic from N Pacific; killed by natives on Hawaii.
Cook, Mount, or **Aorangi,** highest mountain of New Zealand; in Southern Alps, South Isl. Height 3762 m (12,349 ft); part of Mt. Cook National Park.
Cook Islands, isl. group of SC Pacific Ocean. Area 240 sq km (93 sq mi); pop. 26,000; main isl. Rarotonga. Produce fruit, copra. Admin. by New Zealand from 1901, self-governing from 1965; formerly called Hervey Isls.
Coolidge, [John] Calvin (1872-1933), American statesman, Republican president (1923-9). Vice-president (1921-3), took office on death of Harding and pursued conservative policies.
Cooper, Gary, pseud. of Frank J. Cooper (1901–61), American film actor. Famous for roles as reticent man of conscience, often cowboy, in such films as *Mr Deeds Goes to Town* (1936), *High Noon* (1952).
Cooper, James Fenimore (1789-1851), American novelist. First American novelist to acquire international fame, known for 'Leatherstocking' series about frontiersmen. Novels, greatly influenced by Scott, incl. *The Deerslayer* (1841), *The Last of the Mohicans* (1826).
cooperative movement, term covering

variety of socio-economic organizations. Main type is consumer cooperative, which people join for purchase of goods in retail stores owned by cooperative, or to organize wholesale trade. Producers' cooperatives are rarer, comprise workers joined for common ownership and management of production. Movement began in 19th cent. Britain, developed variously throughout Europe.

coot, freshwater bird of Rallidae family, genus *Fulica*. Black with white forehead; unwebbed feet.

Coote, Sir Eyre (1726-83), Irish soldier. Active in Clive's occupation of Calcutta and victory at Plassey. Won battle of Wandiwash (1760) and captured Pondicherry, ending French attempt to dominate India. Returned to India (1779), defeated Hyder Ali several times.

Copenhagen *(Köbenhavn)*, cap. of Denmark, on E Zealand and N Amagar Isls.; port on Oresund. Pop. 1,251,000. Admin., commercial, cultural centre. Shipbuilding, fishing, brewing, porcelain mfg. Exports dairy produce. Cap. from 1443; British defeated Danes in naval battle (1801). Univ. (1479); Christiansborg Palace (18th cent.).

Copernicus, Nicolaus (1473-1543), Polish astronomer. Set down principles of Earth's axial rotation and position of Sun at centre of solar system, with planets in orbit around it. Provided foundation for work of Kepler and Newton.

Copland, Aaron (1900-), American composer. Much of his work displays American idioms grafted on to European tradition, *eg* the ballets *Rodeo* and *Appalachian Spring*.

copper (Cu), reddish-brown malleable ductile metallic element; at. no. 29, at. wt. 63.54. Occurs free and as sulphide and oxide ores. Excellent conductor of electricity and heat; resists corrosion. Used in electrical wire, boilers, numerous alloys (bronze, brass, *etc*). Compounds used as fungicides and pesticides.

copperhead, *Ancistrodon contortrix*, poisonous snake of pit viper group of E North America and Canada. Name also applied to poisonous Australian *Denisonia superba*.

copra, *see* COCONUT.

Copts, native Christian minority (*c* 10%) of Egypt. Culturally rather than ethnically distinct, they belong to the Coptic Church which was isolated when declared heretical in 451. *See* MONOPHYSITISM.

copyright, exclusive right granted by law to authors, composers, artists, *etc*, to print, publish and sell their works for specified time. Agreement reached (Bern Convention, 1887) by many countries (excluding US) to safeguard rights internationally. Universal Copyright Convention came into force in US (1955), UK (1957).

coral, small marine coelenterate usually living in colonies in warm seas. Individuals (polyps) consist of jelly-like body surrounded by calcareous skeleton. With death of polyp, skeletons accumulate to build reefs.

coral reef, chain of calcareous rocks found in warm, shallow seas. Consists of skeletal material, mainly coral polyps, accumulated *in situ* over long period, together with transported and chemically precipitated organic debris. Forms incl. fringing reefs, barrier reefs, ATOLLS.

Coral Sea, arm of SW Pacific Ocean, between E Papua New Guinea and NE Australia. Incl. Great Barrier Reef. Scene of US-Australian victory (1942) over Japanese.

coral snake, one of various highly poisonous burrowing snakes of S US, subtropical America; related to cobra. Red, yellow and black bands around body.

cor anglais, *see* OBOE.

Corbusier, Le, pseud. of Charles Edouard Jeanneret (1887-1965), French architect, b. Switzerland. Influential innovator, he employed pure geometrical forms in his work, and industrial methods to mass-produce housing. Designs incl. chapel at Ronchamp, UN building. Devised town-planning schemes.

Corday, Charlotte (1768-93), French political assassin. A Girondist sympathizer, she stabbed Marat in his bath, and was guillotined 4 days later.

Cordeliers, radical political club during French Revolution. Estab. 1790, active in overthrow of GIRONDISTS (1792-3). Leaders incl. Danton, Marat.

Córdoba, city of C Argentina, cap. of Córdoba prov. Pop. 791,000. Railway jct., commercial and cultural centre; cars, tractors, textiles, glass mfg. Supplied with h.e.p. from Río Primero. Founded 1573. Old buildings incl. cathedral, univ. (1613).

Córdoba or **Cordova,** city of S Spain, on R. Guadalquivir, cap. of Córdoba prov. Pop. 250,000. Tourism; industs. incl. textile mfg., engineering. Cap. of independent Moorish emirate, later caliphate, from 756; famous gold, silver, leather crafts. Taken by Castile 1236. Much Moorish architecture, esp. mosque (8th cent.), now a cathedral.

corduroy, *see* VELVET.

Corelli, Arcangelo (1653-1713), Italian composer, violinist. In his sonatas and *concerti grossi*, he estab. characteristic style of writing for violin, both as solo and orchestral instrument.

Corfu *(Kérkira)*, isl. of W Greece, in Ionian Sea. Area 637 sq km (246 sq mi). Olives, wine; tourism. Ancient *Corcyra*; settled by Corinth *c* 734 BC. Under Venetian rule 1386-1797, British 1815-64. Cap. is **Corfu,** pop. 27,000. Port, resort.

corgi, small Welsh dog of 2 varieties: Pembrokeshire, short-tailed and red or red and white; Cardiganshire, long-tailed and any colour except white. Stands *c* 30 cm/12 in. at shoulder.

coriander, *Coriandrum sativum*, annual herb of parsley family native to Mediterranean countries. Grown in

Europe and US. Seeds used as flavouring.

rinth *(Kórinthos),* town of SC Greece, on Gulf of Corinth. Pop. 16,000. Port; raisin, wine trade. Founded *c* 1350 BC; traditional rival of Athens. Colonized Syracuse, Corfu; joined Achaean League. Remains incl. citadel. Refounded (1858) after earthquake.

rinth, Gulf of, Greece. Inlet of Ionian Sea between mainland and Peloponnese. Joined to Saronic Gulf by canal (1881-93) across Isthmus of Corinth.

Corinthian capital

rinthian order, most elaborate of the Greek orders of architecture, similar to onic, but distinguished by its inverted bell-haped capital decorated with design of canthus leaves and volutes. Oldest known xample is at Bassae, *c* 420 BC; order was ttle used.

inthians 1 and **2,** epistles of NT, written y St Paul (*c* AD 55) prob. from Ephesus 1) and Macedonia (2). Admonish the eople of Corinth for their notorious nmorality.

iolanus, Gnaeus Marcius (*c* 500-450 C), Roman general. Exiled from Rome or tyrannical aspirations, joined Volcians. Prepared to attack Rome, but issuaded by mother and wife. Put to death y Volscians.

k *(Corcaigh),* county of Munster prov., S ish Republic. Area 7462 sq km (2881 sq i); pop. 258,000. Crossed E-W by ountains; fertile valleys; indented coast cl. Bantry Bay. Agric., dairying; fishing. o. town **Cork,** co. bor. with Cóbh, on R. ee. Pop. 138,000. Exports agric. produce. oollen mfg.; distilling. Protestant, RC athedrals.

k, outer tissue produced by evergreen ork oak, *Quercus suber,* of the lediterranean region to replace pidermis as a protective layer. npervious, compressible and elastic, used r stoppers, floor-coverings, floats, *etc.* rees can be stripped about every 10 years r *c* 150 years.

kwood, *see* BALSA.

m, *see* BULB.

morant, diving seabird of Phalacroracidae family. Long neck and body, ooked bill, mainly black plumage; breeds colonies. Species incl. widespread *halacrocorax carbo* common on N lantic coast.

corn, *see* MAIZE; WHEAT; OATS.

corncrake, *Crex crex,* brown short-billed European game bird of rail family.

cornea, *see* EYE.

Corneille, Pierre (1606-84), French dramatist. Principal formulator of French Classical theatre. Portrayed tragedy within man rather than in external events. Major works incl. *Le Cid* (1637), *Polyeucte* (1641). Finally eclipsed by Racine.

cornet, brass wind instrument created in France (*c* 1825) by adding valves to post horn, although a modern cornet resembles a squat trumpet.

cornflower, *Centaurea cyanus,* hardy annual of daisy family native to Mediterranean regions. Formerly weed in European grainfields, now popular garden flower.

Cornish, *see* CELTIC.

Corn Laws, in Britain, restrictions placed on exports or imports of grain. Acts (1791, 1813) forced up price of grain by protective tariffs on imports, serving interests of landowners. Opposition, esp. among new industrial classes over high food prices, culminated in formation of Anti-Corn Law League (1839), leaders of which incl. Bright, Cobden. Laws repealed 1846 by Peel under mounting public pressure during Irish famine (1845-6).

Cornwall and Isles of Scilly, county of SW England. Area 3546 sq km (1369 sq mi); pop. 177,000; admin. hq. Truro. Interior moorland, *eg* Bodmin Moor in E; rocky, rugged coastline; mild climate. Tourism; dairy farming, fruit, vegetable growing; kaolin indust.; tin mining. *See also* SCILLY ISLES.

Cornwallis, Charles Cornwallis, 1st Marquess (1738-1805), British general. During American Revolution, led retreat from Carolinas to Virginia; his surrender at Yorktown (1781) marked end of fighting. As governor-general of India, quelled Tippoo Sahib.

Coromandel Coast, *see* TAMIL NADU.

corona, *see* SUN.

coronary thrombosis, *see* THROMBOSIS.

Corot, Jean Baptiste Camille (1796-1875), French landscape painter. Sketches from nature noted for their simplicity of form and clarity of light. Later misty landscapes, grey-green in tone, were popular successes.

corporate state, system in which state controls economy, comprised mainly of privately-owned businesses. Political and economic power vested in organization controlling corporations of employers and workers; dates from medieval guild system. Modified form under virtual dictatorships operated in Fascist Italy from 1920s and in Portugal until 1974. Collectivist in principle, use of private capital justified in capitalist context on grounds of national priorities. Post-war Western indust. states have taken on some corporate state characteristics.

Correggio, Antonio Allegri da (*c* 1494-1534), Italian painter. Known for his soft style and use of extreme illusionism in his decorations; late works foreshadow Italian Baroque.

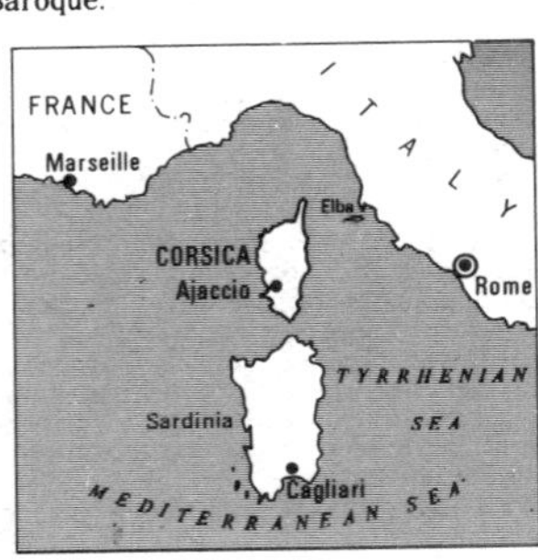

Corsica

Corsica *(Corse),* isl. dept. of France, in Mediterranean Sea, N of Sardinia. Area 8721 sq km (3367 sq mi); cap. Ajaccio. Plains along E coast, mountainous elsewhere, highest peak Monte Cinto (2709 m/8891 ft); extensive scrubland *(maquis).* Tourism, limited agric. (olives), fishing. Settled from Etruscan times, ceded (1768) to France by Genoa. Banditry and blood feuds rife until early 20th cent. Napoleon born in Ajaccio.

Cortés, Hernán or **Hernando Cortez** (1485-1547), Spanish conquistador. Led force of 600 men in conquest of Mexico. Entered Tenochtitlán (Mexico City) in 1519, where he was received by emperor Montezuma as god Quetzalcoatl. Recaptured Tenochtitlán (1521) after Aztec revolt; victory marked fall of Aztec empire. Gradually lost political power; failing to be appointed viceroy.

cortisone, crystalline steroid hormone produced by cortex of adrenal gland. Used to treat inflammatory diseases and allergies, *eg* arthritis, asthma; dangerous side-effects.

Corunna, or **Coruña, La,** city of NW Spain, on Atlantic Ocean, cap. of La Coruña prov. Pop. 190,000. Sardine fishing, cigar mfg. Armada sailed from here (1588). Scene of Peninsular War battle (1809) in which Sir John Moore was killed.

corundum, very hard mineral, form of aluminium oxide. Found chiefly among metamorphosed limestones, shales. Coarser varieties used as abrasives, *eg* EMERY; finer as gems, *eg* RUBY, SAPPHIRE.

corvette, originally, a full-rigged sloop of war, below a frigate in size, carrying up to 20 guns on upper deck. In WWII a small anti-submarine escort vessel.

Cos *(Kos),* isl. of Greece, in the Dodecanese off Turkey. Area 282 sq km (109 sq mi), main town Cos. Cereals, fruit, wine; Cos lettuce originated here. Ancient literary, medical centre (school of Hippocrates).

Cosenza, city of Calabria, SW Italy, on R. Crati. Cap. of Cosenza prov. Pop. 103,0[illegible] Furniture, textiles; fruit market. Cathed[illegible] (12th cent.), castle (13th cent.).

Cosgrave, William Thomas (1880-196[illegible] Irish statesman. After 1922 split of Si[illegible] Fein, headed Irish Free State go[illegible] (1922-32) until defeat by De Valé[illegible] Resigned 1944 as opposition leader. [illegible] son, **Liam Cosgrave** (1920-), was [illegible] (1973-77) at head of Fine Gael go[illegible] Introduced (1976) measures to prevent I[illegible] activities in Republic supporting conflict Northern Ireland.

cosmic rays, high energy radiation reach[illegible] Earth from outer space. Primary cos[illegible] rays consist largely of protons and al[illegible] particles; these collide with particles [illegible] upper atmosphere to produce second[illegible] cosmic rays containing mesons, neutr[illegible] electrons, *etc.* Various subatomic partic[illegible] incl. positron, discovered in cosmic ra[illegible] Source unknown; some rays originate [illegible] solar flares, but most come from bey[illegible] Solar System.

cosmology, science of nature, origin a[illegible] history of universe. Modern cosmol[illegible] theories assume that universe looks sa[illegible] in all directions and from all positi[illegible] General theory of relativity provi[illegible] framework for study of gravitation and shaping effect on universe. Theories origin of universe incl. BIG-BANG and STEA[illegible] STATE theories.

Cossacks, people of S Russia and Sibe[illegible] famous as horsemen. Settled in Don [illegible] Dnepr areas in 15th and 16th cents., h[illegible] privileges of auton. govt. in return military service. Participation unsuccessful peasant revolts in 18th c[illegible] led to loss of some auton. In 19th ce[illegible] organized by Russian govt. into communities spread throughout coun[illegible] Deprived of privileges after many fou[illegible] against Bolsheviks (1918-20).

Costa del Sol, coastline of S Spain, betw[illegible] Almeria and Tarifa. Popular resort regi[illegible] *eg* Malaga, Torremolinos.

Costa Rica, republic of Central Amer[illegible] between Nicaragua and Panama. A[illegible] 50,700 sq km (19,575 sq mi); pop. 2,111,[illegible] cap. San José. Language: Spanish. Relig[illegible] RC. Dormant volcanic mountains [illegible] jungle in N; plains on Caribbean, Pac[illegible] coasts. Mainly agric., coffee, bana[illegible] timber exports. Part of Guatemala un[illegible] Spanish rule until 1821; part of Cen[illegible] American Federation (1823-38).

Costermansville, *see* BUKAVU.

cost of living index, measurement of cos[illegible] goods and services needed to maintai[illegible] specific standard of living. Originally u[illegible] to indicate incidence of poverty, now u[illegible] by govt. as guide to fiscal policy, and basis for wage negotiations.

Côte d'Azur, *see* RIVIERA.

Côte d'Or, range of hills in Burgundy France. Wine-producing region, m[illegible] centres Dijon, Nuits St Georges, Beaune

Cotman, John Sell (1782-1842), Eng[illegible] painter. Noted for landscape watercolo[illegible]

cotoneaster, genus of shrubs of rose fa[illegible]

native to Asia. Most species have glossy green leaves, small pink or white flowers and abundant crimson berries.

otopaxi, mountain of NC Ecuador; world's highest active volcano. Height 5897 m (19,347 ft).

otswold Hills, W England, limestone range mainly in Gloucestershire. Form Severn-Thames watershed. Attractive stone villages. Wool centre until 17th cent.

otton, soft white seed hairs filling pods of various shrubs of genus *Gossypium* of mallow family, native to tropics. Cheapest and most widely used natural fibre. Has been spun, woven and dyed since prehistoric times. Cotton mfg. has been a major industry, esp. in Britain and US (18th and 19th cents.). US, USSR, India, China, Mexico are chief producers.

ottonmouth, *see* WATER MOCCASIN.

ottontail, one of several common non-burrowing American rabbits, genus *Sylvilagus,* with short fluffy tails, white underneath.

uch grass, *Agropyron repens,* perennial weed, troublesome on arable land, with creeping rhizomes of which each broken piece is capable of reproduction. Native to Europe, now common in North America.

ugar, *see* PUMA.

oulomb, Charles Augustin de (1736-1806), French physicist. Used torsion balance to deduce Coulomb's law: force of attraction or repulsion between charged bodies is proportional to product of magnitude of charges and inversely proportional to square of distance between them. SI unit of charge named after him.

uncil for Mutual Economic Assistance (COMECON), E European organization estab. (1949) to coordinate economic policy in Communist bloc. Its 1959 charter gave it same status as European Economic Community, expanded scope to regulate indust. production. Albania expelled (1961) from membership. Mongolian People's Republic joined (1962), Cuba (1972), Vietnam (1978).

uncil of Europe, organization of European states. Estab. (1949) to secure greater unity between its members; to safeguard common political, cultural heritage; facilitate economic, social progress. Members mainly from W and N Europe. European Commission investigates alleged violations of European Convention on Human Rights (signed 1950), submits findings to European Court of Human Rights (estab. 1958).

unterpoint, in music, art of combining two or more independent melodies so that they form a harmonious whole. Dominant feature of much Renaissance and Baroque music.

unter-Reformation, *see* REFORMATION, CATHOLIC.

untertenor or **male alto,** adult male singer with unusually high voice, produced by developing falsetto or head voice. Most often to be heard in Renaissance and Baroque music.

Country Party, National, Australian political party. Origins in 19th cent.; represents agrarian interests. In 20th cent., has often held 3rd party balance of power in alliance with Liberal party, esp. during and after WWI.

county, in England and Wales, main political, social and admin. division. As 'shire', unit of govt. before Norman Conquest (1066); form for most of 20th cent. estab. by Local Government Act (1888). Restructured by new act (1972) resulting in county and district councils. Now 45 counties in England, 6 in Wales. Scottish counties, by extension of legislation (1973), replaced by 9 regions, 3 island areas.

coup d'état, in politics, sudden (usually forcible) overthrow of govt. Differs from revolution, involving radical restructuring of society, in that top level only of govt. or admin. is replaced. Hist. precedents range from Napoleon's rise to power in France to Amin in Uganda (1971) and Pinochet in Chile (1973).

Couperin, François (1668-1733), French composer, harpsichordist. Noted organist; wrote 4 books of harpsichord suites.

Courbet, Gustave (1819-77), French painter. Leader of realist school of French painting, his unidealized scenes from daily life incl. *Funeral at Ornans* (1850). Imprisoned after Paris commune. He lived in Switzerland from 1873.

courgette or **zucchini,** *Cucurbita pepo,* small marrow, 5-20 cm/2-8 in. long. Ridged outer skin; used as vegetable.

coursing, hunting of game, usually hares, by greyhounds trained to follow by sight rather than scent. In competitions, 2 dogs chase a hare and are tested for qualities of speed and agility.

court, in law, person or persons appointed to try cases, make investigation, render judgment. Secular, complex system developed in ancient Rome. In England and Wales, High Court of Justice (estab. by Judicature Act, 1873) comprises chancery; King's (or Queen's) Bench; probate, divorce and admiralty; court of appeal.

Cousteau, Jacques Yves (1910-), French naval officer, underwater explorer. Invented aqualung (1943); helped develop bathyscaphe, underwater filming. Founder of French naval underwater research; has produced many books, films on sea life.

Covenanters, in Scottish history, members of groups bound by oath to defend Presbyterianism. Covenant of 1581 sought to combat RC church in Scotland; National Covenant of 1638 opposed Archbishop Laud's attempts to introduce Book of Common Prayer into Scotland. Supported Puritan Revolution only after English Parliament's acceptance of Solemn League and Covenant (1643), promising estab. of Presbyterianism in England. Resisted coercion after Restoration;

movement ended with Glorious Revolution (1688).

Coventry, city of West Midlands met. county, WC England. Pop. 340,000. Cars, aircraft, hosiery, rayon industs. Medieval weaving town. Centre destroyed in WWII bombing. New cathedral, incorporating old, completed 1962.

Coverdale, Miles (1488-1569), English translator of entire Bible (1535). Collaborated in Great Bible (1539); edited 'Cranmer's Bible' (1540).

cow, mature female of domestic cattle. Name also applied to mature female of other animals, *eg* buffalo, moose, whale.

Coward, Sir Noël (1899-1973), English actor, playwright, composer, film director. Best known for witty comedies incl. *Private Lives* (1930), *Blithe Spirit* (1941), also wrote revues, songs, film scripts *eg Brief Encounter* (1945).

Cowper, William (1731-1800), English poet. Known for religious *Olney Hymns* (1779) incl. 'God moves in a mysterious way'; *John Gilpin's Ride* (1782), *The Castaway* (1803).

cowrie, gastropod mollusc of Cypraeidae family, abundant in tropical seas. Shells, shiny and brightly coloured, sometimes used as money or decoration.

cowslip, *Primula veris,* European plant of primrose family. Has yellow bell flowers.

coyote or **prairie wolf,** *Canis latrans,* small wolf of plains of W North America. Thick fur, bushy tail; largely nocturnal. Omnivorous, hunts singly or in packs.

coypu, *Myocastor coypus,* large herbivorous aquatic rodent of South America, *c* 90 cm/3 ft in length. Introduced into other countries for cultivation of fur (nutria).

crab, one of various crustaceans of suborder Brachyura with 4 pairs of legs, pair of pincers and flattened shell; abdomen reduced and folded under thorax. Many species edible.

crab apple, *Malus pumila,* tree of apple family of Europe and W Asia. Small reddish-yellow fruit with bitter flavour used in preserves. Parent of all cultivated apples.

Crabbe, George (1754-1832), English poet. Known for realistic, anti-pastoral heroic verse, *eg The Village* (1783), *The Borough* (1810) incl. 'Peter Grimes', used by Benjamin Britten as theme of opera.

Crab nebula, gaseous nebula in constellation Taurus, remnant of supernova explosion seen in 1054. Emits radio waves and X-rays; at its centre is a PULSAR.

Cracow, *see* KRAKÓW.

Craigavon, James Craig, 1st Viscount (1871-1940), Irish statesman. Helped organize (1914) Ulster Volunteers to resist Irish Home Rule. First PM of Northern Ireland (1921-40).

cramp, painful spasm of the muscles. May be caused by excessive loss of salt, effect of cold on nervous system, or by continual pressure on particular nerves.

Cranach, Lucas, real name Müller (1472-1553), German artist; known as 'Th[e] Elder'. Early works of religious subjec[ts] noted for their handling of landscap[e]. Later associated with Luther, he wa[s] prolific producer of woodcuts, portrai[ts] and mythological figures, developing ow[n] style in painting erotic female nude[s]. Portraits incl. Luther, Charles V.

Cranberry

cranberry, *Vaccinium oxycoccus,* vine-lik[e] shrub with bitter, crimson berries, nati[ve] to Europe and US. Traditional sauce wi[th] venison and turkey.

Crane, [Harold] Hart (1899-1932), America[n] poet. Known for *White Buildings* (192[6]) influenced by Rimbaud, and *The Brid[ge]* (1930).

Crane, Stephen Townley (1871-190[0]) American author. Best known for Ci[vil] War novel, *The Red Badge of Coura[ge]* (1895).

crane, any of Gruidae family of long-necke[d] long-legged wading birds, fou[nd] everywhere except South Americ[a]. Species incl. grey European comm[on] crane, *Grus grus.*

crane fly or **daddy-long-legs,** slend[er] harmless long-legged fly of Tipulid[ae] family. Larvae, known as leatherjacke[ts] live in ground and are pests of crops.

cranesbill, *see* GERANIUM.

Craniata, subphylum of chordates havi[ng] definite head. Incl. vertebrates, but n[ot] hemichordates or protochordates.

Cranmer, Thomas (1489-1556), Engli[sh] churchman, archbishop of Canterbu[ry] (1533-56). Annulled Henry VIII's marria[ge] to Catherine of Aragon despite pa[pal] opposition (1533). Encouraged translati[on] of Bible into English and its circulati[on] throughout churches. Under Edward [VI] compiled 2 Anglican Prayer Books (15[49,] 1552). Under Mary I, condemned as trai[tor] and heretic, burned at stake.

crannog, in archaeology, lake dwelling bu[ilt] on artificial island of stones, earth, timb[er]. Often surrounded by wooden stocka[de]. Most date from late Bronze Age in Irela[nd,] Scotland.

aps, *see* DICE.

assus, Marcus Licinius (*c* 108-53 BC), Roman soldier and political leader. Amassed fortune by buying confiscated estates. Crushed revolt of slaves under Spartacus (71). Formed 1st Triumvirate with Caesar and Pompey. Given charge of prov. of Syria, killed after defeat by Parthians in Mesopotamia.

ater, bowl-shaped depression in Earth's surface. May be formed by explosion, *eg* at summit of volcanic cone, or impact, *eg* by meteor striking Earth's surface.

awford, Joan, orig. Lucille le Sueur (1906-77), American film actress. Films incl. *Rain* (1932), *A Woman's Face* (1941), *Whatever Happened to Baby Jane?* (1962).

ayfish or **crawfish,** freshwater crustacean, esp. of genus *Astacus,* resembling small lobster; many edible species. Term also applied to crustaceans of Palinuridae family.

écy (-en-Ponthieu), (Eng. *Cressy*), village of Picardy, NE France, near Abbeville. Scene of victory (1346) of Edward III of England over Philip VI of France.

ee, North American Indian tribe formerly inhabiting Manitoba. Plains Cree were buffalo hunters of prairies. Woodland Cree although warlike were friendly to early French and British fur traders around Hudson Bay.

eed, brief statement of religious belief. Examples incl. Nicene, a revised form of that adopted by 1st Council of Nicaea (325) to combat Arianism, used in RC and Eastern Orthodox churches; Apostles', dating from 650 and similar to Nicene, used in RC and Protestant churches; Augsburg Confession (1530) is official Lutheran statement; THIRTY-NINE ARTICLES, basic creed of Church of England, dates from reign of Elizabeth I; Westminster Confession (1645-7) is creed of Calvinist Presbyterian churches. *See also* ATHANASIAN CREED.

mation, ceremonial burning of the dead. Practice in ancient world was prob. based on belief in purifying power of fire. Discontinued in Europe because of Christian belief in resurrection of the body. Subsequently revived with problems of disposal in large cities. First crematorium in US opened 1876; legalized in UK 1884.

mona, town of Lombardy, N Italy, on R. Po. Cap. of Cremona prov. Pop. 84,000. Indust., commercial centre; foodstuffs, textiles. Famous for violin mfg. by Amati, Guarneri, Stradivari. Cathedral (12th cent.), tallest campanile in Italy.

ole, person of European parentage or mixed descent born in West Indies, Central America, tropical South America, or descendant of such a person.

pe or **crêpe,** thin fabric with crinkled texture, originally woven from raw silk.

ss, *Lepidium sativum,* tiny plant of mustard family, native to Persia. Used as a garnish. Different genus from WATERCRESS.

taceous period, final geological period of Mesozoic era; began *c* 135 million years ago, lasted *c* 70 million years. Widespread inundation; extensive chalk formation esp. in latter (upper) half of period. Echinoderms, lamellibranchs, last ammonites; mammals still small and rare, dinosaurs extinct by end of period. Also *see* GEOLOGICAL TABLE.

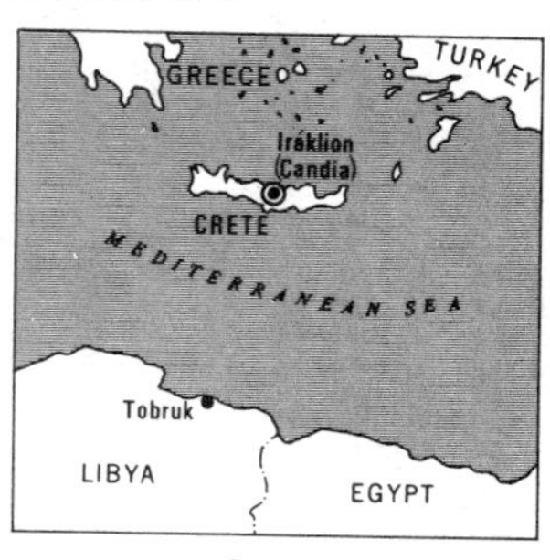

Crete

Crete *(Kriti),* largest isl. of Greece, in E Mediterranean. Area 8332 sq km (3217 sq mi); cap. Iráklion. Mostly mountainous, highest point Mt Ida. Olives, fruit, wine; tourism. Home of Minoan civilization (*fl* 2000-1400 BC); remains incl. KNOSSOS. Turkish from 1669, passed to Greece 1912.

cretinism, congenital deficiency of thyroid hormone secretion, with resulting retardation of physical and mental growth.

Crewe, town of Cheshire, NW England. Pop. 51,000. Major railway jct.; railway engineering.

cribbage, old English card game for two players. Scores are marked with pegs on a board. Invention credited to Sir John Suckling (1609-42).

Crick, Francis Harry Compton (1916-), English biochemist. Shared Nobel Prize for Physiology and Medicine (1962) with Maurice Wilkins and James Watson for work establishing double helix structure of DNA molecule.

cricket, insect of Gryllidae family, related to grasshopper and locust, but with long antennae. Often lives in human habitations, being active at night. Male produces chirping sound by rubbing forewings.

cricket, eleven-a-side game played with bat, ball and wickets. Marylebone Cricket Club (MCC), founded 1787, was governing body of game in England until formation of Cricket Council in 1969. Organized county cricket dates from 1873. Test matches, dating from 1877, played between England, Australia, New Zealand, West Indies, India, Pakistan and, formerly, South Africa.

Crimea, penin. of USSR, in S Ukrainian SSR; extending into N Black Sea. Taken from Turks by Russia (1783); scene of Crimean War (1853-6). Coast is tourist centre.

Crimean War (1853-6), conflict between

Russia and Britain, France and Turkey. General cause was Anglo-Russian dispute, esp. over control of Dardanelles. Pretext was Russian-French quarrel over guardianship of Palestinian holy places. Turkey's rejection of Russian territ. demands prompted latter's occupation of Moldavia and Walachia. Turkey declared war (1853), France and Britain joined (1854), Sardinia (1855). Main campaign, centring on siege of SEVASTOPOL in Crimea, was marked by inept leadership, futile gallantry (*eg* charge of the Light Brigade at battle of BALAKLAVA) and heavy casualties; hospital work by Florence NIGHTINGALE. Settlement at Congress of Paris checked Russian influence in SE Europe.

criminal law, body of law dealing with crimes punishable by state. In Britain developed out of COMMON LAW. Usually, test of criminal liability is intention to commit, so that children (*ie* under 14 years), insane persons, *etc*, are not liable.

criminology, scientific study of crime, criminal(s), subfield of sociology; 19th cent. attempts at definition of criminal 'type' gave way to study of environmental factors. Others have studied crime as business, or as normal learned behaviour.

Crippen, Hawley Harvey (1861-1910), English murderer, b. US. Known as 1st criminal captured through use of radio. Was arrested on board ship attempting to escape to US with mistress after murdering wife.

Cripps, Sir [Richard] Stafford (1889-1952), British politician. Expelled by Labour Party (1939) for urging 'Popular Front' with Communists against Chamberlain's 'appeasement' policy; readmitted 1945. Served in Churchill's war cabinet from 1942 and in Labour cabinet (1945-50); chancellor of exchequer from 1947.

critical mass, in nuclear physics, minimum mass of fissile material, *eg* uranium, that can sustain a chain reaction. If less than critical mass of material is present, reaction dies away.

critical pressure, minimum pressure required to liquefy a gas at its critical temperature.

critical temperature, temperature above which gas cannot be liquefied, regardless of the pressure applied.

Croatia *(Hrvatska),* autonomous republic of NW Yugoslavia. Area 56,524 sq km (21,824 sq mi); cap. Zagreb. Incl. Dalmatia, Istria, Slavonia. Dinaric Alps in W, fertile plain in NE drained by Drava, Sava. Timber, coal, bauxite, most developed region of Yugoslavia; coastal tourism. United with Hungary 1091-1918, part of Yugoslavia from 1918.

Croce, Benedetto (1866-1952), Italian philosopher, historian. Believed ideas are reality, not merely representations. Idealism reflected in *The Philosophy of the Spirit* (1902-17). Minister of education (1920-1) before rise of Fascism.

Crockett, David ('Davy') (1786-1836), American frontiersman. Democrat C[...] gressman from Tennessee. Died at [...] Alamo fighting for independence of Texa[...]

crocodile, large carnivorous reptile of ord[...] Crocodilia, found throughout tropics. Liv[...] in rivers, swamps and on river banks.

Crocodilia (crocodilians), order of lar[...] reptiles with powerful jaws, elongat[...] snout. Four-chambered heart, uniq[...] among reptiles. Body covered with scal[...] bony plates. Order incl. crocodile, gavi[...] alligator.

crocus, genus of spring-flowering plants [...] iris family with fleshy corms and yell[...] purple or white flowers. Over 80 speci[...] native to S Europe.

Croesus (d. *c* 546 BC), king of Lyd[...] Completed conquest of Ionian cities of A[...] Minor. Allied himself with Babylonia a[...] Egypt to resist Persia, but was defea[...] and captured by Cyrus the Gre[...] Proverbial figure of great wealth.

crofting, system used esp. in highlands a[...] islands of Scotland, where tenant rents a[...] cultivates small holding or croft, produc[...] food and raising animals for his own nee[...]

Cro-Magnon man, prehist. human being [...] Upper Palaeolithic period (*c* 30,000 ye[...] ago). Remains found (1868) in rock shel[...] of Cro-Magnon in Dordogne area [...] France. Of same species as modern *Ho[...] sapiens*, but taller.

Cromarty, *see* ROSS AND CROMARTY.

Crompton, Samuel (1753-1827), Engl[...] inventor. Devised (1779) spinning mule, [...] improvement of Hargreaves' spinn[...] jenny, which spun fine yarn suitable [...] muslin.

Cromwell, Oliver (1599-1658), Engl[...] soldier and statesman. Leading Puritan[...] Parliament before Civil War, assum[...] command of anti-royalist forces a[...] victories at Edgehill (1642), Marston M[...] (1644). Demanded execution of Charle[...] after Naseby (1645). Cromwell decla[...] republic after king's execution (1649) [...] crushed Irish resistance; defeated roya[...] Scots under Charles II (1651). Dissol[...] 'Rump' Parliament (1653) and es[...] Protectorate, which he ruled as [...] protector (1653-8). Refused crown (16[...] introduced constitution to strengthen [...] powers. Warred with Dutch (1652-4) a[...] 1651 Navigation Act, and Spain (165[...] Military genius but his govt. was mar[...] by cruelty and intolerance. Succeeded [...] his son, **Richard Cromwell** (1626-1712) [...] lord protector; he resigned 1659 w[...] Commonwealth was re-estab.

Cromwell, Thomas, Earl of Essex [...] 1485-1540), English statesman. Secretar[...] Cardinal Wolsey, whom he succeeded [...] Henry VIII's chief adviser and [...] chamberlain (1539). Instrumental in [...] with papacy, carried out suppression [...] monasteries. Failure of Henry's marri[...] to Anne of Cleves, which he had negotia[...] to secure German alliance, resulted in [...] execution for treason.

Cronus, in Greek myth, youngest of [...] TITANS. Led revolt against father Ura[...]

ɔecame ruler of the world. Married his ɜister Rhea, fathered the OLYMPIAN GODS. Despite attempt to avoid fate by destroying ɿis own children, was overthrown by son ZEUS. Identified with Roman Saturn.

oquet, outdoor game in which players use nallets to drive wooden balls through a series of hoops placed in the ground. Believed to have originated in France, where it had become popular by 17th cent.

osby, Harry Lillis ('Bing') (1904-1977), American singer, actor. World's most successful singer in terms of record sales, made 1st recording in 1926; famous for relaxed style. Also appeared in many films, esp. with Bob Hope.

ɔss, symbol found in many societies, *eg* in ancient India, among American Indians, but esp. important in Christianity in remembrance of Christ's crucifixion. May take several forms, *eg* Latin, St Andrew's, ona. Crucifix is cross with a representation of the dying Christ; used in RC church.

ossbill, bird of finch family. European crossbill, *Loxia curvirostra,* inhabits coniferous forests. Crossed bill used to extract seeds from fruit, cones.

ossbow, a bow fixed to a wooden butt and ired like a musket, the string being pulled back by a lever or winding gear and released by a trigger. Used mainly in the 12th-13th cent.

ɔw, North American Indian tribe. Nomadic hunters in Yellowstone R. area. Allied with whites *v* Sioux in 1870s.

ɔw, any of Corvidae family of perching birds. Often intelligent, with thick beak, mainly black plumage; worldwide distribution. Species incl. carrion crow, *Corvus corone,* and RAVEN, ROOK, MAGPIE.

wberry, *Empetrum nigrum,* small prostrate trailing shrub. Found on moorland in temperate regions. Black edible berries.

wfoot, name loosely applied to many species of plants of genus *Ranunculus* of buttercup family. Deeply divided leaves resembling crow's foot.

wn, the, in UK govt., monarch as head of state. Formal powers incl. royal assent, needed for all parliamentary legislation, and royal prerogative. Latter incl. domestic duties, *eg* appointment of ministers, creation of peers, summoning and dissolution of Parliament, pardoning criminals; foreign duties, *eg* right to make war, treaties, receive and send ambassadors *etc.* Royal prerogative extends to other Commonwealth countries, and to colonial governors in certain areas. Most crown powers, in practice, delegated to ministers.

wn jewels or **regalia,** symbols of British royal authority, kept in Tower of London. Present set dates from Restoration; incl. replica of crown of St Edward the Confessor (used at coronation), imperial state crown (worn on state occasions), swords of state, orb and sceptre.

ydon, bor. of S Greater London, England. Pop. 321,000. Created 1965 from former co. bor. and residential areas of N Surrey.

Crozet Islands, archipelago of *c* 20 isls. in SW Indian Ocean, forming part of French Southern and Antarctic Territs. Area 300 sq km (116 sq mi). Site of meteorological station.

Cruciferae, family of flowering plants, with *c* 220 genera incl. the mustards, cabbages, cresses. Cross-like arrangement of 4 petals. Annuals or biennials.

crucifixion, death imposed by hanging from wooden cross, used widely in Near East, adopted by Romans for slaves and most despised criminals. Romans used T-shaped cross until abolition when Christianity became a lawful religion in empire under Constantine I. JESUS CHRIST died by crucifixion.

Cruikshank, George (1792-1878), English caricaturist and illustrator. Popular political cartoonist, he satirized politicians, Prince Regent, *etc.* Illustrated works of Dickens.

cruise missile, subsonic guided missile carrying small nuclear warhead. Can fly low to avoid enemy radar. Developed in US in late 1970s.

Cruiser of World War II

cruiser, originally a ship of war larger than a frigate. In modern navies, a fast, lightly armoured but heavily armed vessel used mainly for engaging enemy raiders and escorting convoys.

Crusades, series of wars by W European Christians (11th-14th cent.) to recover Holy Land from Moslems, so called from cross worn as badge by crusaders. **First Crusade** (1095-9) followed speech by Pope Urban II urging Christians to fight to recover Holy Sepulchre. Led by great nobles, monarchs of Europe, culminated in capture of Jerusalem (1099); followed by estab. of Latin Kingdom of Jerusalem, and orders of Knights Hospitallers and Knights Templars. These orders were mainstay of later crusades. Turkish reconquests of Christian territ. occasioned later Crusades, beginning with unsuccessful **Second Crusade** (1147-9). Capture of Jerusalem by Saladin (1187) provoked **Third Crusade** (1189-92), led by Richard I of England, Philip II of France and Emperor Frederick I. Ended without recapture of Jerusalem, but trucial rights. **Fourth Crusade** (1202-4), proclaimed by Innocent III, was diverted from purpose by political ambitions of Venetians and ended in sacking of Constantinople by Crusaders and estab. of Latin Kingdom thereof. **Children's Cru-**

sade (1212) followed, ending in children being enslaved, or dying of hunger, disease. Innocent III preached **Fifth Crusade** (1217-21), directed at Egypt, with no positive conclusion. **Sixth Crusade** (1228-9) led by Emperor Frederick II, gained truce, partial surrender of Jerusalem, crowning of emperor as king thereof. Moslems soon reoccupied Jerusalem, and wars broke out again. **Seventh, Eighth** and **Ninth Crusades** were abortive attempts to stem decline of Christian power in Holy Land, ending with fall of last Christian stronghold, Acre (1291). There were also crusades, proclaimed by pope, against pagans, heretics, *eg* Wends, Hussites, Albigenses.

Crustacea (crustaceans), class of arthropods, incl. crabs, lobsters, barnacles, shrimps, water fleas. Mainly aquatic; 2 pairs of antennae, pair of mandibles, other appendages for walking, swimming, *etc.* Body sometimes covered by carapace.

cryogenics, study of production of very low temperatures and of their effect on properties of matter.

crypt, subterranean chamber or vault, esp. under a church floor. Crypts developed when early Christians built churches over tombs of martyrs or saints.

crystal, solidified form of a substance in which atoms or molecules are arranged in ordered geometrical patterns repeated regularly in space. Structure can be studied by examining diffraction patterns produced by passing beams of X-rays through specimens.

Crystal Palace, building of glass and iron, designed by Joseph Paxton to house Great Exhibition of 1851. Erected in Hyde Park, London, it was moved to Sydenham (1852-3); destroyed by fire (1936).

Cuba, isl. republic, largest of West Indies; incl. Isle of Pines (now named Isla de la Juventad). Area 114,524 sq km (44,218 sq mi); pop. 9,728,000; cap. Havana. Language: Spanish. Religion: RC. Mainly low-lying; mountainous in interior and SE. Sugar is main crop and export; tobacco growing (cigar mfg.), fruit growing; timber from inland forested mountains. Settled by Spanish in 16th cent. after Columbus' discovery (1492). Spanish-American War (1898) led to independence in 1902. Castro estab. Communist govt. after 1958 revolt; US-Soviet confrontation over missile installation in Cuba (1962).

cubism, art movement of early 20th cent., derived from work of Cézanne; subjects were portrayed, not as they appear, but by analysis into series of planes. Traditional perspective was abandoned and several different views of subject were often combined. Originated by Picasso and Braque, its formative period was 1907-14.

Cuchulain, hero of Celtic myth. Central to cycle based on exploits, in association with uncle, Conchobar, king of Ulster.

cuckoo, any of Cuculidae family of mainly insectivorous birds. Long slender body, greyish-brown on top, curved beak. Some species parasitic, laying eggs in othe birds' nests, *eg* common European cucko *Cuculus canorus.*

cuckoo flower, *Cardamine pratens* bittercress cress bearing white or purp flowers. Common in N temperate marshe

cuckoo-spit, *see* FROGHOPPER.

cucumber, *Cucumis sativus,* creeping pla of gourd family, native to NW Indi Widely grown in temperate regions f elongated, edible fruit. Gherkin is one of related species.

Cuernavaca, town of C Mexico, cap. Morelos state. Pop. 313,000. Health, touri resort.

cuirass, originally a leather jerkin. Fro medieval times, metal armour protecti the body above the waist, esp. in t 'cuirassiers' or heavy cavalry of the 17 cent.

Culdees, ancient order of monks of Celt church in Ireland and Scotland. La community, at Armagh, disbanded in 154

Culloden Moor, near Inverness, Highla region, N Scotland. Scene of defeat (174 of Bonnie Prince Charlie's Jacobite forc by Duke of Cumberland's Hanoveri army.

Cultural Revolution (1966-9), period ferment in China initiated under Mao Ts tung, resulting in purge of leadersh within Communist Party and state burea cracies in effort to recreate revolutiona spirit. Top officials removed incl. Chu Te Teng Hsiao-ping; radicals in army a youth (latter known as Red Guards), led Lin Piao, Chiang Ching (Mao's wif sparked open conflict, mass ralli Continuing chaos led Chou En-lai to restc order under army. Leaders discredit after Mao's death.

Cumae, ancient city of Campania, W Ita near Naples. Strabo calls it earliest Gre colony in Italy (founded *c* 750 BC). Tak 5th cent. BC by Samnites. Many remai incl. cavern of Cumaean Sybil.

Cumberland, William Augustus, Duke (1721-65), British army officer, son George II. Commanded the allied forces the Netherlands in the War of the Austr Succession, and crushed the 1745 rebell at Culloden with notorious sever earning himself the title 'Butcher'.

Cumberland, former county of NW Engla now in Cumbria; co. town Carlisle. L Dist. in S; drained by Derwent, Esk. Pl of Carlisle in N. Dairying, livest farming; granite, slate quarries.

Cumbernauld, town of Strathclyde, Scotland. Pop. 32,000. Created as 'n town' 1955; well-designed layout.

Cumbria, county of NW England. Area 6 sq km (2628 sq mi); pop. 472,000; admin. Carlisle. Created 1974, incl. Cumberla Westmorland, N Lancashire.

cumin, *Cuminum cyminum,* small ann plant of parsley family grown in Egypt Syria. Small white or pink flow Aromatic seeds used as flavouring.

Cummings, E[dward] E[stlin] (1894-19

Cumin

American poet, painter. Known for poems of typographical experiment, novel *The Enormous Room* (1922).

mulus cloud, *see* CLOUD.

neiform, from Latin meaning 'wedge-shaped', writing developed in Tigris-Euphrates basin, consisting of wedge-like marks impressed on clay tablets. Used by Babylonians and Assyrians.

nninghame-Graham, Robert Bontine (1852-1936), Scottish writer. Known for travel books, *eg A Vanished Arcadia* (1907) on Latin America. Involved in politics as liberal, socialist; first president Scottish Nationalist Party (1928).

pid, Roman god of love, identified with Greek Eros and Roman Amor. Represented as irresponsible cherub with bow and arrow.

pro-nickel, alloy of copper and nickel; ductile, resists corrosion. Used in coinage.

raçao, largest isl. of Netherlands Antilles, n S Caribbean. Area 461 sq km (178 sq mi); pop. 144,000. Has cap. of isl. group, Willemstad. Agric., incl. sisal, citrus fruit growing; famous liqueur mfg.; refining of oil from Venezuela. Discovered by Spanish 1499); Dutch occupation from 1634.

rare, alkaloid from bark of plants of genus *Strychnos.* Used by Amazon Indians as arrow poison. Causes paralysis. Limited medicinal use to relax muscles.

rassow, any of Cracidae family of arboreal birds of tropical America. Black or brown plumage, erect crest; resembles chicken. Species incl. great curassow, *Crax rubra.*

rie, Pierre (1859-1906), and **Marie Curie,** née Sklodowska (1867-1934), French scientists. Pierre studied effect of heat on magnetic substances, showing that magnetic properties are lost above certain temperature (Curie point); investigated PIEZOELECTRIC effect. Marie worked on uranium, radioactive element in pitchblende. Together they discovered radium and polonium and shared Nobel Prize for Physics (1903) with Becquerel. Later Marie pioneered medicinal use of radioactivity; isolated metallic radium, winning Nobel Prize for Chemistry (1911). *See also* JOLIOT-CURIE.

curium (Cm), transuranic element of actinide series; at. no. 96, mass no. of most stable isotope 247. Prepared 1944 by bombarding plutonium with alpha particles.

curlew, large wading bird with downward-curved bill, brownish-grey plumage. *Numenius arquata* is largest European wader.

curling, game played on ice, usually by two teams of four players, in which heavy stones are slid towards a target circle at far end of rink. Played in Scotland, North America and parts of Europe.

currant, shrub of genus *Ribes* of saxifrage family, native to W Europe. Fruit of black currant, *R. nigrum,* and red currant, *R. rubrum,* eaten fresh or made into conserves.

currency, *see* MONEY.

current, *see* ELECTRICITY.

curry, condiment originating in India made from turmeric, coriander, black and cayenne pepper, *etc.* Usually eaten with rice, meat, vegetables.

Curtin, John Joseph (1885-1945) Australian statesman, PM (1941-5). Leader of Labor Party from 1935.

Curzon, George Nathaniel, 1st Marquess Curzon of Kedleston (1859-1925), British statesman. Reform viceroy of India (1899-1905), pacified North West. Conservative foreign secretary, presided at Lausanne Conference (1922-3).

Custer, George Armstrong (1839-76), American army officer. Fought with distinction in the Civil War. Commanded a cavalry unit against the Indians and was killed with all his men by the Sioux at Little Bighorn.

customs, *see* TARIFFS.

Cuthbert, St (*c* 634-87), English missionary. Preached in Northumberland and Scottish borders. Bishop of Lindisfarne (685-7).

cuttlefish, any cephalopod mollusc of Sepioidea family. Ten tentacles around head, parrot-like beak. Flattened shell, or cuttlebone, is internal. Protects itself by ejecting cloud of brown 'ink'.

Cuvier, Georges Léopold Chrétien Frédéric Dagobert, Baron (1769-1832), French zoologist, geologist. Regarded as founder of comparative anatomy and palaeontology. Proposed 4-phylum system of animal classification based on inner structure.

Cuyp, Aelbert (1620-91), Dutch painter. Did landscapes, still lifes, town and river scenes; noted for his handling of light and atmosphere.

Cuzco, town of SC Peru, alt. 3400 m (11,200 ft). Pop. 121,000. Sugar cane, rice products from irrigated region; woollen textiles mfg. Cap. of Inca empire, its numerous palaces and temples, incl. Temple of the Sun, were destroyed by Spaniards under Pizarro. Many ruins remain.

Cwmbran, urban dist. and admin. hq. of Gwent, SE Wales. Pop. 41,000. Designated 'new town' in 1949. Steel, metal working industs.; bricks, tiles mfg.

cyanide, salt of hydrocyanic acid (hydrogen cyanide or prussic acid, HCN). Potassium and sodium cyanide are intensely poisonous white crystalline solids, with odour of bitter almonds; used in extracting gold from low-grade ores, electroplating, steel hardening.

Cybele, in Greek and Roman myth, 'mother of the gods'. Nature goddess, often associated with ATTIS.

cybernetics, science dealing with comparative study of operations of electronic computers and human nervous system. Defined by Norbert Wiener (1948) as 'the study of control and communication in the animal and the machine'.

Cyclades, rocky isl. group of SE Greece, in Aegean Sea. Area 2576 sq km (995 sq mi). Incl. Delos, Naxos, Syros (has chief port Hermoupolis). Wine, tobacco. Turkish from 1566; passed to Greece 1829.

cyclamen, genus of plants of primrose family, native to Mediterranean region. Heart-shaped leaves, flowers white to deep red with reflexed petals.

cycling, sport of bicycle riding. Various competitive events incl. road racing, time trialling, pursuit racing and sprints. Esp. popular in France, Belgium, Netherlands, where professional long-distance races such as Tour de France are held.

cyclone, area of relatively low atmospheric pressure together with surrounding wind system. Tropical cyclone is violent storm, *eg* hurricane, typhoon; temperate latitude cyclone now referred to as a DEPRESSION. Wind circulation is clockwise in S hemisphere, anti-clockwise in N hemisphere.

Cyclopes, in Greek myth, gigantic one-eyed beings. In Homer, race of shepherds, one of whom Odysseus blinds (*see* POLYPHEMUS). In Hesiod, they are craftsmen, sons of Uranus and Gaea.

cyclops, small freshwater crustacean of subclass Copepoda. Enlarged antennae used as oars; single median eye.

Cyclostomata (cyclostomes), class of marine chordates with eel-like body, jawless sucking mouth; no bone or scales. Attach themselves by mouth to fish, rasping flesh and sucking blood. Incl. LAMPREY and HAGFISH.

cyclotron, in physics, a kind of ACCELERATOR.

cymbals, orchestral untuned percussion instrument, of oriental origin; made of 2 concave metal discs which are clashed together or struck with a stick.

Cynics, Greek school of philosophy founded (4th cent. BC) by Antisthenes. Held desires to be impediment to happiness, hence self-sufficient ascetic life of followers, *eg* DIOGENES. Basis of STOICISM.

cypress, family of coniferous trees, Cupressaceae, native to Mediterranean regio[n] Asia and North America. Dark gree[n] needle leaves in overlapping pairs, wood[y] cones. Distinctive symmetrical form.

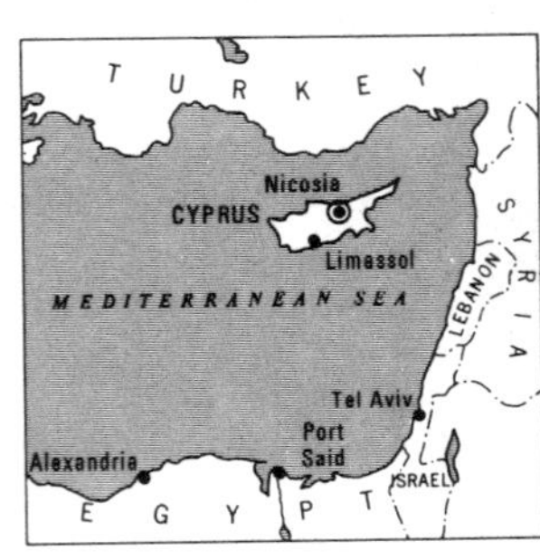

Cyprus

Cyprus (Gk. *Kypros*), isl. republic of Briti[sh] Commonwealth, in E Mediterranean. Ar[ea] 9270 sq km (3572 sq mi); pop. 616,000, 80 being Greek Cypriots; cap. Nicos[ia]. Languages: Greek, Turkish. Religio[n] Eastern Orthodox, Islam. Irrigated pla[in] between 2 mountain ranges. Pasto[ral] economy; grain, wine, olives grow[n]. Minerals incl. iron, copper. Ancient Bron[ze] Age culture; subsequently ruled by Assyr[ia] Persia, Rome, Turkey, Britain (1878-196[0]). Bitter conflict (1950-64, 1974) betwe[en] Greek, Turkish Cypriots; Turkish invasi[on] 1974, followed by partition.

Cyrano de Bergerac, Savinien (1619-5[5]) French author. Satirized society in *Histo[ire] comique des états et empires de la lu[ne]* (1657-62). Inspiration for Rostan[d's] dramatic hero, as longnosed poet-soldi[er] skilled dueller.

Cyrenaica, region of E Libya. Incl. fert[ile] coastal strip, Libyan Desert, Kufra oas[is]. First settled 7th cent. BC by Greeks, w[ho] founded Cyrene. Under Romans, Ara[bs] prior to Turkish rule from 16th ce[nt.] colonized by Italy 1911-42. Federal pr[ov.] (cap. Benghazi) 1951-63.

Cyrenaics, ancient Greek school [of] philosophy holding pleasure to be [the] greatest good, virtue to be the ability [to] enjoy. Thus opposed to Cynics in fi[rst] coherent statement of HEDONISM. Found[ed] by Aristippus (*c* 530-*c* 468 BC).

Cyril, St (*c* 827-69), Greek Christi[an] missionary. With his brother, **St Methodi[us]** (*c* 815-84), sent (863) to convert Moravia despite opposition of German rule[rs]. Cyrillic alphabet, used in Bulgaria, Russ[ia], Serbia, possibly invented by Cyril.

Cyrus the Great (d. 529 BC), founder [of] Persian empire. Overthrew Astyages [of] Media (551) and gained control of A[sia] Minor with defeat of Croesus (54[6]). Captured Babylon (539). Ruled w[ith] toleration, respecting local custo[ms] allowed exiled Jews to return to Palestine.

czar, *see* TSAR.

Czechoslovakia *(Ceskoslovensko),* republic of EC Europe. Area 127,842 sq km (49,360 sq mi); pop. 15,138,000; cap. Prague. Languages: Czech, Slovak. Religion: RC. Comprises plateau of Bohemia (W); lowland of Moravia (C); highlands of Slovakia (E) incl. W Carpathians, High Tatra. Agric. in fertile valleys (esp. cereals, sugar beet, hops); timber, coal, iron industs.; textiles, engineering. Formed (1918) from parts of Austria-Hungary. Occupied in stages by Germans (1938-45). Coup estab. Communist state (1948); liberalization movement suppressed by Soviet invasion (1968).

Czestochowa, city of S Poland, on R. Warta. Pop. 201,000. Railway junction. Iron and steel works, chemicals indust., textile, paper mfg. Monastery on Jasna Góra hill is pilgrimage centre.

Czechoslovakia

D

dab, *Limanda limanda,* food fish of flounder family, found in N Atlantic.

dabchick, bird of grebe family. European species, *Podiceps ruficollis,* is diving bird.

Dacca, cap. of Bangladesh. Pop. 1,730,000. Commercial, indust. centre on R. Dhaleswari. Textiles, jute products, chemicals; muslin mfg. centre until late 19th cent. Mogul cap. of Bengal in 17th cent.

dace, *Leuciscus vulgaris,* small freshwater fish of carp family with silver colouring.

Dachau, town of S West Germany, near Munich. Pop. 30,000. Site of Nazi concentration camp.

dachshund, small German dog, with long body, drooping ears and short legs. Short-haired coat; stands 20-25 cm/8-10 in. at shoulder.

dada or **dadaism,** literary, artistic movement of period 1916-22. Replaced rationality with deliberate madness, chaos in art. Dadaists incl. poet Breton, artists Arp, Duchamp. Developed into SURREALISM.

daddy-long-legs, *see* CRANE FLY.

Daedalus, in Greek myth, craftsman and inventor. Built Labyrinth to contain Minotaur in Crete (*see* MINOS). Made wings of feathers and wax to escape from Crete with son Icarus. Icarus flew too near the sun, the wax melted and he was drowned in the sea.

daffodil, various plants of genus *Narcissus* of amaryllis family with trumpet-like flower. Name usually restricted to common yellow daffodil or lent lily, *N. pseudonarcissus.*

Dagenham, part of Barking, E Greater London, England. Former mun. bor. of Essex. Has Ford motor plant, clothing, chemical mfg.

Daghestan, auton. republic of S European RSFSR, USSR; between E Great Caucasus and Caspian Sea. Area *c* 50,250 sq km (19,400 sq mi); pop. 1,627,000; cap. Makhachkala. Mainly mountainous, with coastal plain along Caspian. Stock raising; grain, cotton, fruit cultivated. Minerals largely undeveloped; some oil, natural gas.

Daguerre, Louis Jacques Mandé (1789-1851), French scene painter, physicist. Invented daguerrotype, photograph produced on copper plate treated with silver iodide; 1st practical method of photography.

dahlia, genus of perennial, tuberous-rooted late-flowering plants of daisy family. Native to Mexico and Central America. Widely cultivated for brightly coloured showy flowers.

Dahomey, *see* BENIN.

Dáil Eireann, legislative, popularly elected assembly of Republic of Ireland. First assembled (1919) in Dublin. After creatio of Irish Free State (1921), upper hous Seanad Eireann, created, which, with Dá (lower house) constitutes state legislature

An early Daimler model

Daimler, Gottlieb (1834-1900), Germa engineer, inventor. Improved intern combustion engine, furthering car indu Founded (1890) Daimler Motor Company.

Dairen, *see* LU-TA.

dairying, business of producing ar distributing milk and milk products. most countries, milk is consumed in liqu form. In others, *eg* Denmark, Ne Zealand, transportable milk products su as butter, cheese and dried milk domina dairy indust.

daisy, *Bellis perennis,* small perennial he of COMPOSITAE family, native to Europe a W Asia.

Dakar, cap. of Senegal, on Cape Ver penin. Pop. 799,000. Admin., commerci centre; port, exports groundnuts, anim products; univ. (1949), Pasteur Institu Former centre of slave trade.

Daladier, Edouard (1884-1970), Fren statesman. Premier (1933, 1933-4, 1938-4 forced to resign (1934) after Stavisky affa signed Munich Pact (1938) enabling Ge many to occupy Sudetenland. Interned Vichy govt. (1940), deported to Germa (1943-5).

Dalai Lama, head of Lamaist religion Tibet and Mongolia. Considered divir reincarnation of his predecessor; 5th Da Lama was given (1640) temporal rule ov all Tibet. During 1959 Tibetan rev against Chinese Communists 14th Da Lama went into exile in India.

Dali, Salvador (1904-), Spanish surrea artist. Influenced by Freud, he paint irrational dream world in a detai academic style; later work, in more :raditional style, incl. religious subjects.

llas, city of NE Texas, US; on Trinity R. Pop. 2,544,000. Commercial, indust. centre. Oil refining; important cotton market; aircraft, electronic equipment, chemical mfg. Settled 1841. President J. F. Kennedy assassinated here (1963).

lmatia, region of Yugoslavia, in Croatia, on Adriatic coast. Mountainous, incl. Dinaric Alps. Resorts incl. Dubrovnik, Split, Zadar. Passed from Austria to Yugoslavia (1919); Zadar and isls. ceded by taly (1947).

lmatian, breed of dog developed in Dalmatia. Short-haired, black spots on white coat; stands 48-55 cm/ 19-23 in. at houlder.

lton, John (1766-1844), English chemist. Proposed theory that all matter is omposed of indestructible atoms; atoms of same element were identical and differed from those of other elements only n weight. Prepared table of atomic weights and devised law of partial pressures of gases (Dalton's law).

n, barrier built across river to store water r regulate its flow for irrigation or to upply power. (*See* HYDRO-ELECTRIC POWER.)

man (*Damao*), former Portuguese enclave in W India. Pop. 69,000. Captured y Portuguese (1559), seized by India in 961. Part of union territ. of Goa, Daman nd Diu.

mascus (Arab. *Esh-Sham*), cap. of Syria. Pop. 1,097,000. Famous for silks and metalware. Early Christian centre under Romans; taken by Arabs (635), seat of aliph (661-750).

mocles, in classical legend, courtier of yracuse who, to show him the perils of a uler's life, was seated at a banquet by Dionysius I under a sword suspended by a ngle hair.

npier, William (*c* 1651-1715), English uccaneer, explorer. Took part in several uccaneering expeditions to Africa, panish America (1679-91). Commanded aval expedition to W and N Australia, ew Guinea, New Britain (1699-1701). ater piloted voyage round world (1708-11).

nson, *see* PLUM.

naë, in Greek myth, daughter of Acrisius, ng of Argos. Imprisoned by her father ecause of an oracle that she would bear a n who would kill him. Zeus entered the rison as a shower of gold and fathered ERSEUS.

Nang, port of central Vietnam on S China a. Pop. 492,000. Major US military base uring Vietnam war.

by, Thomas Osborne, Earl of 631-1712), English statesman. Impeached r treasonable negotiations with France n Charles II's behalf); imprisoned 679-84). Joined Whigs in inviting William Orange to replace James II; served as ng's chief minister (1690-5).

ce, the art of rhythmical, expressive ovement of the body, often to music. Developed from early ritual, *eg* fertility dances and mimetic dances illustrating movements of planets, events in battle, *etc.* Dancing is still part of the ritual of several ecstatic religious groups, *eg* dervishes, Hasidic Jews. In Greece, became part of drama. Allegorical forms developed in medieval Europe, *eg* dance of death. Division into court and folk dances stemmed from late Middle Ages with the *volta* becoming source of modern ballroom dances. BALLET first appeared in 16th-cent. Italian courts. In 20th cent. many dance crazes have been associated with jazz and rock music.

dandelion, several plants of genus *Taraxacum,* esp. *T. officinale,* wild, European plant, cultivated in Asia and North America. Leaves used in salads and as diuretic.

Daniel, apocalyptic book of OT, prob. written *c* 168 BC. Story of Daniel, a Jew living in 6th cent. BC. Captured and taken to Nebuchadnezzar's court, where he was famous for his wisdom.

Danish, language of N Germanic group of Indo-European family. Official language of Denmark, spoken also in Greenland, Faeroes, Iceland, Virgin Isls. Developed from Old Norse. Literature in existence since *c* 850.

D'Annunzio, Gabriele (1863-1938), Italian author, soldier. Belief that sensual pleasure alone gives meaning to life reflected in works, *eg* play *La Gioconda* (1898), poetry. Hero of nationalism, held Fiume for 15 months (1919-20), later pro-Fascist.

Dante [Alighieri] (1265-1321), Italian poet. Best known for *Divine Comedy,* long epic poem giving comprehensive view of human destiny, temporal and eternal; divided into journeys through Hell (*Inferno*) and Purgatory (guided by Vergil) and Paradise (guided by Beatrice). Other works incl. *La Vita Nuova* (1292), prose-linked lyrics addressed to idealized love, Beatrice.

Danton, Georges Jacques (1759-94), French revolutionary. Influential orator, took part in overthrow of Louis XVI (1792). Leader of revolutionaries in new National Convention, advocated spread of Revolution's ideas throughout Europe by war. Member of Committee of Public Safety (1793), eventually opposed REIGN OF TERROR. Guillotined after power struggle with extremists led by Robespierre.

Danube, river of C and SE Europe. Flows 2815 km (1750 mi) from Black Forest (West Germany) to Black Sea (Romania). Tributaries incl. Inn, Sava, Tisza, Prut. Ports incl. Vienna, Belgrade. Navigable below Ulm, passage controlled by commission based in Budapest.

Danzig, *see* GDAŃSK.

Daphne, in Greek myth, nymph loved by Apollo. In trying to flee from him, she was changed into a laurel tree.

daphne, genus of small evergreen flowering shrubs, native to Europe and Asia.

Daphnia, *see* WATER FLEA.

Danube

Dardanelles

Dardanelles (anc. *Hellespont*), narrow str. separating European and Asiatic Turkey; 64 km (40 mi) long, connects Aegean Sea and Sea of Marmara. Of great strategic and commercial importance; Troy stood nearby. In Turkish hands by 1402, it controlled entrance to Constantinople and Black Sea. Focus of conflict in decay of Ottoman Empire and also in WWI (*see* GALLIPOLI).

Dar-es-Salaam, cap. of Tanzania, on Indian Ocean. Pop. 517,000. Admin., commercial centre; port, exports sisal, cotton, diamonds; oil refining. Univ. (1961). Founded 1862.

Darién scheme, Scottish plan to set up a colony on Darién Isthmus, Panama, and gain access to trade in Pacific. Suggested by William PATERSON. Two expeditions (1698, 1699) to Darién failed through illness and Spanish opposition; great losses suffered by Scottish investors hastened Act of Union (1707).

Darius [I] the Great (d. 486 BC), Persian king (521-486). Estab. authority by suppressing revolts of usurpers in early years of reign, then organized personal representatives (satraps) to administer vast empire. Sent unsuccessful expedition to punish Greeks for supporting revolt Ionian city states (492). Second expediti defeated at Marathon (490).

Darjeeling, resort town of West Bengal, N India. Pop. 43,000. In Himalayan foothills alt. of over 1830 m (6000 ft). Nearby t plantations.

Darling, river of E Australia. Flows *c* 27 km (1700 mi) SW from W Great Dividi Range to Murray R. at Wentworth. Fl variable; Menindee Lakes storage scher controls water supply, irrigation, h.e.p.

Darlington, town of Durham, NE Englar Pop. 86,000. Woollens, engineering indus Stockton-Darlington was 1st passenger ra way line (1825).

Darmstadt, city of WC West Germany. Pc 136,000. Indust. centre, esp. railw engineering, chemicals. Former cap. Hesse-Darmstadt duchy.

Darnley, Henry Stuart, or **Stewart, Lo** (1545-67), English nobleman, 2nd husba of Mary Queen of Scots, father of James of Scotland. Joined in murder (1566) David Rizzio, Mary's favourite. Murder prob. at instigation of Earl of Bothw Mary's next husband.

Dartford, town of Kent, SE England, on Darent. Pop. 50,000. Cement, chemi mfg. Tunnel under Thames to Purfl (1963).

Dartmoor, moorland area of Devon, England; features large granite mas ('tors'). Mostly in national park; livestc rearing; wild ponies. Prison estab. 1806 French captives, used for convicts fr 1850.

Dartmouth, mun. bor. of Devon, England. Pop. 6000. Port; Royal Naval C (1905).

Darwin, Charles Robert (1809-82), Engl naturalist. His observations and ex rations during the *Beagle*'s voyages in Pacific led to theory of evolution known Darwinism, recorded in *On the Origin Species* (1859) and *The Descent of M* (1871). Theories on man's ancestry principle of natural selection bitte contested by contemporaries on th logical grounds.

Darwin, cap. of Northern Territ., Austra on N shore of Port Darwin. Pop. 41, Port, exports uranium, iron ore. Sett (1869) as Palmerston; renamed 1911, wh passed under federal control. Sever damaged in 1942 Japanese air raids, ag by cyclone (1974).

date palm, *Phoenix dactylifera,* tree gro widely in N Africa and W Asia. N cultivated in S California and Mexi Nutritious brown fruit eaten raw.

dating, in archaeology, assessment of ag remains. Methods incl. RADIOACTIVE DATI

Daubigny, Charles François (1817- French landscape painter. Associated w Barbizon school, influenced Monet.

Daumier, Honoré (1808-79), French ar Caricatured bureaucrats, politicians, b geoisie; imprisoned for representing L Philippe as 'Gargantua'. Painti describing contemporary life or on Don Quixote theme, incl. *Third Class Carriage*.

auphin, title of eldest son of kings of France. Prob. derives from dolphin device adopted (12th cent.) by counts of Vienne, first to bear the title. Title passed to French royal family in 1350.

auphiné, region and former prov. of SE France, cap. Grenoble. Mountainous in E; main rivers Drôme, Isère. Tourism, h.e.p., vines, silk mfg. Part of kingdom of Arles (10th-13th cent.), annexed by France (1456). Rulers took title DAUPHIN.

avao, seaport of Philippines, on Davao Gulf, SE Mindanao isl. Pop. 516,000 Centre of region producing hemp, timber, coffee. Underwent great indust. growth in 1960s.

avid or **Dewi, St** (d. *c* 588), patron saint of Wales. First abbot of Menevia (now St David's). Founded several monasteries in Wales. Feast day is 1st March.

avid (*c* 1060-*c* 970 BC), king of Israel; Hebrew national hero. Traditionally, harpist to King Saul and slayer of Philistine giant Goliath. Anointed king after death of Saul and Jonathan (*c* 1012). Captured Jerusalem, making it his cap.

avid I (1084-1153), king of Scotland (1124-53). Supported his niece, Matilda, in her struggle with Stephen for the English crown. Invaded England in 1138, defeated by Stephen at Northallerton. Promoted Anglo-Norman aristocracy in Scotland, encouraged trade, church.

avid II (1324-71), king of Scotland (1329-71), son of Robert the Bruce. Lived in France from 1333 after English victory, returned to Scotland 1341. Invaded England for French (1346), defeated and imprisoned till 1357. Succeeded by nephew, Robert II.

avid, Gerard (d. 1523), Flemish painter of Bruges school. Influenced by earlier Flemish masters, he painted religious scenes in a style which became obsolete in his lifetime. Works incl. *The Judgment of Cambyses*.

avid, Jacques Louis (1748-1825), French painter. Treated heroic and republican themes in austere neo-Classical manner; ardent supporter of Napoleon, he painted pictures glorifying his exploits. Works incl. *Death of Marat*.

avies, Peter Maxwell (1934-), English composer. Music employs mediaeval and Renaissance techniques set in modern context, often using parody. Works incl. opera *Taverner*.

Vinci, *see* LEONARDO DA VINCI.

avis, Jefferson (1808-89), American statesman. Secretary of war (1853-7); withdrew as senator for Mississippi at state's secession (1861). President of Confederacy (1861-5), criticized for centralizing policies which contradicted Southern cause of states' rights. Captured and confined by Federal troops (1865-7), never prosecuted.

vis or **Davys, John** (1550–1605), English navigator. Made 3 voyages (1585-7) in search of Northwest Passage, reached Baffin Bay via strait named after him. Killed by Japanese pirates in East Indies.

Davis, Miles (1926-), American jazz musician. Noted for cool style in playing trumpet and flugelhorn, working with small groups in 1950s and 1960s.

Davis Strait, arm of N Atlantic between Baffin Isl. and W Greenland. Length 640 km (*c* 400 mi); width at narrowest point 290 km (*c* 180 mi).

Davitt, Michael (1846-1906), Irish revolutionary. Joined FENIANS in 1865; imprisoned for treason-felony (1870). Released 1877, founded Land League with Parnell (1879). Imprisoned several times for involvement in land agitation. MP 1895-9.

Davy, Sir Humphrey (1778-1829), English chemist. Studied electrolysis, isolating sodium, potassium, boron, calcium, magnesium and barium. Discovered use of nitrous oxide as anaesthetic and identified chlorine as an element. Invented miner's safety lamp and electric arc.

Dawes, Charles Gates (1865-1951), American statesman. Author of Dawes Plan (1924) to facilitate German payment of reparations after WWI; shared Nobel Peace Prize (1925). Vice-president under Coolidge (1925-9).

Dawson, town of W Yukon Territ., Canada; on Yukon R. Pop. 1100. Tourist centre. Founded 1896 during Klondike gold rush, when pop. rose to *c* 20,000. Territ. cap. until 1951.

Dayan, Moshe (1915-), Israeli military leader. Army chief of staff (1953-8). As defence minister (1967-74), largely responsible for Israeli victory over Arab states (1967). Blamed for early reverses in 1973 October War. Resigned. Foreign minister (1977-9); involved in peace negotiations with Egypt.

Day-Lewis, C[ecil] (1904-72), English poet, b. Ireland. Member of left-wing literary movement of 1930s. Collections incl. *The Magnetic Mountain* (1933), *Overtures to Death* (1938). Wrote detective novels under pseud. Nicholas Blake. Created poet laureate 1968.

daylight saving time, time reckoned (usually 1 hour) later than standard time. Adopted in many countries as wartime measure; continued after WWII as 'summer' time by turning clocks ahead in spring and back in autumn.

Dayton, city of SW Ohio; on Great Miami R. Pop. 836,000. Machine tools, refrigerators, aircraft mfg. Wright brothers estab. aircraft research centre (1911). Centre of US military aviation development.

D-Day, term for the day in WWII on which the Allied invasion of Europe began; 6th June, 1944.

DDT, dichloro-diphenyl-trichloroethane, white powder used as insecticide, effective on contact. Developed during 1940s, it helps control insect-borne diseases, *eg* malaria, typhus, yellow fever. Use has been restricted because of harmful effects on animals caused by its accumulation in plants.

deadly nightshade, *see* NIGHTSHADE.

Dead Sea, salt lake on Jordan-Israel border, *c* 70 km (45 mi) long, 394 m (1292 ft) below sea level. Evaporation yields potash, bromide.

Dead Sea Scrolls, collection of ancient Jewish religious writings, found in caves NW of Dead Sea (1947 and later). Written during 1st cents. BC and AD, possibly by a community of ESSENES, they are of importance in study of origins of Christianity.

deafness, total or partial inability to hear. May be caused by accumulated wax, growth of bone in middle ear, diseases affecting foetus in early pregnancy, injury. Electronic hearing aids are used to amplify sound and alleviate deafness.

Dean, Forest of, Gloucestershire, W England. Ancient royal forest. Early indust. region (wood, coal, iron ore exploitation); largely deforested by 17th cent.

death, end of life and cessation of all vital functions in animal or plant. Heart may beat after cessation of breathing and resuscitation is sometimes possible through stimulation of nervous system shortly after cessation of heartbeat. In humans there is danger of brain damage if delay exceeds 4 mins.

death cap or **death cup,** *Amanita phalloides,* toadstool with pale yellow cap, white gills. Appears in autumn in deciduous woods. Deadly poisonous with no known antidote.

death penalty, *see* CAPITAL PUNISHMENT.

death's head hawk moth, *Acherontia atropos,* brown and yellow moth with skull-like mark on abdomen. Found in Europe, Africa; largest British moth with wingspan 13-15 cm/5-6 in.

Death Valley, arid basin of SE California, US; part of Great Basin region. Very high temperature in summer. Incl. W hemisphere's lowest point (*c* 86 m/282 ft below sea level).

death watch beetle, *Xestobium rufovillosum,* small brown beetle of Anobiidae family which attacks seasoned wood. Noted for sound made by head knocking against hard surface.

Deauville, town of Normandy, N France, at mouth of R. Touques. Pop. 6000. Resort with casino, racecourse.

Debrecen, city of E Hungary. Pop. 192,000. Railway jct.; agric. market, machinery. Calvinist coll. (1550), now univ. Seat of revolutionary govt. (1849).

Debs, Eugene V[ictor] (1855-1926), American socialist leader. President of American Railway Union, imprisoned (1894) for disobeying court order in Pullman strike. Pacifist, imprisoned (1918) under Espionage Act. Socialist candidate for Presidency 5 times.

Debussy, Claude (1862-1918), French composer. Works incl. piano music, *eg Clair de Lune,* orchestral pieces, *eg La Mer,* and opera *Pelléas et Mélisande.* Althoug impressionistic, his works are innovativ harmonically.

Decalogue, *see* TEN COMMANDMENTS.

decathlon, ten-event athletic contes comprising 100, 400, 1500 m runs, 110 hurdles, javelin and discus throws, shot pu high jump, long jump and pole vault.

Deccan, triangular plateau of SC Indi enclosed by Eastern and Western Ghats.

Decembrist Revolt, uprising in Petersburg, Russia, on accession Nicholas I in Dec. 1825. Group mainly army officers plotted to replace Nichol by his brother Constantine and obtain constitution. Its failure ended with hangi of some leaders.

decibel, in acoustics, numerical expressi of relative loudness of a sound: differen in decibels of 2 sounds is 10 times t common logarithm of the ratio of the power levels. Symbol dB.

decimal system, system of computati based on powers of 10. Decimal fractio are fractions having some power of 10 denominator; denominator is not usual written but is expressed by decimal poi Thus 25.03 is 2503/100. Used in metr system of weights and measures, mo national currencies.

Declaration of Independence, *see* INDEPE DENCE, DECLARATION OF.

decorated style, name given to seco period of English Gothic architectu which followed Early English in late 13 and 14th cents. Characterized by use of b tracery in window design, and complicat vaulting.

deductive method, *see* INDUCTIVE METHOD.

Dee, several rivers of UK. **1,** NE Scotla flows 140 km (87 mi) from Cairngorms North Sea at Aberdeen. **2,** In Wales a England, flows 113 km (70 mi) fr Gwynedd to Irish Sea via Cheshire.

deer, any of Cervidae family of rumina mammals, incl. deer, elks, reinde moose. Worldwide distribution exce Australia. Antlers, confined to ma except for reindeer and caribou, usua branched and shed annually.

defence mechanism, in psychiat unconscious behaviour pattern designed avert painful or anxiety-provoking feelin Forms incl. repression of distress or sublimation into useful forms, regression infantile behaviour, *etc.*

deflation, *see* INFLATION.

Defoe, Daniel (1660-1731), English auth Best known as author of novels *Robins Crusoe* (1719), *Moll Flanders* (1722) amo 500 works, mainly non-fiction. Also wr prolifically on politics, economics in thrice-weekly *Review* (1704-13).

Degas, [Hilaire Germain] Edg (1834-1917), French painter, sculpt Associated with the impressionists, sought to unite Classical art w immediacy of impressionism. W achieves spontaneity by asymmetric co position and cut-off views. Themes incl. racecourses, ballet scenes.

e Gaulle, Charles André Joseph Marie (1890-1970), French military and political leader, president (1958-69). Opposed armistice with Germany (1940) and formed Free French forces in Britain. Served as interim president (1945-6). Recalled (1958) as premier, elected 1st president of newly-created Fifth Republic. Ended French colonial power in Algeria; withdrew French forces from NATO (1966); vetoed British attempts to join EEC. Policies marked by nationalism and desire for European economic and military independence from US. Resigned after referendum defeat.

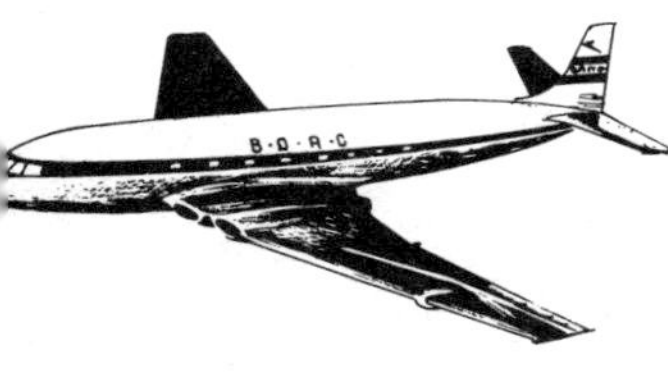

The De Havilland Comet (1949), the world's first jet airliner

e Havilland, Sir Geoffrey (1882-1965), English aircraft designer. Designed WWI fighters, WWII *Mosquito* fighter-bomber and the post-war *Comet,* 1st jet airliner.

eirdre, in Irish myth, beautiful woman whom Conchobar, King of Ulster, desired for his wife. She eloped with Naoise and had many adventures before being allowed to return. On return Naoise and his 2 brothers were treacherously killed, and Deirdre took her own life.

ists, those who believe in the existence of God on purely rational grounds without reliance on revelation or authority. Term esp. used for 17th and 18th cent. rationalists, *eg* Voltaire, Rousseau, Ben Franklin, who held that proof of existence of God was to be found in nature. Also known as freethinkers.

kker or **Decker, Thomas** (*c* 1572-1632), English dramatist. Known for comedies of London life, *eg, The Shoemaker's Holiday* (1600).

lacroix, [Ferdinand Victor] Eugène (1798-1863), French painter. Major painter of Romantic movement, he used historical, literary, Arab themes. Works incl. *Liberty Leading the People.*

La Mare, Walter (1873-1956), English author. Known for fantasy and children's verse, *eg The Listeners* (1912), *Peacock Pie* (1913).

laware, group of closely related North American Indian tribes. Migrated to Atlantic from NW. Made treaty with William Penn (1682), but Iroquois attacks drove them into Ohio. Survivors of massacre (1782) in Pennsylvania fled to Ontario, where their descendants now live.

Delaware, state of E US, on Atlantic. Area 5328 sq km (2057 sq mi); pop. 582,000; cap. Dover; largest city Wilmington. Mainly low-lying, hilly in N. Agric. incl. fruit, vegetable growing; poultry rearing, fishing important. Chemical indust. English settlement (1664); one of original 13 colonies of US. Remained in Union during Civil War (1861-5) despite being slave state.

Delft, town of W Netherlands, on Schie canal. Pop. 81,000. Ceramics ('delftware') mfg. begun 16th cent. Gothic churches. Birthplace of Vermeer.

Delhi, union territ. of N India. Area 1484 sq km (573 sq. mi); pop. 3,647,000. Old Delhi, on R. Jumna, important railway centre; textile mfg., gold and silver filigree work. Reconstructed in 17th cent. by Shah Jehan; fort contains Imperial Palace (1638-48) and Jama Masjid mosque. Interim cap. of India (1912-31), succeeded by neighbour **New Delhi,** which became cap. of republic (1947). Pop. 293,000. Univ. (1922).

Delian League, union of Greek states founded at Delos (478 BC) under Athenian leadership; later developed into an Athenian empire. Disbanded at end of Peloponnesian War (404 BC). Confederation revived to resist Spartan aggression (378 BC); lasted until defeat by Philip of Macedon (338 BC).

delirium, brain disturbance marked by extreme excitement, hallucinations, confused speech. May result from disease, high fever, *etc.* Delirium tremens is form of delirium associated with chronic alcoholism.

Delius, Frederick (1862-1934), English composer. Work is both romantic and impressionist with an individual harmonic quality. Best-known pieces incl. orchestral works, *eg, Brigg Fair,* and choral work *Sea Drift.*

della Robbia, *see* ROBBIA.

Delos (*Dhilos*), small isl. of SE Greece, in Cyclades. Traditional birthplace of Apollo, Artemis, important religious remains.

Delphi (*Delphoi*), ancient city of C Greece, in Phocis, at foot of Mt. Parnassus. Site of Delphic oracle and Pythian games. Remains incl. temple to Apollo.

delphinium, genus of hardy plants of buttercup family. Spikes of spurred, irregular flowers, usually blue, on tall stalk. Also called larkspur.

delta, roughly triangular area of alluvial deposits formed at mouth of a river. Consists of complex of distributary channels, lagoons, marshes. Usually very fertile, many support large agric. pop.

Demerara, river of Guyana. Rises in Guiana Highlands, flows N *c* 320 km (200 mi) to enter Atlantic at Georgetown. Used to transport bauxite.

Demeter, in Greek myth, earth goddess of corn, harvest, fruitfulness. Daughter of Cronus and Rhea; mother by Zeus of PERSEPHONE. She and her daughter were leading figures in Eleusinian mystery cults, representing seasonal cycle. Identified with Roman Ceres.

De Mille, Cecil B[lount] (1881-1959), American film producer-director. Known for adventure films in 1930s-40s, *eg The Plainsman* (1936), and later for biblical epics, *eg The Ten Commandments* (1956).

democracy, govt. in which the people hold power either directly or through elected representatives, rather than by class, group or individual. In Greek city states, democracy took direct form of plebiscite or popular assembly, with exclusion of slaves. Modern democracy evolved out of demands for political and legal equality, later economic and social equality; such demands provoked American and French revolutions. Modern Western democracy is based on competing party system, with emphasis on rule of law and freedom of expression.

Democratic Party, in US, one of the two major political parties. Origins in Democratic Republican Party founded by Jefferson (1800) in opposition to Hamilton's Federalists. Name changed to present one under Jackson (1828). Splits, created by slavery issue and Civil War, led to eclipse of party; revived with support of South after RECONSTRUCTION (1876). In 20th cent., attracted Negro and ethnic minorities. Identified with reform, esp. after F.D. Roosevelt's NEW DEAL (1932).

Democritus (*c* 460-*c* 370 BC), Greek philosopher. Developed atomistic theory of matter. Held that truth could be discovered by thought and that perceptions lead to confusion.

demography, science of statistics dealing with distribution, density, data of birth, marriage, death of populations. Used to determine rates of birth, death, *etc*, in analysis of social systems.

Demosthenes (*c* 384-322 BC), Athenian statesman, orator. Advocated resistance to growing power of Philip of Macedon in series of orations, *Philippics* and *Olynthiacs*, but Philip triumphed at battle of Chaeronea (338). After death of Alexander the Great, organized unsuccessful revolt against Antipater; took poison to avoid capture.

demotic writing, Egyptian flowing (cursive) script, derived from HIERATIC in 7th cent. BC and lasting until 5th cent. AD. Written from right to left.

Denbighshire, former county of N Wales, now in Clwyd. Mountainous in S; scenic, fertile valleys. Coalmining (centred on Wrexham); slate quarrying; agric. Co. town was **Denbigh,** mun. bor. in Vale of Clwyd. Pop. 8000.

Deng Xiaoping, *see* TENG HSIAO-PING.

denim, strong coarse twill-weave cotton fabric, first made in Nîmes, France. Name derives from *serge de Nîmes*.

Denis or **Dionysius of Paris, St** (d. *c* 258), patron saint of France. First bishop of Paris. Traditionally a missionary sent into Gaul *c* 250 and martyred at Montmartre ('Martyr's Hill').

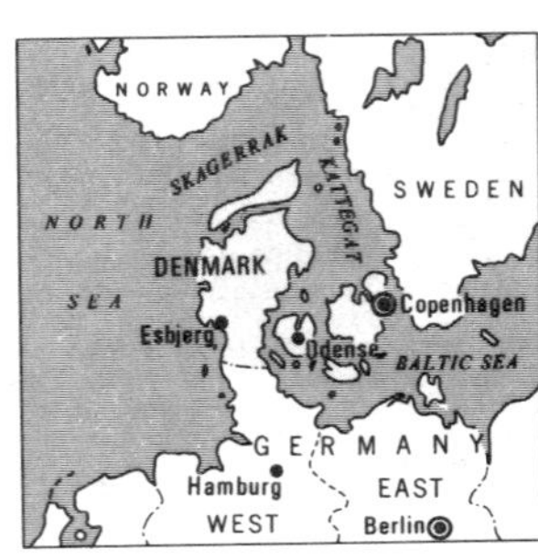

Denmark

Denmark (*Danmark*), kingdom of N Europe. Area 43,022 sq km (16,611 sq mi); pop. 5,104,000; cap. Copenhagen. Language: Danish. Religion: Lutheranism. Comprises Jutland penin., Baltic isls. incl. Zealand, Laaland, Fyn, Bornholm. Overseas terrs. incl. Greenland, Faeroes. Agric., esp. dairying, livestock; fishing. United with Sweden (1397-1523), with Norway (1397-1814); lost Norway in Napoleonic wars, Schleswig-Holstein to Prussia (1864). Under German occupation (1940-5). Joined EEC in 1973.

density, in physics, mass per unit volume of a substance; usually measured in grams per cubic cm. Density of water is 1 gram per cc at 4°C.

dentistry, care and treatment of teeth and gums. Egyptian writings of *c* 16th cent. BC describe dental care, but professional dentistry dates from 19th cent. Important developments incl. use of X-rays, high speed drills, local anaesthetics and taking of fluoride to reduce dental caries.

dentition, number and kind of teeth and their arrangement in mouths of vertebrates. Most lower vertebrates are homodonts (teeth are all similar); in heterodonts, several different types of teeth are present (incisors, canines, premolars and molars).

Denver, cap. of Colorado, US; on South Platte R. Alt. 1609 m (5280 ft). Pop. 1,417,000. Transport jct.; mining machinery, meat produce, air defence industries. Recreation centre. Founded 1859. Cap. from 1867.

deodar, *Cedrus deodara,* species of cedar native to Himalayas with fragrant, durable light-red wood. Cultivated as ornamental.

depreciation, in accounting, reduction in value of CAPITAL through wear, deterioration or obsolescence. Allowance is made for this in book-keeping so that income is not overestimated.

depression, in economics, period of crisis characterized by falling prices, contraction of production, restricted credit, unemployment, bankruptcies. Usually interpreted as overproduction of goods

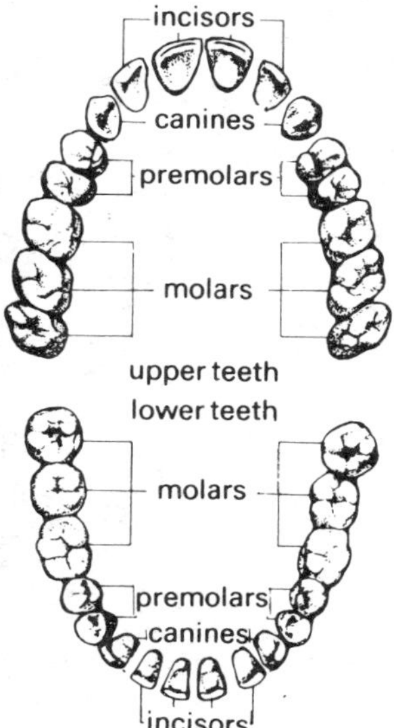

Dentition of a human adult

linked with decreased demand; the resulting fall in consumer purchasing power tends to give cumulative effect. Before 18th cent. usually had non-economic causes, *eg* crop failure. Subsequently, causes mainly indust. or commercial. The Great Depression of 1930s followed 1929 crash of New York stock market.

pression, in meteorology, area of relatively low atmospheric pressure, characteristic of temperate latitudes. Formed by warm tropical air meeting and rising above cold polar air, with associated formation of fronts. May be very extensive; brings unsettled, rainy weather. Also *see* CYCLONE.

pression, in psychiatry, emotional condition characterized by feeling of hopelessness, inadequacy, loss of vigour. May be neurotic or psychotic, *eg* manic-depressive psychosis. Some forms are treated by drugs or electric shock therapy.

Quincey, Thomas (1785-1859), English essayist. Known for *Confessions of an English Opium Eater* (1822).

rain, André (1880-1954), French painter. Prominent member of fauve group, his early work is characterized by use of patches of vibrant pure colour. Later influenced by Cézanne and cubism, reverted to sombre neo-Classical style.

rby, Edward George Geoffrey Smith Stanley, 14th Earl of (1799-1869), British statesman, PM (1852, 1858-9, 1866-8). As Whig colonial secretary, sponsored bill abolishing slavery in British Empire (1833). Joined Tories under Peel; later headed protectionist Tories after split over Peel's free trade policies (1846).

Derby, English horse race, founded (1780) by Earl of Derby, run over course 1.5 mi (2.4 km) long at Epsom, Surrey, in May or June. Also *see* KENTUCKY DERBY.

Derbyshire, county of NC England. Area 2631 sq km (1015 sq mi); pop. 896,000; admin. hq. Matlock. Peak Dist. in NW; lowland in S, E. Mineral springs (*eg* Buxton); stock rearing; coalmining. Co. bor. **Derby,** former co. town, on R. Derwent. Pop. 215,000. Railway jct.; aircraft engines; famous porcelain mfg.

dermatitis, inflammation of skin. Atopic dermatitis or eczema, characterized by an itchy rash, is often associated with allergies such as hay fever. Contact dermatitis is allergic reaction to substances touching skin.

Derry, *see* LONDONDERRY.

dervish, mendicant monk of ISLAM. Various sects are characterized by extreme methods of producing ecstatic states, *eg* whirling and howling dervishes. Strongly antinomian, claiming special favour with God. Theology based on SUFISM.

Derwentwater, lake of Cumbria, NW England. In Lake Dist.; length 5 km (3 mi).

Desai, [Shri] Morarji Ranchhodji (1896-79), Indian political leader, PM (1977-79). Leader of opposition to Mrs Gandhi (1969-77), imprisoned under emergency powers. Led Janata coalition govt. 1977-79.

Descartes, René (1596-1650), French philosopher, mathematician. Started from position of universal doubt, tempered only by dictum 'I think, therefore I am'. Created system known as Cartesian dualism, based on distinction between spirit and matter, in *Discours de la Méthode* (1637). Also regarded as founder of analytical geometry, developed algebraic notation. Contributed much to science of optics.

desert, any barren, unproductive region where rainfall is less than 25 cm/10 in. per year. Surface may be sandy or stony, sometimes with poor scrub vegetation; pop. is scant, specially adapted. Deserts may be hot (*eg* Sahara, Arabian), cool mid-latitude (*eg* Gobi) or cold and perpetually ice-covered (as in N Canada, Siberia).

Des Moines, cap. of Iowa, US; at confluence of Des Moines and Raccoon rivers. Pop. 328,000. Commercial, transport centre in Corn Belt. Coal mining, printing and publishing industs., agric. machinery mfg. Became cap. 1857.

Despenser, Hugh le (1262-1326), English courtier. Chief adviser to Edward II, joined at court by his son, **Hugh le Despenser** (d. 1326). Both were banished by the barons (1321-2), but on return held real power over England, dominating Edward until his overthrow (1326) by Isabella and MORTIMER. Despensers then executed.

Des Prés or **Desprez, Josquin** (*c* 1440-1521), Flemish composer. Developed counterpoint to great expressive ends in Masses, motets and secular songs.

destroyer, a warship originally built (1893) as a defence against fast boats carrying the newly-invented torpedo. Used in WWII for anti-submarine work, escort and reconnaissance, it has now been largely superseded by the smaller frigate.

détente, relaxation of international tensions and hostilities, manifested in treaties or trade agreements. Détente was estab. as policy between US and USSR in mid-1970s, esp. in fields of strategic arms and influence in Third World. Under strain since Soviet invasion of Afghanistan (1979).

detergent, substance used to improve cleansing power of water, *eg* soap. Acts by emulsifying oil on dirty surfaces, thus allowing water to dislodge exposed dirt particles. Synthetic detergents produce no scum, but phosphate present in some is source of pollution.

determinism, in philosophy, doctrine that phenomena are conditioned by preceding data, *eg* denial of moral choice in ethics. Also finds support in psychoanalysis, which denies existence of causeless acts. Opposite of FREE WILL.

detonator, explosive compound, *eg* mercuric fulminate, capable of rapid decomposition. Shock waves created used to set off more inert explosives.

Detroit, port of SE Michigan, US: on Detroit R. between L. St Clair and L. Erie. Pop. 4,669,000. Major shipping, rail centre. World's leading automobile producer (Ford, General Motors, Chrysler). Other industs. incl. food processing, chemicals, steel mfg., shipyards, oil refining. Settled by French (1701).

Dettingen, village of Bavaria, SC West Germany, on R. Main. Scene of Allies' victory (1743) over French in War of Austrian Succession.

deuterium (D), isotope of hydrogen; mass no. 2. Constituent of HEAVY WATER (D_2O). Deuteron is name given to deuterium nucleus.

Deuteronomy (Gk.,=second law), in OT, fifth book of Pentateuch. Contains core of Jewish law, ascribed traditionally to Moses.

De Valéra, Eamon (1882-1975), Irish statesman, b. US. Participant in Easter Rebellion, imprisoned (1916). Became head of Sinn Fein (1917) and of revolutionary Dáil. Left Dáil (1922) over exclusion of Northern Ireland after creation of Irish Free State; returned (1927) at head of Fianna Fáil party. PM (1937-48, 1951-4, 1957-9), kept Ireland neutral in WWII; president (1959-73).

devaluation, deliberate lowering of value of currency in terms of gold or other currencies, so that its exchange rate falls. Resulting increase in cost of imports and fall in price of exports may check deficit in BALANCE OF PAYMENTS through sale of more goods abroad.

Devil, the, *see* SATAN.

devil fish, name given to manta ray a[nd] type of American octopus.

devil's coach horse, *Staphylinus olens,* lar[ge] carnivorous beetle of W Europe. Ho[lds] abdomen erect; emits offensive odo[ur] when threatened.

Devil's Island, *see* FRENCH GUIANA.

devolution, delegation of specific powers [of] authority by nation's central govt. to lo[cal] governing units. Devolved pow[ers] restricted to education, health, transpo[rt] *etc.* Often adopted as constitutio[nal] response to national self-determinati[on] movements. Differs from FEDERALISM [in] that sovereignty in all areas remains w[ith] central govt. and legislature.

Devolution, War of (1667-8), war arising [out] of Louis XIV's claim to Spani[sh] Netherlands. France opposed by Tri[ple] Alliance of United Provinces, Swed[en,] England. Peace concluded with Treaty [of] Aix-la-Chapelle.

Devon, county of SW England. Area 6715 [sq] km (2592 sq mi); pop. 948,000; admin. [town] Exeter. Hilly, over 610 m (2000 ft) [on] Dartmoor; rich agric. lowlands. Livesto[ck] rearing, dairy farming (esp. crea[m]) fishing; mining; tourism. Sea ports w[ere] hist. important (esp. Plymouth).

Devonian period, fourth geological per[iod] of Palaeozoic era; began *c* 395 mill[ion] years ago, lasted *c* 50 million yea[rs]. Formation of Old Red Sandstone, sha[le;] climax of Caledonian mountain buildi[ng] period. Fauna incl. ammonoid cepha[lo]pods, jawed fish, crinoids, last graptoli[tes;] flora incl. treefern forests. Also [see] GEOLOGICAL TABLE.

dew, water deposited on surfaces wh[en] decreasing temperature causes saturat[ion] of water vapour in air. Dew point [is] temperature at which dew forms; if be[low] freezing point, dew freezes and hoar fr[ost] results.

Dewar, Sir James (1842-1923), Scot[tish] chemist. Researched in low temperat[ure] physics; first to liquefy and soli[dify] hydrogen. Developed vacuum flask [for] insulating fluids, forerunner of Thermos.

diabetes, disease characterized by excess[ive] secretion of urine. *Diabetes melli[tus],* caused by insulin deficiency, leads [to] excess glucose in blood and urine. Mar[ked] by loss of weight; acidosis and coma m[ay] follow. Treatment by controlled diet [and] insulin injections.

Diaghilev, Serge Pavlovich (1872-19[29]), Russian ballet impresario. Revi[ved] Russian ballet, making it serious [art] involving leading dancers, musicia[ns,] artists of day, incl. Pavlova, Nijins[ky,] Stravinsky, Fokine, Bakst. Founded Bal[lets] Russes (1909) which toured in W Euro[pe,] Americas, profoundly influencing ba[llet] everywhere except Russia.

dialect, form of speech peculiar to a local[ity,] community, or social group which devia[tes] from the postulated standard speech [of] users' native language.

ialectical materialism, method of hist. analysis, formulated by Marx and Engels, which applies Hegel's dialectic method to observable social processes and natural phenomena. Following FEUERBACH, they substituted materialism for ideas as the basis of the thesis-antithesis-synthesis process. In society, control of means of production determines social structure of classes; conflict between them results in hist. change.

ialysis, in chemistry, separation of colloidal particles from substances in true solution. Technique involves dissolved molecules passing through a membrane more rapidly than larger colloid molecules. Artificial kidney purifies blood by dialysis.

iamagnetism, property of certain substances, *eg* bismuth, of being repelled by magnetic fields. Results from substance being weakly magnetized in direction opposite to external field.

iamond, hardest known mineral, a crystalline form of carbon. Occurs in alluvial deposits and ultrabasic igneous rocks. Gem forms are transparent, brilliant and colourless; others may be yellow, blue, black, *etc.* Flawless crystals used in jewellery; largest is 'Cullinan' in British crown; indust. diamonds used in cutting tools, abrasives. Major source of gem diamonds is South Africa; indust. diamonds mainly from Zaïre, Brazil, Ghana.

iana, in early Roman myth, goddess of the moon, hunting, women in childbirth. Identified with Greek Artemis. Worshipped in Rome as Virgin goddess; her temple at Aricia associated with fertility cult.

arrhoea, frequent discharge of watery faeces. Often caused by inflammation of intestine by bacteria, viruses, *etc,* or by nervous stress. May be treated by drugs or absorbents such as kaolin.

atom, microscopic plant of ALGAE group with silica-containing shell, found in fresh or salt water in Arctic and other cold regions. Diatomaceous earth and diatomite, formed from shells of dead diatoms, are used industrially, esp. for insulating against heat.

az or **Dias, Bártolomeu** (d. 1500), Portuguese navigator. First European to voyage around Cape of Good Hope (1488), opening up sea route to India.

az, Porfirio (1830-1915), Mexican statesman. President (1877-80, 1884-1911). Lost power during revolt under Madero, went into exile.

az de Vivar, Rodrigo (*c* 1040–99), Spanish soldier, national hero, called 'El Cid Campeador' (Lord Champion). Banished from Castile (1081) by Alfonso VI; became soldier of fortune, fighting both Moors and Christians. Captured Valencia (1094), ruling it until his death. Subsequently celebrated in literature, folklore; adopted as heroic leader of *reconquista* of Spain from Moors.

e, small cubes usually of ivory or bone, sides of which are marked by different numbers of dots (so that opposite faces total 7). Several games of chance, incl. craps, poker dice and backgammon, are played with dice.

Dickens, Charles [John Huffam] (1812-70), English novelist. Began as journalist, soon started serial works attacking social abuses, often blending sentiment with humorous caricature, *eg Pickwick Papers* (1836-7), *Nicholas Nickleby* (1838-9). Major works incl. *Great Expectations* (1860-1), *Our Mutual Friend* (1864-5). Known for detailed, realistic creation of world and inhabitants.

Dickinson, Emily [Elizabeth] (1830-86), American poet. Lived in seclusion. Poetry (first pub. 1890) noted for intense, idiosyncratic style.

dictator, in ancient Rome, magistrate appointed in times of emergency to rule with absolute power. In modern usage denotes ruler with absolute power, authority, esp. one exercising it tyrannically. Characteristically, rule tends to TOTALITARIANISM.

dictionary, book of alphabetically listed words in a language, with definitions, derivations, pronunciations, *etc.* Bilingual dictionaries provide equivalents of words in another language. Early English dictionaries incl. Samuel Johnson's *Dictionary of the English Language* (1755). In America, Noah Webster's *Dictionary of the English Language* (1806) is 1st example.

Diderot, Denis (1713-84), French philosopher. Chief editor of *Encyclopédie* (1747-72).

Dido, founder-queen of Carthage in Roman legend. Best known through Vergil's use of legend in *Aeneid,* in which love between her and AENEAS almost causes him to betray his duty to found Rome. When he leaves, she kills herself.

Diefenbaker, John George (1895-79), Canadian statesman, PM (1957-63). Leader of Progressive Conservatives (1956-67).

dielectric, substance which does not conduct electricity but can sustain an electric field. Used to separate plates in capacitors.

Dien Bien Phu, *see* INDO-CHINESE WAR.

Dieppe, town of Normandy, N France, on English Channel. Pop. 30,000. Port, ferry service to Newhaven (England); resort, fishing, shipbuilding. Scene of Allied commando raid (1942).

diesel engine, type of INTERNAL COMBUSTION ENGINE invented by German engineer Rudolf Diesel (1858-1913). Air drawn into cylinder is heated by compression, then ignites fuel oil injected into cylinder; resulting explosion provides power stroke. Though initially more expensive than equivalent petrol engine, uses cheaper fuel. Patented 1892.

Dietrich, Marlene, orig. Maria Magdalene von Losch (*c* 1902-), American film actress, cabaret singer, born Germany. Achieved fame in *The Blue Angel* (1930).

differential calculus, mathematical study

of rates of change of continuously varying functions. Devised independently by Newton and Leibnitz to study problems in dynamics and geometry. Important applications in physics where many phenomena are described by laws dealing with rate of change; leads to study of differential equations.

diffraction, breaking up of ray of light into bright and dark bands or coloured bands, observable after ray has passed through narrow slit or over sharp edge of opaque object. Caused by INTERFERENCE. Effect used in diffraction grating to produce spectra; grating usually consists of glass plate or polished metal surface ruled with equidistant parallel lines.

diffusion, in chemistry, intermingling of liquids or gases by continuous thermal motion of their molecules or ions. Gases spread out and mix by diffusion.

digestion, process by which food is broken down by enzymes into forms which can be used in METABOLISM. In man, carbohydrates are broken down by ptyalin in saliva and by amylase in intestine; protein by pepsin in stomach; fats by action of lipase and bile salts.

Diggers, members of 17th cent. English socio-religious sect, offshoot of LEVELLERS; *fl* 1649-50. Led by Gerrard Winstanley, combined communistic and egalitarian principles; estab. colony on common land in Surrey, destroyed (1650) by a mob.

digital computer, *see* COMPUTER.

digitalis, genus of Old World plants of figwort family. Incl. FOXGLOVE.

Dijon, city of Burgundy, E France, cap. of Côte-d'Or dept. Pop. 203,000. Road and railway jct., engineering, food processing, wine trade; univ. (1722). Hist. cap. of Burgundy, passed to France (1477). Medieval cultural centre. Cathedral (13th cent.).

dill, *Anethum graveolens,* European annual or biennial herb of parsley family. Aromatic seeds used in flavouring.

diminishing returns, law of, in economics, prediction that, after a certain point, an increase in one factor of production (other factors being constant) will yield relatively decreasing returns. Applied to indust. production and exploitation of land.

Dimitrov, Georgi (1882-1949), Bulgarian political leader. Arrested in Berlin on charge of setting fire to REICHSTAG (1933). Acquitted, went to Soviet Union; secretary-general of Comintern (1934-43). Returned to Bulgaria (1944) to lead Communist Party; premier (1946-9).

Dinaric Alps (*Dinara Planina*), mountain range of W Yugoslavia. Separates Dalmatia from Bosnia and Hercegovina. Name also applied to all limestone ranges between Julian Alps (NW) and Balkan system (SE).

dingo, *Canis dingo,* wolf-like wild dog, only indigenous carnivore of Australia. Erect ears, bushy tail; preys on sheep herds. Probably descended from domestic dogs introduced to Australia in prehist. times.

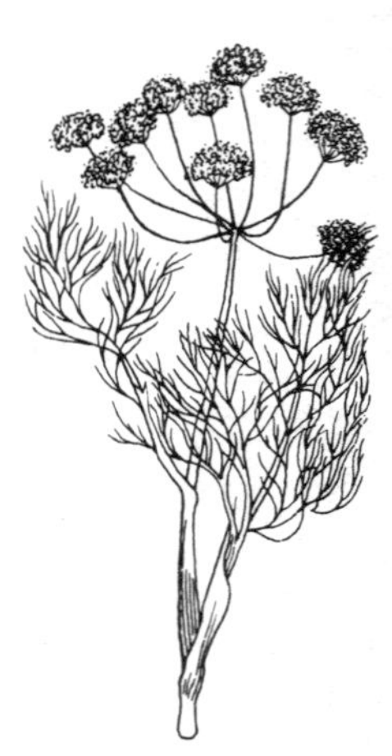

Dill

dinosaur, any of large group of extin mainly terrestrial reptiles of Mesozoic e Reached lengths of 27.5 m/90 ft. Mair herbivorous; later species of Cretacec period carnivorous, with larger brains, tyrannosaur.

Diocletian, full name Gaius Valeri Diocletianus (245-313), Roman emper (284-305), b. Dalmatia. Appointed Ma mian joint emperor (286) and Galerius a Constantius sub-emperors (292) to he defend empire. Persecuted Christia severely. Abdicated in favour of Galerius

diode, in electronics, thermionic val consisting of evacuated tube containing electrodes. Electrons are emitted heated cathode and migrate to positiv charged plate (anode). Used in conversi of alternating current to direct current, in radio and television receivers.

Diogenes (*c* 412-323 BC), Greek philosoph Cynic and ascetic, pupil of Antisthen Said to have lived in a tub.

Diomedes, in Greek myth, Thracian ki son of Ares. Fed his horses on human fle Killed by Heracles (8th Labour), who th took horses to Mycenae.

Dionysius the Elder (*c* 430-367 BC), Gre political leader in Sicily. Became tyrant Syracuse (405) and carried out 2 success wars against Carthage. Defeated d astrously in 3rd war. Succeeded by his s **Dionysius the Younger** (*fl* 350 BC), w was driven out of Syracuse by Di Returned after latter's murder (354) t expelled 344.

ionysus (Roman name Bacchus), Greek god of wine, fertility, son of Zeus and Semele. His worship originated in Thrace and Asia Minor, accompanied by ecstasy in worshippers (esp. women) called Maenads or Bacchantes. Worshipped with Apollo at Delphi, and in countryside as god of vegetation.

ior, Christian (1905-57), French fashion designer. Estab. fashion houses in Paris (1946) and New York (1948). Introduced 'New Look' (1947), extravagant style contrasting sharply with wartime fashions.

ioscuri, in Greek and Roman myth, joint name for Castor and Polydeuces (Lat. Pollux), according to Homer, twin sons of LEDA by Zeus. Placed by him among stars as constellation Gemini.

phtheria, acute infectious disease of throat and other mucous membranes caused by bacteria. Characterized by formation of membranous crust in air passages; toxin produced by bacteria can produce local paralysis.

plodocus, genus of extinct semi-aquatic herbivorous dinosaurs, division Sauropoda. Similar in size and appearance to BRONTOSAURUS. Fossils have been found in Jurassic rocks of US.

plomatic service, body of representatives of a govt. responsible for conduct of relations with foreign govts. Estab. systematically by Italians in 15th cent., esp. by Venice. Soon imitated by leading European states. By 1815 classes, *ie* ambassadors, envoys, ministers resident and chargés d'affaires, recognized. Diplomatic immunity, *ie* diplomat being placed outside law of accredited country, estab. 16th-17th cent. Diplomat is responsible to his own foreign minister, negotiates with foreign ministry of country to which he is accredited.

per or **water ouzel,** any of Cinclidae family of aquatic perching birds. Able to walk under water in pursuit of insects, larvae.

ptera, order of 2-winged flies. Mouthparts lengthened into proboscis for piercing, sucking. *See* FLY.

rac, Paul Adrien Maurice (1902-), English physicist. Introduced relativity theory into study of wave mechanics, extending de Broglie's ideas of wave nature of electron. Predicted existence of positron (discovered 1932). Shared Nobel Prize for Physics (1933) with Schrödinger.

ect current (DC), electric current flowing always in same direction. Produced by batteries.

ectory, executive body of five men, appointed by the two legislative chambers, which governed France (1795-9). Overthrown by coup of 18 Brumaire by which Bonaparte became first consul.

igible balloon, *see* AIRSHIP.

armament, reduction of armed forces and armaments, *eg* to limit set by treaty. Since WWI international attempts have been made to restrict weapons, *eg* Disarmament Conference (1932-7). After 1945, nuclear weapons made problem more serious. Charter of United Nations provided for disarmament planning in Security Council. Commission set up (1946), reached impasse (1948). Geneva Conference (1955) led to conferences on test-ban treaty and moratorium on testing until 1961. Moscow Agreement (1963) banned tests in atmosphere, under water, outer space. USSR and US drafted non-proliferation treaty (1968), approved by UN. *See* also STRATEGIC ARMS LIMITATION TALKS (SALT).

Disciples, Twelve, *see* TWELVE DISCIPLES.

discrimination, accordance of differential or prejudicial treatment, esp. actions or policies directed against welfare of certain groups, minorities. Can be on racial, religious, sexual or class grounds. In UK prohibited under law on grounds of sex or race.

disinfectant, substance used to destroy harmful microbes. First used was phenol (carbolic acid), introduced by Lister (1867). Disinfectant applied to living things usually called an antiseptic.

Disney, Walt[er Elias] (1901-66), American film producer, famous for animated cartoons. Created character Mickey Mouse in 1928, Donald Duck in 1936. First full-length cartoon was *Snow White and the Seven Dwarfs* (1938).

Dis Pater, *see* PLUTO.

dispersion of light, breaking up of light into its component colours, *eg* by a prism.

Disraeli, Benjamin, 1st Earl of Beaconsfield (1804-81), British statesman, PM (1868, 1874-80). Opposed repeal of Corn Laws and helped defeat Peel's ministry after their repeal (1846). Chief figure in revitalized Conservatives after passage of 1867 Reform Bill extending franchise; succeeded Derby as PM (1868). Second term (1874-80) marked by aggressive imperial and military policy; secured controlling interest in Suez Canal for Britain (1875). Had Victoria crowned empress of India (1876). Also known for novels, *eg Coningsby* (1844), *Sybil* (1845).

dissenter or **nonconformist,** in UK, one who adheres to the form of a religion other than that of the Established Church. Applied esp. to those who failed to accept Act of Uniformity (1662). Denotes more popularly the Protestant dissenter, *eg* Presbyterians, Baptists, Methodists, referred to in Toleration Act (1689).

distemper, any of several infectious catarrhal diseases of animals, esp. canine distemper, virus disease of young dogs. Controlled by vaccination.

distillation, vaporization of a liquid followed by condensation back into liquid form. Used to separate mixtures of liquids of different boiling points or to purify liquid contaminated by non-volatile impurities.

District of Columbia (DC), federal admin. dist. of E US; on Potomac R. Area 180 sq km (*c* 70 sq mi); pop. 916,000. Co-extensive with cap. Washington.

Diu, former Portuguese enclave in W India. Pop. 20,000. Taken by Portuguese (1534), seized by India (1961). Part of union territ. of Goa, Daman and Diu.

Black-throated diver

diver, fish-eating bird of N hemisphere of Gavidae family. Short legs, webbed feet.

divine right, doctrine supporting hereditary kingship on grounds that it is according to divine and natural law, and cannot be set aside without breaking such law. Claimed by James I and Charles I of England, lost importance with 1688 Revolution and Parliament's growing power.

diving, sport in which competitor projects himself into water from an elevated position, possibly executing somersaults before entering water. Divided into springboard and platform or high diving.

division of labour, in economics, organization of workers so that different groups have specialized roles in production. May be geographical, *eg* region concentrates on one product, or occupational, *eg* on modern production line. First examined as concept by Adam Smith.

divorce, decree of dissolution of marriage granted by court. Distinct from nullity, decree that marriage was originally illegal. In UK, irretrievable breakdown of marriage is now only ground. Also *see* ALIMONY.

Diyarbakir, (anc. *Amida*), city of EC Turkey, on R. Tigris. Pop. 170,000. Commercial centre; trade in wool, grain. Became Roman colony AD 230, then under Persian and Arab rule. Taken by Turks (1515). Devastated by earthquake (1966).

Djajapura, cap. of Irian Jaya (West Irian), Indonesia. Pop. 16,000. Formerly known as Hollandia, Kotabaru and Sukarnapura.

Djakarta or **Jakarta,** cap. of Indonesia, on coast of NW Java. Pop. 4,576,000. Commercial, transport and cultural centre. Major export port at nearby Tanjungpriok. Founded (1619) as Batavia by Dutch, renamed 1949.

Djerba or **Jerba,** isl. of SE Tunisia, on Gulf of Gabès. Area 510 sq km (197 sq mi). Tourist resort; olive, date growing; sponge fishing. Traditionally Homer's isl. of the lotus-eaters.

Djibouti, republic of E Africa, on Str. of Bab-el-Mandeb. Area 22,000 sq km (8500 sq mi); pop. 113,000; cap. Djibouti. Official language: Arabic. Religion: Islam. Mainly stony desert; nomadic pastoralism, exports cattle, hides, salt. Colony from 1896 a French Somaliland; later known as Frenc Territory of the Afars and the Issa Became independent as Djibouti (1977).

Djibouti or **Jibuti,** cap. of Djibouti, on Gu of Tadjoura. Pop. 62,000. Port, railway Addis Ababa.

DNA or **deoxyribonucleic acid,** fu damental genetic material found in th chromosomes of cell nuclei. Molecul consists of 2 interwound helical strand each strand composed of long chain of nu leotides (derived from a nitrogenous bas a sugar and phosphate group). Sequence bases in molecule constitutes genetic coc which determines proteins and enzymes be synthesized by cell. At cell divisio DNA replicates itself, thus ensuring th hereditary information is passed to ne cells.

Dnepr

Dnepr or **Dnieper,** river of USSR. Rises Smolensk region, flows *c* 2250 km (1400 r generally S through Byelorussian a Ukrainian SSR into N Black Sea. Navigal above Zaporozhye (Dneproges dam).

Dneproges, *see* ZAPOROZHYE.

Dnepropetrovsk, city of USSR, EC Ukr nian SSR; on R. Dnepr. Pop. 1,066,0 Indust. centre, producing iron, steel a manganese.

Dnieper, *see* DNEPR.

Doberman pinscher, breed of large d used as police or guard dog. Short-hair smooth coated; stands 61-71 cm/24-28 in. shoulder.

dock or **sorrel,** any of genus *Rumex* perennial herbs native to temper regions. Large leaves, stout taproots, sm green or brown flowers; popular antid to nettle stings. Common sorrel, *R. aceto* is used in salads.

dodder, several species of *Cuscuta,* parasitic genus of bindweed family. La leaves, roots and chlorophyll; draw n rishment from host through suckers.

Dodecanese (*Dhodhekánisos*), isl. group Greece, in SE Aegean Sea. Area 2720 sq (1050 sq mi); cap. Rhodes. Incl. Rhoc Cos, Kárpathos. Olives, fruit, spong

Dodecanese

Turkish from 1522, taken by Italy 1912; passed to Greece 1947.

Dodge City, SW Kansas, US; on Arkansas R. Pop. 15,000. Hist. trading post on Santa Fé trail and wild cattle town (Wyatt Earp). Wheat, livestock distribution centre.

Dodgson, C. L., *see* CARROLL, LEWIS.

dodo, *Raphus cucullatus,* flightless bird of Mauritius, resembling turkey. Became extinct in 17th cent. through persecution by man.

Dodoma, town of EC Tanzania. Pop. 15,000. Agric. centre; designated (1975) future national cap.

Doenitz, Karl, *see* DÖNITZ, KARL.

Dofar, alternative form of Doha; *see* QATAR.

dog, *Canis familiaris,* domestic carnivore of Canidae family. Numerous varieties developed from wolf by selective breeding since *c* 8000 BC. Dogs classified as sporting, non-sporting, hounds, terriers, working or toys.

doge, chief magistrate in medieval and Renaissance Venice and Genoa. In 14th cent. held office for life; later, office made elective for 2 year terms.

dogfish, small shark of several families of warm and temperate seas. Lesser spotted dogfish, *Scyliorhinus canicula,* found in European waters.

Dogger Bank, large sand bank in North Sea, off Northumberland, England. Cod fisheries; scene of WWI naval battle (1915).

dogtooth violet, any plant of genus *Erythronium* of lily family.

dogwood, any of genus *Cornus* of trees and shrubs. Esp. *C. sanguinea,* a European flowering shrub.

Doha, *see* QATAR.

Dollfuss, Engelbert (1892-1934), Austrian statesman. Christian Socialist chancellor (1932-4), in conflict with German-backed National Socialists over maintenance of Austrian independence. Assumed dictatorial powers (1933), estab. corporate state (1934). Assassinated by Austrian Nazis.

dolmen, Neolithic burial chamber, usually consisting of 2 or more upright standing stones, topped by capstone, probably covered originally by round or oval cairn. Many examples in Wales and Ireland.

Dogwood

dolomite, greyish-white mineral, carbonate of calcium and magnesium. Also a rock, consisting of over 20% mineral dolomite. Rock may be metamorphosed into dolomitic marble. Used as building stone.

Dolomites, range of NE Italy, in the Alps. Highest point Marmolada (3340 m/10,965 ft). Named from rock which forms them. Tourist area.

dolphin, any of Delphinidae family of toothed whales, of worldwide distribution. Incl. common dolphin, *Delphinus delphis,* KILLER WHALE and BOTTLE-NOSED DOLPHIN.

Domagk, Gerhard (1895-1964), German chemist and pathologist. Discovered effect of dye Prontosil in treating streptococcal infections; its active constituent, sulphanilamide, was 1st sulphonamide drug. Awarded Nobel Prize for Physiology and Medicine (1939).

dome, vaulted roof, usually hemispherical in shape and circular in plan. Ancient domes incl. Mycenaean 'Treasury of Atreus' of 14th cent. BC, constructed in concentric rings of stones. Romans developed concrete dome, *eg* Pantheon in Rome. Other famous domes incl. those of St Peter's, Rome, and St Paul's, London.

Domesday Book (1085-6), record of intensive survey of England made by order of William I (the Conqueror). Main aim was to aid taxation through knowledge of economic resources. Covered ownership of land and its value, and pop. Basic source in medieval history.

Dominic, St, orig. Dominigo de Guzmán (*c* 1170-1221), Spanish churchman, founder of DOMINICANS.

Dominica, largest isl. of SE West Indies, in Windward Isls. Area 750 sq km (290 sq mi);

pop. 81,000; cap. Roseau. Mainly mountainous with much volcanic activity (hot springs, gases). Fruit growing; rum, copra exports. Successive French, British occupation, then British colony; became associate state 1967. Independent in 1978.

Dominican Republic, republic of West Indies, occupying E Hispaniola. Area 48,734 sq km (18,816 sq mi); pop. 5,124,000; cap. Santo Domingo. Language: Spanish. Religion: RC. Mountains in interior; agric. land in E; sugar, coffee, cacao, tobacco produce. Bauxite, rock salt mining. Discovered by Columbus (1492); settled by Spanish; independence gained 1844; US military rule 1916-24; dictatorship under Trujillo (1930-61).

Dominicans, in RC church, order of preaching friars founded (1216) by St Dominic. Emphasize study; prominent in medieval universities. Officially the Order of Preachers, popularly called Black Friars because of black and white habit. Aquinas was most notable Dominican theologian.

Domitian, (Titus Flavius Domitianus) (AD 51-96), Roman emperor (81-96). Son of Vespasian, succeeded brother Titus. After crushing revolt of Roman troops in Upper Germany (89), ruled despotically until stabbed to death.

Don, rivers of UK. **1,** in Yorkshire, flows 112 km (70 mi) from Pennines via Sheffield to R. Ouse. **2,** in Scotland, flows 129 km (80 mi) from Grampians to North Sea; famous for salmon fishing.

Don, river of USSR. Rises in C European RSFSR, flows SE and then SW, *c* 1900 km (1200 mi) to Sea of Azov. Joined by canal to R. Volga near Volgograd.

Donald Bane or **Ban,** king of Scotland (1093, 1095-7). Succeeded brother Malcolm III.

Donatello, orig. Donato di Niccolo di Betto Bardi (*c* 1386-1466), Italian painter and sculptor. Most influential sculptor of 15th cent. Pioneer in use of perspective and humanist expression, he introduced shallow relief technique into sculpture. Masterpieces incl. bronze *David.*

Donbas or **Donets Basin,** region of USSR in plain of R. Donets, E Ukrainian SSR. Largest coalfields of USSR support major indust., incl. iron and steel mfg.

Doncaster, town of South Yorkshire met. county, N England, on R. Don. Pop. 286,000. Coalmining; railway engineering; has famous racecourse. On Roman site (*Danum*).

Donegal, county of Ulster prov., N Irish Republic. Area 4830 sq km (1865 sq mi); pop. 122,000; co. town Lifford. Rocky, indented coast incl. Malin Head, most N point of Ireland; hilly interior. Fishing; livestock; woollen, tweed mfg.; h.e.p. **Donegal,** town on Donegal Bay. Pop. 2000.

Donetsk, city of USSR, E Ukranian SSR. Pop. 1,021,000. Indust. centre of Donbas; coal mining, iron and steel industs. Named Yuzovka then Stalino before 1961.

Dönitz, or **Doenitz, Karl** (1891-1980), German naval officer. In WWII, commanded submarine activity; chief of naval staff (1943). Named to succeed Hitler, ordered German surrender to Allies (May, 1945). Imprisoned (1946-56) after Nuremberg trials.

Donizetti, Gaetano (1797-1848), Italian composer. Wrote many tuneful operas, incl. *Lucia di Lammermoor* and *Don Pasquale.*

donkey, *see* Ass.

Donne, John (*c* 1572-1631), English poet, divine. Greatest of metaphysical school. Work, characterized by irony, intellectual 'conceits', incl. early love poetry, *eg Songs and Sonnets,* later religious verse, *eg* 'Death be not proud'. Noted for sermons preached as Dean of St Paul's from 1621.

Doppler, Christian Johann (1803-53), Austrian physicist. Predicted Doppler effect: apparent change in frequency of sound or electromagnetic radiation caused by relative motion of source and observer. Observed frequency is higher than emitted frequency as observer and source approach, lower as they recede. Effect used by astronomers to determine relative velocity of heavenly body and Earth.

Dorchester, town and admin. hq. of Dorset, S England, on R. Frome. Pop. 14,000. Roman *Durnovaria,* many remains. 'Casterbridge' of Hardy's novels.

Dordogne, river of WC France. Flows *c* 465 km (290 mi) from Auvergne Mts. to R. Garonne, forming the Gironde estuary. Tourism, vineyards, h.e.p.

Doré, Gustave (1832-83), French artist. Illustrated Dante's *Inferno, Don Quixote,* the Bible; drew pictures of poor quarters of London (1869-71). Work is noted for his love of the grotesque.

Dorians, people of ancient Greece. Entered Greece from N and overthrew Mycenean Civilization *c* 1150-1000 BC.

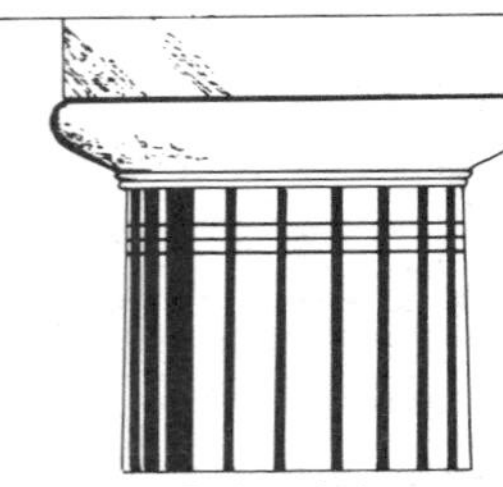

Doric capital

Doric order, earliest and most used of the Greek orders of architecture. Characterized by its lack of base, massive tapering shaft with 20 flutes, simple capital. Parthenon in Athens shows the perfected order.

dormouse, small squirrel-like arboreal rodent of Gliridae family, widely distributed in Old World. Diet of seed, berries, *etc.* European species undergo long hibernation. Species incl. common dormouse, *Muscardinus avellanarius*, only British variety.

Dorpat, *see* TARTU.

Dorset, county of S England. Area 2654 sq km (1024 sq mi); pop. 586,000; admin. hq. Dorchester. Chalk downs (sheep); lowlands (dairying); Portland stone quarried. Coastal resorts *eg* Weymouth. Ancient remains incl. MAIDEN CASTLE.

Dortmund, city of W West Germany, in Ruhr. Pop. 624,000. Port, connected by Dortmund-Ems canal to North Sea; brewing, coal, steel, engineering industs. Member of Hanseatic League. Badly damaged in WWII.

dory, marine fish of Zeidae family. John dory, *Zeus faber*, yellow or golden with spiny dorsal fin, is common in Mediterranean.

Dos Passos, John Roderigo (1896-1970), American novelist. Works incl. trilogy *U.S.A.* (1930-7); mixed 'newsreel', biog. techniques to form composite picture of society.

Dostoyevski, Feodor Mikhailovich (1821-81), Russian novelist. Combined vivid realistic narrative with psychological insight. Major works, incl. *Crime and Punishment* (1866), *The Idiot* (1868), *The Brothers Karamazov* (1879-80), reflect concern with guilt, religious faith.

Dou or **Douw, Gerard** or **Gerrit** (1613-75), Dutch portrait and genre painter. Pupil of Rembrandt, he developed a minute detailed technique.

Douala, city of Cameroon, on Bight of Biafra. Pop. 458,000. Railway terminus and port, exports tropical hardwoods, cocoa, bananas. Former cap. of German colony of Kamerun.

Douay Bible, English version of the Bible translated from the Latin Vulgate edition for the use of RCs. NT pub. at Rheims (1582); OT at the RC college for English priests in Douai (1610).

double bass, four-stringed low-pitched instrument, considered either a survivor of VIOL family or lowest member of violin family. Played with bow in orchestra and plucked to supply bass line in jazz.

Douglas, Clifford Hugh (1879-1952), Scottish economist, engineer. Early theorist of SOCIAL CREDIT. Chief reconstruction adviser to Social Credit govt. of Alberta (1935-6).

Douglas, Gavin (*c* 1474-1522), Scottish poet, bishop. Known for version of *Aeneid* (1513), most sustained poetic achievement in Scots language.

Douglas, Sir James de Douglas, Lord of (*c* 1286-1330), Scottish nobleman, called Black Douglas. After losing estates by order of Edward I, terrorized borders. Later joined Robert the Bruce, with whom he fought at Bannockburn.

Douglas, cap. of Isle of Man, UK. Pop. 20,000. Seaport, resort on E coast. Admin. and legislative buildings.

Douglas fir, *Pseudotsuga taxifolia*, evergreen tree of W North America. Timber exported in large quantities as lumber and plywood.

Douglas-Home, Alexander Frederick, Baron Home of the Hirsel (1903-), British statesman, PM (1963-4). Conservative foreign secretary (1960-3), renounced titles (originally 14th earl of Home) to become PM in succession to Macmillan. Lost ensuing election. Again foreign secretary (1970-4), made life peer (1974).

Douro (Span. *Duero*), river of Spain and Portugal. Flows *c* 770 km (480 mi) from NC Spain, W to Atlantic Ocean near Oporto. Used for irrigation, h.e.p.

Douw, Gerrit, *see* DOU, GERARD.

dove, medium-sized bird of same family (Columbidae) as pigeon. Short neck and legs, cooing cry; seed eater.

Dover, town of Kent, SE England. Pop. 34,000. Ferry port, shortest cross-Channel route (to Calais, 35 km/22 mi). Has Roman lighthouse; Norman castle; one of Cinque Ports.

Dover, cap. of Delaware, US. Pop. 17,000. Fruit canning indust. Settled 1683; became cap. 1777.

Dover, Strait of (Fr. *Pas de Calais*), between SE England and NE France, links English Channel with North Sea. At narrowest only 34 km (21 mi) wide.

Dowding, Hugh Caswall Tremenheere Dowding, 1st Baron (1882-1970), British air marshal. During Battle of Britain, he was chief of Fighter Command (1939-42).

Dowland, John (1563-1626), English composer and lutenist. Wrote plaintive lute songs. Lutenist to Danish and British courts.

Down, former county of SE Northern Ireland. Hilly, incl. Mourne Mts. in SE; Ards Penin., Strangford Lough in E. Agric., linen mfg., tourism. Co. town was DOWNPATRICK.

Downing Street, London street off Whitehall, in which are located official residences of British PM (number 10) and chancellor of exchequer (number 11).

Downpatrick, town of SE Northern Ireland. Pop. 8000. Former co. town of Down. Its cathedral is reputed to have remains of Irish saints Patrick, Columba, Bridget.

Downs, S England. Chalk ranges running W-E. North Downs (up to 294 m/965 ft) of Surrey and Kent end at white cliffs of Dover. South Downs (up to 264 m/865 ft) of Sussex end at Beachy Head. Sheep pasture land. Hampshire, Berkshire, Marlborough downs further W.

Down's syndrome, *see* MONGOLISM.

Doyle, Sir Arthur Conan (1859-1930), English doctor, author, b. Scotland. Created detective Sherlock Holmes in *A Study in Scarlet* (1887). Along with many Holmes stories, also wrote adventure stories, historical romances.

Draco (*fl c* 623 BC), Athenian statesman. Devised code of laws noted for their severity, as almost all crimes carried death-penalty hence 'Draconian'.

Dracula, *see* STOKER, BRAM.

dragon, fabulous monster of Christian, Chinese, Japanese and other folklore. Usually represented as huge, fire-breathing, winged reptilian quadruped. Sometimes used in Christian art, literature to symbolize forces of evil.

dragon fish, any of Pegasidae family of small flying fish of Indian, Pacific oceans. Long snout, body covered with bony plates.

Dragonfly

dragonfly, any of Odonata order of insects with 2 pairs of membranous wings, large eyes and long, thin brightly-coloured body. Feeds on small insects seized in flight. Wingspan of some fossil varieties *c* 60 cm/2 ft.

dragoon, cavalry soldier trained to fight on foot. The name comes from the short musket, called a dragon, carried by French cavalry *c* 1600.

Drake, Sir Francis (*c* 1540-96), English naval officer. In 1570-3 took part in raiding expeditions to the Spanish Main and in the *Golden Hind* was 1st English mariner to circumnavigate the globe (1577-80), for which he was knighted by Elizabeth I. In 1585 he commanded a marauding fleet off Spanish America, and in 1587 destroyed the Spanish fleet at Cádiz. In 1588 helped defeat Spanish Armada.

Drakensberg Mountains or **Quathlamba,** range of South Africa. Extends *c* 1125 km (700 mi) SW-NE from Cape Prov. to Transvaal; rises to 3481 m (11,425 ft) in Lesotho.

drama, artistic form traditionally combining speech and action to tell story, but also incl. monologue, mime. Western drama originated in Greek Dionysiac festivals, leading to classical TRAGEDY. Popular COMEDY developed alongside, using stock characters. Renaissance revived classical theories while in Italy popular COMMEDIA DELL'ARTE flourished. Fusion of classical and popular traditions led to Elizabethan and Jacobean drama in England. Restoration drama was largely artificial and gave way to sentimental and then romantic drama. Realism introduced in 19th cent. leading to deeper psychological interest. Forms diversified widely in 20th cent.

draughts or **checkers,** game of skill for 2 persons played with 24 round pieces on a board divided into 64 alternate light and dark squares. Played in Europe from 16th cent.

Drava, river of EC Europe. Flows *c* 725 km (450 mi) from S Austria through Yugoslavia to Danube near Osijek. Forms part of Yugoslav-Hungarian border.

Dravidian, major group of inhabitants of India, before Aryan invasion, therefore name for S India group possibly descended from pre-Aryan stock. Also name for family of languages mainly in S India and Sri Lanka, incl. Telugu, Tamil, Kannada and Malayalam.

dreams, sequences of sensations, images, thoughts, *etc*, occurring during SLEEP. Shown to be necessary in restorative process of sleep. Considered important in ancient times and among primitive peoples. Psychological significance recognized by Freud and Jung.

Drenthe, prov. of NE Netherlands. Area 2644 sq km (1021 sq mi); cap. Assen. Infertile heathland, reclamation in W. Rye, potatoes, cattle; oil, natural gas.

Dresden, city of SE East Germany, on R. Elbe. Pop. 509,000. River port, railway jct.; produces machine tools, optical instruments. 'Dresden' pottery made at Meissen. Cap. of Saxony 1485-1918. Cultural centre with noted art collections, Baroque buildings; many destroyed in devastating air raid in WWII.

Dreyfus affair (1894-1906), scandal arising out of trial of French army officer, **Alfred Dreyfus** (1859-1935), for treason. Accused of selling military secrets to Germany, he became centre of case arousing anti-Semitic tirades in press and dividing France into groups of royalists, militarists, Catholics on one side, and republicans, socialists, anti-clerics on the other. Dreyfus, a Jew, was imprisoned on Devils Isl.; pardoned (1899), declared innocent (1906) after long struggle by supporters, incl. Zola, to show evidence against him was based on forgery. Affair discredited monarchists and army, united left wing.

drift, in geomorphology, transported material deposited during glaciation of a region. Consists of clay, sand, gravel, boulders. *See* also BOULDER CLAY.

drill, *see* MANDRILL.

Drogheda, town of Co. Louth, NE Irish Republic, on R. Boyne. Pop. 23,000. Exports cattle; linen, cotton mfg. Captured (1649) by Cromwell, massacre followed.

dromedary, *see* CAMEL.

dropsy, *see* OEDEMA.

drugs, chemical substances taken for prevention or alleviation of disease. Types in use incl. antibiotics, sulphonamides, barbiturates, amphetamines. Name also applies to habit-forming narcotics, *eg* heroin, opium.

Druids, ancient religious body of priests, soothsayers, poets in Celtic Gaul and Britain. Taught immortality of soul; held oak and mistletoe sacred. Exercised political power through federation extending across tribal divisions. Druidism declined in Gaul by 1st cent. and soon after in Britain.

drum, percussion instrument; consists of a skin stretched over a hollow cylinder, which resonates when the skin is struck. Timpani or kettledrums produce notes of definite pitch and can be tuned, but other drums are of indefinite pitch.

drumlin, elongated, oval ridge consisting of BOULDER CLAY. Formed by deposition and moulding of material by ice-sheet flowing over area. Commonly occurs in swarms, *eg* Down, Northern Ireland.

Druses, secret religious sect in S Syria and Lebanon. Basically Moslem, but believe in the divinity of the Caliph Hakim (11th cent.).

Dryads, in Greek myth, NYMPHS who lived in trees. Died together with trees which had been their home.

dry cell, *see* CELL, VOLTAIC.

Dryden, John (1631-1700), English poet. Known for *Absalom and Achitophel* (1681) written in heroic couplets, plays esp. *All for Love* (1678), prose criticism, translations of Vergil. Poet laureate (1668-89).

drypoint, method of engraving by drawing on metal printing plate with sharp hard needle. Quality of drypoint lies in 'burr' of metal shavings turned up at side of furrow made by needle; ink collects in burr and gives richness to the print. Technique was used by Dürer, Rembrandt, Whistler.

dry rot, fungal disease of seasoned timber resulting in its eventual crumbling; often occurs in humid unventilated conditions. Prevented by application of creosote or fungicides.

Dubai, seaport of Dubai sheikdom, United Arab Emirates, on Persian Gulf. Pop. 207,000.

Dubček, Alexander (1921-), Czechoslovakian political leader. First secretary of Communist Party (1968-9), chief figure in 'liberalizing' movement in Czech politics, soon crushed by Soviet military intervention (1968). Later deprived of political office.

Dublin, county of Leinster prov., E Irish Republic. Area 922 sq km (356 sq mi); pop. 983,000; co. town DUBLIN. Mountainous in S; elsewhere lowland. Agric., livestock.

Dublin (*Baile Atha Cliath*), cap. of Irish Republic, co. town of Dublin, on R. Liffey and Irish Sea. Pop. 544,000; Admin. and commercial centre, seaport; brewing, distilling, textile mfg. Trinity Coll. (1591), Univ. Coll. (1851). Has RC pro-cathedral, 2 Protestant cathedrals, Abbey Theatre (1904). Scene of Easter Rising (1916).

Dubrovnik (Ital. *Ragusa*), town of Dalmatia, SE Yugoslavia, on Adriatic Sea. Pop. 23,000. Port, resort. Founded 7th cent. by Greeks; rich medieval republic rivalling Venice until 16th cent. Under Austian rule 1814-1919. Cathedral (17th cent.), ancient walls.

Duchamp, Marcel (1887-1968), French painter. Pioneer of the DADA group, he is known for his 'ready-mades', *eg* urinal, mounted bicycle wheel. Most famous painting is *Nude Descending a Staircase*.

duck, aquatic bird of Anatidae family with webbed feet, long neck and long flat bill. Plumage waterproofed by oil from gland near tail.

duckbilled platypus, *Ornithorhynchus anatinus*, semi-aquatic, egg-laying mammal (monotreme) of Australia, Tasmania. Thick fur, webbed feet, duck-like bill; poison spur on heel.

ductless glands, *see* ENDOCRINE GLANDS.

Dudley, John, *see* NORTHUMBERLAND.

Dudley, Robert, *see* LEICESTER.

Dufay, Guillaume (*c* 1400-74), Flemish composer. Served in papal choir and at court of Burgundy. Leading composer of *chansons* and church music.

Dufy, Raoul (1877-1953), French artist. Work marked by calligraphic style and brilliant colour; subjects include racecourses and seaside scenes.

Dugong

dugong, *Dugong dugong,* whale-like herbivorous mammal of Red Sea and Indian Ocean. Brownish or greyish, reaches lengths of *c* 3 m/10 ft. Slow-moving and defenceless; much hunted, now rare. Also called sea cow.

duiker, any of several small antelopes of African bush S of Sahara. Species incl. common grey duiker, *Sylvicapra grimmia*.

Duisburg, city of W West Germany, at confluence of Rhine and Ruhr. Pop. 582,000. Major port; steel, engineering, textile industs. Member of Hanseatic League. Heavy bombing in WWII.

dulcimer, a musical instrument in which strings stretched over a wooden frame are struck by mallets held in the hands. Originated in East in medieval times, lives on in E European folk music.

Dulles, John Foster (1888-1959), American statesman. Eisenhower's secretary of state (1953-9), pursued foreign policy based on collective security of US and Allies and development of nuclear weapons to retaliate in event of attack. His brother, **Allen Welsh Dulles** (1893-1969), was director of Central Intelligence Agency (1953-61).

dulse, *Rhodymenia palmata*, edible seaweed.

Solitary or tufted red fronds grow on rocks, shellfish or other seaweeds.

duma, Russian house of representatives, granted by Nicholas II after Revolution of 1905. Legislative powers restricted by tsar's prerogative. Last duma (1912-17) ended by March revolution.

Dumas, Alexandre, (père) (1802-70), French author. Known for *c* 300 vols. of swashbuckling romance, esp. *The Three Musketeers* (1844), *Count of Monte Cristo* (1845). His son, **Alexandre Dumas (fils)** (1824-95) known for plays esp. *La Dame aux Camélias* (1852), basis of Verdi's opera *La Traviata*, film *Camille*.

Dumbarton, town of Strathclyde region, W Scotland, on R. Clyde. Pop. 26,000. Former royal burgh and co. town of Dunbartonshire. Shipbuilding, engineering industs.; whisky distilling. Cap. of ancient Strathclyde kingdom, centred on Dumbarton Rock and castle.

Dumfries and Galloway, region of SW Scotland. Area 6369 sq km (2459 sq mi); pop. 144,000. Created 1975, incl. former Dumfriesshire, Kirkcudbrightshire, Wigtownshire. Admin. hq. **Dumfries**, former royal burgh on R. Nith. Pop. 29,000. Tweed mfg. Old Bridge (1280); Burns Mausoleum (1815).

Dumfriesshire, former county of S Scotland. Southern Uplands in N; plain of R. Solway in S; Annan, Nith valleys run N-S. Sheep, cattle rearing, root crops; coalmining. Co. town was Dumfries.

Dunant, Jean Henri (1828-1910), Swiss philanthropist. Horrified by experience of tending wounded at battle of Solferino, promoted estab. of International Red Cross (1863). Shared 1st Nobel Peace Prize (1901).

Dunbar, William (*c* 1460-*c* 1520), Scottish poet. Influenced by Chaucer and Scottish traditions, but with vigorous personal voice expressed in technically innovative verse. Poems incl. 'Lament for the Makaris'.

Dunbar, town of Lothian region, E Scotland. Pop. 5000. Fishing port, resort. Scene of battle (1650) in which Cromwell defeated Scots.

Dunbartonshire, former county of W Scotland, now in Strathclyde region. Mountainous in N; incl. Loch Lomond (tourism); industs. along Clyde estuary and Vale of Leven, incl. shipbuilding, bleaching, dyeing. Co. town was DUMBARTON.

Duncan I, king of Scotland (1034-1040), succeeded maternal grandfather, Malcolm II. Murdered by Macbeth.

Duncan II, king of Scotland (1093-4). Son of Malcolm III.

Duncan, Isadora (1878-1927), American dancer. Developed own concept of dance, inspired by ancient Greek art, with free and expressive movements.

Dundalk, co. town of Louth, E Irish Republic, on Dundalk Bay. Pop. 25,000. Exports agric. produce. Railway engineering; linen, hosiery mfg.

Dundee, John Graham of Claverhouse, 1st Viscount (*c* 1649-89), Scottish nobleman, known as 'Bonnie Dundee'. Hated by Covenanters, whom he attempted to suppress (1678-88). Raised force to restore James II, killed leading Jacobite victory at Killiecrankie.

Dundee, city and admin. hq. of Tayside region, E Scotland, on Firth of Tay. Pop. 192,000. Seaport; jute indust., clocks, jam, confectionery mfg., publishing.

Dunedin, city of SE South Isl., New Zealand, on Otago Harbour. Pop. 82,000. Port, exports wool, meat; engineering, woollen mills. Founded 1848 by Scottish settlers; grew rapidly in 1861 gold rush. Has Anglican, RC cathedrals; Univ. of Otago (1869).

Dunfermline, town of Fife, E Scotland. Pop. 50,000. Silk, rayon mfg.; engineering. Has palace of Scottish kings; royal tombs in 11th cent. abbey.

dung beetle, insect of scarab beetle family that rolls ball of animal dung in which to lay eggs and provide food for larvae.

Dunkirk (*Dunkerque*), town of Nord, N France, on Str. of Dover. Pop. 165,000. Port, shipbuilding, major iron and steel indust. Under English rule (1658-62). Scene of evacuation (1940) of *c* 300,000 Allied troops.

Dún Laoghaire, bor. of Co. Dublin, E Irish Republic, on Dublin Bay. Pop. 54,000. Resort; port, ferry service to Holyhead (Wales). Formerly called Kingstown.

Dunlop, John Boyd (1840-1921), Scottish veterinary surgeon. Patented (1888) Dunlop version of pneumatic tyre, producing it commercially in Belfast.

Duns Scotus, John (*c* 1265-1308), Scottish philosopher. A Franciscan, opposed theories of Aquinas. Challenged harmony of reason and faith by showing limits of human reason. Known as 'Doctor Subtilis'.

Dunstable, John (d. 1453), English composer. Travelled abroad in service of English regent of France. Compositions, mainly for the Church, had great influence on European music.

Dunstan, St, (*c* 924-88), English prelate, statesman. Began revival of regularized monasticism in England. As archbishop of Canterbury from 961, drew up national code for monasteries based on Benedictine rule. Principal adviser to all contemporary Wessex kings, virtual ruler of England under Edred and Edgar.

duodenal ulcer, *see* PEPTIC ULCER.

Durazzo, *see* DURRËS.

Durban, city of Natal, South Africa, on Indian Ocean. Pop. 843,000. Major port, exports minerals, grain, fruit; indust. centre, resort. Has part of Univ. of Natal (1909). Founded 1835.

Dürer, Albrecht (1471-1528), German artist. Prolific master of woodcuts, copper engravings and drawings; following visits to Italy, he was largely instrumental in introducing discoveries of Italian Renaissance into North. Works incl. series of woodcuts for *Apocalypse*, watercolours of alpine scenery; few paintings incl. *Four Apostles.* Influenced by writings of Luther.

Durham, John George Lambton, 1st Earl of (1792-1840), British statesman. Promoted liberal measures, *eg* 1832 Reform Bill, earning nickname 'Radical Jack'. Governor-general of Canada, prepared report (1839) advocating responsible self-govt.

Durham, county of NE England. Area 2435 sq km (940 sq mi); pop. 604,000. Pennines in W (sheep), fertile valleys; coastal plain in E, coalfield. Coalmining, iron and steel, shipbuilding industs., chemicals mfg. Admin. hq. **Durham,** city on R. Wear. Pop. 25,000. Castle (1072) now site of univ. (1832). Cathedral (1093) has Bede's remains.

Durkheim, Emile (1858-1917), French sociologist. Stressed importance of collective mind of society in creating personal morality, with loss of social controls leading to deep unhappiness (*anomie).*

Durrell, Lawrence George (1912-), English author, b. India. Best known for 'The Alexandria Quartet' of *Justine* (1957), *Balthazar* (1958), *Mountolive* (1958), *Clea* (1960), using multiple viewpoints.

Durrës, (Ital. *Durazzo*), town of W Albania, on Adriatic. Pop. 53,000. Country's main seaport, exports olive oil, tobacco. Founded 7th cent. BC; important Roman port (*Dyrrachium*).

Dushanbe, city of USSR, cap. of Tadzhik SSR. Pop. 493,000 Cotton and silk mfg.; meat packing. Called Stalinabad (1929-61).

Düsseldorf, city of W West Germany, on R. Rhine, cap. of North Rhine-Westphalia. Pop. 615,000. Iron, steel, vehicles, textiles mfg. Cultural centre. Chartered 1288, residence (14th-16th cent.) of dukes of Berg.

dust bowl, area where exposed top soil is raised by strong winds into dust storms and blown away. Occurs after removal of protective vegetation cover by ploughing. Term applied in particular to W prairies of US, severely affected in late 1930s.

Dutch, language of W Germanic group of Indo-European family. Written and spoken language diverge greatly, since former developed from sophisticated Flemish of 15th cent. Flanders, Brabant, latter from vernacular of Holland.

Dutch East Indies, *see* INDONESIA.

Dutch elm disease, virulent and widespread disease of elms caused by a fungus, *Ceratocystis ulmi,* carried by the ambrosia beetle. Produces wilting and drying of the leaves and ultimately death of the tree.

Dutch Guiana, *see* SURINAM.

Dutch Wars, three naval wars, arising from commercial rivalry, fought between England and Netherlands. First war (1652-4) was precipitated by seizure of Dutch merchant fleet and passage of NAVIGATION ACT (1651). Second conflict (1664-7) sparked by continued threat to English sea power and trade. Settlement of Treaty of Breda incl. favourable change in trade laws for Dutch. Third war (1672-4) formed part of Louis XIV's campaign against Netherlands (1672-8). England allied with France by terms of Treaty of Dover (1670); made peace 1674.

Dvořák, Antonin (1841-1904), Czech composer. Encouraged by Brahms, much of his work was influenced by Czech folksong. Taught in America (1892-5). Compositions incl. 9 symphonies (best known is 9th, *From the New World),* string quartets, choral works, 2 cello concertos, violin concerto, piano concerto, operas.

dwarf, in plants and animals, term applied to specimens which do not attain normal height. In humans, dwarfism may result from deficiency of pituitary hormone or from achondroplasia, hereditary disorder resulting in defective growth of limbs.

dyestuffs, materials used to impart colour to textiles or other substances. Originally obtained from natural materials, *eg* plant roots, best known being indigo and alizarin. Synthetic dyes manufactured from distillation products of coal tar and known as aniline colours.

Dyfed, county of SW Wales. Area 5765 sq km (2226 sq mi); pop. 325,000; admin. hq. Carmarthen. Created 1974, incl. former Pembrokeshire, Cardiganshire, Carmarthenshire.

Dylan, Bob, orig. Robert Zimmerman (1941-), American singer, composer. Leading exponent in 1960s of 'folk rock' fusing folk and rock idioms. Songs of social protest influenced many young musicians.

dynamics, branch of physics dealing with motion of bodies under action of given forces. Also *see* STATICS.

dynamite, powerful explosive discovered by Alfred Nobel (1866). Consists of NITROGLYCERINE absorbed in porous substance, *eg* wood pulp; varying amounts of ammonium or sodium nitrate added. Activated by detonator.

dynamo, device for converting mechanical energy into electrical energy. Simplest type consists of powerful magnet between whose poles an armature (laminated iron core with wire wound around it) is rotated. *See* ELECTROMAGNETIC INDUCTION.

dyne, unit of force in C.G.S. SYSTEM; 1 dyne acting on mass of 1 gram will produce acceleration of 1 cm/sec^2.

dysentery, any of various intestinal inflammations, characterized by intense diarrhoea, usually accompanied by blood and mucus. Amoebic dysentery is caused by parasitic protozoon *Entamoeba histolytica*; bacterial by a bacillus of *Shigella* group.

dyslexia, inability to read properly due to brain disorder which causes letters, or order of letters, to be confused. Sufferers usually of normal intelligence and can be helped by special teaching.

dysprosium (Dy), soft metallic element of lanthanide group; at. no. 66, at. wt. 162.5. Discovered (1886).

E

eagle, carnivorous bird of Accipitridae family with long talons, feathered neck and head. Powerful flier, with keen eyesight; usually nests on cliffs, mountains.

Ealing, bor. of W Greater London, England. Pop. 292,000. Created 1965 from Ealing, Acton, Southall mun. bors. Film studios famous for 'Ealing Comedies' of 1950s.

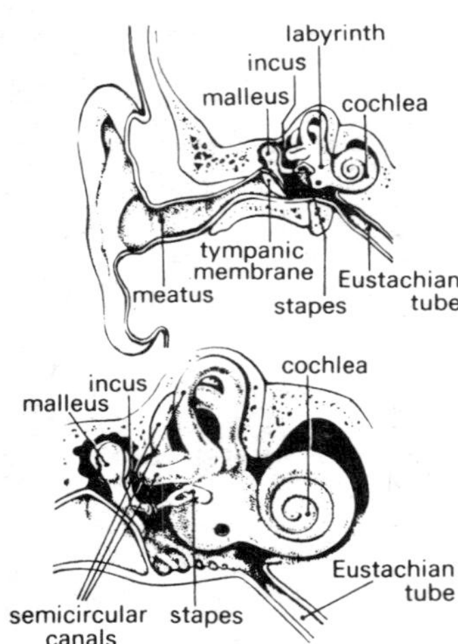

Structure of human ear; lower diagram shows inner ear in more detail

ear, organ of hearing. Human ear consists of: external ear and auditory canal, ending at ear drum; middle ear, cavity containing 3 small bones which communicate vibrations of ear drum to inner ear, a labyrinthine structure in temporal bone; cochlea, containing auditory nerve endings, and 3 fluid-containing semicircular canals, important for balance, are found in inner ear.

Earhart, Amelia (1897-1937), American aviator. First woman to make solo flight of Atlantic (1932). Lost in Pacific during attempt to fly around the world.

Early English, name given to first period of English Gothic architecture (13th cent.). Characterized by pointed arches, long narrow windows without mullions.

Earth, the, fifth largest planet of solar system, third in distance from Sun; mean distance from Sun *c* 150,000,000 km (93,000,000 mi). Revolves in elliptical orbit about Sun, taking 365¼ days to complete orbit, its inclination producing change of seasons. Earth is slightly flattened at poles; equatorial radius *c* 6378 km (3963 mi), polar radius *c* 6357 km (3950 mi). Believed to have central core of iron and nickel, surrounded by mantle of silicate rocks which support thin outer crust.

earthquake, shaking or trembling of the Earth's crust originating naturally below the surface. Consists of series of shock waves which may cause changes in level, cracking or distortion of surface. Associated with younger fold-mountain regions of Earth, esp. fault lines; prob. the result of stresses caused by movement of crustal plates (*see* PLATE TECTONICS). Severity measured by various scales, *eg* Richter. Main zones of activity: (1) Pacific area incl. W coast of America, Alaska, Japan, Philippines, New Zealand; (2) S Europe, NE Africa, Iran, Himalayas, East Indies; (3) mid-oceanic ridges.

earthworm, any of number of round, segmented worms that burrow in soil, class Oligochaeta. Common species of N hemisphere is *Lumbricus terrestris,* important for aerating and fertilizing soil.

earwig, any of Dermaptera order of widely distributed insects. Short stiff forewings, conspicuous forceps at end of abdomen; omnivorous.

East Anglia, E England. Rich agric. area incl. Norfolk, Suffolk; flat, artificially drained. Crops incl. wheat, barley, sugar beet. Ancient kingdom (6th cent.) of Angles. Earldom from 10th cent.

East Bengal, *see* BENGAL.

Eastbourne, town of East Sussex, S England. Pop. 70,000. Coastal resort.

East China Sea, arm of Pacific Ocean, bordering on China and extending from Taiwan to Japan.

Easter, annual Christian festival commemorating resurrection of Jesus. Instituted *c* AD 68. In the West, falls on 1st Sunday after full moon after vernal equinox, between 22nd March and 25th April. In Eastern Orthodox Church, calculated from Julian calendar.

Easter Island (Span. *Isla de Pascua),* isl. off Chile, in E Pacific. Area 199 sq km (46 sq mi); pop. 1600. Agric. incl. livestock rearing, tobacco, sugar cane growing. Has mysterious statues, undeciphered wooden tablets. Discovered 1722; annexed by Chile 1888.

Eastern Orthodox Church, collective name for independent Christian churches of E Europe and W Asia. Rejected authority of Roman See under Pope Leo IX in 1054.

Originally made up of 4 patriarchates (Constantinople, Alexandria, Antioch, Jerusalem), now also incl. certain autonomous churches of USSR, Greece, Romania.

Easter Rebellion, uprising in Dublin (24-29 April, 1916) against British rule in Ireland. Forcibly suppressed, leaders executed. Hardened nationalist feeling.

East Germany, *see* GERMANY.

East India Company, English company chartered (1600) by Elizabeth I for trade with East. Activities largely confined to India after 1623, where it thrived on export of textiles. After Clive's victories over French rivals, became virtual ruler of India. Trade monopoly withdrawn by govt. acts of 1813, 1833. British govt. assumed direct control after Indian Mutiny (1858), company dissolved 1874.

East Indies, vague term which once referred to SE Asia, incl. India, Malay and Indo-Chinese archipelagos; later referred to Netherlands East Indies (now Indonesia).

East Kilbride, town of Strathclyde region, WC Scotland. Pop. 64,000. Created 'new town' in 1947. Aircraft equipment, electronics, printing industs.

East London, city of SE Cape Prov., South Africa, on Indian Ocean. Pop. 123,000. Port, exports grain, fruit; fishing; indust. centre, resort. Founded 1847, formerly called Port Rex.

East Lothian, former county of E Scotland, now in Lothian region. Formerly known as Haddingtonshire. Low-lying in N; Lammermuir Hills in S. Agric., mainly sheep rearing; coalmining. Coastal resorts incl. North Berwick. Co. town was Haddington.

East Pakistan, *see* BANGLADESH.

East Riding, *see* YORKSHIRE.

East Sussex, *see* SUSSEX.

eau de Cologne, perfume made from alcohol and aromatic oils. Production began in Cologne *c* 1709.

ebony, trees or shrubs of genus *Diospyros* of Ebenaceae family. Grows in tropical and subtropical climates. Black hardwood used for cabinet work is derived largely from *D. ebenum* of S India and Sri Lanka. Other species bear edible plum-like fruit known as persimmons.

Ebro, river of NE Spain. Flows *c* 925 km (575 mi) from Cantabrian Mts., N Spain, via Saragossa to Mediterranean Sea near Tortosa. Used for irrigation, h.e.p.

Ecclesiastes, book of OT, written (prob. 3rd cent. BC) by a man of high station in Jerusalem (formerly ascribed to Solomon). Finds philosophical consolation in futility of the world.

Ecclesiasticus or **The Wisdom of Jesus,** apocryphal book of OT written (*c* 200-175 BC) by Jesus, son of Sirach. Celebrates value of wisdom.

echidna or **spiny anteater,** spiny-backed burrowing MONOTREME of Australasia. Long, toothless snout; extensile tongue used to catch ants, termites. Eggs hatched in pouch. Species incl. *Tachyglossus setosus* of Tasmania.

echo, in physics, repetition of sound by reflection of sound waves from a surface. Ships measure depth of water with an echo sounder which indicates time taken for sound pulse to echo off sea bed. *See* SONAR.

eclipse, in astronomy, partial or complete obscuring of one celestial body by another as viewed from a fixed point. Solar eclipses occur when shadow of Moon falls on Earth; *c* 2 or 3 seen per year. Lunar eclipses occur when shadow of Earth falls on Moon; at most 2 seen per year.

ecology, interdisciplinary study of plants and animals in relation to their environment, esp. interdependence of all parts within whole system.

economics, study of production, distribution and consumption of commodities. First attempts at analysis were by ancient Greeks, *eg* Plato *(Republic)* and Aristotle. Development of modern economics began with advocacy of LAISSER-FAIRE by PHYSIOCRATS, and was elaborated by classical economists, *eg* Adam Smith (*Wealth of Nations*, 1776), Ricardo and J.S. Mill; founded on belief in inflexible natural laws governing exchange and production of goods. Challenged in 19th cent. by socialists, esp. Karl Marx (*Das Kapital*, 1867), who threw light on weaknesses of classical market economy such as crisis recurrence. Classical form re-estab. (1870s) and applied mathematically by Alfred Marshall. KEYNES' theories on planning and spending increased govt. interventionist role in West's national economies; resisted from 1970s by monetarists (*see* FRIEDMAN) who believe in controlling money supply.

Ecuador, republic of NW South America, incl. offshore Galápagos Isls. Area 283,561 sq km (109,483 sq mi); pop. 7,814,000; cap. Quito, chief port Guayaquil. Language: Spanish. Religion: RC. Pacific coast plain rises to volcanic Andes. Bananas, coffee are main crops; subsistence agric. in mountains. Spanish colony from 16th cent.; part of viceroyalty of Peru until liberated 1822; independence 1830 at dissolution of Greater Columbia.

ecumenical council, in Christianity, convocation of duly constituted authorities of whole church. Modern RC canonists recognize 21 such councils incl. Nicaea (325), Ephesus (431), Basle (1431), TRENT (1545), Vatican II (1962). Eastern Orthodox churches recognize the first 7 of the 21.

ecumenism, term for movement aimed at unification of Christian churches. Early attempts incl. the Evangelical Alliance (UK 1846, US 1867). World Council of Churches (1948) brought together more than 200 Protestant, Orthodox and Old Catholic churches. Since 2nd Vatican Council (1962), RC Church has been increasingly involved in quest for Christian unity.

eczema, *see* DERMATITIS.

Edam, town of NW Netherlands. Pop. 8000.

Market for Edam cheese; earthenware mfg.

Eddy, Mary Baker (1821-1910), American religious leader. Founder and 1st pastor of Church of Christ, Scientist, in Boston. Formulated CHRISTIAN SCIENCE doctrine.

Edelweiss

edelweiss, *Leontopodium alpinum,* small perennial flowering plant of daisy family. Native to high mountains of Europe and C Asia. Dense woolly white flowers.

Eden, [Robert] Anthony, 1st Earl of Avon (1897-1977), British statesman, PM (1955-7). Conservative foreign secretary (1935-8), resigned over Chamberlain's 'appeasement' policy towards Germany. Again foreign secretary (1940-5, 1951-5). Resigned as PM after SUEZ CRISIS.

Eden, Garden of, in OT, first home of man. Created by God as home for ADAM and Eve; contained trees of life and knowledge. They were banished after tasting the forbidden fruit of the tree of knowledge (Genesis 2:3).

Edgar (*c* 943-75), king of all England (959-75). Called the Peaceful, allowed Danes limited autonomy in Danelaw. Restored monasticism with Dunstan.

Edgar, king of Scotland (1097-1107). Son of Malcolm III.

Edinburgh, Philip [Mountbatten], Duke of (1921-), consort of Elizabeth II of Great Britain, b. Greece. Son of Prince Andrew of Greece and Princess Alice, great-granddaughter of Queen Victoria. Married Elizabeth in 1947.

Edinburgh, cap. city of Scotland, admin. hq. of Lothian region, on S side of Firth of Forth. Pop. 457,000. Admin., commercial centre; printing, publishing; brewing, distilling. Has univ. (1583). Seaport at Leith. Annual arts festival from 1947. Buildings incl. castle, St. Giles Church (mostly 15th cent.), Holyrood Palace (royal residence from time of James IV); Georgian architecture (esp. Adam) in 18th-19th cent. New Town.

Edirne, town of Turkey, in Thrace; formerly Adrianople. Pop. 46,000. Silk, cotton mfg. Founded by Hadrian in AD 125; scene of decisive defeat of Romans by Visigoths (378). Twice fell to Russians in 19th cent.; taken by Turks in 1913.

Edison, Thomas Alva (1847-1931), American inventor. Contributed to wireless telegraphy, telephony and generation of electricity. Invented phonograph (1878) and 1st practicable electric light. Developed 1st distribution system for electric lighting (built in New York, 1881-2). His companies, holding *c* 1300 patents, were consolidated as General Electric Company.

Edmonton, prov. cap. of Alberta, Canada; on N Saskatchewan R. Pop. 554,000. Transport, indust. centre in agric. and oil producing region; furs, oil refining, meat packing. Has Univ. of Alberta (1906).

Edmund Ironside (d. 1016), king of England (1016). Led English opposition to Canute. Canute gained whole kingdom on Edmund's death.

education, process of training and developing knowledge, skill, mind, character, *etc,* esp. by formal schooling or study. Formal education began in Greece, with training in mathematics, music, Homer, philosophy. During Dark Ages, learning preserved by monks; became more general with estab. of monastic schools and univs. (11th-13th cents.). Education limited to clergy, nobility (training in chivalry), and future craftsmen. Renaissance brought widening of whom and what was taught, introducing classics to curriculum. After Reformation many more schools were estab. Important extension of popular education was a feature of late 19th cent. By late 20th cent., most countries in world provided universal, free education, often with private or religious organizations paralleling state-run schools. Also *see* COMPREHENSIVE EDUCATION.

Edward I (1239-1307), king of England (1272-1307). Fought for father Henry III against rebel barons 1264-7, was chief agent in their defeat. Conquered Wales, but failed in long campaigns to subdue Scots. Noted for legal reforms, esp. Statutes of Westminster. Summoned MODEL PARLIAMENT (1295).

Edward II (1284-1327), king of England (1307-27). Continued father Edward I's attempts to subjugate Scotland, but defeated by Robert the Bruce (1314). Favours to Piers Gaveston led to barons' revolt, and alienated his wife, Isabella. Later favourites, the Despensers, were virtual rulers until Isabella and her lover Mortimer invaded from France. They deposed and later murdered Edward.

Edward III (1312-77), king of England (1327-77). Son of Edward II, overthrew (1330) regency of his mother Isabella and her lover Mortimer. Reign dominated by

Hundred Years War, beginning 1337, in which he and son Edward the Black Prince were prominent. Reign also marked by Black Death (1347), consequent social changes, and religious unrest, esp. through teachings of Wycliffe.

Edward IV (1442-83), king of England (1461-70, 1471-83). Son of Richard, duke of York, became king on defeat of Lancastrians at Mortimer's Cross. Fled to Holland after quarrel with Warwick, who briefly restored Henry VI. Recovered throne with victories at Barnet and Tewkesbury (1471).

Edward V (1470-83), king of England (1483). Son of Edward IV, imprisoned with brother Richard, duke of York, in the Tower of London by their uncle, duke of Gloucester. Gloucester took throne as Richard III when they were declared illegitimate; he is said to have had them murdered.

Edward VI (1537-53), king of England (1547-53). Son of Henry VIII and Jane Seymour. Succeeded father under council of regents controlled by uncle, Edward SEYMOUR. Reign saw growth of Protestantism and introduction of Book of Common Prayer. Seymour was overthrown by NORTHUMBERLAND who gained right of succession for Lady Jane GREY.

Edward VII (1841-1910), king of Great Britain and Ireland (1901-10). Eldest son of Queen Victoria, known for his love affairs and sporting activities. Promoted Entente Cordiale with France.

Edward VIII (1894-1972), king of Great Britain and Ireland (1936). Eldest son of George V, forced to abdicate to avoid constitutional crisis over proposed marriage to American divorcée, Wallis Warfield Simpson. Married her (1937) after becoming duke of Windsor.

Edward the Black Prince (1330-76), eldest son of Edward III of England. Notable as protagonist in Hundred Years War, esp. in victory at Poitiers (1356). Opposed brother, John of Gaunt, who held power at end of Edward's reign. Died before father, who was succeeded by Black Prince's son, Richard II.

Edward the Confessor (d. 1066), king of England (1042-66). Grew up in Normandy until he succeeded Harthacanute. Showed favours to Normans, thereby increasing strife with Earl Godwin of Wessex, which led to exile of Godwin and son Harold. After reconciliation, Harold became Edward's heir, though previously Edward had prob. promised William of Normandy succession. Succession crisis resolved by Norman Conquest.

Edwin (*c* 585-632), king of Northumbria. Extended rule over all of England except Kent. Converted to Christianity 627.

EEC, *see* EUROPEAN COMMUNITIES.

eel, any of order Anguilliformes of snake-like bony fish. Naked skin or minute scales; no pelvic fins. Species incl. common eel, *Anguilla anguilla,* born in Sargasso Sea; crosses Atlantic in larval state to mature in European rivers.

eelgrass, *Zostera marina,* flowering plant of the pondweed family. Grows underwater with long grass-like leaves. Found in Europe and North America in shallow salt water.

EFTA, *see* EUROPEAN FREE TRADE ASSOCIATION.

Egbert (d. 839), king of Wessex (802-39). United most of England under his rule by 829.

egg, in biology, *see* OVUM.

eggplant, *see* AUBERGINE.

eglantine, *see* BRIAR.

Egmont, Lamoral, Count of (1522-68), Flemish statesman. Stadholder of Flanders and Artois (1559-67) under Philip II of Spain, he protested against Spanish governorship of Netherlands. Arrest and execution by duke of Alva aroused Netherlands to revolt.

ego, in psychoanalysis, term used to denote personal consciousness, which mediates between impulses of the ID, standards of the SUPEREGO and the outside world.

egret, slender heron-like wading bird with white plumage, genus *Egretta.*

Egypt *(Misr),* republic of NE Africa. Area 1,001,000 sq km (386,500 sq mi); pop. 41,000,000; cap. Cairo, chief port Alexandria. Language: Arabic. Religion: Islam. Largely desert, Qattara Depression in NW, Sinai penin. in NE. Pop. concentrated in fertile Nile valley (Upper Egypt), delta (Lower Egypt). Produces cotton, rice, cereals; petroleum, phosphates. Ancient Egypt ruled by 30 dynasties grouped into 3 'kingdoms' 3100-332 BC. Conquered by Alexander the Great; ruled successively by Ptolemys, Rome, Arabs, Mamelukes, Ottoma . Turks. Home of early Christian leaders 1st-6th cent.; Islam introduced 7th cent. by Arabs. Dominated by British, French in 19th cent.; made British protect. (1914). Constitutional monarchy from 1923, sovereign state from 1936. Republic proclaimed 1953; formed United Arab Republic 1958 with Syria, Yemen, disintegrated 1961; called Arab Republic of Egypt after 1971. Has led 4 Arab wars against Israel (1948, 1956, 1967, 1973) without success, leaving most of Sinai penin. under Israeli occupation. until returned after 1979 peace treaty.

Ehrlich, Paul (1854-1915), German bacteriologist. Discovered means of staining and identifying tuberculosis bacilli; also discovered drug arsphenamine, 1st effective treatment against syphilis. Shared Nobel Prize for Physiology and Medicine (1908) for theory of antibodies' role in immunity.

Eichendorff, Joseph, Freiherr von (1788-1857), German poet. Known for lyrical poetry celebrating countryside, much of it set to music by Schumann, Brahms.

Eichmann, [Karl] Adolf (1902-62), German Nazi official. Chief of Gestapo's Jewish section (from 1939); promoted use of gas chambers. Escaped after WWII. Abducted

(1960) from Argentina by Israeli agents, tried and executed in Israel.

eider duck, *Somateria mollissima,* large sea duck of N regions. Eiderdown used for stuffing quilts, pillows.

Eiffel, Alexandre Gustave (1832-1923), French engineer. Designed Eiffel Tower, 400 m (984 ft) high, built for 1889 Paris Exhibition.

Eiger, mountain of SC Switzerland, height 3973 m (13,042 ft). Notorious North Face, where many climbers have died.

Eilat, port of S Israel, at head of Gulf of Aqaba. Pop. 12,800. Oil pipeline (opened 1957) bypasses Suez Canal. Biblical Elath.

Eindhoven, town of S Netherlands. Pop. 363,000. Rapid 20th cent. growth from radio, television indust.

Einstein, Albert (1879-1955), American physicist, b. Germany. In 1905, enunciated special theory of relativity and gave theoretical explanation of Brownian motion and photoelectric effect. Published (1916) general theory of RELATIVITY, a geometric theory of gravitation superseding that of Newton. Awarded Nobel Prize for Physics (1921). Attempted to find unified theory of gravitation and electromagnetism.

einsteinium (Es), transuranic element of actinide group; at. no. 99, mass no. of most stable isotope 254. Discovered (1952) in debris of thermonuclear explosion.

Eire, *see* IRELAND, REPUBLIC OF.

Eisenhower, Dwight David (1890-1969), American general and statesman, president (1953-61). During WWII, chief of Allied forces in N Africa (1942-3), supreme commander of Allied invasion of Europe (1944). As Republican president, fostered anti-Communist alliances in SE Asia, Latin America.

Eisenstein, Sergei Mikhailovich (1898-1948), Russian film director. Pioneered cinematic techniques. Won fame with *Battleship Potemkin* (1925), later made epics on Russian history, *eg Alexander Nevsky* (1938).

Eisteddfod, traditional Welsh festival for the encouragement of bardic arts, esp. music, poetry, by competition. Dates from before 12th cent. but discontinued 17th-19th cents. Now meets annually in August.

El-Aaiún, *see* WESTERN SAHARA.

eland, either of 2 large antelopes. Giant eland, *Taurotragus derbianus,* of C and S Africa, is largest species of antelope. Cape eland, *T. oryx,* found in S Africa.

elasticity, in physics, property in materials of returning to their original shape and dimensions after being deformed by external forces. Material is permanently distorted if applied forces exceed elastic limit.

Elath, *see* EILAT.

Elba, isl. of W Italy, separated from Tuscany by Str. of Piombino. Area 223 sq km (86 sq mi). Fishing, tourism; iron ore mining from Etruscan times. Principality (1814-15) under exiled Napoleon.

Elbe (Czech. *Labe*), river of C Europe. Flows 1167 km (725 mi) from NW Czechoslovakia via East and West Germany to North Sea at Hamburg. Navigable for *c* 800 km (500 mi); canal links with Rhine, Weser rivers.

Elberfeld, *see* WUPPERTAL.

Elbrus or **Elbruz, Mount,** massif in Caucasus Mts., USSR, W Georgian SSR. Incl. highest peak 5633 m (18,481 ft) in Europe.

Elburz Mountains, mountain range in N Iran, running parallel to S Caspian Sea. Rise to 5771 m (18,934 ft) at Mt. Demavend.

Leaves, flowers and berries of elder

elder, any of genus *Sambucus* of deciduous bushy trees of honeysuckle family. Esp. *S. nigra,* common in Europe, with small, strong-smelling white flower and red or black berries, used to make wine.

Eleanor of Aquitaine (*c* 1122-1204), queen of Henry II of England. Married Henry after annulment of marriage to Louis VII of France. Her sons, Richard I, John, became kings of England. Estab. own court at Poitiers and aided sons in unsuccessful revolt (1173) against Henry.

election, selection of persons for office by vote. Used occasionally in ancient Greece, regularly in Rome to appoint tribunes. Elections regularized in England (1688) although Commons elected in some manner since 14th cent. SUFFRAGE extended by REFORM BILL (1832). Ballot Act (1872) introduced secret ballot. In UK, general (*ie* national) election always follows dissolution of Parliament, at least every 5 years.

electoral college, in US politics, body of electors from each state with formal duty of choosing president and vice-president. Electors of each state, equal in number to its members in Congress, expected to vote for candidates selected by popular vote in state. President need not obtain majority of popular vote in country.

electors, number of princes within Holy Roman Empire who had theoretical right to elect head of empire; in reality, in all elections after 1438 except one, a Habsburg became emperor. In 1356 number set at 7, usually archbishops of Mainz, Trier, Cologne, king of Bohemia, duke of Saxony, margrave of Bradenburg and electors of the Palatinate. Dismissed on dissolution of Empire (1806).

Electra, in Greek myth, daughter of AGAMEMNON and Clytemnestra. Helped brother ORESTES avenge Agamemnon's death in tragedies of Aeschylus, Sophocles, Euripides.

Electra complex, *see* OEDIPUS COMPLEX.

electrical engineering, branch of ENGINEERING dealing with generation and transmission of electrical power and with the devices that use it. *See* ELECTRONICS.

electric fish, one of various fish capable of generating electricity by muscular contraction. Uses shocks for navigation, defence or killing prey. Incl. electric eel, electric ray, stargazer.

electricity, general term for physical phenomena associated with electric CHARGE. Flow of electric charge in conductors constitutes electric current. Charge can be generated by friction, by chemical means (*eg* in a cell) or by electromagnetic induction.

electric light, light produced by electrical means. Electric light bulb contains inert gas (*eg* nitrogen) and wire filament; current passing through filament heats it to white heat. First practical form developed by Edison (1879).

electric motor, device for converting electrical energy into mechanical energy. Simplest type consists of current-carrying coil or armature placed between poles of powerful magnet; mechanical force acting on armature causes it to rotate.

electrocardiograph, instrument used to diagnose heart disorders by tracing changes in electric current and voltage produced by contractions of heart.

electroconvulsive therapy, treatment of certain psychotic conditions by passing electric current through brain to induce convulsions or coma.

electrode, terminal by which electric current enters or leaves conducting substances, *eg* liquid in electrolytic cell or gas in electrical discharge tube. Positive electrode is the anode, negative is the cathode.

electroencephalograph, instrument used to record electrical activity of nerve cells in the brain. Used to diagnose brain disorders, esp. epilepsy.

electrolysis, decomposition of chemical compound (electrolytes) by passage of electric current through compound in solution or in molten state. Electrolyte dissociates into positive and negative ions; ions move to electrodes of opposite charge and give up their charge. Technique used in electroplating of metals.

electromagnetic induction, production of electromotive force in a circuit by variation of a magnetic field. Phenomenon forms basis of DYNAMO.

electromagnetic radiation, radiation propagated through space by variation in electric and magnetic fields. Such radiation consists of waves travelling at speed of light, nature of which depends on frequency. Incl. heat rays, radio waves, light, gamma rays and X-rays.

electromotive force, force of electric pressure that causes electric current to flow in circuits. Equivalent to difference in potential between points in circuit.

electron, elementary particle of matter which by convention carries one negative unit of charge. Electrons are constituents of atoms, assumed to move in orbits about the atomic nucleus; number of protons in nucleus equals number of circulating electrons. Movement of free (*ie* detached from their atomic orbit) electrons constitutes electric current.

electronic music, *see* MUSIC, ELECTRONIC.

electronics, branch of electrical engineering dealing with controlled movement of electrons through thermionic valves and semiconductors and with the devices that use them. Incl. technology of computers, radio circuitry, *etc.*

electron microscope, microscope using beam of electrons to obtain greatly enlarged images of objects. Electron beam passes through thin film of material under investigation and is focused by magnetic or electrostatic fields to form image on fluorescent screen.

electronvolt, unit of energy used in nuclear physics; equals work done on an electron to pass it through potential difference of 1 volt. 1 GeV (BeV in US) = 10^9 electronvolts.

elegy, lyrical poem in contemplative tone lamenting the dead.

element, in chemistry, substance which cannot be decomposed by chemical means into simpler substances. Elements consist of atoms of same atomic number; traditionally 93 occur in nature and 12 more have been made in the laboratory.

elementary particles, in physics, subatomic particles which are basic components of matter. Incl. electron, proton, neutrino which are stable, and neutron, various mesons and many other particles which are unstable. Each elementary particle has corresponding anti-particle, with same mass but opposite charge, spin, *etc.* Recent theories suggest that all elementary particles are composed of QUARKS and LEPTONS.

elephant, thick-skinned mammal of order Proboscidea, with flexible, strong trunk. Indian elephant, *Elephas maximus,* often domesticated, is used for heavy work in India, Burma, Sri Lanka. African elephant, *Loxodonta africana,* larger than Indian, with larger ears. Both species live in itinerant herds.

elephantiasis, chronic disease characterized by gross thickening of skin and connective tissue, esp. of legs and genitals. Caused by blockage of lymphatic vessels, usually by infestation with filaria worms.

elephant seal, *see* SEA ELEPHANT.

Eleusis, ancient city near Athens with shrine of DEMETER. Home of Eleusinian mystery cults celebrating cycle of fertility and death through worship of Demeter, Persephone.

El Ferrol, *see* FERROL, EL.

Elgar, Sir Edward (1857-1934), English composer. First major figure in British music since Purcell. *Enigma Variations* estab. him in 1899. Other works incl. oratorio *The Dream of Gerontius* and marches *Pomp and Circumstance.*

Elgin, town of Grampian region, N Scotland, on R. Lossie. Pop. 16,000. Former royal burgh and co. town of Morayshire. Market town, distilling; port at Lossiemouth. Has ruined cathedral (13th cent.).

Elgin Marbles, ancient sculptures removed from the Parthenon, Athens and acquired by Lord Elgin from the Turks. Brought to England (1803-12), bought by govt. and deposited in British Museum (1816).

El Greco, *see* GRECO, EL.

Elijah, Hebrew prophet of 9th cent. BC. Violently censured the spread of idolatrous worship during reign of King Ahab. Major prophet of Jewish tradition.

Eliot, George, pseud. of Mary Ann or Marian Evans (1819-80), English novelist. Works deal with moral, social problems of her day, *eg The Mill on the Floss* (1860), *Silas Marner* (1861), *Middlemarch* (1872).

Eliot, Sir John (1592-1632), English parliamentary leader. Led impeachment proceedings against duke of Buckingham (1626). Pressed Charles I to accept Petition of Right (1628). Died in prison.

Eliot, T[homas] S[tearns] (1888-1965), English poet, b. US. Poetry, *eg Prufrock and Other Observations* (1917), *The Waste Land* (1922), *The Four Quartets* (1936-43), reflect classical, intellectually conservative attitude to culture. Verse dramas incl. *Murder in the Cathedral* (1935), *The Cocktail Party* (1949), on religious themes. Wrote influential criticism. Awarded Nobel Prize for Literature (1948).

Elisabethville, *see* LUBUMBASHI.

Elisha, Hebrew prophet, successor of ELIJAH.

Elizabeth I (1533-1603), queen of England (1558-1603). Daughter of Henry VIII and Anne Boleyn, succeeded to throne after perilous early life. Re-estab. Protestantism by acts of Supremacy and Uniformity (1559). Persecuted Catholics in later years of reign after series of plots which aimed to replace her by MARY QUEEN OF SCOTS; signed Mary's death warrant (1587). Reign marked by growth of commerce, beginning of colonization of North America, defeat of Spanish Armada (1588), flourishing of drama, literature, music.

Elizabeth II (1926-), queen of Great Britain and Northern Ireland (1952-). Daughter of George VI, married (1947) Philip Mountbatten, Duke of EDINBURGH. Eldest son and heir apparent is CHARLES. Other children are Anne (1950-), Andrew (1960-), Edward (1964-).

Elizabethan drama, name given to plays written between *c* 1570 and 1600 combining traditions of English comedies, chronicle plays with Renaissance classicism. Examples incl. blank verse plays of Shakespeare, Marlow, Jonson, ranging from tragedy to sophisticated comedy.

Elizabethan style, in architecture transitional style of English Renaissance; combined aspects of perpendicular Gothic with Italian Renaissance ideas and Flemish decoration.

elk, *Alces alces,* largest deer of Europe and Asia. Inhabitant of marshland. American variety is MOOSE. In America elk is alternative name for WAPITI.

Ellesmere, most N isl. of Canada, in NE Franklin Dist., Northwest Territs; largest of Queen Elizabeth Isls. Area 213,000 sq km (82,000 sq mi). Ice-cap in S and E; mountainous. Eskimo pop.

Ellice Islands, *see* TUVALU.

Ellington, Edward Kennedy ('Duke') (1899-1974), American pianist, composer. Major composer in jazz music, he also wrote many famous songs.

ellipse, in geometry, curve traced by point which moves so that sum of its distances from 2 fixed points (its foci) is constant. One of the CONIC SECTIONS.

Ellis, [Henry] Havelock (1859-1939), English writer, psychologist. Known for *Studies in the Psychology of Sex* (7 vols., 1898-1928).

English elm

elm, family (Ulmaceae) of deciduous trees with rough oval leaves, native to N temperate regions. Esp. denotes genus *Ulmus.* See DUTCH ELM DISEASE.

El Paso, border city of SW Texas, US, opposite Juárez (Mexico) on Rio Grande

Pop. 424,000. Travel jct., tourist and commercial centre. Copper smelting, oil refining. Settled 1827.

El Salvador

El Salvador, republic of Central America. Area 21,393 sq km (8260 sq mi); pop. 4,365,000; cap. San Salvador. Language: Spanish. Religion: RC. Pacific coastline rises to fertile plain (coffee, cotton growing; cattle rearing); volcanic mountains. World's main source of balsam. Spanish rule (1524-1821); member of Central American Federation until independence in 1838.

Elsinore, *see* HELSINGÖR.

Ely, Isle of, region of Cambridgeshire, EC England, former admin. county. Fen drained to yield agric. land. **City of Ely,** on R. Ouse. Pop. 10,000. Agric. market. Cathedral (11th cent.).

Elysium or **Elysian Fields,** in Greek myth, paradise for heroes favoured by the gods. In Homer, it lies on the most W edge of the world. Later tradition had it as part of underworld for all blessed dead.

Emancipation, Edict of (1861), proclamation freeing all Russian serfs (*c* ⅓ of pop.) issued by Alexander II. Complex procedures for land purchases by peasants and abuse of edict by landlords helped provoke Russian Revolution.

Emancipation Proclamation, in US history, edict freeing slaves in rebellious Confederate states. Issued by Lincoln (Sept. 1862), became law 1 Jan. 1863.

embryo, in zoology, animal in earliest stages of its development, before it emerges from egg membranes, or in viviparous animals, from uterus of mother. Name foetus is often applied to later stages of embryo's development. Also *see* SEED.

emerald, gem form of BERYL. Green colour is due to presence of chromium compounds. Major sources in Colombia, Brazil, US.

Emerson, Ralph Waldo (1803-82), American phiiosopher, poet. Founded transcendentalism, *ie* belief that man has intuitive knowledge of 'world soul'. Ideas formulated in *Nature* (1836). Wrote essays, lyrics, often in free verse form.

emery, finely granular form of CORUNDUM, containing some magnetite. Used as an abrasive.

Emilia-Romagna, region of N Italy, cap. Bologna. Apennines in S; fertile Po valley in C and N. Agric., food processing. Adriatic resorts, *eg* Rimini.

Eminence Grise, *see* JOSEPH, FATHER.

Emmet, Robert (1778-1803), Irish nationalist. Went to France (1800) to enlist support for an Irish uprising. Led small group of followers in insurrection (July, 1803). Captured and hanged.

emotion, in psychology, complex response to stimulus, with both physiological and psychological effects, *eg* changes in rate of breathing, gland secretion, strong feelings of excitement, which usually involve impulse to definite action.

Empedocles (*c* 495-*c* 435 BC), Greek philosopher. Held matter to be composed of 4 elements: earth, water, fire, air. Explained motion as resolution of opposed forces of harmony and discord.

emphysema, disease involving abnormal distention of air sacs of lungs. Occurs with old age or at an advanced stage of chronic bronchitis. Symptoms incl. difficulty in breathing, coughing with sputum.

Empire State Building, New York City, formerly tallest building in world, 380 m (1250 ft) high. Built 1930-1, it has 102 storeys and is a tourist attraction in Manhattan. *See* SKYSCRAPER.

Empire style, mode of furniture design and interior decoration popular in France *c* 1804-30; combined neo-Classical designs with Egyptian motifs. In women's costume, term refers to high-waisted gowns with flowing skirt and short, puffed sleeves.

empiricism, philosophical belief, opposed to RATIONALISM, that all knowledge is derived from experience. Denies innate ideas and *a priori* truth. Dominant tradition in British philosophy since Locke.

Empty Quarter (*Ar Rub Al Khālī*), desert of S Saudi Arabia.

Ems Telegram (July, 1870), incident which led to Franco-Prussian War. William I of Prussia refused to assure French ambassador that no Hohenzollern would seek Spanish throne. Bismarck successfully provoked French govt. to declare war by publishing version of William's telegram reporting interview to Bismarck.

emu, *Dromaius novaehollandiae,* second largest living bird; flightless, capable of running fast. Found in Australia. Brown body; reaches height of 1.5 m/5 ft.

emulsion, colloidal suspension of 2 immiscible fluids, *eg* milk. Emulsions may be stabilized by emulsifying agents; milk is stabilized by casein.

enamel, vitreous glaze, coloured by metallic oxides, which can be fused to surfaces of metals, glass or pottery. Of ancient origin, art of enamelling was perfected by Byzantines in 10th cent. Limoges, France, was main centre of European enamelling from 12th to 16th cents.

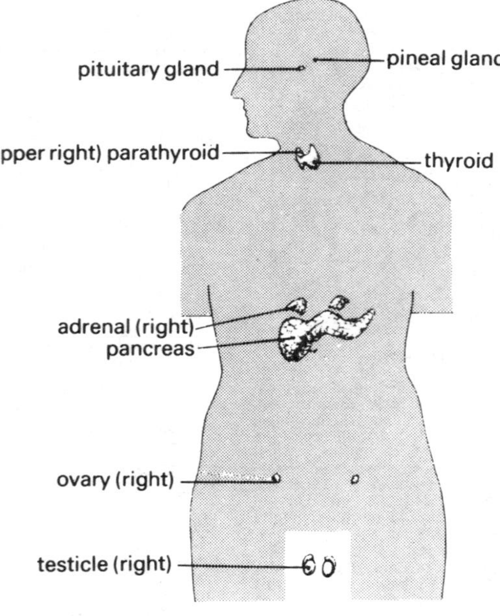

Endocrine glands

encephalitis, name for viral inflammation of the brain, *eg* rabies, poliomyelitis.

enclosure, in English history, practice of fencing off land formerly subject to common rights (open field system). Caused serious hardship, leading to rebellions in Tudor period. New wave of enclosures from 1750 to 1800 forced landless workers to move to cities.

encyclopedia, a book, or set of books, containing articles, usually arranged alphabetically, covering a general or specific area of knowledge. Earliest extant example is Pliny the Elder's *Historia Naturalis* (1st cent. AD). *The Encyclopaedia Britannica* dates from 1768. *See also* ENCYCLOPEDISTS.

Encyclopedists, 18th cent. contributors to Diderot's *Encyclopédie,* incl. Voltaire, Montesquieu, Rousseau.

Enderbury Island, *see* CANTON AND ENDERBURY ISLANDS.

endive, *Cichorium endiva,* plant of daisy family, similar to dandelion. Native to Europe but widely cultivated in US, where it is known as chicory. Leaves used in salads.

endocrine glands or **ductless glands,** organs in body which secrete hormones directly into bloodstream; concerned with metabolism, growth and sexual functions. Principal glands are thyroid, pituitary, parathyroid, adrenals, testicles and ovaries, islets of Langerhans in pancreas.

endorphins, class of pain-killers, incl. enkephalin, found naturally in the brain and pituitary gland. May play a role in mental disorders, acupuncture and behaviour associated with addiction to opiates.

energy, in physics, the ability to do WORK. A body may have potential energy because of its position or kinetic energy because of its motion. It was believed that energy can neither be created nor destroyed, but can be converted from one form into another, *eg* electrical energy into heat energy. Einstein's law $E = mc^2$ (where c = speed of light) now shows that mass and energy are equivalent; energy obtained from annihilation of mass accounts for nuclear energy and power of stars. Energy sources incl. oil, coal, gas, wood, HYDRO-ELECTRIC POWER, NUCLEAR REACTORS, SOLAR ENERGY, wind and tidal power.

Enfield, bor. of N Greater London, England. Pop. 260,000. Created 1965.

Engels, Friedrich (1820-95), German philosopher. Collaborated with Marx in evolving Communist doctrine, notably in *The Communist Manifesto* (1848). Lived in England after 1850, edited much of Marx's *Das Kapital.* His own works incl. *The Origin of the Family, Private Property and the State* (1884).

ngineering, science of putting scientific knowledge to practical use esp. in design and construction of engines, machines and public works. Field divided into civil, mechanical, chemical.

:ngland, constituent country of UK, in S part of GREAT BRITAIN. Area 130,357 sq km (50,331 sq mi); pop. 46,351,000; cap. London. Major cities Birmingham, Liverpool, Manchester. Comprises 39 counties, 6 met. counties, Greater London. Main rivers Thames, Severn, Humber, Tees, Tyne. Pastoral uplands in NW (Pennines, Lake Dist.); lowland (agric., dairying) in SE. Indust. centred in Midlands (coal, iron), Lancashire, Yorkshire (textiles), NE (shipbuilding, engineering). Roman occupation (AD 43-5th cent.) followed by Saxon, Viking, Norman invasions. Successive royal dynasties Plantagenet, Lancaster, York, Tudor, Stuart, Orange, Hanover, Windsor. Church of England split from Rome under Henry VIII. Indust. Revolution began here (18th cent.), made England world's leading indust. nation in 19th cent. Estab. large overseas Empire (Commonwealth after 1931). United with Wales 1536, with Scotland 1707, with Ireland 1801 (partition 1921) to form UNITED KINGDOM.

:ngland, Church of, established church in England. Henry VIII withdrew allegiance to Pope and declared sovereign to be head of English church; confirmed by Act of Supremacy (1543). Under Mary, England was again RC, but Elizabeth I restored Protestantism, Thirty-nine Articles adopted as basic doctrine. Act of Supremacy (1559) restored ecclesiastical jurisdiction to the crown. Presbyterianism substituted for episcopacy by Long Parliament (1646); episcopacy restored (1660). High Church tradition emphasizes ritualism and apostolic succession, Low Church stresses Bible and preaching. Archbishop of Canterbury is chief primate of Church of England and of unestablished Episcopal Church in Scotland, Church of Ireland, Church in Wales, Anglican Church of Canada, Church of England in Australia and Church of the Province of New Zealand.

:nglish, language of W Germanic group of Indo-European family. Second only to Mandarin Chinese in number of speakers in world. First language in Britain, US, Australia, New Zealand. One of official languages of United Nations. Incl. many dialects. Developed from languages of 5th-cent. Germanic invaders of Britain, which became regional dialects. West Saxon (of Wessex) became dominant in 9th cent. (*see* ANGLO-SAXON LITERATURE). Language of this period termed Old English. Norman Conquest (1066) brought change, Norman French being used as official, polite language. Development continued, Middle English (*c* 1150-*c* 1500) becoming standard in 14th cent. Important literature incl. *Gawayne and the Greene Knight, Piers Plowman.* Modern English developed from London dialect pre-1500, language of CHAUCER. Subsequent change mainly loss of inflections, gain of loan-words from other languages.

English Channel (Fr. *La Manche*), arm of Atlantic between England and France; length 563 km (350 mi), width varies from 160 km (100 mi) to 34 km (21 mi) at Strait of DOVER. Many resorts on both coasts; ferry services.

engraving, process of cutting, etching or drawing marks on metal plates, wooden blocks, *etc,* for purpose of reproducing prints. Three main types: relief, incl. woodcutting; intaglio, incl. ETCHING, DRYPOINT; surface printing, *eg* LITHOGRAPHY.

enkephalin, *see* ENDORPHIN.

Enlightenment or **Age of Reason,** European movement of 18th cent., characterized by rationalism, learning, 'scientific' (*ie* sceptical), empirical approach. Based on work of Newton, Descartes, Locke in 17th cent. and expressed esp. in Diderot's *Encyclopédie,* and writings of Voltaire, Rousseau, Hume, Kant. Manifested by social reforms of 'enlightened despots', *eg* Frederick II of Prussia, Catherine II of Russia, and revolutionary movements in France, America.

Ennis, co. town of Clare, W Irish Republic. Pop. 6000. RC pro-cathedral.

Enniskillen, town of SW Northern Ireland. Pop. 7000. Former co. town of Fermanagh. Agric. market. Scene of defeat of James II's forces (1689).

Ennius, Quintus (239-*c* 169 BC), Roman author. First major Latin classical poet. Works incl. epic *Annales.*

Ensor, James Ensor, Baron (1860-1949), Belgian painter. Work has fantastic and macabre quality; used masks, skeletons, ghosts in scenes of everyday life. Precursor of expressionism.

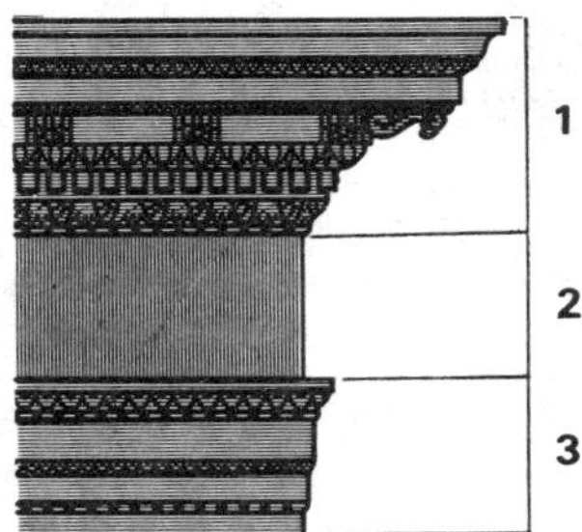

Entablature (Corinthian style): 1. cornice; 2. frieze; 3. architrave

entablature, in classical architecture, horizontal superstructure supported by columns. Consists of architrave, surmounted by frieze, with cornice on top.

Entebbe, town of S Uganda, on N shore of Victoria Nyanza. Pop. 11,000. Commercial centre, international airport. Cap. of British Uganda (1894-1962).

Entente Cordiale, *see* TRIPLE ENTENTE.

enteritis, inflammation of the intestine, esp. small intestine. Common form is gastroenteritis, characterized by abdominal pains, diarrhoea, vomiting; caused by bacterial food poisoning, viruses.

entomology, branch of zoology dealing with insects. Important aspect of entomology is need to control insects which spread disease to man and animals or destroy crops, and stored produce.

entrepreneur, in economics, person who assumes risk and management of a business organization. Fully differentiated from ordinary capitalist by 19th-cent. economists who saw him as coordinator and innovator necessary for corporate indust.

entropy, in thermodynamics, term describing degree of disorder of a system. Entropy never decreases in an isolated system. When it increases the ability of the total energy in system to do useful work diminishes.

Enugu, city of SE Nigeria. Pop. 187,000. Indust. centre; coalmining, engineering, sawmilling. Former cap. of Eastern Region; cap. of Biafra (1967-70) in civil war.

Enver Pasha (1881-1922), Turkish general, political leader. Leader in Young Turks' revolution (1908); became virtual dictator after coup (1913). Instrumental in bringing Turkey into WWI. Killed leading anti-Soviet forces in Bukhara.

enzymes, large group of proteins, produced by plant and animal cells, which act as catalysts in specific chemical reactions vital to life. A few are found in natural secretions, such as digestive juices pepsin and trypsin.

Eocene epoch, second geological epoch of Tertiary period. Alpine mountain building continued. Further evolution of primitive mammals which began in Palaeocene epoch. Increase in temperature, causing widespread subtropical conditions. Also *see* GEOLOGICAL TABLE.

Eos, in Greek myth, goddess of dawn. Identified by Romans with Aurora.

ephedrine, alkaloid drug extracted from certain Chinese plants or synthesized. Used to relieve nasal congestion and asthma.

Ephesians, epistle of NT, traditionally written to Christians at Ephesus by St Paul (*c* AD 60) during his Roman imprisonment, but possibly by a later writer. Uses metaphor of mystical body of Christ as a plea for Christian unity.

Ephesus, ancient Ionian city, on W coast of Asia Minor. Taken by Romans (133 BC), became cap. of Roman Asia. Had famou[s] temple of Diana (Artemis), one of Seve[n] Wonders of the World. Destroyed (262) b[y] Goths.

epic, long narrative poem dealing wit[h] exploits of one or more heroic individual[s,] historical or legendary, usually in exalte[d] style and moral tone. Examples incl. Ilia[d,] Odyssey, Aeneid (classical); BEOWULF (O[ld] English); *Chanson de Roland* (French[);] *Paradise Lost* (English).

Epictetus, (*fl c* AD 100), Greek Stoi[c] philosopher. Taught in Rome before bein[g] banished. Advocated life free of desire[,] trust in providence.

Epicurus, (*c* 340-*c* 270 BC), Gree[k] philosopher. Founder of the Epicurea[n] school of philosophy. Advocated relianc[e] on the senses. Saw freedom from pain o[r] anxiety as greatest good, achieved b[y] simple living.

Epidaurus, ancient city of Greece, in N[E] Peloponnese. Site of temple of Asclepiu[s.] Has best preserved ancient Greek theatre[.]

epiglottis, triangular flap of cartilage behin[d] the tongue. Folds back over windpip[e] during swallowing, thus preventing foo[d] from entering lungs.

epilepsy, group of chronic disorders of th[e] brain characterized by fits. Classified a[s] *petit mal,* in which there is momentar[y] loss of consciousness, or *grand mal,* i[n] which there is loss of consciousness an[d] muscle stiffening for a few minute[s.] Treatment by sedatives and drugs.

Epiphany, Christian feast, celebrated on 6t[h] Jan. Commemorates baptism of Jesus, vis[it] of wise men to Bethlehem, miracle o[f] changing water to wine at Cana.

epiphyte or **air plant,** general name fo[r] plant which grows on another plant but i[s] not a parasite and produces its own food b[y] photosynthesis, drawing water fro[m] atmosphere. Incl. orchids.

Epirus *(Ipiros),* region of NW Greece an[d] SW Albania, between Pindus Mts. an[d] Ionian Sea. Famed for cattle, horses. *Fl* 3r[d] cent. BC under Pyrrhus.

episcopacy, system of church govt. b[y] bishops, used in all pre-Reformation an[d] some post-Reformation churches. Estab[.] by end of 1st cent. and not challenged unti[l] Luther's rejection of the powers of bishops[.] Calvin rejected system as major abuse[.] Degrees of authority are pope, patriarch[,] archbishop, bishop.

Episcopal Church (Protestant), *see* ANGLI[-]CAN COMMUNION.

epistles, in NT, 21 letters, traditionally as[-]cribed to 5 of the Apostles (Paul, Peter[,] James, Jude, John), addressed to some o[f] the new churches and individual member[s] of them.

Epsom and Ewell, town of Surrey, SE England. Pop. 72,000. Epsom Down[s] racecourse nearby (Derby). Has 17th cent[.] spa (Epsom salts).

Epsom salts, hydrated magnesium sulphat[e] ($MgSO_4.7H_2O$), used as a purgative.

Epstein, Sir Jacob (1880-1959), Britis[h]

sculptor of Russo-Polish descent, b. New York. Works frequently aroused violent criticism; influenced by African art and vorticist movement.

quation, in chemistry, expression of chemical reaction by means of formulae and symbols. The equation $2H_2 + O_2 = 2H_2O$ states that 2 molecules of hydrogen combine with 1 oxygen molecule to form 2 of water.

:quator, imaginary line around the Earth, equidistant from both poles and perpendicular to axis. Forms a GREAT CIRCLE; divides globe into N and S hemispheres.

:quatorial Guinea, republic of WC Africa, on Gulf of Guinea. Area 28,000 sq km (10,800 sq mi); pop. 346,000; cap. Rey Malabo. Languages: Bantu, Spanish. Religions: native, RC. Comprises Río Muni (mainland), Bioko isl. (Macías Nguema Biyoga). Hot, wet climate: exports coffee, cocoa, hardwoods. Colony as Spanish Guinea from 18th cent.; independent from 1968.

questrianism, competitive sport for horse and rider. Divided into 3 events: dressage, which tests horse's training; show jumping; 3-day event, consisting of show jumping, dressage and cross-country phases.

quinox, time of year when Sun appears directly overhead at the Equator at noon. Night and day are thus of equal length throughout the world. Occurs twice a year: around 21 March (vernal equinox), 22 Sept. (autumnal equinox).

quity, in law, resort to general principles of fairness and justice when existing law is inadequate. In UK, developed to supplement COMMON LAW.

quivalent weight, in chemistry, number of grams of an element which will combine with or replace 1 gram of hydrogen or 8 grams of oxygen. Product of equivalent weight and valency of element equals its atomic weight. Equivalent weight of an acid is weight of acid containing 1 gram of hydrogen replaceable by a metal.

:rasmus, Desiderius (*c* 1466-1536), Dutch philosopher, humanist. Wrote Latin translation of New Testament (1516), satire *The Praise of Folly*. Believed in rational piety, took critical attitude to superstition. Opponent of religious bigotry, refused to condemn Luther, though remained RC. Influenced English humanists, esp. Thomas More.

:rastus, Thomas, orig. Lüber or Liebler (1524-83), Swiss Protestant theologian, physician. Held that punishment of sin should be left to civil authorities; doctrine known as Erastianism.

rbium (Er), metallic element of lanthanide group; at. no. 68, at. wt. 167.26. Discovered (1843).

Erfurt, city of SW East Germany, on R. Gera. Pop. 204,000. Machinery, electrical goods, agric. market. Former univ. (1392-1816), cathedral (15th cent.).

rg, unit of work or energy in c.g.s. system: 1 erg represents work done when force of 1 dyne acts through distance of 1 cm.

ergonomics, the study of relationship between people and their environment, esp. the science that seeks to adapt work or working conditions to the worker.

ergot, parasitic fungus, *Claviceps purpurea,* of cereal grains, esp. rye. Contains toxic alkaloids which cause hallucinations but can be used medicinally to limit bloodflow.

Erhard, Ludwig (1897-1977), West German statesman. As minister of economics, laid foundation of German 'economic miracle' with currency reforms of 1948. Succeeded Adenauer as Christian Democrat chancellor (1963-6).

Ericaceae, family of flowering plants. Mostly evergreen, with woody, creeping stems. Incl. heaths and rhododendrons.

Ericsson, Leif, *see* LEIF ERICSSON.

Eric the Red (*fl* 10th cent.), Norse chieftain. Discovered and colonized Greenland. Father of Leif Ericsson.

Erie, port of NW Pennsylvania, US; on L. Erie. Pop. 273,000. Coal, timber, grain, petroleum shipping; paper, electrical equipment mfg. Estab. by French as Fort Presque (1753); passed to US (1785).

Erie, Lake, shallowest of Great Lakes, C Canada-US. Area 25,745 sq km (9940 sq mi). Trade route connecting L. Huron and L. Ontario. Chief ports Cleveland, Buffalo, Toledo. Icebound from December-March.

Erin, poetic name for Ireland.

Erinyes, *see* EUMENIDES.

Eritrea, prov. of N Ethiopia, on Red Sea. Area 118,500 sq km (45,750 sq mi); cap. Asmara, chief port Massawa. Arid, rugged region with narrow coastal strip. Nomadic pastoralism, hides, coffee, cereal products. Colonized 1890 by Italy, base for Italian invasions of Ethiopia 1896, 1935. Under British military rule from 1941; united federally with Ethiopia 1952, fully integrated 1962. Guerilla separation movement active since 1970s.

Erivan, *see* YEREVAN.

Erlangen, town of SC West Germany. Pop. 101,000. Indust. centre, esp. textiles, beer; univ. (1743).

ermine, *see* STOAT.

Ernst, Max (1891-1976), German painter. A founder of DADA in Cologne (1919) and surrealist movement in Paris (1924). Developed *frottage* technique and used collage and photomontage.

Eros, in Greek myth, god of love, son of Aphrodite. Represented as beautiful but irresponsible in his infliction of passion. Also worshipped as fertility god. Identified by Romans with CUPID.

erosion, process by which features of Earth's surface are worn away. Results from mechanical action of transported debris, *eg* windborne particles may erode a cliff. Types incl. wind, river, marine, glacial erosion.

Erse, *see* GAELIC.

Erzurum, city of NE Turkey, in Armenia, at an alt. of 1920 m (6300 ft). Pop. 163,000. Of strategic importance, held by Armenians,

Byzantines and Persians; taken by Turks (1515).

Esau, in OT, son of Isaac, older twin brother of JACOB, who tricked him into selling his birthright.

Esbjerg, town of W Jutland, Denmark, on North Sea. Pop. 68,000. Chief Danish fishing port; exports dairy produce. Ferry services to England.

escape velocity, minimum velocity required by a body to escape gravitational influence of a planet. Depends on mass and diameter of planet. For Earth, escape velocity is *c* 11.2 km/sec.

Escorial or **Escurial,** town of C Spain, near Madrid. Site of building complex incl. monastery, palace and mausoleum built 1563-84 by Philip II.

Esdras 1 and **2,** apocryphal books of OT dating from *c* 100 BC-*c* AD 100. Mainly transcripts of EZRA. Esdras 2 is apocalyptic account of Ezra's revelation. In some canons, term is used for books of Ezra and Nehemiah, the apocryphal books then being Esdras 3 and 4.

Esfahan, *see* ISFAHAN.

Eskimo, people of Arctic and Labrador coasts. Pop. (1963) *c* 55,000, incl. *c* 1600 Chukchi Eskimos of NE Siberia. Six main cultural groups: most build stone or earth winter huts (igloos are comparatively rare) and have skin summer tents. Economy depends on hunting. Live in loose, voluntary association under most skilled hunter. Origins thought to be Asian via Aleutian Isls.

Eskisehir (anc. *Dorylaeum*), city of WC Turkey, in Asia Minor. Pop. 260,000. Railway jct.; agric. trade, textile mfg. Has meerschaum deposits and sulphur springs nearby.

esparto, two kinds of tall, coarse grass, *Stipa tenacissima* and *Lygeum spartum,* native to S Spain and N Africa. Used to make cordage and paper.

Esperanto, language for international use, invented (1887) by Polish oculist, Dr L. L. Zamenhof (1859-1917). Uses word bases common to main European languages. Has self-evident parts of speech (*eg* all nouns end in *-o*), single and regular conjugation of verbs and simplified inflections.

espionage, clandestine procuring of information, esp. military intelligence. Not illegal under international law. Origins of modern military intelligence attributed to Frederick II of Prussia; by WWI, European powers had developed espionage systems. Recent trends incl. increased use of diplomatic officials, reconnaissance from satellites.

essay, short literary composition dealing in discursive way with its subject from a personal point of view. Genre estab. by Montaigne (1580), Bacon (1597), developed in periodicals of Addison, Steele (18th cent.).

Essen, city of W West Germany, in Ruhr. Pop. 670,000. Major indust. centre from estab. of Krupp steelworks (early 19th cent.); coal, chemicals, engineering, h.e.p. Badly damaged in WWII.

Essenes, Jewish community (2nd cent. BC-2nd cent. AD). Condemned slavery, trading; emphasized ceremonial purity. Subsisted by simple agric., handicrafts. Possibly referred to in Dead Sea Scrolls.

essential oils, volatile substances of vegetable origin, which impart characteristic flavour or odour to plant of origin. Mostly benzene derivatives or terpenes. Used as perfumes and flavouring agents.

Essex, Robert Devereux, 2nd Earl of (1567-1601), English nobleman. Favourite of Elizabeth I; incurred royal displeasure through secret marriage (1590). Politically ambitious but failed to take power from Burghley; lord lieutenant of Ireland (1599), unable to quell Irish revolt under Tyrone. Excluded from court after unauthorized return to England. Executed for intriguing against govt.

Essex, county of SE England. Area 3673 sq km (1418 sq mi); pop. 1,436,000; admin. hq Chelmsford. Mainly lowland, low hills in N. Agric. (N), dairying (S), fishing, oysters. Coastal resorts *eg* Southend-on-Sea, seaports *eg* Tilbury. Oil refineries. Ancient Saxon kingdom.

estate, in law, degree, nature, extent and quality of interest or ownership person has in land. Real estate is interest in freehold land, personal estate any other kind of property. Since feudal times, term also used to refer to each of 3 social classes having specific political powers: 1st estate was Lords Spiritual (clergy); 2nd estate was Lords Temporal (nobility); 3rd estate was Commons (bourgeoisie).

Estates-General or **States-General,** French national assembly (1302-1789). Three ESTATES were represented as separate bodies in it. Powers were never clearly defined; merely approved monarch's legislation. Did not meet (1614-1789) until Louis XVI called it to resolve govt financial crisis. Commons and radicals in other 2 estates dominated it in move to make it legislative body. In June, 1789 declared themselves National Assembly, defying king. *See* FRENCH REVOLUTION.

ester, organic compound formed by replacing hydrogen of an acid by an organic radical. Many fats and oils are esters; others used as artificial fruit flavours.

Esther, historical book of OT. Story of Esther, Jewish wife of Ahasuerus (Xerxes I), king of Persia (486-465 BC), who prevented massacre of Jews.

Estonian Soviet Socialist Republic *(Eesti)*, constituent republic of W USSR. Area *c* 45,000 sq km (17,400 sq mi); pop. 1,466,000; cap. Tallinn. Bounded by Gulf of Finland to N; generally low-lying, with extensive forests. Agric., dairying. Under Swedish control in 17th cent., Estonia passed to Russia in 1721. Independent 1920-40; occupied by Germany (1941-4).

etching, process of engraving a metal plate usually of copper. Plate is covered with acid-resistant resin and design is drawn on this with a needle, exposing underlying metal. Plate is bathed in acid so that its exposed parts are eaten away, thus transferring design to plate.

ethane (C_2H_6), gaseous hydrocarbon of paraffin series. Found in natural gas; used as fuel and in organic synthesis.

ethanol or **ethyl alcohol** (C_2H_5OH), colourless inflammable liquid, the active ingredient of alcoholic drinks. Prepared by fermentation of sugar or by various indust. processes. Used as fuel and in organic synthesis. *See* PROOF SPIRIT.

Ethelbert or **Aethelbert** (*c* 552-616), Anglo-Saxon ruler. Became king of Kent (560). Converted to Christianity by St Augustine.

Ethelred or **Aethelred the Unready** (956-1016), king of England (978-1016). Rule constantly threatened by Danes after 991, when he began levies of Danegeld. Fled country after defeat (1013) by Sweyn. Restored on Sweyn's death (1014), succeeded by his son Edmund Ironside.

ether, in chemistry, organic compound in which two hydrocarbon radicals are linked by an oxygen atom. Name usually refers to diethyl ether ($C_2H_5OC_2H_5$), prepared by action of concentrated sulphuric acid on ethanol; used as anaesthetic and solvent.

ether, in physics, hypothetical medium, pervading all space, once believed necessary for transmission of electromagnetic radiation, *eg* light. Einstein's relativity theory showed ether was unnecessary concept.

Etherege, Sir George (*c* 1635-91), English playwright, poet. Known for complex Restoration comedies, *eg Love in a Tub* (1664); masterpiece *The Man of Mode* (1676).

ethics, in philosophy, the study of standards of conduct and moral judgment. Classical works incl. Plato's *Republic,* Aristotle's *Nicomachean Ethics.* Christian ethics draw mainly on New Testament and Aristotle. Subsequently, debate has centred on extent to which morality is imposed from outside individual, with 'intuitionists' (*eg* Rousseau) holding that conscience is innate and 'empiricists' (*eg* Locke) holding that it is acquired.

Ethiopia or **Abyssinia,** republic of NE Africa. Area 1,222,000 sq km (472,000 sq mi); pop. 29,705,000; cap. Addis Ababa. Language: Amharic. Religions: Coptic Christianity, Islam. High plateau, bisected from NE-SW by Great Rift Valley, incl. L. Tana, source of Blue Nile. Subsistence agric.; exports coffee, hides; gold mining, salt indust. Aksumite empire *fl* 1st-7th cent.; declined after Moslem incursions, dissolved into rival principalities. Reunited 19th cent., defeated invading Italians 1896. Occupied by Italy 1936; taken by British 1941, regained independence. United federally with ERITREA 1952, fully integrated 1962. Emperor Haile Selassie I deposed 1974 by military coup. Wars with Somalia and Eritrean rebels since late 1970s.

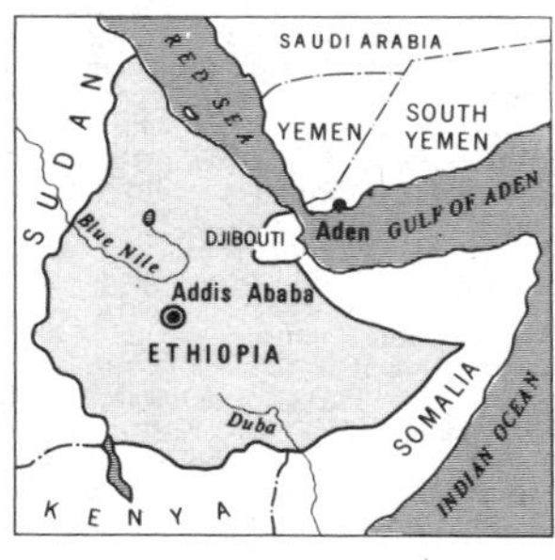

Ethiopia

ethnology, branch of anthropology which deals comparatively with cultures, their distribution, social systems, *etc.*

ethyl alcohol, *see* ETHANOL.

ethylene (C_2H_4), colourless inflammable gas of olefine series. Obtained by catalytic cracking of petroleum. Used as an anaesthetic, in manufacture of polythene and to speed ripening of fruit.

Etna, volcano of E Sicily, Italy. Height 3261 m (10,705 ft); isolated peak with *c* 200 minor cones. Lower slopes densely pop., used for growing fruit, olives, almonds. Major eruptions 1669, 1928, 1971, 1979; city of Catania twice destroyed.

Etruria, ancient region of NW Italy, incl. Tuscany, part of Umbria. Home of ancient Etruscans.

Etruscans, ancient people of NC Italy, believed to have emigrated from Asia Minor in 12th cent. BC. Distinctive culture emerged in 8th cent. BC; at height of civilization in 6th cent. BC. Wealth partly based on knowledge of metalworking; noted for sculpture, tomb paintings and architecture. Declined in 5th and 4th cents. BC in face of Gallic invasion from N and Roman conquests. Spoke non-Indo-European language, which has not been interpreted.

Etsch, *see* ADIGE.

etymology, branch of LINGUISTICS that deals with the origin and development of words. Concerned with changes in both meaning and sound.

Euboea *(Evvoia),* isl. of E Greece, in Aegean Sea. Area 3800 sq km (1467 sq mi); cap. Chalcis. Mountainous. Cereals, vines, livestock. Road bridge to mainland. Turkish till 1830.

eucalyptus, genus of evergreen trees of myrtle family, native to Australia. Pendent leaves, pink or white flowers. Yields timber, gums and aromatic oils.

Eucharist, Christian SACRAMENT in which bread and wine are consecrated and received as body and blood of Jesus. In RC and Orthodox churches, the elements are regarded as miraculously becoming the substance of God (transubstantiation); in most Protestant churches, the rite is regarded as symbolic and is known as the Lord's Supper. Also known as Holy Communion.

Euclid (*fl c* 300 BC), Greek mathematician. Compiler of *Elements*, collection of all geometric knowledge of his time. Esp. noted for its emphasis on deductive reasoning; definitions are given, axioms stated and theorems deduced logically. Also contains important results in number theory. Taught at Alexandria.

Eugène de Savoie-Carignan, Prince [François] (1663-1736), Austrian general, b. France. Joined Marlborough in War of Spanish Succession, defeating the French at Blenheim (1704), Oudenarde (1708), Malplaquet (1709). He fought with further success against the Turks in 1716-17, winning decisive victory at Belgrade.

Eugénie, née Eugenia María de Montijo de Guzmán (1826-1920), empress of the French, consort of Napoleon III; b. Spain.

Euler, Leonhard (1707-83), Swiss mathematician. Made numerous contributions to all branches of mathematics, esp. calculus of variations, number theory, hydrodynamics, mechanics and lunar motion. Many theorems bear his name.

Eumenides (Gk., = kindly ones), in Greek religion, the Furies who tortured conscience of evil-doers, esp. those who killed their own kindred. 'Eumenides' is a propitiatory euphemism for Erinyes ('Terrible Ones').

euphonium, low-pitched brass instrument with 4 valves, used in brass bands.

Euphrates, river of SW Asia. Length *c* 2740 km (1700 mi). Rises in E Turkey, flows SE through Syria, Iraq; merges with R. Tigris to form Shatt-al-Arab. Irrigates large agric. area.

Euratom, *see* EUROPEAN COMMUNITIES.

Eureka Stockade (1854), armed rebellion of miners on Ballarat goldfield, Australia. Causes were resentment of high cost of mining licences, lack of political representation, Chinese competition on field. Rebellion put down swiftly, but legislation followed to satisfy miners' main grievances. Incident since acclaimed as beginning of democracy in Australia.

eurhythmics, method of training response to music through harmonious movement of the body. Developed by Jaques-Dalcroze, influenced ballet, acting.

Euripides (*c* 484-406 BC), Greek tragic poet. Noted for innovations, incl. sympathetic portrayal of common people and women, social criticism, religious unorthodoxy, realistic characterization and language. Wrote over 80 plays, 18 extant, incl. *Alcestis, Medea, Trojan Women, Electra.*

Eurocommunism, policies of W European Communist parties, esp. in Italy and France. Incl. nonalignment with Russia or China, belief in working within parliamentary democracy.

Europa, in Greek myth, daughter of Phoenician King Agenor. Zeus, in the shape of a bull, abducted her to Crete where she bore him Minos, Rhadamanthus and Sarpedon.

Europe, smallest mainland continent. Area *c* 10,360,000 sq km (4,000,000 sq mi); pop. *c* 690,000,000. Forms penin. of Eurasia projecting into Atlantic, separated from Asia by Ural and Caucasus Mts., Black and Caspian Seas. Crossed W-E by ranges incl. Pyrenees, Alps, Carpathians, Balkans, Caucasus. Main rivers Don, Dnepr, Danube, Oder, Elbe, Rhine, Rhône, Loire, Tagus, Volga. Many isls. incl. Iceland, Great Britain, Ireland, Corsica, Sicily, Sardinia. Main penins. incl. Balkan, Italian, Iberian. Fertile N European plain extends France-Poland. Major focus of civilization from *c* 1500 BC. Greek, Roman empires followed by spread of Christianity, agric., commerce in Middle Ages, Renaissance, colonization of New World, rise of nation states. Rapid indust. progress in 18th-19th cents. spurred colonialism, spreading European culture to America, Africa, India. Scene of many wars throughout hist., focus of 2 WWs in 20th cent. Basic political division from 1945 into communist (E), capitalist (W) blocs.

European Communities, international organization with aims of economic integration, political unity. Originally 6 W European countries (Belgium, France, West Germany, Italy, Luxembourg, Netherlands) under Treaty of Rome (1957) estab. 3 communities: European Coal and Steel Community (ECSC), **European Economic Community** (EEC or Common Market), European Atomic Energy Community (Euratom). Merged executives in 1967 to form one Commission. UK, Denmark, Irish Republic joined 1973; Greece in 1981. Spain to join in 1983. Governed by Commission, Council of Ministers, European Parliament. Court of Justice regulates treaties' application, advisory committees monitor social, labour conditions, consumer affairs, *etc.* EEC estab. (1958) with goals of customs union (achieved 1968), common policies on trade, agric.; talks on foreign policy initiated 1970. ECSC estab. 1952 to achieve common market for coal, iron ore, scrap, steel. Harmonized external tariff, regulated internal competition, aided workers in contracting coal indust.; has eventual goal (with Euratom) of Common Energy Policy. Euratom estab. 1958 to promote peaceful uses of nuclear energy; coordinates and promotes research, pools information, promotes training of scientists, technicians.

European Economic Community, *see* EUROPEAN COMMUNITIES.

European Free Trade Association (EFTA), customs union and trading group estab. 1960 by Austria, Denmark, Norway, Portugal, Sweden, Switzerland, UK. Finland became associate member (1961), Iceland joined 1970. UK and Denmark left 1972 to join EEC.

europium (Eu), metallic element of

lanthanide series; at. no. 63, at. wt. 151.96. Occurs in monazite. Discovered (1896).

Europoort, *see* ROTTERDAM.

Eurydice, *see* ORPHEUS.

Eustachian tube, narrow canal connecting middle ear and throat.

Evans, Sir Arthur John (1851-1941), English archaeologist. Began excavations at Knossos, Crete, in 1899; in course of 30 years' work, he revealed an ancient culture which he named MINOAN CIVILIZATION.

Evans, Dame Edith (1888-1976), English actress. Known in many major roles incl. Nurse in *Romeo and Juliet*, Lady Bracknell in *The Importance of Being Earnest*.

evaporation, conversion of a liquid into vapour, without boiling point of liquid necessarily being reached. Rate of evaporation increased by application of heat and by lowering pressure above liquid.

Eve, *see* ADAM.

Evelyn, John (1620-1706), English diarist. Known for *Diary* of 1641-1706 (pub. 1818).

Everest, Mount, highest mountain in world, on Nepal-Tibet border; height 8848 m (29,028 ft). First climbed in 1953, by Hillary and Tensing.

Everglades, subtropical swampy region of S Florida US. Area 12,950 sq km (*c* 5000 sq mi). Notable plants, wildlife, in National Park.

evergreen, tree or plant which remains in foliage throughout the year. In the tropics many broadleaved angiosperms are evergreen, whereas in colder areas evergreens are mainly conifers.

everlasting flowers, blossoms which keep colour and shape when dried by hanging upside down. Often of Compositae family. Incl. flowers of *Xeranthemum, Helipterum, Waitzia* genera.

Everyman (*c* 1500), anon. English morality play. Dramatizes late medieval Christian view of human nature and destiny.

Evesham, town of Hereford and Worcester, WC England, on R. Avon. Pop. 14,000. In fertile Vale of Evesham; fruit, vegetable growing. Agric. market, canning. Simon de Montfort killed in battle here (1265).

evolution, in biology, theory that all species of animals and plants developed from earlier forms by hereditary transmission of slight variations in genetic composition to successive generations. Theory of evolution by natural selection is due to Darwin (1859); earlier theories incl. Lamarck's inheritance of acquired characteristics.

Excalibur, *see* ARTHURIAN LEGEND.

excise, tax or duty on the manufacture, sale or consumption of various commodities within a country. Distinct from customs, paid on goods entering country from abroad. Developed in 17th cent. by Holland. Usual goods subject to such tax are tobacco, alcoholic beverages, luxury goods, *etc*.

excommunication, act of formally excluding a person from the sacraments, rights and privileges of a religious body, usually to punish the person expelled and to protect remaining members from his influence. Retained esp. in RC church. Excommunicates are free to return to the church on repentance.

excretion, elimination of useless or harmful metabolic products; organs mainly concerned being kidneys and large intestines of vertebrates, Malpighian tubes of insects, nephridia of invertebrates and stomata of plants.

executive, in politics, that part of govt. concerned with admin. of laws, incl. bureaucracy and officials who direct it. and carrying them out. Also *see* SEPARATION OF POWERS.

executor, in law, person appointed by testator to carry out provisions and directions of will. May be appointed by court to collect assets, settle debts if deceased died intestate.

Exeter, city and admin. hq. of Devon, SW England, on R. Exe. Pop. 95,000. Railway jct.; agric. market. Has 11th cent. cathedral, guildhall, univ. (1955).

existentialism, philosophical movement which holds that there is no fixed human nature, that man is free to act as he will and that this is the source of his anguish. Derived from Kierkegaard, exponents incl. SARTRE, Jaspers.

Exmoor, moorland of SW England, national park in Devon, Somerset. Formerly forested; sheep, wild deer, ponies.

Exodus (Gk., = going out), in OT, 2nd book of Pentateuch. Covers period of Jewish history during which Israelites, under Moses, escaped from bondage in Egypt. Deals with founding of the Jewish nation, incl. Moses receiving the TEN COMMANDMENTS and other laws.

exorcism, ritual act of driving evil spirits from person, places or things in which they are believed to dwell. Occurs in primitive societies and in sophisticated religious practice. Officially recognized in RC church.

expansion, thermal, increase in size of body due to increase in temperature. Caused by increased activity of component molecules. Gases expand by *c* 1/273 of their volume at 0°C for each degree rise in temperature.

explosive, substance which, when heated or otherwise excited, undergoes rapid decomposition with production of large volume of gas; rapid increase of pressure in confined space caused by gas produces explosion. High explosives, incl. TNT, dynamite and nitroglycerine, require detonators to set them off.

expressionism, term for art which tries to give objective expression to inner experience. In 20th-cent. painting, associated with artists such as Soutine, Kokoschka, Rouault and the Blaue Reiter, Brücke movements; characterized by distortion of form, violent non-naturalistic colour. Precursors of style incl. van Gogh,

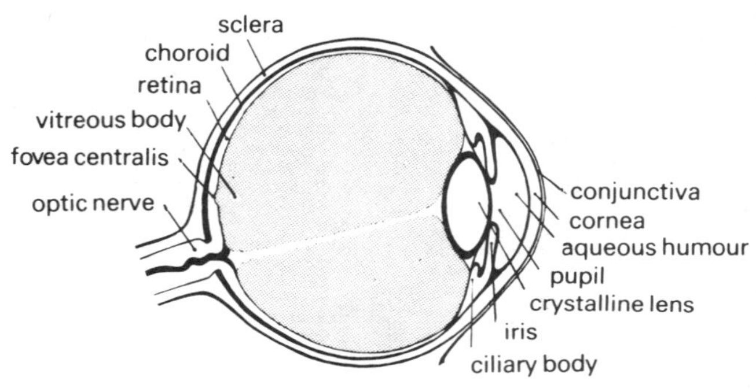

Human eye

Munch. In literature, Strindberg was important forerunner; movement (esp. strong in Germany) incl. plays of Toller, poetry of Benn, novels of Kafka. In cinema, Weine's *Cabinet of Dr Caligari* is masterpiece. Term also embraces early music of Schoenberg, Berg.

extrasensory perception (ESP), faculty of perception other than by known sense organs. Belief in existence of ESP is not widely accepted.

extreme unction, sacrament in RC and Orthodox churches of anointing and giving absolution of sins to the dying.

extroversion and **introversion,** in psychology, terms coined by JUNG to denote opposite types of personality. Extrovert personality directs his interest and activity outwards, depends on environment, other people, while an introvert directs his activity inwards to self, and is less affected by surroundings.

extrusive rock, any rock formed by solidification of molten material forced out at Earth's surface. All extrusive rocks are thus IGNEOUS ROCKS; they incl. volcanic lava and pyroclastic material.

Eyck, Hubert van (*c* 1370-1426) and **Jan van Eyck** (*c* 1390-1441), Dutch painters, brothers, who founded Flemish school. Hubert's work is characterized by descriptive realism conveyed in minute detail. Jan is famous for his portraits, incl. *Arnolfini and his Wife*.

eye, organ of sight. Human eyeball has opaque white outer layer (sclera) with transparent bulge (cornea) in front. IRIS is located behind cornea and lens behind this; watery aqueous humour fills space between these and jelly-like vitreous humour rest of eye. Light-sensitive RETINA lines inner surface of sclera and transmits sensation of light through optic nerves to brain.

Eyre, Lake, salt lake of NE South Australia. Area *c* 9100 sq km (3500 sq mi); falls to 12m (39 ft) below sea level. Much of it is perennially dry.

Eyre Peninsula, peninsula of S South Australia, between Spencer Gulf and Great Australian Bight.

Eysenck, Hans Jurgen (1916-), British psychologist, b. Germany. Known for advocacy of behaviour therapy rather than Freudian psychoanalysis, and for belief in absolute measurability of intelligence.

Ezekiel, prophetical book of OT. Recounts visions of priest, Ezekiel (*fl* 592 BC). Focuses on fall of Jerusalem, but foretells restoration of its glory.

Ezra, historical book of OT, opening with return of Jews from exile in Babylon to Jerusalem (538 BC) and covering 80 years of life and teachings of Ezra, Hebrew prophet and scribe; incl. rebuilding of Temple.

F

abergé, Peter Carl (1846-1920), Russian goldsmith. His workshops were famous for exquisite masterpieces, incl. flowers, animals and Easter eggs.

abian Society, British socialist organization, founded 1884. Aims to achieve socialism through gradual reformist strategy rather than revolutionary action. Instrumental in estab. British Labour Party. Prominent members have incl. G.B. Shaw, Sidney and Beatrice Webb.

abius Maximus, Quintus (d. 203 BC), Roman soldier. Called *Cunctator* ('Delayer') for his successful delaying tactics employed against Hannibal after defeat at L. Trasimene.

ble, short moral tale, with animals, inanimate objects as characters. Best-known exponents incl. Aesop, La Fontaine.

actory Acts, legislation enacted by British Parliament to regulate conditions and hours of work, safety and sanitary provisions in factories and workshops. First was Health and Morals of Apprentices Act (1802); Cotton Mills Act (1819) forbade employment of children under 9 and reduced hours of labour for under-16s. Act of 1845 banned night-work for women, and that of 1847 introduced 10 hour working day. Factory inspectors appointed 1833. Offices, shops, *etc*, covered 1963.

eces, waste matter expelled from intestines. Consists of undigested food, bacteria, water and mucus.

eroes, isl. group of Denmark, in N Atlantic. Area 1399 sq km (540 sq mi); pop. 40,000; cap. Thorshavn. Rugged, treeless. Sheep; fishing. Passed from Norway to Denmark (1380); auton. legislature from 1948.

hrenheit, Gabriel Daniel (1686-1736), German meteorological instrument maker. Pioneered use of mercury in thermometers and devised Fahrenheit scale of temperature in which water freezes at 32° and boils at 212°.

nting, temporary unconsciousness caused by inadequate flow of blood to brain. May be treated by stretching out victim or lowering his head.

irbanks, Douglas (1889-1939), American film actor. Famous for roles as gallant swashbuckler, and for marriage to Mary PICKFORD. Their son, **Douglas Fairbanks, Jnr** (1909-), also became a film star, known for debonair roles.

irbanks, town of C Alaska, US; on Tanana R. Pop. 15,000. Terminus of Alaska Highway. Founded after 1902 gold strike.

irfax, Thomas, 3rd Baron Fairfax of Cameron (1612-71), English general. Commanded New Model Army which defeated Charles I at Naseby (1645). Refused to preside over trial of Charles as he doubted the judges' impartiality. Resigned command rather than invade Scotland (1650).

Fair Isle, small isl. in Shetlands, N Scotland. Famous knitwear mfg. Has bird observatory.

fairy, in folklore, supernatural being with magical powers. Concept has existed from earliest times but has greatly varied: described as demonic, mischievous, loving, bountiful. National variations incl. Arab djinns, SW English pixies, German elves, Scandinavian trolls.

Faisal, *see* FEISAL.

Falange, orig. *Falange Española,* fascist movement and party in Spain. Founded (1933); became only legal party in Spain under leadership of Franco (1937). Power waned, esp. after new constitution (1966) and death of Franco (1975).

falcon, bird of prey of Falconidae family. Long pointed wings, powerful hooked beak; diet of birds, insects, small mammals. Some falcons trained for hunting small game. Species incl. peregrine, kestrel, merlin.

falconry, *see* HAWKING.

Falkirk, town of Central region, C Scotland. Pop. 38,000. Large iron foundries. Scene of Edward I of England's victory over Wallace (1298).

Falkland Islands (Span. *Islas Malvinas*), crown colony of UK, in S Atlantic Ocean. Comprise East and West Falkland, *c* 200 small isls. Area 12,100 sq km (4700 sq mi); pop. 2500; cap. Stanley. Sheep rearing. Dependencies incl. South Georgia, South Orkney, South Shetland, South Sandwich Isls., Graham Land. Entire area claimed by Argentina.

Falla, Manuel de (1876-1946), Spanish composer. Influenced by Spanish folk music. His few compositions incl. Nights in the Gardens of Spain for piano and orchestra, ballet *The Three-cornered Hat.*

Fallopian tubes, in female mammals, tubes leading from ovaries to the uterus, in which fertilization takes place.

fallout, radioactive material deposited on Earth's surface following nuclear explosions. May cause genetic damage or various diseases, *eg* leukaemia. Strontium 90 present in fall-out is very dangerous as it may replace calcium in body.

fallow deer, *Dama dama,* European deer of Mediterranean region, rare in wild state. Usually reddish-brown with white spots; also dark varieties. Introduced into many parts of N Europe, North America as park animal.

Fallow deer

Famagusta, port of E Cyprus. Pop. *c* 40,000. Exports citrus fruits, potatoes; holiday resort.

family planning, *see* CONTRACEPTION.

Fangio [y Cia], Juan Manuel (1911-), Argentinian racing driver. World champion 5 times (1951, 1954-7). Retired 1958.

FAO, *see* FOOD AND AGRICULTURE ORGANIZATION.

Faraday, Michael (1791-1867), English chemist and physicist. Studies in electrochemistry led to discovery of 2 quantitative laws of electrolysis (Faraday's laws). Discovered principle of electromagnetic induction, effect utilized in dynamo. His concept of electric and magnetic fields of force became basis of Maxwell's electromagnetic theory. Discovered benzene (1825).

Far East, vague term for countries of E Asia, incl. China, Japan, Korea and Mongolia. Sometimes also taken to incl. countries of SE Asia and Malay Archipelago.

Farne Islands, *c* 30 isls. off Northumberland, NE England. Chapel to St Cuthbert (d. 687).

Faro, town of S Portugal, cap. of Algarve prov. Pop. 19,000. Port, exports wine, figs, cork; sardine, tuna fishing; tourism.

Faroe Islands, *see* FAEROES.

Farouk I (1920-65), king of Egypt (1936-52). Exiled after military coup under Naguib and Nasser (1952). Succeeded by son Fuad, who was deposed in 1953.

Farquhar, George (1678-1707), English dramatist, b. Ireland. Developed Restoration comedy into more sentimental mode. Works incl. *The Recruiting Officer* (1706), *The Beaux' Stratagem* (1707).

fascism, political ideology of totalitaria militarist and nationalistic charact Advocates govt. by one-party dictatorsh and centralized control of private ecc omic enterprise (*see* CORPORATE STAT Nationalism most extreme in rac suppression of minorities, *eg* an Semitism; strong police measures used maintain law and order, oppc democracy, Communism. Originated wi Mussolini's Fascist party which held pow in Italy (1922-43). Fascism had spread 1936 to Germany (Nazis), Japan, Spa (Falange), most of E Europe.

Fashoda Incident (1898-9), Anglo-Fren dispute over control of upper Nile regi French forces took Fashoda (now Kodc in S Sudan, but, fearing war, withdrew up British insistence. Peaceful settleme marked end of French claims in area.

Fates (Gk. *Morai*), in Greek myth, thr goddesses who controlled course of hum life; Clotho spun the thread of life, Lache measured it, Atropos cut it. The Rom Fates (*Parcae*) were Nona, Decun Morta.

Fathers of the Church, term for Christi teachers and writers of the early Chur whose work is considered orthodox. West, incl. those up to and incl. St Gregc the Great, and to St John of Damascus East.

Fatimites or **Fatimids,** Moslem dynas claiming descent from Mohamme daughter, Fatima, which ruled in N Afr and Egypt (909-1171). Also conquer Sicily, W Arabia, Palestine and Syria. Ca became Fatimite cap. (969). Rule enc with Saladin's conquest of Egypt.

fats, group of naturally occurring substan found in plants and animals. Consist mixtures of esters of glycerol with hig fatty acids, *eg* stearic, palmitic, oleic ac Excellent source of energy in food.

Faulkner or **Falkner, William** (1897-19 American novelist, short story writ Created imaginary county in Deep Sou populated with vivid characters complex, decaying society. Novels ir *The Sound and the Fury* (1929), *Light August* (1932). Awarded Nobel Prize Literature (1949).

fault, in geology, fracture in rock str along which movement has occurred displace sides relative to each oth Movement may be upward, sideways, both.

Fauré, Gabriel (1845-1924), French c poser. His delicate and sensitive mu incl. nocturnes for piano, chamber mu operas, a Requiem, songs.

Faust, hero of several medieval legen Based on historical figure (d. *c* 1540) philosopher who was said to have sold soul to the Devil in exchange knowledge and power. Story, first pub the *Faustbuch* of 1587, inspired Marlo Goethe, Thomas Mann, Gounod and m others.

fauvism (Fr. *fauve* = wild beast), short-li modern art movement (*c* 1905-8). U

›old distortion of form and brilliant pure olour. Exponents incl. Matisse, Derain, /laminck, Marquet.

wkes, Guy (1570-1606), English conpirator. Catholic convert, involved in Gun›owder Plot (5 Nov. 1605) to blow up Iouses of Parliament during opening of ew session by James I. Plot exposed, 'awkes and other leaders executed.

I, *see* FEDERAL BUREAU OF INVESTIGATION.

oruary Revolution, *see* REVOLUTION OF 848, RUSSIAN REVOLUTION.

deral Bureau of Investigation (FBI), ranch of US Dept. of Justice. Estab. (1908) › investigate all violations of Federal laws xcept those, *eg* currency, tax, postal laws, ealt with by other Federal agencies.

eralism, system of govt. dividing nation's overeign powers between central federal) authority and constituent subivisions (states, provinces). Central govt. owers usually incl. foreign relations, deence, commerce, coinage; states usually ontrol their internal affairs. Arbitration of isputes often delegated to courts with eference to written constitution and recedents. US, West Germany, USSR, anada, Australia have federal govt. strucires.

leralist Party, in US history, political arty (estab. *c* 1791) under leadership of lexander Hamilton and John Adams. dvocated strong central govt., expansion f commerce, anti-French foreign policy. ost power to Jeffersonians after 1800. Iational significance lost by 1817.

sal I or **Faisal I** (1885-1933), king of Iraq 1921-33). Joined with T.E. Lawrence in evolt against Turkey (1916). Proclaimed ing of Syria (1920), deposed by French iandatory powers. British, who held iandate in Iraq, supported him in fight for 'aqi throne.

sal II or **Faisal II** (1935-58), king of Iraq 939-58). Killed in military coup which stab. republic.

sal, Ibn Al-Saud (1905-75), king of Saudi rabia (1964-75). Succeeded brother Saud s king. Reign marked by pro-Western olicies, increasing wealth and chnological advances, based on vast oil xports. Assassinated by a nephew. icceeded by half-brother Khaled.

Ispars or **felspars,** group of rock›rming aluminium silicate minerals. istinct types contain calcium, potassium, odium or, very rarely, barium. Comprise *c*)% of Earth's crust; found in igneous ›cks, *eg* granite, basalt. Clay is product of eathering of feldspars.

lini, Federico (1920-), Italian film irector. Noted for sympathy for victims of olence, greed or apathy. Films incl. *La rada* (1954), *La Dolce Vita* (1960), *8½* 963), *Satyricon* (1969).

cing, sport of combat with swords. Three pes of sword used: foil, a light weapon; ›ée, derived from duelling sword; sabre, a it-and-thrust weapon.

iians, secret revolutionary society

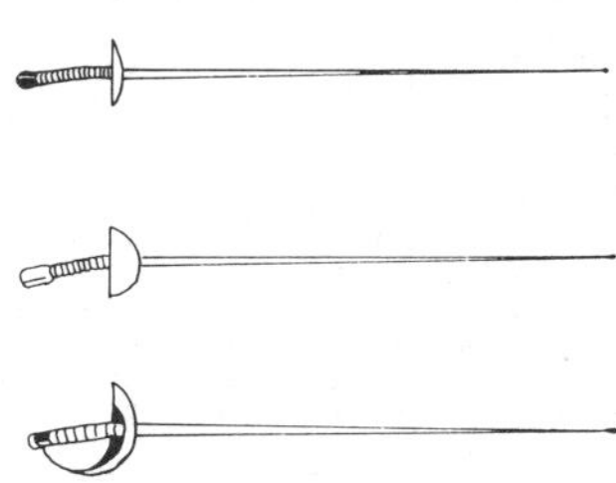

Fencing: foil, epée and sabre (top to bottom)

formed (*c* 1858) to secure Irish independence from Britain. Promoted risings and terrorism suppressed by British, thus drawing attention to Irish problems. Group of Irish emigrants in US attempted invasion of Canada (1866); invasion ended in failure but encouraged Canadian confederation. *See* also SINN FEIN.

fennec, *Fennecus zerda,* small fawn-coloured fox of desert areas of N Africa, Arabia. Large ears.

fennel, name for several herbs, esp. those of genus *Foeniculum* in parsley family, used to flavour fish sauces and salad dressings.

Fens, The, flat low-lying area of E England, W and S of The Wash, within Cambridgeshire, Lincolnshire, Norfolk. Formerly bay of North Sea, silting created marsh. Draining begun 1621. Now fertile, rich agric. incl. cereals, sugar beet, fruit.

fer-de-lance, *Bothrops atrox,* highly venomous snake of pit viper group of tropical America, West Indies. Reaches lengths of *c* 1.8 m/6 ft.

Ferdinand I (1503-64), Holy Roman emperor (1558-64). Claimed kingdoms of Bohemia and Hungary on death of brother-in-law, Louis II (1526), leading to war until 1538. Negotiated Peace of Augsburg (1555) before succeeding his brother, Charles V.

Ferdinand II (1578-1637), Holy Roman emperor (1619-37). A fervent Catholic, his deposition as king of Bohemia (1619) by Bohemian Protestants marked beginning of THIRTY YEARS WAR. Reimposed Catholicism in Bohemia by force after victory at White Mountain (1620). Failed to sustain early successes.

Ferdinand (1861-1948), tsar of Bulgaria (1908-18). German prince, elected prince of Bulgaria (1887). Proclaimed Bulgarian independence from Ottoman Empire (1908). Defeated in 2nd Balkan War (1913); joined Central Powers in WWI. Abdicated.

Ferdinand I [the Great] (d. 1065), king of Castile (1035-65) and León (1037-65). Began reconquest of Spain from the Moors.

Ferdinand V [the Catholic] (1452-1516), king of Aragón and Castile. Married his cousin Isabella of Castile (1469); they ruled

Castile jointly (1474-1504) until her death. Became Ferdinand II of Aragón (1479), thus uniting all of Spain except Granada. In 1492, reconquered Granada and expelled Jews from Spain. Rivalled Portuguese colonial expansion, notably by financing Columbus.

Fergusson, Robert (1750-74), Scottish poet. Known for lively, humane satires of urban life, written in Scots, incl. 'Auld Reikie', 'Leith Races'. Died in lunatic asylum.

Fermanagh, former county of SW Northern Ireland. Hilly in NE, SW; bisected by Upper and Lower Lough Erne. Agric.; cattle rearing. Co. town was Enniskillen.

Fermat, Pierre de (1601-65), French mathematician. Anticipated Descartes' discovery of analytical geometry and certain features of differential calculus. Famed for work on number theory; his famous 'last theorem' remains unproved, despite his claims.

fermentation, chemical change caused by enzyme action. Yeast enzyme system causes alcoholic fermentation of sugar, with production of ethyl alcohol and carbon dioxide.

Fermi, Enrico (1901-54), American physicist, b. Italy. Awarded Nobel Prize for Physics (1938) for work on neutron bombardment, esp. use of absorbing materials to slow down neutrons. Headed Univ. of Chicago group which achieved first controlled nuclear reaction (1942).

fermions, in physics, elementary particles, incl. electron, proton, which conform to Fermi-Dirac statistics and obey Pauli exclusion principle. Divided into baryons and leptons. Number of fermions taking part in nuclear interactions appears to be conserved.

fermium (Fm), transuranic element; at. no. 100, mass no. of most stable isotope 257. Discovered in debris of nuclear explosion (1953).

fern, any of a class, Filicineae, of flowerless perennial plants. Distinctive frond-shaped leaves. Reproduces by spores rather than seeds. More than 6000 species, widely distributed esp. in tropics. Fossils indicate many early varieties.

Fernando Po, *see* BIOKO ISLAND.

Ferrara, city of Emilia-Romagna, NC Italy, cap. of Ferrara prov. Pop. 155,000. Agric. market, food processing; univ. (1391). Cultural centre 13th-16th cent. under Este family; incorporated 1598 into Papal States.

ferret, domesticated albino variety of polecat, genus *Mustela*. Tamed to hunt rabbits and rats.

Ferrier, Kathleen (1912-53), British contralto. Her rich, full voice rapidly brought her international fame after WWII; career cut short by cancer.

Ferrol (del Caudillo), El, town of Galicia, NW Spain, on Atlantic Ocean. Pop. 88,000. Chief Atlantic naval base; fish processing. Birthplace of Franco ('El Caudillo').

ferromagnetism, property of certain metals, esp. iron, cobalt and nickel, of having high susceptibility to acquir magnetism. Such materials exh HYSTERESIS and may be used as perman magnets.

fertility drugs, substances used to incre possibility of conception. Male inferti sometimes treated by thyroid and pituit hormones. Failure to ovulate in female be treated by drug clomiphene, but may cause multiple births.

fertilization, union of male sperm cell w female egg cell (ovum) to form a zyg which develops to form new individual. *also* POLLINATION.

fertilizer, substance put on soil to impr quantity and quality of plant grov usually by supplying necessary nitrog phosphorus and potassium. Orga fertilizers incl. animal manure and b meal; inorganic incl. nitrates and am nium compounds, superphosphates basic slag.

fescue, any of genus *Festuca* of peren grasses. Many used in temperate regi for lawns or pasture.

fetishism, worship of inanimate ob believed to have supernatural power. TABOO, TOTEMISM.

feudalism, economic, political, social sys of medieval Europe. In ideal syst ownership of all land was vested in k who granted it to highest nobles in ret for military, personal service; they in t granted land to lesser nobles, and so until lowest level (serf) reached. Local was manor, whose lord (seigneur) gran land to and protected peasants, ville serfs, in return for service. Church ow ship of land worked in parallel. Sys declined with growth of money econo rise of mercantile classes.

Feuerbach, Ludwig Andreas von (1804- German philosopher. Abandoned Hege idealism for naturalistic materialism. *The Essence of Christianity* (1841) alysed religion anthropologically, asser God to be man's projection of his nature.

fever, abnormally high body temperat usually a symptom of infection or dise Believed to be caused by stimulatior temperature-control centre of brain du destruction of bacteria.

feverfew, *Chrysanthemum parthen* perennial herb of daisy family. D leaves and flowers used to make medic tea.

Feydeau, Georges (1862-1921), Fre playwright. Known for ingeniously trived farces.

Fez (Fr. *Fès*), city of N Morocco. 426,000. Route centre; carpet mfg., lea goods. Founded 808; sacred city of Is with *c* 100 mosques; has ancient Mos univ.

Fezzan, region of SW Libya. Mainly des some oases; produces dates. Federal p 1951-63.

Fianna Fáil, Irish political party, estab. by opponents of Irish Free State. Ur eadership of DE VALÉRA, controlled govt. 'rom 1932, demanding separation from 3ritain. Opposed by FINE GAEL.

re, thread-like tissue capable of being spun into yarn. Animal fibres, composed nainly of protein, incl. silk, wool, hair of goats, rabbits, *etc;* vegetable fibres, composed mostly of cellulose, incl. cotton, kapok, hemp. Modern synthetic fibres are usually polymers, *eg* nylon and various polyesters.

re optics, branch of optics dealing with ransmission of light along very narrow lexible glass cables. Technique used to ocate faults in machinery, investigate uman body, and in communications.

:hte, Johann Gottlieb (1762-1814), German philosopher. Wrote *Critique of Religious Revelation* (1792), developing Kantian ethics. *Addresses to the German People* (1808) stirred national feeling gainst Napoleon's domination.

dler crab, small burrowing crab, genus *Uca,* of salt marshes and sandy beaches. Male has one claw much larger than other.

ld, John (1782-1837), Irish composer, pianist. Worked mainly in Russia. Devised *nocturne* form, later developed by Chopin.

dfare, *Turdus pilaris,* European bird of thrush family, with grey head, brown back.

lding, Henry (1707-54), English author. Important in development of English novel. First novels, *eg Joseph Andrews* 1742), burlesqued Richardson's *Pamela,* as well as using powerful social satire. Best known for *Tom Jones* (1749), complex comic masterpiece.

ld mouse, *see* MOUSE.

ld of the Cloth of Gold, place near Calais, France, where Henry VIII of England met Francis I of France (1520) to discuss possible alliance against Charles V. Name given because of lavish display of wealth.

lds, Gracie, orig. Grace Stansfield 1898-1979). English comedienne, music-hall singer. Songs associated with her incl. Sally'.

lds, W. C., orig. Claude William Dukenfield (1880-1946), American film actor. Famous as gravel-voiced, alcoholic, intolerant comedian. Films incl. *The Bank Dick* (1940).

d theory, in physics, means of representing effect of physical phenomena throughout space. Magnetic, electric and gravitational forces may all be represented by fields.

e, region of E Scotland, between firths of Tay and Forth. Area 1305 sq km (504 sq mi); pop. 343,000; admin. hq. Glenrothes. Created 1975 from former Fife county. Lomond Hills in W. Rich agric. (esp. cereals); coalmining; fishing.

h column, collaborationist group, native of one country but working for another. Term first used by Spanish Nationalist General Mola (1936) who, besieging Madrid with 4 columns, boasted of having a fifth column' already within.

Fig

fig, any of genus *Ficus* of mulberry family, esp. *F. carica,* broad-leaved cultivated tree bearing soft, many-seeded, edible fruit. Prob. grown first in Arabia; spread to Mediterranean countries and US.

fighting fish, *Betta splendens,* small brightly coloured freshwater fish of S Asia. Males, very aggressive to each other, bred in Thailand for fighting.

figwort, perennial plant of genus *Scrophularia* with square stem.

Fiji Islands, country of SW Pacific Ocean, comprising *c* 320 isls of which *c* 100 inhabited. Area 18,350 sq km (7080 sq mi); pop. 607,000; cap. Suva. Main isls. Viti Levu, Vanua Levu. Produces sugar cane, rice, fruit and gold; tourist centre. Discovered (1643) by Tasman; British colony from 1874 until independence 1970. Large Indian pop., descendants of plantation workers imported 19th cent. Member of British Commonwealth.

Fillmore, Millard (1800-74), American statesman, president (1850-3). Whig vice-president, succeeded Zachary Taylor as president. Supported 'compromise' view on slavery issue.

film, *see* CINEMA.

finch, any of Fringillidae family of small short-beaked, seed-eating birds. Incl. canary, sparrow, goldfinch.

Fine Gael, Irish political party, estab. 1933. Has held power three times, in coalition with Labour Party. Opposed by FIANNA FÁIL.

Fingal's Cave, cavern in Staffa, (isl. of Inner Hebrides), W Scotland, lined by hexagonal basalt columns similar to those of GIANT'S CAUSEWAY. Fingal is identified with FINN

MACCUMHAILL. Inspired Mendelssohn's overture

fingerprint, impression of lines, whorls on inner surface of end joint of finger. Used by police for identification since 1901, impression being thought unique and permanent for each individual.

Finisterre, Cape, headland of La Coruña prov., most W point of Spanish mainland. Scene of two English naval victories (1747, 1805) over French.

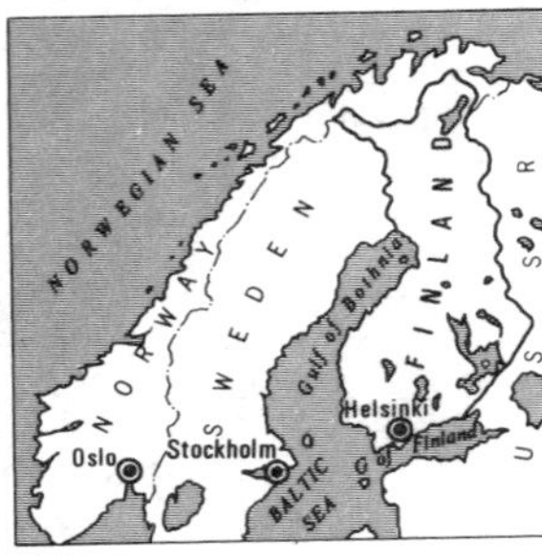

Finland

Finland (*Suomi*), republic of NE Europe. Area 337,010 sq km (130,120 sq mi); pop. 4,752,000; cap. Helsinki. Languages: Finnish, Swedish. Religion: Lutheran. Tundra in N (Lapland), lakes, forests in S. Mostly low-lying; main rivers Torne, Kemi, Oulu. Forestry (pulp, paper), h.e.p., some agric. Conquered (12th cent.) by Eric IX of Sweden, Swedish culture estab. in Middle Ages. Ceded to Russia 1809. Independence followed Russian Revolution (1917), republic estab. 1919. Lost territ. (incl. Karelia) after war with USSR (1939-40).

Finland, Gulf of, arm of Baltic Sea, between Finland and USSR. Frozen in winter. Main ports Helsinki, Leningrad, Tallinn, Vyborg.

Finn Maccumhaill or **MacCool,** hero of Gaelic mythology. Leader of the Fianna, band of warriors with whom he had many adventures defending Ireland. His son was OSSIAN.

Finno-Ugric or **Finno-Ugrian,** language group within Uralic family. Incl. Estonian, Finnish, Lapp, Hungarian (Magyar).

fir, general name for any of the tall, widely distributed, coniferous, evergreen trees of genus *Abies*, and for other similar trees.

firearms, weapons discharging projectiles by use of explosives. Primitive cannon were first used *c* 1300; hand-guns followed half a century later. The most rapid improvements came with the invention of the percussion cap, breech loading and the magazine in the 19th cent. Automatic weapons appeared *c* 1900.

fireclay, clay composed mainly of alumina and silica, capable of resisting intense heat. Used to make firebrick for lining kilns and metallurgical furnaces.

firefly, any of Lampyridae family luminescent beetles, most numerous tropics. Light, produced by chemic action in special organs on abdomen, us as communication between sexes. Larva and wingless females called glow-worms.

Firenze, *see* FLORENCE.

fireworks, preparations of explosives us for display purposes. Thought to have or inated in China, introduced to Europe (1 cent.). Potassium nitrate and potassiu chlorate commonly used with vario metal salts to give range of colours.

First World War, *see* WORLD WAR I.

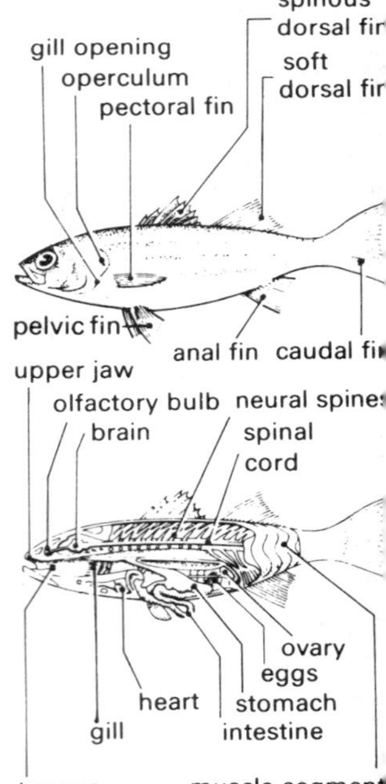

Organs of a bony fish (striped bass)

fish (Pisces), cold-blooded aquatic v tebrate. Gill-breathing, finned; body usu covered with scales. Diet of plankt plants and aquatic animals. ICHTHYOLOGY.

Fisher, Geoffrey Francis, Baron Fisher Lambeth (1887-1972), English churchm Archbishop of Canterbury (1945- Promoted ecumenical movement, visit pope in 1960; president of World Counci Churches (1946-54).

her, St John (1459-1535), English hurchman, scholar. Imprisoned (1534) for pposing Henry VIII's divorce from atherine of Aragon; Pope Paul III conequently made him cardinal (1535). Henry ad him beheaded. Canonized 1935.

her, John Arbuthnot, 1st Baron 1841-1920), British admiral. As first sea ord (1904-10) introduced the *Dreadnought* lass of battleships. Recalled to the same ffice in 1914, but resigned because of ifferences with Churchill over the ardanelles campaign (1915).

her or **pekan,** *Martes pennanti,* large Iorth American carnivore of marten amily.

heries, industry of catching, processing, nd selling fish. Most fish are caught by rawling, seining, drifting or by baited nes. Most highly developed fisheries are hose of N Atlantic, esp. around Iceland, Iewfoundland and Labrador. Modern inensive methods of fishing incl. use of actory ships which quickly freeze or can heir catch. Term also incl. fish farming.

hguard and Goodwick, urban dist. of yfed, SW Wales. Pop. 5000. Railway erminus; ferry services to Cork, Rosslare Ireland).

sion, in biology, form of asexual eproduction occurring in various plants, rotozoa, bacteria, *etc,* in which parent rganism splits into 2 or more pproximately equal parts, each becoming n independent individual.

sion, nuclear, splitting of heavy atomic uclei (*eg* uranium or plutonium) into 2 ragments of approximately equal mass, ccompanied by release of nuclear energy nd neutrons. May occur spontaneously or e caused by impact of neutrons. *See* CHAIN EACTION.

zgerald, F[rancis] Scott [Key] 1896-1940), American author. Works eflect despair of 'lost generation' in 1920s merica, *eg* novels *The Great Gatsby* 1925), *Tender is the Night* (1934).

zherbert, Maria Anne, née Smythe 1756-1837), wife of George, Prince of ales (later George IV). Married George 1785); marriage deemed illegal as she was Catholic and he a minor. Relationship ontinued until 1803.

me, *see* RIJEKA-SUSAK.

s, handball game played by 2 or 4 ompetitors in a special court. Chiefly onfined to Britain, esp. to public schools.

e Year Plan, Soviet economic proramme, first introduced in USSR by Stalin 928) to impose collectivization of agric. nd enhance industrialization. Ruthlessly nforced, caused much suffering. Other rogrammes followed; practice has been dopted elsewhere, *eg* Cuba, China.

ellants, term applied to severely ascetic hristian groups who practised public agellation as a penance. Widespread in th-cent. Europe. Prohibited (1349) by ope Clement VI, but heretical groups ersisted. Still survive in South America.

flamingo, any of Phoenicopteridae family of large gregarious wading birds. Long thin legs, webbed feet, sinuous neck; red or pink plumage. Found in tropical and temperate zones.

Flanders (Flem. *Vlaanderen*), region of SW Belgium and NE France. Former county of Low Countries. Medieval cloth centre (Bruges, Ghent); now indust. area based on coalfields. Battleground in many wars. In Belgium, divided into East, West Flanders provs.; in France, part of Nord region. Distinct Flemish language.

flatfish, any of order Pleuronectiformes of fish with compressed, asymmetric bodies. Larvae normal, but during growth eyes migrate to same side of head. Eyed side of fish camouflaged, other side unpigmented. Species incl. turbot, halibut, flounder, sole, plaice.

Flaubert, Gustave (1821-80), French novelist. Famous works, *eg Madame Bovary* (1857), *L'Education sentimentale* (1869), reveal perfection of form, extreme impersonality of style, despite tragic material.

Flax

flax, any plant of genus *Linum,* esp. *L. usitatissimum* with slender leaves and small blue flowers, of worldwide distribution. Stems are source of LINEN and seeds of LINSEED oil.

flea, any of Aphaniptera order of wingless, flattened insects. Long hind legs adapted for jumping. Adult sucks blood of mammals, birds; transmits disease, esp. bubonic plague and endemic typhus.

fleabane, any plant of genus *Erigeron,* of Compositae family.

Fleet Street, term for British national newspapers, since most are located in or around street of that name in London.

Fleming, Sir Alexander (1881-1955), Scottish

bacteriologist. Discovered penicillin in a mould contaminating bacterial culture, but did not develop its large-scale antibiotic use. Shared Nobel Prize for Physiology and Medicine (1945) with Chain and Florey for work on penicillin.

Flemish, language of W Germanic group of Indo-European family. Usually thought to be Belgian variant of DUTCH, not distinct language. Spoken in N Belgium, France.

Fletcher, John (1579-1625), English dramatist. Wrote majority of 52 plays pub. with BEAUMONT. True collaborations incl. tragicomedies *Philaster, A King and No King*. Also collaborated with Massinger, Shakespeare.

Flinders, Matthew (1774-1814), English naval officer, hydrographer. Surveyed and charted Australian coasts. First to circumnavigate Tasmania (1798), also circumnavigated Australia (1801-3).

Flinders Island, *see* FURNEAUX ISLANDS.

flint, hard, fine-grained rock, a variety of quartz. Often found in chalk and limestone, dates from upper Cretaceous and Tertiary periods. May be shaped by flaking; widely used in Stone Age for making tools, weapons.

Flintshire, former county of NE Wales, now in Clwyd. Clwydian Hills in W, Dee estuary to E. Coalmining; agric.; coastal resorts. Main indust. centre **Flint,** mun. bor. on R. Dee. Pop. 15,000.

FLN, *see* NATIONAL LIBERATION FRONT.

Flodden, hill of Northumberland, NE England. Scene of battle in which James IV of Scotland defeated, killed by English (1513).

Flora, Roman goddess of flowers and fertility.

Florence (*Firenze*), city of NC Italy, on R. Arno, cap. of Tuscany. Pop. 464,000. Indust., tourist centre; railway jct. Etruscan, then Roman settlement. Scene of Guelph-Ghibelline conflict (12th-13th cent.). Under Medici family became centre of Renaissance art, architecture; its famous artists incl. da Vinci, Donatello, Giotto, Michelangelo, Raphael. Birthplace of Dante. Buildings incl. Pitti palace, Ponte Vecchio, Uffizi gallery, domed cathedral. Cap. of Italy 1865-70. Damaged in WWII, 1966 floods.

Florey, Howard Walter, Baron Florey (1898-1968), British pathologist, b. Australia. With E. B. CHAIN, developed methods of purifying penicillin and producing it on a large scale for use during WWII. Shared Nobel Prize for Physiology and Medicine (1945) with Chain and Fleming.

Florida, state of SE US; mainly on penin. separating Atlantic and Gulf of Mexico. Area 151,670 sq km (58,560 sq mi); pop. 8,421,000; cap. Tallahassee; chief cities Jacksonville, Miami. Generally low-lying, swampy (Everglades); subtropical climate. Agric. esp. citrus fruits; fishing; aero-space industs. Major tourist region, resorts incl. Miami, Palm Beach. Spanish colonized area in 16th cent.; purchased by US 1821. Admitted to Union as 27th state (1845).

Florida Keys, chain of small isls., S Florida, US. Largest are Key West and K Largo. Linked by highway. Resort game fishing.

flounder, *see* FLATFISH.

flour, finely ground and sifted meal cereal, esp. wheat and rye, consisti mainly of starch and gluten. Differe grades of flour make bread, past macaroni, *etc.*

flower, part of seed plant containi reproductive organs, *ie* the male stame bearing pollen in anthers, and the ovary gynaecium, the whole surrounded petals and sepals.

flugelhorn, brass instrument similar shape to bugle, with 3 valves like trumpet, but producing a fuller, m mellow sound. Played in brass bands most characteristically in jazz.

fluke, any of order Trematoda of parasi flatworms, with 2 suckers used for hesion. Life cycle involves several lar forms and one or more hosts. Some spec parasitic in humans.

fluorescence, property of certain materi of absorbing light of short wavelength violet or ultra violet) and emitting light longer wavelength (such as visible lig In fluorescent lamp, ultraviolet lig produced by passing current throu mercury vapour, is converted to visi light by fluorescent substance on walls glass tube.

fluoridation, addition of metallic fluorid esp. sodium fluoride, to drinking water reduce incidence of dental decay.

fluorine (F), pale yellow gaseous elemen halogen family; at. no. 9, at. wt. 18. Very chemically active, not found f occurs in cryolite and fluorspar. First p pared (1886) by electrolysis. Used manufacture of FLUOROCARBONS.

fluorite or **fluorspar,** crystalline mine composed of calcium fluoride. Tra parent, sometimes fluorescent; colour but tinted by impurities. Used glassmaking, as flux in metallurgy; sou of fluorine.

fluorocarbons, group of synthetic orga compounds obtained by replacing some all of the hydrogen atoms of hydrocarb by fluoride atoms. Chemically stable, u in manufacture of oils, plastics (*eg* Tefl refrigerants and aerosol propellants.

fluorspar, *see* FLUORITE.

Flushing (*Vlissingen*), town of Netherlands, on Walcheren Isl. at mout Western Scheldt. Pop. 39,000. Oil refin fishing, shipbuilding. Scene of Al invasion (1944).

flute, woodwind instrument of metal or w with range of 3 octaves, played by blow across small aperture near one end. flute sounds a fourth lower than con flute and bass flute an octave lower. piccolo sounds an octave higher.

fly, any of order Diptera of insects wi pair of functional membranous wi ʌany flies transmit disease by blood-ucking or carrying germs on body. ·pecies incl. MOSQUITO, HORSEFLY, TSETSE FLY. ʌame applied esp. to HOUSE FLY and also to ·ther orders of insect.

catcher, any of Muscicapidae family of mall birds with thin curved beak. Catches ısects while in flight.

'ing Dutchman, legendary spectral ship, elieved to haunt Cape of Good Hope. :aptain is doomed to sail forever. Subject f opera by Wagner.

ing fish, any fish capable of leaping from ʌater, using enlarged pectoral fins to glide nrough air; mainly tropical. Species incl. ıtlantic flying fish, *Exocoetus volitans.*

ing fox, one of several fruit-eating bats, ɔund in tropics from Asia to Australia, enus *Pteropus.* Malayan kalong, *P. ampyrus,* has wingspan of *c* 1.5 m/5 ft, ırgest of all bats.

ing lemur, any of order Dermoptera of rboreal nocturnal mammals of SE Asia. ɪembrane stretched between legs enables to make gliding leaps. Also called colugo.

American flying squirrel

ng squirrel, any of several nocturnal ɔecies of squirrel. Uses fold of skin :retched from forelegs to hind legs to lide from tree to tree. Various species ccur in North America, Scandinavia, Asia.

nn, Errol (1909-59), Australian film actor. :nown for roles as adventurous omanizer, as in *The Sea Hawk* (1940).

see MODULATION.

:h, Ferdinand (1851-1929), French gen-ral. Forestalled the initial German dvance at the Marne (1914) and stinguished himself at the battles of pres (1915) and the Somme (1916). Allied ıpreme commander (1918).

ıs, in optics, point at which rays of light :flected by a mirror or refracted by a ns meet (real focus), or would meet if ɔntinued back through lens or mirror 'irtual focus). Focal length of thin lens is stance from its optical centre to point at hich rays of light parallel to its principal xis are focused.

:us, mammalian embryo in later stages ' its development when main features of lly developed animal are recognizable; in an, embryo is considered as foetus after months of gestation.

fog, mass of water droplets suspended in the air, obscuring vision for any distance up to 1 km/0.62 mi. Formed by water vapour condensing on minute dust particles. Mixture of smoke and fog, common in indust. areas, results in smog.

Foggia, city of Apulia, SE Italy, cap. of Foggia prov. Pop. 155,000. Major wheat market; flour, cheese. Cathedral (12th cent.).

Fokine, Michel (1880-1942), American choreographer, dancer, b. Russia. One of founders of modern ballet, working with Diaghilev in most brilliant period of Ballets Russes (1909-14). Ballets incl. *The Firebird, Petrouchka.*

Folkestone, town of Kent, SE England. Pop. 44,000. Cross-Channel ferry services. One of Cinque Ports.

folklore, traditional beliefs, legends, customs, *etc,* of a people. Regarded as important by anthropologists as the imaginative expression of a society's cultural values.

Fontainebleau, town of Ile-de-France, N France, in forest of Fontainebleau. Pop. 20,000. Resort; NATO hq. (1945-67). Château, built by Francis I, was former residence of French kings.

Fontenoy, village of Hainaut prov., Belgium. Scene of French victory (1745) over British, Dutch, and Austrian forces.

Fonteyn, Dame Margot, orig. Margaret Hookham (1919-), English ballerina. Long-time *prima ballerina assoluta* of the Royal Ballet. Acclaimed for roles in such ballets as *The Sleeping Beauty, Giselle.*

Foochow, cap. of Fukien prov., SE China on R. Min. Pop. 680,000. Fishing port; steel, chemical mfg. One of 5 original treaty ports, formerly major tea exports. Educational centre, summer resort.

food, any substance taken into and assimilated by a plant or animal, which enables it to grow and repair tissue and provides source of energy. Human food should contain: protein, necessary for building and repairing tissue; carbohydrates and fats, which provide energy; minerals, *eg* iron, calcium and phosphorus; vitamins.

Food and Agriculture Organization (FAO), specialized agency of UN, estab. 1945; hq. in Rome. Aims to help nations increase efficiency of farming, forestry and fisheries. Operations incl. research and development, financial and technical assistance, information services.

food poisoning, sickness caused by eating food contaminated by bacteria, *eg* salmonellae, or by toxin produced by bacteria, *eg* staphylococci, present in food before cooking. Also caused by inorganic compounds, *eg* those of lead, or organic compounds present in certain animals and plants, *eg* toadstools.

foot, end part of leg on which person or animal stands or moves. Human foot has 26 bones: 14 phalanges in toes, 7 tarsal bones forming the heel and 5 metatarsals in the ball of foot.

foot, in measurement, British unit of length: 1 ft = 0.3048 m.

Foot, Michael (1913-), British politician. Labour Party leader (1980-).

foot-and-mouth disease, contagious virus disease of cloven-footed animals *eg* cattle, deer. Characterized by fever and blisters in mouth and around hoofs. Controlled by slaughter and strict quarantine.

football, *see* AMERICAN FOOTBALL; ASSOCIATION FOOTBALL; AUSTRALIAN RULES FOOTBALL; GAELIC FOOTBALL; RUGBY FOOTBALL.

force, in mechanics, agency which alters state of rest or motion of a body, producing acceleration in it. SI unit of force is the newton. By Newton's law of motion, force is proportional to rate of change of momentum of body.

Ford, Gerald Rudolph, orig. Leslie Lynch King (1913-), American statesman. Republican president (1974-7). Vice-president (1973-4), president after Nixon's resignation.

Ford, Henry (1863-1947), American industrialist. Pioneer automobile manufacturer, developed mass-production techniques. Ford Motor Company by *c* 1915 was world's largest automobile producer.

Ford, John (1586-*c* 1640), English dramatist. Best known for *'Tis Pity She's a Whore* (*c* 1627), reflecting typical Jacobean concern with sexual corruption.

Ford, John, orig. Sean O'Fearna (1895-1973), American film director. Made over 125 feature films; early human dramas incl. *The Informer* (1935), but best known for westerns *eg Stagecoach* (1939).

Foreign Legion, French force of foreign mercenaries under French officers and senior NCOs. Formed by Louis Philippe (1835) mainly to keep the peace in Algeria. Hq. now in Corsica.

Forester, C[ecil] S[cott] (1899-1966), English novelist. Best known for 'Horatio Hornblower' novels about British naval officer in Napoleonic wars. Other novels incl. *The African Queen* (1935), *The Ship* (1943).

forestry, science of planting, tending and managing timber as a crop. Major producers of coniferous wood, used for construction, pulp and paper, are USSR, US, Canada, Sweden and Finland. Broad-leaved woods are important in Brazil, Indonesia, India, China.

Forfar, town of Tayside region, E Scotland. Pop. 11,000. Former royal burgh and co. town of Angus. Jute, linen mfg.

forgery, act of imitating documents, signatures, works of art, *etc,* with intent to deceive. In law, crime limited to written documents.

forget-me-not, any annual or perennial plant of widely-distributed genus *Myosotis.* Oval leaves with blue, white, or yellow flowers.

Forli, city of Emilia-Romagna, NC Italy, cap. of Forli prov. Pop. 110,000. Textiles,

Forget-me-not

furniture. Medieval cathedral, citadel.

formaldehyde (HCHO), pungent produced by oxidation of metha Dissolves readily in water, 40% solu being known as formalin. Used disinfectant and preservative, and manufacture of plastics.

formic acid (HCOOH), colourless liq found in nettles and ant and bee sti Manufactured from steam and car monoxide by catalysis. Used in dyeing.

Formosa, *see* TAIWAN.

formula, in chemistry, representation nature and number of atoms wh constitute single molecule of chem compound by means of letters and figu Structural formula indicates arrangem of atoms and nature of chemical bo linking them. Empirical formula indic only relative proportions of atoms and necessarily their actual numbers.

Forrest, John Forrest, 1st Ba (1847-1918), Australian explorer, politic Led expedition from Perth to Adel (1870). First premier (1890-1901) Western Australia.

Forster, E[dward] M[organ] (1879-19 English author. In novels, *eg Howard's* (1910), *A Passage to India* (1924), stre need for sincerity and sensitivity in hu relationships.

forsythia, *Forsythia suspensa,* decidu shrub with olive-brown twigs and ye flowers which appear before leaves.

Fortaleza, Atlantic port of NE Brazil, ca Ceará state. Pop. 1,110,000. Impor sugar refining, flour milling; carnauba cotton exports; textile, soap mfg. Fou 1609.

Fort-de-France, cap. of MARTINIQUE.

Forth, river of C Scotland. Flows 105 km mi) from Central region into Firth Forth. Ports incl. Grangemouth, L Firth crossed by rail bridge (1890), bridge (1964). Linked to W coast by dis Forth and Clyde Canal.

Fort Knox, *see* LOUISVILLE.

Fort Lamy, *see* NDJAMENA.

ortuna, Roman goddess of fortune. Originally associated with fertility, later identified with Greek Tyche (chance). Represented with cornucopia and ship's rudder.

ort William, *see* THUNDER BAY.

ort William, town of Highland region, NW Scotland, on Loch Linnhe. Pop. 4000. Near Ben Nevis; tourist centre.

ort Worth, city of NE Texas, US; on Trinity R. tributary. Pop. 393,000. Railway jct.; grain, livestock market; meat packing, aircraft mfg., oil and gas industs. Army fort estab. 1847.

rum, market and meeting place of Roman towns, usually surrounded by public buildings and colonnades. Forum in Rome extended from Capitoline Hill almost to Colosseum and contained various triumphal arches, basilicas, temples.

ssil, remains or impressions of animal or plant life preserved in rocks of Earth's crust. Study of fossils is called palaeontology. Can aid dating and correlating of geological strata, and study of evolution.

oucault, Jean Bernard Léon (1819-68), French physicist. Calculated speed of light through air and other media by arrangement of mirrors. Demonstrated rotation of Earth by turning of plane of oscillation of long pendulum.

ouquet, Nicolas, Marquis de Belle-Isle (1615-80), French statesman. Superintendent of finance (1653-61) during Louis XIV's minority, acquired great personal wealth by embezzlement. Imprisoned for life (1664).

ourier, [François Marie] Charles (1772-1837), French social philosopher. Evolved system of utopian communism. Aimed to reorganize society into small, self-sufficient cooperative units.

ourier, Jean Baptiste Joseph, Baron (1768-1830), French mathematician. Famed for *Théorie analytique de la chaleur*, in which he developed Fourier series (representation of functions by infinite series of sines and cosines). This method is of fundamental mathematical importance.

ournier, Henri Alban, *see* ALAIN-FOURNIER.

ur stroke (cycle) engine, *see* INTERNAL COMBUSTION ENGINE.

owles, John (1926-), English novelist. Works, *eg The French Lieutenant's Woman* (1969), combine erudition and experiment with form of novel.

ox, Charles James (1749-1806), English statesman, orator. Opposed Lord North's policy in America. Demanded British abstention during French Revolution. Advocated political rights for dissenters and Catholics; as foreign secretary (1806), urged abolition of slave trade (achieved 1807).

ox, George, *see* SOCIETY OF FRIENDS.

x, wild carnivore of dog family, common in N hemisphere. Nocturnal predator, diet of small animals, fruit; lives in burrows. European red fox, *Vulpes vulpes,* red-brown above, white below.

Foxe, John (1516-87), English Protestant clergyman. Famous for *Actes and Monuments* (1563), known as *Book of Martyrs,* celebrating piety and heroism of Protestants martyred under Mary Tudor.

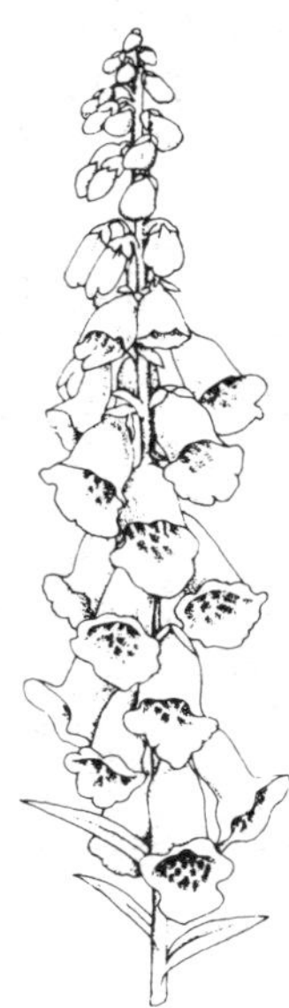

Foxglove

foxglove, *Digitalis purpurea,* perennial of figwort family, native to W and C Europe. Tapering spikes with purple, pink or white, bell-shaped flowers. Leaves yield poisonous alkaloid, digitalin, used in medicine.

fox terrier, small terrier with smooth or wire-haired coat, originally bred for chasing foxes from hiding. Stands 38 cm/15 in. at shoulder.

Foyle, river of Northern Ireland. Flows through former Co. Tyrone to Atlantic via Lough Foyle (navigable inlet *c* 24 km/15 mi long), below Londonderry.

f.p.s. system of units, British system of physical units based on fundamental units of foot, pound and second.

fractions, in mathematics, *see* RATIONAL NUMBER.

Fragonard, Jean Honoré (1732-1806), French painter. Painted frivolous, gallant and sentimental subjects which typified court life of Louis XV.

France, Anatole, pseud. of Jacques Anatole François Thibault (1844-1924), French author. Novels incl. political satires *L'Ile des pingouins* (1908), *La Révolte des anges* (1914). Awarded Nobel Prize for Literature (1921).

France, republic of W Europe. Area *c* 547,000 sq km (211,000 sq mi); pop. 53,278,000; cap. Paris. Language: French. Religion: RC. Comprises 95 admin. depts., incl. Corsica. Mountainous regions incl. Vosges, Jura (E), Alps (SE), Massif Central (SC), Pyrenees (SW); fertile lowlands in Aquitaine, Paris Basin. Main rivers Seine, Loire, Rhône. Mainly agric. until recently, esp. cereals, livestock, vineyards. Indust. centred on NE coal and iron ore deposits (Nord, Lorraine). Tourism, esp. along S coast. Exports wines, luxury goods, motor cars. Roman prov. of Gaul until 5th cent.; Frankish kingdom estab. 9th cent. under Charlemagne, consolidated 10th-14th cent. by Capet dynasty. Regained much territ. from England in Hundred Years War. Revolution (1789) and Napoleonic Wars followed by brief restorations of monarchy, succession of republics. Fifth Republic created 1958 by De Gaulle. Suffered heavy losses in WWI, German occupation (Vichy regime) in WWII. Retains close ties with former overseas possessions, formed FRENCH COMMUNITY (1958). Member of EEC.

Francesca, Piero della, *see* PIERO DELLA FRANCESCA.

Franche-Comté, region and former prov. of E France, hist. cap. Besançon (Dôle until 1678). Incl. parts of Jura, Vosges; forests, agric. esp. dairying. United in 9th cent. as Free County of Burgundy, part of Holy Roman Empire from 1034; under Spanish Habsburgs in 16th-17th cent. Ceded to France (1678).

Francis I (1768-1835), emperor of Austria (1804-35). Succeeded father Leopold II as Holy Roman emperor as **Francis II** (1792). Unsuccessful in wars with France (1792-1809). After assuming Austrian title, forced to dissolve Holy Roman Empire (1806). Daughter, Marie Louise, married (1810) Napoleon. Joined Allies against Napoleon (1813); presided over Congress of Vienna.

Francis I (1494-1547), king of France (1515-47). Succeeded father-in-law, Louis XII. Continually at war in Italy with Emperor Charles V, who had won imperial election over Francis (1519). Campaigns largely unsuccessful; captured at Pavia (1525). Noted Renaissance patron.

Francis Ferdinand (1863-1914), Austrian archduke. Heir apparent to Francis Joseph; assassinated with wife in Sarajevo by Gavrilo Princip, Serbian nationalist. Death led to Austrian ultimatum to Serbia and outbreak of WWI.

Franciscans or **Grey Friars,** in RC church, members of several orders following the rule of ST FRANCIS OF ASSISI, incl. Capuchins and Conventuals. Noted missionaries, educators and preachers.

Francis Joseph or **Franz Josef** (1830-1916), emperor of Austria (1848-1916). Succeeded on abdication of his uncle, Ferdinan Subdued independence movements i Hungary, Sardinia (1849). Lost Lombard (1859), Venetia (1866) to Italy. Reorganize empire into Austro-Hungarian Monarch to placate Hungarian nationalists, b coming king of Hungary (1867). Reign sa growth of Slav nationalism in empire.

Francis of Assisi, St, orig. Giovanni Bernardone (*c* 1182-1226), Italian fria Attracted following by preaching; founde Franciscan order of friars in Rome (1209 its rule based on brotherhood, absolu poverty and concern for poor and sic Many stories told of his simple lif gentleness with animals.

Francis of Sales, St (1567-1622), Frenc Jesuit preacher. Bishop of Geneva (1602 converted many Huguenots. With St Jan Frances of Chantal, founded Order of th Visitation for women unable to underg the austerity of the established orders.

Francis Xavier, St (1506-52), Basque Jesu missionary, called 'Apostle to the Indie With ST IGNATIUS OF LOYOLA, founded S ciety of Jesus (Jesuits). Estab. missions India, Japan and China, where he died.

francium (Fr), extremely unstab radioactive element of alkali metal grou at. no. 87, mass no. of most stable isoto 223. Discovered (1939) as decay product actinium.

Franck, César Auguste (1822-90), Belgia composer. Lived mostly in Paris teacher and organist. Leader of 19th-cer French Romantic school. Best known f orchestral and organ works.

Franco [Bahamonde], Francis (1892-1975), Spanish military and politic leader. Rose to power before SPANISH CIV WAR, led Fascist revolt with German ar Italian support, becoming head insurgent govt. (1936). Dissolved a political parties but FALANGE and bega authoritarian rule. Despite agreemen with Hitler, Mussolini, kept Spain neutral WWII. Restored monarchy by law succession (1947), retaining post of rege until his death. Chose JUAN CARLOS successor and king.

Franco-Prussian War (1870-1), confli between German states and Franc Napoleon III provoked into declaring w by Bismarck's EMS TELEGRAM. France lo decisive battle of Sedan, Napole captured. French resistance continu briefly, peace concluded with Treaty Versailles (1871); Paris Commune held o against Prussian siege until suppressed French army. Results of war incl. Germ unification under Prussia, French loss Alsace-Lorraine, estab. of Third Repub in France.

Frank, Anne (1929-*c* 1945), Dutch author *The Diary of a Young Girl* (194 recording experiences while hiding fro Nazis in Amsterdam 1942-44. Died Belsen concentration camp.

Frankfort, cap. of Kentucky, US; Kentucky R. Pop. 22,000. Whisky distillir trade.

ankfurt (-am-Main), city of W West ;ermany, on R. Main. Pop. 626,000. Transport, commercial centre; publishing, :hemicals, vehicles. Trade fairs held from : 1240. Founded 1st cent. by Romans; free mperial city 1372-1806. Seat of German :onfederation (1815-66); Cathedral.

ankfurt-an-der-Oder, town of East ;ermany on R. Oder. Pop. 58,000. Food rocessing, esp. frankfurter sausages. Ianseatic League member.

.nkincense, aromatic resin from NE African trees of genus *Boswellia*. Used as ncense.

anklin, Benjamin (1706-90), American tatesman, scientist, writer. Colonial eader, presented plan for union at Albany :ongress (1754), helped draft Declaration f Independence (1776). Ambassador in :urope (1776-85), negotiated French ecognition of new republic (1778) and eace with Britain (1781-3). Active in 'ederal Constitutional Congress (1787). among many scientific experiments, flew ite in thunderstorm, proving presence of lectricity in lightning; invented lightning onductor.

anklin, Sir John (1786-1847), English aval officer, explorer. Led expeditions to :anadian Arctic. Searched for Northwest 'assage (1845), but entire expedition was ost.

anks, group of Germanic tribes who ettled along lower Rhine in 3rd cent. alian Franks invaded Gaul in 4th-5th ents. under their leader Clovis, who ccepted Christianity and united all the 'ranks. Frankish empire expanded to incl. nuch of France, W Germany, Switzerland, ustria and parts of Italy by 9th cent.

anz Ferdinand, *see* FRANCIS FERDINAND.

anz Josef, *see* FRANCIS JOSEPH.

anz Josef Land, Arctic archipelago of 'SSR, N of Novaya Zemlya. Comprises *c* 80 ninhabited isls., largely ice covered; site f meteorological stations.

aser, [John] Malcolm (1930-), Aus-ralian politician, PM (1975-). Became eader of Liberal Party (1975). Appointed 'M of interim govt. (Nov. 1975) by overnor-general, Sir John Kerr, replacing Vhitlam's Labor admin. Won 2 ensuing lections.

aser, chief river of British Columbia, anada. Rises in E Rocky Mts., flows NW, hen SW 1370 km (*c* 850 mi) to Str. of eorgia, S of Vancouver. Salmon. 'avigable to Yale *c* 130 km (*c* 80 mi) from nouth.

ud, in law, intentional deception to cause erson to give up property or other legal ght. If contract is based on fraud, injured arty may void it and claim damages.

azer, Sir James George (1854-1941), cottish classicist, anthropologist. Best nown for *The Golden Bough* (1890), an xhaustive study of magic, superstition, rimitive religion.

derick I [Barbarossa] (*c* 1122-90), erman king (1152-90), Holy Roman emperor (1155-90). As king, pacified Germany. When emperor, conducted 4 Italian campaigns against Lombard League and papacy. At first successful, was defeated at Legnano (1176), conceded Lombard League's demands at Peace of Constance (1183); excommunicated by Pope Alexander III. Drowned in Cilicia on Third Crusade.

Frederick II (1194-1250), Holy Roman emperor (1220-50). Received (1197) Sicily from Pope Innocent III. Crusade, really state visit, resulted in cession of Jerusalem, Nazareth, Bethlehem to Christians, and his crowning (1229) as king of Jerusalem. Latter gave rise to long conflict with papacy, and his excommunication (1245).

Frederick IX (1899-1972), king of Denmark (1947-72). Succeeded by his daughter Margarethe.

Frederick I (1657-1713), king of Prussia (1701-13). Succeeded father Frederick William as elector of Brandenburg (1688). Became 1st king of Prussia.

Frederick [II] the Great (1712-86), king of Prussia (1740-86). Initiated (1740) War of Austrian Succession against Maria Theresa, securing Silesia. His leadership and military genius in wars during rule made Prussia a leading European power. Further enlarged kingdom through 1st partition of Poland (1772). Prolific writer, composer, patron of arts, had noted association with Voltaire. Became symbol of German nationalism.

Frederick Barbarossa, *see* FREDERICK I.

Frederick William (1620-88), elector of Brandenburg (1640-88), known as the 'Great Elector'. Rebuilt army and territ. after Thirty Years War, enlarging possessions at Peace of Westphalia (1648). Laid foundation of powerful Prussian state.

Frederick William I (1688-1740), king of Prussia (1713-40). Laid foundations of efficient admin. and army; avoided wars, built up treasury by careful economy.

Frederick William III (1770-1840), king of Prussia (1797-1840). Tried to remain neutral in Napoleonic Wars. Defeated by Napoleon at Jena (1806); forced to accept Treaty of Tilsit (1807), which greatly reduced his territ. Rebelled against Napoleon's domination (1813-14).

Frederick William IV (1795-1861), king of Prussia (1840-61). At first, gave in to 1848 revolutionaries' demands, later crushed them. Belief in divine right to rule led him to refuse offer of imperial crown from Frankfurt parliament (1849). Mental disturbance (1857) led to regency of his brother William I.

Fredericton, cap. of New Brunswick, Canada; on St John R. Pop. 44,000. Timber, leather products.

Free Church of Scotland, *see* SCOTLAND, CHURCH OF.

free enterprise, economic practice in which relationship of supply and demand is allowed to regulate economy without govt. control. *See* LAISSER-FAIRE.

Freemasonry, principles and rituals of Free and Accepted Masons, international secret society practising brotherliness, charity and mutual aid. Masons claim roots in ancient times but order prob. derives from English and Scottish fraternities of stonemasons and cathedral builders in Middle Ages. Organized in self-governing national authorities known as grand lodges; first opened in London (1717), others in all European countries by 1800. Members must be male and believe in a higher being.

free port, port or zone within port free of customs regulation (*see* TARIFF). Estab. in late Middle Ages, *eg* by Hanseatic League. Present ones incl. Hong Kong, Singapore, parts of most international airports.

freesia, genus of bulbous plants of iris family, native to South Africa. Fragrant, usually white or yellow, funnel-shaped flowers.

freethinkers, *see* DEISTS.

Freetown, cap. of Sierra Leone, on Sierra Leone Penin. Pop. 214,000. Admin., commercial centre; good natural harbour, exports diamonds, iron ore, palm products. Settled (1787-92) by freed slaves.

free trade, international trade conducted without restrictions, *eg* quotas on imports, protective tariffs, export bounties. Advocates hold that system allows each country to specialize in goods it can produce most cheaply. EEC aims to abolish protective tariffs between members.

free will, in theology, doctrine that man can choose between good and evil independently of the will of God. Problematic when held alongside belief in God's omniscience. In philosophy, concept of free will is denied by DETERMINISM.

freezing, conversion of liquid into solid form. For given pressure, freezing occurs at fixed temperature; this temperature may be lowered by dissolving substances in fluid.

Frege, Gottlob (1848-1925), German philosopher, mathematician. Founder of modern symbolic logic.

Freiburg, *see* FRIBOURG, Switzerland.

Freiburg (-im-Breisgau), city of SW West Germany, on W edge of Black Forest. Pop. 175,000. Textiles, paper mfg. Held by Austria 1368-1805. Gothic cathedral, univ. (1457).

Fremantle, city of SW Western Australia, at mouth of Swan R. Pop. 25,000. Outport for Perth, exports oil, wheat, wool, minerals. Founded 1829.

French, John Denton Pinkstone, Earl of Ypres (1852–1925), British general. Commanded British Expeditionary Force to France (1914-15). Lord-lieutenant of Ireland (1918-21).

French, Romance language belonging to Italic branch of Indo-European family. One of official languages of United Nations. Developed from vernacular Latin, with Celtic and Germanic elements in vocabulary. Historically divided into Old Fren (9th–13th cent.), Middle French (14th–16 cent.), Modern French (from 17th cent.).

French and Indian War (1754-60), Nor American conflict between Britain a France, part of SEVEN YEARS WAR. Aided Iroquois Indians, British attacked Fren forts and cities, finally taking Québ (1759). Treaty of Paris (1763) end French claims to Canada.

French Antarctica, *see* FRENCH SOUTHE AND ANTARCTIC TERRITORIES.

French Community, political union (esta 1958) comprising France, its overse depts. and territs., and 6 independe African states: Central African Repub Chad, Congo (People's Republic), Gab Djibouti, Senegal. Promotes econom defensive and cultural cooperati Originally incl. all former French colon in Africa; most withdrew in 1962.

French Equatorial Africa, former Fren overseas territ. Comprised present-d CENTRAL AFRICAN REPUBLIC, CHAD, Peopl Republic of the CONGO, GABON. Estab. 19 cap. Brazzaville; dissolved 1958.

French Guiana, overseas region of Fran NE South America. Area 91,000 sq k (35,135 sq mi); pop. 60,000; cap. Cayen Rises from Atlantic coast to tropi forests and mountains of Inini ter Largely undeveloped; main exports go timber, rum. Site of former penal colon incl. Devil's Isl.

French Guinea, *see* GUINEA.

French horn

French horn, brass instrument of coi tubing, whose bore widens into a fla bell-shape.

French India, group of 5 former Fren settlements in India, incl. Pondicherry. transferred to India by 1954.

French Polynesia, overseas territ. France, in S Pacific Ocean. Compri Gambier, Marquesas, Society, Tuam Tubuai isl. groups. Area 4000 sq km (1 sq mi); pop. 146,000; cap. Papeete (Tah Produce fruit, copra, pearl shell; tou indust. Acquired by France during 1 cent.

French Revolution, political upris

egun 1789. Product of 18th-cent. liber- lism and assertion of capitalist class gainst outdated feudal system. Immediate ause was state's vast debt. To raise ioney, LOUIS XVI convened ESTATES- ENERAL (May, 1789), which demanded weeping political, social and fiscal eforms and declared itself National ssembly. Louis yielded, but dismissal of ECKER led to mob's storming of Bastille. ational Guard organized, feudal rivileges abolished, and commune estab. s govt. of Paris. Louis imprisoned (1791) fter attempt to flee country, forced to ccept new constitution. Republican IRONDISTS and extremists controlled gislative assembly; their desire to spread evolutionary ideas and Austrian threats to estore Louis to absolute power served as retext for FRENCH REVOLUTIONARY WARS. fter abortive insurrections, National Con- ention (estab. 1792) abolished monarchy, et up First Republic (Sept. 1792), onvicted and executed Louis for treason an. 1793). Royalist backlash led to REIGN F TERROR. DIRECTORY estab. 1795; corrupt dmin. led to Napoleon's coup d'état of 18 rumaire and Consulate (1799).

nch Revolutionary Wars, general Euro- ean conflict (1792-1802), precipitated by rench Revolution. Austrian and Prussian tention to restore Louis XVI to former ower, and French desire to spread revolu- on throughout Europe, led France to eclare war on Austria. After early everses, France invaded Germany, etherlands and Italy (where Napoleon ame to prominence). By beginning of 19th ent., Austria and its Russian allies had ithdrawn from war, leaving Britain alone gainst France. Short-lived peace (1802) llowed by Napoleonic Wars (1803-15). *See* APOLEON I.

nch Southern and Antarctic Terri- ries, French overseas territ. Area 0,000 sq km (158,000 sq mi). Formed 1955 om Adélie Land (Antarctica) and erguelen, Amsterdam, St Paul and Crozet ls. (Indian Ocean).

nch Sudan, *see* MALI.

nch West Africa, former French over- as territ. Comprised present-day BENIN, UINEA, IVORY COAST, MALI, MAURITANIA, IGER, SENEGAL, UPPER VOLTA. Estab. 1895, ip. Dakar; dissolved 1958.

uency, in physics, number of periodic cillations, vibrations or waves per unit of ne; usually measured in cycles per cond. For wave motion, frequency uals wave velocity divided by wave- ngth.

co, method of wall-painting with atercolours on ground of wet plaster. echnique was perfected in Italy in 16th ent.

ud, Sigmund (1856-1939), Austrian ychiatrist, founder of PSYCHOANALYSIS. His ork on hysteria led him to believe that mptoms were caused by early trauma, id were expressions of repressed sexual ergy. Devised 'free association' tech- nique and dream Interpretation to discover repressed experiences. Emphasized importance of infantile sexuality in personality's development in later life. Influenced Jung and Adler, who later opposed him. Works incl. *The Interpretation of Dreams* (1900), *The Ego and the Id* (1923).

Freya, in Norse myth, goddess of love, marriage and fertility. Wife of Odin, her worship became merged with that of FRIGG.

Fribourg (Ger. *Freiburg*), town of W Switzerland, cap. of Fribourg canton. Pop. 40,000. Chocolate mfg. Cathedral (13th cent.); univ. (1889).

friction, force opposing motion of one surface over another; heat produced by friction accounts for inefficiency of machinery.

Friedman, Milton (1912-), American economist. A leading monetarist, he rejected Keynesian theories; advocated strict control of money supply. In UK, theories applied by Conservative govt. (1979-). Awarded Nobel Prize for Economics (1976).

Friedrich, Caspar David (1774-1840), German romantic painter. Specialized in melancholy forest and mountain scenes, portrayed in strange light of dusk or moonlight.

Friendly Islands, *see* TONGA.

Friesland (anc. *Frisia*), prov. of N Netherlands. Area 3432 sq km (1325 sq mi); cap. Leeuwarden. Incl. W Frisian Isls. Noted for Friesian cattle. Distinct dialect, still widely spoken. Medieval region under counts of Holland, joined United Provs. 1579. East Friesland (N West Germany) separate from 1454.

18th-century frigate

frigate, originally a narrow-hulled oared sailing vessel in the Mediterranean. In the 18th cent. a full-rigged warship of up to 50 guns. In WWII a ship specially designed for convoy and anti-submarine work, superseding the destroyer.

frigate bird, any of Fregatidae family of large tropical seabirds with webbed feet, large hooked beak.

Frigg or **Frigga,** in Germanic myth, mother

goddess, wife of Odin, mother of Balder. Worshipped as deity of household and love. *See* FREYA.

Frisian Islands, offshore group of *c* 30 isls. in North Sea, stretching from Wadden Zee to Jutland. Comprise W Frisians (Netherlands), E Frisians (West Germany), N Frisians (Denmark, West Germany). Low-lying, sandy; cattle, fishing.

Friuli-Venezia Giulia, region of NE Italy. Alps in N, fertile plain in S; chief city Venice, cap. Trieste. Part (Istria) ceded to Yugoslavia 1947.

Frobisher, Sir Martin (*c* 1535-94), English navigator. Made 3 unsuccessful attempts (1567-8) to find Northwest Passage; discovered Frobisher Bay. Joined Drake in West Indies expedition (1585). Knighted for part in defeating Spanish Armada (1588).

Froebel, Friedrich Wilhelm August (1782-1852), German educator. Founded KINDERGARTEN system, estab. 1st kindergarten in 1837.

frog, tailless amphibian of order Anura. Mainly aquatic or semi-aquatic, with webbed feet; arboreal forms have enlarged webbed hands, feet. Sticky tongue used to seize prey. Young, known as tadpoles, have fish-like form.

frogbit, *Hydrocharis morsus-ranae,* floating pond weed with kidney-shaped leaves, white flowers.

froghopper, any of Cercopidae family of leaping insects. Larvae enveloped in froth (cuckoo-spit) secreted from anus; often seen on plants. Also called spittle bug.

Froissart, Jean (*c* 1338-*c* 1410), French chronicler, poet, traveller. Wrote *Chronicles,* lively and invaluable, though sometimes inaccurate, record of Europe 1325-1400.

Fronde, name given to French civil wars during Louis XIV's minority (1648-53). First, caused by quarrels between Parlement of Paris and royal authority over taxation, was suppressed by MAZARIN and CONDÉ. Second, caused by attempt of nobles to limit power of Mazarin, was led by Condé.

front, in meteorology, line at Earth's surface marking boundary between cold and warm air masses. As warm air is lighter, it ascends the frontal plane or surface above cold air. Cold front results from advancing cold air mass; warm front from advancing warm air mass. Associated with DEPRESSIONS.

Frontenac, Louis de Buade, Comte de (*c* 1622-98), French governor of New France in Canada (1672-82, 1689-98). Authority disputed by Jesuits; recalled to France (1682). Reappointed 1689 to counter Iroquois aggression.

Frost, Robert Lee (1874-1963), American poet. Most famous verse in *North of Boston* (1914), *West-running Brook* (1928). Known for clear, simple, moral poetry, close to rural life and nature, which can also express irony, bitterness, despair.

frost, weather condition occurring when air temperature falls to 0°C or below. Exists 2 main forms: (1) hoarfrost, produc when water vapour crystallizes directly white coating on ground; (2) ground black frost, produced when sub-ze temperatures cause water to freeze.

frostbite, damage to skin and tiss resulting from exposure to intense c Caused by lack of blood circulation a formation of ice crystals; nose, hands, fe and ears most often affected.

fructose or **fruit sugar,** crystalline su found in ripe fruit and honey.

fruit, mature, fertilized ovary of flow varying in form from tufted seed dandelion to cultivated apple. Edible fr classified as tree, *eg* apple, orange; bu *eg* strawberry, blackcurrant; stone, plum; pip, *eg* grape; berry, *eg* raspbe and nut, *eg* walnut.

fruit bat, any of suborder Megachiroptera large fruit-eating bats of Old World trop Species incl. FLYING FOX.

fruit fly, insect of Trypetidae family, wh larvae bore into fruit, other plants.

Frunze, city of USSR, cap. of Kirghiz S Pop. 533,000. Centre of fertile agric. regi produces machinery, textiles. Forme called Pishpek.

Fry, Christopher (1907-), English dra tist. Known for witty verse plays, *eg* *Lady's Not for Burning* (1948), *Venus served* (1950).

Fry, Elizabeth, née Gurney (1780-18 English prison reformer, philanthropist Quaker, she improved conditions women in Newgate and other prisons.

Fuad I, orig. Ahmed Fuad Pasha (1868-19 king of Egypt (1922-36). Ruled as su (1917-22) before becoming king w British protect. in Egypt ended.

Fuchs, Sir Vivian Ernest (1908-), Eng geologist, explorer. Led, with Sir Edm Hillary, Commonwealth Trans-Antar Expedition (1957-8), 1st overland cross of Antarctic.

fuchsia, genus of colourful shrubs willowherb family with red or pur flowers. Most species native to trop America. Widely cultivated ornamental

Fugger, Jacob (1459-1525), German m chant, member of great Augsburg trad family. Helped finance Maximilian I, to secure election of Charles V. Fa patronized arts, learning.

fugue, piece of music in a set numbe parts or voices, each of which foll separate yet interrelated melodic line fugue begins with each voice statin theme in turn but thereafter is confined to a set pattern.

Fujiyama or **Fuji-san,** highest mountai Japan, in C Honshu isl.; alt. 3776 m (12 ft). A dormant volcano, last active in Place of pilgrimage, sacred to Japanese

Fukien, prov. of SE China on Formosa Area 119,000 sq km (46,000 sq mi); (est.) 24,000,000; cap. Foochow. Mount ous, forested; lumber resources. Form great tea exports, famous preserved fru

ukuoka, seaport of Japan, on Kyushu isl. Pop. 1,022,000. Shipbuilding, textile mfg.

ulani, pastoral nomads of W Africa, found throughout area between Upper Nile and Senegal. Moslem; reached height of power in 19th cent., during which they conquered Hausa states of Nigeria.

uller, Richard Buckminster (1895-), American architect, engineer. Constructor of geodesic dome, spherical structure of light but extremely strong triangular members.

lmar, *Fulmarus glacialis,* large grey seabird of petrel family of Arctic and subarctic regions. Visits land only to breed.

ulton, Robert (1765-1815), American engineer, inventor. Built *Clermont* (1807), 1st successful American steamship.

mitory, any plant of Fumariaceae family, esp. widely distributed species *Fumaria officinalis* with fern-like leaves and pink, spurred flowers.

unchal, cap. of Madeira Isls., Portugal. Pop. 100,000. Commercial centre; port, exports Madeira wines; tourism.

nction, in modern mathematics, rule which associates to each member of a set a member of another set. More familiarly, functions are expressed by formulae which express variation of 1 quantity (dependent variable) in terms of variation of other quantities (independent variables).

nctionalism, in art and architecture, 20th-cent. principle emphasizing unity of form and purpose, and rejecting all inessential ornament. Promiment exponents of the style were members of Bauhaus school and Le Corbusier.

ndamentalism, conservative, mainly Protestant, religious movement of 20th-cent. Upholds literal interpretations of Bible against modern textual criticism and scientific theory (*eg* Darwinism).

undy, Bay of, arm of N Atlantic, SE Canada; 270 km (*c* 170 mi) long; separates New Brunswick from Nova Scotia penin. Has tides up to 12-15 m (40-50 ft) high.

lnen, *see* FYN.

ngus, any of many plants of division Thallophyta. Lacking CHLOROPHYLL, they depend on organic matter for growth. Saphrophytes feed on dead organisms, parasites on living. Reproduction by SPORE rather than seed. Incl. mushrooms, toadstools, yeasts.

fur, soft thick hair covering the skin of many mammals, *eg* sable, mink, ermine, chinchilla. Valued for both warm and luxurious clothing.

Furies, *see* EUMENIDES.

Furneaux Islands, isl. group in Bass Str., off Tasmania, SE Australia. Largest is Flinders Isl. (area 2072 sq km/800 sq mi). Intensive cattle and sheep raising.

furze, *see* GORSE.

Fuseli, Henry, orig. Johann Heinrich Füssli (1741-1825), Anglo-Swiss painter, b. Zurich. He produced highly imaginative works, depicting horrific and fantastic scenes. Works incl. *The Nightmare* and illustrations of Milton and Shakespeare.

Fushun, city of Liaoning prov., NE China. Pop. 1,080,000. Major indust. centre; extensive open cast coal mines, oil shale refining; engineering, automobile mfg.

fusion, nuclear, nuclear reaction in which two light atomic nuclei fuse to form heavier nucleus, with release of enormous energy, *eg* deuterium and tritium nuclei fuse to form helium nucleus. Nuclei must have sufficient kinetic energy to overcome repulsive forces; extremely high temperatures provide this energy. Potential source of useful energy; basis of stellar energy and hydrogen bomb.

Futuna Island, *see* WALLIS AND FUTUNA ISLANDS.

futurism, artistic and literary movement inaugurated (1909) by Italian poet Marinetti. Adherents incl. Italian painters Boccioni, Balla, Carra. They sought to eliminate conventional form and to express vital dynamism of machine age. Influenced constructivism, dada, vorticism. Later became assimilated in fascist ideology.

Fyn (*Ger. Fünen*), isl. of Denmark. Area 2976 sq km (1149 sq mi); main town Odense. Dairying. Situated between Jutland and Zealand.

Fyne, Loch, sea loch of Strathclyde region, W Scotland. Length 64 km (40 mi). Noted for herring, kippers.

G

gabbro, coarse-grained, plutonic igneous rock. Consists of plagioclase feldspar and pyroxene. Dark coloured and heavy; formed by slow cooling of large underground masses.

Gabès, town of SE Tunisia, on Gulf of Gabès. Pop. 41,000. Fishing port; exports dates, fruit.

Gable, Clark (1901-60), American film actor. Star for nearly 30 years, known as 'king' of Hollywood. Best known for *Gone With the Wind* (1939).

Gabo, Naum (1890-1977), American sculptor, b. Russia. Leading constructivist. Used modern synthetic materials in space-constructions; pioneer of kinetic art.

Gabon

Gabon, republic of WC Africa. Area 268,000 sq km (103,500 sq mi); pop. 538,000 cap. Libreville. Languages: Bantu, French. Religions: animist, RC. Coastal plain, interior plateau; largely tropical rain-forest. Exports petroleum, manganese, hardwoods. Reached *c* 1485 by Portuguese; slave trade 17th-19th cent. Part of French Congo from 1886; territ. of French Equatorial Africa from 1908; independent republic from 1960. Member of French Community.

Gabor, Dennis (1900-), British physicist, b. Hungary. Awarded Nobel Prize for Physics (1971) for invention of principle of HOLOGRAPHY (1948).

Gaborone, cap. of Botswana. Pop. 37,000.

Gabriel, archangel, messenger of God. Appears several times in Bible, notably to tell Virgin Mary she will bear child to be called Jesus. In Islam, revealed Koran to Mohammed. Christian tradition regards him as trumpeter of Last Judgment.

Gadafy, Muammar al-, *see* QADDHAFI.

gadfly, name used for various blood-sucking flies, *eg* horsefly, that attack livestock.

gadolinium (Gd), metallic element (lanthanide series; at. no. 64, at. wt. 157.2 Some isotopes used in nuclear reactors t absorb neutrons.

Gaea, or **Gaia,** in Greek myth, goddess earth. Emerged from primeval chaos ar gave birth to Uranus, the sky. Her childre by Uranus were the TITANS.

Gaelic or **Goidelic,** subgroup of CELT branch of Indo-European language famil Incl. Irish Gaelic (Erse), Scottish Gaeli extinct Manx. Irish Gaelic divided into O (7th–9th cent.), Middle (10th–16th cent and Modern periods. Revived in 20th cen as national language of Eire. Scottis Gaelic identical with Irish until 17th cent.

Gaelic football, fifteen-a-side team gam played with a round ball, combining a pects of soccer and rugby. Mainly confine to Ireland.

Gaelic literature, literature of Gaeli speaking Ireland and Scotland. N separated nationally until 17th cen therefore divided into Old Irish (befo 900), Middle Irish (until 1350), Late Midd or Early Modern Irish (until 1650) ar Modern Irish and Scottish Gaelic (fro 1650). Old Irish works incl. Book Leinster. Middle Irish works divided into cycles of heroic tales, *ie* Red Branch Ulster cycle (pagan), and Fenian (late more complex, Christian), incl. work poet OSSIAN. Modern Irish period saw ri of prose, less formal poetry. Scottish Gael poetry stimulated by events of 1745, as poetry of Alexander MacDonald, and *Ossian* of James MACPHERSON. Gael revival in late 19th-cent. Ireland.

Gagarin, Yuri Alekseyevich (1934-68), Ru sian cosmonaut. First man to orbit Ear (April, 1961). Killed in aeroplane acccider

Gaia, *see* GAEA.

Gainsborough, Thomas (1727-88), Englis painter. Painted elegant portraits, *eg Bl Boy, Mrs Siddons,* members of Roy Family; also first authentically Englis landscapes.

Gaitskell, Hugh Todd Naylor (1906-6 British politician. Labour chancellor exchequer (1950-1). Leader of parliame tary Labour Party (1955-63), adopt moderate stance on nationalization a disarmament issues.

Galahad, *see* ARTHURIAN LEGEND.

Galápagos Islands or **Colón Archipelag** isl. group of Ecuador, in E Pacific Ocea Area *c* 7800 sq km (3000 sq mi); chief is San Cristóbal (Eng. Chatham) and Isabe (Albemarle). Unique flora and fauna, in giant tortoise; visited (1835) by Darw now nature reserve.

Galatea, *see* PYGMALION.

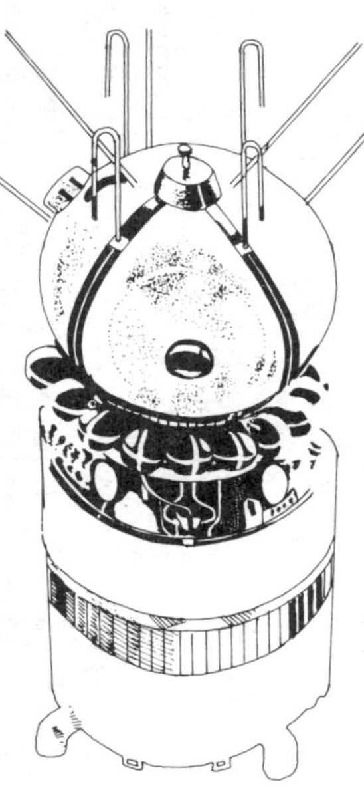

The Vostok spacecraft in which Gagarin made the first manned space flight

lati, city of E Romania, on R. Danube. ᵓop. 239,000. Naval base; port, exports ;rain, timber.

latia, ancient region of C Asia Minor, ıround modern Ankara. Came under Roman rule in 2nd cent. BC.

latians, St Paul's Epistle to the, book of NT, possibly written *c* AD 48 at Ephesus. Exposition of how Christianity superseded aw of Moses.

laxy, large grouping of stars, gas and dust ıeld together by mutual gravitational ıttraction. Milky Way is galaxy containing olar system. Most galaxies are elliptical r spiral shaped; *c* 1000 million are thought o exist.

lbraith, J[ohn] K[enneth] (1908-), American economist, b. Canada. Adviser to .F. Kennedy; US ambassador to India 1961-3). Advocate of using nation's wealth or public projects rather than consumer goods; early critic of dependence on economic growth. Works incl. *The Affluent Society* (1958).

len (*c* 130-*c* 200), Greek physician. Systematized contemporary medical knowledge in series of treatises; authority remained unchallenged until 16th cent.

Galicia (Pol. *Galicja,* Ukr. *Halychyna),* region of SE Poland and W Ukraine. Incl. plains in N, N Carpathians in S; main rivers Dnestr, Vistula. Chief cities Kraków, Lvov. Hist. duchy, part of Poland from 14th cent.; ceded to Austria by 1772 partition. Polish again after WWI; part to USSR after WWII.

Galicia, region and former kingdom of NW Spain. Mountainous with deep valleys, indented coast; drained by R. Miño. Stock raising, fishing. Main towns La Coruña, Vigo, Santiago de Compostela. Voted for autonomy in 1980 referendum.

Galilee, Sea of, lake of NE Israel. Length 23 km (14 mi), area *c* 166 sq km (64 sq mi). Lies below sea level, fed by hot mineral springs. Fisheries since Biblical times. Also known as L. Tiberias.

Galileo Galilei (1564-1642), Italian astronomer and physicist. Constructed first astronomical telescope (1609) and discovered 4 brightest satellites of Jupiter. Investigated motion of falling bodies, his findings contradicting Aristotle's teaching. Supported Copernican theory; later forced by Inquisition to renounce this belief. His use of observation, experiment and mathematics helped lay foundation of modern science.

gall bladder, membranous sac which stores and concentrates bile from liver in most vertebrates. In humans, attached to underside of liver; contracts to eject bile into duodenum to aid digestion.

Galleon

galleon, a square-rigged warship of the 16th cent. with narrow hull, beaked bow and rectangular forecastle, carrying usually 2 tiers of guns. Used by Spanish to bring treasure from Americas.

galley, long, low-built vessel propelled by oars and sail. Used in ancient and medieval times, esp. in Mediterranean. Rowers were generally slaves.

Gallic Wars, campaigns of Julius Caesar during his proconsulship in Gaul (58-51 BC). Conquest of Gaul was completed when Caesar crushed rebellion led by Vercingetorix.

Gallipoli *(Gelibolu),* penin. of European Turkey, between Gulf of Saros and Dardanelles. Scene of unsuccessful landings by Allies to capture Constantinople via Dardanelles (1915-16).

gallium (Ga), soft metallic element; at. no. 31, at. wt. 69.72. Used to make high temperature thermometers and alloys of low melting point. Discovered spectroscopically in 1875.

gallon, unit of liquid measure. British Imperial gallon is volume occupied by 10 pounds of water under specified conditions; equals *c* 4.546 litres. US gallon is *c* 5/6 of Imperial gallon.

Galloway, area of SW Scotland, in Dumfries and Galloway region. Rhinns of Galloway penin. in SW, with Mull of Galloway at S end (most S point in Scotland). Dairying; black Galloway cattle.

Galsworthy, John (1867-1933), English author. Known for novel sequence *The Forsyte Saga* (1906-22) portraying Edwardian moneyed class. Also wrote plays. Awarded Nobel Prize for Literature (1932).

Galton, Sir Francis (1822-1911), English scientist. Founded and coined term for eugenics, movement to improve species through control of hereditary factors. Developed statistical correlation and questionnaire techniques.

Galvani, Luigi (1737-98), Italian physician. Discovered contraction of frog's muscles produced by contact with 2 different metals. Ascribed source of electricity to animal tissue; theory discredited by Volta.

galvanization, plating of iron or steel sheets with zinc to protect them from atmospheric corrosion. Sheets usually immersed in molten zinc; zinc can also be deposited by electrolysis.

galvanometer, device used to measure or detect small electric currents. Usually consists of current-carrying coil suspended between poles of permanent magnet; magnetic field produced by current interacts with field of magnet, causing coil to move.

Galveston, port and tourist resort of SE Texas, US; on Galveston Isl. in Gulf of Mexico inlet. Pop. 62,000. Shipyards; exports sulphur, cotton, wheat. Oil, cotton processing; chemical, hardware mfg.

Galway, county of Connacht prov., W Irish Republic. Area 5939 sq km (2293 sq mi); pop. 168,000. Indented coast, mountains in W; incl. scenic Connemara, Aran Isls. Agric., fishing; marble quarrying. Co. town **Galway,** on Galway Bay. Pop. 37,0 Fishing port, univ. coll. (1849).

Gama, Vasco da (*c* 1469-1524), Portugue navigator. Discovered sea route to Ind via Cape of Good Hope (1497-9), opening East Indian trade and leading to dev opment of Portuguese empire. Made further voyages to India; briefly vicer (1524).

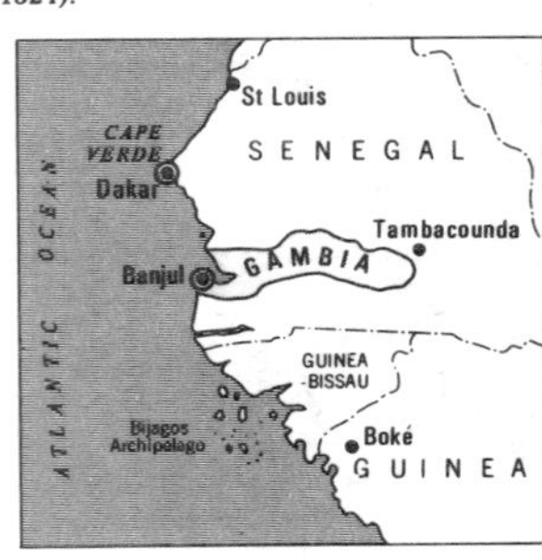

Gambia

Gambia, republic of W Africa. Area 10,360 km (4000 sq mi); pop. 569,000; cap. Banj Official language: English. Religio animist, Islam. Surrounded by Seneg extends *c* 320 km (200 mi) along Gambia. Exports groundnuts, hides. Fi discovered in 15th cent. by Portugue British colony from 1843; independe (1965). Member of British Commonwealt

Gambier Islands, archipelago of S Paci Ocean, part of French Polynesia. Main Mangareva. Produce copra, coffee, pe shell. Acquired by France (1881).

gamete, in biology, reproductive cell, usua sexually differentiated. Male gamete (sp matozoon) unites with female game (ovum) to form the cell (zygote) wh develops into new individual.

gamma rays, high frequency electrom netic radiation, similar to X-rays. Emitt by atomic nuclei during radioactive dec great penetrating power.

Gandhi, Indira (1917-), Indian stat woman, PM (1966-77, 1979-). Daughter Nehru, succeeded Shastri as leader Congress Party and PM. Declared war Pakistan (1971) in support of Banglade independence (estab. 1971). Proclaim state of emergency (1975-7); retair premiership, suspending most democra processes, imprisoning opponents. L ensuing election; subsequently fac corruption charges. Re-elected 1979.

Gandhi, Mohandas Karamcha (1869-1948), Indian political and religi leader. Known as *Mahatma* (great soule Campaigned for independence from 19 Asserted Hindu ethics by abstaining fr Western ways, practising ascetici Imprisoned (1930) by British for c disobedience campaigns, employing p

;ive resistance and fasting as political veapons. Prominent in conferences eading to independence (1947), disappoin-ed by partition into Hindu and Moslem ;tates. Shot by Hindu nationalist fanatic.

nesa, in Hindu religion, god of wisdom ınd patron of literature. Son of Siva and Parvati; usually represented with head of ın elephant.

nges, river of N India and Bangladesh. Rises in Himalayan Uttar Pradesh, flows *c* .500 km (1560 mi) through Allahabad, Varanasi and Patna to form delta at Bay of Bengal. Major irrigation source. Sacred to Hindus.

ng of Four, the, radical faction within Chinese Communist party that emerged as political force in Spring 1976 and was uppressed in following October. Members vere Chang Ch'un-ch'iao, Wong Hung-wen, Yao Wen-yan, and Chiang Ch'ing (Mao's vidow). Convicted on political charges 1980).

ıgrene, decay of tissue in injured part of ody caused by loss of blood supply to that art. Gas gangrene occurs when certain acteria invade wounds, destroying nearby ealthy tissue and forming gas. Damaged issue must be removed surgically.

ngtok, cap. of SIKKIM.

ınet, large marine bird of Sulidae family, ound on all coasts except Antarctica. Nests in colonies on cliffs.

nymede, in Greek myth, son of Tros, king f Troy. Because of his great beauty, Zeus, n the form of an eagle, carried him to Mt. Olympus to be cup-bearer of the gods.

rbo, Greta, orig. Greta Gustafsson 1905-), Swedish film actress. Spent most f her career in US. Became symbol of loof allurement, enhancing this by early etirement. Films incl. *Queen Christina* 1933), *Camille* (1936), *Ninotchka* (1939).

rcía Lorca, Federico (1898-1936), Spanish oet. Major poet of his generation, murder-d by Falangists in Civil War. Revived panish ballad form with *Romancero itano* (1929), expressing preoccupation vith death. Also known for plays, esp. ragedy *Blood Wedding* (1933).

rda, Lake, N Italy, mainly in Lombardy. argest lake in Italy, area 370 sq km (149 q mi).

den city, planned residential and indust. own designed to combine advantages of own and country. Features incl. encircling ural belt, predetermined max. pop., ommunity ownership of land. Examples ıcl. Letchworth and Welwyn Garden City.

denia, genus of evergreen trees and hrubs of madder family. Native to ubtropical S Africa and Asia. Glossy eaves, highly fragrant white or yellow, vaxy flowers.

rdiner, Stephen (*c* 1493-1555), English hurchman. Lord high chancellor under Mary I, pursued anti-Protestant policies.

rfield, James [Abram] (1831-81), American statesman, Republican president 1881). Assassinated.

gargoyle, water spout in form of grotesque figure, human or animal, projecting from the gutter of a building. Many examples found on Gothic cathedrals.

Garibaldi, Giuseppe (1807-82), Italian soldier and patriot. Major figure of RISORGIMENTO. Fought in South American wars (1836-48) after involvement in unsuccessful republican plot. Returned to Italy, fought for Sardinia against Austria (1848) and for Roman Republic against France (1849). With 1000 volunteer 'Red Shirts', conquered Sicily and Naples (1860), making Victor Emmanuel king of Italy. Twice attempted (1862, 1867) to unite Papal States with new kingdom.

Garlic

garlic, *Allium sativum,* perennial plant of lily family, native to Asia. Pungent, bulbous root is used as flavouring.

garnet, crystalline silicate mineral. Hard, colours incl. red, white, green, brown, yellow. Found in metamorphic rocks, esp. gneiss, mica, hornblende schists. Red, transparent variety is semi-precious gem-stone; others used as abrasives.

Garonne, river of SW France. Flows *c* 645 km (400 mi) from Spanish Pyrenees via Toulouse to join R. Dordogne near Bordeaux, forming Gironde estuary.

Garrick, David (1717-79), English actor-manager. Manager of Drury Lane Theatre (1747-76). Did much to revive Shake-speare's popularity.

Garter, [Most Noble] Order of the, oldest British order of knighthood, estab. *c* 1344. Limited to 25 knights and members of royal family. Has motto, *Honi soit qui mal y pense.*

garter snake, small, harmless, striped snake of genus *Thamnophis,* common in North America.

gas, state of matter in which molecules move freely, causing matter to expand indefinitely to fill its container.

Gascony *(Gascogne),* region and former prov. of SW France, hist. cap. Auch. Incl. sandy Landes, hilly Armagnac, part of Pyrenees; agric., vineyards, brandy. Duchy created 7th cent., incorporated (11th cent.) into Aquitaine. Under English rule

(1154-1453). Basque language and customs survive in some areas.

Gaskell, Elizabeth Cleghorn, née Stevenson (1810-65), English novelist. Works, incl. *Mary Barton* (1848), *Cranford* (1853), *North and South* (1855), deal with social, moral problems of Victorian age. Wrote life of Charlotte Brontë (1857).

gasoline, *see* PETROLEUM.

Gaspé, penin. of E Québec, Canada, extending into Gulf of St Lawrence. Mountainous interior; wooded. Coastal fishing, lumbering, pulp milling; tourism.

gastric ulcer, *see* PEPTIC ULCER.

Gastropoda (gastropods), class of molluscs with distinct head, eyes and tentacles. Large flattened foot used for motion. Incl. snail, limpet.

Gateshead, town of Tyne and Wear met. county, NE England, on R. Tyne. Pop. 214,000. Opposite Newcastle, linked by tunnel, bridges. Shipbuilding, engineering industs., chemicals mfg.

Gaudier-Brzeska, Henri (1891-1915), French sculptor. Member of vorticist group, he worked in London from 1911. Work incl. fluid drawings of animals and sculpture influenced by African art.

Gaudí, Antoni (1852-1926), Spanish architect. His exotic art nouveau buildings are known for their undulating façades and decorations of ceramics. Designed church of Sagrada Familia in Barcelona, which remains unfinished.

Gauguin, [Eugène Henri] Paul (1848-1903), French painter. Began painting in impressionist manner, became leading artist of synthesist style. His work is characterized by use of pure unnaturalistic colours applied in flat areas. Rejecting Western civilization, he went to live in Tahiti. Works incl. *The Yellow Christ*. Great influence on 20th-cent. art.

Gaul *(anc. Gallia),* hist. region of W Europe, mainly coextensive with modern France. Originally comprised Cisalpine Gaul (Italy N of Apennines) conquered 3rd cent. BC by Romans, and Transalpine Gaul (modern France) conquered by Julius Caesar in Gallic Wars (58-51 BC).

gaur, *Bibos gaurus,* wild ox of forested hills of India, Burma. Largest of wild cattle.

Gauss, Karl Friedrich (1777-1855), German mathematician. Made numerous contributions to mathematics, incl. number theory, algebra, geometry; discovered a form of non-Euclidean geometry. Worked on terrestrial magnetism, electromagnetism; invented an electric telegraph with Weber (1833).

Gautier, Théophile (1811-72), French author. Poetry, with its emphasis on form, provided model for Parnassians. Novels incl. *Mlle de Maupin* (1835).

Gaveston, Piers (d. 1312), courtier, favourite of Edward II of England. The king allowed him great power, incl. regency in own absence, which roused anger of barons. They banished Gaveston twice, and finally had him beheaded.

gavial, *Gavialis gangeticus,* animal of crocodile group, distinguished by lon[g] narrow snout. Diet of fish; not dangerous [to] man. Found in large rivers of Ind[ia,] Burma.

Gawain or **Gawaine,** *see* ARTHURIAN LEGEN[D]

Gay, John (1685-1732), English poet, pla[y]wright. Remembered as author of *T[he] Beggar's Opera* (1728) satirizing litera[ry] conventions, political figures.

Gay-Lussac, Joseph Louis (1778-185[0]) French chemist, physicist. Discover[ed] independently Charles' law of expansion [of] gases. Stated law of combining g[as] volumes: volumes of gases which combi[ne] to give gaseous product are in ratio [of] small whole numbers to each other and [to] volume of product.

Gaza, city of NE Egypt, on Mediterrane[an] Sea. Pop. 118,000. Port; admin., commerc[ial] centre of Gaza Strip coastal regi[on.] Formerly one of chief cities of Philistin[e;] taken by Alexander the Great 332 B[C.] Battlefield in WWI (1917). Under Egy[pt] from 1949; occupied by Israel from 1967.

Grant's gazelle

gazelle, small swift-running antelope [of] Africa, Asia, genus *Gazella*. Usually fa[wn] coloured, with backward-pointing horns.

Gaziantep, city of S Turkey, near Syr[ian] border. Pop. 301,000. Agric. centre; tex[tile] mfg. Strategically important, taken [by] Saladin in 1183. Fell to French (1921) af[ter] siege during their Syrian mandate; [re]turned (1922). Formerly called Aintab.

Gdańsk (Ger. *Danzig*), city of N Poland, [on] Gulf of Gdańsk, cap. of Gdańsk prov. P[op.] 427,000. Port, exports coal, timber, gra[in;] shipbuilding, food processing. Hansea[tic] League member; under Prussian r[ule] 1793-1919. Free city under League [of] Nations from 1919; annexed by Germa[ny] 1939, returned to Poland 1945.

Gdynia, city of N Poland, on Gulf of Gdań[sk.] Pop. 224,000. Port, exports coal, timb[er,] grain; naval base, shipbuilding. Develo[ped] after 1924 from fishing village to repl[ace] free city of Danzig (Gdańsk) as ma[in] Polish port.

gearbox, box containing system of toot[hed] wheels which are used to transmit mo[tion] from one part of a machine to another. Different ratios of diameters of driving and driven wheels can be used to vary speed and torque.

ecko, any of Gekkonidae family of harmless lizards of tropical and subtropical regions. Many can walk vertically on smooth surfaces, using adhesive pads on feet. Catches insects with extensile tongue. Tail can break off when seized; new one grows.

eelong, city of S Victoria, Australia, on Corio Bay. Pop. 132,000. Port, exports wheat, wool, meat products; textile mfg., oil refining. Founded 1838.

eiger counter, device used to detect and measure ionizing radiation, esp. alpha, beta and gamma rays. Consists of positively charged wire inside negatively charged metal cylinder. Ions, formed by incoming radiation, migrate to electrodes and produce electrical pulse.

elatin, colourless, clear, water-soluble animal protein obtained from animal tendons, ligaments, *etc.* Used in food preparation and preservation, photography, as culture medium for bacteria, *etc.* Glue is impure form.

elderland, prov. of EC Netherlands. Area 5017 sq km (1937 sq mi); cap. Arnhem. Drained by Ijssel, Waal, Lower Rhine. Medieval duchy.

elignite, blasting explosive consisting of nitroglycerine, nitrocellulose, wood pulp and potassium nitrate.

ell-Mann, Murray (1929-), American physicist. Awarded Nobel Prize for Physics (1969) for contributions and discoveries concerning elementary particles and their interactions. Worked on theory of 'strange' particles; devised system of particle classification ('eight-fold way'). Introduced concept of QUARK as building block for elementary particles.

elsenkirchen, city of W West Germany, on Rhine-Herne canal. Pop. 318,000. Major coalmining centre of Ruhr coalfield; grew rapidly after 1850. Heavily bombed in WWII.

emini, *see* ZODIAC.

mstone, mineral which when cut and polished may be used as a gem. Hard, normally transparent and crystalline. Precious varieties incl. diamond, emerald, ruby, sapphire; semi-precious incl. amethyst, aquamarine, garnet.

ne, unit of hereditary material. Genes are arranged into linear sequence to form chromosomes, each gene occurring at a specific point. Composed of DNA; changes in structure of DNA cause mutation of genes, leading to changes in inheritable characteristics.

neral Agreement in Trades and Tariffs (GATT), United Nations agency estab. 1948). Aims to reduce tariffs *etc,* assist rade of developing countries.

neral strike, withdrawal of labour by workers in an entire indust. or throughout region or country. Often politically motivated in that it seeks govt. concessions or overthrow of govt. Examples incl. that in Russia (Oct. 1905), resulting in granting of democratically elected DUMA, and in Northern Ireland (May, 1974) which brought down power-sharing executive. In Britain, the **General Strike** (May, 1926) was called by TUC in response to national lockout of coalminers. Less than half the workers responded and govt. was able to keep most services running. TUC capitulated, miners remained on strike until Nov.

Genesis, in OT, 1st book giving an account of the creation of the world and of man. Traces Hebrew history from Abraham to Joseph. Generally thought to have been compiled after the Exile, but contains much Babylonian and Egyptian folklore, *eg* Flood, Creation myths.

Genet, Jean (1910-), French dramatist. Convicted criminal, became leading exponent of ABSURD drama. Plays incl. *The Maids* (1948), *The Balcony* (1956). Other works incl. novel *Our Lady of the Flowers* (1949).

genet, cat-like carnivore of genus *Genetta*, related to civet. Preys nocturnally on rodents, birds; found in Africa, S Europe.

genetics, branch of biology dealing with heredity and variation in similar or related animals and plants. Documented studies on sweet pea by Mendel were foundation. Modern developments are based on genetic code, which describes various arrangements of nitrogenous bases that constitute DNA, the fundamental genetic material.

Geneva *(Fr Genève,* Ger. *Genf),* city of SW Switzerland, on R. Rhône and L. Geneva, cap. of Geneva canton. Pop. 323,000. Cultural, commercial centre; watches, optical instruments; confectionery. Prehist. then Roman site; part of Holy Roman Empire during Middle Ages. Joined Swiss Confederation 1815. Centre of Reformation; Calvin's Academy (1559) became univ. (1873). Palais des Nations was seat of League of Nations 1920-46, now used by UN agencies. Red Cross hq.

Geneva, Lake (Fr. *Lac Léman,* Ger. *Genfersee),* on Swiss-French border. Rhône enters at E, leaves SW. Area 578 sq km (223 sq mi).

Geneva Convention, an international agreement (1864) regulating the treatment of wounded in war. Later extended to cover treatment of sick and prisoners and protection of civilians in war-time. Revised (1906, 1929, 1949).

Genghis Khan or **Jenghiz Khan** (*c* 1167–1227), Mongol chieftain. Conquered Mongolia (1206), most of Chin empire in China (1213-15), Turkestan, Transoxania, and Afghanistan (1218-24), and invaded SE Europe. He ruled finally over all lands between the Yellow and the Black seas. His grandson Kublai Khan conquered the rest of China.

Genoa *(Genova),* town of NW Italy, on Ligurian Sea, cap. of Liguria and of Genoa prov. Pop. 795,000. Port, shipbuilding; engi-

GEOLOGICAL TABLE: TIME SCALE

Estimated ages in millions of years

	ERA	PERIOD	EPOCH	TIME BEGAN	MAJOR EVENTS	ANIMAL AND PLANT LIFE
PHANEROZOIC EON	CENOZOIC	**Quaternary**	Holocene Pleistocene	*c* 10,000 yrs *c* 2	Retreat of ice; present landscape formed. Major Ice Ages; pluvials	Rise of man; beginning of extinction of mammals *eg* mammoths, sabre-tooth carnivores.
		Tertiary	Pliocene Miocene Oligocene Eocene Palaeocene	*c* 13 *c* 25 *c* 36 *c* 58 *c* 65	Alpine-Himalayan mountain building. Shallow seas in Europe; extensive clay plains formed.	Proliferation of mammals; ancestors of modern fauna. Vegetation of modern types.
	MESOZOIC	**Cretaceous**		*c* 135	Extensive inundation; chalk formation.	Echinoderms, lamelli-branchs, last ammonites. Dinosaurs become extinct.
		Jurassic		*c* 195	Widespread limestone formation.	Ammonites, brachio-pods, lamellibranchs, insects. 1st birds. Dinosaurs reach max. size.
		Triassic		*c* 225	Extensive arid, semi-arid areas. Red sands in North America.	Ammonites, crinoids, lamellibranchs. 1st mammals, dinosaurs.
	PALAEOZOIC	**Permian**		*c* 280	Increasing aridity; salt beds formed. Marls, sand-stones, evaporites developed.	Last trilobites. Increasing ammonites, reptiles. More advanced conifers.
		Carbonifer-ous Pennsylvan-ian Mississippian		*c* 345	Formation of coal measures. Shallow seas over continents, vast swamps.	Crinoids, brachiopods; increasing fish, amphibians, insects. 1st reptiles. Club mosses, horsetails.
		Devonian		*c* 395	Climax of Caledonian mountain building; formation of Old Red Sandstone.	Cephalopods, jawed fish, crinoids, last graptolites. Treefern forests.
		Silurian		*c* 435	Extensive seas; Caledonian mountain building continues.	Graptolites, trilobites, brachiopods, cephalopods. Jawless fish. 1st land plants.
		Ordovician		*c* 500	Extensive seas; beginning of Caledonian mountain building.	Graptolites dominant; also trilobites, crinoids, corals. 1st vertebrates (fish) in North America.
		Cambrian		*c* 570	Europe largely submerged. Large shallow seas covered North America.	Trilobites dominant; also graptolites, brachiopods. Some algae, lichens.
		PRECAMBRIAN ERA		*c* 4500	Formation, consolidation of continental shields *eg* Canadian, African, Australian.	Rare traces of rudimentary life, found only in Late Precambrian. Fore-runners of trilobites, worms, sponges, jellyfish. Some algae, fungi.

neering; univ. (1243). Medieval maritime republic, *fl* during Crusading era.

enre, style of painting in which subjects or scenes from everyday life are treated realistically. Genre painting was prominent in 17th-cent. Dutch art; its exponents incl. Steen, Vermeer, de Hooch.

ent, *see* GHENT.

entian, family, Gentianaceae, of low-growing mountain plants of worldwide distribution, esp. those of genus *Gentiana* with many species popular in rock gardens.

entile da Fabriano (*c* 1370-1427), Italian painter. A leading exponent of International Gothic style, his masterpiece is *Adoration of the Magi* (Florence).

enus, in biology, *see* CLASSIFICATION.

eoffrey of Monmouth (*c* 1100-54), British chronicler. Wrote *Historia Regum Britanniae,* which provided basis for the Arthurian cycles.

eography, study of the similarities, differences, and relationships between regions of the Earth's surface. Falls into 2 sections: physical geography (incl. study of climate, landforms, soils) and human geography (incl. economic, political, urban, historical geography). First developed by Greeks; regional description advanced by Strabo in Roman times. Arabs maintained study through Middle Ages until new impetus came from Spanish, Portuguese exploration of 15th-16th cents. Modern systematic (*ie* topical) and regional approaches to geography estab. by Humboldt and Ritter respectively. 20th cent. has seen ascendancy of systematic approach and quantitative techniques in analysing geographical data.

eology, study of the composition, structure and history of the Earth, and the processes resulting in its present state. Study of composition incl. crystallography, mineralogy, petrology and geochemistry; study of structure incl. structural geology and geophysics; study of history incl. historical geology, stratigraphy and palaeontology. Physical geology studies processes of change. Study of Earth dates back to Greek times. Modern geology pioneered by Hutton's theory of uniformitarianism (1795); 20th-cent. research in atomic structure, radioactivity, *etc,* has greatly advanced geology.

eological Table, *see* page 186.

eometry, branch of mathematics that deals with points, lines, surfaces and solids. Elementary geometry is based on exposition given by EUCLID. Analytic geometry uses algebraic methods to study geometry. Later developments incl. differential geometry, which uses calculus to study surfaces, projective geometry and non-Euclidean geometry.

eorge, St (*c* 4th cent.), patron saint of England. Traditionally, Palestinian soldier martyred in Asia Minor. In art, literature, represented as slayer of a dragon. Cult brought to England in Crusades. His red cross is on the Union Jack. No longer considered saint by RC church. Feast day 23rd April.

George I (1660-1727), king of Great Britain and Ireland (1714-27). Elector of Hanover (1698-1727), became king under terms of Act of SETTLEMENT. Left admin. of govt. to ministers, practice which initiated cabinet govt. in Britain.

George II (1683-1760), king of Great Britain and Ireland (1727-60). Son of George I, whose policy of ministerial govt. he continued. Last British king to lead troops in battle (Dettingen, 1743).

George III (1738-1820), king of Great Britain and Ireland (1760-1820). Succeeded grandfather George II. Ruled through sympathetic ministers (Bute, North) in attempt to assert authority until younger Pitt's ministry curbed ambitions. Chief event of reign was AMERICAN REVOLUTION, result of North's coercive policies. Intermittent insanity led to regency of his son (later George IV).

George IV (1762-1830), king of Great Britain and Ireland (1820-30). Served as prince regent during insanity of his father, George III (1811-20); leader of dissolute social set. Personally unpopular, esp. through attempts to divorce his wife, Caroline of Brunswick.

George V (1865-1936), king of Great Britain and Ireland (1910-36). Second son of Edward VII. Played role as moderator in constitutional crisis over Parliament Act of 1911. Married Mary of Teck (1867-1953). During WWI, changed name of royal house from Saxe-Coburg-Gotha to Windsor.

George VI (1895-1952), king of Great Britain and Northern Ireland (1936-52). Became king when his brother, Edward VIII, abdicated. Married Elizabeth Bowes-Lyon (1900-), now known as the Queen Mother. Elder daughter succeeded him as Elizabeth II.

George II (1890-1947), king of Greece (1922-3, 1935-47). Deposed, went into exile. After restoration, allowed METAXAS to take dictatorial powers. Exiled during German occupation, returned after plebiscite (1946) in favour of monarchy.

George, Stefan (1868-1933), German poet. Influenced by Nietzsche and French symbolists, saw poet as priest with duty to people as well as self.

George Cross, highest British civilian award for acts of courage. Instituted 1940.

George Town, Malaysia, *see* PENANG.

Georgetown, cap. of CAYMAN ISLANDS.

Georgetown, cap. of Guyana, Atlantic port at mouth of Demerara R. Pop. 182,000. Sugar, rice, bauxite exports.

Georgia, state of SE US. Area 152,489 sq km (58,876 sq mi); pop. 4,970,000; cap. Atlanta. Large areas of swamp and forest; Atlantic coastal plain rises gradually to Appalachians. Subtropical climate. Agric. produce incl. peanuts, cotton, maize, tobacco. Minerals esp. kaolin clay. Cotton milling, wood processing. British colony estab.

after struggle with Spanish (1754). One of original 13 colonies of US.

Georgian Soviet Socialist Republic, constituent republic of W USSR. Area *c* 69,700 sq km (26,900 sq mi); pop. 5,016,000; cap. Tbilisi. Bounded by Black Sea in W, Greater Caucasus in N and Lesser Caucasus in S. Tea, citrus fruit, tobacco grown on Black Sea coast; rich manganese deposits. Region contained ancient kingdom of Colchis, legendary home of Golden Fleece. As independent kingdom, *fl* in 12th and 13th cent., but accepted Russian protection in 18th cent. Joined USSR (1922), becoming constituent republic (1936).

Georgian style, name given to English architecture during reigns of George I, II and III (1714-1820). Revival of Palladianism, led by Colen Campbell, Earl of Burlington and W. Kent, dominated first half of period. Neo-Classicism of Adam, Soane, *etc,* dominated second half.

geranium, family, Geraniaceae, of widely distributed plants, esp. those of genera *Geranium* and *Pelargonium* native to S Africa. Cranesbill geranium grows wild in Americas.

gerbil, small burrowing rodent of desert regions of Africa, Asia. Large hind legs used for leaping. Mainly nocturnal, with large eyes and long tail; diet of seeds, grain. Popular as pet.

geriatrics, branch of medicine dealing with diseases and care of old people.

Géricault, [Jean Louis André] Théodore (1791-1824), French painter. Regarded as a founder of French Romantic school; painted many horse and racing subjects. Realistic treatment of *The Raft of the Medusa* (1819) provoked public protest.

German, W Germanic language of Indo-European family. Official language of Federal Republic of Germany, German Democratic Republic, Austria, and most common language in Switzerland. First language for many elsewhere, important as second esp. in commerce. Divided into High German (spoken in southern areas), Low German (northern lowlands). Modern standard German descends from German used for Luther's translation of Bible, a High German dialect.

germander, any plant of genus *Teucrium* of mint family. Worldwide distribution.

Germanic languages, branch of Indo-European family of languages. Divided into East, North and West Germanic groups. East incl. Gothic, Burgundian, Vandalic, all dead. North, also called Scandinavian, incl. Danish, Norwegian, Swedish, Icelandic; all descend from Old Norse. West incl. English, Dutch, German.

germanium (Ge), soft metalloid element; at. no. 32, at. wt. 72.59. Semiconductor, used in transistors; also used as a rectifier.

German measles, *see* RUBELLA.

German shepherd, *see* ALSATIAN.

Germany *(Deutschland),* country of NC Europe, now divided into East and West Germany. Language: German. Religions:

Germany

Protestant, RC. Low, sandy plain in N block mountains, forests in C; Rhine valley in W; Bavarian Alps in S. Main rivers Rhine, Elbe, Oder, Danube; extensive cana system. Industs. centred in Ruhr (W) Saxony (E). Separated from France or death of Charlemagne (AD 814), principalities formed Holy Roman Empire (962-1806). Confederation from 1815 under Prussian hegemony, empire estab. 1871 Colonial expansion in late 19th cent Nationalist, expansionist aims contributed to WWI, after which Weimar Republic proclaimed. Rise of Hitler led to WWI much territ. lost (incl. E Prussia), occupation by 4 allied powers 1945 followed by partition 1949. **East Germany** *(Deutsche Demokratische Republik),* occupied by USSR after WWII; communist govt. member of Warsaw Treaty Organization COMECON. Area *c* 108,000 sq km (42,000 sq mi); pop. 16,756,000; cap. East Berlin. **West Germany** *(Bundesrepublik Deutschland),* occupied by UK, USA, France after WWI federal govt., member of NATO, EEC. Area *c* 249,000 sq km (96,000 sq mi); pop 61,310,000; cap. Bonn.

germination, process whereby plan embryo within seed resumes growth after period of dormancy. This period varie from a few days (most grasses) to over 40 years (Indian lotus). Process require water, oxygen and in many cases light Temperature is also critical.

Germiston, city of S Transvaal, South Africa Pop. 281,000. Railway jct., importan goldmining and refining, indust. centre i Witwatersrand. Founded 1887, after discovery of gold.

germ warfare, the use of disease bacteria biological poisons, hormones, *etc* as weapon of war. Employed in crude form (pollution of water supplies, deliberate planting of contaminated material, *etc*) fo many years. It has been avoided in moder warfare despite much research.

Gershwin, George (1898-1937), America composer. Treated jazz idiom in symphon ic form. Works incl. *Rhapsody in Blue, A American in Paris* and Negro opera *Porg* *and Bess.* Also composed many tuneful songs for Broadway musicals.

Gestalt, in psychology, affirmation that experience consists of organized wholes (*gestalten*) rather than of sum of distinct parts.

Gestapo (*Geheime Staatspolizei*), secret police in Nazi Germany (1933-45). Combined with Hitler's SS after 1936 under Himmler. Carried out ruthless policy of investigation, torture and extermination. Indicted as one body at Nuremberg war crimes trials (1945-6).

Gethsemane, traditional site of Jesus' betrayal in garden at foot of Mount of Olives near Jerusalem.

Gettysburg, bor. of S Pennsylvania, US. Pop. 7000. Scene of Federal repulse of Confederate's advance into North during Civil War (1863); also of Lincoln's famous Address (1863), which contained famous statement of the principles of American govt. 'of the people, by the people, for the people'.

geyser, spring from which columns of superheated water and steam are intermittently ejected. Caused by hot lava heating water which has percolated into geyser's central tube; found in active or recently active volcanic areas. Famous geyser regions are Iceland, New Zealand, and Yellowstone Park, US.

Ghana, republic of W Africa, on Gulf of Guinea. Area 238,500 sq km (92,100 sq mi); pop. 10,969,000 cap. Accra. Official language: English. Religions: animist, Christianity. Largely forest, with savannah in N; main river Volta. Cocoa, hardwoods, palm products; also gold, diamonds, manganese. Former centre of slave trade; British Gold Coast colony estab. 1874. Ghana formed as independent state (1957) from Gold Coast, Ashanti, Togoland, Northern territs. Republic from 1960. Member of British Commonwealth.

Ghats, two mountain ranges of S India: Eastern Ghats (E coast), av. height *c* 450 m (1500 ft); Western Ghats, av. height *c* 900 m (3000 ft). Together enclose Deccan plain.

Ghent (Flem. *Gent,* Fr. *Gand),* city of WC Belgium, on R. Scheldt, cap. of East Flanders prov. Pop. 219,000. Port, canal to Terneuzen; industs. incl. textiles, steel. Hist. cap., cultural centre of Flanders. Castle, cathedral (12th cent.); Cloth Hall (14th cent.); univ. (1816).

gherkin, *see* CUCUMBER.

ghetto, section of a city inhabited mainly by members of racial or religious minority group and characterized by social deprivation. Originally applied to early medieval European cities in which segregation of Jews into autonomous community was voluntary. First compulsory segregation began late 14th cent. in Spain and Portugal; others incl. Frankfurt (1460), Venice (1516). Nazis estab. Jewish ghettos, *eg* in Warsaw.

Ghibellines, *see* GUELPHS AND GHIBELLINES.

Ghiberti, Lorenzo (1378-1455), Florentine sculptor. Best known for bronze doors of Baptistery in Florence.

Ghirlandaio or **Girlandaio, Domenico** (1449-94), Florentine fresco painter. Noted for his ability to portray contemporary life and manners, as in his *Calling of the Apostles* (Sistine Chapel, Rome). Michelangelo was apprenticed to him.

Giacometti, Alberto (1901-66), Swiss sculptor, painter. Known for elongated and emaciated statues of isolated figures.

giants, in myth and folklore, man-like beings of more than human size and strength, but lacking supernatural status of gods, civilization of men. In Greek myth, attempted unsuccessfully to conquer Olympian gods in revenge for defeat of TITANS; in Scandinavian myth, regarded as first of world's inhabitants. Perpetuated in allegories and folk stories, *eg* 'Jack the Giant Killer'.

Giant's Causeway, headland of N Northern Ireland, in former Co. Antrim. Comprises many levels of hexagonal basalt columns. In legend, built as giant's route to Scotland.

Gibbon, Edward (1737-94), English historian. Author of panoramic *The History of the Decline and Fall of the Roman Empire* (6 vols., 1776-88), inspired by visit to Rome. Attacked for criticism of rise of early Christianity.

Gibbon

gibbon, smallest of anthropoid apes, genus *Hylobates,* found in SE Asia. Arboreal, uses long arms to swing through branches.

Gibbons, Grinling (1648-1721), English woodcarver, sculptor, b. Rotterdam. Famous for carvings of fruit, flowers, and animals.

Gibbons, Orlando (1583-1625), English organist, composer. Organist at Westminster Abbey. Composed anthems, madrigals, *eg Silver Swan,* instrumental pieces.

Gibraltar, City of, city of S Iberian penin., on Str. of Gibraltar. Area 6.5 sq km (2.5 sq mi); pop. 30,000; rises to 425 m (1400 ft). Free port, heavily fortified naval base, tourist resort. Rock of Gibraltar was one of the ancient 'Pillars of Hercules'. Held by Moors from 8th cent., by Spain 1462-1704. Captured by Britain 1704; British crown colony 1830-1969. Still politically associated with Britain. Long claimed by Spain.

Gibraltar, Strait of, channel connecting Mediterranean Sea and Atlantic Ocean. Narrowest width *c* 13 km (8 mi); separates S Spain from N Africa. Headlands at Rock of Gibraltar (N) and Ceuta (S) formerly called Pillars of Hercules.

Gide, André (1869-1951), French author. Works reflect own struggle for self-development, balancing hedonism with asceticism. Novels incl. *La Porte étroite* (1909), *Les Faux-monnayeurs* (1926). Nobel Prize for Literature (1947).

Gielgud, Sir [Arthur] John (1904-), English stage, film actor, producer. Played many leading roles in Sheridan and Shakespeare (esp. Hamlet).

Gierek, Edward (1913-) Polish statesman. Succeeded Gomulka as first secretary of Politburo (1970). Resigned 1980 in face of widespread strikes in favour of free trade unions. Succeeded by Kania.

Gijón, city of Asturias, NW Spain, on Bay of Biscay. Pop. 188,000. Port, exports coal and iron ore; iron and steel, glass industs.

gila monster, *Heloderma suspectum,* venomous lizard of deserts of SW US and Mexico. Body covered in bands of orange and black.

Gilbert, Sir W[illiam] S[chwenck] (1836-1911), English author. Known as librettist of SULLIVAN's light operas, *eg Trial by Jury* (1875), *The Pirates of Penzance* (1879), *The Mikado* (1885). Also wrote humorous, cynical *Bab Ballads* (1869).

Gilbert and Ellice Islands, *see* TUVALU, KIRIBATI.

Gilgamesh, hero of Babylonian epic. Earliest known written epic (*c* 2000 BC) found on clay tablets in ruins of Nineveh. Gilgamesh story prob. much older, of Sumerian origin, tells of his search for immortality after friend Enkidu dies.

gill, organ in aquatic animals for absorption of oxygen dissolved in water. Consists of membrane or outgrowth of body surface through which oxygen passes into blood and carbon dioxide into water. Fish have internal gills; external gills found on amphibian larvae, molluscs, *etc.*

Gillray, James (1757-1815), English caricaturist. Satirized family of George III, the French, politicians and social customs of his day.

gin, alcoholic spirit distilled from grain and flavoured with juniper berries. Major producers are Netherlands, where it originated in 17th cent., Britain and US.

ginger, *Zingiber officinale,* perennial plant. Originally from S China. Hot, spicy root is sliced and preserved in syrup as confection. Ground ginger is used as spice.

ginkgo or **maidenhair tree,** *Ginkgo biloba,* deciduous tree, native to China. Fan-shaped leaves, fleshy seeds in edible kernel. Survivor of prehistoric era. Widely cultivated as ornament.

Ginsberg, Allen (1926-), American poet. Best known for *Howl* (1956) lamenting sickness of American society.

ginseng, aromatic plant of genus *Panax.* Aromatic root has sweetish taste and is valued medicinally.

Giorgione [da Castelfranco], orig. Giorgio Barbarelli (*c* 1477-1510), Venetian painter. Work has poetic, evocative quality, based on new effects of light and colour.

Giotto [di Bondone] (*c* 1266-*c* 1337), Florentine artist. Regarded as founder of modern painting, he broke with formula of Byzantine art and introduced new naturalism into his figures. Works incl. fresco cycles in churches in Padua, Assisi, Florence.

gipsy, *see* GYPSY.

gipsy moth, *Lymantria dispar,* European moth, extinct in Britain since *c* 1850. Introduced into North America, has become serious pest in forests.

Giraffe

giraffe, hoofed long-legged mammal of African grasslands. Tallest of animals (reaches height of 5.5 m/18 ft), uses long neck to eat leaves of trees. Two species genus *Giraffa.*

Girl Guides and **Girl Scouts,** *see* BOY SCOUTS.

Gironde, estuary of W France, *c* 72 km (45 mi) long, formed by jct. of Garonne and

Dordogne rivers near Bordeaux.

Girondists, French political party during Revolution. Moderate republicans, instrumental in estab. of First Republic (1792-3). Favoured European war to spread revolutionary ideas. Overthrown by extremist Jacobins and Cordeliers.

Giscard d'Estaing, Valéry (1926-), French statesman, president (1974-). Finance minister (1962-6, 1969-74). Leader of Independent Republicans (allied with Gaullists).

Gish, Dorothy, orig. Dorothy de Guiche (1898–1968), American silent film actress. Famous for roles in D.W. Griffith's films from 1912. Appeared with her sister, **Lillian Gish,** orig. Lillian de Guiche (1896-), in *Orphans of the Storm* (1922).

Gîza, El, or **Gizeh,** city of N Egypt, on R. Nile opposite Cairo. Pop. 893,000. Produces cotton textiles, cigarettes, footwear. Nearby are Great Pyramid of Khufu (Cheops) and the Sphinx.

glacier, moving mass of snow and ice formed in high mountains and polar regions. Compaction turns snow into névé then to granular ice. Types incl. mountain or valley glacier, piedmont glacier, ice sheet.

gladiators, the professional fighters of ancient Rome, who engaged in mortal combat as a public spectacle, using sword and shield or sometimes trident and net.

gladiolus, genus of corm-based plants native to S Africa. Member of Iridaceae family. Widely cultivated as garden plant. Sword-like leaves, spikes of funnel-shaped flowers.

Gladstone, William Ewart (1809-98), British statesman, PM (1868-74, 1880-5, 1886, 1892-4). Renowned orator, policies based upon strong religious and moral convictions. As chancellor of the exchequer, promoted free trade and progressive taxation policy. Headed Liberal govts. which achieved Irish land acts, civil service and army reforms, development of education. Last ministry, dominated by Irish problems, ended after defeat of HOME RULE bill.

Glamorgan, former county of S Wales. 1,299,000; co. town Cardiff. Mountainous in N; fertile Vale of Glamorgan in S; Gower Penin. in SW. Main rivers Taff, Neath. Major indust. area; rich coal deposits (Rhondda, Merthyr Tydfil); iron and steel works (Swansea, Port Talbot). From 1974 divided into **Mid Glamorgan** (area 1018 sq km/393 sq mi; pop. 538,000; admin. hq. Cardiff), **South Glamorgan** (area 416 sq km/161 sq mi; pop. 386,000; admin. hq. Cardiff), and **West Glamorgan** (area 816 sq km/315 sq mi; pop. 367,000; admin. hq. Swansea).

gland, organ which builds up chemical compounds from the blood and secretes them. Most glands discharge through ducts either to outer surface of skin, *eg* sweat glands, or to an inner surface, *eg* digestive glands secreting into gut. Ductless or ENDOCRINE GLANDS secrete hormones directly into the blood.

Glasgow, largest city of Scotland, admin. hq. of Strathclyde region, on R. Clyde. Pop. 810,000. Major port; industs. incl. shipbuilding, engineering, textiles, brewing, whisky distilling. Founded 6th cent. by St Kentigern; royal burgh, grew mainly 18th-19th cents. through tobacco, cotton trade. Has 12th-cent. cathedral; 2 univs. (1451, 1964).

glass, hard brittle substance, usually made by fusing sand (silica) with lime and soda or potash; molten mass is rapidly cooled to prevent crystallization. Other metallic oxides, *eg* lead, barium or aluminium, are added to increase durability, impart colour or provide special optical properties.

glass fibre, fine filaments of glass which may be woven into a cloth and impregnated with hard-setting resins. The resulting material is extremely strong, lightweight and corrosion resistant. Used in boat and vehicle-body construction.

Glastonbury, town of Somerset, SW England. Pop. 7000. In legend, site of 1st English Christian church estab. by Joseph of Arimathea; reputed burial place of King Arthur. Has ruined 8th-cent. abbey.

glaucoma, disease of the eye characterized by abnormally high pressure within eyeball; often results in impaired vision or blindness. Usually requires surgery or treatment by drugs.

Gleiwitz, *see* GLIWICE.

Glencoe, valley of Highland region, W Scotland. Scene of massacre (1692) of Macdonalds by Campbells and English.

Glendower, Owen (*c* 1359-*c* 1416), Welsh chieftain. Led series of revolts in Wales against Henry IV, defeating king's forces in campaigns of 1400-2. Lost ground after 1405, the revolt being effectively over by 1409.

Glenrothes, town and admin. hq. of Fife region, Scotland. Pop. 27,000. Founded as new town (1948).

gliding, sport of flying heavier-than-air machine without engine power, using air currents to gain height, and gravity to maintain forward motion. First gliders were developed by Otto Lilienthal in 1890s and also by the Wright brothers.

Glinka, Mikhail Ivanovich (1804-57), Russian composer. Created characteristic 'Russian' style. Best-known works are operas *A Life for the Tsar* and *Russlan and Ludmilla*.

Gliwice (Ger. *Gleiwitz*), city of S Poland. Pop. 199,000. Coalmining, steel works, engineering. Under Prussian rule 1742-1945.

glockenspiel, tuned percussion instrument consisting of set of steel bars of different lengths, which player hits with hammers. Produces bell-like sound.

Glorious Revolution (1688-9), in English history, overthrow of Catholic James II by united Whig and Tory opposition. William of Orange was petitioned by Whig and

Tory leaders to rule as William III jointly with his wife Mary, James' Protestant daughter. Their acceptance of Bill of Rights assured Parliament's authority in place of 'divine right of kings'.

Gloucester, Thomas of Woodstock, Duke of (1355-97), English nobleman. Led baronial opposition to Richard II, but reconciled (1389); later arrested for further intrigues and prob. murdered.

Gloucestershire, county of W England. Area 2638 sq km (1018 sq mi); pop. 495,000. Cotswold Hills in E (sheep); lower Severn valley in C (dairying, fruit); Forest of Dean in W (coal). Admin. hq. **Gloucester,** on R. Severn. Pop. 91,000. City, river port; timber trade. Hist. Roman town; has cathedral (15th cent.) on site of abbey (681).

glow-worm, *see* FIREFLY.

Gluck, Christoph Willibald von (1714-87), German composer, active in Paris, Vienna. Reformed opera by stressing importance of drama, simplicity. Works incl. *Orfeo, Alceste.*

glucose, crystalline sugar, occurring in fruit and honey. Sugars and other carbohydrates are converted into glucose in body; its oxidation to carbon dioxide and water is major energy source. Produced commercially by hydrolysis of starch.

gluten, sticky protein substance, found in wheat and other grain; gives dough its elastic consistency.

glutton, *see* WOLVERINE.

glycerol or **glycerin[e],** colourless viscous alcohol, obtained by hydrolysis of fats during manufacture of soap. Glycerides, its esters with fatty acids, are chief constituents of fats and oils. Used in manufacture of explosives, resins, foodstuffs, toilet preparations and as antifreeze.

glycogen or **animal starch,** carbohydrate formed from glucose and stored in animal tissues, esp. liver and muscles. Can be reconverted into glucose to supply body's energy needs.

glycol or **ethylene glycol,** colourless viscous liquid, used in manufacture of polyester fibres (Dacron, Terylene) and as antifreeze.

gnat, two-winged fly of mosquito family with piercing mouthparts and long antennae.

gneiss, coarse-grained, crystalline rock, resembling granite. Formed by metamorphism of igneous and sedimentary rock; displays alternate bands of constituents, *eg* feldspar, hornblende, mica.

Gnosticism, system of belief combining ideas from Christian theology, Greek philosophy and diverse mystic cults. Arose during 1st cent. Followers believed in salvation through direct spiritual knowledge rather than faith. Declared heretical by early Christians.

gnu or **wildebeest,** large antelope of E and S Africa, with buffalo-like head, hairy mane, beard and tail. Two species, genus *Connochaetes.*

Goa, former Portuguese enclave of W India. Area *c* 3500 sq km (1350 sq mi); pop. 537,000; cap. Panjim. Captured by Portuguese (1510), seized by India (1961). Part of Union Territ. of Goa, Daman and Diu.

goat, hollow-horned ruminant, genus *Capra,* related to sheep. Usually coarse-haired males bearded. Domesticated varieties kept for nutritious milk, flesh, hair; wild goats incl. IBEX.

Gobelins, Manufacture Nationale des, French tapestry manufactory. Founded in 15th cent. as dye works, purchased 1662 by Louis XIV. Now state-controlled.

Gobi Desert, sandy region of C Asia (China, Mongolia). Area *c* 1,295,000 sq km (500,000 sq mi); av. alt. 1200 m (4000 ft). Grassy fringes inhabited by pastoral Mongols.

goby, any of Gobiidae family of spiny-finned carnivorous fish. Pelvic fins joined to form suction disc, used to cling to rocks. Freshwater and saltwater varieties.

God, in the three major monotheistic religions (Judaism, Christianity, Islam), creator and ruler of the universe. Regarded as eternal, infinite, immanent, omniscient. Often given attributes of goodness, love, mercy. In Christianity, believed to have lived on earth in person of Jesus Christ. *See* TRINITY.

Godavari, river of SC India. Flows *c* 1440 km (900 mi) SE from Western Ghats (Maharashtra) across the Deccan to Bay of Bengal. Sacred to Hindus.

Godiva (*fl c* 1040–80), wife of Leofric, earl of Mercia. According to legend, she rode naked through the streets of Coventry so that her husband would grant her request to relieve the people of his heavy taxes.

Godolphin, Sidney Godolphin, 1st Earl of (1645-1712), English statesman. Noted for financial expertise, served as first lord of treasury (1684-9, 1700-1, 1702-10). Close associate of Marlborough. Dismissed (1710) by Queen Anne.

Godthaab, cap. of Greenland, on Godthaab Fjord. Pop. 9000. Port; founded 1721, first Danish colony on Greenland.

Godunov, Boris (*c* 1551-1605), tsar of Russia (1598-1605). Ruled as regent during reign of Feodor I (1584-98) before succeeding him. Prob. had Dmitri, Feodor's brother and heir, murdered. Died while opposing pretender who claimed to be Dmitri.

Godwin (d. 1053), earl of Wessex, chief adviser to Canute and Edward the Confessor. Helped Edward to the throne (1042) and married his daughter Edith to him. Led opposition to king's French favourites, for which he and sons were exiled. Invaded England (1052), forced Edward to reinstate him. His son Harold succeeded Edward for 4 months.

Godwin, William (1756-1836), English writer. Best known for *An Enquiry Concerning Political Justice* (1793) arguing that best society would be one of rational individualists. Theories influenced Romantic poets. Wrote novel, *Caleb Williams* (1794). Husband of Mary WOLLSTONECRAFT.

Godwin-Austen, Mount, *see* K2.

Bar-tailed godwit

godwit, migrant wading bird of sandpiper family, genus *Limosa*. Inhabits northern regions.

Goebbels, Paul Joseph (1897-1945), German political leader. Nazi propaganda minister (1933-45); noted orator. Committed suicide during fall of Berlin.

Goering or **Göring, Hermann Wilhelm** (1893-1946), German political leader. Took part in Hitler's Munich *Putsch* (1923). Nazi air minister (1933); controlled German economy (1937-43). Responsible for expansion of Luftwaffe and air war against Britain (1940-1). Committed suicide after being sentenced to death at Nuremberg trials.

Goes, Hugo van der (d. 1482), Flemish painter. Works incl. *Portinari Altarpiece* (Florence), large work depicting the Adoration of the Shepherds.

Goethe, Johann Wolfgang von (1749-1832), German author. Leading figure in STURM UND DRANG movement, also held important cabinet post at Weimar and researched into plant biology and optics. Known for romantic novel *The Sorrows of Young Werther* (1774). Later classical works incl. plays *eg Iphigenia in Tauris* (1787), novel *Wilhelm Meister* (vol. 1, 1796). Later works indicate regained sympathy with Romanticism. *Faust* (Part I, 1808; Part II, 1832) remains his masterpiece, a symbolic representation of the human search for knowledge and experience.

Gogh, Vincent van (1853-90), Dutch painter. Early work, dark and heavy in form, replaced by lighter impressionist technique in Paris (1886). Settled at Arles (1888), where he was briefly joined by Gauguin. From 1888, subject to fits of insanity, he produced portraits and landscapes, painted in bold colour with swirling brushstrokes. Committed suicide.

Gogol, Nikolai Vasilyevich (1809-52), Russian author. Works, mixing stark realism with grotesque caricature and fantasy, incl. short story 'The Overcoat' (1842), satirical comedy *The Inspector General* (1836), novel *Dead Souls* (1842).

goitre, enlargement of thyroid gland producing swelling on front of neck. Simple goitre is caused by iodine deficiency; incidence is reduced by adding iodine to table salt. Exophthalmic goitre or Grave's disease, caused by over-activity of thyroid, is accompanied by protrusion of eyeballs.

Golan Heights, mountain ridge of SW Syria. Great strategic importance; taken by Israelis in 1967 war; after 1973 war occupied by UN forces.

gold (Au), ductile, malleable metallic element; at. no. 79, at. wt. 196.97. Chemically inert; resists corrosion; found free. Used in coinage, jewellery and dentistry (alloyed with silver or copper).

Gold Coast, *see* GHANA.

goldcrest, *Regulus regulus,* smallest European bird, with yellow crown, olive green upper-parts. Found in coniferous woods.

Golden eagle

golden eagle, *Aquila chrysaetos,* large eagle of mountainous regions of N hemisphere. Dark plumage with golden tinge on head.

Golden Fleece, in Greek myth, fleece of winged ram which carried Phrixus and Helle from the intrigues of their father's concubine. Phrixus sacrificed ram; fleece guarded by dragon at Colchis. Later recovered by JASON.

Golden Gate Bridge, suspension bridge over Golden Gate waterway, San Francisco, US. Opened 1937, its total length is 2824 m (9266 ft); main span 1280 m (4200 ft) is one of world's longest bridges.

Golden Horde, Mongol warriors of Batu Khan, so-called from the splendour of his camp. Their empire was estab. in mid-13th cent. and comprised most of Russia. They took part in Kublai Khan's Chinese conquests. Empire broke up into autonomous khanates after 1405, finally crushed by IVAN III (1487).

Golden Horn, *see* BOSPORUS.

goldenrod, any of genus *Solidago* of perennial plants of Compositae family, with spikes of yellow flowers. Native to Europe and North America. Formerly thought to have medicinal properties.

goldfinch, *Carduelis carduelis,* Eurasian finch with scarlet face, black and yellow wings.

goldfish, *Carassius auratus,* small freshwater fish of carp family, of Asiatic origin. Many domestic varieties; often kept in ponds, fishbowls.

Golding, William Gerald (1911-), English novelist. Best known for first novel, moral allegory *Lord of the Flies* (1954). Other novels incl. *Pincher Martin* (1956), *The*

Spire (1964), *Rites of Passage* (1980).

Goldoni, Carlo (1707-93), Italian dramatist. Known for comedies on everyday subjects *eg La Bottega del caffè* (1751), *La Locandiera* (1753).

Goldsmith, Oliver (1730-74), English author, b. Ireland. Known for humorous pastoral novel *The Vicar of Wakefield* (1766). Also wrote poem *The Deserted Village,* regretting rural enclosures, and comedy *She Stoops to Conquer* (1773).

gold standard, system whereby a unit of currency is equal to and redeemable in a specified quantity of gold. Used as international reference for currencies in late 19th cent. International gold standard broke down in WWI. Many currencies now fixed to US dollar.

golf, game played with ball and clubs over outdoor course. Origins can be traced back to 15th cent. in Scotland. Original 13 rules were drawn up by Royal and Ancient Club, St Andrews, Scotland (1754). Great growth as leisure activity and as professional sport, esp. in US, dates from 1920s. Standard golf course comprises 18 holes of varying length (total *c* 4500-5000 m/5000-6000 yd).

Golgotha, Aramaic name for CALVARY.

Goliath, in OT, giant champion of Philistines, enemies of Israel. Killed by David with a stone from his sling (1 Samuel 17).

Gomulka, Wladyslaw (1905-), Polish political leader. Became leader of Polish Communist Party (1943), expelled (1949) for 'nationalist deviations'. Reinstated after Poznań riots (1956). Resigned during 1970 riots over massive food price increases; succeeded by Gierek.

gong, percussion instrument of Oriental origin, consisting of free-hanging metal disc with turned-in edges; struck with mallet.

gonorrhoea, acute infectious inflammation of mucous membranes of genital passages; caused by a gonococcus transmitted during sexual intercourse. Symptoms are pain in passing water and discharge of pus from urethra. Treated by antibiotics, *eg* penicillin.

Good Friday, the Friday before Easter Sunday, observed by Christians as commemoration of Jesus' crucifixion.

Good Hope, Cape of, headland of SW Cape Prov., South Africa, on W side of False Bay. Rounded (1488) and named 'Cape of Storms' by Bartolomeu Dias; renamed by Henry the Navigator.

Goodman, Benjamin David ('Benny') (1909-), American band leader, clarinettist. Organized his own orchestra from 1933, and contributed to development of swing music.

Goodwin Sands, sandbars off Kent, SE England. Length 16 km (10 mi); shipping hazard, marked by lightships.

Goodyear, Charles (1800-60), American inventor. Developed vulcanization process for rubber (1839).

goose, long-necked web-footed bird, related to duck and swan. Two genera, *Anser* being grey, *Branta* black. Domestic goose bred from greylag goose, *Anser anser.* Wild goose is migratory, breeding in tundra regions of N hemisphere.

Gooseberry

gooseberry, shrub of genus *Ribes* of saxifrage family. Esp. *R. uvacrispa,* native to cool, moist climates. Berry used in preserves.

gopher, small burrowing rodent of Geomyidae family of North America. Carries food in fur-lined cheek pouches.

Gordon, Charles George (1833-85), British soldier and administrator, known as 'Chinese' Gordon. Suppressed TAIPING REBELLION in China. Governor of Sudan (1877-80); killed after 10-month siege of Khartoum, having been sent to evacuate it during MAHDI's revolt.

Gordon, Lord George (1751-93), English politician. Led mob which marched on Houses of Parliament to petition for repeal of Catholic Relief Act, which had lifted civil restrictions on Catholics. March degenerated into week-long destructive 'Gordon Riots' (1780). Tried for treason, acquitted.

Gorgons, in Greek myth, three sisters (Euryale, Medusa, Stheno) with snakes instead of hair. Their gaze turned people to stone. Medusa, only mortal one, slain by Perseus.

gorilla, *Gorilla gorilla,* largest of anthropoid apes, reaching height of 1.8 m/6 ft; found in forest of W equatorial Africa. Terrestrial, walks on all fours using knuckles; vegetarian diet.

Göring, *see* GOERING.

Gorki, Maksim, pseud. of Aleksei Maksimovich Peshkov (1868-1936), Russian author. Early works, *eg* play *The Lower Depths* (1902), autobiog. *Childhood* (1913-14), draw on wide variety of experiences to express humanist ideals. After Revolution, formulated concept of 'socialist realism'.

Gorky or **Gorki,** city of USSR, C European RSFSR; major port at confluence of Volga and Oka. Pop. 1,344,000. Indust. centre, producing textiles, automobiles, chemicals. Founded as Nizhni Novgorod.

Görlitz, town of SE East Germany, on R. Neisse. Pop. 89,000. On Polish border; engineering, textiles.

orse or **furze,** spiny evergreen bush of Leguminosae family. Fragrant yellow flowers followed by black, hairy seed pods. Species incl. common *Ulex europaeus.*

orton, John Grey (1911-), Australian statesman, Liberal PM (1968-71).

oshawk, *Accipiter gentilis,* hawk of Eurasia, North America. Trained for falconry.

ospels of Matthew, Mark, Luke and **John,** first 4 books of NT. First 3 (known as Synoptic Gospels) agree in subject matter and order of events of life, death and teachings of Jesus. Gospel according to John is a more philosophical book demonstrating Jesus as the vital force in the world.

osport, town of Hampshire, S England. Pop. 76,000. Port on Portsmouth Harbour; yacht building; has naval barracks.

ossaert, Jan, *see* MABUSE, JAN.

öta Canal, waterway of S Sweden. Length *c* 385 km (240 mi), from Göteborg via R. Göta, Lakes Vänern, Vättern to Baltic Sea near Söderköping. Opened 1832.

öteborg or **Gothenburg,** city of SW Sweden, icefree port on Kattegat at mouth of R. Göta. Pop. 693,000. Fishing; marine engineering. Founded (1619) by Gustavus Adolphus; cathedral, univ. (1891).

othenburg, *see* GÖTEBORG.

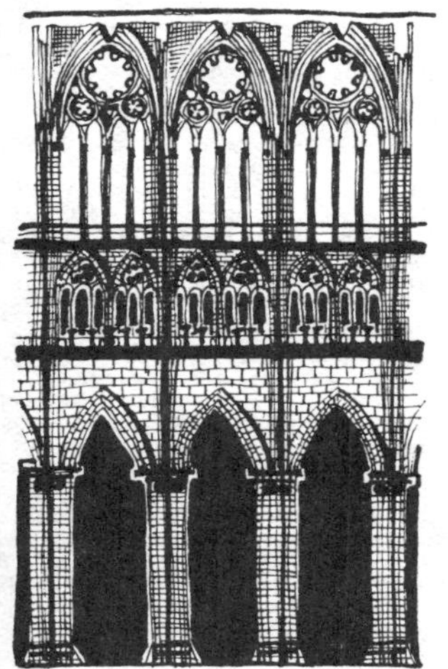

Gothic: detail of Amiens Cathedral

othic, style of architecture which developed in France (12th cent.) and was dominant in W Europe until 16th cent. Characterized by use of flying buttresses, ribbed vaulting, pointed arches. English Gothic is divided into Early English, decorated and perpendicular.

Gothic novel, literary genre characterized by gloom, the grotesque and the supernatural. Originated with Horace Walpole's *Castle of Otranto* (1764). Other Gothic writers incl. Ann Radcliffe.

Gothic revival, in architecture, revival of Gothic style in late 18th and 19th cents., esp. in Britain and US. Influential writings of Pugin and Ruskin made it dominant in Victorian era, esp. for design of churches.

Goths, Germanic people, originally inhabiting the Vistula basin, who invaded E parts of Roman empire in 3rd and 4th cents. Divided into 2 branches: West Goths or VISIGOTHS; East Goths or OSTROGOTHS.

Gotland, Baltic isl. of SE Sweden. Area 3173 sq km (1225 sq mi); cap. Visby. Cereals, sugar beet; tourism. Trade centre from Stone Age. Taken by Sweden (1280); held by Danish (1570-1645).

Göttingen, city of NE West Germany, on R. Leine. Pop. 124,000. Precision instruments, machinery mfg. Hanseatic League member from 1351. Univ. (1724).

gouache, method of painting which mixes watercolours with gum arabic, thus rendering them opaque.

Gouda, town of W Netherlands. Pop. 59,000. Market for Gouda cheese; pottery. Gothic town hall.

Gounod, Charles (1818-93), French composer. Outstanding works are operas *Faust* and *Romeo and Juliet.*

gourami, *Osphronemus goramy,* freshwater food fish of SE Asia. Brightly coloured varieties popular as aquarium fish.

gourd, member of Cucurbitaceae family of trailing plants with succulent, usually edible fruit *eg* squash, melon, pumpkin; mostly of Asian and Mexican origin. Esp. *Cucurbita maxima,* a globular yellow gourd which weighs up to 110 kg/240 lb.

gout, metabolic disease confined mainly to males. Characterized by excess of uric acid in blood and deposition of sodium urate crystals in joints. Results in painful and tender inflammation of affected parts (often big toe). Treatment by drugs and dietary control.

Gower, John (d. 1408), English poet. Friend of Chaucer, known for moral and didactic works, *eg Confessio Amantis* (1390).

Gowon, Yakubu (1934-), Nigerian military, political leader. Emerged as head of federal military govt. after 1966 coups. Crushed Biafran attempt to secede (1967-70). Overthrown by coup (1975) after period of economic mismanagement.

Goya [y Lucientes], Francisco José de (1746-1828), Spanish painter. Court painter to the king (1786), his paintings of royal family show his contempt for their stupidity. Produced series of etchings incl. 'Caprices', 'Bullfight', 'Disasters of War'. Macabre 'black paintings' of later years incl. *Saturn Devouring his Children.*

Gozo, *see* MALTA.

Gracchus, Tiberius Sempronius (163-133 BC), Roman politician. As tribune (133), introduced law to redistribute land; killed during subsequent riots. His brother, **Gaius Sempronius Gracchus** (153-121 BC), was elected tribune (123, 122), reintroduced Tiberius' agrarian reforms and reduced power of aristocracy. Killed during election riots.

Grace, W[illiam] G[ilbert] (1848-1915), English cricketer. Greatest cricketer of his times, he scored over 54,000 runs, incl. 126 centuries, and took over 2800 wickets in his first-class career. Captained England 13 times.

grace, in Christian theology, the unmerited love and favour of God towards man, which redeems his original sin and allows him to enjoy eternal life. Most theologies retain man's freedom in accepting grace, but CALVINISM holds that grace is irresistible but only offered to those whose salvation is predestined.

Graces, in Greek myth, three sister goddesses, daughters of Zeus. Personification of charm and beauty in human life and nature. They are Aglaea (Brilliance) Euphrosyne (Joy), Thalia (Bloom).

graft, in surgery, *see* TRANSPLANTATION.

grafting, in horticulture, practice of uniting two plants and growing them as one. The stock may be a mature plant or a root, the scion (part to be grafted on) may be a bud or a cutting.

Graham, Martha (1895-), American choreographer, dancer. One of most important figures in modern dance.

Graham, William Franklin ('Billy') (1918-), American evangelist. Has used revivalist techniques with success in US and abroad from 1949.

Grahame, Kenneth (1859-1932), British author. Remembered for children's classic *The Wind in the Willows* (1908).

Graham Land, mountainous penin. of Antarctica, lying between Bellingshausen and Weddell seas. Part of British Antarctic Territ. from 1962.

Grail, Holy, in medieval legend and literature, variously depicted as chalice, dish, stone, or cup. Many pagan elements in legend, but best-known version is Christian one, identifying Grail as cup used in Last Supper, later used by Joseph of Arimathea to catch crucified Christ's blood. Carried by Joseph to England. Became subject of quest by Arthur's knights, would be revealed only to pure knight. *See* ARTHURIAN LEGEND.

Grainger, Percy Aldridge (1882-1961), Australian composer, pianist. Known for arrangements of folk music, *eg Shepherd's Hey, Country Gardens.* Settled in US (1914).

gram, unit of mass in c.g.s. system; 1000 grams = 1 kilogram = 2.20462 pounds.

grammar school, in UK, state-financed secondary school, attended by pupils selected on academic ability. Also *see* COMPREHENSIVE EDUCATION.

gramophone or **phonograph,** instrument fo[r] reproducing sound that has bee[n] mechanically transcribed in a spira[l] groove on a disc or cylinder. Needl[e] following the groove in rotating disc o[r] cylinder picks up and transmits the soun[d] vibrations. First built (1878) by Thoma[s] Edison; use of discs introduced (1887) b[y] Emile Berliner. Subsequent development[s] incl. electronic reproduction, stereo.

Grampian, region of NE Scotland. Area 870[0] sq km (3360 sq mi); pop. 464,000. Admin. hq Aberdeen. Created 1975, incl. forme[r] Morayshire, Banffshire, Aberdeenshire Kincardineshire.

Grampians, mountain system of Scotland, N of line joining Helensburgh and Stone haven, and S of Great Glen. Incl. Be[n] Nevis, Cairngorms.

grampus, *see* KILLER WHALE.

Gramsci, Antonio (1891-1937), Italian polit[i]cal thinker. Helped found Italian Commu[]nist party. Developed Marxist concept o[f] hegemony to show how dominant clas[s] projects its economic, political and socia[l] attitudes, so that these are accepted a[s] natural order; thus revolution involve[s] creation of alternative hegemony as wel[l] as transfer of political and economi[c] power.

Granada, city of S Spain, cap. of Granad[a] prov. Pop. 203,000. Agric. market, touris[t] centre, univ. (1531). Cap. of Moorish King[]dom from 1238; last Moorish stronghold i[n] Spain, fell to Castile 1492. Mooris[h] architecture incl. Alhambra palace (13t[h] cent.); cathedral (16th cent.) contain[s] tombs of Ferdinand and Isabella. Univ (1531).

Gran Chaco, *see* CHACO.

Grand Alliance, War of the (1688-97[)] conflict between France and Europea[n] coalition known as League of Augsbur[g] (Grand Alliance after 1689), begun whe[n] Louis XIV invaded Palatinate. England ha[d] sea victories, but Alliance was defeated i[n] land battles. Concluded by Treaty o[f] RYSWICK.

Grand Banks, *see* LABRADOR CURRENT.

Grand Canal *(Yun-ho),* waterway of [E] China. Extends from Peking to Hangchow *c* 1600 km (1000 mi) long. Navigab[le] throughout year by junks, small steamer[s]. Begun in 6th cent. BC taking 2000 years t[o] complete. Economic importance now re[]duced after silting.

Grand Canyon, gorge of NW Arizona, US; o[f] Colorado R. Length 349 km (217 mi); widt[h] 6.4-29 km (4-18 mi); depth 1.6 km (*c* 1 mi[)]. Has spectacular scenery. Popular touris[t] region of geological importance. Part o[f] Grand Canyon National Park.

Grand National, annual English steeple[]chase, run since 1839 in March or April a[t] Aintree, Liverpool, over course 4.5 mi (7 km) long.

Grand Rapids, town of WC Michigan, US; o[n] Grand R. Pop. 564,000. Agric. market [in] fruit-growing area; furniture, paper, ele[c]trical goods mfg.

Grand Remonstrance, list of protests against autocratic rule of Charles I of England, drawn up by Long Parliament (1641). Demanded parliamentary control of appointment of royal ministers, church reform.

Grangemouth, town of Central region, C Scotland; on Firth of Forth at E end of Forth and Clyde Canal. Pop. 25,000. Port; oil refining, chemicals mfg.

granite, coarse-grained, crystalline, igneous rock. Whitish-grey in colour, hard; consists mainly of quartz, feldspar, mica. Formed at depth, occurs as dykes, sills, batholiths; often exposed by erosion of overlying rocks. Used in building. Commonest of plutonic rocks.

Gran Paradiso, mountain of NW Italy, in Graian Alps. Highest peak (4059 m/13,323 ft) in Italy.

Grant, Cary, orig. Archibald Leach (1904-), British film actor. Star since early 1930s as suave, often humorous, hero of such films as *Bringing up Baby* (1938), *Arsenic and Old Lace* (1944).

Grant, Ulysses Simpson (1822-85), American general and statesman, president (1869-77). Commanded Union army (1864-5) in Civil War after success of his Vicksburg campaign. Wore down Confederate army by sustained war of attrition, forcing Lee's surrender at Appomattox Courthouse (1865). Republican admin. characterized chiefly by bitter partisan politics and corruption.

grape, smooth-skinned juicy berry of many vines of genus *Vitis*. Globular or oblong shaped, colours vary from green to white, black to purple; grows in clusters. Numerous hybrids and varieties of Old and New World types. Since ancient times eaten both fresh and dried (raisins, currants, sultanas) as fruit, and fermented to produce wine.

grapefruit, *Citrus paradisi,* edible fruit widely cultivated in tropical areas. Round in shape, growing in clusters, with bitter yellow rind and acid juicy pulp.

Grape hyacinth

grape hyacinth, any plant of genus *Muscari,* hardy bulbous perennial of lily family. Spikes of small blue flowers. Over 40 species native to Europe and Asia Minor.

graphite, soft crystalline form of carbon, known as plumbago or black lead. Occurs naturally. Used as lubricant, in electrical machinery and in making 'lead' pencils.

graptolites, extinct colonial animals, whose skeletons are found as fossils in Cambrian, Ordovician and Silurian rocks. Classified among Protochordata.

Grass, Günter (1927-), German author, sculptor. Novels incl. *The Tin Drum* (1959), *Dog Years* (1963), *Local Anaesthetic* (1969), reflect political concerns. Other works incl. plays, poetry.

grass, any plant of Gramineae family. Long, narrow leaves, jointed stems, flowers in spikelets, seed-like fruit, *eg* wheat, sugar cane, bamboo. Also incl. hay and pasture grasses. Worldwide distribution.

grasshopper, insect of order Orthoptera, with hind legs adapted for jumping, thickened forewings, membranous hind wings. Two families: short-horned and long-horned. Males make chirping noise by rubbing body parts.

grass of parnassus, *Parnassia palustris,* perennial plant with solitary, delicate, white buttercup-like flower. Found in European marshland.

grass snake, *Natrix natrix,* harmless snake common in Europe. Good swimmer, often found near water; diet of mice, fish, frogs. Normally greenish-brown with yellow collar.

Grattan, Henry (1746-1820), Irish politician, patriot. Led opposition which secured (1782) right of Irish parliament to initiate legislation; gained vote for Catholics in Ireland. Supported Catholic Emancipation; opposed Act of Union (1800) ending Irish parliament.

Graubünden, *see* GRISONS.

gravel, coarse sediment, precisely defined in geology as having particle size between 2 mm and 4 mm. Commonest constituent is quartz. Term also used loosely for mixture of pebbles and rock fragments, used in roadbuilding *etc*.

Graves, Robert Ranke (1895-), English author. Known for autobiog. *Good-bye to All That* (1929) giving account of WWI experiences, historical novels of classical Rome, *eg I, Claudius* (1934), mythography, esp. *The White Goddess* (1948), and poetry in *Collected Poems* (1965).

Gravesend, town of Kent, SE England, on R. Thames. Pop. 54,000. Yachting centre; customs and pilot station.

gravitation, universal force of attraction between bodies. Newton's law of gravitation states that any 2 particles attract each other with force proportional to product of their masses and inversely proportional to distance between them. Gravity is gravitational force between Earth and bodies near its surface; accounts for weight of a body and its tendency to fall to earth. Modern gravitational theories are based on Einstein's general theory of relativity, in which distribution of matter determines the structure of SPACE-TIME CONTINUUM.

gravitational collapse, in astronomy, tendency of a star to contract under influence of its own gravitation as its store of nuclear fuel becomes depleted. Depending on mass of star, may become white dwarf, supernova or neutron star; for sufficiently large mass, BLACK HOLE may be formed.

Gray, Thomas (1716-71), English poet. Famous for 'Elegy Written in a Country Churchyard' (1751).

grayling, *Thymallus thymallus,* grey-coloured freshwater fish of salmon family, widely distributed in Europe.

Gray's Inn, *see* INNS OF COURT.

Graz, city of SE Austria, on R. Mur, cap. of Styria prov. Pop. 249,000. Produces iron, steel, textiles, paper. Gothic cathedral, univ. (1586).

Great Artesian Basin, artesian water-bearing basin of E Australia. Largest in world, area c 1,735,000 sq km (670,000 sq mi); mainly in SW Queensland.

Great Australian Bight, large bay of S coast of South and Western Australia, part of Indian Ocean. Extends *c* 1125 km (700 mi) E-W.

Great Barrier Reef, coral reef off NE coast of Australia, extends *c* 2000 km (1250 mi) from Torres Str. to Tropic of Capricorn.

Great Bear Lake, W Mackenzie Dist., Northwest Territs., Canada. Area 31,800 sq km (*c* 12,275 sq mi). Drained by Great Bear R. into Mackenzie R. Navigable only 4 months of year.

Great Britain, largest isl. of British Isles, comprising ENGLAND, SCOTLAND, WALES, and isls. governed with mainland (but not N Ireland, Isle of Man, Channel Isls.). Area 230,608 sq km (89,038 sq mi). Bounded by Atlantic, Irish Sea (N, W), English Channel (S), North Sea (E). Highland in N, W (Scottish Highlands, Lake Dist., Pennines, Wales); lowlands in SE. Maritime temperate climate. Political unit from 1707, extended to Ireland 1801. UNITED KINGDOM formed by partition of Ireland (1921).

great circle, circle described on surface of a sphere by a plane which passes through centre of sphere. Shortest distance between 2 points on a sphere lies on great circle passing through them.

Great Dane, breed of large powerful dog with short dense coat. Stands *c* 76 cm/30 in. at shoulder.

Great Dividing Range, mountain system of E Australia, running parallel to coast from Cape York Penin. to S Victoria. Incl. Blue Mts., Snowy Mts.

Great Exhibition, first modern, international indust. exhibition. Held 1851 under patronage of Prince Albert in CRYSTAL PALACE. Had aim of encouraging craftsmanship, indust. design.

Great Glen, fault valley of N Scotland. Length *c* 97 km (60 mi) runs SW-NE from Loch Linnhe to Moray Firth.

Great Lakes, in C North America; 5 freshwater lakes between Canada and US. They are lakes Superior, Michigan, Huron, Erie, Ontario. Form important transport route with St Lawrence Seaway to E. Mai[n] cargoes iron ore, coal, grain. Also hav[e] important commercial fisheries, touris[t] resorts.

Great Plains, grassy plateau region of W[ ] US-Canada. Extend from Rocky Mts. t[o] prairies of Mississippi valley, S to Texa[s] Oklahoma. Mainly stock-grazing land.

Great Rift Valley, fault system of SW Asi[a] and E Africa. Extends *c* 4800 km/3000 m[i] from R. Jordan valley (Syria) to C Mozam-bique; divides into W, E sections in [ ] Africa, filled by many lakes.

Great Salt Lake, inland salt lake of N Utah US. Area 2590 sq km (*c* 1000 sq mi). Sa[lt] extracts; size has varied greatly.

Great Schism, *see* SCHISM, GREAT.

Great Slave Lake, S Mackenzie Dis[t] Northwest Territs., Canada. Area 28,400 s[q] km (*c* 10,980 sq mi). Drained by Mackenzi[e] R. Named after Slave Indians who onc[e] lived on its shores.

Great Trek, *see* TREK, GREAT.

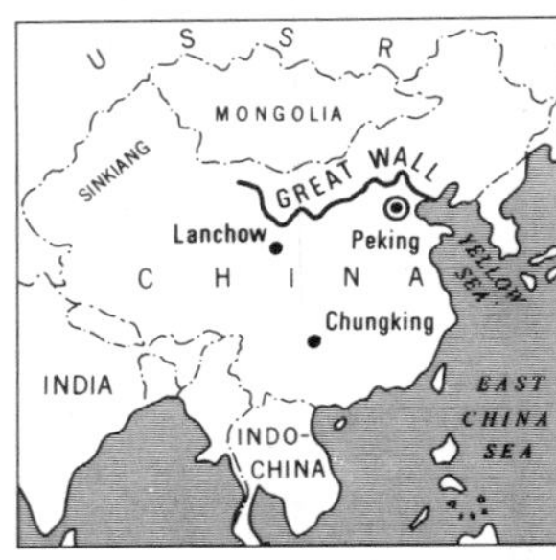

Great Wall of China

Great Wall of China, fortification across [ ] China running *c* 2400 km (1500 mi) along edge of Mongolian plain from Kansu pro[v.] to Hopeh prov. on Yellow Sea. First built i[n] 3rd cent BC as protection against hosti[le] nomadic tribes.

Great Yarmouth, town of Norfolk, England. Pop. 50,000. Coastal reso[rt] herring indust.

grebe, any of Podicipedidae family [of] freshwater diving birds with short ta[il] partially webbed feet; worldwide distri-bution.

Greco, El, pseud. of Domenicos Theotoc-poulos, (*c* 1541-1614), Greek-Spanis[h] painter, b. Crete. Trained in Venice. [In] Toledo, painted visionary religious wor[k] in highly mannerist style, characterized b[y] vivid colour, harsh light, elongated figures.

Greece *(Ellas, Hellas),* republic of S Europe, incl. S Balkan penin., Aegean an[d] Ionian isls. Area 132,000 sq km (50,900 s[q] mi); pop. 9,360,000; cap. Athens. Languag[e] Greek. Religion: Eastern Orthodox. Pind[us] Mts. run N-S; fertile valleys. Agric. bac[k]ward (tobacco, currants, olives); touri[sm] indust. Home of Minoan, Mycenaean civilizations; powerful city-states (*eg* Athens, Sparta, Corinth) from 6th cent. BC. Centre of literature, art, science. Weakened by city state rivalry (*eg* Peloponnesian War), conquered 338 BC by Philip II of Macedon. Fell to Romans 146 BC. Turkish from 1453, revolts led to independence 1829, monarchy from 1832. Territ. gained in Balkan Wars (1913), WWI. Influx of refugees from Turkey in 1920s. Unsuccessful Italian invasion (1940); occupation by German forces (1941-4), followed by civil war until 1949. Coup (1967) exiled king, estab. military govt. until 1974. Member of EEC from 1981.

reek, branch of Indo-European language family. Ancient Greek language associated with major civilization, literature. Of many dialects, Attic (dialect of Athens) was dominant. From Attic, *koinē* (common language) developed, used all over Mediterranean. NT written in *koinē*, and Modern Greek descended from it. Latter divided into written form and vernacular.

reek Church, *see* EASTERN ORTHODOX CHURCH.

reen algae, any of the division Chlorophyta of ALGAE in which the chlorophyll is not masked by any other pigment. Considered ancestral type from which higher green plants evolved. Aquatic, mainly freshwater, or terrestrial in moist areas.

reenaway, Kate (1846-1901), English watercolour painter. Illustrated children's books.

reene, [Henry] Graham (1904-), English author. Novels, concerned with individuals faced with moral dilemmas, incl. *Brighton Rock* (1938), *The Power and the Glory* (1940). Also wrote 'entertainments', *eg Our Man in Havana* (1958), essays and plays.

reenfinch, *Carduelis chloris,* common European songbird. Male is olive-green, with yellow on wings and tail.

reenhouse effect, the retention of heat from sunlight at the Earth's surface, caused by atmospheric carbon dioxide that admits shortwave radiation but traps longwave radiation emitted by the Earth. Some posit that, because of enormous amounts of carbon dioxide released through man's activities, Earth will suffer continuous heating-up.

reenland, isl. of Denmark, in N Atlantic, mostly N of Arctic Circle. Area 2,176,000 sq km (840,000 sq mi); pop. 51,000; cap. Godthaab. Icecap covers most of interior, up to 2450 m (8000 ft) thick. Cryolite mining at Ivigtut; sheep in SW; cod, halibut industs. US air bases at Thule, Sondre Stromfjord. Discovered (*c* 982) by Eric the Red, Norse colonies up to 15th cent.; modern colonization begun *c* 1721. Danish colony until 1953. Self-government of internal affairs since 1979.

reenland Sea, arm of Arctic Ocean, connecting it with the Atlantic; lies between Greenland and Spitsbergen. Largely covered with drifting pack-ice.

reen Mountain Boys, *see* ALLEN, ETHAN.

Greenock, town of Strathclyde region, WC Scotland. Pop. 69,000. Container port, shipbuilding, sugar refining.

Greenwich, bor. of SE Greater London, England, on R. Thames. Pop. 205,000. Created 1965, incl. former Greenwich, Woolwich met. bors. Original site of Royal Observatory (1675) now in Herstmonceux; on prime meridian (long. 0°), source of Greenwich Mean Time. Has Royal Naval Coll.; maritime museum.

Greenwich Village, *see* NEW YORK CITY.

Gregorian chant, *see* PLAINSONG.

Gregory [I] the Great, St (*c* 540-604), Roman monk, pope (590-604). Extended and defined papal authority, promoting monasticism, missions to England. Refusal to recognize patriarch of Constantinople furthered split with Eastern Church. Responsible for major doctrinal pronouncements, changes in liturgy and contribution to development of plainsong (Gregorian chant).

Gregory VII, St, orig. Hildebrand (d. 1085), pope (1073-85). As Benedictine monk, initiated Hildebrandine reform, attacking simony, lay investiture, clerical unchastity. Carried on reforms as pope, causing strife with Henry IV of Germany, who sided with party which resented papacy's domination in temporal sphere. Henry, excommunicated twice, captured Rome (1083), forcing Gregory into exile.

Gregory XIII, orig. Ugo Buoncompagni (1502-85), Italian churchman, pope (1572-85). Prominent in Council of Trent (1562-3), became cardinal 1565. Supported Jesuits. Introduced Gregorian calendar.

Grenada, isl. state of SE West Indies, in Windward Isls. Area 311 sq km (120 sq mi); pop. 97,000; cap. St. George's. Cacao, limes, fruit, spice exports; cotton, rum mfg. British colony from 1783, became independent (1974).

Grenadines, isl. group of SE West Indies, in Windward Isls. Admin. by Grenada and St Vincent.

Grenoble, city of SE France, on R. Isère, cap. of Isère dept. Pop. 389,000. Tourist, winter sports centre; glove mfg., metals indust. based on h.e.p., nuclear research; univ. (1339). Hist. cap. of Dauphiné. Medieval cathedral.

Grenville, George (1712-70), British statesman, PM (1763-5). Began (1763) prosecution of John WILKES. His policy of internally taxing America (Stamp Act, 1765) antagonized colonists. His son, **William Wyndham Grenville, Baron Grenville** (1759-1834), was also PM (1806-7). Served as foreign secretary (1791-1801) before forming coalition of 'all the talents' which secured abolition of slave trade.

Grenville, Sir Richard (*c* 1542-91), English admiral. As commander of the *Revenge* he continued to engage a large Spanish fleet off the Azores although mortally wounded and deserted by rest of squadron.

Gresham, Sir Thomas (*c* 1519-79), English

financier. Founder of Royal Exchange. Name given to Gresham's law, *ie* that 'bad' (i.e. debased) money tends to drive 'good' money from circulation.

Grey, Charles Grey, 2nd Earl (1764-1845), British statesman, PM (1830-4). Foreign secretary (1806-7), resigned over George III's opposition to measure of Catholic Emancipation. His admin. was noted for REFORM BILL of 1832.

Grey, Edward, 1st Viscount Grey of Fallodon (1862-1933), British statesman. Liberal foreign secretary (1905-16), worked in vain to prevent war. Achieved accord with Russia (1907), completing TRIPLE ENTENTE.

* **Grey, Sir George** (1812-98), British colonial administrator. Governor of South Australia (1841-5), then of New Zealand (1845-53, 1861-8). Premier of New Zealand (1877-9).

Grey, Lady Jane (*c* 1537-54), English noblewoman. Married Lord Guildford Dudley, son of NORTHUMBERLAND, who persuaded Edward VI to make Jane his successor, rather than Mary Tudor. She was actually proclaimed queen (July, 1553), imprisoned after 9 days and beheaded.

greyhound, breed of tall, slender hound, once used to hunt small game; racing of greyhounds popularized in early 20th cent. Stands *c* 66 cm/26 in. at shoulder.

grey whale, *Eschritius glaucus,* migratory whalebone whale of Arctic; winters on N Pacific coast. Reaches lengths of 13.7 m/45 ft. Almost extinct in 19th cent., now protected.

Grieg, Edvard Hagerup (1843-1907), Norwegian composer. Work combines romantic with national idioms. Works incl. piano concerto, *Peer Gynt* suite.

griffin, mythical creature with body and hind legs of a lion and head and wings of an eagle. Originated in ancient Middle Eastern legend.

Griffith, Arthur (1872-1922), Irish statesman. Leader of SINN FEIN separatist movement. Became 1st president of Irish Free State (1922).

Griffith, D[avid] W[ark] (1880-1948), American film director-producer, Pioneered cinematic techniques, *eg* flashback, cross-cutting, close-up; best remembered for *Birth of a Nation* (1915), *Intolerance* (1916).

Grimm, Jakob Ludwig (1785-1863) and his brother, **Wilhelm Karl Grimm** (1786-1859), German philologists and literary scholars. Famous for collection of folk tales *Grimm's Fairy Tales* (1812-15). Jakob considered founder of comparative philology, famous for Grimm's law, theory of sound changes in Indo-European languages.

Grimsby, town of Humberside, E England, at mouth of Humber. Pop. 96,000. Major fishing port; boat building.

Grisons (Ger. *Graubünden),* canton of E Switzerland. Largest Swiss canton, area 7110 sq km (2745 sq mi); cap. Chur. Forested mountains; glaciers; headwaters of Inn, Rhine; resorts. Joined Swiss Confederation 1803.

gritstone, durable, coarse variety of SANDSTONE.

Grivas, George (1898-1974), Greek Cypriot revolutionary. Led the EOKA terrorist movement against British rule in Cyprus from 1954 until the settlement of 1959. Launched further terrorist campaign (1971).

grizzly bear, *Ursus horribilis,* brown bear of Alaska, W Canada and Rocky Mts. Most carnivorous of bears, nearly exterminated for attacking livestock.

Gromyko, Andrei Andreyevich (1909-), Soviet diplomat. Foreign minister (1957-80).

Groningen, prov. of NE Netherlands. Area 2328 sq km (899 sq mi). Dairying, large natural gas deposits. Cap. **Groningen** pop. 200,000. Railway jct., agric. market, chemicals. Univ. (1614).

Gropius, Walter (1883-1969), German architect. Leading functionalist architect, his early factory designs, constructed with modern industrial materials, were pioneering works in modern style. Founder-director of the Bauhaus (1919-28). Lived in UK, then US from 1930s.

Grossglockner, highest mountain of Austria, in Hohe Tauern. Height 3796 m (12,460 ft); mountainside road reaches 2346 m (770[illegible] ft).

Grossmith, George (1847-1912) and his brother, **Weedon Grossmith** (1853-1919), English actors. Known for their collaboration in *Diary of a Nobody* (1892), satirizing lower middle class life.

Grosz, George (1893-1959), German artist. Associated with dadaism, satirized bourgeoisie, militarism.

ground ivy, *Glechoma hederacea,* creeping aromatic perennial plant of mint family.

groundnut, *see* PEANUT.

groundsel or **ragwort,** any plant of *Senecio* genus of Compositae family. Esp. *S. vulgaris* of temperate areas of Europe, with small yellow flowers and deeply cut leaves.

ground squirrel, one of various burrowing mammals of temperate zones of N hemisphere, genus *Citellus.*

grouse, gamebird of moorlands of N hemisphere with mottled feathers, round body. Species incl. PTARMIGAN, CAPERCAILLIE and red grouse, *Lagopus lagopus,* common in Scotland.

Grozny, city of USSR, cap. of Checheno-Ingush auton. republic, S European RSFSR. Pop. 375,000. Major oil centre.

Grünewald, Matthias (*c* 1470-1528), German painter. Famous for *Isenheim Altarpiece,* dramatic depiction of the Crucifixion painted in late Gothic style.

Gruyères (Ger. *Greierz),* town of W Switzerland. Pop. 1000. Famous cheese first made here.

Guadalajara, city of WC Mexico, cap. of Jalisco state. Pop. 2,076,000. Commercial and route centre, famous glass, pottery industs. Settled 1542. Univ. (1792), 16th-17th cent. cathedral. Popular health resort o[illegible] plateau *c* 1500 m (5000 ft) high.

Guadalajara, town of C Spain, cap. of Guadalajara prov. Pop. 32,000. Agric. market. Scene of Republican victory (1937) in Civil War. Infantado palace (15th cent.).

Guadalcanal, largest of Solomon Isls., in SW Pacific. Area *c* 6500 sq km (2500 sq mi); pop. 24,000; main town Honiara. Copra exports. Discovered 1788; occupied by Japan in WWII, retaken by US (1943) after intensive fighting.

Guadalquivir, river of Spain. Rises in Sierra de Segura, Jaén prov.; flows SW 580 km (360 mi) through Cordoba, Seville. Navigable below Seville. Used for irrigation, h.e.p.

Guadeloupe, overseas region of France, in Leeward Isls., West Indies. Area 1779 sq km (687 sq mi); pop. 329,000; cap. Basse-Terre (pop. 16,000). Comprises 2 islands (Guadeloupe, Grande-Terre), 3 dependencies and N half of ST MARTIN. Fruit, coffee, rum, cacao products. Settled by French in 17th cent.

Guam, largest of Mariana Isls., W Pacific Ocean, territ. of US. Area 540 sq km (210 sq mi); pop. 113,000; cap. Agana. Subsistence farming; economy dominated by US military base. Discovered (1521) by Magellan; taken from Spain by US (1898). Occupied by Japanese (1941-4).

guanaco, *Lama huanacos,* American mammal of camel family, found in arid regions of Andes. Thought by some to be ancestor of domesticated llama; woolly, resembles long-legged sheep.

guano, accumulated excrement of seabirds, found esp. on isls. off coast of Peru. Rich in phosphate and nitrogen, it was formerly an important fertilizer.

Guareschi, Giovanni (1908-68), Italian journalist. Known for humorous stories, *eg The Little World of Don Camillo* (1950), about friendly feud between parish priest and communist mayor.

Guarneri or **Guarnerius,** family of Italian violin makers in Cremona. Founded by **Andrea Guarneri** (*c* 1626-98).

Guatemala, republic of Central America. Area 108,889 sq km (42,042 sq mi); pop. 6,621,000, mostly Indian; cap. Guatemala City. Languages: Spanish, Indian dialects. Religion: RC. Volcanic mountains near Pacific coast; jungle in N (Péten). Agric. economy; coffee, cotton, banana growing. Hist. civilizations incl. Maya-Quiché; Spanish conquest 1524; gained independence 1821; basis of Central American Federation (1825-38). Frequent earthquakes, esp. 1976.

Guatemala City, cap. of Guatemala, alt. 1520 m (*c* 5000 ft). Pop. 717,000, largest city in Central America. Coffee exports, textiles, cement, soap mfg. Founded 1776 as cap., rebuilt after 1917-18 earthquakes, badly damaged in 1976 earthquake. Univ. (1676).

guava, *Psidium guajava,* small tree of tropical America. Yellowish, pear-shaped, edible fruit is used in preserves.

Guayaquil, port of W Ecuador, at mouth of Guayas R. Pop, 823,000. Bananas, cacao, coffee exports; iron founding, textile mfg. Linked by rail and road with Quito. Founded *c* 1535. Suffered from fire and earthquake damage.

gudgeon, *Gobio gobio,* small European freshwater fish with 2 barbels; used for bait.

guelder rose or **snowball,** *Viburnum opulus,* bush of honeysuckle family. Native to N temperate regions. Grows to *c* 2 m/6 ft, with spherical clusters of white flowers.

Guelphs and Ghibellines, rival political factions in late medieval Europe. Rivalry began with strife between Guelphs or Welfs and the Hohenstaufen emperors, to whom Ghibellines were loyal, in 12th cent. Germany. Continued in 13th-14th cent. Italy after Hohenstaufen line died out, with Guelphs at first loyal to papacy and Ghibellines to Holy Roman emperor; later broke up into petty feuds.

Guernica, town of Basque prov., N Spain. Pop. 15,000. Hist. meeting place of Basque parliament. Destruction (1937) by German bombing during Civil War inspired painting by Picasso.

Guernsey, second largest of Channel Isls., UK. Area 62 sq km (24 sq mi); pop. incl. dependencies 54,000; cap. St Peter Port. Fruit, vegetables, flower growing; Guernsey cattle; tourism.

Guevara, Ernesto ('Che') (1928-67), Cuban revolutionary, b. Argentina. Guerrilla leader in Cuban invasion (1956), economic adviser in Castro govt. (1959-65). Went to Bolivia to further Communist revolution; captured while leading guerrilla band, executed. Exploits inspired many left-wing revolutionary movements.

Guiana, region of NE South America, bounded by Negro, Orinoco, Amazon rivers and Atlantic in E. Mainly highlands, with humid coastal strip. Incl. Guyana, Surinam, French Guiana, parts of Venezuela, N Brazil.

Polaris guided missile

guided missile, type of ROCKET or jet-propelled missile with explosive warhead, controlled in flight by radio or automated guidance system. Developed by Germans in WWII (esp. V-2, using gyroscopic control). Advances in electronics have led to great accuracy in control over thousands of miles. US Minuteman, Polaris and Titan missiles are key strategic weapons.

Guienne, *see* GUYENNE.

Guildford, admin. hq. of Surrey, SE England. Pop. 57,000. Cathedral (1936); Univ. of Surrey (1966).

guilds or **gilds,** associations of people within same craft or trade, powerful in medieval W Europe. They had local control over craft or trade, set standards for craftsmen to work to, and prices of goods, protected trade from taxation and estab. status of members in society. Disappeared with Industrial Revolution.

guillemot, long-billed diving bird, abundant on N Atlantic coasts. Nests in large colonies on cliffs. Species incl. common guillemot, *Uria aalge,* and black guillemot, *Cepphus grylle.*

Guinea, republic of W Africa. Area 246,000 sq km (95,000 sq mi); pop. 4,763,000; cap. Conakry. Language: French. Religion: Islam. Humid, marshy coastal plain rises to interior highlands. Cattle raising important; exports bananas, iron ore, alumina. Former French Guinea estab. 1895; part of French West Africa from 1904; became independent 1958.

Guinea, Equatorial, *see* EQUATORIAL GUINEA.

Guinea, Gulf of, inlet of Atlantic Ocean off W Africa. Extends from Cape Palmas (Liberia) to Cape Lopez (Gabon). Incl. bights of Benin and Bonny.

Guinea-Bissau

Guinea-Bissau, republic of W Africa. Area 36,130 sq km (13,950 sq mi); pop. 777,000; cap. Bissau. Language: Portuguese. Religions: animist, Islam. Coastal mangrove swamp, tropical forest; produces palm oil, hardwoods, copra, groundnuts. Centre of slave trade 17th-18th cent.; became Portuguese colony (1879), overseas prov. (1951). Independence gained 1974. Claims right to Cape Verde Isls.

guinea fowl, *Numida meleagris,* turkey-like domestic fowl of African origin.

guinea pig, domesticated form of South American cavy. Popular as pet, also used in laboratory experiments.

Guinness, Sir Alec (1914-), English stage, film actor. Best known for parts in films, *eg Kind Hearts and Coronets, The Bridge on the River Kwai.* On stage, remembered for modern-dress Hamlet (1958).

Guise, Claude de Lorraine, 1st Duc de (1496-1550), French nobleman. Given title by Francis I; founder of Guise family. His daughter, Mary of Guise, married James V of Scotland and was mother of Mary Queen of Scots. His sons, **François de Lorraine, 2nd Duc de Guise** (1519-63) and **Charles de Lorraine, Cardinal de Guise** (*c* 1525-74), shared control of France during reign of Francis II, husband of Mary Queen of Scots. Led militant Catholic party which provoked civil war with Huguenots. François was assassinated. His son, **Henri de Lorraine, 3rd Duc de Guise** (1550-88), was largely responsible for Saint Bartholomew's Day Massacre. Formed Catholic League (1576) to oppose Huguenots. Assassinated at king's instigation after leading revolt against HENRY III.

guitar, six-stringed, flat-backed instrument with frets on the fingerboard. Popular in 17th-18th cent., interest in guitar music renewed in 20th cent. Electric guitar, introduced to amplify the sound, has become an instrument in its own right in the hands of rock musicians.

Gujarat, state of W India. Area 190,000 sq km (72,000 sq mi); pop. 26,687,000; cap. Ahmedabad. Mainly fertile plain; incl. Kathiawar penin. and marshy Rann of Kutch. Cereals, cotton grown. Formed (1960) from N and W parts of former Bombay state.

Gulbenkian, Calouste Sarkis (1869-1955), British industrialist, diplomat, b. Turkey. He made a vast fortune in oil, and estab. Gulbenkian Foundation for advancement of arts, science, education.

Gulf Stream, warm ocean current of N Atlantic. Flows from Gulf of Mexico NE up US coast. Off Newfoundland merges with the North Atlantic Drift, tempering climate of W and N Europe.

gull, any of Laridae family of web-footed seabirds. White or grey in colour; usually nests on cliffs, rocky coasts. Black-headed gull, *Larus ridibundus,* breeds inland on marshes, moors. HERRING GULL is commonest coastal gull.

gullet, *see* OESOPHAGUS.

gumbo, *see* OKRA.

gum tree, *see* EUCALYPTUS.

gun, *see* ARTILLERY, FIREARMS, PISTOL, MACHINE GUN.

gunboat, originally a small, shallow-draught fighting ship built to operate on rivers. Since WWII a high-speed coastal patrol vessel.

gunpowder, an explosive made from potassium nitrate, sulphur and carbon. Believed to have been invented in 9th-cent. China and introduced to Europe in 14th cent., its use as a propellant revolutionized warfare, but it is now seldom used except in fireworks.

unpowder Plot, *see* FAWKES, GUY.

uppy, *Lebistes reticulatus,* small tropical freshwater fish of South America and Caribbean. Many brightly coloured varieties bred for aquaria.

urkha, certain predominantly Hindu tribes of Nepal. Famed for their fighting qualities, they provided the British army with 10 regiments in WWI, and in WWII fought with distinction in N Africa, Malaya and Burma.

ustavus I (1496-1560), king of Sweden (1523-60). Elected king after leading peasant rebellion which achieved Swedish independence from Denmark. Estab. Lutheran National Church (1527), gained economic freedom from German-dominated Hanseatic League.

ustavus [II] Adolphus (1594-1632), king of Sweden (1611-32). Championed Protestant cause in THIRTY YEARS WAR. Brilliant commander, gained series of victories while campaigning in Germany (1630-2). Defeated WALLENSTEIN at Lützen, but was killed.

ustavus V (1858-1950), king of Sweden (1907-50). Maintained Sweden's neutrality in WWI, WWII.

ustavus VI (1882-1973), king of Sweden (1950-73). Succeeded by grandson Carl XVI Gustaf.

utenberg, Johann (*c* 1397-1468), German printer. Regarded as inventor of printing from movable type (*c* 1437). Prob. printed *Mazarin Bible* (1456).

uthrie, Sir [William] Tyrone (1900-71), British actor, producer. Administrator of Old Vic and Sadler's Wells theatres (1939-45). Helped found Canada's Shakespeare Festival at Stratford, Ontario (1953).

utta-percha, rubber-like gum produced from LATEX of several SE Asian trees of *Palaquium* and *Payena* genera. Used in electrical insulation, manufacture of golf balls.

uyana, country of NE South America, member of British Commonwealth; formerly British Guiana. Area 215,000 sq km (83,000 sq mi); pop. 820,000; cap. Georgetown. Language: English. Religions: Hinduism, Islam, Christianity. Mainly jungle with cultivable coastal strip. Chief products sugar (demerara), rice, bauxite. Settled by Dutch in 17th cent.; British occupation (1796); independence (1966) as Guyana.

Guyenne or **Guienne,** hist. region of SW France, cap. Bordeaux. Formed, with Gascony, duchy of Aquitaine; under English rule (1154-1453).

Gwent, county of SE Wales. Area 1376 sq km (531 sq mi); pop. 438,000; admin. hq. Cwmbran. Created 1974, formerly known as Monmouthshire.

Gwyn or **Gwynne, Eleanor ('Nell')** (1650-87), English actress. Principally remembered as mistress of Charles II.

Gwynedd, county of NW Wales. Area 3868 sq km (1493 sq mi); pop. 226,000; admin. hq. Caernarfon. Created 1974, incl. former counties Anglesey, Caernarvonshire, Merionethshire.

gymnastics, performance of athletic exercises, whose competitive form can be traced to ancient Greek Olympics. Modern form was developed in early 19th cent. in Germany. Events incl. vaulting and pommel horse, rings, parallel and asymmetric bars, beam and floor exercises.

Gymnophiona, order of limbless, worm-like amphibians. Functionless eyes hidden under skin. Found in Asia, Africa, Central America. Formerly called Caecilia.

gymnosperm, botanical term for seed plants in which ovules are not enclosed in an ovary. They incl. cycads and conifers.

gynaecology, branch of medicine concerned with ailments specific to women, esp. those of reproductive system.

gypsum, hydrous calcium sulphate mineral. Soft, white or grey; found among clays and limestones. Occurs in various forms, *eg* alabaster, selenite. Used in cement, fertilizers, plaster of Paris.

gypsy, gipsy or **Romany,** member of nomadic tribe, believed to have originated in NW India. Entered Europe in early 15th cent. Spread throughout Europe and North America but mostly found in Balkans, Spain, Italy. Have their own language (Romany) which belongs to Indo-Iranian group. Traditionally earned living by metalworking, fortune telling, horse trading. Est. numbers *c* 5 million.

gyroscope, wheel mounted so that it is free to rotate about any axis. When wheel is spun, its support may be turned in any direction without altering wheel's original plane of motion. Used in gyrocompass, as control device for guided missiles, and, in large form, as ship stabilizer.

H

Haag, Den, *see* HAGUE, THE.

Haakon VII (1872-1957), king of Norway (1905-57). Second son of Frederick VIII of Denmark. Elected king after Norway achieved independence from Sweden. Led resistance to German occupation (1940-5) from Britain.

Haarlem, city of W Netherlands, on R. Spaarne, cap. of North Holland prov. Pop. 229,000. Centre of bulb, flower indust.; printing, chocolate. Church (15th cent.), Frans Hals museum.

Habakkuk, prophetic book of OT, possibly written *c* 600 BC. Consists of set of poems on triumph of divine justice and mercy over evil.

habeas corpus, in law, writ or order from judge to custodian of detained person requiring that person be brought before court at stated time, place, for decision on legality of his detention. Serves as chief safeguard against illegal detention.

Haber, Fritz (1868-1934), German chemist. Known for Haber process by which ammonia is produced catalytically from hydrogen and nitrogen at high pressures; used in fertilizer manufacture. Awarded Nobel Prize for Chemistry (1918).

Habsburg or **Hapsburg,** ruling house of Austria (1282-1918), also of Hungary and Bohemia (1526-1918), Spain (1516-1700). Austria became hereditary possession under RUDOLPH, count of Habsburg. From 1438, all Holy Roman emperors but one belonged to Habsburg house. Acquired Low Countries through Maximilian I's marriage (1477) to Mary of Burgundy. Reached greatest height as world power under Emperor CHARLES V, who brought Spain into Habsburg dominions. Hungary and Bohemia incorporated (1526) through marriage of Charles' brother, FERDINAND I. Habsburgs lost some territ., *eg* Spain, through wars of succession in 18th cent. With FRANCIS II's assumption of title emperor of Austria (1804), family history became synonymous with that of Austria (AUSTRO-HUNGARIAN MONARCHY after 1867). After death of Charles I, who abdicated 1918, claims to dynasty passed to his son, Archduke Otto.

Hackney, bor. of NC Greater London, England. Pop. 191,000. Created 1965, former met. bor. Incl. Shoreditch, Stoke Newington.

haddock, *Melanogrammus aeglefinus,* marine fish of Gadidae family, similar to cod but smaller; conspicuous black lateral line. Found on N Atlantic coasts.

Hades, in Greek myth, home of the dead, ruled by Pluto (or Hades) and Persephone. Separated from living world by rivers Styx (hateful), Lethe (forgetfulness), Phlegethon (fiery), Cocytus (wailing), Acher[on] (woeful). Dead ferried across Styx [by] CHARON. Entrance was guarded [by] CERBERUS.

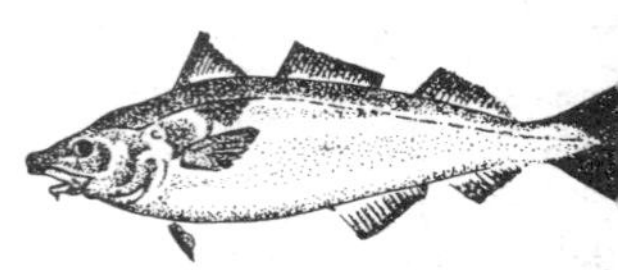

Haddock

Hadrian (AD 76-138), Roman emper[or] (117-38), b. Spain. Estab. Euphrates as frontier of empire, abandoning Trajan['s] conquests in Mesopotamia. Adopt[ed] defensive policy, building walls [in] Germany and across Britain from Tyne [to] Solway Firth (126).

hadrons, class of ELEMENTARY PARTICL[ES] which experience the STRONG NUCLE[AR] INTERACTION. Incl. protons, neutron[s], mesons. Hadrons are held to be compose[d] of QUARKS, unlike LEPTONS, the other bas[ic] class of elementary particles.

Haeckel, Ernst Heinrich (1834-191[9]) German biologist. Principal Germa[n] exponent of Darwinism; his biogenetic la[w] that each organism in its developme[nt] repeats stages through which its ancesto[rs] passed in course of evolution, was infl[u]ential in 19th cent.

haematite (Fe_2O_3), iron ore minera[l]. Consists of ferric oxide; occurs as reddis[h] brown earthy masses or dark gre[y] crystals. Found among all types of rock[s] often causing reddish colour. Importa[nt] source of iron. Major sources in U[SA], Canada, Australia.

haemoglobin, red colouring matter of re[d] blood cells of vertebrates. Consists [of] protein (globin) combined with iro[n]-containing haem. Carries oxygen fro[m] lungs to tissues in form of easil[y] decomposed oxy-haemoglobin and carri[es] carbon dioxide back to lungs.

haemophilia, condition in which one [of] normal blood-clotting factors is absen[t]. Characterized by prolonged bleeding fro[m] minor injuries and spontaneous intern[al] bleeding. Inherited only by males throug[h] mother.

haemorrhage, escape of large quantities [of] blood from blood vessels. Blood from c[ut] artery is bright red and comes in spurt[s]; blood from veins is much darker and flow[s] smoothly.

haemorrhoids or **piles,** painful swelling

veins in region of the anus. May occur during pregnancy, as a result of constipation, *etc*.

afnium (Hf), metallic element; at. no. 72, at. wt. 178.49. Resembles zirconium; found in zirconium minerals. Used in manufacture of tungsten filaments. Discovered (1923).

lagen, city of W West Germany, in Ruhr. Pop. 226,000. Indust. centre (iron, steel, chemicals, vehicles).

agfish, any of Myxinidae family of saltwater CYCLOSTOMES, with worm-like body; reaches lengths of 60 cm/2 ft. Lives in mud on sea bottom, feeding on worms, crustaceans; parasitic on fish.

aggada, *see* TALMUD.

laggai, prophetic book of OT, written *c* 520 BC in Jerusalem after return from the Exile. Consists of exhortations to rebuild the Temple.

laggard, Sir [Henry] Rider (1856-1925), English novelist. Known for adventure stories in African setting, esp. *King Solomon's Mines* (1885).

lague, The *(Den Haag, 's-Gravenhage),* city of W Netherlands, cap. of South Holland prov., seat of Dutch govt. Pop. 673,000. Seat of International Court of Justice (1913).

ague Conferences, two international peace conferences held 1899, 1907. Failed to achieve aim of arms reduction, but set up arbitration procedures, conventions respecting rules of war. First conference estab. Hague Tribunal, Permanent Court of Arbitration on international disputes. Superseded (1945) by International Court of Justice.

lahn, Otto (1879-1968), German physical chemist. Discovered several radioactive isotopes, incl. protactinium (with Lise Meitner). Awarded Nobel Prize for Chemistry (1944) for inducing nuclear fission in uranium by bombardment with neutrons.

laifa, port of NW Israel, on Mediterranean. Pop. 360,000. Indust. centre; oil refining, chemicals, textiles. Rail jct. and international airport. Seat of Technion (Israel Institute of Technology).

laig, Douglas Haig, 1st Earl (1861-1928), British army officer. Commanded 1st Army Corps in France (1914); commander-in-chief of British forces (1915-17). His costly strategy of prolonged trench warfare provoked criticism, but he was architect of final victory.

ail, hard pellets of ice, often associated with thunderstorms. Nucleus, *eg* dust particle, is carried upward by air current until layer of ice coats it; gathers further layers on descent. Hailstones can cause damage.

laile Selassie, orig. Tafari Makonnen (1891-1975), emperor of Ethiopia (1930-74). Led resistance to Italian invasion (1935), fled to England (1936). Regained throne (1941). Leader of pan-African movement. Deposed (1974) by military coup.

lainan, isl. of Kwangtung prov., S China. Area *c* 33,670 sq km (13,000 sq mi); pop. 2,800,000; cap. Kiungshan. Produces timber, rubber, coffee, iron ore. Large naval base at Yulin.

Haiphong, chief seaport of NE Vietnam. Pop. 1,191,000. Naval base near mouth of Red R. Commercial, indust. centre; cement, textile, chemical industs. Heavily bombed by US in Vietnam war.

hair, filamentous outgrowth of the skin, consisting mainly of keratin. Grows from small depression (follicle) at whose side is a sebaceous gland, providing oil for skin. Hair is characteristic of mammals.

Haiti, republic of West Indies, occupying W HISPANIOLA. Area 27,713 sq km (10,700 sq mi); pop. 4,833,000, mainly Negro; cap. Port-au-Prince. Languages: French, Creole dialect. Religion: RC. Consists of 2 penins. and 2 isls. Largely wooded mountains; tropical climate. Subsistence agric.; commercial crops incl. coffee, sugar, sisal; timber, bauxite. Spanish ceded possession in 17th cent. to French sugar planters. Independence 1804; hist. ruled by despots, esp. Duvalier (1957-71).

hake, marine food fish of Merlucciidae family, related to the cod; long-bodied, with projecting lower jaw. Species incl. European *Merluccius merluccius,* now scarce through overfishing.

Halakah, *see* TALMUD.

half-life, time taken for half the atoms of a radioactive substance to disintegrate. Uranium 238 has half-life of 4.5×10^9 years.

half-tone, *see* PHOTOENGRAVING.

halibut, *Hippoglossus hippoglossus,* largest flatfish, reaching lengths of 2.4 m/8 ft; found in N Atlantic. Popular food fish. Related species in N Pacific.

Halicarnassus, ancient city of SW Asia Minor (modern Turkey). Site of mausoleum, built (*c* 350 BC) in memory of King Mausolus of Caria by his wife: one of Seven Wonders of the World.

Halifax, cap. of Nova Scotia, Canada; Canada's principal ice-free Atlantic port. Pop. 268,000. Shipbuilding, oil refining, food processing (fish). Founded 1749 as naval base; important during both WWs. Has Dalhousie Univ. (1818).

Halifax, town of West Yorkshire met. county, N England. Pop. 91,000. Woollens, carpets mfg.

Halle, town of SC East Germany, on R. Saale. Pop. 236,000. Railway jct.; salt (saline springs), lignite mining. Former Hanseatic League member; univ. (1694).

Halley, Edmund (1656-1742), English astronomer. Astronomer Royal after 1720. Studied motion of comets and predicted return of comet of 1682 (Halley's comet); it returns every 75 or 76 years (expected again in 1986).

Halloween, eve of ALL SAINTS' DAY. Esp. celebrated in countries with strong Celtic influence; prob. derives from pre-Christian feasts to mark beginning of winter. Associated with supernatural activity.

Hallstatt, village of C Austria. Site of early Iron Age remains; gave name to Hallstatt

Urn of the Hallstatt period

culture in archaeology (*c* 800-500 BC).

hallucination, false sensory impression which invents or misinterprets external phenomena. May occur during schizophrenia or be induced by certain drugs, *eg* mescaline, cannabis or LSD.

halogens, in chemistry, the 5 elements fluorine, chlorine, bromine, iodine and astatine (unstable). Chemically similar, monovalent and highly reactive.

Hals, Frans (*c* 1580-1666), Dutch genre and portrait painter. His bold brushstrokes give impression of gaiety to individual portraits, *eg Laughing Cavalier*, captures fleeting expressions in his large groups.

Hälsingborg or **Helsingborg,** town of S Sweden, on Öresund. Pop. 101,000. Port, ferry service to Helsingör (Denmark). Copper refining; textiles. Contested by Denmark until 1710.

Hamburg, city of N West Germany, on R. Elbe, cap. of Hamburg state. Pop. 1,699,000. Major port (outport at Cuxhaven), transshipment trade, shipbuilding, chemicals industs.; cultural, broadcasting centre. Founded by Charlemagne, archbishopric from 834. Alliance (1241) with Lübeck formed basis of Hanseatic League. Rapid growth in 19th cent., incorporated Altona 1938. Severely damaged in 1842 fire, WWII.

Hameln (Eng. *Hamelin*), town of NW West Germany, on R. Weser. Pop. 49,000. Food processing indust. Scene of the legend of the Pied Piper.

Hamersley Range, mountain range of NW Western Australia. Highest peak Mt. Bruce (1226 m/4024 ft). Extensive high-quality iron ore deposits.

Hamilcar Barca (d. 228 BC), Carthaginian soldier. Commander in Sicily during First Punic War (247-241), but was defeated and forced to withdraw. Virtual dictator of Carthage after 237. Led successful invasion of Spain (237-228) but was killed. Father of Hannibal.

Hamilton, Alexander (1755-1804), American statesman, b. West Indies. Dominated President Washington's cabinet as 1st secretary of the treasury (1789-95), pursued centralization of finances, stabilization of economy. Leader of FEDERALIST PARTY. Supported Jefferson in presidential ballot (1800) against Aaron Burr, who later killed him in duel.

Hamilton, Lady Emma, née Lyon (1765-1815), English courtesan. Became mistress, later wife (1791), of Sir William Hamilton, British ambassador to Naples. Became mistress (1798) to Horatio Nelson, bearing (1801) him a daughter. Died in poverty.

Hamilton, cap. and chief port of Bermuda on Bermuda isl. Pop. 3000. Tourist resort.

Hamilton, port of S Ontario, Canada; at W end of L. Ontario. Pop. 529,000. Railway jct.; mfg. centre; steel works, auto and rai machinery. Founded 1813. Has McMaste Univ. (1930).

Hamilton, town of N North Isl., New Zealand. Pop. 75,000. Agric. market, foo processing; has Waikato Univ.

Hamilton, town of Strathclyde region, WC Scotland. Pop. 46,000. Coalmining area engineering, textiles industs.

Hammarskjöld, Dag (1905-61), Swedish statesman. As secretary-general of the UN (1953-61) increased its influence. Influentia in Suez Crisis (1956), active in attempts to solve Congo problem (1960-1) until hi death in plane crash. Nobel Peace Prize (posthumously awarded, 1961).

Hammerfest, town of Kvaloy Isl., N Norway most northerly in Europe. Pop. 7000. Ice free port, whaling, sealing.

hammerhead shark, any of genus *Sphyrna* of medium-sized sharks that have hammer like lobes on head, with eyes and nostrils a extremities.

Hammersmith and Fulham, bor. of W Greater London, England. Pop. 167,000.

Hammerstein, Oscar (1895-1960), American librettist, lyricist. Famous for musical created with composer Richard Rodgers *eg Oklahoma, Carousel, South Pacific.*

Hammurabi (*fl* 18th cent. BC), king o Babylon (*c* 1792-1750 BC). Founded ancien Babylonian empire. Best remembered fo his legal code.

Hampden, John (*c* 1594-1643), English statesman. Became focus of resentmen against Charles I through imprisonmen for refusal (1636) to pay 'ship money' tax One of five MPs whose attempted arrest by Charles (1642) was a cause of Civil War.

Hampshire, county of S England. Area 377 sq km (1456 sq mi); pop. 1,453,000; admin hq. Winchester. Incl. New Forest; downs in N, SE; fertile lowland. Crops incl. cereals root crops; livestock rearing. Indust. in ports of Southampton, Portsmouth.

Hampstead, part of Camden, NC Greate London, England. Former met. bor. unti 1965. Nearby is Hampstead Heath park.

Hampton Court, English palace on R Thames, built by Cardinal Wolsey (1514) a his private residence. Later passed to Henry VIII and became royal residence.

hamster, rat-like burrowing rodent o Europe and W Asia, with internal chee pouches to carry food. Common hamster *Cricetus cricetus*, is grey or brown. Golde hamster, *Mesocricetus auratus*, is popula pet; also used for medical research.

Hamsun, Knut Pederson (1859-1952)

Norwegian novelist. Work, *eg Hunger* (1899), *The Growth of the Soil* (1917), affirms elemental values of nature. Awarded Nobel Prize for Literature (1920).

an, dynasty of China (202 BC-AD 220), broken by Hsin dynasty (AD 9-25). Noted for territ. expansion and artistic development; ink and paper came into use, making of porcelain began. Buddhism introduced.

ınd, prehensile extremity of arm. Human hand contains 27 bones: 8 carpal bones in wrist, 5 long metacarpals, and 14 phalanges forming the fingers and thumb (3 in each finger, 2 in thumb).

ındball, eleven-a-side team game played by catching, passing and throwing an inflated round ball. Aim is to score by throwing ball into goal. First played in Germany, *c* 1890.

andel, George Frideric (1685-1759), German composer. Settled in England under patronage of George I. Tried to introduce Italian opera to London, then turned to oratorio. Numerous works incl. *concerti grossi,* keyboard suites, oratorios *Messiah* (1742), *Judas Maccabaeus,* miscellaneous orchestral music, *eg Water Music.*

angchow, cap. of Chekiang prov., E China. Pop. 960,000. Port on R. Tsientang. Famous for silk weaving. Indust. centre, producing iron and steel, chemicals, *etc.* Cap. of S China during 12th and 13th cent., it was centre of learning and trade.

anging Garden of Babylon, terraced building planted with gardens, constructed by Nebuchadnezzar II (d. 562 BC). One of the Seven Wonders of the World.

ankow, *see* WUHAN.

annibal (247-182 BC), Carthaginian soldier. Commander in Spain (221); his capture of Saguntum led Rome to declare war on Carthage (218). Crossed Alps to invade Italy; defeated Romans at L. Trasimene (217) and Cannae (216), but had insufficient support to capture Rome. Recalled (203) to defend Carthage, defeated by Scipio Africanus at Zama (202). After peace, became ruler of Carthage; Romans forced him to flee to Syria (196). Took poison in Bithynia to avoid being surrendered to the Romans.

anoi, cap. of Vietnam. Pop. 1,444,000. Port on Red R.; rail jct.; agric., indust., cultural centre. Hist. cap. of Annam and Indo-China. Damaged by US during Vietnam war.

anover (*Hannover*), city of N West Germany, on R. Leine, cap. of Lower Saxony. Pop. 547,000. Indust., commercial centre; univ. (1879). Hanseatic League member from 1386; cap. of electorate of Hanover from 1692. Badly damaged in WWII.

anover, House of, British royal house. Succession claimed through Sophia, granddaughter of James I and wife of Elector Ernest Augustus of Hanover. Act of SETTLEMENT (1701) made their son, George, heir to Queen Anne, thus excluding Catholic Stuart line. Hanoverian monarchs were George I, II, III and IV and William IV. Lost right to British crown with Victoria (1837) because women barred from throne of Hanover.

Hansard, official report of British parliamentary proceedings. Luke Hansard began (1774) printing accounts of debates. Made official in 1803, remained in family to 1889. Now pub. by Her Majesty's Stationery Office.

Hanseatic League, medieval trading organization of N German towns. From groups of individual *hansa,* an association of merchants trading to foreign countries, league became a great confederation by 14th cent., with companies at most seaports on the Baltic and North seas. Provided trading privileges and protection of its own army. Declined steadily until dissolution in 17th cent.

Hanyang, *see* WUHAN.

Hapsburg, *see* HABSBURG.

hara-kiri, traditional Japanese honourable suicide. Involves ritual self-disembowelment with dagger. Originally practised among warrior class to avoid dishonour of capture; *c* 1500 became privileged alternative to execution. Still occasionally practised. Also known as *seppuku.*

Harald [III] Hardrada (d. 1066), king of Norway (1046-66). Joined with Tostig to invade England (1066), and was killed by Harold of England at Stamford Bridge.

Harappa, *see* INDUS VALLEY CIVILIZATION.

Harbin, cap. of Heilungkiang prov., NE China. Pop. 1,670,000. Main port on R. Sungari; major railway jct. Railway engineering; aircraft, tractor mfg. Developed by Russians (1896-1924).

Hardicanute, *see* HARTHACANUTE.

Hardie, [James] Keir (1856-1915), British socialist, b. Scotland. Founder, 1st president (1893-1900) of Independent Labour Party. Influential in formation (1906) of Labour Party, leading it in House of Commons (1906-7).

Harding, Warren Gamaliel (1865-1923), American statesman, Republican president • (1921-3). Admin. known for inefficiency, corruption.

hardness, in mineralogy, resistance a substance offers to being scratched. Measured by Mohs scale ranging from softest (1) to hardest (10), each number being represented by a standard mineral, *eg* calcite (3), topaz (8), diamond (10).

hard water, water containing dissolved calcium and magnesium salts which interfere with lathering and cleansing properties of soap. Fatty acids in soap form insoluble precipitates (scum) with these salts. Temporary hardness, caused by dissolved bicarbonates, can be removed by boiling; permanent hardness, caused by sulphates, is removed by addition of soda (sodium carbonate) or zeolite.

Hardy, Thomas (1840-1928), English novelist, poet. Novels, set in native 'Wessex' (SW England), *eg The Mayor of Casterbridge*

(1886), *Tess of the D'Urbervilles* (1891), *Jude the Obscure* (1896), reflect vision of human possibilities destroyed through malevolent destiny. Later turned solely to poetry.

Hare, William, *see* BURKE, WILLIAM.

hare, swift rabbit-like mammal, but non-burrowing and with longer ears and hind legs than rabbit. Formerly classed as rodent, now put with rabbits in order Lagomorpha. Species incl. European brown hare, *Lepus europaeus,* and mountain hare, *L. timidus,* whose coat turns white in winter.

harebell, *see* BLUEBELL.

harelip, congenital cleft of one or both lips, but usually only the upper one; often occurs with associated cleft palate. May be corrected by early surgery.

Hargreaves, James (*c* 1720-78), English engineer. Built 'spinning jenny' (1764) enabling one person to spin several threads simultaneously.

Haringey, bor. of N Greater London, England. Pop. 227,000. Created 1965 from mun. bors. of Middlesex.

Harlem, *see* NEW YORK CITY.

Harlequin

Harlequin, stock character of COMMEDIA DELL'ARTE, became buffoon of French, then English pantomime. Traditionally wears mask, particoloured tights.

Harley, Robert, 1st Earl of Oxford (1661-1724), British statesman. Tory lord treasurer (1711-14), became chief minister to Queen Anne. Instrumental in Peace of Utrecht (1713). Imprisoned (1715) over dealings with Jacobites.

harmonica or **mouth organ,** simple musical instrument consisting of enclosed box containing tuned metal reeds with holes through which air is blown or sucked.

harmonium, small organ in which the sound is produced by forcing air through reeds. Pressure is raised by pumping bellow with the feet.

harmony, in music, the combining of note to form CHORDS in ways that are musical correct or interesting. It is a domina feature of Western music, often of gre emotional significance.

Harmsworth, Alfred, *see* NORTHCLIFFE.

harness racing, *see* HORSE RACING.

Harold (*c* 1022-66), king of England (1066 Son of GODWIN, was recognized as heir throne by Edward the Confessor, but ha earlier been forced to swear to suppo William of Normandy's claim. On death Edward, defeated and killed brother Tost and Harald III of Norway, who invaded England, but was defeated and kille himself by William at Hastings.

Harold Harefoot (d. 1040), king of Englan (1037-40). Bastard son of Canute, h claimed throne on father's death (1035 and was elected king after conflict wi half-brother Harthacanute.

harp, stringed musical instrument, wi triangular frame; player plucks the string Modern orchestral harp has range of 6 octaves and each string can play any of notes at the touch of a pedal.

Harpers Ferry, *see* BROWN, JOHN.

Harpies, in Greek myth, repellent birds wi the faces of women. Associated with th powers of the underworld and believed carry off people who had disappeared. Als said to devour everything in sight.

harpsichord, string keyboard music instrument, in which the strings ar plucked mechanically. Popular from abo 1550 to 1800, but then replaced by th piano. Now revived for authent performances of Baroque music.

harrier, hawk of genus *Circus,* with broa wings and long legs and tail. Worldwic distribution.

Harris, Sir Arthur Travers (1892- British airforce officer. Acquired th nickname 'Bomber Harris' as commande in-chief of Bomber Command (1942-5).

Harris, Joel Chandler (1848-1908 American author. Known for 'Brer Rabbi Negro folk collections in authentic dialec *eg Uncle Remus: His Songs and His Sayin* (1880). Also wrote novels.

Harris, *see* LEWIS WITH HARRIS.

Harrisburg, cap. of Pennsylvania, US; o Susquehanna R. Pop. 427,000. In co mining region. Steel, bricks, clothing mf Serious leak at nearby nuclear react (1979).

Harrogate, town of North Yorkshire, England. Pop. 62,000. Spa from 159 holiday centre.

Harrow, bor. of NW Greater London, En land. Pop. 197,000.

hartebeest, large red-brown Africa antelope with short curved horns. Ca hartebeest, *Alcelaphus caama,* found in Africa.

Hartford, cap. of Connecticut, US; c Connecticut R. Pop. 731,000. Commercia insurance centre. Industs. incl. firearm typewriters mfg. Settled 1635-6.

arthacanute or **Hardicanute** (d. 1042), king of Denmark (1035-42) and of England (1040-2). Son of Canute, gained English throne on death of half-brother Harold Harefoot, leaving it to Edward the Confessor.

artlepool, town of Cleveland, NE England, on Hartlepool Bay. Pop. 97,000. United with West Hartlepool 1967. Fishing, shipbuilding industs.

arun al-Rashid (*c* 763-809), Abbasid caliph of Baghdad. Made Baghdad centre of Arab culture; idealized in *Thousand and One Nights*.

arvard University, *see* CAMBRIDGE, Mass.

arvest mouse, *Micromys minutus*, small red-brown European field mouse that builds its nest among stalks of plants, esp. growing grain.

arvey, William (1578-1657), English anatomist, physiologist. Discovered circulation of blood; demonstrated flow of blood from heart through arteries and back to heart through veins.

arwich, town of Essex, SE England. Pop. 15,000. Port; ferry services to N Europe.

aryana, state of N India. Area *c* 44,000 sq km (17,000 sq mi); pop. 9,971,000; cap. Chandigarh. Mainly flat, dry and barren. Formed (1966) from Hindi-speaking parts of Punjab.

arz Mountains, forested range of C Germany, in both German republics. Highest peak BROCKEN.

ashish, *see* HEMP.

asidism, beliefs of Jewish mystical movement founded (18th cent.) in Poland by BAAL-SCHEM-Tov. Spread rapidly among uneducated; still exerts some influence in Jewish life.

assan II (1929-), king of Morocco (1961-). Introduced constitutional monarchy (1963).

astings, Warren (1732-1818), British colonial administrator. First governor-general of India (1773-84). In spite of financial, admin., judicial reforms and strengthening British position in India, he met opposition in Britain. After return (1785), impeached (1787) on charges of malpractice. Acquitted (1795).

astings, town of East Sussex, SE England. Pop. 72,000. Seaside resort. Norman victory over Saxons near by (1066). Chief of Cinque Ports.

astings, Battle of, confrontation between invading William, duke of Normandy (William the Conqueror), and Harold, king of England (14 Oct. 1066). Fought at Senlac Hill, near Hastings, England, until Harold was killed. First, most decisive victory of Norman Conquest.

athaway, Anne (1556-1623), English farmer's daughter. Married Shakespeare in 1582.

aughey, Charles James (1925-), Irish statesman. Held various posts in Fianna Fáil govts. from 1961 to 1970, when forced to resign over alleged gun-running for IRA, though acquitted by court. Succeeded Lynch as PM (1979-).

Hausa

Hausa, people of N Nigeria, S Niger. Farmers and far-ranging traders. Hausa languages are basically Hamitic but people mainly Negroid. Predominantly Moslem.

Havana (*La Habana*), cap. of Cuba, on Gulf of Mexico. Pop. 1,861,000. Port, exports sugar, cotton, tobacco. Commercial centre; textiles, cigars, chemicals, rum mfg. Founded 1514; cap. from 1552. Tourism declined after Castro's coup (1959). Has 18th cent. cathedral.

Havering, bor. of NE Greater London, England. Pop. 240,000. Created 1965 from Romford, Hornchurch (both in Essex).

Havre, Le, *see* LE HAVRE.

Hawaii, volcanic isl. group and state of US; in C Pacific. Area 16,706 sq km (6450 sq mi); pop. 887,000; cap. Honolulu. Incl. Hawaii (area 10,456 sq km/4037 sq mi), Oahu, Maui, Kauai, Molokai isls. Coral reefs, several large active volcanoes. Extensive fishing. Agric. incl. sugar cane, pineapple production. Important tourist industs. International air and shipping base; naval base at Pearl Harbor, Oahu (attacked by Japanese in 1941 bringing US into WWII). Pop. of Japanese, Caucasian, Polynesian origin. Known as Sandwich Isls. after discovery by Cook in 1778; native rule until annexed by US (1898); was territ. (1900-59). Admitted to Union as 50th state (1959).

Haw-Haw, Lord, *see* JOYCE, WILLIAM.

hawk, name for several birds of prey with short, rounded wings, hooked beak and claws. Incl. kites, buzzards, harriers; excl. falcons.

Hawke, Edward Hawke, 1st Baron (1705-81), British admiral. Defeated French squadron off Cape Finisterre (1747) and by annihilation of French fleet at Quiberon Bay (1759) removed threat of invasion.

hawking or **falconry,** sport of hunting game, using trained hawks or falcons. Practised in Arabia, Persia, India since ancient times, became popular in medieval Europe. Trained bird is carried on gloved wrist of falconer; unhooded and released on sight of prey.

Hawkins or **Hawkyns, Sir John** (1532-95), English privateer. Made slaving expeditions (1562-7) to Guinea. Treasurer and comptroller of navy (1573), rear admiral in defeat of Spanish Armada (1588). Died at sea.

hawk moth, any of Sphingidae family of moths with thick body and long pointed forewings. Long proboscis used to suck flower nectar.

hawthorn, any of genus *Crataegus* of thorny shrubs or small trees of rose family. Native to Eurasia and North America. Clusters of fragrant white or pink flowers, small red fruits called haws.

Hawthorne, Nathaniel (1804-64), American author. Known for novel, *The Scarlet Letter* (1850), on themes of Puritanism, secret sin. Other works incl. *The House of Seven Gables* (1851) and *Tanglewood Tales* (1853), for children.

Haydn, [Franz] Joseph (1732-1809), Austrian composer. Estab. classical forms of the sonata and symphony. Prolific composer, wrote over 100 symphonies, 84 string quartets, piano sonatas, operas and choral works, *eg The Creation, The Seasons.*

Hayes, Rutherford Birchard (1822-93), American statesman, Republican president (1877-81).

hay fever, inflammation of mucous membranes of eyes or nose. Usually caused by allergic reaction to plant pollen. Characterized by sneezing, watering of eyes.

hazel, any of genus *Corylus* of shrubs and trees of birch family. Native to Eurasia. Yields useful elastic wood. Edible fruit variously known, according to variety, as hazelnut, cob, filbert, Barcelona nut.

Hazlitt, William (1778-1830), English essayist. Known for perceptive criticism of Romantic poets, Elizabethan drama, *eg Characters of Shakespeare's Plays* (1817). Noted prose stylist. Also wrote on philosophy and politics.

health insurance, plan by prior payment to provide services or cash for medical care in times of illness or disability. Can be part of voluntary or compulsory national insurance scheme connected with SOCIAL SECURITY scheme. Early forms were in Germany (1883), most comprehensive scheme coming in UK (*see* NATIONAL HEALTH INSURANCE ACT).

heart, muscular organ which maintains blood circulation in vertebrate animals. Human heart is divided into 2 halves by muscular wall; each half is divided into 2 chambers, upper atrium and lower ventricle. Oxygenated blood from lungs enters left atrium and is pumped into left ventricle by contraction of heart, then into arteries. Venous blood enters right atrium, is pumped into right ventricle and then into lungs to regain oxygen.

heart attack, sudden instance of heart failure, esp. that associated with coronary thrombosis.

heat, internal energy of substance produced by vibrations of constituen molecules, and which passes from place of higher temperature to those of lowe temperature. Transmitted by conductio convection and radiation. SI unit of heat i joule; quantity of heat held by body i product of its mass, specific heat an temperature. Increase in heat of a bod may result in increase in temperature o change of state (*eg* from liquid to gas). *Se* LATENT HEAT.

Heath, Edward Richard George (1916- British statesman, PM (1970-4). Electe leader of Conservative Party in 1965. Su cessfully pursued policy of British entr into EEC (achieved 1973). Admin. marke by bad relations with trade unions culmi ating in miners' strike. Replaced as part leader (1975) after leadership election.

Heath

heath or **heather,** any of genera *Erica* an *Calluna* of shrubs of Ericaceae famil Found on temperate moorlands throughou world. Plants have bell-shaped hangin flowers.

heatstroke, illness caused by exposure t excessive heat. May cause cramp an collapse from salt loss, or faintin Extreme rise in body temperature ma result if body's temperature-regulatin mechanism breaks down.

heaven, in Judaeo-Christian theolog dwelling place of God and his angel where the blessed will live after deat Similar beliefs exist in Islam, Mahayan Buddhism and Hinduism.

Heaviside, Oliver (1850-1925), Englis physicist. Independently of Kennell predicted existence of KENNELLY-HEAVISID LAYER.

heavy spar, *see* BARITE.

heavy water (D_2O), water composed o deuterium and oxygen, found in ordinar water at concentration of 1 part in 500 Used as moderator in nuclear reactor Name also applies to water containin substantial quantities of D_2O or HDO.

Hebe, in Greek myth, goddess of yout Daughter of Zeus and Hera, wife o Heracles after his deification. Cupbearer o the gods before GANYMEDE.

Hebrew, NW Semitic language of Afr Asiatic family. From 586 BC to 19th cent preserved by Jews in religion, learning, their vernacular languages being Aramaic, Yiddish. Rise of Zionism in 19th cent. caused adoption as national language, which it became with estab. of Israel (1948).

ebrews, epistle of NT, traditionally ascribed to St Paul but not now accepted as his. Written before AD 90. Exhorts Christians not to return to Judaism under pressure of persecution.

ebrides, *c* 500 isls. off NW Scotland. Formerly admin. by Argyllshire, Inverness-shire, Ross and Cromarty. Mild, wet climate; crofting, fishing, tourism, tweed mfg. Depopulation (*c* 100 isls. inhabited). Under Norwegian rule 6th-13th cents. **Inner Hebrides** incl. Coll, Colonsay, Iona, Islay, Jura, Mull, Rhum, Skye, Tiree. **Outer Hebrides** incl. Barra, Benbecula, Lewis with Harris, St Kilda, North and South Uist. Now admin. by WESTERN ISLES isl. authority. Outer Hebrides are separated from mainland and Skye by the Minch and Little Minch.

ebron (Arab. *Al Khalil*), town of W Jordan. Pop. 43,000. Sacred to Jews and Moslems; traditional site of tomb of Abraham and his family.

ecate, in Greek myth, goddess of witchcraft, ghosts.

ctare, metric unit of area, equal to 10,000 square metres; 1 hectare = *c* 2.47 acres.

ector, in Greek legend, eldest son of King Priam and husband of Andromache. Greatest hero of Trojan troops during Trojan War. Killed by Achilles.

ecuba, in Greek legend, wife of King Priam of Troy and mother of Hector, Paris, Troilus, Cassandra.

dgehog, any of Erinaceidae family of spiny-backed insectivores widely distributed in Old World. Protects itself by curling up into ball with spines standing outwards. Hibernates in winter.

dge sparrow, *Prunella modularis,* small European bird with reddish-brown back, grey head and white-tipped wings. Also called dunnock.

donism, in ethics, theory that pleasure or happiness of self or society is object of actions. Exponents incl. Aristippus, Epicurus, J. S. Mill.

egel, Georg Wilhelm Friedrich (1770-1831), German philosopher. Formulated concept of historical dialectic: fusion (synthesis) of opposite concepts (thesis and antithesis). Activating principle is 'world spirit' (*Weltgeist*) in universe of continuous self-creation. Works incl. *Phenomenology of Mind* (1807), *Science of Logic* (1812-16). Greatly influenced subsequent philosophers of history, esp. Marx.

gemony, leadership or dominance, esp. of one state or nation over another. Usage in 20th cent. extended by GRAMSCI to incl. cultural dimension.

gira or **hejira,** the flight of Mohammed from Mecca to Medina in AD 622. The Mohammedan era is dated from 16 July of that year, with (in West) AH after year number, *ie* After Hegira.

Heidegger, Martin (1889-1976), German philosopher. Link between Kierkegaard and later existentialists. Major work, *Being and Time* (1927).

Heidelberg, city of WC West Germany, on R. Neckar. Pop. 129,000. Precision instruments, printing industs.; wine, fruit, tourism. Residence of Electors Palatine 13th-18th cent. Famous univ. (1386) centre of German Reformation (16th cent.); ruined 13th cent. castle. Remains of prehist. 'Heidelberg man' found nearby.

Heilbronn, city of SW West Germany, on R. Neckar. Pop. 112,000. River port, railway jct., indust. centre.

Heilungkiang, prov. of NE China. Area *c* 705,000 sq km (272,000 sq mi); pop. 33,000,000; cap. Harbin. Wheat, soya beans grown; major timber indust. Indust. centres in S, minerals (oil, coal, gold).

Heine, Heinrich, pseud. of Chaim Harry Heine (1797-1856), German poet. Settled in Paris (1831). Known for romantic lyric poetry in *Book of Songs* (1827).

Heinkel, Ernst (1888-1958), German aircraft designer. Developed jet aircraft (*c* 1939) independently of Whittle. His company was Germany's largest producer of warplanes in WWII.

Heisenberg, Werner Karl (1901-76), German physicist. Developed form of quantum theory based on matrix methods. His uncertainty principle states that certain pairs of quantities (*eg* position and momentum of particle) cannot both be measured completely accurately. Awarded Nobel Prize for Physics (1932).

Hekla, volcano of S Iceland. Height 1520 m (5000 ft). Many eruptions recorded, most recent 1970.

Helen, in Greek myth, beautiful wife of King Menelaus of Sparta; daughter of Zeus by Leda. Her abduction to Troy by Paris instigated Trojan War. Reconciled to Menelaus after fall of Troy.

Helena, cap. and tourist resort of Montana, US. Pop. 23,000.

helicopter, aircraft with horizontal rotating wings (rotors) which enable it to take off and land vertically, to move in any direction (by inclining axis of rotor) and to hover. Mainly used for short-range transportation, air-sea rescue, firefighting. *See* SIKORSKY.

Heligoland (*Helgoland*), isl. of West Germany, in North Sea, off W Schleswig-Holstein. Exchanged (1890) by UK for Zanzibar.

Heliopolis, ancient ruined city of N Egypt. Centre of sun-worship.

Helios, in Greek myth, sun god, son of TITANS Hyperion and Theia. Crossed the sky daily from east to west in chariot drawn by 4 horses.

heliotrope, any plant that turns to face the sun, esp. genus *Heliotropium* of plants of borage family with clusters of white or purple flowers.

helium (He), inert gaseous element; at. no. 2, at. wt. 4.003. Found in natural gas in Texas and in atmosphere. Used in balloons and airships because of lightness and non-flammability; low boiling point makes it useful in cryogenics. First discovered in Sun (1868), abundant in stars.

Hell, in Christian theology, dwelling place of devils to which sinners are doomed to eternal punishment after death. Often represented with images of fire. Similar concepts occur in Greek myths (Hades), Islam, Judaism.

hellebore, any of genus *Helleborus* of winter-blooming perennials of the buttercup family. Found in Europe and Asia, frequently cultivated as ornamental, esp. Christmas rose, *H. niger*.

Hellespont, *see* DARDANELLES.

Helmholtz, Hermann von (1821-94), German physician, scientist. Developed concept of conservation of energy. Pioneer of physiological optics and acoustics; extended Young's theory of colour vision. Invented ophthalmoscope (1851).

Helsingborg, *see* HÄLSINGBORG.

Helsingfors, *see* HELSINKI.

Helsingör or **Elsinore,** town of NE Zealand, Denmark, on Öresund. Pop. 42,000. Port, ferry service to Hälsingborg (Sweden). Kronborg Castle is scene of Shakespeare's *Hamlet*.

Helsinki (Swed. *Helsingfors*), cap. of Finland, on Gulf of Finland. Pop. 825,000. Admin., cultural centre; univ. (moved from Turku 1828). Chief port, kept open in winter by ice-breakers, exports timber, paper, wood products. Founded 1550, cap. from 1812.

Helvetia, region now within W Switzerland, formerly occupied by Celtic Helvetii (2nd cent. BC-5th cent. AD). Name still used poetically for Switzerland, and on Swiss postage stamps.

Hemel Hempstead, town of Hertfordshire, EC England. Pop. 69,000. Designated new town 1946; light industs.

Hemingway, Ernest Miller (1899-1961), American author. Member of 'lost generation' of expatriates as described in *The Sun Also Rises* (1926). Works, *eg A Farewell to Arms* (1929), *For Whom the Bell Tolls* (1940), novella *The Old Man and the Sea* (1952), celebrate physical courage in terse, dramatic understatement. Nobel Prize for Literature (1954).

hemlock, *Conium maculatum,* biennial umbelliferous herb of N hemisphere. Source of alkaloid poison coniine used medicinally and by ancient Greeks as instrument of capital punishment, notably in case of Socrates.

hemp, *Cannabis sativa,* tall Asiatic herb of nettle family. Stems yield fibre for rope, coarse cloth, paper. Seeds used as birdfood and oil extracted from them as base of paints and soaps. Resin from female flower yields cannabis or marijuana, or whole flower may be processed as hashish. These, when smoked or eaten, may cause mild hallucinations and sense of euphoria

Hemlock

henbane, *Hyoscyamus niger,* poisono plant of nightshade family, native to O World. Source of alkaloid drugs sc polamine and hyoscamine.

henge, in archaeology, ritual monument early British Bronze Age. Usually consist of circular or oval earthen bank with o or two surrounding patterns of pos stones or pits. Examples at Stoneheng Avebury.

henna, *Lawsonia inermis,* small Old Wor tropical shrub. Fragrant white or r flowers; leaves yield reddish-brown d used as hair or body dye.

Henrietta Maria (1609-69), queen conso (1625-49) of Charles I of England. Daught of Henry IV of France. Aroused popular r sentment against Charles through attemp to aid Catholic cause.

Henry III (1017-56), Holy Roman emper (1046-56). The empire reached the peak its power during his reign.

Henry IV (1050-1106), Holy Roman emper (1084-1105). Son of Henry III. Conflict wi Pope Gregory VII over his right to ele bishops; invaded Italy and depos Gregory (1084). Crowned emperor antipope, Clement III. Forced to abdicate

Henry V (1081-1125), Holy Roman emper (1111-25). Forced abdication of his fathe Henry IV. Continued father's struggle wi papacy over election of bishops un compromise reached in Concordat Worms (1122).

Henry I (1068-1135), king of Engla (1100-35). Youngest son of William I, seiz crown on death of brother, William excluding his elder brother Robert II, du of Normandy. Later seized Norman (1105) and imprisoned Robert for li Attempted to secure throne for daught MATILDA.

Henry II (1133-89), king of England (1154-8 By marriage with Eleanor of Aquitai gained huge tracts of land in Franc Named as successor by mother Matild invaded England and forced Stephen name him as heir. Estab. power of thro by subduing barons, strengthening roy courts. Attempted to extend power ov

Church; entered long controversy with Thomas à Becket, ending in Becket's murder. Struggles with sons ended in defeat by son, Richard I. Reign saw beginning of English conquest of Ireland.

enry III (1207-72), king of England (1216-72). Son of John, came to power (1227) after regency. Expensive, unsuccessful campaign in France and autocratic rule led to Barons' War (1263). Simon de MONTFORT, barons' leader, defeated Henry at Lewes and summoned Parliament. Order restored by Henry's son, later Edward I.

enry IV (1367-1413), king of England (1399-1413). Son of John of Gaunt; exiled 1398-9 by Richard II. Returned and forced Richard to abdicate; claim to throne upheld by Parliament. Reign, marked by barons' uprisings and revolt in Wales, left crown in serious debt.

enry V (1387-1422), king of England (1413-22). Son of Henry IV; claiming French throne, reopened Hundred Years War. Defeated French at Agincourt (1415) and seized Normandy. Married Catherine of Valois; recognized as heir to French throne by her father, Charles VI.

enry VI (1421-71), king of England (1422-61, 1470-1). Succeeded father Henry V in infancy. His claims to French throne were unrecognized by the French, whose victories under Joan of Arc and Charles VII drove English from France. Dominated by his wife Margaret of Anjou. Subject to insanity after 1453, became pawn in struggle between Houses of York and Lancaster. Deposed by Edward IV (1461). Briefly restored 1470. Imprisoned in Tower of London, where he died.

enry VII (1457-1509), king of England (1485-1509); until accession, Henry Tudor, Earl of Richmond. Became head of house of Lancaster after death of Henry VI (1471) and fled to France. Invaded England (1485), seized throne from Richard III after victory at Bosworth Field. United houses of York and Lancaster by marrying (1486) Elizabeth, daughter of Edward IV. Defeated Yorkist impostors Lambert Simnel, Perkin Warbeck. Centralized govt. and finances, estab. Tudor tradition of autocratic rule.

enry VIII (1491-1547), king of England (1509-47). Son of Henry VII. Married (1509) brother's widow, Catherine of Aragon. Govt. dominated by WOLSEY until he failed to secure annulment of marriage from pope. This initiated split from Rome, culminating in estab. of Henry as 'supreme head' of Church of England (1534). With chief minister T. CROMWELL, carried out dissolution of monasteries, confiscating wealth. Executed 2nd wife, Anne Boleyn (1536) on charge of adultery, married Jane Seymour (1537) who bore him Edward VI. Successive marriages were to Anne of Cleves (1540), Catherine Howard (1542), Catherine Parr (1543). Wars with Scotland, Ireland, France left crown in debt.

enry II (1519-59), king of France (1547-59). Son of Francis I. Continued wars against Emperor Charles V, England (winning Calais, 1558), Spain. Married (1533) Catherine de' Medici.

Henry III (1551-89), king of France (1574-89). Reign marked by continuing Catholic-Huguenot strife and conflict with Catholic League led by de Guise. Expelled from Paris (1588) by revolt inspired by de Guise. Made alliance with Huguenot leader, Henry of Navarre (later Henry IV), to regain city. Had de Guise murdered; assassinated by fanatic monk.

Henry IV, orig. Henry of Navarre (1553-1610), king of France (1589-1610), king of Navarre (1572-89). Became leader of Huguenots (1569) and legal heir to French throne (1584); fought 10 year war to estab. rule after death of Henry III. Became Catholic as political move (1593). Estab. religious tolerance with Edict of Nantes (1598). Assassinated by fanatic.

Henry, Joseph (1797-1878), American physicist. Independently of Faraday, discovered principle of electromagnetic induction. Developed electromagnet and invented electromagnetic telegraph. Discovered self-inductance and invented an electric motor.

Henry, Patrick (1736-99), American revolutionary. Renowned orator, led opposition to British rule.

Henry the Navigator (1394-1460), Portuguese prince, son of John I. Patron of navigation and exploration of W Africa, laying basis for development of Portuguese overseas empire.

Henryson, Robert (*c* 1430–*c* 1505), Scottish poet. Best known for *Testament of Cresseid,* a severe moral treatment of 'Troilus' story.

Henze, Hans Werner (1926-), German composer. Much of his early work was highly abstract and used 12-note technique; now concentrates on music concerned with social values. His operas incl. *The Bassarids, The Young Lord.*

hepatica, *see* LIVERWORT.

hepatitis, inflammation of liver. Two common forms, transmitted by viruses: serum hepatitis, conveyed by traces of blood on hypodermic needles *etc,* and infectious hepatitis.

Hepburn, Katharine (1907-), American stage and film actress. Known for clipped voice, cool acting. Films incl. *Bringing up Baby* (1938), *The African Queen* (1951).

Hephaestus, in Greek myth, lame god of fire, son of Zeus and Hero, patron of smiths and craftsmen. Married to Aphrodite. Identified by Romans with Vulcan.

Hepplewhite, George (d. 1786), English cabinet maker, furniture designer. Developed light elegant style, esp. in his chairs.

Hepworth, Dame Barbara (1903-75), English abstract sculptor. Early work was carved directly in stone and wood; later work in bronze.

Hera, in Greek myth, daughter of Cronus

Hepplewhite-style dressing table

and Rhea; sister and wife of Zeus. Patron of sexual life of women and marriage. Jealous, she persecuted Zeus' mortal offspring. Sometimes identified with Roman Juno.

Heracles, in Greek myth, son of Zeus and Alcmene. Known as Hercules by the Romans. Popular hero famed for strength and courage. Driven mad by Hera, he killed his wife and children. To expiate this crime served King Eurystheus of Tiryns for 12 years, achieving 12 labours: (1) brought back skin of Nemean lion, (2) killed the Hydra, (3) captured the Cerynean hind and (4) the Erymanthian boar, (5) cleaned the stables of Augeas, (6) destroyed the Stymphalian birds, (7) captured the Cretan bull and (8) the man-eating mares of Diomedes, (9) stole the girdle of Queen Hippolyte of the Amazons, (10) brought back the cattle of Geryon, (11) stole the apples of the Hesperides, (12) captured Cerberus from Hades. Also involved in many other adventures incl. Argonauts' quest. On death he obtained immortality, married Hebe.

Heraclitus (*c* 535-*c* 475 BC), Greek philosopher. Believed that all things imply their opposites, that change is the only reality, permanence an illusion. Held fire to be underlying universal substance.

Herakleion, *see* IRÁKLION.

heraldry, system of inherited symbols (traditionally displayed on shield, surcoat) used for identification of individuals, families, institutions. Prob. originated in Germany (12th cent.); in Middle Ages, rules for personal devices such as coats of arms, badges, crests, were regularized. In UK, controlled by College of Arms since 1483.

herb, any seed plant whose stem withers back to the ground after each season's growth, as distinguished from a tree or shrub whose woody stem lives from year to year. Also any plant used as a medicine or seasoning, *eg* thyme, basil.

Herbert, George (1593-1633), English po[e]
Best known for collection of metaphysic[al]
religious poems *The Temple* (1633).

herbivore, name applied to any animal, es[p.] mammal, which feeds entirely or main[ly] on vegetation.

Hercegovina, *see* BOSNIA AND HERCEGOVINA.

Herculaneum (Ital. *Ercolano*), ancient ci[ty] of SW Italy, near Naples. Roman reso[rt] buried (AD 79) with POMPEII in eruption [of] Vesuvius. Site discovered 1709.

Hercules, *see* HERACLES.

heredity, process whereby characteristics [of] living organisms are transmitted fro[m] parents to offspring by means of gen[es] carried in chromosomes. Mutation [of] chromosomes can result in changes [in] inherited characteristics. Studied scient[if]ically as genetics.

Hereford and Worcester, county of [W] England. Area 3927 sq km (1516 sq m[i]); pop. 610,000; admin. hq. Worcester. Creat[ed] 1974, comprises former Herefordshir[e,] Worcestershire.

Herefordshire, former county of [W] England. Malvern Hills in E; Wye Valley [in] C; Black Mts. in SW. Hereford beef catt[le,] fruit growing, esp. apples, pears. Co. tow[n] was **Hereford,** city on R. Wye. Pop. 47,00[0]. Agric. market. Has 11th cent. cathedral.

Herero, nomadic BANTU people of Namibia.

Hereward the Wake (*fl* 1070), Engli[sh] chieftain. Led Anglo-Saxon rebelli[on] against William the Conqueror (1070-[1]). Took Isle of Ely as his stronghold but w[as] defeated (1071).

hermaphrodite, animal or plant possessi[ng] both male and female reproducti[ve] systems, *eg* earthworms. Name sometim[es] applied to humans possessing physic[al] characteristics of opposite sex due [to] hormone imbalance.

Hermes, in Greek myth, messenger of t[he] gods; son of Zeus and Maia. Patron [of] merchants, travellers, roads and thieve[s]. Represented with staff, winged shoes a[nd] broad hat. Identified by Romans wi[th] Mercury.

Hermes Trismegistus, Greek name f[or] Egyptian god THOTH, supposed author [of] the 17 treatises of *Corpus Hermeticu[m]*, prob. compiled in 3rd cent. AD, whic[h] describe the mystical harmonies of t[he] universe.

hermit crab, type of crab of Pagurid[ae] family that protects its soft abdomen [by] living in empty mollusc shell which [it] drags around when walking.

hernia or **rupture,** abnormal protrusion [of] an organ through a tear in wall [of] surrounding structure, esp. loop [of] intestine into top of thigh. Usually treat[ed] by surgery.

Hero, in Greek myth. priestess of Aphrodi[te] at Sestos. Her lover, Leander, used to swi[m] the Hellespont nightly to visit her. S[he] allowed the light with which she guid[ed] him to blow out and he drowned. In despa[ir] she threw herself into the sea.

ro or **Heron of Alexandria** (*fl* AD 2nd ent.), Greek mathematician, inventor. eveloped double force pump, water rgan and steam devices. Investigated perations of screws, wheels, levers and ulleys.

od Antipas (d. *c* AD 40), tetrarch of alilee and Peraea. Married Herodias, other of Salome; banished by Caligula AD 39) after seeking title of king. xecuted John the Baptist; ruled at time of esus' death.

odotus (*c* 484-*c* 424 BC), Greek historian, alled the 'Father of History'. Travelled idely through known world, observing nd recording customs and beliefs. Major ork is *History of Graeco-Persian Wars.*

od the Great (*c* 74-4 BC), king of Judaea. eclared king of Judaea through Mark ntony's influence (40). Estab. his cap. at erusalem (37), where he rebuilt Great emple. According to St Matthew, ordered assacre of male infants in Bethlehem to revent survival of Jesus.

oin or **diacetyl morphine,** white rystalline powder derived from morphine. troduced as supposed non-addictive ainkilling substitute for morphine, it roved to be a powerfully addictive narotic.

on, long-legged, long-necked wading bird f Ardeidae family. Breeds in colonies or eronries high in trees.

pes, name given to 2 different virus seases, characterized by eruption of mall blisters on skin and mucous embranes. *Herpes simplex* is group of flamed blisters (cold sores) often around outh. *H. zoster* or shingles is painful fection of sensory nerves.

rick, Robert (1591-1674), English poet. nown for collection, *Hesperides* (1648), cl. religious verse, love lyrics.

ring, *Clupea harengus,* common food fish f N Atlantic. Once fished in great umbers, stocks greatly depleted in some reas. Related species in N Pacific.

ring gull, *Larus argentatus,* common arine bird of N hemisphere. Scavenger round harbours; feeds on fish.

schel, Sir Frederick William 1738-1822), British astronomer, b. ermany. Considered founder of modern stronomy, he discovered planet Uranus 1781), 2 of its satellites (1787), and 2 atellites of Saturn. Constructed powerful eflecting telescopes and discovered umerous nebulae and double stars. His on, **Sir John Frederick William Herschel** 1792-1871), extended his study of heavenly odies.

tfordshire, county of EC England. Area 634 sq km (630 sq mi); pop. 947,000. Lowing; Chiltern Hills in NW. Cereals, arket gardening, dairy farming. Admin. q. **Hertford,** town on R. Lea. Pop. 20,000.

tz, Heinrich Rudolf (1857-94), German hysicist. Confirmed (1888) existence of ectromagnetic waves predicted by laxwell and showed that they obey same laws as light. Unit of frequency named after him, equal to one cycle per second.

Hertzog, James Barry Munnik (1866-1942), South African soldier, politician, PM (1924-39). Organized anti-British National party (1913). Advocated neutrality in WWI, WWII.

Herzegovina, *see* BOSNIA AND HERCEGOVINA.

Herzl, Theodor, *see* ZIONISM.

Hesiod (*fl c* 8th cent. BC), Greek poet. Earliest of Greek poets after Homer. Wrote didactic poem *Works and Days* on farming. May have written *Theogony,* concerning origin of world and genealogies of gods.

Hesperides, in Greek myth, daughters of Evening who, with the help of dragon Ladon, guarded the golden apples of the tree given by Gaea to Hera on her marriage to Zeus. Heracles killed Ladon, stole apples as his 11th labour.

Hess, Rudolf (1894-), German Nazi leader, b. Egypt. Hitler's deputy from 1933. In apparent peace bid, flew stolen plane to Scotland (1941); imprisoned. Sentenced to life imprisonment at Nuremberg trials (1946).

Hesse, Hermann (1877-1962), German author. Best-known novels, *eg Demian* (1919), *Steppenwolf* (1927), *The Glass-Bead Game* (1943), reflect interest in Indian mysticism, psychoanalysis. Swiss citizen from 1921. Nobel Prize for Literature (1946).

Hesse *(Hessen),* state of WC West Germany, cap. Wiesbaden. Mainly forested uplands; agric., vine growing, minerals. Resorts incl. several spas, *eg* Bad Homburg. Region incl. parts of former Hesse-Nassau prov. and Hesse-Darmstadt duchy.

Heyerdahl, Thor (1914-), Norwegian ethnologist. Known for practical demonstrations of feasibility of early racial migrations. Works incl. *Kon Tiki* (1950) on voyage from Peru to W Pacific isls. by balsa raft, *The Ra Expeditions* (1971) on crossing Atlantic by Egyptian-style papyrus boat.

hibernation, winter sleep of certain animals in temperate regions. Complete hibernation involves temperature drop, no food, spring awakening; practised by some mammals, most amphibians. Partial hibernation, practised by *eg* bats, involves periodic awakening for food.

hibiscus, genus of ornamental plants of mallow family, comprising *c* 150 herbs, shrubs and trees. Found in tropical and warm temperate areas.

hiccup or **hiccough,** involuntary spasm of diaphragm followed by intake of air which is halted by sudden closing of glottis. Most hiccup attacks pass quickly.

hickory, any of genus *Carya* of timber and nut-producing trees of walnut family. Native to E Canada and US. Species incl. PECAN.

hieratic, Egyptian cursive script derived from hieroglyphics for purpose of writing on papyrus. Gave way to DEMOTIC from 7th cent. BC but survived longer as religious script.

hieroglyphics, ancient Egyptian pictographic writing developed in pre-dynastic times, *ie* before 3100 BC. Used 3 classes of symbol: ideograms or pictograms, representing words in pictorial form; phonograms, representing sounds of words; determinatives, to indicate sense. *See* ROSETTA STONE.

Highland, region of N Scotland. Area 25,141 sq km (9709 sq mi); pop. 186,000. Admin. hq Inverness. Created 1975, incl. former Sutherland, Caithness, Ross and Cromarty, Inverness-shire, Nairnshire.

Highlands, area of Scotland, N of line joining Helensburgh and Stonehaven. Mainly uplands, mountains rising to 1342 m (4406 ft) at Ben Nevis; many sea, freshwater lochs; bisected by Great Glen. Crofting, fishing, distilling, tourist industs. Oil discovered off N, E coasts; h.e.p.

highwayman, formerly, robber on horseback, who robbed travellers on highway. Esp. prevalent in UK in 17th-18th cent., leading to estab. of Bow Street Runners. Most famous was Dick Turpin.

hijacker, originally, one who steals goods, esp. truck and contents, in transit. Term applied from late 1960s to one who forces pilot of aircraft to fly to non-scheduled landing point. Became tactic of international guerrilla warfare.

Hildebrand, *see* GREGORY VII, ST.

Hill, Sir Rowland (1795-1879), English reformer. Responsible for introduction of pre-paid penny-stamp post (1840).

Hillary, Sir Edmund Percival (1919-), New Zealand mountaineer, explorer. He and **Tensing Norkay** (1914-), were first to reach summit of Mt. Everest (May, 1953), as part of British Everest Expedition. Joint-leader of Commonwealth Trans Antarctic Expedition (1957-8).

Hilliard, Nicholas (*c* 1547-1619), English painter, goldsmith. First true miniaturist in England, he was court painter to Elizabeth I and James I.

Hillingdon, bor. of W Greater London, England. Pop. 228,000. Created 1965 from Middlesex towns incl. Uxbridge.

Hilversum, town of WC Netherlands. Pop. 112,000. Resort; textiles, electrical goods. Chief Dutch broadcasting centre.

Himachal Pradesh, state of N India. Area *c* 56,000 sq km (21,600 sq mi); cap. Simla. Pop. 3,424,000. In W Himalaya, bordering on Tibet. Produces timber. Formed (1948) from former Hill States; more areas from Punjab added in 1966.

Himalaya, world's highest mountain system, stretching *c* 2400 km (1500 mi) across C Asia; forms natural barrier between Tibet and India, Nepal, and Bhutan. Peaks incl. Mt. Everest, Kanchenjunga, Nanga Parbat.

Himmler, Heinrich (1900-45), German Nazi leader. Became head of SS (1929), commander of entire police force (1936), minister of interior (1943). Responsible for enforcement of extermination policies. Captured by Allies; committed suicide.

Hindemith, Paul (1895-1963), Germ composer. Output large, varied, moderr style. Works incl. symphonies and ope *eg Mathis der Maler*. Also a noted mu theorist. Music banned by Nazis, after 1 lived in US, Switzerland.

Hindenburg [und Beneckendorff], P von (1847-1934), German military, politi leader. Became supreme commander Central Forces (1916), directing Germ war effort until end of WWI. President Reich (1925-34); appointed Hitler chan lor (1933).

Hindi, Indic language in Indo-Iranian bra of Indo-European family. Official langu of India. Variant of Hindustani.

Hinduism, Western term for the religion social system of loosely related se which incl. most of India's pop. Has single founder but grew over period o 5000 years, assimilating many beliefs. Hindus traditionally subscribe to CA system and the sacredness of V scriptures.

Hindu Kush, mountain range, mainly in Afghanistan, separated from W Himal by Indus valley. Tirich Mir in Pakis height 7692 m (25,236 ft), is highest peak.

Hindustani, group of Indic languages Indo-Iranian branch of Indo-Europ family. Some use term only for spo forms of Hindi and Urdu, others incl. Indian vernaculars. Developed from PR RIT. Lingua franca in modern India.

hinny, *see* ASS.

hip, *see* BRIAR.

Hipparchus, tyrant of Athens. *See* HIPPIAS

Hipparchus (2nd cent. BC), Greek astro mer. Made catalogue of hundreds of st and discovered precession of equino first to use trigonometry.

Hippias, tyrant of Athens (527-510 BC). of Pisistratus, shared rule of Athens w his brother Hipparchus, until latt murder. Deposed by Alcmaeonidae fam with aid of Sparta.

Hippocrates (*c* 460-*c* 370 BC), Greek ph cian, known as the 'Father of Medici Leader of school of medicine on isl. of C whose members emphasized scient basis of medicine, distinguishing it fr philosophy and religion. Hippocratic o taken by medical graduates, said represent his ethical ideas.

Hippolyte, *see* AMAZONS.

Hippolytus, *see* PHAEDRA.

hippopotamus, heavy thick-skinned herbi rous mammal common to rivers of Afr Large tusks in lower jaw source of iv Two species: *Hippopotamus amphibius* C Africa, and pygmy hippopotam *Choeropsis liberiensis*, of Liberia.

Hirohito (1901-), emperor of Ja (1926-). Reign marked by Sino-Japan (beginning 1937) and defeat in W Became constitutional emperor (19 renounced claims to imperial divinity.

Hiroshima, seaport of Japan, SW Honshu Pop. 842,000. Shipbuilding, car and te

Hippopotamus

nfg. Devastated by 1st atomic bomb (6 Aug. 1945), with loss of *c* 80,000 lives.

ispaniola, isl. of Greater Antilles, West ndies, lying between Cuba and Puerto Rico. Area 76,483 sq km (29,530 sq mi). Comprises Haiti in W, Dominican Republic n E. Discovered by Columbus in 1492.

tamine, white crystalline substance found n animal tissue. Released when tissue is njured or during allergic reactions. Dilates blood vessels and stimulates gastric ecretion.

tory, systematic study of the past, recording, analyzing, correlating and interpreting past events. Sources incl. buildings, rtifacts as well as chronicles, contemporary written records. Herodotus considered st historian; Thucydides began tradition of ccuracy, continued by Tacitus in Roman eriod. Story-telling element stressed by Xenophon, Livy. Medieval historians reoccupied with theological interpretation of world's history, or with simply hronicling events (as by Saxo Grammaticus, Matthew Paris). Renaissance brought mphasis on textual criticism, esp. in 16th-7th cent. Accuracy was again combined with moral, social concern with 18th-cent. writers, incl. Voltaire, Montesquieu. 19th ent. saw emergence of archaeology, philology, and develpoment of history into cademic discipline. Philosophy of history nfluenced by HEGEL, MARX, TOYNBEE.

chcock, Alfred [Joseph] (1899-1980), British film director. Famous for suspense hrillers. Films incl. *Blackmail* (1929), *The Lady Vanishes* (1938), *Psycho* (1960).

tler, Adolf (1889-1945), German dictator, . Austria. Founded (1921) National Socialist (Nazi) Party. During imprisonment 1923) for attempted coup (beer hall putsch') in Munich, wrote *Mein Kampf* my struggle), statement of ideology. Economic depression after 1929 brought mass support, making (1932) Nazis largest party in Reichstag. Hitler was appointed hancellor (Jan. 1933), estab. dictatorship March, 1933) by attributing Reichstag fire o Communists. Estab. (1934) Third Reich, ssuming title of Führer. Political opponents, Jews, socialists were persecuted, imprisoned or killed. Aggressive foreign policy and Anglo-French 'appeasement' led to MUNICH PACT (1938). Invaded Poland (1939) beginning WWII. Personal command of Russian campaign (1941) led to Stalingrad defeat. Survived assassination attempt (1944) by high-ranking officers. Faced with total defeat, committed suicide (April, 1945) with his wife, Eva Braun.

Hittites, people inhabiting Asia Minor and Syria from 3rd to 1st millennium BC. At peak of power 1450-1200, when they challenged Assyria and Egypt. Spoke one of earliest recorded Indo-European languages. Thought to be among 1st peoples to smelt iron.

Hobart, cap. of Tasmania, Australia, on Derwent estuary. Pop. 162,000. Admin. centre; port with fine natural harbour, exports fruit, timber, metals; food processing, metal refining; univ. of Tasmania (1890). Founded 1804.

Hobbema, Meindert (1638-1709), Dutch painter. Painted quiet landscapes, specializing in watermills and woodland scenes.

Hobbes, Thomas (1588-1679), English philosopher. Best-known work, *Leviathan* (1651), argued that humans are naturally violent, self-seeking, only to be controlled in totalitarian state, ruled by absolute monarch. Theories attacked by Locke.

hobby, *Falco subbuteo,* small European falcon with long wings, short tail.

Ho Chi Minh, orig. Nguyen That Thanh (1890-1969), Vietnamese political leader. Helped found French Communist Party (1920) and Vietnamese Communist Party (1930). Organized and led Viet Minh, fighting guerrilla war against Japanese in WWII; headed provisional govt. after war. Gained complete control of North Vietnam after Indo-Chinese War (1946-54) against French. Geneva settlement divided Vietnam, Ho given control N of 17th parallel. Pursued militant policy in effort to reunite Vietnam through guerrilla war with South.

Ho Chi Minh City, city of S Vietnam; formerly Saigon. Pop. 3,461,000. Indust. centre with neighbouring Cholon, with canal link to R. Mekong. French colonial cap. from 1887 until independence in 1954; cap. of S Vietnam 1954-76. Hq. of US and South Vietnamese forces in Vietnam war; seriously damaged in guerrilla fighting.

hockey, game played on field or ice. Field hockey, an eleven-a-side game played with ball and stick, developed in England, becoming popular in 1870s. Ice hockey, six-a-side game played with stick and rubber puck, originated in Canada in 1870s.

Hockney, David (1937-), English artist. Early work related to pop art. Later style is more realistic and colourful; excels in depiction of water and in naturalistic portraiture.

Hodgkin, Dorothy Mary Crowfoot (1910-), British biochemist, Used X-rays to determine structure of vitamin B_{12}, insulin, penicillin. Won Nobel Prize for Chemistry (1964).

Hoek van Holland, *see* HOOK OF HOLLAND.

Hoffmann, E[rnst] T[heodor] A[madeus] (1776-1822), German author, composer. Influential during Romantic period through literary style; stories used by Offenbach for libretto of *Tales of Hoffmann.*

Hofmannsthal, Hugo von (1874-1929), Austrian writer. Abandoned lyric poetry for mythological drama *eg Elektra* (1903). Wrote libretti for Richard Strauss's operas, incl. *Rosenkavalier* (1911).

hog, name applied to several members of pig family. Species incl. red river hog, *Potamochoerus porcus,* of C and S Africa, pygmy hog, *Sus salvanius,* of Nepal, and WART HOG.

Hogarth, William (1697-1764), English painter, engraver. Painted series of morality pictures, incl. *The Rake's Progress,* which satirized social abuses; engravings of these were popular successes.

Hogg, James (1770-1835), Scottish author. Known as 'The Ettrick Shepherd'. Wrote *The Private Memoirs and Confessions of a Justified Sinner* (1824) dealing with Calvinist doctrine of predestination. Also wrote poetry.

Hoggar Mountains, *see* AHAGGAR.

Hohenstaufen, German princely family, originating as dukes of Swabia. Holy Roman emperors (1138-1208, 1214-54); kings of Sicily (1194-1268).

Hohenzollern, German dynasty, founded by Frederick of Hohenzollern in Nuremberg (1192). His sons estab. 2 lines of family in Prussia and Bavaria, adding (1415) electorate of Brandenburg. Kings of Prussia (1701-1918); emperors of Germany (1871-1918).

Hokkaido, isl. of N Japan, separated from Honshu isl. by Tsugaru Str. Area *c* 78,000 sq km (30,000 sq mi). Forested, with mountainous interior; harsh climate in winter. Fishing main indust.; produces coal, timber. Originally inhabited by aboriginal Ainus, settled by Japanese in 16th cent.

Hokusai, Katsushika (1760-1849), Japanese painter and designer. Master of wood-block print, he is famous for his imaginative landscapes; his simplified design and dramatic composition influenced Western art.

Holbein, Hans, ('the Younger') (*c* 1497-1543), German painter. Leading realist portrait painter of the N European Renaissance. Court painter to Henry VIII, his portraits incl. many of Erasmus, and the *Ambassadors.*

Holinshed, Raphael (d. *c* 1580), English chronicler. Wrote *Chronicles of England, Scotland and Ireland* (1577), used as source for plots by Shakespeare.

Holland, Sir Sidney George (1893-1961), New Zealand statesman, PM (1949-57). Leader of National Party from 1946.

Holland, hist. region of W. Netherlands. County from 10th cent., held Zeeland, pa of Friesland during Middle Ages. Prospe ty at height 15th-16th cents. throu commerce, cloth indust. Led Dut independence struggle, chief of Unit Provs. 1579-1795. Divided 1840 into Nor and South Holland provs. North Holla incl. some Frisian Isls. Area 2631 sq k (1016 sq mi); cap. Haarlem, chief ci Amsterdam. South Holland, area 2810 km (1085 sq mi); cap. The Hague, ch towns Rotterdam, Leiden. Name also us for the Netherlands.

Holly

holly, any of genus *Ilex* of evergree smooth-leaved trees and shrubs. Speci incl. European holly *I. aquifolium* with r berries. Traditional Christmas decoratior

hollyhock, *Althaea rosea,* biennial plant mallow family. Native to China, n widely cultivated garden plant. Lar showy flowers on long spikes. Grows up *c* 3 m/10 ft.

Hollywood, suburb of Los Angeles, U Centre of American film industry.

holmium (Ho), metallic element lanthanide group; at. no. 67, at. wt. 164. Discovered (1878).

Holocene or **Recent epoch,** second a current geological epoch of Quaterna period. Began *c* 11,000 years ago. Wh Pleistocene glaciers melted, climate w for a time warmer than now; prese landscape formed, *eg* lakes, deserts. M dominant; culture developed throu Mesolithic and Neolithic, Bronze and Ir Ages to present level of civilization. A *see* GEOLOGICAL TABLE.

holography, means of producing dimensional images without use of lens Light from a laser is split into 2 beams, o of which falls directly onto photograph plate. Other beam illuminates subject to reproduced and then recombines w reference beam to form interferen pattern (hologram) on plate. 3-dimensional virtual image can be seen shining laser light through developed film

Holst, Gustav (1874-1934), British compos Work incl. opera *The Perfect Fool,* cho work *Hymn of Jesus,* orchestral suite *T Planets.*

Holt, Harold Edward (1908-67), Australi

statesman, Liberal Party leader and PM (1966-7). Drowned.

ͻly Alliance, treaty signed (1815) by emperors of Russia, Austria, Prussia, with all European sovereigns eventually signing except George IV of Britain, pope, and sultan of Turkey. Estab. to preserve 1815 status quo, suppressed revolutions until Revolution of 1848 rendered it ineffective.

ͻly Communion, *see* Eucharist.

ͻly Ghost, *see* Trinity.

ͻly Grail, *see* Grail, Holy.

ͻlyhead, port of Gwynedd, NW Wales, on Holy Isl. Pop. 11,000. Tourist resort; has ferry services to Irish Republic.

ͻly Island, *see* Lindisfarne.

ͻly Land, *see* Israel.

ͻlyoake, Sir Keith Jacka (1904-), New Zealand statesman, PM (1957, 1960-72). National Party leader (1957-72). Governor general (1977-).

ͻly Roman Empire, revival of ancient Roman Empire of the West, founded by Charlemagne (800). After period of decline and disunity, empire was revived by coronation of Otto I (962), who united Lombardy with Germany. Dominions incl. Germany, Austria, Bohemia, Belgium and, until 1648, Switzerland and Netherlands. Habsburgs became hereditary rulers after 1438. Opposed Protestant Reformation in 16th cent. Influence declined after Thirty Years War (1618-48), power thereafter being wielded by Spanish and Austrian branches. Dissolved (1806) after Napoleon's conquests.

ͻlyrood House, royal palace in Edinburgh, Scotland, built *c* 1500 by James IV on site of 12th-cent. abbey. Almost destroyed by fire (1650) and rebuilt by Charles II in 1670s.

ͻly Week, in Christian calendar, week preceding Easter, commemorating Jesus' passion and death.

ͻme, Sir Alec Douglas-, *see* Douglas-Home.

ͻme Guard, in UK, originally the Local Defence Volunteers, formed (1940) as makeshift anti-invasion force, became efficient army of *c* 2 million by 1945.

ͻmeopathy, system of therapeutics introduced by German physician Samuel Hahnemann (1755-1843). Based on belief that cure of disease is effected by minute doses of drugs capable of producing in a healthy individual symptoms of the disease being treated.

ͻmer (*fl. c* 8th cent. BC), Greek epic poet. Traditionally regarded as author of Iliad and Odyssey, although opinions differ over single authorship, with some doubt over his existence. Said to have been blind wanderer.

ͻme Rule, in Irish history, slogan used by Irish nationalists in 19th cent. who wished to obtain self-govt. for Ireland within British empire. Home Rule movement began in 1870s under leadership of Parnell. Gladstone's 1st Home Rule Bill (1886) defeated; 2nd (1893) thwarted by House of Lords; 3rd (1912) never put into effect because of WWI and Irish pressure for independent republic.

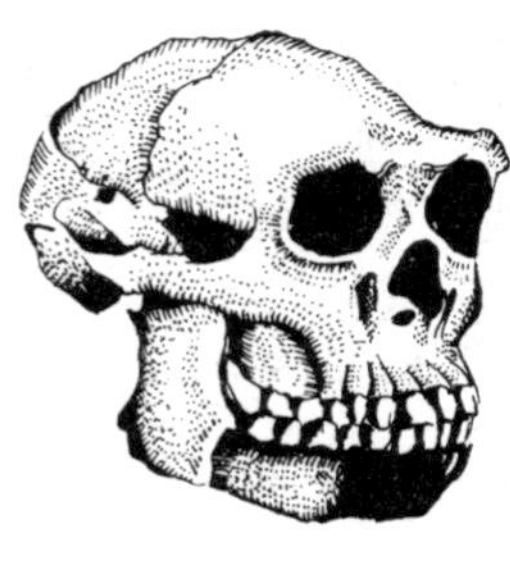

Homo erectus: reconstructed skull

Homo erectus, extinct species of man, incl. Java man and Peking Man. Recent finds suggest that *Homo erectus* may have existed more than 2 million years ago in E Africa.

homosexuality, sexual attraction towards individuals of same sex. In women, commonly called lesbianism. Acceptance varies from culture to culture, male homosexual practices being illegal until recently in Britain.

Homs (anc. *Emesa),* city of WC Syria. Pop. 292,000. Agric. centre; oil refining, textile mfg.

Honan, prov. of EC China. Area 168,350 sq km (65,000 sq mi); pop. 70,000,000; cap. Chengchow. Sparsely pop. in mountainous W, agric.; indust. in E; cereals, cotton, coal mining. Crossed by Hwang Ho.

Honduras, republic of Central America, incl. off-shore Bay Isls. Area 112,088 sq km (43,277 sq mi); pop. 3,439,000; cap. Tegucigalpa. Language: Spanish. Religion: RC. Humid Caribbean coast (banana plantations); Mosquito Coast in NE; mainly forested mountains in interior with important silver mines. Visited by Columbus (1502), colonized by Spanish; gained independence 1821; member of Central American Federation 1825-38. Disastrous floods in 1974.

Honecker, Erich (1912-), East German political leader. Secretary of Communist Party (1971-), succeeding Ulbricht.

honesty or **moonwort,** *Lunaria annua,* European flowering plant with distinctive silver moon-shaped seed pods. Purple or white flowers in spring.

honey, sweet sticky fluid manufactured by honey bees from nectar taken from flowers, and stored in honeycombs as food. Consists of various sugars produced by action of enzymes on sucrose in nectar. Colour and flavour depend on type of flower from which nectar was collected.

honey bee, *Apis mellifera,* social bee of Old World origin. Builds nests of wax, storing honey in hexagonal cells; often kept in hives by man to supply honey.

honeysuckle, any of genus *Lonicera* of wild and cultivated, erect or climbing shrubs. *L. periclymenum,* best known in Europe, has fragrant yellow or white flowers. Name often used for family Caprifoliaceae, incl. viburnums, elder, as well as true honeysuckle.

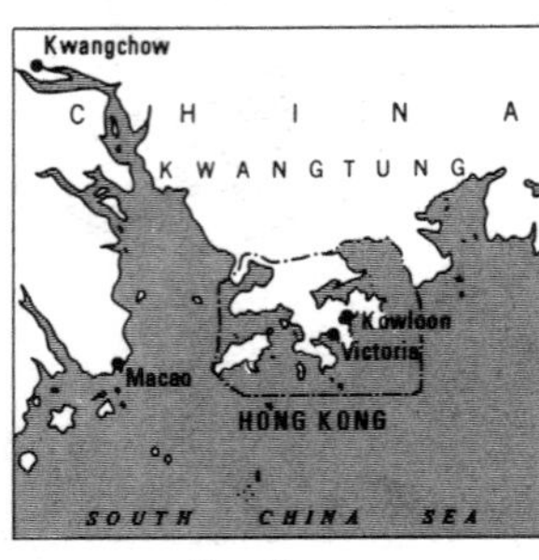

Hong Kong

Hong Kong, British crown colony of SE Asia, connected to S China. Area 1034 sq km (398 sq mi); pop. 4,606,000; cap. Victoria. Incl. Hong Kong isl. (ceded to Britain 1941), Kowloon penin. (joined by tunnel 1972), and New Territ. (leased from China for 99 years in 1898). Major textile, garment industs.; shipbuilding, electrical equipment mfg. Important link for Chinese trade. Free port, with fine harbour.

Honolulu, cap. and chief port of Hawaii, US; on SE Oahu isl. Pop. 705,000. Financial, tourist centre; sugar processing, pineapple canning. Cap. from 1845.

Honshu, chief isl. of Japan. Area *c* 230,000 sq km (89,000 sq mi). Mountainous (Fujiyama), little arable land; rivers short and rapid. Densely populated; indust. centres incl. Tokyo, Yokohama, Nagoya, Osaka.

Honthorst, Gerard van (1590-1656), Dutch artist. Painted biblical, mythological and genre scenes.

Hooch or **Hoogh, Pieter de** (1628-*c* 1684), Dutch genre painter. Remembered for his depiction of interiors and courtyards; his rendering of effects of light is esp. fine.

Hooghly or **Hugli,** river of W Bengal, NE India; *c* 260 km (160 mi) long. Most westerly and most important arm of Ganges. Constant dredging of it maintains Calcutta's access to ocean.

Hooke, Robert (1635-1703), English physicist. A noted experimenter, he formulated Hooke's law of elasticity and invented the spiral spring for watches.

Hook of Holland *(Hoek van Holland),* town of SW Netherlands, on North Sea. P[illegible] 3000. Ferry to Harwich (England).

hookworm, minute parasitic roundwo[illegible] infecting humans, common in trop[illegible] Larvae in soil penetrate skin and migr[illegible] to intestine; blood-sucking causes anaem[illegible] *Ancylostoma duodenale* is comm[illegible] species.

hoopoe, *Upupa epops,* insectivorous bird [illegible] Old World, with slender bill and erec[illegible] headcrest. Solitary, timid.

Hoover, Herbert Clark (1874-1964), Ame[illegible] can statesman, Republican presid[illegible] (1929-33). Term marked by loss of pub[illegible] confidence on stock-market crash and s[illegible] sequent Depression.

Hoover, J[ohn] Edgar (1895-197[illegible] American public official. Director [illegible] Federal Bureau of Investigation (1924-72[illegible]

Hoover Dam, on Colorado R., US; [illegible] Arizona-Nevada border. Built 1931-6; one [illegible] world's largest dams, forming L. Me[illegible] Supplies h.e.p. and irrigation over la[illegible] area. Formerly named Boulder Dam.

hop, *Humulus lupulus,* perennial climbi[illegible] vine of hemp family. Grown for the co[illegible] like female flowers (hops), which are dr[illegible] and used in flavouring beer.

Hope, Bob, orig. Leslie Townes Ho[illegible] (1903-), American comedian, b. Brita[illegible] Associated with Bing Crosby, Doro[illegible] Lamour in 'Road' films, *eg Road [illegible] Morocco* (1942).

Hopeh, Hopei or **Chihli,** prov. of NE Chi[illegible] on Pohai gulf. Area *c* 194,250 sq km (75,[illegible] sq mi); pop. 50,000,000; cap. Shihkiachwa[illegible] Cereals, cotton, stock raising. Indu[illegible] around Peking.

Hopi, *see* PUEBLO INDIANS.

Hopkins, Gerard Manley (1844-89), Engl[illegible] poet, Jesuit priest. Works, displayi[illegible] metrical inventiveness, deal with religi[illegible] nature. *Poems* (pub. 1918) incl. 'The Wre[illegible] of the Deutschland'.

Horace, full name Quintus Horatius Flacc[illegible] (65-8 BC), Roman lyric poet, satir[illegible] Achieved fame with *Satires, Epodes,* [illegible] best known for *Odes, Epistles* and *A[illegible] Poetica.*

horehound or **hoarhound,** *Marrubi[illegible] vulgare,* herb of mint family with bit[illegible] aromatic juice. Grows wild in Europe, A[illegible] and US. Used as flavouring and for cou[illegible] mixtures and lozenges.

hormone, substance formed in endocri[illegible] glands of higher animals. Carried by blo[illegible] to other organs and tissues to control t[illegible] body's metabolism. May be a steroid, [illegible] oestrogen, a protein, *eg* insulin, or sim[illegible] organic compound, *eg* adrenaline.

Hormuz, Strait of, passage off S Iran, c[illegible] necting Persian Gulf and Gulf of Om[illegible] Also called Strait of Ormuz.

horn, a brass instrument with a funn[illegible] shaped mouthpiece and a long, coni[illegible] tube wound into a coil with a flaring bell. [illegible] natural horn sounds only the notes [illegible] hunting calls; FRENCH HORN has valves [illegible] produce all notes.

Horn, Cape, rocky headland of S Chile

Tierra del Fuego, most S point of South America. Notorious for stormy seas.

ornbeam, any of genus *Carpinus* of small trees of birch family. Found in US, Europe and Asia. Bears clusters of light-green nuts and yields very hard white wood.

ornbill, any bird of Bucerotidae family of Asian and African tropics. Has large curved bill with brightly coloured horny growth.

ornblende, dark green or black mineral of amphibole group. Glassy in appearance; found widely among igneous and metamorphic rocks.

ornet, name given to several species of large social wasps, esp. European *Vespa crabro.*

oroscope, *see* ASTROLOGY.

orse, *Equus caballus,* herbivorous hoofed mammal. Earliest known ancestor is dog-sized *Eohippus* of *c* 50 million years ago. *E. przewalskii* of Mongolia only surviving wild horse. Horses are classed as draught, light and ponies. Light horses such as Arabian and racehorses used for driving or riding.

orse chestnut, *Aesculus hippocastanum,* deciduous tree, native to temperate Eurasia. Large leaves, white flowers followed by glossy brown seeds ('conkers') growing in green spiky burrs.

orsefly, large fly of Tabanidae family, the female of which sucks blood of livestock. Also called cleg or gadfly.

orsepower, British unit of power; equals rate of working at 550 foot-pounds/sec; 1 horsepower = 745.7 watts.

orse racing, contest of speed between horses over designated course. Saddle racing incl. flat or thoroughbred races and steeplechases (over obstacles). In harness racing (trotting) horse pulls two-wheeled sulky. In England, Jockey Club (founded 1750) controls horse racing. Famous events are Epsom Derby, St Leger Stakes, One and Two Thousand Guineas, Oaks and Grand National.

orseradish, *Armoracia rusticana,* perennial herb of mustard family, native to S Europe and naturalized in North America. Grated, pungent root is used as relish.

orseshoe bat, bat of Europe and Asia, of Rhinolophoidae family. Has horseshoe-shaped membranous outgrowths of skin (nose-leaves) around nose, used for navigation.

orsetail, any of genus *Equisetum* of rush-like plants related to fern and club moss. Survivor of primitive group of plants.

orthy [de Nagybánya], Nicholas (1868-1957), Hungarian statesman, admiral. Led counter-revolutionary 'white' forces against Béla Kun's Communist govt. (1919-20). Became regent of Hungary (1920). Forced to resign, deported by occupying Germans (1944).

orus, in ancient Egyptian religion, god of the sun, light and goodness; son of Osiris and Isis. Represented with head of falcon.

osea, prophetic book of OT written by Hosea (8th cent. BC). Largely a sermon against moral decadence.

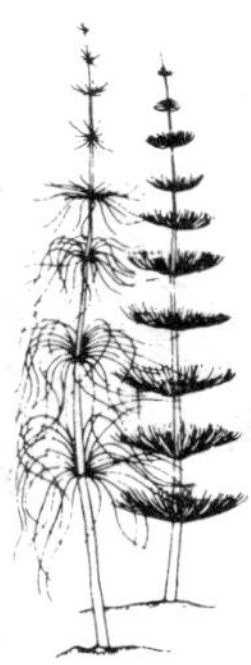

Giant horsetail

Hospitallers, *see* KNIGHTS HOSPITALLERS.

Hotspur, *see* PERCY, HENRY.

Hottentot, people of Namibia and NW Cape Prov. Pastoral nomads prob. related to Bushmen. Numbers diminished, pop. (est. 1963) 24,000.

Houdini, Harry, pseud. of Erich Weiss (1874-1926), American escapologist. Renowned for spectacular escapes from ropes, handcuffs, *etc.*

Hounslow, bor. of W Greater London, England. Pop. 201,000. Created 1965 from Middlesex towns. Has Heathrow airport.

house fly, *Musca domestica,* two-winged fly of worldwide distribution. Vomits digestive juice on food before eating it, spreading disease germs. Breeds in manure or decaying matter.

House of Commons, lower chamber of British PARLIAMENT. Composed of members (MPs) popularly elected by single-ballot system, each representing specific constituency of UK; presided over by Speaker. More powerful of 2 Houses, govt. (*see* CABINET) depending on majority in it and answerable to it for all actions. Initiates all major legislation, controls national finance.

House of Lords, upper chamber of British PARLIAMENT. Composed largely of hereditary peers, with Anglican archbishops, bishops, life peers. Derived from medieval king's council. Presided over by Lord Chancellor. Powers curtailed by PARLIAMENT ACTS (1911, 1949). Also acts as UK's final court of appeal.

House of Representatives, lower house of US CONGRESS. Composed of members elected by populace for 2-year terms on proportional basis; presided over by Speaker. Originates revenue bills, has power to impeach president.

Housman, A[lfred] E[dward] (1859-1936), English poet, scholar. Known for collection

Cross-Channel hovercraft

of pessimistic lyric poems, *A Shropshire Lad* (1896).

Houston, port of SE Texas, US; on canal with access to Gulf of Mexico. Pop. 2,482,000. In important oil, sulphur mining region; exports cotton, chemicals, petroleum. Cap. of Texas republic (1837-9). Has NASA space centre; Rice Univ. (1912).

Hove, town of East Sussex, SE England. Pop. 73,000. Resort, adjoins Brighton.

hovercraft, amphibious vehicle developed (1959) in UK by Sir Christopher Cockerell (1910-). Supports itself on cushion of air, usually generated by horizontal fan; forward motion provided by propellers or jets. First commercial service was Rhyl to Wallasey (UK) passenger ferry (1962).

hover fly, any of Syrphidae family of 2-winged insects. Resembles wasp with yellow and black bands on abdomen.

Howard, Catherine, *see* HOWARD, THOMAS.

Howard, John (1726-90), English reformer. Tour of English prisons led to 2 acts of Parliament (1774) improving prison conditions. Howard League for Penal Reform (founded 1866) continues his work.

Howard, Thomas, 3rd Duke of Norfolk (1473-1554), English nobleman. A Catholic, had influence at Henry VIII's court through niece, Anne Boleyn, Henry's 2nd wife. Avoided execution for treason (1547) only by death of Henry; imprisoned throughout reign of Edward VI. His other niece, **Catherine Howard** (*c* 1521-42), was Henry's 5th wife; she was executed primarily to remove Howard family influence. His son, **Henry Howard, Earl of Surrey** (*c* 1517-47), was a poet, introducing sonnet forms, also iambic blank verse. Arrested with his father and executed. His son, **Thomas Howard, 4th Duke of Norfolk** (1536-72), favourite of Elizabeth I, was executed after failure of plot to free Mary Queen of Scots. His cousin, **Charles Howard of Effingham, 1st Earl of Nottingham** (1536-1624), became lord high admiral (1585), commanding English fleet against Spanish Armada (1588).

Howe, Richard Howe, 1st Earl (1726-99 English admiral. Commanded Chann fleet in Seven Years War, British fle during American Revolution. Defeate French off Ushant ('Glorious First of June 1794). His brother, **William Howe, 5 Viscount Howe** (1729-1814), became Britis commander-in-chief in America afte victory at Bunker Hill (1775). Defeate Washington at Brandywine (1777 Resigned 1778.

howler monkey, largest of New Worl monkeys, genus *Alouatta,* of forests tropical America. Noted for howling noise

Hoxha, Enver (1908-), Albania statesman. Led radical resistance agains Italians (1939-44), founded Albania Communist Party (1941). Premier Albanian Republic (1944-54), first secretar of party (1954-). Supported China durin and after Sino-Soviet split (1961).

Hoy, isl. of Orkney, N Scotland. Has 'Old Ma of Hoy' rock stack (137 m/450 ft high).

Hoyle, Sir Fred (1915-), Englis astronomer, author. Developed math matical form of steady-state theory universe.

Hua Kuo-feng or **Hua Guofeng** (*c* 1921- Chinese political leader. Premier (1975-80 Succeeded Mao Tse-tung as part chairman (1976-).

Huascarán, highest mountain of Peru; in Andes. Height 6768 m (22,205 ft). Avalanch in 1962 killed 3,000 people in foothi villages.

Hubble, Edwin Powell (1889-1953 American astronomer. Formulated la that distant galaxies are receding wit velocities proportional to their distance following observations of red shift in thei spectra; this expansion of universe explained by big-bang theory.

Huddersfield, town of West Yorkshire me county, N England. Pop. 132,000. Woollen carpets mfg; textile machinery.

Hudson, Henry (*c* 1550-1611), Englis explorer. In search of Northwest Passag explored Hudson R. and Hudson Bay. Disappeared after being cast adrift by mutinous crew.

ıdson, river of E New York, US. Rises in Adirondack Mts. Flows S 510 km (*c* 315 mi) to New York City harbour. Major commercial route linked to Great Lakes, St Lawrence Seaway.

ıdson Bay, inland sea of EC Canada, in SE Northwest Territs. Area 1,230,000 sq km (*c* 475,000 sq mi). James Bay in S. Fur trade. Churchill is main port. **Hudson Strait** provides access to the Atlantic.

ıdson's Bay Company, chartered 1670 for purpose of obtaining furs for the English market. Its vast territories, known as Rupert's Land, incl. all land drained by rivers flowing into Hudson Bay, were sold to Canadian govt. (1869). In 20th cent. its operations were diversified into retailing and mfg.

ıé, city of C Vietnam. Pop. 209,000. Market centre; cement mfg. Cap. of hist. kingdom of Annam. Palaces and tombs of Annamese kings destroyed during North Vietnam's Tet offensive of 1968.

ıelva, town of SW Spain, on penin. between mouths of Odiel and Tinto, cap. of Huelva prov. Pop. 106,000. Port, exports copper, iron ores; fishing, tourism.

ıesca, town of NE Spain, cap. of Huesca prov. Pop. 33,000. Agric. market, pottery mfg. Cap. of Aragón 1096-1118. Cathedral (13th cent.), royal palace.

ıghes, Ted (1930-), English poet. Poetry, powerfully conveying sense of brute forces in man and nature, incl. *Lupercal* (1960), *Crow* (1970).

ıghes, William Morris (1864-1952), Australian statesman, b. England, PM (1915-22). Headed Labor, then National wartime govts.

ıgo, Victor Marie (1802-85), French poet, dramatist, novelist, leader of Romanticism. Introduced flexibility, melody into French verse, *eg* in play *Hernani* (1830), verse collections *Odes et ballades* (1826), *Les Rayons et les ombres* (1840). Novels, incl. *Notre Dame de Paris* (1831), *Les Misérables* (1862), reflect compassion for common man.

ıguenots, Calvinist Protestants of France, protagonists in Wars of Religion (1562-98), ending with Edict of Nantes. Many emigrated after its revocation (1685).

ıhehot, cap. of Inner Mongolia auton. region, N China. Pop. 530,000. Centre of trade routes to Mongolian People's Republic; chemicals, motor vehicle mfg.

ıll or **Kingston-upon-Hull,** city and admin. hq. of Humberside, NE England, on Humber estuary. Pop. 272,000. Port; ferry services to Europe; fishing. Univ. (1954).

ımanism, movement in thought and literature, originally applied to Italian Renaissance. Involved reaction against medieval religious authority, rediscovery of secular Classical ideals and attitudes. Notable humanists incl. Sir Thomas More, Colet.

Humber, estuary of NE England, of rivers Trent, Ouse. Length *c* 60 km (37 mi); ports incl. Hull, Grimsby.

Humberside, county of NE England. Area 3512 sq km (1356 sq mi); pop. 845,000; admin. hq. Hull. Created 1974, comprising former East Riding of Yorkshire, N Lincolnshire.

humble bee, *see* BUMBLE BEE.

Humboldt, [Friedrich Heinrich] Alexander von (1769-1859), German explorer, scientist, geographer. Expedition to Central and South America (1799-1804) resulted in greater understanding of scientific factors in geography. Explored Russia and C Asia (1829). Wrote *Kosmos* (1845-62), physical description of the Earth.

Humboldt Current, cold current of S Pacific, flowing N along coasts of Chile, Peru.

Hume, David (1711-76), Scottish philosopher. Took ideas of Locke, Berkeley to logical extension of SCEPTICISM. Held that reason could only be subject to passions and rejected any rational theology. Works incl. *Treatise of Human Nature* (1739), *An Enquiry Concerning Human Understanding* (1748), *History of Great Britain* (1754).

humidity, *see* RELATIVE HUMIDITY.

hummingbird, any of Trochilidae family of small brightly coloured New World birds. Feeds on insects and nectar, hovering over flowers with rapidly-vibrating wings. Bee hummingbird, *Mellisuga helenae,* of Cuba is world's smallest bird.

humus, amorphous, black organic matter in soil. Humification is process of decomposition of plants and animals into elements useful in maintaining soil fertility. Sometimes extended to incl. partially decomposed matter in soil.

Hunan, prov. of SC China. Area *c* 207,000 sq km (80,000 sq mi); pop. 51,000,000; cap. Changsha. Leading rice producer. Major lead, zinc, antimony mines.

Hundred Years War (1337-1453), conflict between England and France, resulting from commercial and territ. rivalries. Begun when EDWARD III claimed French throne (1337). English successes at Sluis, Crécy, Poitiers were countered by later French victories under du Guesclin; French recovered most of their lost territ. by 1377. War was renewed by HENRY V who conquered much of Normandy after victory at Agincourt (1415). JOAN OF ARC began French recovery after 1429; by 1453 Calais was only English possession in France.

Hungary *(Magyar Népköztársaság),* republic of EC Europe. Area 93,012 sq km (35,912 sq mi); pop. 10,699,000; cap. Budapest. Language: Magyar. Religions: RC, Protestant. Danube runs N-S; to E is Alföld plain; to W is Bakony Forest (hilly), L. Balaton. Agric. (esp. cereals) on collective system; indust. developing (coal, petroleum, bauxite). Kingdom estab. by St Stephen (11th cent.); ruled by Ottoman Turks until 1683; part of Habsburg empire

Hungary

until 1848 revolt; part of 'dual monarchy' (Austria-Hungary) 1867-1918, then independent republic. Joined Axis in WWII. Communist govt. estab. 1948. Revolt (1956) suppressed by USSR.

Huns, nomadic pastoralists of NC Asia who invaded E Europe *c* 370, forcing the Ostrogoths and Visigoths to migrate westwards. Under their leader Attila, overran Balkans and forced Emperor Theodosius to pay tribute. When tributes ceased Huns invaded Gaul but were defeated at Châlons (451). Subsequent invasion of Italy was abandoned (452).

Hunt, [James Henry] Leigh (1784-1859), English poet, essayist. Wrote essays on music, painting, Italian literature. Imprisoned for attacking Prince Regent in *The Examiner* (1813).

Hunt, William Holman (1827-1910), English painter. Founder member of Pre-Raphaelite Brotherhood with Rossetti and Millais; work is noted for its detail, harsh colour and laboured symbolism. Works incl. *Light of the World.*

Hunter, John (1728-93), Scottish surgeon, physiologist. Made studies in comparative anatomy and introduced new techniques in surgery.

Huntingdonshire, former county of EC England, now part of Cambridgeshire. Low-lying, Fens in NE; pasture, market gardening, cereals. Co. town was **Huntingdon (and Godmanchester),** on R. Great Ouse. Pop. 17,000.

Hupeh or **Hupei,** prov. of EC China. Area *c* 186,000 sq km (72,000 sq mi); pop. 45,000,000; cap. Wuhan at jct. of Yangtze and Han rivers. C part is low-lying, with many lakes and rivers. Grains, cotton, rice grown. Steel complexes.

hurling, fifteen-a-side team game played with sticks and ball, mainly in Ireland. Played for several cents. prior to formation of Gaelic Association standardized rules (1884).

Huron, confederation of 4 North Americ Indian tribes. Lived in Ontario in 17th ce Numbered *c* 20,000. Farmers, crops in tobacco. Defeated and dispersed Iroquois in 1649. Remaining membe settled near Detroit and in Ohio, and lat in Oklahoma.

Huron, Lake, 2nd largest of Great Lakes, Canada-US border. Area 59,596 sq k (23,010 sq mi). Bounded by Ontar (Canada), Michigan (US). Georgian Bay NE extension; Saginaw Bay in S. Tra route connecting L. Superior, L. Michig with L. Erie, used by oceangoing and la vessels. Ice-bound winter.

hurricane, violent cyclonic storm occurri in tropical areas. Consists of high-spe wind system revolving around a calm, lo pressure centre or 'eye'. Common Caribbean, Gulf of Mexico areas; occur Pacific as 'typhoons' or 'tropical cyclone Term also used to describe winds velocity over 120 kmh (75 mph), *ie* force on Beaufort Scale.

Hus or **Huss, Jan** (*c* 1370–1415), Bohemi religious reformer. Influenced by views Wycliffe, his preaching against cleric privilege attracted popular support and l to his excommunication (1410). Grant safe conduct to explain views to Council Constance (1414), he was tried a condemned for heresy. Death by burni led to HUSSITE WARS.

Husák, Gustav (1913-), Czechoslov statesman. Succeeded Dubček as fi secretary of Communist party (1969) aft Soviet invasion. President since 1975.

hussars, originally Hungarian cavalry in t 15th cent., the name was later applied light horse regiments in many Europe armies.

Hussein I (1935-), king of Jordan (1952- Moderate pro-Westerner, but led Jord against Israel in 1967 Arab-Israeli w After loss of territ. W of R. Jordan, confli arose with Palestinian guerrillas, leadi to 1970 war. Although victorious, ceded Bank to PLO (1974).

Husserl, Edmund, *see* PHENOMENOLOGY.

Hussite Wars, conflicts in Bohemia a Moravia begun when supporters of Jan H opposed succession of SIGISMUND as king Bohemia (1419). Hussites defeated crusa ing forces sent against them. Peace trea (Compactata) drawn up at Council of Bas was accepted by moderate Hussit Conflict broke out again after Compacta was revoked (1462).

Hutton, James (1726-97), Scottish geologi Originated several basic principles modern geology, notably theory UNIFORMITARIANISM.

Huxley, Thomas Henry (1825-95), Engli biologist. Foremost British exponent Darwin's theory of evolution; his writin deal with conflict of traditional religi and science. His grandson, **Sir Juli Sorell Huxley** (1887-1975), English biolog and author, was active in populariz science. His brother, **Aldous Leona Huxley** (1894-1963), was a novelist a ɘssayist. Known for novels of ideas, *eg* *Point Counter Point* (1928), anti-Utopian *Brave New World* (1932), *Eyeless in Gaza* (1936). Essays on religion, philosophy incl. *Heaven and Hell* (1956).

ıygens, Christiaan (1629-95), Dutch mathematician, physicist, astronomer. Developed Huygens' principle in wave theory of light which explained polarization, reflection and refraction.

vang Ho or **Yellow,** river of N China. Flows *c* 4800 km (3000 mi) from Tsinghai prov. into Pohai gulf.

acinth, any of genus *Hyacinthus* of plants of lily family. Native to Mediterranean and S African regions. Narrow, channelled leaves, spikes of bell-shaped flowers.

aena, carnivorous wolf-like mammal of Africa and Asia, with bristly mane, short hind legs and powerful jaws. Feeds on carrion but will attack other animals.

brid, offspring produced by crossing 2 individuals of unlike genetic constitution, *eg* those of different race or species. Hybrid may be fertile or infertile. Hybridization is used in agric. to achieve greater vigour, growth in offspring, *eg* mule, hybrid corn.

de, Douglas, known in Irish as An Craoibhin Aoibhinn (1860-1949), Irish scholar, statesman, president of Irish Republic (1938-45). Instrumental in revival of Irish language; 1st president of Gaelic League (1893-1915).

de, Edward, *see* CLARENDON.

derabad, cap. of Andhra Pradesh, SC India. Pop. 1,796,000. Transportation centre; textile mfg. Wall encloses old city Cap. of former princely state of Hyderabad (1724-1948).

derabad, city of SE Pakistan. Pop. 628,000. Textile, machinery mfg. Cap. of Sind (1768-1843) until taken by British.

der Ali (1722-82), Indian military leader, ruler of Mysore (1766-82). In Anglo-French conflict sided with French until defeat by British (1781). Succeeded by his son, Tippoo Sahib.

dra, in Greek myth, many-headed monster. When 1 head was cut off 2 grew in its place. The 2nd labour of Heracles was to kill the monster, which he did by burning the stump of neck after cutting off each head.

dra, solitary freshwater coelenterate polyp, class Hydrozoa, which lacks free-swimming medusa stage. Tube-like body with tentacles around mouth; reproduces asexually by budding.

drangea, genus of flowering shrubs of saxifrage family, native to Americas. White, blue or pink flowers.

draulic press, device consisting of 2 liquid-filled cylinders of unequal diameter connected by a pipe and fitted with pistons. By Pascal's law, a force exerted on smaller piston will result in a greater force (proportional to quotient of the surface areas of pistons) on larger piston. Invented by J. Bramah (1795).

Hydrangea

hydraulics, branch of ENGINEERING dealing with mechanical properties of water and other liquids. Divided into hydrostatics dealing with liquids at rest, *eg* in hydraulic presses, and hydrokinetics dealing with problems of friction and turbulence in moving liquids.

hydrocarbon, organic compound containing hydrogen and carbon only. Petroleum and coal gas largely consist of such compounds.

hydrocephalus, enlargement of an infant's head caused by accumulation of fluid in the cranium. Damage to the brain and mental retardation may result.

hydrochloric acid, strong corrosive acid formed by dissolving hydrogen chloride HCl in water. Used in ore extraction, metal cleaning and as chemical reagent.

hydrocyanic acid (HCN), weak, highly poisonous acid with smell of bitter almonds, formed by dissolving hydrogen cyanide in water. Used as fumigant and in organic synthesis. Also called prussic acid.

hydro-electric power, electrical energy obtained from generators driven by water-turbines. Source of water may be natural (waterfall) or artificial (river-damming). Amount of power is proportional to rate of water flow and vertical distance through which it falls.

hydrofoil, wing-like device which produces upward lift when moved through water. Watercraft which use such devices to lift hull above water are capable of high speeds because of low drag.

hydrogen (H), colourless gaseous element; at. no. 1, at. wt. 1.008. Lightest known substance, its molecule consists of 2 atoms. Burns in oxygen to form water. Occurs in water, organic compounds, petroleum, coal, *etc.* Obtained by electrolysis, decomposition of hydrocarbons, or from water gas. Used in manufacture of ammonia, margarine and synthetic oils. Deuterium and tritium are isotopes important in nuclear research.

hydrogen bomb, nuclear weapon operating on principle of nuclear FUSION. Consists of atomic bomb surrounded by layer of lithium deuteride; intense heat produced by atomic fission causes nuclei of hydrogen isotopes to fuse into helium nuclei, with resultant release of enormous quantity of energy.

hydrogen ion concentration, in chemistry, number of grams of hydrogen ions per litre in an aqueous solution. The pH-value of a solution is the common logarithm of the reciprocal of the hydrogen ion concentration and acts as a measure of acidity or alkalinity. Pure water has pH-value of 7; acids have values from 0 to 7, alkalis from 7 to 14.

hydrogen peroxide (H_2O_2), viscous liquid, often used in aqueous solution as a bleach and disinfectant. Powerful oxidizing agent; in concentrated form, used as rocket propellant.

hydrolysis, in chemistry, decomposition by water. Hydrolysis of organic compounds may be effected by aqueous alkalis or dilute acids, *eg* esters of higher fatty acids are hydrolyzed in presence of alkalis to form soap. Inorganic salts undergo hydrolysis into acids and bases through action of hydrogen and hydroxyl ions in water.

hydrometer, instrument for measuring specific gravity of a liquid. Liquid is placed in graduated tube, which is then immersed in water. Depth to which tube sinks shows the specific gravity.

hydrophobia, *see* RABIES.

hydroponics, science of growing plants in solutions of the necessary minerals instead of in soil. Developed *c* 1860. Increasingly used commercially since 1930s.

hydroxide, compound consisting of element or radical joined to hydroxyl (OH) radical, *eg* potassium hydroxide KOH.

hyena, *see* HYAENA.

hygrometer, instrument for measuring RELATIVE HUMIDITY of atmosphere.

Hymettus *(Imittos),* mountain group of Attica, SE Greece. Highest point Mt. Hymettus (1027 m/3370 ft). Famous honey; marble quarries.

hymn, song in praise or honour of a deity. Christian hymn developed as metrical form in 4th cent.; polyphonic settings evolved in 13th-16th cents. Lutheran CHORALE developed after Reformation. Dissenters of 18th cent. began English hyn tradition with collections such as those Isaac Watts, John Wesley.

hyperbola, in geometry, curve traced point which moves so ratio of its distan from a fixed point to distance from fix line is a constant greater than 1. Curve h 2 branches; it is also a conic section.

hypermetropia or **long sight,** defect of e in which images are focused behind t retina, so that distant objects are se more clearly than near objects. Caus because lens of eye is too short or refractive power too weak. Corrected glasses with convex lenses.

hyperons, in physics, elementary partic of baryon group with mass intermedia between that of neutron and deuter Decay rapidly into neutrons and protons.

hypertension, abnormally high blo pressure. May be symptom of disease, kidney disease, arteriosclerosis, but cau is sometimes unknown.

hypnosis, sleep-like condition induced subject by monotonous repetition of wor and gestures. Subject responds only operator's voice and returns to norm consciousness when told to. Sometim used to treat neurosis as repress memories can be recalled under hypnosi

hyrax, any of order Hyracoidea of rabb sized hoofed mammals of Africa and S Asia.

hyssop, *Hyssopus officinalis,* small perenn aromatic plant, native to Mediterrane region. Blue flowers. Used in folk medici as tonic.

hysterectomy, surgical removal of uter usually necessitated by presence of fibr tumours or cancer.

hysteresis, in magnetism, lag magnetization when ferromagnetic body magnetized. Body retains residual ma netism when external field is removed.

hysteria, form of neurosis in whi sustained anxiety expresses itself as bod disturbance. May result in appare paralysis of a limb or simulation blindness.

I

şi *(Ger. Jassy)*, city of NE Romania. Pop. 202,000. Industs. incl. textiles, metal goods. Cultural centre; univ. (1860).

adan, city of SW Nigeria. Pop. 847,000. Admin., indust. centre; trade in cacao, cotton, palm oil; univ. (1962). Centre of Yoruba culture.

eria, penin. of SW Europe, comprising Spain and Portugal.

ex, any of several species of mountain goats with backward-curving horns, found in Europe and Asia. Incl. Alpine ibex, *Capra ibex*.

is, wading bird of Threskiornithidae family, related to stork, found mainly in tropical regions. Sacred in ancient Egypt.

iza, *see* IVIZA.

n Saud *(c* 1880-1953), king of Saudi Arabia. Captured Riyadh (1902) and took control of Nejd. Annexed kingdom of Hejaz (1924). United Nejd and Hejaz (1932) to form kingdom of Saudi Arabia.

n Sina, *see* AVICENNA.

o, people of SE Nigeria. Number *c* 7 million. Constitute most of pop. of Biafra (*see* NIGERIA).

sen, Henrik Johan (1828-1906), Norwegian dramatist. Works stress importance of individuals' joy in living rather than conventional society's needs. Best-known plays incl. verse *Peer Gynt* (1867); social tragedies *A Doll's House* (1879), *Ghosts* (1881), *Hedda Gabler* (1890); symbolic drama *The Wild Duck* (1884).

arus, *see* DAEDALUS.

e, water in solid state, formed by cooling below freezing point. As water expands on freezing, ice is less dense than liquid water.

e ages, glaciations of PLEISTOCENE EPOCH when ice sheets and glaciers periodically advanced to cover large areas of America, Asia and Europe. Four major advances normally distinguished, most recent ending *c* 11,000 years ago. Greatly affected landscape formation. Believed to have been caused by perturbations in Earth's orbit about Sun.

eberg, mass of ice broken off from a glacier or ice barrier and floating in the sea. Normally only *c* 1/9th total mass is visible above the surface. Hazard to shipping.

e hockey, *see* HOCKEY.

eland *(Island)*, isl. republic of Europe, in N Atlantic. Area 102,950 sq km (39,750 sq mi); pop. 224,000; cap. Reykjavik. Language: Icelandic. Religion: Lutheran. Uninhabited C plateau; over 100 volcanoes (many active; *see* HEKLA, SURTSEY), springs, icefields. Rugged coastline; mild, wet climate, stunted vegetation. Fishing (esp. cod, herring), h.e.p., grazing. Colonized 9th cent. by Norwegians; first parliament in Europe (930); united with Denmark (1380-1918). Independent republic from 1944.

Icelandic, *see* GERMANIC LANGUAGES.

I Ching or **Book of Changes,** one of five Chinese Confucian classics, originally written *c* 1027-256 BC. Contains system of divination based on 64 hexagrams.

ichneumon, *Herpestes ichneumon,* river-side-dwelling mongoose found in S Spain and throughout Africa. Sacred in ancient Egypt.

ichthyology, branch of zoology dealing with fish, their structure, classification and life history. Fish are divided into 3 main classes: jawless fish (Cyclostomata), incl. lampreys and hagfish; cartilaginous fish (Chondrichthyes), incl. sharks and rays; bony fish (Osteichthyes), comprising majority of fish.

ichthyosaur, large extinct aquatic reptile, known from fossils of Jurassic period. Dolphin-like, with 4 paddle-shaped flippers and long snout.

icon, image or picture of Christ, Virgin Mary or a saint, venerated in Eastern Orthodox church. In common use by end of 5th cent., few survived outbreak of iconoclasm in 8th and 9th cents. Following fall of Constantinople, icon-making *fl* in Russia until the Revolution.

Iconium, *see* KONYA.

id, term used by Freud to denote that part of personality which is unconscious, primitive, instinctual, dynamic, as opposed to the EGO and SUPEREGO.

Ida, Mount *(Psiloríti)*, mountain of C Crete, Greece. Height 2455 m (8058 ft).

Idaho, state of NW US. Area 216,413 sq km (83,557 sq mi); pop. 831,000; cap. Boise. Dominated by Rocky Mts.; crossed by Snake, Salmon rivers. Timber, agric. in S (potato, wheat, sugar beet); silver, lead, antimony mines. Settled in 1860s. Admitted to Union as 43rd state (1890).

idealism, in philosophy, theory that nothing outside ideas has any reality. The only reality of objects is in the impression they make on the mind. Normally implies the existence of absolutes, *eg* good, truth. Developed along separate lines by *eg* Plato, Berkeley, Kant, Hegel.

Ife, city of SW Nigeria. Pop. 176,000. Trade in cacao, palm and kernels; univ. (1961). Hist. religious centre of Yoruba tribe.

Ifni, region of SW Morocco. On edge of Sahara; fruit growing, coastal fishing. Overseas prov. of Spain from 1860, cap. Sidi Ifni; returned to Morocco 1969.

Ignatius of Loyola, St, (1491-1556), Spanish monk. Gave up military career after severe wounds. Planned and organized Jesuit order, approved by pope (1540). Elected (1541) 1st general of order.

igneous rocks, rocks formed by cooling and solidification of molten magma. Consist of mass of interlocking crystals due to different rate of cooling of constituent minerals. May be either EXTRUSIVE or INTRUSIVE ROCKS.

Iguaçu or **Iguassú Falls,** waterfall on border between Brazil and Argentina, on Iguaçu river. About 4 km (2.5 mi) wide, 82 m (269 ft) high. H.e.p. supplies.

iguana, any lizard of Iguanidae family of tropical America. Common species is *Iguana iguana* of Mexico and N South America; greenish, with row of spines from neck to tail.

iguanodon, two-legged herbivorous dinosaur, reaching lengths of 7.6 m/25 ft. Fossils found in Cretaceous rocks.

Ijsselmeer or **Ysselmeer,** shallow freshwater lake of NW Netherlands, fed by R. Ijssel. Created from former ZUIDER ZEE by dam (31 km/19 mi long) completed 1932. Four polders reclaimed, giving rich agric. land; also fishing.

Ikhnaton or **Akhenaton,** orig. Amenhotep IV (d. *c* 1354 BC), Egyptian pharaoh (*c* 1372-*c* 1354 BC), husband of Nefertiti. Built Akhetaton (modern TEL-EL-AMARNA) as centre of new religion devoted to worship of sun god Aton, in whose honour he changed his name.

Ile-de-France, hist. region of France, in centre of Paris basin. Agric. area, providing Paris with food; drained by rivers Seine, Oise, Marne.

Iliad, Greek epic in 24 books, attributed to Homer, prob. composed *c* 8th cent. BC, written *c* 6th cent. BC. Set in Trojan War (Ilium=Troy), theme is wrath of Achilles and course of war.

Ilium, *see* TROY.

Illinois, state of NC US. Area 146,676 sq km (56,400 sq mi); pop. 11,229,000; cap. Springfield; major city Chicago. Mississippi R. forms W border. Mainly plains; agric. important esp. livestock, corn, maize, wheat. Large mineral resources in S *eg* coal, oil. Mfg. and indust. concentrated on L. Michigan shore around Chicago (meat packing, oil refining). French estab. missions in 17th cent.; passed to British 1763; taken by US in Revolution. Admitted to Union as 21st state (1818).

Illyria, region on Adriatic coast of Yugoslavia and N Albania. Ancient tribal kingdom estab. 3rd cent. BC, partly conquered (34 BC) by Romans. Name revived by Napoleon (1809), Austria (1816-49).

image, in optics, visual likeness of object produced by reflection from a mirror or refraction by a lens. Real image is formed by light rays actually meeting at a point and entering observer's eye; may be shown on a screen. Virtual image is seen at point from which rays appear to come and cannot be shown on a screen.

imagists, group of poets incl. Richa Aldington, T.S. Eliot, Hilda Doolittle, An Lowell, who followed leadership of T. Hulme, Ezra POUND in reacting agair stultified Georgian romanticism. Wor characterized by total precision presentation of each image within sho free verse form. Active 1910-18.

imam (Arab., =leader), in Islam, a recognized leader incl. successors Mohammed. Esp. used by SHIITES f succession of religious leaders, regarded divinely inspired. *See* MAHDI. Imam al refers to leader of prayers in mosque.

immanence, in theology, the presen throughout natural universe of a spiritu principle. Opposed to transcendence, *ie* t existence of a spiritual principle outsi the natural universe. Three ma monotheistic religions believe that God both immanent and transcendent.

immunity, natural resistance of organism to specific infections. Presen of microbes in body stimulates formati of antibodies which provide tempora immunity for subsequent attacks of particular disease. Can be induced by u of vaccines.

impala, *Aepyceros melampus,* medium-siz reddish antelope of S and E Africa. Ma has long lyre-shaped horns. Noted f extraordinary leaping ability.

impeachment, bringing of public offic before proper tribunal on charge of wron doing. In UK, trial is before House of Lor on Commons' accusation. Rare. WARR HASTINGS case (1788-95) was one of last Britain. In US, House of Representativ has right of impeachment, Senate tri cases. Impeachment procedure beg (1974) against Nixon, who resigned.

Imperial Conference, *see* COMMONWEALT BRITISH.

imperialism, extension of rule by o country over another by diplomat military or economic means. Esp. appli to European expansion (late 19th cen into Asia and Africa. Modern concept neo-imperialism refers to economic political domination of affairs of le developed countries.

impetigo, contagious disease of the sk caused by staphylococci. Characterized eruption of isolated pus-filled blisters hands, neck, face. Treated by antibiotics.

impressionism, school of painting, whic originated in France *c* 1870. At fir Impressionist Exhibition (1874) ma exponents were Monet, Pissarro, Sisle but Cézanne, Manet, Renoir and Deg were originally associated with movemer Their aim was to capture a momenta glimpse of a subject, reproducing changir effects of light in short strokes of pu colour.

incarnation, the assumption of human for by a god. Concept occurs in ma religions, *eg* ancient Egyptian and India beliefs that certain kings were divine i carnations; also Greek belief that go used human forms to communicate wi men. Christians believe Jesus to be both wholly divine and human.

ncas, name ordinarily given to the pop. of Peru before conquest by Pizarro (1533), but properly restricted to ruling caste, ruler himself being the Inca. Civilization, centred at Cuzco, may go back to 1200. Achieved high level of culture as shown by social system, knowledge of agric., roadmaking, ceramics, textiles, buildings.

ncendiary bomb, canister containing highly inflammable substance. Often dropped from aircraft in conjunction with explosive bombs.

ncest, sexual relations between people of close kinship. Prohibited by law or custom in most societies. Definitions of kinship, often complex, vary among societies.

nchon, seaport of NW South Korea. Pop. 797,000. Ice-free harbour on Yellow Sea. Commercial and indust. centre; produces steel, textiles, chemicals, coke.

ncome tax, govt. tax on individual or corporate incomes. Modern form introduced in Britain by Pitt (1799) to raise funds for Napoleonic Wars; permanent tax adopted (1874).

ndependence, town of W Missouri. Pop. 112,000. Hist. starting point on Santa Fé and Oregon trails.

ndependence, American War of, *see* AMERICAN REVOLUTION.

ndependence, Declaration of, formal statement adopted (4 July, 1776) by 2nd Continental Congress declaring the 13 American colonies free and independent of Britain. Almost entirely written by Thomas Jefferson, document sets out principle of govt. under theory of natural rights.

India

ndia *(Bharat),* republic of SC Asia. Area *c* 3,268,000 sq km (1,262,000 sq mi); pop. 638,388,000; cap. New Delhi. Official language: Hindi; religions: Hinduism, Islam. Indian penin. bounded by Himalayas, Pakistan and Bangladesh. Largely plains, cut by Ganges, Brahmaputra, Godavari rivers. Climate mainly tropical monsoon; agric. economy (esp. rice, cotton, tea, timber). Divided into 22 states and 9 union territs. Major cities Bombay, Calcutta. Hinduism estab *c* 1500 BC, Buddhism and Jainism introduced in 6th cent. BC. Country, apart from some princely states, united under Moguls (16th-18th cent.); East India Co. rule (1757-1858) transferred to Britain after Indian Mutiny. Independence struggle led by Gandhi; independence achieved (1947) with creation and partition of Pakistan; republic estab. 1950. All princely states, except Kashmir, incorporated in India or Pakistan. Member of British Commonwealth.

Indiana, state of NC US. Area 93,994 sq km (36,290 sq mi); pop. 5,302,000; cap. Indianapolis. Mainly rolling plains; agric. esp. maize, wheat, livestock, coal mining, limestone quarrying. Settled by French; ceded to British 1763; captured by US 1779; became territ. 1800. Admitted to Union as 19th state (1816).

Indianapolis, cap. of Indiana, US; on White R. Pop. 1,139,000. Transport jct.; grain, livestock market. Meat packing; produces motor car and aircraft parts. Annual motor races ('500').

Indian corn, *see* MAIZE.

Indian Mutiny (1857-8), revolt of native soldiers (sepoys) in Bengal army of British East India Co. Troops resented annexation of Oudh (1856), homeland of many of them, and were angered by issue of cartridges coated with fat of cows (sacred to Hindus) and of pigs (forbidden to Moslems). Revolt, beginning Feb. 1857, spread over NC India; Delhi captured, Lucknow besieged, British garrison massacred at Kanpur. Mutiny subdued by March, 1858. Resulting reforms incl. transfer of rule from East India Co. to British Crown.

Indian National Congress, Indian political party, founded (1885) to increase Indian involvement in formation of British policy in India. Became more militant after 1919, adopting policy, advocated by Gandhi, of civil disobedience and passive resistance to British rule. Under Nehru, became ruling party of India and maintained power except period 1977-9.

Indian Ocean, smallest of 3 world oceans, lying between Antarctica, Africa, Asia and Australia. Area *c* 73,430,000 sq km (28,350,000 sq mi). Reaches greatest depth in Java Trench (7725 m/ 25,344 ft). Main isls. Madagascar, Sri Lanka. Arms incl. Arabian Sea, Bay of Bengal. Seasonal winds (monsoons) yield rain in S and SE Asia.

Indians, American, *see* AMERICAN INDIANS.

Indic, largest group of languages in Indo-Iranian branch of Indo-European family. Incl. ancient forms Vedic, Sanskrit, Prakrit; modern Punjabi, Sindhi, Hindi, Urdu, Assamese, Bengali, Gujarati, Singhalese, Marathi.

indigo, any plant of genus *Indigofera* of Leguminosae family. *I. tinctoria* is source of colourless indican which is oxidized to blue dye, indigo.

indium (In), soft metallic element; at. no. 49, at. wt. 114.82. Found in traces in zinc ores. Used in dental alloys and to protect bearings. Discovered (1863).

Indo-China, former federation of SE Asian states, comprising French colony of Cochin China and French protects. of Laos, Cambodia, Tonkin and Annam. Republic of Vietnam formed from Cochin China, Tonkin and Annam in 1949.

Indo-Chinese War, conflict fought (1946-54) between Viet Minh (coalition of nationalist and Communist groups under Ho CHI MINH) and the French after failure of negotiations for Vietnamese independence. Decisive battle fought at Dien Bien Phu (1954) broke French resistance. Subsequent Geneva Conference divided Indo-China into North and South Vietnam, Laos and Cambodia.

Indo-European, language family with more speakers than any other, *ie c* half of world's pop. Similarities in vocabulary and grammar point to ancient parent language, originating pre-2000 BC. Differences postulated to have arisen as migration separated groups speaking it. Major branches are Anatolian, Baltic, Celtic, Germanic, Greek, Indo-Iranian, Italic, Slavic, Thraco-Illyrian, Thraco-Phrygian, Tokharian.

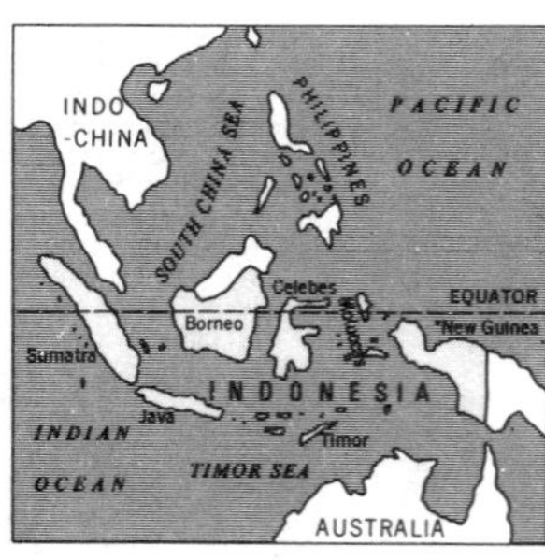

Indonesia

Indonesia, republic of SE Asia. Area *c* 1,904,000 sq km (736,000 sq mi); pop. 145,100,000; cap. Djakarta. Official language: Bahasa Indonesian. Religion: Islam. Comprises former Dutch East Indies, consisting of *c* 3000 isls., incl. Java, Sumatra, Borneo, Lesser Sundas, Moluccas, Irian Jaya. Most islands mountainous; equatorial climate with heavy rainfall. Rice main crop; exports rubber, spices, petroleum. Hinduism and Buddhism introduced under Indian influence; Islam dominant by end of 16th cent. Colonized by Dutch East India Co. (17th cent.). Independence proclaimed 1945, sovereignty transferred 1949.

Indore, city of Madhya Pradesh, C India. Pop. 543,000. Chemical, textile mfg. Cap. of former princely state of Indore.

Indra, in early Hindu religion, god of war and storms. Represented as an amoral, boisterous god.

inductance, electrical, property of a electric circuit by which a changi electric current in it produces varyi magnetic field. This magnetic field m induce voltages in same circuit (se induction) or in neighbouring circui (mutual induction).

induction, in physics, name given to phenomena in electricity and magnetis Electrostatic induction is production charge on a body when another charg body is brought near. Magnetic induction production of a magnetic field ferromagnetic material by extern magnetic field. *See* also ELECTROMAGNET INDUCTION.

inductive method, logical procedu formulated by Francis Bacon of arguir from particular observations to gener principles. Opposite of deduction whic argues from known principles to particul applications. Whereas deduction infallible if original proposition is tru induction can only attain a high degree probability. Both methods central scientific research.

indulgence, in RC Church, total or parti remission of temporal or purgatori punishment for sin. Granted by the Churc providing the sin has already bee forgiven and sinner is in a state of grac System was once notoriously abused wi sale of indulgences, and violently oppose by Luther. Council of Trent (156 outlawed sale of indulgences but approve the system in moderation.

Indus, river of SC Asia. Rises in SW Tibe flows *c* 2700 km (1700 mi) SW throug Kashmir and Pakistan to Arabian Se Irrigates plains of Sind; little used f navigation. *See* INDUS VALLEY CIVILIZATION.

Industrial Revolution, social and econom change resulting from replacement hand tools by machine and power too advent of steam engine, and th development of large-scale indus production; applied esp. to this change Britain (from about 1760). Founded c widening overseas markets, developme of banking, and invention of machines ar new processing methods. Accompanied b population increase and transport deve opments, it turned Britain fro predominantly agric. country into leadir indust. nation of world. Rapid chang spread to Germany, US (after 1860), Japa USSR, and others in 20th cent.

Indus Valley civilization, ancient cultu which *fl c* 2500-1500 BC in valley of R. Indu (area now in Pakistan). Two chief towr were Harappa, in Punjab, and Mohenj Daro in Sind; excavations carried out these sites since 1920s have found evidenc of organized agric., flourishing art ar well-planned architecture.

inert gases, the elements helium, neo argon, krypton, xenon, radon. As the external electron shells are complete, the are virtually chemically inert, b compounds with fluorine have bee produced. Also called noble or rare gases.

ertia, in physics, the tendency of a body to preserve its state of rest or uniform motion unless acted upon by an external force. Forms basis of Newton's first law of motion.

fantile paralysis, *see* POLIOMYELITIS.

fantry, branch of the army trained, equipped and organized to fight on foot. Became dominant in European warfare after invention of firearms.

fection, in medicine, invasion of body by micro-organisms, *eg* bacteria, viruses, protozoa. After period of incubation, inflammation of tissue follows and more widespread effects may result from toxins released by bacteria.

feriority complex, in psychiatry, neurotic state resulting from real or imagined physical or social inadequacy. Behavioural patterns may be dictated by attempts to compensate for it.

finity, in mathematics, term used loosely to denote numerical value of a non-finite quantity. A sequence is said to 'tend to infinity' if it increases beyond all bounds.

flammation, in medicine, defensive reaction of body to injury, infection or irritation. Heat, redness, swelling and pain are signs of inflammation, caused by increased flow of blood and lymph fluid. White blood cells engulf and destroy invading bacteria, forming pus when they die.

flation, in economics, increase in amount of money in circulation resulting in a sudden and relatively sharp fall in its value and hence rise in price of goods and services. Wars have been common cause; govt. borrows and issues paper money, domestic production is incapable of meeting consumer demand thus causing prices to rise. Other instances of inflation incl. hyper-inflation in Germany in 1923, worldwide inflation from 1970s caused by limited supply of oil-related products. Its opposite is **deflation,** condition characterized by decline in prices, business and employment.

fluenza, virus infection, usually of mucous membranes of air passages. Accompanied by muscular pains, weakness and fever. Sometimes occurs in worldwide epidemics; different strains of influenza virus minimize possibility of gaining immunity.

frared radiation, electromagnetic radiation whose wavelength is longer than that of the red part of the visible spectrum but shorter than that of radio waves. Emitted by hot bodies; it has penetrating heating effect. Film sensitive to infrared radiation is used to photograph in total darkness or in haze.

gres, Jean Auguste Dominique (1780-1867), French painter. Pupil of David, he upheld rigid classicism against the Romantic movement led by Delacroix. Works incl. portraits, nudes and Oriental scenes.

itiative, *see* REFERENDUM.

jection, method employed in medicine to introduce liquid into body. Usually administered by means of fine needle and syringe. May be subcutaneous (into skin), intravenous (into vein), intramuscular (into muscle), spinal (into spinal tissue).

injunction, in law, formal written order of court ordering or prohibiting some action. Courts have broadened interpretation from original prohibitive injunction to incl. positive commands.

ink, coloured liquid used in printing and writing. Blue and black writing inks usually consist of tannin extract with iron salts added; coloured writing inks use dissolved dyes. Printing ink consists of pigment mixed with linseed varnish, resins, *etc.*

Inkerman, suburb of Sevastopol, USSR, on Crimean penin. Scene of French and British victory over Russians in Crimean War (1854).

Inland Sea, sea between Japanese isls. of Honshu (on N) and Kyushu and Shikoku (on S). Notably scenic region, rich in fish.

Inner Hebrides, *see* HEBRIDES.

Inner Mongolia, auton. region of N China. Area *c* 425,000 sq km (164,000 sq mi); pop. 18,000,000; cap. Huhehot. Mainly steppe, becoming increasingly arid towards Gobi Desert in W. Stockraising; cereals grown in bend of Hwang Ho. Valuable mineral deposits.

Inner Temple, *see* INNS OF COURT.

Innocent III, orig. Giovanni Lotario di Segni (1161-1216), Italian churchman, pope (1198-1216). Estab. papal supremacy over temporal rulers by asserting will in political affairs. Named Stephen LANGTON as archbishop of Canterbury (1206) in defiance of King John; excommunicated John, and forced him to submit to papal authority. Proclaimed 4th Crusade (1202-4) and crusade against Albigensians (1208). Presided over Fourth Lateran Council (1215).

Innsbruck, city of W Austria, on R. Inn, cap. of Tyrol prov. Pop. 123,000. Tourist centre, esp. winter sports. Castle (15th cent.), Hofkirche (1563), univ. (1677).

Inns of Court, four London legal societies having exclusive right to admit persons to practise at the bar in England (*see* BARRISTER). They are Lincoln's Inn, Gray's Inn, Inner Temple, Middle Temple. Date from before 14th cent.

inoculation, method of immunization against disease. Active inoculation consists of injection of weak strain of infecting microbe and consequent formation of antibodies to provide immunity. Passive inoculation, used to gain short-term immunity, consists of injection of antitoxins from previously infected subjects.

inquest, in law, any inquiry, but esp. coroner's investigation, into cause of a death. Only necessary in cases in which cause is in doubt, or is sudden or violent.

Inquisition, in RC Church, general tribunal estab. (1233) by Gregory IX for the discovery and suppression of heresy and punishment of heretics (at that time ALBIGENSIANS). Notorious for torture of the accused and other abuses esp. when secular rulers used system to their own gain. Continued until 19th cent. The Spanish Inquisition was an independent institution estab. (1478) by Ferdinand V and Isabella of Spain and controlled by the Spanish kings. Infamous for its rigour under TORQUEMADA.

insanity or **lunacy,** legal and colloquial terms, rather than medico-scientific, used for those forms of mental disorder which relieve individual of responsibility for certain acts, and which may lead to his being confined in an institution.

Insecta (insects), largest class of arthropods, with *c* 800,000 species. Adult has body divided into head, thorax and abdomen. Head bears pair of antennae; thorax has 3 segments with 3 pairs of legs and usually 2 pairs of wings. Usually 4-stage life history involving egg, larva, pupa, adulthood.

insecticide, chemical used to destroy insect pests. In 19th cent. inorganic compounds, esp. of arsenic and copper, used. Modern organic chemicals, incl. DDT, highly effective; use sometimes restricted because of cumulative toxic effect on animals and contamination of food.

Insectivora (insectivores), order of small insect-eating mammals, incl. shrews, hedgehogs and moles.

insectivorous plants, plants which supplement nitrogen supply by digesting small insects caught in cavities of plant, *eg* PITCHER PLANT, by viscidity of leaves, *eg* Portuguese fly catcher, or by movement, *eg* VENUS' FLYTRAP. Mainly found in bogs where nitrogen content of soil is low.

instinct, innate, often complex behaviour pattern of animals, developed without any learning process; common to all members of species. Example is nest-building behaviour of birds.

insulation, electrical, resistance to passage of electric current exhibited by certain substances, *eg* dry air, rubber, wax.

insulin, hormone formed in pancreas and secreted into bloodstream. Regulates amount of glucose in blood; lack of insulin causes glucose to accumulate and spill over into urine. *See* DIABETES,

insurance, system of compensating individuals or companies for loss arising, *eg* by accident, fire, theft, *etc.* Payment is made from fund to which those who are exposed to similar risks have made payments (premiums) in return for cover. System practised from ancient times, *eg* in Phoenician trade. Shipping insurance almost universal in Europe by 14th cent., dominated by LLOYD'S of London by 17th cent.; fire insurance arose in Germany (15th cent.); life insurance in England (16th cent.). Since late 19th cent. the state has been prominent in social insurance (*see* SOCIAL SECURITY).

intaglio, design or figure carved, incised or engraved into a hard material so that it is below the surface. Commonest example engraved seal-ring. Also used as method producing printing plates.

integer, in mathematics, any positive negative whole number or zero, *eg* 3 or -5

integral calculus, mathematical stu inverse to differential calculus; involv reconstruction of a function given form its derivative. Used in finding area volumes, *etc,* and solving differenti equations.

integrated circuit, electronic circu consisting of several circuit elements ar amplifying devices formed on single un esp. silicon chip. Used in calculators, cor puters, *etc.*

intelligence, ability of organisms to lea from experience and adapt responses new situations; capacity to understand ar relate concepts; measurement of gener factor underlying individual's performanc on varied specific mental tasks. Product genetic potential and influence of enviro ment, but relative importance of the factors is matter of controversy. Intel gence tests measure over range of inte lectual problems, with scales based norms for specific age groups.

intelligence quotient (IQ), ratio of ment age, as measured by intelligence tests, chronological age, expressed as percentage.

interest, money paid for use of borrowe capital. Usually at fixed percentage ra paid yearly, half-yearly or quarterly. Ma be simple or compound (*ie* interest on a cumulated interest). Usury, in legal term is interest charged on a loan abov specified level, first legislated against England (1545).

interference, in physics, interaction of combining wave motions of sam frequency. Waves reinforce or neutrali one another according to their relativ phases on meeting. Two light beams ca combine to give alternate light and dar bands (interference fringes); two sounds nearly equal frequency can produce bea (alternate increases and decreases loudness).

interferon, a protein produced by viru invaded animal cells to inhibit replicatic of the virus. The possibility of artificial stimulating production of the protein as cure for virus diseases is being tested.

Interlaken, town of WC Switzerland, on Aare. Pop. 6000. Tourist centre of Bernes Oberland, between Lakes Thun (W), Brier (E).

internal combustion engine, engine whic derives its power from the explosion of fuel-air mixture in a confined space. typical 4-stroke automobile engine, fuel-a mixture is drawn into cylinder b downward movement of reciprocatir piston (connected to a crank) and cor pressed as piston returns upwards. At to of stroke SPARKING PLUG ignites mixture ar the rapid expansion drives pisto downwards giving power stroke. The bur gases are exhausted from cylinder b

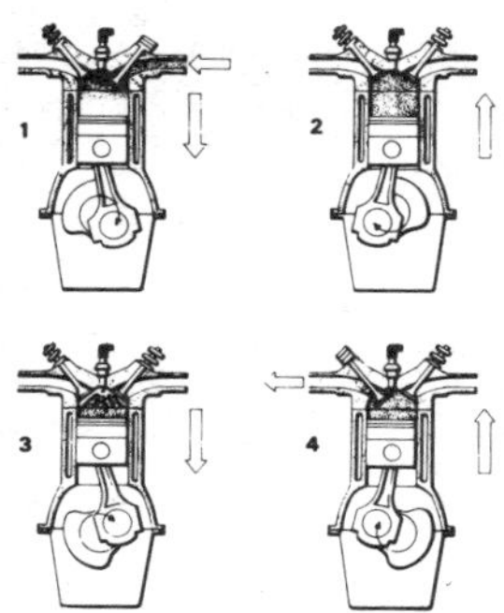

Four-stroke cycle in internal combustion engine: 1. induction stroke; 2. compression stroke; 3. power stroke; 4. exhaust stroke

upward return of piston and the cycle begins again. Arrangement of valves, opened and closed by engine-driven cam shaft, allows mixture to be drawn in, compressed and exhausted. Two stroke engine has arrangement of valves allowing power stroke every two instead of four strokes. *See* Diesel engine, Wankel rotary engine.

ternational Atomic Energy Agency, agency of UN, estab. (1957) to promote peaceful use of atomic energy.

ternational Bank for Reconstruction and Development (World Bank), agency of UN, estab. 1945; hq. Washington. Funded by UN members, serves as loan agency for member states and private investors.

ternational Brigade, volunteer force, largely drawn from Communist sympathizers, which fought for the Republicans during Spanish Civil War.

ternational Civil Aviation Organization (ICAO), agency of UN estab. (1947) at Montréal. Promotes international safety codes and symbols and investigates accidents.

ternational Court of Justice, court estab. (1945) as advisory or arbitrational judicial organ of UN. Replaced Permanent Court of International Justice. Comprises 15 justices; normally sits at The Hague. Renders decisions binding on member states on matters of international law. Advises on request of UN General Assembly.

ternational Criminal Police Commission (INTERPOL), organization estab. (1923) to coordinate police activities of participating nations. Has Paris hq.

ternational date line, imaginary line drawn N and S through Pacific Ocean, roughly following 180° meridian of longitude. Used to mark start of calendar day; 24 hours are lost when crossing it W to E and gained E to W.

International Finance Corporation (IFC), agency of UN, estab. 1956 as an affiliate of International Bank for Reconstruction and Development to encourage growth of productive enterprise in member states, esp. in underdeveloped areas.

International Labour Organization (ILO), agency concerned with conditions of work in its member countries. Estab. by Treaty of Versailles, affiliated to League of Nations (1919-45), then to UN (1946).

international law, rules generally observed and regarded as binding in relations between nations. By late 19th cent., Hague conferences were frequently resorted to for arbitration of disputes.

International Monetary Fund (IMF), agency of UN, estab. 1945; hq. Washington. Facilitates discharge of international debt by enabling member states to buy foreign currencies.

International Red Cross Committee, *see* Red Cross.

International [Workingmen's Association], called First International, organization estab. (1864) in London under leadership of Marx; aimed to unite workers and achieve political power according to principles of *Communist Manifesto*. Dissolved (1876) after conflict with anarchists. Second or Socialist International (estab. 1889) was dominated by German and Russian Social Democrat parties; broke up during WWI. Third International (*see* Comintern) created in 1919. Fourth International formed in 1938 by followers of Trotsky.

Interpol, *see* International Criminal Police Commission.

intestine, lower part of alimentary canal extending from stomach to anus, where latter stages of digestion and collection of waste products take place. Consists of convoluted upper part (small intestine), shorter but wider large intestine, and rectum.

introversion, *see* extroversion.

intrusive rock, any rock formed by solidification of molten material below the Earth's surface. All intrusive rocks are thus igneous rocks, forced into or between solid rocks while molten. May be formed at great depth, *ie* plutonic (*eg* granite), or moderate depth, *ie* hypabyssal (*eg* porphyry).

Invercargill, city of S South Isl., New Zealand, on inlet of Foveaux Str. Pop. 47,000. Fishing, food processing, sawmilling; outport at Bluff Harbour.

Inverness-shire, former county of N Scotland, now in Highland region. Mainly mountainous (Ben Nevis), crossed by Great Glen; incl. S Outer Hebrides, Skye. Livestock rearing, forestry, fishing, h.e.p., tourist industs. Co. town was **Inverness,** town and admin. hq. of Highland region, at NE end of Great Glen. Pop. 35,000. Distilling, woollens, tourism.

invertebrate, any animal without a vertebral column.

iodine (I), non-metallic element of halogen family; at. no. 53, at. wt. 126.9. Consists of grey-black crystals which sublimate to form violet vapour. Compounds found in seaweed and Chile saltpetre. Essential to functioning of thyroid gland. Compounds used in medicine, photography and organic synthesis.

ion, electrically charged atom or group of atoms; positively charged ion (cation) results from loss of electrons, negatively charged ion (anion) from electron gain. Ions can be created by collisions with charged particles, high energy radiation (X-rays, gamma rays) or by dissolving suitable compounds (electrolytes) in water.

Iona, small isl. of Inner Hebrides, W Scotland, in Strathclyde region. Centre of Celtic Christianity after St Columba founded monastery (563). Has 13th-cent. cathedral (restored 20th cent.), reputed royal burial ground.

Ionesco, Eugène (1912-), French playwright, b. Romania. Leading exponent of ABSURD in plays, *eg The Bald Prima Donna* (1950), *Rhinoceros* (1959).

ion exchange, chemical process by which ions held on porous solid material (usually synthetic resin or zeolite) are exchanged for ions in a solution surrounding the solid. Used in water softening, desalination of sea water, extraction of metals from ores.

Ionia, region of W coast of Asia Minor, incl. Aegean Isls. Colonized by ancient Greeks (Ionians) *c* 1000 BC; based on a religious league of 12 cities, prospered commercially. Conquered by Persians (6th cent. BC), revolt of cities (500 BC) led to Persian Wars. Important part of Roman and Byzantine empires, declined under Turks.

Ionian Islands, isl. chain of W Greece, in Ionian Sea. Incl. Corfu, Cephalonia, Levkas, Zakinthos. Mainly mountainous; wine, fruit, olives. Venetian 15th-18th cent.; British protectorate until 1864.

Ionian Sea, part of Mediterranean Sea, between SW Greece and SE Italy. Connected to Adriatic by Strait of Otranto.

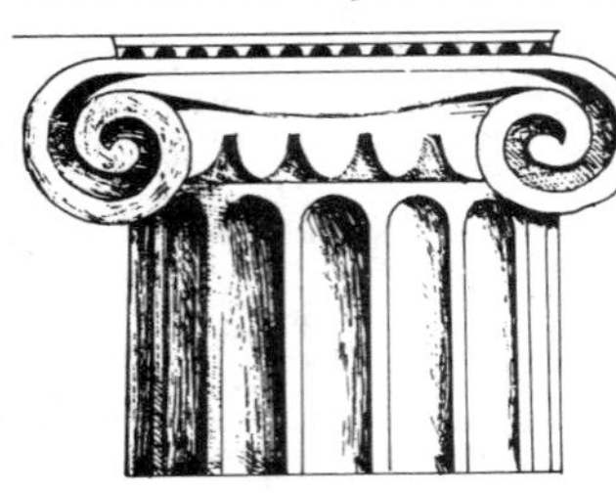

Ionic capital

Ionic order, one of the Greek orders of architecture, characterized by its slender column and 2 ornamental scrolls (spir volutes) on the front of the capital and 2 c the back. Developed in Greek colonies Asia Minor in 6th cent. BC.

ionization chamber, device used measure intensity of ionizing radiation, e gamma rays, or disintegration rate radioactive substances. Usually consists gas-filled chamber containing 2 electrode between which electric potential maintained; current flows when gas ionized by incoming radiation.

ionosphere, region of upper atmospher starting *c* 50 km above ground, in which a appreciable concentration of ions an electrons is produced by solar radiatio Divided into 3 layers, incl. Kennell Heaviside and Appleton. Important radio transmission as it reflects radi waves back to Earth.

Iowa, state of NC US. Area 145,791 sq kı (56,290 sq mi); pop. 2,870,000; cap. De Moines. Mainly rolling plains; lyin between Missouri, Mississippi rivers; hil in NE. Major agric. region; wheat, dair livestock farming. Region explored b French fur traders in 17th cent.; purchase by US as part of Louisiana Purchase (1803 Admitted to Union as 29th state (1846).

Iphigenia, in Greek myth, daughter Agamemnon and Clytemnestra. Sacrifice by her father in order to end the contrar winds which were delaying the Gree ships heading for the Trojan War.

Ipswich, town and admin. hq. of Suffolk, England, on R. Orwell. Pop. 123,000. Agri machinery; food processing industs brewing.

IQ, *see* INTELLIGENCE QUOTIENT.

Iquitos, town of NE Peru, at head navigation on Amazon R. Pop. 110,00 Coffee, cotton, timber exports.

IRA, *see* IRISH REPUBLICAN ARMY.

Iráklion *(Herakleion)* or **Candia,** town of N Crete, Greece, cap. of Iráklion admin. dis Pop. 64,000. Port, exports olive oil, wine.

Iran, republic of SW Asia; formerly Persi Area 1,648,000 sq km (636,000 sq mi); po 35,213,000; cap. Tehran. Language: Persia Religion: Shia Islam. Consists of C platea surrounded by Elburz Mts. in N, Zagr Mts. in S and W. Produces wool for carp mfg., rice, cotton; economy based on ric oil resources. Divided into 13 provs. Centr of ancient Persian empire under Cyru conquered by Alexander the Great (*c* 33 BC). Object of British-Russian rivalry (19t 20th cent.), intensified by oil finds. Pahle dynasty founded (1925); name changed Iran 1935. Shah deposed (1979); Islam republic estab. under Ayatollah Khomeir Conflict with Iraq (1980-).

Iranian, group of languages belonging Indo-Iranian branch of Indo-Europea family. Divided into East and We subgroups, incl. Baluchi, Pashtu, Kurdis Persian. Spoken in Iran, Afghanistan, Pa istan, parts of USSR.

Iraq (Arab. *Iraqia),* republic of SW Asi Area *c* 435,000 sq km (168,000 sq mi); po 12,327,000; cap. Baghdad. Languag

Arabic. Religion: Islam. Drained by R. Tigris, R. Euphrates. Mountainous N rich in oil; cotton and dates grown in irrigated SE. Borders correspond to ancient MESOPOTAMIA. Ottoman domination until WWI. Kingdom (1921-58); became republic after military coup. Conflict with Iran (1980-).

Ireland, isl. of British Isls., separated from Great Britain by Irish Sea. Area *c* 84,000 sq km (32,450 sq mi); pop. 4,576,000. Fertile C lowland with highland rim (Mourne, Wicklow, Kerry, Ox mountains). Main rivers Shannon, Erne, Foyle. Irregular W coast incl. many isls., inlets. Mild, damp climate favours vegetation, esp. grass; led to name 'Emerald Isle'. Partitioned (1921) into NORTHERN IRELAND, and **Republic of Ireland** *(Eire)*. Area *c* 70,000 sq km (27,000 sq mi); pop. 3,365,000; cap. Dublin. Languages: Irish, English. Religion: RC. Comprises 26 counties in 4 provs. (Connacht, Leinster, Munster, Ulster). Main towns Cork, Limerick. Mainly agric., esp. dairying; fishing; tourism. Long struggle for independence from UK ended with estab. of Irish Free State (1921). Republic proclaimed (1949), left Commonwealth. Joined EEC (1973).

Ireton, Henry (1611-51), English parliamentary army officer in Civil War. Fought at Edgehill (1642) and Naseby (1645). Married Cromwell's daughter (1646); as lord-deputy in Ireland (1650) assisted in Cromwell's repressive measures before dying there of plague.

Irian Jaya (West Irian), prov. of Indonesia, occupying W half of New Guinea. Area *c* 414,000 sq km (160,000 sq mi); cap. Djajapura. Exports timber, oil. Known as Netherlands New Guinea until transfer to Indonesia (1963), when named Irian Barat. Present name dates from 1973.

iridium (Ir), brittle metallic element; at. no. 77, at. wt. 192.2. Hard and chemically resistant; found in platinum ores. Alloys used in pen points, watch and compass bearings.

Iris, in Greek myth, goddess of the rainbow and a messenger of the gods.

iris, in anatomy, round pigmented membrane in front of eye, between cornea and lens. Its muscles adjust width of pupil, which it surrounds, and regulate amount of light entering eye.

iris, genus of perennial plants of Iridaceae family, native to temperate regions. Sword-shaped leaves, flowers composed of 3 petals and 3 drooping sepals.

Irish language, *see* GAELIC.

Irish Republican Army (IRA), para-military organization which developed after Dublin Easter Rebellion (1916), pressing for an Irish republic which would incl. whole of Ulster. After being declared illegal by De Valéra (1936) became underground terrorist movement. Sectarian militancy and 'civil rights' disturbances in late 1960s sparked off resurgence of activity by the IRA, now with 2 wings, 'official' and 'provisional', the latter for some years source of systematic terrorist campaign in Northern Ireland. *See* SINN FEIN.

Irish Sea, between Ireland and Great Britain. Connected to Atlantic Ocean by North Channel (N), St George's Channel (S).

Irish wolfhound, breed of large hound with rough grey coat. Tallest of dogs, stands *c* 86 cm/34 in. at shoulder.

Irkutsk, city of USSR, SC Siberian RSFSR; port at confluence of Angara and Irkut. Pop. 550,000. Indust.; produces aircraft, automobiles, machine tools. Founded 1652 as Cossack fortress.

iron (Fe), malleable ductile metallic element, easily magnetized; at. no. 26, at. wt. 55.85. Occurs in various ores, incl. magnetite, haematite and pyrites. Manufactured in blast furnace from oxide ores, limestone and coke. Usually converted (*see* BESSEMER) into wrought iron or steel, their properties depending on amount of carbon present. Compounds essential to higher forms of animal life.

Iron Age, archaeological period following Bronze Age, characterized by use of iron to make tools, weapons. Iron-working techniques were developed by Hittites in 2nd millennium BC but prob. kept secret. Knowledge spread to Middle East and Europe on collapse of Hittite empire (1200 BC). In Europe, iron-working is associated with HALLSTATT and LA TÈNE cultures.

Iron Curtain, term used to describe ideological barrier between countries of Soviet bloc and rest of Europe.

iron lung, device used to maintain artificial respiration in a person who has difficulty in breathing, *eg* as a result of poliomyelitis. Effects expansion and contraction of lungs by mechanical changes in air pressure.

iron pyrites, *see* PYRITE.

ironwood, any of various trees with extremely hard, heavy wood, esp. HORNBEAM.

Iroquois, five North American Indian tribes (Mohawk, Oneida, Onondaga, Cayuga, Seneca). Iroquois Confederacy founded (*c* 1570) by the Onondaga, led by Hiawatha. Estab. advanced culture in New York state. Settled hunters and farmers; lived in palisaded long houses. Dispersed Huron tribes in 1649. Strongly hostile to French but pro-British even during American Revolution. There were *c* 25,000 Iroquois left by 1970s.

Irrawaddy, chief river of Burma. Rises in NW and flows through Mandalay to Andaman Sea; *c* 2100 km (1300 mi) long.

irrigation, artificial distribution of water to soil to sustain plant growth in areas of insufficient rainfall. Methods used incl. sprinkler systems, flooding areas from canals and ditches, and running of water between crop rows. Irrigation has been used since ancient times.

Irving, Sir Henry, orig. John Henry Brodribb (1838-1905), English actor-manager. Leading man to Ellen Terry for many years.

Irving, Washington (1783-1859), American author. Known for comic essays, tales, *eg* 'Rip Van Winkle'.

Isaac, in OT, only son of ABRAHAM and Sarah. Offered by his father as sacrifice to God but saved by divine intervention. Father by Rebecca of Esau and Jacob.

Isabella (1296-1358), queen consort of England. *See* EDWARD II and III.

Isabella I (1451-1504), queen of Castile (1474-1504). Married (1469) Ferdinand II of Aragón, who ruled both Aragón and Castile with her as FERDINAND V.

Isaiah, prophetic book of OT, attributed to Isaiah (*fl* 710 BC), possibly incl. other writings. Warns of the power of Assyria and foretells the destruction and redemption of Israel.

Iseult, *see* TRISTAN AND ISOLDE.

Isfahan or **Esfahan** (anc. *Aspadana),* city of C Iran, cap. of Isfahan prov. Pop. 672,000. Carpet, textile mfg; notable silver filigree work. Cap. of Persia (17th cent.); magnificent architecture.

Isherwood, Christopher [William Bradshaw] (1904-), English author. Known for novels depicting decadence of Weimar Republic, *eg Mr Norris Changes Trains* (1935), *Goodbye to Berlin* (1939).

Ishmael, in OT, son of Abraham and Hagar. Exiled in desert with mother through Sarah's jealousy. Regarded by Moslems as ancestor of Arabs.

Ishtar, Babylonian and Assyrian goddess of fertility, love and war. Went to the underworld to recover her lover TAMMUZ, during which time all fertility ceased on earth. Cult was widely assimilated throughout W Asia. Identified with Astarte.

Isis, ancient Egyptian nature goddess. Sister and wife of OSIRIS; mother of Horus. Represented with cow's head. Her cult persisted in Roman Empire.

Islam or **Mohammedanism,** monotheistic religion in which supreme deity is Allah and chief prophet and founder is MOHAMMED. Based on revelations of Mohammed in *Koran.* Concepts of god, heaven and hell akin to Judaeo-Christian beliefs, with recognition of OT prophets and Jesus (as prophet). Religious duties incl. sincere profession of the creed, prayer 5 times daily, generous alms-giving, observance of Ramadan fast and pilgrimage to Mecca. Main sects are Sunnites and Shiites who are divided over caliphate. Faith spread rapidly after foundation (7th cent.) and today incl. N Africa, the Middle East, Iran, Pakistan, Indonesia and isolated pockets of SE Europe, USSR, China and S Pacific. There are *c* 350 million faithful, called Moslems or Muslims.

Islamabad, cap. of Pakistan, NW of Rawalpindi. Pop. 77,000. Built in 1960s as new cap.

island, land mass surrounded by water. Island-forming processes incl. upward movement of Earth's crust, lowering of sea level, volcanic action, deposition o sediments, coral formation. Sea isls. ma be continental, *ie* formed by separatio from mainland, or oceanic, *ie* formed i the ocean. Two isls., Australia an Antarctica, are continents; largest true is is Greenland.

Islay, isl. of Inner Hebrides, W Scotland, i Strathclyde region. Area 609 sq km (235 s mi); main town Port Ellen. Agric., fishing distilling.

Isle of Man, *see* MAN, ISLE OF.

Isle of Wight, *see* WIGHT, ISLE OF.

Islington, bor. of N Greater London England. Pop. 166,000.

Ismail Pasha (1830-95), khedive of Egyp (1863-79). Encouraged building of Sue Canal; after incurring serious debt, force to sell his canal shares to Britain (1875) Placed country's finances under Anglo French management (1876). Abdicated.

isobar, line on a map connecting points o equal atmospheric pressure. Sinc pressure varies with altitude, pressur values used for weather charts ar reduced to sea-level equivalents befor isobars are drawn.

Isolde, *see* TRISTAN AND ISOLDE.

isomerism, in chemistry, existence of 2 o more compounds with same molecula formula whose physical and chemica properties differ through distinc arrangements of atoms in the molecule, *e* urea ($CO(NH_2)_2$), ammonium cyanat (NH_4CNO).

isotherm, line on a map connecting points o equal temperature. May represent value a one time or average readings over period. Since temperature varies with altitude, values are normally reduced to sea level equivalents before isotherms ar drawn.

isotopes, atoms of same element whic differ in mass number, possessing differen numbers of neutrons in their nuclei. Hav essentially similar chemical propertie but may differ in physical properties. Mos elements consist of mixtures of variou isotopes.

Israel, in OT, name given to JACOB a eponymous ancestor of the Israelites.

Israel, republic of SW Asia, o Mediterranean. Area, *c* 21,000 sq km (810 sq mi); pop. 3,689,000; cap. Jerusalem Language: Hebrew. Religion: Judaism Fertile coastal plain (citrus fruit) rises in N to Galilee (grain) and in S to Negev deser (irrigation schemes, co-operative farm *kibbutzim*). Part of hist. PALESTINE, regio disputed by neighbours after Hebrews con solidated it (*c* 1000 BC). Subsequent occu pations incl. Roman (70 BC-AD 636 Ottoman (1516-1917). British mandat (1920-48) ended in estab. of Israel as Jewis home. Fought Arabs in wars of 1948, 1956 1967, 1973; occupied Sinai from 1967 gradually returned after 1979 peace treat with Egypt.

Istanbul, city of NW Turkey, on both sides o Bosporus, at entrance to Sea of Marmara

Pop. 2,547,000. Major port; cultural, indust. and trade centre; starting point of Baghdad railway. Anc. *Byzantium* founded 658 BC by Greeks. Rebuilt as Constantinople by Constantine I (4th cent. AD) as new Roman imperial cap. Later cap. of Byzantine empire; often attacked, fell to soldiers of 4th Crusade (1204) and finally to Turks (1453). Ottoman and Turkish cap. until 1923; name changed 1930. Harbour is in Golden Horn. Notable architecture incl. Church of St Sophia, built by Justinian in 6th cent.; became a mosque after Turkish conquest. Usküdar (Scutari) is indust. suburb; Florence Nightingale ran hospital here in Crimean War.

Istria *(Istra),* penin. of NW Yugoslavia, in Adriatic Sea. Ceded to Italy after WWI; all except Trieste to Yugoslavia 1947.

Italian, Romance language in Italic branch of Indo-European family. Official language of Italy, and one of Switzerland's. Developed from Latin, Florentine dialect becoming dominant in 14th cent., giving rise to modern standard Italian.

Italic, branch of Indo-European family of languages. Subdivided into 2 groups: ancient Italian, incl. Latin; ROMANCE LANGUAGES, all developed from Latin.

Italy

Italy *(Italia),* republic of S Europe. Comprises penin., isls. incl. Sardinia, Sicily. Area 301,165 sq km (116,280 sq mi); pop. 56,697,000; cap. Rome. Language: Italian. Religion: RC. Chief cities Milan, Naples, Turin, Genoa. Member of EEC. Alps in N, fertile Po basin in NE, Apennines run NW-SE. Volcanic, earthquake activity in S. Indust. based in N and Po basin, using h.e.p. from Alps. Barren S has some agric. (fruit, wine, olives), slow indust. growth. Major tourist indust. Settled by Etruscans, Greeks before rise of Imperial ROME 5th cent. BC; fell to Ostrogoths AD 5th cent. Part of Holy Roman Empire from 962; later medieval growth of city republics, *eg* Florence, Venice, *fl* in Renaissance period. United by Cavour, Garibaldi as kingdom (1861). Fascist rule under Mussolini led to expansion (Abyssinia, Albania) and alliance with Germany in WWII. Colonies lost, republic created 1946.

Ithaca *(Itháki),* isl. of W Greece, one of Ionian Isls. Area 85 sq km (33 sq mi); main town Ithaca. Home of Homer's Odysseus.

Ivan [III] the Great (1440-1505), Russian ruler, grand duke of Moscow (1462-1505). Conquered Novgorod (1478) and expanded territ. of Muscovy by conquest and treaty. Threw off domination of Tartars of the Golden Horde (1480).

Ivan [IV] the Terrible (1530-84), Russian tsar (1547-84). Began eastward expansion with conquest of Kazan (1552) and Astrakhan (1556). Unbalanced after 1560, became a harsh tyrant; in a rage, killed his son Ivan (1581). Broke political power of boyars in reign of terror.

Ives, Charles Edward (1874-1954), American composer. Anticipated many later developments in music, incl. complex combinations of rhythms and keys.

Iviza *(Ibiza),* third largest of Balearic Isls., Spain. Area 572 sq km (221 sq mi); main town Iviza. Tourism, agric.

ivory, hard white substance, a form of dentine, making up tusks of elephants, walruses, *etc.* Used for piano keys, cutlery handles, decorative carvings.

Ivory Coast *(Fr. Côte d'Ivoire),* republic of W Africa, on Gulf of Guinea. Area 322,500 sq km (124,500 sq mi); pop. 7,613,000; cap. Abidjan. Official language: French. Religions: animist, Islam. Savannah in N, tropical forest in C, coastal swamps in S. Railway link with Upper Volta. Produces coffee, cotton, bananas, tropical hardwoods. Former centre of slave, ivory trade. French colony from 1893, part of French West Africa from 1904; independent 1960.

ivy, *Hedera helix,* evergreen climbing shrub of Araliaceae family, native to Europe. Woody stem, greenish flowers in autumn, poisonous berries in spring. Climbs walls and trees by tiny roots. *See* POISON IVY.

Iwo, city of SW Nigeria. Pop. 214,000. Agric. centre, esp. cocoa, coffee, palm products; cotton mfg. Former cap. of Yoruba kingdom, *fl* 17th-19th cent.

Iwo Jima, *see* VOLCANO ISLANDS.

Izhevsk, city of USSR, cap. of Udmurt auton. republic, E European RSFSR. Pop. 549,000. Metallurgical centre; steel mills and ammunition factories estab. early 19th cent.

Izmir, port of W Turkey, on Gulf of Izmir; formerly Smyrna. Pop. 637,000. Naval base; exports tobacco, cotton. Colonized by Ionians, prosperous under Roman rule; early Christian centre. Taken by Turks in 1424. Held by Greeks (1919-22); Greek pop. expelled (1923).

J

jacana, any of Jacanidae family of tropical and subtropical birds. Has long toes enabling it to walk on floating plants, *eg* lily leaves. Also called lilytrotter.

Jacaranda

jacaranda, genus of tropical American trees of bignonia family. Finely divided foliage, large clusters of lavender flowers.

jackal, wolf-like wild dog. Hunts nocturnally in packs, taking carrion or living prey. Species incl. oriental jackal, *Canis aureus,* of N Africa and S Asia.

jackdaw, *Corvus monedula,* black bird of crow family, found in Europe and W Asia.

jack rabbit, large North American hare, genus *Lepus.*

Jackson, Andrew (1767-1845), American general and statesman, Democratic president (1829-37). Gained victory over British at New Orleans (1815) after formal conclusion of War of 1812. Estranged South in conflict with South Carolina over taxation rights. Successfully opposed attempts to re-charter Bank of the United States. Jacksonian democracy brought SPOILS SYSTEM of political rewards and strengthened the executive.

Jackson, Thomas Jonathan ('Stonewall') (1824-63), American Confederate general. Fought in Civil War, victorious in Shenandoah Valley campaign (1862) and 2nd battle of Bull Run (1862). Mortally wounded at Chancellorsville.

Jackson, cap. of Mississippi, US; on Pearl R. Pop. 285,000. Railway jct., indust. and commercial centre; cotton, textiles mfg. Estab. as cap. 1821.

Jacksonville, deep-water port of NE Florida, US; on St John's R. Pop. 693,000. Commercial, transport centre; timber, fruit exports. Tourist resort.

Jack the Ripper, popular name fo notorious murderer, never identified, of women prostitutes in E London in 1888.

Jacob, in OT, twin brother of Esau. Gaine Esau's birthright and their father's dyin blessing by trickery. Fled to escape hi brother's anger. During flight, had vision c angels ascending and descending ladder t heaven. On return, after marrying Lea and Rachel, wrestled with angel, receive name Israel. The 12 tribes of Israel wer descended from his sons.

Jacobean, term applied to Englis architecture and decoration characteristi of reign of James I. Classical features wer used more widely and elaborat decoration employed.

Jacobean drama, term used for play written in, and reflecting spirit of, reign c James I. Comedies were generally satire of human folly, *eg* Jonson's *Volpon* Tragedies characterized by emphasis o human, esp. sexual, corruption, often wit revenge theme, *eg* Webster's *The Whit Devil, The Duchess of Malfi,* Tourneur' *The Revenger's Tragedy.*

Jacobins, French society of radica democrats, formed 1789. Originally inc GIRONDISTS, whose support of wa throughout Europe later caused spli Became increasingly radical and, unde Robespierre, instituted REIGN OF TERRO Influence ended by Robespierre's fall an execution (1794).

Jacobite Church, Christian church of Ira Syria, parts of India. Founded (6th cent.) b Jacob Baradaeus. Regarded as heretical b RC and Orthodox churches (*see* MON PHYSITISM).

Jacobites, supporters of claims of house o STUART to English throne after 1688. Sough restoration of James II and hi descendants. Aided by France and Spain raised rebellion of 1715 in support of Jame Edward Stuart. Charles Edward Stuart le last Jacobite rebellion from Scotlan (1745-6), defeated at Culloden.

Jacquard, Joseph Marie (1752-1834 French inventor. Developed (1801-6 Jacquard loom, first to weave figure patterns; used system of punched cards.

jade, either of 2 silicate minerals used a gem: jadeite and nephrite. Normally gree in colour, may be white, yellow, pink. Use in ornamental carving, jewellery.

Jaén, town of S Spain, cap. of Jaén prov. Pop 79,000. Produces olive oil, wine, leathe goods. Moorish kingdom until 124 Cathedral (16th cent.).

Jaffa, *see* TEL AVIV.

jaguar, *Panthera onca,* large cat of Centra and South America. Resembles leopar

Jaguar

with black spots and yellow coat; nocturnal hunter.

Jainism, Indian religion. Arose (6th cent. BC) with Buddhism as protest against formalism of Hinduism. Doctrine based on belief in eternity of all living things, stresses asceticism, respect for all forms of life. The soul retains identity through transmigration and eventually attains NIRVANA. Adhered to by *c* 2 million Indians.

Jaipur, cap. of Rajasthan state, NW India. Pop. 615,000. Commercial centre; famous for jewellery. Enclosed by wall, has maharajah's palace. Cap. of former princely state of Jaipur.

Jakarta, *see* DJAKARTA.

Jamaica, isl. republic of West Indies, member of British Commonwealth. Area 10,962 sq km (4232 sq mi); pop. 2,133,000; cap. Kingston. Language: English. Religion: Protestant. Blue Mts. in E (coffee growing). Tropical climate. Agric. economy (sugar, fruit, spice, tobacco growing); bauxite exports. Important tourism. Discovered by Columbus (1494); captured from Spanish by English (1655); slavery abolished (1833). Gained independence after it seceded from Federation of West Indies (1962). Republic (1980).

James [the Elder], St (d. *c* AD 44), one of the Twelve Disciples, son of Zebedee. In NT, put to death with brother John by Herod Agrippa. Traditionally, body moved to Santiago de Compostela, Spain, site of famous shrine.

James [the Younger], St (*fl* 1st cent. AD), one of the Twelve Disciples, son of Alphaeus.

James I (1566-1625), king of England, Scotland and Ireland (1603-25). Succeeded to Scottish throne (1567) as James VI on abdication of mother, Mary Queen of Scots, and to English throne on death of Elizabeth I. Reign marked by conflict with Parliament, influence of his favourites (*eg* BUCKINGHAM), exercise of royal prerogative, raising of revenue. Antagonized Puritans at Hampton Court Conference (1604), which commissioned translation of Bible (Authorized Version).

James II (1633-1701), king of England, Scotland and Ireland (1685-8). A convert to Catholicism, subject to Whig attempts to exclude him from succession, which were frustrated by his brother, Charles II. After succession, put down Monmouth's rebellion; alienated subjects by autocratic rule, pro-Catholic policies. Fled country after William of Orange had been invited to become king. His restoration bid was foiled by defeat at the Boyne in Ireland (1690).

James I (1394-1437), king of Scotland (1424-37). Sent by his father to France (1406), he was captured by English and held until 1424. Tried to suppress power of his nobles and maintain peace; murdered by group of nobles.

James II (1430-60), king of Scotland (1437-60). Succeeded father James I. Took over govt. in 1449, and ended conflict with Douglas clan with victory at Arkinholm. Killed by misfire of own cannon while taking Roxburgh castle from English.

James III (1451-88), king of Scotland (1460-88). Succeeded father James II. Gained Orkney and Shetland by marriage with Margaret of Denmark. Killed at battle of Sauchieburn fighting rebel nobles.

James IV (1473-1513), king of Scotland (1488-1513). Reign marked by stability and beginnings of prosperity. As part of alliance with France, invaded England but was defeated and killed at Flodden. Marriage to Margaret Tudor (1503) formed basis of Stuart succession to English throne.

James V (1512-42), king of Scotland (1513-42). Succeeded father James IV. Took real power in 1528. Resisted urgings of Henry VIII of England to break with France and Rome. Henry invaded Scotland and defeated Scots at Solway Moss; James died soon after. Succeeded by daughter, Mary Queen of Scots.

James VI, *see* JAMES I.

James, Jesse [Woodson] (1847-82), American outlaw. With brother, **[Alexander] Frank[lin] James** (1843-1915), led notorious outlaw gang which robbed banks and trains in midwest during 1870s. Jesse was killed by a gang member.

James, Henry (1843-1916), American novelist. Novels deal with social relationships between Old World and New, *eg The Europeans* (1878), *The Portrait of a Lady* (1881), *The Bostonians* (1886). Short stories incl. *The Turn of the Screw* (1898). Settled in England (1877), became British national (1915). His brother, **William James** (1842-1910), was a philosopher and psychologist. Opposed 'pure' metaphysical philosophy, argued for practical philosophy, *ie* pragmatism, and relativity of truth. Works incl. *The Principles of Psychology* (1890).

James, in NT, epistle traditionally ascribed to St James the Less. Propounds general points of practical morality.

James Bay, arm of SE Hudson Bay, Canada; between Ontario and Québec.

Jameson, Sir Leander Starr (1853-1917), British colonial administrator. Led unauthorized Jameson raid (1895) into Boer colony of Transvaal to support 'Uitlanders' (largely British settlers); captured, briefly imprisoned by British. Premier of Cape Colony (1904-8).

Jamestown, ruined village of E Virginia, US, on James R. First permanent English settlement in America (1607).

Jammu and Kashmir, state of N India. Area *c* 142,000 sq km (55,000 sq mi); pop. 4,615,000; cap. Srinagar (summer), Jammu (winter). Almost entirely mountainous. Famous for goats' wool (cashmere). At 1947 partition this Hindu-ruled Moslem region disputed by Pakistan and India. Jammu and Kashmir declared part of India 1956; Pakistan retained Azad Kashmir.

Jamshedpur, city of Bihar state, NE India. Pop. 357,000. Major iron and steel works. Founded 1909 by industrialist Tata family.

Janáček, Leoš (1854-1928), Czech composer. Wrote music in national style. Works incl. rhapsody *Taras Bulba* and operas, *eg Jenufa, The Cunning Little Vixen.* Orchestral works incl. *Sinfonietta.*

Janissaries, elite corps of the Turkish army formed in the 14th cent. from press-ganged Christians and prisoners of war. Liquidated by Mahmud II (1826) after a mutiny.

Jansen, Cornelis (1585-1638), Dutch theologian. Attempted to reform RC church by returning to teachings of St Augustine. Attacked orthodox Jesuit teaching, advocating austerity, belief in predestination similar to Calvin's but within Catholicism. Leading followers (Jansenists) set up community at Port Royal, France. Condemned in papal bulls of 1705 and 1713. Noted Jansenists incl. Pascal.

Jansenism, *see* JANSEN, CORNELIS.

Janus, in Roman religion, god of doorways and hence of the beginnings of enterprises. One of principal gods, regarded as custodian of the universe. Represented with double-faced head so that he could look to front and back.

Japan *(Nippon),* country of E Asia, archipelago with 4 main isls. Honshu, Hokkaido, Kyushu and Shikoku, separated from mainland Asia by Sea of Japan. Area *c* 372,000 sq km (142,000 sq mi); pop. 114,898,000; cap. Tokyo. Language: Japanese. Religion: Shinto, Buddhism. Mountainous with active volcanoes, frequent earthquakes; monsoon climate, abundant rainfall. Intensive cultivation yields rice, cereals, soya beans; major fisheries. Massive industrial output. Buddhism, Chinese culture introduced 6th cent AD; was feudal society under warrior leaders (shoguns) until 19th cent. European contacts estab. in 16th cent. Became world power after defeating China (1894-5), Russia (1904-5); 2nd Chinese war merged with WWII after Japanese attack on Pearl Harbor (1941). Surrendered 1945; imperial power curtailed (1946). Rapid economic growth after WWII.

Japanese, language of Japan. Appears to be unrelated to any other language, although grammar similar to Korean. Written language adapted from Chinese since 3rd–4th cent., with simplified phonetic characters added since WWII.

japonica or **flowering quince,** spiky Asiatic shrub of genus *Chaemoneles.* Pink or red flowers, hard yellow fruit used in preserves.

Winter jasmine

jasmine, any of genus *Jasminum* of shrubs of olive family. Native to Asia, South America and Australia. Popular as garden plant for fragrant flowers of yellow, red or white. Used in perfumes or for scenting tea.

Jason, in Greek myth, leader of the ARGONAUTS. Promised his right to throne of Iolcus by the usurper Pelias if he could recover the GOLDEN FLEECE. Secured the fleece from King Aeëtes of Colchis, whose daughter MEDEA helped him in return for promise of marriage. On return to Iolcus, Medea tricked Pelias' daughters into murdering their father, but Jason failed to retain kingdom. Reigned with Medea over Corinth until he broke faith with her. For this, condemned to exile by gods.

jasper, impure, cryptocrystalline QUARTZ used as gem. Opaque, usually red, yellow or brown in colour.

Jaspers, Karl (1883-1969), German philosopher. Interpreter of German EXISTENTIALISM. Held man to be encompassed in continual struggle of love and hate.

jaundice, condition characterized by yellow discoloration of skin. Caused by excess bile pigment in blood. May result from infectious hepatitis, blockage of bile ducts.

Jaurès, Jean Léon (1859-1914), French politician. Advocated democratic socialism and international pacifism. Founded socialist journal *L'Humanité* (1904). Assassinated while trying to prevent outbreak of WWI.

Java, most important isl. of Indonesia. Area *c* 132,000 sq km (51,000 sq mi). Narrow, crossed by volcanic mountains; humid, tropical vegetation. Produces rice, rubber, coffee. Densely populated; has ⅔ of Indonesian pop. and cap. Djakarta.

Java man, forerunner of modern man whose

fossilized remains were found in Java (1891). Considered to be an example of *Homo erectus*.

aw, either of 2 bones which hold the teeth and frame the mouth in most vertebrates. Upper jaw (maxilla), a component of skull, does not move; lower jaw (mandible), hinged to skull, is movable.

ay, brightly coloured bird of crow family. Eurasian jay, *Garrulus glandarius*, has pinkish-brown body, blue-back wings.

azz, music that originated in US at turn of 19th cent., deriving from American Negro music. Key features are use of improvisation and rhythmic drive. Several styles are still current, *eg* traditional, swing and bop, but contemporary jazz is merging both with rock and avant-garde music.

ean Paul, *see* RICHTER, JOHANN PAUL.

edburgh, town of Borders region, SE Scotland. Pop. 4000. Former royal burgh and co. town of Roxburghshire. Tweed, woollen, rayon mfg. Has ruined 12th-cent. abbey.

eddah, *see* JIDDAH.

efferson, Thomas (1743-1826), American statesman, president (1801-9). Wrote much of Declaration of Independence (1776). As secretary of state (1790-3) in Washington's cabinet, opposed centralizing Federalists led by Alexander HAMILTON. Elected president by House of Representatives after tie with Aaron Burr. Admin. highlighted by Louisiana Purchase (1803). Much of subsequent Democratic Party doctrine derived from Jeffersonian Republicans.

efferson City, cap. of Missouri, US; on Missouri R. Pop. 32,000. Agric. processing. Lincoln Univ. founded (1866) for Negroes.

effreys, George, 1st Baron Jeffreys of Wem (*c* 1645-89), English judge. Notorious for harshness at 'Bloody Assizes' after Monmouth's rebellion (1685), hanging *c* 200 and flogging, transporting many more. Lord chancellor under James II.

ehovah, mistaken reconstruction of the ineffable name of God (YHWH) in OT. The form *Yahweh* is now regarded as more correct.

ehovah's Witnesses, *see* RUSSELL, CHARLES TAZE.

ellicoe, John Rushworth Jellicoe, 1st Earl (1859-1935), British admiral. Commanded Grand Fleet (1914-16), notably in battle of Jutland (1916).

ellyfish, free-swimming medusa form of certain coelenterates. True jellyfish, class Scyphozoa, have gelatinous bell-shaped bodies and tentacles with stinging cells for capturing prey.

ena, town of SW East Germany, on R. Saale. Pop. 84,000. Precision engineering, incl. Zeiss optical instruments. Univ. (1558). Scene of Napoleon's victory (1806) over Prussians.

enghiz Khan, *see* GENGHIS KHAN.

enkins' Ear, War of (1739-41), conflict between Britain and Spain, which merged into the War of AUSTRIAN SUCCESSION. Robert Jenkins, a master mariner, claimed to have had his ear cut off by the Spanish; his story so aroused public opinion that Walpole was forced to declare war.

Jenner, Edward (1749-1823), English physician. Made 1st successful vaccination (1796) against smallpox by immunizing patient with cowpox virus.

Jerba, *see* DJERBA.

Jerboa, fawn-coloured nocturnal rodent of Dipodidae family from desert regions of N Africa and Asia. Uses very long back legs for jumping.

Jeremiah, prophetic book of OT, taking place during reign of Josiah. Tells story of priest Jeremiah who was imprisoned for foretelling fall of Jerusalem. Went into Egypt with the remaining Jews when prophecy fulfilled (586 BC).

Jerez (de la Frontera), city of Andalusia, S Spain. Pop. 150,000. Produces wine, sherry (named after town).

Jericho, ancient city of NW Jordan, at N end of Dead Sea. Thought to date from *c* 8000 BC. Canaanite city captured by Joshua and Israelites; often destroyed, rebuilt.

Jerome, Jerome K[lapka] (1859-1927), English author. Known for comic novels, esp. *Three Men in a Boat* (1889).

Jerome, St, full name Sophronius Eusebius Hieronymus (*c* 347-*c* 419), Dalmatian churchman, scholar. Served Pope Damasus I in Rome before retiring (386) to monastery in Bethlehem. His Latin translations of Bible from Hebrew served as basis for the VULGATE.

Jersey, largest of Channel Isls., UK. Area 116 sq km (45 sq mi); pop. 73,000; cap. St Helier. Tourism; Jersey cattle; potato, tomato growing.

Jersey City, in NE New Jersey, US; opposite New York City on Hudson R. Pop. 261,000. Shipping terminal; meat packing, oil refining; foundry and paper products, chemicals mfg. Settled by Dutch in 1620s.

Jerusalem, cap. of Israel, hist. cap. of Palestine. Pop. 336,000. Partitioned 1948 between Israel (new city) and Jordan (old city). Latter contains most of Jewish, Christian, Moslem holy sites. Enclosed by Turks (16th cent.). Sacred sites are Wailing Wall, Mosque of Omar, Church of Holy Sepulchre, monastries, Mt. of Olives. Old city occupied by Israelis after 1967.

Jerusalem artichoke, *see* ARTICHOKE.

Jervis Bay, inlet of Tasman Sea, SE Australia. Shore area (73 sq km/28 sq mi) became federal territ. 1915; proposed as port for Australian Capital Territory. Naval base.

Jesse, in OT, father of David. Name later symbolized royal line and its Messianic associations, *eg* Jesse's Rod (Jesus) and Jesse's Root (Virgin Mary).

Jesuits, *see* JESUS, SOCIETY OF.

Jesus, Society of, or **Jesuits,** RC religious order for men founded (*c* 1534) by IGNATIUS OF LOYOLA. Approved by pope (1540). Original aims were educational and missionary work. Characterized by disciplined organization and long, rigorous training. Political involvement (18th cent.) resulted in expulsion from France, Portugal, Spain and its dominions. Suppressed by Pope Clement XIV (1773). Revived (1814) as worldwide order.

Jesus Christ (*c* 4 BC-*c* AD 29), Jewish religious leader, founder of Christianity. Born in Bethlehem. Believed by Christians to be Son of God and to have been miraculously conceived by the Virgin Mary, wife of Joseph of Nazareth. After baptism by his cousin, John the Baptist, Jesus became a wandering teacher accompanied by band of disciples. Attracted great crowds with miracles and preaching, proclaiming coming of the Kingdom of God. His Sermon on the Mount (Matthew 5:8), which preaches love, humility and charity, aroused hostility of Pharisees. Govt.'s fear of his power led to arrest in Jerusalem after betrayal by Judas Iscariot. Tried and convicted of blasphemy by the ecclesiastical court. Crucified by order of Pontius Pilate. According to Gospels, arose 3 days later. Book of Acts relates that, 40 days later, in sight of his disciples, he ascended to Heaven. *See* TRINITY.

jet, hard, black variety of LIGNITE. May be highly polished and used in jewellery.

jet propulsion, forward movement achieved by reaction caused by expanding gases ejected rearwards. Usually air is compressed, mixed with fuel and burnt. This combustion provides rapid expansion of the gas which produces the rearward jet and also drives the intake compressor.

Jewish Autonomous Region, *see* BIROBIDZHAN.

Jews, people regarded as descended from the ancient Hebrews of Biblical times, whose religion is JUDAISM. In OT, lineage traced from Abraham and 12 tribes of Israel. Originally in Canaan, then Egypt; persecution resulted in Exodus led by Moses. Resettled in Canaan under Saul after period of wandering in desert. First Temple built by Solomon. Kingdom then split into Israel and Judah. Temple destroyed by Babylonians (586 BC), people exiled until their return was allowed by Cyrus the Great and Temple rebuilt (516 BC). Jerusalem destroyed by Romans (AD 70). After fall of Roman Empire, Jews appeared in W Europe but were widely persecuted from 12th-18th cent. Capitalism and 19th-cent. revolutionary movements improved their conditions. Emancipation led to cultural assimilation and ZIONISM. New wave of persecution spread from Russia after assassination (1881) of Alexander II. Rise to power of Nazis in Germany resulted in extermination of 6 million Jews before and during WWII. Refuge sought in Palestine, resulting in formation of Jewish state of Israel (1948) by UN.

Jezebel (d. *c* 846 BC), wife of Ahab, king of Israel. Introduced worship of Baal into Israel and persecuted the prophets. Vigorously denounced by Elijah, wh[o] prophesied her death; executed afte[r] Jehu's defeat of Ahab.

Jiang Qing, alternative spelling of Chian[g] Ch'ing; *see* GANG OF FOUR.

Jibuti, *see* DJIBOUTI.

Jiddah or **Jeddah,** port of W Saudi Arabi[a] on Red Sea coast of Hejaz. Pop. 561,00[0]. Provides sea access to Mecca fo[r] thousands of pilgrims.

Jinnah, Mohammed Ali (1876-1948), India[n] statesman. President of Moslem Leagu[e] after 1934, successfully advocated partitio[n] of India into separate Hindu and Mosle[m] states at independence (1947). Firs[t] governor-general of Pakistan.

Joan of Arc, St (*c* 1412-31), French nationa[l] heroine. Claimed to hear voices urging he[r] to aid the dauphin in struggle agains[t] English. Led army which raised siege o[f] Orléans (1429), then persuaded the dauphi[n] to be crowned as Charles VII at Rheim[s]. Captured at Compiègne (1430) by th[e] Burgundians and delivered to the Englis[h]. Tried and condemned by court of Frenc[h] ecclesiastics at Rouen as heretic an[d] sorceress; burned at stake.

Job, poetical book of OT, of unknow[n] authorship, prob. written 600-400 B[C]. Criticizes the association of sin wi[th] suffering by telling of the sufferin[g] inflicted on the righteous Job by God.

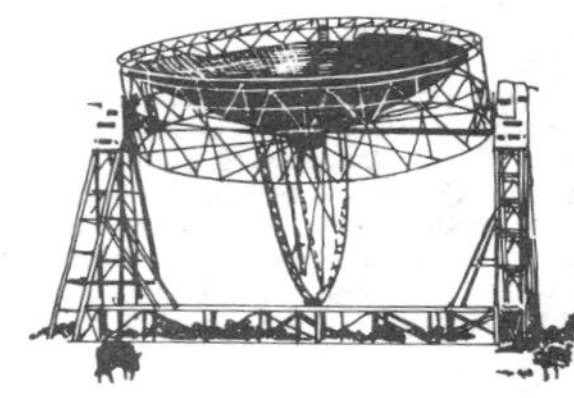

Jodrell Bank radio telescope

Jodrell Bank, site of large radio telescop[e] near Macclesfield, Cheshire. Has steerabl[e] parabolic dish, 76m in diameter.

Joel, prophetic book of OT, predicting plagu[e] of locusts in Judah. Promises th[e] forgiveness of God upon repentance of sin.

Joffre, Joseph Jacques Césaire (1852-1931[)], French marshal. Commanded Frenc[h] armies on Western Front (1914-16) unt[il] outmoded strategy (notably at Verdu[n] 1916) led to his replacement.

Johannesburg, city of S Transvaal, Sout[h] Africa, in Witwatersrand. Pop. 1,433,00[0]; country's largest city. Major indust[rial] commercial centre in world's riche[st] goldmining region; engineering, chemica[l] mfg., diamond cutting. Two univs. Founde[d] 1886.

John [the Divine] or **[the Evangelist], S[t]**

(AD 1st cent.), one of Twelve Disciples, son of Zebedee and brother of James the Elder. Traditionally regarded as the unnamed disciple 'whom Jesus loved' and to whom he entrusted the care of his mother on his death. Regarded as author of 4th Gospel and *Revelations*.

ohn XXIII, orig. Angelo Giuseppe Roncalli (1881-1963), Italian churchman, pope (1958-63). Promoted reform within Church, reconciliation with other Christian churches and world peace. Despite opposition to Communism, advocated socialist reforms. Summoned influential 2nd Vatican Council.

ohn (1167-1216), king of England (1199-1216). Tried to usurp his brother, Richard I, during his absence on 3rd Crusade. Lost most of his French dominions to king of France. Had to yield to papal authority in dispute over Stephen LANGTON. Forced to sign MAGNA CARTA (1215).

ohn III [Sobieski] (1624-96), king of Poland (1674-96). Leader of Christian campaigns against Turks; acclaimed a hero after relieving Turkish siege of Vienna (1683).

ohn, Augustus Edwin (1878-1961), Welsh painter. Influenced by post-impressionism and Rembrandt, he painted portraits of many leading personalities of his day; later society portraits failed to realize his early promise. Works incl. *The Smiling Woman* and portraits of Shaw and Hardy.

ohn Balliol, *see* BALLIOL, JOHN.

ohn Bull, popular personification of England. Depicted as bold, honest but hot-tempered man. First appeared (1712) in *The History of John Bull*, a collection of pamphlets by John Arbuthnot.

ohn, Gospel according to St, fourth of NT gospels, traditionally attributed to St John the Divine. Prob. written *c* AD 100. Most philosophical of gospels, propounding concept of LOGOS.

ohn, three epistles of NT, ascribed to apostle John the Divine; discourses setting forth the nature of Christian fellowship.

ohn Birch Society, extreme right-wing American anti-Communist organization (founded 1958). Named after John Birch, an intelligence officer killed by Chinese Communists (1945).

ohn Chrysostom, St (*c* 347-407), Greek churchman, theologian, patriarch of Constantinople (398-403). Renowned preacher; author of influential commentaries.

ohn dory, *see* DORY.

ohn of Austria, Don (1545-78), Spanish soldier, illegitimate son of Emperor Charles V. Commanded Venetian and Spanish fleets which defeated Turks at Lepanto (1571).

ohn of Gaunt, Duke of Lancaster (1340-99), English nobleman. Fourth son of Edward III, became effective ruler of England during last years of Edward and minority of Richard II.

ohn of the Cross, St, orig. Juan de Yepis y Alvarez (1542-91), Spanish mystic, poet. Friend of St Theresa of Avila. A founder of reformed order of Discalced Carmelites. Known for mystical poetry and treatises on mystical theology.

John O'Groats, in Highland region, N Scotland. Point of mainland Britain farthest from LAND'S END, England.

John Paul I, orig. Albino Luciani (1912-78), Italian churchman, pope (1978). Died one month after succeeding Paul VI.

John Paul II, orig. Karol Wojtyla (1920-), Polish churchman, pope (1978-). First non-Italian pope since 1522.

Johnson, Amy (1903-41), English flier. Made several record flights incl. those to Australia (1930) and to Cape Town and back (1936).

Johnson, Andrew (1808-75), American statesman, president (1865-9). A Democrat, elected vice-president (1864); became president on Lincoln's assassination. Post-Civil War RECONSTRUCTION programme impeded by radical Republicans. Narrowly acquitted in Senate vote over impeachment charge arising from attempt to remove secretary of war, Edwin Stanton, from office (1868).

Johnson, Lyndon Baines (1908-73), American statesman, Democratic president (1963-9). Elected vice-president (1960), became president on Kennedy's assassination. Legislative record of social reform offset by escalation of Vietnam war.

Johnson, Samuel (1709-84), English writer. Known for *A Dictionary of the English Language* (1755), *Rasselas* (1759), *Lives of the Poets* (1783), many miscellaneous essays in the *Rambler* and the *Idler*. Edited Shakespeare with critical prefaces. In 1763 met Boswell who wrote his biog. Founded (1764) famous Literary Club. Tour of Hebrides produced *A Journey to the Western Islands of Scotland* (1775).

John the Baptist, St (d. *c* AD 29), Jewish prophet. In NT, son of Zacharias; cousin of Jesus. Called on people to repent in preparation for the Messiah whom he recognized in Jesus and baptized. Beheaded by Herod Antipas at instigation of SALOME.

joint, in anatomy, place of union between 2 bones, usually one which admits of motion of one or both bones.

Joliot-Curie, Irène (1897-1956), daughter of Pierre and Marie Curie, and her husband **Jean Frédéric Joliot-Curie** (1900-58), were French scientists. Discovered artificial radioactivity by producing radioactive phosphorus isotope by alpha particle bombardment of aluminium; shared Nobel Prize for Chemistry (1935).

Jonah, prophetic book of OT, relating story of Jonah's missionary journey. Incl. story of Jonah being swallowed by a fish. A parable to warn Jews of the dangers of being inward-looking.

Jones, Inigo (1573-1652), English architect. Influenced by Palladio, he brought Italian classicism to England. Designed Queen's House, Greenwich (1616-35) and Banqueting House, Whitehall (1619-22). Also designed scenery and costumes for court masques.

Jones, John Paul (1747-92), American naval officer, b. Scotland. During American Revolution, raided coast of Britain. Later served as admiral in Russian navy.

Jönköping, town of SC Sweden, at S end of Lake Vättern. Pop. 109,000. Match mfg.; paper mills; iron foundries.

jonquil, *see* NARCISSUS.

Jonson, Ben (1572-1637), English author. Known for 'comedies of humours', *eg Everyman in His Humour* (1599), *Volpone* (c 1605), *The Alchemist* (1610). Also wrote tragedy *Sejanus* (1603), court masques, classical verse.

Jordaens, Jacob (1593-1678), Flemish painter. Remembered for boisterous genre scenes of drinking peasants.

Jordan

Jordan, kingdom of SW Asia. Area *c* 98,400 sq km (38,000 sq mi); pop. 2,984,000; cap. Amman. Language: Arabic. Religion: Sunni Islam. Mountains, arid desert; limited cultivation (wheat, fruit). Part of Ottoman empire (16th cent.-1918), mandated to Britain as Transjordan; full independence 1946. Defeated by Israelis (1967), who subsequently occupied territ. W of R. Jordan.

Jordan, river of Palestine. Length *c* 320 km (200 mi). Rises in Anti-Lebanon Mts., flows S to Sea of Galilee and Dead Sea. Used in irrigation schemes. After 1967 Israeli victory formed part of *de facto* border with Jordan.

Joseph, in OT, favourite son of Jacob and Rachel. Sold into slavery in Egypt by his envious brothers where he rose to position of governor under the pharaoh. Saved his father and brothers when they were driven by famine into Egypt.

Joseph, St (*fl* 1st cent. BC -AD 1st cent.), Jewish carpenter, husband of Virgin Mary. Patron of RC church and of dying.

Joseph II (1741-90), Holy Roman emperor (1765-90). One of the 'benevolent despots', ruled solely after death (1780) of his mother, MARIA THERESA. Cut feudal power of nobles by abolishing serfdom, restricted Church's power, extended education.

Joseph, Father, orig. François Leclerc d Tremblay (1577-1638), French Capuchi monk, known as 'Eminence Grise'. Con fidant of Richelieu, advocated anti-Habs burg policy.

Josephine, full name Marie Josèphe Tasche de la Pagerie (1763-1814), empress o France, b. Martinique. First husband Alexandre de Beauharnais, was guillotine (1794). Married Napoleon (1796), who ha marriage annulled (1809) because of he alleged sterility.

Joseph of Arimathea, St (*fl* AD 1st cent.) wealthy member of Jewish Sanhedrin whc according to NT, provided tomb for Jesus Traditionally visited Glastonbury, Englanc *See* GRAIL, HOLY.

Josephus, Flavius, orig. Joseph be Matthias (AD 37-*c* 95), Jewish historian soldier. Governor of Galilee during wa with Rome. When his stronghold fell h won Vespasian's favour, adopting nam Flavius. Works incl. *The Jewish Wa Antiquities of the Jews.*

Joshua, historical book of OT, describin invasion and occupation of Palestine b the Hebrews under Moses' successor a leader, Joshua. Incl. story of the fall c Jericho.

Josiah, king of Judah (*c* 639-*c* 609 BC) Reformed religious worship afte discovery of lost book of the law (possibl Deuteronomy) in the Temple.

Jotunheim Mountains, range of W Norway. Rises to Galdhöpiggen an Glittertind (both *c* 2465 m/8100 ft). Nam from Norse 'Home of the Giants'.

Joule, James Prescott (1818-89), Englis physicist. Discovered law describin heating effect of electric current. Worke on interchangeability of mechanica energy and heat energy. Calculate mechanical equivalent of heat.

joule, SI unit of work or energy, defined a work done on an object by force of newton acting through distance of 1 metre Also measured as work done per sec b current of 1 ampère flowing throug resistance of 1 ohm. Named after Jame Prescott Joule.

journalism, gathering, writing, editing, an publishing of news, through newspaper magazines, radio, TV, film, *etc.* Develope first as offshoot of politics, business, at en of 18th cent. With technological advance emphasis on quick reporting of event rather than polemic has encourage growth of news agencies, wire service *etc.*

Jove, *see* JUPITER.

Joyce, James Augustine Aloysiu (1882-1941), Irish novelist. Works inc greatly influential *Portrait of the Artist a a Young Man* (1916), *Ulysses* (1922), *Fi negans Wake* (1939). Used complex allusive language combining naturalism symbolism. Leading prose innovator o 20th cent.

Joyce, William (1906-46), British Na

propagandist, b. US. Went to Germany at outbreak of WWII and regularly broadcast German propaganda to Britain, gaining nickname Lord Haw-Haw. Hanged for treason.

uan Carlos (1938-), king of Spain (1975-). Heir-designate from 1969, assumed monarchy on Franco's death.

uan Fernández Islands, small isl. group of Chile, 640 km (*c* 400 mi) W of Valparaiso. Lobster fishing. Believed to be scene of Daniel Defoe's *Robinson Crusoe*.

uárez, Benito Pablo (1806-72), Mexican statesman. After overthrow of Santa Anna (1855), revised law to restrict power of church and army. Became president in 1858. Thwarted Napoleon III's attempt to re-estab. empire under Maximilian (1864-7). Died while resisting revolution of Díaz.

uárez, border town of N Mexico, on Rio Grande, opposite El Paso, Texas. Pop. 545,000. Commercial, agric. centre; cotton processing, tourism.

udaea, *see* JUDAH.

udah, hist. kingdom of S Israel ruled by house of David (931 BC-586 BC). At time of Jesus, it was Roman prov. of Judaea.

udaism, religious beliefs and observances of the JEWS; oldest of the monotheistic religions and fundamental to Christianity and Islam. Based primarily on OT, TALMUD and TORAH. Observances incl. male circumcision, daily services in Hebrew, observance of Sabbath (7th day of week) and the 3 principal festivals, Passover, Pentecost and Tabernacles. Movements in Judaism have incl. Pharisees, Sadducees and Essenes of NT times. Hasidism (18th cent.). In West, the 3 modern branches (Orthodox, Conservative, Reform) evolved in Germany (19th cent.). Festivals celebrated in SYNAGOGUE or in home. Minister known as rabbi.

udas Iscariot (*fl* 1st cent. AD), Disciple of Jesus. According to NT, in return for a bribe, betrayed Jesus by kissing him, thus identifying him to Romans. Hanged himself after the Crucifixion.

ude, epistle of NT. Traditionally ascribed to Disciple St Jude, brother of James the Younger, between AD 65-80. Warns against false prophets and heresy.

udge, public official with authority to hear legal disputes, pronounce sentence in court of law. In UK, appointed by lord chancellor on govt. nomination; must be barrister of several years' standing.

udges, historical book of OT. Describes govt. of the 'judges' (*ie* tribal leaders) who ruled Israel before union of the tribes. Recounts repeated apostasy of Israel from God, consequences at hands of alien nations and God's eventual creation of a deliverer in Saul.

udiciary, in politics, that part of govt. concerned with admin. of justice, comprising judges and law courts. Also *see* SEPARATION OF POWERS.

udith, Apocryphal book of OT. Describes attack on Jewish city of Bethulia by Holofernes. Judith enters enemy camp and kills Holofernes.

judo, combat sport developed (1882) in Japan, based on practices of JU-JITSU. A coloured belt worn indicates level of proficiency (black being highest).

Juggernaut or **Jaganath,** in Hindu religion, an incarnation of VISHNU. Cult centres on Puri, India, where his image is annually hauled through the streets. Devotees reputedly threw themselves under wheels of the cart. Has come to denote any irresistible force.

Jugoslavia, *see* YUGOSLAVIA.

jugular vein, either of 2 large veins in the neck. Larger internal jugular vein carries most blood from brain back to heart; smaller external jugular vein receives blood from face and scalp.

Jugurtha (d. 104 BC), king of Numidia. Waged war with Rome (111-106). Captured (106), died in prison in Rome.

ju-jitsu or **jiu-jitsu,** method of weaponless self-defence, from which JUDO is derived, developed in ancient Japan. Systematized forms date from 16th cent. Strength and weight of opponent are used against him.

jujube, edible, date-like fruit of several trees and shrubs of genus *Zizyphus*, esp. *Z. jujuba*; known when preserved in syrup as Chinese dates. Used to make confectionery.

Juliana (1909-), queen of Netherlands (1948-80). Succeeded on abdication of mother, Queen Wilhelmina. Married Prince Bernhard of Lippe-Biesterfeld (1937). Abdicated in favour of daughter Beatrix.

Julian calendar, *see* CALENDAR.

Julian the Apostate (*c* AD 331-63), Roman emperor (361-3). Influenced by the Athenian philosophy of his teachers, renounced Christianity in favour of paganism. Proclaimed emperor by his troops (360), became sole ruler on death of Constantius II. Attempted to reintroduce paganism.

Julius II, orig. Giuliano della Rovere (1443-1513), Italian churchman, pope (1503-13). Restored Papal States to Church. Called 5th Lateran Council (1512) to counter French influence. Patronized Raphael, Michelangelo.

Julius Caesar, *see* CAESAR, GAIUS JULIUS.

July Revolution or **Revolution of 1830,** French coup d'état which deposed Charles X. Liberal opposition to reactionary govt. led to issue of July Ordinances, dissolving chamber of deputies and restricting press freedom. Ensuing fighting led to Charles' abdication and Louis Philippe's succession.

Jumna, river of NC India. Rises in Himalayas of Uttar Pradesh, flows *c* 1370 km (850 mi) through Delhi and Agra to join Ganges near Allahabad.

Juneau, cap. of Alaska, US; in Alaskan Panhandle. Pop. 14,000. Ice-free port; salmon canning indust., sawmilling. Settled in 1880s gold rush; became cap. 1906.

Jung, Carl Gustav (1875-1961), Swiss psychologist. One of founders of analytical psychology, worked with Freud until Jung's divergent view of libido as asexual, primal energy, forced split. Later diverged further from Freud in postulating 'collective unconscious', *ie* innate 'memory' common to all, revealed in dreams, myths, and containing archetypal features. Also formulated extrovert, introvert types.

Jungfrau, mountain of WC Switzerland, in Bernese Oberland. Height 4156 m (13,642 ft); first climbed 1811. Highest railway in Europe to Jungfraujoch (3456 m/11,340 ft).

juniper, any of genus *Juniperus* of small evergreen shrubs of cypress family. Native to temperate regions throughout world. Needle-like foliage, aromatic wood; small berry-like cones used to flavour gin.

Junkers, privileged land-owning class in Prussia, who formed large part of the military elite in Prussian army.

Juno, in Roman religion, wife and sister of Jupiter. Like Greek Hera, patron of women, esp. in their sexual life. Later became major goddess of the state, worshipped (with Jupiter and Minerva) on Capitol.

junta, name given to group of military men in power after coup d'état. Name was applied to military regimes in Greece (1967), Chile (1973).

Jupiter or **Jove,** in Roman religion, the supreme god in the pantheon, identified with Greek Zeus. Originally god of rain and agriculture, later became prime patron of state with temple on Capitol.

Jupiter, largest planet of solar system, *c* 778,340,000 km from Sun; diameter 142,800 km; circles Sun in 11 years 315 days; 12 known satellites. Surface temperature *c* -125° C; shrouded in clouds, only permanent feature is oval marking, 'Great Red Spot'. Largely or entirely composed of gases (hydrogen, helium, ammonia and methane).

Jura, limestone mountain range of E France, W Switzerland, SW West Germany. Part of Alpine system; source of Doubs, Ain rivers. Forests, pastures; tourism, h.e.p.

Jurassic period, second geological period o Mesozoic era; began *c* 195 million year ago, lasted 60 million years. Extensiv limestone formation. Flora incl. conifers ferns, cycads. Fauna incl. ammonites brachiopods, lamellibranchs, insects dinosaurs reached max. size, 1st bird evident. Also *see* GEOLOGICAL TABLE.

jury, in law, group of people (usually 12 sworn to hear evidence, inquire into fact in a case, and give decision on basis o findings. Has origin in Germanic custom introduced into England by Normans. B 18th cent., took form known today. Juror selected from voters' roll, with certai excepted classes.

justice of the peace (JP), local magistrat appointed by special commission to tr minor cases, commit others to highe courts, grant licences to publicans, *etc.*

Justinian I (483-565), Byzantine empero (527-65). Recovered N Africa from th Vandals and Italy from Ostrogoths b victories of his generals BELISARIUS an Narses. Codified Roman law in *Corpu Juris Civilis*, basis of much Europea jurisprudence. Built many churches, incl Hagia Sophia in Constantinople.

jute, natural fibre from tropical annua plants of genus *Corchorus*. Main source are 2 species grown in valleys of Gange and Brahmaputra. Known in W since 1830. Coarse fibre used for sacking, rope carpet backing, *etc.*

Jutes, Teutonic people originally inhabitin areas around mouths of the Rhine. Settle in 5th cent. in S England, esp. Kent, Isle o Wight.

Jutland *(Jylland)*, penin. of N Europe, incl parts of Denmark, N Germany. Mai towns Aarhus, Aalborg. Low-lying, san dunes in W. Agric., esp. dairying, in E Large, indecisive WWI naval battle fough off NW coast (1916).

Juvenal, full name Decimus Junius Juvenali (AD *c* 60-*c* 130), Roman poet. Famous fo *Satires* attacking degenerate Rome fo criminality, sexual corruption and tyranny

K

2 or **Mount Godwin-Austen,** N Kashmir, world's second highest mountain, height 8611 m (28,250 ft). First climbed by Italian expedition (1954).

aaba, in Islam, the most sacred of all Moslem shrines, in the Great Mosque at Mecca. Small cubic building enclosing Black Stone said to have been given to Abraham by the angel Gabriel. Centre of Moslem world and prime goal of pilgrimage, towards which believers face when praying.

abbala, *see* CABALA.

abul, cap. of Afghanistan, on R. Kabul. Pop. 588,000. Indust. and cultural centre; 1800 m (5900 ft) above sea level. Of strategic importance, many great invading forces have passed through. Became cap. 1773.

ádár, János (1912-), Hungarian political leader. First secretary of Hungarian Socialist Workers' party from 1955, he was also twice premier (1956-8, 1961-5). Formed pro-Soviet govt. during 1956 revolt and later had revolt's leaders executed.

affirs or **Kafirs,** name applied by Europeans to members of certain Bantu-speaking tribes of SE Africa. Name often used contemptuously by Europeans for all black Africans.

afka, Franz (1883-1924), German author, b. Czechoslovakia. Novels, *eg The Trial* (1925), *The Castle* (1926), short story *Metamorphosis* (1915), depict world, both real and dream-like, of threatening absurdity, futility.

airouan, town of NC Tunisia. Pop. 82,000. Rug and carpet indust., leather goods. Founded 670; seat of Arab governors of W Africa until 800, of Aghlabid dynasty until 909. Moslem holy city, has 9th-cent. Sidi Okba mosque.

alahari, desert of Botswana and NE South Africa. Av. height over 920 m (3000 ft); mainly grass, scrubland. Peopled by nomadic hunters; cattle and sheep rearing, national park in SW.

ale or **cole,** *Brassica oleracea acephala,* hardy variety of CABBAGE with curly leaves which do not form a head. Grown as winter vegetable; also used as animal fodder.

algan, *see* CHANGKIAKOW.

ali, in Hindu myth, black goddess of death and destruction; as Parvati, she is consort of Siva. Personifies mother goddess devouring life she has produced. Represented as garlanded with skulls and bearing bloody sword. Patron of THUGS.

alimantan, Indonesian part of BORNEO. Area *c* 539,000 sq km (208,000 sq mi). Occupies C and S region of isl.

alinin, Mikhail Ivanovich (1875-1946), Russian revolutionary, 1st president of the USSR (1919-38). He founded (1912) the newspaper *Pravda,* prominent in the October Revolution.

Kalinin, city of USSR, WC European RSFSR; port on R. Volga. Pop. 412,000. Rolling stock, machinery, textile mfg. Founded in 12th cent. as Tver, rivalled Moscow in importance in 14th cent.; renamed (1931).

Kaliningrad (Ger. *Königsberg),* city of USSR, in W European RSFSR enclave on Baltic. Pop. 355,000. Naval base; indust. centre. Founded 1255 as fortress of Teutonic Knights. Hist. cap. of East Prussia. Suffered heavy damage in WWII. Transferred to USSR 1945.

Kama, river of USSR. Flows generally S *c* 1930 km (1200 mi) through E European RSFSR to join Volga below Kazan. Chief tributary of Volga; used to transport timber.

Kamchatka Peninsula, arm of extreme E USSR, between Bering Sea and Sea of Okhotsk. Mountainous, with active volcanoes; fishing and fur trapping main occupations.

kamikaze, name given to Japanese suicide pilots, who during WWII intentionally crashed bomb-laden planes on their targets.

Kampala, cap. of Uganda, on N shore of Victoria Nyanza. Pop. 331,000. Admin., commercial, educational centre; food processing, clothing mfg.; Makerere Univ. (1961). Former seat of kings of Buganda; cap. of Uganda from 1962.

Kampuchea, state of SE Asia. Area *c* 181,300 sq km (70,000 sq mi); pop. 8,574,000; cap. Phnom Penh. Language: Khmer. Religion: Hinayana Buddhism. Large plain drained by Mekong. Mainly agric. (rice); Tonlé Sap is base for fisheries. Formerly French protect. (1863-1955) of Cambodia, part of INDO-CHINA. Independent constitutional monarchy of Cambodia (1955), Khmer Republic estab. 1970. Involved in Vietnam War with US invasion (1970). Five-year civil war ended in 1975 by victory of Communist Khmer Rouge forces. Renamed Kampuchea (1976). Khmer Rouge regime overthrown by Vietnamese-backed forces (1979).

Kananga, city of SC Zaïre, on R. Lulua, cap. of Kasai prov. Formerly called Luluabourg. Pop. 601,000. Cotton market, on Port Francqui-Lubumbashi railway. Rebel cap. (1960-1) during secession of Kasai prov.

Kanchenjunga, world's third highest mountain, in Himalayas on Nepal-Sikkim border; height 8579 m (28,146 ft). First climbed 1955 by British expedition.

Kandahar, city of S Afghanistan. Pop. 149,000. In fruit growing region; has fruit processing plants. Occupied by many forces throughout its history, incl. British (1879-81). National cap. in 18th cent.

Kandinsky, Wassily (1866-1944), Russian painter. Credited with painting 1st purely abstract work (1910). A founder of Blaue Reiter group (1911). Later work was more geometric and explored basic elements of design; taught at Bauhaus (1922-33).

Kandy, city of C Sri Lanka. Pop. 101,000. Centre of tea trade. Has Temple of Tooth, said to contain a tooth of Buddha. Has nearby Univ. of Sri Lanka (1942).

Great grey kangaroo with young in her pouch

kangaroo, large herbivorous marsupial of Australasia with short forelegs, large hind legs and thick tail. Great grey kangaroo, *Macropus major,* reaches heights of 1.8 m/6 ft. Young do not leave mother's pouch for first 6 months. Hunted relentlessly in some areas for hide and flesh.

Kania, Stanislau (1927-), Polish statesman. Succeeded Gierek as first secretary of Politburo (1980) in wake of strikes in favour of free trade unions.

Kannada, *see* DRAVIDIAN.

Kano, city of N Nigeria. Pop. 399,000. Indust. centre agric. market, esp. for groundnuts, cotton, hides. Ancient Hausa city state, hist. caravan route centre. Taken (1903) by British.

Kanpur or **Cawnpore,** city of Uttar Pradesh, NC India, on R. Ganges. Pop. 1,275,000. Important transport jct. Indust. centre; textile, chemical mfg. Ceded to British (1801), scene of massacre of British garrison (1857) during Indian Mutiny.

Kansas, state of C US. Area 213,064 sq km (82,264 sq mi); pop. 2,310,000. cap. Topeka; other major city Wichita. Mainly prairie; major wheat production, also sorghum, cattle. Oil, natural gas, coal resources; quarrying. Region disputed by French, Spanish until bought by US as part of Louisiana Purchase (1803). Admitted to Union as 34th state (1861).

Kansas City, two cities of C US, opposite each other in Kansas (pop. 168,000) and Missouri (pop. 473,000) at jct. of Kansas and Missouri rivers. Railway yards; grain, livestock market and distribution centre; meat packing, flour milling industs.

Kansas-Nebraska Bill, in US, legislation introduced by Stephen A. Douglas (1854), by which territs. of Kansas and Nebraska were created out of that part of Louisiana Purchase closed to slavery by Missouri Compromise (1820). Territs. had right of self-determination on slavery which intensified conflict between North and South.

Kansu, prov. of NC China. Area *c* 777,000 sq km (300,000 sq mi); pop. 19,000,000; cap. Lanchow. Mountainous; fertile soil but little rain. Oil, coal, ores.

Kant, Immanuel (1724-1804), German philosopher. Wrote *Critique of Pure Reason* (1781), *Foundations of the Metaphysics of Ethics* (1785). Distinguished between the world of objects as we know them (phenomena) and world of objects in themselves (noumena). In ethics, posited 'categorical imperative' (*ie* that one should act as if the maxim on which one acts were to become a universal law) as basis of moral action. Profoundly influenced 19th-cent. philosophy.

Kaohsiung, chief seaport of S Taiwan. Pop. 1,115,000. Exports sugar, rice, salt. Indust. centre; produces textiles, petroleum products.

kaolin, *see* CHINA CLAY.

kapok, silky fibres around seeds of several tropical trees of bombax family, esp. *Ceiba pentandra.* Used for stuffing sleeping bags, life jackets, *etc.*

Karachi, chief seaport of Pakistan, on Arabian Sea. Pop. 3,499,000. Exports cotton, hides. Commercial, transport and mfg centre. Became British (1843) with capture of Sind. Cap. of Pakistan (1947-59).

Karaganda, city of USSR, C Kazakh SSR. Pop. 572,000. Coalmining centre; iron and steel mfg. Developed after 1928 to supply coal to Urals indust. region.

Karakoram Range, mountain system of Kashmir, N India, N Pakistan. Separated from W Himalayas by R. Indus, extends 480 km (300 mi) NW-SE. Its peaks incl. K2.

Karakorum, ruined city of C Mongolia. Founded *c* 1220 when Genghis Khan made it his capital. Abandoned 1267 by Kublai Khan. Discovered (1889).

Kara Kum, desert of S USSR, Turkmen SSR between Caspian Sea and R. Amu Darya. Agric., esp. cotton growing, possible through irrigation by Kara Kum canal.

Karamanlis, Constantinos (1907-), Greek politician. Premier 3 times between 195[illegible] and 1963. In exile after 1963, opposed military junta estab. in 1967. Returned as premier 1974 after restoration of democratic govt.

Kara Sea, part of Arctic Ocean, lying N of Siberia. Bounded by Severnaya Zemlya in E, Novaya Zemlya in W. Receives R. Ob through Gulf of Ob.

karate, method of unarmed self-defence developed in Japan. Involves use of hands and feet to deliver sharp blows to vulnerable parts of body. Considered part of the discipline of Zen Buddhism.

Karelia, auton. republic of NW European RSFSR, USSR. Area *c* 172,000 sq km (67,000 sq mi); pop. 736,000; cap. Petrozavodsk.

Has numerous lakes, marshes; heavily forested. Lumbering, wood product mfg. and fishing main occupations. Iron ore mined; h.e.p. derived from rivers. Karelians, known since 9th cent., are of Finnish origin; region annexed by Russia (1721), increased by land ceded by Finland (1940).

Kariba, Lake, artificial lake on Zimbabwe-Zambia border, along R. Zambezi. Length *c* 280 km (175 mi). Created by construction of Kariba Dam, built 1955-9, height 128 m (420 ft); provides h.e.p. for Zimbabwe and Zambia.

Karl-Marx-Stadt, city of S East Germany, known as Chemnitz until 1954. Pop. 306,000. Textile centre; mining (coal, lignite). Badly damaged in WWII.

Karlsruhe, city of SW West Germany. Pop. 277,000. Indust., admin. centre; has Federal Court of Justice, univ. (1825). Founded 1715, cap. of duchy of Baden from 1771.

karma, in Indian religion and philosophy, sum of an individual's actions which are carried forward from one existence to next, determining incarnation for good or bad. Differing interpretations are found in Hinduism, Buddhism and Jainism.

Temple gateway at Karnak

Karnak, village of C Egypt, on R. Nile. Occupies part of site of ancient city of THEBES. Noted for temple of Amon (14th cent. BC).

Karnataka, maritime state of SW India. Area *c* 192,000 sq km (74,000 sq mi); pop. 29,260,000; cap. Bangalore. Formerly known as Mysore state, renamed 1973. Mainly on S Deccan plateau, with coastal plain on Arabian Sea. Largely agric. economy; coffee, rice, cotton. Forests provide sandalwood. Iron and manganese ore; major gold-mining region.

Karroo, semidesert plateau of Cape Prov., South Africa. Little Karroo (S) rises to 610 m/2000 ft; Great Karroo (C) rises to 915m/3000 ft; Northern Karroo (N), alternative name for High Veld, rises to 1830 m/6000 ft. Sheep, goat rearing; fruit, cereal growing.

Karst *(Kras),* arid limestone plateau of NW Yugoslavia, in Dinaric Alps. Area of ridges, potholes, caves (*eg* Postojna), underground channels. Name also generally applied to all limestone areas with similar topography.

Kasai (Port. *Cassai*), river of Angola and Zaïre. Flows *c* 2090 km (1300 mi) from C Angola to R. Congo. Trade artery; rich in alluvial diamonds. Forms part of Angola-Zaïre border; main S tributary of R. Congo.

Kasavubu, Joseph (1917-69), Congolese political leader. First president of independent Congo (1960-5), he was involved in power struggle with LUMUMBA. Deposed in MOBUTU's 2nd coup.

Kashmir, *see* JAMMU AND KASHMIR.

Kassel or **Cassel,** town of EC West Germany, on R. Fulda. Pop. 202,000. Railway engineering, optical instrument mfg. Formerly cap. of Hesse-Kassel electorate and of Hesse-Nassau prov. Heavily bombed in WWII.

Katanga, region of SE Zaïre, main town Lubumbashi. Fertile plateau, rich in minerals (esp. cobalt, copper, uranium). Seceded (1960-3) after independence of Congo, rejoined after UN intervention. Prov. from 1967, renamed Shaba (1972).

Kathiawar, penin. of Gujarat state, W India, between Kutch and Gulf of Cambay.

Kathmandu, cap. of Nepal. Pop. 210,000. Has 16th-cent. wooden temple. Captured (1768) by Gurkhas; became their cap.

Katowice *(Ger. Kattowitz),* city of SC Poland, cap. of Katowice prov. Pop. 346,000. Mines produce coal, iron, lead, zinc; engineering, metal industs. Chartered 1865; passed from Germany to Poland 1921.

Kattegat, str. between Denmark and Sweden. Connects with North Sea via Skagerrak (N), with Baltic Sea via Oresund (S).

Kaunda, Kenneth David (1924-), Zambian statesman. Founded (1960) United National Independence party; successfully opposed inclusion of Northern Rhodesia (Zambia) in Federation of Rhodesia and Nyasaland. Elected president (1964) at independence.

Kawasaki, port of Japan, on Tokyo Bay, SE Honshu isl. Pop. 1,025,000. Shipbuilding, engineering, steel and textile mfg.

kayak, an Eskimo canoe made of skins, esp. sealskins, stretched over a frame of wood to cover it completely except for opening where paddler sits. Now widely popular; usually made of fibreglass.

Kayseri, city of C Turkey. Pop. 207,000. Agric. centre; carpet, textile mfg. As *Caesarea Mazaca* was cap. of ancient kingdom of Cappadocia.

Kazakh Soviet Socialist Republic, constituent republic of SC USSR. Area 2,720,000 sq km (1,050,000 sq mi); pop. 14,685,000; cap. Alma-Ata. Mainly dry steppe land, rising to Altai Mts. in E and S. Wheat in N, sheep and cattle raising in C; mineral resources incl. coal, oil, copper. Came under Russian rule (1730-1820); constituent republic (1936).

Kazan, city of USSR, cap. of Tatar auton. region, E European RSFSR; on Volga. Pop. 993,000. Indust. and cultural centre. Cap. of Tartar khanate in 15th cent.; taken by Ivan the Terrible in 1552.

Kazantzakis, Nikos (*c* 1883-1957), Greek author. Works, incl. novels *Zorba the Greek* (1946), *Christ Recrucified* (1954), *Freedom and Death* (1957), deal with duality of man as flesh and spirit.

kea, *Nestor notabilis*, yellowish-green parrot of mountainous regions of New Zealand. Feeds on carrion, insects, berries; can injure sheep.

Kean, Edmund (*c* 1788-1833), English tragic actor. Best-known roles incl. Shylock, Richard III, Othello, which he played with wild emotion.

Keaton, Buster, pseud. of Joseph Francis Keaton (1895-1966), American silent film comedian. Famous for unsmiling persistence in face of disaster. Acted in, directed classics *eg The General* (1926).

Keats, John (1795-1821), English poet. Leading Romantic lyricist. Works incl. sonnets, *eg* 'On First Looking into Chapman's Homer', Horatian odes, *eg* 'Ode on a Grecian Urn', 'Ode to a Nightingale', unfinished blank-verse epic *Hyperion*. Died of tuberculosis.

Keble, John (1792-1866), English clergyman, poet, hymn writer. Inspired OXFORD MOVEMENT with his 'National Apostasy' sermon (1833).

Keeling Islands, *see* COCOS ISLANDS.

Keflavik, town of SW Iceland, on Faxa Bay. Pop. 6000. Fishing port; international airport from WWII, US air force base.

Kekkonen, Urho Kaleva (1900-), Finnish statesman. Three times PM before becoming president (1956). Fifth term of office as president began 1978.

Kekulé [von Stradonitz], Friedrich August (1829-96), German chemist. His work on composition of carbon compounds was of basic importance to modern chemistry. Devised theory that structure of benzene is hexagonal ring.

Keller, Helen [Adams] (1880-1968), American author, lecturer. Blind and deaf from age of two, she was taught to read, write and speak by companion, Anne Sullivan Macy. She graduated from Radcliffe Coll. (1904), and became famous for work for handicapped.

Kellogg, Frank Billings (1856-1937), American statesman. Secretary of state (1925–9), advocated peaceful settlement of international disputes. Promoted Kellogg-Briand Pact against war, signed by 15 nations in 1928. Awarded Nobel Peace Prize (1929).

Kells, Book of, illustrated 8th-cent. manuscript, found in monastery founded 6th-cent. by St Columba at Kells, Co. Meath, Ireland; now in Trinity Coll. library, Dublin.

Kelly, Edward ('Ned') (1854-80), Australian bushranger. Notorious for bank robberies in SE region, captured (1880) and hanged.

kelp or **tangle,** general terms for larg seaweeds of the BROWN ALGAE. Used source of alginates and formerly of iodin Name also applies to ashes of seawee from which potassium salts were onc obtained.

kelpie, *see* COLLIE.

Kelvin, William Thomson, Baron (182 1907), British physicist. Formulated 2r law of thermodynamics; supported Joule theories of interchangeability of heat ar mechanical energy. Introduced absolu scale of temperature, named Kelvin sca in his honour.

Kemal Pasha, Mustafa, *see* ATATURK.

Kemble, John Philip (1757-1823), acto manager of Drury Lane and Cove Garden. Important roles incl. Haml Brutus, Coriolanus. His sister was Sar Kemble SIDDONS. His niece, **Frances An ('Fanny') Kemble** (1809-93), was high successful in tragedy, comedy, *eg* as Julie

Kempis, *see* THOMAS À KEMPIS.

Kennedy, John Fitzgerald (1917-63), Ame can statesman, Democratic preside (1961-3). Son of diplomat and industrialis Joseph Kennedy, who was US ambassad to Great Britain (1937-40). Formed Pea Corps, initiated Medicare health insuran scheme. Criticized for allowing aborti invasion of Cuba by Cuban exiles (196 forced Soviet withdrawal of nucle weapons from Cuba (1962). Expand American military role in Vietna Assassinated in Dallas (Nov. 196 allegedly by Lee Harvey Oswald. H brother, **Robert Francis Kenne** (1925–68), was attorney general (1961– Assassinated while campaigning for Dem cratic presidential nomination. Anoth brother, **Edward Moore Kenne** (1932-), was Democratic senator f Massachusetts after 1962 election; ma unsuccessful bid for presidenti nomination (1980).

Kennedy, Cape, *see* CANAVERAL, CAPE.

Kennelly, Arthur Edwin (1861-1939), Ame can electrical engineer, b. India. Predict existence of layer of ionized particles upper atmosphere (1902), independently Heaviside. This layer was discovered Appleton.

Kennelly-Heaviside Layer, layer of ION SPHERE, between 90 and 150 km abo Earth's surface, from which radio wav can be reflected. Electron concentrati decreases during night and reach maximum at noon.

Kenneth MacAlpin, *see* MACALPIN.

Kensington and Chelsea, royal bor. of W Greater London, England. Pop. 153,0 Created 1965 from met. bors. H Kensington Palace; Albert Hall; museu incl. Victoria and Albert.

Kent, William (1685-1748), English archite painter and landscape gardener. Ass ciated with Earl of Burlington in develo ment of neo-Palladianism in England. H naturalistic gardens were designed harmonize with the country house.

nt, county of SE England. Area 3732 sq km 1440 sq mi); pop. 1,449,000; admin. hq. Maidstone. N Downs in N, curving SE to Dover; Weald in SW; elsewhere low-lying. Orchards, hops, market gardening ('Garden of England'). Chalk, gravel industs.; ports incl. Chatham, Dover; resorts incl. Margate, Broadstairs. Roman conquest 55 BC; Anglo-Saxon kingdom; Christianity estab. at Canterbury (AD 597).

ntigern, St. *see* MUNGO, ST.

ntucky, state of EC US. Area 104,623 sq km (40,395 sq mi); pop. 3,428,000; cap. Frankfort; major city Louisville. Ohio R. forms N border. Bluegrass region (horse breeding); hilly plains; tobacco, corn; coal mining; bourbon whisky distilling. British claimed region from French (1763); frontier explored by Daniel Boone. Admitted to Union as 15th state (1792); slave state, remained in Union in Civil War (1861-5).

ntucky Derby, American horse race held annually since 1875 at Churchill Downs, Louisville, Kentucky. Run in May over course 1¼ mi (2 km) long.

Kenya

nya, republic of E Africa. Area 583,000 sq km (225,000 sq mi); pop. 14,856,000; cap. Nairobi. Languages: Swahili, English. Religions: animist, Christian. Coastal strip; arid plains in N, highlands in W; incl. Great Rift Valley, part of Victoria Nyanza. Produces coffee, tea, sisal, grain, cattle; large game reserves (*eg* Tsavo); unexploited minerals. Coast controlled by Portuguese, then Arabs, until British trade exploration 19th cent.; leased by UK from Zanzibar 1887, became Kenya Protectorate 1920. Interior became crown colony 1920. Discontent among Kikuyu natives led to Mau Mau terrorism 1952-6. Coast and interior united at independence 1963; republic from 1964. Member of British Commonwealth.

nya, Mount, peak of C Kenya. Snow-capped extinct volcano with many glaciers; height 5197 m (17,058 ft). First climbed 1899.

nyatta, Jomo (*c* 1893-1978), Kenyan statesman. Imprisoned (1953-9) for alleged involvement in Mau Mau revolt. Elected president of Kenya African National Union (1960). Became PM (1963) at Kenyan independence and president in 1964.

Kepler, Johannes (1571-1630), German astronomer. A founder of modern astronomy, he deduced 3 laws of planetary motion from Brahe's detailed observations. These laws were basis of Newton's law of universal gravitation and showed that the Sun controls motion of planets.

Kerala, maritime state of SW India on Malabar Coast. Area *c* 38,850 sq km (15,000 sq mi); pop. 21,280,000; cap. Trivandrum. Largely plains, with hills in E; grows rice, rubber, coconuts. Created (1956) out of Travancore-Cochin state.

keratin, tough protein forming principal matter of hair, nails, horns, wool, *etc.*

Kerensky, Aleksandr Feodorovich (1881-1970), Russian politician. A moderate socialist, he succeeded Prince Lvov as premier (July, 1917); supported Russian role in WWI. His indecisive policies ended in overthrow by Bolsheviks in Nov. 1917. Lived in US after 1940.

Kerguelen Islands, group of isls. in S Indian Ocean, forming part of French Southern and Antarctic Territs. Area *c* 7000 sq km (2700 sq mi). Comprises one large volcanic isl. (Kerguelen or Desolation), which rises to 1865 m (6120 ft), and over 300 small isls.

Kermanshah, city of W Iran. Pop. 291,000. Market centre for rich agric. area; oil refinery. Founded by Sassanids (4th cent.).

kerosene, *see* PARAFFINS.

Kerouac, Jack (1922-69), American author. Novels, *eg On the Road* (1957), *Big Sur* (1962), *Desolation Angels* (1965), came to represent contemporary youth.

Kerr, Sir John Robert (1914-), Australian lawyer, public official. Governor-general from 1974, precipitated constitutional crisis (1975) by dismissing Whitlam as PM after refusal by Senate to work with Labor govt. Replaced him with Malcolm FRASER.

Kerr effect, phenomenon by which an applied electric field makes certain transparent media capable of double refraction. Effect utilized in Kerr cell, a high-speed shutter capable of opening or closing in 10^{-8} seconds.

Kerry, county of Munster prov., SW Irish Republic. Area 4701 sq km (1815 sq mi); pop. 120,000; co. town Tralee. Mountains incl. Macgillicuddy's Reeks; Lakes of Killarney inland; indented coast incl. Dingle Bay. Agric., fishing, tourism.

kestrel, *Falco tinnunculus,* small brown and grey European hawk. Hovers against wind before swooping on prey of mice, insects.

Keswick, town of Cumbria, NW England. Pop. 5000. In Lake Dist.; tourism.

ketone, organic compound containing divalent carbonyl group (CO) and 2 hydrocarbon radicals. Formed by oxidation of secondary alcohols. Simplest ketone is ACETONE.

kettledrums, *see* DRUM.

Kew Gardens, site of Royal Botanic Gardens, S London, England. Area *c* 117 ha/288 acres. Founded 1761, opened to public 1841. Has botanical research centre.

key, *see* SCALE.

keyboard instruments, musical instruments which produce sound when player depresses levers set in a row at front. Group incl. pipe and reed organs, harpsichord (virginals and spinet), clavichord, pianoforte and celesta.

Keynes, John Maynard Keynes, 1st Baron (1883-1946), English economist. Outlined economic fallacies of Versailles treaty in *The Economic Consequences of the Peace* (1919). After Depression (1929), advocated govt. planned spending and intervention in market to stimulate employment and national purchasing power. *The General Theory of Employment, Interest, and Money* (1936) profoundly affected capitalist economic attitudes.

Key West, *see* FLORIDA KEYS.

KGB (Komitet Gosudarstvennoye Bezhopaztnosti), security police or intelligence agency of USSR, estab. 1954 to replace notorious NKVD; known for terror tactics in carrying out security operations.

Khabarovsk, city of USSR, indust. centre of SE Siberian RSFSR; on R. Amur. Pop. 528,000. Fur trade; oil refining. Founded (1652) as fort.

Khachaturian, Aram Ilich (1903-1978), Russian composer. Influenced by Armenian folk music. Works incl. ballet *Spartacus,* piano and violin concertos.

khaki, term first applied to uniform worn by British army in Indian Mutiny (1857). Similar uniform came into general use during the Boer War.

Khaled [ibn Abdul Aziz] (1913-), king of Saudi Arabia (1975-). Succeeded on assassination of half-brother Feisal.

Khama, Sir Seretse (1921-80), Botswanan politician. Returned from exile to Bechuanaland (1956) after renouncing claims to tribal chieftaincy because of marriage to Englishwoman. Became (1965) premier of Bechuanaland and president (1966) of new Botswana republic.

Kharkov, city of USSR, railway centre of E Ukrainian SSR. Pop. 1,444,000. Machinery mfg., engineering. Cap. of Ukraine 1920-34. Damaged in WWII.

Khartoum *(El Khartûm),* cap. of Sudan, at confluence of Blue Nile and White Nile. Pop. 334,000. Admin., commercial centre, railway jct., cotton trade, univ. (1951). Founded (1822) by Mohammed Ali. Destroyed after siege (1885) by Mahdists, in which Gordon was killed; recovered (1898) by Kitchener. **Khartoum North** lies opposite Khartoum, across Blue Nile. River port, dockyards; cotton trade. Conurbation also incl. OMDURMAN; combined pop. 633,000.

Khmer Republic, *see* KAMPUCHEA.

Khmer Rouge, *see* KAMPUCHEA.

Khomeini, Ruholla (1901-), known as Ayatollah Khomeini, Iranian Muslim religious leader. Deposed Shah of Iran (1979) and instituted an Islamic republic.

Khrushchev, Nikita Sergeyevich (18
1971), Soviet political leader. Emerged dominant figure secretary of Commun Party (1953); premier (1958). Denounc Stalin and his repressive internal polic (1956); adopted policy of peaceful existence with West. Withdrew missi from Cuba after confrontation with (1962). Policies embittered China. Depos 1964.

Khufu or **Cheops** (*fl c* 2900 BC), Egypti pharaoh, founder of 4th dynasty. Fam for building of Great Pyramid at Giza.

Khyber Pass

Khyber Pass, mountain pass, betw Afghanistan and NW Pakistan, link Peshawar and Kabul. Hist. route invading armies and trade, *c* 45 km (28 long; now carries a railway and road.

Kiangsi, prov. of SE China. Area *c* 171,000 km (66,000 sq mi); pop. 31,000,000; c Nanchang. Mountainous, drained by ma rivers incl. navigable Kan flowing NE to Poyang. Major rice producer; cultivation. Produces tungsten, kaolin porcelain.

Kiangsu, prov. of E China, on Yellow S Area *c* 106,000 sq km (41,000 sq mi); p 58,000,000; cap. Nanking. Rich agric. reg consisting mainly of alluvial plain of Yangtze. Silk mfg., cotton. Dens populated, with many large cities, ir Shanghai.

kibbutz, *see* COLLECTIVE FARMING.

Kidd, William (*c* 1645-1701), Scottish pira known as Captain Kidd. Commissioned governor of New York (1695) to prot English ships from pirates, he turned piracy himself. Arrested (1699), he claim his actions had official support. Tried a convicted (1701), hanged.

Kidderminster, town of Hereford a Worcester, WC England, on R. Stour. P 47,000. Carpet mfg., begun 18th cent. Flemish immigrants.

kidnapping, illegal seizure and detention removal of person by force or fraud, of for ransom or political ends.

kidneys, in vertebrates, pair of excret organs; in humans, located near verteb olumn in small of the back. Separate 'aste products, *eg* urea, toxins, from the lood and excrete them as urine through ie bladder. Also regulate acidity of body uids and secrete a hormone. *See* DIALYSIS.

l, city of NE West Germany, at E end of iel Canal, cap. of Schleswig-Holstein. Pop. 59,000. Shipbuilding, engineering, fishing; niv. (1665). Hanseatic League member om 1284, major German naval base 371-1945.

l Canal, Schleswig-Holstein, N West Ger- any. Waterway 98 km (61 mi) long, from orth Sea to Baltic Sea. Built 1887-95.

rkegaard, Sören Aabye (1813-55), Dan- h philosopher. Attacked organized relig- n, believing that man must work out own elationship with God. Influenced 20th- ent. existentialists. Works incl. *Either/Or* 843), *Stages on Life's Way* (1845).

v, city of USSR, cap. of Ukrainian SSR; on nepr. Pop. 2,144,000. Indust. and cultural entre. Cap. of powerful medieval Kievan ate (*fl* 10th-13th cent.); early centre of reek Church in Russia. Under Russian ontrol in 17th cent. Hist. buildings incl. lth-cent. cathedral of St Sophia, mon- stery of St Michael. City devastated in WII.

ali, cap. of Rwanda. Pop. 90,000. Admin. entre; trade in cattle, hides, coffee.

oma-Ujiji, town of W Tanzania, on L. anganyika. Pop. 33,000. Terminus of ailway to Dar-es-Salaam; trade with urundi, Zaïre. Former slave and ivory entre. Stanley met Livingstone at Ujiji 871).

uyu, African people, belonging to BANTU roup. Largest Kenyan tribal group. Led y Jomo KENYATTA, fought British in Mau lau uprising. Mainly agric. economy.

dare, county of Leinster prov., EC Irish epublic. Area 1694 sq km (654 sq mi); pop. 7,000; co. town Naas. Mainly agric., incl. og of Allen, Curragh (racecourse, horse- aining). Main rivers Liffey, Barrow. **ildare,** market town, pop. 3000. athedral, abbey ruins.

imanjaro, mountain of NE Tanzania, ighest in Africa. Permanently snow- apped extinct volcano, height 5892 1/19,340 ft. First climbed 1889. Also called huru Peak.

kenny, county of Leinster prov., SE Irish epublic. Area 2062 sq km (796 sq mi); pop. 9,000. Hilly; main rivers Nore, Barrow. oalmining; black marble quarrying; agric. o. town **Kilkenny,** on R. Nore. Pop. 10,000. ncient cap. of Ossory (kingdom to 1110). astle (12th cent.), abbeys (13th cent.), rotestant, RC cathedrals.

larney, town of Co. Kerry, SW Irish epublic. Pop. 8000. Lakes of Killarney earby; tourist centre.

er whale or **grampus,** *Orcinus orca,* argest of dolphin group, reaching length of .1 m/30 ft. Voracious predator on seals, orpoises, birds; will attack other whales. Vorldwide distribution.

liecrankie, Pass of, in Tayside region, C Scotland. Scene of battle (1689) in which William III's forces were defeated by 'Bonny' Dundee (who was killed).

Kilmarnock, town of Strathclyde region, W Scotland. Pop. 49,000. Coalmining area; engineering, carpets, distilling.

Kimberley, city of NE Cape Prov., South Africa. Pop. 104,000. Major diamond-mining and cutting centre, metal working; railway jct. Founded 1870; besieged 1899-1900 by Boers.

Kincardineshire or **The Mearns,** former county of E Scotland, now in Grampian region. Hilly in W (sheep); fertile along coast and Howe of the Mearns (cereals, root crops). Fishing; whisky distilling. Co. town was Stonehaven.

kindergarten, a school or class for children before official school age (usually 3-5), using informal games, exercises, crafts to prepare them for later school. Theory and 1st kindergarten formed by FROEBEL.

kinetic art, term referring to sculptured works which involve moving parts, shifting light, *etc.* Examples incl. mobiles of Calder and complex machines of Jean Tinguely.

kinetic theory of gases, explanation of behaviour of gases, which assumes that gas molecules are elastic spheres in continuous motion; their kinetic energy depends on the gas temperature. Impact of molecules on walls of containing vessel accounts for gas pressure. Theory explains all experimental gas laws (Boyle's law, Charles' law, *etc*).

King, Martin Luther (1929-68), American clergyman, civil rights leader. Founded Southern Christian Leadership Council after leading successful boycott of segregated buses in Montgomery (1955-6). Chief advocate of non-violent action against segregation of blacks. Awarded Nobel Peace Prize (1964). Assassinated in Memphis.

King, William Lyon Mackenzie (1874-1950), Canadian statesman, Liberal PM (1921-6, 1926-30, 1935-48). Helped draw up Statute of WESTMINSTER (1931).

King Charles spaniel, *see* SPANIEL.

king cobra, *see* COBRA.

kingfisher, any of Alcedinidae family of fish-eating birds with long sharp bill, short tail. European kingfisher, *Alcedo atthis,* has iridescent blue-green plumage.

King James Bible, *see* AUTHORIZED VERSION.

Kings, book of OT, called 1st and 2nd Kings in Authorized Version. Relates history of Hebrews from death of David until fall of Judah. Incl. reign of Solomon, division of kingdom into Israel and Judah, and lives of prophets, Elijah and Elisha.

King's [or Queen's] Bench, in UK, one of three divisions of High Court of Justice. Formerly, supreme court of common law.

King's Counsel, *see* BARRISTER.

Kingsley, Charles (1819-75), English clergyman, author. Known for historical romances *Westward Ho!* (1855), *Hereward the Wake* (1866), moral fantasy *The Water Babies* (1863). Christian socialist, involved in controversy with J.H. NEWMAN.

Kingston, port of SE Ontario, Canada; at NE end of L. Ontario. Pop. 62,000. Locomotives mfg., textiles. Founded as Fort Frontenac (1673); destroyed 1758, resettled 1782; cap. of United Canada (1841-4). Has Queen's Univ. (1841) and Royal Military Coll.

Kingston, cap. of Jamaica. Pop. 573,000. Port with deep harbour. Hq. of coffee trade; tobacco produce, exports; textile, brewing, food processing industs. Founded 1692; became official cap. (1872).

Kingston-upon-Hull, *see* HULL.

Kingston-upon-Thames, royal bor. of SW Greater London, England, on R. Thames. Pop. 136,000. Created 1965 from Surrey residential bors. Saxon kings crowned here.

Kingstown, cap. of ST VINCENT.

Kinross-shire, former county of E Scotland, now in Tayside region. Important agric. area. Co. town was **Kinross,** on Loch Leven. Pop. 3000. Textile mills.

Kinsey, Alfred C. (1894-1956), American zoologist. Famous for questionnaire-based report *Sexual Behaviour in the Human Male/Female* (1948-53) showing permissiveness was more widespread than previously thought.

Kinshasa, cap. of Zaïre, on R. Congo. Pop. 2,008,000. Admin., commercial centre, univ. (1954). River port. Founded (1881) by Stanley as Léopoldville; cap. of Belgian Congo from 1929; renamed 1966.

Kintyre, Mull of, penin. of Strathclyde region, W Scotland. Extends 68 km (40 mi) SSW from Tarbert. Hilly; main town is Campbeltown.

Kipling, [Joseph] Rudyard (1865-1936), English author, b. India. Works incl. novels, *eg Kim* (1901), poetry, *eg* 'Mandalay', 'Gunga Din', 'If', in *Barrack Room Ballads* (1892), popular children's books, *eg The Jungle Book* (1894), *Puck of Pook's Hill* (1906). Reflected British imperialism in India. Nobel Prize for Literature (1907).

Kirchner, Ernst Ludwig (1880-1938), German artist. An originator of the Brücke group, painted in an expressionist style employing bright colour and simplified form. Also made many powerful woodcuts.

Kirghiz Soviet Socialist Republic, constituent republic of SC USSR. Area *c* 199,000 sq km (76,500 sq mi); pop. 3,529,000; cap. Frunze. Mountainous, with Tien Shan range along Chinese border. Stock raising, esp. sheep; cotton, wheat grown in valleys. Annexed to Russia by 1876.

Kiribati, state of W Pacific, incl. Gilbert and Phoenix Island groups, Banaba (Ocean Island) and 3 Line Islands. Area 790 sq km (305 sq mi); pop. 63,000; cap. Tarawa. Language: English. Religion: Christian. Produces copra, phosphates; fishing, tourist industs. Formerly part of Gilbert and Ellice Islands protectorate (1892), colony (1915-75). Line, Phoenix groups joined 20th cent. Fully independent 1978.

Kirin, prov. of NE China. Area *c* 186,500 sq km (72,000 sq mi); pop. 24,000,000; cap. Changchun. On fertile Manchurian pl[...] soya beans, grain grown. Major source[...] timber, coal, iron, *etc.* Cities incl. Ki[...] pop. 1,200,000.

Kirk, Norman Eric (1923-74), New Zeal[...] politician. PM at head of Labour g[...] (1972-4), also served as foreign minister.

Kirkcaldy, town of Fife region, E Scotla[...] on Firth of Forth. Pop. 50,000. P[...] linoleum, textiles mfg.; engineering.

Kirkcudbrightshire, former county of [...] Scotland, now in Dumfries and Gallow[...] region. Uplands in N, W; slopes S to Solw[...] Firth. Cattle, sheep rearing; tourism. [...] town was **Kirkcudbright,** former ro[...] burgh. Pop. 3000. Market town.

Kirkwall, town and admin. hq. of Orkney [...] authority, N Scotland, on Mainland isl. P[...] 5000. Fishing port, exports agric. produ[...] whisky distilling; oil indust. service ba[...] Has St Magnus' cathedral (1137).

Kirov, Sergei Mironovich (1888-19[...] Soviet political leader. Close aide of St[...] and member of Politburo from 1930, [...] assassination was excuse for mass [...] Communist Party purges and trials dur[...] 1930s.

Kiruna, town of N Sweden. Pop. 23,[...] Mining centre of high-grade iron [...] transported by rail to Luleå (Swede[...] Narvik (Norway).

Kisangani, city of NC Zaïre, on R. Con[...] Pop. 311,000. River port, trade in cot[...] rice; univ. (1963). Founded (1883) [...] Stanleyville, renamed 1966. Rebel g[...] estab. here briefly during civil [...] (1960-4).

Kishinev (Romanian *Chişinău*), city [...] USSR, cap. of Moldavian SSR. Pop. 503,[...] Centre of rich agric. region; f[...] processing. Scene of pogrom (1903). Par[...] Romania (1918-40).

Kissinger, Henry Alfred (1923-), Am[...] can govt. official, b. Germany. Secretar[...] state (1973-7), he negotiated withdrawa[...] American troops from Vietnam, end[...] Arab-Israeli war (1973) and Isr[...] withdrawals from Arab territ. Awar[...] Nobel Peace Prize (1973).

Kitakyushu, indust. city of Japan, N Kyu[...] isl. Pop. 1,064,000. Produces iron and st[...] textiles, machinery, chemicals. Form[...] (1963) from 5 towns (Kokura, Wakama[...] Yawata, Moji and Tobata).

Kitasato, Shibasaburo (1852-1931), Japan[...] bacteriologist. Authority on infecti[...] diseases, discovered plague bacillus (18[...] Also isolated bacilli of tetanus [...] developed antitoxin for diphtheria.

Kitchener, Horatio Herbert Kitchener, Earl (1850-1916), British field marsh[...] statesman, b. Ireland. After reconquer[...] Sudan, became its governor-general (18[...] As commander-in-chief (1900-2), introdu[...] successful tactics against Boers, negotia[...] peace. Secretary of state for war (1914-[...] supervised expansion of British ar[...] Drowned en route to Russia.

kite, bird of hawk family, with long poin[...] wings and forked tail. Feeds on carr[...]

and small animals. Species incl. European red kite, *Milvus milvus*.

thara or **cithara,** lyre-like musical instrument of the ancient Greeks, with 5 to 7 strings stretched between a crossbar at the top and a sound box at the bottom. Played by plucking.

ttiwake, *Rissa tridactyla,* gull of Arctic and N Atlantic. Inhabits open sea, breeding on cliff faces.

itwe, city of NC Zambia. Pop. 251,000. Indust. and commercial centre in copperbelt mining region. Founded 1936.

ivu, region of E Zaïre, main town Bukavu. Coffee, cotton, rice growing; gold, tin mining. Incl. Albert (or Virunga) National Park, Ruwenzori Mts.; rain forest (W). Scene of heavy fighting in civil war (1960-4).

Kiwi

wi, nocturnal insectivorous New Zealand bird, genus *Apteryx,* with small functionless wings, hair-like feathers, and long curved bill.

izil Kum, *see* KYZYL KUM.

lagenfurt, town of S Austria, at E end of Wörthersee, cap. of Carinthia prov. Pop. 74,000. Winter sports centre in mountain lakeland. Produces textiles and leather goods.

lee, Paul (1879-1940), Swiss painter. Began as a graphic artist; later associated with Blaue Reiter group. Works characterized by love of fantasy and calligraphic line. Taught at Bauhaus for many years.

leist, [Bernt] Heinrich [Wilhelm] von (1777-1811), German author. Known for plays, *eg* comedy *The Broken Jug* (1803), tragedy *Prinz Friedrich von Homburg* (1821), novella *Michael Kohlhaas* (1808).

lemperer, Otto (1885-1973), German conductor. Left Nazi Germany and settled in US in 1933, where he became conductor of Los Angeles Symphony Orchestra. Toured Europe, America extensively; best known for interpretations of Beethoven.

limt, Gustav (1862-1918), Austrian painter. Leading exponent of art nouveau in Vienna and co-founder of Vienna Secession group, he is known for his richly ornamented female portraits.

Klondike, *see* DAWSON.

knapweed, any of genus *Centaurea* of perennial plants of composite family, esp. *C. nigra,* with purple flowers resembling those of thistle.

knee, joint formed between lower end of femur and upper end of tibia, protected by kneecap or patella. Powerful ligaments and muscles maintain stability.

Kneller, Sir Godfrey, orig. Gottfried Kniller (*c* 1646-1723), English painter, b. Germany. Court painter from time of Charles II to George I. Employed large studio to produce numerous fashionable portraits.

knighthood, form of feudal tenure involving both a property qualification and code of conduct termed CHIVALRY. Reached zenith at time of Crusades (12th-13th cents.). Feudal landholders who held land directly of the crown were required to provide given number of knights for service in field. Military or religious orders of knighthood, independent of feudal obligations, also existed, *eg* Knights Templars, Knights Hospitallers.

Knights Hospitallers, members of religious military order founded in Jerusalem during 1st Crusade to protect pilgrims. Driven from Holy Land (1291), they estab. themselves in Rhodes (1310), which they held against Turks until 1522. Moved to Malta (1530) where they continued their wars against Turks. Expelled from Malta (1798) by Napoleon.

Knights Templars, members of military order founded *c* 1118 to protect pilgrims to Holy Land. Driven from Jerusalem (1187), they estab. their hq. in Acre, which they held until 1291. Resentment over their powerful banking role in Europe led to their persecution and dissolution (1314).

Knossos or **Cnossus,** ancient city of N Crete, Greece, near Iráklion. Centre of MINOAN CIVILIZATION. In Greek legend, home of King Minos and site of labyrinth. Palace excavated by EVANS.

knot, unit of speed used by ships and aircraft, being one NAUTICAL MILE per hour.

Knox, John (1505 or 1515-72), Scottish religious leader. Converted to Protestantism under influence of George WISHART. Exiled in Geneva (1544) where he conferred with Calvin. Invited to lead Reformation in Scotland (1559), succeeded in estab. Presbyterianism after abdication of Mary Queen of Scots. Proposed organization of CHURCH OF SCOTLAND in *The First Book of Discipline* (1560).

Knut, *see* CANUTE.

koala, *Phascolarctos cinereus,* arboreal bear-like Australian marsupial with large ears, grey fur. Tailless, *c* 60 cm/2 ft long; diet of eucalyptus leaves. Protected since 1936, following intensive hunting.

Kobe, seaport of Japan, on Osaka Bay, SW Honshu isl. Pop. 1,364,000. Produces iron and steel, textiles, ships, chemicals.

Köbenhavn, *see* COPENHAGEN.

Koblenz or **Coblenz,** city of W West Germany, at confluence of Rhine and

Koala

Moselle. Pop. 117,000. Centre of wine trade; furniture, piano mfg. Roman *Confluentes*, founded *c* 10 BC. Held by archbishops of Trier 1018-1794; cap. of Rhine prov. 1824-1945.

Koch, Robert (1843-1910), German bacteriologist. Developed methods of identifying, classifying and growing bacteria which estab. modern science of bacteriology. Discovered (1876) anthrax bacillus and studied its life cycle. Discovered (1882) tubercule bacillus causing tuberculosis, for which work he received Nobel Prize for Physiology and Medicine (1905).

Kodály, Zoltán (1882-1967), Hungarian composer. With Bartók, collected Hungarian folk tunes. Works, national in idiom, incl. *Háry János, Psalmus Hungaricus, Dances of Galanta*.

Kodiak bear

Kodiak bear, *Ursus middendorffi*, brown bear of Kodiak Island and other Alaskan islands. Largest land-dwelling carnivore: may weigh over 680 kg (1500 lb) and exceed 3 m (10 ft) in length.

Kodiak Island, off S Alaska, US; in Shelikof Str. Area 13,890 sq km (5363 sq mi). Hil and forested, indented coastline. Salmo fishing, canning.

Koestler, Arthur (1905-), British writer, Hungary. Works, incl. essays, novels, *Darkness at Noon* (1940), studies in histo of ideas, *eg The Sleepwalkers* (1959 reflect scientific background, disillusio ment with Communism.

kohlrabi, *Brassica oleracea caulorapa,* pla of cabbage family. Grown for edib bulbous portion of stem.

Kokoschka, Oskar (1886-1980), Austria painter, dramatist. Early work incl. viole expressionist landscapes and portrai expressing psychological tension.

Kokura, *see* KITAKYUSHU.

kola, *see* COLA.

Kola Peninsula, region of USSR, European RSFSR, between Barents an White seas. Tundra in NE, forested in SV Rich mineral resources. Chief tow Murmansk.

Köln, *see* COLOGNE.

Kolwezi, town of S Zaïre in Katanga pro Pop. 48,000. Commercial and transpo centre for copper, cobalt mining regio Site of massacre of Europeans an Africans by Katangese rebels; led French, Belgian armed intervention (1978

Kolyma, river of USSR, NE Siberian RSFS Rises in Kolyma Range; flows N *c* 2550 k (1600 mi) to East Siberian Sea. Pass through important goldfields.

Komodo dragon, *Varanus komodoens* world's largest lizard, reaching lengths 3.7 m/12 ft. Discovered (1912) on Ind nesian island of Komodo.

Konakry, *see* CONAKRY.

Königsberg, *see* KALININGRAD.

Kon-tiki, legendary sun king supposed have migrated from Peru to the Pacif Isls. *See* HEYERDAHL.

Konya (anc. *Iconium),* city of SC Turkey, rich agric. region. Pop. 247,000. Textil carpet mfg. Cap. of sultanate of Iconium Rum under Seljuk Turks in 11th cen Religious centre of Whirling Dervish from 13th cent.

kookaburra, *Dacelo gigas,* large Australia kingfisher, with loud laughing cry. Al called laughing jackass.

Koran (Arab., *quran,*=recitation), sacr book of Islam. Written in classical Arabi regarded as word of God revealed MOHAMMED by angel Gabriel. Derived some extent from Jewish scripture. Th canonical version was estab. *c* 652.

Korea *(Choson),* historical country of E Asi divided (1948) into North and South Kore Mountainous penin., forested in N (go iron deposits), agric. in S (rice, barle with tungsten, coal resources. Languag Korean. Religion: Confucianism. Kingdo 1392-1910 until Japanese annexatio Liberation after WWII led to Russian (N US (S) occupation and KOREAN W (1950-3). **North Korea** (People's Repub of Korea) estab. under Communist go Area *c* 120,500 sq km (47,000 sq mi); po

Korea

17,072,000; cap. Pyongyang. **South Korea** (Republic of Korea) dependent on US aid after invasion by North Korea (1950). Area *c* 98,500 sq km (38,000 sq mi); pop. 37,019,000; cap. Seoul.

orean, language of Korea and part of Japan. Appears to be unrelated to any other language, although syntax similar to Japanese. Literature dates from 7th cent. AD.

orean War, conflict fought (1950-3) between Communist and non-Communist forces in Korea. Invasion of South Korea by North Korean troops (later backed by Chinese) led UN to authorize support for South Korea by international military force under US command. Ceasefire negotiations (begun 1951) led to 1953 armistice ending war.

órinthos, *see* CORINTH.

os, *see* COS.

osciusko, Tadeusz (1746–1817), Polish national hero. Led nationalist revolutionaries against Russian invasion (1794), was captured but freed (1796) to live in exile.

osciusko, Mount, highest peak of Australia, in Snowy Mts., S New South Wales. Reaches 2229 m/ 7316 ft.

osher, term for food complying with Jewish dietary laws. Meat must be that of animals which chew cud and have cloven hooves; must be slaughtered by specially trained Jew and cleansed of all traces of blood, and must not be cooked or eaten with milk products.

ošice, city of E Czechoslovakia. Pop. 181,000. Indust. centre, esp. machinery, textiles, food processing. Gothic cathedral (14th cent.). Part of Hungary until 1920.

ossuth, Lajos (1802-94), Hungarian revolutionary hero. Instrumental in precipitating Hungarian nationalist uprising against Austria (1848). President of short-lived republic (1849); fled to Turkey after Russia came to Austria's aid.

osygin, Aleksei Nikolayevich (1904-80), Soviet politician. Succeeded (1964) Khrushchev as premier and chairman of council of ministers, sharing power with Leonid Brezhnev, secretary of Communist Party.

Kotabaru, *see* DJAJAPURA.

Kowloon, seaport and penin. of Hong Kong. Pop. (city) 2,195,000. Adjoins Kwangtung prov., S China. Main indust. area of Hong Kong; linked by rail to Kwangchow, tunnel to Hong Kong isl.

Kozhikode, seaport of Kerala state, SW India, on Malabar Coast. Pop. 334,000. Exports coconut goods. Formerly called Calicut, once renowned for calico. Site of many European trading posts 16th-18th cent.; ceded to British 1792.

Krakatoa, small Indonesian isl., between Java and Sumatra. Violent volcanic eruption in 1883, greatest in recorded history, caused much destruction; thousands killed by resulting tidal waves.

Kraków (Eng. Cracow), city of S Poland, on R. Vistula, cap. of Kraków prov. Pop. 833,000. Iron, steel industs.; trades in timber, agric. produce; educational and cultural centre, univ. (1364). Founded 8th cent., cap. of Poland 1305-1609. Under Austrian rule 1795-1919, except 1815-46 (independent republic). Cathedral (14th cent.) contains royal tombs.

Krasnoyarsk, city of USSR, indust. centre of C Siberian RSFSR. Pop. 796,000. Railway engineering, textiles; centre of goldmining region; major h.e.p. plant on R. Yenisei.

Krebs, Sir Hans Adolf (1900-), British biochemist, b. Germany. Described Krebs or citric acid cycle, series of biochemical reactions governing the oxidation of foodstuffs and release of energy. Shared Nobel Prize for Physiology and Medicine (1953).

Krefeld or **Crefeld,** city of W West Germany, on R. Rhine. Pop. 226,000. Textile centre, formerly linen (estab. by Huguenots), now silk and rayon. Also produces steel.

Kreisky, Bruno (1911-), Austrian political leader, chancellor (1970-). Helped negotiate treaty (1955) achieving Austrian independence and neutrality. Formed (1970) 1st single party govt. in Austria since WWII after socialist electoral victory.

kremlin, fortified citadel in several Russian towns. Best known is that in Moscow, much of it dating from 15th cent. Contains palaces, cathedrals, bell towers. Now centre of Soviet govt.

krill, small shrimp-like crustacean, main food of toothless whales. Also now being developed as protein concentrate for animals and humans.

Krishna, in Hindu religion, eighth incarnation of VISHNU. As adolescent, represented as erotic, often sporting with milkmaids. As adult, he is hero of epic *Mahabharata.*

Krivoi Rog, city of USSR, SC Ukrainian SSR; on R. Ingulets. Pop. 650,000. Iron mining centre; produces iron and steel, chemicals.

Kronstadt, port and naval base of USSR, on Kotlin Isl. in Gulf of Finland, W European RSFSR. Pop. *c* 50,000. Taken from Sweden (1703) by Peter the Great and later fortified. Served as port for St Petersburg but importance declined after canal built to latter (1875-85).

Kropotkin, Piotr Alekseyevich, Prince (1842-1921), Russian anarchist. Arrested for spreading nihilist propaganda in Russia (1874). Fled Russia (1876); lived in England for 30 years until returning to Russia after 1917 Revolution.

Kruger, [Stephanus Johannes] Paul (1825-1904), South African statesman. Secured independence of Transvaal (1881) in the Pretoria Agreement with Britain. As president (1883-1900), opposed Rhodes's policies of unifying South Africa under British rule. Tried to maintain Boer supremacy by excluding non-Boers from franchise. Policies contributed to outbreak of Boer War.

Krupp, Alfred (1812-87), German industrialist. Built up famous iron and steel works at Essen. His son, **Friedrich Alfred ('Fritz') Krupp** (1854-1902), specialized in armaments. His daughter Bertha married **Gustav von Bohlen und Halbach** (1870-1950), who adopted the name Krupp and manufactured almost the entire output of German armaments in WWI. Krupp works was centre for German rearmament in period after 1933. Gustav's son, **Alfred Felix Krupp** (1907-), was imprisoned as a war criminal for using slave labour; he subsequently rebuilt the organization into an international concern.

krypton (Kr), inert gaseous element; at. no. 36, at. wt. 83.80. Found in minute traces in atmosphere (*c* 1 part per million). Used in fluorescent lights. Discovered (1898) in residue of liquid air.

Kuala Lumpur, cap. of Malaysia. Pop. 452,000, mainly Chinese. Commercial, transport centre for tin mining and rubber growing area.

Kublai Khan (1216-94), Mongol emperor of China. Grandson of Genghis Khan; succeeded to empire on death of his brother Mangu Khan (1259). Completed Mongol conquest of China with defeat of Sung dynasty (1279). Invasions of Java and Japan were unsuccessful. Visited by Marco Polo.

Kuching, cap. of Sarawak state, East Malaysia. Pop. 63,000. Port on R. Sarawak.

kudu, *Strepsiceros strepsiceros,* large African antelope, with long spiral horns and striped grey coat.

Kuibyshev, city of USSR, E European RSFSR; port on Volga. Pop. 1,216,000. Indust. centre; aircraft, tractor, textile mfg. Founded (1586) as Samara to protect trade on Volga; renamed 1935.

Ku Klux Klan, in US history, 2 distinct secret societies; original Ku Klux Klan founded (1866) to maintain white supremacy in South. Disbandment ordered (1869), but local organizations continued. Second Ku Klux Klan (founded 1915) added intense hatred of foreigners, anti-Catholicism, anti-Semitism to its white supremacy policy. At its peak in 1920s, influence has declined, even in South.

Kulturkampf (Ger., = culture struggle struggle in Germany to restrict power Catholic church in politics, as represent through Centre party. Govt. und Bismarck passed series of laws from 18 incl. measures to remove church control school system and introduction of ci marriage. Ceased when Bismarck, feari rise of Socialism, rescinded anti-Cathol policies.

Kumasi, city of SW Ghana, cap. of Ashan region. Pop. 345,000. Commercial centr market town in cocoa-producing dist.; uni (1961). Former cap. of Ashanti confeder tion, captured (1896) by British.

Kumquat

kumquat, any of genus *Fortunella* of shru native to China and Japan. Bear sma citrus fruits with soft pulp and sweet rin often candied as sweetmeat.

Kun, Béla (1886-*c* 1937), Hungarian po tician. After becoming Bolshevik in Russi headed short-lived Communist dictatorsh in Hungary (1919). Fell from power aft defeat by Romanian troops intervening counter-revolution (1919). Returned USSR where he is thought to have died party purges.

kung-fu, Chinese system of self-defenc similar to KARATE, but emphasizing c cular rather than linear movements.

Kunlun, mountain range of C Asia betwe Tien Shan and Himalayas along Tib border. Length *c* 1600 km (1000 m Highest point 7724 m (25,340 ft) at Ulu Muztagh.

Kunming, cap. of Yunnan prov., S Chin Pop. 1,100,000. Commercial, transport ce tre; coal, steel complex. Ancient wall city.

Kuomintang, Chinese nationalist politic party, organized (1912) in accordance wi principles of SUN YAT-SEN. Strengthen (1922-4) with aid of Communists. Und leadership of CHIANG KAI-SHEK, Kuominta troops captured Peking (1928) and set govt. in Nanking. Engaged in civil war wi Communists after 1927. Authoritarian ru lasted until Communist victories forc Chiang and Nationalists to set up govt. Taiwan (1950).

Kurdistan, hist. region of SE Turkey, a parts of Iran, Iraq, Syria. Inhabited pastoral nomads. Revolts in Turkey suppressed (1920s, 1946); Kurds have been in rebellion in Iraq from 1960s, in Iran from 1979.

uril or **Kurile Islands** (Jap., *Chischima*), isl. chain of USSR, stretching from Kamchatka penin. to Hokkaido isl. (Japan). Area *c* 15,600 sq km (6000 sq mi). Of volcanic origin, with several active volcanoes; main occupations lumbering, fishing. Japanese possession (1875-1945). Japan claims southernmost 2 isls.

urosawa, Akira (1910-), Japanese film director. Known for dramatic treatments of historical, legendary stories, *eg Rashomon* (1950), *The Seven Samurai* (1954).

uro Shiwo or **Japan Current,** warm ocean current of W Pacific. Flows N past E Taiwan and Japan, moderating climate of both.

utch, Rann of, salt marsh region of Gujarat state, W India. Area disputed by India and Pakistan; scene of fighting between their forces (1965).

utuzov, Mikhail Ilarionovich, Prince (1745-1813), Russian army officer. Superseded Barclay de Tolly as commander after the defeat at Smolensk (1812), and devised the tactics which reversed the French advance and turned it into the disastrous retreat from Moscow.

uwait, independent sheikdom of SW Asia, at head of Persian Gulf. Area *c* 18,000 sq km (6950 sq mi); pop. 1,119,000. Mainly desert; major oil producer. British protect. (1899-1961). Shares control of Neutral Territory with Saudi Arabia. **Kuwait** or **Al-Kuwait** is cap. and port. Pop. 775,000.

uznetsk Basin, region of USSR, SC Siberian RSFSR. Area *c* 69,900 sq km (27,000 sq mi). Richest coalfield in USSR with reserves of iron ore.

wajalein, atoll in Ralik Chain of Marshall Isls., W Pacific Ocean. Incl. many islets. Formerly dist. hq. of US trust territ. of the Pacific Isls.; missile station. Japanese base in WWII, taken by US (1944).

Kwangchow or **Canton,** cap. of Kwangtung prov., S China. Pop. 2,300,000. Major port on R. Chukiang delta. China's centre for external trade, site of twice-yearly trade fair. Shipyards, textile mfg., steel complex.

Kwangju, city of SW South Korea. Pop. 606,000. Agric., commercial centre; rice milling, cotton and silk mfg.

Kwangsi (-Chuang), auton. region of S. China. Area *c* 220,000 sq km (85,000 sq mi); pop. 34,000,000; cap. Nanning. Mainly hills with basin of Si Kiang. Major producer of sugar cane, manganese, tin.

Kwangtung, maritime prov. of S China, incl. Hainan isl. Area *c* 231,500 sq km (89,400 sq mi); pop. 55,000,000; cap. Kwangchow. Coast has enclaves MACAO, HONG KONG. Fishing, agric., major sugar cane producer, oil refining.

Kweichow, prov. of SC China. Area *c* 171,000 sq km (66,000 sq mi); pop. 26,000,000; cap. Kweiyang. High plateau region. Produce incl. rice, cereals, timber. Minerals incl. mercury, coal.

Kweiyang, cap. of Kweichow prov., SC China. Pop. 660,000. Rail, indust. centre. Important coalfields nearby. Textile and fertilizer mfg.

Kyd, Thomas (1558-94), English playwright. Estab. vogue for revenge tragedy with *The Spanish Tragedy*.

Kyoto, city of Japan, SC Honshu isl. Pop. 1,462,000. Many craft industs. Founded in 8th cent., hist. cap. of Japan 794-1868 (political power resided in Tokyo after 1603). Buddhist centre. Univ. (1897).

Kyushu, isl. of SW Japan. Area *c* 35,600 sq km (13,800 sq mi). Mountainous; mild subtropical climate favours agric. Indust. concentrated in N around country's largest coalfield.

Kyzyl Kum or **Kizil Kum,** desert of USSR, in Uzbek SSR and Kazakh SSR, between Amu Darya and Syr Darya.

L

labelled compound, compound in which radioactive isotope of an element replaces normal stable atom. Used to trace paths of compound through mechanical or biological systems.

Labiatae, family of flowering plants. Characterized by square stem, hairy leaves, grouping of flowers on stem, hooded petals, *eg* lavender, thyme, sage, mint.

labour, in economics, factor of PRODUCTION. In perfect competition, price of labour (wages) is elastic and depends on demand.

labour, division of, *see* DIVISION OF LABOUR.

Labour Party, in UK, political party organized to implement socialist policies, as advocated by Fabian Society, on evolutionary basis, supported by most of trade union movement. Formed (1906), adopted socialist programme (1918). Rose rapidly in elections, sharing major party status with Conservatives from 1922. Prominent figures incl. MacDonald, Attlee, Bevan, Wilson. Elsewhere, grouping of socialists and trade unions characterize labour parties, *eg* N Europe, Australia, New Zealand. Labour links with European SOCIAL DEMOCRACY reflect similar policies and means of implementation.

Labrador, mainland territ. of Newfoundland, E Canada. Area 292,000 sq km (*c* 113,000 sq mi). Separated from Newfoundland Isl. by Str. of Belle Isle. Tundra in N; forests in S. Cod fishing, iron ore industs. H.e.p. supplies from Churchill R. Inhabited by Eskimos in N. British gained control (1763); joined Newfoundland 1809.

Labrador Current, cold ocean current of W Atlantic. Flows S past W Greenland, E Canada, meets Gulf Stream off Newfoundland. Shallow waters at junction of currents known as Grand Banks; frequent fogs, cod fisheries.

Labrador retriever, large dog with short black or golden coat. Stands *c* 55 cm/22 in. at shoulder.

laburnum, genus of deciduous trees of Leguminosae family. Native to S and C Europe. Clusters of yellow flowers followed by pods of poisonous seeds.

Laccadive, Minicoy and Amindivi Islands, *see* LAKSHADWEEP.

lace, openwork fabric woven in ornamental designs. Finest lace is made from linen. Lace became fashionable in 16th cent. and reached height of production in Flanders in 18th cent. Machine-made lace first appeared *c* 1760. Chief modern centres are France, Belgium, Britain, Ireland and Italy.

Lachlan, river of S New South Wales, Australia. Flows *c* 1480 km (920 mi) from Great Dividing Range via Wyangala Dam to Murrumbidgee R. Provides irrigation.

lacquer, solution of film-forming substanc dissolved in volatile solvents, applied decorate or protect surfaces. Commone forms use cellulose esters. Lacquer wo was highly developed in art of China a Japan.

lacrosse, ten-a-side outdoor sport play with ball and netted stick. Originated North American Indians, it was named French settlers; 1st games played by whi men date from 1840s.

lactic acid, *see* LACTOSE.

lactose, white crystalline sugar found mammalian milk; less sweet than ca sugar. Bacterial fermentation of lactose milk produces lactic acid. Lactic acid al formed by splitting of glucose in anim cells, with consequent release of use body energy.

Ladakh, region of NE Kashmir, Ind bordering on Tibet. Incl. highest Karakoram Mts.; traversed by upp reaches of Indus. Claimed by Chinese, w occupied parts in 1962.

Ladoga, Lake, largest lake in Europe, USSR, NW European RSFSR. Area *c* 18,2 sq km (7000 sq mi). Outlet is R. Nev flowing to Gulf of Finland.

ladybird, any of Coccinellidae family small beetles; red or yellow with bla spots. Larvae and adults feed on aphids.

Lady Day, *see* ANNUNCIATION.

Lady of the Lake, *see* ARTHURIAN LEGEND.

Ladysmith, town of W Natal, South Afric Pop. 33,000. Railway jct., engineerin textiles. Besieged 1899-1900 by Boe relieved by British force.

lady's slipper, any of various plants ORCHID family whose flowers resemble slipper, esp. of genus *Cypripedium* nati to Americas.

Laënnec, René Théophile Hyacinth (1781-1826), French physician. Invent stethoscope, which he used to diagno disorders of the chest.

Lafayette, Marie Joseph Paul Yves Ro Gilbert du Motier, Marquis (1757-1834), French soldier. Went America in 1777 to fight for the colonis Elected to the French National Assemb (1789) and commanded the Fren National Guard (1789-92), but his modera views antagonized the Jacobins and he fl the country. Imprisoned by the Austrian he was released by Napoleon. Led mo erates in the July Revolution (1830).

La Fontaine, Jean de (1621-95), Fren author. Known for *Fables choisi* (1668-94), adaptations of ancient fabl affectionately ridiculing human folly.

lager, a light beer, stored for several mont

for ageing. Most beers in Europe, many in America are lagers.

gos, cap. of Nigeria, on Bight of Benin. Pop. 1,477,000. Built on several isls. and mainland, linked by bridges. Admin., indust. centre; railway terminus and port, exports palm produce, groundnuts, cocoa; univ. (1962). Formerly notorious slave market; ceded (1861) to UK, became colony (1886) until merged with Southern Nigeria (1906). Site near Abuja, C Nigeria, designated for new cap.

grange, Joseph Louis, Comte (1736-1813), French mathematician. Famed for *Mécanique analytique* (1788), purely analytic study of mechanics; contributed to calculus of variations.

hore, city of N Pakistan. Pop. 2,165,000. Indust., transport centre; railway engineering. Cap. of Mogul, then Sikh empires; captured by British (1846). Has Shah Jehan's Shalamar gardens (1637); univ. (1882).

ibach, *see* LJUBLJANA.

ing, Ronald David (1927-), Scottish psychiatrist. Work, notably *Sanity, Madness and the Family* (1964), assumes mental illness does not exist clinically.

isser-faire or **laissez-faire,** in economics, doctrine that economic system functions best without govt. interference and that, unregulated by artificial means, natural economic order tends to favour maximum good of individual and community as a whole. First formulated by PHYSIOCRATS in reaction to MERCANTILISM, later adapted by Adam Smith, Bentham and Mill. Basis of Western economic activity in 19th cent., but development of monopolies led to govt. regulation in 20th cent.

ke (Scot. *loch*, Irish, *lough*), body of water surrounded by land. May form naturally in depression caused by glacial, volcanic or tectonic action, or artificially by damming. Normally freshwater; high evaporation causes salt lakes.

ke District, Cumbria, NW England. National Park (area 2242 sq km/866 sq mi) of lakes (incl. Windermere, Coniston Water, Ullswater, Derwent Water) and mountains (incl. Scafell Pike, Helvellyn, Skiddaw).

ke dwelling, in archaeology, habitation built on artificial platform, usually supported by piles driven into lake bottom. Examples incl. Iron Age one at Glastonbury, England, Neolithic and Bronze Age sites in Switzerland, Germany. Also *see* CRANNOG.

kshadweep, union territ. of India, comprising group of 27 isls. in Arabian Sea off coast of Kerala state. Area 32 sq km (12 sq mi); pop. *c* 32,000; cap. Kavaratti Isl. Formerly known as Laccadive, Minicoy and Amindivi Islands (till 1973).

maism, form of Buddhism practised in Tibet, Bhutan and Mongolia. Derived from Mahayana Buddhism but incorporating erotic mysticism, many animistic elements. Introduced into Tibet in 8th cent. Monastery estab. near Lhasa (*c* 750). Spiritual head, DALAI LAMA, ruled in Tibet until 1959.

Lamarck, Jean Baptiste, Chevalier de (1744-1829), French naturalist. Proposed evolutionary theory (Lamarckism) that modifications induced in an individual by the environment are transmitted to individual's descendants. His *Histoire naturelle des animaux sans vertèbres* (1815-22) founded modern invertebrate zoology.

Lamartine, Alphonse Marie Louis de (1790-1869), French poet, statesman. Major Romantic. Works incl. *Les Méditations poétiques* (1820), *Histoire des Girondins* (1847). One-time Royalist politician, led provisional govt. of Revolution (1848).

Lamb, Charles (1775-1834), English essayist. Works incl. *Specimens of English Dramatic Poets* (1808), collection *Essays of Elia* (1823). Children's books incl. *Tales from Shakespeare* (with sister, 1807). Friend of Coleridge and other Romantics.

Lambeth, town of SC Greater London, England. Pop. 272,000. Created 1965 from met. bor., incl. part of Wandsworth. Has Lambeth Palace (residence of Archbishop of Canterbury).

Lamentations, prophetic book of OT, traditionally attributed to Jeremiah but written after fall of Jerusalem (*c* 586 BC). Consists of 5 poems mourning the fall of the city.

lammergeier, *Gypaetus barbatus*, bird of vulture family, found in remote mountain ranges of Europe and Asia. Also called bearded vulture.

lamprey, primitive marine or freshwater CYCLOSTOME. Species incl. Atlantic lamprey, *Petromyzon marinus*.

Lanarkshire, former county of SC Scotland, now in Strathclyde region. Lowther Hills in S (sheep); low-lying, fertile in C (market gardening); heavy industs. based on iron, coal deposits in N. Chief city Glasgow. Co. town was **Lanark,** former royal burgh on R. Clyde. Pop. 9000. Market town; textiles mfg. Owen's New Lanark model town (1784) nearby.

Lancashire, county of NW England. Area 3043 sq km (1175 sq mi); pop. 1,370,000; admin. hq Preston. Pennine moors in N, E; fertile lowlands in C, SW. Coal mining; textile indust. (once famous for cotton); engineering.

Lancaster, city of Lancashire, NW England, former co. town on R. Lune. Pop. 50,000. Textiles, furniture mfg. Has univ. (1964); 13th-cent. castle on site of Roman camp.

Lancaster, House of, English royal family. Founded by Edmund ('Crouchback'), son of Henry III, created earl of Lancaster in 1267. John of Gaunt became duke (1362) through marriage into Lancaster family and his son became 1st Lancastrian king as Henry IV. Others were Henry V and Henry VI. Rivalry with House of York led to Wars of the Roses.

Lancelot, *see* ARTHURIAN LEGEND.

Lanchow, cap. of Kansu prov., NC China. Pop. 1,450,000. On Hwang Ho. Major oil refinery, plutonium processing plant. Hist. and modern transport hub. Petrochemical, plastic and fertilizer industs.

Landes, coastal region of SW France, between Médoc and R. Adour. Formerly wasteland of dunes, lagoons, moorland; pine forests now yield lumber, resins *etc.*

Land League, Irish organization, formed 1879 under leadership of PARNELL and Michael Davitt, which sought to improve conditions of land ownership for Catholics and to fight evictions. By operation of boycott, influenced passage of Gladstone's Land Act (1881), which fixed fair rents and secured tenure.

Landor, Walter Savage (1775-1864), English poet. Works incl. *Gebir* (1798), *Hellenics* (1847). Also wrote prose *Imaginary Conversations* (1824-8).

Landseer, Sir Edwin Henry (1802-73), English painter. Specialized in sentimental paintings of animals, incl. *The Monarch of the Glen*. Modelled lions at base of Nelson's Column, London.

Land's End, granite headland of Cornwall, SW England. Most W point of England.

landslide, mass movement of earth and rock down a slope. Normally occurs along definite interface, when water-saturated material detaches from impermeable material underneath. Also caused by earth tremors, undercutting of cliff face, *etc.*

Lanfranc (d. 1089), Italian churchman and scholar. Archbishop of Canterbury (1070-89), instituted many church reforms incl. replacing English bishops with Normans.

Langland, William (*c* 1331-*c* 1400), English poet. Probable author of *Piers Plowman*, Middle English religious allegory.

Langton, Stephen (d. 1228), English churchman, theologian. Elected archbishop of Canterbury, in defiance of King John, through influence of Pope Innocent III (1207). Assumed see (1213) after John submitted to papal authority. Supported barons in struggle leading to Magna Carta.

Langtry, Emilie Charlotte ('Lillie') (1853-1929), English actress, known as 'Jersey Lily'. Famous for beauty, friendship with Prince of Wales (later Edward VII).

language, systematically differentiated sounds used in significant sequences as means of communication. May be represented by further system of written signs (*see* ALPHABET). Considered a defining attribute of mankind. *See* LINGUISTICS.

Languedoc, region and former prov. of S France, hist. cap. Toulouse. Cévennes in E; fertile Garonne plain in W. Agric., vineyards. Under medieval counts of Toulouse until incorporated (1271) into France. Name derived from *Langue d'oc* (medieval Provençal dialect).

Lansbury, George (1859-1940), English politician. Led parliamentary Labour Party (1931-5) but resigned leadership because of pacifist views.

Lansing, cap. of Michigan, US; on jct. Grand and Cedar rivers. Pop. 445,00 Railway centre; has important motor c indust. Cap. from 1847.

lantern fish, any of Myctophidae family deep-sea fish, with light-producing orga on body and head.

lanthanides or **rare earths,** group of ra metallic elements with atomic numbe from 57 to 71 inclusive. Have simil chemical properties and are difficult separate.

lanthanum (La), metallic element lanthanide series; at. no. 57, at. wt. 138.9 Discovered (1839).

Laocoön, in Greek legend, Trojan priest Apollo. He warned against admitting th Greek wooden horse within the city wal Angered Apollo (Athena in some version who sent sea serpents to strangle him ar his 2 sons.

Laoighis or **Leix,** county of Leinster prov., Irish Republic. Area 1720 sq km (664 mi); pop. 50,000; co. town Port Laoighis Mainly flat, with Slieve Bloom Mts. in Agric., dairying. Formerly called Queen County.

Laos, republic of SE Asia. Area *c* 236,800 km (91,500 sq mi); pop. 3,546,000; ca Vientiane. Languages: Laotian, Frenc Religion: Buddhism. Forested (teak mountainous terrain apart from Mekor valley; principal crop rice; maize, tobacc coffee grown. French protect. 1893-194 Communist Vietminh forces invade withdrew with French 1954. Civil war fro 1960; neutral govt. estab. 1962; fightir resumed 1967 with involvement of Nor Vietnamese forces. Ceasefire (1973 Monarchy abolished 1975 and Communi control estab.

Lao-tze or **Lao-tzu** (*fl* 6th cent. BC), Chine philosopher. Traditionally held to b founder of Taoism and author of *Tao T Ching*.

La Paz, admin. cap. of Bolivia, cap. of La P dept.; near L. Titicaca. Pop. 655,000. Seat govt. Has airport at 3960 m (*c* 13,000 f Tanning, brewing, flour milling; texti chemical mfg. Founded by Spanish (1548).

lapis lazuli, silicate mineral, a semi-precio gemstone. Opaque, azure blue in colour.

Laplace, Pierre Simon, Marquis d (1749-1827), French mathematician an astronomer. Formulated nebul hypothesis of origin of solar syste (planets formed by shrinkage of gaseo nebula surrounding Sun).

Lapland, region of Arctic Europe, in Norway, Sweden, Finland, NW USS Forest in S, tundra in N. Nomadic Lap form indigenous pop.; reindeer herdin fishing, hunting. Area has rich miner resources, esp. iron ore at Kirun Gällivare (Sweden).

La Plata, city of E Argentina, cap. of Buen Aires prov. Pop. 479,000. Exports agr produce from pampas region through port, Ensenada. Meat packing, oil refinir Called Eva Perón (1952-5).

Lapp

Lapps, N Scandinavian people, concentrated largely in Norway (called Finns there). Semi-nomadic reindeer herdsmen, hunters, some fishers. Origins believed to be C Asian. Speak Finno-Ugric language. Pop. *c* 30,000.

Laptev Sea, part of Arctic Ocean, lying N of Siberia. Bounded by Severnaya Zemlya in W, New Siberian isls. in E. Receives R. Lena.

lapwing, *Vanellus vanellus,* large greenish-black and white plover of Europe and C Asia, noted for erratic flight during breeding season. Also called peewit.

larch, any of genus *Larix* of tall deciduous coniferous trees of pine family. Found mainly in N hemisphere. Used in building.

lares and penates, Roman gods of the home. Lares represented ancestral spirits. Penates were guardians of the store-cupboard.

Largs, town of Strathclyde region, W Scotland, on Firth of Clyde. Pop. 10,000. Tourist resort. Scene of battle (1263) in which Alexander III of Scotland defeated Haakon IV of Norway.

Larisa or **Larissa,** town of E Greece, on R. Peneus, cap. of Larisa admin. dist. Pop. 56,000. Railway jct., agric. market. Cap. of ancient Thessaly.

lark, any of Alaudidae family of mainly Old World songbirds. Skylark, *Alauda arvensis,* noted for song as it hovers or ascends.

Larkin, Philip Arthur (1922-), English poet. Collections, *eg The Less Deceived* (1955), *The Whitsun Weddings* (1964), *High Windows* (1975), estab. 'new poetry' as reaction against romanticism, political enthusiasms.

larkspur, *see* DELPHINIUM.

Larne, port of E Northern Ireland. Pop. 18,000. In former Co. Antrim. Bauxite refining; linen mfg.; has ferry service to Stranraer (Scotland).

La Rochefoucauld, François, Duc de (1613-80), French author. Known for *Maximes* (1665), bitter epigrams illustrating belief that self-interest is main human motivation.

La Rochelle, town of W France, on Bay of Biscay, cap. of Charente-Maritime dept. Pop. 95,000. Port, fishing, shipbuilding. Huguenot stronghold in 16th-17th cent., successfully besieged (1627-8) by Richelieu. Medieval buildings, 18th-cent. cathedral.

larva, free-living form of animal emerging from egg, usually distinct from adult and incapable of sexual reproduction. Undergoes metamorphosis into adult, *eg* tadpole into frog or caterpillar into butterfly.

larynx, organ of speech at entrance to windpipe (trachea); contains vocal cords; visible on outside as Adam's apple. Composed mainly of cartilage and muscle. Inflammation of lining causes laryngitis; accompanied by hoarseness, coughing and sore throat.

La Salle, René Robert Cavelier, Sieur de (1643-87), French explorer. Built forts and developed fur trade in North America. Claimed Mississippi valley for France after journeying down river (1682); later attempt to find its mouth from sea ended in mutiny and murder by his own men.

Lascaux, site of caves in SW France decorated with animal paintings of Upper Palaeolithic Age, dating from *c* 20,000-14,000 BC. Discovered 1940, cave had to be closed following deterioration of paintings.

laser (light amplification by stimulated emission of radiation), source of intense narrow beam of coherent light. Atoms of gas or crystalline solid (*eg* ruby) are stimulated into excited states by light beams. They return to ground state with emission of pulses or continuous beams of highly coherent light. Used in cutting and welding metals, in surgery and holography.

Laski, Harold Joseph (1893-1950), British political scientist. Influential Fabian, he taught at London School of Economics from 1920. Chairman of Labour Party (1945-6). Works incl. *Liberty in the Modern State* (1930).

Las Palmas, *see* PALMAS, LAS.

La Spezia, *see* SPEZIA, LA.

Lassalle, Ferdinand (1825-64), German socialist and writer. Influenced by Marx. Founded General German Workers' Union (1863), forerunner of Social Democratic party. Died after a duel.

Lassus, Orlandus or **Orlando di Lasso** (*c* 1530-94), Flemish composer. Produced over 2000 vocal works, both secular and religious, in high polyphonic style. Settled in Munich after travelling widely in Europe.

Last Supper, *see* EUCHARIST.

Las Vegas, resort of S Nevada, US. Pop. 331,000; state's largest town. In ranching area; entertainment centre with famous gambling casinos. First settled by Mormons.

Latakia (*El Ladhiqiya*), port of NW Syria, on Mediterranean. Pop. 191,000. Exports famous tobacco, cotton. Prospered under Romans and Crusaders, but declined 16th cent. Revived with tobacco trade.

La Tène, shallows at E end of L. Neuchâtel, Switzerland. Site of discovery of Iron Age remains of Celtic people; name now given to European Iron Age (2nd period), *c* 5th cent. BC-1st cent. AD.

latent heat, heat required to change state of a substance from solid to liquid, or from liquid to gas, without increase in its temperature. During a change of state the addition of heat causes no rise in temperature until the change of state is complete.

Lateran Treaty, agreement signed (1929) between Church and state in Italy. Confined papal sovereignty to independent Vatican City. Recognized Roman Catholicism as state religion and guaranteed religious teaching in schools.

laterite, reddish soil composed mainly of hydrated iron oxide. Formed by decomposition of underlying rocks, *eg* granite, basalt, in areas with distinct wet and dry seasons. Used as building material, source of iron.

latex, milky fluid found in several plants, *eg* rubber tree, poppy. Consists of an emulsion of various resins and proteins. Latex of Pará rubber tree is worked into various types of rubber.

Latimer, Hugh (*c* 1485-1555), English churchman. Converted to Protestantism (1524). Appointed bishop of Winchester (1535); resigned (1539). Under Edward VI, preached against corruption among clergy. With Ridley, burned at stake for heresy under Mary I.

Latin, language in Italic branch of Indo-European family. Standard language of Roman empire. Divided into Classical Latin and Vulgar (vernacular) Latin. Latter gave rise to Romance languages. Now dead, but Classical form still used in Roman Catholic church. Was European lingua franca till *c* 18th cent.

Latin America, term denoting countries of Central and South America, S of US-Mexico border; excl. British West Indies. Refers esp. to Spanish, Portuguese-speaking countries.

latitude, in geography, angular distance north or south of the Equator of any point on Earth's surface, measured from Earth's centre. Parallels are lines of latitude encircling the Earth parallel to the Equator (0°).

Latium (*Lazio*), region of C Italy, cap. Rome. Coastal plain in W, Apennine foothills in E; much reclaimed marshland, *eg* Pontine Marshes. Agric., fishing, tourism, h.e.p. Ancient Latium fell to Romans 3rd cent. BC.

La Tour, Georges de (1593-1652), French painter. Worked all his life in Lorraine.

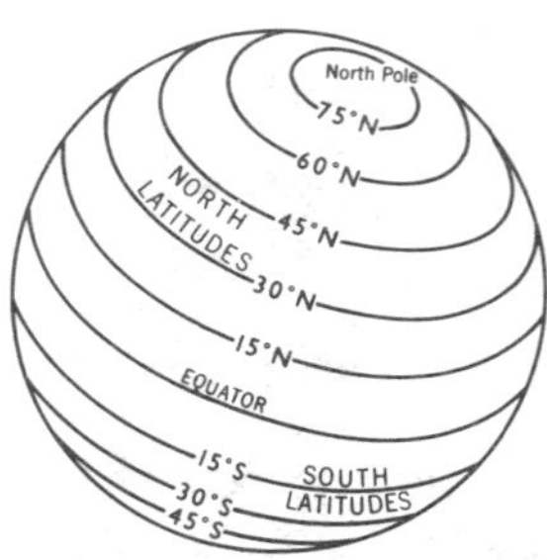

Parallels of latitude

Specialized in nocturnal religious an genre scenes dramatically illuminated b concealed source of light.

Latter Day Saints, *see* MORMONS.

Latvian Soviet Socialist Republi constituent republic of W USSR. Area 66,600 sq km (25,600 sq mi); pop. 2,521,00 cap. Riga. Mainly low-lying plain wit extensive forests; dairy products, timbe textiles produced. Hist. controlled b Sweden, Poland and Russia (from 1721 independent (1918-40) until annexed b USSR.

Laud, William (1573-1645), English churc man, archbishop of Canterbury (1633-45 Supported Charles I in struggle with Parli ment. Attempted to eradicate Puritanism Attempt to impose the Prayer Book o Scotland (1638) was resisted by forc Impeached by Parliament (1640 imprisoned and executed.

Laue, Max Theodor Felix von (1879-1960 German physicist. Awarded Nobel Priz for Physics (1914) for prediction tha atomic lattice of a crystal would act a diffraction grating for X-rays.

laughing gas, *see* NITROUS OXIDE.

laughing jackass, *see* KOOKABURRA.

Launceston, city of N Tasmania, Australi at head of Tamar estuary. Pop. 63,00 Port, exports agric. produce, timber.

Bay laurel

laurel, any of genus *Laurus* of evergree trees or shrubs; esp. bay laurel, *L. nobili* with greenish flowers, black berries, glossy leaves used as flavouring (as bay leaves) and in wreaths. Name also applied to certain similar trees and shrubs.

aurel and Hardy, American comedians, known for numerous short films in which everything they do ends in chaos. They were Stan Laurel (1890-1965) and Oliver Hardy (1892-1957).

aurentian Shield or **Plateau,** mainly in N Ontario, C Canada. Oldest rock formation of North America with dotted lake pattern formed by glacial action. Tundra in N; forested areas in S. Has rich mineral, timber, fur resources.

aurier, Sir Wilfrid (1841-1919), Canadian Liberal statesman. First French-Canadian PM of Canada (1896-1911).

ausanne, city of SW Switzerland, on L. Geneva, cap. of Vaud canton. Pop. 227,000. Printing, woodworking, leather, tourism. Cathedral (12th cent.); coll. (1537) became univ. (1890).

ausanne Conference, peace treaty (1922-3) between Allies and Turkey resolving problems raised by Treaty of SÈVRES, which had not been recognized by new Turkish govt. under Ataturk. Status of Dardanelles was decided and E Thrace recovered by Turkey.

va, molten rock from interior of Earth which has reached surface through volcanic vents and fissures. 'Acid lavas', with high silica content, are thick and slow moving; 'basic lavas', with low silica content, are very fluid. Rock froth formed on surface of lava flow is called pumice.

aval, Pierre (1883-1945), French politician. Premier and foreign minister (1931-2, 1935-6). Created vice-premier of Pétain's Vichy govt. (1940) and all-powerful premier (1942). Executed for treason following liberation.

vender, any of genus *Lavandula* of fragrant European plants of mint family, esp. *L. officinalis,* with spikes of pale purple flowers used in making perfumes.

avoisier, Antoine Laurent (1743-94), French chemist. A founder of modern chemistry, he introduced rational nomenclature, distinguished between elements and compounds, and made quantitative investigations of reactions. Explained role of oxygen in combustion and respiration. Estab. composition of water.

aw, Andrew Bonar (1858-1923), British statesman, b. Canada. Elected leader of Conservative Party (1911), he served in coalitions under Lloyd George (1915-21). PM (1922-3) after withdrawing from coalition; resigned because of poor health.

aw, John (1671-1729), Scottish financier. Founded 1st bank in France (1716). He acquired (1717) monopoly of trade in Louisiana, estab. vast stock company. Excessive speculation led to frenzied selling and ruin of thousands, incl. Law.

w court, *see* COURT.

wn tennis, *see* TENNIS.

awrence, D[avid] H[erbert] (1885-1930), English novelist, poet. Works reflect belief in sex, primitive subconscious and nature as cures for destructive effects of modern indust. society. Novels incl. semi-autobiog. *Sons and Lovers* (1913), *Women in Love* (1920), *Lady Chatterley's Lover* (1928).

Lawrence, Sir Thomas (1769-1830), English painter. Succeeded Reynolds as painter to the king (1792); leading portraitist of his time.

Lawrence, T[homas] E[dward] (1888-1935), British soldier, scholar, b. Wales. Known as 'Lawrence of Arabia'. Joined Arab revolt against Turks (1916), secured Arab cooperation for Allenby's campaign. As colonial adviser on Arab affairs, failed to realize his pro-Arab objectives and withdrew into obscurity. His experiences are recalled in *Seven Pillars of Wisdom* (1926).

lawrencium (Lr), transuranic element of actinide series; atomic no. 103, mass no. of most stable isotope 256. Lawrencium 257 first prepared (1961) by bombarding californium with boron nuclei.

Lazio, *see* LATIUM.

lead (Pb), soft metallic element; at. no. 82, at. wt. 207.19. Occurs as galena (PbS); obtained by roasting this ore. Used in accumulators, alloys, plumbing and roofing, and as shield against radiation; compounds used in paint. Lead tetraethyl used in petrol to prevent knocking.

leaf, outgrowth of stem of plant. Usually consists of broad blade, petiole (stalk), and stipules. Functions incl. food mfg. through assimilation of carbon dioxide and absorption of light, *see* PHOTOSYNTHESIS, releasing water to atmosphere, *see* TRANSPIRATION. Chlorophyll gives green colour. Evergreen leaves are termed persistent, those which fall annually, deciduous.

leaf insect, tropical insect of same family (Phasmidae) as stick insect. Wings shaped and coloured to resemble leaves among which it lives.

League of Nations, first major organization of world's countries dedicated to preservation of peace and international cooperation; hq. Geneva. Founded (1920) as part of Treaty of VERSAILLES, largely on initiative of Woodrow Wilson. Members incl. (at some time) all major nations except US; Germany and Japan withdrew 1933. Although successful in humanitarian actions, it failed to act against aggression by some of its members, *eg* Japan (1931), Italy (1935). Dissolved itself (1946) and transferred services and property to UN.

Leakey, Louis Seymour Bazett (1903-72), British anthropologist, b. Kenya. Discovered fossil remains in East Africa, incl. those of *Zinjanthropus,* proto-man *c* 1,750,000 years old, estab. man to have existed earlier than previously supposed.

Leamington Spa, Royal, town of Warwickshire, C England. Pop. 45,000. Engineering; saline springs, popular health resort from 18th cent.

Leander, *see* HERO.

Lear, Edward (1812-88), English humorist, artist. Famous for nonsense verse, esp. limericks, sometimes reflecting alienation and melancholy, *eg* 'The Jumblies', *A Book of Nonsense* (1846), *The Owl and the Pussycat* (1871), illustrated by himself.

leather, durable material prepared from hide or skin of animals by removal of flesh and hair and subsequent tanning. Tanning helps prevent decay and gives leather flexibility and toughness.

Leavis, F[rank] R[aymond] (1895-1978), English literary critic. Editor of influential periodical *Scrutiny* (1932-53). Works, *eg The Great Tradition* (1948), *The Common Pursuit* (1952), reflect belief that literature should have moral value and meet standards of intellectual elite.

Lebanon, republic of SW Asia, E Mediterranean. Area *c* 10,000 sq km (3860 sq mi); pop. 3,012,000; cap. Beirut. Language: Arabic. Religions: Islam, Maronite Christian. Fertile Beqa valley (grain, fruit) lies between Lebanon Mts. and Anti-Lebanon. Centre of ancient Phoenician empire; part of Syria under Romans, Byzantines, Turks until French mandate (1920); independent 1945. Destructive religious and civil strife from mid-1970s.

Leconte de Lisle, Charles Marie René (1818-94), French poet. Wrote austere, pessimistic poetry, *eg Poèmes antiques* (1852), *Poèmes tragiques* (1884).

Le Corbusier, *see* CORBUSIER, LE.

Leda, in Greek myth, wife of Tyndareus. Seduced by Zeus who visited her in form of a swan. She bore 2 eggs; one contained DIOSCURI, other Helen and Clytemnestra.

Lee, Robert E[dward] (1807-70), American army officer, commander of the Confederate forces in the Civil War. Won 2nd battle of Bull Run (1862) and Chancellorsville (1863), but was defeated at Gettysburg (July, 1863) and, ultimately outnumbered, surrendered to Grant (April, 1865).

leech, any of Hirudinea class of annelids. Body segmented, with sucker at each end; most species suck blood. Lives in water or wet earth. *Hirudo medicinalis* once used medicinally to bleed patients.

Leeds, city of West Yorkshire met. county, N England, on R. Aire. Pop. 499,000. Textiles; engineering industs. Has univ. (1904). Woollen indust. from 14th cent.

leek, *Allium porrum,* biennial plant of same genus as ONION. Cylindrical stem and flat leaves. Used as vegetable and in soups. National emblem of Wales.

Lee Kuan Yew (1923-), Singapore statesman. Became 1st PM of Singapore (1959-). Withdrew country from Federation of Malaysia (1965) which it had joined in 1963. Expanded economic base of country.

Leeuwenhoek, Antony van (1632-1723), Dutch naturalist. Developed single lens microscope, which enabled him to discover protozoa, spermatozoa and bacteria and study red blood cells.

Leeward Islands, archipelago of E We Indies, N Lesser Antilles. Extend SE fro Puerto Rico to Windward Isls. Incl. Virgi Isls. (US); ex-British colonies Antigua, Kitts-Nevis-Anguilla, Montserrat, Britis Virgin Isls.; Guadeloupe (French); Eustatius (Dutch), St Martin. Is discovered by Columbus (1493).

Léger, Fernand (1881-1955), French painte Associated with cubism, he later created style employing machine-like forms.

Leghorn, *see* LIVORNO.

Roman legionary

legion, fighting unit of Roman army varyin from 3000 to 4000 foot soldiers (divided in 10 cohorts) with additional cavalrymen.

legislature, in politics, that part of gov empowered to make laws for a country c state, usually comprising elected repr sentatives. British Parliament and U Congress were important in developmer of legislatures as check on judiciary an executive. Also *see* SEPARATION OF POWERS.

Leguminosae, family of flowering plan and trees. Characterized by having see pods and nitrogenous nodules on roo which allow NITROGEN FIXATION in soil. Inc laburnum, gorse, CLOVER. Many specie have tendrils which twine around support *eg* PEA.

Lehár, Franz (1870-1948), Hungarian con poser. Works, mostly operettas, incl. *Th Merry Widow* (1905).

Le Havre, city of N France, at mouth of F Seine. Pop. 264,000. Major port wi passenger and cargo traffic. Oil refinin Founded in 1576 by Francis I.

Leibnitz, Gottfried Wilhelm, Baron vo (1646-1716), German philosopher, mat ematician. Posited universe of uni (monads) which follow a harmony esta by God. Thus this becomes the 'best of a possible worlds'. Devised form of calculu independently of Newton.

Leicester, Robert Dudley, Earl of (*c* 1532-88), English courtier. Favourite of Elizabeth I, he was once considered her most likely choice of husband. Led unsuccessful expedition to the Netherlands (1585-7).

Leicestershire, county of EC England. Area 2553 sq km (986 sq mi); pop. 833,000. Mainly low-lying; uplands in E. Dairying; coal mining in W. Co. town was **Leicester,** on R. Soar. Pop. 277,000. Hosiery, shoe mfg. Has univ. (1957); Roman *Ratae,* remains incl. Jewry Wall; Norman castle (12th cent.); cathedral (1926).

Leichhardt, [Friedrich Wilhelm] Ludwig (1813-48), German explorer, scientist. Explored N and E Australia. Disappeared on trans-continental expedition (1848).

Leiden or **Leyden,** city of WC Netherlands, on R. Old Rhine. Pop. 171,000. Produces textiles, machinery. Univ. (1575).

Leif Ericsson (*fl c* 1000), Norse explorer, son of Eric the Red. Thought to have reached North America; the 'Vinland' he discovered has not been precisely delimited, perhaps New England or Newfoundland.

Leinster, prov. of E Irish Republic. Area 20,331 sq km (7850 sq mi); pop. 1,742,000. Comprises cos. Carlow, Dublin, Kildare, Kilkenny, Laoighis, Longford, Louth, Meath, Offaly, Westmeath, Wexford, Wicklow. Ancient kingdom.

Leipzig, city of S East Germany, at confluence of Pleisse, White Elster. Pop. 565,000. Indust. centre, annual trade fair; centre of German fur trade and publishing until WWII. Univ. (1409). Badly damaged in Thirty Years War and WWII; scene of Napoleon's defeat (1813).

Leith, town of Lothian region, E Scotland, on Firth of Forth. Part of Edinburgh from 1920. Major Scottish seaport; fishing, whisky distilling.

Leitrim, county of Connacht prov., NW Irish Republic. Area 1526 sq km (589 sq mi); pop. 28,000; co. town Carrick-on-Shannon. Many lakes; hilly in N. Cattle, dairying.

Leix, *see* LAOIGHIS.

Léman, Lac, *see* GENEVA, LAKE.

Le Mans, city of NW France, on R. Sarthe, cap. of Sarthe dept. Pop. 185,000. Railway jct., agric. market, engineering. Annual 24-hour motor race. Hist. cap. of Maine. Site of final French defeat by Prussia (1871). Cathedral (11th cent.).

Lemberg, *see* LVOV.

Lemming, small thick-furred rodent, resembling vole, of Arctic and subarctic regions. Norwegian lemming, *Lemmus lemmus,* noted for mass migration during times of overpopulation and food scarcity.

Lemnos (*Limnos*), isl. of Greece, in N Aegean Sea. Area 482 sq km (186 sq mi); main town Kastron. Fertile valleys; fruit, cereals.

Lemon, *Citrus limon,* evergreen tree bearing bitter yellow fruit. Grown in Mediterranean regions, S US and South Africa. Juice used in cooking, rind in candied peel.

Lemon

lemon sole, *Microstomus kitt,* edible flatfish of eastern N Atlantic.

Ring-tailed lemur

lemur, primitive arboreal primate, found mainly in Madagascar. Usually nocturnal, with large eyes and long non-prehensile tail. Diet of insects, fruit. Species incl. ring-tailed lemur, *Lemur catta.*

lemures, in Roman religion, malevolent ghosts of the dead. Propitiated in Lemuria rites.

Lena, longest river of USSR. Rises in Baikal Mts. W of L. Baikal, flows NE *c* 4250 km (2650 mi) through EC Siberian RSFSR to Laptev Sea. Gold and other minerals obtained along its course.

Lend-Lease Act, legislation passed (1941) by US Congress, empowering president to sell, lend or lease US war supplies to countries whose defence was considered vital to defence of US. Countries such as Britain provided reciprocal programmes.

Lenin, Vladimir Ilyich, orig. Ulyanov (1870-1924), Russian revolutionary. Exiled twice for anti-govt. activity, engineered split (1903) between BOLSHEVIKS and Mensheviks in Social Democrats. Returned to Russia after outbreak of RUSSIAN REVOLUTION to overthrow Kerensky's govt. (Nov. 1917), estab. Council of People's Commissars. Civil war (1918-20) ended with founding of the Soviet Union. Exercised dictatorial powers as chairman of the council and chairman of the Communist

Party. Instrumental in creation of COMINTERN world socialist movement. Differed from orthodox MARXISM in his actions and writings, advocating violent revolution, instigated by professional revolutionaries.

Leningrad, city of USSR, W European RSFSR; at mouth of R. Neva. Pop. 4,588,000. Major port; cultural and indust. centre; shipbuilding, exports timber. Founded (1703) as St Petersburg by Peter the Great. Intersected by numerous canals; spaciously planned, buildings incl. Winter Palace and cathedral; has Hermitage art gallery (1852) and univ. (1819). Scene of revolutions (1905, 1917). Replaced as cap. by Moscow (1918). Called Petrograd (1914-24).

Lenôtre, André (1613-1700), French landscape gardener. Designed parks and gardens for Louis XIV, in particular those at Versailles.

lens, portion of transparent medium, *eg* glass, bounded by curved or plane surfaces, which causes light rays to converge or diverge on passing through it. Convex lens causes parallel beam of light to converge and produce real image, concave lens causes divergence of light and produces virtual image. ABERRATION is defect of lens.

Lent, Christian period of 40 days of penance and fasting before Easter (Ash Wednesday to Easter Sunday).

lentil, *Lens culinaris,* small branching plant of Leguminosae family. Cultivated for its round flat seeds which are dried and used in cooking. Native to Old World.

Leo I, St (*c* 400-461), Italian churchman, pope (440-61). Estab. authority over bishops. Dissuaded (452) Attila from sacking Rome.

Leo X, orig. Giovanni de' Medici (1475-1521), Italian churchman, pope (1513-21). Patron of the arts. Excommunicated Luther (1521).

Leo, *see* ZODIAC.

León, city of C Mexico, in Guanajuato state; alt. 1700 m (*c* 5600 ft). Pop. 526,000. Agric., mining centre; shoe, textiles, cement mfg. Founded 1576.

León, city of W Nicaragua. Pop. 81,000. Cultural, agric. and trade centre. National cap. until 1855. Destroyed by earthquake, moved to present site (1610). Has part of National Univ.

León, region and former kingdom of NW Spain. Chief cities Salamanca, Valladolid. Cantabrian Mts. in N, elsewhere plateau; drained by R. Douro. Agric., stock raising, mining, forests. Formed, with Asturias, Christian kingdom from 866; united with Castile 1230. Hist. cap. **León,** pop. 119,000, cap. of modern León prov. Agric., commercial centre. Gothic cathedral (13th cent.).

Leonardo da Vinci (1452-1519), Italian artist, scientist, engineer. Regarded as epitome of Renaissance creativity, his extant works are few and often unfinished. Paintings incl. *Adoration of the Magi, Last Supper* fresco, *Mona Lisa, Virgin of the Rocks.* Produced notebooks covering problems in hydraulics, mechanics, anatomy, *etc.*

Leonidas (d. 480 BC), Spartan king. Althoug heavily outnumbered, he and his Sparta troops defended pass of Thermopylae (48 BC) against Persians under Xerxe defeated and killed.

leopard or **panther,** *Panthera pardu* mammal of cat family, found in Africa an Asia. Yellow-buff coat, with blac markings. Black panther is all-blac variety.

Leopold I (1640-1705), Holy Roman emperc (1658-1705). Reign was marked by wa with France and the Turks.

Leopold II (1747-92), Holy Roman emperc (1790-2). Allied with Prussia to resto Louis XVI to French throne.

Leopold I (1790-1865), king of Belgiun Having refused Greek throne (1830), h was elected king of Belgium on i separation from Netherlands (1831).

Leopold II (1835-1909), king of Belgiur (1865-1909). Financed Stanley's explor tions (1879-84) in the Congo, leading t formation of Congo Free State (188 which Leopold ruled personally. His rut less exploitation of the territ., by which h amassed a fortune, drew much hostility.

Leopold III (1901-), king of Belgiu (1934-51). Led Belgian resistance to th German occupation in WWII. Surrendere unconditionally in 1940; imprisoned un 1945. Accused of cooperating with th Germans, he remained in exile until 195 abdicated in favour of his son Baudouin.

Léopoldville, *see* KINSHASA.

Lepanto, *see* NAUPAKTOS.

Lepidoptera, order of insects, comprisin moths and butterflies, with *c* 150,0 species.

leprosy, chronic infectious disease of th skin and nerves, caused by bacteriu *Mycobacterium leprae.* Lepromatous for causes ulcerous blotches on fac tuberculoid form causes loss of sensatio in skin. Advanced leprosy may result i loss of fingers, toes. Most prevalent i tropical regions. Treated with sulphon drugs.

leptons, elementary particles which do no experience strong nuclear interaction. present, those known are electron, muon, types of neutrino and corresponding an particles.

Le Puy (en Velay), town of SC France, ca of Haute-Loire dept. Pop. 30,000. Liqueu mfg., hist. lace indust. Medieval pilgrimag centre. Romanesque cathedral (12 cent.).

Lermontov, Mikhail Yurevich (1814-41 Russian author. Wrote lyric poetry, class novel of 'superfluous man' *A Hero of Ou Time* (1840).

Lerwick, port and admin. hq of Shetlan Island Authority, N Scotland, on Mainlar isl. Pop. 6000. Fishing, knitwear, offsho oil industs.

Le Sage, Alain René (1668-1747), Frenc author. Best known for picaresque novel manners, *Gil Blas* (1715-35).

lesbianism, *see* HOMOSEXUALITY.

Lesbos or **Mytilene,** isl. of Greece, in E Aegean Sea. Area 1632 sq km (630 sq mi); cap. Mytilene. Wheat, olives, fruits. Cultural centre *c* 6th cent. BC, home of Aristotle, poets Sappho, Alcaeus. Member of Delian League.

Lesotho, kingdom of S Africa, surrounded by Republic of South Africa. Area 30,300 sq km (11,700 sq mi); pop. 1,279,000, mainly Basuto tribe; cap. Maseru. Languages: Sesotho, English. Religions: animist, Christian. Drakensberg Mts. in E, elsewhere tableland; main rivers Orange, Caledon. Main occupation stock rearing; exports wool, mohair, diamonds. Many Basuto tribesmen work in South African mines. British Protect. of Basutoland from 1868, independent from 1966. Member of British Commonwealth.

Lesseps, Ferdinand Marie, Vicomte de (1805-94), French diplomat, engineer. Negotiated concession for Suez Canal and supervised its construction (1859-69). Began work on Panama Canal (1881), but company went bankrupt.

Lessing, Doris May, née Taylor (1919-), English author, b. Persia. Known for semi-autobiog. 'Children of Violence' novel sequence, dealing with her African childhood, political activism, psychological development; also wrote *The Golden Notebook* (1962).

Lessing, Gotthold Ephraim (1729-81), German aesthetician, dramatist. Known for theoretical works, *eg Laokoon* (1766) demarcating subject matter of painting, poetry, *Hamburg Dramaturgy* (1767-8) attacking neo-classical formalism. Best-known dramas incl. *Emilia Galotti* (1772), *Nathan the Wise* (1779).

Lethe, in Greek myth, one of rivers of HADES. Water drunk by the dead to gain forgetfulness of previous existence.

Lettuce, *Lactuca sativa,* vegetable widely grown for its crisp leaves used raw in salads. Varieties incl. asparagus lettuce *(angustana),* cabbage lettuce *(capitata)* and Cos *(longifolia).*

Leukaemia, cancer-like disease of white blood cells resulting from disorder of bone marrow and other blood-forming tissue. Accompanied by anaemia and enlargement of lymph nodes, liver, spleen. Generally fatal, though has been cured in children; may be relieved or controlled by X-rays and drugs.

Levant, name given to coastlands of E Mediterranean in Turkey, Syria, Lebanon and Israel.

Levellers, extreme republican and democratic party in English Civil War period. Advocated religious and social equality, sovereign House of Commons elected by universal manhood suffrage. Gained some support in army rank and file from 1647; suppressed by Cromwell (1649).

Leven, Loch, two lochs of Scotland. **1,** in Highland region, extends 14 km (9 mi) E from Loch Linnhe to Kinlochleven. **2,** in Fife region, with isl. castle in which Mary Queen of Scots was imprisoned (1567-8).

Leverhulme, William Hesketh Lever, 1st Viscount (1851-1925), English industrialist. Founded Lever Bros. Ltd. (1886), international soap manufacturers, which later became Unilever. Estab. (1888) model village, Port Sunlight, as part of benefits to employees.

Lévesque, René (1922-), Canadian politician. Left Liberal Party to found Parti Québecois (1967) with aim of Québec's secession from Canada. Became premier of Québec (1976).

Lévi-Strauss, Claude (1908-), French anthropologist, b. Belgium. Founded 'structural' method of analyzing cultures. Works incl. *Totemism* (1962), *The Raw and the Cooked* (1969).

Levites, in OT, descendants of Levi, son of Jacob and Leah. Hereditary religious caste, bearers of the Ark of the Covenant.

Leviticus, in OT, third book of Pentateuch, detailing duties and ceremonies of priests and Levites.

Lewes, town and admin. hq of East Sussex, SE England. Pop. 14,000. Has ruined 11th-cent. priory, Norman castle. Scene of defeat of Henry III by Simon de Montfort (1264).

Lewis, C[ecil] Day, *see* DAY-LEWIS, C[ECIL].

Lewis, C[live] S[taples] (1898-1963), English author, b. Ireland. Known for criticism, *eg The Allegory of Love* (1936), Christian apologetics, esp. *The Screwtape Letters* (1942), children's books, *eg The Lion, the Witch, and the Wardrobe* (1950).

Lewis, [Harry] Sinclair (1885-1951), American novelist. Known for satires of American life, *eg Main Street* (1920), *Babbitt* (1922). Nobel Prize for Literature (1930).

Lewis, [Percy] Wyndham (1884-1957), English painter, author, b. US. Leader of vorticist painting movement. Edited magazine *Blast* (1914-15) with Ezra Pound. Wrote novels, *eg The Apes of God* (1930), *The Childermass* (1928).

Lewis, *see* LEWIS WITH HARRIS.

Lewis and Clark Expedition, exploring expedition (1803-6) across North America led by Meriwether Lewis (1774-1809) and William Clark (1770-1838). They followed Missouri R. to its source, crossed continental divide, and explored Columbia R. from its source to Pacific.

Lewisham, bor. of SE Greater London, England. Pop. 240,000.

Lewis with Harris, largest isl. of Outer Hebrides, NW Scotland, in WESTERN ISLES. Area 2137 sq km (825 sq mi); main town Stornoway. Mainly peat bog, moorland. Crofting, fishing industs.; Harris Tweed mfg.

Lexington, *see* BOSTON.

Leyden, *see* LEIDEN.

Lhasa, cap. of Tibet auton. region, SW China. Pop. 120,000. Alt. 3600 m (11,800 ft). Trade, religious centre; Lamaist temple, monasteries, palace of Dalai Lama.

Liaoning, maritime prov. of NE China. Area *c* 230,500 sq km (89,000 sq mi); pop.

28,000,000; cap. Shenyang. Heavily industrialized; major coal, iron ore, paper producer. Soya beans major crop.

libel, in law, one of two types of defamation (exposure to hatred, contempt, ridicule or material loss), other being slander. Libel must take permanent form, *eg* writing, picture, tape, film, whereas slander consists in utterance (by speech, gesture, *etc*) of defamatory statement. Both, to be actionable, must affect living individual (*eg* relative of defamed deceased). Slander is a civil offence, libel may be criminal, *eg* if likely to cause breach of the peace. Defences incl. truth, fair comment, qualified privilege.

liberalism, philosophy or movement advocating individual freedom. Theory based on LOCKE's doctrine involving freedom from restraint on life, health, liberty, property. In politics, manifested in parties pressing for democratic govt. and gradual reform of social institutions. Influence of utilitarians (esp. Bentham, Mill) enabled movement to promote state-controlled social measures in early 19th cent. Economic policies founded on opposition to state regulation. In UK, **Liberal Party** developed from WHIG PARTY after Reform Bill (1832), declining in 20th cent. with rise of Labour Party. Prominent leaders incl. Palmerston, Gladstone, Lloyd George. Liberalism in W Europe associated with nationalist movements in 19th cent. In British Commonwealth, Liberal parties achieved major party status, often forming govts., *eg* Canada (formed in 1850s) and Australia (founded 1944).

Liberia

Liberia, republic of W Africa. Area 111,300 sq km (43,000 sq mi); pop. 1,742,000; cap. Monrovia. Languages: tribal, English. Religions: animist, Islam. Coastal plain, inland plateaux; extensive rain forest. Main food crop rice; exports iron ore, gold, diamonds. Major rubber-producing indust. from 1925; large merchant fleet using 'flag of convenience'. Founded (1822) as colony for freed American slaves; independent republic from 1847.

libido, in psychology, term used by Freud to denote energy of sexual and creative instincts, as opposed to death instinct destructive drive.

Libra, *see* ZODIAC.

library, organized collection of books and other written material. Earliest known library was collection of clay tablets in Babylonia (21st cent. BC). Noted ancient examples incl. that of Assurbanipal (d. 626 BC) at Nineveh and those at Alexandria and Pergamum. Public libraries estab. in Greece (330 BC) and at Rome. Oldest existing public library of Europe is that of Vatican (15th cent.) with many univ. libraries estab. earlier, *eg* Sorbonne (1257). Modern libraries incl. Bodleian (Oxford), Bibliothèque Nationale (Paris), British Library (London), Library of Congress (Washington).

Libreville, cap. of Gabon, on estuary of R Gabon. Pop. 186,000. Port, exports timber palm oil; commercial, admin. centre. Founded (1848) by freed slaves.

Libya

Libya, republic of N Africa. Area 1,759,500 sq km (679,350 sq mi); pop. 2,748,000; cap. Tripoli. Language: Arabic. Religion: Islam. Fertile coastal strip; interior mainly desert (Libyan, Sahara) with some oases. Grain, fruit growing; major producer of oil, natural gas. Under Turkish rule from 16th cent.; taken by Italy 1912. Scene of heavy fighting in WWII; under Franco-British military govt., then UN rule, 1943-51. Federal kingdom of Libya estab. 1951 comprising Cyrenaica, Fezzan, Tripolitania provs.; unitary state from 1963. Republic proclaimed (1969) after military coup.

lichee, *see* LITCHI.

lichen, any of large group (Lichenes) of dual plants composed of a particular alga (blue-green or green) and particular fungus growing in SYMBIOSIS. The algal cells manufacture food sugars while the fungus forms a protective shell. Typically greyish-green, grows on rocks or trees from Arctic to tropical regions.

Lichtenstein, Roy (1923-), American painter, sculptor. A leading exponent of pop art, uses magnification of coarsel

Lichen

screened picture to bring out round dots and primary colours. Works incl. *Whaam!*, based on comic strips.

icorice, *see* LIQUORICE.

idice, village of W Czechoslovakia. Wholly destroyed in Nazi massacre after assassination of local Nazi leader (1942). Rebuilt after war.

ie, Trygve Halvdan (1896-1968), Norwegian statesman. First secretary-general of the UN (1946-53).

iebig, Justus von (1803-73), German chemist. Developed methods of quantitative organic analysis. Pioneer of chemical methods in physiology and agric.

iebknecht, Wilhelm (1826-1900), German politician. Founded (with August Bebel) German Social Democratic Labour Party (1869). His son, **Karl Liebknecht** (1871-1919), formed communist Spartacus party (1916). Led, with Rosa LUXEMBURG, Spartacist insurrection against govt. Killed after arrest by army officers.

Liechtenstein

iechtenstein, independent principality of WC Europe, in Rhaetian Alps. Area 166 sq km (64 sq mi); pop. 25,000; cap. Vaduz. Language: German. Religion: RC. Cereals, wine; tourism. Created 1719 from union of Vaduz, Schellenberg countships; independent 1866; joined Swiss customs union 1923.

iège (Flem. *Luik*), city of E Belgium, on R. Meuse and Albert Canal, cap. of Liège prov. Pop. 433,000. Coal region; machinery, arms mfg.; univ. (1817). Centre of Walloon culture.

Liffey, river of E Irish Republic, flows 80 km (50 mi) from Wicklow Mountains via Dublin to Dublin Bay; 3 power stations on river.

Lifford, co. town of Donegal, N Irish Republic, on R. Foyle. Pop. 1000.

ligament, short band of tough fibrous tissue connecting 2 bones at a joint, or holding an organ, *eg* liver, spleen, in position.

light, electromagnetic radiation which is detectable by the eye; variation in its wavelength produces sensation of colour. According to quantum theory, light consists of discrete bundles of energy (photons) and the energy of each photon is proportional to frequency of the light. In this theory, light exhibits both wave-like and particle-like properties. Speed of light is 3×10^{10} cm/sec (186,000 mi/sec).

lighthouse, structure in or adjacent to navigable waters, equipped to give optical or, more recently, radio-electrical guidance to ships (*see* RADIO RANGE). Identified by characteristic light flashes, fog sirens, radio signals. Now largely automatic. First lighthouse was Pharos of Alexandria (*c* 280 BC); first British was Eddystone (1698).

lightning, electrical discharge in the atmosphere. May be from one part of cloud to another, from cloud to cloud, or from cloud to Earth. Types incl. forked, sheet lightning; both are accompanied by thunder. Much rarer ball lightning sometimes seen as moving luminous ball, which may disintegrate explosively.

light year, distance travelled by light in 1 year; equals *c* 9.46×10^{12} km (5.88×10^{12} mi). Measure of distance in astronomy.

lignite or **brown coal,** soft, brownish-black fossil fuel intermediate between peat and COAL. Has low carbon content, burns with smoky flame and has low heat-producing capacity.

lignum vitae, hard wood of tropical American evergreen trees of genus *Guaiacum*. Used for pulleys, chopping boards; contains resin used medicinally.

Liguria, region of NW Italy, cap. Genoa. Alps in W, Apennines in E, Italian Riviera in S. Olives, vines, fruit, flowers; shipbuilding, chemicals. Celtic inhabitants conquered by Romans 2nd cent. BC; dominated by Genoa in Middle Ages; annexed by Sardinia 1815.

Ligurian Sea, arm of Mediterranean Sea, between Liguria, Tuscany, and Corsica. Incl. Gulf of Genoa; Italian Riviera on N shores.

lilac, any of genus *Syringa* of trees or shrubs of olive family, esp. *S. vulgaris* native to Europe and Asia. Has cone-shaped clusters of blue, pink or white fragrant flowers and very hard wood.

Lilith, Jewish female demon. In some traditions, 1st wife of Adam; later folklore makes her a vampire child-killer.

Lille, city of N France, cap. of Nord dept. Pop. 929,000. Forms conurbation with Roubaix, Tourcoing; major textile mfg., engineering centre; coalfield nearby. Citadel, univ. (1808).

Lilongwe, cap. of Malawi. Pop. 103,000. Admin. centre, agric. coll. Founded 1947.

lily, any of genus *Lilium* of perennial, bulbous plants. Native to N temperate zones. Showy, trumpet-shaped flowers. Name also used for many unrelated lily-like flowers esp. of AMARYLLIS genus.

lily of the valley, *Convallaria majalis*, perennial plant of lily family. Native to Europe, N Asia and US. Dark green leaves with bell-shaped, fragrant, white flowers.

Lima, cap. of Peru, with Pacific port at Callao. Pop. 3,303,000. Commercial, indust. centre; oil refining, textile mfg. Founded by Pizarro (1535), centre of Spanish colonial power in South America until 19th cent. Has cathedral, univ. (1551).

Limbo, in some Christian theologies, region bordering on hell, where unbaptized children and righteous people who lived before Jesus dwell after death.

lime or **linden,** any of genus *Tilia* of tall deciduous trees native to N temperate regions. Heart-shaped leaves, white fragrant flowers. Common lime, *T. europaea,* yields whitewood used in furniture. Also, small, thorny, semitropical tree, *Citrus aurantifolia,* bearing small, lemon-shaped, greenish-yellow citrus fruit rich in vitamin C.

lime, quicklime or **calcium oxide** (CaO), white solid made by heating calcium carbonate (limestone). Combines with water to form calcium hydroxide (slaked lime). Used to make mortar, cement and to neutralize acidic soil.

Limerick (*Luimneach*), county of Munster prov., SW Irish Republic. Area 2686 sq km (1037 sq mi); pop. 157,000. Galty Mountains in SE; has part of fertile Golden Vale. Agric., salmon fishing. Co. town **Limerick,** on Shannon estuary. Pop. 61,000. Port, shipbuilding; tanning, curing industs. Once cap. of Munster kingdom. Norman castle; Protestant, RC cathedrals.

limerick, humorous, usually epigrammatic poem of 5 lines of mixed iambic and anapestic metre with rhyme scheme aabba. Popularized by Edward Lear.

limestone, sedimentary rock composed wholly or mainly of calcium carbonate. Formed from remains of marine organisms, *eg* shells, skeletons, by chemical precipitation, or by mechanical deposition. Varieties incl. chalk, dolomite, marble; used as building stone, in lime and cement mfg.

Limoges, city of C France, on R. Vienne, cap. of Haute-Vienne dept. Pop. 165,000. Enamelling indust. (estab. 13th cent.); porcelain mfg. (estab. 18th cent.) using local kaolin. Cathedral (13th cent.), univ.

limonite, iron ore mineral, any of several mixtures of iron oxides and iron hydroxides. Normally brownish with yellow streak; formed by weathering o iron-rich minerals. Used as source of ochre pigment, iron.

limpet, marine gastropod mollusc wit flattened cone-shaped shell. Uses flesh foot to adhere to rocks. Used for bait an food.

Limpopo or **Crocodile,** river of SE Africa Flows *c* 1600 km (1000 mi) from Transvaal South Africa to Indian Ocean in S Mozambique. Forms part of South Africa Botswana border, all of South Africa Zimbabwe border.

Linacre, Thomas (*c* 1460-1524), Englis humanist, physician. Founder of Roya College of Physicians (1518).

Lincoln, Abraham (1809-65), America statesman, president (1861-5). Electe president shortly before secession o Southern states and outbreak of CIVIL WAR Tenure marked by conflicts over policies but he eventually acquired almos dictatorial control. Morally justified Unio cause with EMANCIPATION PROCLAMATIO freeing slaves and GETTYSBURG Addres (1863). After re-election (1864), opposed b Republican radicals for policy seeming t favour leniency towards the South. Assassinated (April, 1865) by John Wilkes Booth.

Lincoln, cap. of Nebraska, US. Pop. 182,000 In prairie region; industs. incl. foo processing, flour milling.

Lincolnshire, county of E England. Are 5885 sq km (2272 sq mi); pop. 530,000. Wold in E; Fens in S; elsewhere fertile lowlanc Agric., livestock; fishing; iron, steel industs Co. town **Lincoln,** on R. Witham. Pop 72,000. Agric. processing, machinery. Wa Roman *Lindum;* 11th-cent. cathedral.

Lincoln's Inn, *see* INNS OF COURT.

Lindbergh, Charles Augustus (1902-74 American aviator. Made 1st sol transatlantic, non-stop flight (1927). His so died (1932) in prominent kidnapping.

linden, *see* LIME.

Lindisfarne or **Holy Island,** off Northum berland, NE England. Causeway t mainland. Monastery estab. 635 by S Aidan; priory (1083); Lindisfarne Gospel (7th cent.) now in British Museum.

Line Islands, group of coral isls. in C Pacifi Ocean. Christmas, Fanning, Washingtc isls. part of Kiribati. Kingman Reef, Jarvi Palmyra isls. admin. by US. Remainde disputed by US, UK.

linen, fabric made from fibre of FLAX plan Uneven texture, durable and cris Introduced to N Europe by Romans, widel used in Middle Ages. Ireland is chie producer of fabric; Belgium produce finest fibre.

ling, large edible fish of cod family. Commo ling, *Molva molva,* found in Europea waters. Name also applied to burbot.

lingua franca, spoken language allowin communication between people mutually unintelligible languages. Origina ly applied to hybrid language (inc Turkish, French, Spanish, Arabic e ements) used by traders in E Mediterr nean. Modern examples incl. use of English in science and commerce.

linguistics, science of LANGUAGE, concerned both with its structure (synchronic analysis) and its hist. development (diachronic). In 19th cent., comparative philology estab. generic relations between languages, *eg* Indo-European family. SAUSSURE developed structural, synchronic approach to language which has subsequently predominated. *See* CHOMSKY, PHONETICS, SEMANTICS.

Linköping, town of SE Sweden. Pop. 111,000. Railway jct., engineering; textiles; tobacco. Cathedral (13th cent.).

Linnaeus, Carolus, orig. Karl von Linné (1707-78), Swedish taxonomist. Estab. binomial nomenclature principle of botanical and zoological classification.

linnet, *Acanthis cannabina,* small songbird of finch family, found in open countryside of Europe and W Asia.

Lin Piao (1908-71), Chinese military and political leader. Became defence minister (1959). Ranked second to Mao Tse-tung in Communist Party hierarchy; considered Mao's political successor. Said to have died in plane crash in Mongolia; may have been removed in party purge.

linseed, seed of common FLAX plant which yields an oil used in paint, varnish and linoleum. After oil extraction, residue is used in cattle feed as linseed cake.

Linz, city of N Austria, on R. Danube, cap. of Upper Austria prov. Pop. 208,000. River port; produces iron, steel, machinery.

lion, *Panthera leo,* large carnivore of cat family; once widespread, now found in Africa S of Sahara and NW India. Yellow to brown in colour; male usually has black or tawny mane. Social, lives in group called pride. Hunts zebras, wildebeeste, *etc*; old or wounded animals may attack man.

Lipari Islands or **Aeolian Islands,** isl. group of SW Italy, in Tyrrhenian Sea. Incl. active volcanoes (Stromboli, Vulcano). Exports pumice stone, wine. Traditional home of Aeolus, the wind god.

Lippi, Fra Filippo (*c* 1406-69), Italian painter. Master of colour and line; masterpiece is fresco series in the choir of Prato Cathedral (1452-*c* 1465). His son, **Filippino Lippi** (*c* 1457-1504), was also a Florentine painter. Work incl. frescoes in Florence and Rome.

liquefaction of gases, process of changing gases to liquid state. Gases can be liquefied by application of pressure provided their CRITICAL TEMPERATURE is not exceeded.

liquid, state of matter intermediate between gas and solid. In a liquid, molecules are free to move with respect to each other but are restricted by cohesive forces from unlimited expansion as in a gas.

liquorice or **licorice,** dried root of leguminous plant, *Glycyrrhiza glabra,* of Europe and Asia. Used in confectionery and medicine.

Lisbon (*Lisboa*), cap. of Portugal, at mouth of R. Tagus. Pop. 1,612,000. Indust., commercial centre; port, exports wine, olive oil, cork. Taken from Moors 1147; cap. from 1260. Rebuilt after 1755 earthquake; floods 1967. Univ. (1290).

Lisburn, town of W Northern Ireland, on R. Lagan. Pop. 29,000. In former Co. Antrim. Linen mfg. Has 17th-cent. Protestant cathedral.

Lister, Joseph, 1st Baron Lister (1827-1912), English surgeon. Founded antiseptic surgery; used carbolic acid (1865) and heat to sterilize instruments to prevent septic infection of wounds.

Liszt, Franz (1811-86), Hungarian pianist, composer. Protégés incl. Wagner, who married his daughter Cosima. His music is highly romantic and incl. many virtuoso piano pieces, *eg* 'Hungarian Rhapsodies', as well as songs, choral and orchestral music (esp. symphonic poems).

Li Tai Po or **Li Po** (*c* 700-62), Chinese poet. Wrote great number of poems (mostly lost) celebrating natural beauty, wisdom found in drunkenness, rejection of duty, preferment.

litchi, lychee or **lichee,** *Litchi chinensis,* Chinese tree, now grown in Florida and California. Cultivated for pulpy fruit enclosed in thin, brittle shell.

literature, all writings in prose or verse, esp. those of imaginative or critical character, often distinguished from scientific writing, news reporting, *etc*. Historically chief vehicle for transmitting and conserving culture of society, enabling much more complex and complete records to be kept than society relying on oral, pictorial transmission.

lithium (Li), soft metallic element, lightest metal known; at. no. 3, at. wt. 6.94. Chemically similar to sodium, but less active. Used in alloys; compounds used in nuclear research.

lithography, process of printing from a flat stone or metallic plate. Design is applied to surface with greasy material and surface is then wetted. Greasy ink is applied and is absorbed by greasy parts of surface but repelled by wet parts. Prints are then taken from the surface. Most modern lithography is offset, design being transferred from metal plate to rubber-covered cylinder, then to the paper. Technique invented by Aloys Senefelder (1796).

Lithuanian Soviet Socialist Republic, constituent republic of W USSR. Area *c* 65,200 sq km (25,200 sq mi); pop. 3,399,000; cap. Vilnius. Largely flatland, drained by R. Neman; formerly mainly agric., indust. development from 1940. In 13th cent. was grand duchy formed to oppose Teutonic knights; became powerful and expanded in 14th cent. Merged with Poland (1569); passed to Russia after Polish partition (1795). Independent (1918-40) until incorporated into USSR.

litmus, colouring matter obtained from various lichens. Used as acid-base indicator in chemical analysis; acids turn it red, bases blue.

litre, unit of liquid capacity in metric system. Originally defined as volume occupied by 1 kilogram of water at 4° C; now defined as 1000 cubic cm; 1 litre = *c* 1.76 pints.

Little Bighorn, *see* CUSTER.

Little Rock, cap. of Arkansas, US; on Arkansas R. Pop. 348,000. Commercial centre; cotton, bauxite, coal trade centre; clothing mfg.

Liu Shao-chi (*c* 1898-*c* 1974), Chinese political leader. Chairman of Chinese People's Republic (1959-68); deposed during Cultural Revolution.

liver, large gland of vertebrates. In man, opens off beginning of small intestine. Functions incl. formation and secretion of bile, storage of glucose in form of glycogen, synthesis of blood proteins, storage of iron, and breakdown of haemoglobin from worn-out red blood cells.

Liverpool, Robert Banks Jenkinson, 2nd Earl of (1770-1828), British statesman, PM (1812-27). Early years of his Tory admin. were marked by introduction of Corn Laws and repressive measures against unrest (1815-20). Later took more liberal line.

Liverpool, city of Merseyside met. county, NW England, on R. Mersey. Pop. 561,000. Major seaport; indust. centre; road tunnel to Birkenhead. Has Anglican, RC cathedrals; univ. (1903).

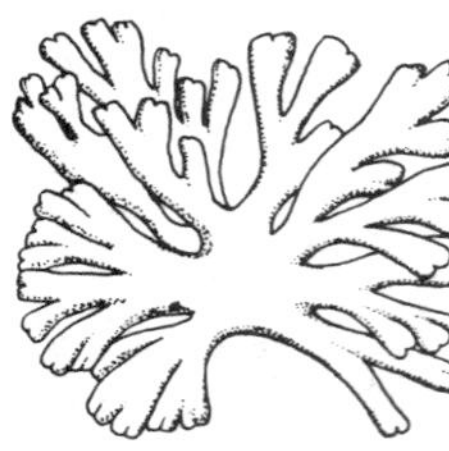

Liverwort

liverwort, any plant of class Hepaticae of flowerless, moss-like plants. Grows on moist ground or tree-trunks. Name is also applied to unrelated flowering plants of buttercup family of genus *Hepatica*.

Livingstone, David (1813-73), Scottish missionary and explorer. Journeyed extensively in C and S Africa; believed in ending slave trade by estab. Christianity and legitimate commerce in its place. Reached L. Ngami (1849), R. Zambezi (1851); led 3 expeditions, discovering Victoria Falls (1855), L. Nyasa (1859). Set out (1866) to seek Nile's source; met by H.M. Stanley at Ujiji (1871).

Livingstone, *see* MARAMBA.

Livonia, region of NE Europe, comprising modern Estonian SSR and N Latvian SSR. Conquered by Livonian Brothers of the Sword in 13th cent., later disputed by Sweden, Russia and Poland; ceded t Russia in 1721.

Livorno (Eng., Leghorn), town of Tuscany NW Italy, on Ligurian Sea. Cap. of Livorn prov. Pop. 178,000. Port, exports wine, oliv oil, marble; resort; naval academy.

Livy, full name Titus Livius (59 BC–AD 17) Roman historian. Wrote *History of Rom* in 142 volumes, covering period fron arrival of Aeneas to death of Drusus (BC). Only 35 volumes survive.

lizard, reptile of suborder Lacertilia, incl gecko, iguana, monitor. Scaly skin, lon body and tail; usually 4-legged, but som species legless, *eg* snake-like slow-worm.

Lizard Point, headland of Cornwall, SV England. Most S point in England.

Ljubljana (Ger. *Laibach*), city of NV Yugoslavia, on R. Sava, cap. of Slovenia Pop. 213,000. Cultural, indust. centre; univ (1595). Under Habsburgs from 1277.

llama, *Lama peruana,* South America hoofed mammal of camel family Humpless, stands *c* 1.2 m/4 ft high a shoulder. Used as pack animal and fo wool, meat. Vicuña and guanaco ar related species.

Llandrindod Wells, spa town and admin. h of Powys, C Wales. Pop. 3500.

Llandudno, urban dist. of Gwynedd, N Wales. Pop. 19,000. Seaside resort.

Llanos, prairie of C Venezuela and Colombia, in Orinoco basin. Cattle.

Llewelyn ap Gruffydd (d. 1281), prince o North Wales. Succeeded his uncle as rule (1246). Recovered much of South an North Wales during Barons' War i England; recognized as prince of Wale (1267). Lost most of his lands in invasion c Edward I (1277).

Lloyd George, David, 1st Earl Lloyd George of Dwyfor (1863-1945), Britis statesman, PM (1916-22). Libera chancellor of the exchequer (1908-15 Rejection by House of Lords of his 190 budget, seeking to finance old-ag pensions, led to Parliament Act (1911) cu tailing power of Lords; also introduce health and unemployment insurance (*se* NATIONAL INSURANCE ACT). As PM c wartime coalition, unified Allied wa command; worked with Clemenceau an Wilson to draw up Treaty of VERSAILLE (1919). Achieved victory in 1918 electio but reliance on Conservatives led t disintegration of his support. Remained i Parliament until 1944.

Lloyd's, association of English insuranc underwriters, originally covering marin risks only, now issuing many types c insurance policy. Name derived from th coffee house, kept by Edward Lloyd in 18 cent., used as meeting place. *Lloyd Register of Shipping* is annual publicatio detailing information on world shipping.

loach, any of Cobitidae family of sma freshwater fish with several barbe around mouth. Found in Europe, Asia, Africa.

loam, type of soil, composed of sand, sil

clay and humus. Porous, retains moisture well, has good air circulation. Easily worked and fertile.

Lobachevski, Nikolai Ivanovich (1793-1856), Russian mathematician. Discovered a form of non-Euclidean geometry.

lobelia, genus of annual or perennial plants of bellflower family. Native to temperate regions. Small, rounded leaves with blue, red, yellow or white irregular flowers.

Lobito, port of W Angola, on Atlantic Ocean. Pop. 98,000. Exports minerals, coffee, maize. Terminus of trans-African railway from Mozambique.

lobotomy, surgical operation to treat certain severe psychoses. Consists of severing fibres between prefrontal lobes and rest of brain.

lobster, edible marine crustacean of Homaridae family with 5 pairs of jointed legs, 1st pair having pincer-like jaws. Greenish or grey when alive, turns red when boiled.

Locarno, town of S Switzerland, on L. Maggiore. Pop. 14,000. Tourism.

Locarno Pact, series of treaties concluded among European nations (1925) at Locarno, Switzerland, guaranteeing German borders in W, as designated by Treaty of Versailles (1919). Germany also agreed to demilitarize Rhineland and was promised League of Nations membership.

Locke, John (1632-1704), English philosopher. Leading empiricist, wrote *Essay concerning Human Understanding* (1690), holding knowledge to be based on sense experience, not innate ideas. Opposed Hobbes in belief in equality of men and happiness of original natural state. *Two Treatises on Government* (1689) influenced framers of US Constitution.

lockjaw, *see* TETANUS.

Locomotive: Stephenson's Rocket (1829)

locomotive, powered vehicle designed to push or pull railway train. First practical example built by Trevithick (1804); other early models incl. Stephenson's *Rocket* (1829), all with steam as driving force. Electric locomotives (introduced *c* 1895) obtain power from 3rd rail or overhead wire. Diesel electric locomotives (*c* 1925), in which electric generator is driven by diesel engine, have extensively replaced steam locomotives.

locust, insect of short-horned grasshopper family (Acrididae). Often migrates in swarms, devastating large areas of crops. Species incl. migratory locust, *Locusta migratoria,* of Africa and S Asia.

lodestone, *see* MAGNETITE.

Łódź, city of C Poland, cap. of Łódź prov. Pop. 1,087,000. Major textile centre; electrical, metal industs.; univ. (1945). Under Russian rule 1815-1919.

loess, fine-grained, yellowish soil transported and deposited by wind. Originates as dust from arid areas or margins of ice-sheets; forms porous, well-graded, very fertile soils. Major deposits in N China, C Europe, C US. With high humus content, forms BLACK EARTH soils of USSR.

Lofoten Islands, isl. group of NW Norway, incl. Vesteralen Isls. Within Arctic Circle. Rich cod, herring fisheries.

Logan, Mount, in St Elias Mts., SW Yukon, Canada. Highest mountain in Canada, rising to 6050 m (19,850 ft).

loganberry, hybrid BLACKBERRY, *Rubus loganobaccus,* developed from American blackberry and raspberry. Acid, purplish-red fruit.

logarithm, power to which a given number b (base of logarithm) must be raised to produce that number; thus if $b^n = c$, n is said to be logarithm of c to base b, written $\log_b c$. Tables of logarithms used extensively to reduce problems in multiplication and division to easier problems in addition and subtraction; base of common logarithms is 10. Invented by John Napier.

logic, the science of correct reasoning. Aristotle founded systematic logic using SYLLOGISM and deductive method (reasoning from general to particular). His system still finds general acceptance, although attacked by medieval nominalists who argued that logic merely reflects structure of mind, not reality. Formal logic is not to be confused with truth as it requires no reference to content. More recent developments have been made by *eg* Boole, Russell, Wittgenstein.

logical positivism, modern school of philosophy which believes that the work of the philosopher is to clarify concepts rather than to make metaphysical speculations. Holds that for a proposition to be meaningful, it must be scientifically testable. Originated in Vienna Circle of 1920s. Exponents incl. Carnap, WITTGENSTEIN. *See* POSITIVISM.

logos (Gk., =word), in Greek philosophy, any immanent ordering principle in universe. In Christian theology, the link between God and man manifested in God's word becoming flesh in Jesus. Specifically stated in St John's Gospel.

Lohengrin, in medieval German legend, knight of Holy GRAIL who is led by a swan to save Princess Elsa from an unwanted suitor. Story is basis of Wagner's opera (1850).

Loire, longest river of France. Flows *c* 1005 km (625 mi) from Cévennes Mts. via Orléans, Tours, Nantes to Bay of Biscay at St Nazaire. With tributaries, incl. Allier, Cher, Vienne, drains much of France; limited navigation, seasonal flooding. Loire valley famous for wines and hist. châteaux.

Loki, in Norse myth, personification of evil and trickery.

Lollards, followers of John WYCLIFFE. Sect in England who anticipated some Reformation doctrines, *eg* the individual's direct responsibility to God, use of vernacular Bible as only reliable guide to faith. Attacked ecclesiastical wealth and monasticism; denied transubstantiation. Their persecution led to a minor rebellion in 1414, but movement had declined by 16th cent.

Lombards, Germanic people who originally inhabited lower basin of the Elbe. Under Alboin, invaded N Italy (568) and estab. kingdom of Lombardy. After threatening the power of the popes, they were conquered by Charlemagne, who took control of Italy.

Lombardy, region of N Italy, cap. Milan. Mountains, lakes, Alpine passes in N; tourism, h.e.p. Lombard Plain (Po basin) in S; irrigated agric. esp. maize, wheat, rice, flax; dairying. Italy's main indust. area, esp. textiles, chemicals, iron and steel. Taken by Romans 3rd cent. BC, by Charlemagne 774. Cities formed Lombard League in 12th cent., defeated Frederick I at Legnano (1176). Later ruled by Spain, France, Austria; annexed 1859 by Sardinia.

Lomé, cap. of Togo, on Bight of Benin. Pop. 135,000. Port, exports cocoa, coffee, copra; univ. of Benin (1970).

Lomé Convention, agreement on trade and economic cooperation between EEC and various Third World countries, signed in 1975.

Lomond, Loch, largest lake of Scotland, between Central, Strathclyde regions. Length 35 km (22 mi); tourist and recreation area.

London, Jack, full name John Griffith London (1876-1916), American author. Known for adventure novels incl. *The Call of the Wild* (1903), *White Fang* (1906).

London, cap. city of England and UK, on R. Thames. Greater London area 1579 sq km (610 sq mi); pop. 6,918,000. Major admin., commercial, indust., cultural centre; has univ. (1836). Governed from 1965 by Greater London Council; comprises City of London (pop. 5000), 32 bors.; incl. Middlesex, parts of Kent, Essex, Surrey, Hertfordshire. Roman *Londinium;* chief English city from reign of Alfred. Buildings incl. Tower of London, Westminster Abbey, St Paul's Cathedral (1710), Buckingham Palace (1703), Houses of Parliament (1852) GPO Tower (1964). Extensively rebuil after Great Plague, Fire (1665-6); damage in WWII air raids.

London, town of S Ontario; on Thames R Pop. 270,000. Railway jct.; indust. an commercial centre; food produce, textil mfg. Settled 1826. Seat of Univ. of Wester Ontario.

Londonderry or **Derry,** former county of N Northern Ireland. Hilly in S incl. Sperri Mts.; rivers incl. Foyle, Bann. Agric. distilling, fishing. Co. town wa **Londonderry,** on R. Foyle. Pop. 52,000 Port; shipbuilding; clothing mfg. Ha Protestant, RC cathedrals. Withstood sieg (1688-9) by James II. Scene of continuin religious conflict.

Long Beach, port of S California, US. Pop 359,000. Major oil, defence industs. Touris resort.

Longfellow, Henry Wadsworth (1807-82) American poet. Known for sentiment lyrics, narrative poems, *eg Evangelin* (1847), *Song of Hiawatha* (1855).

Longford, county of Leinster prov., C Iris Republic. Area 1044 sq km (403 sq mi); pop 31,000. Low-lying, peat bogs. Cattle, dairy ing. Co. town **Longford,** pop. 4000. Castl (17th cent.), RC cathedral.

Long Island, SE New York, US, separate from mainland by Long Isl. Sound. Lengt 190 km (118 mi); width 19-32 km (12-20 mi) Extends E from New York City (inc Brooklyn, Queen bors., Coney Isl. resort) Mainly residential and resort area, esp. i E. Has Kennedy, La Guardia airports.

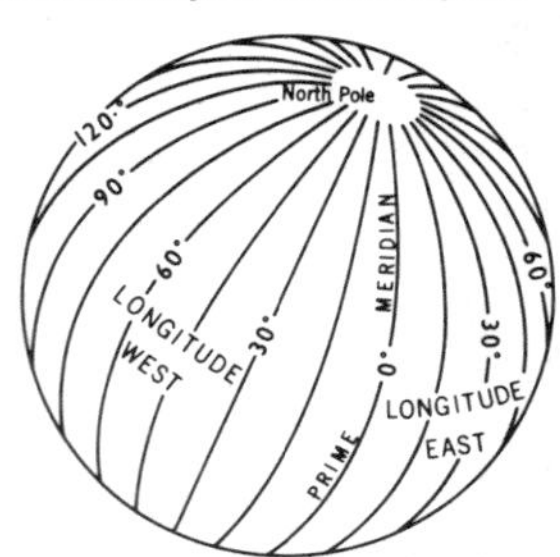

Degrees of longitude

longitude, in geography, angular distanc east or west of prime meridian of any poin on Earth's surface, measured from Earth centre. By international agreement, prim meridian (0°) runs through Greenwich England.

Long March, journey from Kiangsi prov. t Shensi prov., *c* 9600 km (6000 mi), mad (1934-5) by *c* 90,000 Chinese Communis soldiers, women and children. Under con stant threat of attack from Nationalis forces, less than half of them survive Mao Tse-tung estab. himself as Communis leader during march.

ong Parliament, name given to English Parliament (1640-60) whose opposition to Charles I led to Civil War. After expulsion of Presbyterian members (Pride's Purge, 1648), was known as Rump Parliament. Dissolved (1653) by Cromwell; reassembled (1659) and finally dissolved at Restoration (1660).

ong sight, *see* HYPERMETROPIA.

oofah, skeleton of dishcloth gourd of genus *Luffa*. Used as bath sponge.

oom, frame machine used for weaving cloth. Power loom was introduced (1785-7) by Cartwright. An attachment invented by J. M. Jacquard (1804), using punched cards and needles, made it possible to weave intricate patterns.

ope de Vega, *see* VEGA.

oquat, *Eriobotrya japonica,* small evergreen tree of rose family, native to China and Japan. Yellow fruit known as Japanese plum.

orca, Federico García, *see* GARCÍA LORCA.

ords, House of, *see* HOUSE OF LORDS.

ord's Prayer or **Pater Noster,** most widely known and used Christian prayer. Taught by Jesus to his disciples; part of Sermon on the Mount (Matthew 6: 9-13).

ord's Supper, *see* EUCHARIST.

orelei, rock on E bank of Rhine, West Germany, midway between Bingen and Koblenz. In legend, home of a siren who lured sailors onto reef below.

orenz, Konrad (1903-), Austrian zoologist. Estab. science of ethology, *ie* study of group behaviour patterns in animals. Works incl. *On Aggression* (1966). Nobel Prize for Physiology and Medicine (1973).

orient, town of Brittany, NW France, on Bay of Biscay. Pop. 106,000. Port, fishing indust.; naval base.

oris, tailless arboreal mammal of lemur group, genus *Loris*, found in SE Asia, India and Sri Lanka. Nocturnal, with large eyes and furry body.

orraine, Claude, *see* CLAUDE LORRAINE.

orraine (Ger. *Lothringen*), region and former prov. of E France, hist. cap. Nancy. Low plateau, rising to Vosges Mts. in E. Main rivers Meuse, Moselle. Rich iron ore deposits; coalmining in Saar basin. French prov. from 1766. Ceded with Alsace to Germany (1871), returned (1918). Again annexed during WWII.

ory or **lorikeet,** small brightly coloured parrot of Australasia with brush-tipped tongue used to gather nectar.

os Alamos, *see* SANTA FÉ.

os Angeles, city of S California, US; near Pacific. Pop. 2,727,000, with extensive suburbs 10,350,000; state's largest city. Shipping, communications centre; agric. trade, business centre; defence, film industs. Founded by Spanish Franciscan monks (1781). Became cap. of Mexican California (1845); captured by US forces (1846). Growth boosted with railway development and oil discovery. Has part of Univ. of California (1919).

ot, river of S France. Flows *c* 480 km (300 mi) from Cévennes via Cahors to R. Garonne. Fertile valley; vineyards.

Lothair I (795-855), Holy Roman emperor (840-55). From 817 ruled as joint emperor with his father, Louis I, on whose death empire was divided between Lothair and his brothers, Charles and Louis the German. Lothair's attempts to reunite empire were resisted by his brothers.

Lothian, region of EC Scotland. Area 1753 sq km (677 sq mi); pop. 750,000; admin. hq Edinburgh. Created 1975, incl. former East Lothian, Midlothian, West Lothian.

lotus, various tropical African and Asiatic water or pond lilies. Species incl. Egyptian lotus, *Nymphaea lotus,* with white flowers, and Indian lotus, *Nelumbo nucifera*. Blossom symbolic in Indian art and religion.

Loughborough, town of Leicestershire, EC England. Pop. 46,000. Engineering; hosiery; bell foundry. Technological univ. (1964); teachers' coll.

Louis [I] the Pious (778-840), Holy Roman emperor (814-40). Succeeded father, Charlemagne.

Louis VII (*c* 1120-80), king of France (1137-80). Led disastrous 2nd Crusade (1147-9).

Louis [IX], St (1214-70), king of France (1226-70). Led 7th Crusade to Egypt, but was captured (1250) and did not return to France until 1254.

Louis XI (1423-83), king of France (1461-83). Successfully curtailed power of great nobles, led by Charles the Bold of Burgundy.

Louis XIII (1601-43), king of France (1610-43). Assumed power in 1617 following regency of mother, Marie de' Medici. Policy controlled by her protégé, Richelieu, from 1624.

Louis XIV (1638-1715), king of France (1643-1715). During his minority, France was ruled by MAZARIN. Known as the 'Sun King', Louis assumed absolute control after 1661; rule marked by territ. expansion with development of army and economic reform until death of COLBERT. Louis' ambitions in Europe led to numerous wars (1683-1715), esp. with Spain, Holland and England. War of Spanish Succession (1701-14), by which he secured Spanish throne for his grandson, led to military weakness and huge debts. Under his patronage, arts and sciences flourished; had magnificent palace built at Versailles.

Louis XV (1710-74), king of France (1715-74). During minority, left govt. to duke of Orléans (d. 1723) and Cardinal Fleury. After Fleury's death (1743), attempted to rule alone but was dominated by mistresses such as Mme de Pompadour. Lost possessions in Canada and India after Seven Years War (1756-63). Personal extravagance and expenditure on war left France on verge of bankruptcy.

Louis XVI (1754-93), king of France (1774-92). Dominated by wife, Marie Antoinette, and his court. Forced to recall Estates-General (1789), opening way for French Revolution. At first still popular with the people, weakened his position by attempting to flee country (1791); recaptured; agreed to become constitutional monarch. Deposed (Sept. 1792); tried for treason and guillotined.

Louis XVII (1785-*c* 1795), titular king of France. Son of Louis XVI, he was imprisoned from 1792 until his death.

Louis XVIII (1755-1824), king of France (1814-24). Lived in exile (1791-1814); assumed royal title on death of Louis XVII. On fall of Napoleon (1814), ascended throne; expelled (1815) during Hundred Days. Restored by allies (June, 1815). Ruled moderately until 1820, after which he fell under control of reactionary ultra-royalists.

Louisiana, state of S US, on Gulf of Mexico. Area 125,675 sq km (48,523 sq mi); pop. 3,928,000; cap. Baton Rouge; chief city New Orleans. Coastal plain dominated by Mississippi delta (subject to floods). Forestry; agric. incl. cotton, rice, sugar cane; salt, petroleum, sulphur mining. Claimed by France in 17th cent.; part of Louisiana Purchase by US in 1803. Admitted as 18th state (1812).

Louisiana Purchase, land bought from France by US in 1803 for 15 million dollars. Extended from Mississippi to Rocky Mts., and from Gulf of Mexico to Canada.

Louis Napoleon, *see* NAPOLEON III.

Louis Philippe (1773-1850), king of France (1830-48), known as the Citizen King. As Duc d'Orléans, supported deposition of Charles X (1830) and was chosen king. Reign, known as 'July Monarchy', characterized by middle-class ideals. Increasing opposition turned him from liberalism to absolutism. Forced to abdicate after Revolution of 1848. Fled to England.

Louisville, city of N Kentucky, US; on Ohio R. Pop. 888,000. Tobacco, whisky processing; meat packing, chemical mfg. Has annual Kentucky Derby horse race. Nearby is Fort Knox (US gold bullion stores).

Lourdes, town of SW France, at foot of Pyrenees. Pop. 18,000. Site of St Bernadette's vision of the Virgin (1858); now major pilgrimage centre.

Lourenço Marques, *see* MAPUTO.

louse, small wingless insect with sucking mouthparts. Divided into 2 orders: Anoplura, blood-sucking lice, parasitic on most mammals; Mallophaga, biting lice, parasitic mainly on birds. Species incl. *Pediculus capitis,* human head louse.

Louth, county of Leinster prov., NE Irish Republic. Area 821 sq km (317 sq mi); pop. 86,000; co. town Dundalk. Flat, low-lying. Dairying, fishing.

Louvain (Flem. *Leuven*), town of C Belgium, on R. Dyle. Pop. 86,000. Brewing, lace mfg. Medieval cloth centre, cap. of Brabant 11th-15th cents. RC univ. (1426).

Louvre, former French royal palace in Paris, opened to the public as an art museum in 1793. Contains one of the fines[t] collections in world.

love bird, small Old World parrot, es[p.] African genus *Agapornis.* Frequently kep[t] as cage bird.

love-in-a-mist, *Nigella damascena,* annua[l] garden plant of buttercup family. Feather[y] leaves, blue or white flowers.

Lovelace, Richard (1618-58), English poe[t.] Known for Cavalier lyrics, esp. 'T[o] Lucasta, Going to the Wars', 'To Althea from Prison'.

Low, Sir David (1891-1963), British politica[l] cartoonist, b. New Zealand. Create[d] 'Colonel Blimp', TUC horse.

Low Countries, region of NW Europe. Inc[l.] NETHERLANDS, BELGIUM, LUXEMBOURG. Als[o] *see* BRABANT, FLANDERS, HOLLAND.

Lowell, prominent American family of Ne[w] England. **James Russell Lowell** (1819-91[)] was a poet. Wrote *Biglow Papers* (1848) i[n] Yankee dialect, *The Vision of Sir Launfa[l]* (1848), *A Fable for Critics* (1848). **Perciva[l] Lowell** (1855-1916) was an astronome[r.] Founded Lowell Observatory, Arizon[a] (1894). Predicted existence of planet Pluto[.] His sister, **Amy [Lawrence] Lowel[l]** (1874-1925), was a poet, a member of th[e] IMAGISTS.

Lowell, Robert [Traill Spence] (1917-77[)] American poet. Works incl. *Lord Weary['s] Castle* (1946), *The Mills of the Kavanaugh[s]* (1951), verse, prose autobiog. *Life Studie[s]* (1959).

Lower California, *see* BAJA CALIFORNIA.

Lower Hutt, city and indust. centre of S[W] North Isl., New Zealand, on Por[t] Nicholson. Pop. 59,000. Engineering, foo[d] processing, car assembly.

Lowestoft, town of Suffolk, E England. Pop[.] 52,000. Port, resort on North Sea. Fishing[,] yachting.

Lowry, Laurence Stephen (1887-1976[)] English artist. Known for his seemingl[y] naive paintings of the industrial landscap[e] and its inhabitants.

Loyalists, *see* UNITED EMPIRE LOYALISTS.

Loyalty Islands (Fr. *Îles Loyauté*), isl. grou[p] of SW Pacific Ocean, dependency of Ne[w] Caledonia. Area *c* 2070 sq km (800 sq mi[)] main isls. Lifu, Maré, Uvéa. Chief crop[s] copra, rubber, sugar cane.

Loyola, St Ignatius of, *see* IGNATIUS.

LSD, *see* LYSERGIC ACID DIETHYLAMIDE.

Luanda, São Paulo de, cap. of Angola, o[n] Atlantic Ocean. Pop. 475,000. Admin[.] commercial centre; port, exports coffe[e,] cotton, minerals; oil refining. Founde[d] 1575.

Lübeck, city of N West Germany, on R[.] Trave. Pop. 230,000. Linked by canal (190[0)] to R. Elbe; port, shipbuilding, foo[d] processing. Chief city of Hanseatic Leagu[e] (1241-1630). Medieval buildings incl. ca[-] thedral, town hall.

Lublin, city of SE Poland, cap. of Lubli[n] prov. Pop. 277,000. Railway jct., agri[c.] machinery, textile mfg.; univ. (1944[)] Under Russian rule 1815-1919.

lubricants, substances used to reduc[e]

friction between moving surfaces. May be liquid (oil), semi-solid (grease), solid, *eg* colloidal graphite in water (aquadag) or oil (oildag). Recently gas at pressure has been used in high speed machinery.

Lubumbashi, city of SE Zaïre, cap. of Shaba region. Pop. 404,000. Mineral refining centre in Katanga mining dist.; food processing, RC cathedral. Founded (1910) as Elisabethville, renamed 1966.

Lucan, full name Marcus Annaeus Lucanus (AD 39-65), Roman poet, b. Spain. His epic *Pharsalia* deals with war between Caesar and Pompey.

Lucas van Leyden (1494-1533), Dutch painter, engraver. Influenced by Dürer in woodcuts and engravings; paintings reflect beginnings of Dutch genre art.

Lucerne (Ger. *Luzern*), town of C Switzerland, on L. Lucerne, cap. of Lucerne canton. Pop. 158,000. Tourism, printing, machinery. Joined Swiss Confederation 1332.

Lucerne, Lake (Ger. *Vierwaldstättersee*), in C Switzerland. Area 111 sq km (43 sq mi).

lucerne, *see* ALFALFA.

Lucian (*fl* 2nd cent.), Greek prose writer. Wrote scathing indictments of contemporary conditions, beliefs, *eg Dialogues of the Dead*.

Lucifer, in OT book of Isaiah, figurative reference to king of Babylon, misconstrued to mean fallen angel; hence became a term for Satan. Also Roman name for Venus as morning star.

Lucknow, cap. of Uttar Pradesh, NC India. Pop. 749,000. Railway engineering; paper, carpet mfg. Cap. of Oudh kingdom (1775-1856). British besieged in city for 5 months during Indian Mutiny until relieved in Nov. 1857.

Lucretius, full name Titus Lucretius Carus (*c* 95-*c* 55 BC), Roman poet. Known for *De rerum natura* expounding Epicurean philosophy.

Luddites, in English history, name given to those taking part in machine-wrecking riots (1811-16). Rioters were protesting against low wages and unemployment attributed to introduction of textile-making machines. Named after mythical Ned Ludd.

Ludendorff, Erich (1865-1937), German general. Chief of staff in WWI, ably supporting Hindenburg's military successes. Backed Hitler's 'beer-hall putsch' (1923).

Ludwig I (1786-1868), king of Bavaria (1825-48). Initially a liberal, but later reactionary policies and scandalous affair with Lola MONTEZ led to enforced abdication.

Ludwig II (1845-86), king of Bavaria (1864-86). A liberal romantic, he lavished a fortune on the composer Wagner and the building of fairy-tale castles. Declared insane, and drowned himself.

Ludwigshafen, city of W West Germany, on R. Rhine, opposite Mannheim. Pop. 166,000. River port, major chemical indust., dyes, plastics.

Lugano, town of S Switzerland, on L. Lugano, near Italian border. Pop. 22,000. Tourist centre.

Lugansk, *see* VOROSHILOVGRAD.

lugworm or **lobworm,** tube-dwelling annelid worm, genus *Arenicola*, with bristly appendages on body; burrows into mud and sand. Used as bait.

Luik, *see* LIÈGE.

Luke, St (*fl* AD 1st cent.), Gentile physician, friend of St Mark and St Paul. Credited with authorship of 3rd Gospel of NT and Acts of the Apostles.

Luke, Gospel according to St, third of NT Gospels, attributed to St Luke. Longest and historically most detailed of the Gospels.

Luleå, town of NE Sweden, on Gulf of Bothnia at mouth of R. Lule. Pop. 67,000. Exports iron ore from Kiruna and Gällivare; timber, reindeer hides.

Lully, Jean Baptiste (1632-87), French composer, b. Italy. Court composer to Louis XIV. Pioneered opera in France; also helped to estab. ballet in his comedy-ballets, in association with Molière.

Luluabourg, *see* KANANGA.

lumbago, pain in the small of the back, often associated with pain down the leg. May be caused by back strain or pressure on nerves by a 'slipped disc'.

Lumière, Louis Jean (1864-1948), French cinema pioneer. With his brother, **Auguste Marie Louis Nicholas Lumière** (1862-1954), invented cinematograph in 1895, 1st device to project moving pictures onto screen.

luminosity, in astronomy, measure of actual quantity of light emitted by a star, irrespective of its distance from Earth. *See* MAGNITUDE.

luminous paint, paint containing a phosphorescent sulphide, usually of barium or calcium. After exposure to light it appears luminous in dark. The type used on watch faces is excited radioactively and does not need exposure to light.

Lumumba, Patrice Emergy (1925-61), Congolese politician. Became premier at independence of Congo. Involved in power struggle with Kasavubu. Arrested by Mobutu and murdered.

lunacy, *see* INSANITY.

Lund, town of SW Sweden. Pop. 78,000. Paper, furniture mfg.; printing, publishing. Cathedral (12th cent.). Univ. (1668).

Lüneburg Heath (*Lüneburger Heide*), sandy heath of NE West Germany, between Elbe and Aller rivers. Sheep grazing, potato growing. Site of German surrender (1945).

lungfish, any of various fish which have lungs as well as gills. Six freshwater species known, considered living fossils. Found in S America, Africa, Australia.

lungs, respiratory organs in air-breathing vertebrates. In humans, occupy most of thorax and are separated by heart. Carbon dioxide in blood is exchanged for oxygen as blood circulates through the air sacs (alveoli) of the lungs.

lupin, any of genus *Lupinus* of plants of Leguminosae family. Native to Mediterranean region and North America. Flowers, borne on long spike, may be a variety of colours.

Lusaka, cap. of Zambia. Pop. 401,000. Admin., commercial, communications centre; agric. market; univ. of Zambia (1966). Replaced Livingstone as cap. of Northern Rhodesia (1935).

Lushun, *see* LU-TA.

Lusitania, British liner sunk without warning off Irish coast by German submarine on 7th May, 1915. Almost 1200 people were killed, over 100 of them American. This act aroused considerable American hostility to Germany and helped bring US into WWI.

Lu-ta or **Lushun-Talien,** municipality of Liaoning prov., NW China comprising Lushun (formerly Port Arthur) and Talien. Pop. 1,650,000. Soya bean, grain, coal exports; oil refining. Important naval base and ice-free port at end of Liaotung penin. Part of Kwanfung lease (1898-1945) under Japanese; finally reintegrated into China 1955.

lute, string instrument shaped like half pear, with fretted finger-board; the strings, usually 6 in number, are plucked. Popular (15th-17th cents.), both as a solo instrument and for accompanying singers.

lutetium (Lu), metallic element of lanthanide series; at. no. 71, at. wt. 174.97. Discovered (1907).

Luther, Martin (1483-1546), German religious leader. Augustinian friar, teacher at Univ. of Wittenberg. Campaigned against sale of indulgences; nailed 95 theses to Wittenberg church door (regarded as start of Protestant Reformation). Initially sought reform within Church but excommunicated in 1521. Fled to Wartburg after refusing to retract statements at Diet of Worms. Translated NT into German. Endorsed Melanchthon's Augsburg Confession (1530), basis of Lutheranism.

Lutheranism, Protestant doctrine founded on teachings of Martin LUTHER and formulated in confessional Book of Concord (1580). Regards the Bible as only necessary guide to faith; holds the individual to be directly responsible to God and salvation to come through faith alone. Rejects transubstantiation and has no unified liturgical order. Flourishes primarily in Germany, Scandinavia and US.

Luthuli, Albert John (1899-1967), South African political leader. Openly opposed *apartheid*, advocating non-violent resistance. Kept under restriction after 1952; arrested for treason (1956) but acquitted (1959). Awarded Nobel Peace Prize (1960).

Luton, town of Bedfordshire, C England, on R. Lea. Pop. 166,000. Engineering, esp. car indust.; airport.

Lutyens, Sir Edwin Landseer (1869-1944), English architect. Designed countr houses, churches, office blocks *etc.* Work incl. imperial capital of India at New Delh

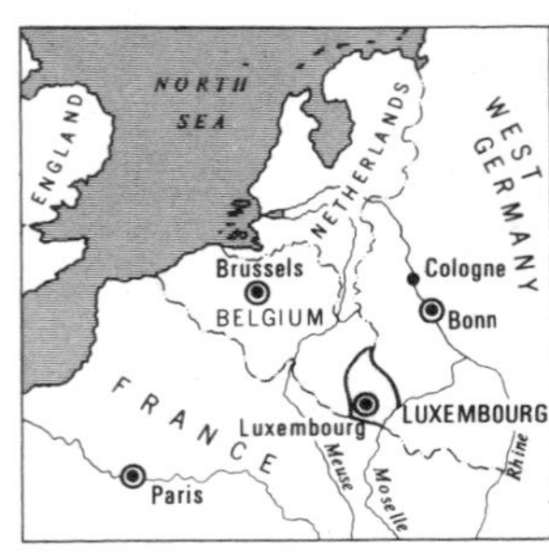

Luxembourg

Luxembourg, grand duchy of NW Europe Area 2587 sq km (999 sq mi); pop. 358,00 Language: Letzeburgesch (Ger. dialect Religion: RC. Agric., cattle; iron mining Duchy from 1354 (Habsburg from 15t cent.); grand duchy within Netherland from 1815; independent 1890. Occupied b Germans in both WWs. In Benelux custom union from 1948; member of EEC. Cap **Luxembourg,** on R. Alzette. Pop. 78,00 Cultural centre. Iron, steel indust. Hq. c ECSC, European Court of Justice. Palac (16th cent.); cathedral.

Luxemburg, Rosa (1870-1919), Germa revolutionary, b. Poland. A Marxist, sh founded the Spartacus League (1916) wit Karl LIEBKNECHT. Arrested and killed afte leading Spartacist insurrection.

Luxor, town of C Egypt, on R. Nile. Pop 30,000. Occupies part of site of ancient cit of THEBES.

Luzern, *see* LUCERNE.

Luzon, largest isl. of Philippines. Area 105,000 sq km (40,400 sq mi). Largel mountainous, rising to 2928 m (9606 ft Rich agric. areas produce rice, sugar can hemp; minerals incl. chromite, nicke copper. Chief city Manila. Scene of heav fighting in WWII.

Lvov, Prince Georgi Evgenyevic (1861-1925), Russian statesman. Le provisional govt. (Feb.-July, 1917) afte February uprising. Succeeded b Kerensky.

Lvov (Ger. *Lemberg*), city of USSR, W Ukrainian SSR. Pop. 667,000. Indust. centre oil refining, machinery mfg. Taken b Poles (1349), became cap. of Austria Galicia (1772-1919). Returned to Polan ceded to USSR (1945).

lychee, *see* LITCHI.

Lydgate, John (*c* 1370-*c* 1452), English poe monk. Very famous in own time but no eclipsed by his friend Chaucer. Prolifi writer, works incl. *The Fall of Princes.*

Lydia, *see* SARDIS.

Lyell, Sir Charles (1797-1875), Scottish geologist. Author of standard text *The Principles of Geology* (1830-3), expounding uniformitarianism theory of James HUTTON.

lymph, colourless fluid derived from blood plasma which has filtered through the capillary walls. Carried by lymphatic vessels to various parts of body where it distributes nutrients and oxygen to the tissues. Lymph nodes are organs in lymphatic vessels which collect bacteria from lymph; also produce lymphocytes, class of white blood cells important in formation of antibodies.

Lynch, John ('Jack') (1917-), Irish politician. Was finance minister in Fianna Fáil cabinet before succeeding Sean Lemass as PM (1966-73, 1977-9).

lynching, murder of accused person by mob action, without lawful trial. Practice of pioneers in US before rule of law as penalty for, *eg,* horse-stealing, rape. Common in S US after Civil War.

lynx, any of genus *Lynx* of wildcats with short tail, tufted ears. European lynx, *L. lynx,* found in N Europe and Siberia, now rare. Largest North American variety is Canadian lynx, *L. canadensis. See* BOBCAT.

Lyons, Joseph Aloysius (1879-1939), Australian statesman, PM (1932-9). Helped estab. United Australia party (1931), headed coalition govt.

Lyons (*Lyon*), city of EC France, at confluence of Rhône and Saône, cap. of Rhône dept. Pop. 1,152,000. River port, transport jct.; banking centre, major textile indust. (esp. silk, rayon), univ. (1808). Roman *Lugdunum,* founded *c* 43 BC. Cathedral (12th cent.).

lyre, ancient Greek stringed musical instrument, like a small portable harp but played with a plectrum. Also known in other ancient civilizations, incl. Assyria and Egypt, and in medieval Europe.

lyrebird, brightly coloured Australian bird, genus *Menura.* Male displays lyre-shaped tail during courtship dance, performed on specially built mound.

Lyrebird

Lysander (d. 395 BC), Spartan general. Commanded fleet which inflicted final defeat on Athens at Aegospotamos (405); captured Athens (404).

lysergic acid diethylamide or **LSD,** alkaloid synthesized from lysergic acid, which is found in the fungus ergot. Powerful hallucinogenic drug, capable of inducing delusions resembling those occurring in psychotic state.

M

Maas, *see* MEUSE.

Maastricht, city of SE Netherlands, on R. Maas, cap. of Limburg prov. Pop. 145,000. Railway, canal jct.; produces textiles, ceramics. Pop. massacred by Spanish 1579.

Mabuse, Jan, orig. Jan Gossaert (*c* 1478-*c* 1533), Flemish painter. Adopted style based on Italian Renaissance forms.

McAdam, John Loudon (1756-1836), Scottish engineer. Introduced (*c* 1815) improved roads made of crushed stone; known as 'macadam' roads.

MacAlpin, Kenneth (d. *c* 860), king of the Scots. Succeeded father in 832 or 834. United kingdoms of Scots and Picts *c* 844.

Macao, Portuguese colony of SE Asia on Chukiang (Pearl) estuary. Area 15 sq km (6 sq mi); pop. 276,000. Chief town Macao is largely coextensive with colony. Free port; trade, tourism centre; textile indust., gambling casinos. Leased by Portuguese (1557), *fl* as trade post until rise of neighbouring Hong Kong.

macaque, monkey of genus *Macaca* found mainly in India and SE Asia. Species incl. barbary ape of Gibraltar and rhesus monkey.

macaroni, *see* PASTA.

MacArthur, Douglas (1880-1964), American general. Chief of general staff (1930-5). Commanded US and Allied forces in SE Asia during WWII. Directed post-war occupation of Japan. Recalled (1951) from post as UN commander in Korea for public disagreement with President Truman.

Macaulay, Thomas Babington, Baron Macaulay of Rothley (1800-59), English historian. Known for Whig interpretation of history in *The History of England from the Accession of James the Second* (1849-61). Also wrote poetry, *Lays of Ancient Rome* (1842) and numerous essays.

macaw, brightly coloured long-tailed parrot of tropical Central and South America. Species incl. scarlet macaw, *Ara macao.*

Macbeth (d. 1057), king of Scotland. Killed Duncan I and took crown (1040). Defeated and killed by Duncan's son, Malcolm III.

Maccabees, Jewish family (*fl* 2nd cent. BC) founded by priest Mattathias (d. 166 BC). With sons, led opposition against Syrians. **Judas Maccabeus** (d. 161 BC) reoccupied Jerusalem, rededicated the Temple. **Simon Maccabeus** (d. 135 BC) estab. peace in Palestine.

Maccabees, last two books of OT Apocrypha. Covers history of MACCABEES.

McCarthy, Joseph Raymond (1909-57), American politician. As Republican senator for Wisconsin (1947-57), he claimed (1950) that state dept. had been infiltrated by Communists. Held Senate investigations

Macaw

of people suspected of subversion, accuse[d] many of Communist sympathies. Censure[d] by Senate (1954).

Macclesfield, town of Cheshire, W Englan[d]. Pop. 44,000. Textiles mfg.

McDiarmid, Hugh, pseud. of Christophe[r] Murray Grieve (1892-1978), Scottish poe[t]. Attempted to create a contemporary Sco[ts] poetic in *A Drunk Man Looks at the Thist[le]* (1926). 'Hymns to Lenin' (1931, 1935) refle[ct] Marxist views.

Macdonald, Flora (1722-90), Scottis[h] heroine. After Jacobite defeat at Cullode[n] (1746), she aided Prince Charles Edwar[d] Stuart's escape to France by disguisin[g] him as her Irish maidservant and escortin[g] him to Skye. Briefly imprisone[d] afterwards.

Macdonald, Sir John Alexander (1815-91[)], Canadian statesman, b. Scotlan[d]. Conservative PM (1867-73, 1878-91[)]. Promoted Canadian Confederatio[n]; became 1st PM of Dominion of Canada.

MacDonald, [James] Ramsay (1866-1937[)], British statesman, PM (1924, 1929-35[)]. Leader of parliamentary Labour Par[ty] (1911-14) until removed over pacifist stan[d] at outbreak of WWI. First Labour P[M] (1924), lost ensuing election aft[er] publication of ZINOVIEV letter. PM minority govt. (1929), split in cabinet led to formation of Conservative-dominated National govt. (1931) with MacDonald as nominal head.

acdonnell Ranges, mountain system of S Northern Territory, Australia. Highest peak Mt. Zeil (1510 m/4955 ft). Cut by many gorges; Alice Springs built near gap in E mountains.

ace, *see* NUTMEG.

acedonia, region of SE Europe, in Greece, Yugoslavia, Bulgaria. Mainly mountainous, rising to over 2450 m (8000 ft). Sheep, goats; wheat, tobacco. Ancient Macedon reached imperial zenith under Philip II, Alexander the Great (4th-3rd cent. BC). Later held by Romans, Slavs, Turks until 1912. Hist. cap. of Greek Macedonia is Salonika. Yugoslav Macedonia is autonomous republic, cap. Skopje.

aceió, Atlantic port of NE Brazil, cap. of Alagôas state. Pop. 324,000. Sugar, cotton processing; textile, soap mfg.

acgillicuddy's Reeks, range of Co. Kerry, SW Irish Republic, near Lakes of Killarney. Incl. CARRANTUOHILL.

cGonagall, William (1830-1902), Scottish poet. Known for doggerel verse displaying unconsciously ludicrous rhyme, disregard for rhythm, unintentional bathos.

ach, Ernst (1838-1916), Austrian physicist and philosopher. Emphasized that scientific laws are generalizations of numerous observations, not *a priori* truths. Rejected ideas of absolute space and time implicit in Newtonian mechanics; his views were vindicated by Einstein's theory of relativity. *See also* MACH NUMBER.

achiavelli, Niccolò (1467-1527), Italian writer, statesman. Prominent figure in Florentine republic from 1498. Ruined by restoration of the Medici (1512). Retired to country estate where he wrote *The Prince* (*c* 1517), which argues that ideal of unified Italy under strong ruler justifies means of achieving it; had enormous influence.

achine gun, firearm with mechanism allowing rapid and continuous fire. R.J. Gatling developed multi-barrel type in US (1862) but earliest in general use was belt-fed, recoil-powered Maxim (1884) issued to British army in Boer War. In WWI, Lewis light machine gun was a standard infantry weapon, while specialized machine gun tasks were allotted to the medium, water-cooled Vickers. Lewis still in use in WWII, although superseded by the Bren.

achine tools, term for large power-driven tools esp. lathe, drill, planer. Operate by removing material from object being machined, *eg* in turning (shaping cylindrical external contours), milling (shaping flat surfaces), drilling, boring, threading (cutting external screw thread) and tapping (cutting internal screw thread).

ach number, ratio of speed of a body in some medium (*eg* air) to speed of sound in same medium. Mach number greater than 1 indicates supersonic speed.

achu Picchu, ruined Inca city, *c* 80 km (50 mi) NW of Cuzco, Peru. Discovered 1911; terraced slopes descend to Urubamba R.; major tourist attraction.

Macias Nguema Biyoga, *see* BIOKO ISLAND.

Macintosh, Charles (1766-1843), Scottish chemist. Developed waterproof fabric ('mackintosh').

Mackenzie, Sir Alexander (*c* 1755-1820), Scottish explorer, fur trader. Journeyed in Canada from Great Slave L. via Mackenzie R. to Arctic Ocean (1789). Became 1st European to cross continent N of Mexico (1793).

Mackenzie, Sir Compton, orig. Edward Montague Compton (1883-1972), British author. Works incl. *Sinister Street* (1913), comic novel *Whisky Galore* (1947).

Mackenzie, William Lyon (1795-1861), Canadian journalist, b. Scotland. Organized short-lived REBELLION OF 1837, failing in attempt to seize Toronto. Fled to US; returned to Canada (1849).

Mackenzie, river of Northwest Territs., Canada. Flows NW from Great Slave L. 1800 km (1120 mi) to Beaufort Sea. Tributaries incl. Liard, Athabaska, Peace, Slave. With Slave, Peace, Finlay rivers, forms the longest river system in Canada. Natural gas fields in delta region.

mackerel, *Scomber scombrus,* food fish of N Atlantic and Mediterranean. Swims in large schools near surface, often inshore.

McKinley, William (1843-1901), American statesman, president (1897-1901). Republican admin. dominated by expansionist policy; Philippines acquired after Spanish-American War (1898) and Hawaii annexed. Shot by anarchist.

McKinley, Mount, mountain of SC Alaska, US; in Alaska Range and Mt. McKinley National Park. Height 6194 m (20,320 ft). Highest peak in North America.

Mackintosh, Charles Rennie (1868-1928), Scottish artist, architect, furniture designer. Influenced by Celtic art, he was a major exponent of art nouveau. Buildings incl. Glasgow School of Art.

McLuhan, [Herbert] Marshall (1911-80), Canadian writer, academic. Known for controversial communication theories, *eg* 'the medium is the message'. Works incl. *The Gutenberg Galaxy* (1962), *Understanding Media* (1964).

MacMahon, Marie Edmé Patrice Maurice de (1808-93), French army officer, statesman. Defeated Austrians at Magenta (1859). Defeated and captured by Prussians at Sedan (1870); on release, suppressed Paris Commune (1871). A monarchist, chosen president of the republic (1873); forced to resign (1879).

Macmillan, [Maurice] Harold (1894-), British statesman, PM (1957-63). Foreign secretary (1955), chancellor of the exchequer (1955-7); headed Conservative govt. after Eden's resignation. Period of office marked by recognition of many colonies as independent states. Resigned soon after PROFUMO affair.

MacNeice, Louis (1907-63), English poet, b.

Ireland. Works incl. *Blind Fireworks* (1929), *Solstices* (1961). Also translated Aeschylus, Horace, Goethe.

Mâcon, town of Burgundy, EC France, on R. Saône. Cap. of Saône-et-Loire dept. Pop. 39,000. Burgundy wine trade.

Macpherson, James (1736-96), Scottish poet. Known for *The Works of Ossian* (1765), which he claimed were translations from 3rd-cent. bard. His sources were never produced but work considerably influenced Romantic movement in Britain, Germany.

Macquarie Island, volcanic isl. of Australia, in SW Pacific Ocean *c* 1600 km (1000 mi) SE of Tasmania.

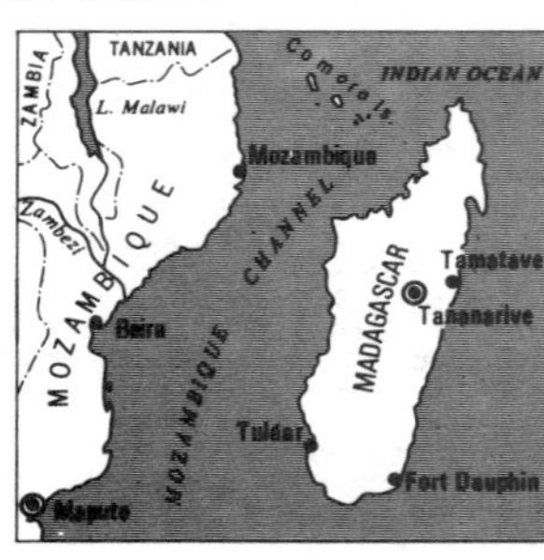

Madagascar

Madagascar, isl. republic of W Indian Ocean, separated from Africa by Mozambique Channel. Area 587,000 sq km (226,600 sq mi); pop. 8,289,000; cap. Tananarive. Languages: Malagasy, French. Religions: Christian, animist. Pop. divided into Indonesian and black African ethnic groups. Main isl. Madagascar, also incl. Nossi-Bé, Sainte-Marie Isls. Narrow coastal strip; mainly C highland, now largely deforested. Unique flora and fauna. Crops incl. sugar, coffee, rice; cattle raising. French colony from 1896 until independence in 1960. Known as Malagasy Republic till 1975.

madder, any of genus *Rubia* of perennial herbs, esp. Eurasian vine, *R. tinctorum,* cultivated for red madder dye extracted from root.

Madeira Islands, archipelago of N Atlantic, forming Funchal dist. of Portugal. Area 790 sq km (305 sq mi); cap. Funchal. Only 2 inhabited isls.: Madeira, Porto Santo. Largest isl. is Madeira, rising to 1860 m (6106 ft). Health, tourist resort. Madeira (fortified wine), fruit, fishing.

Madhya Pradesh, state of C India. Area *c* 443,400 sq km (171,200 sq mi); pop. 41,650,000; cap. Bhopal. Mainly on N Deccan plateau; monsoon climate aids largely agric. economy; dense forests provide teak. Coalmining; major source of manganese.

Madison, James (1751-1836), American statesman, president (1809-17). Leading figure in drafting US Constitution (1787 Democratic-Republican secretary of sta (1801-9).

Madison, cap. of Wisconsin, US; on isthm between Monona and Mendota lakes. Po 302,000. Centre of farming region. Founde as territ. cap. (1836). Has Univ. Wisconsin (1848).

Madras, cap. of TAMIL NADU, SE India. Po 2,470,000. Major seaport, exports cotto hides. Textile, clothing mfg. Founded Fort St George by British (1639 University (1857).

Madrid, cap. of Spain and Madrid prov., c R. Manzanares. Pop. 3,170,000. Admi indust., transport centre on the Casti plateau. Fortress, taken from Moors Castile (1083); cap. from 1561. Besieg 1936-9 by Nationalists in Civil Wa Buildings incl. Bourbon palace, Prado a gallery; univ. (1508).

madrigal, musical composition written f two or more singers and usually perform unaccompanied. First flourished in Italy 14th cent., and then again in Italy ar England in more elaborate form in 16 and 17th cents.

Madurai, city of Tamil Nadu, S India. Po 548,000. Textile, brassware mfg. Dat from 5th cent. BC. Ceded to British (1801).

Maelström, channel off NW Norway, in Lofoten Isls. Area of whirlpools, dangero currents. Term now applied to a whirlpools.

Maeterlinck, Maurice, Count (1862-1949 Belgian author. Known for anti-naturalist dramas, *eg Pelléas et Mélisande* (1892 *L'oiseau bleu* (1909). Also wrote dream-lik verse studies of plant, animal life. Nob Prize for Literature (1911).

Mafeking, town of NE Cape Prov., Sou Africa. Pop. 8000. Agric. trade centr Scene of 7-month siege of British by Boe 1899-1900. Extra-territ. cap. of Bechuan land until 1965.

Mafia, originally, name given to secr groups in Sicily and S Italy, opposed landowners and process of law. Es powerful 19th-early 20th cent., suppress by Fascist govt. in 1920s, turned industry, commerce after WWII. Broug to US by immigrants, long suspected controlling illegal operations. Also know as 'Cosa Nostra'.

Magadha, ancient Indian kingdom, situate in modern Bihar state. Prominent in 7 cent. BC, came under Mauryan empire 320 BC; recovered importance in 5th cer AD under Gupta dynasty. Scene development of Buddhism and Jainism.

Magdalena, river of Colombia. Rises in Andes, flows N 1600 km (*c* 1000 mi) Caribbean near Barranquilla. Importa trade route; oilfields.

Magdalene, *see* MARY MAGDALENE.

Magdalenian, in archaeology, final phase Upper Palaeolithic Age, centred on S France; lasted from *c* 15,000 to 10,000 B Magdalenians are known for their cave a (*eg* that at Altamira) and refined tools.

agdeburg, city of WC East Germany, on R. Elbe. Pop. 278,000. Railway jct., canal link with R. Weser; industs. incl. sugar refining, textiles, glass, chemicals. Former Hanseatic League member.

agellan, Ferdinand, English form of Fernão de Magelhães (*c* 1480-1521), Portuguese navigator. In service of Spain, sailed W (1519) to find S passage to Pacific. Explored Río de la Plata estuary; rounded South America via Str. of Magellan (1520). Killed by natives in Philippines. One of ships, under del Cano, completed 1st global circumnavigation (1522).

agellan Strait, narrow channel of extreme S Chile, between mainland and Tierra del Fuego. Connects Atlantic and Pacific. Discovered by Magellan (1520).

agenta, town of Lombardy, N Italy. Pop. 18,000. Scene of battle (1859) in which French and Sardinians defeated Austrians.

aggiore, Lake, Lombardy, NW Italy, N tip in Switzerland. Area 212 sq km (82 sq mi). In mountainous region; vines, olives. Resorts incl. Locarno, Stresa.

aggot, legless worm-like larva of certain insects, *eg* house fly.

aghreb or **Maghrib,** Arabic term for NW Africa. Incl. N areas of Morocco, Algeria, Tunisia and, sometimes, Libya.

agi, priestly caste in ancient Media and Persia, reputed to possess supernatural powers. ZOROASTER was prob. a Magus. Term also refers to Wise Men of the East in NT who brought gifts to newborn Jesus.

agic (from MAGI), attempt to manipulate world by supernatural means. Practice depends on theory of underlying, unseen forces. Concept occurs in many cultures, incl. fetishism, totemism, necromancy. Malevolent magic called 'black' magic.

aginot Line, a fortification system built in 1930s along French frontier. It failed to deter German flanking action (1940) in WWII.

agma, molten material beneath the solid crust of the Earth. Solidifies when cooled to form IGNEOUS ROCKS, occasionally reaching surface as lava.

agna Carta, charter signed by King John of England (1215) in face of demands by barons. Secured feudal rights and estab. areas over which king had no jurisdiction. Interpreted throughout English history as guaranteeing certain political and civil liberties.

agnesium (Mg), light silver-white metallic element; at. no. 12, at. wt. 24.31. Burns with intense white flame. Occurs in magnesite, dolomite and sea water. Used in lightweight alloys, photographic flash bulbs; compounds used in medicine.

agnetic pole, either of 2 points on a magnet where its magnetism appears to be concentrated and from which magnetic lines of force emanate. Magnetic poles exist only in pairs (north and south poles); freely suspended magnet turns so that its south pole points N (principle used in compass). Like poles repel each other, unlike poles attract. Force acting between poles is inversely proportional to the square of the distance between them.

magnetic poles, in geography, 2 points on Earth's surface corresponding to poles of a magnet, towards which needle of magnetic compass points and where magnetic force is vertically downwards. N and S magnetic poles do not coincide with geographical poles; positions vary, following circular paths.

magnetic tape, thin plastic ribbon coated with ferromagnetic particles (usually an oxide of iron or chromium). In TAPE RECORDER particles are aligned in varying degrees according to amplitude and frequency of signal. Also used to store information in computers.

magnetism, branch of physics dealing with magnets and magnetic phenomena. Magnetic force results from electricity in motion. Magnetic properties of materials such as iron result from unbalanced electron spin in the atom, giving rise to magnetic moment of atom. Overall magnetism follows when individual magnetic moments of atoms are aligned together.

magnetite (Fe_3O_4), iron ore mineral. Hard, black in colour; consists of magnetic iron oxide (variety called lodestone is natural magnet).

Magnitogorsk, town of USSR, W Siberian RSFSR. Pop. 406,000. Major metallurgical centre based on magnetite ore; iron and steel, coke, chemical mfg. Built 1929-31.

magnitude, in astronomy, measure of star's apparent brightness. Stars of any one magnitude are 2.512 times brighter than stars of next magnitude; thus stars of 1st magnitude are brightest and are 2.512 times brighter than those of 2nd. Faintest stars visible are approximately of 6th magnitude.

magnolia, genus of trees and shrubs with showy, fragrant flowers. Native to North America and Asia. Large white, pink, purple or yellow showy flowers.

magpie, long-tailed, black and white bird of crow family, genus *Pica*. Common magpie *P. pica* found in North America, Europe.

Magritte, René (1898-1967), Belgian surrealist painter. His work examines nature of reality, often depicting familiar objects in disturbing juxtapositions or unfamiliar settings.

Magyars, people constituting main ethnic group of Hungary. Originally nomadic, migrated from Urals to Caucasia (5th cent.). Forced W, settled in Hungary in 9th cent. Magyar language belongs to Finno-Ugrian group.

Mahábhárata, great Sanskrit epic of India, compiled *c* 400 BC-AD 200. Main story is struggle for succession to kingdom of Bháratas. Incl. BHAGAVAD-GITA and an abridgment of RAMAYANA. Rest of book contains mix of folklore, myth, philosophy.

Maharashtra, state of WC India. Area *c* 307,000 sq km (118,500 sq mi); pop. 50,335,000; cap. Bombay. Mainly on Deccan plateau, with coastal plain on Arabian Sea. Mainly agric. economy; cotton, rice, groundnuts. Textile mfg.

Mahayana, branch of BUDDHISM which arose in NW India before 6th cent. Stresses disinterested love, salvation of others as route to the individual's own salvation. Developed extensive pantheon and changed concept of NIRVANA to denote salvation or damnation in afterlife resulting from nature of one's actions.

Mahdi, leader and prophet expected by Moslems to appear on earth before the world ends to restore justice. In Sunnite Islam he is a descendant of Mohammed's daughter Fatima. In Shiite Islam he is a hidden IMAM. There have been many claimants, notably **Mohammed Ahmed** (1848-85), who led rebellion against Egyptian rule in Sudan. Died after capturing Khartoum. His followers, the Mahdists, were defeated (1898) by British.

Mahler, Gustav (1860-1911), Austrian composer. Wrote music often classic in form but highly romantic and expressive in style. Works incl. 9 symphonies, song cycle *Das Lied von der Erde*. Also renowned as a conductor.

mahogany, any of genus *Swietenia* of tropical trees. Dark, heavy wood valued for furniture, esp. that of *S. mahogani* of tropical America. Name also applied to various similar woods.

Mahrattas or **Marathas,** people of WC India who speak Marathi language. Supplanted Moguls in 18th cent., controlling the Deccan and much of S India. Lost most of their territ. to the British by 1818.

Maiden Castle, well-preserved site of Iron Age hill fort near Dorchester, Dorset, England. Occupied from 3rd cent. BC. Captured by Romans (AD 43).

maidenhair, any of genus *Adiantum* of ferns native to tropical and warm temperate regions. Delicate, green fronds. Cultivated as potplant.

maidenhair tree, *see* GINKGO.

Maidenhead, town of Berkshire, SC England, on R. Thames. Pop. 45,000. Boating centre; electronic equipment mfg.

Maidstone, mun. bor. and co. town of Kent, SE England, on R. Medway. Pop. 71,000. Hops market, brewing.

Mailer, Norman (1923-), American author. Novels incl. *The Naked and the Dead* (1948) in WWII setting.

Main, river of C West Germany. Flows *c* 500 km (310 mi) from N Bavaria via Würzburg, Frankfurt to R. Rhine at Mainz. Navigable for *c* 355 km (220 mi); canal link to R. Danube.

Maine, region and former prov. of NW France, cap. Le Mans. Agric., stock raising. County from 10th cent., united with Anjou (1126). Returned to French crown (1584).

Maine, state of extreme NE US. Area 86,027 sq km (33,215 sq mi); pop. 1,084,000; cap. Augusta; chief town Portland. Forested lakeland; hilly in W; crossed by many rivers Main occupations lumbering, farming, fishing (esp. lobsters); some mini (stone, clay). Part of Massachusetts colo in 17th-18th cent. Admitted to Union 23rd state (1820).

Maintenon, Françoise d'Aubigr Marquise de (1635-1719), second wife Louis XIV. Married Louis XIV secretly 1685).

Mainz (Fr. *Mayence*), city of WC We Germany, at confluence of Rhine a Main, cap. of Rhineland-Palatinate. Po 184,000. River port, chemica engineering; major wine centre. Rom. camp; 1st German archbishopric (74 Early printing centre, home of Gutenbe Univ. (1477-1798, 1946).

maize or **Indian corn,** *Zea mays,* cultivat American cereal plant of grass fami Grain borne on cobs enclosed in hus Naturalized in S Africa, India, China, Europe and Australia. Cobs may be roast or boiled. When coarsely milled, call hominy or polenta; with gluten remov becomes cornflour.

majolica or **maiolica,** variety of potte which grew to prominence in 15th-ce Italy, after being introduced from Spa Produced by applying tin enamel earthenware; on firing it forms wh opaque surface, on which design is paint Object is then glazed and fired again.

Majorca (*Mallorca*), largest of Balearic Isl Spain. Area 3639 sq km (1405 sq mi); ca and chief port Palma. Mountainous in N Tourism, fruit growing, wine mfg., fishir Kingdom from 1276, united with Arag 1343.

Makarios III, orig. Michael Christedou Mouskos (1913-77), Cypriot churchma political leader. Leader of Greek Cypri movement for union with Greece (Enosi exiled by British (1956-7). Elect president on estab. of republic (195 Deposed by Greek-inspired coup (1974) b took up presidency again after Turki invasion.

Makassar, *see* UJUNG PANDANG.

Malabar Coast, coastal region of SW Ind extending from Goa to Cape Comorin. Nc mainly in Kerala state.

Malabo, cap. of Equatorial Guinea, on Bio Isl. Pop. 37,000. Commercial, adm centre; port, exports cacao, coffee; fi processing. Formerly called Santa Isabel.

Malacca, cap. of Malacca state, SW We Malaysia. Pop. 86,000. Seaport on Str. Malacca. Trade declined after rise Singapore. Held by Portuguese, th Dutch, until ceded to Britain (1824).

Malachi, prophetic book of OT, sometim attributed to Ezra. Castigates priests a the people for their laxity. Foretells juc ment and coming of a Messiah.

malachite, copper ore mineral. Soft, gre in colour; consists of basic copp carbonate. Found in oxidized zones copper deposits, sometimes as cement sandstones. Used as gem, source pigment.

Málaga, city of S Spain, on Mediterrane

Sea, cap. of Málaga prov. Pop. 403,000. Resort; port, exports wine, fruit. Founded 12th cent. BC by Phoenicians; chief port of Moorish Granada, taken by Spain 1487. Moorish citadel, 16th-cent. cathedral.

Malagasy Republic, *see* MADAGASCAR.

malaria, infectious disease caused by parasitic protozoon, genus *Plasmodium*, which feeds on red blood cells. Transmitted by bite of female mosquito of *Anopheles* group. Characterized by intermittent attacks of fever and shivering. Formerly treated by quinine, now by synthetic drugs.

Malawi, republic of EC Africa. Area *c* 118,000 sq km (45,250 sq mi); pop. 5,669,000; cap. Lilongwe. Languages: Bantu dialects, English. Religions: animist, Christian. Great Rift Valley runs N-S, filled by L. Malawi; elsewhere plateau, incl. Shiré Highlands (SW). Produces tea, cotton, tobacco, sugar cane, groundnuts. Area of L. Malawi visited by Livingstone (1859); British protect. estab. 1891; called Nyasaland (1907-64). Formed federation with Rhodesia (1953-62); independent 1964, republic 1966. Member of British Commonwealth.

Malawi, Lake, lake of EC Africa, between Malawi, Tanzania, Mozambique. Length *c* 580 km (360 mi); part of Great Rift Valley. Drained to S by R. Shiré into Zambezi. Major trade artery. Explored (1859) by Livingstone; called L. Nyasa until Malawi's independence (1964).

Malaya, region of SE Asia, corresponding to West Malaysia, comprising former British colonies of Malay penin. Area *c* 131,400 sq km (51,000 sq mi). Mountainous interior flanked by plains; densely forested. Equatorial climate. World's leading rubber, tin producer. Called Federation of Malaya (1948-63); independence from Britain 1957.

Malay Archipelago, group of isls. between SE Asia and Australia. Incl. Indonesia, Philippines.

Malaysia

Malaysia, federated state of SE Asia in British Commonwealth. Area *c* 332,650 sq km (128,500 sq mi); pop. 12,960,000; cap. Kuala Lumpur. Language; Malayan. Religion: Islam. Formed (1963) from MALAYA (West Malaysia) and SABAH, SARAWAK (East Malaysia). Singapore seceded in 1965.

Malcolm III [Canmore] (d. 1093), king of Scotland (1057-93). Defeated and succeeded MACBETH (1057). Married (1070) St MARGARET. Killed while invading England.

Malcolm IV (1142-65), king of Scotland (1153-65). Grandson of David I. Treaty of 1157 with Henry II fixed Anglo-Scottish border at Tweed and Solway. Succeeded by brother William the Lion.

Maldive Islands, republic in N Indian Ocean, SW of Sri Lanka; comprises *c* 2000 coral isls. Area 298 sq km (115 sq mi); pop. 140,000; cap. Malé. Language: Divehi. Religion: Islam. Agric. economy based on coconuts, fruit. British protect. from 1887, independent in 1965; became republic (1968).

Mali, republic of W Africa. Area 1,240,000 sq km (478,000 sq mi); pop. 6,290,000; cap. Bamako. Languages: French, various African. Religions: Islam, animist. Desert in N, elsewhere semidesert; main rivers Senegal, Niger. Swamp, marsh SW of Timbuktu; irrigation at Ségu. Main crops groundnuts, cotton, rice, maize; cattle raising. Economy severely affected by drought in early 1970s. Occupied by French in late 19th cent.; became colony (1904), called French Sudan from 1920. Part of Mali Federation (1959-60) with Senegal; independent 1960.

Malines, *see* MECHELEN.

mallard, *Anas platyrhynchos,* wild duck of N hemisphere, from which most domestic ducks are descended. Male has green head and white band around neck.

Mallarmé, Stéphane (1842-98), French poet. Formulated theories of SYMBOLISTS. Works incl. *L'Après-midi d'un faune* (1876).

Mallorca, *see* MAJORCA.

mallow, any of genus *Malva* of herbs native to N temperate regions. Large dissected leaves, purple, pink or white flowers.

Malmö, city of SW Sweden, on Öresund. Pop. 454,000. Port, exports timber, grain, dairy produce; shipbuilding. Ferry to Copenhagen. Held by Denmark until 1658.

malnutrition, deficiency of essential component of diet. May be caused by inadequate food or insufficient vitamins in food. May also be caused by failure to assimilate food during illness.

Malory, Sir Thomas (d. 1471), English writer. Known for *Le Morte d'Arthur* (*c* 1469), last medieval English treatment of the ARTHURIAN LEGEND.

Malplaquet, village of Nord, N France. Scene of battle (1709) in which Marlborough defeated French in War of Spanish Succession.

Malraux, André (1901-76), French author, politician. Novels incl. *La Condition humaine* (1933), *L'Espoir* (1937).

malt, grain, chiefly barley, which has been partially germinated and then dried in kilns. Used in brewing. Contains nutritional carbohydrates and protein.

Malta, republic of S Europe, in Mediterranean Sea S of Sicily, comprising isls. of Malta, Gozo, Comino. Area 316 sq km (122 sq mi); pop. 340,000; cap. Valletta. Languages: Maltese, English. Religion: RC. Tourist resort; agric. incl. cereals, potatoes, fruit. Taken by Norman Sicily 1090; given to Knights Hospitallers 1530. Annexed by Britain 1814; independent from 1964. Formerly major naval base; heavily bombed during WWII. Member of British Commonwealth, UN.

Malthus, Thomas Robert (1766-1834), English economist, churchman. Suggested in *An Essay on the Principle of Population* (1798) that poverty is inevitable as population increases geometrically while food supply increases arithmetically.

Maluku, *see* MOLUCCAS.

Malvern, town of Hereford and Worcester, W England, on E slopes of Malvern Hills. Pop. 29,000. Resort, spa.

Malvinas, Islas, *see* FALKLAND ISLANDS.

mamba, large arboreal snake, genus *Dendraspis,* of C and S Africa. Aggressive, with large fangs; venom can be fatal.

Mamelukes, members of military caste, originally made up of slaves, used as soldiers of caliphate. Mameluke sultanate was estab. in Egypt (1250) and dominated Middle East until absorbed into Ottoman empire (1517). Mamelukes retained actual control of Egypt until 1811.

mammals (Mammalia), class of warm-blooded vertebrates with hair on body, lungs for respiration, 4-chambered heart. Offspring fed on milk secreted by female mammary glands. Divided into 3 subclasses: primitive egg-laying monotremes, pouch-bearing marsupials and more advanced placentals.

Mammoth

mammoth, extinct large elephant of Eurasia and North America, with hairy skin and long upward-curving tusks. Known from fossil remains of Pleistocene period, frozen corpses in Siberia, and cave paintings.

man, *Homo sapiens,* sole surviving member of the hominid family. Precise evolution of modern man from more primitive form *eg* AUSTRALOPITHECUS and HOMO ERECTUS, i unclear and subject to controvers NEANDERTHAL and CRO-MAGNON man ar considered early forms of *H. sapiens.*

Man, Isle of, isl. of UK, in Irish Sea. Area 58 sq km (227 sq mi); pop. 56,000; ca Douglas. Hilly (Snaefell, 620 m/2034 ft mild climate. Crops, livestock; tourism Hist. dependency of Norway, Scotlan passed to UK 1828. Parliament ('Tynwald' Manx language now little used.

Manado or **Menado,** cap. of N Sulawes prov. (Celebes), Indonesia. Pop. 170,00 Seaport; exports coffee, copra.

Managua, cap. of Nicaragua, on L. Managu Pop. 500,000. Admin., indust., trade centr textiles, cement, cigarette mfg. Becam cap. 1855. Destroyed by earthquakes (193 1972).

manatee, herbivorous aquatic mamma genus *Trichechus,* with rounded tail and front flippers. Found in shallow coast waters of West Indies, South America, W Africa. Numbers reduced by over-hunting.

Manáus, inland port of NC Brazil, cap. o Amazonas state; on Negro R. near jct. wit Amazon. Pop. 389,000. Timber, rubber, nu exports; jute milling, oil refining. Gre during early 20th-cent. rubber boom.

Mancha, La, arid treeless plateau of S Ne Castile, Spain. Made famous by Cervante in *Don Quixote de la Mancha.*

Manche, La, *see* ENGLISH CHANNEL.

Manchester, city of Greater Mancheste met. county, NW England. Met. count pop. 2,675,000; city 492,000. Linked to sea b Ship Canal (1894); major seaport. Textile (hist. cotton mfg.), chemicals mfg. Ha univ. (1880). Roman *Mancunium;* mediev wool trade.

Manchu, Chinese imperial dynast (1644-1912). Strong rulers up till end of 18t cent. expanded empire, adding Turkesta Mongolia, Manchuria. Later reigns marke by numerous rebellions and increase pressure of European powers fo profitable trading terms. Dynast overthrown by revolution led by Sun Ya sen.

Manchukuo, puppet state set up i Manchuria (1932) by the Japanese afte their occupation of country (1931). Rule by Pu-yi, last emperor of all China Manchukuo returned to China after WWII.

Manchuria, region of NE China. Comprise Liaoning, Kirin, Heilungkiang provs Mountains surround fertile C plain, draine by Liao, Sungari rivers; major agric. an mfg. centre of China. Important timbe and mineral resources. Occupied b Japanese 1931-45.

Mandaeans, ancient Gnostic sect still exta in Iran and S Iraq. Beliefs drawn fro Babylonian astrology and cults of the Magi

Mandalay, city of C Burma, on th Irrawaddy. Pop. 418,000. Transport an commercial centre. Old walled city largel destroyed by Japanese (1942); numerou pagodas.

Mandarin, *see* CHINESE.

mandoline or **mandolin,** musical instrument of lute family, with 4 or 5 pairs of strings, each pair tuned to same note. Played with a plectrum.

mandrake, *Mandragora officinarum,* poisonous plant of nightshade family. Short stem, purple flowers. Fleshy, forked root thought to resemble a human form, long believed to have supernatural properties. Used as narcotic in Middle Ages.

mandrill, *Mandrillus sphinx,* large fierce baboon of W Africa with red nose, blue cheeks. Drill, *M. leucophaeus,* less colourful.

manes, in Roman religion, deified souls of the dead.

Manet, Edouard (1832-83), French painter. His portrayal of commonplace scenes, using light and dark shadows, pioneered a new style; he greatly influenced the impressionists. In 1870s, adopted a lighter, more colourful manner. Works incl. *Déjeuner sur l'herbe, Bar at the Folies-Bergère.*

manganese (Mn), hard brittle metallic element; at. no. 25, at. wt. 54.94. Occurs as pyrolusite (MnO_2), from which it is obtained by reduction with aluminium. Used in making alloys, esp. very hard manganese steel. Manganese dioxide is used in dry cells, in glass manufacture and as an oxidizing agent.

mangelwurzel, *see* MANGOLD.

mango, *Mangifera indica,* tree bearing edible fleshy yellowish-red fruit, native to Malaya and West Indies.

mangold or **mangel-wurzel,** *Beta vulgaris,* variety of beet, native to Europe. Formerly cultivated as cattle food.

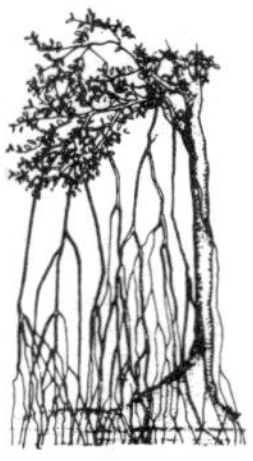

Mangrove

mangrove, any of genus *Rhizophora* of tropical evergreen trees found in swampy areas and on river banks.

Manhattan, *see* NEW YORK CITY.

manic-depressive psychosis, form of severe mental disturbance, characterized by alternate bouts of mania and depression. Treatment incl. shock therapy for depression, lithium compounds for mania.

Manichaeism, dualist religious philosophy (*fl* 3rd cent.-7th cent.) based on teachings of Mani (b. Persia, *c* 216-76). Combined elements of Zoroastrianism, Gnostic Christianity and Platonism. Persecuted by orthodox Zoroastrians. Term came to be used in medieval Church for all dualist heresies.

Manila, cap. and chief seaport of Philippines, SW Luzon isl. Pop. 1,436,000. Exports hemp, sugar; cigarette, textile mfg. Founded 1571. Replaced as cap. by Quezon City (1948-77). Divided by R. Pasig into old Spanish walled city *(Intramuros)* and modern section. Has Univ. of St Thomas (1611). Spanish fleet destroyed by US under Dewey (1898) in Manila Bay.

Manila hemp, strong cord-like fibre obtained from abacá (Manila hemp plant); used to make rope, paper, clothing.

manioc, *see* CASSAVA.

Manipur, state of NE India. Area *c* 22,300 sq km (8600 sq mi); pop. 1,070,000; cap. Imphal. Bounded on E by Burma; largely mountainous. Forests provide teak.

Manitoba, Prairie prov. of WC Canada. Area 638,466 sq km (246,512 sq mi); pop. 1,030,000; cap. Winnipeg. Tundra in N (Laurentian Shield); lakes in C; farmland in S watered by Red, Assiniboine rivers. Mainly agric. (esp. wheat, oats, barley growing); timber; mining (gold, copper, zinc). Meat packing, flour milling industs. Chartered 1670 to Hudson's Bay Co.; British control from 1763; became prov. 1870 after purchase by Canada.

Manitoba, Lake, SW Manitoba, Canada. Area 4076 sq km (1817 sq mi). N end is connected to L. Winnipegosis; drained by Dauphin R. into L. Winnipeg.

Manitoulin Islands, chain of Canada-US, in N L. Huron. Most are in Canada, incl. Manitoulin Isl., the world's largest lake isl.

Manley, Norman Washington (1893-1969), Jamaican politician, PM (1959-62). Founded socialist People's National Party (1938), leader while Jamaica was in West Indies Federation (1958-62). His son, **Michael Norman Manley** (1924-), was PM 1972-80.

Mann, Thomas (1875-1955), German author. Preoccupied with duality of artistic and practical life. Novels incl. *Buddenbrooks* (1901), *Death in Venice* (1913), *The Magic Mountain* (1924), *Dr Faustus* (1948). Settled in US (1939). Nobel Prize for Literature (1929).

manna, in OT, food provided by God for the Israelites in the wilderness. Various natural explanations proposed, *eg* edible lichen, *Lecanora esculenta.*

mannerism, in art and architecture, 16th-cent. style, originating in Italy as reaction against classical perfection of high Renaissance style of Raphael, *etc.* Painting characterized by contorted figures, lack of classical balance, vivid colour. Exponents incl. Parmigianino, Tintoretto.

Mannheim, city of WC West Germany, at confluence of Rhine and Neckar, opposite Ludwigshafen. Pop. 309,000. Vehicles, machinery mfg. Seat of Electors Palatine from 1720, became centre of music, theatre (*eg* Mannheim orchestra). Has baroque buildings, palace.

manometer, instrument used to measure pressure of gases. Simplest type consists of U-shaped tube partially filled with liquid.

manor, *see* FEUDALISM.

Mans, Le, *see* LE MANS.

Mansard or **Mansart, François** (1598-1666), French architect. Considered outstanding exponent of French 17th-cent. Classicism. Type of roof designed to give higher interior space named after him.

Mansfield, Katherine, pseud. of Kathleen Mansfield Beauchamp (1888-1923), British author, b. New Zealand. Known for short stories *eg Bliss* (1920).

manslaughter, unlawful killing of human being, distinguished from murder in being without premeditated malice. Usually divided into voluntary (intentional killing but done in heat, *eg* in sudden affray) and involuntary (unintentional; resulting from culpable negligence, *eg* reckless driving).

Mansûra, city of N Egypt, on Nile delta. Pop. 238,000. Cotton mfg. centre, railway jct. Scene of Mamelukes' victory (1250) over Crusaders under St Louis.

Mantegna, Andrea (*c* 1431-1506), Italian painter. His figures have sculptural quality and display extreme foreshortening. Paintings reflect interest in classical antiquity. Works incl. frescoes in Mantua.

mantis or **mantid,** any of Mantidae family of elongated slender insects. Seizes insect prey with pincer-like forelegs, often held up together as if praying.

Mantua (*Mantova*), town of Lombardy, N Italy, cap. of Mantova prov. Pop. 67,000. Renaissance cultural centre under Gonzaga family; ducal palace (14th cent.). Birthplace of Vergil nearby.

Manu, in Hindu myth, survivor of great flood and ancestor of mankind.

Manx, *see* GAELIC.

Manx cat, short-haired tailless variety of domestic cat.

Maori, aboriginal inhabitants of New Zealand, of Polynesian stock. Traditional economy based on agric., fishing, hunting, gathering. Originally divided into tribes, with frequent intertribal wars. On British colonists' attempts to settle large tracts of land, began Maori Wars (1861-71). Now comprise 10% of pop., with 4 Maori electorates sending representatives to Parliament.

Mao Tse-tung (1893-1976), Chinese political leader. Helped found Chinese Communist Party; after Communist split with KUOMINTANG (1927), organized Red Army and consolidated authority during LONG MARCH (1934-5). Prolonged civil war of 1930s and 1940s ended in triumph over Chiang Kai-shek's Nationalists and estab. of People's Republic of China (1949) with Mao as chairman of govt. council (1949-59). Retained post as Party chairman, instigating CULTURAL REVOLUTION in 1966, purging leadership in effort to recreate revolutionary spirit. Widely influential, esp. in his writings, as exponent of revolution and guerrilla warfare.

map, two-dimensional representation of the Earth's surface or part of it. Sphere cannot be represented on flat surface without some distortion of shape, area or direction. Various map projections may be used to preserve one of these qualities at expense of others; types incl. conic, cylindrical, azimuthal. Also *see* CARTOGRAPHY.

maple, any of genus *Acer* of deciduous trees or shrubs, native to N temperate regions. Various species cultivated as ornamentals, for timber or for sap which is source of maple syrup. Leaf is emblem of Canada. Also *see* SYCAMORE.

Maputo, cap. of Mozambique, on Delagoa Bay. Pop. 384,000. Admin., commercial centre; port, exports hardwoods, cotton, sugar, tobacco, mineral ores; transit trade, rail links with South Africa, Zimbabwe, Swaziland; univ. (1962). Cap. from 1907, formerly called Lourenço Marques, renamed after Mozambique's independence (1975).

maquis, term applied to robber bands widespread in Corsica until early 20th cent., later to French underground resistance movement during German occupation of WWII. Originally word for drought-resistant scrub vegetation of W Mediterranean region.

marabou, *Leptoptilus crumeniferus,* large billed stork of Africa, SE Asia. Green back plumage, bald head; tail feathers highly prized. Also called adjutant stork.

Maracaibo, port of NW Venezuela, on outlet of L. Maracaibo. Pop. 792,000. Coffee exports; major oil refining industry. Founded 1571.

Maracaibo, Lake, NW Venezuela, connected by waterway with Gulf of Venezuela. Area 13,210 sq km (*c* 5100 sq mi). Major oil deposits discovered 1917.

Marajó, isl. of N Brazil, in Amazon delta. Length 240 km (*c* 150 mi). Swampy rain forest in W (timber, rubber products), grassland in E (cattle rearing).

Maramba, town of S Zambia, on R. Zambezi near Victoria Falls. Pop. 52,000. Tourist, commercial and trade centre. Cap. of Northern Rhodesia 1911-35. Formerly Livingstone (till 1972).

Marat, Jean Paul (1743-93), French revolutionary, b. Switzerland. Founded and edited journal *L'Ami du peuple* (1789), in which he denounced those in power. Elected to National Convention (1792), he led campaign against Girondists. Stabbed to death while in his bath by Charlotte Corday, a Girondist sympathizer.

Marathon, village of SE Greece, on Plain of Marathon. Here Athenians defeated (490 BC) Persians under Darius.

marathon race, long distance race derived from run of Pheidippides from Marathon to Athens to announce defeat of Persians (490 BC). Olympic event since 1896; distance standardized to 42.18 km (26 mi 385 yd).

arble, crystallized variety of LIMESTONE. Formed by metamorphism under heat and pressure; colour varies due to different impurites. Can take on high polish; used in building and sculpture.

arc, Franz (1880-1916), German painter. Leading member of the Blaue Reiter group; noted for symbolic compositions of animals.

arceau, Marcel (1923-), French mime. Known as creator of clown Bip.

arches, The (*Marche*), region of EC Italy, cap. Ancona. Apennines in W (h.e.p.); cereals, vines, livestock in river valleys, coastal plain. Name derives from frontier (march) fiefs estab. here (10th cent.) by Holy Roman Empire. Name also applied to border areas between England and Wales or Scotland.

arconi, Guglielmo, Marchese (1874-1937), Italian physicist. Famous for development of wireless telegraphy; made use of an aerial to improve transmission. Transmitted long-wave signals (1895), transatlantic signals (1901). Shared Nobel Prize for Physics (1909).

arcos, Ferdinand Edralin (1917-), Philippine political leader. President of Philippines from 1965. Suppressed political opposition; declared martial law (1972) in face of alleged Communist subversion.

arcus Aurelius Antoninus, orig. Marcus Annius Verus (AD 121-80), Roman emperor (161-80), Stoic philosopher. Defended empire against Parthians and Germans. Persecuted Christians as enemies of empire. Wrote *Meditations,* an expression of his Stoic philosophy.

arcuse, Herbert (1898-1979), American philosopher, b. Berlin. Applied theories of Marx and Freud to analyse modern indust. society, holding that new revolutionary elite will be drawn from skilled technical workers. Works incl. *Eros and Civilization* (1955), *One Dimensional Man* (1964).

ardi Gras, French name for SHROVE TUESDAY. Celebrated in festivals, notably in New Orleans, Rio de Janeiro, Nice.

arduk, chief god of Babylonian pantheon. Creator of mankind, god of fertility. Identified with Bel in OT.

arengo, village of Piedmont, NW Italy. Scene of battle (1800) in which French under Napoleon defeated Austrians.

are's tail, *Hippuris vulgaris,* aquatic perennial herb with erect stem, whorls of slender leaves and minute green flowers. Native to Europe, Asia and N Africa.

argaret, St (*c* 1045-93), Scottish queen. Grand-daughter of Edmund Ironside, went to Scotland after Norman conquest; married MALCOLM III. Through her influence, Roman form of Christianity replaced earlier Celtic rites in Scotland. Helped introduce English ways into Scotland.

argaret, Maid of Norway (1283-90), queen of Scotland. Daughter of Eric II of Norway, inherited throne on death (1285) of her grandfather Alexander III. Marriage was arranged between her and Edward, prince of Wales. Died on crossing to Scotland, provoking war over succession.

Margaret of Anjou (*c* 1430-82), queen consort of England. Married Henry VI (1445); when Henry became insane, she opposed the protector, Richard, duke of York. Strengthened her position with birth of son Edward (1453), whose cause she supported during conflict between houses of York and Lancaster (beginning 1455). Captured (1471) at Tewkesbury; returned to France.

Margaret [Rose], Countess of Snowdon (1930-), British princess. Second daughter of George VI. Married (1960) Antony Armstrong-Jones. Has 2 children, David (1961-) and Sarah (1964-). Divorced (1978).

margarine, butter substitute prepared from hydrogenated vegetable oils and skim milk; vitamins A and D are usually added. Developed in 1860s using animal fats.

Margate, town of Isle of Thanet, Kent, SE England. Pop. 50,000. Seaside resort.

Margrethe II (1940-), queen of Denmark (1972-). Daughter of Frederick IX.

marguerite, several cultivated flowers of genus *Chrysanthemum* of composite family, esp. *C. frutescens* (Paris daisy) with single flower of white petals surrounding yellow centre.

Mari, auton. republic of EC European RSFSR, USSR; in middle Volga valley. Area *c* 23,300 sq km (8960 sq mi); pop. 703,000; cap. Yoshkar-Ola. Extensively forested; main indust. lumbering, wood product mfg. The Mari, a Finno-Ugrian people, were conquered by Ivan the Terrible in 16th cent.

Mariana Islands, isl. group of W Pacific Ocean. Main isls. GUAM, Saipan, Tinian; all except Guam formerly part of US trust territ. of the Pacific Isls.; commonwealth of US since 1978. Produce copra, sugar cane. Discovered (1521) by Magellan; all except Guam, which was ceded to US, sold by Spain to Germany (1899). Japanese from WWI, taken by US (1944).

Mariana Trench, deepest known depression on Earth's surface (11,033 m/36,198 ft), in W Pacific. Lies to E of Mariana Isls. Bottom has been reached by bathyscaphe.

Maria Theresa (1717-80), Austrian empress. Ruled (1745-65) through husband, Emperor Francis I, and (1765-80) through son, Joseph II. Succeeded (1740) to Habsburg lands by terms of PRAGMATIC SANCTION. Right to do so was opposed by European alliance in War of Austrian Succession (1740-8); lost Silesia to Prussia. Alliance with France to regain Silesia led to SEVEN YEARS WAR.

Marie Antoinette (1755-93), Austrian princess, queen consort of Louis XVI of France. Her extravagance, involvement in scandal, attempts to influence policy in favour of Austria, opposition to economic reform, all made her unpopular. Sought Austrian military intervention (1792) in

French Revolution. Convicted of treason, guillotined.

Marie Byrd Land or **Byrd Land,** region of Antarctica, E of Ross Sea and S of Amundsen Sea. Claimed for US by R.E. Byrd (1929).

Marie de' Medici, *see* MEDICI.

Marie Louise (1791-1847), Austrian princess. Married (1810) Napoleon I, after he had divorced Josephine. She bore him a son (1811) before returning to Austria after his 1st abdication (1814).

marigold, several plants of genus *Calendula* with orange or yellow flowers. So-called African marigold, *Tagetes erecta,* is unrelated species, native to Mexico.

marijuana, *see* HEMP.

marimba, musical instrument, resembling a xylophone, but with larger resonators and usually made of metal. Played with soft-headed mallets. Of African origin, it is popular in South America.

marines, troops trained and organized for service at sea or on land. In UK, Royal Marines (founded 1664) constitute main commando force, as do Marine Corps (1775) in US. Traditional roles incl. spearheading beach attacks.

Maritimes, region in E Canada. Comprise Atlantic provs. of New Brunswick, Nova Scotia, Prince Edward Isl.

Mariupol, *see* ZHDANOV.

Marius, Gaius (*c* 155-86 BC), Roman soldier, politician. Involved in civil war against Sulla from 88, seized Rome (87) during Sulla's absence and ruthlessly destroyed his enemies.

Marivaux, Pierre Carlet de Chamblain de (1688-1763), French dramatist. Known for stylized comedies of love.

marjoram, several plants of mint family of genera *Origanum* or *Marjorana,* esp. *M. hortensis* (sweet marjoram), grown for its aromatic leaves used in cooking.

Mark, St, orig. John Mark (*fl* 1st cent. AD), disciple of Jesus, friend of St Peter and St Paul. Traditional author of 2nd Gospel and 1st bishop of Alexandria. Patron saint of Venice.

Mark, Gospel according to St, second of NT Gospels, attributed to St Mark; written *c* AD 70. Shortest of Gospels, recounts life of Jesus.

Mark Antony, *see* ANTONY, MARK.

markhor, *Capra falconeri,* largest of wild goats, found in Afghanistan and Himalayas. Shaggy goat and corkscrew-spiralling horns.

marl, calcareous mudstone, consisting of clay with calcium carbonate. Sedimentary, laid down by fresh or sea water. Crumbles easily; 'marling' is spreading marl on poor soils to reduce acidity, promote nitrification.

Marlborough, John Churchill, 1st Duke of (1650-1722), English army officer, statesman. Supported William of Orange in deposing James II. Gained power through influence of his wife, Sarah Jennings (1660-1744), over Queen Anne. Famed for victories over French at Blenheim (1704 Ramillies (1706) and Malplaquet (1709 Dismissed from office (1711) after wife quarrel with Anne and return of Tories power. Reinstated on George I's accessior

marlin, large oceanic gamefish with spea like snout. Species incl. blue marli *Makaira nigricans,* and white marli *Tetrapturus albidus,* of American Atlant coast.

Marlowe, Christopher (1564-93), Englis dramatist, poet. Powerful plays, e *Tamburlaine the Great, The Jew of Malt Dr Faustus, Edward II,* estab. blank vers as Elizabethan dramatic form. Life ende mysteriously in tavern brawl.

Marmara or **Marmora, Sea of** (an *Propontis*), sea between European ar Asiatic Turkey. Links Black Sea (b Bosporus) to Aegean Sea (by Dardanelles

Marmoset

marmoset, small squirrel-like social monke of Callithricidae or Hapalidae family, four in Central and South America. No prehensile tail, claws on fingers and toes.

marmot, any of genus *Marmota* of squirre like rodents found in mountainous areas temperate N hemisphere. Short leg coarse thick fur; lives in burrows.

Marne, river of NE France. Flows *c* 525 k (325 mi) from Langres Plateau v Châlons, Epernay to R. Seine near Par Linked by canals to many rivers, inc Aisne, Rhine. Scene of unsuccessf German WWI offensives (1914, 1918).

Maronites, Christian sect chiefly Lebanon, with patriarch recognized by th pope. Distinct community since 7th cer when they adopted MONOTHELETISM; r entered Roman communion in 12th cent.

Marprelate controversy, 16th-cent. Engli religious argument. Seven Puritan-inspir pamphlets, pub. (1588–9) under pseudonym of Martin Marprelate, scurrilously attacked authoritarianism of Church of England.

arquesas Islands, archipelago of C Pacific Ocean, part of French Polynesia. Comprise N group (Washington Isls.) and S group (Mendaña Isls.); main isl. Hiva Oa. Mountainous; fertile, produce fruit, copra, cotton. Acquired by France (1842).

arquetry, decorative technique in which ornamental woods, bone, metal, tortoiseshell, *etc*, are inlaid in veneer and then fixed to surface of furniture.

arrakesh (Fr. *Marrakech*), city of C Morocco, in foothills of Atlas Mts. Pop. 436,000. Commercial centre, agric. market; carpets, leather goods mfg.; tourist indust. Founded 1062, *fl* in Middle Ages as terminus of Saharan caravan routes.

arram grass, coarse perennial grass of genus *Ammophila* grown on sandy shores to bind sand.

arriage, union, sanctioned by custom and religion, of persons of the opposite sex as husband and wife. In most societies, sanctified by rite or sacrament. Normally limitations are placed on choice of mate, *eg* exogamy (marriage outside group), or endogamy (marriage within group). Exchange of property is often a concomitant of marriage. *See* POLYGAMY.

arrow, soft pulp in interior cavities of bones. Red marrow, in which blood cells originate, fills all bones at birth. Replaced in long bones of adults by yellow marrow, containing mainly fat.

ars, in Roman religion, god of war, identified with Greek Ares. Father of Romulus and greatest god after Jupiter.

ars, planet 4th in distance from Sun; mean distance from Sun *c* 227.9 × 10^6 km; diameter 6790 km; mass *c* 11% that of Earth. Solar orbit takes 687 days; period of axial rotation 24 hrs 37 mins. Thin atmosphere composed mainly of carbon dioxide; temperature varies from -70° C to 30° C during day. Viking space mission (1976) showed polar caps were ice but found no evidence of life.

arsala (anc. *Lilybaeum*), town of W Sicily, Italy. Pop. 79,000. Fishing; Marsala wine. Major Carthaginian fortress from 4th cent. BC; Roman naval base. Garibaldi began Sicilian campaign here (1860).

arseilles (Fr. *Marseille*, anc. *Massilia*), city of Provence, SE France, on Gulf of Lions. Cap. of Bouches-du-Rhône dept. Pop. 1,004,000. Major port and naval base, linked to Rhône by tunnel; soap, margarine mfg., chemicals, oil refining. Founded *c* 600 BC by Greeks; free city until passing to France in 1481.

arshall, Alfred (1842-1924), English economist. Updated formulations of classical economists, developed marginal utility theory. Chief work, *Principles of Economics* (1890).

arshall, George Catlett (1880-1959), American army officer, statesman. Army chief of staff (1939–45). As secretary of state (1947–9), he initiated (1947) European Recovery Program (Marshall Plan) giving economic aid to European countries. Awarded Nobel Peace Prize (1953).

Marshall Islands, archipelago of W Pacific Ocean, formerly part of US trust territ. of the Pacific Isls; joined Caroline Isls. to form Federated States of MICRONESIA (1978). Area 180 sq km (70 sq mi); comprise Ralik (W), Ratak (E) chains; main town Jaluit. Produce coffee, copra, sugar cane. German from 1885; occupied by Japanese from WWI. Taken (1944) by US; BIKINI ATOLL site of US atomic bomb tests.

Marshall Plan, *see* MARSHALL, GEORGE.

marsh gas, *see* METHANE.

marsh mallow, *Althaea officinalis*, perennial herb with pink flowers, native to Europe, Asia and N Africa. Found in marshes. Root yields mucilage used in confectionery.

marsh marigold, *Caltha palustris*, perennial herb of buttercup family with yellow flowers and round leaves. Native to Europe, Asia and North America.

Marston Moor, Yorkshire, England. Scene of battle (1644) in which Parliamentarians defeated Royalists in Civil War.

marsupial mole, *Notoryctes typhlops*, mole-like Australian marsupial with silky golden hair. Lives underground, burrowing for insects.

marsupials (Marsupialia), subclass of primitive mammals incl. kangaroo, wombat, found mainly in Australasia but with species, *eg* opossum, in America. Young, born small and underdeveloped, are nourished by mammary glands in female's pouch.

martello towers, circular forts, modelled on one at Mortella in Corsica, built around S and E coasts of England as defence against Napoleon's projected invasion.

marten, any of genus *Martes* of weasel-like arboreal carnivores with long body, short legs and valuable fur. Pine marten, *M. martes*, is European variety, with dark brown coat.

Martha's Vineyard, isl. off SE Massachusetts, US. Area 260 sq km (*c* 100 sq mi). Atlantic summer resort. Settled 1643; hist. important whaling, fishing industs.

Martial, full name Marcus Valerius Martialis (*c* AD 40-*c* 104), Roman poet, b. Spain. Known for epigrams, modern concept of which derives from his. Based works on sharply observed contemporary society.

Martin, St (*c* 316-397), bishop of Tours, b. Illyria. Originally a soldier, traditionally left army giving his cloak to a beggar. Evangelized Gaul, estab. many monastic communities.

Martin, John (1789-1854), English painter. Known for his enormous paintings of visionary religious scenes and landscapes.

martin, small bird of swallow family that feeds on insects caught in flight. Species incl. house martin, *Delechon urbica*, which builds mud nest under eaves.

Martini, Simone (*c* 1284-1344), Italian painter of Sienese school.

Martinique, overseas region of France; isl. of SE West Indies; in Windward Isls. Area 1100 sq km (425 sq mi); pop. 374,000; cap. Fort-de-France (pop. 99,000). Mountainous (Mont Pelée); of volcanic origin. Agric. incl. sugar cane, coffee; rum mfg. Colonized by French 1635; overseas dept. 1946-72.

martyr (Gk., = witness), in Christian church, one who chooses to die rather than give up the Christian faith; 1st recorded Christian martyr is St Stephen (Acts 6: 7).

Marvell, Andrew (1621-78), English poet. Known for metaphysical lyrics incl. 'To his Coy Mistress', 'The Garden', 'The Definition of Love'. Also wrote political pamphlets.

Marx, Karl Heinrich (1818-83), German philosopher. Journalist and radical leader; with ENGELS, pub. *Communist Manifesto* (1848). After Revolution of 1848, spent much of his life in London and helped found (1864) association which became First INTERNATIONAL. In his theory of social change adapted Hegel's thesis to produce DIALECTICAL MATERIALISM, involving conflict of economic classes, first expressed in *The German Ideology* (1846). Major work, *Das Kapital* (1867; vols. II, III edited by Engels 1885-94), was basis for much subsequent doctrine of modern COMMUNISM and SOCIALISM. Also *see* MARXISM, SOCIAL DEMOCRACY.

Marx Brothers, American comedians, originally in vaudeville, but best known for films. They were Leonard ('Chico') (1891-1961), Adolph ('Harpo') (1893-1964), Julius ('Groucho') (1895-1977), and Herbert ('Zeppo') (1901-79), who left after 1st 5 films. Anarchic, wise-cracking films incl. *Duck Soup* (1933), *A Night at the Opera* (1936).

Marxism, political and economic system of thought, developed from philosophy of Karl MARX; also known as economic determinism. Method of analysis is DIALECTICAL MATERIALISM, from which was derived assertion that social change results from class struggle over control of means of production with the working class (proletariat) ultimately triumphing and leading to classless society. Marxism spread in late 19th-cent. Europe through INTERNATIONALS and socialist parties (*see* SOCIAL DEMOCRACY), eventually dividing between those who believed struggle would be evolutionary and those led by Lenin advocating violent revolution if necessary. Success of Russian Revolution (1917) made permanent split between Socialists and Communists (*see* COMMUNISM, MODERN). Orthodox Marxism subsequently esp. influential in Third World countries with mainly agrarian workers.

Mary, the Virgin (1st cent. BC-1st cent. AD), mother of Jesus, wife of Joseph of Nazareth. RC, Orthodox and Anglican churches teach doctrine of her perpetual virginity. In RC church she is regard with Christ, as co-redeemer of mankind.

Mary I (1516-58), queen of England (1553 Daughter of Henry VIII and Catherine Aragon; accession was resisted NORTHUMBERLAND. Restored papal supre acy in England and married Philip II Spain (1554). Sanctioned persecution Protestants, thus earning nickna 'Bloody Mary'.

Mary II (1662-94), queen of Engla (1689-94). Daughter of James II, s married (1677) William of Orange (Willia III of England). After 'Glorious Revoluti (1688), they ruled jointly until her death.

Maryland, state of E US, on Atlantic. Ar 27,394 sq km (10,577 sq mi); pop. 4,137,0 cap. Annapolis; chief city Baltimo Almost divided by Chesapeake Bay; rolli upland in interior. Agric. (esp. poul rearing); food processing, meta shipbuilding industs.; fishing in Chesapea Bay. Settled early 17th cent.; one original 13 colonies of US.

Mary Magdalene or **Magdalen** (1st ce AD), Christian saint. In NT, demoni healed by Jesus; present at Crucifixion a one of those who found the tomb em and to whom the risen Christ appear Traditionally identified with the repenta prostitute who anointed Jesus' feet Luke's Gospel.

Mary Queen of Scots (1542-87), queen Scotland (1542-67). Daughter of James she was brought up in France. Marri Francis II of France; returned to Scotla (1561) after his death. Married her cou DARNLEY (1565), who was murdered (156 Mary then married BOTHWELL, suspected being Darnley's murderer. Ensuing ci war forced her abdication in favour of s by Darnley, James VI. Fled to Engla after defeat at Langside (1568); imprison by Elizabeth. Involved in several Catho plots to place her on English thro Executed for implication in Babingto plot.

Masaccio, orig. Tommaso Guidi (140 1428), Italian painter. His revolutiona handling of perspective and use of light define forms profoundly influenced s sequent painters of the Renaissance. major extant work is fresco series Brancacci Chapel, Florence.

Masai, nomadic E Africa people, of Hami origin. Mainly in Kenya and Tanzan Formerly noted as warriors. Liveliho depends largely on cattle rearing.

Masaryk, Thomas Garrigue (1850-193 Czech statesman, philosopher. Ca paigned for Czech independence fr Austria. Became president (1918) of n republic; resigned 1935, succeeded Beneš. His son, **Jan Masaryk** (1886-194 was foreign minister (1945-8). Said to ha committed suicide after Soviet-organiz coup of 1948.

Mascarene Islands, group of isls. in Indian Ocean, E of Madagascar. In Réunion, Mauritius, Rodriguez.

Masefield, John [Edward] (1878-196

English poet, playwright. Works incl. *Salt Water Ballads* (1902), narrative poems, *eg The Everlasting Mercy* (1911). Also wrote verse dramas, sea adventure stories. Poet laureate (1930-67).

maser (microwave amplification by stimulated emission of radiation), device for creation of intense, narrow beam of high frequency radio waves; waves produced have same frequency and are in phase. Depends on excitation of atoms of a crystal or gas by incoming radiation. Hydrogen maser is basis of highly accurate atomic clock. LASER is maser operating at optical frequencies.

Maseru, cap. of Lesotho, on R. Caledon. Pop. 29,000. Railway links with South Africa.

Mashhad or **Meshed,** city of NE Iran, cap. of Khurasan prov. Pop. 670,000. Pilgrimage centre for Shiite Moslems. Cap. of Persia in 18th cent.

Mashonaland, region of NE Zimbabwe. Fertile plain and tableland, inhabited mainly by Mashona tribe.

Mason-Dixon Line, boundary between Maryland and Pennsylvania, US, fixed (1763-7) by Charles Mason and Jeremiah Dixon to resolve border disputes. Regarded, before Civil War, as separating free states from slave states and now North from South.

Masons, *see* FREEMASONRY.

Masorah, collection of Jewish annotations concerning the correct Hebrew text of the Holy Scriptures. Compilation ceased in 15th cent.

masque, form of dramatic entertainment in which spectacle, music are emphasized, usually based on mythological, allegorical theme. Reached height with court masques contrived by partnership of Ben Jonson, Inigo Jones for James I.

Mass, liturgical service of RC church, incl. celebration of EUCHARIST. Low Mass is spoken; High Mass is more elaborate ritual, chanted and sung. Term also used by Anglo-Catholics; in Eastern churches the terms 'Holy Liturgy' or 'Offering' are used for a similar service. Formerly RCs used medieval Latin liturgy; vernacular adopted since 2nd Vatican Council.

mass, in physics, the quantity of matter in a body. More precisely, inertial mass of body is determined by acceleration produced in it by applied force. Mass is distinct from weight, which is measure of gravitational force of attraction on body. By theory of relativity, inertial mass increases as velocity increases, so that a given force produces smaller acceleration with increasing velocity (only appreciable at velocities approaching that of light). Einstein's equation $E = mc^2$ shows that mass and energy are equivalent (where c = speed of light).

Massachusetts, New England state of US. Area 21,386 sq km (8257 sq mi); pop. 5,778,000; cap. Boston. Berkshire Hills in W; Atlantic resort area (Cape Cod, Martha's Vineyard, Nantucket). Agric., livestock rearing, fisheries. Main industs. shipbuilding, machinery, textile, paper mfg. Education, research centre. Pilgrim Fathers landed at Plymouth Rock in *Mayflower* (1620); Puritan theocracy estab. Focus of pre-Revolution protest (1776). One of original 13 colonies of US.

Massey, William Ferguson (1856-1925), New Zealand statesman, b. Ireland, PM (1912-25). Estab. 'Reform Party' (1903).

Massif Central, large plateau region of SC France. Area *c* 85,000 sq km (33,000 sq mi); highest peak Puy de Sancy (1885 m/6187 ft). Incl. volcanic Auvergne, limestone Cévennes. Stock rearing; coal, kaolin mining. Source of many rivers, incl. Allier, Dordogne, Loire.

Massine, Léonide (1896-1979), American ballet dancer, choreographer, b. Russia. Worked with Diaghilev. Staged *The Three-cornered Hat, La Boutique fantasque.*

mass number, in chemistry, number of protons plus neutrons in atomic nucleus.

mass spectrometer, instrument which uses electric and magnetic fields to arrange streams of ionized particles into order depending on their charge to mass ratio. Used to determine atomic weights of individual isotopes of an element and to find relative abundance of isotopes in sample of an element.

Mastiff

mastiff, large powerful smooth-coated dog, used as watchdog. Stands *c* 76 cm/30 in. at shoulder.

mastodon, extinct elephant-like mammal that flourished from Oligocene epoch onwards. Differed from elephant in larger size and in structure of teeth; some had 4 tusks.

Masurian Lakes, group of *c* 2700 lakes, Mazury region, NE Poland. Scene of Russian defeats in WWI (1914, 1915).

Matabeleland, region of SW Zimbabwe. Inhabited mainly by Matabele tribe.

Mata Hari, orig. Margaretha Geertruida Zelle (1876-1917), Dutch-Indonesian dancer. Joined German secret service (1907). Betrayed Allied secrets to Germans in WWI. Executed by French.

Matapan, Cape, headland of Greece, S extremity of Peloponnese. Scene of British naval victory (1941) over Italians.

match, small strip of wood, cardboard, *etc*, tipped with composition which catches fire by friction. Modern match-heads contain phosphorus sulphide and oxidizing agent. Safety match-head contains antimony trisulphide and potassium chlorate; striking surface contains red phosphorus.

maté or **Paraguay tea,** dried leaves of South American evergreen tree, *Ilex paraguariensis.* Popular bitter beverage, drunk from special calabashes, is made from it.

materialism, in philosophy, system of thought which takes matter as only reality. Early materialist philosophies incl. Democritus' atomistic theory, Epicureanism, Stoicism. Subsequent exponents incl. Hobbes, Mill, Marx.

mathematics, study of numbers, spatial relations and axiomatic systems. Branches of mathematics under early investigation incl. arithmetic, geometry (esp. by Greeks) and algebra. Seventeenth cent. saw beginning of standard algebraic methods and introduction of calculus, prob. most frequently applied mathematical method. Axiomatic development of mathematics began in 19th cent., which also saw perfection of techniques to solve classical problems. Twentieth cent. has seen greater subdivision of major areas of research, *eg* geometry now divided into topology, differential geometry, algebraic geometry, *etc,* as well as development of abstract mathematical systems, originally arising out of specific problems, but now studied in their own right, *eg* group theory.

Matilda or **Maud** (1102–67), queen of England. Daughter of HENRY I; married Emperor Henry V, and, after his death Geoffrey Plantagenet. Her cousin, Stephen, seized throne (1135) but was challenged (1139) by Matilda. Captured Stephen (1141) and was elected 'lady of the English'. Later withdrew claim to throne in favour of son, Henry II.

Matisse, Henri (1869-1954), French painter, sculptor. Leader of fauves, he developed bright, often stylized design. His characteristic decorative works, influenced by Near Eastern art, juxtaposed brilliant colours and employed distorted perspectives. He painted long series of odalisques and still lifes.

Mato Grosso, forested area of WC Brazil. Heavy rainfall, cattle raising in SW upland; mineral resources unexploited (manganese mining near Corumba). Region mainly in Mato Grosso state. Indian pop. in Amazon basin.

matriarchy, form of social organization in which the mother is head of family or group, descent and kinship being traced through mother rather than father. Often associated with polyandry (*see* POLYGAMY). Found in South Sea Isls. and among certain North American Indians.

matrimony, *see* MARRIAGE.

matrix, in mathematics, rectangular array of numbers, arranged into rows and columns. Matrix is said to be square if it has same number of rows and columns. Used in all branches of mathematics, esp. in solution of systems of linear equations.

Matterhorn (Fr. *Mont Cervin,* Ital. *Mont Cervino*), peak of Pennine Alps, on Swiss Italian border. Height 4475 m (14,690 ft). First climbed 1865 by Edward Whymper.

Matthew, St (*fl* 1st cent. AD), tax gatherer o Capernaum, one of Twelve Disciples. Firs Gospel usually attributed to him. Traditionally said to have been martyred.

Matthew, Gospel according to St, first o NT Gospels, traditionally attributed to S Matthew since 2nd cent. Gives account o Jesus' life stressing that he was Messiah a foretold in OT.

Maugham, W[illiam] Somerset (1874-1965) English author, b. France. Novels incl autobiog. *Of Human Bondage* (1915), *Th Moon and Sixpence* (1919), *Cakes and Al* (1930). Also wrote masterly short stories plays, often using tropical setting.

Mau Mau, secret terrorist organization active 1952-60, whose members, drawn from Kikuyu tribe, took oath to drive white settlers from Kenya. Also attacke Africans who opposed Mau Mau. Finall offered free pardon by Kenya govt. (1963).

Maundy Thursday, Thursday before Easter when British sovereign distributes Maundy money to the poor. Relic of ceremony commemorating Jesus' washing Apostles feet.

Maupassant, Guy de (1850-93), French author. Known for naturalistic short storie pessimistically depicting ironies of life, *e* 'Boule de Suif', 'La Parure'. Also wrot novels incl. *Une Vie* (1883).

Mauretania, ancient region of N Africa, incl present-day N Morocco, W Algeria Kingdom under Numidian control in 2n cent. BC; became Roman prov. Overrun b Vandals in 5th cent.

Mauriac, François Charles (1885-1970) French novelist. Preoccupied with sin salvation. Novels incl. *Thérèse Desqueyroux* (1927), *Vipers' Tangle* (1932) Nobel Prize for Literature (1952).

Mauritania

Mauritania, republic of NW Africa. Are 1,031,000 sq km (398,000 sq mi); pop 1,544,000; cap. Nouakchott. Languages Arabic, French. Religion: Islam. Mainly i

Sahara, pop. mostly nomadic herdsmen; limited agric. (maize, millet) in S along R. Senegal. Exports iron ore, copper ore, gum arabic, dried and salted fish. French protect. from 1903; became colony (1920), admin. from St Louis (Senegal) until 1957. Independent from 1960.

Mauritius

auritius, isl. state of W Indian Ocean, part of Mascarene Isls. Has 3 dependencies incl. Rodriguez isl. Total area 1860 sq km (720 sq mi); pop. 924,000; cap. Port Louis. Languages: English, French. Religions: Hinduism, Christianity. Majority of pop. of Indian descent. Hilly, largely volcanic; economy dominated by sugar cane. Discovered (1505) by Portuguese; held by Dutch (1598-1710), by French (1715-1810), by British from 1815. Independent from 1968. Member of British Commonwealth.

aurois, André, pseud. of Emile Herzog (1885-1967), French author. Known for biographies, *eg Ariel* (1923) on Shelley, *Don Juan* (1930) on Byron.

aximilian I (1459-1519), Holy Roman emperor (1493-1519). Acquired Low Countries by marriage to Mary of Burgundy (1477). Involved in wars to defend his new territ. against French. Opposed French expansion in Italy but lost Milan to French (1516).

aximilian [Joseph Ferdinand] (1832-67), emperor of Mexico (1864-7). Younger brother of Francis Joseph of Austria; accepted crown offered (1863) by French-dominated Mexican assembly. After French military support was withdrawn through American pressure, he lost power. Refused to leave country; was captured and shot.

axwell, James Clerk (1831-79), Scottish physicist. His 4 equations concerning electric and magnetic fields described interaction between electricity and magnetism and unified all previous observations about the 2 phenomena. Deduced that light is electromagnetic in nature and predicted existence of electromagnetic (radio) waves, detected by Hertz. Contributed to kinetic theory of gases.

aya, pre-Columbian South American civilization of Yucatán Penin., S Mexico, Guatemala and Honduras. Relics of Classic period (*c* AD 317-889) incl. pyramidal temples. Hieroglyphic inscriptions and calendars indicate knowledge of mathematics, abstract astronomy. Culture declined after 9th cent. with Spanish conquest (1546) completing its destruction.

Maya, in Hindu religion, term for goddess Devi, consort of SIVA. Also used as term for illusory world of the senses, often personified as a woman.

Mayakovski, Vladimir Vladimirovich (1893-1930), Russian poet. Leading futurist. Works incl. propagandist *Ode to the Revolution* (1918), *150,000,000* (1920), satirical plays *eg The Bedbug* (1928).

May Day, first day of May. Important European festival, originating from pre-Christian fertility ceremonies. Traditions incl. maypoles, election of May king or queen. In Scotland, Ireland, day is called Beltane, celebrated with bonfires. May Day designated (1889) by Second Socialist International as international labour holiday.

Mayence, *see* MAINZ.

Mayflower, *see* PILGRIM FATHERS.

mayflower, name applied to several spring-blooming plants. In Britain name given to blossoms of HAWTHORN.

mayfly, any of order Ephemeroptera of insects with 4 gauzy wings and 3 long tail filaments. Larvae live several years in ponds, streams, eventually changing into dull brown winged insect (subimago). Subimago moults rapidly to form shiny adult; adult dies within a few hours, being unable to feed.

Mayo, county of Connacht prov., NW Irish Republic. Area 5398 sq km (2084 sq mi); pop. 114,000; co. town Castlebar. Rugged terrain in W; more fertile E has agric., livestock.

Mazarin, Jules, orig. Giulio Mazarini (1602-61), French statesman, b. Italy. Created cardinal (1641), he succeeded his patron, Richelieu, as chief minister of France (1642). Exercised great power during Louis XIV's minority. Negotiated end of Thirty Years War at Westphalia (1648). Autocratic rule, taxation policies provoked Fronde revolt (1648–53).

Mazzini, Giuseppe (1805-72), Italian nationalist. Worked, primarily while in exile, to unify Italy under republican govt. by revolutionary action. Founded secret society 'Young Italy' (1830) dedicated to these aims. Headed short-lived republic in Rome (1849).

Mbabane, cap. of Swaziland. Pop. 24,000. Railway to Mozambique. Tin, iron mining nearby.

Mead, Margaret (1901-78), American anthropologist. Extended scope of anthropology by relating culture to personality. Works incl. *Coming of Age in Samoa* (1928).

mead, alcoholic beverage made from fermented honey and water flavoured with spices. Mead drinking was an important social activity in Anglo-Saxon communities.

meadow grass, see BLUEGRASS.

meadow saffron or **autumn crocus,** *Colchicum autumnale,* native to Europe and N Africa. Widely cultivated for purple crocus-like flowers in autumn. Corms yield the alkaloid colchicine used in genetic experiments and as treatment for gout.

meadowsweet, any of genus *Filipendula,* esp. *F. ulmaria,* perennial herb of rose family, native to Europe and Asia, with pink or white flowers. Name also used for several species of genus *Spiraea.*

mealybug, insect of Coccidae family, whose body is covered with waxy secretion. Some species injurious to trees and plants.

mean, in mathematics, number between smallest and largest values of some set of numbers, obtained by some prescribed method. Usually refers to arithmetic mean, *ie* sum of numbers in a group divided by number of members in the group; geometric mean of *n* positive numbers is *n*-th root of their product.

meander, curve in course of a river winding from side to side over flat land. By erosion, river may cut off its own meanders, forming ox-bow or mort lakes.

Mearns, The, see KINCARDINESHIRE.

measles, infectious viral disease spread by airborne droplets. Most common in childhood. Characterized by blotchy body rash preceded by running nose, watery eyes, fever. Incubation period 10-14 days.

meat, flesh of animals, esp. sheep, pigs and cattle, used as food. Composed mainly of muscle and connective tissue. Contains fat, vitamin B, minerals such as iron, and large amounts of protein. Cooking meat helps coagulate blood and albumen, improve flavour, soften and sterilize it.

Meath, county of Leinster prov., E Irish Republic. Area 2339 sq km (903 sq mi); pop. 91,000; co. town Trim. Undulating terrain, drained by R. Boyne. Agric., livestock. Ancient kingdom (larger than present county); antiquities (*eg* at Kells, Tara).

Mecca (*Makkah*), cap. of Hejaz region, W Saudi Arabia. Pop. 367,000. Birthplace of Mohammed. Islam's holiest city and pilgrimage centre. Goal of pilgrimage is the Kaaba, cubical stone building, contained in Great Mosque. Kaaba contains sacred Black Stone, kissed by pilgrims.

mechanical engineering, branch of ENGINEERING dealing with machines, engines and power plants. Divided into heat utilization (in engines, *etc*) and machine design.

mechanics, branch of physics dealing with effect of forces acting on bodies. Usually divided into statics and dynamics.

Mechelen (Fr. *Malines*), town of NC Belgium, on R. Dyle. Pop. 78,000. Railway jct., industs. incl. furniture, textiles, vehicles. Cathedral (14th cent.).

Mecklenburg, region of N East Germany. Large, low-lying fertile plain with lakes, forests. Crops incl. rye, potatoes, suga beet. Hist. cap. Schwerin; chief por Rostock, Wismar, Stralsund. Imperi duchy from 1348, divided into 2 duchie 1621; both joined German empire 187 Reunited as state 1934.

Medan, city of Indonesia, cap. of Nort Sumatra prov. Pop. 636,000. Trade centr dealing in tobacco, rubber; tourism. Has univs.

Medawar, Sir Peter Brian (1915- English biologist, b. Brazil. With Si Macfarlane Burnet awarded Nobel Priz for Physiology and Medicine (1960) fo showing that animals can be induced overcome their tendency to reje transplanted tissue or organs.

Medea, in Greek myth, sorceress wh helped JASON obtain Golden Fleece. Whe Jason wished to marry Creusa, Medea se her a poisoned wedding dress whic burned her to death. Killed her ow children by Jason and married Kin Aegeus.

Medellín, city of NW Colombia, in Andes; al 1520 m (*c* 5000 ft). Pop. 1,159,000. Importa textile industs., coffee exports; gold minin Founded 1675. Has 3 univs.

Medes, ancient people of W Asia, in are now NW Iran. Subjects of Assyria in 9 cent. BC, they gained their independenc in 7th cent. BC. Defeated by Cyrus th Great *c* 550 BC, after which they merge with Persians.

Medici, Italian family of merchants an bankers, who ruled Florence (15th-18 cent.) and were famous patrons of the ar during the Renaissance. **Cosimo d Medici** (1389-1464) was first of family rule Florence. Greatly extended family banking interests; encouraged study Greek. Patron of Donatello, Brunellesch His grandson, **Lorenzo de' Medi** (1449-92), called 'Il Magnifico', was a lavis patron of Greek and Latin learning, a and literature. His son, Giovanni d Medici, became pope as LEO X. Giulio d Medici became pope as CLEMENT VI **Alessandro de' Medici** (1510-37) wa created hereditary duke of Florence afte period of exile. His tyrannical rule ende in his assassination. Succeeded by **Cosim de' Medici** (1519-74), who became gran duke of Tuscany. **Catherine de' Medi** (1519-89), consort of Henry II of Franc was regent for her son Charles I (1560-74); instigated St Bartholomew's Da massacre of French Protestants (1572 **Marie de' Medici** (1573-1642), was queen Henry IV of France. Acted as regent fo her son, Louis XIII, after Henry's dea (1610); ultimately exiled by Louis whe Richelieu became his chief minister (1630

medicine, art and science of diagnosi treatment, curing and prevention disease. Hippocrates (*c* 400 BC) esta rational basis of observation in medicin rejecting superstition and magic. Galen anatomical writings (AD 2nd cent. preserved by Moslem physicians in Midd Ages, dominated medical thought un more accurate studies of Vesalius appeared in 16th cent. Harvey's discovery of circulation of blood (1628) was also important. Medicine revolutionized in 19th cent. by use of antiseptics, anaesthetics and by Pasteur's findings on microbes. Advances in 20th cent. incl. use of antibiotics, inoculation with vaccine, blood transfusion, organ transplants.

Medina, city of Hejaz region, W Saudi Arabia. Pop. 198,000. Mosque contains Mohammed's tomb, pilgrimage centre. Mohammed fled here from Mecca in 622.

Mediterranean Sea

Mediterranean Sea (anc. *Mare Internum*), inland sea bounded by S Europe (N), W Asia (E), and N Africa (S). Area *c* 2,512,300 sq km (970,000 sq mi). Linked to Atlantic by Str. of Gibraltar; to Black Sea by Dardanelles; to Red Sea by Suez Canal. Main isls. Balearics, Corsica, Sardinia, Sicily, Crete, Cyprus. Focus of ancient and classical civilizations. Declined from 15th cent. until Suez Canal opened (1869). Strategic, commerical importance; tourism.

medium, *see* SPIRITUALISM.

medlar, *Mespilus germanica,* deciduous, sometimes thorny tree of rose family, native to Europe and Asia. Small, apple-shaped fruit eaten when partly decayed.

Médoc, region of SW France, between Bay of Biscay and Gironde. Famous vineyards.

Medusa, *see* GORGONS.

medusa, free-swimming generation of coelenterates, resembling bell or umbrella. Usually produced asexually by budding of polyps, itself reproducing sexually to form polyps. In class Scyphozoa, incl. common jellyfish, medusa stage is dominant.

Medway, river of SE England, flows 113 km (70 mi) from Surrey, Sussex through Kent to Thames estuary. Medway conurbation incl. Chatham, Gillingham, Rochester.

meerkat, *see* MONGOOSE.

meerschaum, soft, white clay-like mineral, consisting of hydrous magnesium silicate. Absorbent, heat-resistant; used for tobacco pipes, cigar-holders, *etc.* Also called sepiolite.

The Temple of Mnaidra, a megalithic structure on Malta

megalithic, form of building using large stones, common in tomb construction in Neolithic and early Bronze Age periods. Megalithic structures incl. menhirs and stone circles, *eg* those at Avebury and Stonehenge.

Mehemet Ali, *see* MOHAMMED ALI.

meiosis, in biology, method of nuclear division in formation of gametes (sex cells) in animals and spores of most plants, by which number of chromosomes is reduced by half. Usually consists of 2 successive divisions, each resembling MITOSIS.

Meir, Golda (1898-1978), Israeli political leader, b. Russia. Founder member of Labour party. Premier (1969-74), she resigned in aftermath of 4th Arab-Israeli war.

Meissen, town of SE East Germany, on R. Elbe. Pop. 51,000. From 1710 'Dresden' china made here, from local kaolin.

Meistersinger (Master singers), members of German guild of poets or musicians (14th-16th cents.). Drawn from craftsmen and traders, they aimed to preserve traditions of medieval MINNESINGER.

Meknès, city of N Morocco. Pop. 403,000. Trade centre in agric. region; carpets, leather goods, pottery mfg. Former cap. of Morocco.

Mekong, river of SE Asia. Rises in SC China (Tsinghai prov.), flows *c* 4180 km (2600 mi) SE along Laos border into Cambodia and forms large (*c* 194,000 sq km/75,000 sq mi) rice-growing delta in S Vietnam.

Melanchthon, orig. Philip Schwarzerd (1497-1560), German humanist scholar. Friend and follower of Luther, explained Reformation principles in *Loci communes* (1521); wrote Augsburg Confession (1530). After Luther's death, was influenced by Calvin. Helped create German school system.

Melanesia, one of three divisions of Pacific isls., S of equator. Incl. Admiralty Isls., Bismarck Archipelago, Solomon Isls., New Hebrides, New Caledonia and Fiji. Also *see* MICRONESIA, POLYNESIA.

Melanesians, peoples of S and SW Pacific isls., of Australoid stock. Language is

Malayo-Polynesian. Main groups are the Papuans and taller, finer featured 'true' Melanesians.

melanin, dark brown pigment found in skin, hair and other tissues. Protects body from harmful ultraviolet solar radiation.

Melbourne, William Lamb, 2nd Viscount (1779-1848), British statesman, PM (1834, 1835-41). Second Whig admin. marked by Chartist agitation, trouble in Ireland. Acted as trusted adviser to young Queen Victoria. His wife, **Lady Caroline Lamb** (1785–1828), is chiefly remembered for tempestuous love affair with Byron.

Melbourne, city of SE Australia, on Yarra R., cap. of Victoria. Pop. 2,604,000. Admin., commercial, indust. centre; exports (via Port Melbourne) minerals, agric. produce, wool; 3 univs. First settled 1835; cap. of Victoria from 1851, of Australia 1901-27.

Melchites, Arabic-speaking Christians of Egypt, Israel and Syria. Members of part of Eastern Orthodox Church which reunited with Rome. Their head (under the pope) is patriarch of Antioch.

Melilla, Spanish enclave in N Morocco, on Mediterranean Sea. Pop. 65,000. Port, exports iron ore; fishing. Spanish from 1470.

melodrama, originally sensational drama with musical accompaniment. Now any play which exaggerates emotions, conflicts, at cost of psychological depth or development of characters.

melody, a sequence of notes having a distinctive musical shape. May form the tune of a song or short instrumental piece, or serve as a theme from which a longer work is developed.

melon, *Cucumis melo,* sweet juicy, edible fruit of gourd family, native to S Asia but widely cultivated in tropical and subtropical countries. Varieties incl. musk melon, honeydew and cantaloupe, a hard-shelled Mediterranean variety. *See* WATERMELON.

Melos or **Milos,** isl. of S Greece, in the Cyclades. Area 158 sq km (61 sq mi). Venus de Milo statue found here 1820.

Melville, Herman (1819-91), American author. Known for symbolic adventure novel on whaling, *Moby Dick* (1851). Also wrote *Billy Budd* (pub. 1924), short stories.

Melville Island, isl. of Northern Territ., Australia, separated from mainland by Clarence Str. Area *c* 5700 sq km (2200 sq mi); mainly wooded hills, mangrove swamp. Aboriginal reserve in N; lumbering, pearling, fishing.

Melville Island, W Franklin Dist., Northwest Territs., Canada; largest of Parry Isls. Area 42,500 sq km (*c* 16,400 sq mi).

membrane, pliable sheetlike material; may be artificial or natural. Semi-permeable membrane forms barrier in OSMOSIS. Mucous membrane is form of animal tissue that lines internal passages and acts as connective tissue.

Memling or **Memlinc, Hans** (*c* 1430-94), Flemish painter, b. Germany. Influenced by van der Weyden, he painted serene religious subjects.

memory, in psychology, term for capacity to retain and consciously recall past experience, therefore underlying all learning. Most accurate when individual is interested in subject of memory. Early childhood memories can often only be recalled in psychoanalysis, as they have been repressed.

Memphis, ancient city of N Egypt, on R Nile. Traditionally founded by 1st pharaoh Menes; cap. (*c* 3100-*c* 2250 BC) of united Egypt. Ruins incl. temple of Ptah, palaces, pyramids; nearby is SAKKARA.

Memphis, city of SW Tennessee, US; on Mississippi R. Pop. 867,000; state's largest city. Port, railway jct. Cotton, timber, livestock market. Settled *c* 1820, boomed as river port.

Menai Strait, channel (24 km/15 mi long) between NW Wales coast and Anglesey. Spanned by road bridge built by Telford (1826), rail bridge by Stephenson (1850).

Menander (*c* 342-291 BC), Greek comic poet. Known mainly through Latin adaptations of his plays by Plautus and Terence. Only complete play in existence is *Misanthrope*.

Mencius, Latin form of Meng-tse (*c* 371-*c* 288 BC), Chinese scholar. Taught that man is innately compassionate and that only poor material conditions drive him to be self-seeking. Thus urged rulers to follow doctrines of Confucius to ensure the happiness of their subjects.

Mencken, H[enry] L[ouis] (1880-1956), American journalist. Attacked America's complacent bourgeois mores as co-editor of *Smart Set* (1914-23) and as founder-editor of *American Mercury* (1924-33). Compiled *The American Language* (1919).

Mendel, Gregor Johann (1822-84), Austrian monk and botanist. Pioneer of modern genetics; his experiments in cross-breeding peas led to theory of organic inheritance determined by dominant and recessive traits.

Mendeleev or **Mendelejeff, Dmitri Ivanovich** (1834-1907), Russian chemist. Developed periodic classification of elements by atomic weight (now atomic number is used); predicted existence and properties of then unknown elements scandium, gallium and germanium.

mendelevium (Md), transuranic element; at. no. 101, mass no. of most stable isotope 258. First prepared (1955) by bombarding einsteinium with alpha particles.

Mendelssohn [-Bartholdy] [Jakob Ludwig] Felix (1809-47), German composer. Romantic in style but often classical in form, his music has great charm and lyricism. Works incl. overture to *A Midsummer Night's Dream,* oratorio *Elijah,* chamber music, violin concerto, 5 symphonies.

Mendicant Orders, name for 4 orders of RC church which subsist mainly on alms, *ie* Augustinian Hermits, Carmelites, Dominicans, Franciscans.

Mendip Hills, limestone range of Somerset, SW England. Extend *c* 37 km (23 mi), rising to 325 m (1068 ft) in Blackdown. Cheddar Gorge; caves with prehist. remains.

Menelaus, in Greek myth, king of Sparta, husband of Helen. Abduction of Helen by Paris instigated Trojan War. Reconciled with Helen after fall of Troy.

Menelik II (1844-1913), emperor of Ethiopia (1889-1913). Gained throne with aid of Italy. Thwarted Italian invasion (1895-6), thus ensuring Ethiopian independence.

Menes (*fl* 3200 BC), founder of 1st dynasty of ancient Egypt. Traditionally, united Upper and Lower Egypt and founded Memphis.

Meng-tse, *see* MENCIUS.

menhir, tall upright standing stone, found singly or in groups. Famous examples found at Carnac, Brittany. Some believed to have importance in prehist. astronomical calculations.

meningitis, inflammation of meninges, membranes surrounding brain and spinal cord. Results from infection by viruses or bacteria. Symptoms incl. fever, severe headache, muscular spasms in neck or back.

Mennonites, fundamentalist, pacifist Protestant sect. Originally Swiss, developed under influence of teachings of Anabaptist Menno Simons (*c* 1496-1561). Now found chiefly in Canada, US. Amish and Herrite churches are conservative branches of Mennonites.

menopause, permanent cessation of menstruation, commonly occurring between ages of 40 and 50. Results from changes in pituitary and ovarian hormones. Also called change of life or climacteric.

Menorca, *see* MINORCA.

Menshevism, *see* BOLSHEVISM.

menstruation, discharge of cells and blood from the uterus through the vaginal opening. Occurs approximately every 4 weeks when lining of uterus is shed and regenerated. Begins in puberty and ends at menopause.

mental illness, *see* NEUROSIS, PSYCHOSIS, PSYCHOSOMATIC DISEASE.

mental retardation, lack since birth of certain mental functions present in normal individual. Caused by infection of foetus during pregnancy, birth injury, hormone disturbance, *etc.*

menthol, white crystalline solid with characteristic smell. Found in oil of peppermint; used in medicine, cosmetics.

Menton (Ital. *Mentone*), town of SE France, on Côte d'Azur. Pop. 25,000. Resort. Part of Monaco until 1848, then independent republic until ceded to France in 1860.

Menuhin, Yehudi (1916-), American violinist. Debut made at age seven. Famed for interpretations of Elgar and Beethoven concertos.

Menzies, Sir Robert Gordon (1894-1978), Australian statesman. PM (1939-41, 1949-66). In 1944 initiated formation of Australian Liberal Party.

Mephistopheles, in German legend, personification of the Devil to whom FAUST sold his soul.

mercantilism, economic policy founded on principle that national wealth and power are best served by accumulating large reserves of bullion. Aim achieved by encouraging export and levying high duties on imports. Predominated during period (16th-18th cents.) of W European warfare with need to maintain armies. Supplanted during Industrial Revolution by LAISSER-FAIRE theories.

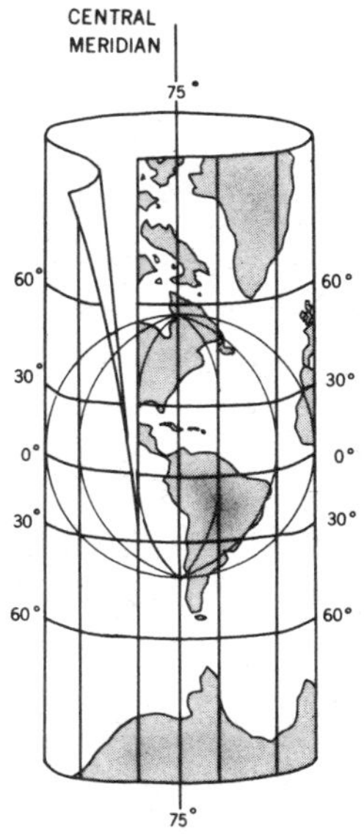

Mercator projection

Mercator, Gerardus, Latinized form of Gerhard Kremer (1512-94), Flemish cartographer, mathematician. Developed map projection (1569) named after him. Produced world atlas (3 vols., 1585-94).

Mercury, in Roman religion, god of commerce. Usually identified with Greek HERMES.

Mercury, planet nearest to Sun and smallest in Solar System. Mean distance from Sun 57.91×10^6 km; diameter 4840 km. Solar orbit takes 88 days; period of axial rotation 59 days. Almost no atmosphere; daytime temperatures reach *c* 430° C.

mercury or **quicksilver** (Hg), metallic element, only common metal liquid at room temperature; at. no. 80, at. wt. 200.59. Occurs as cinnabar (HgS); prepared by roasting ore in air. Used in thermometers, barometers and other scientific instruments and in mercury vapour light; alloys (amalgams) used in dentistry. Compounds, which are extremely poisonous, used in medicine, as detonators, *etc*.

Meredith, George (1828-1909), English author. Known for novels incl. *The Egoist* (1879). Also wrote poetry, *eg Modern Love* (1862).

merganser, diving sea duck of N hemisphere, with thin hooked beak. Species incl. common merganser or goosander, *Mergus merganser*.

meridian, line of LONGITUDE. All meridians converge at the poles, cutting Equator at right-angles.

Mérimée, Prosper (1803-70), French author. Known for short novels esp. *Carmen* (1845) which inspired Bizet's opera.

merino, breed of sheep, originally from Spain, noted for fine silky wool. Comprises 70% of Australian sheep population.

Merionethshire, former county of NW Wales, now in Gwynedd. On Cardigan Bay, drained by R. Dee. Mainly mountainous, many lakes. Livestock rearing; slate quarrying. Co. town was Dolgellau.

Merlin, *see* ARTHURIAN LEGEND.

merlin, *Falco columbarius*, small falcon of N hemisphere. Male slate-blue above with reddish striped underparts.

mermaid, in folklore, sea creature with head and upper body of a beautiful woman and tail of a fish. Often represented as luring sailors to their death.

Merovingians, Frankish dynasty (5th-8th cents.). First important member was CLOVIS (*c* 466-511), who estab. Frankish monarchy (481). Kingdom divided at his death. Childeric III, last Merovingian king, deposed (751) by PEPIN THE SHORT.

Mersey, river of NW England. Flows 113 km (70 mi) to Irish Sea. Estuary 26 km (16 mi) long, incl. ocean ports of Liverpool, Birkenhead; Ship Canal to Manchester.

Merseyside, met. county of W England. Area 652 sq km (252 sq mi); pop. 1,562,000. Created 1974, comprises Liverpool and suburbs; incl. N Wirral penin.

Merthyr Tydfil, town of Glamorgan, S Wales, on R. Taff. Pop. 55,000. Coalmining, light industs.

Merton, bor. of S Greater London, England. Pop. 163,000. Created 1965 from residential N Surrey; incl. Wimbledon (tennis championships).

mesa (Span., = table), flat-topped, tableland area with steep sides. Formed by hard-capped, horizontal strata resisting denudation. Over time, erosion of sides of mesa produces a butte. Both are common in SW US.

mescal or **peyote,** *Lophophora williamsii*, species of cactus native of N Mexico and SW US. Button-like tops are source of hallucinogenic drug mescaline.

Meshed, *see* MASHHAD.

Mesmer, Friedrich Anton (1734-1815), German physician. Developed theory of animal magnetism (mesmerism) for curing disease. His cures of psychosomati ailments by suggestion caused bri sensation, but were soon discredited.

Mesolithic, transitional period betwee Palaeolithic and Neolithic, beginning wit withdrawal of ice sheets *c* 10,000 years ag Nomadic hunting and collecting econom was replaced by localized, specialize methods. Lasted longest in N Europe.

mesons, group of unstable elementar particles with mass intermediate betwee that of electron and proton. Existenc predicted by Yukawa to explain force holding atomic nucleus together; firs observed in cosmic rays (1947), severa different types are now known.

Mesopotamia, region of SW Asia, betwee R. Tigris and R. Euphrates; mainly i modern Iraq. Cradle of several ancier civilizations esp. at Ur, Babylon, Nineveh.

Mesozoic or **Secondary era,** geological er intermediate between Palaeozoic an Cenozoic eras. Duration *c* 160 millio years. Comprises Triassic, Jurassic, Cr taceous periods. Extensive deposition c limestone and chalk; fauna incl. mollusc ammonites, brachiopods, giant reptiles; 1s mammals and birds. Also *see* GEOLOGICA TABLE.

Messiaen, Oliver (1908-), Frenc composer. Works incl. *Turangali* symphony, *Vingt Regards sur l'enfar Jésus* for piano, many works for organ.

Messiah (Heb., = the anointed), in Judaisn the leader promised by God to restore th kingdom of David. Christians regard Jesu as Messiah.

Messina (anc. *Zancle*), town of NE Sicily Italy, on Str. of Messina. Cap. of Messin prov. Pop. 267,000. Port, exports olive oi wine, fruit; univ. (1549). Greek colon founded 8th cent. BC. Badly damaged b earthquakes 1783, 1908.

Messina, Strait of, channel between Ital and Sicily, linking Tyrrhenian and Ionia Seas. Length *c* 32 km (20 mi). Currents whirlpools gave rise in ancient times t legends of Scylla and Charybdis.

metabolism, chemical processes associate with living organisms, largely controlle by enzymes. Divided into 2 parts: catabo ism, breaking down of complex substance into simpler ones or waste matter, wit release of energy for vital processes anabolism, building up of comple substances from simpler material, wit storage of energy.

metallurgy, science of metals, incl. thei extraction from ores and purification formation of alloys, and study of thei properties and behaviour.

metamorphic rocks, igneous or sedimen tary rocks transformed in character an appearance by any of the processes o METAMORPHISM. Examples incl. granite int gneiss, limestone into marble, shale int slate.

metamorphism, in geology, processes caus ing change in character and appearance c rocks in Earth's crust. Caused by hea pressure, or chemically active fluids. Com monest types of metamorphism are thermal (heat only), dynamic (pressure only), regional (heat and pressure, always associated with mountain-building).

metamorphosis, period of transformation of animal from larval to adult form. Insects placed in 2 divisions according to type of metamorphosis: Endopterygota, those undergoing complete metamorphosis with pupal stage, and Exopterygota, without pupal stage. *See* PUPA, NYMPH.

metaphor, figure of speech in which word or phrase ordinarily denoting one thing is made to stand for another, *eg* 'My love is a red, red rose', whereas **simile** states the comparison explicitly by using 'like' or 'as', *eg* 'My love is like a red, red rose'.

metaphysical poetry, early 17th-cent. English verse genre, marked by complexity, compression, use of puns, paradox, unusual imagery and syntax. Poets incl. Donne, Herbert, Marvell.

metaphysics, branch of philosophy which deals with first principles and seeks to explain the nature of being (ontology). Epistemology (the study of the nature of knowledge) is a major part of most metaphysical systems. The foundations were laid by Plato, Aristotle, with one of the most complete structures being estab. by St Thomas Aquinas. Since Comte many have regarded metaphysical problems as insoluble. *See* POSITIVISM, LOGICAL POSITIVISM.

Metaxas, Joannis (1871-1941), Greek army officer, statesman. Active in restoration of monarchy (1935), he was premier from 1936; exercised dictatorial powers. Led successful resistance against Italian invasion (1940).

metempsychosis, *see* REINCARNATION.

meteor, small body which enters Earth's atmosphere from outer space; becomes incandescent (shooting star) through friction with air, leaving bright streak as it passes. Most are consumed but some, called meteorites, consisting of metal or stone, reach Earth's surface.

Meteor Crater, hole *c* 1280 m (4200 ft) wide and 180 m (600 ft) deep, in Arizona, US; formed by meteorite impact.

meteorology, study of phenomena in all levels of atmosphere. Incl. WEATHER, one branch of meteorology confined to lower levels. Earliest work is Aristotle's *Meteorologica* (*c* 340 BC); later inventions *eg* thermometer, barometer increased accuracy of observations. Advances incl. use of satellites.

methane (CH_4), colourless inflammable gas, 1st hydrocarbon of paraffin series. Given off by decaying vegetable matter (marsh gas); found in coal mines (firedamp). Occurs in natural gas and coal gas.

methanol or **methyl alcohol** (CH_3OH), colourless liquid, originally obtained by destructive distillation of wood. Used as a solvent, in organic synthesis; as it is poisonous, used to denature ethyl alcohol.

Methodism, Protestant religious denomination. Originated as part of Church of England revival (*c* 1729) led by John WESLEY. Doctrines, influenced by those of ARMINIUS, stress repentance, salvation for all and thus evangelism and lay preaching. Separated from Church of England (1791); now has *c* 13 million followers, mainly in UK and US.

Methodius, St, *see* CYRIL, ST.

Methuselah, in OT, an antediluvian patriarch credited with having lived 969 years.

metre, SI unit of length; 1 metre = *c* 39.37 in., 1000 metres = 1 kilometre = *c* 0.62 miles.

metric system, decimal system of weights and measures in which kilogram, metre and litre are basic units of weight, length and liquid capacity, respectively. Devised in France during revolutionary period (1791-5).

Metternich [-Winneburg], Clemens Wenzel Lothar, Fürst von (1773-1859), Austrian statesman, b. Germany. Foreign minister (1809-48). Formed alliance with Prussia and Russia against France. Chief figure at Congress of VIENNA (1814-15); advocated maintenance of 'balance of power' in Europe. Repressive measures within Austria led to enforced abdication during Revolution of 1848.

Metz, city of NE France, on R. Moselle, cap. of Moselle dept. Pop. 181,000. Centre of Lorraine iron mining; metals, textiles industs. Important city of Roman Gaul; powerful medieval bishopric. Annexed by France in 1552; part of Germany (1871-1918). Gothic cathedral (13th cent.).

Meuse (Flem. *Maas*), river of NE France, S Belgium, and Netherlands. Flows 933 km (580 mi) from Langres Plateau via Namur, Liège, Maastricht to join Rhine delta. Heavy traffic on lower course.

Mexicali, town of NW Mexico, cap. of Baja California state; on US border. Pop. 346,000. Commercial centre in agric. region.

Mexican War, conflict (1846-8) between US and Mexico. Immediate cause was annexation of Texas by US (1845). US military successes led to Treaty of Guadalupe Hidalgo (1848), by which Texas and much of SW US was recognized as American territ.

Mexico (Span. *Mejico*), federal republic of SW North America. Area 1,972,544 sq km (761,600 sq mi); pop. 66,944,000; cap. Mexico City. Languages: Spanish, Indian dialects. Religion: RC. Pacific and Gulf of Mexico coastlines rise to high C plateau dominated by Sierra Madre range. Varied climate. Limited agric. concentrated in irrigated region (many of foodstuffs imported). Mineral wealth incl. silver, lead, iron, coal, oil; tourism. Had ancient Maya, Toltec, Aztec civilizations; Spanish conquest (1519) under Cortés. Independence struggle (1810-21); in Texas revolt (1836) and war with US (1846-8), Mexico ceded all land N of Rio Grande to US. Revolution (1910); civil war estab. new constitution (1917).

Mexico, Gulf of, extensive arm of Atlantic, bounded by US, Mexico. Connected to Atlantic by Str. of Florida, and to

Mexico

Caribbean by Yucatán Channel. Receives Mississippi, Grande rivers.

Mexico City, cap. of Mexico and Federal Dist.; on C plateau, alt. 2380 m (*c* 7800 ft). Pop. 11,943,000. Transport, financial, cultural, indust. centre. Textile, glass mfg.; automobile indust.; gold, silver refining. Built on site of ancient Aztec cap. Tenochtitlán (1521). Has National Univ. (1551), cathedral (1573). Ancient site of Teotihuacán, with famous pyramids and temples.

Miami, city of SE Florida, US; on Biscayne Bay. Pop. 2,288,000. Famous tourist and holiday resort.

mica, group of minerals consisting of silicates of aluminium and potassium. Crystallize into thin plates; flexible and heat resistant. Used in insulators, paints, tiles.

Micah, prophetic book of OT, attributed to prophet Micah (8th cent. BC). Denounces social injustice and hypocrisy but foretells Messianic deliverance.

Michael (1596-1645), tsar of Russia, founder of Romanov dynasty. Election as tsar (1613) ended confusion in finding successor to Boris Godunov.

Michael I (1921-), king of Romania (1927-30, 1940-7). Ruled (1927-30) under regency until replaced by his father, Carol II. When Carol abdicated, regained throne. Overthrew dictatorship of Antonescu (1944) and concluded armistice with Allies. Abdicated in favour of Communist republic (1947).

Michael, archangel in Jewish, Christian and Islamic tradition, guardian of Israel. His feast (Michaelmas) is celebrated on 29th September.

Michaelmas daisy, *see* ASTER.

Michelangelo (Buonarroti) (1475-1564), Italian artist, architect and poet, a major figure of the Renaissance. Sculptures incl. *Pietà* (St Peter's, Rome), *David* (Florence), *Moses* (for tomb of Pope Julius II). Painted fresco cycle on Old Testament themes (1508-12) and *Last Judgment* (1536-41) in Sistine Chapel, Rome. Also did frescoes for Pauline Chapel in the Vatican, and designed sepulchral chapel of Medici [in] Florence. Architect of St Peter's from 154[6].

Michigan, state of NC US. Area 150,779 [sq] km (58,216 sq mi); pop. 9,185,000; ca[p.] Lansing; chief city Detroit. Upper an[d] Lower penins. separated by L. Michiga[n]. Agric., dairying and livestock raisin[g], lumbering in S; iron ore, copper, pe[at], bromine exploitation in N. Leading mot[or] vehicles mfg., machinery, heavy indus[try]. French settlement in 17th cent.; ceded [to] British 1763; passed to US 1783; becam[e] separate territ. 1805. Admitted to Union [as] 26th state (1837).

Michigan, Lake, third largest of Gre[at] Lakes, entirely within NC US. Area 57,4[..] sq km (22,178 sq mi). Chief ports Chicag[o,] Milwaukee.

microbe, microscopic organism, esp. any [of] the bacteria which cause disease.

microfilm, film on which documen[ts,] printed pages, *etc*, are photographed in [a] reduced size for convenience in storag[e]. Enlarged prints may be made or film ma[y] be projected on ground glass screen [of] special viewer. A **microfiche** is a sheet [of] microfilm (10 cm × 15 cm) on whic[h] several pages may be recorded.

micrometer, scientific instrument f[or] making very accurate measurement [of] distances and angles.

Micronesia, one of three divisions of Paci[fic] isls., N of equator. Incl. Caroline, Marian[a,] Marshall, Gilbert isls. (Kiribati) and Naur[u]. Also *see* MELANESIA, POLYNESIA.

Micronesia, Federated States o[f], federation of CAROLINE and MARSHA[LL] ISLANDS formed 1978. Achieved full intern[al] self-govt. and responsibility for forei[gn] affairs, but US retains responsibility f[or] defence.

Micronesians, peoples of Pacific isls. N [of] Melanesia. Of Australoid stock, language [is] Malayo-Polynesian.

microphone, device for converting sou[nd] waves into an electrical signal. Type us[ed] in telephone consists of diaphragm in clo[se] contact with loosely packed carbon grain[s;] sound waves cause diaphragm to vibra[te] and compress grains. Motion of grai[ns] causes variation in current flow throug[h] associated electric circuit.

microprocessor, in electronics, a single CH[IP] or complex of chips assembled to perfor[m] specific functions; used esp. as centr[al] processing unit in calculators a[nd] computers. Has led to increase[d] automation.

microscope, optical instrument used [to] obtain enlarged images of small objec[ts]. Simple microscope uses single convex le[ns] to produce virtual image; compou[nd] microscope uses 2 convex lenses (objecti[ve] and eyepiece) mounted at opposite ends [of] tube. *See* ELECTRON MICROSCOPE.

microwave heating, form of high-frequen[cy] radiation which may be used in very hi[gh] speed cooking. Heat is immediate[ly] generated throughout an object rath[er] than passing in from surface by co[n-]

A modern microscope

duction. Also used in pasteurization, insect destruction.

icrowaves, electromagnetic radiation with wavelength between 1 mm and 30 cm. Ranges from short radio waves almost to infrared rays.

idas, in Greek myth, king of Phrygia. Dionysus gave him power of turning everything he touched to gold. Begged relief of this power when even his food turned to gold. In another legend, given ass's ears as punishment for preferring Pan's music to Apollo's.

iddle Ages, period in W European history considered to have begun with fall of Roman Empire (5th cent.) and ended with early Renaissance in 15th cent. Period marked by unity of W Europe within RC church and prevalence of feudal system.

iddle English, *see* ENGLISH.

iddlesbrough, admin. hq. of Cleveland, NE England. Port; iron, steel indust.; chemicals mfg. From 1968 part of TEESSIDE.

iddlesex, former county of SE England. Mainly absorbed by Greater London 1965, small parts joined to Surrey, Hertfordshire.

iddle Temple, *see* INNS OF COURT.

iddleton, Thomas (1580-1627), English dramatist. Works incl. tragedies, *eg The Changeling* (*c* 1623, with T. Rowley), *Women Beware Women* (*c* 1625).

idge, small 2-winged insect of Ceratopogonidae family with sucking mouthparts. Some species blood-suckers.

id Glamorgan, *see* GLAMORGAN.

idlands, term used for central counties of England, incl. Derby, Nottingham, Leicester, Northampton, Warwick, Stafford.

idlothian, former county of E Scotland, now in Lothian region. Previously called Edinburghshire. Moorfoot Hills (SE), Pentland Hills (SW); low-lying in N. Chief city Edinburgh. Sheep, dairy farming; market gardening; coalmining; fishing.

idnight sun, feature of high latitude regions where, during midsummer period, Sun remains visible above horizon throughout 24 hours. Caused by tilting of Earth's axis.

Midrash, collection of rabbinical commentaries and explanatory notes on the Scriptures. Compiled between *c* 400 BC and *c* AD 1200.

midsummer, the summer solstice, *ie* in N hemisphere *c* 21 June. Midsummer day is 24 June, feast of St John the Baptist. Night before has been occasion for solar ceremonies since ancient times, with vestiges (*eg* bonfires, merrymaking, association with love, lovers) remaining in Europe to present day.

Midway Islands, two isls. of NC Pacific Ocean, admin. by US Dept. of Interior. Area 5 sq km (2 sq mi); pop. 2,000; comprise Eastern, Sand Isls. Discovered by US (1859), annexed (1867). Naval air base estab. 1941; site of US naval victory (1942) over Japan.

Midwest or **Middle West,** C region of US. Incl. prairie states of Illinois, Indiana, Ohio, Iowa, Kansas, Nebraska, Minnesota, Wisconsin, North and South Dakota, and E Montana. Mainly agric. esp. grain production. Large indust. cities concentrated in Great Lakes area.

midwife toad, *Alytes obstetricans,* small dark European toad. After female spawns, male twists strands of eggs round his hind legs, carrying them until tadpoles hatch.

Mies van der Rohe, Ludwig (1886-1969), German architect. Produced designs for all-glass skyscrapers (1921); developed functional style characterized by pure geometric design. Director of Bauhaus (1930-3), later worked in US.

mignonette, any of genus *Reseda* of annual or perennial herbs native to Mediterranean and E Africa. Garden variety *R. odorata* has small spikes of fragrant, whitish flowers.

migraine, extremely severe prolonged headache, often affecting only one side of head. May be accompanied by nausea and disturbed vision. Believed to be caused by excessive expansion and contraction of blood vessels of brain.

migration, movement of animals from one place to another for breeding or finding new food supplies. Some animals, *eg* lemmings, undertake spontaneous migrations resulting from overpopulation. Certain birds and fish migrate seasonally.

Milan (*Milano*), city of N Italy, cap. of Lombardy and of Milan prov. Pop. 1,706,000. Indust., commercial centre, major railway jct., agric. market. Roman *Mediolanum*; member of Lombard League (12th cent.), later medieval duchy under Visconti then Sforza families. Under Habsburgs 1713-1861, passed to Sardinia. Cathedral (1386), La Scala opera house (1778), many art galleries. Badly damaged in WWII.

mildew, any fungus, esp. of families Peronosporaceae and Erysiphaceae that attacks various plants or appears on organic matter, *eg* leather, fabrics, *etc,* when exposed to damp. Characterized by whitish, powdery coating on surface.

mile, unit of linear measure, equal to 1760 yds or 1.609 km.

Miletus, ancient port of Asia Minor, in W Turkey on R. Menderes (Maeander). Most important of 12 Ionian Cities; centre of learning.

milfoil, *see* YARROW.

Milford Haven, town of Dyfed, SW Wales. Pop. 14,000. Fishing port; oil importing and refining.

Milhaud, Darius (1892-1974), French composer. Member of 'les Six' group. Numerous works, often lighthearted in style, were variously influenced by jazz, Latin American rhythms, *etc.*

militia, an organized military force of civilians called upon in national emergency. Known in Europe before formation of regular armies; again raised in Britain when Napoleonic invasions threatened, it later merged with the TERRITORIAL ARMY; in US it merged with the NATIONAL GUARD.

milk, fluid secreted by mammary glands of female mammals for nourishment of young. Almost a complete food, containing fat, carbohydrates, lactose sugar, vitamins A, B, D. Source of calcium and phosphorus.

milkwort, any of genus *Polygala* of herbs native to Europe and North America, with small blue, pink or white flowers.

Milky Way, belt of faint stars encircling the heavens, seen as an arch across sky at night. Now known to be a galaxy containing *c* 10^{11} stars, incl. the Sun.

Mill, James (1773-1836), English philosopher. An associate of Bentham, and advocate of UTILITARIANISM. His son, **John Stuart Mill** (1806-73), was also a philosopher. Introduced more humanitarian ideas into utilitarian theory, favouring democracy and social reform. Emphasized importance of quality, as well as quantity, of pleasure as motivating force in life. Works incl. *Essay on Liberty* (1859), *Utilitarianism* (1863), *Autobiography* (1873).

Millais, Sir John Everett (1829-96), English painter. Founder member of the Pre-Raphaelite Brotherhood; early work was richly coloured and detailed. Later painted trivial genre scenes and fashionable portraits. Works incl. *Christ in the House of his Parents.*

Miller, Arthur (1915-), American playwright. Known for committedly liberal plays, *eg Death of a Salesman* (1947), *The Crucible* (1953). Second wife was Marilyn Monroe.

Miller, Henry (1891-1980), American author. Many works mainly fictionalized autobiog. incl. *Tropic of Cancer* (1934), *Nexus* (1960).

miller's thumb, see BULLHEAD.

Millet, Jean François (1814-75), French painter. Worked at Barbizon after 1849, where he specialized in painting peasant life and rustic scenes. Works incl. *The Gleaners* (1857) and *The Angelus* (1859).

millet, name for several cereal and forage grasses, *eg* common millet, *Panicu[m] miliaceum*, grown in Asia, N Africa and Europe as food crop.

Millipede

millipede, any of class Diplopoda of man[y-] legged arthropods. Cylindrical, segment[ed] body; herbivorous. Differs from centipe[de] in having 2 pairs of legs on each segme[nt] and no poisonous bite.

Milne, A[lan] A[lexander] (1882-195[6]), English author. Known for children's boo[ks] incl. *Winnie-the-Pooh* (1926).

Milos, *see* MELOS.

Milosz, Czeslaw (1911-), Polish writer, [b.] Lithuania. Now resident in America. *T[he] Captive Mind* (1953) studies effects [of] communism on 4 Polish writers. Oth[er] works incl. poetry, novels. Nobel Prize f[or] Literature (1980).

Milton, John (1608-74), English poet. Ear[ly] works incl. 'L'Allegro', 'Il Penseros[o'], masque *Comus* (1634), pastoral ele[gy] *Lycidas* (1637). Blind after 1652, wrote h[is] masterpiece, blank verse epic *Paradi[se] Lost* (1667), attempting to 'justify the wa[ys] of God to men'. Also wrote classical dram[a] *Samson Agonistes* (1671), prose pamphle[ts]. Latin secretary to Commonweal[th] (1649-60).

Milton Keynes, area of Buckinghamshir[e,] SC England, designated new town. Prese[nt] pop. 46,000; planned 250,000. Open Unive[r]sity hq.

Milwaukee, port of SE Wisconsin, US; on [L.] Michigan. Pop. 1,585,000; state's large[st] city. Shipping centre; important brewin[g,] meat packing industs.; heavy machiner[y,] electrical equipment mfg. Trade po[st] estab. 1795.

mimosa, genus of trees, shrubs and herbs [of] Leguminosae family, mostly native [to] tropical and subtropical America. Sever[al] species respond to light and touch, [eg] *Mimosa pudica,* the sensitive plan[t]. Related species incl. ACACIA.

minaret, slender tower attached to corner [of] Islamic mosque from which muezzin ca[lls] the faithful to prayer 5 times a day.

Minch, channel off NW Scotland, separatin[g] Outer Hebrides from mainland. Litt[le] Minch to S separates Inner and Out[er] Hebrides.

mind, presumed seat of consciousness. In philosophy, the concept has been interpreted in various ways, materialists explaining it in terms of matter, dualists holding that the mind exists independently alongside matter, idealists that the mind is the only reality and apparent matter the creation of the imagination.

Mindanao, isl. of S Philippines. Area *c* 94,600 sq km (36,500 sq mi). Mountainous, rising to 2954 m (9690 ft) at Mt. Apo; heavily forested. Produces pineapples, hemp, rice, coffee; gold mined. Underwent rapid population growth in 1960s; scene of fighting against terrorists belonging to large Moslem minority from 1970s.

Mindoro, isl. of Philippines, S of Luzon. Area 9740 sq km (3760 sq mi). Mountainous, with little arable land. Timber produced.

mine, originally explosive-filled tunnel dug under an enemy position. Later, took form of buried canister, detonated by pressure or remote control, laid in systematic patterns as defence against armoured fighting vehicles. Anti-personnel version scatters shrapnel. Naval mine is larger container of explosive detonated by contact, magnetically or by remote control.

mineral, naturally occurring inorganic solid of homogeneous structure and definite composition expressible as a chemical formula. ROCKS are usually a mixture of minerals.

mineralogy, branch of GEOLOGY dealing with the study of minerals. Emphasis in 19th-20th cent. on chemical composition and crystallographic features.

mineral water, water naturally impregnated with metallic salts or gases, often held to have medicinal value. Sulphates, phosphates, carbonates of such metals as iron, magnesium, sodium, barium, or gases such as carbon dioxide or hydrogen sulphide, occur in mineral waters.

Minerva, in Roman religion, goddess of arts, craftsmen and wisdom. Identified with Greek ATHENA.

Ming, Chinese dynasty (1368-1644), founded by Chu Yuan-chang. Empire extended from Korea to Burma at its height. First contacts with Europeans, esp. missionaries, began in Ming period. Noted for literary excellence, fine porcelain. Supplanted by Manchu dynasty.

miniature, very small painting, usually a portrait, executed in gouache or watercolour. Form *fl* in 16th and 17th cent. in hands of such practitioners as Holbein, Hilliard and Cooper.

minimum lending rate, *see* BANK RATE.

mining, process of extracting metallic ores and minerals from Earth's crust. When mineral deposits lie near surface, opencast (open cut) and strip mining are used. Subterranean system of shafts and galleries is used to extract minerals which lie deeper.

mink, semi-aquatic carnivore of weasel family, genus *Mustela*. Species incl. European mink, *M. lutreola* and larger North American, *M. vison*, bred for its soft, thick fur.

Minneapolis, city of E Minnesota, US; contiguous with St Paul ('Twin Cities'), on Mississippi R. Pop. 378,000, with St Paul 2,011,000, state's largest city. Financial, commercial, indust. centre of agric. region; processes grain and dairy produce, clothing mfg. Seat of Univ. of Minnesota (1851).

Minnesinger, poet and musician of Germany in 12th-13th cents. who sang of courtly love; incl. Walther von der Vogelweide, Wolfram von Eschenbach. Corresponded to TROUBADOURS. *See* MEISTERSINGER.

Minnesota, state of N US. Area 217,736 sq km (84,068 sq mi); pop. 4,019,000; cap. St Paul; largest city Minneapolis. N borders with Canada; prairies in S (grain, dairy farming esp. butter production); iron ore, granite mining in Mesabi Range. Drained by Hudson, St Lawrence, Mississippi river systems. E part of region ceded to British by French (1763); obtained by US from British (1783); W part purchased from French (1803). Admitted to Union as 32nd state (1858).

minnow, *Phoxinus phoxinus*, smallest fish of carp family, common in European fresh water. Males brightly coloured at spawning time.

Minoan civilization, Bronze Age civilization of Crete revealed by excavations of Arthur EVANS. During Middle Minoan period (*c* 2000-1600 BC), great palaces were built at Knossos, Phaistos, Mallia, urbanization began and metal-working reached high point. Two pictographic scripts, Linear A and later Linear B (deciphered 1952), were used. Destruction of Knossos *c* 1400 BC marks decline of civilization and growth of Mycenaean power.

Minorca (*Menorca*), second largest of Balearic Isls., Spain. Area 702 sq km (271 sq mi); main town and port Mahón. Mainly low-lying. Tourism, cereals, fruit growing, livestock.

Minos, in Greek myth, king of Crete, son of Zeus and Europa. Had Labyrinth built by Daedalus to house the monstrous Minotaur (man with bull's head), offspring of wife Pasiphaë by a bull. Minotaur was slain by THESEUS. Minos became a judge in Hades after his death.

Minotaur, *see* MINOS.

Minsk, city of USSR, cap. of Byelorussian SSR. Pop. 1,276,000. Indust. and cultural centre; tractor, automobile, textile mfg. Passed from Poland to Russia (1793).

mint, any of genus *Mentha* of aromatic herbs native to Mediterranean area but now widespread. Species incl. garden mint, *M. rotundifolia*, used for sauces; peppermint, *M. piperita*, used in confectionery and medicines and spearmint, *M. spicata*, used in chewing gum and sauces.

Minton, Thomas (1765-1836), English potter. Estab. small pottery at Stoke-on-Trent

(1789). Created celebrated Willow Pattern ware and produced good bone china.

minuet, French dance in triple time. Originally rustic, became fashionable court dance in 18th cent. Used by Haydn, Mozart in sonatas.

Miocene epoch, fourth geological epoch of Tertiary period. Alpine mountain building continued; withdrawal of seas, formation of extensive plains. Mammals still dominant. Decrease in temperature continued from Oligocene. Also *see* GEOLOGICAL TABLE.

Miquelon, *see* ST PIERRE AND MIQUELON.

Mirabeau, Honoré Gabriel Riqueti, Comte de (1749-91), French statesman. A leader in National Assembly (1789), he sought to create constitutional monarchy.

miracle, event which apparently transcends laws of nature and is thus thought to be due to supernatural intervention, esp. that of God. Concept only occurs where natural laws and divine will have been clearly distinguished, *eg* in the 3 major monotheistic religions. Many miracles of Jesus recorded in Gospels. In RC church, attestation of miracles required in process of canonization.

miracle play or **mystery play,** medieval religious drama. Began as simple dramatization of religious stories, later presented with contemporary social realism, humour. Developed into full cycles, performed on feast-days by town guilds.

mirage, optical illusion in the atmosphere. Caused by refraction and reflection of light rays in layers of air of different temperature and density. Occurs most often in deserts, polar seas.

Mirandola, *see* PICO DELLA MIRANDOLA.

Miró, Joan (1893-), Spanish painter. Joined surrealist group in 1925; work has become more abstract and is noted for its use of amoeba-like shapes and bright colours.

miscarriage, *see* ABORTION.

Mishima, Yukio, pseud. of Kimitake Hiraoka (1925-70), Japanese author. Works, *eg Confessions of a Mask* (1949), *The Sailor Who Fell from Grace with the Sea* (1963), celebrate the beauty and violence of traditional Japanese life. Committed ritual suicide after haranguing a demonstration.

Mishnah, *see* TALMUD.

Miskolc, city of NE Hungary, on R. Sajó. Pop. 203,000. Iron, steel indust., railway engineering. Cattle, wine, tobacco market. Medieval church, buildings. Univ. (1949).

missile, *see* GUIDED MISSILE.

missions, organizations with aim of spreading religious knowledge. Early dissemination of Christianity undertaken by missionaries, *eg* St Paul; in early Middle Ages by St Patrick, St Augustine, St Boniface. Further wave of activity (esp. by Jesuits) with opening up of New World. Protestant missions incl. Society for Promoting Christian Knowledge (1698). Since 19th cent., missions have emphasized medical care and education.

Mississippi, state of SE US. Area 123,584 sq km (47,716 sq mi); pop. 2,386,000; cap. Jackson. W border formed by Mississippi R.; mainly on Gulf of Mexico coastal plain. Cotton, soya beans, poultry, livestock farming. Some oil resources, fishing, lumbering. Taken by British from French (1763); gained by US after Revolution. Admitted to Union as 20th state (1817).

Mississippi, river of C US. Rises in N Minnesota, flows S 3780 km (*c* 2350 mi) forming many natural state boundaries. Enters Gulf of Mexico forming delta in SE Louisiana. Tributaries incl. Ohio, Missouri, Arkansas rivers; main ports St Louis, New Orleans. Region explored by French in 17th cent.; US control after Louisiana Purchase 1803; important in 19th-cent. W expansion.

Mississippian period, earlier of 2 subdivisions of Carboniferous period in North America. Began *c* 345 million years ago, lasted 20 million years. Time of large shallow seas, deposition of limestones, sandstones, shales. Typified by brachiopods, crinoids, corals; increasing amphibians, fish, insects; mosses, ferns. Also *see* GEOLOGICAL TABLE.

Missolonghi (*Mesolóngion*), town of WC Greece, on Gulf of Patras. Pop. 11,000. Fish, tobacco trade. Greek stronghold in independence struggle against Turks (1822-6), Byron died here (1824).

Missouri, state of C US, on W bank of Mississippi R. Area 180,487 sq km (69,686 sq mi); pop. 4,822,000 cap. Jefferson City; other major city St Louis. Mainly rolling prairie, crossed by Missouri R. Livestock, grain, dairy farming; lead, barytes mining. Explored by French in 17th cent.; bought by US as part of Louisiana Purchase (1803). Admitted to Union as 24th state (1821). Slave state, remained in Union in Civil War.

Missouri, river of WC US; longest in North America. Rises in SW Montana (Rocky Mts.); flows E 4130 km (*c* 2565 mi), then SE across C plains through North and South Dakota, Missouri to join Mississippi near St Louis. Hist. fur trade route until railway boom. Provides h.e.p., irrigation.

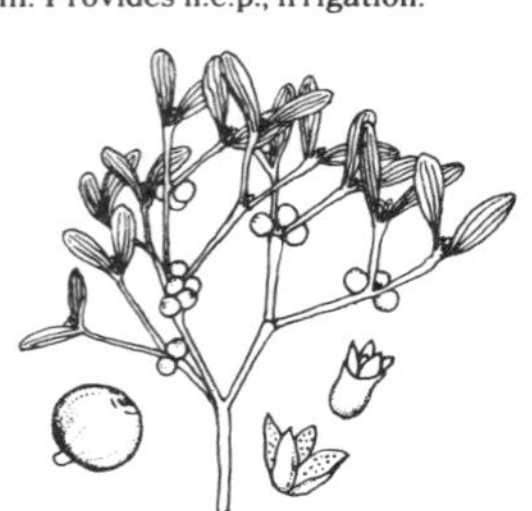

Mistletoe

mistletoe, *Viscum album,* European evergreen plant. Parasitic on trees, has yellowish flowers and white, poisonous berries. Traditional Christmas decoration. Held sacred by Druids.

mistral, cold, dry, often strong N or NW wind which blows in S France, esp. Rhône valley and delta, in winter.

mite, tiny arachnid of order Acarina, with 4 pairs of legs and rounded body. Often parasitic on animals or destructive of food.

Mitford, Nancy Freeman (1904-73), English writer. Known for satirical novels of upper-class manners, *eg The Pursuit of Love* (1945). With Alan Ross edited comic study of social distinctions, *Noblesse Oblige* (1956), coining terms 'U', 'non-U'. Her sister, **Jessica Mitford** (1917-), wrote autobiog. *Hons and Rebels* (1960), *The American Way of Death* (1963).

Mithra, originally, in ancient Zoroastrian myth, god of light and wisdom; by 5th cent. BC principal Persian god. Cult spread into Europe; by 2nd cent. AD major religion of Roman Empire. Mithras (Latin form) worshipped by legions as ideal comrade and soldier. Cult involved rigorous ethics and secret ritual; declined in 3rd cent.

Mithradates [VI] the Great (*c* 132-63 BC), king of Pontus. Expansion of his empire over Asia Minor and into Greece led to series of 3 wars with Rome (88-84, 83-81, 74-63). Finally defeated by Pompey.

mitosis, in biology, method of division of nucleus of body cells, prior to division into 2 new cells. Chromosomes are formed in nucleus and, when nuclear membrane breaks up, they migrate to equator of cell and divide lengthways. The 2 halves move to opposite ends of the cell where 2 new nuclei are assembled around them.

Mitterrand, François Maurice Marie (1916-), French politician. Head of Socialist Party from 1971. Narrowly defeated in presidential elections (1965, 1974) as candidate of Combined Left.

moa, any of Dinornithidae family of extinct flightless birds of New Zealand, hunted by Maoris *c* 500 years ago. Resembled ostrich, reaching heights of 3.7 m/12 ft.

Moab, ancient country of Jordan, in uplands E of Dead Sea. Moabite stone is 9th-cent. BC record of successful revolt against Israel. Discovered 1868.

Mobile, seaport of SW Alabama, US, on Mobile Bay. Pop. 403,000. Shipbuilding indust.; exports cotton, timber. Founded by French (1710). Seized from Spanish by US (1813).

Mobutu, Sese Seko, orig. Joseph (1930-), Zaïrian army officer, politician. Led army coup against 1st Congolese govt. (1960); arrested Lumumba, who was later murdered by Mobutu's troops. In 2nd coup (1965), deposed Kasavubu and Tshombe, becoming head of state.

Moçambique, *see* MOZAMBIQUE.

mockingbird, *Mimus polyglottos,* American bird noted for melodious song and mimicry of other birds.

Model Parliament, parliament summoned (1295) by Edward I of England, so called because it estab. general type of future parliaments. First attempt to be representative, as it drew on all 3 estates.

Modena (anc. *Mutina*), city of Emilia-Romagna, NC Italy, cap. of Modena prov. Pop. 180,000. Agric. machinery, vehicles; univ. (1678). Ruled by Este family 13th-19th cent. Medieval cathedral, ducal palace.

moderator, in physics, substance, *eg* graphite or heavy water, used to slow down high energy neutrons produced during fission in nuclear reactor, thus making them more likely to cause further fission.

modernism, in religion, term for movement in late 19th and 20th cents. which tries to redefine Christian teachings in light of modern science, historical research. In RC Church referred to specific movement condemned by Pius X in 1907.

Modigliani, Amedeo (1884-1920), Italian painter, sculptor. Influenced by African sculpture, cubism and Italian masters such as Botticelli, he painted numerous distinctive elongated portraits.

modulation, in physics, alteration of characteristics, *eg* frequency or amplitude, of a wave in accordance with characteristics of another wave. Amplitude modulation, in which amplitude of radio wave is changed in accordance with signal to be broadcast, is principal mode of radio transmission. Frequency modulation provides radio transmission with reduced noise and outside interference.

Mogadishu (Ital. *Mogadiscio*), cap. of Somalia, on Indian Ocean. Pop. 230,000. Admin., commercial centre; port, exports livestock, bananas. Founded 9th cent. by Arabs. Taken by sultan of Zanzibar (1871); sold to Italy (1905), became cap. of Italian Somaliland.

Mogul, dynasty of Moslem emperors of India. Founded (1526) by BABER. Achieved greatest power under AKBAR. Weakened by wars against MAHRATTAS in 18th cent., later emperors were under control of the British, who dissolved empire in 1857.

Mohammed (*c* 570-632), Arab prophet, founder of ISLAM. A rich merchant, b. in Mecca, where he had vision (*c* 610) calling on him to found a monotheistic religion. Word of God revealed to him by angel Gabriel became text of KORAN. Plot to kill him led to flight (HEGIRA) to Medina (622), where he estab. Islamic theocracy. Conquered Mecca (630), estab. basis for Mohammedan empire.

Mohammed Ahmed, *see* MAHDI.

Mohammed Ali or **Mehemet Ali** (*c* 1769-1849), pasha of Egypt, b. Albania. Suppressed power of MAMELUKES in Egypt (1811). Intervened successfully in Greek war of independence until defeated by European allies at Navarino (1827). Revolted against Ottoman sultan (1831, 1839). Granted hereditary rights to governorship of Egypt, founding royal line.

Mohammedanism, *see* ISLAM.

Mohammed II (1429-81), Ottoman sultan

(1451-81), founder of Ottoman empire. Captured Constantinople (1453). Conquered Greece, Serbia, Albania and the Crimea. Noted linguist and patron of arts and learning.

Mohawk, *see* IROQUOIS.

Mohegan or **Mohican,** North American Indian tribe of SW Connecticut. Supported by British became one of most powerful tribes in S New England. Increase of white settlement led to virtual extinction by 19th cent.

Mohenjo-Daro, one of two centres of INDUS VALLEY CIVILIZATION.

Mohican, *see* MOHEGAN.

Mohorovičić Discontinuity or **Moho,** boundary line between Earth's crust and mantle, av. depth below land surface *c* 35 km (22 mi). Discovered by Andrija Mohorovičić (1857-1936), Croatian geologist.

Mojave or **Mohave,** desert of S California, US; S of Sierra Nevada. Area 38,850 sq km (*c* 15,000 sq mi). Death Valley in N.

molasses, syrup obtained from drainings of raw sugar cane or from sugar during refining (latter syrup being called treacle in Britain). Used in making rum, confectionery and as cattle feed.

Mold, town and admin. hq. of Clwyd, N Wales. Pop. 8000.

Moldau (*Vltava*), river of Czechoslovakia. Flows *c* 435 km (270 mi) from Böhmerwald via Prague to R. Elbe. H.e.p.

Moldavia (*Moldova*), region of NE Romania, fertile plain between rivers Prut, Siret. Principality founded 14th cent., formerly incl. Bukovina, Bessarabia. United with Walachia to form Romania (1859).

Moldavian Soviet Socialist Republic, constituent republic of W USSR, bounded by Ukrainian SSR and Romania. Area *c* 33,800 sq km (13,000 sq mi); pop. 3,948,000; cap. Kishinev. Largely flat, with fertile black-earth soil; extensive vineyards. Created (1940) by merger of former Moldavian ASSR with parts of Bessarabia ceded by Romania.

mole, small burrowing insectivore of Talpidae family, with small weak eyes, pointed snout, clawed feet. European common mole, *Talpa europaea,* has black velvety fur, eats mainly earthworms.

mole (= gram-molecule), in chemistry, quantity containing same number of molecules as number of atoms in 0.012 kg of carbon 12 isotope.

molecular weight, sum of atomic weights of all atoms in a molecule of a substance.

molecule, smallest portion of a substance able to exist independently and retain properties of original substance.

Molière, pseud. of Jean Baptiste Poquelin (1622-73), French dramatist. Known for comedies of manners involving caricatures of human folly, pretentiousness, *eg Tartuffe* (1664), *Le Misanthrope* (1666), *Le Bourgeois Gentilhomme* (1670), *Le Malade imaginaire* (1673).

Mollusca (molluscs), phylum of soft-bodied unsegmented animals often with hard shell. Usually move by means of single muscular foot. Incl. snail, slug, octopus (no shell), squid (small internal shell).

Moloch, pagan Semitic god of fire. Practice of sacrificing first-born children to him condemned by OT prophets.

Moloch

moloch, *Moloch horridus,* agamid lizard of Australian deserts. Brown body covered with spines; feeds on ants. Also called spiny lizard or thorny devil.

Molotov, Vyacheslav Mikhailovich, orig. Skriabin (1890-), Soviet political leader. As foreign minister (1939-49, 1953-6), he negotiated Non-aggression Pact with Germany (1939). Influence declined during Khrushchev's rise, which he opposed. Expelled from party (1964).

Moltke, Helmuth Bernhard, Graf von (1800-91), Prussian army officer. As chief of staff (1858-88) reorganized Prussian army, facilitating victories against Denmark (1864), Austria (1866), France (1870). His nephew, **Helmuth Johannes Ludwig von Moltke** (1848-1916), was also chief of staff (1906-14).

Moluccas, group of isls., forming Maluku prov. of Indonesia. Area *c* 84,000 sq km (32,000 sq mi). Incl. Halmahera, Aru and Tanimbar Isls. Formerly called Spice Isls., nutmeg and cloves originated here. Under Dutch control from 1667 to WWII.

molybdenum (Mo), metallic element; at. no. 42, at. wt. 95.94. Occurs as molybdenite (MoS_2); obtained by reducing oxide with carbon. Used to harden steel; molybdenum disulphide used as a lubricant.

Mombasa, city of E Kenya, on Indian Ocean. Pop. 371,000. Port at Kilindini to SW exports coffee, sisal, hides, tea; handles major part of Kenya, Uganda, Tanzania's trade. Oil refining, cement, glass mfg. Arab trade centre from 11th cent.; held by

Portugal 16th-17th cent. Ceded to UK by Zanzibar 1887.

moment of force, measure of tendency of a force to cause rotation of a body about a point or axis. Measured as product of magnitude of force and perpendicular distance from its line of action to axis of rotation.

momentum, in physics, the product of mass and velocity of a body. In Newtonian mechanics, total momentum of system of bodies on which no external forces act is constant.

Monaco, independent principality of S Europe, enclave within SE France. Area 149 ha. (368 acres); pop. 26,000; cap. Monaco-Ville. Commercial centre La Condamine; tourism in MONTE CARLO. Ruled by Genoese Grimaldi family from 13th cent. Part of France (1793-1814), Sardinia (1815-61). Constitutional monarchy from 1911-59 (restored 1962). Customs union with France.

Monadhliath Mountains, range of NC Scotland, in Highland region; rise to 941 m (3087 ft).

Monaghan, county of Ulster prov., NE Irish Republic. Area 1290 sq km (498 sq mi); pop. 50,000. Undulating terrain; oats, livestock. Co. town **Monaghan,** on Ulster Canal. Pop. 5000. RC cathedral.

monasticism, system of organized community life for those who have retired from world under religious vows. Vows of celibacy, poverty and obedience are typical. Feature of Christianity, Buddhism, Jainism and Islam. Middle Ages in Europe saw rise of great monastic orders, *eg* Benedictines, Cistercians, Carthusians.

Mönchen-Gladbach, city of W West Germany. Pop. 260,000. Centre of cotton indust., also produces paper. Grew around abbey founded 972. Badly damaged in WWII. Called München-Gladbach till 1963.

Monck or **Monk, George, 1st Duke of Albemarle** (1608-70), English soldier. Fought for Charles I in Scotland, captured at the battle of Nantwich (1644) and in 1646 turned parliamentarian. In the unrest which followed Cromwell's death, he intervened with an army from Scotland and engineered Charles II's restoration (1660).

Mond, Ludwig (1839-1909), British chemist, b. Germany. Perfected Solvay process for manufacture of alkali. Devised method for extraction of nickel from its ores using carbon monoxide (Mond process).

Mondrian, Piet (1872-1944), Dutch painter. Chief exponent of neo-plasticism, a strict form of geometric abstraction. Works are characterized by use of straight line grids and rectangles of primary colours.

monetarism, *see* FRIEDMAN.

Monet, Claude (1840-1926), French painter. Leading member of the impressionists, he evolved a broken-colour technique to catch the changing effects of light. Later series of waterlily paintings culminated in almost abstract vision of nature.

money, in economics, unit of value or means of payment. Cattle often used as unit of value in ancient societies with more convenient objects as means of payment. Subsequently both these roles merged in durable, intrinsically valuable metals. State coinage prob. originated in Lydia (7th cent. BC), thus allowing govt. to use currency of higher face value than its commodity value. Paper currency (widely in use since 17th cent.) usually backed by a precious metal until 1930s.

Mongolia, republic of C Asia, formerly Outer Mongolia. Area *c* 1,566,000 sq km (605,000 sq mi); pop. 1,576,000; cap. Ulan Bator. Language: Mongolian. Religion: Lamaist Buddhism. Mainly grazing plateau land (*see* GOBI DESERT) with extremes of climate. Trade in wool, hides, cloth; mineral extraction. Economy based on stock rearing. Nomadic Mongols conquered region under Genghis Khan (*c* 1205). Communism estab. 1924 after break with China.

mongolism or **Down's syndrome,** congenital disease caused by fault in formation of ovum. Characterized by mental retardation and broad face, slanting eyes.

Mongols, nomadic Asiatic tribe who, under GENGHIS KHAN and his sons, conquered much of Asia, incl. China. Also invaded Europe, penetrating as far as Hungary and Poland. Power waned towards end of 14th cent.; Mongol rule in China ended 1368.

mongoose, small Old World carnivore of Viverridae family. Feeds on small mammals, birds' eggs, *etc;* often kept for killing snakes. Species incl. Indian mongoose, *Herpestes edwardsi.* Meerkat, *Suricata suricata,* is South African species.

monism, in philosophy, doctrine that there is only one ultimate substance or principle, whether matter (materialism) or mind (idealism) or some third thing which unifies both.

monitor, any of Varanidae family of large carnivorous lizards of Africa, Asia, Australia. Elongated snout, long neck and extensible forked tongue. Largest species is KOMODO DRAGON.

Monk, George, *see* MONCK.

monkey, group of long-tailed primates; divided into platyrrhines (New World monkeys) of South America and catarrhines (Old World monkeys) of African and Asian tropics. Incl. capuchin, marmoset, macaque.

monkey puzzle or **Chile pine,** *Araucaria araucana*, coniferous tree, native to Chile. Stiff pointed leaves, contorted appearance; grown as ornamental.

monkshood or **aconite,** any of genus *Aconitum* of perennial herbs of buttercup family, esp. *A. napellus,* native to N temperate regions, with hoodshaped flowers. All species are poisonous.

Monmouth, James Scott, Duke of (1649-85), claimant to English throne. Illegitimate son of Charles II by Lucy Walter, he became figurehead for Whig supporters of Protestant succession in opposition to

Catholic duke of York. Fled to Holland after RYE HOUSE PLOT (1683). On accession of James II (1685), returned to England and raised rebellion against him. Defeated at Sedgemoor and executed.

Monmouthshire, former county of SE Wales, on English border, now called Gwent. Hilly in W, incl. part of S Wales coalfield. Main town Newport. Coalmining; iron, steel works; light industs. Co. town was **Monmouth,** at confluence of Wye and Monnow. Pop. 7000.

Monnet, Jean (1888-1979), French economist. President of European Coal and Steel Community (1952-5). Leading advocate of European unity.

Monophysitism, Christian heresy of 5th and 6th cents. Taught that Jesus had only one nature (divine), opposed at Council of Chalcedon (451). Adhered to by Coptic, Jacobite and Armenian churches.

monopoly, in economics, virtual control of supply of commodity or service by one producer, enabling producer to fix price at which consumer must purchase product. Legislation places restraints on monopolistic tendencies; in UK, Monopolies Commission set up 1948. Govt. monopolies (*eg* postal system) operated to facilitate public services. Socialist doctrine extends monopoly principle to all basic industries, *eg* nationalization of steel by British Labour govt. *See* OLIGOPOLY.

monorail, railway with single rail. Usually the rail is elevated with cars suspended from it or running above it. Driving wheels may rotate horizontally making contact with side of rail.

monosodium glutamate, white soluble crystalline salt extracted from grains or beets. Intensifies flavours, used widely in tinned food.

monotheism, belief that there is only one god, as in Judaism, Christianity and Islam.

Monotheletism, Christian heresy of 7th cent. Taught that Christ operated with one will although he had 2 natures. Arose as compromise between MONOPHYSITISM and orthodoxy. Died out except among MARONITES.

monotremes (Monotremata), subclass of primitive egg-laying mammals showing many reptilian features. Echidna and duckbilled platypus only living species, found in Australia and New Guinea.

Monroe, James (1758-1831), American statesman, president (1817-25). Negotiated Louisiana Purchase (1803). Promulgated Monroe Doctrine (1823), opposing European attempts to interfere in affairs of American countries or to recolonize recently independent American colonies; provided basis for much subsequent American foreign policy.

Monroe, Marilyn, orig. Norma Jean Baker or Mortenson (1926-62), American film actress. Known for sex goddess image, her talent for comedy was revealed in *eg The Seven-Year Itch* (1955), *Some Like It Hot* (1959). Committed suicide.

Monroe Doctrine, *see* MONROE, JAMES.

Monrovia, cap. of Liberia, near mouth of R. St Paul. Pop. 172,000. Admin., commercial centre; port, exports rubber, iron ore. Founded (1822) for freed American slaves.

Mons (Flem. *Bergen*), town of SW Belgium, cap. of Hainaut prov. Pop. 97,000. Coalmining, textiles, chemicals. Battleground in both WWs. Town hall (15th cent.), cathedral (16th cent.).

monsoon, wind system involving seasonal reversal of prevailing wind direction. Found most often within tropics, esp. SE Asia. In India, winter monsoon (Nov.-April) is cold, dry N wind; summer monsoon (May-Sept.) is warm, wet SW wind.

Montagu, Lady Mary Wortley, neé Pierrepont (1689-1762), English letter-writer. Known for lively descriptions of Turkish life from viewpoint as wife of British ambassador. Introduced inoculation to England from Turkey.

Montaigne, Michel Eyquem, Seigneur de (1533-92), French writer. Creator of modern essay form. *Essais* (complete edition, 1595) reflect personal scepticism, philosophical interests. Greatly influenced European thought.

Montale, Eugenio (1896-), Italian poet. Known for pessimistic 'hermetic' poetry. Awarded Nobel Prize for Literature (1975).

Montana, state of NW US, in Rocky Mts. Area 381,087 sq km (147,138 sq mi); pop. 766,000; cap. Helena. Bounded in N by Canada; Bitterroot Range in W; plains in E. Main occupations cattle, grain farming; lumbering; copper, zinc, silver, gold mining. Explored by fur traders in 18th, 19th cents.; developed with gold, silver, copper strikes. Admitted to Union as 41st state (1889).

Mont Blanc, peak of Savoy Alps, SE France. Highest in Alps (4808 m/15,781 ft). Part of Mont Blanc massif extending into Italy, Switzerland; incl. several peaks, glaciers. First ascended 1786. Road tunnel (11.3 km/7 mi long) opened 1965, links France with Italy.

montbretia, any of genus *Tritonia* of flowering plants native to S Africa. European garden varieties incl. *T. crocosmiflora* with orange-crimson flowers.

Montcalm, Louis-Joseph de Montcalm-Gozon, Marquis de (1712-59), French general. Commanded French forces in Canada after 1756, capturing Fort William and defending Ticonderoga (1758). Killed in defeat at Québec by British forces under Wolfe.

Monte Carlo, town of Monaco, on Riviera. Resort, gambling casino. Annual car rally and motor racing grand prix.

Monte Cassino, *see* CASSINO.

Montenegro (*Crna Gora*), autonomous republic of SW Yugoslavia. Area 13,838 sq km (5343 sq mi); cap. Titograd. Mountainous, except around L. Scutari; sheep, goats. Mineral resources. Medieval prov. of Zeta, within Serbia; independent after 1389, resisted Turks 14th-19th cent. Yugoslav prov. from 1918, republic from 1946.

Monte Rosa, mountain group of SW Switzerland and N Italy, in Pennine Alps. Highest is Dufourspitze (4636 m/15,217 ft), first climbed 1855.

Monterrey, city of NE Mexico, cap. of Nuevo León state. Pop. 1,725,000. Indust. and rail centre; lead, iron, steel, textile, glass mfg. Founded 1579. Has notable 18th-cent. cathedral.

Montesquieu, Charles Louis de Secondat, Baron de la Brède et de (1689-1755), French political theorist. Wrote satirical *Lettres persanes* (1721). His comparative analysis of govt. in *L'Esprit des Lois* (1748) influenced formulation of American Constitution.

Montessori, Maria (1870-1952), Italian educator, doctor. Developed Montessori Method, emphasizing importance for children of 3-6 years of freedom of choice and action and use of exercises and games in growth of coordination, perceptual skills.

Monteverdi, Claudio Giovanni Antonio (1567-1643), Italian composer. Leading figure in early development of opera with such works as *Orfeo* (1607). Wrote 9 books of madrigals and much church music.

Montevideo, cap. of Uruguay, on Río de la Plata estuary. Pop. 1,230,000. Major seaport, handles most of Uruguay's trade. Wool, hides, meat exports. Meat packing, tanning, flour milling industs. Founded 1726. Became cap. 1828. Has National Univ. (1849). Tourism, in scenic area.

Montez, Lola, real name Maria Gilbert (1818-61), Irish adventuress. Became mistress of Ludwig I of Bavaria. Greatly influenced his policy until banished (1848).

Montezuma II (*c* 1480-1520), Aztec emperor of Mexico (1502-20). Captured by Cortés (1519) during Spanish conquest and held hostage in Mexico City (Tenochtitlán). Persuaded by Cortés to quell an Aztec uprising, he was killed by his own subjects.

Montfort, Simon de, Earl of Leicester (*c* 1208-65), English statesman. Led baronial side against Henry III in Barons' War (1263-7). Victory at Lewes (1264) followed by the Great Parliament, which estab. precedent of representation in England. Defeated and killed at Evesham.

Montgolfier, Joseph Michel (1740-1810), French inventor. With his brother, **Jacques Etienne Montgolfier** (1745-99), invented 1st practical hot-air balloon, in which they made 1st manned flight (1783).

Montgomery, Bernard Law, 1st Viscount Montgomery of Alamein (1887-1976), British field marshal. Given command of British 8th Army in N Africa in 1942, won the victory of El Alamein, followed by successful penetration into Tunisia and final defeat of Axis forces. Commanded land forces in Normandy invasion (1944).

Montgomery, cap. of Alabama, US; on Alabama R. Pop. 250,000. Railway jct.; cotton, livestock produce. First cap. of Confederacy (1861).

Montgolfier's balloon

Montgomeryshire, former county of C Wales, now in Powys. Mountainous. moorland; fertile valleys in E. Sheep rearing, oats; slate, stone quarrying. Co. town was **Montgomery.** Pop. 1000.

Montmartre, *see* Paris.

Montpelier, cap. of Vermont, US; on Winooski R. Pop. 9000.

Montpellier, city of Languedoc, S France, cap. of Hérault dept. Pop. 205,000. Resort, wine trade, chemicals mfg. Purchased (1349) from Aragón; former Huguenot stronghold. Univ. (1289).

Montréal or **Montreal,** largest city of Canada, in SE Québec; on isl. at confluence of St Lawrence, Ottawa rivers, at foot of Mt. Royal. Pop. 2,802,000; mainly French-speaking. Major seaport, commercial, transport, financial centre. Leading grain exports; railway equipment mfg.; iron and steel industs.; fur trade centre. Settled by French (1642); surrendered to British (1760). Seat of McGill Univ. (1821), Montréal Univ. (1876). Site of Expo 1967 fair.

Montreux, town of SW Switzerland, on L. Geneva. Pop. 20,000. Tourism.

Montrose, James Graham, Marquess of (1612-50), Scottish soldier. Leader of Covenanters in Bishops' War (1639-40). Changed sides in Civil War and successfully led Highland army for Charles I against Presbyterians. Defeated at Philiphaugh (1645) and fled abroad. On return, hanged after attempt to raise rebellion.

Mont-St-Michel, rocky isl. of NW France, in Bay of Mont-St-Michel. Tourist centre, linked to mainland by causeway. Abbey (founded 708), used as prison in 19th cent.

Montserrat, isl. of E West Indies, in Leeward Isls. Area 98 sq km (38 sq mi); pop. 13,000; cap. Plymouth. Cotton, fruit exports. Discovered by Columbus (1493). British colony from 17th cent. Volcanic and rugged; subject to earth tremors.

Montserrat or **Monserrat,** mountain of Catalonia, NE Spain. Height 1235 m (4054 ft). On ledge is Benedictine Monastery and church containing shrine of black Virgin.

Monza, city of Lombardy, NW Italy. Pop. 122,000. Textiles, carpets, hats. Cathedral contains iron crown of Lombardy. Motor racing track.

Moon, only natural satellite of Earth; diameter 3476 km (2160 mi). Revolves around Earth at mean distance of 384,000 km once in *c* 27⅓ days (with reference to stars) or *c* 29½ days (with respect to Sun). Shines by reflected light from Sun; said to be full when opposite Sun and new when between Earth and Sun and partly visible. Without atmosphere or water; first visited by American spacemen July, 1969.

moonstone, semi-precious gemstone. Blue-white, translucent; a variety of feldspar.

Moore, George (1852-1933), Irish author. Novels, *eg Esther Waters* (1894), reflect influence of French naturalism. Also wrote several volumes of autobiog.

Moore, G[eorge] E[dward] (1873-1958), English philosopher. Known mainly as rigorous expounder of philosophical problems rather than deviser of a system. Concerned with language, epistemology. Works incl. *Principia Ethica* (1903).

Moore, Henry (1898-), English sculptor. Advocate of direct carving, his work is based on natural forms expressed in stone, wood or bronze. Themes incl. mother and child, reclining figures; also noted for drawings.

Moore, Sir John (1761-1809), British army officer. Commander of expedition sent by Wellington (1808) to assist Spanish army in dislodging Napoleon, was mortally wounded at battle of Corunna, which he had won though greatly outnumbered.

moorhen, *Gallinula chloropus,* olive green water bird of Europe and North America, found near ponds, marshes.

Moors, nomadic people of N Africa of mixed Arab and Berber descent. Became Moslem in 8th cent.; conquered Spain (711) but were defeated in France by Charles Martel (732). Founded caliphate in Spain famed for learning and architectural splendour. Gradually expelled from Spain by Christians, their last stronghold, Granada, falling in 1492.

moose, *Alces americanus,* largest of deer family, found in Alaska, Canada, N US. Huge branching antlers spanning up to 1.8 m/6 ft. Elk is related European species.

moraine, accumulation of ungraded debris, ranging from clay to boulders, transported and deposited by glacier. Types incl. lateral, medial, ground and terminal moraines, classification being dependent on which part of glacier laid them down.

morality plays, didactic late medieval, earl Renaissance verse dramas. Develope from MIRACLE PLAYS, Biblical characters which gave place to personifications vice, virtues, as in EVERYMAN.

Moral Re-Armament or **MRA,** movemen started (1938) by F. Buchman. Follower believe in national spiritual reconstructio starting with the individual.

Moravia, Alberto, pseud. of Albert Pincherle (1907-), Italian novelis Known for realistic novels, *eg The Time Indifference* (1929), *Two Women* (1957).

Moravia (*Morava*), region of Czecho slovakia, between Bohemia (W) an Slovakia (E). Main towns Brno, Ostrav Drained by R. Morava. Agric., coalminin Habsburg domain until 1918, became pro of Czechoslovakia. Combined with Silesi (1927); abolished as political unit (1949).

Moravian Church, evangelical Protestar episcopal sect, founded in Bohemia (145 among followers of Jan HUS. Persecute and driven out of Bohemia; revived i Saxony (18th cent.). Active in all America

Moray, James Stuart, 1st Earl of, *se* MURRAY.

moray eel, any of Muraenidae family c widely distributed marine eels. Aggressiv carnivore, laterally compressed, ofte brightly coloured; hides in rock crevices.

Moray, former county of NE Scotland, no in Grampian region. Previously calle Elginshire. Cromdale Hills in S; low-lyin fertile in N. Livestock rearing, salmo fishing, whisky distilling. Co. town wa Elgin. **Moray Firth,** inlet of North Se between former Moray, Nairnshire an Ross and Cromarty.

mordant, substance used in dyeing to fi colouring matter. Usually consists of basi metal hydroxide (*eg* aluminium hydro ide), which combines with dye to forr insoluble coloured compound (lake) i fibres of fabric.

Mordvinia, auton. republic of E Europea RSFSR, USSR. Area *c* 26,160 sq km (10,10 sq mi); pop. 990,000; cap. Saransk. Foreste steppe; agric., lumbering and wood produc mfg. Mordvinians, a Finno-Ugrian peopl were conquered by Russians in 16th cent.

More, Sir Thomas (1478-1535), Englis statesman, scholar. Friend of Erasmu who exerted strong influence on More humanist ideas. Succeeded Wolsey as lor chancellor (1529-32); resigned over Henr VIII's divorce from Catherine of Aragor Refused (1534) to recognize Henry as hea of Church; executed for treason. Mos famous work, *Utopia* (1516), depicts idea state ordered by reason.

Morecambe (and Heysham), town c Lancashire, NW England, on Morecamb Bay. Pop. 42,000. Resort; port; oil refinery.

morel, any of genus *Morchella* of edibl mushrooms resembling a sponge on stalk. *M. esculenta,* the commonest, i found in deciduous woods and pastures c Europe and North America.

Morel

Morgan, Sir Henry (*c* 1635-88), Welsh buccaneer. Led pirates in West Indies against Spaniards; made daring march across Panama isthmus to capture Panama City (1671). Called to England to answer charges of piracy, he gained royal favour and was later made governor of Jamaica.

Morgan, J[ohn] Pierpont (1837-1913), American financier. Enlarged family fortunes, esp. in railway holdings; formed (1901) US Steel Corporation. Became a symbol of wealth, renowned philanthropist.

Morgan, Thomas Hunt (1866-1945), American biologist. Awarded Nobel Prize for Physiology and Medicine (1933) for chromosome theory of heredity.

morganatic marriage, form of marriage in which man of royalty marries a woman of inferior social status with provision that although children of the marriage will be legitimate, neither they nor the wife may lay claim to his rank or property.

Moriscos, name given to Spanish Moslems who accepted Christian baptism. Edict of 1568 demanded abandonment of all remaining Moorish customs; led to revolt and persecution of Moriscos. Finally expelled from Spain in 1609.

Mormons or **Church of Jesus Christ of Latter-Day Saints,** evangelical religious sect founded in US (1830) by Joseph SMITH after divine revelations. Settled in communities in W Missouri but came into conflict with their neighbours. After death of Smith, Brigham YOUNG became leader and transferred centre of movement to Salt Lake City, Utah. Now worldwide membership of *c* 3 million as result of extensive proselytizing.

morning glory, common name for various twining vines of convolvulus family esp. American *Ipomoea purpurea,* widely cultivated for its purple flowers. Seeds of some varieties contain hallucinogens.

Morocco (Arab. *Al-Mamlaka al-Maghrebia*), kingdom of NW Africa. Area 447,000 sq km (172,500 sq mi); pop. 18,906,000; cap. Rabat. Language: Arabic. Religion: Islam. Largely desert; Atlas Mts. run SW-NE; fertile coast. Produces cereals, fruit, olives, cattle. Minerals incl. phosphates, petroleum, iron ore. Part of Roman MAURETANIA: Arabs brought Islam 7th cent., *fl* under Berber

Morocco

dynasties 11th-14th cents. Settled by Portuguese (1415-1769); became Barbary pirate base. Disputed in 19th cent.; French, Spanish protects. estab. 1912, Tangier internationalized (1923). Independent 1956, constitutional monarchy from 1962.

Moroni, cap. of Comoro Islands, on Grande Comore Isl. Pop. 12,000.

Morpheus, in Greek and Roman myth, shaper of dreams.

morphine, white crystalline alkaloid derived from opium. Used in medicine to relieve pain; continued use leads to addiction.

Morris, William (1834-96), English artist, writer, decorator, printer. Founded firm to produce stained glass, tapestry, furniture and to raise standard of Victorian design. Founded Kelmscott Press (1890) to revive standards of printing. Believed in possibility of improving quality of working life through craftsmanship; his socialist beliefs are reflected in writings.

Morris, William Richard, *see* NUFFIELD.

Morse, Samuel Finley Breese (1791-1872), American inventor, painter. Devised one form of electric telegraph and system of communication, Morse Code, using short and long taps to represent letters of alphabet.

mortar, short-barrelled, large-bore cannon, used in early siege warfare for lobbing missiles over city walls at short range. In WWI and II modern version projected 2 or 3 in. finned bombs (explosive or smoke) as infantry support.

Mortimer, Roger de, 1st Earl of March (*c* 1287-1330), English nobleman. Opposed EDWARD II in baronial wars (1321-2) but was captured (1322); escaped to France (1324) where Edward's wife, Isabella, became his mistress. Together they invaded England, forced Edward's abdication (1326). Ruled England until Edward III had him executed.

mosaic, surface ornamentation by laying small pieces of stone, tile, metal or glass on a bed of cement. Used principally for decoration of floors and walls. Art was first developed by the Romans and perfected by Byzantines (6th cent.); revived by the

Italians in 13th cent., it declined with introduction of fresco.

Mosaic Law, laws by which the Jewish people were governed, contained mainly in Pentateuch and stated in Ten Commandments given to Moses on Mt. Sinai.

moschatel, *see* MUSK.

Moscow (*Moskva*), cap. of USSR and RSFSR; on R. Moskva. Pop. 8,011,000. Indust., cultural and political centre; metal goods, textile mfg. Founded 12th cent.; became national cap. (1547) under 1st tsar Ivan the Terrible; remained so until 1712. Burned during occupation by Napoleon (1812). Cap. again after Revolution (1918). Kremlin (fortified citadel) contains 15th-cent. Uspenski and 16th-cent. Arkhangelski cathedrals, Grand Palace. Lenin's tomb and 16th-cent. St Basil's Cathedral in Red Square. Has 2 univs. (1755, 1953).

Moseley, Henry Gwyn-Jeffreys (1887-1915), English physicist. His work on frequencies of atomic spectra led him to equate charge on atomic nucleus with atomic number.

Moselle (Ger. *Mosel*), river of NE France and NW West Germany. Flows *c* 550 km (340 mi) from Vosges via Metz, Thionville to R. Rhine at Koblenz. Canalized for much of course. Vineyards.

Moses (*fl c* 13th cent. BC), Jewish lawgiver, OT prophet. Led Jews out of captivity in Egypt (Exodus); received Ten Commandments on Mt. Sinai. Estab. organized Jewish religion. Traditional author of Pentateuch.

Moses, Anna Mary Robertson ('Grandma') (1860-1961), American painter. A modern primitive, she is remembered for her popular scenes of rural life.

Moslem League, political organization estab. (1906) to safeguard rights of Moslems in India. Under leadership of Jinnah, demanded creation of separate Moslem state in 1940s; achieved in founding (1947) of Pakistan.

Moslem religion, *see* ISLAM.

Mosley, Sir Oswald (1896-1980), British politician. Held office in Labour govt. of 1929; resigned over economic policy. Organized (1932) British Union of Fascists; led agitation against Jews. Detained 1940-3.

mosque, building for Moslem worship. Main features are: *qibla* wall, with its central *mihrab* or prayer niche which indicates direction of Mecca; a *dikka* (platform for services); a minaret. (from which faithful are called to prayer). Early mosques were adaptations of Christian basilicas.

mosquito, any of Culicidae family of 2-winged insects. Female uses skin-piercing mouthparts to suck blood of animals, often transmitting diseases through its saliva, *eg Anopheles* carries malaria parasite.

Mosquito Coast, belt of land on Caribbean coast, in NE Honduras and E Nicaragua. British protect. (1678-1860), S part annexed by Nicaragua (1894).

moss, any of class *Musci* of small primitive plants. Worldwide distribution. Grows in tufts on moist ground, tree trunks. Important as pioneers of rock surfaces, holding moisture and producing humus, mosses allow seeds of other plants to germinate.

Mossadegh, Mohammed (1880-1967), Iranian statesman. Premier (1951-3), nationalized (1951) British-owned oil indust.; dispute led to breaking-off of diplomatic relations between Iran and Britain. Imprisoned after attempt to overthrow shah.

Mössbauer, Rudolf Ludwig (1929-), German physicist. Awarded Nobel Prize for Physics (1961) for discovery of Mössbauer effect in which gamma rays emitted by certain radioactive isotopes maintain unvarying wavelength if radiating nuclei are held in crystal form. Effect has been widely used.

Mosul (*Al Mawsil*), city of N Iraq, on R. Tigris. Pop. 293,000. Agric. trade centre; rich oilfields nearby. Near ruins of Nineveh.

motet, relatively short, freely contrapuntal piece of vocal music, usually unaccompanied, with Biblical or similar prose text. Early motets were based on plainsong.

moth, insect of order Lepidoptera. Distinguished from butterfly by different antennae, wing arrangement, and night flight.

mother-of-pearl, hard iridescent lining of certain marine shells, *eg* pearl oyster, abalone. Used for decoration, jewellery.

Motherwell (and Wishaw), town of Strathclyde region, C Scotland. Pop. 74,000. Towns united 1920. Coalmining; iron, steel industs.

motion sickness, nausea and vomiting caused by effect of motion on balance organ of inner ear; experienced on ships, motor vehicles, aircraft, *etc.*

motor, *see* ELECTRIC MOTOR.

motor car, *see* AUTOMOBILE.

motorcycle, two-wheeled vehicle propelled by an internal combustion engine. Prob. first built by Gottlieb Daimler (*c* 1885). Engines are usually air-cooled, often 2-stroke (cycle) and generally range from 50-1000 cc.

motorcycle racing, sport dating from introduction of reliable motorcycles in early 1900s. Events incl. annual TT races held in Isle of Man since 1907.

motor racing, competitive sport for motor cars, introduced in France (1894). Present-day international Formula One championship is decided on results of Grand Prix races in over 10 countries. Other events incl. Indianapolis 500 (805 km) in US and Le Mans 24-hr race.

mould, name for various minute fungi forming furry coating mostly on dead organic matter. The blue mould often found on cheese is of *Penicillium* genus, source of penicillin.

Moulmein (*Maulamyaing*), seaport of S

Burma, near mouth of R. Salween. Pop. 175,000. Exports rice, teak.

mountain, natural elevation of Earth's surface, raised relative to surrounding area to height over 305 m/1000 ft. Distinguished from plateau by summit being small in proportion to base. Formed by volcanic action, differential erosion of high land, earth movements, esp. folding and faulting, or combination of all factors. A major mountain-building period is called an orogeny (*see* GEOLOGICAL TABLE).

mountain ash or **rowan,** any of genus *Sorbus* of small trees and shrubs of rose family. Native to N temperate regions. Compound leaves, white flowers followed by red berries.

Mountbatten, Louis Francis Albert Victor Nicholas, 1st Earl Mountbatten of Burma (1900-79), British admiral. In WWII, supreme Allied commander in SE Asia (1943-6). Last viceroy of India (1947), governor-general (1947-8) after partition. Admiral of fleet (1955-9) and chief of defence staff (1959-65). Murdered by IRA.

Mourne Mountains, range of SE Northern Ireland. Highest peak Slieve Donard (852 m/2796 ft).

mouse, small omnivorous rodent of same family (Muridae) as rat, vole. Species incl. house mouse, *Mus musculus,* found worldwide near human habitation, and wood or field mouse, *Apodemus sylvaticus,* of W European countryside.

mouse deer, *see* CHEVROTAIN.

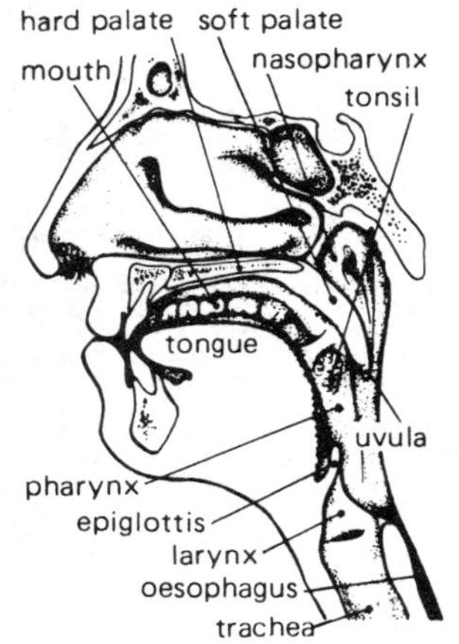

Human mouth

mouth, in anatomy, front opening of the alimentary canal. Roof is formed of hard palate, muscular tongue rests on floor; lined with mucous membrane. Process of digestion is begun in mouth by enzyme in saliva which helps convert starch to sugar.

mouth organ, *see* HARMONICA.

Mozambique

Mozambique or **Moçambique,** republic of SE Africa. Area 783,000 sq km (302,300 sq mi); pop. 11,756,000; cap. Maputo. Languages: Bantu, Portuguese. Religions: animist Christianity. Coastal lowlands; mountains in interior, N and W; main rivers Limpopo, Zambezi. Produces sugar cane, cashew nuts, tea, copra, sisal; h.e.p. at Cabora Bassa. Transit trade with C, S Africa. Reached (1498) by Vasco da Gama; Portuguese settlement followed 15th-19th cent. Became Portuguese East Africa colony (1907). Overseas prov. from 1951. Intense guerrilla warfare by 'Frelimo' nationalists from mid-1960s and fall of govt. in Portugal (1974) resulted in independence (1975).

Mozart, Wolfgang Amadeus (1756-91), Austrian composer. Began to perform in public and compose at age of six. Prolific composer, raised classical music to great heights in his elegance of style and beauty of form. Died in poverty. Over 600 compositions incl. 41 symphonies, 21 piano concertos, string quartets, operas, *eg Marriage of Figaro, Don Giovanni, Così fan tutte, The Magic Flute.*

mucous membrane, skin-like layer lining alimentary canal, genital tract and air passages. Secretes mucus, which has protective and lubricating function.

mudpuppy, aquatic North American salamander, genus *Necturus.* Retains certain larval characteristics, *eg* external gills, underdeveloped legs.

mudskipper, fish of goby family, genus *Periophthalmus* or *Boleophthalmus,* found in tropics. Lives in mud of mangrove swamps, using pectoral fins to hop over mud surface or climb mangrove roots.

Mugabe, Robert (1925-), Zimbabwean statesman. Co-founder of Zimbabwe African National Union (1963). Joint leader with Nkomo of Patriotic Front's guerilla war against white rule. Became PM after 1980 elections.

Muhammad, alternative spelling of MOHAMMED.

Muir, Edwin (1887-1959), Scottish poet. Works, *eg* in *Collected Poems* (1952), draw on dream imagery, archetypal myth.

Mujibur Rahman (1920-75), Bangladeshi political leader. 1st PM of independent Bangladesh (1972-5). Killed in army coup.

Mukden, *see* SHENYANG.

mulberry, any of genus *Morus* of deciduous trees and shrubs, native to N temperate and subtropical regions. Fruit resembles raspberry. Leaves of *M. alba,* white mulberry, used for feeding silkworms.

Muldoon, Robert David (1921-), New Zealand statesman, PM (1975-). Leader of National Party.

mule, *see* ASS.

Mülheim-an-der-Ruhr city of West Germany, in Ruhr. Pop. 188,000. Coalmining, iron and steel mfg., textiles. Coal research institute.

Mulhouse (Ger. *Mülhausen*), city of Alsace, E France, on R. Ill and Rhine-Rhône canal. Pop. 219,000. Textile mfg., chemicals (potash deposits nearby), engineering. Part of Swiss Confederation (1515-1798), voted to join France. Held by Germany (1871-1918).

Mull, isl. of Inner Hebrides, W Scotland, in Strathclyde region. Area 909 sq km (351 sq mi), main town Tobermory. Crofting, fishing, tourism.

mullein, any of genus *Verbascum* of biennial herbs of figwort family. Found in Europe and Asia. *V. thapsus* has woolly leaves and spike of yellow flowers.

Müller, Paul Herman (1899-1965), Swiss chemist. Discovered (1939) DDT's use as insecticide. Awarded Nobel Prize for Physiology and Medicine (1948).

mullet, any of Mugilidae family of grey edible freshwater or marine fish. Feeds on debris in shallow water. Unrelated red mullet or goat fish of Mullidae family is important food fish.

Mullingar, co. town of Westmeath, C Irish Republic. Pop. 6000. RC cathedral.

multiple sclerosis, chronic disease of nervous system, resulting in degeneration of nerve sheaths of brain and spinal cord. Symptoms incl. speech disorder, loss of muscular coordination; cause unknown.

mummy, dead body preserved by embalming, esp. associated with ancient Egypt. Usual method was removal of internal organs, drying of body with natron and wrapping in linen bandages. Human mummies often placed in human-form coffins.

mumps, infectious disease caused by airborne viruses. Symptoms incl. fever and painful swelling of parotid salivary glands. Usually childhood disease; may cause sterility in adult men. Incubation period 2-4 weeks.

Munch, Edvard (1863-1944), Norwegian painter, graphic artist. Forerunner of expressionism; his neurotic works, characterized by distortion and vivid colour, depict anguish and themes of love and death. Works incl. *The Scream, The Sick Child* and numerous woodcuts, lithographs, *etc.*

Part of the coffin lid of an ancient Egyptian mummy

München, *see* MUNICH.

München-Gladbach, *see* MÖNCHEN-GLADBACH.

Münchhausen, Karl Friedrich Hieronymus, Baron von (1720-97), German soldier. Fought for Russians against Turks. Best known as hero of many fantastic adventures, collected and pub. in 1785 by Rudolf Erich Raspe and subsequently expanded by others.

Mungo, St. (d. *c* 612), Scottish churchman, also called St. Kentigern. Missionary in Cumbria; said to have founded church at Glasgow.

Munich (*München*), city of S West Germany, on R. Isar, cap. of Bavaria. Pop. 1,315,000. Cultural, indust. centre; publishing, brewing industs. Tourism, annual *Oktoberfest*. Under Wittelsbachs from 1255, cap. of Bavaria from 1506. Nazi hq. from 1919, scene of Hitler's *Putsch* (1923), Munich Pact (1938). Has museums, art galleries, univ.

Munich Pact, agreement (Sept. 1938) signed by Germany, Italy, Britain and France sanctioning Hitler's annexation of Sudetenland in Czechoslovakia. Represented height of Western appeasement policy towards Nazi Germany; agreement thought then to have averted world war.

Munro, H[ector] H[ugh], *see* SAKI.

Munster, prov. of SW Irish Republic. Area 24,126 sq km (9315 sq mi); pop. 979,000. Comprises cos. Clare, Cork, Kerry, Limerick, Tipperary, Waterford. Ancient kingdom, former cap. Cashel.

Münster, city of NW West Germany, on Dortmund-Ems canal. Pop. 266,000. Metal goods, brewing; univ. (1773). Hanseatic League member; scene of experimental Anabaptist govt. (1533-5) under John of Leiden. Treaty of Westphalia (1648) signed here. Medieval appearance destroyed in WWII.

muntjac, small deer with short antlers, genus *Muntiacus,* found in forests of India and SE Asia. Also called barking deer.

muon or **mu-meson,** elementary particle of lepton family with mass 207 times that of electron and either positive or negative charge. Decays rapidly into electron, neutrino and anti-neutrino.

mural painting, decoration of walls or ceilings by oil paint, ceramics, tempera, fresco, encaustic wax, *etc*.

Murat, Joachim (1767-1815), French marshal, king of Naples (1808-15). Married Napoleon's sister, Caroline (1800). Made king of Naples (1808). Joined Allies (1814) in attempt to retain throne, but supported Napoleon during Hundred Days; defeated by Austrians. Shot after unsuccessful invasion to recover Naples.

Murcia, city of SE Spain, on R. Segura, cap. of Murcia prov. Pop. 244,000. Textiles (hist. silk mfg.), food processing; univ. (1915). From 11th cent. cap. of Moorish kingdom of Murcia, conquered by Castile 1266. Gothic cathedral (14th cent.).

murder, unlawful killing of human being, distinguished from MANSLAUGHTER in that it is malicious, premeditated; also, any killing done while committing another serious crime, *eg* rape, robbery. In some countries, premeditated murder still receives CAPITAL PUNISHMENT.

Murdoch, [Jean] Iris (1919-), English author, b. Ireland. Known for sensitive, intricate, intellectual novels, *eg The Bell* (1958), *The Unicorn* (1963).

Murillo, Bartolomé Estéban (1617-82), Spanish painter. Known for his idealized religious paintings and sentimental genre scenes.

Murmansk, city of USSR, N European RSFSR; on Barents coast of Kola penin. Pop. 381,000. Ice-free port; exports timber; fisheries. Founded 1915, important base in WWII.

Murray or **Moray, James Stuart, 1st Earl of** (*c* 1531-70), Scottish nobleman. One of leaders in Scottish Reformation. Adviser to half-sister, Mary Queen of Scots, on her return to Scotland; appointed regent after her abdication (1567). Assassinated.

Murray, chief river of Australia, flows *c* 2575 km (1600 mi) from Snowy Mts. via Albury, Murray Bridge to Indian Ocean at L. Alexandrina. Main tributaries Darling, Goulburn, Murrumbidgee. Forms most of Victoria-New South Wales border. Provides extensive irrigation, h.e.p.

Murrumbidgee, river of S New South Wales, Australia. Flows *c* 1600 km (1000 mi) W from Snowy Mts. to Murray R. Main tributary Lachlan. Murrumbidgee Irrigation Area (MIA) permits high-yield fruit, rice, livestock farming.

Muscat, cap. of Oman. Pop. 25,000. Port on Gulf of Oman. Exports dates, dried fish, mother-of-pearl.

Muscat and Oman, *see* OMAN.

muscle, body tissue consisting of bundles of cells in the form of fibre which contract or expand under suitable stimulation. Three types of muscle exist: striated or voluntary muscle, which forms flesh and is under conscious control; smooth or involuntary, which is found in walls of alimentary canal, blood vessels, *etc*, and is under control of nervous system; and cardiac or heart muscle.

muscular dystrophy, condition which produces progressive wasting of the muscles, esp. in males. Cause unknown.

Muses, in Greek myth, nine daughters of Zeus and Mnemosyne, goddesses of the arts and literature.

mushroom, fleshy, edible fungi esp. those of family Agaricaceae. Species incl. field mushroom *Agaricus campestris*.

music, art of combining sounds made by musical instruments or human voice. In Europe up to 17th cent., vocal music was dominant form (*see* PLAINSONG; POLYPHONY). In 17th cent., instrumental music developed independent style and OPERA emerged. CONCERTO form dates from early 18th cent.; classical SYMPHONY was estab. in mid 18th cent. and developed to great heights by Haydn, Mozart and Beethoven. Romantic composers of 19th cent. began to break with strict classical forms. Music of 20th cent. has moved away from conventional harmony and tonality, under influence of such innovators as SCHOENBERG. Musical instruments can be divided into 5 main groups: string, wind (woodwind, brass), percussion, keyboard, electronic. Recent developments incl. use of chance and electronic methods.

music, electronic, music produced by electronic circuits. In electronic instruments, *eg* electronic organ and synthesizer, signals are produced by such devices as oscillators, amplified and then fed into loudspeakers. Keyboard of electronic instrument serves as group of switches.

Musil, Robert [Edler von] (1880-1942), Austrian novelist. Chiefly known for monumental masterpiece *The Man Without Qualities* (1930-43), examining cultural collapse through story of year in life of brilliant intellectual.

musk, various plants with musky scent esp. *Mimulus moschatus* of figwort family, with yellow flowers, and moschatel, *Adoxa moschatellina,* with greenish flowers.

musk deer, *Moschus moschiferus,* small solitary deer from highlands of C Asia. Hunted for glandular secretion (musk) from abdomen of male, used in perfumery.

musket, muzzle-loading handgun with matchlock action used by infantry from late 15th cent., later (from *c* 1680) with flintlock. Superseded by breech-loading magazine rifle in 19th cent.

musk ox, *Ovibos moschatus,* hoofed ruminant intermediate between ox and sheep, found in tundra of Canada and Greenland. Long coarse hair, downward curving horns, musky smell.

muskrat or **musquash,** *Ondatra zibethica,* North American aquatic rodent with musky odour. Cultivated for glossy brown fur; introduced *c* 1905 into Europe, proved to be pest.

Muslim religion, see ISLAM.

muslin, group of plain woven cotton fabrics, believed to be named after Mosul, Iraq. Introduced into England in late 17th cent.

musquash, see MUSKRAT.

mussel, marine or freshwater bivalve mollusc. Marine mussels, usually of Mytilidae family, attach themselves to rocks, *etc,* by thread-like secretions. Freshwater mussels of Unionidae family sometimes source of mother-of-pearl and pearls.

Musset, [Louis Charles] Alfred de (1810-57), French poet. Known for introspective love lyrics, *Les nuits* (1835-7). Also wrote plays. Lover of George Sand.

Mussolini, Benito (1883-1945), Italian dictator. Originally a Socialist, he founded (1919) *Fasci di Combattimento,* dedicated to aggressive nationalism and suppression of Socialism and Communism. Organized Fascism into political party (1921). Directed march on Rome (Oct. 1922) which led to his appointment as premier. Assumed dictatorial powers by 1926; reformed govt. according to Fascist principles. Conquered Ethiopia (1935-6), annexed Albania (1939). Entered WW II (1940) in Axis alliance with Hitler. Resigned 1943 after Allied invasion of Italy; rescued from custody by German paratroopers. Shot by partisans.

Mussorgsky, Modest Petrovich (1839-81), Russian composer. Member of 'the Five'. Musical output was restricted by alcoholism. Famed for opera *Boris Godunov and piano work Pictures at an Exhibition.*

Mustafa Kemal, see ATATURK.

mustard, various annual plants of genus *Brassica* with yellow flowers and slender seed pods. Native to Europe and W Asia. Main types are black mustard, *B. nigra,* and white mustard, *B. hirta,* both used in condiment mustard.

mutation, in heredity, sudden change in number or chemical composition of chromosomes. Mutation in gametes can produce inherited change in characteristics of organisms which develop from them and is basis of evolution. Mutations occur naturally at slow rate but can be accelerated, *eg* by exposure to radiation.

Mycenae, ancient city of Greece, in NE Peloponnese, near modern Mikínai. Centre of MYCENAEAN CIVILIZATION.

Mycenaean civilization, late Bronze Age Greek civilization with its centre at Mycenae, which *fl* 1600-1200 BC. Deriving their culture in part from the Minoans of Crete, Mycenaeans gained ascendancy over Crete by 1450 BC and achieved commercial and cultural dominance in Greece (1400-1200 BC). Built strongly walled cities at Mycenae, Tiryns, Pylos and noted beehive tombs. Overthrown by Dorian invaders.

My Lai, small village of South Vietnam, scene of massacre (1968) of over 100 civilians by US troops, who alleged that it was a Viet Cong base.

mynah, Asiatic starling found mainly in India and Sri Lanka. Hill mynah, *Gracula religiosa,* noted for mimicking human speech.

myopia or **short sight,** condition in which images are focused in front of retina, so that distant objects are seen unclearly. Caused because lens of eye is too long or its refractive power too great. Corrected by glasses with concave lenses.

myrrh, aromatic gum resin extracted from small tree, *Commiphora myrrha,* native to Arabia and Ethiopia.

myrtle, any of genus *Myrtus* of evergreen shrubs native to Asia. Common Mediterranean myrtle, *M. communis,* has oval leaves, white flowers, purple berries. Yields extract used in perfumery.

Mysore, city of Karnataka state, SW India. Pop. 356,000. Silk and cotton goods mfg. Former state cap.

mysteries, in Greek and Roman religion, various secret cults. Most important among the Greeks were the Eleusinian (*see* ELEUSIS) and Orphic. Esp. important from 5th cent. BC. Several Asiatic cults were incorporated by the Romans, *eg* those of Isis and Mithras. Possibly many of the cults derived from earlier fertility rituals.

mystery plays, see MIRACLE PLAYS.

mysticism, belief that person can intuitively understand spiritual truths beyond the comprehension of the intellect, *eg* that individual can form a direct relationship with God. Has incl. such movements as neoplatonism, Gnosticism; influenced Quakers.

myth, traditional story of unknown authorship, usually relating supernatural events, actions of gods. May be associated with religious ceremony or offer explanations of natural phenomena, customs, origin of a people, *etc.*

Mytilene (*Mitilini*), cap. of Lesbos isl. Greece. Pop. 26,000. Port; fruit, olive trade.

myxomatosis, infectious virus disease of rabbits spread by mosquitoes and fleas. Characterized by growth of soft tumours in connective tissue. Artificially introduced into Britain and Australia to reduce rabbit population.

N

Naas, co. town of Kildare, EC Irish Republic. Pop. 5000. Former cap. of Leinster.

Nabokov, Vladimir, pseud. of Vladimir Sirin (1899-1977), American author, b. Russia. Works, incl. *Lolita* (1958), *Pale Fire* (1962), use idiosyncratic verbal games.

nacre, *see* PEARL.

nadir, in astronomy, point on celestial sphere directly opposite ZENITH and directly below observer.

Nagaland, state of NE India on Burma border. Area 16,500 sq km (6400 sq mi); pop. 515,600; cap. Kohima. Wild, forested region inhabited by Nagas, headhunters until recently. Formed in 1962.

Nagasaki, major port of Japan, W Kyushu isl. Pop. 447,000. Shipbuilding and engineering indust.; fisheries. Opened to foreign trade in 16th cent. Devastated by 2nd atomic bomb (9 Aug. 1945), with loss of 25,000 lives.

Nagoya, major port of Japan, SC Honshu isl. Pop. 2,080,000. Engineering, chemical and textile mfg.; pottery and porcelain. Has Shinto shrine (2nd cent.), castle (1612).

Nagpur, city of Maharashtra state, C India. Pop. 930,000. Railway jct.; cotton goods, hosiery mfg. Former cap. of Nagpur Mahratta kingdom.

Nagy, Imre (1896-1958), Hungarian political leader. Communist premier (1953-5); critical of Soviet influence in Hungary, removed from office. Recalled to lead new govt. after revolution (1956). Executed after Soviet military occupation.

Nahum, prophetic book of OT, written *c* 650 BC; of unknown authorship. Foretells fall of Nineveh (612 BC).

Naiads, in Greek myth, NYMPHS of springs, lakes and rivers.

nail, in anatomy, horny outgrowth of the outer layer of skin (epidermis) growing at tips of fingers and toes. Grows from fold in skin at base of nail; composed of keratin.

Nairnshire, former county of NE Scotland, now in Highland region. Hilly in S; low-lying, fertile in N. Agric., livestock rearing; fishing. Co. town was **Nairn,** former royal burgh on Moray Firth. Pop. 10,000.

Nairobi, cap. of Kenya, in E African highlands. Pop. 776,000. Admin., commercial, tourist centre on Uganda-Mombasa railway; exports coffee, sisal, hides; has coll., part of Univ. of E Africa. Founded 1899.

Namibia, or **South West Africa,** disputed territ. of SW Africa, admin. by Republic of South Africa. Area 824,000 sq km (318,000 sq. mi); pop. 852,000; cap. Windhoek. Languages: Bantu, Afrikaans, English. Religions: animist, Christian. Namib Desert along coast, plateau inland; salt pans in N. Stock raising, rich in minerals; exports skins, diamonds, copper, lead, manganese. German colony from 1892; admin. after WWI by South Africa under League of Nations mandate. Revocation 1966 by UN disputed by South Africa. Independence was due in 1978, but postponed.

Namur (Flem. *Namen*), town of SE Belgium, at confluence of Meuse and Sambre, cap. of Namur prov. Pop. 33,000. Leather goods, cutlery, glass mfg. Battleground in many wars. Cathedral (18th cent.).

Nanchang, cap. of Kiangsi prov., SE China. Pop. 675,000. Transport, indust. centre on R. Kan; tractor mfg., engineering, large silk complex.

Nancy, city of NE France, on R. Meurthe and Marne-Rhine canal, cap. of Meurthe-et-Moselle dept. Pop. 279,000. Iron and steel mfg., engineering; univ. (1768). Cap. of duchy of Lorraine from 12th cent.

Nanking, cap. of Kiangsu prov., E China. Pop. 2,000,000. Rail jct. on Yangtze; textiles, oil refining, iron and steel mfg. Ming imperial tombs. Cap. of Nationalist govt. (1928-37), until captured by Japanese.

Nansen, Fridtjof (1861-1930), Norwegian explorer, scientist and statesman. Crossed Greenland icefields (1888); attempted to reach North Pole by drifting in ship *Fram* (1893-5), reached further N than anyone before. Awarded Nobel Peace Prize (1922) for work with post-WWI refugees.

Nantes, city of Brittany, NW France, on R. Loire. Cap. of Loire-Atlantique dept. Pop. 433,000. Outport at St Nazaire; oil refining, food processing. Seat of dukes of Brittany (10th-16th cent.). Ducal castle, cathedral; univ. (1460).

Nantes, Edict of, decree issued (1598) by Henry IV of France granting religious freedom and civil rights to Huguenots (French Protestants). Its terms were gradually nullified in 17th cent.; revoked 1685.

Nantucket, isl. off SE Massachusetts, US. Atlantic summer resort. Settled 1659. Hist. whaling centre.

napalm, incendiary material made from petrol or oil and a thickening agent. Used in warfare as it sticks to target while burning.

naphtha, mixture of light hydrocarbons obtained by distillation of petroleum, coal tar, *etc.* Inflammable and volatile; used as cleaning solvent and in making varnish.

naphthalene ($C_{10}H_8$), white crystalline solid with penetrating smell. Obtained from distillation of coal tar. Used in moth balls and manufacture of dyes.

Napier, John (1550-1617), Scottish mathematician. First to publish table of logarithms (1614); introduced calculating rods ('Napier's bones').

Napier, city of E North Isl., New Zealand, on Hawke's Bay. Pop. 40,000. Major wool trade centre; textile, tobacco, food-processing industs. Founded 1855.

Naples (*Napoli,* anc. *Neapolis*), city of S Italy, on Bay of Naples. Cap. of Campania and of Napoli prov. Pop. 1,225,000. Major port, indust. centre; tourism. Greek colony founded 6th cent. BC, Roman resort. Under Normans from 1139; cap. of Kingdom of Naples (1282-1860). Univ. (1224), cathedral.

Napoleon I, full name Napoleon Bonaparte or Buonaparte (1769-1821), French military and political leader, emperor (1804-14), b. Corsica. Revitalized Revolutionary Army in Italian campaign (1796-7), driving out Austrians. Invaded Egypt (1798) as part of plan to take India; campaign became hopeless after Nelson's naval victory at Aboukir. Coup d'état (1799) estab. Napoleon as first consul, effectively dictator. Reorganized state, codified laws in Code Napoléon. Had himself created emperor. In Napoleonic Wars, thwarted European alliance against him by defeating Austria at Austerlitz (1805), Prussia at Jena (1806), Russia at Friedland (1807); ruled virtually entire continent after peace treaty of Tilsit, placing members of his family on several thrones (*see* BONAPARTE). Defeated by Nelson at Trafalgar (1805); failed in attempts to prevent trade with Britain by CONTINENTAL SYSTEM (1806-12). Decline set in with failure of PENINSULAR campaign in Spain and disastrous invasion of Russia (1812), ending in retreat and loss of most of army. Defeated at Leipzig by new European alliance. Abdicated 1814, exiled to Elba. Returned to France, but Hundred Days rule ended in defeat at Waterloo (1815). Exiled to St Helena, where he died.

Napoleon III, orig. Louis Napoleon Bonaparte (1808-73), French political leader, emperor (1852-70). Nephew of Napoleon I, he spent youth in exile. Plotted 2 unsuccessful coups (Strasbourg, 1836; Boulogne, 1840). Elected president of republic after Revolution of 1848. After coup d'état (1851), dissolved legislature and assumed dictatorial powers; proclaimed emperor (1852). Rule marked by military intervention in Crimea, Mexico, Italy; annexed Nice, Savoy. Manoeuvred by Bismarck into war with Prussia (1870); defeated, taken prisoner at Sedan. Exiled to England, where he died.

Napoli, *see* NAPLES.

Nara, town of Japan, SC Honshu isl. Pop. 262,000. Cultural and religious centre; 1st permanent cap. of Japan 709-84.

Narbonne (anc. *Narbo Martius*), town of Languedoc, S France. Wine trade, brandy distilling, sulphur processing. Pop. 40,000. First Roman colony in transalpine Gaul, estab. 118 BC; *fl* in Middle Ages until harbour silted up (14th cent.). Palace, cathedral (both 13th cent.).

narcissism, in psychology, extreme self-love. Regarded by psychoanalysts as early stage in normal psychosexual development.

Narcissus: jonquil

Narcissus, in Greek myth, beautiful youth who rejected love of others. Caused by Aphrodite to become enamoured of his own image in a mountain pool. Pined away and was changed into a flower.

narcissus, genus of bulbous perennial herbs of amaryllis family. Found in Europe, Asia and North America. Erect linear leaves; yellow, white or bicolour flowers, often with trumpet-shaped corolla. Species incl. jonquil, *Narcissus jonquilla,* and DAFFODIL.

narcotic, substance which has depressant effect on nervous system. Used medicinally in small doses to relieve pain, induce sleep, *etc.* Main narcotics are opium and its derivatives (morphine, heroin). Usually addictive.

Narvik, town of NW Norway, on Ofot Fjord. Pop. 13,000. Ice-free port, railway terminus; exports Swedish iron ore. Scene of heavy fighting (1940).

narwhal, *Monodon monoceros,* medium-sized arctic whale. Male has long spiralled tusk, up to 2.4 m/8 ft long, extending from upper jaw. Hunted for oil.

NASA, *see* NATIONAL AERONAUTICS AND SPACE ADMINISTRATION.

Naseby, village of Northamptonshire, C England. Site of Royalists' defeat by Cromwell's Parliamentarians (1645).

Nash, John (1752-1835), English architect, town planner. Works, in classical style, incl. Regent Street and Regent's Park, London.

Nash, Ogden (1902-71), American poet. Known for humorous verse pub. in *New Yorker.*

Nash, Paul (1889-1946), English artist. Official war artist in both World Wars; poetic vision, influenced by surrealism, is revealed in his landscapes.

Nash, Sir Walter (1882-1968), New Zealand statesman, b. England. Labour Party leader and PM (1957-60).

Nashville, cap. of Tennessee, US; on Cumberland R. Pop. 448,000. Road, railway jct.; cotton trade, printing and publishing industs.; centre of recording indust. Seat of Vanderbilt Univ. (1873).

assau, former duchy (from 1806) of WC West Germany, cap. Wiesbaden. Forested and hilly; agric., wine production, spas. Part of Prussian prov. of Hesse-Nassau from 1866, of Hesse from 1945.

assau, cap. and port of Bahamas, on New Providence Isl. Pop. 102,000. Holiday resort. Exports pulpwood, salt, crayfish.

asser, Gamal Abdel (1918-70), Egyptian political leader. Joined in military coup which estab. 1952 republic; became premier (1954), president (1956). Nationalized Suez Canal (1956) and withstood Anglo-French invasion to recover it. Aggressive anti-Israel policy led to war (1967).

asturtium, any of genus *Tropaeolum* of plants, native to South America. Common garden variety is *T. majus* with orange spurred flowers. Also name of genus of WATERCRESS.

atal, smallest prov. of South Africa, in E. Area 91,400 sq km (35,300 sq mi); pop. 2,193,000; cap. Pietermaritzburg. Coastal strip, interior plateau with Drakensberg foothills in W. Sugar, cereals, fruit growing; coalmining. Boer republic founded 1838; annexed by Britain 1843, became UK colony 1856. Absorbed Zululand 1897; prov. of Union of South Africa 1910.

atal, port of NE Brazil, cap. of Rio Grande do Norte state; near mouth of Potengi R. Pop. 344,000. Exports sugar, cotton, salt; textile mfg. International airport nearby.

ational Aeronautics and Space Administration (NASA), US govt. agency (estab. 1958) responsible for space exploration.

ational Assembly, name adopted by Estates-General of France in 1789, marking its defiance of Louis XVI.

ational Country Party, *see* COUNTRY PARTY.

ational debt or **public debt,** indebtedness of govt. expressed in monetary terms. Calculated in many different ways, variously incl. public borrowing from individuals (*eg* loan stocks, bonds, treasury notes) or from foreign govts. or international organizations.

ational Guard, in US, body estab. (1903) to replace state militias. Subject to state jurisdiction in peacetime. Responsible to president in national emergency.

ational Health Insurance Act (1946), in UK, legislation providing for estab. of National Health Service (1948), most comprehensive free medical care scheme of its time.

ational Insurance Act (1911), in UK, legislation devised by LLOYD GEORGE, providing for estab. of compulsory national schemes in areas of old age pensions, sickness and disability insurance, and unemployment. *See* SOCIAL SECURITY.

ationalism, social and political creed expressing common heritage and culture through unification of an ethnic group, manifested either, in estab. nations, as doctrine that national welfare should prevail over international considerations, or, as basis for achieving independence as advocated by separatist groups. Extreme forms incl. FASCISM.

nationalization, transference of ownership or control of land, resources, industs., *etc.*, to national govt. Also refers to acquisition by state of foreign-owned assets.

National Socialism or **Nazism,** ideology of National Socialist German Workers' Party (Nazi Party). Formulated in part by Hitler in *Mein Kampf* (1923) and by Alfred Rosenberg (1893-1946). Founded on principles of racial purity (Aryans representing 'master race'), allegiance to *Führer* (leader), reversal of terms of Versailles Treaty, German territ. expansion, esp. into Slav lands, and eradication of Communists and Jews, who were said to have betrayed Germany in WWI.

National Trust, in UK, non-profitmaking organization founded 1895 and incorporated by Parliament (1907). Aims to promote preservation for the people of lands and buildings of historic or aesthetic value. Has power to acquire land, issue protective orders on private property.

native cat, carnivorous arboreal Australian marsupial of Dasyuridae family.

NATO *see* NORTH ATLANTIC TREATY ORGANIZATION.

natterjack, *Bufo calamita,* small toad of W Europe. Brownish yellow in colour.

natural gas, mixture of gaseous hydrocarbons, esp. methane, occurring naturally as deposits in porous rock, often in association with petroleum. Used as domestic fuel.

natural selection, in evolution, process by which those individuals of a species best-fitted to their specific environment tend to leave more offspring, which inherit those characteristics in which this fitness lies, whereas those less fitted tend to leave less offspring and die out. Thus there is progressive tendency towards greater degree of adaptation. Basis of Darwin's theory of evolution described by him and A.R. Wallace (1859).

Naupaktos (Ital. *Lepanto*), town of WC Greece, on Gulf of Corinth. Pop. 7000. Scene of destruction of Turkish fleet by Holy League in battle of Lepanto (1571).

Nauru, isl. republic of SW Pacific Ocean. Area 21 sq km (8 sq mi); pop. 8000. Extensive phosphate deposits. Discovered (1798), named Pleasant Isl.; admin. by Australia from 1947 until independence (1968). Member of British Commonwealth.

nautical mile, unit of distance used in sea and air travel; equivalent to 1 minute of arc of a great circle of Earth. International nautical mile equals 1852 m (*c* 1.15 mi); UK nautical mile is slightly larger, equalling 6080 ft (1853.18 m).

nautilus, cephalopod mollusc of Indian and Pacific oceans. External coiled shell divided into chambers, animal living in outermost chamber; other chambers filled with gas, giving shell buoyancy.

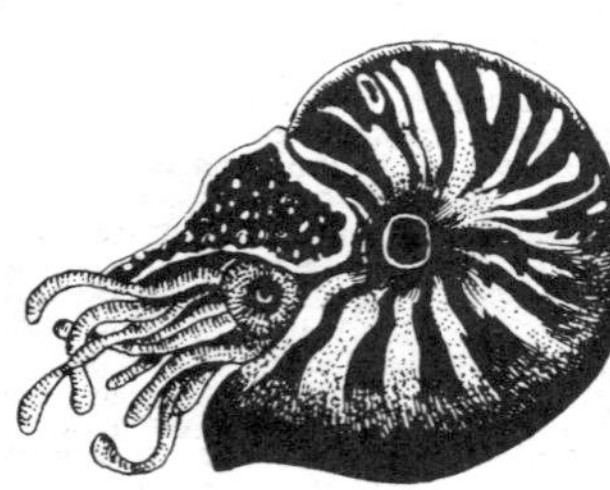

Nautilus

Navaho or **Navajo,** North American Indian tribe. Inhabited NE Arizona in 17th cent. Nomadic hunters, farmers, shepherds.

Navarino, *see* Pylos.

Navarre, region and former kingdom of N Spain and SW France, hist. cap. Pamplona. Mountainous, incl. pass of Roncesvalles; drained by R. Ebro. Pop. mainly Basque. Cereals, livestock, h.e.p. Founded 9th cent.; S part annexed to Spain (1515), N part to France (1589).

navel or **umbilicus,** scar, usually in form of depression in middle of the abdomen, marking place where the umbilical cord was joined to the foetus.

Navigation Acts, English legislation designed to restrict carrying of goods from abroad only to English-owned ships or to ships of country producing the goods. Acts of 1651 were designed to combat Dutch competition in trade with English possessions. Finally repealed 1849.

navy, branch of armed services equipped for maritime warfare. Originated among ancient nations bordering on Mediterranean. With development of air and submarine warfare in 20th cent., size of vessels has given place to speed and mobility, the only large warships being aircraft carriers.

Naxos, isl. of Greece, in Aegean Sea, largest of Cyclades. Area 438 sq km (169 sq mi). Fruits, wine. Ancient centre for worship of Dionysus. In legend, here Theseus abandoned Ariadne.

Nazareth, town of N Israel. Pop. *c* 23,000. Associated with early life of Jesus. Pilgrimage centre.

Nazism, *see* National Socialism.

Ndjamena, cap. of Chad, at confluence of Logone, Shari rivers. Pop. 179,000. Admin. centre, market for salt, dates, livestock. Founded 1900, known as Fort Lamy until 1973.

Ndola, city of NC Zambia. Pop. 229,000. Indust., commercial, railway centre in copperbelt region.

Neagh, Lough, C Northern Ireland. Largest freshwater lake in British Isles: length 29 km (18 mi); width 18 km (11 mi).

Neanderthal man, early form of man, usually considered a representative of *Homo sapiens*. Lived between 100,000 and 40,000 years ago. Had prominent brow ridges, receding chin, sloping forehead but brain similar in size to modern man's.

Nebraska, state of C US; on W bank of Missouri R. Area 200,000 sq km (77,230 sq mi); pop. 1,554,000; cap. Lincoln; chief city Omaha. Mainly prairies; tableland in W. Maize, wheat, sorghum, livestock farming. Agric. related industs. Exploration by Spanish in 16th cent. Region developed after Louisiana Purchase by US (1803). Admitted to Union as 37th state (1867).

Nebuchadnezzar II (d. 562 BC), king of Babylonia (*c* 605-562 BC). Quelled revolt in Judah (597), taking many Jews into exile in Babylon. Destroyed Jerusalem (586) after 2nd revolt. Rebuilt Babylon.

nebula, luminous cloud-like patch seen in night sky, consisting of masses of rarefied gas and dust. Name was formerly applied to extra-galactic systems of stars.

neck, part of man or animal joining the head to the body. In man, column of 7 cervical vertebrae form bones of neck; they are surrounded by systems of muscles which move and support them.

Neckar, river of SW West Germany. Flows 370 km (230 mi) from Black Forest to R. Rhine at Mannheim. Navigable to Stuttgart; canal link to Danube.

Necker, Jacques (1732-1804), French statesman, b. Switzerland. Succeeded Turgot as finance minister (1776) and attempted fiscal reform to restore financial stability; dismissed (1781) by Louis XVI. Recalled 1788, he advised summoning of Estates-General. Subsequent dismissal led to storming of Bastille (14 July, 1789) and reinstatement. Resigned 1790.

nectar, *see* ambrosia.

nectarine, *see* peach.

Nefertiti or **Nefretete** (*fl* 14th cent. BC), Egyptian queen, wife of Ikhnaton. Her beauty is suggested by famous portrait bust.

Negev or **Negeb,** semi-desert of S Israel between Mediterranean and Aqaba. Area 13,310 sq km (5140 sq mi). Minerals, natural gas. Settled by immigrants on cooperative farms.

Nehemiah, historical book of OT. Relates story of Nehemiah, cup-bearer to King Artaxerxes I of Persia. Later governed Jerusalem (from 445 BC). Rebuilt city walls and reformed temple worship.

Nehru, Jawaharlal (1889-1964), Indian statesman and writer, PM (1947-64). Influenced by Gandhi, devoted himself to obtaining Indian independence from Britain. President of Indian National Congress 4 times. Frequently in jail for civil disobedience campaigns of 1930s. First PM of independent Indian state. Maintained influential neutral stand in foreign affairs.

Neisse (*Nysa*), two rivers of E Europe. **Glatzer** or **Silesian Neisse** flows *c* 195 km (120 mi) NE from SW Poland to R. Oder near Brzeg. **Görlitzer** or **Lusatian Neisse**

flows *c* 225 km (140 mi) N from NW Czechoslovakia via Görlitz to R. Oder near Gubin (Poland); forms part of Poland-East Germany border.

Nelson, Horatio, Viscount Nelson (1758-1805), English admiral. Aided Jervis off Cape St Vincent and ended Napoleon's Egyptian campaign by destroying the French fleet at Aboukir Bay (1798). At Naples he put down a Jacobin revolt and formed a liaison with Emma HAMILTON, wife of the British ambassador. In 1801 he destroyed the Danish fleet at Copenhagen, and in 1805 died of wounds at the moment of victory over a combined French and Spanish fleet at Trafalgar.

Nelson, town of South Isl., New Zealand, on Tasman Bay. Pop. 29,000. Port with ferry service to North Isl.

Nematoda (nematodes), phylum of unsegmented roundworms, *eg* threadworms, eelworms. Incl. soil-dwellers, free-swimming forms, and parasites, *eg* hookworm.

Nemertea (nemerteans), phylum of mainly marine worms with unsegmented body and protrusible proboscis used to catch prey. Variable length, reaching 18 m/60 ft. Also called ribbon worms.

Nemesis, in Greek myth, personification of retribution, esp. in cases of human presumption towards the gods.

neo-Classicism, artistic style of 2nd half of 18th cent. which began as reaction to Baroque and rococo styles, and was inspired by antique buildings and archaeological finds. Noted practitioners incl. Adam brothers in architecture.

neodymium (Nd), metallic element of the lanthanide series; at. no. 60, at. wt. 144.24. Compounds used to colour glass.

Neolithic, last period of STONE AGE in which domestication of animals, farming began. Started in SW Asia 8000-6000 BC; ended at different times in different areas, *eg c* 3500 BC in Mesopotamia but later in Europe.

neon (Ne), inert gaseous element; at. no. 10, at. wt. 20.18. Found in traces in atmosphere; obtained by fractional distillation of liquid air. Produces bright reddish-orange glow when electric current is passed through it; used in neon signs.

neoplatonism, philosophy loosely derived from doctrines of Plato, expounded (3rd cent.) by Plotinus. Held that all existence, material and spiritual, emanates from transcendent One through the divine mind (*see* LOGOS) and world soul. Influence continued through Middle Ages, affected 17th-19th cent. writers, poets.

Nepal, kingdom of SC Asia. Area *c* 140,000 sq km (54,600 sq mi); pop. 13,421,000; cap. Kathmandu. Language: Nepali. Religions: Hindu, Buddhism. Formerly remote region in Himalaya, bordered by India and Tibet; rice and grain grown in Nepal valley. Under Gurkha control from 1768; sovereignty recognized by British in 1923.

nephritis, inflammation of the kidneys, often caused by bacterial infection.

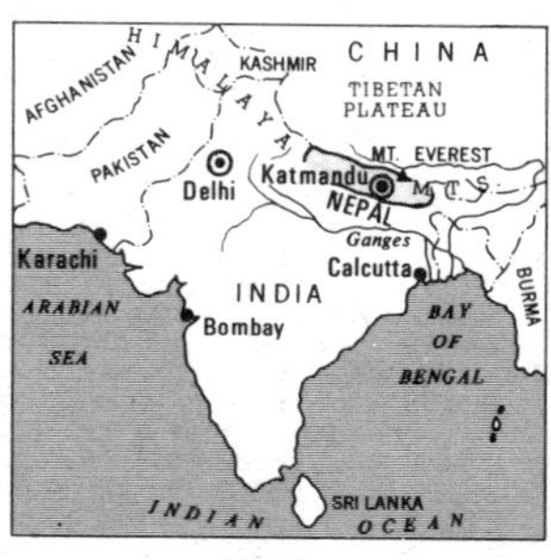

Nepal

Neptune, planet 8th in distance from Sun; mean distance from Sun *c* 4500 × 10^6 km; diameter 44,800 km; mass *c* 17 times that of Earth. Solar orbit takes *c* 165 years. Discovered (1846) by Galle following predictions of Leverrier and Adams.

Neptune, in Roman religion, god of water. Sometimes identified with Greek POSEIDON.

neptunium (Np), transuranic element; at. no. 93, mass no. of most stable isotope 237. First transuranic element, discovered (1940) during neutron bombardment of uranium.

Nereids, in Greek myth, daughters of sea god Nereus; NYMPHS of the Aegean Sea.

Nero [Claudius Caesar Drusus Germanicus] (AD 37-68), Roman emperor (AD 54-68). Adopted as heir to Claudius I through intrigues of his mother Agrippina. After accession, arranged deaths of rightful heir Britannicus, Agrippina, wives Octavia and Poppaea, his adviser Seneca and many others. Suspected of starting great fire of Rome (64), began persecution of Christians, whom he accused of the crime. Committed suicide during revolt.

Neruda, Pablo, pseud. of Neftalí Ricardo Reyes (1904-73), Chilean poet. Nobel Prize for Literature (1971).

nervous system, network of nerves and nerve tissue in animals which conducts impulses to coordinate senses and activities. Basic unit is nerve cell or neuron, consisting of nerve cell body and various thread-like processes. Impulses are transmitted from axons to dendrites at junctions called SYNAPSES. Certain impulses are communicated to brain and spinal cord from receptors (sensory organs inside or outside body), other impulses are communicated to effectors, *eg* muscles or glands.

Ness, Loch, lake of Highland region, N Scotland. Length 39 km (24 mi), forms part of Caledonian Canal. Home of reputed 'monster'.

Nestorians, Christian followers of Nestorius (d. *c* 451). Driven into Persia after Council of Ephesus (431), they suffered much persecution. Modern Nestorian Church is mainly in Iraq.

netball, seven-a-side game for women played mainly in English-speaking countries. Introduced into England (1897) from US as form of BASKETBALL.

Netherlands (*Nederland*), kingdom of NW Europe. Area 41,344 sq km (15,963 sq mi); pop. 13,986,000; cap. Amsterdam, seat of govt. The Hague. Language: Dutch. Religions: Protestant, RC. Low-lying, 25% below sea level; large reclaimed areas. Dairying, bulbs, fishing. Extensive canal system links main rivers (Scheldt, Maas, Rhine), important transit trade. Industs. centred in Amsterdam, Rotterdam (Europe's leading port), Utrecht. Member of EEC. Part of Low Countries until 16th cent.; rebelled against Spanish rule after religious repression. N provinces declared independence 1579. Estab. overseas empire 17th cent. Union with former Austrian Netherlands (Belgium) (1814-30). German occupation in WWII.

Netherlands Antilles, autonomous Dutch isl. groups in Caribbean. Area 960 sq km (370 sq mi); pop. 246,000; cap. Willemstad. Language: Dutch. N group in Leeward Isls. incl. Saba, St Eustatius, S part of St Martin; S group off Venezuela, incl. Curaçao, Aruba, Bonaire. Economy depends on refining of Venezuelan oil on Curaçao and Aruba. Dutch territ. from 17th cent. (known as Curaçao until 1949); granted full autonomy (1954).

Netherlands New Guinea, *see* IRIAN JAYA.

nettle, any of genus *Urtica* of plants with stinging hairs on leaves which cause a rash by injecting histamine into the skin.

Neuchâtel, (Ger. *Neuenburg*), city of W Switzerland, on L. Neuchâtel, cap. of Neuchâtel canton. Pop. 39,000. Chocolate, condensed milk. Academy (1838) now univ.

neuralgia, pain felt along the course of a nerve.

neuritis, inflammation of a nerve or group of nerves. May be caused by viral infection (*eg* shingles) or by bacteria (*eg* leprosy), *etc.*

neuron, *see* NERVOUS SYSTEM.

neurosis, form of mental disturbance merging normal behaviour with genuine derangement. Characterized by one or more of following: anxiety, depression, phobias, compulsions and obsessions.

neutrality, condition of a state abstaining from participation in a war between other states, and maintaining an impartial attitude in dealing with belligerent states.

neutralization, in chemistry, interaction of acid and base to form a salt and water. Solution is said to be neutral when there are equal numbers of hydrogen and hydroxyl ions present.

Neutral Territory, *see* KUWAIT.

neutrino, uncharged elementary particle with zero rest mass. Existence predicted by Pauli in connection with beta-decay. First detected 1956; 2 different types exist, corresponding to electron and to muon.

neutron, uncharged elementary particl[e] with mass slightly greater than that [of] proton, found in nucleus of atom (excep[t] that of hydrogen). Outside nucleus, neutro[n] decays into proton, electron and ant[i]neutrino (half-life *c* 13 mins.). Discovere[d] by Chadwick (1932); neutrons pla[y] important role in nuclear fission.

neutron star, hypothetical state [of] sufficiently massive star which undergoe[s] GRAVITATIONAL COLLAPSE. Gravitationa[l] forces within star would be sufficient t[o] compress the matter composing star int[o] immensely dense ball of neutrons a fe[w] kilometres wide. Pulsars are believed to b[e] rapidly rotating neutron stars.

Nevada, state of W US. Area 286,299 sq kn (110,540 sq mi); pop. 637,000; cap. Carso[n] City. Mainly within arid Great Bas[in] region; Sierra Nevada on W border. Live[]stock rearing esp. cattle, sheep; importar[t] mining (iron ore, copper, gold). Reso[rt] towns incl. Las Vegas, Reno (famous fo[r] gambling casinos). Ceded to US by Mexic[o] (1848). Admitted to Union as 36th stat[e] (1864).

Nevis, isl. of E West Indies, in Leeward Isl[s]. Area 130 sq km (50 sq mi); pop. 48,000 (wit[h] St Kitts); chief town Charlestown. Cotto[n], sugar cane growing. Former British colon[y] with St Kitts, Anguilla; became associat[ed] state 1967.

Nevis, Ben, mountain of Highland region, [W] Scotland, near Fort William. Highest i[n] British Isles, 1342 m (4406 ft).

Newark, city of NE New Jersey, US; o[n] Newark Bay and Passaic R. Pop. 2,057,00[0]; state's largest city. Commercial, indus[t.], shipping centre. Varied mfg. indust[s]. Founded by Connecticut Puritans (1666).

New Bedford, port of SE Massachusetts, U[S]; on Buzzard's Bay. Pop. 167,000. Resor[t], fishing, varied mfg. industs. Hist. importar[t] whaling in 18th, 19th cents. Settled 1652.

New Britain, isl. in Bismarck Archipelag[o], part of Papua New Guinea. Area *c* 36,60[0] sq km (14,100 sq mi); chief town Rabau[l]. Mountainous, with active volcanoe[s]. Exports copra, timber.

New Brunswick, Maritime prov. of S[E] Canada. Area 72,481 sq km (27,985 sq mi); pop. 701,000; cap. Fredericton; chief city S[t] John. Mainly low-lying. Timber, coal, ga[s], h.e.p. resources. Agric. esp. dairy farming. Fishing in Gulf of St Lawrence, Bay o[f] Fundy. French settlement (1604); passed t[o] English (1714). Became one of 4 origina[l] provs. of Canada (1867).

Newbury, town of Berkshire, S Englan[d]. Pop. 24,000. Market town. Has famou[s] racecourse. Two battles of Civil Wa[r] fought here (1643, 1644).

New Caledonia, overseas territ. of France in SW Pacific Ocean. Comprises Ne[w] Caledonia, Loyalty, and other isls. Are[a] 18,700 sq km (7200 sq mi); pop. 144,000; cap. Nouméa. Produces copra, coffee, cotton; deposits of nickel, iron ore, chromium. Discovered (1774) by Cook; French fron[m] 1853.

Newcastle, Thomas Pelham-Holles, Duk[e]

of (1693-1768), British politician, PM (1754-6, 1757-62). Secretary of state (1724-54). Headed Whig admin. dominated by William PITT during Seven Years War.

Newcastle, city of E New South Wales, Australia, at mouth of Hunter R. Pop. 363,000. Major coalmining, iron and steel mfg. centre; port, exports coal, wheat, wool. Has cultural centre, cathedral, univ.

Newcastle-under-Lyme, town of Staffordshire, WC England. Pop. 77,000. In the Potteries; tile mfg. Keele Univ. (1962) nearby.

Newcastle upon Tyne, city and admin. hq of Tyne and Wear met. county, NE England, on R. Tyne. Admin. hq of Northumberland. Pop. 209,000. Major indust. centre; coal, shipbuilding indust., chemicals mfg.; port. Has univ. (1963). Castle (12th cent.); St Nicholas Cathedral (14th cent.).

New Church or **Church of the New Jerusalem,** religious body estab. by followers of SWEDENBORG. First public service held in London (1788).

Newcomen, Thomas (1663-1729), English inventor. In partnership with Thomas Savery (*c* 1650-1715), devised steam engine (1705) used to pump water from mines.

New Deal, US reform programme enacted (1933) during admin. of F.D. Roosevelt. Sought recovery from Depression by extensive economic and social reform and public works projects.

New Delhi, *see* DELHI.

New Democratic Party (NDP), Canadian political party, founded (1961) as union of Co-operative Commonwealth Federation and Canadian Labour Congress.

New Economic Policy (NEP), official economic policy (1921-8) of USSR. Introduced by Lenin to counter unrest. Abolished compulsory labour service, requisition of grain. Provided open market with fixed prices and limited private enterprise. Replaced by FIVE YEAR PLAN.

New England, region of NE US, incl. Maine, New Hampshire, Vermont, Massachusetts, Rhode Isl., Connecticut.

New Forest, woodland heath of Hampshire, S England. National park, area 376 sq km (145 sq mi). Agric.; livestock, ponies. Royal hunting forest of Saxons.

Newfoundland, isl. and prov. of E Canada. Area 404,519 sq km (156,185 sq mi); pop. 574,000; cap. St John's. Prov. comprises isl. (area 106,810 sq km/42,734 sq mi) and mainland Labrador which are separated by Str. of Belle Isle. Timber, iron ore, h.e.p. resources. Fisheries (esp. cod) on Grand Banks. Discovered by John Cabot (1497); British sovereignty estab. 1714; jurisdiction over Labrador 1809. Voted to join Canada as 10th prov. (1949).

Newfoundland dog, breed of large powerful dog, developed in Newfoundland. Coat dense and oily. Stands *c* 71 cm/28 in. high at shoulder.

New Guinea, isl. of SW Pacific, N of Australia. Area *c* 830,000 sq km (320,000 sq mi). Mountainous, rising to over 5000 m (16,500 ft); tropical rain forests. Agric. economy, minerals largely unexploited. Divided into IRIAN JAYA (West Irian) and mainland of PAPUA NEW GUINEA.

Newham, bor. of E Greater London, England. Pop. 227,000. Created 1965 from East Ham, West Ham co. bors., parts of Barking, Woolwich.

New Hampshire, New England state of US. Area 24,097 sq km (9304 sq mi); pop. 853,000; cap. Concord; largest town Manchester. White Mts. in N.; many lakes, woods. Poultry, dairy farming; granite quarrying; timber, h.e.p. resources. Mfg. industs. concentrated in S. First colonized in 1620s. Under Massachusetts jurisdiction until 1679. One of original 13 colonies of US.

New Haven, port of S Connecticut, US; on Long Island Sound. Pop. 414,000. Varied mfg. industs. Settled as Puritan theocracy. Joint cap. with Hartford (1701-1875). Seat of Yale Univ. (1701).

New Hebrides, *see* VANUATU.

New Ireland, isl. in Bismarck Archipelago; part of Papua New Guinea. Area *c* 8600 sq km (3300 sq mi). Mountainous.

New Jersey, state of NE US; on Atlantic. Area 20,295 sq km (7836 sq mi); pop. 7,344,000; cap. Trenton; chief cities Newark, Jersey City. Indust. concentrated in N; farmlands, resorts in S. Shipbuilding, oil refining; machinery, textiles, chemicals mfg. First settled by Dutch, Swedish colonists. English gained control 1664. One of original 13 colonies of US.

Newman, John Henry (1801-90), English churchman. Anglican vicar, joined KEBLE in writing *Tracts for the Times* (1833), inspiring OXFORD MOVEMENT. Became RC in 1845; created cardinal in 1879.

Newmarket, town of Suffolk, E England. Pop. 13,000. Horse racing.

New Mexico, state of SW US. Area 315,115 sq km (121,666 sq mi); pop. 1,196,000; cap. Santa Fé; largest city Albuquerque. Arid plateau crossed by Rio Grande, Pecos R. Agric., incl. cattle, sheep, grain farming; important mining (copper, petroleum, uranium, potash). Spanish colonies opposed by Apache, Pueblo Indians. US control estab. after Mexican War (1846-8); developed with Santa Fé Trail and railway. Admitted to Union as 47th state (1912).

New Orleans, port of SE Louisiana, US; on Mississippi R. Pop. 1,094,000; state's largest city. Major commercial, trade centre. Sugar, oil refining; petroleum, timber, iron and steel exports. Founded by French (1718); French-Creole cultural influence still remains. Hist. cotton, slave trade. Andrew Jackson defeated British here (1815). Seat of Tulane Univ. (1884). Has annual Mardi Gras festival; traditional home of jazz.

Newport, town and admin. hq. of Isle of Wight county, S England. Pop. 22,000.

Newport, resort and naval base of SE Rhode Isl., US. Pop. 35,000. Settled 1639.

Newport, town of Gwent, SE Wales, on R.

Usk. Pop. 108,000. Extensive docks (exports coal); iron, steel indust.

Newport News, seaport of SE Virginia, US; on Hampton Roads (James R.). Pop. 347,000. Has shipyards, drydocks. Coal, petroleum, tobacco exports. Settled by Irish colonists (1621).

New South Wales, state of SE Australia. Area 801,300 sq km (309,400 sq mi); pop. 5,112,000; cap. Sydney. Incl. Lord Howe Isl. dependency. Comprises narrow coastal lowlands; tablelands and mountains of Great Dividing Range; W slopes and plains, incl. Murray-Darling basin. Mainly pastoral, agric. incl. dairying, wheat. Indust. centred in Newcastle, Wollongong, Sydney; h.e.p. in Snowy Mts. Australian E coast called New South Wales by Cook (1770); first colonized 1788. Became federal state (1901).

newspaper, publication usually intended to convey news, issued regularly, *eg* daily or weekly. Developed in 17th cent. with spread of printing. In late 19th cent. achieved mass appeal with growth of literacy, better printing techniques.

Smooth newt

newt, small lizard-like amphibian of salamander family, found in Europe, North America, Asia.

New Testament, second part of the Christian Bible which deals with life and teachings of Jesus Christ (4 Gospels); growth of the Church (Acts of the Apostles); letters to individuals and newly-formed Christian communities (Epistles); vision of the struggle between the Church and its enemies (Revelation). Recorded in Greek in early Christian period.

Newton, Sir Isaac (1642-1727), English physicist, mathematician. Author of *Principia* (1687), in which he enunciated 'inverse square law' of gravitation and 3 laws of motion; application of these laws enabled him to explain planetary motion for 1st time. Discovered that white light is composed of colours of spectrum; invented reflecting telescope. Developed differential and integral calculus independently of Leibnitz.

newton, SI unit of force; defined as force required to impart an acceleration of 1 m/sec^2 in mass of 1 kilogram.

Newtonian mechanics, mechanics described by Newton's 3 laws of motion. Its predictions prove extremely successful for describing motion of bodies at ordinary velocities but must be modified to take account of relativistic effects for velocities close to that of light.

Newtown St Boswells, town of SE Scotland, admin. hq. of Borders region. Pop. 1300.

new town, planned urban community in UK, estab. under New Towns Act of 1946. Created, like GARDEN CITIES, to reduce congestion in major conurbations.

New World, name used for the continent of America, *ie* North, Central and South America.

New York, state of NE US, incl. Long Isl. in SE. Area 128,402 sq km (49,576 sq mi); pop. 17,932,000; cap. Albany; chief cities Buffalo, New York, Rochester. Appalachian Mts. in C; St Lawrence valley in N; crossed by Erie Canal, Mohawk, Hudson rivers. Agric. esp. dairy farming, fruit, cereal growing. Food produce, clothing, machinery mfg., printing and publishing. Indust., shipping concentrated in New York City. E region explored by Hudson (1609), settled by Dutch as New Amsterdam; taken by English (1664). Battleground during Revolution. One of original 13 colonies of US.

New York City, in SE New York state, US; major port on Hudson R. Pop. 7,482,000, with suburbs 16,679,000; largest city in US. Comprises bors. Bronx, Brooklyn, Manhattan, Queen's, Richmond (Staten Isl.). Rail, air, shipping terminal. Varied mfg. industs. esp. consumer goods. Financial centre (Wall Street); major US trade centre. Manhattan Isl. settled by Dutch (1625); seized by English (1664); state cap. until 1797. Harbour dominated by Statue of Liberty; has UN hq., Empire State Building. Notable areas Greenwich Village, Harlem. Seat of 5 univs. incl. Columbia (1754).

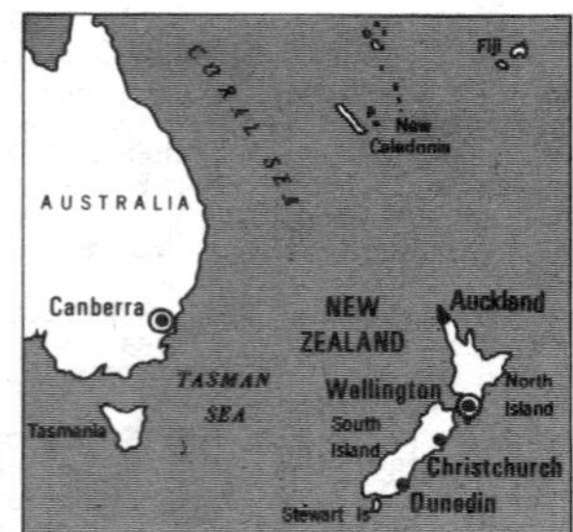

New Zealand

New Zealand, country in SW Pacific Ocean. Area 268,100 sq km (103,500 sq mi); pop. 3,107,000; cap. Wellington. Comprises North, South, Stewart, and several smaller isls. Mountain ranges run NE -SW, rising to Mt. Cook in Southern Alps; many fertile valleys, coastal lowlands, *eg* Canterbury Plains. Economy based on sheep farming, dairying; timber indust., h.e.p.; food processing, engineering in towns. Ancestors of Maoris arrived 10th cent.;

Tasman was 1st white man to reach New Zealand (1642). Under UK rule from 1840; Maori freedom guaranteed by Waitangi Treaty, but land disputes led to series of wars after 1843. Gold discoveries from 1861 accelerated settlement. Dominion from 1907; independent 1931. Member of British Commonwealth.

ey, Michel (1769-1815), French army officer. Won victory of Elchingen (1805), and commanded rearguard in retreat from Moscow (1812). He supported Louis XVIII after Napoleon's abdication but changed side again to lead Old Guard at Waterloo (1815). Condemned as traitor and shot.

iagara Falls, famous waterfalls on Canada-US boundary; on Niagara R. Forms part of border between Ontario and New York State. Goat Isl. separates Canadian (Horseshoe) Falls, 47 m (158 ft) high, 945 m (3100 ft) wide, and American Falls, 50 m (167 ft) high, 329 m (1080 ft) wide. Popular tourist area. H.e.p. supplies.

iamey, cap. of Niger, on R. Niger. Pop. 130,000. Admin., commercial centre. Terminus of trans-Sahara motor route.

ibelungenlied (The Lay of the Nibelungs), medieval German heroic epic written *c* 1200 from older sources. First part tells legend of Siegfried, his love for Kriemhild, wooing of Brunhild on behalf of Burgundian king Gunther, and death at hands of Hagen; second part deals with historical encounter between Burgundians (Nibelungs) and Huns. Wagner used first part for opera-cycle *Ring of the Nibelung.*

icaea (modern *Isnik*), ancient city of Asia Minor, in NW Turkey. Founded in 4th cent. BC as Antigonia, was Roman trade centre. Scene of ecumenical council of AD 325.

icaragua, republic of Central America. Area 128,410 sq km (49,579 sq mi); pop. 2,395,000; cap. Managua. Language: Spanish. Religion: RC. Mountain ranges and interior plateaux flanked by Pacific, Caribbean coasts. Main crops incl. cotton, coffee, sugar; exports timber, gold. Under Spanish rule (1522-1821); member of Central American Federation (1825-38). Earthquake damage (1972).

ice (Ital. *Nizza*), city of Provence, SE France, on Côte d'Azur, cap. of Alpes-Maritimes dept. Pop. 438,000. Port, resort, perfume and soap mfg., fruit and flowers. Greek colony of *Nikaia,* founded 3rd cent. BC. Ceded by Sardinia to France in 1860. Birthplace of Garibaldi.

icene Creed, *See* CREED.

icholas, St (*fl* 4th cent.), Lycian churchman, bishop of Myra (Asia Minor). Patron of children, mariners, pawnbrokers. Origin of Santa Claus.

icholas I (1796-1855), tsar of Russia (1825-55). Crushed Decembrist revolt (1825). Ruled autocratically. Militarist policies helped precipitate Crimean War (1853).

icholas II (1868-1918), tsar of Russia (1894-1917). Suppressed Revolution of 1905 which followed defeat in Russo-Japanese war; later came under influence of RASPUTIN. Maintained autocratic rule of predecessors. Forced to abdicate after failures in WWI and held captive during Russian Revolution. He and his family said to have been shot at Ekaterinburg.

Nicholson, Ben (1894-), English painter. Works are characterized by austere geometric designs and restricted colour range.

nickel (Ni), magnetic metallic element; at. no. 28, at. wt. 58.71. Extremely resistant to corrosion; used in numerous alloys, as a catalyst, in electro-plating, *etc.*

Nicobar Islands, *see* ANDAMAN.

Nicosia (Gk. *Levkosia,* Turk. *Lefkosha*), cap. of Cyprus. Pop. 147,000. Commercial centre, agric. market. Produces leather, textiles, cigarettes. Has 16th-cent. walls built by Venetians.

nicotine, colourless water soluble alkaloid found in leaves of TOBACCO plant. Extremely poisonous, used as basis of insecticides.

Nielsen, Carl August (1865-1931), Danish composer. Works characterized by progressive tonality, esp. in his 6 symphonies.

Nietzsche, Friedrich Wilhelm (1844-1900), German philosopher. Most influential work, *Thus Spake Zarathustra* (1883), characterized by passionate individualism, calls for race of 'supermen' to replace 'slave morality' of Christianity.

Niger, republic of W Africa. Area 1,267,000 sq km (489,000 sq mi); pop. 4,994,000; cap. Niamey. Language: French. Religion: Islam. Sahara desert, Aïr Mts. in N, semidesert in S; drained by R. Niger. Produces groundnuts, cotton, animal products, uranium ore. Territ. of French West Africa from 1904, became independent 1960.

Niger, river of W Africa. Flows *c* 4180 km (2600 mi) from Guinea via Mali, Niger, entering Gulf of Guinea by large delta in S Nigeria. Main tributary is R. Benue. Irrigation, h.e.p.

Nigeria

Nigeria, federal republic of W Africa, on Gulf of Guinea. Area 925,000 sq km (357,000 sq mi); pop. 72,217,000; cap. Lagos; site near

Abuja, C Nigeria, designated for new cap. Main languages: Hausa, English. Main religions: Islam, Christianity, animist. Chief tribes Fulani, Hausa, Ibo, Yoruba. Flat semi-desert in N, savannah plateaux in C, tropical forest in S; main rivers Niger, Benue. Agric. products incl. palm oil, cocoa, groundnuts, cotton, rubber. Major petroleum exporter, found in Niger delta and offshore. Colony and protect. estab. (1914) by merging of Northern and Southern Nigeria and Lagos. Four regions created (1954); independent 1960, republic 1963. Military govt. imposed (1965); 12 states replaced regions (1967), 7 new states added 1976. Secession of Eastern Region (mainly Ibo) as Biafra caused civil war (1967-70). Member of British Commonwealth, UN.

Nightingale, Florence (1820-1910), English nurse, hospital administrator. Took 38 nurses to Crimea (1854); estab. hospital units at Scutari and Balaklava. Greatly reduced death rate among army casualties by imposing high standards of hygiene and care. Founded (1860) nurses' training institution at St Thomas's Hospital, London.

nightingale, *Luscinia megarhynchos,* small migratory songbird of thrush family, with brown upper-parts, whitish brown under-parts. Found in woods of Europe, Asia, N Africa. Male noted for singing at night.

nightjar, any of Caprimulgidae family of small nocturnal birds. Short bill and wide mouth; feeds on insects captured in air.

nightshade, any plant of genera *Solanum* and *Atropa* mainly native to South America and subtropical regions. Extremely poisonous deadly nightshade, *A. belladonna,* has black berries and yields the alkaloid atropine which reduces action of parasympathetic nerves. Formerly used cosmetically to dilate pupils of eyes.

nihilism, in political history, 19th-cent. Russian revolutionary movement. Rejected all estab. institutions, took terrorist action, *eg* arson, assassination; culminated in tsar's murder (1881).

Nijinsky, Vaslav (1890-1950), Russian ballet dancer. One of most famous of Diaghilev's dancers, created leading roles in *L'Après-midi d'un faune, Spectre de la rose.* Career cut short by insanity.

Nijmegen (Ger. *Nimwegen,* Fr. *Nimègue*), city of E Netherlands, on R. Waal. Pop. 216,000. Inland port, with canal link to R. Maas; engineering, chemicals. RC univ. (1923).

Nike, in Greek myth, goddess of victory. Usually represented as winged, carrying wreath or palm branch.

Nile, world's longest river, in NE Africa. Flows *c* 6690 km (4160 mi) from farthest headstream, R. Luvironza (Burundi), to Mediterranean Sea. Nile proper (*c* 3015 km/1875 mi long) formed at Khartoum by union of Blue Nile (rises in Ethiopian Highlands) and White Nile (formed at L. No, Sudan, by jct. of Bahr-el-Ghazal and Bahr-el-Jebel; latter, as Albert Nile, flows *c* 960 km (600 mi) from L. Albert, Uganda). Drops 285 m (935 ft) in 6 cataracts betwe Khartoum and Aswan; joined by R. Atbar Below Cairo enters wide delta, reaches se via Rosetta (W), Damietta (E) channe Seasonal flooding, due to Blue Nile, use for irrigation from *c* 4000 BC; irrigatio h.e.p. developed 20th cent. by series dams (*eg* Aswan) and barrages. Nile valle was focus of ancient Egyptian civilizatio its source legendary until 19th-cen explorations by Bruce, Speke, Stanley.

Nîmes (anc. *Nemausus*), city of Languedo S France, cap. of Gard dept. Pop. 130,0 Tourist centre; wine, fruit, grain trad Founded by Greek colonists; importa Roman remains incl. arena, temple nearby Pont du Gard aqueduct.

Nineveh, ruins of N Iraq, on R. Tigris. Ca of ancient Assyrian empire (*fl* 9th-7th cen BC).

Ninghsia-Hui, auton. region of NC Chin Area *c* 276,000 sq km (106,000 sq mi); po 3,000,000; cap. Yinchuan. Mainly dese rough grazing on Inner Mongolian platea agric. in SE near Hwang Ho. Largely po by Mongols.

Ninian, St (*c* 360-*c* 432), Scottish missionar Founded church at Whithorn (397).

Niobe, in Greek myth, queen of Thebes an daughter of Tantalus. Boasted about he many children compared to Let whereupon Artemis and Apollo (the only children of Leto), killed them all. Turne by Zeus into a stone column which we perpetually.

niobium or **columbium** (Nb), rare metalli element; at. no. 41, at. wt. 92.91. Used alloys which are resistant to hig temperatures.

Nippur, ancient Sumerian city Mesopotamia; religious centre for worshi of god Enlil.

nirvana, in Buddhism and some forms Hinduism, state of annihilation of th worldly self and thus of being free of th cycle of rebirth.

nitrates, salts or esters of nitric acid, th salts being soluble in water. Nitrates in so are source of nitrogen, needed by plan for growth; produced from nitrogen b bacteria. Metallic nitrates used to mak explosives, as fertilizers and in chemica synthesis.

nitric acid (HNO_3), colourless corrosiv liquid; powerful oxidizing agent. Obtaine by catalytic oxidation of ammonia. Used i manufacture of fertilizers, explosives an in organic synthesis.

nitrocellulose or **cellulose nitrate,** any o various esters of nitric acid and cellulose formed by action of mixture of nitric an sulphuric acids on cellulose. Used to mak explosives (guncotton), plastics an lacquers.

nitrogen (N), colourless gaseous elemen chemically inactive; at. no. 7, at. wt. 14.0 Forms *c* 4/5 of atmosphere; occurs in Chil saltpetre (sodium nitrate) and saltpetr deposits. Essential constituent of livin organisms, occurring in proteins an nucleic acids. Used in manufacture of ammonia (Haber process).

trogen cycle, cycle of natural processes by which nitrogen in atmosphere is made available to living organisms. Inorganic nitrogen compounds in soil are absorbed by plants and converted to proteins and nucleic acids; animals absorb proteins by eating plants. Nitrogen compounds re-enter soil by plant decay or as animal excreta; they are broken down by bacteria in soil into form suitable for plant utilization.

trogen fixation, conversion of atmospheric nitrogen into nitrates, which can be used by plants, by action of bacteria or blue-green algae. Bacteria are found in soil or in nodules of certain leguminous plants (peas, clover, *etc*). Part of NITROGEN CYCLE.

troglycerin[e], thick pale yellow oily liquid, prepared by action of concentrated sulphuric and nitric acids on glycerol. Explodes when struck; used to make DYNAMITE, cordite, *etc.*

trous oxide or **laughing gas** (N_2O), colourless sweet-tasting gas, used as light anaesthetic in dentistry. Obtained by heating ammonium nitrate.

iue Island, island of S Pacific, between Tonga and Cook Islands. Area 260 sq km (100 sq mi); pop. 6000. Chief town and port Alofi. Annexed by New Zealand (1901), self-governing from 1974; formerly called Savage Island.

ixon, Richard Milhous (1913-), American statesman, Republican vice-president (1953-61), president (1969-74). Terms marked by US withdrawal from Vietnam, rapprochement with China, economic recession. Investigations into 'Watergate affair' after 1972 revealed widespread govt. corruption in which Nixon was involved. Threatened with impeachment, he resigned; pardoned by successor, President Ford.

izhni Novgorod, *see* GORKY.

komo, Joshua (1917-), Rhodesian politician. President of Zimbabwe African People's Union (1961-). Joint leader with Mugabe of Patriotic Front's guerilla war against white rule. Defeated by Mugabe in 1980 elections.

krumah, Kwame (1909-72), Ghanaian political leader. PM of Ghana (formerly Gold Coast) at its independence (1957), became 1st president (1960) of republic. Overthrown by army coup (1966).

o or **noh play,** highly stylized form of Japanese theatre. Plays mostly written in 15th cent. Characteristic features incl. use of chorus, wooden masks, elaborate costumes, formal acting style using dance.

loah, in OT, builder of the ark which saved human and animal life from the Flood. His sons Shem, Ham and Japheth became the eponymous ancestors of the biblical races of mankind.

lobel, Alfred Bernhard (1833-96), Swedish chemist, philanthropist. Invented dynamite (1866) and perfected other explosives. Bequeathed fund from which annual prizes were to be awarded for work in physics, chemistry, physiology and medicine, literature, and for work in cause of peace. Awards made annually since 1901.

No actor

nobelium (No), transuranic element; at. no. 102, mass no. of most stable isotope 255. Discovered (1957) at Nobel Institute, Stockholm, by nuclear bombardment of curium.

noble gases, *see* INERT GASES.

noble metals, metals such as gold, platinum or silver which resist corrosion and are chemically inactive.

nocturne, short lyrical piece usually for piano; introduced by JOHN FIELD and much used by Chopin.

Nolan, Sidney (1917-), Australian artist. Paintings explore Australian landscape and folklore, *eg* Ned Kelly.

Nolde, Emil, orig. Hansen (1867-1956), German expressionist painter. Painting is characterized by violent colour, simplified form and influence of primitive art.

nomad, member of a tribe of people having no permanent home, moving about constantly in search of food, pasture *etc.*

nominalism, in philosophy, doctrine first current in medieval SCHOLASTICISM that universal concepts have no general reality and are merely conveniences of classification. Opposed to REALISM.

Non-aggression Pact (Aug. 1939), secret agreement between USSR and Germany to divide Poland and E Europe into spheres of Soviet and German influence, and to foil Anglo-French moves to involve USSR in containing German aggression. Ended with German attack on USSR in 1941.

nonconformist, *see* DISSENTER.

non-Euclidean geometry, branch of geometry based on postulates different from those of Euclid. Usually Euclid's 5th or parallel postulate is rejected (that through any point only 1 line can be drawn parallel to another line).

Nonjurors, English and Scottish clergymen who, after Revolution of 1688, refused to take oath of allegiance to William and Mary.

Nordenskjöld, Nils Adolf Erik, Baron (1832-1901), Swedish explorer and geologist, b. Finland. Navigated Northeast

Passage (1878-80); made expeditions to Spitsbergen and Greenland.

Norfolk, Dukes of, *see* HOWARD.

Norfolk, county of E England. Area 5355 sq km (2068 sq mi); pop. 680,000; admin. hq. Norwich. Flat, low-lying; fertile soils; rich agric., poultry; fishing. In E, Norfolk Broads, area of shallow lakes, rivers; yachting.

Norfolk, seaport of SE Virginia, US; on Hampton Roads (Elizabeth R.). Pop. 773,000. Naval base (Atlantic fleet hq.), shipyards; coal, tobacco exports. Founded 1682.

Norfolk Island, territ. of Australia, in S Pacific Ocean *c* 1600 km (1000 mi) NE of Sydney. Area 34 sq km (13 sq mi); pop. 2,000. Tourist resort; whaling; exports fruit. Discovered (1774) by Cook; penal colony until 1855. Transferred from New South Wales to federal govt. 1913.

Norman architecture, form of Romanesque developed in Normandy and England (11th-12th cents.). Characterized by massive construction, semi-circular arches, barrel vaults.

Normandy (*Normandie*), region and former prov. of N France, hist. cap. Rouen. Low-lying, drained by Seine, Eure, Orne: incl. Cotentin penin. Main towns Rouen, Le Havre, Cherbourg. Agric. (cattle, dairying, apples), fishing, tourism. Name derives from Norsemen who invaded area in 9th cent.; Normandy conquered England (1066), colonized S Italy (11th-12th cent.). Part of France from 1450. Scene of Allied invasion in 1944.

Normans, descendants of Viking settlers who conquered N France (Normandy) in 9th cent. Under Duke William, conquered England (1066), displaced Anglo-Saxon nobility, reformed law and social system. Also conquered S Italy and Sicily (11th cent.).

Norns, FATES of Norse myth; determined destiny of gods and men. Usually represented as Urth (past), Verthandi (present), Skuld (future), who spun and wove web of life.

Norse, *see* GERMANIC LANGUAGES.

Norsemen, *see* VIKINGS.

North, Frederick North, 8th Baron (1732–92), British politician, PM (1770-82). Premiership was dominated by influence of George III; carried out taxation policies which led to American Revolution (1776). Resigned after British surrender.

North Africa campaign, conflict (1940-3) during WWII along Egypt-Libya coastal area for control of Mediterranean and Suez Canal. Began with Italian attempts to capture Egypt. German forces under Rommel (Afrikakorps) drove British back into Egypt; advance was halted by British victory under Montgomery at El Alamein (1942). Germans retreated into Tunisia and eventually surrendered to Allies (May, 1943).

Northallerton, town and admin. hq. of North Yorkshire, N England. Pop. 7000. Nearby is site of Battle of the Standard where English defeated Scots (1138).

North America, third largest continent; W hemisphere; comprises US (in[illegible] Alaska), Canada, Mexico. Area *c* 24,346,0[illegible] sq km (9,400,000 sq mi); pop. 301,000,0[illegible] Central plain separates E mountain rang[illegible] (Laurentian, Appalachian) from W Roc[illegible] Mts. River systems incl. Mississippi, [illegible] Lawrence-Great Lakes. Highest point M[illegible] McKinley. Climate varies from Arctic in [illegible] to subtropical in S. Varied agric., pastor[illegible] in plains; extensive mineral resources. [illegible]digenous Indian pop.; European settleme[illegible] from 16th cent.

Northamptonshire, county of C Englan[illegible] Area 2367 sq km (914 sq mi); pop. 516,0[illegible] Wheat growing, cattle, sheep rearing; ir[illegible] ore. Admin. hq. **Northampton,** on R. Ne[illegible] Pop. 151,000. Footwear mfg.

North Atlantic Drift, warm ocean curre[illegible] of N Atlantic Ocean. Continuation of Gu[illegible] Stream, flows NE from off Newfoundlan[illegible] Ameliorates W European winters.

North Atlantic Treaty Organizatio[illegible] (NATO), defence force estab. 1952 [illegible] result of pact (1949) between US, Britai[illegible] Canada, France, Benelux, Denmar[illegible] Norway, Iceland, Italy and Portugal. Lat[illegible] additions were Greece (1952), Turk[illegible] (1952), West Germany (1954).

North Borneo, *see* SABAH.

North Brabant, prov. of S Netherlands. Are[illegible] 4929 sq km (1903 sq mi); cap. 's Hert[illegible]genbosch. Textiles, electrical industs. His[illegible] links with N Belgium (*see* BRABANT).

North Cape *(Nordkapp),* headland [illegible] Norway, on Magerøy Isl. Popularly take[illegible] as most N point of Europe, lat. 71° 10′ N.

North Carolina, state of E US; on Atlanti[illegible] Area 136,200 sq km (52,590 sq mi); po[illegible] 5,515,000; cap. Raleigh; largest ci[illegible] Charlotte. Coastal swamp rises [illegible] Piedmont and Appalachians in [illegible] Tobacco, cotton, peanut growing, mi[illegible] quarrying. Settled 1650 by Virgini[illegible] colonists. One of original 13 colonies of U[illegible] Joined South during Civil War.

Northcliffe, Alfred Charles Willia[illegible] Harmsworth, Viscount (1865-1922[illegible] British journalist, publisher. With h[illegible] brother Harold, later Lord ROTHERMER[illegible] estab. world's largest newspape[illegible] enterprise, the Amalgamated Press. H[illegible] founded the *Daily Mail* (1896), and *Dai[illegible] Mirror* (1903). Acquired *The Times* (1908).

North Dakota, state of NC US; on Canad[illegible] border. Area 183,000 sq km (70,670 sq mi[illegible] pop. 651,000; cap. Bismarck. Mainly plai[illegible] crossed by Missouri R. Barley, whea[illegible] livestock farming; quarrying. Explored b[illegible] French; acquired by US in Louisian[illegible] Purchase (1803). Admitted to Union, jointl[illegible] with South Dakota, as 39th state (1889).

Northeast Frontier Agency, *see* ASSAM.

Northeast Passage, passage from Nort[illegible] Sea to Pacific, along N coast of Europe an[illegible] Asia. Explored 16th-18th cent.; firs[illegible] navigated 1878-9 by Swede Ni[illegible] Nordenskjöld. Soviet shipping route, kep[illegible] open by icebreakers.

Northern Ireland, constituent part of UK. Area 14,146 sq km (5462 sq mi); pop. 1,537,000; cap. Belfast. Comprises former Cos. Antrim, Armagh, Down, Fermanagh, Londonderry, Tyrone (most of ancient ULSTER); divided into 26 dists. (1973). Agric. (cereal, potatoes, livestock); fishing; industs. incl. shipbuilding, textiles (esp. linen). Estab. 1921 after IRELAND partitioned; continuing Protestant-RC conflict led to suspension of Stormont govt. 1972. 'Power-sharing' attempted (1973-4) but direct rule from Westminster restored.

Northern Rhodesia, *see* ZAMBIA.

Northern Territory, self-governing territ. of N Australia. Area 1,349,000 sq km (521,000 sq mi); pop. 118,000, incl. *c* 27,000 aborigines; cap. Darwin. Plains, basins in N, mountain ranges in S; tropical monsoon climate in N, arid in S. Beef cattle raising; mining, esp. copper, manganese, bauxite, iron, lead. Fifteen aboriginal reservations, largest of which is Arnhem Land. Became federal territ. 1911.

North Holland, *see* HOLLAND.

North Island, one of main isls. of New Zealand, separated from South Isl. by Cook Str. Area 114,690 sq km (44,280 sq mi); pop. 2,284,000; main cities Wellington, Auckland. C plateau has active volcanoes, hot springs, geysers. Dairy cattle and sheep in fertile valleys, coastal lowlands.

North Korea, *see* KOREA.

North Ossetia, auton. republic of S European RSFSR, USSR; on N slopes of Caucasus. Area *c* 8030 sq km (3090 sq mi); pop. 597,000; cap. Ordzhonikidze. Mountainous; fruit, grain, cotton grown in valleys. Metal ore (lead, zinc) and oil deposits. Region annexed by Russia by 1806. **South Ossetia** is auton. region of Georgian SSR on S slopes of Caucasus.

North Pole, northern end of Earth's axis; first reached (1909) by Peary. Distinct from north magnetic pole, position towards which needle of magnetic compass points and location of which varies with time.

North Rhine-Westphalia *(Nordrhein-Westfalen),* state of W West Germany. Area *c* 33,930 sq km (13,100 sq mi); cap. Düsseldorf. Highly indust. area (incl. RUHR), main products iron, steel, chemicals, textiles. Formed 1946.

North Riding, *see* YORKSHIRE.

North Sea, between Great Britain and NW Europe, *c* 965 km (600 mi) long N-S, up to 645 km (400 mi) wide. Fishing grounds; gas, oil deposits off Norway, Scotland.

North Star, *see* POLARIS.

Northumberland, Earls of, *see* PERCY.

Northumberland, John Dudley, Duke of (*c* 1502-53), English statesman. As chief minister to Edward VI, he tried to alter succession in favour of his daughter-in-law, Lady Jane Grey, a Protestant, thus excluding Mary Tudor, a Catholic. His plot, lacking popular support, failed; executed for treason.

Northumberland, county of NE England. Area 5033 sq km (1943 sq mi); pop. 289,000; admin. hq. Newcastle. Cheviot Hills (N), Pennines (W). Sheep farming; coal, shipbuilding, engineering industs. on Tyneside. Northumberland National Park (1031 sq km/398 sq mi) incl. Hadrian's Wall.

North Vietnam, *see* VIETNAM.

Northwest Frontier Province, former province of British India on Afghanistan border, created 1901. Became part of Pakistan in 1947. Mountainous region; passes, incl. Khyber, were strategically important.

Northwest Passage, sea route linking Atlantic, Pacific oceans round N North America. Long-sought as possible short route to Orient. Frobisher, Davis, Franklin failed to discover it. First navigated by Amundsen (1903-6).

Northwest Territories, admin. region of N Canada; incl. 4 dists.: Baffin, Inurik, Fort Smith, Keewatin. Area 3,379,699 sq km (1,304,903 sq mi); pop. 43,000, mainly Eskimo, Indian; admin. centre Yellowknife. Drained in W by Mackenzie R.; has many lakes incl. Great Bear, Great Slave. Fur trading; mineral resources. Exploration, trade sponsored by Hudson's Bay Co. (estab. 1670); known as Rupert's Land (incl. Prairies) until ceded to Canada (1869).

North Yorkshire, county of N England. Area 8317 sq km (3211 sq mi); pop. 661,000; admin. hq. Northallerton. Created 1974, comprising mainly former N, W Ridings of Yorkshire.

Norway

Norway (*Norge*), kingdom of NW Europe, in W Scandinavia. Area 324,250 sq km (125,200 sq mi); pop. 4,059,000; cap. Oslo. Language: Norwegian. Religion: Lutheran. Nomadic Lapps in N. Deeply indented coast (ice-free due to N Atlantic Drift), mountainous; partly within Arctic Circle. Important North Sea fishing, forestry, minerals, h.e.p., limited agric.; offshore oil resources developed in 1970s. United with Denmark, Sweden 1397, ceded to Sweden 1814; independent from 1905. Occupied by Germans 1940-5.

Norwegian, N Germanic Indo-European

language. Spoken in Norway and parts of US. Descended from Old Norse.

Norwegian Antarctic Territory, all isls. and mainland S of 60°S and between 20°E and 45°W.

Norwich, city and admin. hq. of Norfolk, E England, on R. Wensum. Pop. 120,000; Agric. market; food processing; footwear mfg. Has Univ. of East Anglia (1963). Norman cathedral (1096).

nose, facial organ containing openings of respiratory passages and organ of smell. Internal cavity is divided by cartilaginous septum into 2 halves which unite in nasal part of PHARYNX.

Nostradamus, Latin name of Michel de Nostredame (1503-66), French astrologer, physician. Wrote *Centuries* (1555), rhymed quatrains of obscure prophecies, long popular.

notochord, skeletal rod, composed of cells, lying between digestive tract and central nervous system in most primitive members of phylum Chordata. Present in embryonic stages of vertebrates, it is later surrounded and replaced by the vertebral column.

Nottinghamshire, county of C England. Area 2164 sq km (836 sq mi); pop. 974,000. Low-lying in Trent Valley, hilly in SW. Cereals, root crops, cattle; coal mining in W. Incl. remains of Sherwood Forest. Admin. hq. **Nottingham,** city on R. Trent. Pop. 281,000. Hosiery, bicycles; Danish town (9th cent.); hist. silk, lace mfg. Has univ. (1948); RC cathedral.

Nouakchott, cap. of Mauritania. Pop. 55,000. Admin., commercial centre on caravan routes; harbour nearby on Atlantic coast.

nova, in astronomy, star whose brightness suddenly increases by several thousand times and then slowly fades to its original intensity. Believed to be caused when star blows off part of its outer layer.

Novalis, pseud. of Friedrich Leopold von Hardenberg (1772-1801), German poet. Leading Romantic, *Hymns to the Night* (1800) express yearning for mystical unity in death.

Novara, city of Piedmont, NW Italy, cap. of Novara prov. Pop. 103,000. Textiles, rice-milling, map-making. Scene of Austrian victory (1849) over Piedmontese.

Nova Scotia, Maritime prov. of SE Canada, incl. CAPE BRETON Island. Area 55,491 sq km (21,425 sq mi); pop. 847,000; cap. Halifax. Rugged coastline has many natural harbours. Fishing (esp. cod), timber, agric. (dairy farming, fruit); coal, metals, salt mining. Settled as ACADIA by French; British gained possession (1714); joined with Cape Breton (1820). One of 4 original provs. of Canada (1867).

Novaya Zemlya, 2 isls. of USSR, between Barents and Kara seas. Area *c* 83,000 sq km (32,000 sq mi). N island permanently ice covered, tundra in S.

novel, long fictional prose narrative. Although antecedents exist in Classical Greece, Rome, medieval Italy, 1st true examples with realistic treatment [of] psychology incl. Cervantes' *Don Quixot[e]*, Richardson's *Pamela*, Fielding's *To[m] Jones*. Influential exponents incl. Ja[ne] Austen (domestic novel of manners), Melville, Flaubert, Dostoyevski, Zo[la] (naturalism), Proust, Joyce.

Novello, Ivor, full name Ivor Novello Davi[es] (1893-1951), Welsh actor-manager, compo[s]er. Known for songs, esp. 'Keep the Hom[e] Fires Burning', plays, *eg The Dancin[g] Years* (1939).

Novgorod, city of USSR, W Europea[n] RSFSR; on R. Volkhov. Pop. 186,000. One [of] oldest Russian cities; Rurik's estab. [a] Prince of Novgorod (862) regarded as fou[n]dation of Russia. Cap. of powerful tradin[g] state in 13th and 14th cent., rivallin[g] Moscow in power. Subjugated by Ivan [III] and devastated by Ivan the Terrible (1570). Has 11th-cent. Cathedral of St Sophia.

Novi Sad (Ger. *Neusatz),* city of N[E] Yugoslavia, on R. Danube, cap. [of] Vojvodina. Pop. 163,000. River por[t], commercial, indust. centre.

Novokuznetsk, city of USSR, SC Siberia[n] RSFSR. Pop. 541,000. Metallurgical centr[e] in Kuznetsk Basin; iron and stee[l], aluminium mfg. Known as Stalins[k] (1932-61).

Novosibirsk, city of USSR, SC Siberia[n] RSFSR; jct. of Trans-Siberian railway on [R.] Ob. Pop. 1,312,000. Founded 1896, grew a[s] indust. centre based on proximity [of] Kuznetsk Basin; agric. machinery, texti[le] mfg.

Nubia, ancient region of NE Afric[a]. Extended from Aswan (Egypt) t[o] Khartoum (Sudan), boundaries poor[ly] defined. Conquered Egypt (7th cent. BC) after being subject to it for cents.; powerfu[l] Christian kingdom 6th-14th cen[t]. Conquered by Egypt in 19th cent. Inc[l]. **Nubian Desert,** barren sandstone platea[u] of NE Sudan, between Nile valley and Re[d] Sea; rises to over 2135 m/7000 ft near coas[t].

nuclear energy, energy released fro[m] atomic nucleus during nuclear reaction[s] esp. FISSION or FUSION. Results fro[m] conversion of matter into energy.

nuclear fission, *see* FISSION.

nuclear fusion, *see* FUSION.

nuclear physics, branch of physics dealin[g] with structure of atomic nuclei, subatomi[c] particles, fission process, radioactiv[e] decay, *etc.*

nuclear reactor, structure in which nuclea[r] fission chain reaction is initiated an[d] controlled to produce energy or furthe[r] fissionable material. Metal rods are used t[o] absorb neutrons produced during fissio[n] and so control rate at which reactio[n] proceeds.

nuclear warfare, hostilities involving use o[f] nuclear warheads, envisaging tota[l] destruction of enemy's war potentia[l] before retaliation is possible. Strategi[c] emphasis is therefore on methods o[f] delivery, which incl. low-level bombers an[d] long range GUIDED MISSILES. Tactica[l] weapons carrying small amounts o[f] nuclear material have also been tested *eg* CRUISE MISSILES.

ıcleic acids, *see* DNA, RNA.

ıcleus, in biology, central body present in most plant and animal cells, enclosed by membrane which separates it from protoplasm of rest of cell. Contains hereditary material in form of chromosomes, which control reproduction, growth, *etc*.

ıcleus, in physics, central part of the atom, consisting of protons and neutrons (except for hydrogen nucleus, which consists of single proton). Mass of atom is concentrated in nucleus, which bears a positive charge.

uffield, William Richard Morris, Viscount (1877-1963), English industrialist, philanthropist. Beginning in 1912, developed Morris Motors Ltd. into major mass-producer of motor cars. His benefactions incl. founding of Nuffield College, Oxford, and Nuffield Foundation for research (1943).

ullarbor Plain, arid limestone tableland of South and Western Australia. Extends *c* 400 km (250 mi) inland from Great Australian Bight. No surface water or trees.

ımbat, *Myrmecobius fasciatus*, small rat-sized Australian marsupial anteater. Long snout and bushy tail. Brown with distinctive white stripes.

umbers, in OT, fourth book of Pentateuch. Contains two censuses of Israelites and continues history of Exodus and journey to Promised Land with rise of Joshua and Caleb as leaders.

umidia, ancient kingdom of NW Africa, corresponding nearly to modern Algeria. United as Roman prov. after defeat (201 BC) of Carthage; *fl* 3rd-1st cent. BC.

umismatics, study of coins and medals. Invention of coinage is attributed to Chinese; in West, first coins were struck by Lydians of Asia Minor *c* 750 BC.

un, member of a religious community of women, esp. one living under monastic vows. *See* MONASTICISM.

uremberg (*Nürnberg*), city of SC West Germany, on R. Pegnitz. Pop. 499,000. Toys, precision instruments, clocks. Medieval commercial centre; centre of German Renaissance. Scene of annual Nazi rallies from 1933. Birthplace of Albrecht Dürer.

uremberg Trials, trial of Nazi leaders and military commanders after WWII by Allied Tribunal. Charges incl. crimes against peace and humanity, war crimes. Those sentenced to death or long terms of imprisonment incl. Goering, Ribbentrop, Speer, Hess and Dönitz. Trial estab. principle of individual responsibility not to carry out criminal orders.

Nureyev, Rudolf (1939-), Russian ballet dancer. Lived in West after 1961. Esp. associated with Dame Margot Fonteyn.

nursing, care of the sick. Practised by various religious orders in the Middle Ages. First hospital training school was estab. at Kaiserswerth, Germany by Theodor Fliedner (1836). School estab. (1860) at St Thomas's Hospital by Florence Nightingale became model for such schools.

Nusa Tenggara, *see* SUNDAS.

nut, dry, one-seeded fruit of various trees and shrubs. Consists of kernel (often edible) in a hard woody shell which is separable from the seed itself, *eg* walnut, hazelnut.

nutcracker, *Nucifraga caryocatactes*, bird of crow family, found in coniferous forests of Europe and Asia. Brown with white speckles.

nuthatch, small sharp-beaked tree-climbing bird of Sittidae family. Nests in holes in trees; diet of insects, nuts.

nutmeg, hard aromatic seed of East Indian tree, *Myristica fragrans*. Grated and used as spice, while outer covering yields the spice mace. Oil derived from seed and covering used in medicine and cosmetics.

nux vomica, poisonous disc-shaped seed of Asiatic deciduous tree, *Strychnos nux-vomica*, of logania family. Contains various alkaloids, incl. strychnine.

Nyasa, Lake, *see* MALAWI, LAKE.

Nyasaland, *see* MALAWI.

Nyerere, Julius Kambarage (1921-), Tanzanian statesman. Became PM at independence (1961) of Tanganyika, then president upon estab. of republic (1962). Pursued socialist policies, with Chinese aid. Negotiated union with Zanzibar which created Tanzania, becoming president (1964).

nylon, name given to group of synthetic long-chain polymeric amides, made into fibres, yarn, moulded plastics, *etc*. Fibre, characterized by strength, elasticity and low absorbency of moisture, is used in mfg. of hosiery and textiles.

nymph, larva of insect undergoing incomplete METAMORPHOSIS (without pupal stage). Resembles adult, but without wings and sexually immature. Winged adult emerges after series of moults.

nymphs, in Greek myth, generic name for large number of minor female deities associated with natural objects. Usually represented as young, beautiful and amorous, *eg* NAIADS, NEREIDS, DRYADS, OREADS.

O

Oahu, volcanic isl. of Hawaii, US. Area 1540 sq km (595 sq mi); main city HONOLULU. Tourism; extinct volcanoes.

oak, any of genus *Quercus* of hardwood trees and shrubs of beech family bearing nuts called ACORNS. Widely distributed in N temperate regions. Wood used in furniture. Bark of cork oak, *Q. suber,* is used commercially as source of cork.

Oakland, port of W California, US; on San Francisco Bay. Pop. 362,000. Naval base; electrical equipment, chemicals, shipbuilding. Connected by bridge with San Francisco.

oarfish or **king-of-the-herring,** marine fish, genus *Regalecus,* with long ribbon-like body and mane-like crest behind head. Reaches lengths of 6.1 m/20 ft or more.

oasis, fertile area in a desert, caused by presence of water. May be natural spring or made by sinking artesian well. Date palm is commonest vegetation.

oat, *Avena sativa,* hardy, widely grown cereal grass, native to Asia. Cultivated as food for man, *eg* oatmeal, and for horses.

Oates, Titus (1649-1705), English Protestant conspirator. Fabricated and testified to 'Popish Plot' (1678), said to involve murder of Charles II, burning of London, and reintroduction of Catholicism. Resulting panic caused judicial murder and persecution of many Catholics. Imprisoned for perjury (1685); pardoned (1688).

Ob, river of USSR. Formed by union of Biya and Katun rivers, flows *c* 3500 km (2200 mi) N and NW through W Siberian RSFSR to Gulf of Ob on Arctic Ocean. Middle course extensively flooded during spring thaw. Trade route in summer; h.e.p. near Novosibirsk.

Obadiah or **Abdias,** shortest prophetic book of OT. Foretells triumph of Israel over Edom. Prob. written before 550 BC.

Oban, town of Strathclyde region, W Scotland. Pop. 7000. Port, tourist resort; fishing industs. Ferry services to Inner Hebrides.

Obeid, El, town of C Sudan. Pop. 66,000. Railway terminus, road jct., trade in gum arabic, cereals, cattle. Scene of Mahdi's victory (1883) over Egyptians.

obelisk, in ancient Egypt, four-sided monolithic slender shaft, tapering towards top, with pyramidical apex. Dedicated to the sun god, they were often placed in pairs about temples. Cleopatra's Needles, now in London, Paris are examples.

Oberammergau, town of S West Germany, on R. Ammer, in Bavarian Alps. Pop. 5000. Woodcarving, tourism, winter sports. Passion Play performed every 10 years (begun 1634) is thanksgiving f deliverance from plague.

Oberhausen, city of W West Germany, c Rhine-Herne canal, in Ruhr. Pop. 235,0 Coalmining, oil refining, zinc smelting.

obesity, excess of body fat. Usually resul from over-eating of carbohydrate fooc Obesity can usually be reduced by eati less sugar and starch and taking mo exercise.

Oboe

oboe, woodwind instrument with double ree and conical bore, developed from mediev shawm or pommer. Attained its prese form in France in *c* 1650. Cor anglais c English horn is similar, but a fifth lower pitch.

Obote, [Apollo] Milton (1924-), Uganda political leader, PM (1962-6). Seize presidency (1966); while absent abroa deposed by Amin (1971). Elected presider (1980) after overthrow of Amin.

obsidian, hard, usually black, volcanic glas Formed by viscous acid lava cooling to quickly for minerals to crystallize. Use esp. in prehist. times for weapon ornaments.

obstetrics, branch of medicine concerne with childbirth and treatment of mothe before and after delivery.

O'Casey, Sean (1880-1964), Irish dramatis Works, reflecting early life in Dubli slums, incl. tragi-comedies *Juno and th Paycock* (1924), *The Plough and the Star* (1926). Also wrote expressionist anti-WW drama, *The Silver Tassie* (1929).

occultism, belief in hidden powers an forces, esp. supernatural. Designate alleged mystic arts, *eg* alchemy, astrolog magic, spiritualism.

ocean, large expanse of salt water on Earth surface. Five usually distinguishec Antarctic or Southern, Arctic, Atlanti Indian and Pacific, the largest. Togethe oceans cover 71% of Earth's surface.

Oceania, general term for isls. of Pacifi belonging to Melanesia, Micronesia an Polynesia groups, and sometimes those o Australasia and the Malay Archipelago.

Ocean Island, isl. of Kiribati. Area 5 sq km (2 sq mi). Heavily exploited phosphate deposits. Former cap. of Gilbert and Ellice Isls. Colony until WWII.

Oceanus, in Greek myth, the great outer stream which encircled the earth. Personified as a TITAN who was father of river gods and sea nymphs (Oceanids).

ocelot, *Felis pardalis,* wild cat of Central and South America; body length *c* 76 cm/30 in. Yellow or grey coat with black spots. Valued for its fur.

Ochil Hills, range of C Scotland, in Central, Tayside, Fife Regions. Rise to 720 m (2360 ft).

ochre or **ocher,** natural earth, mixture of hydrated iron oxide and clay. Ranges in colour from yellow to brown and red. Used as pigment in paints.

O'Connell, Daniel (1775-1847), Irish nationalist leader. Founded (1823) Catholic Association to further Catholic emancipation. Elected to Parliament (1828), although unable to take oaths necessary to assume seat; Catholic Emancipation Act (1829) was passed as a result. After 1841, worked for repeal of union with Britain but his conservative ways lost him popular support.

Octavian, *see* AUGUSTUS.

octopus, cephalopod mollusc with rounded sac-like body, no shell and 8 sucker-bearing arms. Lives mainly on sea bottom, ejecting inky fluid for protection. Species incl. common octopus, *Octopus vulgaris,* of Atlantic and Mediterranean.

ode, originally, Greek poem sung to musical accompaniment. Classical exponents incl. Sappho, Pindar, Horace, Catullus. Revived in 16th cent. in modern period, form no longer necessarily set to music. Exponents incl. Ronsard, Spenser, Milton, Dryden, Keats, Shelley.

Odense, city of Fyn Isl., Denmark. Pop. 168,000. Port, exports dairy produce; shipbuilding; textiles. Founded 10th cent., cathedral (rebuilt in 13th cent.).

Oder (Czech and Pol. *Odra*), river of E Europe. Flows 900 km (560 mi) from NC Czechoslovakia through Poland to Baltic Sea at Szczecin. Forms N Part of Polish-East German border. Navigable below Racibórz, canals to Katowice indust. region.

Odessa, city of USSR, SW Ukrainian SSR; on Black Sea. Pop. 1,046,000. Port; exports grain, timber; indust. centre. Taken in 1789 from Turks by Russia. Scene of workers' revolution led by mutineers from *Potemkin* (1905). Under Romanian occupation (1941-3); large Jewish pop. decimated.

Odin, in Norse myth, the supreme god, creator of earth, sky and mankind. Associated with war and learning. In Germanic myth called Wotan or Woden.

Odovacar or **Odoacer** (*c* 435-93), German chieftain, 1st barbarian ruler of Rome. Proclaimed king by the German mercenaries he led in service of Rome, he deposed the emperor Romulus Augustulus (476), thus ending Western Roman Empire. Defeated by invading Ostrogoths under Theodoric and murdered.

Odysseus, from a Greek amphora of the 5th century BC

Odysseus, in Greek myth, king of Ithaca. A leader of Greeks in TROJAN WAR, noted for his cunning. Devised Wooden Horse scheme. Hero of Homer's ODYSSEY. Known as Ulysses by Romans.

Odyssey, Greek epic in 24 books attributed to Homer. Tells story of ODYSSEUS. After fall of Troy, attempted to return to kingdom Ithaca, but incurred curse of Poseidon which led to 10 years of wandering; rid palace of wife Penelope's suitors with aid of son Telemachus before estab. rule again.

OECD, *see* ORGANIZATION FOR ECONOMIC COOPERATION AND DEVELOPMENT.

oedema or **dropsy,** abnormal accumulation of fluid in body tissues, resulting in swelling. Caused by heart failure, obstruction of lymphatic vessels, kidney disease, *etc.*

Oedipus, in Greek myth, king of Thebes. Abandoned as child when it was prophesied that he would kill his father Laius and marry his mother Jocasta. Brought up in Corinth ignorant of his true parentage. Killed Laius in chance encounter on way to Thebes and married Jocasta after saving kingdom by answering riddle of the Sphinx. Later learned truth, blinded himself; Jocasta committed suicide. Succeeded by Creon and died at Colonus. Children were POLYNICES, Eteocles, ANTIGONE and Ismene. Hero of Sophocles' *Oedipus Rex, Oedipus at Colonus.*

Oedipus complex, in psychoanalytic theory,

sexual desire of son for mother accompanied by conflict with father. May be openly expressed at age 4-5 years, later repressed as son realizes sanctions against incest, but persists in unconscious. Concept developed by Freud. Daughter's desire for father called Electra complex.

Oersted, Hans Christian (1777-1851), Danish scientist. Estab. relationship between electricity and magnetism (1819) by discovery that magnet takes up right-angled position to direction of electric current.

oesophagus or **gullet,** part of alimentary canal connecting the PHARYNX with the stomach. Carries food to stomach by muscular contraction of its walls.

oestrogen, any of group of female hormones, produced synthetically or secreted in ovaries of mammals. Responsible for development of female secondary sexual characteristics and stimulation of ovulation.

oestrus, period of heat (maximum sexual receptivity) in female mammals.

Offa (d. 796), Anglo-Saxon chieftain, king of Mercia (757-96). Estab. Mercian supremacy over most of England S of the Humber. Had defensive earthwork, Offa's Dyke, built on Welsh border.

Offaly, county of Leinster prov., C Irish Republic. Area 1997 sq km (771 sq mi); pop. 57,000; co. town Tullamore. Flat, low-lying, has part of Bog of Allen; Slieve Bloom Mts. in SE. Agric., cattle; peat. Ancient kingdom. Formerly called King's County.

Offenbach, Jacques (1819-80), French composer, b. Germany. Wrote popular light operas, *eg Orpheus in the Underworld,* and serious *Tales of Hoffmann.*

ogam or **ogham,** alphabetic system of writing developed in Britain in 5th cent. AD. Letters are represented by combinations of lines and notches carved along edges of memorial stones.

Ogbomosho, city of SW Nigeria. Pop. 432,000. Trade centre for agric. region, esp. cotton, yams, cassava.

ogham, *see* OGAM.

Oglethorpe, James Edward (1696-1785), English army officer, philanthropist. Estab. (1733) colony of Georgia as refuge for imprisoned debtors.

O'Higgins, Bernardo (1776-1842), Chilean revolutionary. Led opposition to Spanish rule from 1810; defeated at Rancagua (1814), fled to Argentina. Returned with San Martín's army, became ruler after victory at Chacabuco (1817). Exiled to Peru after overthrow (1823).

Ohio, state of N US. Area 106,765 sq km (41,222 sq mi); pop. 10,697,000; cap. Columbus; chief cities Cleveland, Cincinnati. Mainly flat with L. Erie in NE, Ohio R. in S, Allegheny Mts. in E, prairies in W. Important agric. esp. wheat, livestock; mining incl. coal, oil; indust. concentrated in iron and steel, machinery, rubber, motor car, paper mfg. Control of fur trade estab. by British (1763); ceded to US after Revolution (1783). Admitted to Union as 17th state (1803).

Ohio, river of NC US. Flows from W Pennsylvania SW 1579 km (981 mi) to Mississippi R. Forms 5 state borders; drains indust. region of Pittsburgh, Cincinnati, Louisville. Navigable from Pittsburgh; subject to flooding.

Ohm, Georg Simon (1787-1854), German physicist. His work on electrical circuits led him to formulate Ohm's law: potential difference between ends of a conductor is proportional to current flowing. Unit of electrical RESISTANCE named after him.

oils, group of liquids divided into 3 main classes: (1) fatty oils, consisting of mixtures of glycerides of fatty acids, found in animals and plants; (2) mineral oils consisting of mixtures of hydrocarbons obtained from PETROLEUM, shale or coal; (3) ESSENTIAL OILS.

Oise, river of N France. Flows *c* 305 km (190 mi) from Belgian Ardennes via Compiègne to R. Seine NW of Paris. Heavy river traffic, canal links with Sambre, Somme, Escaut (Scheldt).

Okapi

okapi, *Okapia johnstoni,* rare mammal of giraffe family, from Congo forests. Stands *c* 1.5 m/5 ft at shoulder; red-brown in colour, white bands on legs.

Okhotsk, Sea of, arm of NW Pacific, on E Siberian RSFSR. Enclosed by Kamchatka penin., Kuril and Sakhalin isls.

Okinawa, largest of Ryuku Isls., W Pacific. Area 1176 sq km (454 sq mi); cap. Naha. Sugar cane, rice, sweet potatoes grown. Scene of intense fighting between Japan and US (1945). Placed under US military control until returned to Japan in 1972.

Oklahoma, state of SC US. Area 181,090 sq km (69,919 sq mi); pop. 2,817,000; cap. Oklahoma City; other major city Tulsa. Mainly prairie, mountainous in E; chief rivers Red on S border, Arkansas and tributaries. Wheat growing, livestock rearing esp. cattle; oil, natural gas resources. First explored by Spanish; part of Louisiana Purchase (1803); reserved for Indians, redistributed (1889) for white settlers. Admitted to Union as 46th state (1907).

Oklahoma City, cap. of Oklahoma, US; on North Canadian R. Pop. 746,000. Indust., commercial centre in agric., oil producing region; related industs. incl. oil refining, food processing. Founded 1889; became cap. 1910.

okra or **gumbo,** *Hibiscus esculentus,* aromatic bean of mallow family, native to Africa. Grown extensively in S US, India. Used as vegetable.

Olaf II [Haraldsson], St (*c* 995-1030), king of Norway (1015-28). Attempted to convert Norway to Christianity and unify country under his rule. Exiled after rebellion in favour of CANUTE (1028). Killed during invasion to regain crown. Patron saint of Norway.

Olaf V (1903-), king of Norway (1957-). Succeeded his father, Haakon VII.

Oland Island, Baltic isl. of SE Sweden, separated from mainland by Kalmar Sund. Area 1347 sq km (520 sq mi); main town Borgholm. Agric.; limestone quarrying; tourism.

Old Catholics, Christian church estab. by German clergy who rejected decrees of the 1870 Vatican Council, esp. dogma of papal infallibility. Priests are allowed to marry; confession is optional. Survives in Germany, Netherlands, US.

Oldenburg, city of NW West Germany, on R. Hunte. Pop. 135,000. Railway jct., agric. market, textile, dyes. Cap. of former county (duchy from 1777). Source of Danish rulers (1448-1863); part of Denmark 1676-1773.

Oldenburg, Claes (1929-), American sculptor, b. Sweden. Works, derived from advertising and display techniques, are usually classed as pop art; most famous are large, soft renditions of everyday objects.

Old English, *see* ENGLISH.

Oldham, bor. of Greater Manchester met. county, NW England. Pop. 102,000. Textile indust., esp. cotton spinning.

Old Testament, Christian term for Hebrew part of the Bible. Relates story of the Jews from time of Moses to (with APOCRYPHA) cent. before birth of Jesus. Largely based on 3rd cent. BC translation into Greek (SEPTUAGINT). Western Churches adopted the Latin version (VULGATE).

Olduvai Gorge, archaeological site in Tanzania where remains of tool-making precursors of man, *c* 1.8 million years old, were discovered by LEAKEY in 1959. Other fossil hominids have since been found there.

Old World, name used for the continents of Europe, Asia and Africa.

Oleander

oleander, *Nerium oleander,* poisonous evergreen shrub native to Mediterranean region. Lance-shaped leathery leaves, large pink flowers.

oleaster, common name for plants of genus *Elaeagnus*; incl. *E. angustifolia,* ornamental shrub, native to S Europe and W Asia. Yellow flowers and olive-like fruit.

Oligocene epoch, third geological epoch of Tertiary period. Alpine mountain building continued. Mammals dominant; rise of true carnivores, erect primates. Decrease in temperature from Eocene epoch. Also *see* GEOLOGICAL TABLE.

oligopoly, in economics, virtual control of supply of commodity or service by a few producers. While privately-controlled MONOPOLY is rare, oligopoly is relatively usual in form of CARTEL or interlocking directorates.

olive, *Olea europaea,* European evergreen tree, native to Asia Minor. Cultivated since ancient times for fruit, eaten either unripe (green) or ripe (black), or used as source of oil. Wood prized for ornamental work.

Oliver, Isaac (*c* 1565-1617), English painter. Worked under Hilliard; continued art of miniature painting, but portraits are in more naturalistic style.

Olives, Mount of or **Olivet,** ridge E of Jerusalem visited many times by Jesus. Garden of Gethsemane on W slope.

Olivier, Laurence [Kerr], Baron Olivier of Brighton (1907-), English actor, director. Famous for appearances at Old Vic and in films, *eg Rebecca, Richard III, Hamlet.* Director of UK's National Theatre (1962-73).

Olomouc (Ger. *Olmütz*), town of C Czechoslovakia, on R. Morava. Pop. 80,000. Food processing. Former cap. of Moravia. Cathedral (14th cent.). Univ. (1573).

Olympia, ancient city of Greece, in W Peloponnese. Founded *c* 1000 BC; centre for worship of Zeus, temple had Phidias' statue of Zeus. OLYMPIC GAMES first held here.

Olympia, cap. and port of Washington, US; at end of Puget Sound. Pop. 23,000. Exports fish, timber. Founded 1850; became territ. cap. 1853.

Olympian gods, in Greek myth, the twelve major gods who lived on Mt. Olympus. Succeeded the TITANS as rulers of universe. Headed by Zeus and his sister and wife, Hera.

Olympic games, ancient Greek festival consisting of contests in athletics, poetry and music held every 4 years at Olympia. First records kept from 776 BC; abolished AD 393. Games were revived (1896) by Pierre de Coubertin; women participated from 1912. Winter Olympics estab. 1924.

Olympus (*Olimbos*), mountain range of NE Greece, near Aegean coast. Rises to 2915 m (9570 ft), highest point in Greece. Legendary home of ancient gods.

Omagh, town of WC Northern Ireland. Pop. 12,000. Former co. town of Tyrone. Agric. market; dairy produce.

Omaha, city of E Nebraska, US; on Missouri R. Pop. 573,000; state's largest city. Railway, insurance centre. Livestock market, meat packing, machinery mfg. Founded 1854; territ. cap. 1855-67.

Oman, independent sultanate of SW Asia, SE Arabian penin., along Gulf of Oman. Area *c* 212,000 sq km (82,000 sq mi); pop. 839,000; cap. Muscat. Coastal plain (dates) backed by mountains, arid plateau. Linked by treaty with Britain. Called Muscat and Oman until 1970.

Omar (*c* 581-644), Arab ruler. One of Mohammed's ablest advisers, he succeeded Abu Bakr (634) as 2nd caliph. Greatly extended Islamic empire with victories in Persia, Syria, Egypt.

Omar Khayyam (*fl* 11th cent.), Persian poet, mathematician. Famous in West for *Rubáiyát* through Edward Fitzgerald's English translation (1859); series of independent epigrammatic stanzas. Famous in East as astronomer and mathematician, assisted calendar reform.

Omayyads, Arab dynasty of caliphs. Founded 661 by Muawiya, whose cap. was Damascus. Overthrown by Abbasids (750), who massacred Omayyad family. A survivor escaped to Spain, where he founded emirate of Córdoba (756-929) later a caliphate (929-1031).

ombudsman, public official appointed to investigate citizens' complaints against local or national govt. agencies for infringement of rights of individual. Introduced into Sweden (1809). Appointed in New Zealand (1962), UK (1966).

Omdurman, city of C Sudan, on White Nile opposite Khartoum. Pop. 299,000. Trade in livestock, hides, cotton goods. Mahdi's cap. 1884, site of his tomb. Scene of Kitchener's victory (1898) over Khalifa's forces.

Omsk, city of USSR, W Siberian RSFSR; at confluence of Om and Irtysh. Pop. 1,014,000. Automobile, agric. machinery mfg; oil refining. Founded 1716 as fort.

onager, *Equus hemionus onager,* wild ass o India and Persia.

Onega, Lake, second largest lake of Europe, in USSR, NW European RSFSR. Area *c* 9840 sq km (3800 sq mi). Outlet is R. Svir flowing into L. Ladoga. Important fisheries

O'Neill, Eugene [Gladstone] (1888-1953) American dramatist. Experimented with technique, combining myth, symbolism expressionism. Plays incl. trilogy *Mourning Becomes Electra* (1931), *The Iceman Cometh* (1946), *Long Day's Journey into Night* (pub. 1956). Nobel Prize for Literature (1936).

onion, *Allium cepa,* biennial plant of lily family, native to SW Asia. Widely cultivated fo edible bulb with pungent smell and flavour

Ontario, prov. of C Canada. Area 1,068,587 sq km (412,582 sq mi); pop. 8,500,000; cap Toronto; other major cities Ottawa Hamilton. Forests, lakes in N (Laurentian Shield with nickel, uranium, iron, coppe resources. Indust., agric., pop. concentrated in S around Great Lakes (trade transport focus of Canada). French fu traders settled region in 17th cent., British control from 1763; area named Uppe Canada (1791); became one of 4 origina provs. of Canada (1867).

Ontario, Lake, smallest of Great Lakes, EC Canada-US. Connects L. Erie with S Lawrence Seaway. Area 19,529 sq km (754 sq mi); chief port Toronto. Important trade link; commercial fishing (affected by recent pollution).

onyx, semi-precious form of CHALCEDONY Differs from agate only in having straigh parallel, regular bands of colour.

oolite, sedimentary rock composed o spherical nuclei surrounded by concentri layers, normally of calcium carbonate Oolitic LIMESTONE is chemically precipitated; term formerly applied to uppe Jurassic period in Europe.

Oostende, *see* OSTEND.

opal, hydrated amorphous form of silica Impurities determine colour; gem opal pearly and translucent, with red, green an blue tints.

op or **optical art,** style of abstract paintin developed in 1960s which uses geometri patterns to create optical illusions o movement. Exponents incl. Bridget Riley and Vasarely.

OPEC, *see* ORGANIZATION OF PETROLEU EXPORTING COUNTRIES.

Open University, Milton Keynes, UK, estab 1969 to provide tuition for non-qualifie part-time adult students throug correspondence courses integrated wit radio, TV broadcasts, summer schools, an counselling and tutorial system. Has 90,00 students.

opera, stage drama in which singing largel or totally takes place of speech. Develope in West as Italian court entertainmen from *c* 1600 (MONTEVERDI being earlies master of form). Rigidity of resultin conventions led to reaction in favour o dramatic expression *c* 1750. In 19th cent., grand opera, spectacular and serious, contrasted with entertaining light operas. Most operas of 20th cent. retain earlier musical forms, but are often more subtle or symbolic in content.

operetta, short light OPERA, usually with some spoken dialogue, esp. works of Offenbach, Johann Strauss, Gilbert and Sullivan.

opium, narcotic drug obtained from unripe seed capsules of OPIUM POPPY. Derivatives incl. morphine, heroin, codeine, used medicinally as sedative, but strictly controlled as they are addictive.

opium poppy, *Papaver somniferum,* annual plant native to Asia and Asia Minor. Cultivated as source of OPIUM.

Opium Wars (1839-42, 1856-8), wars between China and Britain, resulting from Chinese refusal to allow importation of opium from India. Hong Kong ceded by China after British victory (1842). British-French victory in 2nd war estab. free trade in Chinese ports and legalization of opium trade.

Oporto *(Pôrto),* city of W Portugal, on R. Douro. Pop. 1,315,000. Seaport, exports port wine; artificial harbour for large ships at nearby Leixões; textiles, pottery mfg. Univ. (1911). Roman *Portus Cale,* gave name to Portugal.

opossum, any of Didelphidae family of mainly arboreal American marsupials with long prehensile tails. Noted for habit of feigning death when in danger -'playing possum'. Name also applied to Australian HONEY MOUSE.

Oppenheimer, J[ohn] Robert (1904-67), American physicist. Directed research at Los Alamos (1942-5) leading to production of 1st atomic bomb; opposed decision to develop hydrogen bomb. Considered security risk, he was deprived of membership of US Atomic Energy Commission (1953). Rehabilitated 1963.

Ops, in Roman religion, wife of Saturn; mother of Jupiter and Juno. Goddess of the harvest. Identified with Greek Rhea.

optical fibres, *see* FIBRE OPTICS.

optics, science of light and principles underlying phenomena of light and vision, divided into physical and geometrical optics. Former studies nature of light and its wave properties, latter treats reflection, refraction, *etc,* by ray aspect of light.

oracle, in Greek religion, answer given by particular gods, usually through priest or priestess, to human questioner. Name also applied to shrine where such responses were given. Most famous were those of Zeus at Dodona and of Apollo at Delphi.

Oran, city of NW Algeria, on Gulf of Oran. Pop. 485,000. Port, exports wine, wheat, wool; food processing. Founded 10th cent.; alternated between Spain, Turkey after 1509, taken by France (1831). Severely damaged by earthquake (1791). Scene of British destruction of French fleet (1940), to prevent capture by Germans. Univ. (1967).

Orange, House of, ruling family of the Netherlands. Name derives from principality in SE France inherited (1544) by William the Silent, of house of Nassau. His successors were stadholders of Dutch republic. William VI, prince of Orange, became 1st king of Netherlands in 1815.

Orange, town of Provence, SE France. Pop. 26,000. Tourist centre. Hist. cap. of Orange principality. Roman remains incl. arch, amphitheatre.

Orange, river of S Africa. Flows *c* 2100 km (1300 mi) W from N Lesotho via South Africa to Atlantic Ocean at Alexander Bay. Forms part of South Africa-Namibia border. Large irrigation, h.e.p. scheme; alluvial diamond deposits.

orange, evergreen tree of genus *Citrus,* bearing round, reddish-yellow fruit. Native to China but widely cultivated. Species incl. *C. sinensis,* common sweet orange used esp. in production of orange juice, and *C. aurantium,* bitter or Seville orange used in marmalade.

Orange Free State, prov. of EC South Africa. Area 129,250 sq km (49,900 sq mi); pop. 1,682,000; cap. Bloemfontein. Mainly plateau, bounded by R. Orange (S), R. Vaal (N). Sheep rearing, fruit, cereal growing; mines produce gold, diamonds, coal. Settled after 1836 Trek by Boers; republic created 1854. Annexed by Britain in Boer War, became Orange River Colony 1900. Prov. of Union of South Africa from 1910.

Orange Order, militant Irish Protestant organization; named after William of Orange, whose victory at battle of Boyne (1690) estab. Protestant succession. Formed (1795) to maintain Protestant supremacy over Catholics.

Orangutan

orangutan, *Pongo pygmaeus,* large anthropoid ape of forests of Borneo and Sumatra. Long arms, short legs and reddish-brown hair; male up to 1.5 m/5 ft tall. Mainly arboreal; vegetarian diet.

oratorio, musical setting of text (usually religious) for soloists, chorus and orchestra, first introduced by St Philip Neri at his Oratory in Rome *c* 1550. Examples are Handel's *Messiah* and Bach's *Christmas Oratorio*.

oratory, art of eloquence. Originated in ancient Greece and Rome as branch of rhetoric concerned with effective delivery of speeches. Noted classical exponents incl. Demosthenes and Cicero; Aristotle wrote on theory of oratory. Classical models influenced medieval sermons, and with rising importance of parliaments, 18th-cent. political speakers.

orbit, in astronomy, path described by one body (*eg* planet, spacecraft) round a heavenly body (*eg* star, planet). In physics, path of electron round atomic nucleus. In anatomy, eye socket in vertebrate animals.

orchestra, large group of players of musical instruments, usually under direction of a conductor. Developed in West from *c* 1600. Modern symphony orchestra evolved in course of 18th and early 19th cents. and consists of 4 sections: strings, brass, woodwind and percussion.

orchid, any of family Orchidaceae of perennial plants. Worldwide distribution but most of *c* 450 genera native to humid tropical regions. Some species are epiphytic. Flowers usually showy and of all colours.

Orczy, Emmuska, Baroness (1865-1947), English author, b. Hungary. Remembered for romantic adventure story of French Revolution, *The Scarlet Pimpernel* (1905), and many sequels.

ordeal, ancient method of trial. Accused exposed to physical dangers, *eg* fire. If he survived, was thought to have done so through divine intervention and therefore was innocent.

order in council, in UK, govt. decree of the sovereign issued with advice of the Privy Council. Survival of sovereign's sole power to govern. Used by Victoria to abolish (1870) purchase of army commissions, thereby avoiding opposition of House of Lords. Still used as subordinate legislation to issue new constitution for overseas territ.

orders of architecture, several classical styles of structure distinguished chiefly by the type of column (incl. base, shaft, and capital) and entablature. The 5 orders are IONIC, DORIC and CORINTHIAN, developed in Greece, and Tuscan and Composite, developed in Italy.

Ordnance Survey, official UK mapping agency. Estab. 1791 under Board of Ordnance, produced 1st map 1801. Also *see* CARTOGRAPHY.

Ordovician period, second geological period of Palaeozoic era; began *c* 500 million years ago, lasted *c* 65 million years. Extensive seas; beginning of Caledonian mountain building period. Typified by graptolites, trilobites, crinoids, corals; earliest vertebrates (fish) in North America. Also *see* GEOLOGICAL TABLE.

ore, mineral or rock from which one or more metals may be profitably extracted.

Oreads, in Greek myth, NYMPHS of the mountains.

Örebro, town of SC Sweden, at W end of Lake Hjalmaren. Pop. 117,000. Railway jct. shoe mfg. Isl. castle scene of many hist diets *eg* when Bernadotte chosen king of Sweden (1810).

Oregon, state of NW US, on Pacific. Area 251,181 sq km (96,981 sq mi); pop. 2,385,000 cap. Salem; largest city Portland. Columbia R. forms N border, Willamette R. divides W Coast and Cascade ranges. Important timber production, industs. Agric. in valleys (wheat, fruit, vegetables, livestock). Contested by Britain, US until 1846; territ 1848, settlement began in 1840s via Oregon Trail. Admitted to Union as 33rd state (1859).

Orel or **Oryol,** city of USSR, SW European RSFSR; on R. Oka. Pop. 305,000. Market centre; textile machinery mfg. Founded 1564 as outpost against Tartars.

Orestes, in Greek myth, only son of AGAMEMNON and Clytemnestra. Avenged father's murder by killing Clytemnestra and her lover, Aegisthus, with aid of sister Electra. Pursued by Eumenides to Athens. Acquitted of matricide by the Areopagus. Story is treated by Aeschylus, Sophocles and Euripides.

Öresund (Eng. The Sound), str. between Denmark and Sweden, links Kattegat with Baltic Sea. Minimum width 5 km (2 mi).

Orff, Carl (1895-), German composer. Known for his highly rhythmic choral compositions incl. *Carmina Burana* (1937) based on medieval Latin and German verse.

organ, keyboard instrument, sound of which is produced by air forced through a pipe or past a metal reed (*see* HARMONIUM). Modern instruments generally have 2 or 3 keyboards (great, swell and choir) controlling different sets or ranks of pipes, and a set of foot pedals. The electronic organ contains electrical circuits that create electric signals when the keys are pressed; signals are amplified and fed to a loudspeaker to produce sound.

Organization for Economic Cooperation and Development (OECD), body of 24 nations, founded 1961; hq. in Paris. Aims incl. promotion of economic growth among its member countries, expansion of world trade, coordination and improvement of development aid.

Organization of African Unity (OAU), group of 30 African states estab. 1963 in Addis Ababa. Aims incl. African solidarity, elimination of colonialism, coordination of economic, cultural, health, defence policy. Now has over 40 member states.

Organization of American States (OAS), body of 24 American countries, estab. 1948; hq. in Washington. Aims incl. promotion of peace and economic development. Expelled Cuba (1962) and began trade boycott against it; some member countries have resumed trade with Cuba.

Organization of Petroleum Exporting Countries (OPEC), body of 11 countries which export large quantities of crude oil. Founded 1960 in Baghdad; aims to unify petroleum policies of member countries, which incl. Saudi Arabia, Iran, Libya, Algeria.

rientale, region of N Zaïre, main town Kisangani. Goldmining; cotton, coffee growing. Secession attempted after independence of Congo, became centre of rebel forces (1960-3). Renamed Haut-Zaïre 1972.

rienteering, sport combining cross-country running with navigation by map and compass. Introduced (1918) in Sweden.

rigen [Adamantius] (*c* 185-*c* 254), Egyptian theologian. Head of catechetical school of Alexandria. Compiled parallel text of 6 Hebrew and 2 Greek versions of Bible. Wrote defence of Christianity, *Contra Celsum*.

riginal sin, in Christian theology, tendency to sin considered innate in mankind as a result of Adam's sin of rebellion. Thus salvation can only be obtained through divine GRACE.

rinoco, river of Venezuela. Rises in Guiana Highlands, flows NW to Colombia, then NE across Venezuela into Atlantic creating wide delta. Length 2735 km (1700 mi). Navigable for 435 km (*c* 270 mi) as far as Ciudad Bolívar.

riole, any of Oriolidae family of brightly coloured songbirds of Europe and Asia. Species incl. golden oriole, *Oriolus oriolus*; male yellow with black wings. Name also applied in US to genus *Icterus*.

rion, in Greek myth, giant and hunter of Boeotia loved by Artemis. She accidentally killed him and in grief placed him in heavens as a constellation.

rion, in astronomy, constellation located at celestial equator, containing bright stars Rigel and Betelgeuse. Incl. gaseous Orion nebula, visible to unaided eye as faint patch of light.

rissa, maritime state of E India. Area *c* 156,000 sq km (60,000 sq mi); pop. 21,935,000; cap. Bhubaneswar. Mainly hilly with fertile coastal strip; agric. economy based on rice. Iron and manganese ore, coalmining. Under British control (1803).

rizaba, resort town of EC Mexico. Pop. 112,000. Agric. industs., major textile mfg. centre. To N is volcanic **Orizaba,** highest mountain in Mexico. Height 5700 m (18,700 ft).

rkney, isl. authority of N Scotland, comprising Orkney Isls. Area 975 sq km (376 sq mi); pop. 18,000.; admin. hq Kirkwall. Only 20 of *c* 70 isls. inhabited, incl. Mainland, South Ronaldsay, Hoy. Lowlying, treeless. Dairy, poultry farming; fishing; oil indust. services base on Flotta. Have prehist. remains incl. SKARA BRAE. Isls. passed from Norway to Scotland 1471.

rléans, Philippe, Duc d' (1674-1723), French nobleman. Acted as regent for Louis XV after annulling terms of Louis XIV's will. Rule was noted for corruption; notorious for his profligacy. Encouraged financial methods of John LAW. His great-grandson, **Louis Philippe Joseph, Duc d'Orléans** (1747-93), known as Philippe Egalité, achieved prominence as liberal during French Revolution. Guillotined after eldest son (later LOUIS PHILIPPE) deserted French army.

Orléans, town of Orléanais, NC France, on R. Loire, cap. of Loiret dept. Pop. 205,000. Road and railway jct., wine and grain trade, textile mfg., univ. (1312). From 10th cent. second residence after Paris of French kings; duchy from 1344. Besieged by English (1428-9), saved by Joan of Arc; again by Catholics (1563) as Huguenot stronghold. Gothic cathedral.

ormer, *see* ABALONE.

ormolu, copper and zinc alloy used in imitation of gold. Much used in France in 18th cent. to decorate furniture and clocks.

Ormonde, James Butler, 1st Duke of (1610-88), Irish soldier. Appointed lieutenant-general of troops in Ireland (1640), he fought against Irish rebels. As lord lieutenant of Ireland, came to terms with rebels (1647). Left for France after Cromwell's conquest of Ireland (1649). Lord lieutenant twice more; finally removed from office (1684) by intrigue.

Ormuz, *see* HORMUZ.

ornithology, branch of zoology dealing with birds.

orogenesis, process of mountain building, resulting in formation of mountain ranges. *See* also MOUNTAIN.

Orpheus, in Greek myth, poet and musician, son of muse Calliope by Apollo. His music charmed animals, trees and rivers. After wife Eurydice's death, went to Hades to recover her. The gods, persuaded by his music, released her on condition that he should not look at her until they reached upper world. He could not resist and she vanished. He was later torn to pieces by Thracian women; head floated, still singing, down R. Hebrus and reached Lesbos.

Orphic mysteries, religious cult of ancient Greece, traditionally founded by Orpheus. Followers believed in dual nature of man; Dionysian (divine) and Titanic (evil). Stressed strict ethical code.

Orr, John Boyd, *see* BOYD ORR.

orris root or **orrice,** root of *Iris florentina,* a European IRIS. Powdered and used in perfumery, dentifrices.

Orthodox Church, *see* EASTERN ORTHODOX CHURCH.

orthopaedic surgery, branch of surgery concerned with diagnosis and treatment of injuries, deformities and diseases of bones, joints, muscles, *etc.*

Orvieto, town of Umbria, WC Italy. Pop. 25,000. Market town, wine, pottery. Cathedral (13th cent.); Etruscan remains.

Orwell, George, pseud. of Eric Arthur Blair (1903-50), English author, b. India. Known for novels reflecting independent socialist commitment, esp. allegory of Russian Revolution *Animal Farm* (1946), anti-Utopia *1984* (1949). Also wrote many important literary, political essays.

Oryol, *see* OREL.

oryx, any of genus *Oryx* of long-horned African and Asian antelopes, inhabiting semi-desert areas.

Osaka, major seaport of Japan, on Osaka Bay, SW Honshu isl. Pop. 2,750,000. Indust. and commercial centre; exports cotton goods, machinery. Textiles, chemical and steel mfg. Has rebuilt 16th cent. castle, Buddhist and Shinto temples. Univ. (1931).

Osborne, John [James] (1929-), English playwright. Plays incl. *Look Back in Anger* (1956), creating archetype of the 'angry young man', *The Entertainer* (1957).

oscillograph, instrument for displaying or recording, in form of curve, waveforms of alternating currents and high frequency oscillations, *eg* sound waves. **Oscilloscope** is type of oscillograph which displays waveforms on fluorescent screen of cathode ray tube.

Oshawa, port of SE Ontario, Canada; on N shore of L. Ontario. Pop. 135,000. Car mfg., leather goods, plastics industs.

osier, *see* WILLOW.

Osiris, ancient Egyptian god of underworld; husband and brother of Isis. Treacherously slain by brother, Set. Associated with fertility and immortality.

Oslo, cap. of Norway, on Oslo Fjord. Pop. 645,000. Admin., commercial centre; ice-free port; timber, electrical, clothing industs., shipbuilding. Founded 1048, medieval Hanseatic town. Rebuilt after fire (1624), called Christiania 1624-1925. Seat of Nobel Institute. Buildings incl. Storting (parliament), Akershus fortress (13th cent.).

Osman or **Othman I** (1259–1326), Turkish sultan, founder of Ottoman dynasty. Asserted his independence from Seljuk Turks by estab. own sultanate (*c* 1299). Conquered NW Asia Minor.

osmium (Os), hard metallic element; at. no. 76, at. wt. 190.2. Densest substance known; occurs in natural alloy osmiridium with iridium. Forms hard alloys with platinum and iridium, used in pen points.

osmosis, tendency of solvent to pass through a semi-permeable membrane (permeable to solvent but not to dissolved substance) into solutions of higher concentrations. Makes possible absorption of water by plant roots and cells of animal bodies.

osprey, *Pandion haliaetus,* large bird of hawk family of Europe, Asia, North America. Dark plumage with white underparts. Found near water; feeds on fish.

Ossetia, *see* NORTH OSSETIA.

Ossian or **Oisin,** semi-legendary Irish bard of 3rd cent. Supposedly son of Finn MacCumhaill who lived to tell tales of his father to St Patrick. *See* MACPHERSON, JAMES.

Ossory, ancient Irish kingdom, with cap. at Kilkenny. Ruled by kings until early 12th cent.

Ostend (Flem. *Oostende),* town of W Belgium, on North Sea. Pop. 58,000. Resort port, ferry to Dover, canal to Bruges Ghent. Fishing, fish processing, shipbuilding.

osteoarthritis, *see* ARTHRITIS.

osteomyelitis, infection of bone, with formation of pus in the marrow. Usually caused by bacteria carried in the bloodstream; treated by antibiotics.

osteopathy, medical practice based on theory that ailments result from 'structural derangements' of bones and muscles which can be corrected by manipulation. Pioneered by Andrew Still (1828-1917).

Ostia, ancient city of WC Italy. Once port for Rome, at mouth of Tiber, *fl c* AD 100-300. Now 5 km (3 mi) from sea. Extensive ruins.

Ostrava or **Moravská Ostrava,** city of N Czechoslovakia, on Moravian side of R. Ostravice. Iron, steel indust., railway engineering. Opposite is Slezská Ostrava, on Silesian side, coalmining centre. Combined pop. 279,000.

Ostrich

ostrich, *Struthio camelus,* fast-running flightless bird of Africa and Arabia. Long sparsely feathered neck, long legs with 2 toes on each foot; largest of all birds, *c* 2 m/8 ft tall. Male is black with white wing and tail feathers.

Ostrogoths, branch of GOTHS who were conquered by the Huns *c* 370. Gained their independence *c* 450 and settled in Pannonia (modern Hungary). Under Theodoric, invaded and conquered Italy (488-93). Lost their separate identity after defeat by Byzantine forces of Justinian (552).

Oswiecim (Ger. *Auschwitz),* town of S Poland. Pop. 39,000. Railway jct.; agric. machinery, chemical indust. Site of Nazi concentration camp in WWII, where *c* 4 million people died.

Otago, region of S South Isl., New Zealand. Area 66,120 sq km (25,530 sq mi); pop. 294,000; chief city Dunedin. Southern Alps, glacial lakes, fjords in W; valleys, coastal lowlands in E. Sheep, dairy farming, tourism, h.e.p. Pop. rose rapidly during gold rush of 1860s.

Othman I, *see* OSMAN I.

Otranto (anc. *Hydruntum*); town of Apulia, SE Italy, on Str. of Otranto between Italy and Greece, Albania. Pop. 5000. Roman port; destroyed 1480 by Turks, never recovered.

Ottawa, cap. of Canada, in SE Ontario; on Ottawa R. Pop. 693,000. Connected to L. Ontario by Rideau Canal. Political, social, cultural centre. Important lumber indust.; major pulp and paper mills. Founded 1827 as Bytown, renamed 1854; chosen as cap. (1858). Has Parliament buildings, Ottawa Univ. (1866), Carleton Univ. (1942).

Ottawa, river of EC Canada. Flows from W Québec, SE 1130 km (*c* 700 mi) to St Lawrence R. near Montréal. Forms extensive part of S Québec-Ontario border. Many lakes, rapids along its course. Connected with L. Ontario by Rideau Canal.

Otter, any of genus *Lutra* of aquatic carnivorous mammals, of worldwide distribution. Long flattened tail, webbed feet used for swimming. Usually lives beside fresh water, feeding on fish; SEA OTTER is marine variety.

Otto [I] the Great (912-73), king of Germany (936-73) and Holy Roman emperor (962-73). Succeeded his father Henry the Fowler. Extended realm over much of Germany and Lombardy. Defeated Magyars at Lechfeld (955). Crowned emperor by Pope John XII (962). Deposed John (963) and had his own choice elected pope.

Ottoman Empire, Islamic empire estab. in Asia Minor by OSMAN I and his descendants following collapse of Seljuk Turk empire. Under Mohammed II, Constantinople captured (1453). Under Suleiman the Magnificent, empire reached its peak, incl. Turkey, Syria, Hungary, Egypt, Persia, most of Greece and Balkans. After unsuccessful siege of Vienna (1683), its European power declined. Gradually dismembered by Russia and European powers (19th-early 20th cent.).

Otway, Thomas (1652-85), English playwright. Wrote Restoration tragedies, *eg The Orphan* (1680), *Venice Preserved* (1682).

Ouagadougou, cap. of Upper Volta. Pop. 169,000. Admin., commercial centre. Railway to Abidjan (Ivory Coast); trade in groundnuts, millet, livestock. In Ivory Coast (1933-47).

Oudenaarde (Fr. *Audenarde*), village of W Belgium, on R. Scheldt. Scene of French defeat (1708) by British and Austrians in War of Spanish Succession.

Oudh, former province of British India, now part of Uttar Pradesh. Annexation by Britain (1856) a cause of Indian Mutiny (1857-8).

Oudjda, *see* OUJDA.

Ouessant, *see* USHANT.

Oujda or **Oudjda,** city of NE Morocco. Pop. 349,000. Railway jct., agric. trade centre for E Morocco, W Algeria. Occupied by French 1907-56.

Oulu (Swed. *Uleåborg*), town of W Finland, on Gulf of Bothnia. Pop. 85,000. Port, exports timber products; shipbuilding. Univ. (1958), cathedral.

ounce, in measurement, British unit of weight; equal to *c* 28.35 grams.

ounce, *see* SNOW LEOPARD.

Ouse, rivers of England. **1,** in Yorkshire, flows 97 km (60 mi) to R. Trent, forming Humber estuary. **2,** in Sussex, flows 48 km (30 mi) through S Downs to English Channel at Newhaven. **3,** Great Ouse, flows 257 km (160 mi) from Northamptonshire across the Fens to the Wash.

Outer Hebrides, *see* HEBRIDES.

Outer Mongolia, *see* MONGOLIA.

outlawry, originally deprivation by law of person's legal rights, property, protection, as punishment for crime. Killing of outlaw was not an offence.

ouzel, name applied to birds of DIPPER family and RING OUZEL.

ovary, either of 2 female reproductive organs (ductless glands) which produce germ cells or ova, and, in vertebrates, sex hormones.

ovenbird, *Seiurus aurocapillus,* North American bird of wood warbler family, that builds oven-shaped grass nest on ground. Name also applied to birds of Furnariidae family from Central and South America that build similar clay nests.

overture, prelude for orchestra before opera or choral work, or independent orchestral work in similar style.

Ovid, full name Publius Ovidius Naso (43 BC-*c* AD 18), Roman poet. Known for erotic *Ars Amatoria,* and *Metamorphoses,* series of tales from ancient mythology. Latter profoundly influenced European literature from medieval times on. Later wrote *Tristia,* poems of exile after banishment.

Oviedo, city of N Spain, cap. of Oviedo prov. Pop. 164,000. Indust. centre in coal and iron mining area; armaments mfg., chemicals; univ. (1604). Cap. of Asturias 9th-10th cent. Gothic cathedral; 9th-cent. Cámara Santa contains famous relics.

ovum or **egg,** in biology, female gamete or reproductive cell. When fertilized by male sperm, develops into new member of same species.

Owen, Robert (1771-1858), British social reformer. Estab. model indust. community for mill workers at New Lanark, Scotland. Improved housing and working conditions, opened schools and shops. Similar scheme at New Harmony, Indiana, unsuccessful. In 1830s, advocated that trade unions should run industs. along cooperative lines. Ideas inspired COOPERATIVE MOVEMENT.

Owen, Wilfred (1893-1918), English poet. Known for *Poems* (1920, collected by Sassoon) expressing horror of war. Killed in WWI.

Owen Falls, waterfall of SE Uganda, on Victoria Nile near Victoria Nyanza. Site of dam (1954) which controls floods, supplies h.e.p. to Uganda and Kenya.

Owens, John Cleveland ('Jesse') (1913-80), American athlete. Only man to win 4 track and field gold medals (100m, 200m, long jump, 4 × 100m relay) in single Olympics (1936). In an athletics meeting in 1935 he broke 6 world records within 45 mins.

owl, any of order Strigiformes of widely distributed nocturnal birds of prey. Broad head and forward-facing eyes surrounded by disc of stiff feathers; short hooked beak. Feeds on rodents and small birds.

ox, name for several members of Bovidae family. Name specifically applies to castrated bull of domesticated breeds, esp. *Bos taurus.*

oxalic acid, white crystalline poisonous solid occurring in small quantities in wood sorrel and rhubarb leaves. Used in ink manufacture, dyeing and bleaching.

Oxalis: European wood sorrel

oxalis or **wood sorrel,** any of genus *Oxalis* of creeping plants with five-parted flowers, clover-like leaves.

ox bow lake, *see* MEANDER.

Oxenstierna, Count Axel Gustafsson (1583-1654), Swedish statesman. Appointed chancellor (1612), administered country during Gustavus Adolphus' absence at war. Continued Swedish involvement in Thirty Years War after Gustavus' death; made alliance with France after defeat at Nördlingen (1634). Virtual ruler of Sweden during minority of Queen Christina.

Oxford Movement, term for movement (from 1833) to revive Church of England through a return to practices of early Christianity. Held Anglicanism to be middle ground between Roman Catholicism and evangelicalism. First led by NEWMAN who wrote, with Keble and Pusey, *Tracts for the Times* (1833-41). Movement lost ground with entry c Newman and others into RC church. Als called Tractarianism, Anglo-Catholicism.

Oxfordshire, county of SC England. Are 2611 sq km (1008 sq mi); pop. 542,00 Cotswolds in W, Chilterns in SE; elsewher fertile clay vale. Cereals, livestock. Admin hq **Oxford,** on R. Thames (Isis). Pop 115,000. Cars, electrical goods indust Univ. (oldest in UK) grew as medieva centre of learning from 1249. Building incl. Bodleian Library, Ashmolea Museum. Scene of several medieva parliaments. Royalist hq. in Civil War.

oxidation, in chemistry, originally, proces by which oxygen combines with o hydrogen is removed from a substance More generally, process in which electron are removed from atoms or ions.

oxlip, *Primula elatior,* perennial plant o primrose family. Yellow flowers in spring.

Oxus, *see* AMU DARYA.

oxyacetylene welding, form of meta welding using mixture of oxygen an ACETYLENE. Gases are sent through high pressure system and burn with extremel hot flame.

oxygen (O), gaseous element; at. no. 8, at. wt 16.00. Forms *c* 1/5 of atmosphere; mos abundant of all elements on Eart Chemically active, it combines with mos elements. Necessary in respiration an combustion. Obtained by fractiona distillation of liquid air; used in weldin flames; liquid oxygen used as rocke propellant.

oyster, edible marine bivalve mollusc, esp of genera *Ostrea* and *Crassostrea.* She made of 2 unequal halves with rough oute surface. Lives on sea bed or adheres t rocks in shallow water. May be cultivate as food or for pearls in artificial beds.

oyster catcher, any of Haematopodida family of wading birds of Europe, and th Americas. Lives on sea shores, feeding o limpets, oysters, *etc.* Species incl. *Haema topus ostralegus,* with black and whit plumage, red legs and beak.

Ozark Mountains, plateau of SC US; mainl in S Missouri and NW Arkansas. Averag height 610 m (2000 ft). Important lea barytes deposits; many mineral spring Tourist area.

ozone (O_3), unstable allotropic form o oxygen, with 3 atoms in molecule rathe than usual 2. Pale blue gas wit penetrating odour; powerful oxidizin agent. Formed by silent electric discharge through oxygen or, naturally, b action of ultraviolet light; used a bleaching agent and germicide.

ozonosphere, layer of upper atmospher between 15 and 30 km above Earth surface, in which there is an appreciab concentration of ozone. It absorbs much c Sun's ultraviolet radiation, which would b harmful to animal life.

P

pacemaker, electronic device connected to the wall of the heart which provides small regular electronic shocks to restore normal heartbeat.

Pacific Islands, Trust Territory of the, isls. of Pacific Ocean, held (1947-78) by US under trusteeship from UN. Incl. Caroline, Mariana (except Guam), Marshall Isls. In 1978 Caroline and Marshall Isls. formed Federated States of MICRONESIA, Northern Mariana Isls. became Commonwealth of US.

Pacific Ocean, world's largest and deepest ocean; stretches from Asia-Australia (W) to the Americas (E), from Antarctica to the Bering Strait. Area *c* 180,000,000 sq km (70,000,000 sq mi). Reaches depth of 11,033 m (36,198 ft) in Mariana Trench. Many volcanic and coral isls. in S and W, esp. Polynesia, Melanesia and Micronesia. Ocean currents circulating in Pacific incl. Equatorial, Kuroshio, East Australia, Humboldt, California.

pacifism, individual or collective opposition to the use of armed force, esp. between nations; more generally, opposition to any violence. Religious reasons for pacifism found in Christianity, Buddhism, Confucianism, *etc.*

pack rat, North American rodent, genus *Neotoma,* often with bushy tail. Noted for habit of collecting shiny objects to decorate nest.

Paderewski, Ignacy Jan (1860-1941), Polish pianist, statesman. Famed performer, esp. of Chopin. Best-known composition is *Minuet in G.* Active in cause for Polish independence, became premier for 10 months in 1919.

Padua (*Padova*), city of Venetia, NE Italy, cap. of Padova prov. Pop. 242,000. Indust., transport centre. Roman *Patavium*; *fl* in Middle Ages under Carrara family and Venice. Univ. (1222), basilica (13th cent.).

Paganini, Niccolò (1782-1840), Italian violinist, composer. His virtuoso playing revolutionized violin technique. Compositions feature brilliant effects.

pagoda, Buddhist temple in form of pyramidal tower, built in superimposed storeys tapering towards top. Common in India and China, they were imitated in 18th-cent. European architecture.

Pahlavi, Mohammad Reza (1919-80), shah of Iran (1941-79). Succeeded on abdication of father. Followed policy of rapid westernization, inspiring widespread opposition. Forced into exile (1979).

pain, sensation arising from excessive stimulation of sensory nerve ends and conveyed by nerve fibres to the brain. Relieved by analgesics, narcotics, *etc.*

Paine, Thomas (1737-1809), American writer, b. England. Argued for immediate independence of American colonies in pamphlets *Common Sense* (1776), *The American Crisis* (1776-83). Defended French Revolution in *The Rights of Man* (1791-2). Accused of treason in England, fled to France (1792).

paint, pigment in suspension with oil, water or other medium (often with additional thinners) used to decorate or protect a surface. After application, dries to adhesive film by evaporation of thinner or oxidation of medium. One of commonest media is linseed oil with turpentine as thinner, but many specialized synthetic paints increasingly used.

painted lady, *Vanessa cardui,* widely distributed butterfly with brownish-black and orange wings.

painting, one of the fine arts, practised from earliest times. Examples of palaeolithic animal paintings survive at Lascaux. Frescoes were important in art of ancient Egypt and Rome. Oil colour, portraiture and use of perspective were developed in 15th cent., landscape in 16th and 17th cents. Impressionism was major innovation of 19th cent. Abstract painting began in early 20th cent.

Paisley, town of Strathclyde region, WC Scotland. Pop. 95,000. Textiles industs. esp. thread; once famous for Paisley shawls. Has 12th-cent. abbey.

Paiute or **Piute,** North American Indian tribes related to Aztecs. N group of Idaho and Nevada opposed white settlers of 1860s. S group of Great Basin, Nevada were sedentary root gatherers.

Pakistan

Pakistan, republic of SC Asia, on NW India boundary. Area *c* 804,000 sq km (311,000 sq mi); pop. 76,770,000; cap. Islamabad. Language: Urdu. Religion: Islam. Mountains in

N and W; population concentrated in plains watered by Indus and its tributaries; desert in SW. Agric. economy (esp. grains, rice, cotton). Major cities Karachi, Lahore. Divided into 4 provs. (Baluchistan, Punjab, Sind, Northwest Frontier). Created 1947 out of India following Moslem agitation led by Jinnah; became republic 1956. Long-standing dispute with India over possession of Kashmir led to fighting (1965). East Pakistan became independent republic of BANGLADESH (1972) following civil war and Indian military intervention.

Palaeocene epoch, first geological epoch of Tertiary period. Beginning of Alpine mountain building. Replacement of dinosaurs by primitive mammals, ancestors of cat, dog, horse, elephant; modern vegetation *eg* seed-bearing plants. Also *see* GEOLOGICAL TABLE.

Palaeolithic or **Old Stone Age,** prehist. period beginning *c* 1.8 million years ago during which modern man, *Homo sapiens,* evolved from 1st tool-making predecessors, *eg* AUSTRALOPITHECUS. Usually subdivided into Lower, Middle and Upper periods. Lower period, earliest division, saw development of simple stone tools, *eg* hand axes. Middle period, represented by culture of Neanderthal man, saw introduction of flint tools. In Upper period, *H. sapiens* emerged, and specialized tools, *eg* burins, were developed.

palaeontology, branch of geology dealing with the study of prehist. life, based on fossil remains. Incl. palaeobotany, palaeozoology; yields information on evolution, adaptation of organisms to changing environment.

Palaeozoic or **Primary era,** geological era intermediate between Precambrian and Mesozoic eras. Duration *c* 350 million years. Cambrian, Ordovician, Silurian periods form Lower Palaeozoic; time of trilobites, graptolites, brachiopods, earliest fish. Devonian, Carboniferous, Permian periods form Upper Palaeozoic; time of amphibians, reptiles, corals, crinoids, earliest terrestrial flora. Also *see* GEOLOGICAL TABLE.

palate, term for roof of human mouth. Front portion, hard palate, joins tooth ridge; back portion, soft palate, is fibrous muscular arch which closes back of nose during swallowing. Uvula projects from centre of arch.

Palatinate (*Pfalz*), two regions of West Germany, hist. linked under Wittelsbach family (1214-1918). **Lower** or **Rhenish Palatinate** (*Rheinpfalz*), lies between R. Rhine and French border; now part of Rhineland-Palatinate state. Fertile, produces wines; main towns Neustadt, Kaiserslautern. **Upper Palatinate** (*Oberpfalz*), now part of Bavaria prov. Agric., cattle raising. Counts Palatine were imperial electors from 1356; territ. called Electoral Palatinate (*Kurpfalz*).

pale, hist. term for restricted region within a country, where different system of law and govt. prevailed. In Irish history, denotes region around Dublin where English rule was enforced (12th-17th cent.).

Palembang, city of Indonesia, cap. of South Sumatra prov., port on R. Musi. Pop. 583,000. Trade centre for nearby oilfields; exports petroleum products, rubber.

Palermo (anc. *Panormus*), town of N Sicily, Italy, on Tyrrhenian Sea. Cap. of Sicily and Palermo prov. Pop. 679,000. Port, exports fruit, wine, olive oil; indust. centre; univ. (1805). Founded by Phoenicians, later held by Carthage, Rome, Byzantium. *Fl* under Arabs, Normans (esp. 12th-13th cents.). Cathedral (12th cent.).

Palestine, *see* ISRAEL.

Palestrina, Giovanni Pierluigi da (*c* 1525-94), Italian composer. Wrote mainly sacred works for unaccompanied voices, incl. over 100 Mass settings. Considered master of counterpoint and polyphony.

Pali, vernacular dialect of classical SANSKRIT. The language of S Buddhist scriptures, has become religious language of Buddhism.

Palladio, Andrea (1508-80), Italian architect. Known for theoretical writings on harmonic proportion in architecture, esp. Roman. Designed villas with classical temple front. Greatly influenced neo-Classical work of 17th and 18th cents.

palladium (Pd), white metallic element; at. no. 46, at. wt. 106.4. Occurs with platinum and iridium. Used as catalyst in hydrogenization and in alloys with gold, platinum, silver.

Pallas Athena, *see* ATHENA.

palm, any of family Palmae of tropical and subtropical trees or shrubs. Woody, branchless trunk, large evergreen feather-like or fan-shaped leaves growing in bunch at top. Economically important species incl. date, coconut, raffia and sago.

Palma (de Mallorca), cap. of Majorca and Baleares prov., Spain, on Bay of Palma. Pop. 267,000. Chief city and port of Balearic Isls., exports agric. produce; tourist resort. Roman colony. 13th-cent. cathedral.

Palmas, Las, city of Grand Canary, Canary Isls., Spain, cap. of Las Palmas prov. Pop. 328,000. Tourist resort; outport at Puerto de la Luz, exports fruit, wine; fishing. Cathedral (18th cent.).

Palmer, Samuel (1805-81), English painter. Influenced by Blake, he is remembered for the visionary landscapes of his 'Shoreham Period' (1826-35).

Palmerston, Henry John Temple, 3rd Viscount (1784-1865), English statesman, PM (1855-8, 1859-65). As Whig foreign secretary (1830-41, 1846-51), secured Belgian independence and supported Turkish territ. integrity against plans of Russia and France. As PM, continued Crimean War, supported Italian nationalism, put down Sepoy revolt in India (1857-8).

Palmerston North, city of S North Isl., New Zealand, on Manawatu R. Pop. 90,000.

palm oil, fatty, orange-red oil obtained from fruit of many palms, incl. oil palm *Elaeis guineensis.* Used in soap, candles, *etc.*

alm Sunday, Christian holy day commemorating Jesus' entry into Jerusalem. Celebrated on Sunday before Easter.

almyra, ancient city of C Syria. Rose to prominence (AD 130-270) until destroyed by Romans in 273.

alomar, Mount, mountain of S California, US; near San Diego. Height 1867 m (6126 ft). Has world's largest reflecting telescope, 508 cm (200 in.) in diameter.

amirs, mountainous region of C Asia, mainly in USSR, E Tadzhik SSR, but extending into Afghanistan and China. Consists of high mountain valleys bordered by mountain ranges; highest peak is Kongur Shan 7719 m (25,326 ft) in China.

ampas, large grassy plain of NC Argentina. Cattle raising, dairy farming; wealth from related industs., *eg* meat packing.

ampas grass, several giant perennial South American grasses of genera *Cortaderia* and *Gynerium*. Grown as ornamentals.

amplona, city of N Spain, at foot of Pyrenees, cap. of Navarra prov. Pop. 169,000. Agric. market, iron, lead-smelting. Basque kingdom founded 824, was cap. of kingdom of Navarre until union with Castile (1515). Cathedral (14th cent.).

an, in Greek myth, god of flocks and shepherds. Represented as partly goat-like in form. Played musical pipes. Identified with Faunus by Romans.

anama, republic of Central America. Area 75,650 sq km (29,210 sq mi); pop. 1,860,000; cap. Panama City. Language: Spanish. Religion: RC. Volcanic mountains in W and E; fertile lowlands in C (bananas, coffee, mahogany exports). Also important fishing industs., esp. shrimps. Pop. mainly mestizo (mixed). Explored by Balboa (1513); became part of Colombia after break with Spain (1821); independent 1903.

anama Canal, waterway across Isthmus of Panama, connecting Caribbean and Pacific; 64 km (40 mi) long. Built by US (1904-14), admin. by US govt. agency.

anama Canal Zone, former admin. region of US comprising *c* 16 km (10 mi) wide canal strip in C Panama. Area 1432 sq km (553 sq mi); admin. hq. Balboa. Under 1979 treaty, most of area transferred to Panama; US maintained control of Canal.

anama City, cap. of Panama, on Gulf of Panama. Pop. 428,000. Clothing, shoes, beer mfg. Founded 1519; rebuilt 1673 at new site after destruction by pirates under Henry Morgan. Became cap. 1903.

ancreas, gland found in mesentery, near duodenum, of vertebrates. Secretes alkaline mixture of digestive enzymes through a duct into duodenum. Cell groups (islets of Langerhans) also secrete hormones insulin and glucagon.

anda, arboreal, mainly vegetarian mammal of order Carnivora. Giant panda, *Ailuropoda melanoleuca,* found in Tibet and SW China, feeds mostly on bamboo shoots; black and white, resembles bear. Lesser panda, *Ailurus fulgens,* of Himalayas, resembles raccoon; reddish-brown fur, long bushy tail.

Pandora, in Greek myth, first woman on earth. Fashioned from clay by Hephaestus at command of Zeus as vengeance on man because of Prometheus' stealing of fire from the gods. Sent to Epimetheus, brother of Prometheus, carrying box which she opened, releasing all evils on world, while hope alone remained in box.

Pangolin

pangolin or **scaly anteater,** any of order Pholidota of toothless mammals of Africa and tropical Asia. Body and tail protected by horny scales; feeds on ants, termites caught by sticky tongue.

Pankhurst, Emmeline, née Goulden (1858-1928), English suffragette. Founded Women's Social and Political Union (1905), whose members used militant methods in cause of women's suffrage. Imprisoned (1912-13) and released after hunger strikes. Supported by daughters, **Christabel Pankhurst** (1880-1958) and **Sylvia Pankhurst** (1882-1960).

panpipes, ancient musical instrument made of several pipes of different length bound together and played by blowing across open upper ends. Used in folk music, *eg* that of Romania.

Pan-Slavism, doctrine of 19th cent. urging political and cultural unity of all Slavs. First Pan-Slav conference (1848) favoured Austrian protection of Slavs. Russia later seen as champion, but widely believed to use doctrine for expansion into Austrian and Turkish empires.

pansy, *see* VIOLET.

pantheism, system of belief which identifies God in all things. Found in all periods, *eg* in Brahmanism, and in much nature poetry.

pantheon, originally building for worship of all gods. Pantheon at Rome was built by Agrippa (27 BC) and rebuilt *c* AD 120 by Hadrian. Term also denotes building in which illustrious men are buried.

panther, *see* LEOPARD.

pantomime, originally type of drama without speech. In 18th cent. term used for mimed scenes, spectacles, based on Italian *commedia dell'arte*. Now a typically British Christmas entertainment, with comedy, songs, dancing.

papacy, office of the pope as bishop of Rome and head of RC church. Estab., according to RC doctrine, when Jesus gave Peter primacy of Church.

Papadopoulos, George (1919-), Greek political leader. Became premier after leading 1967 military coup. Abolished monarchy (1973) and became president. Overthrown by military coup amidst popular unrest (1973). Sentenced to death for treason (1975); sentence commuted.

Papal States, former independent territ. of C Italy, cap. Rome. Originated in 'Patrimony of St Peter' given to popes in 4th cent.; grew to max. extent 16th cent. (incl. Latium, Umbria, the Marches, E Emilia-Romagna). Italian unification (1861) absorbed all but Rome (annexed 1870). Also *see* VATICAN CITY.

papaw, *see* PAWPAW

papaya, *Carica papaya,* tropical American tree. Large, edible melon-like fruit.

Papen, Franz von (1879-1969), German politician. Member of Catholic Centre Party, made chancellor by Hindenburg (1932). On resignation, helped secure Hitler's chancellorship and served as his deputy (1933–4). Acquitted of war crimes at Nuremberg.

paper, thin material consisting of sheets of cellulose derived from vegetable fibres. Most paper is made from wood pulp freed from non-cellulose material; higher grade made from cotton rags. Invented in China *c* AD 105, it was spread to rest of world by the Arabs in 8th cent.; paper mfg. in Europe began in Spain in 12th cent. Leading producers incl. Canada, USSR, Scandinavia.

paprika, *see* PEPPER.

Papua New Guinea, country of SW Pacific, member of British Commonwealth. Area 463,000 sq km (178,000 sq mi); pop. 3,000,000; cap. Port Moresby. Consists of E part of New Guinea isl., Bismarck Archipelago, Bougainville and other isls. Timber exports; minerals incl. gold, copper. Country formed from Australian territ. of Papua and former German colony of New Guinea, mandated to Australia by League of Nations in 1920. Became independent 1975.

Papyrus

papyrus, *Cyperus papyrus,* tall sedge of Africa and Asia. Ancient Egyptians used stem for boats, cloth and to make sheets o[f] writing material, also called papyrus.

parabola, in geometry, curve described by [a] point which moves so that its distanc[e] from a fixed point (focus) equals it[s] distance from fixed line (directrix). Als[o] described by intersection of cone wit[h] plane parallel to one side.

Paracelsus, Philippus, orig. Theophrastu[s] von Hohenheim (*c* 1493-1541), Swiss physi[-] cian, alchemist, chemist. Forerunner o[f] scientific medicine, advocated use o[f] experiment, study of anatomy, drugs.

parachute, umbrella-shaped nylon or sil[k] canopy (developed 18th cent.) reducin[g] speed of falling body through air. Used i[n] military and sporting activity; also a[s] brake for aircraft and spacecraft durin[g] landing.

Paraclete, in Christian theology, the Hol[y] Spirit, considered as comforter, intercesso[r] or advocate.

Paradise, term denoting Garden of Ede[n] before the Fall; also used to denote heave[n] or intermediate stage for righteous soul[s] between death and final judgement.

paraffins, hydrocarbons of general formul[a] C_nH_{2n+2}; chemically inactive. First members of paraffin series, incl. methane are gases, used as fuels. Next 11 are liquid which form principal constituents of para[f-] fin oil (kerosene), a fuel obtained i[n] distillation of petroleum. Other member[s] are wax-like solids, chief constituents o[f] paraffin wax.

Paraguay, republic of SC South America Area 406,752 sq km (157,047 sq mi); pop 2,888,000; cap. Asunción. Languages Spanish, Guariní. Religion: RC. Unexploi[t-] ed Chaco in W; concentration of pop. an[d] indust. between Paraguay, Paraná rivers Cotton, maté growing; cattle rearing (mea[t] packing). Settled in 16th cent. by Spanish gained independence 1811. Extende[d] Chaco frontier in war (1932-5) with Bolivia

Paraguay, river of SC South America. Rise[s] in E Mato Grosso (W Brazil), flows S 210[0] km (*c* 1300 mi) through Paraguay to joi[n] Paraná R. Forms part of Argentina-Braz[il] border.

parakeet, any of several small parrots wit[h] long tails. BUDGERIGAR is common species.

parallax, in astronomy, apparent differenc[e] in position of heavenly body wit[h] reference to some point on surface o[f] Earth and some other point, *eg* centre o[f] Earth (diurnal parallax) or centre of Su[n] (annual parallax). Caused by Earth's ro[-] tation and revolution about Sun. Used t[o] measure distance from Earth to heavenl[y] body.

parallel, in mapping, *see* LATITUDE.

paralysis, loss of voluntary movemen[t] usually caused by disorders of nervou[s] system. Damage to spinal cord or brai[n] stroke, poliomyelitis may result i[n] paralysis.

paramagnetism, property of certai[n] materials, *eg* platinum and aluminium, [of] being weakly attracted by magnets. D[e-] gree of paramagnetism may be increased in some substances by decrease of temperature.

'aramaribo, cap. of Surinam, port near mouth of Surinam R. Pop. 151,000. Rum, bauxite, coffee exports. Many canals.

'araná, port of EC Argentina, cap. of Entre Ríos prov. on Paraná R. Pop. 128,000. Grain, cattle produce. Cap. of Argentina 1853-62. Has cathedral.

'araná, river of S Brazil. Formed by Paranaíba-Rio Grande rivers, flows SW 3200 km (*c* 2000 mi) along Paraguay border, through Argentina to Uruguay R. at La Plata estuary.

aranoia, in psychiatry, mental disorder associated with delusions of persecution or grandeur. Often occurs with schizophrenia; true paranoia, in which personality remains intact, is rare.

arasite, plant or animal that lives on or in an organism of another species from which it derives nourishment or protection without benefiting the host and usually harming it. Ectoparasites, *eg* lice, live on surface of host; endoparasites, *eg* tapeworms, inside host's body.

arathyroid, one of usually four small glands on or near the thyroid gland. They secrete a hormone, parathormone, which regulates calcium and phosphate concentration of blood.

archment, writing material prepared from stretched untanned animal skins. First used in Pergamum (*c* 150 BC).

'aris, in Greek myth, son of Priam of Troy. Chosen to settle dispute over APPLE OF DISCORD which led to his abduction of HELEN, thus instigating Trojan War. In war, killed Achilles and was killed by Philoctetes.

'aris (anc. *Lutetia*), cap. and dept. of France, on R. Seine. Pop. 2,290,000, greater Paris 9,863,000. River port, transport focus; admin., commercial, indust. centre (esp. luxury goods, clothing); tourism. Dominates France culturally and economically. Gaulish, then Roman settlement; made cap. of France in 987 by Capet. Medieval scholastic, religious centre; *fl* as literary, artistic centre 17th-19th cent. Focus of revolutions in 1789, 1830, 1848, 1871. Places of interest incl. Notre Dame Cathedral (12th-13th cent.), Sainte Chapelle, Arc de Triomphe, Eiffel Tower (300 m/984 ft), Montmartre (artistic quarter), Palais d'Elysée (president's residence), Sorbonne univ. (12th cent.), Louvre art gallery. Modern Paris planned (19th cent.) by Haussmann.

'aris Commune (18 March-29 May, 1871), Parisian revolutionary govt. Set up at end of FRANCO-PRUSSIAN WAR after premier Adolphe Thiers' attempt to crush armed national guard of Paris. Socialist govt. elected (26 March). Thiers' siege succeeded, and *c* 20,000 prisoners killed.

'aris, Congress of, conference held (1856) to negotiate settlement of Crimean War. Russian-Turkish boundary restored to prewar status, Black Sea declared neutral, Moldavia and Walachia (later Romania) became auton.

Paris Peace Conference, *see* VERSAILLES, TREATY OF.

Paris, Treaty of, name of several treaties signed in Paris. That of 1763, signed by Britain, France and Spain, ended Seven Years War. By treaty of 1783, Britain acknowledged independence of US. Treaty of 1814 gave France favourable settlement of Napoleonic wars after Napoleon's abdication but that of 1815, after French defeat at Waterloo, was much harsher.

parity, conservation of, in physics, principle that there is no fundamental difference between left and right; thus laws of physics should be valid for both left-handed and right-handed systems of co-ordinates. Lee and Yang showed (1956) principle was violated by certain types of beta-decay of atomic nuclei.

Park, Mungo (1771-1806), Scottish explorer. Explored and estab. much of course of R. Niger (1795-6); drowned on 2nd expedition after attack by natives.

Park Chung Hee (1917-79), South Korean political leader. Seized power in army coup (1961); became president (1963). Estab. dictatorial powers, ostensibly to withstand threats of North Korean invasion. Assassinated.

Parker, Charlie ('Bird'), orig. Charles Christopher Parker (1920-55), American jazz musician. Noted for his saxophone improvisations, he was a leader in the movement away from swing to the 'bop' style of the late 1940s.

Parkinson's disease, disturbance of voluntary movements caused by degeneration of the basal ganglia of the brain. Characterized by rhythmic body tremors and muscular rigidity. Usually occurs in later life.

Parliament, bicameral legislature of UK, consisting of HOUSE OF LORDS, HOUSE OF COMMONS. Executive power rests in sovereign, who in reality acts only on advice of ministers, *ie* PRIME MINISTER and CABINET. Modern development began in 13th cent. with frequent assemblies, influence of DE MONTFORT; MODEL PARLIAMENT esp. important. Its political power grew under Plantagenets, marked by deposition of 2 kings and growth of Parliament's control of national finance. Commons' drafting of statutes replaced petitions (1414). Tudors generally dominated both Houses, but under Charles I traditional conflict between sovereign's prerogative and parliamentary privilege exaggerated into absolutism *v* popular govt. Led to CIVIL WAR. Parliament's power affirmed by Bill of RIGHTS (1689). Party system developed after Civil War, became important in 19th cent. Reform Bill (1832) reconstituted Commons, extended SUFFRAGE. Parliament Acts (1911, 1949) estab. predominance of Commons, esp. with power in finance bills.

Parliament Act (1911), legislation restricting veto power of House of Lords.

Arose from rejection of 1909 finance bill by Lords. In case of financial legislation, Lords stripped of rights to amend or reject; right to delay other legislation limited to two years, reduced to one year under 1949 Parliament Act.

Parma, city of Emilia-Romagna, NC Italy, cap. of Parma prov. Pop. 178,000. Agric. market, textiles, Parmesan cheese mfg. Medieval cultural centre; under Farnese family 1545-1731. Romanesque cathedral (11th cent.), univ. (1502).

Parmigianino, orig. Francesco Mazzola (1503-40), Italian painter, etcher. An early mannerist, his elegant graceful work is marked by its elongation of figures.

Parnassus, Mount, peak of Boeotia, C Greece. Height 2456 m (8061 ft). Sacred to Apollo, Dionysus, the Muses. Delphi lies on slopes.

Parnell, Charles Stewart (1846-91), Irish nationalist leader. Led obstructive tactics of Irish nationalists in Parliament from 1877. Directed campaign for land reform in Ireland; imprisoned (1881) for obstructing provisions of new land act; released (1882). Supported Gladstone's Home Rule bill (1886). Career ruined after involvement in divorce scandal with Kitty O'Shea (1889-90).

Páros, isl. of Greece, in Aegean Sea, one of Cyclades. Area 166 sq km (64 sq mi). Tourism. Famous for marble.

Parr, Catherine (1512-48), English queen consort, 6th wife of Henry VIII. Married Henry in 1543. After Henry's death, married Lord Thomas Seymour (1547).

parrot, hook-billed, often brilliantly coloured bird of Psittacidae family. Widely distributed, esp. in Australasia and South America. Noted for speech mimicry. Species incl. cockatoo, macaw, parakeet, lory.

Parry, Sir William Edward (1790-1855), English explorer, naval officer. Led several expeditions (1818-25) in search of Northwest Passage; attempted to reach North Pole by sledge (1827).

Parseeism, *see* ZOROASTRIANISM.

Parsifal, figure in ARTHURIAN LEGEND, sometimes called Percival, often identified with Gawain. Story basis of medieval poems.

parsley, *Petroselinum hortense,* biennial herb with aromatic curled leaves, used as flavouring, yellow umbelliferous flowers.

parsnip, *Pastinaca sativa,* biennial plant of parsley family. Long, fleshy edible root.

parthenogenesis, biological reproduction from unfertilized ovum. Occurs naturally in some organisms; male drones of ants, bees and wasps are produced by parthenogenesis. Can be artificially induced in rabbits, frogs, *etc,* but resulting offspring rarely reach maturity.

Parthenon, temple of Athena on Acropolis, Athens. Built by Callicrates and Ictinus (447-432 BC) in Doric style; Phidias supervised the sculpture. Middle section destroyed by Venetian bombardment 1687. *See* ELGIN MARBLES.

Parthia, ancient kingdom of SW Asia corresponding to Khurasan, NE Iran. Once part of Assyrian and Persian empires. Parthian kingdom founded in 248 BC. Reached greatest power under Mithradates I and II, controlling regions between Euphrates and Indus.

partridge, medium-sized European game bird with plump body, short tail. Common European partridge, *Perdix perdix,* has mottled brown above with grey speckled breast.

Pasadena, residential town of S California, US; near Los Angeles. Pop. 113,000. Has California Institute of Technology.

Pascal, Blaise (1623-62), French philosopher, scientist. Worked on mathematical theory of probability and differential calculus. Developed hydraulic press, formulating law on application of pressure on contained fluids. Religious writings incl. *Lettres provinciales* (1656) defending Jansenism, and famous collection, *Pensées,* stating his belief in inadequacy of reason.

pasha or **pacha,** title formerly used in Turkey and N Africa for military leaders and provincial governors. Abolished in Turkey (1934), in Egypt (1952).

Pasiphaë, *see* MINOS.

pasqueflower, *see* ANEMONE.

Passchendaele, village of W Belgium. Scene of WWI battle (1917) forming part of unsuccessful British offensive.

passionflower, any of genus *Passiflora* of climbing vines native to tropical America. Showy flowers; small, edible, yellow or purple egg-like fruits.

Passion play, dramatic representation of the suffering, death and resurrection of Jesus; a form of miracle play. Most famous staged at Oberammergau, Bavaria, every 10 years from 1634.

Passover, Jewish religious festival commemorating deliverance of Israelites from Egypt (although based on much older festival). Celebrated late March or early April; lasts 7 days.

pasta, preparation of glutinous wheat (semolina) and eggs, originating in Italy. Forms incl. macaroni, spaghetti, vermicelli.

pastel, drawing medium consisting of powdered pigment mixed with gum, usually moulded into sticks. Used in Italy in 15th cent.; major exponents of medium incl. Chardin and Degas.

Pasternak, Boris Leonidovich (1890-1960), Russian author. Wrote lyric, narrative poetry, novel *Dr Zhivago* (pub. in West 1958). Forced to refuse Nobel Prize for Literature (1958).

Pasteur, Louis (1822-95), French chemist. Showed that fermentation is caused by micro-organisms and that similar micro-organisms present in air are responsible for infection of wounds. Pasteurization process for sterilization of food is based on his work on fermentation of beer and wine. Eliminated disease of silkworms; produced vaccines against rabies and anthrax.

Patagonia, region of S Argentina, from Colorado R. to Tierra del Fuego (incl. S Chile). Mainly semi-arid grassy plateau, mountains in SW; sheep rearing, some cattle in W; oil, gas resources, iron ore deposits S of Río Negro.

patent, govt. document conferring MONOPOLY right to produce, sell, or get profit from an invention for a certain number of years. Rights extend only within state granting patent, but since first signing (1883) of International Convention for the Protection of Industrial Property, many countries give external rights.

Pater Noster, *see* LORD'S PRAYER.

Pathans, semi-nomadic Moslem people of W Pakistan and Afghanistan. Noted as fierce fighters. Former occupants of Northwest Frontier Prov.

pathology, branch of medicine concerned with cause, origin and nature of disease, incl. changes resulting from disease.

Patmos, isl. of Greece, in Aegean Sea, in the Dodecanese. Area 34 sq km (13 sq mi). St John the Divine wrote the Revelation here. Monastery (11th cent.).

Patna, cap. of Bihar state, NE India. Pop. 473,000. Railway jct.; centre of rice growing region. Dates from 6th cent. BC.

Patras (*Pátrai*), town of W Greece, in NW Peloponnese, on Gulf of Patras. Pop. 121,000. Port; exports currants, olive oil, wine. Greek War of Independence began here (1821).

patriarch, in OT, one of the founders of the ancient Jewish families, *eg* Abraham, Jacob. Also bishops of Eastern Orthodox Church who hold authority over other bishops.

patricians, members of privileged class of ancient Rome, descended from original citizens. Unlike the plebeians, they were entitled to hold public office. By 3rd cent. BC, almost all public offices were open to plebeians, and term patrician became an honourable title.

Patrick, St (*c* 385-461), patron saint of Ireland. Prob. born in Britain but enslaved in Ireland. Escaped and returned as Christian missionary, effected conversion of country. Writings incl. *Confessions.* Feast day is 17 Mar.

Patton, George Smith (1885-1945), American general. Commanded 3rd Army, playing leading role in liberation of France (1944), C Europe (1945).

Pau, town of SW France, cap. of Pyrénées-Atlantiques dept. Pop. 126,000. Resort, wine trade, textile mfg., univ. (1724). Hist. cap. of Béarn; residence from 1512 of kings of Navarre.

Paul, St, Jewish name Saul (d. *c* AD 67), Christian missionary, b. Tarsus. Jewish nationalist. Was converted while on road to Damascus to help suppress Christianity (prob. *c* AD 35). Became 'Apostle to the Gentiles'; travelled as missionary throughout Greek world and Near East. Prob. martyred in Rome under Nero. Epistles, attributed to him, contain fundamental statements of Christian doctrine.

Paul III, orig. Alessandro Farnese (1468-1549), Italian churchman, pope (1534-49). During his pontificate, Catholic Reformation began. Attempted to introduce reforms into the church; convened Council of TRENT (1545). Approved founding of Jesuit order (1540).

Paul VI, orig. Giovanni Battista Montini (1897-1978), Italian churchman, pope (1963-1978). Improved relations with communist countries. Reconvened 2nd Vatican Council and implemented its reforms. Reaffirmed Church's ban on contraception in encyclical *Humanae Vitae* (1968).

Pauli, Wolfgang (1900-58), Austro-American physicist. Awarded Nobel Prize for Physics (1945) for discovery of Pauli exclusion principle of quantum theory: no 2 electrons in atom can have same 4 quantum numbers. Principle has been extended to other elementary particles (fermions).

Pauling, Linus Carl (1901-), American chemist. Awarded Nobel Prize for Chemistry (1954) for work on nature of chemical bond; also worked on structure of protein molecules. Widely known for advocacy of vitamin C in treatment of common cold. Awarded Nobel Peace Prize (1962) for opposition to nuclear tests.

Pavlov, Ivan Petrovich (1849-1936), Russian physiologist. His experiments on stimulation of salivation in dogs by ringing of bells led to theory of the conditioned reflex. Awarded Nobel Prize for Physiology and Medicine (1904) for work on digestion.

Pavlova, Anna Matveyevna (*c* 1882-1931), Russian ballet dancer. Danced with Diaghilev's Ballets Russes. Famous in *The Dying Swan,* created for her by Fokine.

Pawnee, North American Indian tribe. Moved from Texas to S Nebraska in 16th cent. Warlike tribe but allied to US govt.; moved to reservation in Oklahoma (1876).

pawpaw or **papaw,** *Asimina triloba,* tree native to S US. Oblong, yellowish, edible fruit with many seeds. Name also applied to PAPAYA.

Pax, in Roman religion, goddess of peace. Identified with Greek Irene.

Paxton, Sir Joseph (1803-65), English architect, landscape gardener. Known for his innovatory design of the Crystal Palace, built for 1851 Great Exhibition.

pea, *Pisum sativum,* annual climbing leguminous herb, widely cultivated for edible pod-borne seeds, used as vegetable. Also *see* CHICKPEA, SWEET PEA.

Peace, river of Canada. Rises in N British Columbia, Canada; flows NE 1923 km (1195 mi) through Alberta to join Slave R. near L. Athabaska.

Peace Corps, agency of US govt. Estab. (1961) to send trained workers to Third World with aim of helping in education, health care, agric. and technology.

peach, *Prunus persica,* small tree of rose family with decorative pink blossom and sweet, velvety-skinned fruit. Native to China, now cultivated throughout warm temperate regions. The nectarine, *P. persica nectarina,* is a smooth-skinned variety.

Peacock, Thomas Love (1785-1866), English author. Known for novels satirizing intellectual fashions of his day, *eg Nightmare Abbey* (1818).

Peacock

peacock, *Pavo cristatus,* male game bird native to India and SE Asia, introduced elsewhere as ornamental bird. Erects long iridescent tail feathers into fan shape as courtship display.

Peak District, national park of S Pennines, C England, mainly in Derbyshire. Area 1404 sq km (542 sq mi). Limestone in S, many caves.

Peake, Mervyn (1911-68), English novelist, poet, illustrator, b. China. Known esp. for trilogy of Gothic fantasies, *Titus Groan* (1946), *Gormenghast* (1950), *Titus Alone* (1959).

peanut or **groundnut,** *Arachis hypogaea,* spreading annual vine of Leguminosae family. Yellow flowers, underground seedpods. Native to Brazil but widely cultivated in tropical and subtropical regions for edible seeds; also used to make oil and peanut butter.

pear, any of genus *Pyrus* of rose family, esp. European *P. communis,* widely cultivated in temperate regions for edible fruit.

pearl, hard, rounded secretion found in certain shellfish, esp. pearl oyster and pearl mussel; used as a gem. Colours incl. white, pink, black. Formed by layers of calcite or aragonite encircling an irritant, *eg* grain of sand, parasite; composition same as flat 'mother-of-pearl', or nacre, layer on inside of shell.

Pearl Harbor, *see* HAWAII.

Pearse, Patrick Henry (1879-1916), Irish patriot, educator. Leading figure in revival of Gaelic. Led Irish forces in Easter Rebellion (1916); executed.

Pearson, Lester Bowles (1897-1972), Canadian statesman, Liberal PM (1963-8). Secretary of state for external affairs (1948-57). Awarded Nobel Peace Prize (1957) for negotiating compromise to Suez crisis.

Peary, Robert Edwin (1856-1920), American explorer, naval officer. Led expeditions (1886-95) to N Greenland, proving it to be an island. Made several attempts to reach North Pole, generally regarded as 1st man to succeed (April, 1909).

Peary Land, penin. of N Greenland. Mountainous, terminates at Cape Morris Jesup, world's most N point of land (710 km/440 mi from N Pole).

Peasants' Revolt, rising of English peasants (1381), led by Wat TYLER and John BALL, resulting from low wages, heavy taxes and desire to reform feudal system. Rebels entered London and, after meeting Richard II, were promised end of serfdom. Rebellion quickly suppressed after Tyler's murder.

peat, partly decomposed vegetable matter, found in marshy lands in temperate zones, mainly where there is no limestone to neutralize the acids formed by decomposition. Early stage in formation of coal. Used dried as fuel and as mulch in horticulture.

pecan, *Carya illinoensis,* hickory tree of S and C US, producing edible nut similar to walnut.

peccary, small New World wild pig, genus *Tayassu,* with scent glands and sharp tusks. Two species, collared peccary, *T. angulatus,* found from SW US to Argentina, and white-lipped peccary, *T. pecari.*

Pechora, river of USSR, N European RSFSR. Rises in N Urals, flows *c* 1750 km (1100 mi) N and W to enter Barents Sea.

Pecos, river of S US. Rises in N New Mexico, flows SE 1480 km (926 mi) through SW Texas to join Rio Grande. Extensive water supplies for irrigation from dams.

Pécs (Ger. *Fünfkirchen*), city of S Hungary. Pop. 165,000. Indust. centre in coalmining area; leather, tobacco, wine. Cathedral (11th cent.); 1st Hungarian univ. (1367-1526, 1921). Under Turkish rule (1543-1686).

Pedro I (1798-1834), emperor of Brazil (1822-31). Son of John VI of Portugal, escaped with family to Brazil on Napoleon's invasion; remained as regent. Proclaimed Brazil independent (1822); abdicated 1831. Succeeded by his son **Pedro II** (1825-91), who ruled benevolently (1831-89) until abdication in favour of republic. Abolished slavery (1888).

Peeblesshire or **Tweeddale,** former county of S Scotland, now in Borders region. In Southern Uplands; sheep rearing; woollen goods mfg. Co. town was **Peebles,** former royal burgh on R. Tweed. Pop. 6000.

Peel, Sir Robert (1788-1850), British statesman, PM (1834-5, 1841-6). As home secretary, secured Catholic Emancipation Act (1829), created London police force (1829); opposed Reform Bill of 1832

Statement of policy in his Tamworth Manifesto (1834) held to mark beginning of Conservative Party. Split party over removal of import duties and repeal of Corn Laws (1846).

peewit, *see* LAPWING.

Pegasus, in Greek myth, winged horse sprung from blood of Medusa when she was slain by Perseus. Captured by BELLEROPHON.

pegmatite, very coarse-grained, igneous rock. Composition similar to granite; contains large crystals of quartz, mica, feldspar. Source of rare elements, tin, tungsten, gemstones.

Pegu, city of S Burma, on R. Pegu. Pop. 255,000. Cap. of united Burma in 16th cent. Many temples incl. Shwe Mawdaw pagoda.

Peiping, *see* PEKING.

Peipus, Lake (*Chudskoye Ozero*), lake of USSR, on Estonian-RSFSR border. Area *c* 3540 sq km (1360 sq mi). Scene of Alexander Nevsky's victory (1242) over Livonian Knights.

Pekinese or **Pekingese,** Chinese breed of small dog introduced to Europe in 1860. Long silky coat, pug nose; stands 15-23 cm/6-9 in. at shoulder.

Peking or **Peiping,** cap. of China, special municipality (area *c* 17,000 sq km/6564 sq mi) of Hopeh prov. Pop. 7,570,000. Indust., transport centre. Imperial centre (Forbidden City), cap. 1421-1911; cap. again after Communist victory (1949). Noted Ming and Ching architecture; several univs.

Peking man, fossil remains of proto-human *Homo erectus* found near Peking (1927). Originally dated as 350,000 years old. Recent finds of almost identical fossils in E Africa, dated as 1.5 million years old, have introduced new problems into study of man's evolution.

Pelagius (*c* 360-*c* 420), British monk. Rejected predestination; denied existence of original sin and individual's need of GRACE. Spread teachings in N Africa, Palestine. These, regarded as heresy (Pelagianism), were condemned at Council of Ephesus (431).

Pelé, real name Edson Arantes do Nascimento (1940-), Brazilian footballer. Considered one of the greatest forwards ever.

Pelham, Henry (1696-1754), British statesman, PM (1743-54). Served in Walpole's govt. from 1721, then headed Whig admin. until his death.

pelican, any aquatic bird of tropical and warm-water family Pelicanidae. Very large bill with pouch suspended underneath where it stores fish.

pellagra, disease caused by lack of niacin, vitamin of B group. Symptoms incl. sore tongue, diarrhoea, skin rash, disturbance of nervous system. Occurs in areas where diet consists mainly of maize.

Peloponnese (*Peloponnisos*), penin. of S Greece, joined to C Greece by Isthmus of Corinth. Formerly called Morea. Main towns Patras, Corinth. Mountainous; rugged coast. Currants, vines, olives; livestock; tourism. Dominated by Sparta until defeat by Thebes (4th cent. BC).

Peloponnesian War (431-404 BC), struggle between Athens and Peloponnesian Confederacy led by Sparta. After eventual victory, Sparta replaced Athens as dominant Greek power. THUCYDIDES wrote famous account of war.

pelota, name for several games played with ball and racket, glove, hand or bat. Originated in the Basque provs. of Spain and France.

pelvis, basin-shaped bony structure composed of lower part of backbone and 2 hip bones. Hip bone consists of pubis, ilium and ischium, on which body rests when sitting. Female pelvis is larger to aid childbirth.

Pemba, isl. of Tanzania, in Indian Ocean. Area 980 sq km (380 sq mi); cap. Chake Chake. Exports cloves, copra. Part of sultanate of Zanzibar from 1822.

Pembrokeshire, former county of SW Wales, now in Dyfed. Co. town was Haverfordwest. Hilly NE; rugged coast is national park. Potato growing, dairy farming; fishing; tourism. Early centre of Celtic Christianity. **Pembroke,** with Pembroke Dock, is town. Pop. 14,000.

Penal Laws, legislation enacted after English Reformation banning Roman Catholics from civil office and penalizing them for not conforming to Church of England. Laws were extended to Nonconformists after Restoration. Ended by Catholic Emancipation Act (1829).

penance, in RC and Eastern Orthodox churches, sacrament involving confession of sin, repentance and submission to the satisfaction imposed, followed by absolution by a priest.

Penang or **George Town,** cap. of Penang state, NW West Malaysia. Pop. 270,000. Leading seaport of Malaysia, on Penang Isl.

penates, *see* LARES AND PENATES.

Penelope, in Greek myth, wife of Odysseus. Despite many suitors, she remained faithful during Odysseus' absence, agreeing to marry only when she had finished weaving father-in-law Laertes' shroud, which she unravelled nightly.

penguin, any bird of order Sphenisciformes, of S hemisphere. Flightless, wings form strong flippers for swimming and diving; nests in large colonies.

penicillin, group of antibiotic substances produced by *Penicillium* moulds, esp. *P. chrysogenum* and *P. notatum.* Antibacterial effect noted by A. Fleming (1929); purified and used medicinally (1941).

Peninsular War, campaign fought (1808-14) against French in Iberian penin. by Britain, Portugal and Spanish guerrillas. Began when Napoleon invaded Portugal (1807) and then provoked revolts in Spain by placing his brother Joseph on Spanish throne (1808). British intervened in

Portugal, defeated French at Vimeiro and then invaded Spain. Following Sir John Moore's retreat, Sir Arthur Wellesley (later Duke of Wellington) led defensive campaign centred on Torres Vedras, invaded Spain, and routed French at Vitoria (1813). Napoleon abdicated after British advanced into France (1814).

penis, in males of higher vertebrates, organ which emits sperm in copulation. In mammals, also provides a urinary outlet.

Penn, William (1644-1718), English religious leader, founder of Pennsylvania. Became a Quaker (1667), then preached and wrote in favour of religious toleration. Obtained charter to estab. colony in Pennsylvania, (1682). As its governor, drew up liberal constitution.

Pennine Alps, mountain range of S Switzerland, NW Italy. Peaks incl. Matterhorn, Monte Rosa. Main resort is Zermatt.

Pennines, England. Hills running N-S from Cheviots to Peak Dist. Watershed of N English rivers; rises to 893 m (2930 ft) at Cross Fell. Rough pasture; tourism. 'Pennine Way' footpath 400 km (250 mi) long.

Pennsylvania, state of NE US. Area 117,412 sq km (45,333 sq mi); pop. 11,804,000; cap. Harrisburg; chief cities Philadelphia, Pittsburgh. Mainly in Appalachian Mts. Drained by Ohio R. in W, Susquehanna R. in E. Agric., indust.; mineral wealth, esp. coal, oil, iron ore. Settled by Dutch, Swedish, English colonists. English colony estab. under William Penn (1682). Centre of activity in Revolution, Civil War. One of original 13 colonies of US.

Pennsylvanian period, later of 2 subdivisions of Carboniferous period in North America. Began *c* 325 million years ago, lasted *c* 45 million years. Fauna incl. freshwater lamellibranchs, 1st reptiles, giant dragonflies, spiders. Luxuriant vegetation, formation of vast swamps; development of European, North American coal measures. Also *see* GEOLOGICAL TABLE.

pension, payment made regularly to a person, or dependents, who has fulfilled certain conditions of service or reached a certain age. Pension plan is paid for prior to retirement and can be part of voluntary scheme or compulsory national scheme, connected with SOCIAL SECURITY provisions.

Pentagon, the, building in Arlington, Virginia in which main offices of US Department of Defense are situated. Consists of 5 concentric buildings connected by corridors. Term also applied to military leadership of US.

Pentateuch, first five books of OT. Known in Judaism as the Torah.

pentathlon, five-event athletic contest for women comprising 100 m hurdles, shot put, high jump, long jump and 200 m.

Pentecost (Gk., *pentekoste* = 50th), Jewish religious festival celebrating end of grain harvest, 50 days after Passover. Also Christian festival celebrating descent of Holy Ghost upon Disciples on 50th day after Jesus' resurrection. Also known as Whit Sunday.

Pentland Firth, strait off N Scotland, separating former Caithness from Orkney Isls. Notorious for rough seas.

Penzance, town of Cornwall, SW England, on Mount's Bay. Pop. 19,000. Fishing port; resort.

Peony

peony or **paeony,** any of genus *Paeonia* of perennial herbs or shrubs of buttercup family. Native to Eurasia and W US. Large scarlet, pink or white flowers.

Pepin the Short (*c* 714-68), king of Franks (751-68). Son of Charles Martel, he deposed last Merovingian king, Childeric III, thus founding Carolingian dynasty. Father of Charlemagne.

pepper, *Piper nigrum,* tropical vine yielding fruit dried as condiment; ground as black pepper or (without seed cover) as white pepper. Also condiments (sometimes known as paprika) prepared in similar way from tropical American *Capsicum frutescens* or chili. *See* CAYENNE, PIMENTO.

peppermint, *see* MINT.

peptic ulcer, erosion of lining of stomach (gastric ulcer) or duodenum (duodenal ulcer). Aggravated by action of acidic gastric juices. Symptoms incl. stomach ache, nausea, heartburn. Cause unknown; possibly related to stress.

Pepys, Samuel (1633-1703), English diarist, naval official. Famous for his *Diary* (pub. 1825), recording, in cipher, personal life, public affairs of 1660s.

Perceval, Spencer (1762-1812), British statesman, Tory PM (1809-12). Assassinated in lobby of House of Commons.

perch, any of genus *Perca* of freshwater food fish with spiny dorsal fins.

percussion instruments, musical instruments struck to produce sound. Most produce no definite notes and their function is chiefly rhythmic, *eg* drum, triangle, cymbals, though some do produce notes of definite pitch, *eg* xylophone, timpani, glockenspiel.

Percy, Henry, 1st Earl of Northumberland (1342-1408), English nobleman. Helped secure throne for Henry IV from Richard II. Later, took part in plot led by his son, **Sir Henry Percy** (1366-1403) (known as 'Hotspur') and Owen Glendower to overthrow king. Plan to crown Edmund de Mortimer ended with Hotspur's death at Shrewsbury. **Thomas Percy, 7th Earl of Northumberland** (1528-72), plotted release of Mary Queen of Scots and restoration of Roman Catholicism to England; beheaded after revolt failed.

peregrine falcon, *Falco peregrinus,* swift falcon of Europe, Asia, North America; much used in falconry. Male has slate-grey upper-parts, buff under-parts.

perennial, *see* ANNUAL.

perfume, fragrant essence prepared from essential oils of plants or synthetic compounds, mixed with fixatives such as musk or ambergris. The ingredients are generally dissolved in alcohol.

Pergamum or **Pergamus** (modern *Bergama*), ancient city of Asia Minor, now in W Turkey on R. Caicus. Cap. of kingdom of Pergamum (3rd-2nd cent. BC); under Roman rule (133 BC).

Pericles (*c* 495-429 BC), Athenian statesman. Dominant figure in Athens from *c* 460, at time of city's political and cultural zenith. Created empire out of Delian league, successfully defending it against Persia, Sparta. Patronized arts and literature; responsible for building of Parthenon. Onset of Peloponnesian War brought his overthrow (430); reinstated before he died.

perigee, in astronomy, point nearest Earth in orbit of celestial bodies, *eg* Moon and artificial satellites. Opposite is apogee.

Périgueux, town of SW France, on R. Isle, cap. of Dordogne dept. Pop. 35,000. Famous for pâté, truffles. Hist. cap. of Périgord (incorporated into France 1589). Roman remains.

perihelion, in astronomy, point nearest Sun in orbit of celestial bodies, *eg* planets and comets. Opposite is aphelion.

periodic table, arrangement of chemical elements according to their atomic numbers to illustrate periodic law: properties of elements are in periodic dependence upon their atomic numbers. Formulated by MENDELEEV (1869-71). Law reflects way in which successive electron shells are filled; elements with same number of electrons in their outer shell have similar properties, *eg* alkali metals have one such electron. *See* VALENCY.

periscope, optical instrument which enables observer to see objects not directly visible from his position, esp. those above eye level. Consists of long tube at each end of which is a prism or mirror, which reflects light to observer's eye. Used esp. in submarines.

peritoneum, membrane lining abdominal cavity and enclosing in its folds the internal organs.

periwinkle, small marine mollusc with conical spiral shell, genus *Littorina*. Species incl. European edible periwinkle, *L. littorea*.

periwinkle, any of genus *Vinca* of mostly trailing, evergreen plants of dogbane family, esp. European *V. minor* with light lilac-blue, pink or white flowers.

Perm, city of USSR, E European RSFSR; railway jct. and port on R. Kama. Pop. 999,000. Centre of Urals indust. area; agric. machinery, timber products. Univ. (1916).

permafrost, permanently frozen subsoil. Found in high latitudes where rainfall is low and mean annual temperature is below 0°C. Topsoil may thaw for part of year.

Permian period, final geological period of Palaeozoic era; began *c* 280 million years ago, lasted *c* 55 million years. Increasing aridity; swamps dried up, salt beds formed, marls, sandstones, evaporites developed. Increasing reptiles, ammonites, more advanced conifers; last trilobites. Also *see* GEOLOGICAL TABLE.

Perón, Juan Domingo (1895-1974), Argentinian political leader. Elected president (1946) after taking part in military coup (1943). Made series of reforms based on nationalism, populism and state socialism. Career aided by popularity of 2nd wife, **Eva Duarte Perón** (1919-52). Lost support after her death; deposed by army coup (1955), went into exile. Returned 1973, re-elected president. His 3rd wife, **María Estela ('Isabel') Martínez 'de' Perón** (1931-), succeeded him as president on his death. Deposed by military junta (1976).

perpendicular, name given to final phase of English Gothic architecture (late 14th to middle 16th cent.). Characterized by vertical tracery for walls and windows, fan vaulting.

Perpignan, city of S France, on R. Têt, cap. of Pyrénées-Orientales dept. Pop. 114,000. Wine, fruit trade; tourist centre. Cap. of Spanish Roussillon (17th cent.). Cathedral (14th cent.), castle.

Persephone, in Greek myth, daughter of Zeus and Demeter. Abducted by Pluto to underworld and required to spend winter months of year there. Return symbolized start of vegetative growth. Her cult was celebrated in the Eleusinian mysteries; also worshipped at Rome as Proserpina.

Persepolis, cap. of ancient Persian empire, now ruined, in SC Iran. Ruined palaces, royal tombs. Partially destroyed by Alexander the Great in 331 BC.

Perseus, in Greek myth, son of Zeus and Danaë. Slew Medusa, used her head to turn ATLAS into a mountain. Married Andromeda whom he rescued from sea-monster. Accidentally killed his grandfather, Acrisius, in discus contest thus fulfilling a prophecy at his birth.

Pershing, John J[oseph] (1860-1948), American army officer, commander-in-chief of American Expeditionary Force in WW I (1917-8).

Persia, *see* IRAN.

Persian cat, small domestic cat with long silky hair, originally raised in Persia and Afghanistan.

Perseus slaying Medusa, from a Greek carving of the 6th century BC

Persian Gulf

Persian Gulf, arm of Indian Ocean, between Iran and Arabian penin. Connected to Arabian Sea by Str. of Hormuz and Gulf of Oman.

Persian Gulf States, *see* UNITED ARAB EMIRATES; BAHRAIN; QATAR.

Persian Wars, struggles (500-449 BC) between Greek city states and Persian Empire. Begun by Greek support for revolt of Ionian cities of Asia Minor against Persian rule. Persian expedition under Darius I was defeated at Marathon (490). Later expedition led by Xerxes I, son of Darius, successfully invaded Greece but Persian fleet was destroyed at Salamis (480) and army crushed at Plataea (479). Wars dragged on but Greek cities had estab. their freedom.

persimmon, *see* EBONY.

perspective, system of representing 3-dimensional space in spatial recession on flat surface. Geometric system based on converging lines was formulated by Alberti and Brunelleschi in 15th cent. and developed by Uccello, Piero della Francesca, *etc.*

Perspex [UK] or **Plexiglass** [US], trademark for transparent polyacrylic plastic. May be moulded while hot. Tough, unsplinterable; many uses.

perspiration, *see* SWEAT.

Perth, city of SW Australia, on Swan R., cap. of Western Australia. Pop. 805,000. Admin., commercial centre; exports (via Fremantle) agric. produce, minerals, esp. gold. Founded 1829; has Univ. of Western Australia (1911).

Perthshire, former county of C Scotland, now in Central and Tayside regions. Grampian Mts., Trossachs; lochs incl. Earn, Tay, Katrine; fertile lowland. Agric.; deer forest, sheep rearing; h.e.p. at Pitlochry; tourist industs. Co. town was **Perth,** former royal burgh on R. Tay. Pop. 43,000. Insurance centre; whisky distilling. Cap. of Scotland (12th-15th cents.).

Peru

Peru, republic of W South America. Area 1,285,210 sq km (496,220 sq mi); pop. 16,819,000: cap. Lima. Languages: Spanish, Quechua, Aymará (Indian). Religion: RC. Pacific coastal plain in W rises to 2 Andean ranges in interior. Important mineral resources (zinc, silver, copper); subsistence agric. esp. cotton; sheep, llamas, alpacas raised for wool. Anchovy, fish meal industs. Well-organized Inca empire was destroyed by Spanish following Pizarro's invasion (1532); independence obtained under Bolívar, Sucre (1824). S region lost in war with Chile (1879-84).

Perugia, city of Umbria, C Italy, cap. of Perugia prov. Pop. 138,000. Indust. centre, chocolate mfg. Etruscan, Roman remains. Centre of Umbrian school of painting (13th-16th cents.). Univ. (1276).

Perugino, orig. Pietro di Vanucci (*c* 1445-1523), Italian painter of Umbrian school. Executed fresco *Christ Giving the Keys to St Peter* in Sistine Chapel. Raphael was his pupil.

Pescara, city of Abruzzi e Molise, EC Italy, on Adriatic Sea at mouth of R. Pescara. Cap. of Pescara prov. Pop. 137,000. Port, resort; mfg.

Peshawar, town of N Pakistan, near Khyber Pass. Pop. 268,000. Centre for trade between Pakistan and Afghanistan. Taken by British (1848).

Pestalozzi, Johann Heinrich (1746-1827), Swiss educational reformer. Laid foundation of modern educational theory.

stressing importance of relating words, ideas to concrete things.

Pétain, Henri Philippe (1856-1951), French military, political leader. In WWI, halted German advance at Verdun (1916). Premier at time of France's collapse in WWII, concluded armistice with Germans. Headed Vichy govt., serving as figurehead for LAVAL after 1942. Death sentence for collaboration (1945) commuted.

Peter, St, orig. Simon (d. *c* AD 67), leader of Twelve Disciples. He and brother, St Andrew, were fishermen in Galilee when called by Jesus. Given charge of Church by Jesus after resurrection; regarded as 1st pope. Prob. martyred during Nero's rule.

Peter [I] the Great (1672-1725), tsar of Russia (1682-1725). Joint tsar with brother Ivan V, became sole ruler on Ivan's death (1696). Introduced policy of westernizing Russia. Reorganized army and civil admin., encouraged trade, indust. and science. Gained access to Baltic through war with Sweden (1700-21). Built new cap. at St Petersburg.

Peter III (1728-62), tsar of Russia (1762). Forced to abdicate in face of plot led by the Orlovs, favourites of his wife and successor, Catherine II. Assassinated.

Peter 1 and **2,** epistles of NT, traditionally ascribed to St Peter.

Peterborough, city of Cambridgeshire, E England, on R. Nene. Pop. 70,000. Railway jct.; engineering, brick mfg. Has cathedral (12th cent.).

Peterloo Massacre, incident at St Peter's Field, Manchester, England (1819). Large meeting, petitioning for parliamentary reform, dispersed by yeomanry and hussars; 11 people killed. Resulting indignation accelerated reform movement.

Peter's pence, annual tax of one penny paid to papal see by English households before Reformation. Now annual voluntary donation made by RCs.

Petition of Right (1628), document containing constitutional demands presented by English Parliament to Charles I. Declared taxation without parliamentary approval illegal, reaffirmed principle of habeas corpus, *etc.* Acceptance by Charles resulted in restoration of subsidies to him.

Petra, ancient city of SW Jordan. Edomite cap. from 4th cent. BC until capture by Romans in AD 106. Ruins, discovered 1812, incl. temples and tombs carved in rock.

Petrarch or **Francesco Petrarca** (1304–74), Italian poet. First Renaissance humanist, began revival of spirit of antiquity, profound influence on later European writers. Famous for songs and sonnets expressing love for Laura in *Canzoniere,* also allegorical poem *Trionfi.*

petrel, one of various small seabirds of 2 families: Hydrobatidae, storm petrels; Pelecanoididae, diving petrels. Noted fliers, returning to land only to breed.

petroleum, naturally occurring liquid mixture of hydrocarbons, with varying amounts of sulphur and nitrogen compounds. Fractional distillation yields petrol (gasoline), paraffin oil (kerosene), diesel oils, heavy fuel oils and bitumens, *etc.* Formed millions of years ago from remains of animals and plants buried and compressed. Main petroleum producing areas incl. Middle East, USSR and US.

petrology, branch of geology dealing with study of all aspects of rocks. Incl. study of origins (petrogenesis), systematic description of rocks (petrography).

Petropavlovsk, city of USSR, N Kazakh SSR; jct. on Trans-Siberian railway. Pop. 207,000. Meat packing, flour milling.

Petropavlovsk (-Kamchatski), city of USSR, E Siberian RSFSR; on SE Kamchatka coast. Pop. 215,000. Naval base; fisheries, shipbuilding, sawmilling.

Petrozavodsk, city of USSR, cap. of Karelian auton. republic, NW European RSFSR; on L. Onega. Pop. 234,000. Shipyards, fisheries, sawmilling.

petunia, genus of perennial herbs of nightshade family, with funnel-shaped flowers of various colours. Native to tropical America. Cultivated widely.

Pevsner, Antoine (1886-1962), Russian sculptor. With brother Naum Gabo, leading exponent of constructivism.

pewter, any of several alloys of tin, with lead, copper or antimony added to improve malleability. Used from Roman times to make domestic utensils until replaced by china in 18th and 19th cents.

peyote, *see* MESCAL.

Phaedra, in Greek myth, daughter of Minos and wife of Theseus. Fell in love with stepson Hippolytus, but was rejected by him and hanged herself.

Phaethon, in Greek myth, son of Helios (the sun). Attempted to drive father's chariot, but unable to control horses. Killed by Zeus' thunderbolt.

phalanger, arboreal Australasian marsupial of Phalangeridae family. Thick fur, prehensile tail; nocturnal. Flying phalangers use membrane stretched between limbs to glide through trees. Also called possum.

phalarope, small aquatic bird of Phalaropodidae family. Male, smaller and less brightly coloured than female, incubates eggs.

phallicism or **phallism,** worship of image of male reproductive organ as symbol of regenerative powers of nature. Occurs in many primitive societies, also in cult of Priapus in classical Greece and of Cybele and Attis in Rome. In India, the deity Siva is often represented as a phallic symbol.

Phanerozoic eon, all geological time from beginning of the Palaeozoic era to the present. Contrasts with Precambrian times in possessing sedimentary accumulations in which are found abundant remains of plants and animals. Also *see* GEOLOGICAL TABLE.

Pharisees, one of two main Jewish sects which originated in Maccabean age (other being their opponents, SADDUCEES). Insisted on strictest observance of Mosaic Law.

pharmacy, preparation and dispensing of medicines and drugs. **Pharmacology** is the scientific study of drugs, their chemistry, effects on the body.

Pharos of Alexandria, lighthouse which stood on an isl. off Alexandria, Egypt. Completed *c* 280 BC under Ptolemy II, it was destroyed in 14th cent. by earthquake. One of the Seven Wonders of the ancient World.

Pharsala, ancient city of Thessaly, EC Greece. Here in 48 BC Caesar defeated Pompey.

pharynx, muscular cavity of alimentary canal leading from mouth and nasal passages to the oesophagus. Top part, nasopharynx, is concerned only with breathing; middle part, oropharynx, is passage for food and air; lower part, laryngeal pharynx, is for swallowing only.

pheasant, game bird of Phasianidae family. Males brilliantly coloured, with long tapering tail. Mainly terrestrial, building nest on ground.

phenols, aromatic compounds having hydroxyl (OH) radicals directly attached to benzene ring. Commonest is carbolic acid (C_6H_5OH), white crystalline solid produced from coal tar; used as disinfectant and in manufacture of plastics.

phenomenology, movement in philosophy founded by Austrian philosopher Edmund Husserl (1859-1938). Aims to study objects of consciousness without any preconceptions about the objects themselves and thus apprehend phenomena directly. Influential in early development of EXISTENTIALISM.

Phidias (active *c* 475-430 BC), Athenian sculptor, architect. None of his original work remains. Works incl. colossal statues of Athena on the Parthenon, Athens, and Zeus at Olympia, one of Seven Wonders of the ancient World.

Philadelphia, port of SE Pennsylvania, US; on Delaware R. Pop. 5,643,000; state's largest city. Shipping, commercial centre. Exports coal, grain, timber. Imports raw materials. Varied industs. incl. oil refining, shipbuilding. Founded 1682 by Quakers. Focus of activity in Revolution; federal cap. (1790-1800). Has many hist. famous buildings esp. Independence Hall, scene of Constitutional Convention (1787). Univ. of Pennsylvania (1740).

philately, collection and study of postage stamps. Collecting began after issue of first stamps in 1840s; 1st catalogues printed *c* 1861. Largest collection is in British Museum, London.

Philemon, Epistle to, NT epistle written by St Paul. Consists of request to Philemon asking him to forgive his slave, Onesimus, for escaping.

Philip, St (*fl* AD 1st cent.), one of Twelve Disciples. Possibly preached in Phrygia.

Philip [II] Augustus (1165-1223), king of France (1180-1223). Abandoned 3rd Crusade after quarrel with Richard I of England.

Philip [IV] the Fair (1268-1314), king of France (1285-1314). Quarrel with Boniface VIII over right to tax clergy ended in pope's deposition by Philip, who secured Clement V's election (1305) and transfer of see to Avignon (1309). Supplemented treasury by persecution of KNIGHTS TEMPLARS (1308-14).

Philip VI (1293-1350), king of France (1328-50). Elected regent on death of cousin, Charles IV, invoking Salic law to exclude claims of Edward III of England (1328). Crowned first of Valois kings (1328). Disputes with Edward led to Hundred Years War and English victory at Crécy (1346).

Philip II (382-336 BC), king of Macedonia (359-336 BC). Began conquest of Greece, culminating in defeat of Athens and Thebes at Chaeronea (338). Assassinated. Father of Alexander the Great.

Philip II (1527-98), king of Spain (1556-98). Succeeded his father, Emperor Charles V. His dominions incl. Netherlands, Naples, Sicily, and much of New World. Championed orthodox Catholicism, persecuting heretics. His repression provoked major revolt in Netherlands (1567). Annexed Portugal (1580). Economy drained by wars, Spanish power declined after destruction of Armada (1588). Husband of Mary I of England.

Philip V (1683-1746), king of Spain (1700-46). Grandson of Louis XIV, his accession as 1st Bourbon king of Spain provoked War of Spanish Succession.

Philip Mountbatten, *see* EDINBURGH, DUKE OF.

Philip the Good (1396-1467), duke of Burgundy (1419-67). Allied with English attempt to secure French throne for Henry V, but later supported Charles VII of France. Made Low Countries centre of commerce and culture.

Philippi, ancient city of Macedonia, N Greece. Here Octavian and Antony defeated Brutus and Cassius (42 BC).

Philippians, epistle of NT, written by St Paul from captivity in Rome to Christians at Philippi, Macedonia.

Philippines, republic of SE Asia, isl. group incl. Luzon, Mindanao. Area *c* 300,000 sq km (115,000 sq mi); pop. 46,351,000; cap. Manila. Language: Filipino. Religion: RC, Islam. Mountainous, densely forested; tropical monsoon climate on larger isls. Mainly agric. economy; produces rice, corn, hemp, sugar, timber; minerals incl. chromite, gold. Discovered by Magellan (1521); under Spanish control (1564-1898) until ceded to US after Spanish-American War. Total independence gained in 1946. Occupied by Japanese in WWII. Islamic insurgents active from 1970.

Philistines, non-Semitic people, prob. of Cretan origin, who inhabited S Palestine from 12th cent. BC. Constantly at war with Israelites; conquered by David and under Solomon incorporated into Israel.

Philippines

Regained independence, finally accepted Assyrian domination (8th cent. BC).

'hillip, Arthur (1738-1814), British colonial administrator. First governor of New South Wales (1786-92), estab. penal settlement at Sydney (1788).

hilology, *see* LINGUISTICS.

hilosophy (Gk., = love of wisdom), theory or logical analysis of principles underlying the ultimate nature of the universe (ontology, metaphysics) and related fields, incl. conduct (ethics), thought (logic), knowledge (epistemology). In the West, tradition springs from classical Greece (esp. Plato, Aristotle) and was reinterpreted in Christian terms by medieval scholastics. Modern rationalism begins with Descartes; modern empiricism with Locke. Other disciplines are critically examined for basic principles and concepts, *eg* philosophy of science, history. Eastern philosophy, though often rigorous, tends to be regarded as part of mystical theology.

hlebitis, inflammation of a vein, usually associated with blockage of vein by blood clots (thrombophlebitis). May occur after childbirth or surgery. Blood clots, usually in leg, may dislodge and travel to lungs.

hloem, vascular tissue of a plant which distributes synthesized foods, *eg* proteins and sugars.

hlox, genus of herbs native to North America, cultivated for showy flowers.

'hnom Penh or **Pnom Penh,** cap. of Kampuchea. Pop. 2,000,000. Trade centre, port on R. Mekong. Stronghold of government forces during civil war (1970-5). Became cap. of Cambodia 1867.

hoenicians, Semitic people descended from the Canaanites who occupied the coastal areas of modern Syria and Lebanon (Phoenicia). Exercised maritime and commercial power *c* 1200-600 BC throughout the Mediterranean area, founding colonies in Sicily, Malta, Cyprus, N Africa (*eg* Carthage), and Spain. Chief cities were Tyre and Sidon.

hoenix, cap. of Arizona, US; on Salt R. Pop. 1,221,000. Commercial centre in irrigated agric. region producing fruit, cotton. Health resort. Became cap. 1889.

phoenix, in ancient Egyptian myth, beautiful lone bird which lived in the Arabian desert for 500 years and then consumed itself in fire, new phoenix arising from ashes. Used as symbol of death, resurrection.

Phoenix Islands, group of 8 coral isls. in C Pacific Ocean. Incl. CANTON AND ENDERBURY ISLS.; other 6 isls. part of Kiribati.

phonetics, study of system of LANGUAGE sounds. Branches incl. study of speech sounds using written symbols to transcribe accurately their differences, and phonemics, the study of significant differences between groups of roughly similar sounds.

phonograph, *see* GRAMOPHONE.

phosphates, salts or esters of phosphoric acid (H_3PO_4). Calcium superphosphate used as fertilizer, sodium phosphate (Na_3PO_4) used in detergents.

phosphorescence, property of certain substances of giving off lingering emission of light following excitation by radiation, *eg* light or X-rays. Causes certain minerals, *eg* zinc sulphide, to glow in dark.

phosphorus (P), non-metallic element; at. no. 15, at. wt. 30.97. Occurs in various allotropic forms: white form is waxy poisonous solid which ignites spontaneously in air; red form is non-poisonous and less reactive, obtained by heating white form. Occurs widely in phosphate minerals; essential to life, occurs in blood, bones, *etc.* Compounds used in fertilizers, detergents, matches.

photochemistry, study of influence of light and other radiant energy on chemical reactions; photochemical effects are utilized in photography and photosynthesis.

photoelectric effect, emission of electrons from surface of certain substances when exposed to light of suitable frequency. **Photoelectric cell** uses effect to convert light into electrical energy. Commonest type contains electric circuit with 2 electrodes separated by light-sensitive semiconductor; current flow in circuit increases when light strikes semiconductor. Used to open automatic doors, as burglar alarm, *etc.*

photoengraving, photomechanical process used for printing illustrations. Subject to be reproduced is photographed and its image is transferred through the negative to a metal plate coated with light-sensitive chemical. Coating unaffected by light is removed and underlying metal plate etched away. Half-tone is form of photoengraving using dots of varying size to obtain variations in tone.

photography, process of reproducing optical image on light-sensitive substance (silver bromide or chloride) under controlled conditions in CAMERA. Developer produces metallic silver on those parts of photographic plate previously exposed to light. Fixing agent, *eg* 'hypo', dissolves remaining silver salts, leaving negative image. Positive image is obtained by placing negative on light-sensitive paper and then repeating developing and fixing process.

photon, fundamental quantum of electromagnetic energy, the energy of light. Sometimes regarded as uncharged elementary particle of zero rest mass, travelling at speed of light. Its energy is product of Planck's constant and frequency of electromagnetic wave.

photosynthesis, process by which plants make food by transformation of carbon dioxide and water into carbohydrates. Occurs in green part of plants and utilizes energy from sunlight. The green pigment CHLOROPHYLL is necessary for the reaction.

Phrygians, ancient people of Asia Minor. Spoke Indo-European language. Culture *fl* 8th to 6th cents. BC, marked by impressive architecture. Phrygian cap. Gordion destroyed by Cimmerians (676 BC). Later subject to Lydians, Persians.

pH-value, in chemistry, *see* HYDROGEN ION CONCENTRATION.

physical anthropology, branch of ANTHROPOLOGY concerned with physical characteristics of peoples. Studies evolution of body types and development of racial groups using statistical methods.

physics, science concerned with fundamental relationships between matter and energy. Classical physics, developed in 19th cent., deals with electricity, magnetism, heat, optics, mechanics, *etc.* Quantum physics of 20th cent., which assumes that energy exists in discrete bundles, explains atomic and nuclear phenomena.

physiocrats, group of 18th-cent. French economic theoreticians headed by François Quesnay (1694-1774). Among first to study economics systematically. Saw land and agric. as basis of wealth. Believed in natural economic laws which must be allowed to operate freely. Influenced Adam Smith and other laisser-faire economists.

physiology, study of functions and vital processes of living organisms, both plants and animals.

physiotherapy, method of treating illness and injury by physical means such as massage, exercise, heat and electricity.

pi (π), symbol used to denote ratio of circumference of a circle to its diameter; π = 3.14159 (to 5 decimal places; runs to infinite number of decimal places).

Piaf, Edith, orig. Edith Giovanna Gassion (1915-63), French singer, known as 'the Little Sparrow'. Renowned for her passionate songs of unhappiness.

Piaget, Jean (1896-1980), Swiss psychologist. Known for unique contributions to theories of cognitive development in children.

piano or **pianoforte,** keyboard instrument having compass of 7 octaves, keys of which operate hammers which strike the strings. First appeared mid-18th cent.

Picardy (*Picardie*), region and former prov. of N France, hist. cap. Amiens. Fertil area, drained by R. Somme; agric., textil indust. Part of France from 1477.

Picasso, Pablo (1881-1973), Spanish artis Dominant figure in 20th-cent. art. In hi 'blue' period (1901-4), painted expressiv scenes of human poverty and degradatior in 'rose' period (1905-7), painted circu scenes. Influenced by Cézanne and negr sculpture, evolved cubist style with Braqu in Paris; *Les Demoiselles d'Avignon* (1907 marks beginning of cubist phase. Late turned to monumental classical nude sculptures, pottery. Famous wor *Guernica* (1936) expresses his horror a outrages of Spanish Civil War.

Piccard, Auguste (1884-1962), Belgia physicist, b. Switzerland. Made 1st balloo ascents into stratosphere (1931 Constructed bathyscaphe which reache depth of 10,900 m (35,800 ft).

piccolo, small woodwind instrument; pitche an octave higher than FLUTE.

Pickford, Mary, orig. Gladys Smit (1893-1979), American film actress, Canada. Became famous as 'America sweetheart' through silent films.

Pico della Mirandola, Giovanni, Con (1463-94), Italian philosopher, humanis Sought to reconcile Platonism ar Christianity in series of theses, prefaced b *On the Dignity of Man*.

Picts, Iron Age people inhabiting Scotland, Ireland. First described by Romans in A 297, they resisted Roman conquest an maintained their independence unt absorbed into kingdom of the Scots *c* 850.

pidgin, lingua franca, not 1st language speakers, with restricted vocabular simple syntax. Originally applied to variet of English spoken by Chinese trading wi English, extended to incl. pidgi developed from Portuguese, Frenc Spanish, Malay *etc,* in Africa, West Indies.

Piedmont (*Piemonte*), region of NW Ital cap. Turin. H.e.p., livestock in mountainou W; wheat, rice in fertile Po valley. Rule by house of Savoy from 12th cent; part Sardinia from 1720 to unification (1860 Annexed to France 1798-1814.

piedmont, area of land lying at foot mountains or upland. May also describ particular feature *eg* piedmont plain.

Pierce, Franklin (1804-69), America statesman, Democratic president (1853-7 Alienated North by appeasing the South c slavery issue.

Piero della Francesca (*c* 1420-92), Italia painter. Known for geometric perfectic of his forms and mastery of perspectiv Work incl. fresco series *The Legend of th True Cross* at Arezzo.

Pierre, cap. of South Dakota, US; on Missou R. Pop. 10,000. Livestock market, shippin industs. Founded 1880; became cap. 1889.

Pietermaritzburg, cap. of Natal, Sou Africa. Pop. 159,000. Admin., indus railway centre in stock rearing area; ha part of univ. of Natal (1909). Founde (1838) by Boer leaders. Two cathedrals.

Pietism, movement in Lutheran church favouring devotion rather than dogmatism. First leader was German theologian, Philip Jakob Spener (1635-1705). Declined in late 18th cent. Influenced Kant, Kierkegaard.

piezoelectric effect, property exhibited by certain crystals of developing electric charge on their surface when subjected to pressure. Crystals also expand and contract in response to alternating current. Piezoelectric crystals are used in microphones, loudspeakers, *etc.*

pig, any of Suidae family of hoofed mammals. Omnivorous, canine teeth often lengthened into tusks. Domestic pig developed from wild boar, *Sus scrofa*; source of pork, lard. Wild species incl. babirussa, wart hog.

pigeon, bird of Columbidae family, widely distributed in tropical and temperate regions. Wood pigeon or ring dove, *Columba palumbus,* with greyish plumage, is largest European species. Domesticated breeds derived from rock dove, *C. livia*; noted for homing ability.

Pigmy, *see* PYGMY.

Pigs, Bay of, inlet of S Cuba. Scene of unsuccessful invasion by Cuban exiles backed by US forces in attempt to overthrow Communist Castro regime (1961).

pika, small tailless mammal, genus *Ochotona,* of same order (Lagomorpha) as rabbit. Found in rocky mountains of Asia and North America.

pike, *Esox lucius,* carnivorous freshwater fish of N temperate regions. Voracious predator, feeding on fish, water birds, *etc.* Reaches lengths of 1.5 m/5 ft.

Pikes Peak, mountain of C Colorado, US. Height 4301 m (14,110 ft). Most famous peak in Rocky Mts.

Pilate, Pontius (*fl* AD 1st cent.), Roman procurator of Judaea (*c* 26-36). Fearing Jewish recrimination, allowed execution of Jesus. Trad. committed suicide in Rome.

pilchard, *Sardina pilchardus,* small marine food fish of herring family, common in Mediterranean and off Portuguese coast. Sardine is young pilchard.

piles, *see* HAEMORRHOIDS.

pilgrimage, journey made to a shrine or holy place as a religious act. Occurs in many religions, *eg* in Hinduism to Ganges, in Islam to Mecca, in Judaism to Temple at Jerusalem, in Christianity to Jerusalem, Bethlehem, Nazareth. Important in medieval Europe, with major centres at Canterbury (England), Santiago de Compostela (Spain). In RC church, pilgrimage is still fostered with Rome being the major centre.

Pilgrimage of Grace (1536), rising of English Roman Catholics, esp. in Lincolnshire and Yorkshire, protesting against abolition of papal supremacy and suppression of monasteries by Henry VIII. Rebels dispersed peacefully, but many executed after further rebellion in 1537.

Pilgrim Fathers, name given to those English emigrants who sailed in *Mayflower* (1620) to found Plymouth Colony in Massachusetts. About ⅓ of them had previously migrated to Holland in search of religious freedom.

Pill, the, popular name for oral contraceptive which interferes with menstrual cycle, preventing ovulation by hormone action.

Pillars of Hercules, *see* GIBRALTAR, STRAIT OF.

pilot fish, *Naucrates ductor,* spiny-finned marine fish, often found accompanying sharks, turtles.

Pilsen *see* PLZEŇ.

Pilsudski, Joseph (1867-1935), Polish military and political leader. Active in cause of Polish independence from Russia before WWI. Led Polish troops against Russia in support of Austria in WWI. Became head of state of independent Poland (1919). Retired 1922, returned as virtual dictator (1926-35) after coup d'état.

Piltdown man, skull fragment found at Piltdown, Sussex (1912). Believed to be oldest human species found in Europe until proved to be a hoax (1953).

pimento, *Pimenta officinalis,* tree of myrtle family, native to West Indies. Dried fruits used as spice.

pimpernel, any of genus *Anagallis* of annual herbs of primrose family; esp. scarlet pimpernel, *A. arvensis,* with red, white or blue flowers which close in bad weather.

Pindar (518-438 BC), Greek poet. Wrote choral lyrics, incl. *Epinikia,* odes celebrating athletic victories.

Pindus Mountains (*Píndhos*), range of NC Greece, runs N-S between Epirus (W), Thessaly (E). Highest point Smólikas (2636 m/8652 ft).

pine, any of genus *Pinus* of evergreen conifers, widely distributed in N hemisphere. Needle-shaped leaves. Yields timber, turpentine, resin.

pineal body, small cone-shaped projection from centre of brain of all vertebrates. In certain amphibians and reptiles, it is sensitive to light and is remnant of central eye. Function in humans unknown, but believed to secrete hormone which influences sexual development.

pineapple, *Ananas comosus,* plant native to tropical America, now grown chiefly in Hawaii. Edible, juicy fruit develops from flower spike.

pine marten, *Martes martes,* nocturnal carnivore of forests of N Europe and W Asia. Omnivorous, often catching squirrels. Has dark brown fur, bushy tail.

Pines, Isle of, isl. off W Cuba. Area 3056 sq km (1180 sq mi). Fishing, agric., marble quarrying; covered by pine forests. Has large prison for political prisoners. Awarded to Cuba over US claims (1925).

ping-pong, *see* TABLE TENNIS.

pink, any of genus *Dianthus* of annual or perennial plants native to temperate regions. White or red flowers with ragged

Pink: sweet william

edges. Species incl. sweet william, *D. barbatus. See* CARNATION.

Pinkie, Battle of, Scottish defeat by English forces (1547). Caused Scots to send Mary (later Mary Queen of Scots) to France to avoid marriage to Edward VI. Battle site is near Musselburgh.

Pinochet [Ugarte], Augusto (1916–), Chilean political leader. Took control of govt. after overthrowing Marxist regime of Allende (1973). Suppressed left-wing opposition.

Pinter, Harold (1930-), English dramatist. Known for menacing comedies, *eg The Caretaker* (1959), *The Homecoming* (1964).

pion or **pi-meson,** elementary particle with mass *c* 270 times that of electron. Discovered (1947) in cosmic radiation; plays important role in forces which bind atomic nucleus.

pipistrelle, small insectivorous bat of wide distribution, genus *Pipistrellus.*

pipit, songbird of Motacillidae family, genus *Anthus.* Brown plumage; insectivorous.

piracy, taking of ship or contents on the high seas, distinct from privateering in that pirate holds no commission, does not fly national flag. Formerly common, esp. in Spanish Main, Barbary coast, Chinese and Malay waters. Famous pirates incl. Henry Morgan, Edward Teach (Blackbeard). Also *see* HIJACKER.

Piraeus, *see* ATHENS.

Pirandello, Luigi (1867-1936), Italian author. Known for plays dealing with relationship between illusion, reality incl. *Six Characters in Search of an Author* (1921), *Henry IV* (1922). Also wrote novels, short stories. Nobel Prize for Literature (1934).

Piranesi, Giovanni Battista (1720-78), Italian architect, engraver. His numerous etchings of Roman antiquities greatly influenced Romantic concept of Rome. Famous for *Carceri d'Invenzione*, series of fantastic imaginary prisons.

piranha, South American freshwater fish with sharp teeth and powerful jaws. Lives in schools which can attack large animals. Species incl. *Pigocentrus piraya,* up to 60 cm/2 ft in length.

Pisa, city of Tuscany, WC Italy, on R. Arno. Cap. of Pisa prov. Pop. 104,000. Medieval republic, warred with Florence, defeated (1284) by Genoa. Cathedral (12th cent.) leaning tower (1173, height 55m/180 ft).

Pisano, Andrea (*c* 1290-1348), Italian sculptor, architect. Continued Giotto's work on cathedral and campanile in Florence; most famous work is bronze doors of Baptistery at Florence, begun 1330.

Pisano, Nicola (*c* 1220-*c* 1280), Italian architect, sculptor. Leading figure in rebirth of sculpture in Italy. His works incl. pulpits at Pisa and Siena, are marked by synthesis of Gothic and classical styles. His son, **Giovanni Pisano** (*c* 1250-*c* 1314) continued revival of sculpture. Works incl. pulpit of Pisa cathedral.

Pisces, *see* ZODIAC.

Pisistratus (*c* 605-527 BC), tyrant of Athens. Leader of popular party, he seized power *c* 560. Twice exiled, he returned (541) and estab. his personal rule until his death.

Pissarro, Camille (1830-1903), French painter, b. West Indies. A leading impressionist, enormously prolific, he influenced early work of Cézanne and Gauguin.

pistachio, *Pistacia vera,* small tree native to Mediterranean region and Asia. Fruit contains greenish, edible nut.

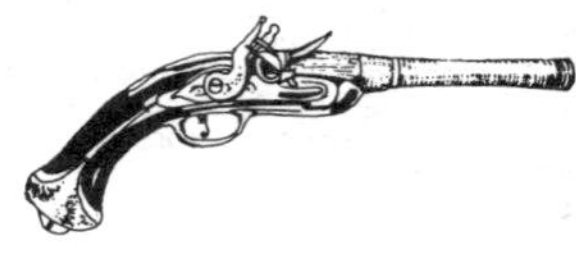

Flintlock pistol of c 1680

pistol, small, short-barrelled firearm designed to be fired with one hand. Originally made in Italy (16th cent.), REVOLVER made in 19th cent. and 'automatic' repeating pistols in 20th cent.

Pitcairn Island, isl. of SC Pacific Ocean, admin. by UK. Area 5 sq km (2 sq mi); pop. 65. Fruit growing. Colonized (1790) by mutineers from HMS *Bounty* and Tahitian women; pop. removed 1856, some later returned.

pitch, dark sticky substance, liquid when heated, solid when cold. Obtained as residue from distillation of petroleum, coal tar, wood tar. Used in waterproofing, road construction.

pitch, quality of a musical sound dependent on rate of vibrations producing it. The greater the number of vibrations per second, the higher the note. Instruments are tuned to a standard pitch in which the A above middle C is equal to 440 vibrations per second.

pitchblende, uranium ore mineral, a form of uraninite. Consists of uranium oxide with various impurities. Source of uranium; also radium, lead, thorium, some rare-earth elements. Major sources in US, Canada, Australia, Zaïre.

pitcher plant, any of genus *Sarracenia,*

insectivorous bog herbs of North America. Leaves in form of pitcher.

Pitman, Sir Isaac (1813-97), English inventor. Developed improved system of phonetic shorthand.

Pitt, William, 1st Earl of Chatham (1708-78), English statesman. Chief figure in coalition with duke of Newcastle (1757-61), architect of military defeat of French in India and Canada (1759). Forced to resign by George III. Retired because of ill health from 2nd coalition (1766-8). Broke with Whigs over colonial policy in America, favouring conciliation. His son, **William Pitt** (1759-1806), was Tory PM (1783-1801, 1804-6). Reformed finances to help fund national debt, introduced new taxes. Failed to anticipate war with France; his various coalitions had little success on land against French. Suppressed political reformers. Solved Irish question by passing Act of Union (1800), but resigned when George III vetoed Catholic emancipation. Second ministry ended with his death soon after defeat of Allies by Napoleon at Austerlitz.

Pittsburgh, city of SW Pennsylvania, US; at point where Allegheny and Monongahela rivers form Ohio R. Pop. 2,322,000. In rich coal mining region. Iron and steel, oil refining, machinery mfg. industs. Settled in 1760 as Fort Pitt (formerly French Fort Duquesne). Has univ. (1787).

pituitary gland, endocrine gland situated at base of brain. Composed of 2 lobes. Anterior lobe secretes important hormones whose functions incl. maintenance of growth, stimulation of thyroid and sex organs, *etc.* Posterior lobe secretes hormone which regulates flow of urine.

pit viper, any of Crotalidae family of venomous snakes, incl. rattlesnake, sidewinder, with heat-sensory pits on each side of head. Found in Asia and New World.

Pius V, St, orig. Michele Ghislieri (1504-72), Italian churchman, pope (1566-72). Furthered the Catholic Reformation by implementing the decrees of the Council of Trent. Excommunicated Elizabeth I (1570). Organized alliance against the Turks, which led to victory at Lepanto (1571).

Pius VII, orig. Barnaba Chiaramonti (1740-1823), Italian churchman, pope (1800-23). Signed Concordat (1801) with Napoleon to re-estab. Church in France. Taken prisoner (1809-14) by French on occupation of papal states.

Pius IX, orig. Giovanni Mastai-Ferretti (1792-1878), Italian churchman, pope (1846-78). Refused to recognize new kingdom of Italy. Proclaimed dogma of Immaculate Conception (1854); convened 1st Vatican Council which enunciated papal infallibility.

Pius XI, orig. Achille Damiano Ratti (1857-1939), Italian churchman, pope (1922-39). Responsible for Lateran Treaty (1929) estab. Vatican City state. Condemned Nazism in 1937 encyclical.

Pius XII, orig. Eugenio Pacelli (1876-1958), Italian churchman, pope (1939-58). Worked to limit extension of WWII, while taking ambiguous stand towards Axis powers. Excommunicated Hungary, Romania, Poland in 1953.

Piute, *see* PAIUTE.

Pizarro, Francisco (*c* 1476-1541), Spanish conquistador. With partner, Almagro, led expedition to Peru (1530) in search of fabulous wealth of Incas. Seized Inca ruler Atahualpa (1532) and had him murdered after receiving his enormous ransom (1533). Captured Cuzco (1533), completing conquest of Peru. Founded Lima (1535). Dispute between Almagro and Pizarro led to execution of Almagro (1538), whose followers later assassinated Pizarro.

placenta, organ consisting of embryonic tissue by which the embryo of most mammals is nourished. Attached to lining of mother's uterus. Oxygen and nutrients are carried to it by mother's blood.

plague, contagious disease caused by bacterium *Pasteurella pestis*; carried by fleas from infected rats. Form known as bubonic plague is characterized by swollen lymph nodes (buboes); pneumonic plague infects lungs. Occurred sporadically in Europe, notably in Black Death (1346-9).

plaice, *Pleuronectes platessa,* marine flatfish, commercially important in Europe. Light brown body with orange spots.

Plaid Cymru, *see* WELSH NATIONALIST PARTY.

plain, large area of relatively flat land usually at low altitude. Commonest types are glacial plains, flood plains, coastal plains. Often grass-covered *eg* pampas, steppes, savannah.

plainsong, religious chant that developed in early Christian church and survives in RC liturgy. Consists of single melodic line sung in unison, usually unaccompanied. Developed into POLYPHONY in late Middle Ages. Also known as Gregorian chant.

Planck, Max Karl Ernst Ludwig (1858-1947), German physicist. Attempts to explain distribution of black-body radiation led to his hypothesis that vibrating atoms absorb or emit radiant energy only in discrete bundles (quanta) whose magnitude is product of Planck's constant and frequency of radiation. Founder of modern quantum theory. Nobel Prize for Physics (1918).

plane, any of genus *Platanus* of deciduous trees native to temperate regions. Palmate leaves, pendulous burr-like fruit.

planet, heavenly body in orbit round the Sun, which shines by reflected sunlight. Minor planet is called an ASTEROID. *See* SOLAR SYSTEM.

planetarium, arrangement for projecting images of heavenly bodies on inside of large hemispherical dome by means of system of optical projectors which is revolved to show celestial motion.

plankton, general term for minute organisms found drifting near surface of sea or lakes. Incl. protozoa, crustacea, algae and other invertebrates.

plant, member of vegetable group of living organisms. Generally manufactures own food by PHOTOSYNTHESIS (but *see* FUNGUS); has an unlimited growth (*ie* old tissue remains in place and new tissue grows away from it); has cells with more or less rigid walls; has no means of independent locomotion. Divided into 4 main divisions: Thallophyta (algae, lichens, fungi); Bryophyta (mosses, liverworts); Pteridophyta (ferns, club mosses, horsetails); Spermophyta (conifers, flowering plants). *See* CLASSIFICATION.

Plantagenet, name applied to English royal house, whose monarchs were Henry II, Richard I, John, Henry III, Edward I, II, III, Richard II. After Richard II's deposition (1399), house divided into houses of York and Lancaster.

plantain, *Musa paradisiaca,* tropical plant. Produces long yellow-green banana-like fruit. Name also applies to any of genus *Plantago* of plants with rosettes of leaves and spikes of greenish flowers.

plasma, in biology, clear fluid forming 55% of blood. Composed mainly of water, with dissolved proteins, inorganic salts, urea and sugar.

plasma, in physics, high-temperature ionized gas, composed almost entirely of equal numbers of electrons and positive ions. Excellent electrical conductor and responsive to magnetic fields; study of plasma is important to achievement of controlled thermonuclear reactions.

Plassey, village of West Bengal, NE India. Scene of Clive's victory over Nawab of Bengal (1757) giving Britain control of Bengal.

plaster of Paris, fine white powder produced by heating gypsum. When mixed with water, forms paste which sets and hardens. Used for casts, moulds, *etc.*

plastics, materials which are stable in normal use but are plastic in some part of their production and can be moulded by heat and pressure. Most plastics are synthetic polymers. The 2 main groups are thermoplastic materials, which can be melted and reset, and thermosetting materials, which cannot be remoulded.

plastic surgery, surgery dealing with repair of lost or damaged tissue, or cosmetic improvements. Skin grafting is used to cover extensive burns or other injuries.

Plata, Río de la (River Plate), wide estuary of SE South America, formed at confluence of Uruguay and Paraná rivers. Chief ports Buenos Aires, Montevideo. Explored by Magellan (1520). Scene of naval battle (1939) in which German battleship *Graf Spee* was scuttled.

Plataea, ancient city of Boeotia, SE Greece. Scene of Greek naval victory (479 BC) over Persians.

Plate, River, *see* PLATA.

plateau, elevated area of land with relatively level surface. Causes incl. basalt lava flows, faulting, erosion. Types incl. tableland, bordered by steep sides all around, and dissected plateau, where different rates of erosion eventually leave only isolated peaks.

plate tectonics, study of the main structural features of the Earth's crust in terms of several great crustal regions, or plates which change their positions through time. Mountain ranges, faults, trenches, mid-oceanic ridges result from plate movements. CONTINENTAL DRIFT theory derives from plate tectonics, continents being embedded in shifting plates.

Plath, Sylvia (1932-63), American poet. Known for intense, highly personal verse in collections *The Colossus* (1960), *Ariel* (1965). Also wrote a novel, *The Bell Jar* (1971). Committed suicide.

platinum (Pt), metallic element; at. no. 78, at. wt. 195.09. Malleable and ductile; resists corrosion by air and acids; excellent conductor of electricity. Used in electrical apparatus, jewellery and chemical catalysis.

Plato (*c* 427-*c* 347 BC), Greek philosopher, pupil of Socrates. Founded (387 BC) Academy near Athens to educate ruling elite. Author of *Republic* advocating ideal state based on rational order, ruled by philosopher kings. Propounded independent reality of universal ideas (esp. idea of the good), and ideal forms which man could come to perceive through dialectic method of inquiry. Held that virtue, reason, happiness were one. Dialogues incl. *Apology, Phaedo, Laws.* Most noted student was Aristotle.

Platyhelminthes (flatworms), phylum of bilaterally symmetric invertebrates. Reproduction by complex hermaphroditic system. Divided into 3 classes: Cestoda, tapeworms; Trematoda, parasitic flukes; Turbellaria, free-swimming aquatic worms.

platypus, *see* DUCKBILLED PLATYPUS.

Plautus, Titus Maccius (*c* 254–184 BC), Roman comic poet. Adapted Greek New Comedy for Roman stage; works incl. *Aulularia, Miles Gloriosus.* Profound influence on later European literature.

playing cards, cards used in gaming, divination and conjuring. Originated in the Orient, reaching Europe in 14th cent. Symbols for the 4 suits and 52-card deck were introduced in France in 16th cent.

plebeians, members of unprivileged class of ancient Rome, originally excluded from holding public office. Secured political equality with patricians from *c* 500-300 BC.

plebiscite, expression of people's will by direct ballot on political issue, as in referendum. Since 18th cent., used for deciding between independent nationhood or affiliation with another nation.

Pleiades, in Greek myth, seven daughters of Atlas and nymph Pleione. Pursued by Orion and turned into constellation which bears their name.

Pleiades, star cluster in constellation Taurus. Six stars are readily visible but cluster contains several hundred.

Pleistocene epoch, first geological epoch of Quaternary period. Began *c* 2 million years ago, lasted until *c* 11,000 years ago. Incl. 4 major glaciations, or Ice Ages, accompanied in warmer equatorial regions by high rainfall (pluvial) periods. Fauna incl. mastodons, mammoths, sabre-tooth carnivores, wolves, bison. During this epoch, man evolved from primitive ape-like creatures, *eg* Java, Peking man, to present form; time of Palaeolithic culture. Also *see* ICE AGES and GEOLOGICAL TABLE.

Plekhanov, Georgi Valentinovich (1857-1918), Russian revolutionary. Influential in introducing Marxist thought to Russia. Broke with Bolsheviks after 1903 split in Social Democratic Party; his view that Russia was not ready for Socialism was adopted by Mensheviks.

plesiosaur, extinct marine reptile of Jurassic period and later, order Plesiosauria. Long thin neck, 4 paddle-like limbs, long tail. Reached lengths of 15 m/50 ft.

pleurisy, inflammation of pleura, the membrane enclosing the lung. Usually caused by infection by bacteria or viruses; often occurs with pneumonia. Characterized by difficulty in breathing and collection of fluid around lungs.

Pleven or **Plevna,** city of N Bulgaria. Pop. 112,000. Agric. centre; textiles; wine. Taken by Russia from Turks after siege (1877).

Plexiglass, *see* PERSPEX.

Pliny the Elder, full name Gaius Plinius Secundus (AD *c* 23-79), Roman scholar. Wrote *Historia naturalis,* encyclopedic collection of scientific knowledge in 37 books. His nephew, **Pliny the Younger,** full name Gaius Plinius Caecilius Secundus (AD *c* 62-*c* 113), was consul. Wrote letters of literary and historical importance.

Pliocene epoch, final geological epoch of Tertiary period. End of Alpine mountain building. Continuing decrease in temperature caused extinction of many mammals, migration of others. Beginning of Lower Palaeolithic culture. Also *see* GEOLOGICAL TABLE.

Ploeşti, city of SC Romania. Pop. 195,000. Petroleum indust., pipelines to Bucharest, Constanza.

Plotinus (*c* AD 205-70), Greek philosopher, b. Egypt. Settled (AD 244) in Rome, founding neoplatonist school. Developed concept of creation by Emanation from God rather than directly by God.

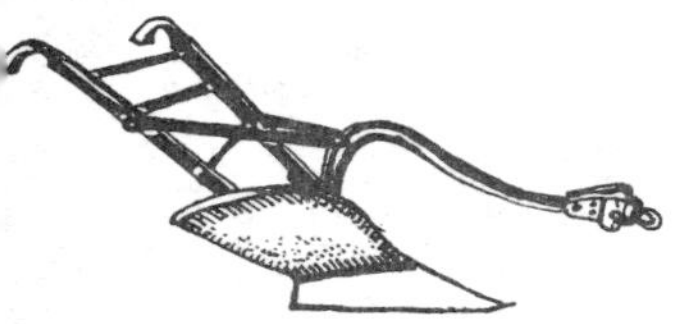

Horse-drawn walking plough

plough, farm implement used to cut, break and turn over soil. First ploughs were wooden wedge tipped with iron, pushed or pulled by men or oxen. Modern plough incorporates: coulter, blade or disc, which makes vertical cuts in soil; share, which cuts horizontally through undersoil; mouldboard, which turns over soil.

Plovdiv (anc. *Philippopolis*), city of C Bulgaria, on R. Maritsa. Pop. 303,000. Agric. centre, esp. cereals, wine, attar of roses; textiles; tobacco. Taken by Philip II of Macedonia, renamed; cap. of Roman Thracia, and 19th-cent. Eastern Rumelia.

plover, wading bird of Charadriidae family. Species incl. golden plover, *Pluvialis dominica*.

plum, small tree or shrub of genus *Prunus,* native to Asia Minor. Oval, smooth-skinned, edible fruit with flattened stone. Commercially cultivated plums incl. varieties of *P. domestica* (*eg* greengage, damson).

Plutarch (AD *c* 46-*c* 120), Greek biographer, essayist. Best known for *Parallel Lives,* paired biographies of Greeks and Romans, with vivid characterization, anecdotes. Popular in Elizabethan England through translation by Sir Thomas North, source for Shakespeare's Roman plays.

Pluto, in Greek myth, son of Cronus and Rhea; ruler of HADES. Worshipped as god of dead and of earth's fertility. Identified with Roman Orcus or Dis Pater.

Pluto, planet 9th in distance from Sun; mean distance from Sun *c* 5900×10^6 km; diameter *c* 5800 km; period of rotation about Sun *c* 248 years. First detected 1930. Has surface of frozen methane.

plutonic rock, igneous rock formed at great depth below Earth's surface. Commonly occurs as INTRUSIVE ROCK; slow cooling produces coarsely crystalline texture, *eg* granite.

plutonium (Pu), transuranic element; at. no. 94, mass no. of most stable isotope 244. Plutonium 239, produced by irradiating uranium 238 with neutrons, is used as fuel in nuclear reactors and in nuclear weapons.

Plymouth, city of Devon, SW England, at head of Plymouth Sound. Pop. 251,000. Seaport, naval base; boatbuilding, fishing. Medieval *Sutton,* hist. seafaring base (Drake, Raleigh, 'Pilgrim Fathers'). Has RC cathedral. Damaged in WWII air raids.

Plymouth, town of SE Massachusetts, US; on Plymouth Bay. Pop. 19,000. Site of Pilgrim landing in 1620 after sailing from England on *Mayflower*.

Plymouth Brethren, evangelical sect founded in Dublin by John Nelson Darby (1827). Spread to Europe and North America. Movement follows literal interpretation of Bible, has no ministers.

Plzeň (Ger. *Pilsen*), city of W Czechoslovakia. Pop. 163,000. Agric. market; breweries; metallurgy, munitions.

pneumoconiosis, disease of the lungs resulting from inhalation of mineral dust, esp. asbestos and silica. Usually affects miners, sand-blasters, *etc.* Causes lung inflammation and growth of fibrous scar tissue.

pneumonia, inflammation of the air sacs (alveoli) of the lungs, caused by bacterial or viral infection. Bronchial pneumonia is confined to area close to air passages, lobar pneumonia affects whole lobe. Bacterial form characterized by fever, pain in chest, blood-stained sputum; treated by antibiotics.

Pnom Penh, *see* PHNOM PENH.

Po (anc *Padus*), river of N Italy. Flows *c* 650 km (405 mi) E from Alps to delta on Adriatic Sea. Po basin is most fertile region of Italy.

Pocahontas (*c* 1595-1617), American Indian princess. Said to have saved John Smith, English colonist in Virginia, from execution. Married another colonist, James Rolfe (1614). Died in England.

pochard, *Aythya ferina,* European diving duck. Male has black chest, grey body, chestnut head and neck. Name also applied to several other diving ducks.

pocket borough, in Great Britain before Reform Bill (1832), borough in which representation in Parliament was controlled by one family or person.

Poe, Edgar Allan (1809-49), American author. Known for short stories creating atmosphere of suspense, *eg The Fall of the House of Usher.* Poetic works incl. *The Raven and Other Poems* (1845). Also wrote detective stories, *eg The Murders in the Rue Morgue* (1841).

poet laureate, office of court poet in Britain. Ben Jonson first held position although Dryden first held title. Poets laureate incl. Wordsworth, Tennyson, Betjeman.

poetry, in literature, term for imaginative, concentrated writing esp. using metrical and figurative language. Verse may be rhymed or un-rhymed (blank).

pogrom, Russian word, originally meaning 'destruction'; later applied to organized attacks on Jews, often carried out with connivance of tsarist govt. Pogroms of 1881-2 and 1903 were esp. severe.

Pohai, Gulf of, arm of Yellow Sea. Indents NE China coast. Formerly called Gulf of Chihli.

Poincaré, Raymond (1860-1934), French statesman, president (1913-20). Demanded strict treatment of Germany after WWI. As premier (1922-4, 1926-9), ordered armed occupation of Ruhr to enforce payment of war reparations (1923). His cousin, **Jules Henri Poincaré** (1854-1912), was a mathematician. Did pioneering research on topology of surfaces. Anticipated parts of relativity theory.

poinsettia, *Euphorbia pulcherrima,* plant native to Mexico and tropical America. Yellow flowers surrounded by tapering red leaves resembling petals.

pointer, short-haired hunting dog; usually white with brown spots. Hunts by scent and will 'point' to game with tail and muzzle outstretched. Stands *c* 66 cm/26 in. a shoulder.

pointillism, technique of painting in whic tiny dots of pure colour blend together t form intense colour effects at a distanc Developed by the neo-impressionists, inc Seurat and Signac.

poison, substance having a dangerous c fatal effect on living things when drunl absorbed, *etc.* Some are corrosive, e acids, disinfectants; others interfere wi body chemistry, *eg* cyanide.

poison gas, corrosive or poisonous gas c vapour-forming liquid or solid. Fir employed in WWI. Incl. chlorine whic affects lungs, mustard gas which affec skin, and nerve gases which attack centr nervous system.

poison ivy, any of genus *Toxicodendron* cashew family. Leaves of 3 leaflet greenish flowers, ivory-coloured berrie Can cause severe skin rash on contact.

Poitiers, town of W France, cap. of Vienn dept. Pop. 79,000. Wine and wool trad metal, chemical industs., univ. (1431). His cap. of Poitou. Scene of victory (1356) c Black Prince over John II of Franc Baptistery (4th cent.), cathedral (12t cent.).

poker, card game, with two basic variation draw and stud poker; usually played fc financial stakes. Originated in US, growin popular after 1870.

Poland

Poland (*Polska*), republic of EC Europe Area *c* 312,600 sq km (120,700 sq mi); pop 35,010,000; cap. Warsaw. Language: Polish Religion: RC. Forested N Carpathians in S elsewhere fertile plain; main rivers Oder Vistula. Agric. incl. cereals, livestock Indust. centred in Silesia, Warsaw, Łódź coal, iron, lead mining, textile mfg. engineering. First united 10th cent. medieval colonization by Teutonic Knights whom the Poles defeated at Tannenberg (1410). Disappeared completely after partitions (1772, 1793, 1795) between Austria, Prussia, Russia; re-formed 1918-21 Conflict with Germany over Danzig led to WWII; occupied by Germans and Russians Jewish pop. almost wholly exterminated

Territ. lost to USSR, gained from Germany after WWII. From 1947 ruled by communist govt.; member of COMECON.

polar bear, *Thalarctos maritimus,* large creamy white bear of Arctic Circle. Good swimmer, lives on floating ice; preys on seals, young walruses. Reaches lengths of 2.7 m/9 ft.

Polaris, star of constellation Ursa Minor, less than 1° from the north celestial pole and thus important navigationally. Also called North Star or Pole Star.

polarized light, light whose transverse vibrational pattern is confined to a single plane. Polarizing agents incl. crystals and Nicol prism.

polder, Dutch term for land reclaimed from sea or fresh water. Normally flat, lying below sea level; protected by dykes, drained by pumps. Makes fertile agric. land. *See* ZUIDER ZEE.

pole, in geography, extremity of Earth's axis. *See* NORTH POLE, SOUTH POLE, MAGNETIC POLES.

polecat, *Mustela putorius,* carnivorous mammal of N Europe and Asia, related to weasel. Dark brown outer fur; feeds on rodents, reptiles. Scent glands emit fetid odour for protection. Ferret is domesticated polecat.

Pole Star, *see* POLARIS.

police, force, or body of persons, estab. and maintained for keeping order, enforcing law and preventing, detecting and prosecuting crimes. First instituted as official body in Britain by Peel (1829) with reorganization of SCOTLAND YARD. In UK, police administered by Home Office in England, Scottish Office in Scotland.

poliomyelitis or **infantile paralysis,** virus infection of the grey matter of spinal cord. Affects nerve cells which control muscular contraction, sometimes causing paralysis. Immunity became possible with Salk vaccine (1955) and Sabin vaccine (1961).

Polish, language in W Slavic branch of Indo-European family. Official language of Poland.

Polish Corridor, strip of land, lying between East Prussia and rest of Germany, which gave Poland access to Baltic. Formerly German territ., awarded to Poland (1919). German agitation to recover it led to invasion of Poland and WWII (1939).

Politburo, policy-making committee of Soviet Communist Party, the effective govt. of USSR. Term also applied to similar bodies in other Communist states.

Polk, James Knox (1795-1849), American statesman, Democratic president (1845-9). Annexation of Texas led to Mexican War (1846-8), by which California and much of SW were acquired.

polka, lively Bohemian dance in 2/4 time, originating *c* 1830. Popular in Europe for about 50 years.

pollen, fine, yellowish dust, produced in anthers of flowering plants. Mature grains containing male element unite with female element in ovule to produce embryo which becomes SEED.

pollination, process allowing FERTILIZATION in seed plants. Pollen is transferred to stigma by wind, bees or other insects.

Pollock, Jackson (1912-56), American painter. Leading abstract expressionist; chief exponent of ACTION PAINTING.

pollution, harm caused to environment as a result of man's emission of substances which are non-biodegradable, or which, when broken down, become dangerous. Atmospheric pollutants incl. sulphur gases, hydrocarbons and solid waste from smoke and automobile emissions, which become esp. dangerous in smog; also fluorocarbons, used as aerosol propellants, which reduce OZONOSPHERE's capacity to protect Earth from ultraviolet radiation. Water pollutants incl. sewage, indust. effluent (often containing poisonous heavy metals, *eg* mercury, cadmium, lead), detergents, pesticides (*see* DDT), oil spills. Any may kill living things in water by poisoning or deoxygenation, or be ingested and passed to higher organisms, incl. man, in food-chain. Pollution of seas now one of concerns of UN Environmental Programme which also admins. international monitoring, controls on heavy indust. Also *see* GREENHOUSE EFFECT.

Pollux, *see* DIOSCURI.

Polo, Marco (*c* 1254-*c* 1324), Venetian traveller. Journeyed with father and uncle to Far East (1271-5). Reached court of Kublai Khan, who later employed him on diplomatic missions. Returned to Venice (1292-5), captured while fighting Genoa. While in prison, dictated valuable accounts of his travels.

polo, outdoor game, prob. originating in Persia, played between teams of 4 on horseback. Long-handled sticks used to hit wooden ball into the opponents' goal. Brought by British army officers from India to England, where it was first played competitively in 1871.

polonaise, stately Polish dance in 3/4 time at a moderately fast tempo. Best known are those by Chopin.

polonium (Po), radioactive element; at. no. 84, mass no. of most stable isotope 209. Formed by decay of radium; discovered (1898) in pitchblende by the Curies. Powerful source of alpha particles.

Poltava, city of USSR, NC Ukrainian SSR. Pop. 279,000. Centre of fertile agric. region producing sugar beet, fruit, grain. Peter the Great defeated Charles XII of Sweden nearby (1709).

poltergeist, name given to force, often supposed to be supernatural, responsible for unexplained rappings, movement of furniture, flying about of small objects in house.

polyanthus, *Primula polyantha,* hardy perennial herb of primrose family. Derived from hybrid of common primrose and cowslip. Grown as garden plant.

Polybius (*c* 201-*c* 120 BC), Greek historian. Taken as a prisoner to Rome (168), he enjoyed patronage of the Scipio family. Wrote history of years 220-146 BC in 40 books, 5 of which survive.

polyethylene, *see* POLYTHENE.

polygamy, state or practice of having 2 or more husbands (polyandry) or wives (polygyny) at same time. Polyandry is found in South Sea Isls. and among some North American Indian and Eskimo tribes. In Tibet, takes form of marriage to several brothers. Often associated with MATRIARCHY. Polygyny is more widespread esp. among hunting peoples, *eg* in Africa. Often confined to ruling caste. Has occurred in certain Christian sects. Practised by Moslems (limit of 4 wives).

polygon, in geometry, closed plane figure bounded by 3 or more sides; triangle is 3-sided polygon. Designated a regular polygon if all sides have equal length.

polyhedron, solid figure having polygons for its faces. Designated a regular polyhedron if faces are all congruent regular polygons; only those with 4, 6, 8, 12 and 20 faces can exist (formerly called the 'Platonic solids').

polymer, chemical compound consisting of giant molecules formed by linkage of smaller molecules (monomers). In addition-polymerization, giant molecules are multiples of monomer molecule; in condensation-polymerization, they are formed from monomers by chemical reaction involving elimination of some by-product, *eg* water. Cellulose is natural polymer; nylon and rayon are synthetic.

Polynesia, one of three major divisions of Pacific isls., to E of Melanesia and Micronesia. Bounded by New Zealand, Hawaii and Easter Isl., incl. Samoa, Tonga, Line, Cook, Tuvalu, Phoenix isls. and groups forming French Polynesia.

Polynesians, people of Pacific isls. between Hawaii, New Zealand and Easter Isls., of Malayo-Polynesian linguistic stock. May have come from Malaysia or South America.

Polynices or **Polyneices,** in Greek myth, son of Oedipus. After banishment of father, agreed to rule Thebes alternately with brother Eteocles. When Eteocles refused to relinquish throne Polynices led 'Seven against Thebes' expedition. All were killed except Adrastus. Story basis of tragedies by Aeschylus, Euripides.

polyp, sedentary form of coelenterate with tube-like body and mouth surrounded by tentacles. Either solitary (*eg* Hydra) or colonial (*eg* coral-forming polyps). Some reproduce asexually, forming free-swimming medusae by budding; others reproduce sexually to form new polyps.

polyp, in medicine, tumour growing from mucous membrane, to which it is attached by a stalk. Found in intestines, uterus, *etc*; removed if malignant.

Polyphemus, in Greek myth, a Cyclops, son of Poseidon. In Homer's *Odyssey,* imprisoned Odysseus and his men in cave. They escaped after Odysseus had blinded him with burning stake.

polyphony, style of musical composition in which separate melodic lines are harmonically interrelated *eg* in a round. Developed in West in medieval times when extra parts were added to plainsong. Reached great heights in music of Bach and Palestrina.

polystyrene, *see* STYRENE.

polytheism, belief in or worship of more than one god. Usually each god is distinguished by a particular function but is represented in myth as related to other members of cosmic family. Prob development of primitive ANIMISM.

polythene or **polyethylene,** thermoplastic material made by polymerization of ethylene. Used to make translucent plastic film, moulded objects and in electrical insulation.

polyvinyl chloride (PVC), colourless thermoplastic material formed by polymerization of vinyl chloride. Resistant to water, acid, alcohol. Used for flooring, coated fabrics, cable covering.

pomegranate, *Punica granatum,* small tree native to subtropical Asia. Scarlet flower followed by many-seeded, pulpy, edible fruit.

Pomerania (Pol. *Pomorze,* Ger. *Pommern*), region of NC Europe, on Baltic coast extending from Stralsund (East Germany) in W to R. Vistula (Poland) in E. Flat, low lying; agric., livestock, forestry. In 1945, all Pomerania E of R. Oder passed to Poland.

Pomeranian, breed of small dog with long silky hair, erect ears, tail curved over back. Stands *c* 15 cm/6 in. at shoulder.

Pompadour, Antoinette Poisson, Marquise de (1721-64), mistress of Louis XV of France. Acquired great power with Louis; encouraged alliance with Austria leading to French involvement in Seven Years War. Patron of Voltaire.

Pompeii, ancient city of Campania, S Italy near Bay of Naples. Roman port, resort buried (AD 79) with Herculaneum in eruption of Vesuvius. Site discovered 1748. Many public buildings and villas, with well preserved murals, have been uncovered.

Pompey, full name Gnaeus Pompeius Magnus (106-48 BC), Roman soldier. Made consul (70). Defeated Mithradates in Asia Minor (65). Joined Caesar and Crassus in 1st Triumvirate (60). Later opposed Caesar, championing senatorial party. Defeated by Caesar in civil war at Pharsala (48); fled to Egypt, where he was murdered.

Pompidou, Georges Jean Raymond (1911-74), French statesman, president (1969-74). Premier (1962-8), dismissed by De Gaulle soon after 1968 student-labour unrest. Elected president after De Gaulle's resignation, pursued similar policies.

Pondicherry, union territ. of S India. Area 474 sq km (183 sq mi); pop. 471,000; cap. Pondicherry. Comprises former French India (founded 1674); transferred to India (1954). Became union territ. 1962.

Ponta Delgada, *see* AZORES.

Pontiac (*fl* 18th cent.), American Indian,

chief of Ottowa tribe. Led widespread uprising of Indian tribes against British (1763-6).

ontine Marshes, area of WC Italy, between Tyrrhenian Sea and Apennines. Fertile, populous in Roman times; abandoned due to malaria. Drainage completed 1920s, agric. settlement followed.

ontius Pilate, *see* PILATE, PONTIUS.

ontoon, card game. *See* VINGT-ET-UN.

ontormo, Jacopo, orig. Jacopo Carrucci (1494-1556), Italian painter. Style represents transition between late classicism and early mannerism.

ontus, region of Asia Minor, now in NE Turkey. Became kingdom *c* 300 BC and *fl* under Mithradates until defeat by Romans under Pompey (65 BC).

ony express, mail service running from St Joseph, Missouri to Sacramento, California, US. Riders covered distance of *c* 3200 km (2000 mi) in 8 days. Inaugurated 1860, replaced by telegraph in 1861.

oodle, breed of dog probably developed in Germany. Thick frizzy or curly coat usually trimmed in standard style (introduced in France). Stands over 38 cm/15 in. at shoulder. Miniature poodles are 25-38 cm/10-15 in. at shoulder and toy poodles are under 25 cm/10 in.

ool, *see* SNOOKER.

oole, town of Dorset, S England, on Poole Harbour. Pop. 113,000. Port, resort; boatbuilding; pottery mfg.

oona, city of Maharashtra state, W India. Pop. 1,135,000. Cotton, paper mfg.

oor Laws, legislation providing public relief and assistance for poor. English law (1601), 1st state intervention on behalf of destitute, made them responsibility of parish. Poorhouses built, work provided, local levies raised. Workhouses estab. (18th cent). Speenhamland System (1795) attempted to help by subsidizing low wages. Abuses aroused discontent in agric. workers and employers, led to Poor Law amendment (1834). This act granted relief only to able-bodied poor in strictly regulated workhouses, introduced strong central authority. Harsh effects helped rise of CHARTISM. Complete reform achieved 1930. Poor Law abolished, replaced by National Assistance Board (1948).

op art, art style, appearing in late 1950s, which uses subjects and techniques derived from commercial art and popular culture. Subject matter incl. assemblages of cans, replicas of food, enlarged photographs and comic book characters. American exponents incl. Warhol, Oldenburg, Lichtenstein.

ope, Alexander (1688-1744), English poet. Known for skilled use of heroic couplet, poems incl. discussion of classical values, *An Essay on Criticism* (1711), mock heroic *The Rape of the Lock* (1714), satirical *Dunciad* (1728), deistic *Essay on Man* (1733-4), 'Epistle to Dr Arbuthnot' (1735).

ope, *see* PAPACY.

opish Plot, *see* OATES, TITUS.

Poplar

poplar, any of genus *Populus* of trees of willow family. Native to N temperate regions. Soft fibrous wood, flowers in catkins.

Popocatépetl, dormant volcano of C Mexico, overlooking Mexico City. Height 5452 m (17,887 ft).

Popper, Sir Karl Raimund (1902-), British philosopher, b. Austria. Wrote classic *The Logic of Scientific Discovery* (1935) on the problem of induction and demarcation of science. Other works incl. *The Open Society and Its Enemies* (1945) attacking Marxist doctrine.

poppy, any of genus *Papaver* of annual and perennial plants. Showy red, violet, yellow or white flowers. Incl. commercially important OPIUM POPPY. Corn poppy, *P. rhoeas,* is found in Europe.

Popular Front, in French history, term for alliance in 1930s between left-wing political parties. Socialists, Communists, and Radical Socialists united under Léon Blum and formed Popular Front govt. (1936-8) which carried out series of social reforms. Term is also applied to any similar political grouping.

Populism, American agrarian political movement of late 19th cent. Discontent among farmers led to formation (1891) of Populist Party, whose presidential candidate polled over 1 million votes in 1892 election. Majority of populists had joined Democrats by 1896.

porcelain, hard, white, non-porous variety of pottery which is translucent; made of kaolin, feldspar and quartz or flint. First made by the Chinese during T'ang period, it was refined during Sung period. European forms incl. Sèvres, Limoges (France), Chelsea, Bow, Staffordshire (England), Meissen, Dresden (Germany).

porcupine, rodent covered with sharp erectile spines in addition to hair. Two families: New World Erethizontidae (partly arboreal) and Old World Hystricidae (mainly terrestrial).

porphyry, igneous rock comprising large

crystals embedded in fine-grained groundmass. Term refers to any such texture, not composition. Red porphyry, *ie* feldspar crystals in purplish groundmass, was valued by ancient Egyptians.

porpoise, small toothed whale of Phocaenidae family. Common porpoise, *Phocaena phocaena,* found in N Atlantic, is smallest species, reaching lengths of 1.8 m/6 ft. Feeds on fish, crustaceans.

Porsena, Lars, *see* TARQUINIUS SUPERBUS.

port, sweet fortified wine made in Douro valley of Portugal. May be ruby, tawny or white.

Port Arthur, China, *see* LU-TA.

Port-au-Prince, cap. of Haiti, major port on Gulf of Gonaïves. Pop. 703,000. Rum distilling, sugar refining, brewing. Founded 1749; became cap. 1770. Has Univ. of Haiti (1944); 18th-cent. cathedral.

Port Elizabeth, city of S Cape Prov., South Africa, on Algoa Bay. Pop. 469,000. Port, exports minerals, fruit, wool; car assembly works. Founded (1820).

Porter, Cole (1893-1964), American composer of musicals. Songs, of which he wrote both words and music, incl. 'Night and Day', 'Anything Goes'.

Port Harcourt, city of SE Nigeria, on Niger delta. Pop. 242,000. Railway terminus and port, exports palm oil, groundnuts, cocoa; commercial and indust. centre, esp. oil refining, metal products, tyre mfg., vehicle assembly. Founded (1912).

Portland, William Henry Cavendish Bentinck, 3rd Duke of (1738-1809), English statesman. Headed coalition govt. of North and Fox in 1783; again PM (1807-9).

Portland, port of NW Oregon, US; on Willamette R. Pop. 1,083,000; state's largest city. Railway jct.; shipyards. Timber, grain exports, wood industs.

Portland, Isle of, penin. of Dorset, SW England. Famous for quarrying of Portland stone, fine building material.

Port Laoighise, co. town of Laoighis, C Irish Republic. Pop. 4000. Formerly called Maryborough.

Port Louis, cap. of Mauritius. Pop. 141,000. Admin. centre; port, exports sugar. Founded 1735; has Anglican and RC cathedrals.

Port Moresby, cap. of Papua New Guinea, in SE New Guinea isl. Pop. 113,000. Exports rubber, gold.

Pôrto, *see* OPORTO.

Pôrto Alegre, city of S Brazil, cap. of Rio Grande do Sul state; at N end of Lagôa dos Patos. Pop. 1,044,000. Meat, hides, wool exports. Settled by German, Italian immigrants in 19th cent. Has 2 univs.

Port of Spain, cap. of Trinidad and Tobago, on NW Trinidad isl. Pop. 350,000. Sugar produce, oil refining, rum distilling. Receives iron, bauxite shipments from Venezuela, Guianas. Has Anglican, RC cathedrals. Became cap. 1783.

Porto Novo, cap. of Benin, on coastal lagoon near Bight of Benin. Pop. 104,000. Admin. centre; port, exports palm oil, kap cotton. Former seat of a native kingdo became colonial cap. 1900.

Port Phillip Bay, inlet of Bass Str., Australia. Ports incl. Melbourne a Geelong; resorts on sandy E shores.

Port Said (*Bûr Saîd*), city of NE Egypt, Mediterranean entrance to Suez Can Pop. 349,000. Major port and fuelli station, exports cotton; salt, chemi industs. Founded 1859.

Portsmouth, city on Portsea Isl., Hampshi S England. Pop. 200,000. Main UK na base. Has Cathedral (12th cent.); Nelso flagship *Victory*.

Portsmouth, port of SE Virginia, US; Hampton Roads (Elizabeth R.). P 111,000. Naval depot; shipyards. Expo cotton, tobacco; varied mfg.

Port Sudan, city of NE Sudan, on Red Se Pop. 133,000. Sudan's chief port, expo cotton, gum arabic, hides, salt.

Port Talbot, town of Glamorgan S Wales, Swansea Bay. Pop. 51,000. Ore termin new harbour (1970) serve large steelwor

Portugal

Portugal, republic of SW Europe, on Iberian penin. Incl. Azores, Madeira Is Area 92,000 sq km (35,500 sq mi); po 9,798,000; cap. Lisbon. Languag Portuguese. Religion: RC. Mountainous N, E; main rivers Minho, Douro, Tagu Agric., wine, cork, fishing (sardines, tuna Subtropical in S (tourism). Part of Rom *Lusitania,* fell to Visigoths, Moo Independent from 12th cent.; acquir overseas empire 15th-16th cent. Und Spanish rule 1580-1668. Suffered in War Spanish Succession, Peninsular War; lo Brazil 1822. Republic estab. 19 dictatorships followed, esp. Salaz (1928-68). Democracy restored aft military uprising 1974; followed decolonization programme.

Portuguese, Romance language in Ita branch of Indo-European family. Spoken 1st language in Portugal, Madeira, t Azores, Brazil. Developed from Latin, b also influenced by Arabic.

Portuguese East Africa, *see* MOZAMBIQUE.

Portuguese Guinea, *see* GUINEA-BISSAU.

Portuguese man-of-war, *Physalia physalis,* colonial marine coelenterate of open Atlantic. Floating bladder bears medusae and polyps with diverse functions, *eg* reproduction, feeding. Long tentacles with poisonous stinging organs.

Portuguese Timor, *see* TIMOR.

Portuguese West Africa, *see* ANGOLA.

Poseidon, from a greek statue of c 200 BC

Poseidon, in Greek myth, brother of Zeus and god of the sea. Represented as vengeful god carrying a trident with which he could cause earthquakes. Identified by Romans with Neptune.

Posen, *see* POZNAŃ.

positivism, system of philosophy basing knowledge solely on observable scientific facts and their relations to each other. Rejects metaphysics. Founded by Auguste Comte. *See* LOGICAL POSITIVISM.

positron, anti-particle of electron, possessing same mass but positive electric charge. Positron-electron pairs can be produced by conversion of energy into matter, but the 2 particles annihilate each other.

possum, *see* OPOSSUM, PHALANGER.

postal service, arrangement for delivery of mail to members of public. Early systems estab. in Persian, Roman empires. In Britain, Charles I estab. acceptance of public mail, extending services of royal couriers; flat-rate penny post instituted by Rowland Hill in 1840. Air mail started in 1918. Universal Postal Union regulates international harmony (estab. 1875).

post-impressionism, term used to describe work of those French painters who rejected impressionism in favour of greater emphasis on the subject or the formal structure and style of the painting. Most important exponents were Gauguin, van Gogh, Cézanne.

potash or **potassium carbonate** (K_2CO_3), compound used as fertilizer and in manufacture of glass and soap.

potassium (K), soft metallic element; at. no. 19, at. wt. 39.10. Highly reactive; combines with water to produce strong alkali potassium hydroxide. Occurs in wide variety of silicate rocks and mineral deposits; essential to life processes. Compounds used in soap, glass, fertilizers.

potato, *Solanum tuberosum,* plant of nightshade family. Native to South America but widely cultivated for edible tubers. Introduced into Europe *c* 1570.

Potemkin, Grigori Aleksandrovich, Prince (1739-91), Russian army officer. Took part in the annexation (1783) of the Crimea, where he governed ably. He reformed the army, built the Black Sea fleet, estab. the port of Sevastopol. Favourite of Catherine II.

potential, in physics, work done against force exerted by field in bringing unit physical quantity (*eg* mass, electric charge, magnetic pole) from infinity to some specified point. Used as measure of strength of field at any point.

Potomac, river of E US; forms Maryland's S border. Flows E 459 km (285 mi) past Washington DC to Chesapeake Bay. Shenandoah R. (Civil War battleground) is main tributary.

Potosí, town of SW Bolivia, cap. of Potosí dept. Alt. 4200 m (*c* 13,780 ft). Pop. 77,000. Leading mining centre; tin, copper, tungsten. Founded 1545. Has 19th-cent. cathedral; univ. (1571).

Potsdam, city of C East Germany, on R. Havel. Pop. 120,000. Produces precision instruments, chemicals. Residence successively of Brandenburg, Prussian, German rulers. Scene of Potsdam Conference (1945).

Potsdam Conference, meeting (July, 1945) of Allied leaders to implement agreement of YALTA CONFERENCE. Estab. American, British, French and Soviet occupation zones in Germany, to be supervised by Allied Control Council. Redistributed German territ. to Poland and USSR; laid economic and political basis of post-WWII Germany.

Potter, [Helen] Beatrix (1866-1943), English author and illustrator of children's books incl. *The Tale of Peter Rabbit* (1902), *The Tale of Jemima Puddle-Duck* (1908).

Potteries, The, area of Staffordshire, NC England, in Trent Valley. Pottery indust. founded 1769 by Wedgwood. Incl. Stoke-on-

Trent, Newcastle-under-Lyme.

pottery, general term for objects made of clay and baked hard. Originally hand made, pottery was fashioned on wheels in Egypt before 4000 BC; glazes were also developed in Egypt in 2nd millennium BC. Red and black figured vases produced in Greece *c* 600-450 BC represent high point of art and provide valuable historic record. Chinese developed own advanced pottery techniques which were emulated when Chinese pottery was introduced into Europe in 16th cent. Islamic potters of Syria, Persia, Turkey produced brilliantly coloured and glazed work from 9th-16th cents., which also influenced European style. Also *see* PORCELAIN.

Poulenc, Francis (1899-1963), French composer, pianist. Member of 'les Six' group of composers. Works, often witty in nature, incl. ballet music, and piano, orchestral, chamber works.

Pound, Ezra (1885-1972), American poet, lived in Europe after 1907. Influenced modern poetry as imagist, vorticist and friend, patron, of younger poets. Works incl. allusive, erudite *Hugh Selwyn Mauberley* (1920), *Cantos* (1925-69). Fascist sympathizer during WWII.

pound, in measurement, British unit of weight; equal to *c* 0.4536 kilograms.

Poussin, Nicolas (1594-1665), French painter. Dominant influence on French classical painting. Developed classical landscape in 1640s, austere and constructed with geometric precision. Works incl. 2 series of *Seven Sacraments* and *Landscape with Diogenes*; spent most of his life in Rome.

power, in physics, the rate of doing work. SI unit of power is the watt.

Powys, inland county of E Wales. Area 5077 sq km (1960 sq mi); pop. 106,000; admin. hq Llandrindod Wells. Created 1974, incl. former Breconshire, Montgomeryshire, Radnorshire.

Poynings' Law, act of Irish Parliament (1494). Stated that approval of English legislature was required for summoning of Irish Parliament and for passing of any legislation. Repealed 1782.

Poznań (Ger. *Posen*), city of W Poland, on R. Warta, cap. of Poznań prov. Pop. 522,000. Railway jct.; engineering and chemical industs.; univ. (1919). Seat of Polish primate from 1821. Under Prussian rule 1793-1919.

Prado, Spanish national museum of painting and sculpture, in Madrid, opened to the public in 1819.

Praetorians, body guard of Roman emperors, first organized in reign of Augustus. Played important part in accession of certain emperors. Disbanded by Constantine I.

Pragmatic Sanction, 1) decree issued (1438) by Charles VII of France, limiting papal authority over Church in France; 2) decree issued (1713) by Emperor Charles VI, extending right of succession in Austrian Empire to female line. On his death, led to War of Austrian Succession (1740-8).

pragmatism, movement in philosophy which determines the validity of concepts by their practical results. Opposed to RATIONALISM. Exponents incl. C. S. Peirce William James.

Prague (*Praha*), cap. of Czechoslovakia, on R. Moldau. Pop. 1,176,000. Admin. commercial centre. Metal working textiles; food processing; printing publishing. Univ (1348); Hradčany Palace St Vitus cathedral. Centre of 15th-cent. Hussite movement. Czech cap. from 1918 German occupation 1939-45. Focus of 1968 liberalization movement, suppressed by Soviet forces.

prairie, area of gently undulating, treeless natural grassland. Applies esp. to such areas in North America between Rockies in W and Great Lakes and Ohio R. in E former grazing land now extensively cultivated for cereals.

prairie dog, *Cynomys ludovicianus* burrowing squirrel-like rodent of North American plains. Lives in large colonies barks like a dog.

prairie wolf, *see* COYOTE.

Prakrit, languages other than Sanskrit and Vedic of Indic group of Indo-Iranian branch of Indo-European family. Incl modern vernaculars. Some scholars hold PALI to be a Prakrit.

praseodymium (Pr), metallic element of lanthanide series; at. no. 59, at. wt. 140.91 Compounds used to colour glass and enamel. First isolated 1904.

Prato, city of Tuscany, NC Italy. Pop 156,000. Woollen indust. Cathedral contains works by Donatello and Filippo Lippi.

prawn, any of various edible shrimp-like crustaceans, widely distributed in fresh and salt waters. Common prawn, *Palaemon serratus*, is 7.5-10 cm/3-4 in. long.

Praxiteles (*fl c* 350 BC), Athenian sculptor With Phidias, considered greatest sculptor of ancient Greece. Marble *Hermes* at Olympia is only surviving work. Copies of other statues incl. *Aphrodite of Cnidus*.

Precambrian or **Archaean era,** earliest geological era, incl. all time from consolidation of Earth's crust to beginning of Palaeozoic era. Duration *c* 4000 million years. Sometimes divided into Early and Late Precambrian. Largely metamorphic rock, exposed as continental shields, *eg* Canadian, African, Australian. Rare traces of rudimentary life; forerunners of trilobites, worms, sponges, jelly fish; some algae, fungi. Also *see* GEOLOGICAL TABLE.

precession of the equinoxes, westward movement of equinox along the ecliptic. Caused by gravitational pull of Sun and Moon on Earth's equatorial bulge; Earth's axis describes cone returning to original position every 26,000 years.

precious stone, *see* GEMSTONE.

predestination, in Christian theology doctrine that God foreordained all events esp. the salvation of certain souls. Follows from belief in omniscience and omnipotence of God; formulated by St

Augustine. RC doctrine allows the co-existence of free will, while Calvin taught absolute predestination of souls. Occurs also in Judaism and Islam.

pregnancy, period of development of fertilized ovum in the uterus. In humans, lasts on average 40 weeks.

prelude, initially an introductory movement in music; later a short piano piece. Preludes of Bach and Chopin use single theme and complete cycle of keys.

premier, *see* PRIME MINISTER.

Pre-Raphaelite Brotherhood, society, nucleus of which was 3 English artists, D.G. Rossetti, Millais and Holman Hunt, formed 1848 to revive painting with a fidelity to nature they considered characteristic of Italian art before Raphael. Associated painters incl. Ford Madox Brown, Burne-Jones. Dissolved by 1853.

Presbyterianism, system of Christian church govt. by elders (presbyters), elected by the congregation rather than by bishops. Instituted by CALVIN it is the system of most reformed churches. The Church of Scotland is the only Presbyterian church estab. by law.

president, chief EXECUTIVE of a republic, acting as both head of state and govt. In republic with parliamentary govt. has little or no executive power, head of govt. usually being prime minister or premier. In US and France, president has substantial powers.

Presley, Elvis (1935-77), American singer. Leading exponent of rock-and-roll in 1950s with such songs as 'Heartbreak Hotel', 'Blue Suede Shoes' and 'Hound Dog'.

press gang, a naval party empowered by law to force men to serve in British fleet. Initiated by Edward III, it was chief method of naval recruitment from Elizabethan times down to Napoleonic wars, after which it was discontinued though still legal.

pressure, in physics, force per unit area acting on a surface. Atmospheric pressure is pressure due to weight of Earth's atmosphere; at sea level, this pressure supports column of mercury *c* 76 cm high.

Prester John, legendary Christian priest and ruler of a great empire, originally thought to be in Asia, later associated with Ethiopia. Legend first arose in 12th-cent. chronicles.

Preston, former co. town of Lancashire, NW England, on R. Ribble. Pop. 97,000. Port; textiles esp. cotton; engineering.

Prestonpans, town of Lothian region, EC Scotland. Pop. 3000. Scene of battle (1745) in which Jacobite forces defeated English.

Pretender, Old, *see* STUART, JAMES FRANCIS EDWARD.

Pretender, Young, *see* STUART, CHARLES EDWARD.

Pretoria, admin. cap. of South Africa and cap. of Transvaal. Pop. 562,000. Admin., indust. centre; railway engineering, large steelworks; univ. (1930). Founded 1855; cap. of Boer confederation from 1860, of Union of South Africa from 1910.

Prévost d'Exiles, Antoine François (1697-1763), French author, known as Abbé Prévost. Known for novel *Manon Lescaut* (1731).

Priam, in Greek legend, king of Troy during Trojan War. Chief wife was Hecuba; his children incl. Hector, Paris, Cassandra. Slain at fall of Troy.

Priapus, in Greek myth, son of Dionysus and Aphrodite. Fertility god of gardens. Statues of him as little man with enormous phallus were used as scarecrows.

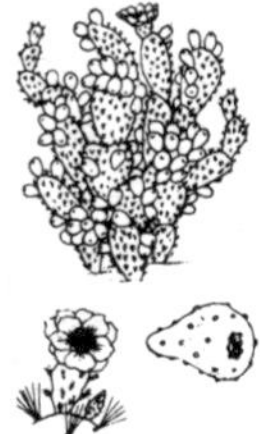

Prickly pear

prickly pear, common name for various species of genus *Opuntia* of cacti with flattened, jointed, spiny stems. Native to Mexico; naturalized in S Europe, N Africa, Australia. Pear-shaped fruits of several species are edible.

Pride, Thomas (d. 1658), English soldier. Colonel on Parliamentary side during Civil War. Carried out purge (1648) of Presbyterian members of House of Commons (believed to be royalist sympathizers). Resulting Rump Parliament pursued prosecution of Charles I.

Priestley, J[ohn] B[oynton] (1894-), English author, critic. Known for novels incl. *The Good Companions* (1929), *Angel Pavement* (1930). Also wrote plays.

Priestley, Joseph (1733-1804), English chemist, theologian. Discovered oxygen (1774); prepared and studied various other gases incl. sulphur dioxide, ammonia.

primary school, institution at which children of up to *c* 11 years old are taught basic subjects, *eg* reading, arithmetic.

primates, order of mammals, incl. monkeys, apes, man. Primarily arboreal, with 5 digits on hands and feet; well-developed vision and large brain. Order also incl. more primitive lemurs and tarsiers.

prime minister or **premier,** chief member of CABINET, responsible to parliament. In UK and Commonwealth, holds executive power; appoints cabinet and is leader of governing party.

prime number, integer that can be evenly divided only by itself and 1. Each integer can be written as a product of prime numbers.

Primo de Rivera, Miguel (1870-1930), Spanish military and political leader. Estab. military dictatorship (1923) with support of Alfonso XIII. Continued as leader of civil admin. from 1925. Resigned 1930. His son, **José Antonio Primo de Rivera** (1903-36), founded FALANGE party. Executed by Loyalists.

primrose, *see* PRIMULA.

primula, large genus of perennial herbs with white, yellow and pink flowers, found in temperate regions of N hemisphere. Main European varieties are common primrose, *Primula vulgaris,* COWSLIP, OXLIP and cultivated POLYANTHUS. Himalayan primrose, *P. denticulata,* has lilac-coloured flowers on long stem.

Prince Edward Island, Maritime isl. prov. of SE Canada. Area 5657 sq km (2184 sq mi); pop. 123,000; cap. Charlottetown. Agric.; stock raising, dairy farming; fishing (esp. lobsters). Settled in 17th cent. by French; ceded to Nova Scotia 1763; became separate colony 1769; prov. 1873.

Principe, *see* SÃO TOMÉ AND PRINCIPE.

printed circuit, electronic circuit in which wiring is printed on an insulating base. May be prepared by attaching copper foil to base, drawing circuit pattern on foil with wax and then etching away untreated foil.

printing, method of reproducing words or illustrations in ink on paper or other material by mechanical means. Block printing was used in China in 8th cent. and movable type was introduced there in 11th cent. GUTENBERG is credited with the European invention of movable type (*c* 1437). In England, Caxton set up 1st printing press in London (1476). Modern commercial printing uses such processes as LITHOGRAPHY and PHOTOENGRAVING.

Pripet Marshes, forested marshland of USSR, C Byelorussian SSR. Formerly natural defence barrier between Poland and Russia. Crossed by R. Pripet, which rises in NW Ukrainian SSR and flows *c* 800 km (500 mi) to join R. Dnepr.

prism, in optics, transparent body whose ends are congruent triangles in parallel planes and whose 3 sides are parallelograms. Glass prisms change direction of light passing through them; triangular prisms disperse white light into colours of spectrum.

prison, place where convicted criminals are confined. Became important in late 18th cent., replacing capital punishment, mutilation, *etc.* Work of JOHN HOWARD influenced reform, esp. in US, where 1st cellular prison estab. (1790), and Pennsylvania system of discipline developed. In UK, Quaker group, esp. Elizabeth FRY, led reform. Modern prisons seek rehabilitation, *eg* by use of specialist staff, open prisons, although punitive treatment, *eg* chain gangs, solitary confinement, still exists. *See* PROBATION.

prisoners of war, members of the regular or irregular armed forces of a nation at war held captive by the enemy. Hague Conference of 1907 and Geneva Conventions of 1929 and 1949 laid down rules governing their treatment.

privateers, privately owned war vessels having govt. commission to seize enemy shipping (1589-1815). The system was subject to much abuse as a cover for piracy and was abolished (1856).

privet, any of genus *Ligustrum* of shrubs and small trees of olive family. Widely cultivated for hedges.

privy council, body of advisors or counsellors appointed by or serving head of state, esp. in UK and Commonwealth. Comprises cabinet, members of judiciary (in UK incl. archbishops). Acted as executive arm of govt. until 1688, superseded by cabinet.

probability theory, mathematical study of laws of chance. Event whose probability is 0 will never occur, one whose probability is 1 is certain to occur. Probability that tossed coin will fall as a head is $\frac{1}{2}$.

probation, system whereby sentence on convicted offender is suspended on condition of good behaviour, regular reporting to probation officer.

process engraving, *see* PHOTOENGRAVING.

Proconsul, extinct primate of Miocene period, known from fossils found in Kenya. Possible ancestor of chimpanzee, gorilla.

production, in economics, creation or manufacture for sale of goods and services with exchange value. Factors of production are regarded as land, labour, capital.

profit, in economics, return on CAPITAL.

Profumo, John Dennis (1915-), British politician. Conservative secretary of state for war, he resigned after his involvement in prostitution scandal was revealed.

progression, in mathematics, series of numbers, each formed by a specific relationship to its predecessor. In arithmetic progression, successive terms differ by a fixed amount (common difference) *eg* 1,3,5,7,9....; in geometric series, ratio of successive terms is constant (common ratio) *eg* 1,2,4,8,16....

Progressive party, in US, name of three 20th cent. political organizations, active at different presidential elections. First was 'Bull Moose' party, estab. (1911) by Republicans dissatisfied with W.H. Taft; supported (1912) Theodore ROOSEVELT. Second had socialist programme, supported La Follette in 1924 campaign. Third was again left-wing, challenged Democrats in 1948 election, nominating Henry Wallace.

prohibition, method of legally regulating manufacture, sale and transporting of alcoholic beverages. In US, refers to period (1920-33) of absolute ban on such manufacture and sale. Widespread. bootlegging led to repeal.

Prokofiev, Sergei Sergeyevich (1891-1953), Russian composer. His music has an individual harmonic quality often allied to great lyricism. Works incl. operas, 7 symphonies, concertos, film music

Alexander Nevsky; wrote orchestral fairy tale *Peter and the Wolf*.

proletariat, term used for class of wage earners existing on their own labour, esp. in indust. environment. In Marxist theory, proletariat is exploited by capitalist class, from which it must take power to achieve classless society.

Prometheus, in Greek myth, stole fire from the gods and gave it to mankind. Chained by Zeus to rock in Caucasus, where his liver was eternally devoured by an eagle. Released by Heracles.

promethium (Pm), radioactive element of lanthanide series; at. no. 61, mass no. of most stable isotope 145. Obtained in nuclear reactors from fission of uranium.

pronghorn or **prongbuck,** *Antilocapra americana,* antelope-like North American ruminant, only member of Antilocapridae family. Hollow branched horns cast annually. Long persecuted by man, now protected.

proof spirit, alcoholic spirit containing 49.28% alcohol by weight or 57.1% by volume. Spirit said to be 70° proof or 30° under proof contains 0.7 × 57.1 = 39.97% alcohol by volume.

propaganda, technique of moulding public opinion by spreading information through all media to gain religious, social or political ends in area of controversy. Important in dissemination of information in wartime, and by political parties in both democratic and totalitarian countries.

Propertius, Sextus (54/48-*c* 16 BC), Roman poet. Friend of Virgil, Ovid. Early poetry dominated by affair with Cynthia, a courtesan; later poetry continued theme of love and women.

prophets, in OT, Jewish religious leaders regarded as chosen by God to guide the people, esp. during kingdom of Palestine and the Captivity. Incl. Isaiah, Jeremiah, Ezekiel and Daniel. Term applied collectively to the books of OT bearing their names.

proportional representation (PR), system of voting giving numerical reflection of voting strength of each party in representative assembly. Advocated by J.S. MILL, in order to allow minorities voice in govt. Best-known system is **single transferable vote,** in which elector has only one vote, but may indicate order of preference on list of candidates. Candidate elected on minimum quota of votes, after which surplus votes go to next on list, *etc.*

prose, ordinary form of spoken or written language, without metrical structure, as opposed to poetry or verse. Usual form of expression in novel, biography, essay.

Proserpina, *see* PERSEPHONE.

prostate gland, partially muscular gland surrounding urethra at base of urinary bladder in males. Secretes part of seminal fluid. Enlargement of prostate is common disorder of middle and old age; removal by surgery allows free flow of urine.

prostitution, offering oneself, or another, for sexual intercourse for money, material gain. In many societies, prostitution was religious act, *eg* in ancient Babylon, W Asia. Tolerated in Middle Ages, became problem with spread of venereal disease (16th cent), and legally suppressed by Protestant reformers. Police regulation, attempt to close or license brothels in 19th cent. Subsequent concern more with suppression of associated crimes, diseases.

protactinium (Pa), radioactive element of actinide series; at. no. 91, mass no. of most stable isotope 231. Occurs in uranium ores. Discovered 1918.

Protectorate, govt. of England (1653-9) estab. by Cromwell after he had dissolved Rump Parliament. Cromwell assumed title of lord protector and, with army support, ruled as dictator. His son, Richard Cromwell, succeeded him as lord protector (1658); resigned 1659.

proteins, large group of complex nitrogen-containing organic substances essential to living organisms. Made up of 20 amino acids, linked together in numerous ways to form large molecules. Synthesis of protein from amino acids is essential to growth and tissue maintenance.

Protestantism, religion of all Christian churches except RC and Eastern Orthodox. Most originated during REFORMATION. Stresses individual responsibility to God rather than to ecclesiastical authority.

Proteus, in Greek myth, wise old man of the sea with power of assuming various forms to escape questioning. If caught and held would foretell the future.

proton, stable elementary particle possessing charge equal but opposite to that of electron; mass *c* 1836 times that of electron. Occurs in nucleus of all atoms, usually joined with neutrons.

protoplasm, essential living matter of plant and animal cells, consisting of colloidal solution of proteins, lipoids, carbohydrates and inorganic salts. Carries out essential processes of reproduction, absorption of food, waste excretion, *etc.* In cell, differentiated into central nucleoplasm and surrounding cytoplasm.

Protozoa, phylum of all unicellular animals, consisting of naked mass of protoplasm surrounded by membrane. Reproduction often by fission but some parasitic varieties, *eg* malaria parasite, have complicated life cycle involving several hosts.

Proudhon, Pierre Joseph (1809-65), French social theorist. Condemned private property in *What is Property?* (1840) for maintaining inequality and injustice. Favoured theory of mutualism, whereby association of owner-producers cooperate for common good.

Proust, Marcel (1871-1922), French novelist. Influenced by Bergson's theory of subjective nature of time. Known for semi-autobiog. roman-fleuve, *A la recherche du temps perdu* (16 vols., 1913-27), detailing narrator's changing reactions to experience.

Provençal, variety of French. Considered by some to be dialect(s), by others a separate language. Spoken in Provence and other areas of S France. Developed as *langue d'oc* of Middle Ages, vehicle of troubadour literature. *Langue d'oc* unsuccessfully revived in 19th cent.

Provence, region and former prov. of SE France, hist. cap. Aix. Largely mountainous, Rhône valley in W, coastal plain (incl. Camargue) in S. Wine, fruit, silk, cattle, h.e.p. Tourism, esp. along Riviera. Settled 7th cent. BC by Greeks, became Roman prov. Part of France from 1486. Also *see* PROVENÇAL.

Proverbs, poetic book of OT, collection of moral maxims traditionally attributed to Solomon. Prob. from various sources and collected 9th-2nd cent. BC.

Providence, seaport and cap. of Rhode Isl., US; on arm of Narragansett Bay. Pop. 904,000. Machinery, jewellery, silverware mfg. Founded on free worship basis (1636). Joint cap. with Newport until 1900. Seat of Brown Univ. (1764).

prune, plum that has been dried without fermentation taking place. Prepared mainly on Pacific coast of US.

Prussia

Prussia (*Preussen*), hist. region and former state of Germany. Comprised much of NE Germany, cap. Berlin. Teutonic Knights conquered heathen Prussians in 13th cent.; their territ. became hereditary duchy in 16th cent. and passed to electors of Brandenburg (1618). Kingdom of Prussia was created from Brandenburg dominions in 1701. Frederick the Great (1740-86) began period of expansion, acquiring Silesia and W parts of Poland. Further territ. gains made after Napoleonic Wars. Under Bismarck, assumed leadership of German states (1860s); William I of Prussia became 1st emperor of Germany (1871). Reduced in size after WWI. Dissolved (1947) after WWII.

prussic acid, *see* HYDROCYANIC ACID.

Przewalski's horse, *Equus caballus przewalskii,* only surviving wild horse, confined to Mongolia and Sinkiang. Tan coloured with black mane; stands 1.4m/4.5 ft at shoulders.

Psalms, poetical book of OT, traditionally attributed to David. Prob. by many authors and collected 6th-1st cent. BC.

Pskov, city of USSR, W European RSFSR near L. Peipus. Pop. 176,000. Centre of flax growing region; linen mfg. Cap. of powerful commercial city state (1348-1510) until annexed by Moscow.

Psyche, in Greek myth, a beautiful girl and the personification of human soul, loved by Cupid. He forbade her to look at him but she disobeyed and he left her. After a long search, she was made immortal and united with him forever.

psychiatry, medical study and treatment of disorders of the mind, incl. psychosis, neurosis. Gained prominence in late 19th cent., esp. with Freud's development of psychoanalysis.

psychical research, study of supernormal phenomena. Estab. as serious study by British Society for Psychical Research (founded 1882), which investigated mediums, poltergeists, *etc.* Extra-sensory perception (ESP), *ie* telepathy, precognition, has been researched in 20th cent.

psychoanalysis, term coined by Freud to denote system of psychology and method of treatment of mental disorders (*see* NEUROSIS). Lays emphasis on importance of unconscious mind, inducing its expression and evading conscious mind's censorship through analytic techniques of free association, dream interpretation.

psychology, science of the mind, more specifically the studies of all interaction between living organisms and the environment. Allied to biological and sociological sciences, but distinguished by its concentration on individual's behaviour, both through mental and emotional processes. Specific concerns are abnormal behaviour, cognition and cognitive development, *etc.* Modes of approach incl. PSYCHOANALYSIS, BEHAVIOURISM, GESTALT.

psychosis, name given to certain severe mental disorders which involve loss of contact with reality. Functional psychoses without apparent organic cause, are mainly of schizophrenic or manic-depressive type; organic psychoses are caused by brain damage or disease.

psychosomatic disease, physical disorder of body resulting from disturbance of the mind. Asthma, duodenal ulcers, high blood pressure, certain heart disorders, *etc,* are considered partly psychosomatic in origin.

psychotherapy, treatment of mental disorder by psychological means, involving communication between trained person and patient. Methods incl. suggestion, hypnosis and psychoanalysis.

ptarmigan, bird of grouse family, genus *Lagopus,* of mountains of N hemisphere. Toes and legs feathered; winter plumage is white.

Pteridophyta, division of plants comprising fern, horsetail and club moss groups. Incl. many ancient fossil varieties.

Pterodactyl

erodactyl, any of order Pterosauria of extinct flying reptiles of Mesozoic era. Membranous wings stretched between hind limb and greatly elongated fourth digit of forelimb.

tolemy I [Soter] (d. 284 BC), Macedonian general under Alexander the Great. Given control of Egypt during partition of Alexander's empire. Estab. new Egyptian dynasty (305). Descendant, **Ptolemy XII** (d. 47 BC), ruled Egypt jointly with sister (and wife) Cleopatra. Forced by Caesar to accept her reinstatement after he had deprived her of power. Drowned in Nile. His brother, **Ptolemy XIII** (d. 44 BC), was then made joint ruler with Cleopatra by Caesar. She had him murdered.

tolemy or **Claudius Ptolemaus** (*fl* AD 140), Greco-Egyptian astronomer, geographer. Described geocentric solar system in which Sun and planets revolved in circular orbits about stationary Earth; influential until superseded by works of Copernicus. Also wrote *Geography* incl. atlas of maps of known world.

uberty, stage of child's development when sexual maturity begins. Generally, age 11-14 in girls and 12-16 in boys. Hormones from pituitary gland stimulate gonads to form fertile sperm or ova and to secrete hormones which control secondary sex characteristics.

ublic ownership, another term for NATIONALIZATION.

ublic school, in UK, secondary school, run on fee-paying (private) basis and having academic curriculum. Famous examples incl. boys' boarding schools Eton, Harrow, Winchester. Elsewhere, public schools are free to all pupils.

ublishing, trade concerned with creation and distribution of books and other reading matter. Closely allied to printing and bookselling.

'uccini, Giacomo (1858-1924), Italian composer. Renowned for operas *Manon Lescaut, La Bohème, Tosca, Madame Butterfly* and *Turandot*. Combined great dramatic expression with strong melody.

'uebla, city of C Mexico, cap. of Puebla state. Pop. 499,000. Onyx quarrying, cotton milling, pottery industs. Has cathedral (1649); univ. (1537).

Pueblo, group of North American Indian tribes living in SW US. Distinguished by custom of living in adobe communal longhouses *(pueblos)*. Reached high level of civilization, esp. in agric., sand paintings, pottery *etc*. Successfully resisted Spanish colonization in 17th cent. Groups incl. Hopi, Zuni. Some 20,000 still live on reservations in Arizona, New Mexico.

puerperal fever, infection by bacteria of womb after childbirth. Caused many deaths in 19th cent. Virtually eliminated by antisepsis and antibiotics.

Puerto Rico, isl. territ. of US, E West Indies, in Greater Antilles. Area 8871 sq km (3425 sq mi); pop. 3,317,000, one of highest pop. densities in world; cap. San Juan. Languages: Spanish, English. Religion: RC. Mainly mountainous; tropical climate. Fertile agric. soil (sugar cane, tobacco growing). Settled by Spanish (1508), ceded to US after 1898 war. Became 'Commonwealth' 1952. Much emigration to US because of unemployment.

puff adder, *Bitis arietans*, highly poisonous viper common in tropical Africa. Short tail, yellow markings on body; reaches lengths of *c* 1.2 m/4 ft.

puffball or **smokeball,** spherical fungus which breaks open when ripe to emit dust-like spores. Common puffball is *Lycoperdon perlatum*.

puffer, tropical fish of Tetraodontidae family. Skin covered with small prickles erected when body is inflated with air or water. Edible if expertly prepared; otherwise poisonous.

puffin, *Fratercula arctica*, small marine bird with black and white plumage. Triangular beak banded with blue, red and yellow. Breeds in colonies on Atlantic coasts, nesting in burrows.

pug, breed of small dog, probably of Chinese origin. Broad flat nose, curled tail; stands *c* 28 cm/11 in. at shoulder.

Pugin, Augustus Welby Northmore (1812-52), English architect, writer. Influential advocate of Gothic revival.

Puglia, *see* APULIA.

Pulitzer, Joseph (1847-1911), American newspaper owner, b. Hungary. Left funds for the **Pulitzer Prizes,** awarded each year since 1917 for achievements in journalism, letters and musical compositions.

pulsars, heavenly bodies which emit short pulses of radio waves at regular intervals. First detected 1967. Believed to be rotating neutron stars, remnants of supernova explosions.

pulse, in physiology, wave of arterial expansion caused by beating of heart. Normal rate in adults is *c* 60–70 beats per min.

puma, *Felis concolor*, large member of cat family, ranging from Argentina to Canada. Yellowish-brown short fur, slender build. Also called cougar or mountain lion.

pumice, *see* LAVA.

pump, machine for raising, transferring or increasing the pressure of water or other fluids (incl. gases). In ancient times the screw type was used for irrigation purposes. Various types exist now, incl. reciprocating, gear and centrifugal pumps.

pumpkin or **squash,** *Cucurbita pepo,* annual vine with large, round, edible fruit. Native to North America, widely cultivated. Name also given to similar plants of genus *Cucurbita.*

Punch and Judy, glove puppet play introduced to England in 17th cent., prob. derived from Italian *commedia dell'arte.* Characters incl. murderous hunchback, Punch, and nagging wife, Judy.

Punic Wars, series of conflicts between Rome and Carthage for dominance of Mediterranean. First Punic War (264-241 BC) resulted in acquisition of Sicily by Rome. During 2nd Punic War (218-201 BC), Hannibal invaded Italy but could not capture Rome. Forced to return to Carthage, he was defeated at Zama by Scipio Africanus Major (202). Third Punic War (149-146 BC) led to total destruction of Carthage by Scipio Africanus Minor.

Punjab, state of N India. Area *c* 75,600 sq km (29,200 sq mi); pop; 13,473,000; cap. Chandigarh. Hist. region of Punjab dominated by Sikhs in 19th cent.; annexed by Britain after Sikh Wars (1845-9). At partition, W Punjab became Pakistani prov. Indian prov. of E Punjab later divided (1966) into states of Haryana (Hindi-speaking) and Punjab (Punjabi-speaking).

Punjabi, Indic language in Indo-Iranian branch of Indo-European family. Spoken in NW India and Pakistan. Close to W Hindi, Urdu.

Punta Arenas, port of S Chile, on Magellan Str. Pop. 68,000. World's most S city. Wool, lamb exports. Coal mining nearby.

pupa, third stage of development of insect undergoing complete METAMORPHOSIS. Involves anatomical changes, often occurring in cocoon or cell. Adult emerges after pupa stage.

pupil, in anatomy, circular opening in centre of iris of eye. Size of pupil varies with intensity of light and is affected by adrenaline in the blood and drugs such as belladonna.

puppet, small figure of human or animal made to perform on miniature stage by unseen operator who speaks dialogue. Types incl. marionette, controlled by wires, and 'glove' puppet. Puppet shows have great antiquity, being familiar in 5th cent. BC Greece.

Purbeck, Isle of, penin. of Dorset, S England. Purbeck marble (limestone) quarried.

Purcell, Henry (1659-95), English composer, organist of Chapel Royal. Works incl. opera *Dido and Aeneas,* music for *The Fairy Queen, King Arthur,* as well as songs, instrumental and church music.

purgative, drug given to induce bowel movement. Vegetable purgatives incl. senna, rhubarb, bran; mineral salts us incl. magnesium sulphate (Epsom salts).

purgatory, in RC and Eastern Orthod theology, place where those who have di in grace of God expiate their unatoned si by suffering. Suffering can be lessened prayers of living.

Puritanism, social and theologic movement in Protestantism in Britain a America. Arose out of pressure for refor of religious establishment (16th cent.). I fluenced by Calvinist theory and aimed less ritualistic forms of worship. By 17 cent., had separated from Church England, and opposed Charles I, pr cipitating Civil War (1640s). Puritanis taken by colonists to New England, whe it exerted a great influence on society.

purslane, *Portulaca oleracea,* annual he native to India. Fleshy, succulent leav sometimes used as salad or pot herb.

pus, thick yellowish-white substance pr duced as result of bacterial inflammatio Composed of white blood cells, tissue flui bacteria and dead tissue.

Pusan, seaport of SE South Korea, on Kor Str. Pop. 2,450,000. Largest Korean po indust., commercial centre; railwa engineering, shipbuilding; produces irc and steel, textiles.

Pusey, Edward Bouverie (1800-82), Englis clergyman, leader in OXFORD MOVEMENT.

Pushkin, Aleksandr Sergeyevic (1799-1837), Russian author. Best-know works incl. verse-novel *Eugene Oneg* (1831), tragedy *Boris Godunov* (183 Poetry incl. Byronic lyrics, narrati poem, *The Bronze Horseman* (1833). Als wrote short story cycle, *Tales of Belk* (1830). Had great influence on subseque Russian literature.

Putney, *see* WANDSWORTH.

Putumayo, river of NW South Americ Rises in Colombian Andes, flows E 1600 k (*c* 1000 mi) forming Colombia-Peru borde then into Brazil to join Amazon as the Içá.

Puy, Le, *see* LE PUY.

Pu-Yi, Henry (1906-67), last Chines emperor (1908-12). Ruled as Hsuan Tun Later, served as emperor (1934-45) Japanese puppet state of Manchukuo.

PVC, *see* POLYVINYL CHLORIDE.

Pygmalion, in Greek myth, king of Cypru Made ivory statue, Galatea. When he fell i love with it Aphrodite brought statue to li and he married her.

Pygmy or **Pigmy,** diminutive, *c* 1.5 m (5 ft Negroid people of Africa, Malaysia an New Guinea. Sometimes called Negrillo (Africa) or Negritos (Far East). Generall hunters and food gatherers living in sma nomadic bands in scrub regions.

Pylos (*Pílos*), town of Greece, in SV Peloponnese. Scene of Athenian victor (425 BC) over Sparta and of battle o Navarino (1827) in which British, French Russian fleet defeated Turks, Egyptian during War of Greek Independence Ruined Mycenaean palace (13th cent. BC).

Pym, John (*c* 1583-1643), English politician

Led Puritan opposition to Charles I in Parliament; instrumental in drawing up Petition of Right (1628). In Long Parliament, moved impeachment of Strafford and Laud. One of 5 members of Commons whom Charles tried to arrest (1642).

'ongyang, cap. of North Korea. Pop. 1,500,000. Indust. centre of coal, iron region. Mfg., heavy engineering. Rebuilt after destruction of Korean War.

'orrhoea, any discharge of pus. Name usually applies to *Pyorrhoea alveolaris*, infection of gums and teeth sockets, usually leading to loosening of teeth.

Aztec pyramid, Mexico

/ramid, in ancient Egypt, monumental stone structure with square base and triangular sides, meeting at an apex. Erected as tombs for kings of Egypt, great period of pyramid building was *c* 2700-2300 BC. Three famous pyramids at Giza incl. Great Pyramid of Khufu (Cheops), one of Seven Wonders of the ancient World. Similar structures built by Aztecs, Mayas.

yramids, Battle of the, defeat by Napoleon (July, 1798) soon after his invasion of Egypt, of an army of 60,000 Mamelukes. Briefly gave him control of the area until defeated at Aboukir.

yramus and Thisbe, in classical myth, Babylonian lovers. Pyramus, mistakenly thinking Thisbe had been killed by a lion, killed himself. When Thisbe found his body, she took her own life with his sword.

yrenees (Sp. *Pirineos*), mountain range of SW France, NE Spain. Extend from Bay of Biscay to Mediterranean. Higher in C, E, rise to 3403 m (11,168 ft) at Pico de Aneto. Passes incl. Roncesvalles. Incl. Andorra. Tourism, h.e.p.

yrethrum, *Chrysanthemum coccineum*, perennial plant native to Persia and Caucasus. Widely cultivated in temperate regions for red, pink or white flowers and commercially for insecticide pyrethrum powder extracted from dried flower heads.

pyrite or **iron pyrites** (FeS_2), yellow mineral, consisting of iron sulphide. Most widespread sulphide mineral; often mistaken for gold (nicknamed 'fool's gold'). Source of iron and sulphur.

pyroclastic rock, fragmented volcanic material thrown into atmosphere by explosive activity. May be solid when ejected or liquid solidified by contact with air. Incl. pumice.

pyrometer, instrument used to measure temperatures beyond range of normal thermometers. Incl. platinum resistance thermometer which utilizes change in resistance with temperature.

pyroxenes, group of rock-forming minerals, composed mainly of silicates of calcium, iron and magnesium.

Pyrrho (*c* 365-270 BC), Greek philosopher. Founder of SCEPTICISM. Taught that every proposition could be maintained or contradicted with equal plausibility, thus knowledge must always be in question.

Pyrrhus (*c* 318-272 BC), king of Epirus (295-272 BC). Invaded Italy (281) to aid Tarentum against Rome. Sustained heavy losses in 2 victories (hence 'Pyrrhic victory') before defeat at Beneventum (275).

Pythagoras (*c* 582-*c* 507 BC), Greek philosopher, b. Samos. Founded religious brotherhood at Crotona. Held that all relationships could be expressed in numbers. Made discoveries in musical intonations. Influenced subsequent work of Euclid. Believed Earth revolved around fixed point ('hearth') of universe. Originated **Pythagoras' theorem,** which states that in a right-angled triangle the square of the hypotenuse equals the sum of the squares of the other two sides.

Pythian games, in ancient Greece, games held at Delphi every 4 years in honour of Apollo. Incl. athletic, literary and musical contests.

python, any of Pythonidae family of constrictor snakes, of Old World tropics. Reaches lengths of 9.1 m/30 ft.

Q

Qaddhafi or **Gadafy, Muammar al-** (1942-), Libyan political leader. Gained power after military coup overthrowing King Idris (1969). Fostered Arab unity; failed in attempt to unite Egypt and Libya (1973). Used Libyan oil wealth to support revolutionary movements, esp. Palestinian guerrillas.

Qatar, penin. of E Arabia, in Persian Gulf. Area *c* 11,400 sq km (4400 sq mi); pop. 201,000; cap. Doha (pop. 130,000). Oil reserves. Sheikdom under British protection until 1971. Allied with United Arab Emirates.

Qattara Depression, arid region of N Egypt, in Libyan Desert. Area *c* 18,130 sq km (7000 sq mi); falls to 133 m (436 ft) below sea level, lowest point in Africa. Has extensive salt marsh. Formed S part of Allied defence line at El Alamein (1942).

Quadruple Alliance, (1) league formed (1718) by Britain, France, Austria and Netherlands to prevent Spain from nullifying terms of Peace of Utrecht. Spain renounced claims to Austrian territ. in Italy in settlement of 1720. **(2)** alliance formed (1814) by Austria, Britain, Prussia and Russia to strengthen coalition against Napoleon.

quagga, *Equus quagga,* extinct South African zebra. Excessively hunted for hide in 19th cent.

quail, any of various small migratory game birds. Only European species is *Coturnix coturnix,* which winters in Africa.

Quakers, *see* SOCIETY OF FRIENDS.

quantum theory, physical theory introduced by Planck that radiation is emitted and absorbed not continuously but only in multiples of indivisible units (quanta). Extended by Einstein to explain photoelectric effect and by Bohr to explain atomic spectra. In 1920s, developed into mathematical theory of wave mechanics which explains many phenomena of atomic physics.

quarantine, restriction of movements on people and animals who may have been exposed to infectious diseases. Arose in 14th-cent. Europe as an attempt to control spread of plague. Often applied to animals to prevent spread of foot-and-mouth disease, rabies, *etc.*

quarks, hypothetical elementary particles, introduced by M. Gell-Mann and G. Zweig, which serve as building blocks for all strongly interacting elementary particles (hadrons). Originally 3 quarks, bearing charges which are fractions of that on electron, were introduced; more may be needed to explain new phenomena.

quarrying, removal of building stone, granite, marble, slate, *etc,* from surface deposits. Stone in broken or crushed for used for cement, road making a concrete aggregate, is removed by drilli and blasting. Blocks of stone suitable f building and ornamental work a machine cut.

quartz, commonest mineral, consisting silicon dioxide (SiO_2). Hard, norma colourless and transparent; coloured impurities. Varieties incl. agate, amethy chalcedony, onyx. Used in jewelle electronics, lenses and prisms.

quartzite, hard metamorphic roc consisting of firmly cemented qua grains. Normally light-coloured; may darker due to mineral impurities. Form by metamorphism of pure quartz san stone.

quasars (quasi stellar radio sources), extr galactic sources of immense quantities light or radio waves. Observed red shift their spectral lines suggests they a receding at velocity close to that of light.

Quasimodo, Salvatore (1901-68), Itali poet. Early works reflect occult, hermet interests. *The Promised Land and Oth Poems* (1958) marks preoccupation wi social, political issues. Nobel Prize f Literature (1959).

Quaternary period, second and curre geological period of Cenozoic era. Began 2 million years ago. Comprises Pleistoce and Holocene (or Recent) epochs. Deter ration of climate, begun in Tertiary, led extensive glaciations; followed by warm climate, formation of modern landscape lakes, deserts. Development of man fro primitive ape-like creature to prese form. Also *see* GEOLOGICAL TABLE.

Quathlamba, *see* DRAKENSBERG MOUNTAINS.

Québec or **Quebec,** prov. of E Canada, inc Anticosti, Magdalen isls. in Gulf of Lawrence. Area 1,553,640 sq km (594,860 s mi); pop. 6,299,000; cap. Québec; large city Montréal. Bounded in N by Hudso Ungava bays. Resources in Laurentia (timber, asbestos, aluminium, iron or h.e.p.). St Lawrence R. valley is agric indust. base. French landed 1534; settle region as New France in 17th cent.; Britis gained control 1763; named Lower Canad 1791; became one of original 4 provs. Canada (1867). French language an customs retained. Separatist moveme grew from 1960s. In 1980 referendu majority rejected Quebec govt.'s desire negotiate for independence.

Québec or **Quebec City,** cap. and major po of Québec prov., Canada; on St Lawrenc R. Pop. 542,000. mainly French speakin Timber produce and exports, shipbuildin clothing mfg. Port icebound in winte French settlement under Champlai

1608); cap. of New France until British ιefeat of French on Plains of Abraham 1759); cap. of Lower Canada (1791). Has :itadel, Laval Univ. (1852).

ébecois, Parti, *see* LÉVESQUE.

een Anne's lace, *see* CARROT.

een Charlotte Islands, archipelago of W ßritish Columbia, Canada. Timber, fishing ndusts. Indian pop. Largest of group is ;raham Isl.; area 6436 sq km (2485 sq mi).

eensberry, John Sholto Douglas, 9th Marquess of (1844-1900), Scottish noble-nan. Patron of the rules of modern gloved oxing drafted by John Chambers (1867).

een's Counsel, *see* BARRISTER.

eensland, state of NE Australia. Area ,727,500 sq km (667,000 sq mi); pop. !,198,000; cap. Brisbane. Great Dividing Range parallels coast, incl. Darling Downs S), Atherton Tableland (N); Great Ar-esian Basin in SW; Barrier Reef off-shore. ugar cane, fruit growing; timber indust.; eef cattle raising; mining, esp. copper, ead, bauxite, oil. Penal settlement estab. 824 at Moreton Bay; Queensland became :olony (1859), federal state (1901).

esnay, François, *see* PHYSIOCRATS.

etzal, crested bird of Trogonidae family, of forests of Central America. Green and ·ed plumage, with long tail feathers.

etzalcoatl, principal god of Toltecs, and ubsequently, Aztecs. Credited with discov-ery of arts and sciences. Represented as plumed serpent.

ezon City, city of Philippines, C Luzon isl. Pop. 995,000. Replaced nearby Manila as :ap. 1948-77. Residential; textile mfg.

icksand, deposit of loose, fine-grained aturated sand particles. May engulf heavy object. Often found near river mouths, along sea shores.

quicksilver, *see* MERCURY.

quietism, form of Christian mysticism which holds that union with God is achieved through complete passivity of soul, annihilation of will and cessation of self-consciousness. Founded (1675) by Spanish priest, Miguel de Molinos. Condemned (1687) by Pope Innocent XI.

Quimper, town of Brittany, NW France, cap. of Finistère dept. Pop. 51,000. Pottery (Quimper or Brittany ware), tourism. Cathedral (13th cent.).

quince, *Cydonia oblongata,* small tree native to Asia. Bears bitter, yellow, pear-shaped fruit used in preserves.

quinine, crystalline alkaloid extracted from cinchona bark. Introduced into Europe from South America, it was formerly used in treatment of malaria.

Quisling, Vidkun (1887-1945), Norwegian fascist leader. Collaborated in German invasion of Norway (1940); headed subsequent puppet govt. after 1942. Shot for treason after War. Name became synonymous with traitor.

Quito, cap. of Ecuador at foot of Pichincha volcano, near the equator. Alt. 2850 m (9350 ft). Pop. 600,000. Brewing, flour milling, major textile mfg. Indian settlement before Spanish conquest (1534). Has univ. (1787); many famous churches.

Qumran, W Jordan, site of discovery of Dead Sea Scrolls (1947). Originally iron-age fort, occupied (2nd cent. BC) by monastic community until AD 68. Dead Sea Scrolls comprise their library.

quoits, outdoor game in which an iron ring is thrown at a peg in an attempt to encircle it. Known in England since 14th cent. Horseshoe pitching, popular in US, is a similar game.

R

Ra, ancient Egyptian sun god. Represented as hawk, lion. Sailed across sky in barge during day. Early Egyptian kings claimed descent from him.

Rabat, cap. of Morocco, at mouth of Bou Regreg. Pop., incl. nearby Salé, 597,000. Admin. centre; textile, carpet industs. Ancient walled town. Univ. (1957). Former cap. of French Morocco (1912-56).

rabbi, originally a scholar and teacher of the Jewish law. Now refers to those trained and ordained as spiritual heads of congregations.

rabbit, *Oryctolagus cuniculus,* burrowing European mammal of hare family, order Lagomorpha. Smaller and less swift than hare; lives in large groups. Serious pest of farmland. Domestic varieties sometimes bred for fur.

Rabelais, François (*c* 1494-1553), French author. Wrote satirical romance, *Gargantua and Pantagruel* (5 vol., 1532-64, last 2 vol. perhaps not by Rabelais), narrating adventures of giant and son in search of wisdom, experience.

rabies or **hydrophobia,** infectious virus disease of mammals, affecting brain and spinal cord. Transmitted in saliva of infected animals, usually by biting; symptoms incl. fever, delirium, muscle spasms, inability to drink, paralysis. Incubation period 10 days to several months. No known treatment; early administration of vaccine usually effective.

Raccoon

raccoon, *Procyon lotor,* medium-sized North American mammal, with mask-like facial markings and black ringed tail. Nocturnal, largely arboreal; classed as carnivore, it is omnivorous.

race, in biology, term used to denote subspecies or variety of species, differing slightly in characteristics from typical species member.

Rachmaninov, Sergei Vasilyevich (1873-1943), Russian composer, pianist. Works, highly romantic in style, incl. symphonies, piano music, *eg* concertos, *Rhapsody on a Theme of Paganini* for piano and orchestra. Lived mainly in after 1917.

Racine, Jean (1639-99), French dramati Famous for classical tragedies of passic *Andromaque* (1667), *Iphigénie en Auli* (1674), *Phèdre* (1677).

rackets or **racquets,** ball-and-racket gar played on enclosed court by 2 or 4 perso Ball is struck against end-wall. Mode form developed in England in 19th cer SQUASH RACKETS is variant played on small court.

Rackham, Arthur (1867-1939), Engli watercolour painter and illustrator. Knov for his illustrations of children's books.

racoon, *see* RACCOON.

radar, system employing transmitted a reflected radio waves to detect presence objects and determine their position, d tance, height or speed. Also used f navigation in ships, aircraft.

Radcliffe, Ann, née Ward (1764-182 English novelist. Known for 'gothic romances, esp. *The Mysteries of Udolpho*

radiant energy, energy which is transmitt in form of electromagnetic energy, heat, light, X-rays. Radiant heat can communicated from source to observ through a vacuum or intervening mediu without heating it.

radiation, *see* ELECTROMAGNETIC RADIATION.

radiation sickness, disease resulting fro exposure to uncontrolled radiation, esp. rays or that resulting from nuclear e plosions. Effects incl. genetic damag cancer of skin and blood cells, *etc.*

radical, in chemistry, group of 2 or mo atoms that acts as single unit ar maintains its identity in chemic reactions; usually incapable of independe existence.

radio, transmission of electric signals b means of electromagnetic radiatic generated by high-frequency alternatir current. Maxwell postulated existence radio waves (1873) and Hertz demo strated their existence (1888); Marco demonstrated their use in communicatio (1895).

radioactive dating, determination of age objects or materials by estimation of i content of radioactive isotopes. Radi active carbon 14, produced in the atmo phere by action of cosmic rays and a sorbed into living tissue, is used to estima age of archaeological specimens.

radioactivity, spontaneous disintegration atomic nuclei of certain elements said be radioactive, *eg* radium, uraniur thorium. Accompanied by emission alpha or beta particles and possib gamma rays. Radioactivity can be induce in elements not naturally radioactive by neutron bombardment in nuclear reactor.

radio astronomy, study of heavenly bodies by analysis of radio waves which they emit (first detected 1932). Emission sources incl. bodies too distant for optical observation as well as non-luminous or dark stars, and larger bodies in Solar System, *eg* Sun, Jupiter.

radiography, use of X-rays to produce images on photographic material. Used in medicine and industry.

radiology, use of radiation in diagnosis and treatment of disease. X-rays are used to photograph living bone and tissue and also to destroy abnormal cells (*eg* cancer cells). Gamma rays from cobalt 60 also used to cure cancer.

radio range, system of application of radio to marine and air navigation. Usually consists of unattended 'beacons' emitting a constant, identifiable radio signal. Ships and aircraft may take bearings on the beacon (using a receiver with a directionally sensitive antenna) and plot their position.

radish, *Raphanus sativus,* annual plant of mustard family, native to Europe and Asia. Pungent, fleshy root eaten raw as relish.

radium (Ra), naturally occurring radioactive element; at. no. 88, mass no. of most stable isotope 226. Occurs in pitchblende and other uranium ores; formed by disintegration of uranium 238. Discovered (1898) by the Curies. Used to treat cancer and in luminous paints.

Radnorshire, former county of EC Wales, now in Powys. Mountainous. Sheep rearing. Co. town was Presteigne.

Radom, city of EC Poland. Pop. 178,000. Railway jct., agric. machinery mfg. Seat of Polish diets 14th-16th cent. Under Russian rule 1815-1919.

radon (Rn), radioactive gaseous element; at. no. 86, mass no. of most stable isotope 222. Formed as immediate disintegration product of radium; one of the inert gases.

Raeburn, Sir Henry (1756-1823), Scottish painter. Influenced by Reynolds, he portrayed many of the leading personalities of Scotland.

Raffles, Sir Thomas Stamford (1781-1826), British colonial official. Served with East India Co.; masterminded capture of Java from the Dutch (1811). Acquired Singapore (1819) and began its settlement.

ragged robin, *Lychnis flos-cuculi,* slender perennial herb native to Europe and N Asia. Pink flowers with ragged-looking petals.

Raglan, Fitzroy James Henry Somerset, 1st Baron (1788-1855), British army officer. Commanded the British expeditionary force in the Crimea, where he won the battle of Inkerman (1854); blamed for the failure to take Sevastopol.

ragtime, style of music using syncopated melodic lines over rigid march-like bass. Introduced in 1890s, became widely popular; lost popularity to jazz in 1920s. Principal composer of piano rags was Scott Joplin.

Common ragweed

ragweed, any of genus *Ambrosia* of plants of daisy family, native to North America.

ragworm, annelid worm of Nereidae family, order Polychaeta. Largely marine, living under stones or burrowing in mud and sand. Commonly used for bait.

ragwort, *see* GROUNDSEL.

Rahman [Putra], Tunku Abdul (1903-), Malaysian politician, PM (1964-70). First PM of Malaya at independence (1957). Advised formation of Malaysia federation (created 1963).

rail, marsh bird of Rallidae family, with short wings and tail. Species incl. water rail, corncrake, coot, moorhen.

railway, transport system running on fixed rails. Early railways were developed for use in mines. Important innovations incl. introduction of iron rails in 18th cent. and building of 1st locomotive to run on rails (Trevithick, 1804). Stockton-Darlington line (1825) was 1st to carry passengers regularly, and Liverpool-Manchester line (1830) was 1st to use steam locomotives exclusively. Railway had important part in development of W North America. In 20th cent., steam gave way to electric and diesel power. Modern developments incl. high-speed trains.

rain, drops of condensed atmospheric water vapour brought to earth by force of gravity. Varieties incl.: orographic, found in mountain areas; cyclonic, associated with depressions; convectional, common in equatorial regions. Rain can be artificially produced by 'seeding' clouds with silver iodide crystals.

rainbow, arc of colours of SPECTRUM seen in sky during rainy weather. Caused by reflection and refraction of sunlight through raindrops. Primary rainbow has red on outside, violet on inside. Secondary rainbow, in which colours are reversed, formed by 2 internal reflections.

Rainier III, orig. Rainier de Grimaldi (1923-), ruling prince of Monaco

(1949-). Married American film actress Grace Kelly (1956).

Rainier, Mount, peak of W Washington, US; highest in Cascade Range, at 4392 m (14,410 ft). In Mt. Rainier National Park.

Rais or **Retz, Gilles de Laval, Seigneur de** (1404-40), French soldier. Accompanied Joan of Arc in her campaigns. Confessed to abusing and murdering over 100 children. Hanged on witchcraft charge. Thought to be original Bluebeard.

raised beach, strip of flat land, formerly beach, raised above sea level by land rising or sea level falling. May be several, producing step-like landscape near coast.

raisin, sun-dried fruit of certain varieties of sweet white grape. Varieties incl. sultana and currant. California, Australia and Mediterranean region are main producers.

Rajasthan, state of NW India. Area *c* 342,000 sq km (132,000 sq mi); pop. 25,724,000; cap. Jaipur. Thar Desert in W borders on Pakistan. Mainly agric. economy; grain, cotton.

Rajputs, land-owning warrior caste, formerly dominant in Rajputana (roughly coextensive with Rajasthan, N India). After British conquest of India, many Rajput princes retained independent states.

Raleigh or **Ralegh, Sir Walter** (*c* 1552–1618), English courtier, navigator, writer; favourite of Elizabeth I. Made unsuccessful attempt to estab. 'Virginia' colony in North America. Introduced tobacco, potatoes into Britain. Under James I, convicted of treason and imprisoned in the Tower (1603), where he began his *History of the World.* Beheaded on original treason charge after failure of voyage to the Orinoco in search of gold (1616).

Raleigh, cap. of North Carolina, US. Pop. 469,000. Tobacco trade; electrical and textile industs. Cap. from 1788.

Ramadan, ninth month of Moslem year; period of daily fasting from sunrise to sunset. Commemorates first revelation of the Koran.

Ramayana, Indian epic. Written in Sanskrit *c* 3rd cent. BC, tells story of Rama (later identified as Vishnu). Immense popularity in India caused adaptation in most vernacular languages.

Rameau, Jean Philippe (1683-1764), French composer. Wrote pioneering treatises on theory of harmony. Noted for operas, opera-ballets, harpsichord pieces.

Rameses or **Ramses II** (d. 1225 BC), Egyptian king (1292-1225 BC). Fought against Hittites. Splendour of his reign marked by building of temples at Karnak and Thebes; temple at Abu Simbel bears 4 colossal figures of him.

Ramillies, village of C Belgium. Scene of French defeat (1706) by British, Dutch and Danish (under Marlborough) in War of Spanish Succession.

Ramsay, Allan (*c* 1685-1758), Scottish poet. Known for pastoral comedy, *The Gentle Shepherd* (1725), collections of Scots song ballads, *eg The Tea Table Miscellan* (1724-37).

Ramsey, [Arthur] Michael (1904- English churchman, archbishop Canterbury (1961-74).

Ramsgate, town of Isle of Thanet, Kent, S England. Pop. 39,000. Resort; fishin yachting. Hoverport.

Rand, The, *see* WITWATERSRAND.

Rangoon, cap. and main port of Burma, nea mouth of R. Rangoon. Pop. 1,586,00 Exports rice, teak, petroleum. Dominate by gold-spired Shwe Dagon pagoda, majo Buddhist shrine. Cap. of region from 175 Taken by British (1824, 1852); cap. of unite Burma (1886).

Ransome, Arthur (1884-1967), Englis author. Known for realistic children' adventure stories, *eg Swallows an Amazons* (1931).

Ranunculaceae, family of dicotyledonou plants with characteristic divided leave Incl. buttercup, anemone, delphinium.

Rapallo, town of Liguria, NW Italy. Po 21,000. Port, resort. Treaties between Ital and Yugoslavia (1920), Russia an Germany (1922) signed here.

rape, several plants of genus *Brassica,* esp *B. napus* and *B. campestris.* Widespread i N hemisphere. Grown extensively fo forage. Seeds yield edible oil and mustar substitute.

Raphael, archangel in Apocryphal OT boo of Tobit.

Raphael, real name Raffaello Sanzi (1483-1520), Italian painter. One of th creators of the High Renaissance, hi works are known for their calm perfectio of line and colour. Works incl. *Th Betrothal of the Virgin, Sistine Madonna* Executed Vatican murals, notably *Th School of Athens* and the *Disputa.*

rare earths, oxides of the lanthanide serie of elements; much alike in physical an chemical properties. Name also applied t LANTHANIDES themselves.

Rarotonga, main isl. of Cook Isls., SC Pacifi Ocean. Area 67 sq km (26 sq mi); mai town Avarua.

raspberry, various shrubs of genus *Rubus* o rose family. Grown in temperate region for soft, edible red or black berries.

Rasputin, Grigori Yefimovich (1872-1916), Russian monk. Gained power over the tsarina who believed he could cure her son, Alexis, of haemophilia. His corrupting influence over state affairs led to his murder by a group of noblemen.

rat, one of many long-tailed rodents of Muridae family, of worldwide distribution. Species incl. BLACK RAT, BROWN RAT.

ratel, nocturnal carnivorous mammal, genus *Mellivora,* with grey pelt above and black below. Resembles badger, but larger. Found in Africa, S Asia. Also called honey badger.

rationalism, in philosophy, doctrine that truth comes wholly from reason without aid from senses or intuition. Opposed to

EMPIRICISM. Implies belief in mind's ability to read the true order of the outside world. Exponents incl. Descartes, Leibnitz, Spinoza.

rational number, number expressed as a quotient of 2 integers; integers are rational numbers whose denominators are 1. Also called fraction.

Ratisbon, *see* REGENSBURG.

rattan, climbing palms of genera *Calamus* and *Daemonorops* native to tropical Asia. Long stems used for Malacca canes and in wickerwork.

Rattigan, Terence Mervyn (1911-1977), English playwright. Known for popular narrative dramas, *eg French without Tears* (1936), *The Winslow Boy* (1946).

rattlesnake, venomous New World snake of pit viper family. Loose horny tail segments produce characteristic rattle when shaken. Diamondback, *Crotalus adamanteus,* is largest and most dangerous.

Ravel, Maurice (1875-1937), French composer. Master of orchestration; works incl. ballet *Daphnis et Chloé,* orchestral pieces, *eg Bolero, Rhapsodie espagnole,* chamber music, piano pieces.

raven, *Corvus corax,* large bird of crow family, found on cliffs and mountains of N hemisphere. Glossy black plumage, large pointed bill.

Ravenna, city of Emilia-Romagna, NC Italy, cap. of Ravenna prov. Pop. 139,000. Indust. centre, agric. market. Cap. of Western Empire from AD 402, Ostrogothic cap. under Odovacer, Theodoric. Many Byzantine buildings, mosaics, *eg* church of St Vitale. Tomb of Dante.

Rawalpindi, city of N Pakistan. Pop. 615,000. Railway engineering, chemical mfg. Interim cap. of Pakistan from 1959 until completion of nearby Islamabad.

ray, any of various cartilaginous fish of order Hypotremata, with flattened body, huge pectoral fins and whip-like tail. Many species carry stinging organs. Families incl. sting rays, eagle rays and mantas or devil rays.

ray, in physics, straight line along which light or other radiation is regarded as propagating from its source. Name also applied to streams of particles emitted by radioactive substances or of electrons in vacuum tubes.

rayon, synthetic fibre made from cellulose, usually obtained from wood pulp. Two most important forms are made either by forcing cellulose acetate through fine holes and allowing solvent to evaporate in warm air or by VISCOSE PROCESS.

razorbill, *Alca torda,* seabird of auk family. Plumage black above, white below; bill crossed by white band. Nests colonially on Atlantic coasts.

razorshell, marine bivalve mollusc with long razor-shaped shell. Burrows rapidly in sand when disturbed. Species incl. *Solen marginatus.*

Reading, town and admin. hq. of Berkshire, S England, at confluence of Thames, Kennet rivers. Pop. 132,000. Railway jct.; biscuits; seed nurseries. Noted agric. work at univ. (1926).

Razorbill

Reagan, Ronald Wilson (1911-), American statesman, Republican president (1981-). Film actor before entering politics. Governor of California (1967-75).

realism, in medieval philosophy, theory that universal concepts have a real existence and are not merely conveniences of classification. Opposed to NOMINALISM. In scholasticism, St Thomas Aquinas is main exponent. Also has specialized use in modern epistemology to denote theory that objects exist independently of our perception, *ie* opposite of IDEALISM.

real number, any number expressible as a possibly infinite decimal. Those expressed by non-repeating decimal are called irrational (*eg* π); those expressed by repeating decimal are called rational (*eg* $\frac{1}{3} = 0.333....$).

Réaumur, René Antoine Ferchault de (1683-1757), French scientist. Invented alcohol thermometer and devised temperature scale in which boiling point of water is 80°. Worked on methods of making steel.

Rebellion of 1837, short-lived uprising in Upper and Lower Canada protesting against British admin. policies in Canada. Most of leaders, incl. W.L. MACKENZIE and L.J. Papineau, escaped to US.

Recife, Atlantic port of NE Brazil, cap. of Pernambuco state. Pop. 1,250,000. Sugar, coffee, cotton exports. Founded 1548.

Recklinghausen, city of W West Germany, in Ruhr. Pop. 122,000. Coalmining, iron founding, brewing.

Reconstruction, term applied to US post-Civil War era, during which programme to reorganize defeated states and reintegrate them into Union was adopted. To enforce Negro enfranchisement in South, Reconstruction Act (1867) passed by Congress estab. 5 military districts. Structure broke down as South was overrun by CARPETBAGGERS. Civil govt. restored by 1876.

recorder, wind instrument of flute type. Blown from end through whistle mouthpiece; usual sizes are descant or soprano, treble or alto, tenor and bass. Developed in medieval times and popular in 16th-18th cents. Revived in 20th cent.

rectifier, in electronics, device for converting alternating current into direct current. Types in use incl. thermionic valve and semiconductors.

rectum, in anatomy, terminal part of large intestine, opening into the anal canal.

Red, river of SC US. Flows 1967 km (1222 mi) from N Texas to Oklahoma border, then SE through Arkansas, Louisiana to join Mississippi R.

red algae, any of division Rhodophyta of ALGAE that contain a red pigment which masks the green chlorophyll. Distinguished by their sexual reproduction. Mostly found as shrubby masses in depths of warm oceans.

Red Army [Worker-Peasant Red Army], official name (1918-45) of Soviet Army.

red blood cell, *see* BLOOD.

Redbridge, bor. of NE Greater London, England. Pop. 227,000. Created 1965 from Ilford, Wanstead, Woodford, part of Dagenham (all in Essex).

Red Cross, international society for relief of suffering in time of war or disaster. International Committee of Red Cross founded (1863) on advocacy of J.H. Dunant (1828-1910). Delegates from 14 countries adopted Geneva Convention (1864), providing for neutrality of personnel treating wounded, *etc.* Over 100 national Red Cross societies now exist. Known as Red Crescent in Islamic countries. Awarded Nobel Peace Prize (1917, 1944, 1963).

red deer, *Cervus elaphus,* deer of temperate Europe and Asia. Branched antlers shed annually, reddish coat.

red giant, large star with relatively low surface temperature, between 10 and 100 times larger than Sun and *c* 100 times brighter. Most normal stars are believed to evolve into red giants as their hydrogen fuel is consumed.

Redgrave, Sir Michael (1908-), English actor. Played at Old Vic, notably in Shakespearian roles. Has also appeared in films. His daughter, **Vanessa Redgrave** (1937-), actress, known for stage, film roles.

Red Guard, *see* CULTURAL REVOLUTION.

red-hot poker, herb of genus *Kniphofia,* native to S Africa. Bright red or orange poker-shaped flowers.

Red Indians, *see* AMERICAN INDIANS.

Redmond, John Edward (1856-1918), Irish political leader. Leader of Irish Nationalists in Parliament after 1900. Supported Home Rule bill (1912). Opposed Easter Rebellion (1916); lost power to more radical Sinn Fein.

redpoll, *Acanthis flammea,* small grey-brown finch with crimson forehead. Found throughout N temperate areas.

Red River Rebellion (1869-70), revolt of Métis (French-Canadian halfbreeds) and Indians after transfer of Red River Settlement from Hudson's Bay Co. to Canada. Provisional govt. set up under Louis Riel (1844-85). Revolt collapsed when troops sent against it.

Red Sea, narrow sea between NE Africa and SW Arabia, in Great Rift Valley. Length *c* 2400 km (1500 mi). Linked to Mediterranean by Gulf of Suez and Suez Canal; to Gulf of Aden by Str. of Bab-el-Mandeb.

redshank, *Tringa totanus,* wading bird, related to sandpiper, of Eurasia and N Africa. Long red legs.

red shift, in astronomy, displacement of spectral lines towards longer wavelengths at red end of spectrum of light from distant galaxies. Explained as a DOPPLER effect due to recession of galaxies; leads to Hubble's law that velocity is proportional to distance of source.

redstart, *Phoenicurus phoenicurus,* European bird of Turdinae family, with red tail and black throat.

reduction, in chemistry, reaction opposite to oxidation. Originally denoted removal of oxygen from a substance or addition of hydrogen; now incl. reactions adding one or more electrons to atom or ion.

redwood, *see* SEQUOIA.

reed, several grasses, esp. of genus *Phragmites.* Cosmopolitan common reed *P. communis,* is tall, stout aquatic grass. Dried stems used in thatching.

reed instrument, musical instrument in which sound derives from vibrating reed. In double reed instruments, *eg* oboe, bassoon, wind is blown between 2 reeds. Clarinet has single reed laid against wind aperture.

reed mace, *see* CATTAIL.

re-entry, return of missile or space vehicle into Earth's atmosphere. Enormous quantities of heat are generated by friction between molecules of air and speeding vehicle; a heat shield is designed to give protection from this heat.

referendum, submission of an issue of public importance (*eg* proposed legislation) to the direct vote of the electorate. An **iniative** is the right of a group of citizens to introduce a matter for legislation either to legislature or to referendum. Switzerland pioneered these techniques. Referendums have been used in UK on Common Market issue (1975) and on proposed Scottish and Welsh assemblies (1979).

refining, process by which impurities are removed from metals, petroleum, sugar, *etc.* Petroleum is refined by fractional distillation and catalytic cracking; metals by electrolysis (*eg* for copper), amalgamation with mercury (*eg* for silver), leaching with cyanide (*eg* for gold).

reflex, in physiology, involuntary response to a stimulus, *eg* a sneeze, determined b nervous impulses. Stimulated receptor area causes sensory neurons to transmit nervous impulses to nerve cells in brain and spinal cord; these in turn transmit impulses to motor neurons which determine action of muscles, glands, *etc*.

Reformation, religious revolution in W Europe in 16th cent. Began as reform movement in RC church, evolved into doctrines of Protestantism. Begun in Germany by LUTHER and in Geneva by CALVIN. KNOX introduced Calvinism to Scotland. In England, Henry VIII rejected papal control and formed Church of England.

Reformation, Catholic, reform movement in RC church in 16th cent. as response to Protestant REFORMATION; popularly known as Counter-Reformation. Attempted to reform abuses within Church in order to protect traditional Roman Catholicism against Lutheranism. Implemented by Council of Trent (1545).

Reform Bills, in British history, legislation passed to liberalize House of Commons' representation. Whigs' **1832** bill enfranchised large indust. towns previously unrepresented, abolished numerous 'rotten boroughs' and extended vote to middle-class men. Derby-Disraeli's **1867** bill more than doubled franchise by giving vote to working men in towns. Gladstone's **1884** bill relaxed rural qualifications.

refraction, in physics, change in direction of ray of light passing from one medium to another; caused by light travelling at different velocities in different media. Snell's law states that ratio of sine of angle of incidence to sine of angle of refraction is a constant called refractive index of that pair of media. The refractive index of a medium is usually given in relation to a vacuum.

refrigeration, process of reducing temperature of substances. In refrigerators, vaporized refrigerant, usually ammonia or Freon, is compressed and forced through a condenser, where it loses heat and liquefies. It vaporizes in coils of refrigeration compartment and draws heat from materials placed there. Refrigerant returns to compressor and cycle is repeated.

Regency, in British history, last 9 years (1811-20) of reign of George III. Because of king's periodic insanity, govt. conducted in name of Prince of Wales, later George IV.

Regensburg (Eng., Ratisbon), city of SE West Germany, at confluence of Danube and Regen. Pop. 132,000. River port, railway jct. Roman *Castra Regina*; episcopal see from 739. Prosperous medieval centre until 15th cent.

Reggio di Calabria (anc. *Rhegium*), city of SW Italy, on Str. of Messina, cap. of Reggio di Calabria prov. Pop. 179,000. Port, resort, agric. market.

Reggio nell'Emilia, city of Emilia-Romagna, NC Italy, cap. of Reggio nell'Emilia prov. Pop. 130,000. Agric., indust. centre, aero engines.

Regina, prov. cap. of Saskatchewan, Canada; on Wascana Creek. Pop. 151,000. Railway jct., wheat trade centre; agric. machinery, car mfg., oil refining. Founded 1882. Cap. of Northwest Territs. (1883-1905).

Regulus, Marcus Atilius (d. *c* 250 BC), Roman soldier. In 1st Punic War, invaded Africa, but was defeated and captured by Carthaginians (255). Sent to Rome to propose peace, but advised continuing war. Returned to Carthage as promised, where he was put to death.

Reich, Wilhelm (1897-1957), Austrian psychiatrist, resident in US after 1939. Works, incl. *The Function of the Orgasm* (1927), stress the importance of frequent sexual release to avoid neurosis. Ideas on therapeutic properties of all-pervading orgone energy led to imprisonment, in which state he died.

Reichstag, name given to lower chamber of federal German legislature (1871-1945). Fire in Reichstag building (1933) gave Hitler pretext to suppress Communists.

Reign of Terror (1793-4), final period of French Revolution. Committee of Public Safety, led by Robespierre, controlled France; effected ruthless elimination of counter-revolutionaries (*c* 2500 guillotined). Ended with overthrow of Robespierre by National Convention.

Reims, *see* RHEIMS.

reincarnation or **metempsychosis,** belief common to several religions that, after death, soul of human being enters another body, human or animal. In Hinduism and Buddhism, moral conduct determines quality of subsequent incarnations. Also occurs in Greek thought, *eg* in Pythagoras, Plato.

Reindeer

reindeer, *Rangifer tarandus,* large deer of Arctic regions of Europe and Asia. Both sexes have long branched antlers. Can be domesticated; milk, flesh and skin valued. Caribou is related species. Numbers greatly reduced by hunting.

Reith, John Charles Walsham, 1st Baron Reith of Stonehaven (1889-1971), British public official. First director-general of British Broadcasting Corporation. Stamped BBC with own personality, ideals.

relative humidity, measure of moisture of atmosphere. Equals ratio of mass of water vapour per unit volume of air to maximum mass of water vapour same volume of air could contain at same temperature; usually expressed as percentage.

relativity theory, physical theory of space, time, energy and gravitation formulated by Einstein. Special theory of 1905 is limited to observers in state of uniform motion relative to each other. It assumes that the laws of physics take same form for all observers and that speed of light is same for all observers, irrespective of their own motion. Its consequences incl. principle that MASS and ENERGY are interchangeable, that it is impossible to travel at speed faster than that of light and that measurement of time depends on observer's motion (there is no absolute time). General theory of 1916 deals with observers not in state of uniform motion and is a geometric interpretation of gravitation. Its consequences incl. fact that light rays are deflected towards large gravitating bodies.

relay, electrical, device by which variations in one electric circuit control switching on and off of current in another circuit. May be mechanical switch operated by electromagnet; used in telegraphy and electrical control.

relics, objects associated with Jesus or saint, venerated in RC and Eastern Orthodox churches. Medieval traffic in relics led to their cult being condemned by Protestant reformers.

religion, expression of belief in powers higher than man. Often involves attempts to explain origin and nature of universe, evolution of techniques to make the inexplicable more acceptable. Ethical concepts were introduced by BUDDHISM, JUDAISM, CHRISTIANITY, ISLAM. Religions are divided into 'revealed' *eg* Christianity where Jesus revealed word of God, and 'natural' *eg* Buddhism which is result of human speculation alone. *See* POLYTHEISM, MONOTHEISM.

Rembrandt [Harmensz van Rijn], (1606-69) Dutch painter, etcher. Estab. himself as successful portrait painter with *Anatomy Lesson of Dr Tulp*. Business declined with death of his wife in 1642; declared bankrupt 1656. His later series of portraits, esp. self-portraits, are masterpieces of psychological insight.

Remonstrants, followers of ARMINIUS who presented a remonstrance in 1610 setting forth their differences from the Calvinism of the Dutch Reformed Church. Originally suppressed, recognized as independent church in 1795.

Remus, *see* ROMULUS.

Renaissance (Fr.,=rebirth), period of cultural and intellectual revival in W Europe (14th-16th cent.). Originated in Italy, where scholarship was stimulated by classical manuscripts, foundation of libraries and academies. Under patronage of popes and nobles, *eg* Medici, men of genius were encouraged to create works of an individuality and humanism unknown in Middle Ages. Study of classical models influenced architecture of Alberti, Brunelleschi; discoveries of laws of perspective by Donatello, Masaccio, *etc*, made painting, sculpture more realistic. Later masters incl. Leonardo da Vinci, Michelangelo, Raphael. Learning spread to other countries in 15th cent., hastened by invention of printing. Other major Renaissance figures incl. Josquin Des Prés in music, Erasmus in humanism, Machiavelli in politics, Cervantes and Shakespeare in literature.

Renfrewshire, former county of WC Scotland, now in Strathclyde region. Hilly in W, SE; elsewhere lowland. Dairying; oats, potatoes. Industs. incl. engineering, chemicals, textile mfg., whisky distilling, centred in Paisley, Greenock (shipbuilding). Co. town was **Renfrew,** port and former royal burgh on R. Clyde. Pop. 19,000. Engineering indust.

Reni, Guido (1575-1642), Italian painter of Bolognese school. Early exponent of Classicism.

Rennes, city of NW France, at confluence of Ille and Vilaine, cap. of Ille-et-Vilaine dept. Pop. 213,000. Agric., trade centre, textile mfg.; univ. (1735). Hist. cap. of Brittany.

rennet, substance extracted from membrane lining stomach of unweaned mammals, esp. calves. Contains enzyme rennin which curdles milk; used to make cheese and junkets.

Reno, resort of W Nevada, on Truckee R. Pop. 145,000. Famous for legal gambling, quick divorces. Univ. (1874).

Renoir, Pierre Auguste (1841-1919), French artist. Leading impressionist, he was a noted figure painter. Later returned to more classical style, devoting himself to well-rounded nudes. His son, **Jean Renoir** (1894-1979), was film director. Works incl. *La Grande Illusion* and *La Règle du jeu*.

reparations, payment made by defeated nation to victorious, to compensate for material losses incurred in war. After WWI, Dawes Plan (1924) awarded loan to Germany which had fallen behind in payments to Allies. Young Plan (1929) sought to ensure payment by mortgaging German railways and estab. Bank for International Settlements. After WWII, payment by Germany to Allies was to be effected by confiscation of assets and equipment.

Representatives, House of, *see* HOUSE OF REPRESENTATIVES.

repression, *see* DEFENCE MECHANISM.

reproduction, process by which all living organisms produce new individuals. May be sexual or asexual. Asexual reproduction found in plants and lower animals; simplest form is by division of single cell (fission).

Sexual reproduction involves union of male and female gamete to form a zygote.

Reptilia (reptiles), class of cold-blooded scaly-skinned vertebrates. Mainly terrestrial, with some aquatic varieties; egg-laying. Dominant animal group in Mesozoic period; fossils show links between birds, mammals. Incl. turtles, tortoises, lizards, snakes, crocodiles, tuatara.

republic, state or nation in which supreme power rests in electorate and is exercised by elected representatives. Govt. of republic may be centralized (*eg* France), or federated (*eg* US).

Republican Party, in US, one of the two major political parties. Hist. linked with Hamilton's Federalists. Founded (1854) in opposition to slavery, consolidated with Lincoln's election (1860). Held power during RECONSTRUCTION, became party of business interest in late 19th cent.; T. ROOSEVELT split party (1912). Conservative policies resulted in blame for Depression (1929), after which held presidency 3 times (1953-61, 1969-77, 1981-).

Requiem, in RC church, Mass for the repose of the souls of the dead. Consists of 8 sections, derived in part from ordinary Mass. Has inspired notable musical settings, *eg* by Mozart, Verdi, Fauré.

resin, substance exuded from various plants, esp. pines and firs. Used in varnish, lacquer and medicines. Synthetic resins are used extensively in plastics indust.

resistance, electrical, property of conductor by which it resists flow of electric current, and converts part of the electrical energy into heat. From Ohm's law, resistance is measured by ratio of potential difference between ends of conductor to size of current flowing.

resolving power, in optics, measure of smallest distance between 2 points in image of an optical system (microscope or telescope) when the 2 points can be distinguished as separate.

resonance, in physics, sympathetic vibration of body in response to vibrations of some external source. Effect is greatest when natural frequency of body is reached by the exciting source.

Respighi, Ottorino (1879-1936), Italian composer. Produced bright, lyrical orchestral music, *eg Fountains of Rome*.

respiration, process by which living organisms take in oxygen from air or water, use it to oxidize carbohydrates, fats, *etc*, with subsequent release of energy, and give off products of oxidation, esp. carbon dioxide. Process describing taking in of oxygen and giving out of carbon dioxide is more properly called breathing.

Restoration, in English history, name given to re-estab. of monarchy on accession in 1660 of Charles II following collapse of Protectorate. Name also applies to entire period of Charles' reign.

Restoration drama, name given to 2 types of play popular in England in late 17th cent.: the heroic play, partly inspired by French classical tragedy, *eg* Dryden's *Conquest of Granada*, and witty, often immoral comedies of manners, *eg* Congreve's *The Way of the World*.

resurrection, rising from death to life. Used esp. for rising of Jesus from the tomb and for rising of all dead at Last Judgment. Belief in resurrection of body also a tenet of Moslem belief.

retina, membrane lining back cavity of eyeball. Light-sensitive nerve endings (rods and cones) convey impulses to the brain via the optic nerve. Visual purple in rods makes them sensitive to dim light, but it is inactivated by bright light. Cones function in bright light and are responsible for colour vision and detailed vision.

Retz, Gilles de, *see* RAIS, GILLES DE.

Réunion, isl. in WC Indian Ocean, overseas region of France. Area *c* 2510 sq km (970 sq mi); pop. 496,000; cap. St Denis. Of volcanic origin, with one active volcano; rises to 3069 m (10,069 ft). Sugar cane leading crop; exports sugar, rum. Settled by French in 1642.

Reuter, Paul Julius, Baron de, orig. Israel Beer Josaphat (1816-99) British news agency founder-owner, b. Germany. Founded Reuters news agency.

Reval, *see* TALLINN.

Revelation, Apocalyptic book of NT, traditionally written by St John the Divine. Consists of prophetic vision of triumph of God and martyrs over evil.

Revere, Paul (1735-1818), American silversmith. Famous for ride (1775) from Charlestown to Lexington to warn Massachusetts patriots of advance by British troops at outbreak of American Revolution.

Revolution of 1848, series of revolts in Europe provoked by February Revolution in France, in which Louis Philippe was overthrown and republic estab. In Germany, popular uprising for united country quelled by Prussian army. In Hungary, attempts to estab. independence from Austria were unsuccessful; led to overthrow of Metternich. In Italy, 1st attempts to expel Austrians and unite country (*see* RISORGIMENTO) were defeated.

revolver, PISTOL with cylindrical breech rotated mechanically and bored with chambers for bullets which are fired in succession. Developed by Samuel Colt (1836).

Reykjavik, cap. of Iceland, on Faxa Bay. Pop. 82,000. Admin., cultural centre. Port, fishing indust. (esp. cod, herring), textiles, publishing; univ. (1911). Founded 874. Natural hot water supply from nearby springs. Lutheran, RC cathedrals.

Reynolds, Sir Joshua (1723-92), English painter. First president of the Royal Academy (1769); his *Discourses* enshrine his advocacy of the Grand Manner. Painted numerous portraits.

Rhaeto-Romanic, Romance group of dialects in Italic branch of Indo-European family. Incl. Romansh, Ladin, Friulian. Former is one of four official languages of

Switzerland, latter two spoken in Italian Tyrol, NE Italy.

Rhea, in Greek myth, a Titan; wife and sister of CRONUS. Helped Zeus overthrow Cronus.

rhea, any of Rheidae family of flightless South American birds, similar to ostrich. Three-toed feet, partially feathered head and neck.

Rhee, Syngman (1875-1965), Korean statesman. Leader of drive for independence during Chinese, Japanese occupations. President of South Korea (1948-60) until exiled. Rule noted for corruption and repression.

Rheims (*Reims*), city of Champagne, NE France, on R. Vesle. Pop. 196,000. Centre of Champagne wine indust. Textile mfg.; univ. (1547). Coronation place of many French kings. Cathedral (13th cent.) badly damaged in WWI.

rhenium (Re), hard metallic element; at. no. 75, at. wt. 186.2. Very rare; found in molybdenum ores. Used in thermocouples and as a catalyst. Discovered 1925.

rheostat, instrument introduced into electric circuit to vary its resistance and control flow of current. Used to regulate brightness of electric lights, *etc.*

rhesus factor (Rh factor), protein present in red blood cells of 85% of people. Those having factor are said to be Rh positive, those without Rh negative. Transfusion of blood from Rh positive person to Rh negative person causes antibodies to form in latter's blood, resulting in agglutination of red blood cells. An Rh negative mother who has a positive baby may experience problems with later pregnancies, unless suitably treated.

rhesus monkey, *Macaca mulatta,* light brown long-haired macaque of SE Asia.

rhetoric, *see* ORATORY.

rheumatic fever, acute inflammatory disease of lining and valves of the heart and of larger joints. Usually affects children and adolescents. Cause unknown, but is always preceded by infection with haemolytic streptococci.

rheumatoid arthritis, *see* ARTHRITIS.

Rh factor, *see* RHESUS FACTOR.

Rhine (Ger. *Rhein,* Dutch *Rijn),* river of WC Europe. Flows 1320 km (820 mi) from SE Switzerland through W West Germany, Netherlands, joining R. Meuse before entering North Sea at Hook of Holland. Tributaries incl. Main, Moselle, Neckar. Forms parts of several national borders, esp. Franco-German. W Europe's main waterway, navigable below Basle; heavy barge traffic; linked to Ruhr indust. area. Vineyards; tourism in Rhine Gorge (Bingen to Bonn). Former E frontier of Roman Gaul; picturesque medieval castles.

Rhineland, area of W West Germany, on both sides of R. Rhine. Incl. parts of North Rhine-Westphalia, Rhineland-Palatinate, Hessen, Baden Württemberg. Occupied by Allies after WWI; demilitarized under treaty of Locarno within 50 km E of Rhine. Refortified by Hitler from 1936.

Rhine

Rhineland-Palatinate, *see* PALATINATE.

Black rhinoceros

rhinoceros, any of Rhinocerotidae family of massive thick-skinned herbivorous mammals of tropical Africa and Asia. One or two upright horns composed of matted hair on snout. Species incl. Indian rhinoceros, *Rhinoceros unicornis,* with 1 horn and black African rhinoceros, *Diceros bicornis,* with 2 horns. Numbers greatly reduced by hunting.

rhizome, creeping stem lying at or under the surface of soil. Differs from root in having scale leaves and leaves or shoots near tip. Produces roots from underside. Unlike root, does not die if cut and may become new plant. Rhizomatous plants incl. common iris, ginger.

Rhode Island, New England state of US. Area 3144 sq km (1214 sq mi); pop. 937,000 cap. Providence. Smallest US state, named after isl. in Narragansett Bay. Mainly low lying; important farming esp. poultry, fishing, tourist, textile industs. Founded (1636). One of 13 original states.

Rhodes, Cecil John (1853-1902), British capitalist, colonial administrator. Acquired fortune through control of Kimberley diamond mines. As part of plan to estab British rule in Africa from Cape to Cairo advised annexation of Bechuanaland (1885), then formed British South Africa

Co. (1889) to exploit area known later as Rhodesia. PM of Cape Colony (1890-5), supported British in Transvaal. Resigned over complicity in JAMESON Raid.

Rhodes (*Rhodos*), isl. of Greece, in SE Aegean Sea, largest of Dodecanese. Area 1404 sq km (542 sq mi); main town Rhodes. Ancient Rhodes *fl* 4th-3rd cent. BC, built 'Colossus of Rhodes' (destroyed by earthquake 224 BC). Held by Knights Hospitallers from 1309 to 1522, when taken by Turks. Occupied by Italy 1912, ceded to Greece 1947.

Rhodesia, *see* ZIMBABWE.

rhodium (Rh), hard metallic element of the platinum group; at. no. 45, at. wt. 102.91. Occurs with and resembles platinum. Resists corrosion; used in alloys, electrical contacts, thermocouples and as a catalyst.

rhododendron, genus of trees and shrubs of heath family, native to Asia but widely cultivated in N temperate regions. Mainly evergreen with red, purple or white flowers. *See* AZALEA.

Rhodope Mountains, range of N Greece and S Bulgaria. Runs NW-SE, rising to 2924 m (9596 ft) in Rila Mts., Bulgaria.

Rhondda, town of Glamorgan, S Wales. Pop. 89,000. Coalmining; light industs.

Rhône, river of W Switzerland and SE France. Flows *c* 810 km (505 mi) from Rhône glacier (Switzerland) via L. Geneva, Lyons, Avignon to delta (Camargue) on Mediterranean. H.e.p. from Génissiat Dam (1948). Vine, fruit, olive growing in fertile valley. Canal link with Rhine. Rhône-Saône corridor a hist. route between N and S France.

rhubarb, any of genus *Rheum* of perennial, large-leaved plants with edible reddish stalks, esp. *R. rhaponticum* and *R. hybridum*. Leaves of all varieties contain poisonous oxalic acid, stalks yield cathartic extract.

Rhum or **Rum,** isl. of Inner Hebrides, W Scotland. Area 109 sq km (42 sq mi). Mainly mountainous. Nature reserve.

rhyme or **rime,** identity or similarity of sound of final accented syllables of words, esp. in vowels and succeeding consonants. Used in poetry esp. at line endings to form audible patterns. First became popular in medieval Latin poetry.

rhyolite, fine-grained acid volcanic rock. Composition similar to granite, but richer in silica. Occurs as highly viscous lava.

rhythm, in music, pattern produced by relative stress and duration of notes. Its use to produce a sense of uplift in both performer and listener is very important.

rib, any of the arched bones attached to the vertebral column and enclosing the chest cavity. In man, there are 12 pairs of ribs, attached to the thoracic vertebrae.

Ribbentrop, Joachim von (1893-1946), German diplomat. As Hitler's foreign minister (1938-45), helped negotiate Russo-German Non-aggression Pact (1939). Hanged as war criminal.

Ribble, river of NW England. Flows 121 km (75 mi) from Pennines via Preston to Irish Sea.

ribbon worm, *see* NEMERTEA.

Ribera, José or **Jusepe** (1591-1652), Spanish painter. Spent his working life in Naples; work is characterized by dramatic contrasts in light and shade and an often gruesome naturalism.

riboflavin or **vitamin B_2,** vitamin of B group found in yeast, liver, milk, *etc.* Lack of riboflavin in diet causes stunted growth, loss of hair, skin lesions, *etc.*

Ricardo, David (1772-1823), English economist. Wrote influential *Principles of Political Economy and Taxation* (1817) setting out theory correlating rent, profit, wages, taxation.

rice, grain of cereal grass *Oryza sativa*. Grown extensively in tropical and subtropical regions of China, India, Japan, Indonesia and SE Asia, which produce *c* 90% of world's rice. Also cultivated in US, Egypt and Europe. Rich in carbohydrate; brown rice, retaining outer husk, has more protein and vitamin value than polished white rice.

Richard [I] the Lion Heart (1157-99), king of England (1189-99). Twice rebelled against father, Henry II, before accession. Leader of 3rd Crusade with PHILIP II of France (1190); helped capture Acre (1191). Captured in Austria during return to England; turned over to custody of Emperor Henry VI and released on payment of great ransom (1194). Killed while fighting Philip in France.

Richard II (1367-1400), king of England (1377-99). Son of Edward the Black Prince, effectively quelled PEASANTS' REVOLT (1381). Power threatened by nobles led by Gloucester until John of Gaunt returned from Spain (1389). Had Gloucester murdered (1397). Deposed after rebellion led by Henry Bolingbroke (HENRY IV). Imprisoned at Pontefract where he died.

Richard III (1452-85), king of England (1483-5). On death of brother Edward IV, he seized Edward's heir, Edward V, and assumed the crown when Parliament declared Edward illegitimate. Suspected of arranging murder of Edward and his brother after he had them imprisoned in the Tower. Defeated and killed at Bosworth by Henry Tudor (HENRY VII).

Richardson, Sir Ralph David (1902-), English actor. Noted roles incl. Sir Toby Belch in *Twelfth Night*; film *Oh! What a Lovely War!*

Richardson, Samuel (1689-1761), English novelist. Helped develop novel form with epistolary works, *eg Pamela* (1740), *Clarissa* (1748), which deal with moral struggles in sentimental terms.

Richelieu, Armand Jean du Plessis, Duc de (1585-1642), French statesman, churchman. Created cardinal 1622. With help of regent Marie de' Medici, became chief minister to Louis XIII (1624) and virtual ruler of France. Sought to reduce Habsburg power by aiding Protestants in Thirty Years War, then brought France into war as ally of Sweden (1635). In France, strengthened royal power to detriment of Huguenots and nobility.

Richmond, cap. of Virginia, US; at head of navigation on James R. Pop. 585,000. Financial, cultural, shipping centre. Tobacco, grain, coal exports; tobacco processing. Settled 1637; cap. from 1779. Cap. of Confederacy during Civil War.

Richmond-upon-Thames, bor. of SW Greater London, England, on R. Thames. Pop. 164,000. Formerly Sheen, created 1965 from Barnes, Twickenham mun. bors. Has Kew Gardens; Hampton Court Palace.

Richter, Johann Paul Friedrich, pseud. Jean Paul (1763-1825), German author. Romantic novels, often humorous, incl. *Hesperus* (1795), *Quintus Fixlein* (1796).

Richthofen, Manfred, Baron von (1892-1918), German airman, known as the 'Red Baron'. Credited with shooting down 80 aircraft during WWI. Died in action.

rickets, disease resulting from vitamin D deficiency, affecting calcium metabolism and causing softening and bending of bones. Caused by insufficient exposure to sunlight or inadequate diet.

Ridley, Nicholas (*c* 1500-55), English clergyman. Worked with Cranmer on Book of Common Prayer; became bishop of London (1550). After accession of Mary I, burned at stake with Latimer.

Riel, Louis, *see* RED RIVER REBELLION.

Riemann, Georg Friedrich Bernhard (1826-66), German mathematician. Riemannian geometry, which describes non-uniform space, has important applications in relativity theory.

Rienzi, Cola di (*c* 1313-54), Italian political leader. Estab. (1347) short-lived Roman republic, but was soon expelled under papal pressure. Returned (1353) to Rome, but his dictatorial rule ended in his murder.

Rif or **Riff, Er,** mountain region of N Morocco; extends from Ceuta (W) to Melilla (E). Rises to over 2450 m/8000 ft. Stronghold of Berber tribes who revolted against French and Spanish rule (1921-6).

rifle, FIREARM with spiral-grooved barrel which imparts spin to bullet. Usually fired from shoulder.

rift valley, natural trough formed by sinking of land between two approximately parallel faults. Associated with volcanic activity. Examples incl. Great Rift Valley of E Africa, Rhine valley.

Riga, city of WC USSR, cap. of Latvian SSR; on Gulf of Riga. Pop. 835,000. Port; exports timber, flax, paper; indust. centre. Founded 12th cent., became centre of Livonian Knights and prosperous Hanseatic trading town. Held by Poland, Sweden and finally Russia (1710). Cap. of independent Latvia (1919-40) until Soviet occupation.

Rights, Bill of, in British history, statute (1689) confirming rights of Parliament and the people previously violated during reign of James II. Estab. political supremacy of Parliament. Embodied terms by which William and Mary succeeded to throne and provided for Protestant succession.

Rights of Man, Declaration of the, hist. French document, drafted 1789; became preamble of French Constitution of 1791. Influenced by Rousseau and American Declaration of Independence, it asserted equality of all men, sovereignty of the people, inalienable rights of the individual to 'liberty, property, security'.

right whale, whalebone whale of Balaenidae family, found in polar waters. Toothless, with large head. Species incl. Greenland whale, *Balaena mysticetus,* reaching lengths of 21 m/70 ft. Now very rare.

rigor mortis, progressive stiffening of muscles of body which occurs several hours after death (depending on atmospheric conditions and state of body). Ended by onset of decomposition after *c* 24 hrs.

Rig-Veda, *see* VEDA.

Rijeka-Sušak (Ital. *Fiume*), town of Croatia, NW Yugoslavia, on the Adriatic. Pop 161,000. Country's largest port; indust centre, oil refining, shipbuilding; tourism. Hungarian from 1779, seized (1919) by D'Annunzio; annexed (1924) by Italy, ceded (1947) to Yugoslavia. Sušak, E suburb Yugoslav from 1919. Roman arch cathedral (14th cent.).

Rilke, Rainer Maria (1875-1926), German poet, b. Prague. Known for intense visionary lyrics, *eg Duino Elegies* (1923) *Sonnets to Orpheus* (1923). Also wrote novel *The Notebooks of Malte Laurids Brigge* (1910).

Rimbaud, [Jean Nicolas] Arthur (1854-91) French poet. Known for decadent verse written between 15 and 19. Intimate of VERLAINE. Works incl. 'Le bateau ivre' (1871), prose piece detailing his spiritual development *Une saison en enfer* (1873).

Rimini (anc. *Ariminum*), city of Emilia Romagna, EC Italy, on Adriatic Sea. Pop 127,000. Port, resort, railway jct.

Rimsky-Korsakov, Nikolai Andreyevich (1844-1908), Russian composer, one of 'the Five'. Music, strongly influenced by folk tunes, displays brilliant orchestration. Works incl. orchestral piece *Scheherezade* opera *Le Coq d'or.* Revised Borodin's *Prince Igor,* Mussorgsky's *Boris Godunov.*

Ring of the Nibelung, *see* NIBELUNGENLIED.

ring ouzel, *Turdus torquatus,* European bird of thrush family. Male has black plumage with white band on chest.

ringworm, contagious skin disease caused by infection with certain microscopic fungi. Characterized by formation of ring shaped eruptive patches and itching. Common sites are between the toes (athlete's foot), scalp and groin.

Río Bravo, *see* RIO GRANDE.

Rio de Janeiro, major port of Brazil, cap. of Guanabara state, on SW shore of Guanabara Bay. Pop. 4,858,000. Transport and communication centre. Coffee, sugar, iron ore exports; flour milling, sugar refining, railway engineering. Touris

Ring ouzel

attractions incl. Sugar Loaf Mt., Corcovado peak (with statue of Christ), Copacabana beach. Has shanty towns on adjacent hills. First settled by French; Portuguese occupation 1567; cap. of Brazil (1763-1960). Seat of Univ. of Brazil (1920).

Río de la Plata, *see* PLATA, RÍO DE LA.

Rio Grande (Mex. *Río Bravo*), river of S US. Flows S 3000 km (1885 mi) from SW Colorado through New Mexico, then SE along Texas-Mexico border to Gulf of Mexico.

Río Muni, mainland area of Equatorial Guinea. Area 26,000 sq km (10,040 sq mi); main town Bata. Narrow coastal plain, interior plateau. Hot, wet climate.

Riot Act, legislation passed (1714) in face of widespread rioting over accession of George I. Under its terms, if an unlawful assembly of 12 or more persons fails to disperse within an hour of reading of prescribed proclamation by a magistrate, those present are guilty of felony and may be dispersed by force.

Ripon, town of North Yorkshire, N England. Pop. 11,000. Cathedral (12th-16th cent.).

Risorgimento (Ital., = resurgence), movement in 19th-cent. Italy for liberation and national unification. Despite failure of 1848-9 insurrections under MAZZINI and CAVOUR, French military intervention against Austria and Garibaldi's conquest of Naples and Sicily enabled Victor Emmanuel of Sardinia to become 1st king of Italy (1861). Unification completed with acquisition of Venetia (1866) and Papal States (1870).

river, natural stream of fresh water draining into sea, lake, inland depression or another river. May flow only intermittently in arid regions.

Rivera, Diego (1886-1957), Mexican artist. Influenced by Communism, depicted Mexican social problems on large murals on public buildings.

Riverina, area of S New South Wales, Australia, between Murray, Murrumbidgee and Lachlan rivers. Fertile, irrigated; produces wheat, sheep, fruit, rice.

Riviera, narrow coastal strip extending from Hyères (SE France) to La Spezia (NW Italy). Italian Riviera divided by Genoa into E and W sections; French Riviera also called 'Côte d'Azur'. Many fashionable resorts *eg* Cannes, Monte Carlo. Vine, flower, fruit growing; fishing.

Riyadh, cap. of Saudi Arabia. Pop. 667,000. Oasis trade centre of Nejd region. Centre of Wahabi Islam since 19th cent.

Rizzio, David (*c* 1533-66), Italian musician, favourite of Mary Queen of Scots. Became Mary's personal secretary. Influence with Mary aroused enmity of group of nobles, incl. her husband, Darnley; stabbed to death at their command.

RNA or **ribonucleic acid,** fundamental genetic material found esp. in protein-making ribosomes in cytoplasm of cells. Molecule consists of long chains of ribose sugar, phosphate groups and nitrogenous bases. One form, messenger RNA, whose synthesis is controlled by DNA in cell nucleus, migrates to ribosomes where it builds up protein molecules. Another form, transfer RNA, arranges sequence of amino acids which determine structure of a particular protein to be built by messenger RNA.

roach, *Rutilus rutilus,* freshwater fish of carp family, found in N Europe. Silvery white with reddish fins.

road, man-made semi-permanent route for wheeled vehicles. Constructed in ancient Persia *c* 500 BC; art developed by Romans, many of whose examples still exist. European road-building neglected from fall of Roman Empire until 19th cent. when TELFORD and MCADAM improved surfaces.

roadrunner, *Geococcyx californianus,* long-tailed, crested desert bird found in SW US. Poor flier, runs with great speed.

robbery, in law, illegal taking of another's property from his person or in his immediate presence by use of violence or intimidation.

Robbia, Luca della (*c* 1399-1482), Florentine sculptor. Head of family workshop which produced glazed terracotta sculpture.

Robert [I] the Bruce (1274-1329), king of Scotland (1306-29). Fought to recover Scottish territ. from English. Forced to flee after defeat at Methven (1307). Successfully resumed campaign after death of Edward I, ultimately defeating Edward II at Bannockburn (1314). Treaty of Northampton (1328) acknowledged Scottish independence.

Robert II (1316-90), king of Scotland (1371-90). Grandson of Robert the Bruce. Founder of the house of Stuart. Regent during uncle David II's minority, later rebelled (1363) when David named Edward III of England his successor (Robert had been granted succession by decree of 1318). Imprisoned, but released to succeed David.

Robert III (*c* 1340-1406), king of Scotland (1390-1406). Succeeded father Robert II. During reign, real power was in hands of brother Robert, earl of Fife, later Duke of Albany. Reign marked by quarrel between Albany and Robert's son David, Duke of

Rothesay; ended with David's mysterious death (1402). Succeeded by other son James I.

Roberts of Kandahar, Frederick Sleigh Roberts, 1st Earl (1832-1914), British field marshall. Successful campaign in Afghanistan (1879) incl. relief of Kandahar. Commander-in-chief (1899-1900) against Boers in South Africa.

Robespierre, Maximilien François Marie Isidore de (1758-94), French revolutionary. Jacobin leader, member of Committee of Public Safety, which instituted Reign of Terror (1793-4). Ousted rivals Hébert and Danton, exercised dictatorial power through Revolutionary Tribunal. Overthrown by the Convention, tried and guillotined.

robin, *Erithacus rubecula,* songbird of thrush family found in Europe and W Asia. Brownish plumage with orange-red face and breast.

Robin Hood, legendary hero of medieval England. Idealized outlaw, lived in Sherwood Forest with Little John, Friar Tuck, Maid Marian and his band. Robbed the rich to help the poor.

Robinson, [William] Heath (1872-1944), English graphic artist. Known for his humorous drawings of complex machinery performing simple tasks.

robot, mechanical device constructed to perform human tasks.

Rob Roy, real name Robert Macgregor (1671-1734), Scottish outlaw. Member of proscribed Macgregor clan, led cattle-stealing raids against duke of Montrose. Submitted voluntarily; sentenced to transportation, was pardoned (1727).

Robson, Mount, mountain in E British Columbia, Canada. Highest peak (3954 m/12,972 ft) in Canadian Rockies.

Rochdale, town of Greater Manchester met. county, NW England. Pop. 91,000. Cotton mfg. (esp. spinning). First co-operative society founded here (1844).

Rochelle, La, *see* LA ROCHELLE.

Rochester, John Wilmot, 2nd Earl of (1647-80), English poet, courtier. Known for amorous lyrics, satires.

Rochester, city of Kent, SE England, on Medway estuary. Pop. 55,000. Indust. centre; engineering. Cathedral (11th cent.); Norman castle (12th cent.); Dickens' home nearby.

Rochester, port of NW New York, US; on L. Ontario. Pop. 971,000. Fruit, market gardening, flower nurseries. Optical, photographic equipment.

rock, naturally occurring substance forming Earth's crust. Consists of one or more types of mineral; may also contain natural glass, decayed organic material, *etc.* Basic types are IGNEOUS, METAMORPHIC and SEDIMENTARY.

Rockefeller, John D[avison] (1839-1937), American industrialist, philanthropist. Ruthlessly built his Standard Oil Co. into largest refining company in US. Philanthropies incl. founding Univ. of Chicago (1892), and Rockefeller Foundation (1913). His son, **John D[avison] Rockefeller, Jr** (1874-1960), carried on father's businesses and philanthropies, estab. Rockefeller Center. His son, **Nelson Aldrich Rockefeller** (1908-79), was Governor of New York (1958-73); vice-president (1974-7).

rocket, popular name for several biennial or perennial plants of mustard family. Esp. dame's violet, *Hesperis matronalis,* with white or purple flowers, and rocket salad, *Eruca sativa,* with leaves eaten in salads.

rocket, projectile driven by its reaction to stream of hot gases it produces by burning propellant. By carrying its own source of oxygen, it operates independently of Earth's atmosphere and can be used in outer space. Propellants used incl. liquid hydrogen and liquid oxygen. Also *see* GUIDED MISSILE, SPACE EXPLORATION.

Rockingham, Charles Watson-Wentworth, 2nd Marquess of (1730-82), British Whig statesman, PM (1765-6, 1782). Headed coalition that repealed Stamp Act (1766). Favoured independence of American colonies.

rock music, form of music popular from mid-1950s. Derives in part from American rhythm and blues, gospel, and country and western music. Early exponents incl. Bill Haley, Elvis Presley, Chuck Berry. Status of rock music as vehicle for artistic expression was enhanced by such performers as the Beatles, Rolling Stones and Bob Dylan in mid-1960s. Modern rock music has absorbed such influences as Eastern music, jazz, electronic and classical music. Punk rock of late 1970s reacted against growing sophistication.

Rocky Mountain goat, *Oreamnos americanus,* ruminant mammal intermediate between goat and antelope, found in remote mountains of NW North America. Thick white coat, short black horns in both sexes.

Rocky Mountains, extensive mountain system of W North America, from Alaska to SW US, E of Coast Ranges. Canadian Rockies form British Columbia-Alberta border (glaciers, resorts). In US incl. scenic Grand Teton Range; Sawatch Mts. rise to Mt. Elbert (4399 m/14,431 ft).

Rocky Mountain sheep, *see* BIGHORN.

rococo, style of architecture and decoration developed in early 18th-cent. from the Baroque. Characterized by elaborate and profuse ornamentation imitating foliage, shell work, scrolls, *etc.* Became popular in Germany, Austria and Italy.

Rodentia (rodents), order of gnawing mammals with large chisel-like incisors which grow continuously. Incl. mouse, rat, squirrel, beaver, porcupine, guinea pig.

rodeo, competitive exhibition of the skills of cowboys. Events incl. bronco-riding (saddled or bareback), bull-riding, calf roping and steer-wrestling. Most famous is annual Calgary Stampede.

Rodgers, Richard Charles (1902-79), American composer. Collaborated with

Lorenz Hart on musicals *eg Pal Joey*, and with Oscar Hammerstein on *South Pacific*, *The King and I*, *The Sound of Music*.

Rodin, Auguste (1840-1917), French sculptor. His powerful realistic sculpture was influenced by Michelangelo and Gothic art. Works incl. *The Thinker*, *The Kiss*, *The Burghers of Calais*.

Rodney, George Brydges Rodney, 1st Baron (1718-92), British admiral. Captured Martinique (1762) in Seven Years War. Famous for victory (1782) over French fleet in American Revolution.

Rodriguez, isl. of Mascarene Isls., W Indian Ocean, a dependency of Mauritius. Area 104 sq km (40 sq mi); main town Port Mathurin. Produces fruit, tobacco, maize. Discovered (1645) by Portuguese; taken (1810) by British.

Roe deer, *Capreolus capreolus*, small Eurasian deer found in woodland. Male has short 3-tined antlers.

Rogation Days, in RC calendar, 4 days (25th April and 3 days preceding Ascension Day) observed by processions asking God's mercy.

Roget, Peter Mark (1779-1869), English physician, lexicographer. Best known for *Thesaurus of English Words and Phrases* (1852).

Röhm, Ernst (1887-1934), German political leader. Organized Nazi storm troops (SA), who enabled him to rival Hitler for political power in 1930s. Executed in purge.

Roland (d. 778), French national hero. His death at hands of Basques while commanding rearguard of Charlemagne's retreating army at Roncesvalles became subject of legend, notably in *Chanson de Roland* (11th cent.).

Rolland, Romain (1866-1944), French author, musicologist. Known for novel series *Jean Christophe* (1904-12, 10 vol.) satirizing modern society. Nobel Prize for Literature (1915).

Roller, jay-like bird of Coraciidae family, found esp. in S Europe and Africa. Noted for tumbling flight in nuptial display.

Roller skating, *see* SKATING.

Rolling Stones, English rock music group formed in early 1960s. Estab. wide following in Europe, North America with songs displaying aggressive rhythm *eg* 'Satisfaction'. Group featured music of Mick Jagger and Keith Richard.

Rolls, Charles Stewart (1877-1910), English pioneer motorist, aviator. First to fly across English channel and back non-stop (1910). Killed in flying accident. With **Sir [Frederick] Henry Royce** (1863-1933), English engineer, formed Rolls-Royce Ltd. (1906), automobile and aeroplane engine manufacturers.

Romains, Jules, pseud. of Louis Farigoule (1885-1972), French author. Works incl. novel cycle *Les Hommes de bonne volonté* (1932-47, 27 vol.).

Roman Catholicism, major division of Christianity. Main tenets incl. recognition of pope as spiritual leader of the church, belief in APOSTOLIC SUCCESSION, conveyance of God's grace through sacraments. Largest Christian denomination with hundreds of millions of adherents around the world. Centre of RC community is Vatican City, Rome.

romance, in Middle Ages, narrative poem (*roman*) on chivalry, love, adventure, derived from short episodes from epics, condensed *chansons de geste*.

Romance languages, only surviving group of Italic branch of Indo-European language family. Spoken mainly in Europe, present and past European colonies. Incl. French, Italian, Portuguese, Romanian, Spanish. Developed from Latin vernacular (Vulgar Latin), after fall of Roman Empire.

Romanesque, style of architecture prevalent throughout Europe from mid-11th to mid-12th cents. Based on Roman forms, style is characterized by rounded arches, massive walls, interior square bays. Also *see* NORMAN ARCHITECTURE.

Romania

Romania or **Rumania,** republic of SE Europe. Area 237,428 sq km (91,671 sq mi); pop. 21,855,000; cap. Bucharest. Language: Romanian. Religion: Eastern Orthodox. Crossed N-S by Carpathians, E-W by Transylvanian Alps. Incl. lower Danube. Agric. mainly grain (lowlands), livestock (highlands), vines. Indust. development rapid, esp. petroleum. Corresponds to Roman *Dacia*; formed by union of MOLDAVIA, WALACHIA (1859); independent from 1878. Gained Transylvania (1920); internal strife, lost territ. (1940). Joined Axis powers (1941-4). Communist govt. estab. 1948. Large minorities in pop., esp. Hungarian, German, Jewish.

Romanian or **Rumanian,** Romance language in Italic branch of Indo-European family. Official language of Romania; also used in USSR, Albania, Greece, *etc*.

Roman law, code of laws of ancient Rome, basis for modern legal system of many countries. Formulated first (*c* 450 BC) as 12 Tables, achieved final form in Tribonian's *Corpus juris civilis*, compiled (AD 528-34) under Justinian I. Outstanding in clarity, comprehensiveness; incl. *jus gentium*, code of international law, and is basis of all European civil law.

Romanov, ruling house of Russia (1613-1917). Dynasty estab. by Michael, descendant of Ivan IV. Ceased to rule with enforced abdication of Nicholas II.

Romans, epistle of NT, written by St Paul to Christians at Rome (*c* AD 58). Fundamental statement of Pauline theology; stresses justification by faith and universality of God's love.

Romansh, *see* RHAETO-ROMANIC.

Romanticism, in the arts, movement emphasizing imagination, emotions rather than intellect and formal restraint. Romantic characteristics incl. philosophic idealism, interest in primitive cultures, revolt against social and cultural conventions esp. in treatment of love. Grew in Europe as revolt against 18th-cent. NEO-CLASSICISM.

Romany, *see* GYPSY.

Rome (*Roma*), cap. of Italy and of Latium, on R. Tiber. Pop. 2,898,000. Admin., indust., commercial, transport centre; film-making; tourism. Traditionally founded (753 BC) on 7 hills by Romulus. Etruscan rulers overthrown *c* 500 BC; republic estab., expanded *eg* by Punic Wars. Empire estab. (31 BC) by Octavian; declined after AD 2nd cent., divided (last Western emperor deposed 476), overrun by Goths, Vandals. Cap. of Papal States throughout Middle Ages; annexed to Italy 1870. Ancient ruins incl. Forum, Colosseum. Many churches, incl. St Peter's. Also *see* VATICAN CITY.

Rome, Treaty of (1957), *see* EUROPEAN COMMUNITIES.

Rommel, Erwin (1891-1944), German army officer. As leader of the Afrika Corps (1941-3) showed brilliant qualities in desert warfare. Suspected of implication in the plot to kill Hitler (1944), he was forced to commit suicide.

Romney, George (1734-1802), English painter. Known for his fashionable portraits, notably Lady Hamilton.

Romney Marsh, low-lying drained coastal marshland of Kent, SE England. Sheep pasturage.

Romulus, legendary founder of Rome; son of Mars and Rhea Silvia, daughter of Numitor, king of Alba Longa. With his twin brother Remus, cast into R. Tiber by Amulius, usurper of Numitor's throne. Survived and suckled by she-wolf. Killed Remus in quarrel when building walls of Rome. Worshipped as god Quirinus.

Roncesvalles (Fr. *Roncevaux*), village of Navarre, NE Spain, in Pyrenees. Mountain pass, height 1056 m (3468 ft), is traditionally scene of defeat of Charlemagne and death of Roland (778).

rondo, form of instrumental music with a recurring section. May be single piece, or last movement of sonata, symphony, concerto.

Ronsard, Pierre de (*c* 1524-85), French poet. Leader of Pléiade group who sought to revitalize French poetry by imitating classical models.

Röntgen or **Roentgen, Wilhelm Konrad** (1845-1923), German physicist. Discovered X-rays while experimenting with cathode rays; showed that these rays affect photographic plates and pass through substances opaque to light. Awarded Nobel Prize for Physics (1901).

Roodepoort-Maraisburg, city of S Transvaal, South Africa. Pop. 114,000. Goldmining and residential centre in Witwatersrand.

rook, *Corvus frugilegus,* gregarious European bird of crow family. Glossy black plumage with bare whitish face.

Roosevelt, Franklin Delano (1882-1945), American statesman, Democratic president (1933-45). Partially crippled by poliomyelitis 1921. Countered Depression with NEW DEAL legislation to aid labour, agriculture, unemployed. Attempted to reorganize Supreme Court which had invalidated several New Deal measures. Elected for unprecedented 3rd term (1940); kept US out of WWII until Japan attacked Pearl Harbor (Dec. 1941). Laid basis for post-war Europe in meetings with Churchill, Stalin. Died after election for 4th term. Wife, **[Anna] Eleanor Roosevelt** (1884-1962), served as US delegate at UN (1945-53, 1961), worked for social reform.

Roosevelt, Theodore (1858-1919), American statesman, president (1901-9). Popular hero after fighting in Cuba (1898). Republican vice-president (1901), succeeded McKinley at latter's death. Vigorously regulated big business by 'trust busting' under Sherman Anti-Trust Act. Pursued militant Latin American policy; secured independence of Panama (1903) to allow building of Panama Canal. Re-elected 1904, awarded Nobel Peace Prize (1906) after mediating to end Russo-Japanese War. Picked successor, W.H. TAFT, whom he later ran against as Progressive candidate (1912).

root, that part of a plant which absorbs moisture and food, provides anchorage and support. May store food. Usually penetrates soil but can grow in air or water.

root, in mathematics, solution of an algebraic equation. Square root of a number is that number which when multiplied by itself gives original number, *eg* 3 and -3 are square roots of 9.

rorqual, toothless whale of worldwide distribution, genus *Balaenoptera.* Small pointed head, well-developed dorsal fin. Species incl. common rorqual, *B. physalus* and blue whale, *B. musculus.*

Rorschach, Hermann (1884-1922), Swiss psychiatrist. Devised test to analyse personality, in which patient describes his interpretations of 10 standardized ink blot designs. His responses are then analysed and interpreted.

Rosaceae, large family of flowering herbs, shrubs and small trees. Incl. rose, bramble, apple, plum and cherry.

Rosario, port of EC Argentina, on Paraná R.

Pop. 807,000. Large railway jct., export depot for wheat, beef from Pampas; sugar refining, flour milling.

Roscommon, county of Connacht prov., WC Irish Republic. Area 2463 sq km (951 sq mi); pop. 54,000. Bounded in E by R. Shannon; lakes, bogland. Cattle, sheep pasture. Co. town **Roscommon,** pop. 2000.

Rose

rose, any of genus *Rosa* of shrubs native to N temperate regions. Spiny stems, five-parted, usually fragrant flowers of various colours. Many varieties, widely cultivated, are derived from wild sweetbriar, *R. rubiginosa,* and dog-rose, *R. canina.*

Rosebery, Archibald Philip Primrose, 5th Earl of (1847-1929), British statesman, Liberal PM (1894-5). His advocacy of imperialist policies in Africa estranged him from much of Liberal Party.

rosemary, *Rosmarinus officinalis,* evergreen shrub of mint family, native to Mediterranean region. Used as culinary herb and in cosmetics.

Rosenberg, Julius (1917-53), American spy. With his wife Ethel (1915-53), was executed for passing atomic secrets to USSR during WWII.

rose of Sharon, *Hibiscus syriacus,* Asian ornamental plant, and *Hypericum calycinum,* evergreen European shrub with large yellow flowers.

Roses, Wars of the, civil wars (1455-85) fought between Houses of Lancaster and York for the English throne. Their badges were red rose and white rose, respectively. Lancastrian king Henry VI was forced to recognize duke of York as his heir but York's claims were set aside on birth of king's son (1454). Fighting began at 1st battle of St Albans (1455). York was defeated and killed at Wakefield (1460) but his son deposed Henry after 2nd battle of St Albans (1461), becoming Edward IV. Henry was briefly restored (1470-1) but was defeated by Edward at Barnet and Tewkesbury. Wars ended when Henry Tudor, a Lancastrian, assumed power as Henry VII after defeating Richard III at Bosworth (1485).

Rosetta stone, ancient Egyptian basalt slab, now in the British Museum, discovered during Napoleon's occupation of Egypt. Bears a decree of Ptolemy V (196 BC) written in hieroglyphics, demotic and Greek, thus enabling hieroglyphics to be deciphered.

rosewood, hard reddish wood obtained from various tropical trees, esp. Brazilian rosewood or jacaranda, *Dalbergia nigra.* Used for cabinet-making, veneering.

Rosicrucians, members of 17th and 18th-cent. occult groups claiming ancient Egyptian origins for their movement. Symbols incl. rose, cross, swastika, pyramid. Prob. derives from works of Johan Andreä (1586-1654) who took pseud. Christian Rosenkreuz. Modern movement adheres to theosophical doctrines.

rosin, residue from distillation of crude turpentine. Hard, brittle resin, usually light-yellow or amber. Used in making varnishes, soaps, and for treating violin bows, *etc.*

Ross, Sir John (1777-1856), Scottish explorer, naval officer. In search of Northwest Passage, discovered Boothia Penin. and King William Land (1829-33). His nephew, **Sir James Clark Ross** (1800-62), made several Arctic expeditions from 1818; located N magnetic pole (1831). Led Antarctic voyage (1839-43), discovered Ross Sea, Ross Isl., Victoria Land.

Ross, Sir Ronald (1857-1932), British physician, b. India. Awarded Nobel Prize for Physiology and Medicine (1902) for discovery of the malaria-causing parasite in the *Anopheles* mosquito.

Ross and Cromarty, former county of N Scotland, incl. some of Hebrides, now in Highland region. Mountains, moorland, lochs; lowland in E (Black Isle). Agric., crofting, sheep farming, deer forests; fishing, tourism. Co. town was Dingwall.

Ross Dependency, New Zealand Antarctic territ., lying S of 60°S and between 160°E and 150°W. Incl. Ross Sea, coastal areas of Victoria, Edward VII and Marie Byrd lands, Ross Isl. (site of Mt. Erebus).

Rossetti, Dante Gabriel (1828-82), English painter, poet. Founded Pre-Raphaelite Brotherhood (1848) with Millais and Hunt. Subjects of paintings were taken from Dante and medieval romance. His poems were attacked on grounds of morality. His sister, **Christina Georgina Rossetti** (1830-94), was also a poet. Wrote religious, often melancholy poetry.

Rossini, Gioacchino Antonio (1792-1868), Italian composer. Noted for melodic and humorous qualities. Wrote 36 operas from 1810-29, incl. *The Barber of Seville, William Tell.* Then virtually abandoned composition, although producing *Stabat Mater.*

Ross Sea, inlet of S Pacific Ocean, E of Victoria Land, Antarctica. Ross Ice Shelf forms S section.

Rostand, Edmond (1868-1918), French poet, dramatist. Best known for verse drama *Cyrano de Bergerac* (1897).

Rostock, town of N East Germany, at head of Warnow estuary. Pop. 215,000. Port; fisheries, shipbuilding, machinery. Hanseatic League member (14th cent.); univ. (1418).

Rostov-on-Don, city of USSR, SW European RSFSR; near mouth of Don on Sea of Azov. Pop. 934,000. Port, exports grain, wool; shipbuilding, agric. machinery mfg. Founded 1761.

Rotherham, town of South Yorkshire met. county, N England. Pop. 85,000. Iron and steel indust.

Rothermere, Harold Sidney Harmsworth, 1st Viscount (1868-1940), English publisher. Provided financial direction in his brother NORTHCLIFFE's publishing firm, at whose death he took control.

Rothesay, town and small port of Strathclyde region, W Scotland, on Isle of Bute. Former county town of Bute. Pop. 7000. Tourist resort.

Rothko, Mark (1903-70), American painter, b. Russia. Known for his large abstract expressionist works.

Rothschild, Mayer Amschel (1743-1812), German banker. Founded family fortune as financial agent in Frankfurt. His sons opened branches in Paris, Vienna and London, where **Nathan Meyer Rothschild** (1777-1836) estab. family branch (1798), supplying British govt. with finances in struggle against Napoleon and making loans to European and South American countries. His son, **Baron Lionel Nathan de Rothschild** (1808-79), further extended family's influence. First Jewish MP.

Rotorua, town of NC North Isl., New Zealand, on L. Rotorua. Pop. 47,000. Major health and tourist centre based on hot springs, geysers, Maori culture.

rotten borough, in English history, parliamentary constituencies which continued to return representatives to Parliament despite virtual disappearance of electorate. Abolished by 1832 Reform Act.

Rotterdam, city of W Netherlands, on R. Nieuwe Maas. Pop. 1,017,000. Chief European seaport, canal links via R. Rhine with NW Germany; entrepôt trade. Indust. centre, incl. shipbuilding, oil refining. Development of Europoort (1960s), massive port, indust. complex. City centre destroyed in WWII.

Rouault, Georges (1871-1958), French painter. Early paintings, employing heavy black outlines, depict injustice and suffering. Later turned to religious painting.

Roubaix, city of Nord, N France. Pop. 109,000. Textile centre, esp. woollens, carpets. Forms conurbation with Lille and Tourcoing.

Rouen, city of N France, on R. Seine, cap. of Seine-Maritime dept. Pop. 389,000. Major port, indust. centre (esp. metals, chemicals, textiles); univ. (1966). Hist. cap. of Normandy. Held by English (1419-49); Joan of Arc burned here (1431). Notable Gothic cathedral. Badly damaged in WWII.

roulette, gambling game played by rolling a small ball around a shallow bowl with an inner disc revolving in the opposite direction. Ball comes to rest in one of 37 (incl. 0) numbered compartments, coloured alternately red and black, determining winning bets.

rounders, nine-a-side English outdoor game played with bat and ball. Similar to baseball, which is prob. derived from it.

Roundheads, name given to members of Parliamentary or Puritan party during English Civil War. So called because of their close-cropped hair.

Round Table, *see* ARTHURIAN LEGEND.

roundworm, *see* NEMATODA.

Rousseau, Henri (1844-1910), French painter, known as 'le Douanier'. Employed a seemingly naive, but direct, imaginative style to depict jungle scenes, exotic subjects, *etc.*

Rousseau, Jean Jacques (1712-78), French philosopher, b. Geneva. Wrote *Discours sur l'origine de l'inégalité des hommes* (1754), an attack on property and the state as causes of inequality. His *Contrat social* (1762) describes ideal state with sovereignty held inalienably by people as a whole; individual retains freedom by submitting to 'general will'. Other works incl. novel on education, *Emile* (1762), autobiog. *Confessions.* Had great influence on theories of French Revolution and 19th-cent. Romanticism.

Rousseau, [Pierre Etienne] Théodore (1812-67), French painter. Leading member of Barbizon school of landscape painters.

rowan, *see* MOUNTAIN ASH.

rowing, sport of propelling a boat by means of oars. Competitive rowing dates from early 19th cent. in England. Annual boat race between Oxford and Cambridge (estab. 1829) is major rowing event in UK.

Rowlandson, Thomas (1756-1827), English caricaturist. Known for satires on the social scene.

Roxburghshire, former county of SE Scotland, now in Borders region. Mainly hilly, Cheviots in S. Teviot, Tweed rivers. Sheep rearing; woollens, tweed mfg. Co. town was Jedburgh.

Royal Academy [of Arts], institution founded (1768) in London by George III to encourage painting, sculpture and architecture.

Royal Air Force, junior of 3 fighting services in UK, formed (1918) by merging Royal Flying Corps and Royal Naval Air Service.

Royal Canadian Mounted Police, federal law-enforcement agency of Canada. Estab. (1873) as North West Mounted Police.

Royal Marines, *see* MARINES.

Royal Navy, *see* NAVY.

royal prerogative, *see* CROWN.

Royal Society (Royal Society of London for Improving Natural Knowledge), British scientific society, founded (1660) to encourage scientific research. Eminent scientists are elected as fellows (FRS).

Royal Society for the Prevention of Cruelty to Animals (RSPCA), British organization founded (1824) in London to promote humane treatment of animals and provide free veterinary treatment.

Royce, Sir Henry, *see* ROLLS.

RSFSR, *see* RUSSIAN SOVIET FEDERATED SOCIALIST REPUBLIC.

Ruanda-Urundi, *see* RWANDA; BURUNDI.

Rub-al-Khali, *see* EMPTY QUARTER.

rubber, elastic substance produced from LATEX, esp. of *Hevea brasiliensis* tree. Most rubber articles are made by treating latex chemically, *eg* by mixing with sulphur and heating (vulcanization). Rubber can be produced synthetically as polymer of isoprene.

rubber plant, *Ficus elastica,* Asian tree of mulberry family. Large, glossy, leathery leaves. Often grown indoors as ornamental.

Rubber tree

rubber tree, various tropical and subtropical trees producing LATEX. Chief source is *Hevea brasiliensis,* native to Amazon but cultivated in SE Asia. Latex is collected from cuts made in bark.

rubella or **German measles,** infectious virus disease, common in childhood. Characterized by pink rash, swelling of lymph nodes behind the ears. In pregnant women, may cause damage to the embryo.

Rubens, Sir Peter Paul (1577-1640), Flemish painter. Court painter to Archduke Albert in Antwerp. Travelled widely as diplomat and painter. Work in exuberant Baroque style is fluent in colour and texture; paintings incl. *Descent from the Cross, Peace and War.*

Rubicon, small river of EC Italy, flowing into Adriatic Sea N of Rimini. In ancient times marked border of Italy and Cisalpine Gaul; crossing (49 BC) by Julius Caesar represented declaration of war on Pompey and Senate.

rubidium (Rb), soft metallic element; at. no. 37, at. wt. 85.47. Extremely reactive member of alkali metal group; ignites spontaneously in air and reacts vigorously with water. Used in photocells.

ruby, precious gemstone, a variety of CORUNDUM. Deep red and transparent; used in jewellery. Finest rubies come from Burma, Thailand.

Rudolf, Lake, lake of NW Kenya and SW Ethiopia, in Great Rift Valley. Length *c* 275 km (170 mi). Has no outlet; gradually diminishing. Now called L. Turkana.

Rudolph I (1218-91), Holy Roman emperor (1273-91). Originally count of HABSBURG, he was founder of the imperial dynasty. Made his sons dukes of Austria and Styria, thus strengthening empire.

Rudolph (1858-89), crown prince of Austria, only son of Emperor Francis Joseph. Found dead at Mayerling with mistress, Maria Vetsera, in mysterious circumstances.

rue, *Ruta graveolens,* European perennial herb. Yellow flowers, blue-green leaves with pungent taste formerly used in medicine.

Ruff

ruff, *Philomachus pugnax,* Eurasian sandpiper, related to plover, male of which has ruff of erectile feathers during breeding season.

Rugby, town of Warwickshire, C England. Pop. 59,000. Railway jct.; engineering; cattle market, cement mfg. Public school (1567).

rugby football, fifteen-a-side team game, played with oval leather ball which may be kicked and handled. Said to have originated at Rugby School, England, in 1823; 1st rules drawn up in 1871; governed by Rugby Union. Differences over payment of players led to formation of professional Rugby League (1895), whose members play thirteen-a-side variation of game.

Ruhr, major indust. area of NW West Germany, based on R. Ruhr (length *c* 230 km/145 mi). Duisburg, Essen, Gelsenkirchen, Bochum, Dortmund form vast conurbation served by extensive system of canals, roads, railways. Major industs. incl. coalmining, iron and steel, chemicals. Heavily bombed in WWII.

Ruisdael or **Ruysdael, Jacob van** (*c* 1628-82), Dutch painter. Major Dutch landscape painter of 17th cent.

Rum, *see* RHUM.

rum, spirit distilled from fermented cane sugar by-products, chiefly molasses. Naturally colourless; brown colour results from storage in casks or addition of caramel. Most export rums are produced in West Indies.

Rumania, *see* ROMANIA.

Rumelia, area of S Balkan Penin. Incl. Thrace, Macedonia. Hist. part of Ottoman Empire; Eastern Rumelia (cap. Plovdiv) autonomous from 1878, annexed by Bulgaria (1885).

Rumford, Benjamin Thompson, Count (1753-1814), British scientist, b. US. His belief that heat is produced by motion of particles helped undermine earlier caloric theory of heat.

ruminant, cloven-hoofed cud-chewing mammal. Four-chambered stomach; food passes first 2 chambers, then is re-chewed and passes to last 2 chambers. Incl. cattle, sheep, goats, deer, giraffes.

rummy, card game played by two to six players. Variations incl. gin rummy and CANASTA.

Rump Parliament, name given to members of Long Parliament remaining after exclusion of army's opponents, carried out in Pride's Purge (1648). Dissolved by Cromwell (1653), who later instituted PROTECTORATE.

Rundstedt, [Karl Rudolf] Gerd von (1875-1953), German field marshal. Commanded in Polish (1939) and French (1940) campaigns. Commanded all German occupation forces in Europe from 1942 until Allied invasion (1944), when he was superseded; reinstated to organize Ardennes offensive.

runes, ancient alphabet, prob. derived from Greek script; used by Scandinavians and other early Germanic peoples from *c* AD 300.

Runnymede, meadow of Egham, Surrey, S England, on S bank of R. Thames. Probable site of sealing of MAGNA CARTA (1215) by King John.

Runyon, Damon (1884-1946), American short story writer. Known for humorous works, *eg Guys and Dolls* (1932), detailing lives of Broadway characters in racy vernacular.

Rupert (1619-82), German prince in military service of uncle, Charles I of England. Commanded Royalist cavalry in Civil War; defeated by Cromwell at Marston Moor (1644). Sponsored founding of Hudson's Bay Co. (1670).

Rupert's Land, hist. territ. of N Canada, held by Hudson's Bay Co. (1670-1869). Comprised drainage basin of Hudson Bay.

rupture, *see* HERNIA.

Rurik (d. 879), traditional founder of first Russian dynasty. Leader of a band of Scandinavian traders, he estab. himself as prince of Novgorod (*c* 862).

Ruse (Turk. *Ruschuk*), city of N Bulgaria, on R. Danube. Pop. 166,000. Indust., commercial centre, exports cereals.

rush, any of genus *Juncus* of long-stemmed plants with small, greenish flowers. Found in marshes of temperate and cold regions. Stems used for making mats, baskets, *etc.* Name also applied to similar plants, *eg* BULRUSH, CATTAIL.

Rushmore, Mount, *see* BLACK HILLS.

Ruskin, John (1819-1900), English critic. His *Modern Painters* (1843-60) started as a defence of Turner but later dealt with politics, social reform, architecture; his *Stones of Venice* (1851-3) reflects advocacy of Gothic architecture.

Russell, Bertrand Arthur William, 3rd Earl Russell (1872-1970), English philosopher, mathematician. Collaborated with A.N. Whitehead on *Principia Mathematica* (1910-13) attempting to estab. logical basis of mathematics. Developed symbolic logic. Other works incl. *History of Western Philosophy* (1945). Leading pacifist spokesman. Nobel Prize for Literature (1950).

Russell, Charles Taze (1852-1916), American clergyman. Founded (1872) evangelical Jehovah's Witnesses. Doctrine centres on belief in imminent 2nd coming of Christ and a millennial period when repentant sinners may be redeemed. Members refuse to participate in warfare or govt.

Russell, John Russell, 1st Earl (1792-1878), British statesman, PM (1846-52, 1865-6). Supported Catholic Emancipation (1829) and helped draft Reform Bill of 1832. Foreign secretary under Palmerston (1859-65).

Russell, Sir William Howard (1821-1907), British journalist, b. Ireland. As *The Times* correspondent covering Crimean War, exposed mismanagement of campaign.

Russia, *see* UNION OF SOVIET SOCIALIST REPUBLICS.

Russian, language in E Slavic branch of Indo-European family. Spoken by *c* 140 million as 1st language in USSR, one of official languages of UN. Uses Cyrillic alphabet.

Russian Orthodox Church, branch of EASTERN ORTHODOX CHURCH. Originally headed by patriarch of Constantinople, patriarchate of Moscow estab. 1589. National church of Tsarist Russia, power and influence declined after Russian Revolution.

Russian Revolution, national uprisings (1905, 1917) against tsarist autocracy. Discontent over agric. and indust. conditions resulted in series (1905) of strikes, mutinies (*eg* battleship *Potemkin* at Odessa); led to limited concessions, such as estab. of *duma* parliament. Further opposition arose after continued Russian losses during WWI. February Revolution (1917) led to estab. of provisional govt. in defiance of tsar, who then abdicated. Socialist opposition to War, led by LENIN and BOLSHEVIKS, culminated in October Revolution. Communist Party estab.; private ownership abolished, Russia withdrew from WWI. Ensuing civil war (1918-20) between Red Army, organized by

Trotsky, and White Army, supported by European nations, ended with Communist consolidation of power and founding (1921) of USSR.

Russian Soviet Federated Socialist Republic (RSFSR), largest constituent republic of USSR. Area *c* 17,070,000 sq km (6,590,000 sq mi); pop. 137,552,000; cap. Moscow. Admin. subdivisions incl. 16 auton. republics and 5 auton. regions. Stretches from Baltic in W to Pacific in E and N to Arctic. Economy, history and culture is that of USSR.

Russo-Japanese War (1904-5), conflict provoked by Russian penetration into Manchuria and Korea. Japan attacked and captured Port Arthur, destroyed Russian fleet at Tsushima. Peace settlement reduced Russian role in E Asia.

Russo-Turkish Wars, series of wars (18th–19th cent.) in which Russia sought to control Black Sea and gain access to Mediterranean at expense of Ottoman Empire. Russian expansion checked by European allies during Crimean War (1853-6). Final settlement dictated at Congress of Berlin (1878).

rust, reddish-brown coating formed on surface of iron or steel exposed to atmosphere. Consists mainly of ferric oxide (Fe_2O_3) and hydroxide. Caused by action of oxygen and moisture.

Ruth, book of OT. Relates story of Ruth, Moabite widow who accompanied her Jewish mother-in-law to Bethlehem and married Boaz. Ancestress of David.

Ruthenia, region of C Europe, in S Carpathian Mts.; now largely in USSR (Ukraine). Part of Austro-Hungarian empire until 1918, then held by Czechoslovakia until 1939. Ceded to USSR in 1945.

ruthenium (Ru), hard brittle metallic element of platinum group; at. no. 44, at. wt. 101.07. Used to make hard alloys with platinum and palladium and as a catalyst.

Rutherford, Ernest Rutherford, 1st Baron (1871-1937), British physicist, b. New Zealand. Developed theory of radioactivity with F. Soddy; awarded Nobel Prize for Chemistry (1908). Discovered atomic nucleus (1909).

Rutland, former county (smallest) of England, now part of Leicestershire. Co. town was Oakham.

Ruwenzori, mountain range of Uganda and Zaïre. Peaks incl. Stanley, Margherita, Alexandra, all *c* 5120 m (16,800 ft). Possibly the ancient 'Mountains of the Moon'.

Rwanda

Rwanda, republic of EC Africa. Area 26,400 sq km (10,200 sq mi); pop. 4,508,000; cap. Kigali. Languages: Bantu, French. Religions: animist, Christian. Mainly high plateau, L. Kivu in W. Cattle rearing, tin mining, exports coffee. Former kingdom, part of German East Africa from 1899; part of Belgian colony of Ruanda-Urundi after WWI; independent as republic from 1962.

Ryazan, city of USSR, C European RSFSR. Pop. 453,000. Trade in agric. produce; agric. machinery mfg. Cap. of medieval principality.

rye, *Secale cereale,* tall Eurasian annual grass grown extensively in Eurasia and North America. Black grain used in making black rye bread, rye whiskey and for livestock feed.

Rye House Plot, conspiracy (1683) to assassinate King Charles II and brother James on London road in Hertfordshire. Plot uncovered, used as excuse to execute several of Charles' opponents.

Ryswick, Treaty of, settlement of War of Grand Alliance (1688-97) thwarting French territ. ambitions; signed (1697) at Ryswick, Netherlands. Dutch gained commercial concessions. Savoy's independence and William III's rule of England acknowledged.

Ryukyu Islands, archipelago of W Pacific Ocean, between Taiwan and Japan. Area 2200 sq km (850 sq mi); pop. 1,235,000; main isl. Okinawa. Sweet potatoes, sugar cane, pineapples, fishing. Part of Japan from 1879, under US jurisdiction from 1945. N group returned to Japan (1953), remainder returned (1972).

S

SA, *see* BROWNSHIRTS.

Saarbrücken (Fr. *Sarrebruck*), city of W West Germany, on R. Saar; cap. of Saarland. Pop. 203,000. Coalmining; machinery, instrument mfg. Ceded to Prussia by France 1815.

Saarland, state of West Germany. Area 2567 sq km (991 sq mi); cap. Saarbrücken. Mainly hilly and forested, incl. R. Saar valley. Rich coalfield, major iron and steel indust. Returned after plebiscites to Germany (1935, 1957) following French occupation.

Sabadell, city of Catalonia, NE Spain. Pop. 159,000. Textile, timber, dye industs.

Sabah, state of East Malaysia. Area *c* 76,500 sq km (29,500 sq mi); pop. 904,000; cap. Kota Kinabulu. Largely mountainous, rising 4100 m (13,455 ft) at Mt. Kinabulu; densely forested. Produces rubber, copra, timber. Was British protect. of North Borneo (1882-1963) until it joined Malaysia.

Sabbath (Heb., = rest), day of rest and worship. Observed by Jews from sunset on Friday to sunset on Saturday, by most Christian denominations on Sunday. Friday is Islamic day of public worship.

Sabines, ancient people of C Italy, from earliest times connected with Rome. According to legend, wives were taken from the Sabines for unmarried followers of Romulus ('rape of Sabine women'). Constantly warred with Romans, but by 3rd cent. BC had amalgamated with them.

sable, *Martes zibellina,* carnivorous mammal of marten family, found in N Asia. Cultivated for valuable fur.

Sable antelope

sable antelope, *Hippotragus niger,* large dark-coloured antelope of S Africa. Long ringed backward-curving horns.

sabre-toothed tiger, extinct cat of Machairodontidae subfamily, with tusk-like canine teeth in upper jaw. Existed between Oligocene and Pleistocene epochs.

saccharin, white crystalline powder produced synthetically from toluene. Slightly soluble in water; *c* 500 times sweeter than sugar. Used as sugar substitute in diabetic diets and as calorie-free sweetener.

Sacco, Nicola (1891-1927) and **Bartolomeo Vanzetti** (1888-1927), Italian anarchists. Tried and convicted (1921) for murder in Massachusetts; case became *cause célèbre* in US, many believing conviction resulted from their reputation as radicals. Despite appeals, both were executed.

sacrament, in Christianity, religious act or ceremony considered esp. sacred and distinct from other rites through institution by Jesus. In RC and Eastern Orthodox churches, 7 sacraments (Eucharist, baptism, penance, confirmation, ordination, matrimony, extreme unction) held to bestow God's grace on man. Most Protestant denominations observe Holy Communion (EUCHARIST) and baptism, but only as symbols of God's grace.

Sacramento, cap. of California, US; on Sacramento R. Pop. 880,000. Railway jct.; food processing, packing. First settled 1839; became cap. 1854. Terminus of 1st transcontinental railway, Pony Express.

sacrifice, the offering of a person, animal or object in homage to a deity. In Bible, occurs in OT, *eg* in story of Cain and Abel; in Greek and Roman religion, among Maya and Aztecs, and many primitive cultures. In NT, Jesus is symbolized as sacrificial lamb. Eucharist is regarded as a form of commemorative sacrifice.

Sadat, Anwar el- (1918-), Egyptian political leader. Succeeded Nasser as president (1970); favoured American diplomacy to gain concessions from Israel after 1973 war. Reduced Soviet influence in country. Signed peace treaty with Israel (1979). Nobel Peace Prize (1978).

Sadducees, smaller of two main Jewish sects which originated in Maccabean age (other being opponents, PHARISEES). Opposed all doctrines not taught in Torah, *eg* resurrection and immortality.

Sade, Donatien Alphonse François, Comte de, known as Marquis de Sade (1740-1814), French author. Cruel sexual practices reflected in novels, *eg Justine* (1791), *Juliette* (1797). Gave name to sadism.

Sadowa, village of N Czechoslovakia, near Hradec Králové. Scene of battle (1866) in which Prussians defeated Austrians.

safety lamp, oil lamp for use in mines, designed not to explode firedamp (methane). First successful type usually attributed to Humphrey Davy (*c* 1816). Uses metal-gauze screen to dissipate heat of flame. Also indicates presence of methane when flame has blue halo. Largely replaced by electric lighting and gas sensing equipment.

saffron, *see* MEADOW SAFFRON.

saga, in Old Norse and Icelandic literature, long prose narrative written 11th-13th cent., usually relating story of historical or legendary hero or important family, incl. battles, legends, *etc*.

sage, *Salvia officinalis*, aromatic herb of worldwide distribution. Grey-green leaves used as seasoning in cookery.

sagebrush, several bushy, deciduous plants of genus *Artemisia*, common in arid regions of W US.

Sagittarius, *see* ZODIAC.

sago, edible starch extracted from pith of various palms esp. *Metroxylon sago* found mainly in Far East. Important food source.

Sahara, desert of N Africa. Largest in world, area *c* 9,065,000 sq km (3,500,000 sq mi); extends from Atlantic Ocean to Red Sea. Largely stony with some sandy areas; interior ranges incl. Ahaggar, Tibesti Mts. Extremely arid climate; inhabited by Sudanese, Negroes, Berbers, Tuaregs. Oases produce dates, fruit; mineral resources incl. salt, iron ore, phosphates, oil and gas.

Saida, seaport of S Lebanon, on Mediterranean. Pop. 24,000. Ancient Sidon of Phoenicia.

Saigon, *see* HO CHI MINH CITY.

sail, area of strong material spread from ship's mast to harness force of the wind as means of propulsion. Sails of papyrus used by ancient Egyptians. Flax and cotton, formerly used in sailmaking, have been replaced by synthetics. Square-rig sail arrangement largely replaced by fore-and-aft rig.

sailfish, any of genus *Istiophorus* of large marine fish. Related to swordfish, has sail-shaped dorsal fin and spear-like upper jaw.

sailing, sport, *see* YACHTING.

sailing ships, wind-propelled vessels prob. first used by ancient Egyptians, later by Greeks and Romans. With introduction of mariner's compass, use of sails in place of oars became general. Reached height of development in 19th-cent. tea clippers. Introduction of steamship (19th cent.) led to gradual disappearance of sailing ships.

saint, *see* CANONIZATION.

St Albans, town of Hertfordshire, EC England. Pop. 52,000. Printing; electronics. Roman *Verulamium*, many remains; has 8th-cent. abbey; Norman cathedral.

St Andrews, town and resort of Fife region, E Scotland. Pop. 12,000. Woollens mfg. Has Royal and Ancient Golf Club (1754); 12th-cent. ruined cathedral; 13th-cent. castle; oldest Scottish univ. (1411).

Saint Bartholomew's Day Massacre, massacre of French Huguenots, instigated by Henri de Guise and Catherine de'Medici; began in Paris on 24th Aug. 1572. Number killed est. at 50,000. Led to resumption of French Wars of Religion.

St Bernard, breed of large dog with dense short hair. Once kept by monks of St Bernard's Hospice in Swiss Alps to rescue travellers. Stands *c* 71 cm/28 in. at shoulder.

St Bernard Passes, two Alpine passes. Great St Bernard (height 2471 m/8110 ft) links Valais canton (Switzerland) with Valle d'Aosta (Italy). Road tunnel, 5.6 km (3.5 mi) long, opened 1964. Little St Bernard (height 2187 m/7178 ft) links Valle d'Aosta with French Savoy. Each pass has hospice founded (11th cent.) by St Bernard of Menthon to aid travellers.

St Catharines, town of S Ontario, Canada; on Welland Ship Canal. Pop. 302,000. In important fruit-growing region. Engineering, food canning industs.

St Christopher, *see* ST KITTS.

St Cloud, suburb of W Paris, France. Horse racing, porcelain mfg. Palace (17th cent., destroyed 1870).

St Denis, suburb of N Paris, France. Engineering, chemical industs. Gothic cathedral contains many royal tombs.

Saint Elmo's fire, visible electric discharge seen at wingtips of aircraft or masts of ships. Caused by static electricity in atmosphere; often observed during electric storms.

St Etienne, city of EC France, cap. of Loire dept. Pop. 335,000. Coalmining centre, iron and steel mfg. Hist. armaments and textiles (esp. silk) industs.

Saint-Exupéry, Antoine de (1900-44), French author, aviator. Novels, *eg Vol de nuit* (1931), *Terre des hommes* (1939, *Wind, Sand and Stars*), reflect humanistic philosophy of endeavour. Also wrote whimsical fantasy *Le Petit Prince* (1943).

St Gall (Ger. *Sankt Gallen*), town of NE Switzerland, cap. of St Gall canton. Pop. 87,000. Indust. centre, esp. silk, cotton. Medieval centre of learning.

St George's Channel, British Isles; between Irish Sea and Atlantic, separating Wales from Ireland. Width 74 km (46 mi) at narrowest point.

Saint-Germain, Treaty of, post-WWI settlement (1919) between Austria and Allies. Austro-Hungarian empire dissolved, Austria gave up parts of its German-speaking territ. to Italy and Czechoslovakia. Independence of Hungary, Yugoslavia, Poland and Czechoslovakia recognized.

St Germain(-en-Laye), suburb of W Paris, France, on R. Seine. Renaissance château.

St Gotthard Pass, mountain pass of S Switzerland, height 2107 m (6916 ft). Road built 1830; railway tunnel (length 14.9 km/9.25 mi) built 1880; road tunnel (length 19.3 km/10.2 mi) opened 1980.

St Helena, isl. of S Atlantic, British crown colony. Area 122 sq km (47 sq mi); pop. 6000; cap. Jamestown. Napoleon's final place of exile (1815-21). Became crown colony 1834.

St Helens, town of Merseyside met. county, NW England. Pop. 105,000. Major glass indust.; iron; chemicals mfg.

St Helier, cap. of Jersey, Channel Isls., UK. Pop. 28,000. Resort; agric. market.

St Ives, town of Cornwall, SW England, on St Ives Bay. Pop. 10,000. Fishing port; resort long favoured by artists.

St James's Palace, in Pall Mall, London, was built by Henry VIII and served as royal residence 1698-1837.

St John, ice-free port of S New Brunswick, Canada; on Bay of Fundy at mouth of St John R. Pop. 113,000. Major timber exports, pulp and paper industs. Estab. as fort in 17th cent.

St John, river of E Canada-US. Rises in N Maine, flows SE 673 km (418 mi) through New Brunswick to Bay of Fundy. Transport link to coast.

St John, Henry, *see* BOLINGBROKE.

St John's, cap. of ANTIGUA.

St John's, cap. and seaport of Newfoundland, Canada; on Avalon penin. Pop. 143,000. Naval and fishing base. Founded 1582.

St John's wort, any of genus *Hypericum* of plants native to Asia and Europe. Speckled leaves, yellow flowers.

Saint-Just, Louis Antoine de (1767-94), French revolutionary. Leading member of Committee of Public Safety during Reign of Terror (1793-4). Arrested and guillotined with his close associate, Robespierre.

St Kilda, small isl. of Outer Hebrides, W Scotland. Uninhabited from 1930; bird sanctuary.

St Kitts or **St Christopher,** isl. of E West Indies, in Leeward Isls. Area 176 sq km (68 sq mi); pop. 60,000 (with Nevis); cap. Basseterre (pop. 16,000). Former British colony with Nevis, Anguilla from 1783; became associate state (1967).

St Laurent, Louis Stephen (1882-1973), Canadian statesman. Liberal PM (1948-57), succeeding Mackenzie King.

St Lawrence, river of E Canada. Flows NE 1197 km (744 mi) from L. Ontario to Gulf of St Lawrence. Forms part of US/Canada border. Main tributaries incl. Ottawa, Saguenay, St Maurice rivers. Forms numerous lakes along course. Major shipping route. Canal system (St Lawrence Seaway) links Great Lakes to Atlantic. Has wide estuary.

St Lawrence, Gulf of, extension of Atlantic, SE Canada; between Québec and Newfoundland. At mouth of St Lawrence R. Has important fishing grounds (esp. cod).

St Louis, city of E Missouri, US; on Mississippi near mouth of Missouri R. Pop. 2,367,000; state's largest city. Commercial, trade, transport centre. Furs, livestock, grain market, meat packing; motor vehicles, aircraft, chemical mfg. Estab. 1764 by French; became river port in 19th cent.

St Lucia, isl. of SE West Indies, in Windward Isls. Area 616 sq km (238 sq mi); pop. 113,000; cap. Castries (pop. 45,000). Scenic mountains with forest-covered slopes. Fruit, coconut exports. Former British colony; became associate state 1967. Independent 1979. Member of British Commonwealth.

St Malo, town of Brittany, NW France, at mouth of R. Rance. Pop. 44,000. Port, fishing, tourism.

St Martin *(Sint Maarten),* isl. of N Leeward Isls., divided between French (Guadeloupe dependency) and Dutch (Netherlands Antilles). Area 96 sq km (37 sq mi). Main export is salt.

St Moritz, town of SE Switzerland, on R. Inn in Engadine Valley. Pop. 3000. Spa; winter sports.

St Nazaire, town of W France, at mouth of R. Loire. Pop. 119,000. Port, outport of Nantes; shipbuilding, food processing. German submarine base in WWII, heavily bombed.

St Paul, cap. of Minnesota, US; contiguous with Minneapolis ('Twin Cities') on Mississippi R. Pop. 310,000. Commercial, indust. centre in agric. region. Livestock trade; automobile, tapes, computers, electronic instrument mfg.

Saint Paul's, Anglican cathedral, London, built (1675-1710) by Sir Christopher Wren on site of old St Paul's which had been severely damaged in Great Fire (1666). Has famous classical dome.

Saint Peter's, Rome, patriarchal basilica of St Peter, in Vatican City. Built mainly between 1506 and 1626, it replaced 4th-cent. basilica built by Constantine over supposed tomb of St Peter. Designed chiefly by Bramante and Michelangelo, with piazza added by Bernini (1629-62). Largest Christian church in world.

St Petersburg, *see* LENINGRAD.

St Petersburg, winter resort of W Florida, US; on Tampa Bay. Pop. 216,000.

St Pierre and Miquelon, overseas isl. dept. of France; off S Newfoundland, Canada. Area 241 sq km (93 sq mi); pop. 6000, cap. St Pierre. Has ice-free harbour; fishing. Settled by French in 17th cent.

St Quentin, town of N France, on R. Somme. Pop. 66,000. Textile mfg., engineering. Scene of French defeat by Prussians (1871), and of German counter-offensive (1918).

Saint-Saëns, [Charles] Camille (1835-1921), French composer. Best known for *The Carnival of the Animals* for 2 pianos and orchestra. Also wrote symphonies, piano concertos, operas.

Saint-Simon, Claude Henri, Comte de (1760–1825), French social theorist. Advocated indust. state directed by science and universal association for common good.

Saint-Simon, Louis de Rouvroy, Duc de (1675-1755), French courtier, author. Wrote bitter account of personalities of Louis XIV's court, pub. as *Mémoires* (1829).

St Tropez, town of Provence, SE France, on

Côte d'Azur. Pop. 6000. Fishing port, fashionable resort.

St Vincent, isl. of SE West Indies, in Windward Isls. Area 388 sq km (150 sq mi); pop. 96,000; cap. Kingstown (pop. 17,000). Mountainous, well forested. Cotton growing, banana exports. British colony from 1763; became associate state 1969. Independent 1979. Member of British Commonwealth.

St Vincent, Cape, headland of SW Portugal. Scene of naval battle (1797) when British under Jervis defeated Spanish fleet.

St Vincent Gulf, shallow inlet of Indian Ocean, South Australia, between Yorke Penin. and Adelaide.

Saint Vitus' dance or **chorea,** condition characterized by irregular involuntary movements of any part of the body. Most common among children. Cause unknown but closely associated with rheumatic fever.

Sakai, indust. city of Japan, on Osaka Bay in SW Honshu isl. Pop. 758,000. Machinery, chemical and textile mfg. Major port in 15th and 16th cents.

saké, alcoholic beverage made from fermented rice. National drink of Japan, where it is served warm.

Sakhalin, isl. of USSR, off E coast of Siberian RSFSR. Area *c* 76,400 sq km (29,500 sq mi). Mountainous, with cold climate; fishing and timber; oil and coal fields. Settled by Russians in 19th cent.; S half, called Karafuto, occupied by Japan (1905-45).

Sakharov, Andrei Dmitriyevich (1921-), Soviet physicist, dissident. Leader in development of Soviet hydrogen bomb. Vigorous advocate of civil liberty and democratic reform in USSR. Awarded Nobel Peace Prize (1975), but refused permission to receive award.

Saki, pseud. of H[ector] H[ugh] Munro (1870-1916), British author, b. Burma. Known for humorous, often macabre short stories in *The Chronicles of Clovis* (1912), novel *The Unbearable Bassington* (1912). Killed in WWI.

Sakkara or **Saqqâra,** village of N Egypt, SW of Cairo. Site of main necropolis of ancient MEMPHIS; step pyramids.

Saladin (*c* 1137-93), Moslem military and political leader, b. Mesopotamia. Became sultan of Egypt (1175). Extended control over Syria (1174-86); led Saracen capture of Jerusalem after defeating Christians at Hattin (1187). Repelled 3rd Crusade led by Richard I of England (1190-2).

Salamanca, city of W Spain, on R. Tormes, cap. of Salamanca prov. Pop. 140,000. Transport jct.; univ. (*c* 1230). Taken from Moors 1085; medieval cultural, religious centre. Scene of Wellington's victory (1812) over French in Peninsular War. Two cathedrals (12th, 16th cent.).

salamander, tailed amphibian of order Urodela. Scaleless with soft, moist skin; teeth in both jaws, no gills.

Salamis, isl. of Greece, in Saronic Gulf. Area 93 sq km (36 sq mi). Scene of naval battle (480 BC) in which Greeks defeated Persians.

Salazar, António de Oliveira (1889-1970), Portuguese statesman. Stabilized country's economy as finance minister before becoming premier (1932-68). Exercised dictatorial power after introducing (1933) new constitution. Suppressed political opposition in Portugal and independence movements in colonies.

Salem, port of NE Massachusetts, US. Pop. 41,000. Settled 1626. Notorious for witchcraft trials of 1692.

Salem, cap. of Oregon, US; on Willamette R. Pop. 80,000. In farming, cattle region; varied agric. related industs., metal goods, paper mfg. Cap. from 1851.

Salerno, city of Campania, SW Italy, on Gulf of Salerno. Cap. of Salerno prov. Pop. 162,000. Port, agric., commercial centre. Medical school founded 9th cent., cathedral (11th cent.). Scene of Allied landings (1943).

Salford, town of Greater Manchester met. county, NW England, on R. Irwell and Manchester Ship Canal. Pop. 126,000. Extensive docks; indust. centre; RC cathedral (1848).

Salic law, law adopted in Middle Ages by certain noble and royal European families, excluding female succession to offices and titles. Applied mainly in France and Spain.

salicylic acid, white crystalline solid obtained from willow bark or phenol. Used in manufacture of aspirin, in food preservation, and as an antiseptic.

Salinger, J[erome] D[avid] (1919-), American novelist. Known for *The Catcher in the Rye* (1951) dealing with adolescent hero's resistance to adult 'phoniness'.

Salisbury, Robert Arthur Talbot Gascoyne-Cecil, 3rd Marquess of (1830-1903), British statesman, PM (1885, 1886-92, 1895-1902). Pursued cautious imperialist policy, trying to arrange territ. expansion in Africa by agreement with European powers.

Salisbury, Robert Cecil, 1st Earl of (1563-1612), English statesman. Succeeded father, Lord Burghley, as Elizabeth's chief minister (1598); arranged James I's accession to throne and admin. his govt.

Salisbury, town of Wiltshire, SW England, on R. Avon. Pop. 35,000. Market town. Built as 'New Sarum' (near ancient 'Old Sarum' fortress). Famous cathedral (13th cent.) has highest spire in England (123 m/404 ft).

Salisbury, cap. of Zimbabwe. Pop. 564,000. Admin., commercial, transport centre in agric. and gold mining region; tobacco indust.; univ. Founded 1890 as Fort Salisbury; cap. of Federation of Rhodesia and Nyasaland 1953-63.

Salisbury Plain, chalk downs of Wiltshire, SW England. Military training area. Incl. STONEHENGE.

saliva, watery secretion of 3 pairs of salivary glands situated around mouth. Contains enzyme ptyalin which begins process of breaking down starch into sugar. Also cleanses mouth and makes sense of taste possible.

Sallust, full name Gaius Sallustius Crispus (86-*c* 34 BC), Roman historian. Wrote histories of the Catiline conspiracy and the wars against JUGURTHA.

salmon, food and game fish, genus *Salmo* or *Oncorhynchus,* which breeds in fresh water. After feeding period of up to 6 years, young migrate to open sea, remaining up to 4 years. Adults return to birthplace to spawn. All Pacific salmon, *Oncorhynchus,* die after spawning but some females of Atlantic salmon, *Salmo salar,* survive.

salmonella, genus of bacteria which incl. causes of typhoid fever and various forms of food poisoning in man and domestic animals.

Salome, traditional name for the daughter of Herodias. In NT, story of how her dancing pleased Herod so much that he granted her request for the head of John the Baptist.

Salonika (*Thessaloníki*), town of NE Greece, on Gulf of Salonika, cap. of Macedonia. Pop. 557,000. Founded 4th cent. BC. Taken by Turks 1430; Greek from 1912.

Salop, *see* SHROPSHIRE.

salsify, vegetable oyster or **oyster plant,** *Tragopogon porrifolius,* plant native to S Europe. Purple flowers, white roots with oyster-like flavour used as vegetable.

SALT, *see* STRATEGIC ARMS LIMITATION TALKS.

salt, in chemistry, compound formed when hydrogen of an acid is wholly or partly replaced by a metal. Salts are formed by reaction of bases with acids. Common salt, sodium chloride ($NaCl$), occurs in sea water and mineral deposits; used in manufacture of chlorine and sodium compounds.

Salt Lake City, cap. of Utah, US; SE of Great Salt L. at foot of Wasatch Range. Pop. 783,000. Transport, commercial, indust. centre. Oil refining, copper smelting; textile, food mfg. Founded 1847 by Brigham Young; Mormon Temple (1893).

saltpetre or **potassium nitrate** (KNO_3), white crystalline salt. Used in fertilizers, gunpowder, glass manufacture, *etc.* Chile saltpetre is sodium nitrate.

saluki, breed of slender hound of ancient origin. Long ears, silky coat; stands up to 71 cm/28 in. at shoulder.

Salvador, Atlantic port of E Brazil, cap. of Bahia state. Pop. 1,237,000. Cocoa, sugar, tobacco exports; sugar refining, flour milling. Founded 1549, cap. of Portuguese territ. until 1763. Formerly named Bahia.

Salvador, *see* EL SALVADOR.

salvage, in maritime law, term used either for act of rescuing life or property from destruction at sea, or for reward to which rescuers are entitled.

Salvation Army, international evangelical and philanthropic movement. Estab. (1865) in London, UK, by William BOOTH, given present name in 1878. Aims to bring Christian religion to those it does not normally reach, as well as bringing practical relief to poor, *eg* soup kitchens, hostels for homeless. Organized on military lines, with uniforms, ranks.

Salween, river of S China and Burma. Rises in Tibet, flows through deep gorges *c* 2800 km (1750 mi) to Gulf of Martaban.

Salzburg, city of NC Austria, on R. Salzach, cap. of Salzburg prov. Pop. 139,000. Cultural, tourist centre. Annual music festival (birthplace of Mozart). Archbishopric from 8th cent.; monastery (8th cent.), medieval castle, cathedral (17th cent.). Univ. (1623).

Samar, isl. of Philippines, SE of Luzon. Area *c* 13,100 sq km (5050 sq mi). Produces bananas, hemp, coconuts.

Samara, *see* KUIBYSHEV.

Samaria, hist. cap. of kingdom of Israel, during 10th-8th cent. BC. Extensive ruins.

Samaritans, descendants of non-Jewish colonists from Babylonia, Syria and elsewhere who were settled in Samaria when Israelites were deported (722 BC). Small number remain in Israel at Nablus and Jaffa. Traditional enemies of Jews; recognized only the Pentateuch.

samarium (Sm), metallic element of lanthanide series; at. no. 62, at. wt. 150.35. Discovered 1879 by spectroscopy; isolated 1901.

Samarkand, city of USSR, E Uzbek SSR. Pop. 476,000. Silk and cotton centre. Ancient city, destroyed by Alexander the Great (329 BC); centre of Arab culture in 8th cent. AD, on trade route between Europe and China. Cap. of Tamerlane's empire 14th cent. Later held by emirs of Bukhara until taken by Russia (1868).

Samoa, isl. group of C Pacific. Mainly volcanic and mountainous. Discovered (1722) by Dutch. Divided (1899) between US and Germany. **American Samoa** is overseas territ. Area 200 sq km (77 sq mi); pop. 31,000; cap. Pago Pago. Fruit growing, tuna fishing. **Western Samoa,** comprising Savaii, Upolu, and smaller isls. is independent state. Area 2850 sq km (1100 sq mi); pop. 151,000; cap. Apia. Produces fruit, copra, cocoa. Taken from Germans by New Zealand in WWI, held by them as UN trust territ. until independence 1962.

Sámos, isl. of Greece, in E Aegean Sea. Area 492 sq km (190 sq mi); cap. Vathi. Mountainous; wine, fruit, tobacco.

Samothrace (*Samothráki*), isl. of Greece, in NE Aegean Sea. Area 181 sq km (70 sq mi). Sponge fishing, goats. Famous *Nike* or *Winged Victory of Samothrace* statue (306 BC) found here 1863.

Samoyed, breed of Siberian dog with thick white or cream coat. Used to pull sleds; stands up to 60 cm/23.5 in. at shoulder.

samphire, *Crithmum maritimum,* European seashore plant of parsley family. Yellowish flowers, pointed, aromatic leaves used in salads.

Samson, one of judges who ruled Israel before estab. of monarchy. Renowned for great strength which depended on his unshorn hair, symbolizing his vows to God. Story of his betrayal to Philistines by

Delilah in OT book of Judges.

Samsun, port of N Turkey, on Black Sea. Pop. 168,000. Situated in major tobacco growing region; exports tobacco. Founded as Greek colony of *Amisus.*

Samuel 1 and **2,** books of OT dealing with estab. of Israel as monarchy and its struggle against Philistines. Covers lives of Samuel, Saul, David. Samuel was last of judges who ruled Israelites; Saul and David were 1st kings.

Samurai warrior

samurai, aristocratic warrior class of feudal Japan with a strict code (bushido) of chivalry. Rose to power in 12th cent. during period of weak govt. and held influence until the Meiji restoration (1868).

Sana, cap. of Yemen. Pop. 448,000. Marketing centre. Noted buildings, esp. Great Mosque; palace of former Imam.

San Antonio, city of SC Texas, US; on San Antonio R. Pop. 982,000. Railway jct., commercial, indust. centre. Cattle, cotton market, oil refining, food processing, brewing. Spanish mission estab. 1718. Taken by Texas (1835); heroic Alamo defence 1836.

sanctions, in international politics, coercive measures adopted in an attempt to enforce a country's fulfilment of its treaty obligations or compliance with international law. Usually economic measures are applied, esp. partial or complete trade boycott.

Sand, George, pseud. of Amandine Lucile Aurore Dupin, Baronne de Dudevant (1804-76), French novelist. Left husband, formed liaisons with Musset, Chopin and others. Novels advocating free love incl. *Indiana* (1832), *Elle et lui* (1859).

sand, sediment composed of rock particles, precisely defined in geology as having particle size between 1/16 mm and 2 mm. Major constituent is quartz; used in production of glass, building materials, abrasives.

sandalwood, several trees of genus *Santalum* incl. Indian *S. album,* white sandalwood. Hard, fragrant wood used for ornamental carving and burned as incense. East Indian red sandalwood, *Pterocarpus santalinus,* yields dye.

sand fly, small 2-winged fly, genus *Phlebotomus,* whose bite spreads diseases, *eg* oriental sore, sand fly fever.

sandhopper, small crustacean with body modified for hopping. Common sandhopper, *Talitrus saltator,* abundant in tidal seaweeds.

Sandhurst, village of Berkshire, S England. Has Royal Military Academy (1799).

San Diego, seaport of S California, US; on San Diego Bay. Pop. 1,585,000. Naval base, defence industs.; fish, cotton, agric. exports. Tuna fishing and canning; aerospace and electronic industs. Spanish mission estab. 1769.

sandpiper, small long-billed shore bird of Scolopacidae family. Species incl. common sandpiper *Tringa hypoleucos,* of Old World.

sandstone, porous sedimentary rock composed mainly of sand grains cemented together. Sand grains usually composed of quartz; cementing material may be calcium carbonate, silica, or iron oxides. Widely distributed; used as building stone.

sandstorm, strong, dry wind carrying clouds of coarse sand. Common in desert areas, esp. N Africa, Arabia, SW US.

Sandwich Islands, *see* HAWAII.

San Francisco, seaport of W California, US; on penin. between San Francisco Bay and Pacific. Pop. 665,000, Bay area 4,592,000. Financial, cultural centre. Exports iron and steel, agric. produce; shipbuilding, oil refining, printing and publishing industs. Founded 1776; grew after 1849 gold rush; destroyed by 1906 earthquake. Known for Golden Gate Bridge. Has parts of Univ. of California.

Sanger, Frederick (1918-), English biochemist. Awarded Nobel Prize for Chemistry (1958) for research on molecular structure of insulin.

Sanhedrin, highest court and council of the ancient Jewish nation, with religious and civil functions.

San José, cap. of Costa Rica, on C plateau. Pop. 234,000. Commercial, indust. centre; coffee, cacao industs., flour milling, fruit canning. Founded 1738. Has univ. (1843); cathedral.

San José, city of W California, US. Pop. 446,000. In fruit-growing area; dried fruit processing, packing; varied mfg. industs.

San Juan, cap. of Puerto Rico, seaport on NE coast. Pop. 515,000. Sugar refining; cigar, textile, drug mfg. Founded 1521. Has cathedral (1512).

San Marino, independent republic of S Europe, enclave within E Italy. Area 62 sq km (24 sq mi); pop. 21,000; cap. San Marino. Silk mfg.; agric. (exports wine, cattle). Quarrying on Mt. Titano. World's smallest republic; traditionally founded 4th cent.

San Martín, José de (1778-1850), Argentinian revolutionary. Played important part in gaining independence for Argentina, Chile and Peru.

San Miguel de Tucumán, city of NW Argentina, cap. of Tucumán prov. Pop. 366,000. Railway jct.; in irrigated agric. region in Andean foothills, producing sugar, rice, grain. Cathedral.

San Remo, town of Liguria, NW Italy, on Riviera. Pop. 63,000. Resort; fruit, flower growing. Cathedral (13th cent.).

San Salvador, small isl. of Bahamas. First sighted by Columbus in discovering Americas (1492). Also known as Watling Island.

San Salvador, cap. of El Salvador. Pop. 366,000. Commercial, indust. centre; meat packing, flour milling, textile industs. Founded 1521. Has National Univ. Has suffered repeated earthquakes.

sans-culottes, term applied during French Revolution to poorer classes, who wore trousers instead of knee breeches worn by aristocracy and bourgeoisie; by extension name was given to extreme republicans.

San Sebastián, city of N Spain, on Bay of Biscay, cap. of Guipúzcoa prov. Pop. 178,000. Port, resort, fishing indust.

Sanskrit, ancient Indic language in Indo-Iranian branch of Indo-European family. Oldest known form is Vedic Sanskrit, language of the Veda (*c* 1500 BC). Became (*c* 400 BC) court language as well as literary, religious language. Used for Hindu literature until AD 1100, still used in liturgy. Many modern Indic languages developed from it.

Santa Anna, Antonio López de (1794-1876), Mexican military, political leader; president (1833-6, 1841-4, 1846-7, 1853-5). Helped overthrow Iturbide (1823); gained power in lengthy struggle. Captured Alamo in attempt to suppress Texas revolt (1836). Defeated in Mexican War (1848).

Santa Cruz, town of C Bolivia, cap. of Santa Cruz dept. Pop. 237,000. Agric., commercial centre; trade in rice, sugar cane.

Santa Cruz de Tenerife, city of Tenerife isl., Canary Isls., Spain; cap. of Santa Cruz de Tenerife prov. Pop. 158,000. Port, exports agric. produce; resort, refuelling station.

Santa Fé, town of EC Argentina, cap. of Santa Fé prov. Pop. 245,000. Linked by canal to Paraná R., transport jct. for grain, livestock trade. Founded 1573.

Santa Fé, cap. and tourist resort of New Mexico, US. Pop. 47,000. Commercial centre in agric. region. Founded by Spanish (1609). W terminus of Santa Fé trail, important 19th-cent. trade route. Los Alamos atomic research centre is *c* 40 km (25 mi) away.

Santa Isabel, *see* MALABO.

Santa Marta, port of N Colombia, on Caribbean. Pop. 151,000. Has deep harbour; banana, coffee exports. Founded 1525.

Santander, city of N Spain, on Bay of Biscay, cap. of Santander prov. Pop. 162,000. Port, resort; iron works, shipbuilding.

Santiago, cap. of Chile, at foot of Andes. Pop. 3,595,000 (with suburbs). Commercial, indust. centre; textile, clothing, iron and steel, chemical mfg. Has railway link with Valparaiso. Founded 1541. Has National Univ. (1842); cathedral (1619).

Santiago (de Compostela), town of Galicia, NW Spain. Pop. 71,000. Tourist resort, pilgrimage centre from 9th cent.; univ. (1501). Cathedral (11th cent.) contains relics claimed to be those of St James.

Santiago de Cuba, major port of SE Cuba. Pop. 316,000. Sugar, tobacco produce; mineral exports. Founded 1514.

Santo Domingo, cap. of Dominican Republic, port on S coast. Pop. 818,000. Sugar, coffee, cacao exports; distilling, brewing, soap mfg. Founded 1496; called Ciudad Trujillo (1936-61). Has univ. (1538); 16th-cent. cathedral.

Santos, Atlantic port of SE Brazil, in São Paulo state. Pop. 396,000. Major coffee, sugar, fruit exports. Ocean access for São Paulo.

São Francisco, river of E Brazil. Rises in SW Minas Gerais plateau, flows NE 2900 km (*c* 1800 mi) to enter Atlantic ocean NE of Aracajú. H.e.p. supplies from Afonso Falls.

Saône, river of E France. Flows *c* 450 km (280 mi) from Vosges via Chalon, Mâcon to R. Rhône at Lyons. Rhône-Saône corridor is hist. route between N and S France; canal links with many rivers, *eg* Rhine, Seine.

São Paulo, city of SE Brazil, cap. of São Paulo state. Pop. 7,199,000 (with suburbs). Leading commercial, transport centre. Exports farm produce via port of Santos. Heavy machinery, motor vehicles, chemicals, textiles mfg. Founded by Jesuits (1554). Has 4 univs.

São Tomé and Principe, republic off W coast of Africa, comprising 2 isls. in Gulf of Guinea. Area 964 sq km (372 sq mi); pop 83,000; cap. São Tomé (pop. 17,000). Exports coffee, cacao, coconut products. Prov. of Portugal from 1522, became independent 1975.

sap, fluid in plants consisting of inorganic salts from soil and carbohydrates manufactured by plant in an aqueous solution. *See* TRANSPIRATION.

sapphire, precious gemstone, a variety of CORUNDUM. Deep blue and transparent; used in jewellery and gramophone styli.

Sappho (*fl* 6th cent. BC), Greek poetess. Began tradition of subjective love lyric. Verse survives only in fragments.

Sapporo, city of Japan, indust. centre of SW Hokkaido isl. Pop. 1,277,000. Flour milling, woodworking and printing industs. Tourist centre.

Saracens, name applied by the Christians during the Middle Ages to their Moslem enemies. Name originally applied to nomadic Arabs inhabiting frontier land between Roman and Persian empires.

Saragossa (*Zaragoza*), city of NE Spain, on R. Ebro, cap. of Saragossa prov. Pop. 547,000. Agric. market; indust., commercial centre; univ. (1587). Roman *Caesarea Augusta*; held by Moors until 1118; cap. of Aragón 12th-15th cent. Surrendered to French after heroic defence (1808-9) in Peninsular War. Moorish castle, 2 cathedrals (12th, 17th cent.).

Sarajevo, city of C Yugoslavia, cap. of Bosnia and Hercegovina. Pop. 271,000. Railway jct.; indust. centre. Scene of assassination (June 1914) of Archduke Francis Ferdinand, led to WWI. Has mosques (Islamic centre); RC, Orthodox cathedrals.

Saratoga Springs, health resort of E New York, US. Pop. 19,000. Scene of heavy fighting in American Revolution (1777).

Saratov, city of USSR, SC European RSFSR; on Volga. Pop. 856,000. Indust. centre, producing agric. machinery, chemicals, locomotives. Oil refining; natural gas fields nearby.

Sarawak, state of East Malaysia. Area *c* 125,000 sq km (48,000 sq mi); pop. 977,000; cap. Kuching. Produces oil, bauxite, rubber. Ceded to James Brooke (1841), whose family ruled as rajahs until 1946; British protect. 1888; joined Malaysia 1963.

sardine, *see* PILCHARD.

Sardinia (*Sardegna*), isl. of Italy, separated from mainland by Tyrrhenian Sea, from Corsica by Str. of Bonifacio. Area 24,092 sq km (9302 sq mi); cap. Cagliari. Mountainous, rising to over 1830 m (6000 ft); pasturage, fishing; zinc, lead mining. Carthaginian, taken by Rome 238 BC; contested by Pisa, Genoa from 11th cent.; papal award to Spain 14th cent. Ruled as Kingdom of Sardinia by Savoy from 1720 until it led move to Italian unification (1861).

Sardis or **Sardes,** ancient city of W Asia Minor, now village in Turkey. Cap. of kingdom of Lydia in 7th cent. BC.

Sargasso Sea, area of still water at centre of ocean currents in N Atlantic between West Indies and Azores. Abundant seaweed covers its surface.

Sargent, John Singer (1856-1925), American painter, b. Florence. Resident in London after 1884, he painted fashionable society portraits with brilliant virtuosity.

Sargon II (772-705 BC), king of Assyria (722-705 BC). Conquered N kingdom of Israel, carrying Jews into captivity. Subdued Babylon (710).

Sark (Fr. *Sercq*), one of Channel Isls., UK. Area 5 sq km (2 sq mi); comprises Great and Little Sark connected by isthmus. Isl. governed by hereditary 'seigneur' or 'dame'.

Sarnia, port of SW Ontario, Canada; on St Clair R. at S end of L. Huron. Pop. 58,000. Oil refineries.

Saronic Gulf or **Gulf of Aegina,** inlet of Aegean Sea, SE Greece. Chief port Piraeus. Joined to Gulf of Corinth by canal (1881-93).

Sarto, Andrea del (1486-1531), Florentine painter. Noted for his rich colour and painterly qualities.

Sartre, Jean-Paul (1905-80), French philosopher. Leading figure in EXISTENTIALISM. Works incl. novels *eg La Nausée* (1938), trilogy *Les Chemins de la liberté* (1945-9), plays *Les Mouches* (1943), *Huis Clos* (1944), philosophical *L'Etre et le néant* (1943), *Critique de la raison dialectique* (1960). Declined Nobel Prize for Literature (1964).

Sarum, Old and **New,** *see* SALISBURY, England.

Saskatchewan, Prairie prov. of WC Canada. Area 651,903 sq km (251,700 sq mi); pop. 957,000; cap. Regina; other major city Saskatoon. Drained in N by Churchill R. Forests, lakeland in N, prairies in S. Mineral resources in N (esp. uranium at Athabaska); timber in C parkland; major wheat production in S. Fur trading area purchased by Canada from Hudson's Bay Co. (1869). Became prov. in 1905.

Saskatchewan, river of C Saskatchewan, Canada; formed by confluence of N Saskatchewan and S Saskatchewan rivers. Flows E 550 km (340 mi) through Cedar L. to L. Winnipeg. Provides h.e.p., irrigation.

Saskatoon, city of SC Saskatchewan, Canada; on S Saskatchewan R. Pop. 134,000. Agric. distribution centre; meat packing, oil refining.

Sassoon, Siegfried Lorraine (1886-1967), English author. Experiences in WWI inspired anti-war *Counter-attack and Other Poems* (1918). Wrote semi-autobiog. novels, *Memoirs of a Fox-Hunting Man* (1928), *Memoirs of an Infantry Officer* (1930).

Satan, in Judaism, Christianity and Islam, the enemy of God and humanity, *ie* a unified personification of evil as opposed to that of good. Also called the Devil. NT developed idea of Satan as prince of demons, enemy of Christ, and describes war in heaven. Central figure of many popular legends, in literature appears as Mephistopheles (*eg* Goethe's *Faust*), Lucifer (*eg* Milton's *Paradise Lost*).

satellite, in astronomy, celestial body in orbit about larger body, usually a planet; Moon is a satellite of the Earth. Russians placed 1st artifical satellite (sputnik) in orbit about Earth (1957). Many have been launched since for communication and espionage purposes and to study upper atmosphere, weather, radiation from outer space, *etc*.

Satie, Erik (1866-1925), French composer. Produced clear and simple music, often ironic or satirical in character. Works incl. ballets, songs, and many piano pieces.

satin, silk or rayon fabric having a smooth finish, glossy on the face and dull on the back. First made in China, popularized in Europe during Middle Ages.

satinwood, close-grained, hard, yellow wood of East Indian tree *Chloroxylon swietenia* and West Indian *Zanthoxylum flavum*. Used in veneers, marquetry, *etc*.

satire, literary work, in prose or poetry, or work of art, *etc,* which ridicules individuals, situations, ideas, esp. with aim of correcting vice. Uses mockery, wit, parody or irony; may be humorous or serious.

Saturn, in Roman religion, god of harvests, later identified with Greek Cronus. Husband of Ops, father of Jupiter, Juno, Ceres, Pluto, Neptune. His festival, Saturnalia, was celebrated near the winter solstice with feasting, revelry and licence for slaves, and was prototype for modern Christmas.

Saturn, in astronomy, 2nd largest planet of Solar System, 6th in distance from Sun; mean distance from Sun *c* 1427 million km; diameter 119,300 km; revolves about Sun in period of *c* 29½ years. Has 10 natural satellites and system of concentric rings of small particles. Has dense atmosphere containing hydrogen, ammonia and methane.

satyr, in Greek myth, minor woodland deity; attendant of Dionysus. Represented with pointed ears, short horns, head and body of man, legs of a goat. Given to riotous merriment and lechery. Similar to Roman faun.

Saudi Arabia, kingdom of SW Asia, occupying most of ARABIA. Area *c* 2,149,690 (830,000 sq mi); pop. 7,866,000; cap. Riyadh. Language: Arabic. Religion: Sunnite Islam. Mainly desert; agric., pastoral economy; great wealth derived from rich oil deposits in E. Has Islamic holy cities Mecca, Medina in Hejaz. State formed 1932 following unification of Nejd and Hejaz under Ibn Saud in 1925.

Saul (d. *c* 1012 BC), first king of Israel. The Bible relates how he was consumed by jealousy for his rival David, whose patron he had previously been. Killed himself after defeat by Philistines at Mt. Gilboa.

Sault Ste Marie, port of SC Ontario, Canada; on international canal link between L. Superior and L. Huron. Pop. 80,000. Timber, steel industs. Estab. as French mission in 17th cent. Opposite is **Sault Ste Marie,** town of Michigan, US. Pop. 15,000.

Saussure, Ferdinand de (1857-1913), Swiss linguist, regarded as father of structural LINGUISTICS. Clearly demarcated synchronic and diachronic ways of studying language. Held that language must be studied as social phenomenon.

Sava or **Save,** river of N Yugoslavia. Flows *c* 940 km (585 mi) from Julian Alps via Zagreb to Danube at Belgrade.

Savage, Michael Joseph (1872-1940), New Zealand statesman, b. Australia. First Labour PM (1935-40).

savanna or **savannah,** natural grassland containing scattered trees and bushes. Found in tropical and subtropical areas with distinct rainy season. Most extensive in Africa; occurs also in *llanos* and *campos* of South America.

Savannah, port of E Georgia, US; near mouth of Savannah R. Pop. 207,000. Naval supplies, cotton exports; shipbuilding, sugar refining, varied mfg. industs.

Savoie, *see* SAVOY.

Savonarola, Girolamo (1452-98), Italian Dominican monk. Through powerful sermons inspired expulsion of Pietro de' Medici from Florence (1494) and ruled as virtual dictator, advocating a return to ascetic Christian values. Excommunicated by Alexander VI (1497). Arrested, convicted of heresy and executed.

savory, any of genus *Satureia* of aromatic herbs of mint family. Native to Europe and used in cooking.

Savoy (*Savoie*), region of SE France, hist. cap. Chambéry. Incl. Savoy Alps, Graian Alps, Mont Blanc massif. Agric., esp. dairying, tourism, h.e.p. Medieval county; duchy from 1416. Ruled by House of Savoy, lost much territ. to France, Switzerland in early 16th cent. Part of Kingdom of Sardinia from 1720; ceded to France (1860).

Savoy, House of, European royal family, sometime rulers of Piedmont, Valois, Bresse, Nice. Acquired Sicily under Peace of Utrecht (1714) and exchanged it for Sardinia (1720). Reign of CHARLES ALBERT, king of Sardinia, saw beginnings of RISORGIMENTO; his son VICTOR EMMANUEL II was 1st king of united Italy. Ruling Italian dynasty from 1861 until abdication of Humbert II (1946).

sawfish, cartilaginous fish with flattened shark-like body, genus *Pristis,* common in tropical seas. Elongated flattened snout with pointed teeth on side used to dig for food.

Saxe, Maurice, Comte de (1696-1750), German soldier in French service. In the War of the Austrian Succession, gained a brilliant victory over European Allies at Fontenoy (1745).

Saxe-Coburg-Gotha (*Sachsen-Coburg-Gotha*), region of West Germany, former duchy created 1826 by union of Saxe-Coburg and Gotha under Ernest I. Ernest's house came to rule Belgium (under his brother, Leopold) and Britain (under his son, Albert, consort of Victoria). Duchy dispersed (1920) into Thuringia and Bavaria.

saxifrage, any of genus *Saxifraga* of mainly perennial plants of N temperate and Arctic regions. Most species grow wild as low, rock plants.

Saxons, Teutonic people originally inhabiting what is now Schleswig (S Jutland). Spread during 5th-6th cent. through NW Germany, N coast of Gaul, S England (in area of later kingdoms of Sussex, Wessex and Essex).

Saxony (Ger. *Sachsen*), region of East Germany, hist. cap. Dresden. Main cities Chemnitz, Leipzig. Duchy from 9th cent.; electorate from 14th cent.; kingdom from 1806, joined German empire 1871. Became East German prov. after WWII (dissolved 1952). Name also applied to region of West Germany, corresponding to state of Lower Saxony (*Niedersachsen*).

saxophone, family of musical wind instruments, varying in range and size but all having single reed and conical tube of brass. Used in military bands, jazz groups and orchestras. Developed by Adolphe Sax in 1840s.

Sayers, Dorothy L[eigh] (1893-1957), English author. Known for detective novels featuring erudite hero, Lord Peter Wimsey, *eg Clouds of Witness* (1926).

scabies, skin disease caused by parasitic mite *Sarcoptes scabiei.* Female burrows under skin, esp. around elbows and groin, to lay eggs. Main symptom is intense itch.

Devil's bit scabious

scabious, any of genus *Scabiosa* of annual or perennial herbs native to Europe, Asia and Africa. Species incl. sweet scabious, *S. atropurpurea,* with white, pink or purple flowers.

Scafell Pike, mountain of Lake Dist., Cumbria, NW England. Highest in England (978 m/3210 ft).

scale, in music, progression in ascending or descending order of related groups of notes. Most pieces of music are based on specific scale, the key of any piece being given by starting note (tonic note) of scale.

scallop, any of Pectinidae family of bivalve molluscs. Two fan-shaped, radially-ribbed shells with wavy outer edge.

Scandinavia, penin. of NW Europe, comprising Norway, Sweden; bounded by Arctic Ocean, Atlantic, Baltic, Gulf of Bothnia. Culturally and hist. also incl. Denmark, Finland, Iceland, Faeroe Isls.

Scandinavian, *see* GERMANIC LANGUAGES.

scandium (Sc), rare metallic element; at. no. 21, at. wt. 44.96. Occurs in several minerals; discovered (1879) by spectroscopic analysis.

Scapa Flow, sea area of Orkney Isls., N Scotland. UK naval base in WWI and II. Interned German fleet scuttled (1919).

scarab beetle, any of Scarabaeidae family of large beetles with club-ended antennae. Incl. dung beetles and chafers. Name particularly applies to Egyptian sacred dung beetle *Scarabaeus sacer* whose image appears on seals or charms.

Scarborough, town of North Yorkshire, NE England. Pop. 44,000. Spa, resort; fishing port. Has remains of 12th-cent. castle.

Scarlatti, Alessandro (*c* 1660-1725), Italian composer. Pioneer of Italian opera. Also wrote masses, cantatas, oratorios. His son, **[Giuseppe] Domenico Scarlatti** (1685-1757), was also a composer. Known for innovative harpsichord music.

scarlet fever or **scarlatina,** contagious disease, esp. of children, caused by bacterium *Streptococcus pyogenes.* Characterized by fever, sore throat, and a scarlet rash. Treated by antibiotics, *eg* penicillin.

scepticism, in philosophy, theory contending that range of knowledge is limited by capacity of mind or inaccessibility of object. Exponents incl. Democritus, Pyrrho, Kant.

Schaffhausen, town of N Switzerland, on R. Rhine, cap. of Schaffhausen canton. Pop. 37,000. Indust. centre using h.e.p. from Schaffhausen Falls.

Scheldt (Fr. *Escaut*; Dutch, Flem. *Schelde*), river of W Europe. Flows 435 km (270 mi) from N France via Belgium (Tournai, Antwerp) to estuary in Netherlands. Connected to many canals.

Schiller, [Johann Christoph] Friedrich von (1759-1805), German poet, dramatist, historian. Associate of Goethe, began with STURM UND DRANG prose dramas, *eg The Robbers* (1781). Later plays more realistic, classical in form, *eg Wallenstein* (1798-9), *Maria Stuart* (1800), *The Maid of Orleans* (1801), *Wilhelm Tell* (1804).

Schism, Great, split in RC church (1378-1417) resulting in rival lines of popes in Avignon and Rome. Following Council of Pisa (1409), there were 3 rival claimants to papacy. Concluded by Council of Constance, when Martin V was elected pope.

schist, metamorphic rock, composed of thin, parallel layers of constituent minerals. Mineral crystals are finer than gneiss, coarser than slate. Types distinguished by dominant mineral *eg* mica schist, hornblende schist, talc schist.

schistosomiasis, *see* BILHARZIA.

schizophrenia, severe mental disorder characterized by separation of thought processes from reality, fragmentation of personality, withdrawal from human contact, bizarre behaviour, delusions and hallucinations. Treated by electric shocks, tranquillizer drugs, psychotherapy.

Schleswig-Holstein, state of N West Germany, in S Jutland penin. Area 15,656 sq km (6045 sq mi); cap. Kiel. Low-lying; main rivers Elbe, Eider, crossed by Kiel Canal. Cereals, potatoes, livestock production; industs. centred in Kiel, Lübeck, Flensburg. Duchies associated with Denmark from 15th cent.; annexed by Prussia (1866) after Austro-Prussian War. N Schleswig returned (1920) to Denmark after plebiscite.

Schliemann, Heinrich (1822-1890), German archaeologist. Discovered 9 superimposed city sites of Troy (1871-90). His excavations at Mycenae (1874-6) revealed remarkable MYCENAEAN CIVILIZATION.

Schmidt, Helmut (1918-), West German politician. Social Democratic chancellor from 1974. Re-elected 1976, 1980.

schnauzer, breed of short-haired German terrier with blunt nose, erect ears. Standard schnauzer, used as guard dog, stands 43-51 cm/17-20 in. at shoulder.

Schoenberg, Arnold (1874-1951), Austrian composer. Early music was romantic. Later developed ATONALITY. From 1921, organized this into system of 12-note composition based on manipulation of rows of notes of the chromatic scale. Lived in US from 1933.

scholasticism, philosophical system of medieval European theologians, esp. St Thomas Aquinas and Duns Scotus. Constituted synthesis of Aristotelian philosophy and Christian revelation, influenced by neoplatonism. Central problem that of universal concepts (*see* NOMINALISM, REALISM).

Schopenhauer, Arthur (1788-1860), German philosopher. Believed man's irrational will to be the only reality, and release from suffering and discord to be achieved only by negation of will. Works incl. *The World as Will and Idea* (1818).

Schrödinger, Erwin (1887-1961), Austrian physicist. Developed mathematical form of quantum theory as wave mechanics. Shared Nobel Prize for Physics with Dirac (1933).

Schubert, Franz Peter (1797-1828), Austrian composer. Noted for his lyrical melody, his work is often underlaid by melancholy. Foremost exponent of German *Lieder*, famous song cycles incl. *Die schöne Müllerin* and *Die Winterreise*. Wrote masterly string quartets, piano pieces. Best-known symphonies are 9th ('Great C major') and 8th ('The Unfinished').

Schuman, Robert (1886-1963), French statesman, premier (1947-8). As foreign minister (1948-53), evolved plan (1950) for European Coal and Steel Community, basis of later European Community.

Schumann, Robert Alexander (1810-56), German composer. Works incl. collections of piano pieces, *Carnaval* and *Kreisleriana*, Piano Concerto in A Minor, and *Spring* and *Rhenish* symphonies. His wife, **Clara Schumann,** née Wieck (1819-96), was renowned pianist.

Schuschnigg, Kurt von (1897-), Austrian statesman. Chancellor from 1934. Forced to resign after Nazis had occupied Austria (March, 1938).

Schütz, Heinrich (1585-1672), German composer. Introduced Italian techniques of vocal writing into Germany. Works incl. madrigals, church music.

Schwarzwald, *see* BLACK FOREST.

Schweitzer, Albert (1875-1965), Alsatian physician, missionary, theologian. From 1913, devoted himself to medical mission at Lambaréné, Gabon. Noted organist; wrote biog. of Bach and edited his organ music. In philosophy, believed in 'reverence for life', respecting all living creatures. Awarded Nobel Peace Prize (1952).

Schwerin, town of NW East Germany, on L. Schwerin. Pop. 109,000. Chemicals, pharmaceuticals mfg. Founded 1160; hist. cap. of Mecklenburg.

Schwyz, town of C Switzerland, cap. of Schwyz canton. Pop. 12,000. Tourist centre near L. Lucerne.

sciatica, pain along the course of the sciatic nerve, esp. affecting back of thigh, calf and foot. Often caused by pressure exerted on spinal nerves by intervertebral discs.

science, system of knowledge, founded on formal axioms or theories constructed from observation and experiment. Sciences such as physics and chemistry, which try to describe and account for natural phenomena, are often studied by theories which express mathematically a principle underlying numerous observations. Ideally, such theories encompass all previous knowledge on the phenomena and can be used to make testable predictions; they are discarded or suitably modified if they are found to be too inaccurate or at a variance with experimental evidence.

science fiction, literary genre drawing on scientific knowledge or speculation to present fantasy. Typical motifs incl. interplanetary travel, artificial intelligence, global cataclysm. Early exponents incl. Jules Verne, H.G. Wells; developed by Isaac Asimov, Ray Bradbury, Arthur C. Clarke.

scientology, religio-scientific movement estab. in US (*c* 1950) by Lafayette Ronald Hubbard (1911-) Members use process similar to psychoanalysis to release energy of subconscious drives. Controversial practices have led to official inquiries in some countries.

Scilly Isles, archipelago off Cornwall, SW England. Incl. *c* 140 granite isls., 5 inhabited (St Mary's, Tresco, St Martin's, St Agnes, Bryher). Area 16 sq km (6 sq mi); pop. 2000; cap. Hugh Town. Mild climate; tourism; early flowers indust.

Scipio, Publius Cornelius ('Africanus Major') (*c* 234-183 BC), Roman soldier. Routed Carthaginian armies in Spain (210-206). Invaded Carthage (204), forcing Hannibal to return from Italy. Defeated Hannibal at Zama (202). His son's adopted son, **Publius Cornelius Scipio ('Africanus Minor')** (*c* 185-129 BC), commanded destruction of Carthage, ending 3rd Punic War (146).

Scone, village of Tayside region, C Scotland. Old Scone was site of Scottish coronations. *See* STONE OF DESTINY.

Scorpio, *see* ZODIAC.

scorpion, any of order Scorpionida of arachnids of warm and tropical regions. Two large pincers in front, long segmented tail with venomous sting.

Scotland, constituent country of UK, in N part of GREAT BRITAIN. Area 78,749 sq km (30,405 sq mi); pop. 5,179,000; cap. Edinburgh; largest city Glasgow.

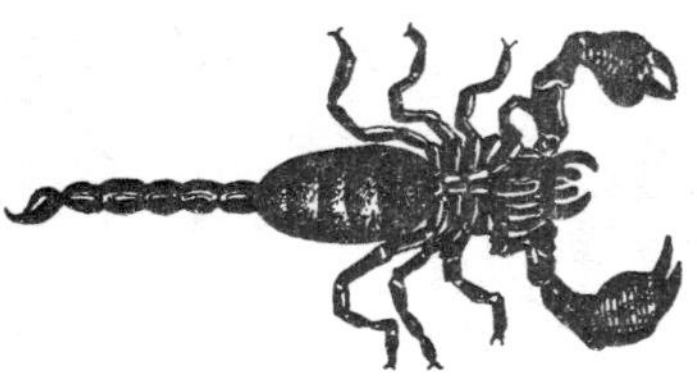

Scorpion

Comprises 9 regions, 3 isl. authorities. Main rivers Clyde, Forth, Tay, Dee. Highlands, isls. in N, W (crofting, fishing, forestry, tourism); uplands in S (sheep rearing). Pop. and industs. mainly concentrated in C lowlands, incl. coalmining, shipbuilding, engineering industs. Offshore oil, gas in E. Christianity spread from 6th cent.; hist. warring with England until union of Crowns under James VI (1603), politically united with England from 1707; Jacobite rebellions in 1715, 1745. Resurgence of nationalism in 20th cent.

Scotland, Church of, established national church in Scotland, presbyterian in govt. Jurisdiction of RC church abolished by Parliament in act of 1560. Under influence of KNOX, reformed church created on self-governing units. Development complicated by periods of episcopacy under Stuart rulers leading to National Covenant (*see* COVENANTERS). Established status confirmed in Act of Settlement (1690) and Act of Union (1707). Secessionary groups incl. Free Church of Scotland (1843).

Scotland Yard, hq. of Metropolitan London police, UK. Name derives from original site in street near Whitehall. Used esp. for Criminal Investigation Dept. (CID) which it houses.

Scott, Sir George Gilbert (1811-78), English architect. Active in Gothic revival, his numerous works incl. St Pancras Station and Albert Memorial, London.

Scott, Robert Falcon (1868-1912), English naval officer, explorer. Led expedition (1901-4) in *Discovery* to explore Ross Sea; discovered King Edward VII Land. Led 2nd expedition in *Terra Nova*, reached South Pole (Jan. 1912) 35 days after Amundsen. He and 4 companions died on return journey.

Scott, Sir Walter (1771-1832), Scottish author. Kindled interest in Scots folklore in ballad collection *The Minstrelsy of the Scottish Border* (1802-3), narrative poems, *eg Lay of the Last Minstrel* (1805), *Lady of the Lake* (1810). Romantic historical novels incl. *Waverley* (1814), *Old Mortality* (1816), *Rob Roy* (1818), *The Heart of Midlothian* (1818), *Ivanhoe* (1820), *Kenilworth* (1821).

Scottish Gaelic, *see* GAELIC.

Scottish Nationalist Party (SNP), political party evolved from Scottish Home Rule Association (formed 1886). Advocates self-govt. for Scotland.

Scottish terrier, breed of dog developed in Scotland in 19th cent. to hunt game. Stands *c* 25 cm/10 in. at shoulder.

Scotus, *see* DUNS SCOTUS, JOHN.

scree, *see* TALUS.

Scriabin, Aleksandr Nikolayevich (1872-1915), Russian composer and pianist. Works, often mystical, incl. tone poem *Prometheus*, piano music.

scribes, term for officials learned in Jewish law. First applied to Ezra (*c* 444 BC); last to Simeon the Just (4th-3rd cent. BC). Work developed into Oral Law of TALMUD.

scrofula, tuberculosis of lymph nodes of neck. Characterized by swelling of nodes and ulceration of overlying skin. Formerly called the King's evil, it was believed to be cured by royal touch.

scrub, thick, stunted vegetation found on tracts of poor, semi-arid land. Types incl. maquis of W Mediterranean area, mallee and mulga scrub of Australia, cactus scrub of E Africa.

Scullin, James Henry (1876-1953), Australian statesman, PM (1929-31). United Labor Party (1928), and was its leader (1928-35).

sculling, sport of propelling a boat by means of sculls (light oars) held in each hand. Competitive sculling races date from 1840s.

sculpture, art of producing 3-dimensional representations of forms. Techniques used incl. carving in wood or stone and modelling in wax or clay for eventual casting in plaster, lead or bronze. Field of sculpture has expanded in 20th cent. to incl. kinetic sculpture, assemblages, welded structures, *etc.*

Scunthorpe, town of Humberside, E England. Pop. 71,000. Iron and steel indust.

scurvy, disease resulting from deficiency of vitamin C in diet. Characterized by weakening of capillaries, haemorrhages in tissue, bleeding from gums. Formerly a problem on long sea voyages when fresh fruit was unavailable, it was treated in 18th cent. by issuing of lime juice.

Scutari, Albania, *see* SHKODËR.

Scutari, Turkey, *see* ISTANBUL.

Scylla, in Greek myth, daughter of Hecate, loved by Poseidon and turned into a monster by Amphitrite. Devoured sailors who passed her cave in Straits of Messina, S Italy. Opposite was **Charybdis,** a monster who had been thrown into sea by Zeus for stealing Hercules' cattle. A whirlpool was created as she sucked and spewed water.

Scythians, nomadic tribe inhabiting the steppes N of Black Sea between the Danube and Don. (7th-2nd cents. BC). Known from their trading contacts with the Greeks. Their expansion was resisted by Persians under Darius (*c* 512 BC). By 2nd cent. BC, had been overwhelmed by Sarmatians.

sea anemone, sedentary marine coelenterate of class Actinozoa. Columnar body without skeleton; mouth surrounded by circles of tentacles. Found attached to rocks, weeds.

Seaborg, Glenn Theodore (1912-), American chemist. Shared Nobel Prize for Chemistry (1951) with E.M. McMillan for discoveries in chemistry of transuranic elements; co-discoverer of americium, curium, berkelium and several other elements.

sea cow, name applied to DUGONG or MANATEE.

sea elephant or **elephant seal,** *Mirounga leonina,* large seal, largest of pinnipeds; reaches lengths of 6 m/20 ft. Male has inflatable proboscis.

seagull, *see* GULL.

seahorse, small fish of Syngnathidae family, esp. genus *Hippocampus.* Elongated snout and prehensile tail; male has pouch for brooding eggs.

seal, carnivorous marine mammal, order Pinnipedia. True seal (Phocidae family) has no external ears and rudimentary hind limbs united to tail. Seals of Otariidae family, incl. sea lion, have external ears and hind limbs used for locomotion. Hunted for skins and oil-yielding blubber.

sea leopard, *Hydrurga leptonyx,* large earless seal of Antarctic. Aggressive predator, feeding on penguins and young seals.

sea lion, eared seal of Otariidae family with smooth coat and no under-fur. Californian sea lion, *Zalophus californianus,* noted for agility, is commonest.

Sealyham, breed of terrier developed in Wales in 19th cent. Coat mainly white; stands 25 cm/10 in. at shoulder.

sea otter, *Enhydra lutris,* web-footed marine carnivore of N Pacific coast. Larger than common otter, with long tail; dark brown fur valued commercially.

sea sickness, *see* MOTION SICKNESS.

sea snake, any of Hydrophidae family of poisonous snakes of Indian and Pacific oceans. Flattened oar-like body.

sea squirt, any of class Ascidiacea of sedentary marine tunicates. Cylindrical or globular body enclosed in skin of cellulose-like material. Contracts body and squirts water when disturbed.

Seattle, seaport of W Washington, US; on Puget Sound between Olympic and Cascade Mts. Pop. 1,822,000. Indust., commercial centre; timber, fish, fruit exports; shipbuilding, aircraft mfg. Settled in 1850s. Has 2 univs.

sea urchin, any echinoderm of class Echinoidea. Globular or disc-shaped; body covered with calcareous plates studded with spines.

seaweed, common name for all types of marine ALGAE, esp. BROWN ALGAE.

Sebastian, St (*fl c* 3rd cent.), Roman martyr. Traditionally, a favourite of Diocletian whom he antagonized by embracing Christianity. Shot with arrows and left for dead; wounds healed but he was eventually battered to death.

Sebastopol, *see* SEVASTOPOL.

secondary school, institution providing for the education of children over the age of 11 years; attendance compulsory until age of 16 years. Types incl. GRAMMAR SCHOOL and secondary modern, both of these being superseded by COMPREHENSIVE EDUCATION.

Second Empire (1852-70), period in French history when Louis Napoleon, after overthrowing Second Republic, ruled as emperor NAPOLEON III. Terminated by Franco-Prussian War.

secretary bird, *Sagittarius serpentarius,* long-legged S African bird of prey with head crest resembling quill pens. Feeds on snakes, insects.

Security Council, *see* UNITED NATIONS ORGANIZATION.

Sedan, town of NE France, on R. Meuse. Pop. 24,000. Textile mfg., metal goods. Huguenot stronghold in 16th-17th cent., passed to France (1642). Scene of decisive Prussian victory (1870) over France; German breakthrough (1940) in WWII.

sedative, drug administered to diminish excitement, nervousness or irritation. Among widely used types are barbiturates. Large doses induce sleep.

Seddon, Richard John, known as 'King Dick' (1845-1906), New Zealand statesman, Liberal PM (1893-1906), b. England.

sedge, any of family Cyperaceae of grass-like plants found on wet ground or in water. Genera incl. *Carex, Cyperus* and *Scirpus,* used in making paper.

Sedgemoor, former marsh of Somerset, SW England. Scene of James II's victory over Duke of Monmouth (1685).

sedimentary rocks, rocks formed by deposition and compaction of sediments. Consist of sand, gravel *etc,* laid down by seas, lakes, rivers, glaciers or wind, and compressed into layers, or strata, of varying thickness. Types incl. limestone, sandstone, shale.

sedum, genus of mainly perennial herbs native to N temperate regions. Found on rocks and walls; fleshy stalks and leaves, white, yellow or pink flowers.

Seebeck effect, in physics, production of current in a circuit when junctions of unlike metals have different temperatures. Also called thermoelectric effect.

seed, fertilized ovule which forms reproductive structure of seed plants. Consists of embryo, stored food and protective covering.

Segovia, Andrés (1893-), Spanish virtuoso guitarist. Pioneered use of guitar as concert instrument.

Segovia, town of NC Spain, cap. of Segovia prov. Pop. 42,000. Tourist centre, pottery mfg. Roman aqueduct still supplies water; Moorish alcazar, Gothic cathedral (16th cent.).

segregation, policy or practice of compelling different racial groups to live apart from each other, go to separate schools, use separate social facilities, *etc.* In Southern states of US, segregation was extensively enforced by 1920; Supreme Court rulings and legislation in 1950s and 60s banned most forms of segregation.

Known as APARTHEID in South Africa.

Seine, river of N France. Flows *c* 770 km (480 mi) from Langres Plateau via Troyes, Paris, Rouen to English Channel at Le Havre. With tributaries (incl. Aube, Marne, Oise), drains most of Paris Basin; navigable by ocean-going vessels to Rouen.

seismology, study of earthquakes and related phenomena. Occurrence and severity of tremors are recorded on a seismograph. Seismological techniques are also used in *eg* mineral prospecting, measuring thickness of ice sheets, depth and shape of ocean floors.

Sekondi-Takoradi, city of SW Ghana, on Gulf of Guinea, cap. of Western Region. Pop. 161,000. Port, exports cocoa, timber, manganese, bauxite. Sekondi was Gold Coast's chief port, superseded by Takoradi deepwater harbour (completed 1928). Towns merged 1946.

Selene, in Greek myth, moon goddess; sister of Helios (the sun). Sometimes identified with Hecate and Artemis.

selenium (Se), non-metallic element of sulphur group; at. no. 34, at. wt. 78.96. Occurs in several allotropic forms; obtained from flue dust produced by burning sulphide ores. Grey metallic form used in photoelectric cells as its conductivity varies with intensity of light. Used in glass and ceramic indust. to impart red colour.

Seleucus I (*c* 358-280 BC), one of Alexander the Great's generals. Founded Seleucid dynasty, line of kings, incl. ANTIOCHUS THE GREAT, who reigned in nearer Asia till 65 BC.

Seljuks, Turkish ruling dynasty, who conquered and controlled most of Near East (11th–13th cents).

Selkirk, Alexander (1676-1721), Scottish sailor. Marooned on Juan Fernández isl. for 4 years. Episode suggested Defoe's *Robinson Crusoe.*

Selkirkshire, former county of SE Scotland, now in Borders region. In Southern Uplands; sheep rearing; woollens, tweed mfg. Co. town was **Selkirk,** Pop. 6000.

semantics, study of the relations between words and meaning. Divided into empirical study of how words are used, philosophic study of nature of meaning itself, and the generation of symbolic formal languages. *See* SEMIOTICS.

Semarang, city of Indonesia, cap. of Central Java prov., on Java Sea. Pop. 647,000. Shipbuilding and mfg. centre. Exports sugar, tobacco, copra.

Semele, in Greek myth, daughter of Cadmus and Harmonia. Loved by Zeus in human form, whom she asked to appear as a god, but was consumed by lightning when he did. Zeus took her unborn son, Dionysus, from ashes and nurtured him in his thigh.

semiconductor, substance whose electrical conductivity is low at normal temperatures but which increases with rising temperature. Conductivity also increases by addition of minute quantities of special impurities. Those in use incl. germanium, silicon and gallium arsenide; important in transistors, rectifiers and photoelectric cells.

semiotics or **semiology,** science of signs in general, incl. SEMANTICS and pragmatics, the study of relationship of signs to their users.

Semiramis, legendary queen of Assyria. Reputedly founded Babylon.

Semite, etymologically a descendant of Shem, son of Noah in Old Testament. Term now used for a linguistic category which incl. Hebrews, Arabs, Syrians, Ethiopians and ancient peoples of Babylon, Assyria, Canaan, Phoenicia.

Semitic, one of two major language groups making up Afro-Asiatic family. Divided into E and W branches, incl. Aramaic, Hebrew, Arabic, Ethiopic.

semolina, cereal food consisting of coarsely ground particles of durum wheat produced during making of fine flour. Used in making macaroni, puddings, *etc.*

Senanayake, Don Stephen (1884-1952), Ceylonese statesman. First PM (1947-52) of independent Ceylon (now Sri Lanka). Succeeded by his son, **Dudley Shelton Senanayake** (1911-73), who was PM (1952-3, 1960, 1965-70).

Senate, in US, upper house of CONGRESS. Composed of senators (2 from each state) serving 6-year terms; presided over by vice-president. Senators were chosen by state legislatures until 17th Amendment (1913) estab. direct popular election. In addition to passing legislation, Senate must ratify treaties and confirm presidential appointments.

senate, governing body in ancient Rome. In early years of republic, censors chose its members. During 3rd and 2nd cent. BC, it controlled foreign affairs, the army, finances, *etc.* Power first challenged by the Gracchi, and by military leaders, *eg* Sulla, Pompey, Julius Caesar. Its authority diminished after Caesar's death, lessening still further during empire.

Sendai, city of Japan, N Honshu isl. Pop. 597,000. Produces chemicals, metal goods, silk. Seat of Tohoku Univ. (1907).

Seneca, [Lucius Annaeus] (*c* 4 BC-AD 65), Roman philosopher, dramatist, statesman. Tutor to Nero, briefly virtual ruler of Rome; later ordered to commit suicide, doing so in manner suited to his philosophy, Stoicism. Best known as writer of tragedies, incl. *Medea, Phaedra, Oedipus,* which greatly influenced Renaissance and later literature.

Senegal, republic of W Africa. Area 196,000 sq km (76,000 sq mi); pop. 5,381,000; cap. Dakar. Language: French. Religion: Islam. Mainly low-lying savannah; stock rearing; exports groundnuts, phosphates. Coastal settlements disputed by France, Portugal 18th-19th cents.; centre of slave trade. Part of French West Africa from 1895; part of Mali Federation 1959-60; independent 1960. Member of French Community.

Senegal, river of W Africa. Flows *c* 1690 km

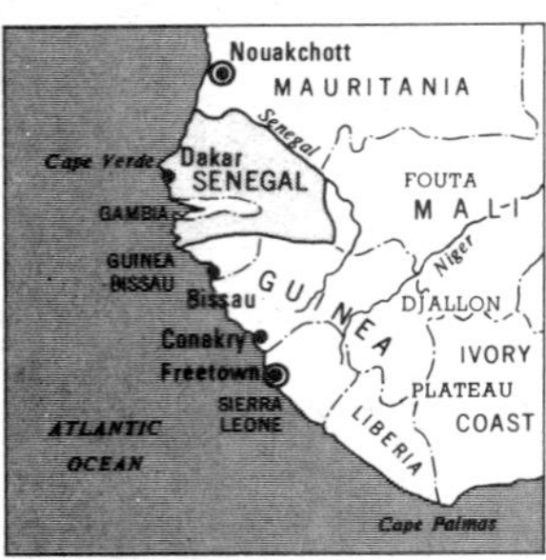

Senegal

(1050 mi) NW from Fouta Djallon highlands to Atlantic at St Louis. Forms Senegal-Mauritania border.

senility, mental deterioration associated with old age. Characterized by loss of memory, confusion, *etc.* Causes incl. degeneration of brain cells and inadequate blood flow to the brain resulting from hardened arteries.

Sennacherib (d. 681 BC), king of Assyria (705-681 BC), son of Sargon II. Destroyed Babylon (689). Rebuilt Nineveh.

sensationalism, in philosophy, belief that all knowledge is acquired through the senses. Central to the philosophies of *eg* Hobbes, Locke, Hume.

sensitive plant, *see* MIMOSA.

Seoul, cap. of South Korea. Pop. 6,879,000. Indust. centre on R. Han; railway engineering, textile mfg. Historical cap. of Korea from 14th cent. Severely damaged during Korean War.

separation of powers, in political theory, principle that executive, legislative and judicial functions of govt. should be independent of each other.

Sepoy Rebellion, *see* INDIAN MUTINY.

Septuagint (Lat., =seventy), most ancient and celebrated Greek version of the Hebrew Scriptures. Traditionally written in 72 days by 72 translators employed by Ptolemy II. Prob. made *c* 250-100 BC.

Sepulchre, Holy, site NW of Calvary, Jerusalem. Traditional site of Jesus' tomb, now covered by Church of the Resurrection, shared by Orthodox, Coptic, Syrian, Armenian and RC churches.

sequoia, two species of large coniferous trees of W US coast. Redwood, *Sequoia sempervirens,* and big tree, *Sequoiadendron giganteum.* Both grow to *c* 100 m (300 ft). Some big trees are *c* 4000 years old.

seraphim, *see* ANGEL.

Serbia *(Srbija),* autonomous republic of E Yugoslavia, incl. Vojvodina autonomous prov., Kosovo autonomous region. Area 88,337 sq km (34,107 sq mi); cap. Belgrade. Mountainous in S; fertile Danubian plain in N (wheat, flax, fruit growing). Medieval kingdom, defeated (1389) by Turks. Independent from 1878, kingdom 1882. Expansionist policy led to Balkan Wars (1912-13), conflict with Austria led to WWI. Nucleus of Yugoslavia 1918, reorganized as republic 1946.

Serbo-Croat, language in S Slavic branch of Indo-European family. Chief official tongue of Yugoslavia.

Serengeti National Park, game reserve of N Tanzania. Mainly grass-covered plain; area 13,000 sq km (5000 sq mi).

serfdom, condition of hereditary semi-bondage characteristic of most peasants under FEUDALISM. Serf usually worked on land of his master, but unlike a slave, retained certain rights and could not be sold. Widespread practice developed throughout Europe during Middle Ages. Disappeared in England towards end of Middle Ages; abolished in France by French Revolution; remained in Russia until Edict of Emancipation (1861).

Seringapatam, town of S India. Pop. 14,000. On isl. in R. Cauvery. Former cap. of Mysore (Karnataka). Fortress captured and Tippoo Sahib killed by British (1799).

serpentine, green or brownish-green mineral, consisting of hydrous magnesium silicate. Chrysotile, a fibrous variety, is major source of asbestos. Name also applied to rock, a mixture of serpentine and other minerals, which may be cut and polished for ornaments.

serum, clear yellowish liquid which separates from blood after clotting. Name also applies to blood fluid containing antibodies of immunity taken from an animal immunized against a specific disease; used as an antitoxin.

Servetus, Michael (1511-53), Spanish theologian. Denied doctrine of Trinity. Fled from Inquisition to Geneva; arrested on Calvin's orders and burnt at stake.

Service, Robert William (1874-1958), Canadian poet, b. England. Known for popular ballads of Yukon gold rush, *eg* 'The Shooting of Dan McGrew'.

servomechanism, automatic device in which small input power controls much larger output power. Output is compared with input through feedback so that difference between the 2 quantities can be used to achieve desired amount of control. Used in aircraft and mfg. machinery.

sesame, *Sesamum indicum,* Asian plant whose flat seeds are used in flavouring and yield edible oil.

Set or **Seth,** in ancient Egyptian religion, god of evil and darkness. Brother and murderer of OSIRIS.

set, in mathematics, collection of objects, *eg* numbers, with some defining property to tell whether a particular object is member of this collection. Operations with sets and their study are important in modern mathematics and logic.

setter, large gun dog trained to find game and point its position. Breeds incl. English, Irish and Gordon setter.

Settlement, Act of, act of English Parliament (1701) regulating succession to throne. Provided that succession should pass to house of Hanover (which it did in 1714) if William III and Anne died without heir. Also declared that only Protestants can succeed to throne.

Seurat, Georges (1859-91), French painter. Devised divisionist (pointillist) technique of painting in small dots of colour. Works incl. *Un Dimanche à la Grande Jatte*.

Sevastopol or **Sebastopol,** seaport of USSR, Ukrainian SSR; on S Crimea coast. Pop. 301,000. Naval base and shipbuilding centre; seaside resort. Site of 5th-cent. BC Greek colony. Captured after 11 month siege (1854-5) by French, British and Turkish troops in Crimean War. Fell to Germans after 8 month siege (1942).

seven deadly sins, in RC theology, capital sins (pride, covetousness, lust, anger, gluttony, envy, sloth).

Seventh Day Adventists, *see* ADVENTISTS.

Seven Weeks War, name for AUSTRO-PRUSSIAN WAR.

Seven Wonders of the World, in antiquity, held to be Great Pyramid of Khufu, Hanging Gardens of Babylon, Statue of Zeus at Olympia, Temple of Artemis at Ephesus, Mausoleum at Halicarnassus, Colossus of Rhodes, Pharos (lighthouse) at Alexandria.

Seven Years War, conflict (1756-63) resulting from formation of coalition by France, Austria, Russia and allies to reduce power of Prussia. Also involved French-British colonial wars in North America (called FRENCH AND INDIAN WARS) and India. Campaigns by Frederick II of Prussia in Bohemia, Saxony and Silesia thwarted by Austria and Russia. Peace treaty of Hubertusburg, although restoring status quo, marked emergence of Prussia as European power. Britain's colonial supremacy settled by Treaty of Paris after victories at Québec (1759) and Plassey (1757).

Severn, river of SW UK. Flows *c* 338 km (210 mi) from C Wales via Worcester, Gloucester to Bristol Channel. Has tidal bore as far as Tewkesbury. Road suspension bridge (1966).

Seville (*Sevilla*), city of SW Spain, on R. Guadalquivir, cap. of Seville prov. Pop. 589,000. River port, fruit, wine trade, mfg. industs.; univ. (1502). Chief city of S Spain under Romans (anc. *Hispalis*), Visigoths; *fl* under Moorish rule 712-1248; New World trade centre (15th-17th cents.). Moorish tower and palace, 15th-cent. cathedral.

Sèvres, suburb of SW Paris, on R. Seine. Porcelain works (Sèvres ware) estab. 1756.

Sèvres, Treaty of, peace settlement (1920) signed at Sèvres between Turkey and Allies. Abolished Ottoman Empire, created new Turkish frontiers. Rejection of treaty by Kemal Ataturk led to LAUSANNE CONFERENCE.

sewing machine, device with mechanically driven needle for sewing of cloth, leather, *etc.* First successful model built (1846) by Elias Howe; developed by Isaac Singer.

sex, either of 2 divisions, male and female, into which animals are divided, depending on their reproductive functions.

sex chromosome, chromosome present in germ cells of most animals and some plants. Such chromosomes are usually designated by letters X and Y. In humans, ova carry an X chromosome, spermatozoa either an X or a Y. An ovum receiving an X chromosome at fertilization develops into a female, and into a male if it receives a Y. Inherited characteristics, *eg* colour blindness, that are determined by genes on the X chromosome are said to be sex-linked.

sextant, instrument for measuring angular distance of celestial bodies from the horizon. Used in navigation, surveying. Developed during 18th cent.

sexton beetle, *Necrophorus humator*, bluish-black burying beetle. Larvae feed on corpses of buried vertebrates.

Seychelles, volcanic isl. group (*c* 90) in W Indian Ocean; member of British Commonwealth. Area *c* 380 sq km (150 sq mi); pop 62,000; cap. Victoria (pop. 14,000) on Mahé Isl. Coconuts, fish, copra, cinnamon, guano exports. French territ. 18th cent., ceded to British 1814. Became independent 1976.

Seymour, Jane (*c* 1509-37), English noblewoman, 3rd wife of Henry VIII. Died after birth of son, Edward VI. Her brother, **Edward Seymour, Duke of Somerset** (*c* 1506-52), became Edward's protector (1547). Sponsored Protestant reforms of Cranmer. Beheaded after losing power to NORTHUMBERLAND.

Sfax, city of E Tunisia, on Gulf of Gabès. Pop. 475,000. Port, exports phosphates, olive oil, sponges; fishing. Former Phoenician then Roman colony.

Sforza, Ludovico (1451-1508), Italian nobleman. Succeeded to duchy of Milan (1494). Driven from power (1499) by Louis XII of France. Patron of Leonardo da Vinci.

's Gravenhage, *see* HAGUE, THE.

Shaba, *see* KATANGA.

Shackleton, Sir Ernest Henry (1874-1922), British explorer, b. Ireland. Accompanied Scott to Antarctic (1901-4); led expedition (1907-9) which located S magnetic pole. Lost ship *Endurance* on expedition (1914-16), journeyed *c* 1300 km (800 mi) by open boat to safety. Died on expedition to Enderby Land.

Shaftesbury, Anthony Ashley Cooper, 1st Earl of (1621-83), English statesman. Gained favour of Charles II after supporting Restoration. Member of CABAL cabinet. Dismissed as lord chancellor after supporting anti-Catholic Test Act (1673). Sought to exclude James II from succession; forced to flee to Holland (1682). **Anthony Ashley Cooper, 7th Earl of Shaftesbury** (1801-85), was social reformer. Tory MP from 1826, promoted factory legislation forbidding employment of women and children in coal mines

(1842), introducing 10-hour working day (1847).

shag, *Phalacrocorax aristotelis,* green-black seabird of cormorant family, found in Europe and N Africa. Nests on cliffs in colonies. Also called green cormorant.

Shah Jehan (*c* 1592-1666), Mogul emperor (1628-58). Conquered much of the Deccan. Built TAJ MAHAL at Agra. Deposed and imprisoned by his son Aurangzeb.

Shakers, popular name for ecstatic religious sect, United Society of Believers in Christ's Second Appearing. Originated among Quakers in England *c* 1747, taken to US (1774). Practised celibacy, separation from society in closed, communal group. Now largely extinct.

Shakespeare, William (1564-1616), English dramatist, poet, b. Stratford-upon-Avon. Spent early years in London as actor, becoming a partner in Globe Theatre (1599). Early plays (written before 1596) incl. histories, *Henry VI* (parts I, II, III), *Richard III;* comedies, *eg Two Gentlemen of Verona, A Midsummer Night's Dream*; tragedy, *Titus Andronicus.* Tragedy, *Romeo and Juliet* (*c* 1595), indicates more developed treatment of character as in later comedies, *eg The Merchant of Venice* (1596), *Much Ado About Nothing* (1598), *As You Like It* (1599), *Twelfth Night* (1599); histories *Henry IV* (parts I, II, 1597), *Henry V* (1598). The 4 great tragedies, *Hamlet* (1600), *Othello* (1602), *King Lear* (1605), *Macbeth* (1606) and classical plays, *eg Julius Caesar* (1599), *Coriolanus* (1608), represent the height of his work. Last period incl. 'problem' plays *Measure for Measure* and *The Tempest* (1611). Verse incl. sonnets, narrative poems, *eg Venus and Adonis* (1593), *The Rape of Lucrece* (1594).

shale, fine-grained, sedimentary rock. Consists mainly of clay compressed or cemented into thin, parallel layers which readily separate. Some shales are sources of oil *eg* in Scotland, US.

shallot, *Allium ascalonicum,* small edible onion with violet-coloured roots and green leaves used as flavouring.

shamanism, religious beliefs and practices of Siberian tribes of N Asia; term also applied to similar practices among Eskimos and North American Indians. Central figure is shaman (priest-magician) who is held to have innate ability to communicate with spirit world.

shamrock, common name for several trifoliate plants, esp. a clover, *Trifolium dubium.* National emblem of Ireland and symbol of Trinity in Christianity.

Shang, Chinese imperial dynasty (*c* 1700 or 1500 -*c* 1000 BC). First historical dynasty, followed semi-legendary Hsia. Period marked by skilled use of bronze.

Shanghai, seaport and largest city of China, special municipality of Kiangsu prov. Pop. 10,820,000. Steel mfg., shipbuilding, heavy engineering, textiles. Open port (1843-1946) with European, American concessions. Univs. incl. Futan (1905). Japanese occupation (1937-45).

Shannon, river of Irish Republic, longest in British Isls. Flows 360 km (224 mi) from Cavan via Lough Derg to Limerick. Long estuary to Atlantic. Provides h.e.p.

Shansi, prov. of NC China. Area *c* 155,000 sq km (60,000 sq mi); pop. (est.) 24,000,000; cap. Taiyuan. High plateau region; low rainfall limits agric. Lumber; coal, iron deposits.

Shantung, prov. of E China on Yellow Sea. Area *c* 140,000 sq km (54,000 sq mi); pop. (est.) 71,000,000; cap. Tsinan. Mountainous in E and C, Hwang Ho delta in W. Agric. limited by low rainfall; wheat, cotton grown. Coal, iron, oil, silk mfg., fishing.

shares, in finance, capital holdings in business enterprise, ownership of which certified by possession of stocks. Bonds are similar certification of ownership but with guaranteed payment if company is liquidated.

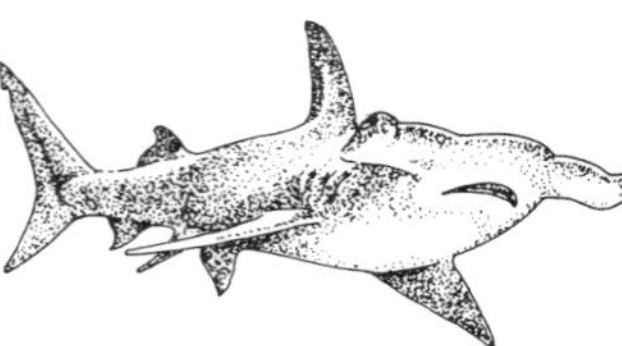

Hammerhead shark

shark, cartilaginous marine fish with slender torpedo-shaped body. Crescent-shaped mouth with numerous pointed teeth. Several families incl. dogfish, whale sharks (largest known fish) and hammerhead sharks. Mainly fish-eating, some species will attack man.

Sharpeville, town of S Transvaal, South Africa, near Vereeniging. Scene of civic disturbances (1960) after police fired shots into black African crowd demonstrating against 'Pass Laws', *c* 70 killed.

Shastri, Lal Bahadur (1904-66), Indian statesman, PM (1964-6). Took office as PM after Nehru's death. Died in Tashkent after signing peace agreement with Pakistan.

Shat-al-Arab, river of SE Iraq, formed at Tigris-Euphrates confluence. Length *c* 193 km (120 mi). Flows into Persian Gulf. Navigable by ocean-going vessels to Basra.

Shaw, George Bernard (1856-1950), British dramatist, critic, b. Dublin. Prominent member of Fabian Society. Early work attacks intellectually complacent London theatre, *eg Plays Pleasant and Unpleasant* (1898) incl. *Candida, Mrs Warren's Profession.* Notable plays with recurring theme of social satire incl. *Man and Superman* (1903), *Major Barbara* (1905), *Pygmalion* (1912), *Saint Joan* (1924). Also wrote many socialist polemics in prefaces to plays and in longer works. Nobel Prize for Literature (1925).

Shawnee, North American Indian tribe.

Settled in Ohio in 18th cent. Warrior tribe. Now settled in Oklahoma.

shearwater, any of genus *Puffinus* of oceanic birds, related to petrel. Slender bill, tube-like external nostrils.

Sheba, OT name for region of S Arabia, incl. Yemen and the Hadramaut. Inhabitants, Sabaeans, estab. highly developed culture *c* 6th-5th cents. BC. The Queen of Sheba who visited Solomon (1 Kings) *fl* 10th cent. BC.

sheep, ruminant mammal of Bovidae family, esp. genus *Ovis*. Domestic sheep, *O. aries*, reared for wool, leather, mutton. Breeds incl. Cotswold and Merino, known for wool; Southdown and Shropshire, kept for wool, mutton. Wild species incl. bighorn, moufflon.

sheepdog, dog trained to herd and guard sheep. Popular breeds incl. COLLIE, old English sheepdog with shaggy blue-grey and white coat; stands 53-64 cm/21-25 in. at shoulder.

Sheffield, city of South Yorkshire met. county, N England, at confluence of Don and Sheaf rivers. Pop. 507,000. Iron and steel indust. Long estab. stainless steel cutlery mfg. Has 15th-cent. church now cathedral; univ. (1905).

Shelburne, William Petty Fitzmaurice, 2nd Earl of (1737-1805), British statesman, PM (1783). Headed ministry that granted US independence at Treaty of Paris.

Shelley, Percy Bysshe (1792-1822), English poet. Romantic works, reflecting radical views on society and religion, incl. *Prometheus Unbound* (1820), *Adonais* (1821). Now best known for short lyrics, *eg* 'Ozymandias', 'To a Skylark', 'Ode to the West Wind'. Drowned while sailing in Italy. His 2nd wife, **Mary [Wollstonecraft] Shelley,** née Godwin (1797-1851), wrote Gothic novel *Frankenstein* (1818).

shell shock, term for severe form of anxiety neurosis which occurred among soldiers in WWI after prolonged exposure to attack.

Shenandoah, *see* POTOMAC.

Shensi, prov. of NC China. Area *c* 197,000 sq km (76,000 sq mi); pop. (est.) 27,000,000; cap. Sian. Wheat, cotton grown; rich coal and iron deposits, oil.

Shenyang or **Mukden,** cap. of Liaoning prov., NE China. Pop. 2,800,000. Rail jct.; heavy engineering; aircraft, machine tools mfg., chemicals. Scene of battle in Russo-Japanese War (1905).

shepherd's purse, *Capsella bursa-pastoris*, annual plant of mustard family. Wide distribution in temperate zones. White flowers. Regarded as troublesome weed.

Sheppey, Isle of, off Kent, SE England, in Thames estuary. Separated from mainland by the Swale.

Sheraton, Thomas (1751-1806), English furniture designer. Wrote *The Cabinet Maker's and Upholsterer's Drawing Book* (1791-4), an influential source of designs. Work characterized by simplicity, straight vertical lines, neo-Classical motifs.

Sheridan, Richard Brinsley (1751-1816), British dramatist, politician, b. Ireland. Known for satirical comedies of manners, *eg The Rivals* (1775) containing Mrs Malaprop, *The School for Scandal* (1777), *The Critic* (1779).

sheriff, in England, officer appointed by Crown to administer county or shire (now honorary); in Scotland, a judge who deals with all but most serious crimes. In US, chief law-enforcement officer of county.

Sheriffmuir, battlefield in Ochil Hills, Tayside Region, C Scotland. Scene of battle (1715) between Jacobites and Hanoverians; both sides claimed victory.

Sherman, William Tecumseh (1820-91), American general. During Civil War, commanded Union push through Georgia (1864); burned Atlanta, devastated countryside.

Sherrington, Sir Charles Scott (1857-1952), English physiologist. Introduced a theory of reflex action. Shared Nobel Prize for Physiology and Medicine (1932).

sherry, fortified wine, originating in Jerez de la Frontera region of Spain. Three main types: fino, dry and light yellow; oloroso, richer and darker in colour; amontillado, darker than fino and less rich than oloroso.

's Hertogenbosch or **Den Bosch,** town of SC Netherlands, cap. of North Brabant prov. Pop. 181,000. Railway jct., cattle market.

Sherwood Forest, ancient royal forest of Nottinghamshire, C England, now largely cleared. Traditional home of Robin Hood.

Shetland, isl. authority of N Scotland, comprising Shetland Isls. Formerly Zetland county. Incl. *c* 100 isls.; area 1429 sq km (552 sq mi); pop. 22,000; admin. hq Lerwick. Main isls. are Mainland, Yell, Unst. Sheep rearing, Shetland ponies; fishing, knitwear mfg. Offshore oil service industs. Oil storage base at Sullom Voe. Acquired from Norway 1472.

Shetland pony, small breed of pony with thick, shaggy coat, mane and forelock. Noted for strength and endurance; stands 1 m/40 in. at shoulder.

Shihkiachwang, cap. of Hopeh prov., NE China. Pop. 800,000. Rail jct.; produces textiles, pharmaceuticals.

Shiites or **Shiahs,** members of the smaller of the 2 main Moslem sects, who upheld right of ALI to succeed Mohammed as 1st caliph and supported later claims of his sons Hasan and Husein to caliphate. Also reject the Sunna, traditional law based on teachings of Mohammed. Predominate in Iran.

Shikoku, isl. of SW Japan, smallest of the 4 major isls. Area 18,770 sq km (7240 sq mi). Mountainous interior, rising to *c* 1980 m (6500 ft); heavily forested. Produces rice, tobacco, tea.

Shillong, cap. of Assam, NE India. Pop. 84,000. Resort, trade centre.

shingles, in medicine, *see* HERPES.

Shinto, term used for native Japanese religious beliefs and practices. Modified under influence of Buddhism and Confucianism, developed as patriotic state Shinto (stressing divinity of emperor, disavowed by Hirohito 1946) and sectarian churches (stressing veneration of ancestors).

shinty, twelve-a-side stick and ball game played in Scottish Highlands. Resembles HURLING, from which it is derived.

ship, term for large sea-going vessel. Used in ancient times by Egyptians, Greeks, Phoenicians and Chinese (propelled by sails and oars). Discovery of Americas led to increase in ship-building. One of first successful steamships was Fulton's *Clermont* on Hudson R. (1807). Steel replaced wood in construction from *c* 1840s. Subsequent developments incl. steam turbines, diesel engine, nuclear power.

ship money, in English history, tax for upkeep of navy and coastal defences. Legality of writs issued by Charles I, levying ship money in peace time and on inland as well as maritime counties, was challenged by John HAMPDEN. Declared illegal 1641.

Shiraz, city of SC Iran, cap. of Fars prov. Pop. 414,000. Produces wines, brocades, rugs. Cap. of Persia at various times.

shire horse, breed of powerful draft horse once common on farms. Bred in Middle Ages to carry knight in full armour.

Shiva, *see* SIVA.

Shkodër, (Ital. *Scutari*), town of NW Albania, on L. Sartari. Pop. 63,000. Wool, grain, tobacco. RC cathedral; Venetian citadel. Cap. of ancient Illyria.

shock, in medicine, disorder resulting from inadequate blood circulation to the tissues. Symptoms incl. decrease in blood pressure, rapid pulse. Causes incl. severe injury, blood loss, emotional trauma, heart damage.

Shockley, William Bradford (1910-), American physicist, b. Britain. His studies in semiconductors led to the invention of the transistor. Shared Nobel Prize for Physics (1956).

shock therapy, method of treating certain mental disorders by chemical agents, *eg* insulin, or by applying electric currents to the brain. Sometimes effective in treating depression.

shoebill, *Balaeniceps rex*, stork-like wading bird with broad shoe-shaped bill. Lives along banks of White Nile.

shogun, title given to hereditary military rulers who controlled Japanese feudal system (1192-1867). Held real power under nominal rule of emperors.

Sholokhov, Mikhail Aleksandrovich (1905-), Russian novelist. Known for masterpiece *And Quiet Flows the Don* (1928-40). Nobel Prize for Literature (1965).

shooting, sport of firing with pistol, rifle or shotgun at moving or stationary targets. Organizations such as British National Rifle Association (formed 1860) standardized rules and held competitions in 19th cent. Events incl. trap or clay pigeon, skeet and small-bore rifle shooting.

shooting star, *see* METEOR.

short circuit, connection, either accidental or deliberate, between 2 points in electrical circuit by path of low resistance, instead of normal high resistance path. Excessive current flow may cause permanent damage to circuit; fuses are designed to avoid effects of short circuit.

shorthand, method of rapid handwriting using strokes, abbreviations or symbols to denote letters, words, phrases. Early systems were orthographic (*ie* using abbreviations for groups of letters but retaining standard spelling). Phonetic system developed (1837) by Isaac PITMAN allows *c* 280 words per minute to be recorded.

short sight, *see* MYOPIA.

Shoshone, North American Indian tribe related to Aztecs. Spread across NW US in 19th cent. Now *c* 4000 live on reservations in California, Idaho, Wyoming.

Shostakovich, Dmitri (1906-75), Russian composer. Works employ modern idioms, often in traditional forms, and incl. 15 symphonies, string quartets. Twice encountered official disapproval of his music.

shoveler, freshwater duck with large broad bill, genus *Anas*. Species incl. *A. clypeata* of N hemisphere; male has green-glossed head, white and brown underparts.

show jumping, *see* EQUESTRIANISM.

shrew, any of Soricidae family of small, solitary, insectivorous mammals, widely distributed in N hemisphere and Africa. Long snout, musk glands; some species secrete poison. Species incl. WATER SHREW and common shrew, *Sorex araneus*.

Shrewsbury, city and admin. hq. of Shropshire, WC England, on R. Severn. Pop. 56,000. Market town; tanning, brewing.

shrike, any of Laniidae family of largely Old World birds. Strong hooked bill; feeds on insects and small animals, impaling bodies on thorns.

shrimp, small free-swimming marine crustacean. Slender elongated body with 5 pairs of legs; many species edible. Species incl. common European brown shrimp, *Crangon vulgaris*.

Shropshire, county of W England. Area 3490 sq km (1347 sq mi); pop. 366,000; admin. hq. Shrewsbury. Hilly in SW (cattle, sheep); flat in N, E (agric., dairying). Known as Salop 1974-80.

Shrove Tuesday, in Christian calendar, day before Lent begins. In England, celebrated by eating pancakes. *See* MARDI GRAS.

shrub, low, perennial woody plant, smaller than TREE and with several permanent stems branching from or near ground rather than single trunk.

Si or **Si-kiang,** river of S China. Length *c* 2000 km (1250 mi). Rises in Yunnan prov., flows E to South China Sea near Kwangchow. Navigable most of its length.

sial, in geology, upper, discontinuous layer of Earth's crust underlying the continents. Consists of relatively light rocks, *eg* granite; named from *si*lica and *al*uminium, the main constituents. Also *see* SIMA.

Siam, *see* THAILAND.

Siam, Gulf of, arm of South China Sea, between Malay penin. and Indo-China.

Siamese cat, breed of short-haired cat with slanting blue eyes. Fawn-coloured coat with darker colour at face and legs.

Siamese twins, twins born with bodies joined by tissue in some way. Surgical separation now often possible. Term derived from male twins, Chang and Eng, b. 1811 in Siam.

Sian, cap. of Shensi prov., NC China. Pop. 1,600,000. Commercial centre. Iron, steel production, textile mfg. Ancient imperial cap. (3rd cent. BC) and religious centre.

Sibelius, Jean Julius Christian (1865-1957), Finnish composer. Music, traditional in form, was often inspired by legends and scenery of Finland. Works incl. tone-poem *Finlandia,* violin concerto, 7 symphonies.

Siberia *(Sibir),* region of C and E USSR, approximating Asiatic part of RSFSR. Area *c* 12,700,000 sq km (4,900,000 sq mi). Plains in W, drained by Ob, Irtysh; plateau in C and S; tundra in N along Arctic Ocean; mainly mountainous in E, incl. Kamchatka Penin. Agric. concentrated in fertile SW plains (main crop wheat); mineral resources incl. oil, coal, gold, iron. Indust., *eg* Kuznetsk basin, has grown rapidly since 1920s. Russian conquest led by Cossacks (16th-17th cent.). Used as political exile colony under tsars; colonization began with Trans-Siberian railway (1892-1905).

Sibylline Books, collection of oracular utterances, written in Greek hexameters, supposedly brought from Greece to Sibyl of Cumae, then to Rome. Consulted by Romans in cases of calamities. Destroyed in burning of capitol, 83 BC.

sibyls, name given by Greeks and Romans to prophetesses of Apollo. *See* SIBYLLINE BOOKS.

Sicilian Vespers, rebellion (1282) in Sicily against French rule of Charles of Anjou; began at time of vespers on Easter Tuesday. Most of French were massacred. Resulted in estab. of Peter III of Aragón as king of Sicily.

Sicily (*Sicilia*), isl. of Italy, separated from mainland by Str. of Messina. Largest Mediterranean isl., area 25,708 sq km (9926 sq mi); cap. Palermo. Mountainous, incl. Mt. Etna; agric., fishing, sulphur, oil. Phoenician, then Greek colony, taken by Rome 241 BC. Under Normans (12th-13th cent.) before forming, with Naples, Kingdom of the Two Sicilies (1815); liberated from Bourbons by Garibaldi (1860).

Sickert, Walter Richard (1860-1942), British artist, b. Munich. His impressionist paintings are sombre in tone. Subjects incl. music hall scenes.

Siddons, Sarah Kemble (1755-1831), English actress, daughter of Roger KEMBLE. Renowned in tragic roles.

sidewinder, *Crotalus cerastes,* desert rattlesnake of SW US. Moves by sideways spiralling action.

Sidi-bel-Abbès, town of NW Algeria, on R. Mekerra. Pop. 151,000. Agric. market. Hq. of Foreign Legion until 1962.

Sidmouth, Henry Addington, 1st Viscount (1757-1844), English statesman, PM (1801-4). Headed Tory govt. which concluded Treaty of Amiens (1802).

Sidney, Sir Philip (1554-86), soldier, writer, leading figure at Elizabeth I's court. Died in battle of Zutphen. Works incl. romance *Arcadia* (pub. 1590), sonnet sequence *Astrophel and Stella* (1591), critiques, *eg The Defence of Poesie* (1595). Considered archetype of Renaissance courtier.

Sidon, *see* SAIDA.

Siegfried or **Sigurd,** hero of N European mythology. Appears in German epics, esp. *Nibelungenlied,* as dragon-killer, lover of Kriemhild, conqueror of Brunhild.

Siemens, [Ernst] Werner von (1816-92), German industrialist, inventor. Invented many commonly used techniques, *eg* Siemens armature. His brother, **Sir William Siemens,** orig. Karl Wilhelm (1823-83), was known for his innovatory work in electricity and application of heat. Developed Siemens-Martin steel-making process.

Siena, town of Tuscany, WC Italy, cap. of Siena prov. Pop. 69,000. Marble, wine; tourism. Medieval cultural, banking centre. Sienese school of painting (13th-14th cent.). Gothic cathedral, town hall. Horse race held annually in Piazza del Campo.

Sierra Leone

Sierra Leone, republic of W Africa. Area 71,700 sq km (27,700 sq mi); pop. 3,292,000; cap. Freetown. Official language: English. Religions: animist, Christianity, Islam. Coastal swamps, rising inland to wooded plateau. Main food crop rice; exports diamonds, iron ore, bauxite, palm products. Freetown area became colony of freed slaves (1808); hinterland incl. in protect. created (1896). Independent from 1961.

Sierra Madre, mountain system of Mexico, dominating much of country. Comprises Sierra Madre Oriental in NE, Occidental in

W and del Sur in S. Rises to 5700 m (18,700 ft) at highest point, Orizaba.

Sierra Nevada, mountain range of S Spain; extends *c* 100 km (60 mi) E-W from Granada to Almeria. Incl. Mulhacén, highest peak in Spain at 3479 m (11,420 ft).

Sierra Nevada, mountain range of E California. Incl. Mt. WHITNEY and Sequoia, Yosemite, Kings Canyon national parks.

Sigismund (1368-1437), Holy Roman emperor (1433-7). Became king of Hungary (1387), Germany (1411). Persuaded the pope to call Council of Constance (1414) to end Great Schism. Granted safe conduct for Jan Hus to attend Council, but Hus was condemned to death there for heresy. Led crusade against Hussites in Bohemia (1420) but was defeated.

Signac, Paul (1863-1935), French neo-impressionist painter. Disciple of Seurat, he adopted the divisionist (pointillist) technique.

Sigurd, *see* SIEGFRIED.

Sihanouk, Norodom (1922-), Cambodian statesman, king (1941-55). Abdicated in favour of father, but continued as premier (1951-70), leading Popular Socialists. Went into exile in China after rightist coup d'état (1970). Returned as head of state in 1975, but resigned and held under house arrest from 1976. Released after overthrow of Khmer Rouge (1979).

sika, *Cervus nippon,* small Japanese deer, introduced into Europe. Chestnut brown coat, white-spotted in summer.

Sikhs, Indian religious community mostly in Punjab. Founded (*c* 1500) by Nanak. Aiming to unite Hindus and Moslems, taught basic identity of all religions. Developed as military power in early 18th cent. against Mogul empire and Islam.

Sikh Wars, conflicts (1845-6, 1848-9) between Sikhs and British, resulting in annexation of Punjab.

Si-kiang, river of China, *see* SI.

Sikkim, state of India, in Himalayas between Nepal and Bhutan. Area 7100 sq km (2700 sq mi); pop. 250,000; cap. Gangtok. Constitutional monarchy under British protection until 1947, became Indian protectorate 1950. Independence and power of king virtually ended 1974, when it became Indian associate state. Became 22nd state of India (1975).

Sikorski, Wladyslaw (1881-1943), Polish general, statesman. After German invasion of Poland (1939), became premier of Polish govt. in exile and commander-in-chief of Polish troops fighting with Allies. Killed in air crash.

Sikorsky, Igor Ivanovich (1889-1972), American aeronautical engineer, b. Russia. Designed, manufactured 1st successful helicopter (1941).

silage, green fodder preserved in airtight silos, used as supplementary feed for cattle, sheep, *etc.*

Silenus, in Greek myth, leader of satyrs and foster father of Dionysus. Represented as inspired, musical and drunken old man.

Silesia (Pol. *Slask,* Ger. *Schlesien,* Czech. *Slezsko*), region of EC Europe, now mainly in Poland; smaller areas in NW Czechoslovakia, SE East Germany. Incl. basin of upper Oder; coal, iron, zinc mining. Chief cities Gliwice, Katowice, Wroclaw. Polish until 14th cent., passed to Bohemia, then to Habsburgs. Annexed by Prussia 1742; divided into Upper, Lower Silesia. Former returned to Poland 1921, latter returned 1945.

silica or **silicon dioxide** (SiO_2), hardy glassy mineral; found free as sand, quartz, flint and as silicates in rocks. Used in manufacture of glass and ceramics.

silicates, salts of silicic acid (H_2SiO_3). Most rocks and many minerals consist of silicates of calcium, magnesium, aluminium and other metals.

silicon (Si), non-metallic element; at. no. 14, at. wt. 28.09. Exists as brown powder and grey crystals; 2nd most abundant element on Earth, occurring in silica and silicate rocks. Obtained by reduction of silica with carbon in electric arc furnaces. Used in alloys, glass making, semiconductor devices.

silicon chip, tiny slice of silicon processed to form miniature INTEGRATED CIRCUIT. Used in electronic circuitry, esp. computers. *See* MICROPROCESSOR.

silicones, group of polymerized organic compounds containing alternate oxygen and silicon atoms with various organic radicals attached to the chain. Characterized by chemical inertness, resistance to electricity and heat; used as lubricants, polishes, waterproofing compounds.

silk, natural fibre produced by silkworms. Usually obtained from cocoon spun by SILKWORM which feeds on mulberry leaves. Silk production began in ancient China, then in 6th cent. spread throughout Asia into Europe (esp. Italy and France).

silk screen printing, method of stencil printing in which paint is squeezed through a piece of fine silk. Parts of design not to be printed are masked by paper or film of lacquer.

silkworm, larva of Chinese silkworm moth, *Bombyx mori.* Spins cocoon of silk fibre, cultivated commercially as source of silk.

silt, sediment composed of rock particles, precisely defined in geology as having particle size between 1/256 mm and 1/16 mm. Commonest constituent is quartz.

Silurian period, third geological period of Palaeozoic era. Began *c* 435 million years ago, lasted *c* 40 million years. Extensive seas; Caledonian mountain building period continued. Typified by graptolites, trilobites, brachiopods, cephalopods; jawless fish, 1st land plants. Also *see* GEOLOGICAL TABLE.

silver (Ag), white metallic element; at. no. 47, at. wt. 107.87. Malleable and ductile; best-known conductor of electricity; resists corrosion by air. Used in coinage, jewellery, mirrors; halogen compounds used extensively in photography as they are light-sensitive.

silverfish, *Lepisma saccharina,* bristletail insect of silvery-white appearance.

sima, in geology, lower continuous layer of Earth's crust underlying ocean floors and continental SIAL. Consists of relatively heavy rocks, *eg* basalt; named from *si*lica and *ma*gnesium, the main constituents.

Simenon, Georges (1903-), French author, b. Belgium. Known for detective novels featuring Inspector Maigret.

Simeon Stylites, St (*c* 390-459), Syrian hermit. Traditionally lived for 36 years on top of pillar from which he taught.

simile, *see* METAPHOR.

Simla, cap. of Himachal Pradesh state, N India. Pop. 43,000. In Himalayas, at height of 2100 m (7000 ft). Summer residence of viceroy and govt. during British rule.

Simnel, Lambert, (*c* 1477-*c* 1535), English imposter. Supported by Yorkists, claimed to be Edward, Earl of Warwick, Edward IV's nephew. Crowned in Dublin as Edward VI. Defeated by Henry VII at Stoke (1487), put to work in royal kitchens.

Simon, St (*fl* 1st cent. AD), one of Twelve Disciples; also called Cananaean, Zealot. Traditionally, martyred with St Jude.

Simonstown, town of SW Cape Prov., South Africa, on False Bay. Pop. 10,000. Major naval base. Founded (1741) by Dutch; ceded to UK (1898), to South Africa (1957).

Simplon Pass, Alpine pass between S Switzerland and N Italy, height 2008 m (6592 ft). Road built by Napoleon (1800-7). Railway tunnel, world's longest (19.7 km/12.25 mi), opened 1906.

Simpson, Sir James Young (1811-70), Scottish obstetrician. Pioneered use of anaesthetics (chloroform, ether) in childbirth (1847).

Simpson, Wallis, *see* WINDSOR, WALLIS WARFIELD, DUCHESS OF.

sin, in Judaism, Christianity and Islam, any transgression of the will of God. Concept does not occur in religions where there is no personal God, *eg* Buddhism. In RC theology, sins are mortal if committed with intent in a serious matter. *See* ORIGINAL SIN, SEVEN DEADLY SINS.

Sinai, barren penin. between Gulf of Suez (W) and Gulf of Aqaba (E). Main town El Arish. Coastal plain in N, El Tih plateau in C; mountainous in S. Nomadic pastoralism, oil drilling, manganese, iron mining. Jebel Musa (possibly Mt. Sinai) has famous Greek Orthodox monastery. Part of Egypt; occupied by Israelis from 1967 war; returned in stages after 1979.

Sind, region of SE Pakistan and former province of British India. Mainly flat, arid land lying in lower Indus valley. Agric. economy. Taken by British (1843).

Singapore, island republic off S end of Malay penin.; in British Commonwealth. Area 583 sq km (225 sq mi); pop. 2,334,000, predominantly Chinese. British colony 1824-1963; joined Malaysia 1963, seceded 1965. City of **Singapore** (pop. 1,240,000) is a major seaport, former British naval base. Commercial centre; exports rubber, tin and copra from Malaysia. Occupied by Japanese 1942-5.

Singer, Isaac Bashevis (1904-), American writer, b. Poland. Writing, ironically treating irrational and grotesque themes, incl. novels *eg The Magician of Lublin* (1960), short stories. Nobel Prize for Literature (1978).

Singer, Isaac Merritt (1811-75), American inventor. Patented (1851) practical sewing machine; became leading manufacturer.

Singhalese, Indic language in Indo-Iranian branch of Indo-European family. Spoken on Sri Lanka.

singing, use of human voice for production of music with or without words. Voices range from female soprano or boy treble, mezzo-soprano, contralto, male and female alto, to male countertenor, tenor, baritone and bass.

Sinkiang(-Uighur), auton. region of NW China, bordering on Mongolia, USSR. Area *c* 1,709,400 sq km (660,000 sq mi); pop. (est.) 12,000,000; cap. Urumchi. Peopled mainly by Turkic Uighurs (Moslems). Grazing on Dzungaria plateau in N. Taklamakan desert covers S. Low rainfall but irrigation schemes allow agric. (cereals, cotton). Mineral, oil resources.

Sinn Fein (Irish, = ourselves alone), Irish separatist national movement founded by Arthur Griffith (*c* 1905). Gained popular political support under leadership of DE VALÉRA; set up Irish assembly in Dublin (1918) and declared independence. Influence declined with formation of Fianna Fáil (1926). Name now applies to political wing of Irish Republican Army.

Sino-Japanese War, First (1894-5), struggle between China and Japan for control of Korea. Japanese victory consolidated by Treaty of Shimonoseki by which China ceded Taiwan and other islands and Liaotung penin.; Korea awarded nominal independence.

Sino-Japanese War, Second (1937-45), struggle prompted by growing Japanese domination of China. Japan annexed Manchuria (1931), set up puppet state of Manchukuo. Hostilities began 1937; Japanese captured most of large Chinese cities and ports by 1938. Chinese, driven W, continued guerrilla warfare. Allies aided China after Japan's entry into WWII. After Japanese surrender (Sept. 1945), Taiwan, Manchuria restored to China.

Sinop (anc. *Sinope*), town of N Turkey, on Black Sea. Founded 8th cent. BC; became important port. Cap. of Pontic empire (2nd cent. BC); prospered under Roman and Byzantine rule.

sinus, name given to any of the various air cavities of the skull opening into the nasal passage. Inflammation of mucous membranes of the sinuses (sinusitis) may occur as a result of colds, allergies; blockage of sinuses by mucus causes headache.

Sioux, seven North American tribes. Gradually driven W, they settled (late 18th cent.) in N Great Plains area. Invasion of their reservation by gold prospectors in

1870s led to uprising in which General Custer perished.

Sirens, in Greek myth, sea nymphs who, by their beautiful singing, lured sailors to their death on rocks. Argonauts were saved by the more beautiful music of Orpheus, while Odysseus stopped ears of his crew with wax.

Sirius or **Dog Star,** brightest star in sky, located in constellation Canis Major. In 1862, observed to have a companion, Sirius B, a white dwarf star.

sirocco, hot, dust-laden S wind originating in Sahara Desert and affecting N Africa, Sicily, S Italy. Occurs mainly in spring.

sisal, strong fibre obtained from leaves of an agave, *Agave sisalana,* native to S Mexico, but now grown throughout the tropics. Used for making rope, sacking.

Sisley, Alfred (1839-99), French painter of English descent. Member of the impressionist group, he devoted himself to landscape.

Sistine Chapel, private chapel of the pope in the Vatican. Built (1473) under Sixtus IV, it is renowned for frescoes of the Creation, Deluge and Last Judgment by Michelangelo.

Sisyphus, in Greek myth, king of Corinth. For his disrespect to Zeus, condemned in Tartarus to roll repeatedly a heavy stone to top of hill; when stone reached top, it rolled down again.

Sitting Bull (*c* 1831-90), American Indian chief. Led Sioux at battle of Little Bighorn (1875) in which Custer and his troops were wiped out. Killed in renewed strife.

Sitwell, Dame Edith (1887-1964), English author. Works incl. poetry, *eg Façade* (1922) set to music by William Walton. Her brother, **Sir Osbert Sitwell** (1892-1969), wrote series of family memoirs incl. *Left Hand, Right Hand!* (1944), poetry. Their brother, **Sir Sacheverell Sitwell** (1897-), poet and art critic, wrote histories of art.

SI units (Système International d'Unités), internationally agreed coherent system of units, which has replaced c.g.s. and f.p.s. systems for scientific purposes. Based on 7 units: metre (m), kilogram (kg), second (s), ampère (A), kelvin (K), mole (mol) and candela (cd). Numerous other units, incl. newton, joule, watt, volt, ohm, are derived from these.

Siva or **Shiva,** in Hinduism, god of destruction and reproduction; one of the supreme trinity. In destructive role, represented with garland of skulls and surrounded by demons. As Natarajah, regarded as Lord of the Cosmic Dance; consort was KALI. Anciently associated with phallic worship.

Sjaelland, *see* ZEALAND.

Skagerrak, str. between SE Norway and NW Denmark, linking North Sea and Kattegat. Width *c* 130 km (80 mi).

Skara Brae, Neolithic village in Orkney, Scotland, uncovered from a sand dune by a storm (1851). Comprises stone houses linked by a roofed-over alleyway.

Siva

skate, large ray, esp. of genus *Raja,* often used as food.

skating, sport of gliding on ice by means of specially-designed metal blades fitted to boots. Used in ice HOCKEY. Forms incl. pair, free, figure and speed skating. Another form, **roller skating,** uses specially-constructed metal skates bearing 4 small roller wheels to glide on smooth surfaces.

skeleton, solid framework which supports and protects soft tissue of an animal body. Vertebrates have skeletal structures composed of bone and cartilage entirely within the organism (endoskeleton); other animals, *eg* arthropods, coelenterates, have skeletons external to living tissue (exoskeletons).

skiing, method of gliding over snow using elongated wooden or metal runners fastened to the feet. Sport of skiing is divided into 2 sections: Alpine, (downhill and slalom), in which competitors race down prepared slopes; Nordic, which incl. cross-country (or langlauf) and ski-jumping events. Competitive skiing began in 19th cent.

Skikda, town of NE Algeria, on Gulf of Stora. Pop. 128,000. Formerly called Philippeville. Port for Constantine, exports incl. fruit, wine, iron ore. Founded (1838) by French.

skin, flexible external covering of body. In humans, consists of outer epidermis and inner dermis. Former is covered by layer of dead cells which are constantly replaced. Latter contains blood vessels, nerve endings, hair follicles, sweat and sebaceous glands. Main functions are to protect, to regulate body temperature and to serve as organ of sense and excretion.

skink, any of Scincidae family of snake-like lizards, found mainly in desert regions. Elongated body, scaly tongue; limbs reduced or absent.

Skinner, B[urrhus] F[rederick] (1904-), American psychologist. Known for extreme BEHAVIOURISM, completely rejecting the unobservable.

skittles, game played with pins and balls or discs. Nine pins are set up in diamond pattern and missile is hurled at the pins with object of knocking them over.

Skopje, city of S Yugoslavia, on R. Vardar, cap. of Macedonia. Pop. 388,000. Transport, indust. centre (iron, steel), univ. (1946). Cap. of Serbia in 14th cent. Badly damaged by earthquake 1963.

skua, any of Stercorariidae family of large gull-like sea birds. Will chase other birds, stealing their food. Species incl. great skua, *Stercorarius skua*, of both polar regions.

skull, bony framework of the head comprising cranium, or brain case, and facial skeleton. Contains more than 20 tightly interlocked bones. Protects brain and sense organs, *ie* nose, eyes and ears.

skunk, bushy-tailed North American carnivore of Mustelidae family. Glossy black fur, usually with white stripe on back; ejects foul-smelling contents of 2 glands at back of tail for defence.

skydiving, sport of jumping from an aircraft and executing free-fall manoeuvres before opening the parachute, often as late as possible.

Skye, largest isl. of Inner Hebrides, W Scotland, in Highland region. Area 1665 sq km (643 sq mi); main town Portree (pop. 1000). Hilly in S (Cuillins). Sheep rearing, crofting; tourist centre.

Skye terrier, terrier originally bred in Skye for hunting. Long silky coat, short legs, long body; stands 25 cm/10 in. at shoulder.

Skylab, *see* SPACECRAFT.

skylark, *see* LARK.

Skyros (*Skíros*), isl. of Greece, in Aegean Sea. Area 205 sq km (79 sq mi). Agric., fishing; chromite.

skyscraper, popular name for many-storeyed building. Originally designed in the US in order to save space, 1st examples were built in Chicago in 1880s. Tallest is Sears Building, Chicago, with 110 stories (473 m/1472 ft high).

slander, *see* LIBEL.

slate, dense, fine-grained metamorphic rock. Formed by compression of SHALE over long period; splits readily into thin, smooth plates. Used as roofing material.

slavery, ownership of a human being by another. Fundamental to social system of Greek city states and Roman empire. Largely replaced in Europe by serfdom under feudal system, but large numbers of African slaves were introduced to Americas as agric. labourers. Attempts at abolition on humanitarian grounds date from early 19th cent. (slave trade banned by UK 1807; slavery in British West Indies abolished 1833). Major issue in US Civil War, being basis of South's plantation economy; abolished after North's victory. Still believed to exist in Middle East.

Slavic or **Slavonic,** branch of Indo-European family of languages. Divided into 3 groups: E Slavic, incl. Russian, Ukrainian; W Slavic, incl. Polish, Czech, Slovak; S Slavic, incl. Serbo-Croat, Slovenian, Bulgarian.

Slavonia, region of N Yugoslavia, between Drava and Sava rivers. Main town Osijek. Low-lying, fertile; cereals, vegetable growing. Passed (1699) from Turkey to Hungary; united with Croatia 1868.

Slavs, Indo-European linguistic group, originally from N Carpathian region. Incl. Russians, Poles, Czechs, Slovaks, Bulgars, Slovenes and Serbo-Croats.

sleep, bodily state of rest when there is little or no conscious thought or voluntary movement. Electrical waves recorded from brain show sleep occurs in cycles of *c* 2 hours; in a cycle there is a period of intense electrical brain activity and rapid movement of eyes under lids (REM) followed by longer session without REM. DREAMS occur during REM.

sleeping sickness, infectious disease of tropical Africa caused by either of 2 trypanosomes transmitted by bite of tsetse fly. Symptoms incl. fever, swollen lymph nodes; lethargy follows later when trypanosomes invade nervous system, and death may follow.

slide rule, mathematical instrument consisting of a ruler with central sliding piece, both being marked with logarithmic scales; used in making rapid calculations by adding and subtracting logarithms.

Sligo, county of Connacht prov., NW Irish Republic. Area 1797 sq km (694 sq mi); pop. 55,000. Indented Atlantic coast; rugged, Ox Mts. in W. Cattle, potatoes; fishing. Co. town **Sligo,** pop. 17,000. RC cathedral.

Slim, William Joseph Slim, 1st Viscount (1891-1970), British field marshal. During WWII, commanded repulse of Japanese in Burma. Governor-general of Australia (1953-60).

slipped disc, *see* VERTEBRA.

sloe, *see* BLACKTHORN.

sloth, slow-moving herbivorous mammal of Bradypodidae family, found in tropical forests of Central and South America. Long coarse hair; lives upside down in trees, using hooked claws to walk along branches. Two genera; *Bradypus*, three-toed sloth; *Choloepus*, two-toed sloth.

sloth bear, *Melursus ursinus*, long-snouted bear of S India and Sri Lanka. Uses long tongue to feed on ants.

Slough, town of Buckinghamshire, SC England. Pop. 87,000. Industs. incl. chemicals; vehicle, aircraft parts; radio, television mfg.

Slovakia (*Slovensko*), region of E Czechoslovakia; main town Bratislava. Mountainous, incl. Tatra. Agric., mining. Part of Hungary (10th cent.-1918), became prov. of Czechoslovakia. Independent ally of Axis in WWII, reunited (1945). Distinctive Slovak language, culture.

Slovenia, autonomous republic of NW Yugoslavia. Area 20,246 sq km (7817 sq mi); cap. Ljubljana. Julian Alps in NW, main rivers Drava, Sava. Agric., forestry, mining.

Under Habsburgs until became (1918) part of Yugoslavia.

slow-worm, *Anguis fragilis,* legless snake-like lizard, widely distributed in Europe and Asia. Found in woods, damp meadows; diet of insects, worms. Also called blindworm.

slug, terrestrial gastropod mollusc, order Pulmonata, with reduced plate-like shell enclosed by its mantle. Herbivorous, often destructive of plants; moves on muscular foot leaving trail of slime.

Sluis or **Sluys** (Fr. *L'Ecluse*), town of SW Netherlands, near Belgian border. Scene of offshore naval battle (1340) in which Edward III of England defeated French.

smallpox, infectious virus disease characterized by prolonged fever and red spots which develop into pus-filled blisters. May cause permanent scarring of the skin. Vaccination has led to complete eradication of the disease in all parts of the world.

smell, one of five senses, less developed in humans than sight, touch, hearing. Perceived through stimulation of olfactory nerves of the nose by particles given off by substances.

smelt, small silvery marine or freshwater food fish of Osmeridae family; spawns in fresh water. Species incl. common smelt, *Osmerus eperlanus,* of Europe.

smelting, process of obtaining metal from its ores by action of heat. Usually involves reduction of metal oxide with carbon.

Smetana, Bedřich or **Frederick** (1824-84), Czech composer. Leader of nationalist Czech music. Works incl. opera *The Bartered Bride,* orchestral cycle *Ma Vlast* ('My Country'), string quartets.

Smith, Adam (1723-90), Scottish economist. Formulated theory of division of labour, defined value as labour expended to make object. Advocated free trade, rejecting MERCANTILISM. His influential *Wealth of Nations* (1776) was 1st systematic formulation of economic theory, became basis of 19th-cent. LAISSER-FAIRE doctrine.

Smith, Frederick Edwin, *see* BIRKENHEAD, 1ST EARL OF.

Smith, Ian Douglas (1919-), Zimbabwean statesman. As PM of Rhodesia (1964-79), issued Unilateral Declaration of Independence from Britain (1965). Set up republic under constitution perpetuating white minority rule (1969). Increasing political and military pressure in 1970s forced him to accept black majority rule.

Smith, John (*c* 1580-1631), English colonist. *See* POCAHONTAS.

Smith, Joseph (1805-44), American religious leader. Claimed to have vision directing him to sacred writings, transcribed as *Book of Mormon* (1829). Founded church (1830) based on revelations. Murdered by mob at Carthage, Illinois. Followers formed MORMONS.

smoke, suspension of solid particles in a gas, esp. particles of carbon and hydrocarbon in atmosphere derived from combustion of carbonaceous fuels. When combined with fog, forms **smog**. Considered health risk, therefore controlled by govt. measures advocating clean air and smokeless zones.

Smolensk, town of USSR, railway jct. of W European RSFSR; port on R. Dnepr. Pop. 276,000. Linen and textile mfg. Founded 9th cent.; became commercial centre, trading with Constantinople. Cap. of principality 12th-14th cent. Occupied by Napoleon (1812) and Germans (1941-3).

Smollett, Tobias [George] (1721-71), Scottish writer, surgeon. Known for energetic picaresque novels *Roderick Random* (1748), *Peregrine Pickle* (1751), *Humphrey Clinker* (1771).

smuggling, offence of importing or exporting goods illegally, esp. those requiring payment of duty. Esp. prevalent in 18th cent. with imposition of duties in UK, North America, Europe; goods smuggled incl. spirits, lace, tobacco, tea. Modern smuggling incl. drugs, illegal immigrants.

smut or **bunt,** various parasitic fungi of order Ustilaginales. Appear as black sooty spores on host plant. Serious threat to cereal crops. Treatment with compounds of sulphur and mercury.

Smuts, Jan Christian (1870-1950), South African soldier, statesman, PM (1919-24, 1939-48). Commanded Boer forces (1901-2) in war against UK, later sought cooperation with British. Joined Botha in creating (1910) Union of South Africa. Member of British war councils during both WWs.

Smyrna, *see* IZMIR.

snail, gastropod mollusc of order Pulmonata with spiral protective shell. Marine, freshwater and terrestrial varieties. Species incl. common garden snail, *Helix aspersa,* and edible or Roman snail, *H. pomatia.*

Snake, river of NW US, rising in Yellowstone National Park (Wyoming). Flows SW 1670 km (1038 mi) through Idaho, then NW along Oregon border to Washington to join Columbia R.

snake, any of suborder Ophidia of limbless elongated reptiles. Horny scales on body, forked tongue; mouth opens wide for swallowing large prey. Poisonous snakes carry venom in salivary glands; venom acts either as nerve poison, paralysing victim, or as tissue poison, destroying cells and causing haemorrhages.

snapdragon, any of genus *Antirrhinum* of perennial plants native to Mediterranean region, esp. garden variety *A. majus* with showy white, crimson or yellow flowers.

sneeze, reflex action consisting of brief indrawn breath followed by forcible expulsion of air through nose. Initiated by irritation of lining of nose.

snipe, wading bird of Scolopacidae family, with long narrow bill used for digging. Species incl. common snipe, *Gallinago gallinago,* of Europe and Asia.

snooker, game played on billiard table with 15 red balls, 6 coloured balls and white cue ball. Derived from BILLIARDS. Similar to US game of pool.

Snow, C[harles] P[ercy], Baron Snow of Leicester (1905-80), English author, scientist. Known for long novel sequence incl. *Strangers and Brothers* (1940), *Corridors of Power* (1963), dealing with ethics of power. Wrote controversial essay, *The Two Cultures* (1959).

snow, precipitation consisting of delicate, hexagonal ice crystals, formed in atmosphere at temperatures below freezing point. Lower limit of permanent snow cover is called 'snow-line'; it reaches sea level at poles.

snow bunting, *Plectrophenax nivalis,* small bird of N regions; in spring, male's plumage is white with black back and tail. Breeds in Arctic, migrating to Europe and America in winter.

Snowdon, Anthony Armstrong-Jones, 1st Earl of (1930-), British designer, photographer. Married (1960) Princess Margaret; divorced in 1978.

Snowdon, mountain of Gwynedd, NW Wales. Highest in England and Wales (1085 m/3560 ft). Rack Railway from Llanberis. Snowdonia national park in surrounding area.

snowdrop, any of genus *Galanthus* of early-blooming, bulbous perennials native to Europe. White flowers.

snow goose, *Anser caerulescens,* white North American goose with black-tipped wings, dark pink bill and legs.

snow leopard or **ounce,** *Uncia uncia,* large cat of mountains of C Asia; reaches lengths of 2.1 m/7 ft. Coat whitish with dark blotches in summer, almost pure white in winter. Feeds on sheep, goats, ibex.

Snowy Mountains, range of SE New South Wales, Australia. Highest point Mt. KOSCIUSKO. Snowy Mts. scheme estab. 1949 to provide h.e.p., irrigation.

snowy owl, *Nyctea scandiaca,* large owl of Arctic and subarctic regions. Largely diurnal and solitary; white plumage with dark brown markings. Feeds on hares, lemmings, fish.

snuff, powdered tobacco sniffed into nostrils or rubbed on to teeth and gums. Snuff-taking was widespread in 18th cent. when elaborately decorated snuff boxes were made.

soap, mixture of sodium salts of fatty acids (esp. oleic, palmitic and stearic acids) or of potassium salts of these acids (soft soaps). Prepared by boiling fats and oils with alkali. Acts most effectively in soft water; hard water causes scum (precipitated calcium or magnesium salts) to form.

soapstone or **steatite,** soft, grey mineral, composed mainly of TALC with other minerals *eg* chlorite, mica, quartz. Used in sculpture and electrical insulators.

soapwort or **bouncing Bet,** *Saponaria officinalis,* European annual or perennial herb. Clusters of pink flowers; sap forms lather with water.

Soares, Mario (1924-), Portuguese political leader. Imprisoned in 1960s for socialist opposition to Salazar regime, exiled (1970-4). Returned after military coup (1974); PM 1976-78.

Soapwort

Sobieski, John, *see* JOHN III [SOBIESKI].

soccer, *see* ASSOCIATION FOOTBALL.

social class, category or grouping of people according to economic, occupational or social status. In Marxist terms, refers exclusively to those persons with common relationship to material production. Traditionally, society divided into upper, middle and working (lower) classes, according to socio-economic grouping.

social contract, theory that society originated out of voluntary association, bringing with it mutual obligations. Formulated by Hobbes and Locke, expanded by Rousseau, had great influence on subsequent development of responsible govt. in democracies.

Social Credit, economic programme, developed from theories of economist C.H. DOUGLAS. Calls for redistribution of purchasing power by issuing dividends (based on estimate of nation's wealth) to all persons to counter economic depression. Adopted by Social Credit Party of Alberta, Canada; elected (1935). Later achieved power in British Columbia.

social democracy, advocacy of socialism within democratic framework, adhering to evolutionary means of achieving power; esp. important in Europe. Split in German Social Democratic party (SPD) at start of 20th cent. reflected dilemma of other European Socialist parties, whether or not to cooperate with bourgeois govts. to achieve gradual reform; Eduard Bernstein (1850-1932) was leading proponent of this 'revisionism', opposing use of violent revolution to gain power for proletariat (*see* MARXISM). Collapse of Internationals during WWI led to increase of reform-conscious Social Democratic parties in Europe, some forming govts., *eg* in Scandinavian countries and Britain (*see* LABOUR PARTY), between WWs. In Germany, SPD revived after WWII; gained power under Brandt (1969). In France, Socialist groups under Blum formed Popular Front govt. in 1930s; formed major opposition party in Fifth Republic.

socialism, any of various economic and

political theories or systems advocating transfer of means of production and distribution from private ownership to community as a whole, with all sharing work, produce. In this sense, can incl. SOCIAL DEMOCRACY as well as MARXISM. Early socialist theorists (*eg* OWEN, SAINT-SIMON) believed in reform of existing society to achieve utopian ideal. Attacked by Marx, who taught inevitability of revolution. By 1870s, Marxist ('scientific') socialism was strong political force in Europe, but internally split into 2 main factions, gradualists and revolutionaries. Schism made permanent with triumph of revolutionary COMMUNISM in Russia (1917).

social security, system by which govt. provides for nation's wage earners and dependants, esp. for their protection in sickness, old age or unemployment. First estab. 1883 in Germany with HEALTH INSURANCE and PENSION schemes. In UK, NATIONAL INSURANCE ACT (1911) added unemployment insurance.

Society Islands, archipelago of SC Pacific Ocean, part of French Polynesia. Comprise Windward Isls. (incl. Tahiti) and Leeward Isls. Produce copra, pearl shell, vanilla. Acquired by France (1843).

Society of Friends or **Quakers,** Christian sect founded (*c* 1650) in England by George Fox (1624-91). Hold that understanding and guidance come directly from 'inward light' of Holy Spirit, and that sacrament and formal worship are unnecessary for Christian life. Colony estab. (1682) in Pennsylvania, US, by PENN.

Society of Jesus, *see* JESUS, SOCIETY OF.

sociology, study of human society, and of social relations, organization and change; specifically the study of the beliefs, values, interrelationships, *etc,* of social groups and of the principles and processes governing social phenomena. Systematic discipline since 19th cent., esp. through work of Auguste Comte, and later Durkheim and Max Weber.

Socotra, isl. of Southern Yemen, in Arabian Sea. Area *c* 3630 sq km (1400 sq mi). Barren plateau with mountainous interior. Part of British protect. of Aden after 1886.

Socrates (469-399 BC), Greek philosopher. Believed knowledge could be approached by question-and-answer sequence (dialectic method), and wisdom to be based on recognition of one's ignorance. Ideas on weakness of democratic govt. unpopular in Athens. Assembly tried and condemned him on charge of corrupting youth; died by drinking poison. Teachings preserved in writings of disciple Plato, and subsequently Aristotle.

soda, name applied to various sodium compounds, incl. sodium carbonate, bicarbonate and hydroxide. Sodium carbonate, manufactured on large scale from common salt, is used to make soap, glass, paper and to soften water. Sodium bicarbonate is used in baking powder and medicine.

sodium (Na), soft silvery white metallic element; at. no. 11, at. wt. 22.99. Reacts violently with water to form strong alkali sodium hydroxide. Occurs combined as chloride (common salt), nitrate (Chile saltpetre); prepared by electrolysis of fused chloride. Used in organic syntheses, *eg* of lead tetraethyl; yellow sodium vapour light used in street lighting.

Sodom and Gomorrah, in OT, two of the cities of the plain, destroyed by God because of their wickedness. Possibly situated SW of Dead Sea.

Sofia (anc. *Sardica*), cap. of Bulgaria. Pop. 965,000. Major route centre in W Balkans. Indust. centre, esp. machinery, textiles. Univ. (1880), Black Mosque. Colonized by Romans; sacked by Huns (447). Cap. of former Turkish Rumelia, of Bulgaria from 1879.

Soho, dist. of City of WESTMINSTER, London, England. Has many foreign restaurants; nightclubs, sex shops *etc.*

soil, loose accumulation of material forming topmost layer of Earth's land surface. Consists of organic material (humus) and inorganic material (weathered rock, incl. clay, silt, sand) together with air and water. Types incl. BLACK EARTH, LOAM, LOESS.

Soissons, town of N France, on R. Aisne. Pop. 30,000. Agric. market. Cathedral (12th cent.); ruined abbey contains tombs of Merovingian kings.

Sokoto, town of NW Nigeria, on R. Kebbi. Pop. 50,000. Cap. of vast Moslem Fulani empire of Sokoto in 19th cent.

Solanaceae, family of plants native to tropical and temperate regions, esp. tropical America. Incl. deadly nightshade, tobacco, potato.

solan goose, another name for GANNET.

solar energy, energy liberated by thermonuclear reactions in Sun and radiated in form of radio waves, X-rays and light. May be utilized by solar cells to generate electricity or by solar furnaces to produce high temperatures.

solar flare, short-lived eruption of Sun's surface, usually associated with sunspots. Accompanied by emission of particles, X-rays, *etc*; causes magnetic and radio disturbances on Earth.

Solar System, name for Sun and collection of bodies in orbit about it. Comprises Sun, 9 major planets (Mercury, Venus, Earth, Mars, Jupiter, Saturn, Uranus, Neptune, Pluto), their satellites, minor planets, comets and meteors.

solar wind, stream of ionized particles, mainly protons and electrons, emitted from Sun's surface, esp. during solar flares and sunspot activity. Particles reaching Earth are trapped by its magnetic field to form Van Allen radiation belt; others cause auroral displays around the poles.

solder, alloy used in joining metal. Soft solders, which have low melting point, contain lead and tin in varying proportions with some antimony.

sole, edible flatfish of Soleidae family, with

worldwide distribution. European *Solea solea* is sold as Dover sole.

Solent, The, channel between Hampshire, S England, and Isle of Wight. Shipping route to Southampton, Portsmouth; yachting.

sol-fa, tonic, *see* TONIC SOL-FA.

Solferino, village of N Italy, near Mantua. Scene of indecisive battle (1859) between French and Austrians which inspired Dunant to form Red Cross.

solicitor, in UK, member of legal profession who is not member of the bar; may not plead cases in superior courts. Advises clients in legal cases, engages barristers for them, *etc.*

solid, state of matter in which constituent molecules or ions possess no translatory movement. Solids possess definite crystalline structure and retain their shape unless deformed by external forces; certain amorphous non-crystalline solids, *eg* glass, may be considered as supercooled fluids.

solid-state physics, branch of physics dealing with matter in solid state. Often refers specifically to study of semiconductors and their use in electronic devices without moving parts or heated filaments.

Solomon (d. *c* 932 BC), king of Israel, son of David and Bathsheba. His peaceful reign was marked by growth of trade and building of the Temple in Jerusalem. Famous for his wisdom.

Solomon Islands, state of SW Pacific, member of British Commonwealth. Area *c* 29,800 sq km (11,500 sq mi); pop. 215,000; cap. Honiara. Consists of all isls. of Solomon Isls. archipelago (incl. Guadalcanal), except Bougainville and Buka, which belong to Papua New Guinea. Formerly known as British Solomon Isls. Protect. (estab. by 1899), independent 1978.

Solon (*c* 639-*c* 559 BC), Athenian statesman. Revised constitution to create limited form of democracy.

solstice, time of year when Sun appears directly overhead at the line marking its furthest distance N or S of the Equator. For N hemisphere, summer solstice (21 June) occurs when Sun reaches Tropic of Cancer, winter solstice (22 Dec.) when Sun reaches Tropic of Capricorn. Day is at max. length at summer solstice, night at winter solstice.

solution, homogeneous molecular mixture of 2 or more substances, *eg* of solid or gas in liquid. Some alloys are solutions of one metal in another.

Solway Firth, inlet of Irish Sea, between SW Scotland and NW England. Fishing.

Solzhenitsyn, Aleksandr Isayevich (1918-), Russian author. Known for novels critical of Soviet regime, *eg One Day in the Life of Ivan Denisovich* (1962), *First Circle* (1964), *Cancer Ward* (1966), *August 1914* (1972). *The Gulag Archipelago* (1974) documents the Soviet system of prison camps. Nobel Prize for Literature (1970). Exiled in 1974.

Somalia or **Somali Democratic Republic,** republic of E Africa. Area 637,700 sq km

Somalia

(246,200 sq mi); pop. 3,443,000; cap. Mogadishu. Language: Somali. Religion: Islam. Coastal lowland, arid interior plateau. Nomadic pastoralism; exports bananas, livestock, hides. Formed 1960 from union of British Somaliland (created 1884, cap. Hargeisa) and Italian Somaliland (created 1889, cap. Mogadishu; from 1950 a UN trust territ.). War with Ethiopia in late 1970s over disputed Ogaden territory.

Somaliland, French, *see* DJIBOUTI.

Somerset, Edward Seymour, Duke of, *see* SEYMOUR, JANE.

Somerset, county of SW England. Area 3458 sq km (1335 sq mi); pop. 411,000; admin. hq. Taunton. Exmoor in W; Mendips in NE; plain in C. Dairying (esp. Cheddar cheese), sheep, cider apples.

Somme, river of N France. Flows *c* 240 km (150 mi) from near St Quentin via Amiens, Abbeville to English Channel. Canal links to Oise, Scheldt. Scene of heavy fighting in WWI (1916).

Somoza, Anastasio (1896-1956), Nicaraguan political leader, president (1937-47, 1950-6). Ruthless rule after gaining dictatorial power in coup (1936). Assassinated. His son, **Anastasio Somoza [Debayle]** (1925-), was also president (1967-72, 1974-9). Oppressive rule led to overthrow by left-wing Sandinista guerillas.

sonar or **asdic,** method of detecting and locating underwater objects, esp. submarines or shoals of fish, by projecting soundwaves through water and registering the vibrations reflected back. Also used in measuring depths.

sonata, piece of instrumental music so named to distinguish it from a cantata for voices and instruments. Developed from *c* 1600 as a composition for a single instrument, esp. a keyboard one, with or without accompaniment. Usually in several movements, first of which is in **sonata form** containing 2 themes subjected to statement, development and recapitulation.

song, vocal form of musical expression, normally setting of lyric. Earliest documented European song dates from

10th cent. Early practitioners were TROUBADOURS, MINNESINGER. Developed by such masters as Machault, DUFAY, LASSUS and English lutanists of 16th-17th cents. Reached peak as vehicle of romantic expression in work of Schubert, Schumann and Brahms in 19th cent. Folk song has survived with little change for centuries.

Song of Solomon, poetical book of OT, traditionally attributed to Solomon, but sometimes dated as late as 3rd cent. BC. Primarily a glorification of pure love or an allegory of God's love for Israel.

songthrush, *Turdus philomelos,* common European songbird with brown back and spotted breast.

sonic boom, noise created by shock waves set up by aircraft travelling faster than sound. Waves are transmitted as variations in atmospheric pressure; when waves touch ground, characteristic double bang is heard.

sonnet, poem of 14 lines, expressing single complete thought or idea, generally written in iambic pentameter. Most common rhyme schemes are the Italian form (*eg* Keats's *On First Looking into Chapman's Homer*) with 8 lines (octave) followed by group of 6 lines (sestet), and Shakespearian form with 3 quatrains followed by couplet.

Soochow or **Wuhsien,** city of Kiangsu prov., E China. Pop. 730,000. On Grand Canal; rail jct. Famous silks, weaving. Former treaty port, opened 1896. Has many canals, gardens and pagodas.

Sophists, term applied in Athens (middle 5th cent. BC) to persons giving lessons in rhetoric, politics and mathematics in return for money. Later Sophists emphasized rhetoric rather than substance of knowledge, becoming known for their ability to conduct specious argument. Condemned by Socrates and Plato.

Sophocles (*c* 496-406 BC), Greek tragic poet. One of three great masters of tragedy, other two being contemporaries Aeschylus and Euripides. Known for use of dialogue rather than lyric, introducing 3rd actor, and use of dramatic irony. Extant plays incl. *Oedipus Rex, Oedipus at Colonus, Antigone, Electra.*

Sophonias, *see* ZEPHANIAH.

soprano, highest singing voice in women and boys, latter also known as treble. Term sometimes applied to high-pitched member of a family of instruments, *eg* soprano saxophone.

Sorbonne, traditional name for Univ. of Paris, France, from 1st college estab. (1253) by Robert de Sorbon.

Sorel, Georges (1847-1922), French social philosopher. Introduced Marxist ideas into France, later becoming anarcho-syndicalist, then Leninist, regarding Marxism, like all extremist social doctrines, as world-changing myth, not science. Known for *Reflections on Violence* (1908), defending role of violence in revolution.

sorghum, genus of grasses with solid stems native to Africa; esp. *Sorghum vulgare,* widely cultivated as forage crop. Variously known as Kaffir corn, durra, Guinea corn, Indian millet.

sorrel, *see* DOCK, OXALIS.

Sorrento, town of Campania, SW Italy, on Bay of Naples. Pop. 29,000. Resort.

Sosnowiec, city of S Poland. Pop. 197,000. Iron and steel industs., engineering.

soul, concept of non-material, immortal life-essence or spiritual identity of individual. Mind and body conceived as its vehicle. Occurs in most religions either as individual attribute (Christianity, Islam) or as general principle or world soul (Hinduism, Buddhism). Denied by materialists.

Sound, The, *see* ÖRESUND.

sound, vibrations in air or some other medium which stimulate the auditory nerves and give sensation of hearing. Travels at *c* 330 m/sec (760 mph) in air; velocity varies with temperature and is greater in solids. Pitch of sound depends on number of vibrations per second; lowest normally audible sound has frequency of *c* 20 cycles/sec, highest *c* 20,000.

Sousse or **Susa,** town of E Tunisia, on Gulf of Hammamet. Pop. 255,000. Tourist resort; port, exports olive oil. Ancient *Hadrumetum,* founded 9th cent. BC by Phoenicians.

South Africa

South Africa, republic of S Africa. Area 1,221,000 sq km (471,500 sq mi); pop. 27,700,000; caps. Pretoria (admin.), Cape Town (legislative), Bloemfontein (judicial). Languages: Afrikaans, English. Religion: Christianity. Comprises Cape Prov., Natal, Orange Free State, Transvaal; controls Namibia despite withdrawal of UN mandate (1966). Mainly plateau, fringed by mountains (*eg* Drakensberg); main rivers Orange, Vaal. Cereals, fruit, sugar cane, vines; great mineral wealth, esp. in Witwatersrand. Dutch settlement estab. 1652 at Table Bay; Cape annexed by UK 1806. Boer dislike of British rule led to 'Great Trek' 1836 to Orange Free State, Transvaal; Boer republics estab. 1850s. Boer War (1899-1902) ended in British victory; Union of South Africa estab. 1910.

Republic from 1960, withdrew from British Commonwealth 1961. Follows controversial policy of separate development (*apartheid*) of blacks and whites; incl. 9 Bantu 'homelands' eventually to become partly independent (*eg* TRANSKEI).

South African War, *see* BOER WAR.

South America, S continent of W hemisphere, bounded by Pacific in W and Atlantic in E. Area *c* 17,819,000 sq km (6,880,000 sq mi); pop. 222,319,000. Dominated in W by Andean cordillera; C plateau incl. Mato Grosso, Pampas; drained by Amazon, Plata, Orinoco river systems. Hist. highly developed Indian civilizations (esp. Incas) *fl* before Spanish, Portuguese exploration and colonization for mineral wealth in 16th cent. Nine Spanish-speaking independent republics estab. under Bolívar, San Martín in 19th cent.; Brazil is Portuguese-speaking. Guiana Highlands comprise Surinam, Guyana, French Guiana. Much political instability in all republics after independence.

Southampton, city of Hampshire, S England, on Southampton Water. Pop. 213,000. Chief English passenger seaport; transatlantic services. Also cargo port. Oil refinery at Fawley. Univ. (1952).

Southampton Island, in E Keewatin Dist., Northwest Territs., Canada; at entrance to Hudson Bay. Area 40,700 sq km (15,700 sq mi). Pop. mainly Eskimo.

South Arabia, Federation of, *see* SOUTHERN YEMEN.

South Australia, state of S Australia. Area 984,500 sq km (380,100 sq mi); pop. 1,294,000; cap. Adelaide. Mainly low-lying, incl. Nullarbor Plain in SW, L. Eyre in N; has Musgrave (N), Flinders and Mt. Lofty (SE) ranges. Produces sheep, wheat, fruit, wine; minerals incl. iron ore, salt. First settled 1836; became crown colony 1842, federal state 1901.

South Carolina, state of SE US, on Atlantic coast. Area 80,432 sq km (31,055 sq mi); pop. 2,878,000; cap. Columbia. Low coastal plain, Savannah R. on S border; plateau in NW. Important agric. (tobacco, cotton, soya beans, maize, stock rearing), related industs.; stone, clay mining. First settled by Spanish (1526); then by English (1670). One of original 13 colonies of US. First secessionist state before Civil War (1860).

South China Sea, part of Pacific Ocean enclosed by SE China, Indo-China, Malay penin., Borneo, Philippines and Taiwan.

South Dakota, state of NC US. Area 199,552 sq km (77,047 sq mi); pop. 688,000; cap. Pierre. Mainly agric. (grains, livestock rearing); plains in E divided from Black Hills in SW (gold mines) by Missouri R. Acquired by US as part of Louisiana Purchase (1803). Territ. estab. (1861); Sioux Indians resisted white settlement (1868-90), deprived of land. Admitted to Union, jointly with North Dakota, as 39th state (1889).

Southeast Asia Treaty Organization (SEATO), former anti-Communist defence alliance (1954-77), consisting of Pakistan, the Philippines, Thailand, Australia, France, New Zealand, UK and US.

Southend-on-Sea, town of Essex, SE England, on N side of Thames estuary. Pop. 162,000. Electrical goods mfg. Resort.

Southern Alps, mountain range of South Isl., New Zealand. Runs SW-NE, highest point MT. COOK. Many snowfields, glaciers.

Southern Cross (Crux), small constellation in S hemisphere whose 4 brightest stars appear to form tips of a cross.

Southern Rhodesia, *see* ZIMBABWE.

Southern Yemen

Southern Yemen, republic of SW Asia. Area *c* 287,500 sq km (111,000 sq mi); pop. 1,853,000; cap. Aden. Coastal strip in S borders Arabian Sea; mountains and plateau in interior. History dates from 1963 estab. of Federation of South Arabia out of states of Aden protect. Southern Yemen proclaimed 1967.

Southey, Robert (1774-1843), English author. One of 'Lake poets'. Known for short poems, *eg* 'Inchcape Rock', and biog. of Nelson (1813). Poet laureate (1813).

South Georgia, *see* FALKLAND ISLANDS.

South Glamorgan, *see* GLAMORGAN.

South Holland, *see* HOLLAND.

South Island, one of main isls. of New Zealand, separated from North Isl. by Cook Str. Area 150,480 sq km (58,100 sq mi); pop. 861,000; chief cities Christchurch, Dunedin. Plateau in SW; Southern Alps form W backbone. Coastal lowland incl. Canterbury Plains. Grain, sheep farming; timber; h.e.p.

South Korea, *see* KOREA.

South Orkney Islands, group of isls. in S Atlantic, SE of Cape Horn, forming part of British Antarctic Territ. from 1962. Area *c* 620 sq km (140 sq mi). Discovered 1821; also claimed by Argentina.

South Pole, point at S end of Earth's axis, latitude 90°S. First reached 1911 by Roald Amundsen.

Southport, town of Merseyside met. county, NW England. Pop. 84,000. Clothing mfg. Seaside resort.

South Sea Bubble, popular name for financial scheme in which South Sea Co. (founded 1711 with monopoly in South

American trade) took over British national debt, exchanging its stock for govt. bonds. After widespread speculation, company became bankrupt (1720); resulting investigation revealed govt. corruption.

South Shetland Islands, group of isls. in S Atlantic, NW of Graham Land, forming part of British Antarctic Territ. from 1962. Area *c* 4700 sq km (1800 sq mi). Discovered 1819.

South Shields, town of Tyne and Wear met. county, NE England, on S side of Tyne estuary. Pop. 101,000. Shipbuilding, engineering, chemicals industs.

South Vietnam, *see* VIETNAM.

Southwark, town of SC Greater London, England. Pop. 220,000. Created 1965 from Bermondsey, Camberwell, Southwark.

South West Africa, *see* NAMIBIA.

South Yorkshire, met. county of NC England. Area 1560 sq km (602 sq mi); pop. 1,304,000; admin. hq. Barnsley. Created 1974 from part of former S Riding of Yorkshire.

sovereignty, in politics, supreme independent power held by state or other govt. unit. Sovereign state can conduct diplomacy, make treaties, war, peace. Internally, it makes laws, controls finances and the military.

Sovetsk, town of USSR, W European RSFSR; port on R. Neman. Pop. 60,000. As Tilsit, site of treaty between Russia, Prussia and France (1807), leading to loss of Prussian territ. Passed from East Prussia to USSR (1945) and renamed.

soviet (Russ., = council), in USSR, any of various governing councils, local, intermediate, national, elected by and representing people. Each forms part of a pyramid govt. structure, with village, town soviets at base, SUPREME SOVIET at apex. Organized first (1905) as strike committees. Re-estab. 1917 by workers, soldiers, became govt. instruments under Lenin (1918).

Soviet Union, *see* UNION OF SOVIET SOCIALIST REPUBLICS.

Soweto, township of S Transvaal, South Africa, near Johannesburg. Black African pop. Scene of anti-govt. riots (1976); *c* 150 killed.

soybean, soyabean or **soja bean,** *Glycine max,* annual plant of Leguminosae family. Native to China and Japan but widely cultivated for seeds which are rich in protein and oil used in glycerine and rubber substitutes.

spacecraft, vehicle designed for travelling in outer space. Pioneered by USSR and US. Early craft were artificial satellites put into orbit round Earth. Subsequent developments incl. manned capsules, docking vehicles steered by rockets, *Skylab* orbiting space station with living quarters for 3 astronauts. Planned developments incl. space shuttle capable of re-landing on Earth and being used many times.

space exploration, navigation in manned spacecraft in regions beyond Earth's atmosphere. Unmanned artificial satellites carried out 1st explorations, relaying to Earth information about atmospheric conditions. Orbital flight by manned vehicle first achieved by Yuri GAGARIN. Subsequent extended flights have incl. manned flights to Moon (US), *eg* that of Apollo XI (1969), and unmanned probes to Venus, Mars, Jupiter and Saturn sending back data to Earth.

space-time continuum, four-dimensional description of the universe, blending three space dimensions with dimension of time. Necessitated by theory of relativity in which time is no longer absolute but depends on relative motion of the observer. The geometry of space-time continuum is determined by gravitation; large gravitating bodies affect its curvature.

spaghetti, *see* PASTA.

Spain

Spain (*España*), kingdom of SW Europe, occupying most of Iberian penin.; incl. Balearic, Canary Isls. Area 505,000 sq km (195,000 sq mi); pop. 37,109,000; cap. Madrid. Language: Spanish. Religion: RC. Distinct languages and cultures in Basque Provs. and Catalonia. Pyrenees in NE; large C plateau between Cantabrian Mts. (N), Sierra Morena (S). Main rivers Douro, Ebro, Tagus. Agric. incl. fruit, olives, wine (S), livestock (N); rich in minerals, tourism. Inhabited from prehist. times, part of Roman Empire after defeat of Carthage. Germanic invasion 5th cent.; Moorish conquest 8th cent. Christian reconquest completed 1492, led by Aragón and Castile (united 1479). Exploration led to colonizing Americas, empire *fl* under Habsburgs, colonies lost 19th cent. Republic proclaimed 1931; Civil War (1936-9) resulted in fascist state under Franco; monarchy restored 1975; democratic elections from 1977.

Spalato, *see* SPLIT.

spaniel, one of various breeds of dog with drooping ears and silky coat. Breeds incl. King Charles, cocker, springer spaniels.

Spanish, Romance language in Italic branch of Indo-European family. Spoken as 1st language in Spain and 18 countries in Central, South America. Developed from Latin, Castilian dialect becoming dominant in early Middle Ages.

Spanish-American War (1898), conflict between US and Spain occasioned by US intervention in Cuban struggle for independence from Spain. Spanish fleet destroyed in Manila; Spanish forces surrendered after defeat at Santiago de Cuba. Treaty of Paris granted Cuba independence under US protection; US acquired Guam, Puerto Rico, Philippines.

Spanish Armada, *see* ARMADA, SPANISH.

Spanish Civil War, conflict (1936-9) precipitated by military opposition to liberal govt. of Spanish republic (proclaimed 1931). Conservative interests, merged under FRANCO, won early victories over Republican (or loyalist) forces. International non-intervention pact (signed 1936) broken; Germany and Italy supplied arms to Franco's Insurgents, USSR supported Republicans. Triumph by Insurgents (Madrid captured, Mar. 1939) led to estab. of Franco's dictatorship.

Spanish fly, *see* BLISTER BEETLE.

Spanish Guinea, *see* EQUATORIAL GUINEA.

Spanish Inquisition, *see* INQUISITION; TORQUEMADA.

Spanish Sahara, *see* WESTERN SAHARA.

Spanish Succession, War of the (1701-14), European conflict over succession to Spanish throne; claimants were Philip, grandson of Louis XIV, and Charles, son of Emperor Leopold I of Austria. England, Holland and Austria, seeking to prevent potential union of Spain and France, allied against France, Spain and Bavaria. Hostilities ended by treaties of Utrecht (1713), Rastaat (1714); Philip recognized as king (Philip V).

Spark, Muriel Sarah, née Camberg (1918-), British novelist. Best known for *The Prime of Miss Jean Brodie* (1961).

sparking plug or **spark plug,** device used in internal combustion engine to ignite fuel-air mixture. Consists of 2 electrodes with a gap of *c* 0.38 mm–1.02 mm between them. When a high voltage is impressed on electrodes a spark is discharged.

sparrow, one of various small short-beaked seed-eating birds, esp. of genus *Passer*. House sparrow, *P. domesticus,* has streaked brown and grey plumage; native of N Europe and Asia.

sparrow hawk, *Accipiter nisus,* small Old World hawk with short rounded wings and long tail. Male has slate-grey upper parts, red-brown barred lower parts.

Sparta (*Spárti*), town of Greece, in SC Peloponnese, on R. Eurotas. Pop. 10,000. Nearby is site of ancient Sparta (*Lacedaemon*), militaristic city state at zenith after defeating Athens in Peloponnesian War. Defeated by Thebes (371 BC), Philip II of Macedon.

Spartacists, radical German Socialist group, founded 1916. Led by Karl Liebknecht and Rosa Luxemburg. Became (1918) German Communist Party. Uprising (Jan. 1919) ruthlessly suppressed by Berlin govt.

Spartacus (d. 71 BC), Roman gladiator, b. Thrace. Organized revolt of escaped slaves in S Italy and defeated 2 Roman armies sent against him. Defeated and killed in battle with Crassus. Many of his followers were crucified.

spastic paralysis, condition in which certain muscles are kept permanently taut, causing loss of voluntary movement and spasms of affected muscles. Congenital form (cerebral palsy) is caused by brain damage and may be accompanied by mental retardation.

species, in biology, *see* CLASSIFICATION.

specific gravity, ratio of material's density to density of water at 4°C.

specific heat, in physics, quantity of heat required to raise the temperature of unit mass of a substance by one degree. Expressed in calories per gm per °C.

spectacles, lenses worn to correct or help defective vision. Concave lenses correct short sight (myopia), convex lenses long sight (hypermetropia), cylindrical lenses astigmatism. Earliest European spectacles date from 13th cent.

spectroscope, optical instrument designed to study spectrum of light. Light is introduced through a slit, its rays made parallel by a collimator, dispersed by a prism or grating, and viewed through a telescope eyepiece. Used to determine chemical composition of substances by examination of spectral lines in light emitted or absorbed, and in astronomy to determine physical and chemical nature of stars. The spectral lines of a substance are fundamental characteristics of it and thus a means of identification.

spectrum, in physics, originally name for coloured bands produced by white light passing through a prism or diffraction grating. Colours seen are red (longest wavelength), orange, yellow, green, blue and violet (shortest wavelength). Now refers to resolution of any electromagnetic radiation into its constituent wavelengths.

speedwell, *see* VERONICA.

Speer, Albert (1905-), German architect, Nazi leader. Became minister of armaments (1942). Pleaded guilty to war crimes (1946); sentenced to 20 years' imprisonment.

Speke, John Hanning (1827-64), English soldier, explorer. Accompanied R. F. Burton on 2 African expeditions (1854, 1857-9). Discovered L. Victoria (1858), returning (1862) to confirm it as source of Nile.

Spence, Sir Basil Urwin (1907-76), Scottish architect. Designed Coventry Cathedral, buildings for Sussex Univ.

Spencer, Herbert (1820-1903), English philosopher. Stated theory of evolution was of universal application, that all change within any structure was of increasing differentiation and, at same time, of increasing integration.

Spencer, Sir Stanley (1891-1959), English painter. Painted religious scenes set in familiar environment of his native village.

Spencer Gulf, inlet of Indian Ocean, South Australia, between Eyre and Yorke penins.

Spender, Stephen Harold (1909-), English poet, critic. Associated with Auden, Day Lewis in 1930s. Later poems indicate more liberal than left-wing attitudes.

Spenser, Edmund (*c* 1552-99), English poet. Works incl. *Amoretti* (1595) on his courtship, *Epithalamion* (1595) on his marriage, *The Shepheardes Calender* (1579). Developed Spenserian stanza for masterpiece, *The Faerie Queene* (1590, 1596), an allegorical epic of moral development, praising Elizabeth I.

sperm or **spermatozoon,** in biology, male gamete or reproductive cell. When female ovum is fertilized by sperm, union develops into new member of same species.

spermaceti, white wax-like substance solidifying from colourless oil in head of sperm whale; significance unknown, but may assist in diving. Used in making cosmetics, candles, *etc.*

Spermatophyta, in botany, term for seed-bearing plants. Subdivided into GYMNOSPERM and ANGIOSPERM.

sperm whale or **cachalot,** *Physeter catodon,* large whale of worldwide distribution, much hunted by whalers. Enormous head, one cavity of which contains SPERMACETI oil; teeth in lower jaw. Feeds on molluscs; reaches lengths of 18.3 m/60 ft.

Spey, river of NE Scotland, flows 172 km (107 mi) from Highland region to Moray Firth at Spey Bay. Salmon fishing.

Spezia, La, city of Liguria, NW Italy, on Ligurian Sea. Cap. of La Spezia prov. Pop. 120,000. Port, oil refining; main Italian naval base. Badly damaged in WWII.

sphagnum, bog moss or **peat moss,** genus of soft mosses. Found mainly on surface of bogs. Used for potting and packing plants and in absorbent dressings.

sphinx, in ancient Egyptian art, sculptural representation of recumbent lion with head of man, ram or hawk. Often taken to symbolize pharaoh as descendant of Ra. Many built, most famous near Gîza, Egypt. In Greek myth, destructive agent of gods, represented as winged woman with body of lion or dog. Either killed itself or was slain by Oedipus after he answered its riddle.

spice, aromatic vegetable product, *eg* pepper, ginger, nutmeg, cinnamon, clove, used in cookery to season or flavour food.

Spice Islands, *see* MOLUCCAS.

spider, any of order Araneida of arachnids. Abdomen bears 2 or more pairs of spinnerets; silk thread produced used for web-making and to enclose cocoons. Most species possess poison glands for killing prey; venom of black widow and Australian funnel-web is dangerous to man.

spider crab, sea crab of Majidae family with triangular body and long thin legs. *Macrocheira kaempferi,* found off Japan, is largest crustacean; leg span of *c* 2.4 m/8 ft.

spider monkey, long-legged South American monkey with long prehensile tail, genus *Ateles.* Diet of fruit.

spin, in nuclear physics, intrinsic angular momentum of an elementary particle or photon, produced by rotation about its own axis.

spina bifida, congenital defect of the vertebrae in which one or more of the vertebral arches does not develop. Resulting damage to spinal cord causes varying amounts of paralysis. Treated by immediate surgery.

spinach, *Spinacia oleracea,* widely cultivated annual plant, native to SW Asia. Dark-green edible leaves are rich in iron and eaten cooked as vegetable.

spinal column, *see* VERTEBRA.

spinal cord, portion of central nervous system extending from brain and enclosed in spinal canal formed by vertebral arches. Consists of outer layer of white matter (nerve fibres), inner layer of grey matter (nerve cells) and central canal containing cerebrospinal fluid. Spinal nerves (31 pairs) connected to it convey sensory and motor impulses to and from brain.

spinet, small harpsichord, popular in 17th cent. Usually triangular in shape, with strings at an angle of 45° to keyboard. Replaced rectangular virginals, in which strings are parallel to keyboard.

spinning, process of drawing out and twisting fibre into continuous thread. Simplest tools used were distaff, a rod on which fibre was wrapped, and spindle, a weighted rod on which fibre drawn from distaff was twisted. Later developments incl. spinning wheel, which revolved spindle, often by means of a treadle. In 18th cent. spinning was mechanized by efforts of Hargreaves, Crompton, Arkwright, *etc.*

Spinoza, Benedict or **Baruch** (1632-77), Dutch philosopher. Influenced by Descartes, developed system chiefly contained in *Ethics* (1677), in which all life is embraced by infinite God (or Nature). Excommunicated (1656) from native Jewish sect.

spiny anteater, *see* ECHIDNA.

spiraea, genus of herbs of rose family found in temperate regions. Dense clusters of small pink or white flowers.

spire, steeply pointed tapering structure topping a tower. First examples appeared in Romanesque architecture of 12th cent.; elaborate spires were developed in Gothic period.

spiritual, religious folk song of American Negroes. Created by black singers and choirs in 19th cent.

spiritualism, belief and practice of communication with spirits of the dead. Common to many cultures, *eg* Haiti, North American Indians. Became popular in West during 19th cent. Practice usually involves a medium, who acts as

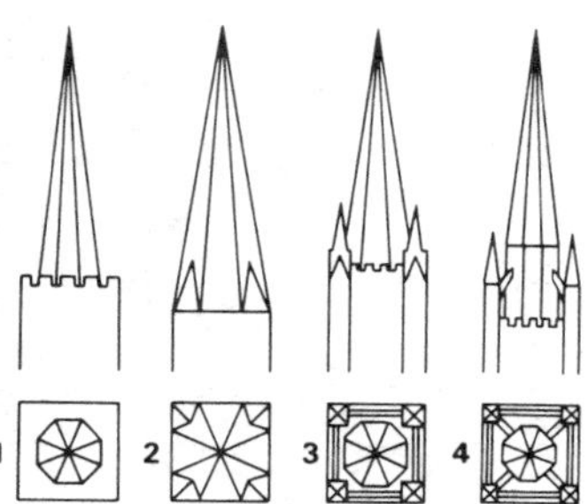

Spires: 1. needle; 2. broach; 3. octagonal; 4. buttress

intermediary between living and dead, at meeting called séance.

Spithead, anchorage in the SOLENT, off Portsmouth, S England. Scene of fleet mutiny (1797).

Spitsbergen (*Svalbard*), isl. group of Norway, in Arctic Ocean. Area *c* 62,150 sq km (24,000 sq mi); main town Longyearbyen. Ceded to Norway 1920. Coalfields shared with USSR.

spittle bug, *see* FROGHOPPER.

spleen, large lymphatic organ on left hand side of abdominal cavity. Destroys old red blood cells and forms certain white cells; acts as reserve blood supply in emergencies. Removable without risk.

Split (Ital. *Spalato*), town of Croatia, W Yugoslavia, on Adriatic Sea. Pop. 184,000. Port, fishing, resort. Ruled by Venice from 1420, by Austria 1815-1918. Has cathedral, baptistery, remains of Roman palace.

Spock, Benjamin McLane (1903-), American pediatrician. Best known for enormously popular *The Common Sense Book of Baby and Child Care* (1945).

Spode, Josiah (1754-1827), English potter. Originated type of bone china, bearing his name, which became standard in England.

spoils system, practice developed in US of rewarding loyal supporters by appointing them to political offices. Corruption incurred by system led to civil service reform in late 19th cent.

Spoleto (anc. *Spoletium*), town of Umbria, C Italy. Pop. 40,000. Agric. market, textiles. Cap of medieval duchy, passed to Papal States (13th cent.). Roman remains; cathedral (12th cent.).

sponge, any of Porifera phylum of sessile aquatic animals. Body-wall usually supported by skeleton of either lime, silica or spongin (used in bath sponges). Sponge feeds by drawing water through pores on body surface.

spontaneous combustion, sudden burning of substance of low ignition point, caused by heat produced through slow oxidation of substance.

spoonbill, wading bird of warm regions with beak flattened and spoon-shaped at tip, genus *Platalea*.

Sporades, isls. of Greece, in Aegean Sea. N Sporades, NE of Euboea, incl. Skyros. S Sporades, or Dodecanese, incl. Sámos, Ikaría.

spore, in botany, non-sexual reproductive cell produced by flowerless plants. Capable of giving rise to new plant.

sprat, *Sprattus sprattus,* small European food fish of herring family. Pale green back with silver underside; lives in large coastal shoals.

spring, natural outlet at ground surface for accumulated underground water. Where WATER TABLE intersects sloping ground surface, 'spring line' occurs; springs also common in limestone areas. Mineral springs may contain sulphur, salt, *etc*; hot springs, *eg* GEYSERS, occur mainly in volcanic areas.

springbok, *Antidorcas marsupialis,* antelope of S Africa, noted for high, stiff-legged leaps in air.

Springfield, cap. of Illinois, US; on Sangamon R. Pop. 181,000. Agric. machinery mfg., food products. Home, burial place of Abraham Lincoln.

Springfield, town of SW Massachusetts, US; on Connecticut R. Pop. 549,000. Plastics, chemical mfg.; printing and publishing industs. US armoury (1794-1966).

spruce, any of genus *Picea* of evergreen trees of N temperate zones. Cultivated as ornamentals and for straight-grained, lightweight timber. Varieties incl. Norway spruce, *P. abies.* Most species yield pulp for paper-making.

sputnik, *see* SATELLITE.

squash, *see* PUMPKIN.

squash [rackets], game similar to RACKETS, played in 4-walled court, normally by 2 people. Originated at Harrow School, England, before 1850.

squid, marine cephalopod mollusc with torpedo-shaped body. Ten tentacles, two being much longer than others, with suckers at ends. Giant squid, genus *Architeuthis,* reaches lengths (incl. tentacles) of 15 m/50 ft.

squill, any of genera *Scilla* and *Urginea* of lily family. Garden varieties cultivated.

squint, disorder of muscles of eye in which both eyes cannot be focused on same point at same time. Treatment incl. corrective glasses and exercise of eye muscles.

squirrel, small, usually arboreal, rodent of Sciuridae family. Species incl. European red squirrel, *Sciurus vulgaris,* which hides food (acorns, nuts) in ground; North American grey squirrel, *S. carolinensis,* now common in Europe.

Sri Lanka, isl. republic, off SE coast of India; member of British Commonwealth. Area 65,600 sq km (25,300 sq mi); pop. 14,346,000; cap. Colombo. Chief language: Sinhalese. Religion: Buddhism. Mountainous centre with broad coastal plain. Agric. economy (rice, rubber, coconuts, tea). Under Dutch control from mid 17th cent. to late 18th

Sri Lanka

cent; annexed by British (1815). Independent as Ceylon (1948), republic (1956); native name adopted in 1972.

Srinagar, summer cap. of Jammu and Kashmir, N India. Pop. 404,000. Resort on R. Jhelum, with many canals.

SS, *see* BLACKSHIRTS.

Staël, Madame de, née [Anne Louise] Germaine Necker (1766-1817), French woman of letters, b. Switzerland. Introduced German Romanticism into France in *De l'Allemagne* (1810). Known for influential salons incl. Chateaubriand, Constant. Also wrote novels, *eg Delphine* (1802).

Staffordshire, county of WC England. Area 2716 sq km (1049 sq mi); pop. 997,000. POTTERIES in N; BLACK COUNTRY in S; R. Trent plain in C. Large coalfields; iron ore, clay also extracted. Admin. hq. **Stafford,** on R. Sow. Pop. 55,000. Footwear mfg.

stag beetle, any of Lucanidae family of beetles with branched antler-like mandibles. Larvae feed on rotting wood.

stagecoach, carriage used from 17th to early 19th cent. for conveyance of passengers, mail, luggage. Drawn by 4 to 6 horses, changed at staging points. Declined after building of railways.

stained glass, coloured glass used in making windows. Designs or figures are made from panes of many colours held together by lead strips which themselves form part of design. Art is of Byzantine origin; best work was executed in medieval Gothic cathedrals.

stalactite, icicle-shaped deposit hanging from ceiling of cave in limestone area. Consists mainly of calcium carbonate, transported to cave in water solution and left behind as water drips from ceiling to floor. Also *see* STALAGMITE.

stalagmite, icicle-shaped deposit rising from floor of cave in limestone area. Consists mainly of calcium carbonate, transported to cave in water solution and left behind as water drips onto floor from ceiling. Also *see* STALACTITE.

Stalin, Joseph, orig. Joseph Vissarionovich Dzhugashvili (1879-1953), Soviet political leader. Elected Communist Party general secretary (1922); shared leadership after Lenin's death (1924) until 1927, when he engineered removal of TROTSKY and Zinoviev. Consolidated power through series of purges in 1930s, becoming premier 1941. Initiated indust. and agric. collectivization with Five Year Plans. Assumed military leadership after Germany invaded USSR (1941). Expanded Soviet power in E Europe in meetings with other Allied leaders and by aggressive post-war foreign policy. His tyrannical methods and personality cult were denounced by Khrushchev (1956).

Stalinabad, *see* DUSHANBE.

Stalingrad, *see* VOLGOGRAD.

Stalinsk, *see* NOVOKUZNETSK.

stamen, male organ of flower. Consists of pollen-bearing anther on filament.

Stamp Act, measure passed by British Parliament (1765), requiring all legal documents in American colonies to bear a revenue stamp. Violently opposed in America on grounds that Parliament did not have right to impose taxation without corresponding representation. Act repealed 1766.

Stanislavsky, Konstantin, pseud. of Konstantin Sergeyevich Alekseyev (1863-1938), Russian actor, producer, dramatic theorist. Co-founder of Moscow Art Theatre, where he implemented 'The Method', influential theory of acting.

Stanley, Edward, *see* DERBY, 14TH EARL OF.

Stanley, Sir Henry Morton, adopted name of John Rowlands (1841-1904), British explorer and journalist, b. Wales. Sent by New York *Herald* to Africa (1871) to find David LIVINGSTONE. In service of Belgium, explored and organized Congo Free State (1879-84).

Stanley Falls, series of cataracts on R. Lualaba, NE Zaïre. Extends *c* 88 km (55 mi) between Ubundi and Kisangani; river drops *c* 60 m (200 ft). Renamed Boyoma Falls.

Stanleyville, *see* KISANGANI.

staphylococcus, any of the genus *Staphylococcus* of spherical bacteria, usually occurring in clusters. *S. aureus* causes boils, abscesses and infection in wounds. Can cause food poisoning by release of toxins.

star, self-luminous gaseous body similar to the Sun, whose energy is derived from thermonuclear reactions which convert hydrogen into helium. Nearest star, other than Sun, is Proxima Centauri, *c* 4 light years away. Stars are grouped into galaxies, those visible from Earth being part of Milky Way. They appear to be fixed, but in fact are in motion about the galaxy. *See* STELLAR EVOLUTION.

Stara-Zagora, city of C Bulgaria. Pop. 122,000. Railway jct., trade centre. Food processing, fertilizers; textiles.

starch, polymeric carbohydrate derived from glucose, found in grain, potatoes, rice, etc. Produced in plants by photosynthesis, it serves as food store. Starch in plants is converted into glucose by animals and is major energy source. Used as stiffener in laundering and in adhesives, foods, *etc.*

Star Chamber, room in king of England's palace, Westminster, so named from stars on ceiling. Name used from 15th cent. for tribunal comprising king's councillors, judges, which met there. Important under Tudors as regular part of law enforcement, became hated when Stuarts used it to enforce unpopular policies, esp. religious. Abolished (1641) by Long Parliament.

starfish, any of class Asteroidea of echinoderms with 5 or more arms radiating from central disc. Skin covered with calcareous plates and spines; moves by tube-feet on underside of arms.

starling, *Sturnus vulgaris,* gregarious European bird with dark metallic plumage. Roosts in woods and city buildings, where it is often regarded as a pest. Introduced into North America.

star-of-Bethlehem, *Ornithogalum umbellatum,* bulbous plant of lily family. Native to Mediterranean region but widely cultivated. Narrow leaves, white star-shaped flowers with green markings.

Staten Island, *see* NEW YORK CITY.

States-General, *see* ESTATES-GENERAL.

static electricity, electric charge at rest, usually produced by friction or electrostatic induction.

statics, in physics and engineering, branch of mechanics dealing with bodies and forces at rest or in equilibrium.

statistics, science of collecting, classifying and interpreting numerical facts and data. Used as method of analysis in sciences, social science, business, *etc.* Concerned both with description of actual events and predictions of likelihood of an event occurring.

statute, law passed by legislature and formally placed on record. In UK, statutes make up written law, distinct from COMMON LAW; in Europe, almost all law is statutory.

Stavanger, town of SW Norway, on Stavanger Fjord. Pop. 90,000. Port, fishing, shipbuilding, offshore oil service indust. Founded 8th cent., cathedral (12th cent.).

Stavisky affair (1934), French financial and political scandal. Serge Alexander Stavisky (1886-1934), floated fraudulent companies, sold forged bonds, gained control of several newspapers, became associate of public figures. When exposed (1933), he fled and was either shot by police or committed suicide. Scandal caused fall of govt. and riots (Feb. 1934).

steady-state theory, in cosmology, theory that universe is in steady state. Although the universe is expanding, matter is continously created and so no overall change can be detected. In this theory, universe has no beginning or end. Rival theory is BIG-BANG THEORY.

steam engine, engine using steam under pressure to supply mechanical energy. When water is converted to steam, it expands *c* 1600 times, producing force capable of mechanical work either on piston or in TURBINE. Experiments first recorded (*c* 130 BC) by Hero of Alexandria. James Watt produced 1st practical version (1769) using separate condenser and valves allowing steam to exert force on piston in both directions.

stearic acid, colourless wax-like fatty acid, found in animal and vegetable fats. Used in manufacture of soap, candles, cosmetics and medicine.

steel, iron containing up to 1.5% carbon. Its properties can be varied by changes in quantity of carbon and other metals present and by heat treatment. Manufactured by Bessemer and open-hearth processes, and more recently in oxygen-blowing or electric furnaces. Corrosion-resistant stainless steel contains up to 25% chromium.

Steele, Sir Richard (1672-1729), English author, b. Ireland. Founded *The Tatler* (1709) and, with ADDISON, *The Spectator* (1711-12), writing witty essays.

Steen, Jan (1626-79), Dutch painter. Known for his genre scenes.

Steer, Philip Wilson (1860-1942), English painter. Founder member of New English Art Club; landscape and figure paintings influenced by impressionists.

stegosaurus, genus of extinct vegetarian dinosaurs. Had small head, double row of defensive bony plates along back, spikes on tail. Length *c* 9 m (30 ft). Lived during Jurassic period.

Stein, Gertrude (1874-1946), American author, settled in Paris (1903). Attempted to create 'cubist' literature, *eg Tender Buttons* (1914). Best known for *Autobiography of Alice B. Toklas* (1933).

Steinbeck, John Ernst (1902-68), American author. Concerned with struggle of poor within dehumanized society. Works incl. short stories, novels *Of Mice and Men* (1937), *The Grapes of Wrath* (1939), *East of Eden* (1952), screenplays. Nobel Prize for Literature (1962).

Steiner, Rudolf (1861-1925), German occultist, b. Austria. Originally leading theosophist, subsequently developed own system of 'anthroposophy' attempting to explain world through nature of man. Schools named after him follow his theories.

stellar evolution, description of life-history of a star. Stars are believed to condense from clouds of gas, mainly hydrogen, which contract under internal gravitational forces. Thermonuclear reactions take place and create energy by fusion of hydrogen into helium; as hydrogen is used up, star expands to become red giant. It then contracts, its final state depending on its size.

Stendhal, pseud. of Marie Henri Beyle (1783-1842), French novelist. Wrote novels treating melodramatic subjects with intense realism, *eg Le rouge et le noir* (1830), *La Chartreuse de Parme* (1839).

Stephen, St (d. *c* AD 36), one of seven deacons of early Church. Stoned to death at Jerusalem, becoming 1st Christian martyr.

Stephen [I], St (*c* 975-1038), king of Hungary (1001-38). Reign marks beginning of Hungarian kingdom. Completed conversion of Magyars to Christianity.

Stephen (*c* 1097-1154), king of England (1135-54). Grandson of William I, usurped throne from Henry I's daughter, MATILDA, whose invasion (1130) of England to regain throne began long period of civil strife. She reigned briefly after Stephen's capture (1141) but he regained throne on release. After death of his son (1153), forced to name Matilda's son, Henry II, as successor.

Stephenson, George (1781-1848), English engineer. Built his 1st locomotive (1814) and 1st locomotive to use steam blast (1815). His famous *Rocket* (1829) was used on Liverpool-Manchester railway.

Stepney, *see* TOWER HAMLETS.

steppe, level, treeless grasslands extending from SE Europe to C Asiatic USSR. Used for grazing, extensive wheat growing. Term also applied to similar mid-latitude grasslands in other continents and to semi-arid areas bordering hot deserts.

stereophonic sound, sound recorded simultaneously by microphones at various distances from sound source. In playback sound emanates from several speakers situated in roughly similar relative positions as original microphones. Gives impression of depth of original sound. Quadrophonic sound uses 4 channels of sound.

sterility, inability to reproduce sexually. Causes in humans incl. glandular imbalance, disease and psychological problems.

sterilization, method of rendering substances free from contamination by bacteria. Immersion in boiling water or alcohol solution, or exposure to radiation are methods used. Term also used for rendering sexual organs incapable of reproduction; in male, VASECTOMY is used, in female, blocking of Fallopian tubes.

Sterne, Laurence (1713-68), English author, b. Ireland. Known for idiosyncratic treatment of thought, feeling, time, as in *The Life and Opinions of Tristram Shandy* (1759-67). *A Sentimental Journey* (1768) burlesques the cult of sentiment.

steroids, group of organic compounds with 4 carbon rings incl. vitamin D, bile acids, male and female sex hormones, adrenal cortex hormones.

stethoscope, instrument used in medicine to detect sounds made by heart and lungs. Consists of chest piece connected by rubber tubes to 2 ear pieces. Devised (1816) by Laënnec to aid diagnosis.

Stettin, *see* SZCZECIN.

Stevenage, town of Hertfordshire, SC England. Pop. 73,000. First 'new town'; furniture mfg.

Stevens, Wallace (1879-1955), American poet. Known for stylish, philosophically speculative verse, *eg Harmonium* (1923), *The Man with the Blue Guitar* (1937), *Notes toward a Supreme Fiction* (1942).

Stevenson, Adlai Ewing (1900-65), American politician. Defeated by Eisenhower as Democractic presidential candidate (1952, 1956). Ambassador to the UN (1961-5).

Stevenson, Robert Louis [Balfour] (1850-94), Scottish author. Works incl. travel books, *eg Travels with a Donkey* (1879), popular novels incl. *Treasure Island* (1883), *Kidnapped* (1886), *The Strange Case of Dr Jekyll and Mr Hyde* (1886), poetry in *A Child's Garden of Verses* (1885).

Stewart, House of, *see* STUART, HOUSE OF.

Stewart, John ('Jackie') (1939-), Scottish motor racing driver. Won 27 world championship Grand Prix victories, taking world championship 3 times. Retired 1973.

Stewart Island or **Rakiura,** volcanic isl. of S New Zealand, separated from South Isl. by Foveaux Str. Area 1375 sq km (670 sq mi); largely mountainous. Resort; fishing.

stick insect, insect of Phasmidae family, commonest in tropical forests. Elongated wingless body resembles twig and matches surroundings.

stickleback, any of Gasterosteidae family of small spiny-backed fish; found in fresh and salt water of N hemisphere.

stilt, wading bird of Recurvirostridae family, mainly inhabiting marshes. Black-winged stilt, *Himantopus himantopus,* with black upper-parts, white under-parts, is found in S Europe, Africa, Asia.

sting ray, *see* RAY.

stinkhorn, *Phallus impudicus,* foul-smelling mushroom. Spores borne in jelly and dispersed by insects attracted by smell.

Stirlingshire, former county of C Scotland, now in Central region. Mountainous in S and W incl. Campsies; fertile lowlands. Agric., coalmining; industs. centred in Falkirk, Grangemouth (oil refining). Co. town was **Stirling,** former royal burgh and market town on R. Forth, now admin. hq. of Central Region. Pop. 30,000. Has univ. (1965); royal castle.

Stoat

stoat, *Mustela erminea,* small carnivore, resembling weasel, with short legs, long body. Reddish-brown coat with black-tipped tail. Found in N Europe, C Asia, North America. Northern varieties turn white in winter, being known as ermine (name also applies to white fur).

stock exchange, organized market for trading in stocks and bonds. Only open to members (brokers) who conduct trade for customers on commission. Board of governors stipulate requirements before stock may be listed for trading. Exists in every major financial centre.

Stockhausen, Karlheinz (1928-), German composer. Early exponent of electronic music. Later work has favoured indeterminacy and oriental mysticism.

Stockholm, cap. of Sweden, between L. Mälaren and Baltic Sea. Pop. 1,375,000. Admin., commercial centre; port; engineering; food processing; chemicals. Founded 1255; associated with Hanseatic League; built partly on isls. Staden Isl. has royal palace (1754).

Stockport, town of Greater Manchester met. county, NW England. Pop. 138,000. Textiles, esp. cotton; machinery.

stocks, *see* SHARES.

Stockton-on-Tees, *see* TEESSIDE.

Stoicism, school of philosophy founded by Zeno of Citium (*c* 315 BC). Exponents incl. Cleanthes, Chrysippus. Saw world as material whole with God as shaping force. Man's true end is active life in harmony with Nature, *ie* God's will. Universal benevolence and justice conceived of as duty, necessitating control of emotion and passions. Followers of stoic doctrine in Rome incl. Seneca, Epictetus, Marcus Aurelius.

Stoke-on-Trent, city of Staffordshire, WC England, on R. Trent. Pop. 258,000. In POTTERIES dist.; formed 1910 from Burslem, Hanley, Fenton, Longton, Tunstall. Pottery indust., coalmining, engineering.

stomach, *see* ALIMENTARY CANAL, DIGESTION.

Stomatopoda (stomatopods), order of burrowing marine crustaceans, sometimes called mantis shrimps. Strong clasping claws on 2nd pair of legs used to crack shells of crabs, *etc.*

Stone Age, period of human culture when stone implements were first used. Usually divided into PALAEOLITHIC, MESOLITHIC and NEOLITHIC periods.

stonefish, highly venomous tropical fish, genus *Synanceja*. Lies motionless in reefs, camouflaged to resemble stone or coral; dorsal fins inject dangerous poison.

Stonehenge, prehist. monument on Salisbury Plain, England. Outer circle of sarsen stone blocks connected by lintels surrounds horseshoe formation of 5 trilithons, each trilithon consisting of 2 upright stones connected by a lintel. This structure dates from *c* 1500-1400 BC. Within it is ovoid structure, which surrounds Altar Stone. A circle of bluestone menhirs was later set between outer circle and trilithons. Believed to have religious or astronomical significance.

Stone of Destiny, stone on which Scottish kings were crowned at Scone. Seized by Edward I of England (1296); placed under coronation chair in Westminster Abbey. Seized by Scottish nationalists (1950), returned 1951.

Stopes, Marie Carmichael (1880-1958), British advocate of birth control. Set up first birth control clinic in Holloway, London (1921).

stork, any of Ciconiidae family of large migratory wading birds. Long legs, neck and bill; tree or roof nesting. Species incl. Old World white stork, *Ciconia ciconia.*

Stormont, parliament of Northern Ireland, formerly responsible for internal affairs. Estab. 1920 at Stormont, Belfast. Suspended 1972 in favour of direct rule by UK Parliament during civil strife.

Stornoway, main town of Lewis with Harris, NW Scotland, admin. hq. of Western Isles. Pop. 5000. Fishing port; Harris tweed mfg.

stout, dark beer made from roasted malt. Similar to porter, but containing higher percentage of hops.

Stowe, Harriet Beecher (1811-96), American novelist. Known for anti-slavery novel, *Uncle Tom's Cabin* (1851-2).

Strabo (*c* 63 BC–*c* AD 24), Greek geographer and historian, b. Asia Minor. Known for *Geographia*, survey of known world.

Strachey, [Giles] Lytton (1880-1932), English biographer. Member of BLOOMSBURY GROUP. Known for psychological, critical biogs., *eg Queen Victoria* (1921), *Eminent Victorians* (1918).

Stradivari, Antonio or **Antonius Stradivarius** (1644-1737), Italian violin maker. Founded renowned Cremona workshop continued by sons. Often considered greatest of violin makers.

Strafford, Thomas Wentworth, 1st Earl of (1593-1641), English statesman. Took efficient, but repressive, measures as lord deputy of Ireland (1632-9), then became Charles I's chief adviser. Impeached by Parliament after unsuccessful campaign against Scots; convicted and beheaded.

Stralsund, town of N East Germany, on Baltic Sea. Pop. 68,000. Port, fishing, shipbuilding. Founded 1209, former Hanseatic League member.

strangeness, in nuclear physics, property of certain elementary particles of decaying much more slowly than would be expected. These particles are created in strong nuclear interactions but decay by weak interactions.

Stranraer, market town of Dumfries and Galloway region, SW Scotland. Pop. 10,000. Fishing industs. Ferry services to Larne, Northern Ireland.

Strasbourg (Ger. *Strassburg*), city of E France, at confluence of Ill and Rhine, cap. of Bas-Rhin dept. Pop. 355,000. Indust., commercial centre of Alsace; major river port. Metal goods, oil refining; tanning, wine trade, pâté mfg. Free city from 13th cent., taken by Louis XIV (1681); part of Germany (1871-1919). Cathedral (11th cent.); univ. (1567). Site of European Parliament.

Strategic Arms Limitations Talks (SALT), series of discussions between US and Soviet Union to limit size of defence forces of the 2 countries. Accord reached in 1972 agreed to restrict antiballistic missile systems. Second treaty limiting offensive nuclear missile systems signed 1979, but not ratified by US Congress following Soviet invasion of Afghanistan.

Stratford, town of SW Ontario, Canada; on Avon R. Pop. 25,000. Has annual Stratford Shakespearian festival.

Stratford-upon-Avon, town of Warwickshire, WC England, on R. Avon. Pop. 19,000. Tourist centre, associations with Shakespeare (birthplace, grave, *etc*), annual festival at Memorial Theatre.

Strathclyde, region of W Scotland. Area 13,849 sq km (5347 sq mi); pop. 2,445,000; admin. hq. Glasgow. Created 1975, incl. former Argyllshire, Ayrshire, Dunbartonshire, Lanarkshire, Renfrewshire. Site of ancient kingdom.

stratification, in geology, arrangement of SEDIMENTARY ROCKS in strata, or layers. Strata are separated by surfaces called 'bedding planes'. Strata need not be horizontal; angle determined by earth movements.

stratosphere, second lowest layer of Earth's ATMOSPHERE, immediately above troposphere. Begins between *c* 9.5 km (6 mi) and 16 km (10 mi) above surface. Temperature low, varies little with height; no clouds or dust. Incl. ozone layer.

stratus cloud, *see* CLOUD.

Strauss, Johann (1804-49), Austrian composer, conductor. Toured many countries with his own orchestra playing Viennese waltzes and other dances. Composed *Radetzky March*. His son, **Johann Strauss** (1825-99), was also a composer and conductor. Wrote over 400 waltzes, such as *Blue Danube, Emperor Waltz*, and operetta *Die Fledermaus* ('The Bat').

Strauss, Richard Georg (1864-1949), German composer. Continued Romantic style of the 19th cent. well into the 20th cent., but with great dramatic and orchestral gifts. Works incl. symphonic poems *Don Juan, Till Eulenspiegel*, operas *Salome* and *Der Rosenkavalier*.

Stravinsky, Igor Fyodorovich (1882-1971), Russian composer. Music is noted for original use of harmony and rhythm. Worked with Diaghilev early in career, for whom he wrote ballets *Rite of Spring, The Firebird, Petrouchka*. In 1920s, wrote such works as *Pulcinella* in neo-Classical style. Took up serial music in 1950s. Left Russia in 1914, living in Paris and eventually settling in US (1939).

strawberry, any of genus *Fragaria* of low perennial herbs of rose family. Native to temperate regions. Valued for fruit. *F. vesca* is the wild strawberry; cultivated strawberry is hybrid.

streptococcus, any of the genus *Streptococcus* of spherical bacteria, usually occurring in chains. Some species cause infection, *eg* sore throats, and pus formation in wounds. Also release toxins which can destroy blood cells and tissue.

Stresemann, Gustav (1878-1929), German statesman, chancellor (1923). As foreign minister (1923-9), negotiated LOCARNO PACT (1925). Shared Nobel Peace Prize (1926) with Briand.

strike, total withdrawal of labour by employees. Chief weapon of labour unions, first used in UK in early 19th cent., *eg* by Luddites. Strike follows union authorization to make it official. Unofficial strike, often local, also known as 'wildcat' strike. Also *see* GENERAL STRIKE.

Strindberg, [Johan] August (1849-1912), Swedish author. Paranoid sensibility reflected in short stories, novels, dramas, incl. *The Father* (1887), *Miss Julie* (1888), *Dance of Death* (1901), *A Dream Play* (1901).

string[ed] instruments or **strings,** group of musical instruments which produce sound from vibrating strings. Strings may be plucked (*eg* harp, guitar, lute), stroked with horsehair bow (*eg* violin, viola) or struck with hammer (*eg* dulcimer, piano, clavichord).

stroboscope, flashing lamp whose frequency can be synchronized with frequency of a rotating object so that the object will appear at rest when illuminated by stroboscope light. Used to study periodic or varying motion.

stroke, *see* APOPLEXY.

Stromboli, *see* LIPARI ISLANDS.

strong nuclear interaction, nuclear force acting between certain elementary particles, *eg* protons, neutrons and certain mesons, when they are less than 10^{-13} cm apart. It lasts *c* 10^{-23} secs and is the strongest known force in nature.

strontium (Sr), metallic element, resembling calcium in its chemical properties; at. no. 38, at. wt. 87.62. Occurs in strontianite and celestine. Compounds impart crimson colour to flames; used in fireworks. Radioactive strontium 90 occurs in fallout; dangerous as it replaces calcium in bones.

structuralism, methodology, originating in linguistics, whose advocates hold that systems, esp. of myths, language, can be regarded as structures which are stable, whole, self-regulating (by a process of exclusion), and which obey internal 'transformation laws' by which whole structure can be deduced from separate elements. Stemming from work of F. de SAUSSURE, developed by LÉVI-STRAUSS, CHOMSKY, Roland Barthes, Michel Foucault. Subsequently extended to other areas incl. biology, mathematics.

strychnine, alkaloid drug obtained from seed of nux vomica tree of genus *Strychnos*. Small doses used as stimulant. Poisonous in large doses; often used as rat-killer.

Stuart or **Stewart, House of,** ruling family of Scotland (after 1371) and of England (after 1603) until death of Anne (1714). James VI of Scotland succeeded to English throne as James I. Two kingdoms united by Act of Union (1707). Subsequent Hanoverian rule challenged by JACOBITES.

Stuart, Charles Edward, *see* STUART, JAMES FRANCIS EDWARD.

Stuart or **Stewart, James Francis Edward** (1688-1766), son of James II, known as the 'Old Pretender'. Claim to English throne frustrated by Act of Settlement (1701) which guaranteed succession to House of Hanover. Accession of 1st Hanoverian, George I, resulted in series of uprisings by James' supporters (Jacobites); landed briefly in Scotland during 1715 Jacobite rebellion. His son, **Charles Edward Stuart** (1720-88), called 'Bonnie Prince Charlie' and the 'Young Pretender', led Jacobite rebellion of 1745. Won victory at Prestonpans; reached Derby in march on London. Retreated into Scotland, defeated at Culloden Moor (1746). Fled to France.

Stuart, John McDouall (1815-66), Scottish explorer. Joined Sturt's expedition to C Australia (1844-6). Made 6 expeditions to interior from 1858, finally reached Van Diemen's Gulf (1862).

Stubbs, George (1724-1806), English painter. Known for his paintings of animals, esp. horses, and sporting scenes.

stucco, plaster or cement, used for surfacing inside or outside walls or for moulded decoration.

sturgeon, fish of Acipenseridae family found in N hemisphere; usually migratory, feeding in sea and breeding in fresh water. Long pointed head, toothless mouth; rows of spiny plates on body. Valued as source of caviare and isinglass.

Sturm und Drang (Ger., = storm and stress), literary movement originating in late 18th-cent. Germany. Emphasized genius of individual as opposed to rationalistic ideal of the Enlightenment. Exponents incl. Goethe, Schiller, Lenz. Great influence in development of ROMANTICISM.

Sturt, Charles (1795-1869), English soldier and explorer, b. India. Explored Murray, Darling, Murrumbidgee river area of SE Australia (1828-30). On 3rd expedition (1844-6), journeyed to interior via L. Eyre and Cooper's Creek.

Stuttgart, city of SW West Germany, on R. Neckar, cap. of Baden-Württemberg. Pop. 633,000. Railway jct.; publishing, precision instruments, motor vehicle mfg.

styrene, colourless aromatic liquid, which polymerizes to polystyrene, a thermoplastic material used as electrical and heat insulator. Styrene is used to make synthetic rubber.

Styria (*Steiermark*), prov. of SE Austria. Area 16,384 sq km (6326 sq mi); cap. Graz. Largely mountainous, main rivers Mur, Enns. Forestry, mining (lignite, iron ore), tourism. S part ceded to Yugoslavia 1919.

Styx, *see* HADES.

Suárez, Adolfo (1932-), Spanish politician. Following Franco's death, appointed premier of interim govt. by Juan Carlos (1976). Won 1977 election as head of Centre Democratic Union, forming 1st democratically elected govt. since 1930s. Re-elected 1979. Resigned 1981.

subatomic particles *see* ELEMENTARY PARTICLES.

subconscious, in psychology, term used for processes of same kind as conscious processes, but occurring outside individual's awareness. Often used loosely as synonym of UNCONSCIOUS.

sublimation, in chemistry, process of changing a substance directly from solid to vapour, by-passing liquid stage.

sublimation, in psychology, term employed, originally by Freud, for an unconscious transformation of socially or personally unacceptable impulse, esp. sexual, into acceptable expression.

submarine, warship that submerges and travels under water. Usually equipped with torpedoes or missiles. In use since 19th cent. Latest are nuclear-powered.

submersible, small underwater research vessel, with pressurized hull, self-contained air supply, power system, *etc.* Bathysphere is lowered from deck of ship by winch. Largely replaced by bathyscaphe (developed 1954 by A. Piccard) which is free-moving. In 1960 a bathyscaphe took 2 men to depth of 35,800 ft (10,900 m) in Mariana trench.

subway, *see* UNDERGROUND.

Suchow, city of Kiangsu prov., E China. Pop. 1,500,000. Rail jct; commercial, indust. centre; produces machine tools, textiles. Called Tungshan (1912-45).

Sucre, cap. of Bolivia, in Chuquisaca dept. Pop. 49,000. Agric. market. Scene of outbreak of South American independence revolt (1809). Founded 1538. Has cathedral, archbishopric; univ. (1624).

sucrose, sugar obtained from sugar cane, sugar beet, maple syrup, *etc.* Consists of glucose and fructose joined together in single molecule.

Sudan

Sudan, republic of NE Africa. Area 2,505,800 sq km (967,500 sq mi); pop. 16,126,000; cap. Khartoum. Language: Arabic. Religions: Islam, animist. Nubian Desert in NE; savannah in C; forest, swamps in S. Main rivers Nile and tributaries. Agric. incl. millet, livestock; exports cotton, gum arabic. Unified (1820-2) by Egyptians; scene of Mahdist revolt (1883-5). Taken by Kitchener (1898); ruled as Anglo-Egyptian condominium until independence (1956).

Sudbury, town of EC Ontario, Canada. Pop. 91,000. Railway jct. In world's major nickel mining region; related industs.

Sudetenland (Czech *Sudety*), mountainous region of N Czechoslovakia, rising to 1602 m (5258 ft). Minerals, timber; spas. German pop. in NW used to justify Hitler's annexation of region (Munich Pact, 1938). Restored to Czechoslovakia (1945).

Suetonius [Tranquillus], Gaius (AD *c* 70-*c* 130), Roman biographer. Extant works are *Lives of the Caesars* and *Concerning Illustrious Men*.

Suez (*El Suweis*), city of NE Egypt, at head of Gulf of Suez and S end of Suez Canal. Pop. 315,000. Port; oil refining. Damaged in Arab-Israeli wars (1967, 1973).

Suez Canal, waterway linking Mediterranean (at Port Said) with Red Sea (at Suez); 166 km (103 mi) long. Built 1859-69 by Ferdinand de Lesseps; formerly managed by Suez Canal Co., in which Britain held majority of shares. Nationalization (1956) by Egypt precipitated SUEZ CRISIS. Closed 1967 after Arab-Israeli war; reopened June, 1975. At S end is Gulf of Suez, NW arm of Red Sea.

Suez Crisis, international incident (1956) begun when Egypt nationalized Suez Canal. In combined operation, Israel invaded Egypt and French and British troops occupied canal area. Under US pressure, invading forces withdrew and were replaced by UN emergency force. Disagreement over British role led to resignation of PM, Anthony Eden.

Suffolk, county of E England. Area 3800 sq km (1467 sq mi); pop. 562,000; admin. hq. Ipswich. Flat, low-lying, with marshy coasts. Crops incl. wheat, barley, sugar beet.

suffrage, right of voting, or exercising of that right. Universal adult suffrage is system whereby every national has vote on reaching age of majority, usually 18 or 21 years. In UK, achieved with Representation of the People (Equal Franchise) Act (1928), which included women over 21 in franchise; culmination of process begun by REFORM BILL of 1832. Also *see* ELECTION; WOMEN'S SUFFRAGE.

suffragettes, *see* WOMEN'S SUFFRAGE.

Sufism, mystical movement of Islam; developed (10th cent.) among Shiites with Neoplatonic, Buddhist and Christian influences. Rejects ritual, emphasizing personal union with God.

sugar, any of class of sweet soluble crystalline carbohydrates, comprising monosaccharides, *eg* fructose, glucose, and disaccharides, *eg* sucrose, lactose, maltose. Name is most commonly applied to SUCROSE.

sugar beet, *see* BEET.

sugar cane, *Saccharum officinarum*, tall, perennial, tropical grass. Cultivated as main source of sugar (*c* 65% of world production). By-products incl. molasses and rum.

Suharto, (1921-), Indonesian military, political leader. Took power after leading army coup that deposed Sukarno (1966). Became president 1968.

suicide, act of voluntary, intentional self-destruction. In UK, until 1961 regarded as crime if committed while of sound mind. Many religions count suicide as murder, although considered honourable in India (SUTTEE), Japan (HARA-KIRI).

Sukarnapura, *see* DJAJAPURA.

Sukarno, Achmed (1901-70), Indonesian political leader, president (1945-66). Active in Indonesian nationalist movement before WWII. Became 1st president of independent republic (1945). His pro-Communist sympathies led to an army coup under Suharto.

Sulawesi, *see* CELEBES.

Suleiman I (1494-1566), Ottoman sultan (1520-66), known as 'the Magnificent'. Brought Ottoman empire to peak of its power; captured Belgrade, Rhodes; annexed much of Hungary. Entered into long-lasting alliance with France (1536). Patronized arts, introduced legal and admin. reforms.

Sulla, Lucius Cornelius (138-78 BC), Roman soldier and political leader. Campaigned successfully against MITHRADATES in Pontus. His return to Italy precipitated civil war with followers of popular party (originally led by MARIUS). Captured Rome and ruled as dictator (82-79). Eliminated opponents; made constitutional reforms.

Sullivan, Sir Arthur Seymour (1842-1900), English composer. With W.S. GILBERT, wrote numerous popular light operas.

Sullivan, Louis (1856-1924), American architect. Formative influence in development of modern style; coined dictum, 'form follows function'. Designed many early skyscrapers.

Sully, Maximilien de Béthune, Duc de (1560-1641), French statesman. Became Henry IV's superintendent of finances (1598), restored country's prosperity.

Sully-Prudhomme, pseud. of René François Armand Prudhomme (1839-1907), French poet. Nobel Prize for Literature (1901).

sulphates, salts or esters of sulphuric acid. Calcium sulphate in form of gypsum used in building or casting. Magnesium sulphate sold as EPSOM SALTS.

sulphonamides, in medicine, range of drugs derived from amide of a sulphonic acid. Developed in 1930s, used extensively to cure infections (except those by viruses) till advent of antibiotics. Still often used where antibiotics are unsuitable.

sulphur (S), non-metallic element, occurring in several allotropic forms; at. no. 16, at. wt. 32.06. Common form is rhombic sulphur, pale yellow solid; occurs free and as sulphide and sulphate minerals. Burns with blue flame to form sulphur dioxide. Used in manufacture of sulphuric acid, carbon disulphide, gunpowder, matches, in vulcanizing rubber and in medicine.

sulphuric acid (H_2SO_4), oily colourless corrosive liquid. Manufactured by catalytic oxidation of sulphur dioxide. Wide indust. use in manufacture of explosives, fertilizers, detergents, dyes and in lead ACCUMULATOR.

Sumatra, isl. of Indonesia, SW of Malay penin. Area *c* 474,000 sq km (183,000 sq mi). Barisan Mts. run parallel to W coast, jungle lowlands in E. Equatorial climate, with heavy rainfall. Produces rice, rubber, tobacco, petroleum. Hindu kingdom estab. 8th cent., Islam introduced by Arab traders in 13th cent. Dutch control started in 17th cent.

Sumerians, people inhabiting S Mesopotamia between 4th and 2nd millennia BC. Began world's 1st urban civilization at such cities as Ur, Lagash and Erech, developed pottery and metalwork. Credited with the invention of cuneiform writing. Eventually conquered by rival Semitic cities.

summer time, *see* DAYLIGHT SAVING TIME.

Sumter, Fort, *see* CHARLESTON, South Carolina, US.

Sun, central body of Solar System around which planets revolve in orbit; it is star nearest Earth, an incandescent sphere composed mainly of hydrogen and helium. Mean distance from Earth *c* 150 million km; diameter *c* 1.4 million km. Temperature at visible surface (photosphere) 6000° C; temperature (photosphere) 6000° C; temperature million° C, enables fusion of hydrogen into helium to take place and supply Sun's energy. Chromosphere, av. temperature *c* 20,000° C, surrounds the photosphere, and the corona, region of extremely high temperature and low density, forms outermost part of Sun's atmosphere.

sun bear, *Helarctos malayanus,* smallest of bears, found in SE Asia. Agile tree climber. Also called honey bear.

Sundas, Greater, isl. group of Indonesia. Comprises Borneo, Sumatra, Java, Celebes, and adjacent isls. **Lesser Sundas** or **Nusa Tenggara,** E of Java, incl. Bali, Lombok, Sumba, Flores and Timor.

Sunday school, organization for giving religious instruction to children, usually attached to church. Robert Raikes began movement in UK, estab. 1st school in 1780; by 1785 over 1000 schools had been founded. At height by end of 19th cent. Movement had immense influence on spread of popular education in UK.

Sunderland, town of Tyne and Wear met. county, NE England, at mouth of R. Wear. Pop. 217,000. Port (coal exports from 14th cent.); shipbuilding, engineering industs.

sundew, any of genus *Drosera* of INSECTIVOROUS PLANTS. Worldwide distribution. Catches and digests prey by sticky tentacles on cup-shaped leaves.

sundial, instrument indicating time of day by position of shadow of upright centre pin (gnomen) cast by Sun on graduated surface. Earliest extant example is Egyptian (*c* 1500 BC).

sunfish, any of various large oceanic fish of Molidae family, esp. ocean sunfish, *Mola mola,* with rounded compressed body.

sunflower, any of genus *Helianthus* of plants of daisy family. Native to New World. Large, yellow daisy-like flowers with dark central discs containing edible seeds from which oil is extracted.

Sung, Chinese imperial dynasty (960-1279). Period noted for growth of large cities, intensive scholarship and development of fine arts. Overthrown by Mongols.

Sunnites or **Sunnis,** members of the larger and more orthodox of the 2 main Moslem sects. They accept historical order of 1st 4 caliphs as rightful line of succession to Mohammed and admit the authority of the Sunna, law based on Mohammed's traditional teachings (as opposed to SHIITES).

sunspot, dark spot appearing on surface of Sun, caused by solar magnetic fields; its temperature is lower than surrounding points on surface. Periods of sunspot activity usually follow cycles of *c* 11 years; associated with magnetic storms on Earth.

Sun Yat-sen (1866-1925), Chinese revolutionary, national hero. Worked outside China from 1895 to bring about revolution. Adopted 'Three People's Principles' of nationalism, democracy, people's livelihood, as his political philosophy (basis of KUOMINTANG party which he led). Returned to China (1911) to serve briefly as president (1912). Set up unofficial govt. of S China at Kwangchow (1921) to oppose warlords in N. Agreed to cooperate with Chinese Communists despite misgivings.

superconductivity, phenomenon exhibited by certain pure metals and alloys, *eg* mercury, cadmium, aluminium, of having almost no electrical resistance at temperatures near absolute zero. Current induced in superconductor will flow almost indefinitely after current source is removed.

superego, in psychoanalysis, that part of the mind which acts as a form of conscience, critical of EGO, and causing guilt and anxiety when ego's thoughts and acts oppose it. At UNCONSCIOUS level, censors unacceptable impulses of ID.

superfluidity, phenomenon exhibited by liquid helium at temperatures below 2.18° Kelvin of flowing without friction and having high thermal conductivity.

Superior, Lake, largest, deepest and most W of Great Lakes, C Canada-US. Area 82,414 sq km (31,820 sq mi). Drained by L. Huron. Important trade route. Canals at Sault Ste Marie enable ships to enter and leave lake. Commercial fishing.

supernova, exploding star whose brightness suddenly increases by up to 10^8 times and then fades away. Only 3 have been observed in our galaxy, in 1054, 1572 (Tycho's nova), 1604 (Kepler's nova). Believed to occur when sufficiently massive star undergoes gravitational collapse as its store of hydrogen becomes depleted.

supply and demand, in classical economics, factors determining price. Supply refers to the amount of a commodity that producers will supply at varying prices (supply falls as price decreases); demand refers to the desire for the commodity (falls as price increases). In perfect competition, price will stabilize at equilibrium of these 2 values.

supreme court, highest organ of JUDICIARY in Federal systems of govt. US Supreme Court is composed of 9 judges, of whom one acts as chief justice. Estab. (1789) by Constitution with status independent of Congress. Greatest bulk of work is as appeal court, also rules on disputes between states, between state and central govts. Interprets Constitution, reviews acts of Congress and state legislation.

Supreme Soviet, highest legislative body of USSR. Consists of 2 equal chambers, Soviet of the Union (members elected on basis of population), and Soviet of Nationalities (members elected on basis of voting by the various republics and auton. regions).

Surabaya or **Surabaja,** city of E Java prov., Indonesia. Pop. 1,556,000. Seaport and major export centre; naval base. Shipbuilding, oil refining, textile mfg.

Surat, city of Gujarat state, W India, on Gulf of Cambay. Pop. 472,000. Important port in 17th cent.; English trading post (1612).

surface tension, force tending to contract surface area of a liquid, due to unequal cohesive forces between molecules near surface. Causes surface to behave like elastic membrane, capable of supporting light objects; also responsible for shape of water droplets and soap bubbles.

surfing, sport of gliding in towards the shore on the crest of a wave, usually on a surfboard. Prob. originated in Polynesia and Hawaii. Developed in early 20th cent.

surgery, branch of medicine concerned with treatment of injury, deformity and disease by means of manual operations with or without instruments. Although practised from ancient times, major advances in this field were not made until the introduction of aseptic techniques and anaesthetics in 19th cent.

Surinam, republic of NE South America. Area 63,037 sq km (163,266 sq mi); pop. 435,000; cap. Paramaribo. Coastal lowlands rise to forested highlands in S. Coffee, rum, timber, bauxite production, exports. Indian, Negro, Indonesian, European pop. Region disputed by English, Dutch; resolved 1815. Named Dutch Guiana; renamed 1948. Ceased being colony (1954), fully independent 1975.

surrealism, in literature and art, movement (esp. 1920s-30s) attempting to draw symbols and images from subconscious mind, influenced by Freud. Founded (1924) by French author André Breton. In literature, confined mostly to France. In painting, international figures incl. Dali, Ernst, Magritte, Miró; in films, Buñuel.

Surrey, Henry Howard, Earl of, *see* HOWARD, THOMAS.

Surrey, county of SE England. Area 1654 sq km (639 sq mi); pop. 994,000; admin. hq. Kingston-upon-Thames. Crossed E-W by North Downs (sheep rearing); dairying, market gardening. London suburbs in NE.

Surtsey, isl. of Iceland, formed 1963-5 by eruption of underwater volcano. Area *c* 325 ha. (800 acres). Nature reserve.

surveying, science of determining relative position of points on the Earth's surface. Such data may then be presented as maps by techniques of cartography. Land surveying incl. both geodesy and plane-surveying, latter not taking account of Earth's curvature; other branches incl. hydrographic (*ie* water) surveying, topographic (*ie* relief) surveying. Surveying by use of air photographs is called photogrammetry.

Susa, *see* SOUSSE.

suspension, in chemistry, system in which small solid particles are dispersed, but not dissolved, in a fluid medium. Differs from a COLLOID in that particles are larger.

Sussex, former county of SE England. South Downs in S, ending at Beachy Head; Vale of Sussex in C; Weald in N. Agric., livestock; extensive woodlands. Coastal resorts incl. Brighton, Worthing. From 1974 divided into **East Sussex** (area 1795 sq km/693 sq mi; pop. 658,000; admin. hq. Lewes) and **West Sussex** (area 2016 sq km/778 sq mi; pop. 630,000; admin. hq. Chichester).

Sutherland, Graham Vivian (1903-80) English painter. Known for his landscapes and studies of natural forms. Other works incl. portraits *Maugham* and *Churchill*; also tapestry for Coventry Cathedral.

Sutherland, former county of N Scotland, now in Highland region. Mountains, moorland; rocky indented coast. Cape Wrath in NW. Deer forest, sheep farming, crofting, fishing, tourism. Co. town was Dornoch.

Sutlej, river of SC Asia. Longest of five rivers of Punjab, rises in Tibet. Flows *c* 1450 km (900 mi) SW through Himachal Pradesh and Indian Punjab to join Indus in Pakistan.

suttee, Hindu custom involving voluntary cremation of widow on husband's funeral pyre. Abolished by British colonial govt. (1829).

Sutton, bor. of S Greater London, England. Pop. 169,000. Created 1965 from N Surrey towns.

Sutton Coldfield, town of West Midlands, England. Pop. 83,000.

Sutton Hoo, site in Suffolk, England, of Saxon ship-burial, dating from *c* AD 650. Excavated in 1939, superb examples of jewellery, coins and weapons were found.

Suva, cap. of Fiji Isls., on Viti Levu isl. Pop. 63,000. Admin. centre; port, exports fruit, sugar, copra, gold; seat of Univ. of South Pacific (1968).

Svalbard, *see* SPITSBERGEN.

Sverdlovsk, city of USSR, W Siberian RSFSR; railway jct. and indust. centre in E Ural foothills. Pop. 1,073,000. Metallurgical indust.; chemical and machinery mfg. Founded in 1721 as Ekaterinburg. Scene of execution of Tsar Nicholas II and his family (1918).

Swabia (*Schwaben*), hist. region of SW West Germany, now in S Baden-Württemberg and SW Bavaria. Incl. source of Danube, Black Forest, Swabian Jura. Duchy under Hohenstaufens from 1079, divided 1268. Cities, incl. Augsburg, formed several Swabian leagues 14th-16th cent.

Swahili, Bantu language of Niger-Congo branch of Niger-Kordofanian language family. Spoken as native tongue in Tanzania, Kenya, Zaïre, Burundi, Uganda, also used as lingua franca by non-indigenous peoples, *etc.* Term also used for many inhabitants of EC Africa, not united ethnic group but defined by common cultures, livelihood, esp. trade, use of language.

swallow, small long-winged migrating bird of Hirundinidae family. Long forked tail; feeds on insects caught in flight. Species incl. *Hirundo rustica,* summer visitor to Europe; builds mud and straw nest on buildings.

swallowtail butterfly, *Papilis machaon,* yellow and black European butterfly whose rear wings have tail-like points. Related species found worldwide.

swamp, tract of water-saturated land, normally with abundant vegetation. Found in low-lying coastal plains, flood plains. Temperate swamps contain grasses, rushes, sphagnum moss; tropical swamps contain cypresses, mangroves.

Swan, Sir Joseph Wilson (1828-1914), English inventor. Made electric lamp (1860). In photography, invented carbon printing, a dry plate process and bromide paper.

swan, large web-footed aquatic bird, genus *Cygnus.* Long slender neck, adult plumage generally white. Species incl. European mute swan, *C. olor,* and Australian black swan, *C. atratus.*

Swansea (*Abertawe*), admin. hq. and port of West Glamorgan, S Wales, on R. Tawe. Pop. 173,000. Exports coal, metal goods, imports ore for iron, steel industs. Oil refining. Has coll. of Univ. of Wales (1920). Famous blue pottery.

swastika, decorative mystic symbol consisting of cross with right-angle extensions at points. Of great antiquity, occurs in many cultures. Adopted as symbol of German Nazi party and Third Reich.

Swaziland, kingdom of SE Africa. Area 17,350 sq km (6700 sq mi); pop. 497,000; cap. Mbabane. Languages: Swati, English. Religions: Christianity, animist. High, middle and low veld areas from W to E; main rivers Komati, Usutu. Crops incl. maize, fruit, sugar, cotton; cattle rearing; iron ore and asbestos mining. Independent from Zulus in 19th cent.; British protect. from 1906 until independence 1968. Member of British Commonwealth.

sweat, weak solution of salt secreted by sweat glands in skin. Heat lost in evaporation of sweat from body helps regulate body temperature.

swede, *see* TURNIP.

Sweden

Sweden (*Sverige*), kingdom of N Europe, in E part of Scandinavian penin. Incl. Baltic isls., Gotland, Oland. Area 449,748 sq km (173,648 sq mi); pop. 8,222,000; cap. Stockholm. Language: Swedish. Religion: Lutheranism. Mountains in N, W; lakes in S. Mainly agric. (wheat, dairying); timber indust.; iron ore; h.e.p. Settled by Germanic tribes, Christianity estab. by 11th cent. United with Norway, Denmark at Kalmar (1397). Independent kingdom from 1523; *fl* under Gustavus Adolphus (17th cent.). United with Norway 1814-1905; neutral in WWs. Increasingly indust.; advanced social welfare system.

Swedenborg, Emanuel, orig. Emanuel Swedberg (1688-1772), Swedish theologian, mystic. Scientific investigations led him to pursue religious studies, believing Second Coming of the Lord had occurred. After his death NEW CHURCH organized by his followers.

Swedish, N Germanic language of Indo-European family. Spoken in Sweden, S Finland, Estonia. Descended from Old Norse.

sweet pea, *Lathyrus odoratus,* climbing annual plant of Leguminosae family, native to Europe. Butterfly-shaped, fragrant flowers.

sweet potato, *Ipomoea batatas,* tropical American trailing, perennial plant. Widely cultivated for edible, sweet-tasting tubers.

sweet william, *see* PINK.

Sweyn (d. 1014), king of Denmark (*c* 986-1014). Led series of raids against England; accepted as king of England (1013). Succeeded by his son, CANUTE.

Swift, Jonathan (1667-1745), English author, b. Ireland. Tory pamphleteer. Known for political, moral satire *Gulliver's Travels* (1726). Other works incl. religious satire

Tale of a Tub (1704), *A Modest Proposal* (1729) on Irish question. Dean of St Patrick's, Dublin (1713-45).

swift, any of Apodidae family of migratory swallow-like birds. Long scythe-like wings, short tail; spends most of time in flight. Species incl. common European swift, *Apus apus,* with black plumage and white throat patch.

swimming, recreation and competitive sport of self-propulsion through water. Four basic swimming styles: front crawl, backstroke, breaststroke, butterfly.

Swinburne, Algernon Charles (1837-1909), English poet. Works notable for technical skill, radical fervour, sensuality, *eg* classical verse play *Atalanta in Calydon* (1865), poetry *Songs before Sunrise* (1871).

Swindon, town of Wiltshire, S England. Pop. 91,000. British Rail workshops.

swine, name given to members of Suidae family, esp. domestic pig.

swing music, style of jazz played by big bands consisting of brass, saxophone and rhythm sections. Originated in US in 1930s and remained popular to 1950s. Exponents incl. Benny Goodman, Count Basie.

Swithin or **Swithun, St** (d. 862), English churchman, bishop of Winchester. According to tradition, weather on his feast day (15 July) guarantees same weather on succeeding 40 days.

Switzerland

Switzerland (Fr. *Suisse,* Ger. *Schweiz,* Ital. *Svizzera*), federal republic of WC Europe. Area 41,285 sq km (15,940 sq mi); pop. 6,346,000; cap. Bern. Main cities Basle, Geneva, Zürich. Languages: French, German, Italian, Romansh. Religions: Protestant, RC. Plateau in C (lakes incl. Geneva, Zürich, Constance); Alps in S, E. Dairy produce (cheese, milk), confectionery; watches, optical instruments; banking, tourism. Part of Holy Roman Empire from 1033, Confederation estab. 1291 for defence against Habsburgs, now comprises 23 cantons. Centre of 16th-cent. Reformation. Full independence from 1648; French occupation (1798-1815). Neutrality estab. by Treaty of Paris (1815).

swordfish, *Xiphias gladius,* large food and game fish (up to 4.6 m/15 ft long), related to tunny, widely distributed in warm seas. Upper jaw extended into flat sword-like structure.

sycamore, *Acer pseudoplatanus,* Eurasian maple tree. Large and deciduous with yellow flowers; planted as shade tree. Name also used for several American PLANE trees. *Ficus sycamorus,* a FIG tree, is sycamore of the Bible.

Sydney, city of SE Australia, on Port Jackson inlet, cap. of New South Wales. Pop. 2,800,000. Admin., commercial centre; major port, exports wool, wheat, meat; industs. incl. coalmining, iron and steel mfg., food processing, car assembly. Settled (1788) as penal colony. Has harbour bridge (1932), opera house (1973), 3 univs.

syenite, coarse-grained igneous rock. Consists of feldspars plus any of various ferromagnesian minerals, *eg* augite, hornblende; similar to granite but contains no quartz.

Syktyvkar, city of USSR, cap. of Komi auton. republic, NE European RSFSR. Pop. 136,000. Timber centre; wood pulp and paper mfg; shipyards.

syllogism, in logic, method of argument drawing a conclusion from 2 premises. Most common form is categorical, made up of 3 statements of fact, *eg* all dogs have 4 feet; a pug is a dog; therefore a pug has 4 feet.

symbiosis, in biology, living together of 2 dissimilar organisms by which each benefits, *eg* cellulose-digesting bacteria present in stomach of cows.

symbolists, group of French poets esp. Rimbaud, Verlaine, Mallarmé, active in late 19th cent., who reacted against realism in literature, feeling that poetry should evoke inexpressible subjective states. Doctrine taken up by painters *eg* Redon, Puvis de Chavannes, Moreau.

symphony, orchestral composition generally in similar form to SONATA. Classical symphony was estab. by Haydn and perfected by Mozart in 18th cent. In 19th cent., composers who developed the form incl. Beethoven, Schubert, Berlioz and Mahler. Symphony has been less dominant in 20th-cent. music; noted 20th-cent. symphonists incl. Sibelius, Shostakovich.

synagogue, in Judaism, building designed for public prayer, religious education and other communal activities. Prob. originated *c* 6th cent. BC among Jews in exile in Babylon, unable to visit TEMPLE in Jerusalem.

synapse, junction between nerve cells where nervous impulses are transmitted from one cell to another. Impulses usually travel down conducting nerve fibre (axon) of nerve cell and, on reaching end of fibre, stimulate release of ACETYLCHOLINE. This excites dendrites of adjacent cell and passes on the impulses.

synchrotron, particle accelerator used to obtain high energy protons, electrons, *etc,* by combination of magnetic field, whose intensity is modulated cyclically, and high frequency electric field.

syndicalism, revolutionary doctrine and plan for post-revolutionary society. Adherents advocate abolition of central govt., replacement by trade unions as decision-makers on production and distribution. Influenced by Proudhon, SOREL.

Synge, J[ohn] M[illington] (1871-1909), Irish dramatist. Known for controversial presentation of peasant life in plays, *eg Riders to the Sea* (1904), *The Playboy of the Western World* (1907).

synthesis, in chemistry and biology, formation of compounds from their constituent elements or simpler materials.

synthetic fibres, artificial, chemically produced fibres, usually derived from long-chain polymers. Woven as fabrics which are generally quick-drying, resistant to creasing and chemical damage; absorb less moisture and are not so warm as natural fibres. Incl. nylon, rayon.

syphilis, infectious disease caused by spirochaete (spiral bacterium) *Treponema pallidum*. Usually transmitted by sexual intercourse or acquired congenitally. In later stages, can affect almost any organ or tissue of the body, esp. mucous membranes, skin and bone, nervous system. Treatment by penicillin effective if applied early enough.

Syracuse (*Siracusa*), city of SE Sicily, Italy, cap. of Siracusa prov. Pop. 109,000. Port; fishing, salt, wine. Founded *c* 734 BC by Greeks, *fl* 5th-3rd cent. BC; taken by Rome 212 BC. Many remains.

Syracuse, town of C New York, US; on Barge Canal. Pop. 197,000. Electrical equipment, typewriter mfg.

Syr Darya (anc. *Jaxartes*), river of SC USSR. Rises as R. Naryn in E Kirghiz SSR and joins Kara Darya in Fergana valley, Uzbek SSR; flows *c* 2100 km (1300 mi) through Kazakh SSR to Aral Sea.

Syria, republic of SW Asia. Area 185,000 sq km (71,000 sq mi); pop. 7,596,000; cap. Damascus. Language: Arabic. Religion: Islam. Bounded by Anti-Lebanon Mts. in W and Syrian desert in S. Agric. in fertile valleys of Euphrates and Orontes; cotton main export; pipelines carrying Iraqi oil provide revenue. Conquered by many peoples, was part of Ottoman Empire (1516-1918). Mandated to France (1920), became completely independent 1944. Joined Egypt in UAR (1958-61).

Syria

Syros (*Síros*), isl. of Greece, in Aegean Sea, most populous of Cyclades. Area 85 sq km (33 sq mi); cap. Syros (Hermoupolis), port, pop. 17,000.

Szczecin (Ger. *Stettin*), city of NW Poland, on R. Oder, cap. of Szczecin prov. Pop. 340,000. Port; shipbuilding, indust. centre; formerly port for Berlin. Hanseatic League member from 1360. Part of Prussian Pomerania 1720-1945.

Szechwan, prov. of SC China. Area *c* 570,000 sq km (220,000 sq mi); pop. (est.) 70,000,000; cap. Chengtu. Isolated region. High mountains in W crossed by Yangtze. Fertile Red basin in C is densely populated and major source of rice, sugar cane, cotton.

Szeged, city of SE Hungary, on R. Tisza. Pop. 130,000. Port in agric. area, food processing; light industs.

T

Table Bay, inlet of Atlantic Ocean, SW Cape Prov., South Africa; *c* 9.7 km (6 mi) across. First Dutch settlement in S Africa estab. 1652 on shores. Overlooked by **Table Mountain,** height 1087 m (3567 ft).

table tennis or **ping-pong,** indoor game played on a rectangular table with hollow celluloid ball and rubber-covered bats. Prob. originated in 1880s in England.

taboo or **tabu,** prohibition, common among primitive peoples, of certain words and actions, usually on religious grounds. Also refers to objects set aside for religious use. Practice occurs esp. in Polynesia.

Tabriz, city of NW Iran, cap. of E Azerbaijan prov. Pop. 599,000. Market centre for fertile agric. area; textile and rug mfg.

Tacitus (AD *c* 55–*c* 120), Roman historian. Author of *Germania,* giving valuable hist. information on Germanic tribes. Wrote biography of Agricola, his father-in-law, and history of the empire (69-97).

Tacoma, port of W Washington, US; on Puget Sound, S of Seattle. Pop. 158,000. Shipyards, lumber, flour mills, copper smelting.

Tadzhik Soviet Socialist Republic, constituent republic of SC USSR. Area *c* 143,000 sq km (55,200 sq mi); pop. 3,801,000; cap. Dushanbe. Largely mountainous, containing Pamir and Alai systems; lowlands in Amu Darya valley. Crops incl. cotton, wheat, fruit; sheep and cattle raising. Region under Russian control by 1895; constituent republic (1929).

Taegu, city of SE South Korea. Pop. 1,309,000. Commercial centre of agric. region (grains, tobacco); textiles produced.

Tafawa Balewa, Alhaji Sir Abubakar (1912-66), Nigerian statesman, 1st PM (1957-66). Assassinated in military coup.

taffeta, light plain-weave fabric with high sheen, originally made of silk.

Tafilelt or **Tafilalet,** oasis of SE Morocco. Largest in Sahara, area *c* 1375 sq km (530 sq mi). Produces dates, leather.

Taft, William Howard (1857-1930), American statesman, Republican president (1909-13).

Tagore, Sir Rabindranath (1861-1941), Indian author, educator. Wrote love lyrics in English and Bengali, *eg* collection *Gitanjali* (1912). Nobel Prize for Literature (1913).

Tagus (Span. *Tajo,* Port. *Tejo*), river of Spain and Portugal. Flows *c* 910 km (565 mi) from Teruel prov., EC Spain to Atlantic Ocean by estuary at Lisbon. Forms part of Spain-Portugal border.

Tahiti, main isl. of French Polynesia, in Windward group of Society Isls. Area 1040 sq km (402 sq mi); cap. Papeete. Mountainous; produces fruit, sugar, copra.

Taimyr Peninsula, most N projection of USSR mainland, on Arctic coast of Siberian RSFSR. N extremity is Cape Chelyuskin.

Tainan, port of SW Taiwan, on Formosa Str. Pop. 513,000. Agric. centre for rice, sugar cane; produces textiles, machinery. Cap. of isl. until 1885.

taipan, *Oxyuranus scutellatus,* large brown dangerously poisonous snake, up to 3 m/10 ft in length. Found in NE Australia and New Guinea.

Taipei, cap. of Taiwan, commercial and indust. centre. Pop. 3,050,000. Founded in 18th cent., replaced Tainan as cap. in 1885.

Taiping Rebellion (1850-64), revolt in China against Manchu dynasty. Led by Hung Hsiu-chuan who declared himself leader of Taiping (Great Peace) dynasty. After initial success, crushed with help of Western troops under C. G. GORDON.

Taiwan (*Formosa*), isl. republic of E Asia, separated from China by Formosa Str. Area *c* 36,000 sq km (13,900 sq mi); pop. 15,500,000; cap. Taipei. Language: Mandarin Chinese. Religion: Buddhism. Crossed N-S by mountain range, reaching *c* 4000 m (13,100 ft); tropical climate, with abundant rainfall. Produces rice, timber, sugar. Settled in 17th cent. by Chinese after expulsion of Dutch. Ceded to Japan (1895-1945). Seat of Chiang Kai-shek's nationalist govt. after 1949; under threat of Chinese invasion, has developed under US economic and military aid. Withdrew from UN (1971), on entry of China.

Taiyuan, cap. of Shansi prov., NC China. Pop. 1,350,000. Indust. centre in major iron and coal area. Ancient walled city.

Taj Mahal, white marble mausoleum near Agra, India. Built 1630-48 by Shah Jehan as tomb for his favourite wife.

Tajo, *see* TAGUS.

Takoradi, *see* SEKONDI-TAKORADI.

Talbot, William Henry Fox (1800-77), English photographic pioneer. Patented various processes for making prints.

talc, softest common mineral; consists of hydrated magnesium silicate. Main constituent of SOAPSTONE. Used in electrical insulators, lubricants, paper mfg., also as talcum powder.

Talcahuano, *see* CONCEPCIÓN.

Talien, *see* LU-TA.

Tallahassee, cap. of Florida, US. Pop. 73,000. Lumber produce. Indian, Spanish settlement prior to territ. cap. (1824).

Talleyrand [-Périgord], Charles Maurice de (1754-1838), French statesman. Bishop of Autun (1789-91), represented clergy in Estates-General (1789); supported moderate reform. Fled abroad on fall of monarchy. Foreign minister under

Directory (1797-9) and under Napoleon (1799-1807). On Napoleon's exile to Elba, secured accession of Louis XVIII and favourable peace terms for French at Congress of Vienna (1814-15).

Tallinn (Ger. *Reval*), city of USSR, cap. of Estonian SSR; on Gulf of Finland. Pop. 430,000. Port; exports timber, paper; shipbuilding; wood products, textile mfg. Founded by Danes (1219); member of Hanseatic League (1285). Taken by Russia from Sweden (1710). Cap. of Estonia (1919-40).

Tallis, Thomas (*c* 1505-1585), English composer. Compositions, noted for contrapuntal skill, incl. motets, anthems, keyboard music.

tallow, solid fat extracted from animals, esp. cattle and sheep. Used to make candles and soap.

Talmud, collection of writings constituting Jewish civil and religious law. Consists of 2 parts, Mishnah (text), and Gemara (commentary). Passages devoted to law itself are known as Halakah; those which contain illustrative parables, legends, *etc*, as Haggadah. Regarded as Oral Law as distinct from Written Law of the Torah.

talus or **scree,** accumulation of rock fragments formed at foot of steep slope. Results from weathering of rock face.

tamarind, *Tamarindus indica,* large evergreen tree of Leguminosae family, native to tropical Africa. Pod contains seeds enclosed in juicy acid pulp, used in beverages and food.

tamarisk, any of genus *Tamarix* of shrubs and small trees native to Mediterranean region and C Asia. Feathery leaves, pink or white flowers.

tambourine, hand-held percussion instrument consisting of circular frame and single drumhead, with circular metal plates or jingles in frame.

Tamburlaine, *see* TAMERLANE.

Tamerlane or **Timur Leng** (*c* 1336–1405), Mongol conqueror. Estab. himself as ruler of Turkestan with his cap. at Samarkand (1369). Conquered Persia, S Russia, India as far as Delhi. Defeated Ottoman Turks at Angora (1402). Patron of learning; notorious for his cruelty.

Tamil, *see* DRAVIDIAN.

Tamil Nadu, maritime state of S India; formerly Madras, renamed 1969. Area *c* 130,000 sq km (50,000 sq mi); pop. 41,103,000; cap. Madras. Plain along Coromandel Coast in E; mountainous in W, reaching alt. of 2400 m (8000 ft) in Nilgiri Hills. Agric. economy; rice, cotton, groundnuts. Under British control by 1800.

Tammuz, in Babylonian and Assyrian religion, god of nature, personification of recreative power of spring. Loved by fertility goddess ISHTAR; killed and restored to life by her.

Tampa, resort and port of W Florida, US; on Tampa Bay. Pop. 1,348,000. Citrus fruit canning indust., phosphates export; breweries, cigar mfg.

Tampere (Swed. *Tammerfors*), city of SW Finland, between Lakes Näsi and Pyhä. Pop. 271,000. Railway jct.; indust. centre, esp. textiles, timber, using h.e.p. from nearby rapids. Has cathedral (20th cent.).

Tamworth Manifesto, election address by Robert PEEL at Tamworth, Staffordshire (1834). Considered manifesto for emerging Conservative Party; accepted Reform Bill of 1832 and proposed careful social and economic reform.

Tana or **Tsana, Lake,** largest lake of Ethiopia, in NW. Area 3625 sq km (1400 sq mi); alt. 1830 m (6000 ft). Source of Blue Nile.

Tananarive, cap. of Madagascar, in C highlands. Pop. 378,000. Admin., commercial centre; univ.; port at Tamatave.

T'ang, Chinese imperial dynasty (618-907). Under second emperor, T'ai Tsung (627-649), China became largest empire on earth. Period marked by prosperity, stability, development of bureaucracy. Poetry and painting flourished.

Tanga, town of NE Tanzania, on Indian Ocean. Pop. 144,000. Railway terminus; port.

Tanganyika, *see* TANZANIA.

Tanganyika, Lake, lake of EC Africa, in Great Rift Valley. Borders on Burundi (NE), Tanzania (E), Zambia (S), Zaïre (W). Area 32,900 sq km (12,700 sq mi); second deepest (1432 m/4700 ft) in world. Reached 1858 by Burton and Speke.

tangerine, small, thin-skinned variety of ORANGE belonging to mandarin orange species, *Citrus reticulata.* Native to SE Asia, now widely grown in tropical and subtropical regions.

Tangier (anc. *Tingis*), city of N Morocco, on Str. of Gibraltar. Pop. 208,000. Port, commercial and tourist centre. Focus of dispute over Morocco in 19th cent., estab. (1923) as international zone. Part of Morocco (1956), declared free port 1961.

tango, dance of Spanish-American origin, internationally popular since *c* 1915. Tempo is moderately slow and rhythm similar to habanera.

Tangshan, city of Hopeh prov., NE China. Pop. (pre 1976) 950,000. Coalmining centre. Iron and steel works, motor vehicle and chemical mfg. Devastated by earthquake (1976), est. 500,000 killed.

tank, heavily armoured vehicle, moving on tracks, mounting a field gun or smaller armament. First used by the British in the Somme (1916). Became major weapon of land warfare in WWII, esp. in N Africa.

Tannenberg (Pol. *Stebark*), village of Olsztyn prov., NE Poland, formerly in E Prussia. Scene of defeat (1410) of Teutonic Knights by Poles and Lithuanians, and defeat (1914) of Russians by Germans.

tannin or **tannic acid,** astringent compound present in many plants, *eg* tea, walnut, gall nuts, hemlock and oak bark. Used in tanning, inks, as dyeing fixative and for clarifying solutions in medicine.

tanning, process by which animal skins are

turned into leather by soaking in tannin. Alum and chrome salts or fats and oils (for chamois leather) are also employed.

tansy, *Tanacetum vulgare,* common European flowering herb of daisy family. Formerly used as stimulant in medicine, now cultivated as garden plant.

Tanta, city of N Egypt, on Nile delta. Pop. 285,000. Railway and commercial centre, cotton indust.

tantalum (Ta), rare metallic element; at. no. 73, at. wt. 180.95. Occurs with niobium in certain minerals. Corrosion resistant, malleable and ductile. Used in surgical instruments, manufacture of hard alloys, and electronic equipment.

Tantalus, in Greek myth, king punished in Hades by being set in pool of water, hungry and thirsty, but unable either to drink from the pool, or to reach fruit tree.

Tantra, group of post-Vedic Sanskrit treatises. Consist of dialogues between SIVA and KALI. Basis of various cults.

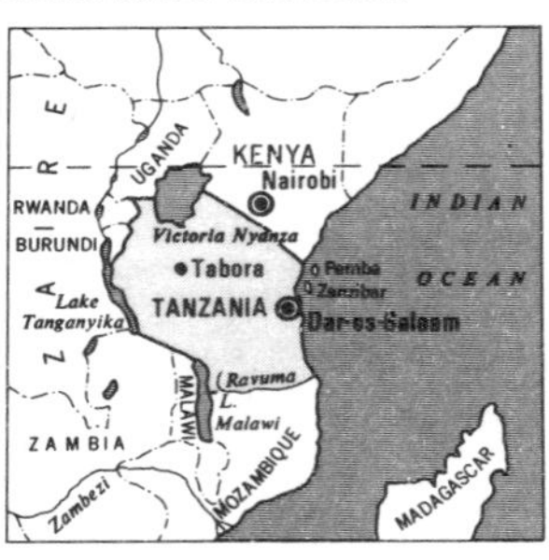

Tanzania

Tanzania, republic of E Africa. Area 945,000 sq km (364,900 sq mi); pop. 16,553,000; cap. Dar-es-Salaam. Languages: Swahili, English. Religions: animist, Islam, Christianity. Narrow coastal plain; interior plateau, with volcanic peaks (*eg* Kilimanjaro), cut by Great Rift Valley. Bordered by L. Tanganyika (W), Victoria Nyanza (N). Exports coffee, cotton, sisal, diamonds; TanZam railway links Zambia with Dar-es-Salaam. Explored 16th cent. by Portuguese; ivory, slave trade under Arabs 18th-19th cent. Part of German East Africa from 1884; mandated to Britain 1916. Independent 1961. Tanzania formed 1964 by union of Tanganyika with Zanzibar.

Taoism, Chinese religion and philosophy. Based on book, *Tao Te Ching,* ascribed to Lao-tze (6th cent. BC) but prob. written 3rd cent. BC. By AD 5th cent., developed into religious system with influences from Mahayana Buddhism. Emphasized effortless action, cessation of all striving. Condemned social philosophy of Confucius.

tape recorder, electromagnetic instrument which records speech and music by interpreting sounds as variations in magnetic field which act on MAGNETIC TAPE. On playback, magnetic patterns reconverted into electrical impulses, in turn converted into audible sound waves.

tapestry, ornamental fabric for covering walls, furniture and for curtains. Made by interweaving of plain warp threads with silk or wool of varying colour and texture. European wool tapestries are extant from 10th cent. Noted centres were Arras (from 14th cent.), Brussels, Beauvais and Gobelins factory, Paris.

tapeworm, long ribbon-shaped segmented parasitic flatworm of class Cestoda. Adults infest intestines of man and other vertebrates, absorbing nutrients through body; life cycle may involve several hosts.

tapioca, *see* CASSAVA.

Malayan tapir

tapir, nocturnal timid pig-like ungulate of tropical America and SE Asia. Flexible snout, resembling small trunk; herbivorous. Species incl. Malayan tapir, *Tapirus indicus,* with black limbs and forequarters, white hindquarters.

tar, dark brown or black viscous liquid obtained from distillation of wood, coal and similar substances. Pitch is more solid form. Used for road-making, as protective coating for wood, *etc.* Distillation of coal tar yields bases for aniline dyes.

Tara, Hill of, Co. Meath, E Irish Republic. Seat of Irish kings until 6th cent.

Taranto (anc. *Tarentum*), town of Apulia, SE Italy, on Gulf of Taranto. Cap. of Ionio prov. Pop. 245,000. Port, naval base; major steelworks. Founded 8th cent. BC by Greeks. Medieval cathedral.

tarantula, name given to various large hairy spiders of Theraphosidae family, with poisonous but rarely fatal bite. Name originally applied to S European *Lycosa tarantula* whose bite was believed to lead to dancing mania in Middle Ages.

Tarbes, town of SW France, on R. Adour, cap. of Hautes-Pyrénées dept. Pop. 54,000. Tourist resort; livestock trade. Romanesque cathedral.

tare, *see* VETCH.

tariffs or **customs,** duties on imported goods intended to protect domestic producers by increasing prices of imports in relation to home-produced goods. Used as protectionist policy by most countries, EEC is leading example of international cooperation on tariffs. Opposed to FREE TRADE.

Tarn, river of S France. Flows *c* 370 km (230

mi) from Cévennes via Albi, Montauban to R. Garonne. Limestone gorges.

tarot, oldest surviving card game, using esoteric designs; now used mainly for fortune-telling.

tarpan, wild horse, once common in Europe and Asia, closely related to Przewalski's horse. Became extinct *c* 1900.

tarpon, *Tarpon atlanticus,* large primitive fish found in warm Atlantic waters; reaches lengths of 1.8 m/6 ft. Popular game fish.

Tarquinius Superbus, Lucius (*fl* 6th cent. BC), last king of Rome. Expelled from Rome (510 BC) because of his despotism; enlisted aid of Etruscan Lars Porsena. Although Porsena captured Rome, Tarquinius was not restored as king.

tarragon, *Artemisia dracunculus,* European perennial WORMWOOD. Long, slender aromatic leaves used as seasoning.

Tarragona, town of NE Spain, on Mediterranean Sea, cap. of Tarragona prov. Pop. 78,000. Port, exports wine. Roman remains. Cathedral (12th cent.).

Tarrasa, city of Catalonia, NE Spain. Pop. 139,000. Major textile centre.

tarsier, small arboreal primate of Tarsiidae family, related to lemur; found in Philippines and East Indies. Rat-sized, with large eyes and ears; long feet and hands equipped with sucker-like discs. Nocturnal, feeds on lizards, insects, *etc.*

Tarsus, town of S Turkey. Pop. 75,000. Agric. trade centre. Has ruins of ancient Tarsus, cap. of Cilicia. Birthplace of St Paul.

tartan, woollen cloth woven in pattern of coloured checks. Tartan kilts and plaids worn by Scottish clans from 15th cent., each clan having own pattern. Illegal (1746-82) after 1745 Jacobite uprising.

tartaric acid, crystalline organic acid, found in vegetable tissue and fruit juices. Salt, potassium hydrogen tartrate, present in grape juice, is deposited as argol in wine casks; used in baking powder (cream of tartar).

Tartars or **Tatars,** name given to peoples who invaded Russia (13th cent.) under Mongol leadership. Known as GOLDEN HORDE, they overran and dominated parts of Eurasia until their empire was lost to Ottomans and dukes of Moscow (15th-16th cents.). In USSR, there are *c* 5 million Tartars, who are Moslems and speak a Turkic language.

Tartu (Ger. *Dorpat*), town of USSR, Estonia SSR. Pop. 104,000. Metalworking, textile, cigarette mfg. Founded in 1030 as Yuryev.

Tashkent, city of USSR, cap. of Uzbek SSR; in oasis of R. Chirchik. Pop. 1,779,000. Cotton textile mfg. Founded 7th cent.; conquered by Genghis Khan and Tamerlane. Taken by Russia in 1865.

Tasman, Abel Janszoon (1603-59), Dutch navigator. Discovered Tasmania, New Zealand, Friendly Isls. (1642-3); proved Australia not united to polar continent.

Tasmania, isl. state of Australia, separated from SE mainland by Bass Str. Area incl. King Isl. and Furneaux Isls. 67,900 sq km (26,200 sq mi); pop. 417,700; cap. Hobart. Large forested C plateau with many lakes and valleys; narrow coastal plains. Fruit, vegetable growing, wool, dairying; timber indust.; h.e.p.; minerals incl. copper, zinc. Discovered (1642) and named Van Diemen's Land by Tasman. First settled (1803) as penal colony, part of New South Wales until 1825; federal state from 1901.

Tasmanian devil, *Sarcophilus harrisii,* burrowing nocturnal carnivorous marsupial of Tasmania. Much hunted, now rare.

Tasmanian wolf or **thylacine,** *Thylacinus cynocephalus,* wolf-like carnivorous marsupial; red-brown coat with dark stripes. Confined to Tasmania, is almost extinct.

Tasman Sea, area of SW Pacific Ocean, between SE Australia and NW New Zealand.

Tasso, Torquato (1544-95), Italian poet, one of most famous of Renaissance. Known for *Gerusalemme Liberata* (*Jerusalem Delivered,* 1575), religious epic on 1st Crusade, and *Aminta* (1573), hedonistic pastoral play.

taste, sensation caused by stimulation of sensory organs (taste buds) in mucous membranes of tongue and palate. Four basic tastes: bitter, salt, sour and sweet. Flavour depends more on smell than taste.

Tatars, *see* TARTARS.

Tatra Mountains (Czech *Tatry*), range on Czech-Polish border, part of Carpathians. High Tatra (N) reach 2662 m (8737 ft); Low Tatra (S) reach 2044 m (6709 ft). Tourism.

Taunton, town and admin. hq. of Somerset, SW England. Pop. 37,000. Clothing mfg.

Taupo, Lake, largest lake in New Zealand, in volcanic region of C North Isl. Area 620 sq km (240 sq mi). Used as h.e.p. reservoir.

Taurus, *see* ZODIAC.

Taurus Mountains, range of S Turkey, running parallel to Mediterranean. Rises to 3734 m (12,251 ft) at Ala Dag. Extends NE as Anti-Taurus. Has important mineral deposits (chromium, copper).

tautomerism, in chemistry, existence of certain compounds as a mixture of 2 isomeric forms in equilibrium; each form may be converted into the other but the equilibrium will tend to be maintained.

Taverner, John (*c* 1490-1545), English composer. Wrote polyphonic church music in elaborate Tudor vocal style.

tawny owl, *Strix aluco,* woodland bird of Europe and Asia; black eyes, no ear-tufts, tawny-brown upper-parts.

taxation, govt. levy to provide revenue. Oldest form is land tax; other means of taxation developed as scope of govt. responsibilities widened, esp. in 19th-20th cent. Direct taxes, graduated according to individual's ability to pay, incl. INCOME TAX, capital transfer and capital gains tax, rates, corporation tax. Forms of indirect taxation incl. sales, purchase and value-added taxes, based on stipulated percentage of retail cost.

Tay, longest river of Scotland, flows 193 km

(120 mi) from Central region via Loch Tay, to North Sea. Estuary crossed by road, rail bridges at Dundee. Salmon fishing.

Taylor, Zachary (1784-1850), American statesman, Whig president (1849-50). Won decisive victory at Buena Vista (1847) in Mexican War. Died in office.

Tayside, region of EC Scotland. Area 7501 sq km (2896 sq mi); pop. 403,000; chief city and admin. hq. Dundee. Created 1975, incl. former Angus, Kinross-shire, most of Perthshire.

Tbilisi (Russ. *Tiflis*), city of USSR, cap. of Georgian SSR; route centre on R. Kura. Pop. 1,066,000. Agric., trade centre; textile, machinery mfg. Founded 4th cent.; prospered on trade route between Europe and Asia. Under Russian rule from 1800. Old section incl. Zion cathedral (5th cent.) and Armenian cathedral (15th cent.).

Tchaikovsky, Piotr Ilich (1840-93), Russian composer. His melodious, romantic music incl. *Pathétique* symphony, ballets *Swan Lake, The Sleeping Beauty,* and fantasies, *eg Romeo and Juliet.* Also wrote *1812* overture, operas, *eg Eugene Onegin,* piano and violin concertos.

tea, *Thea sinensis,* shrub with fragrant white flowers, extensively cultivated in China, Japan, India, Sri Lanka, *etc.* Bitter, aromatic beverage is prepared by infusion of dried leaves in boiling water. Became popular in Britain in 17th cent.

Teach, Edward (d. 1718), English pirate, called 'Blackbeard'. Gained notoriety through his raids on West Indies and coasts of Virginia and the Carolinas. Killed by force sent by governor of Virginia.

teak, *Tectona grandis,* large East Indian timber tree of family Verbenaceae. Now cultivated in W Africa and tropical America. Hard, yellowish wood used in shipbuilding and furniture.

teal, small freshwater duck, genus *Anas.* Species incl. green-winged teal, *A. crecca,* smallest European duck.

tear gas, aerosol, usually bromide compound, inducing temporary loss of sight through excessive flow of tears. Used in warfare and civil disturbances.

Fuller's teasel

teasel, any of genus *Dipsacus* of biennial or perennial herbs native to Europe, Asia and N Africa. Fuller's teasel, *D. fullonum,* is cultivated for its prickly flower heads, used for raising the nap on woollen cloth.

technetium (Tc), radioactive metallic element; at. no. 43, mass no. of most stable isotope 97. First artificially made element, prepared 1937; now obtained as fission product of uranium.

technology, study of methods used in application of science in industry. First technological univ., Ecole Polytechnique, Paris (1794).

tectonics, *see* PLATE TECTONICS.

Tees, river of N England. Flows 113 km (70 mi) from Pennines to North Sea at Middlesbrough.

Teesside, urban area of Cleveland, NE England, at mouth of R. Tees. Pop. 395,000. Heavy industs. Formed 1968 from Middlesbrough, Redcar, Stockton-on-Tees.

teeth, in most vertebrates, hard bone-like structures embedded in upper and lower jaws, serving to bite, tear and chew. Tooth consists of pulp-filled central cavity, surrounded by shell of dentine (ivory) which is coated on crown by enamel and on root by softer cement. In man, early set of 20 deciduous (or milk) teeth is replaced by 32 permanent teeth, beginning in *c* 6th year. On each side of jaw, there are 2 incisors, 1 canine, 2 premolars and 3 molars.

Tegucigalpa, cap. of Honduras, on Choluteca R. Pop. 274,000. Food processing, distilling, cigarette, textile mfg. Founded 1578. Became cap. 1880. Has univ. (1847); 18th-cent. cathedral.

Tehran or **Teheran,** cap. of Iran, S of Elburz Mts. Pop. 4,496,000. Industrial, commercial, transport centre. Became cap. 1788 under Aga Mohammed Khan. Univ (1935).

Tehran Conference, meeting (Nov.-Dec. 1943) at Tehran between Allied leaders Churchill, F.D. Roosevelt and Stalin in WWII. Outlined plans for invasion of Europe and role of UN in peace settlement.

Tehuantepec, isthmus of E Mexico between Campeche and Tehuantepec gulfs. Narrowest part of Mexico.

Teilhard de Chardin, Pierre (1881-1955), French theologian, palaeontologist. A Jesuit, he attempted controversial reconciliation of Christian theology with evolutionary theory. Evolved concept of interaction of psychic and physical energy.

Tejo, *see* TAGUS.

Tel Aviv, city of WC Israel, on Mediterranean. Pop. 1,181,000. Financial, indust. centre; textiles, metals, chemicals. Incorporated Jaffa 1949. Univ. (1953).

telecommunications, long-distance communication by radio, TELEGRAPH, TELEPHONE, *etc.* Formerly relied on cables, now increasingly uses microwaves reflected from artificial satellites.

telegraph, method of sending messages in form of electrical impulses by radio or wire. First practicable system developed by Samuel Morse (*c* 1837). Sophistications incl. reception of messages in printed form (teleprinter), and transmission of photographs (facsimile machine).

Tel-el-Amarna or **Tell-el-Amarna,** site of N Egypt, N of Asyût. City of Akhetaton built here *c* 1365 BC by IKHNATON as new cap. and centre of reformed religion. Ruins, rock tombs.

Telemann, Georg Philipp (1681-1767), German composer. Wrote numerous compositions, incl. motets, 44 passions, oratorios, 600 overtures, 40 operas, keyboard and chamber music.

telepathy, *see* PSYCHICAL RESEARCH.

telephone, device for conveying speech over distances by converting sound into electrical impulses. Invented by Alexander Bell (1876).

telephoto lens, combination of convex and concave lenses, used to increase effective focal length of camera and thus magnify images, without increasing distance between film and camera lens.

telescope, optical instrument for viewing distant objects. Refracting telescope uses 2 convex lenses, objective and eyepiece; reflecting telescope uses concave mirror and eyepiece. A further lens or prism is needed for upright image. Invented (*c* 1608) in Holland, first used for astronomy by Galileo (1609).

television, transmission and reception of visual images using electromagnetic radiation. Pattern of electric impulses from camera reconstructed in receiver to form picture on luminous screen. First developed in UK by John Logie Baird (1926) using mechanical scanning system; later replaced by electronic scanning. TV has become a major form of communication. Also *see* BROADCASTING.

Telford, Thomas (1757-1834), Scottish civil engineer. Built Caledonian Canal (1803-23), *c* 1000 miles of roads. Constructed (1826) Menai Suspension Bridge, Anglesey.

Tell, William (*fl c* 1300), Swiss hero. Traditionally, forced to shoot apple off son's head as punishment for failure to recognize Austrian authority. After his success, he instigated revolt by shooting Austrian bailiff, Gessler.

Teller, Edward (1908-), American physicist, b. Hungary. Aided atomic bomb research during WWII. Called 'father of hydrogen bomb' for contributions to development of H-bomb.

tellurium (Te), semi-metallic element, with properties similar to sulphur; at. no. 52, at. wt. 127.6. Appears as brittle white crystalline solid or amorphous powder. Used to colour glass and ceramics, in vulcanizing rubber and in alloys.

Temesvár, *see* TIMISOARA.

tempera, method of painting in which pigments are mixed with size, casein or egg, esp. egg yolk. Egg tempera was commonest mode of painting easel paintings until 15th cent.; paint dries quickly to produce dull finish.

temperature, measure of degree of hotness of a body, referred to some scale. Celsius (centigrade) scale takes freezing point of water as 0°, boiling point of water as 100°. Fahrenheit scale takes freezing point as 32° and boiling point as 212°. Kelvin or absolute scale takes ABSOLUTE ZERO as its zero point. Kelvin and Celsius degrees are equal, Fahrenheit degree equals 5/9 of Celsius degree.

Temple, three centres of worship successively built by the Jews in ancient Jerusalem: Solomon's, destroyed by Nebuchadnezzar; Zerubbabel's, built after exile in Babylon; and Herod's, destroyed by Romans (AD 70). Wailing Wall survives as part of the last.

tempo, in music, indication of speed at which piece should be played. A description is given often in Italian, *eg largo, andante, allegro, presto,* or a metronome number is given indicating beats per minute.

tench, *Tinca tinca,* European freshwater fish of carp family. Bronze-brown with red eyes.

Ten Commandments or **Decalogue,** in OT, summary of law of God as given to Moses in form of 10 statements on Mt. Sinai. Basis of ethical code of Judaism, Christianity and Islam. Divided into 3 groups dealing with duty to God, personal integrity, proper treatment of others.

tendon, cord of tough fibrous tissue which connects muscle with bone. Achilles tendon attaches muscles of the calf to the heel bone.

Tenerife, largest of Canary Isls., Spain. Area 2060 sq km (795 sq mi); cap. Santa Cruz. Rises to 3712 m (12,192 ft) in volcanic Pico de Teide. Tourist resort; banana, tomato growing.

Teng Hsiao-ping or **Deng Xiaoping** (1904-), Chinese political leader. General secretary of Communist Party (1956-67); removed from office during Cultural Revolution. Restored to office (1973), influence declining with death of Chou En-lai (1975), increasing after death of Mao Tse-tung (1976). Vice-chairman of Communist Party, vice-premier from 1977.

Teniers, David, (The Younger) (1610-90), Flemish painter. Known for his genre scenes of peasant life.

Tennessee, state of EC US. Area 109,412 sq km (42,244 sq mi); pop. 4,292,000; cap. Nashville; largest city Memphis. Mississippi R. forms W border; agric. plain rises to Cumberland Plateau and Appalachians in E. Cotton, tobacco, maize, livestock farming; coal, stone and zinc, phosphate mining; industs. incl. textiles, chemical mfg. Economic development under Tennessee Valley Authority. British estab. claim 1763; admitted to Union as 16th state (1796). Joined Confederacy in Civil War; important battlegrounds.

Tennessee, river of EC US. Formed in E Tennessee, flows 1050 km (650 mi) SW through Kentucky to Ohio R. Series of dams created by Tennessee Valley Authority (estab. 1933) control flooding and provide h.e.p.

tennis or **lawn tennis,** ball-and-racket game played by 2 or 4 players on prepared surface, either indoors or outdoors. Descended from royal game (real tennis) played in France and England in 14th cent. Modern game devised by Major Wingfield in England (1873); 1st Wimbledon championships held 1877. International tournaments restricted to amateur players until late 1960s.

Tennyson, Alfred Tennyson, 1st Baron (1809-92), English poet. Shorter poems incl. 'Ulysses', elegies incl. *In Memoriam* (1850). Longer narrative poems incl. *The Charge of the Light Brigade* (1855), *Idylls of the King* (1859-88) on Arthurian legends. Created poet laureate (1850).

tenor, in singing, high male voice, below alto but above baritone. Also member of family of instruments of similar range, *eg* tenor trombone.

Tensing Norkay, *see* HILLARY.

tepee or **tipi,** *see* WIGWAM.

tequila, Mexican spirit distilled from fermented juice of various agaves.

terbium (Tb), metallic element of lanthanide series; at. no. 65, at. wt. 158.92. Occurs in gadolinite; difficult to isolate.

Ter Borch, Gerard (1617-81), Dutch painter. Known for his small portraits and scenes of prosperous middle-class life.

terebinth, *Pistacia terebinthus,* small European tree. Bark yields turpentine.

Terence, full name Publius Terentius Afer (*c* 195-159 BC), Roman comic poet. Plays incl. *Andria, Hecyra, Eunuchus.*

Teresa, *see* THERESA.

termite, any of order Isoptera of soft-bodied social insects. Lives in colonies composed of several castes: fertile winged forms, sterile workers and soldiers, *etc.* Builds or tunnels large nests; feeds on and destroys wood. Most species are tropical.

tern, migratory seabird of Laridae family, related to gull. Species incl. common tern, *Sterna hirundo,* of Europe and North America; slender body, forked tail.

Terni, city of Umbria, C Italy, cap. of Terni prov. Pop. 113,000. Railway jct., iron and steel, munitions. Founded 7th cent. BC.

terpenes, in chemistry, series of unsaturated hydrocarbons, found in resins and essential oils. Used in perfumes and medicine.

terracotta, hard reddish brick-like earthenware, porous and unglazed. Used since antiquity for statues, figures, vases.

terrapin, name applied to several species of edible aquatic turtles. Species incl. diamond back terrapin, *Malaclemys terrapin,* found in salt marshes of S and E US.

terrier, breed of dog originally used to dig out burrowing animals. Incl. Boston, bull, cairn, fox, Scottish and Skye terriers.

Territorial Army, British volunteer force, estab. 1907. Replaced in 1967 by smaller Territorial and Army Volunteer Reserve.

Terry, Dame Ellen Alice (1847-1928), English actress. Acted opposite Henry Irving. Notable in Shakespearian roles. Famous correspondence with Shaw.

Tertiary period, first geological period of Cenozoic era; began *c* 65 million years ago, lasted *c* 63 million years. Comprises Palaeocene, Eocene, Oligocene, Miocene, Pliocene epochs. Alpine, Himalayan mountain-building period. Evolution of primitive mammals, ancestors of modern fauna, *eg* mammoths, man-like apes; had modern birds. Deterioration of climate toward end of period. Also *see* GEOLOGICAL TABLE.

Test Act, legislation passed (1673) by English Parliament to exclude from office those who refused to take oaths of supremacy and allegiance and to receive communion according to Church of England. Repealed (1828).

test-ban treaty, *see* DISARMAMENT.

testis or **testicle,** either of two oval male sex glands which are suspended in the scrotum. Secretes spermatozoa and testosterone.

testosterone, male steroid sex hormone. Promotes development of male secondary sex characteristics.

tetanus or **lockjaw,** acute infectious disease caused by toxin released by bacterium *Clostridium tetani,* which usually enters body via wounds. Toxin disturbs motor nerve cells, causing muscular spasms, esp. in jaw, face, neck. Prevented by vaccination, treated with tetanus antitoxin.

tetracycline, any of group of broad-spectrum antibiotics derived from bacteria of genus *Streptomyces.*

Tetuán or **Tétouan,** city of N Morocco. Pop. 309,000. Textile, leather industs.; Mediterranean outport at Río Martín exports agric. produce. Cap. of Spanish Morocco (1912-56).

Teutonic Knights, members of medieval German military and religious order, founded *c* 1190 in Holy Land. Undertook conquest of pagan E Prussia (13th cent.), where they estab. their rule. Gradually lost power to the Poles after defeat at Tannenberg (1410).

Tewkesbury, town of Gloucestershire, SW England, on R. Severn. Pop. 9000. Has Norman abbey (12th cent.). Scene of Yorkist victory during Wars of the Roses (1471).

Texas, state of SC US; on Gulf of Mexico. Area 692,408 sq km (267,339 sq mi); pop. 12,808,000; cap. Austin; main cities Houston, Dallas, San Antonio. Prairies in N Panhandle, plains in W, Rio Grande separates Texas from Mexico, Red R. forms NE border. Greatest agric. yield in US. Livestock, major cotton crop, rice, grains; minerals esp. oil, natural gas. Space research indust. Spanish settlement in 18th cent. Americans ousted Mexicans (1835-6). Republic until annexed by US (1845), precipitating Mexican War. Admitted to Union as 28th state (1845). Joined Confederacy in Civil War.

Thackeray, William Makepeace (1811-63), English author, b. India. Masterpiece *Vanity Fair* (1847-8) uses self-seeking adventuress as heroine to expose hypocrisy of social code. Other novels incl. *Pendennis* (1850), *Henry Esmond* (1852).

Thailand, kingdom of SE Asia. Area *c* 514,000 sq km (198,500 sq mi); pop. 45,100,000; cap. Bangkok. Language: Thai. Religion: Hinayana Buddhism. C plain watered by R. Chao Phraya, major rice producing area; S is narrow strip extending down Malay penin. Mainly agric. economy; produces tin, tungsten, rubber, teak. Siamese kingdom dates from 14th cent.; frequent wars with Burmese; lost territ. to British and French in 19th-20th cent. Constitutional monarchy (1932). Formerly Siam, name changed 1939.

Thailand

Thales (*c* 636-*c* 546 BC), Greek philosopher, mathematician, astronomer. Regarded as first Western philosopher. Believed water to be fundamental matter of Nature.

thalidomide, drugs used as a sedative in Europe (1958-61). Withdrawn when found to cause defects of limbs in unborn children if taken during 1st 12 weeks of pregnancy. Discovery led to adoption of stricter regulations in testing of new drugs.

thallium (Tl), rare soft metallic element, similar to lead; at. no. 81, at. wt. 204.37. Obtained from flue dust during processing of pyrites ores. Thallium and its compounds are poisonous; used in insecticides, rat poison, and alloys.

Thames, river of S England. Flows 338 km (210 mi) from Cotswolds via Oxford, Reading, London to North Sea. Tidal to Teddington, W London; hist. major waterway, serving port of London.

Thanksgiving Day, US national holiday. Commemorates 1st harvest of Plymouth Colony and celebration feast held by Pilgrims and neighbouring Indians. Celebrated 4th Thursday in Nov.

Thant, U (1909-74), Burmese diplomat. UN secretary-general (1961-72); granted wide emergency powers. Sought to bring stability to Middle East.

Thar Desert, sandy region of NW India; mainly in Rajasthan, extends into Pakistan.

Thásos, isl. of Greece, in N Aegean Sea. Area 399 sq km (154 sq mi). Olives, vines. Goldmines exploited by Phoenicians. Turkish from 1455, passed to Greece 1913.

Thatcher, Margaret Hilda, née Roberts (1925-), British stateswoman, PM (1979-). Succeeded Edward Heath as leader of Conservative Party (1975); 1st woman PM of UK.

theatre, building for presentation of dramatic performances. Originally an outdoor auditorium for Greek drama, first recorded *c* 5th cent. BC. In Middle Ages, European religious drama performed in churches and in open. Palladio's Teatro Olimpico (1580) was 1st indoor secular theatre. English Elizabethan theatres used courtyard plan, open to the air. By 17th-18th cent., audience separated from performers by raised stage, lights, curtains. 'Theatre in the round', with actors entirely surrounded by audience, is 20th-cent. innovation.

Thebes, ancient city of C Egypt, site now occupied by Karnak and Luxor. *Fl* between XI and XX dynasties (2134-1085 BC) as cap. of Upper Egypt, centre of Amon worship. Many remains, incl. Tutankhamen's tomb (discovered 1922) in nearby Valley of the Kings.

Thebes (mod. *Thivai*), ancient city of Boeotia, SE Greece. Led Boeotian League; fought against Athens in Persian, Peloponnesian Wars. Defeated Sparta at Leuctra (371 BC). Defeated and destroyed (336 BC) by Alexander the Great.

Themistocles (*c* 525-*c* 460 BC), Athenian statesman. Responsible for the building of a strong Athenian navy. During Persian invasion of Greece (480), planned Greek naval victory at Salamis. Exiled by his opponents (471), fled to Persia.

Theocritus (*fl* 270 BC), Greek poet. Regarded as founder of pastoral poetry.

theodolite, portable surveying instrument with telescopic sight. Used to establish horizontal and vertical angles.

Theodoric the Great (*c* 454-526), king of Ostrogoths (*c* 474-526). Encouraged by Roman emperor of the East, Zeno, to invade Italy (488), he completed his conquest with defeat of ODOVACAR at Ravenna (493). Ruled ably after having Odovacar murdered.

Theodosius [I] the Great (*c* 346-95), Roman emperor in the East (379-95). Proclaimed as such by Gratian, he defeated the puppet emperor in the West, Eugenius, and replaced him by his own son Honorius. Empire remained split after his death.

theology, the study of God, his attributes and relation with universe. Systematic theology concerns specific doctrine, *eg* Christianity.

Theophrastus (*c* 370-*c* 285 BC), Greek philosopher. Pupil of Aristotle, later took over his school. His *Characters* is collection of 30 sketches of human types.

theosophy, term for various systems which claim direct mystical contact with divine principle. Esp. doctrines of the Theosophical Society founded by Mme BLAVATSKY to promote study of comparative religions and philosophies.

Theresa, Mother, orig. Agnes Bojaxhiu (1910-), Indian RC missionary, b. Yugoslavia of Albanian parents. Noted for work among starving in Calcutta.

Theresa of Avila, St, orig. Teresa de Cepeda y Ahumada (1515-82), Spanish nun, mystic. Founded (1562) reformed order of (Discalced) Carmelite nuns. Inspired Catholic Reformation. Devotional works incl. *The Way of Perfection* (*c* 1565).

Theresa of Lisieux, St, orig. Thérèse Martin (1873-97), French Carmelite nun, called 'Little Flower of Jesus'. Spiritual autobiog. *The Story of a Soul* (1897) is account of 'little way' of humble goodness.

Thermidor, 11th month of French Revolutionary calendar. Revolution of 9 Thermidor, year 2, (27 July, 1794) saw overthrow of ROBESPIERRE and end of Reign of Terror.

thermionic valve, electronic device consisting of heated cathode which emits electrons, an anode which attracts the electrons, and possibly further perforated grids which control electron flow. Arrangement is placed in glass or metal envelope, usually evacuated or containing gas at low pressure. *See* DIODE, TRIODE.

thermit, mixture of aluminium powder and metal oxide (*eg* iron oxide). Emits tremendous heat when ignited by magnesium ribbon. Used esp. in welding and for incendiary bombs.

thermocouple, device used to measure temperature. Consists of pair of different metals joined at each end; one end is kept at fixed temperature, other is placed at point whose temperature is to be found. Temperature difference causes thermoelectric current to flow which is measured by suitably calibrated galvanometer.

thermodynamics, mathematical study of relation between heat and other forms of energy, and the conversion of one form into another. Based on 3 laws, concerning conservation of energy principle and concept of entropy. Applied to theory of heat engines and chemical reactions.

thermoelectric effect, *see* SEEBECK EFFECT.

thermometer, instrument used to measure temperature. Common type consists of graduated sealed glass tube with bulb containing mercury or coloured alcohol.

thermonuclear reaction, nuclear fusion reaction between atomic nuclei whose energy is derived from thermal agitation. Principle is employed in hydrogen bomb. Controlled thermonuclear reaction for energy production involves problem of containing deuterium and tritium gas at temperatures as high as 5×10^8 °C.

Thermopylae, pass of EC Greece. Here Leonidas' 300 Spartans heroically resisted Persians under Xerxes (480 BC).

thermostat, device employing BIMETALLIC STRIP used to regulate temperature automatically or to activate equipment when temperature changes.

Theseus, in Greek myth, son of Aegeus, king of Athens, or of Poseidon. Heroic deeds incl. killing of Minotaur of Crete (with help of ARIADNE). Abducted Queen Hippolyte who bore him Hippolytus. Married Phaedra, sister of Ariadne. Helped Pirithous abduct Persephone; sent to Hades, but rescued by Heracles. Returned to Athens, found his kingdom in rebellion; sailed to Skyros where he was murdered by King Lycomedes.

Thessalonians, two epistles of NT, written (*c* AD 52) by St Paul from Corinth to church at Thessalonica. Praises faith of Thessalonians but corrects false ideas about general resurrection and the Second Coming.

Thessaloníki, *see* SALONIKA.

Thessaly (*Thessalía*), region of EC Greece. Mountains flank central fertile lowland drained by R. Peneus. United under Jason (374 BC), fell (344 BC) to Philip II of Macedon; part of Roman Macedonia. Turkish from 1355, passed to Greece 1881.

Thetis, in Greek myth, one of Nereids and mother of Achilles. Loved by Zeus and Poseidon but given by them in marriage to mortal Peleus because of prophecy that her son would be greater than his father.

thiamin or **vitamin B_1,** vitamin of B group, found in milk, liver, beans, peas, *etc.* Essential to carbohydrate metabolism; deficiency results in beriberi.

Thiers, [Louis] Adolphe (1797-1877), French statesman. Writings helped precipitate July Revolution (1830); held various offices under Louis Philippe. Later, led opposition to Napoleon III's policies. Negotiated peace after Franco-Prussian War (1871), suppressed Paris Commune. First president of Third Republic (1871-3).

Thieu, Nguyen van (1923-), South Vietnamese political leader, president (1967-75). Helped overthrow Diem (1963). Exercised near-dictatorial powers. Fled country shortly before capitulation of South Vietnam.

Thimbu, *see* BHUTAN.

Third Reich, name given by Hitler to German state under his dictatorship (1933-45). Supposed to last 1000 years.

Third World, name given to technologically underdeveloped nations of Africa, Asia and Latin America. Distinguished from technologically advanced Western nations and those of Soviet bloc. China not usually considered Third World country.

Thirteen Colonies, name applied to British colonies of North America that fought American Revolution and founded United States. They were Massachusetts, New Hampshire, Rhode Island, Connecticut, New York, New Jersey, Pennsylvania, Delaware, Maryland, Virginia, North Carolina, South Carolina and Georgia.

Thirty-nine Articles, basic CREED of Church of England. Originally drawn up (1551-3) revised and adopted by Convocation (1562) Estab. by Act of Parliament (1571).

Thirty Years War, European conflict (1618-48), fought mainly in Germany involving religious and territ. struggle between German princes, variously supported by external powers, and Holy Roman Empire. War precipitated by refusal of Protestant nobles in Bohemia to elect Emperor Ferdinand II king; revolt crushed (1620). War continued in Palatinate; imperial victories led to Danish intervention (1625), effectively crushed by WALLENSTEIN and TILLY (1626-9). Victories of Gustavus Adolphus of Sweden (1631-2) recovered N Germany for Protestants; imperial cause improved with death of Gustavus (1632). War spread beyond Germany after France allied with Sweden (1635). Settlement came with Peace of WESTPHALIA, which broke power of Empire and confirmed French ascendancy.

thistle, any of genera *Onopordum, Cirsium* and *Cnicus* of spiny-leaved plants of composite family. Heads consist of small, purple, yellow, pink, white flowers followed by wind-borne seeds (thistledown). Species incl. Scotch thistle, *O. acanthium.*

Thistlewood, Arthur (1770-1820), English conspirator. Leader in Cato Street conspiracy (1820) to assassinate cabinet ministers. Hanged for treason.

Thomas, St (*fl* 1st cent. AD), one of the Twelve ministers. Doubted Resurrection of Christ until he saw Jesus, touched his side. Traditionally, went to S India or Parthia.

Thomas, Dylan (1914-53), Welsh poet. Wrote intricate life-affirming verse, *eg Deaths and Entrances* (1946), radio play *Under Milk Wood* (1954).

Thomas à Becket, St (*c* 1118-70), English churchman, martyr. Befriended by Henry II, appointed chancellor (1155) and archbishop of Canterbury (1162). Opposed king over taxation. Henry's attempt (1164) to secure jurisdiction over clergy ended in Becket's flight to Rome. Quarrel after return led to murder of Becket in Canterbury Cathedral. Henry did public penance (1174), built shrine.

Thomas à Kempis (*c* 1380-1471), German monk. Augustinian; reputed author of devotional work, *The Imitation of Christ.*

Thomas Aquinas, St (1225-74), Italian philosopher. Major figure of SCHOLASTICISM. Member of Dominican order. Taught at Paris. His system, known as Thomism, became official Catholic theology in 1879. Major work is *Summa theologica* (1267-73).

Thonburi, city of SC Thailand, on R. Chao Phraya opposite Bangkok. Pop. 628,000. Rice milling and sawmilling. Has Wat Arun temple. Cap. of Siam (1767-82).

Thor, in Norse and Teutonic myth, god of thunder, patron of peasants and warriors. Attributes incl. hammer which returned when he threw it.

thorax, in higher vertebrates, part of body between neck and abdomen, containing heart and lungs, protected by ribs. In mammals, diaphragm separates it from abdomen. In insects, thorax consists of 3 segments bearing legs and wings.

Thoreau, Henry David (1817-62), American poet, naturalist, social critic. Associate of EMERSON. Wrote *Walden* (1854) recording observations of nature, thoughts about society, after 2 years spent in isolated cabin. Other works incl. essay 'Civil Disobedience' (1849).

thorium (Th), radioactive metallic element; at. no. 90, at. wt. 232.04. Occurs in monazite sands. Used in filaments and as nuclear fuel; oxide used in gas mantles.

Thorshavn, *see* FAEROES.

Thoth, ancient Egyptian god of wisdom and magic. Credited with invention of hieroglyphics, geometry, *etc.* Represented as human with ibis head. Identified by Greeks with HERMES TRISMEGISTUS.

Thousand and One Nights, *see* ARABIAN NIGHTS.

Thrace (*Thráki*), region of NE Greece. Main town Komotíni. Tobacco, wheat, cotton. Formerly incl. S Bulgaria to R. Danube, European Turkey. Did not accept Greek culture; Greek colonies traded gold, silver. Subdued (342 BC) by Philip II of Macedon; *fl* under Romans. Present borders fixed after Balkan Wars, WWI.

Three Age system, scheme devised (1816-19) by Danish archaeologist C. Thomsen for dividing prehist. into Stone, Bronze and Iron Ages.

Three Rivers, *see* TROIS RIVIÈRES.

thrift, any of genus *Armeria,* esp. *A. maritima,* common thrift or sea pink found on sea cliffs and salt marshes. Cultivated for globe-shaped, papery flowers which may be dried as EVERLASTING FLOWERS.

throat, passage leading from arch of the palate to upper openings of trachea and oesophagus. Incl. PHARYNX.

thrombosis, clotting of blood in an artery or vein. In coronary thrombosis, clot forms in coronary artery or its branches; loss of blood supply may cause death (infarction) of heart tissue. Also *see* APOPLEXY.

thrush, widely distributed songbird of Turdidae family, with dark spots on light breast. Species incl. European mistle thrush, *Turdus viscivorus.*

Thucydides (*c* 460-400 BC), Greek historian. After an unsuccessful command against the Spartans in the Peloponnesian War, he went into exile from Athens (424-404). During his exile, wrote *History of the Peloponnesian War,* an objective and analytical account of war until 411.

Thugs, secret Indian religious sect, incl. both Hindus and Moslems. Worshipped KALI, strangling victims as sacrifices to her. Suppressed by British (1829-48).

Thule, name given by ancients to most N land of Europe, variously identified as Norway, Iceland, Shetland Isls. Modern Thule is settlement (pop. *c* 550) of NW Greenland. US air base nearby.

thulium (Tm), metallic element, rarest of lanthanide series; at. no. 69, at. wt. 168.93.

Thun, town of WC Switzerland. Pop. 37,000. Metal goods, pottery; castle (12th cent.). On R. Aare at NW end of L. Thun, length 18 km (11 mi); tourist area.

thunder, sound following lightning flash. Caused by rapid expansion of air produced by heat of lightning.

Thunder Bay, port of SW Ontario, Canada; on NW shore of L. Superior. Pop. 119,000. Shipping terminus of Great Lakes; exports grain, iron ore. Pulp and paper, flour milling industs. Formed (1970) after amalgamation of Fort William and Port Arthur.

thunderstorm, storm accompanied by thunder, lightning, and often violent gusts of wind, heavy rain or hail. Strong upward currents of moist, rapidly cooling air form deep *cumulonimbus* clouds which produce rain, static electricity.

Thurber, James [Grover] (1894-1961), American humorist. Known for elegant pieces for *New Yorker, eg* 'The Secret Life of Walter Mitty', illustrated by himself. Collections of work incl. *The Seal in the Bedroom* (1932), *Men, Women, and Dogs* (1943).

Thuringia, region of SW East Germany. Main towns Erfurt, Mühlhausen. Hilly, crossed NW-SE by Thuringian Forest; main rivers Saale, White Elster. Agric., esp. cereals, sugar beet. Divided (1485) into several duchies; part of German empire from 1871. East German prov. (1946-52).

Thyestes, in Greek myth, son of Pelops and brother of ATREUS. Seduced Atreus' wife, Aerope. Regained throne of Mycenae with help of his son AEGISTHUS.

thyme, any of genus *Thymus* of shrubby plants or aromatic herbs of mint family. White, pink or red flowers. Used for seasoning.

thymus gland, ductless gland-like body found in base of neck. Shrinks in size after puberty, becoming vestigial. Plays important role in development of infant's immune system.

thyroid gland, ductless gland in front of neck, consisting of 2 lobes on each side of trachea connected by thin tissue. Secretes iodine-containing hormone thyroxine which accelerates carbohydrate metabolism and release of energy.

Tiber (*Tevere*), river of C Italy. Flows 405 km (252 mi) from Tuscan Apennines via Rome to Tyrrhenian Sea.

Tiberias, Lake, *see* GALILEE, SEA OF.

Tiberius [Claudius Nero] (42 BC–AD 37), Roman emperor (AD 14-37). Succeeded his stepfather Augustus. Improved finances of the empire. Lived as tyrannical recluse in Capri towards end of life.

Tibesti Mountains, mountain range of Sahara desert, NC Africa, in N Chad and S Libya. Volcanic in origin, rise to Emi Koussi (3412 m/ 11,200 ft).

Tibet, auton. region of SW China. Area *c* 1,221,700 sq km (471,700 sq mi); pop. 1,700,000; cap. Lhasa. High plateau, *c* 4880 m (16,000 ft), lying between Kunlun Mts. in N and Himalayas in S. Agric. in Tsangpo valley; rough grazing. Largely unexploited mineral resources. Chief religion: Lamaism. Theocratic kingdom under Dalai Lama from 7th cent. Often claimed by China; absorbed 1950. Dalai Lama fled to India after suppression of 1959 revolt.

Ticino (Ger. *Tessin*), canton of S Switzerland. Area 2813 sq km (1086 sq mi); cap. Bellinzona. Mainly mountainous; lakes incl. Maggiore, Lugano. Tourism, vines, tobacco. Pop. is Italian-speaking, RC. Joined Swiss Confederation (1803). Source of **R. Ticino,** flows 257 km (160 mi) via L. Maggiore to R. Po near Pavia (Italy).

tick, parasitic wingless arachnid of order Acarina. Sucks blood of mammals, birds; spreads diseases, incl. forms of typhus.

tide, alternate rise and fall of surface of oceans, seas, bays and rivers. Caused by gravitational pull of Moon and Sun; level rises and falls twice per lunar day (24 hrs., 50 mins.). Spring tides occur when Moon and Sun act together, giving higher high tide, lower low tide; neap tides occur when they act in opposition, reducing amplitude.

Tien Shan, mountain range of C Asia, in Kirghiz SSR and Sinkiang auton. region, China. Reaches 7439 m (24,406 ft) at Mt. Pobeda.

Tientsin, city of NE China in Hopeh prov., admin. directly by central govt. Pop. 4,280,000. International port on Grand Canal and Hai Ho. Chemical, metallurgical, textile industs. Has Nankai Univ. (1919). Treaty port for French and British (1860); walls razed during Boxer Rebellion (1900). Japanese occupation 1937-43.

Tiepolo, Giovanni Battista (1696-1770), Italian painter. Leading exponent of Venetian rococo style, he is renowned for his fresco decorations.

Tierra del Fuego, archipelago of extreme S South America, separated from mainland by Magellan Str. Divided between Chile and Argentina. Main isl. consists of flat tableland (sheep, timber production). Cape Horn is in S. Frequent high winds and heavy rainfall on coast.

Tiflis, *see* TBILISI.

tiger, *Panthera tigris,* large lion-sized cat, widely distributed in Asia. Coat orange-yellow striped with black. Hunts at night.

tiger moth, any of Arctiidae family of moths with brightly striped or spotted wings. Larvae (woolly bears) are brown hairy caterpillars.

Tigris, river of SW Asia. Length *c* 1850 km (1150 mi). Rises in E Turkey, flows through Iraq, merges with Euphrates to form Shatt-al-Arab. Watered ancient Mesopotamia. Large flood control and irrigation scheme near Baghdad. Navigable to Baghdad for shallow draught vessels.

Tijuana, resort of NW Mexico, in Baja California. Pop. 536,000.

Tilburg, city of S Netherlands, in North Brabant. Pop. 214,000. Railway jct.; textile centre, dyeing.

till, *see* BOULDER CLAY.

Tilly, Jan Tserklaes, Count von (1559-1632), Flemish army officer. Commanded Catholic army in Thirty Years War. Died of wounds after defeat at the Lech (1632).

Tilsit, *see* SOVETSK.

Timbuktu (Fr. *Tombouctou*), town of C Mali, near R. Niger. Pop. 10,000. First settled 11th cent.; famous as centre of caravan trade routes, slave market. *Fl* 14th-16th cent. as Moslem commercial, educational centre. Taken by French (1893).

Timişoara (Hung. *Temesvár*), city of W Romania. Pop. 269,000. Railway jct., indust. centre; univ. (1945), 2 cathedrals. Former cap. of the Banat of Temesvár; annexed by Hungary, Turkey, Savoy; passed to Romania (1920).

Timor, isl. of Malay Archipelago, most E of Lesser Sundas. Indonesian Timor in W part of isl. forms prov. of E Nusa Tenggara. Area *c* 15,000 sq km (5700 sq mi); pop. 823,000. Passed to Indonesia from Dutch 1950. Former colony of **Portuguese Timor** comprised E half of isl. and an enclave on NW coast. Area *c* 19,000 sq km (7300 sq mi); pop. 610,000; cap. Dili (pop. 7000). Indonesian intervention in civil war (1975) led to its forcible annexation by Indonesia.

Timor Sea, arm of Indian Ocean between Timor and NW Australia.

Timothy grass

timothy grass, *Phleum pratense,* tall European grass with long cylindrical spikes. Grown in N US and Europe for hay.

Timothy, two epistles of NT, traditionally ascribed to St Paul. Prob. addressed to Timothy, bishop of Ephesus. Gives counsel on the safeguarding of Christian faith.

timpani, *see* DRUM.

tin (Sn), soft metallic element; at. no. 50, at. wt. 118.69. Exists in 3 allotropic forms; malleable, ductile, unaffected by water or air at normal temperatures. Occurs as cassiterite (SnO_2) in Bolivia and Malaysia. Used in tin plating and in alloys (solder, bronze, pewter).

Tintagel Head, cape of Cornwall, SW England. Tintagel Castle traditional birthplace of King Arthur. Has ruined Celtic monastery.

Tintoretto, real name Jacopo Robusti (1518-94), Venetian painter. Leading Venetian mannerist, his works are marked by brilliant brushwork and dramatic use of light and colour.

Tipperary, county of Munster prov., SC Irish Republic. Area 4255 sq km (1643 sq mi); co. town Clonmel. Mountains (Galty, Knockmealdowns); fertile Golden Vale. Admin. divisions North Riding (pop. 58,000), South Riding (pop. 75,000). Towns incl. **Tipperary,** pop. 5000.

Tippett, Sir Michael Kemp (1905-), English composer. Music combines appreciation of early English music and folk song with that of 20th-cent. advances. Works incl. *Fantasia Concertante on a Theme of Corelli,* oratorio *A Child of Our Time,* opera *The Midsummer Marriage.*

Tippoo Sahib (*c* 1750-99), Indian prince, sultan of Mysore (1782-99). Continued French-backed wars of father, Hyder Ali, against British; eventually defeated by Cornwallis at Travancore (1792). Killed when British stormed Seringapatam.

Tirana (*Tiranë*), cap. of Albania. Pop. 192,000. Cultural indust. (textiles, soap, flour) centre; univ. (1957). Founded by Turks (17th cent.); rebuilt as cap. 1920.

Tiresias, in Greek myth, Theban blinded by Hera and given long life and gift of prophecy by Zeus. Consulted by Odysseus; revealed truth about OEDIPUS and warned Creon of consequences of defiance of divine laws. Appears in many myths.

Tirol, *see* TYROL.

Tirpitz, Alfred von (1849-1930), German naval officer. As naval secretary (1897-1916), initiated the naval arms race in Europe and advocated unrestricted submarine warfare in WWI.

Tiryns, ancient town of Argolis, Greece. Occupied by Achaens *c* 2000 BC. Stronghold of MYCENAEAN CIVILIZATION.

tissue, in biology, an aggregate of cells similar in form, such as in nerve, connective, muscle and epithelial tissue in animals, and equivalents in plants.

Tisza (Ger. *Theiss*), river of C Europe. Flows *c* 980 km (610 mi) SW from Ukrainian Carpathians through Hungary to R. Danube in Yugoslavia.

tit or **titmouse,** any of Paridae family of small short-billed songbirds. Species incl. coal tit, *Parus ater,* and blue tit, *P. caeruleus.* Widely distributed.

Titanic, English passenger liner (46,000 tons). On maiden voyage, 14th April, 1912, struck iceberg in N Atlantic and sank with loss of 1513 lives of 2224 aboard. Disaster prompted stricter safety regulations.

titanium (Ti), metallic element resembling iron; at. no. 22, at. wt. 47.9. Compounds widely distributed in nature, but metal difficult to extract. Corrosion resistant, strong and light. Added to various steel alloys and used in aircraft and missiles because of heat-resisting properties.

Titans, in Greek myth, 6 sons and 6 daughters of Uranus and Gaea. Overthrew their father and ruled universe but defeated by OLYMPIAN GODS.

tithes, in Church of England, originally $\frac{1}{10}$th of produce of land paid by inhabitants of parish to support parish church and its incumbent. Commuted to cash payment (1836), abolished 1936.

Titian, real name Tiziano Vecellio (*c* 1487-1576), Venetian painter. Leading artist of High Renaissance, noted for dramatic use of colour. Worked for Emperor Charles V and Philip II of Spain. Developed esp. free handling of colour and form in late paintings. Works incl. religious subjects, portraits, and mythological subjects.

Titicaca, Lake, in WC South America, on Peru-Bolivia border. Area 8290 sq km (3200 sq mi). Drained by Desaguadero R. Highest lake in the world, alt. 3810 m (*c* 12,500 ft). Its ameliorating effect on temperature makes agric. possible.

Tito, Josip Broz (1892-1980), Yugoslav military and political leader, president (1953-80). Led partisan resistance to German occupation in WWII. Became premier of new Communist republic (1945). Withdrew Yugoslavia from Cominform (1948). Favoured policy of nonalignment, resisted Soviet attempts to reimpose hegemony. Sought to maintain national unity in face of Croatian separatists.

titration, process of finding out how much of a certain substance is contained in known volume of solution by measuring how much of a standard solution is required to produce a given reaction.

Titus, epistle of NT, traditionally ascribed to St Paul. Addressed to Titus, bishop in Crete, giving advice on church govt.

Titus [Flavius Sabinus Vespasianus] (AD 39-81), Roman emperor (79-81), son of Vespasian. Captured Jerusalem (70).

Tivoli (anc. *Tibur*), town of Latium, C Italy, on R. Aniene. Pop. 34,000. H.e.p. from nearby waterfalls. Ruins of Hadrian's villa; Villa d'Este (16th cent.).

Tiw or **Tyr,** in Teutonic myth, god of war and athletic events.

TNT or **trinitrotoluene,** high explosive solid, prepared by action of sulphuric and nitric acids on toluene.

toad, tailless amphibian, esp. of genus *Bufo*. Frog-like, but with drier, warty skin, from which it secretes noxious white fluid. Largely terrestrial, lays eggs in water.

toadflax or **butter-and-eggs,** any of genus *Linaria* of European herbs. Esp. *L. vulgaris* with yellow and orange flowers.

toadstool, *see* FUNGUS.

tobacco, any of genus *Nicotiana* of tropical American plants of nightshade family. Now widely cultivated esp. in US, India, China and USSR. Large, sticky leaves, white, greenish or purple flowers. Dried and cured leaves of *N. tabacum* may be rolled into cigars, shredded for cigarettes and pipes, processed for chewing, powdered for snuff.

Tobago, *see* TRINIDAD AND TOBAGO.

tobogganing, sport of sliding down ice-covered slopes on small sleds. Perfected in Switzerland in 1880s using specially prepared runs, *eg* Cresta at St Moritz.

Tobruk, town of NE Cyrenaica, Libya, on Mediterranean Sea. Pop. 28,000. Supply base in WWII; scene of heavy fighting, taken by British 1942.

Tocantins, river of C Brazil. Flows N 2640 km (1640 mi) from E plateau to join Pará R. near Belém.

Tocqueville, [Charles] Alexis de (1805-59), French writer, politician. Wrote *Democracy in America* (1835), in which he foresaw triumph of democracy and social equality in Europe.

Todd, Alexander Robertus, Baron (1907-), Scottish biochemist. Awarded Nobel Prize for Chemistry (1957) for work on structure and synthesis of nucleotides, important contribution in determining structure and function of nucleic acids.

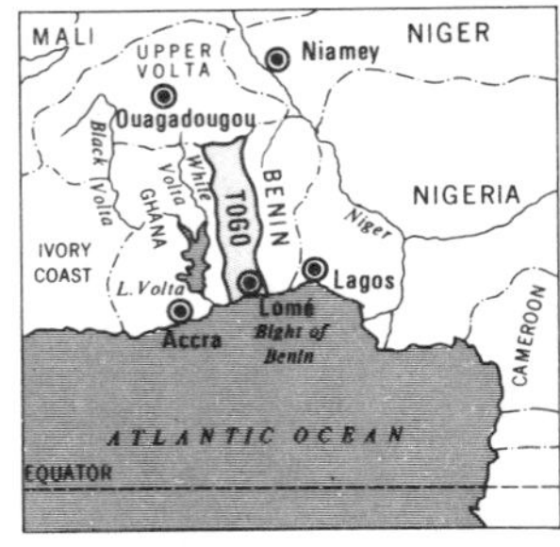

Togo

Togo, republic of W Africa. Area 57,000 sq km (22,000 sq mi); pop. 2,409,000; cap. Lomé. Official language: French. Religions: animist, RC. Tropical forest in N, savannah in S. Exports cacao, coffee, copra, phosphates. Formerly French Togoland, formed (1922) from part of former German protect. of Togoland under League of Nations mandate. Independent 1960.

Togoland, British; French, *see* GHANA; TOGO.

Tojo, Hideki or **Eike** (1884-1948), Japanese military, political leader. Premier (1941-4), provoked US entry into WWII by bombing of Pearl Harbor (Dec. 1941); resigned after sustained losses. Hanged as war criminal.

Tokaj or **Tokay,** town of NE Hungary on R. Tisza. Pop. 5000. Centre of vine-growing area, producing famous Tokay wine.

Tokyo, cap. of Japan, port on Tokyo Bay, SE Honshu isl. Pop. 8,592,000; incl. suburbs, 11,684,000. Major commercial, mfg., indust. centre. Founded 12th cent. as Edo, became cap. of Tokugawa shogunate. Replaced Kyoto as imperial cap. 1868 and renamed as Tokyo ('Eastern Capital'). Rebuilt after extensive damage from 1923 earthquake and bombing in WWII. Site of imperial palace and 4 univs.

Toledo, city of C Spain, on granite hill above R. Tagus, cap. of Toledo prov. Pop. 44,000.

Famous from Moorish times for swords, steel; textile mfg. Seat of Spanish primate. Cap. of Visigothic kingdom from 6th cent., *fl* under Moors from 712. Taken by Castile 1085, cap. of Spain until 1561. Cathedral (13th cent.); home of El Greco.

Toledo, port of NE Ohio, US; at W end of L. Erie. Pop. 779,000. Commercial, indust. centre; exports coal, oil, agric. produce.

Tolkien, J[ohn] R[onald] R[euel] (1892-1973), English author, philologist, b. South Africa. Known for complex fantasies *The Hobbit* (1937), *The Lord of the Rings* (3 vol. 1954-5) using knowledge of Germanic, Celtic myths and language.

Tolpuddle, village of Dorset, S England. 'Tolpuddle Martyrs' were agric. labourers transported for forming a trade union (1834). Public protest forced pardon (1836).

Tolstoy, Leo Nikolayevich, Count (1828-1910), Russian author. Advocated social reform, passivity in opposition to evil forces. In later life evolved own theology of universal love, mysticism, personal deity. Best known for great realistic novels, *eg War and Peace* (1865-9), *Anna Karenina* (1875-7). Also wrote plays, short stories, essays.

Toltec, hist. (*c* 6th-13th cent.) civilization of Mexico. Noted as skilled metal and stoneworkers. Religion centred on deified hero, Quetzalcoatl. Southern expansion (11th-13th cent.) led to domination of MAYA, but eventually supplanted by Aztecs.

toluene (C_7H_8), liquid hydrocarbon of benzene series. Obtained by distillation of coal tar or from petroleum. Used as solvent and in TNT, dyes, *etc.*

tomato, *Lycopersicon esculentum,* annual plant of nightshade family. Native to tropical America but widely cultivated for edible, red or yellow, pulpy fruit. Introduced into Europe in 16th cent.

Tombouctou, *see* TIMBUKTU.

Tomsk, city of USSR, WC Siberian RSFSR; on R. Tom. Pop. 421,000. Engineering, electrical equipment mfg. Cultural centre; univ. (1888). Founded 1604; developed in 19th cent. with discovery of gold.

ton, unit of weight, in UK equal to 2240 pounds, in US 2000 pounds. **Metric ton** or **tonne** is equal to 1000 kg.

Tone, [Theobald] Wolfe (1763-98), Irish nationalist. A founder of society of United Irishmen (1791). Enlisted French aid to invade Ireland and set up independent republic. Captured by British, convicted of treason. Committed suicide.

tone poem or **symphonic poem,** musical composition characteristic of Romantic period, intended as interpretation of literary, dramatic and pictorial elements. Introduced by Liszt.

Tonga or **Friendly Islands,** kingdom of S Pacific Ocean, comprising Tongatabu, Vavau, Haapai isl. groups. Area 675 sq km (260 sq mi); pop. 93,000; cap. Nuku'alofa. Exports copra, fruit. Discovered (1616) by Dutch; named Friendly Isls. by Cook (1773). Under British protection from 1900, independent 1970. Member of British Commonwealth.

tongue, muscular organ attached to floor of mouth in most vertebrates. Covered by mucous membrane in which the taste buds are embedded. Minute projections (papillae) give it rough texture. Used in mastication and swallowing and, in man, articulation of speech.

tonic sol-fa, in music, notation system designed to simplify sight-reading. Notes are *doh, ray, me, fah, soh, lah, te, doh,* indicating position in major scale relative to a given key note.

Tonkin, hist. region of North Vietnam. Area *c* 103,600 sq km (40,000 sq mi). Became French protect. of Union of Indo-China in 1887. With parts of ANNAM formed North Vietnam after 1954.

Tonkin, Gulf of, arm of South China Sea bounded by S China and North Vietnam. Here, in 1964, an alleged attack by North Vietnamese torpedo boats on 2 US destroyers precipitated increased US involvement in Vietnam War.

Tonlé Sap, lake of C Cambodia. Expands from *c* 2850 sq km (1100 sq mi) to *c* 10,360 sq km (4000 sq mi) in wet season. Important fisheries.

tonsil, mass of lymphoid tissue on each side of throat at back of mouth. Tonsillitis is an inflammation of tonsils, usually by streptococci; occurs mostly in childhood.

Toowoomba, city of SE Queensland, Australia. Pop. 64,000. Road and rail jct., trade centre for Darling Downs agric. region; food processing, agric. machinery.

topaz, hard, colourless to yellow mineral; consists of silicate of aluminium and fluorine. Found among acid igneous rocks. Yellow variety used as a gem.

Topeka, cap. of Kansas, US; on Kansas R. Pop. 178,000. Commercial, indust. centre; wheat, cattle shipping; tyre mfg., railway engineering, printing.

topology, mathematical study of surface features which remain unchanged under continuous transformations; it is concerned with structure, rather than size.

Torah, *see* PENTATEUCH.

Torbay, resort town of Devon, SW England. Pop. 109,000. Created 1968 from Torquay, Paignton, Brixham.

Torino, *see* TURIN.

tornado, funnel-shaped, rotating column of air extending downward from *cumulonimbus* cloud. Travels at 30-66 kph (20-40 mph); small in area but destructive. Common E of Rocky Mts., US, and Australia.

Toronto, prov. cap. of Ontario, Canada; on N shore of L. Ontario at mouth of Humber R. Pop. 2,803,000. Natural harbour. Important transport, commercial, education centre. Food processing, printing and publishing, railway industs. Supplied with h.e.p. from Niagara Falls. Founded by French as fort 1749; called York 1793-1834. Has famous City Hall; Univ. (1843).

torpedo, name given to various electric rays

of genus *Torpedo*. Commonest Atlantic species is *T. nobiliana*.

torpedo, underwater explosive missile first developed by Robert Whitehead (1866). Early types were propelled by compressed air or electric motor, later by jet engines with sophisticated guidance systems. Fired from ship, submarine, aircraft.

Torquay, *see* TORBAY.

Torquemada, Tomás de (1420-98), Spanish monk. Appointed (1483) inquisitor general of Castile and Aragón. Responsible for expulsion of Jews from Spain (1492). Notorious for cruelty during INQUISITION.

Torres Strait, channel between S New Guinea and Cape York Penin., NE Australia. Width *c* 130 km (80 mi).

Tôrres Vedras, town of W Portugal. Pop. 6000. Medieval fortress, royal residence. Centre of Wellington's defence lines in Peninsular War.

Torricelli, Evangelista (1608-47), Italian physicist, mathematician. Invented principle of barometer, using mercury-filled tube, and demonstrated existence of air pressure with it. Obtained 1st man-made vacuum by means of his barometer.

tortoise, name given to various land-dwelling turtles, esp. of genus *Testudo*. Widely distributed in warm regions, may hibernate in cool climates; herbivorous. Giant tortoises live up to 150 years.

Toruń (Ger. *Thorn*), city of NC Poland, on R. Vistula. Pop. 150,000. Railway jct., river port; engineering. Founded 1231 by Teutonic Knights; Hanseatic League member. Under Prussian rule 1793-1919. Birthplace of Copernicus.

Tory Party, British political organization. Began (*c* 1680) as group supporting James II. Discredited for pro-Jacobite leanings after accession of George I, spent much of 18th cent. in opposition to Whigs. Traditionally favoured continued influence of Crown and Church of England; supported by country gentry. Revived under younger Pitt, held almost unbroken power until 1830. Evolved into CONSERVATIVE PARTY in 1830s.

Toscana, *see* TUSCANY.

Toscanini, Arturo (1867-1957), Italian conductor. Became musical director at La Scala, Milan (1898), principal conductor of Metropolitan Opera, New York (1908). Also conducted New York Philharmonic and NBC Symphony orchestras.

Tostig, *see* HAROLD.

total internal reflection, in optics, reflection of light ray incident at boundary with medium in which it travels faster. Occurs when angle of refraction predicted by Snell's law exceeds 90°.

totalitarianism, system of absolute govt., in which social and economic activity of state organized hierarchically to eliminate opposition. Highly centralized govt. controlled by single official party. Doctrine usually appeals to nationalist and socialist sentiment. Extreme modern examples incl. Stalinist USSR and Nazi Germany.

totemism, belief of tribe or clan that its distinctive bond is symbolized by a particular animal or plant. This symbol may be represented in tattoos, carvings, *eg* in totem poles of certain North American Indian tribes. Also occurs in Melanesia, Australia.

toucan, any of Ramphastidae family of fruit-eating birds, found in tropical American forests. Black body with bright throat; extremely long brightly coloured beak.

touch-me-not, any of genus *Impatiens* of Eurasian annual plants, esp. *I. noli-me-tangere*. When ripe, pods burst on being touched, scattering seeds.

touchstone, hard, black, fine-grained stone, usually basalt or chert. Formerly used to determine purity of gold, silver from streaks left on it when rubbed with metal.

Toulon, city of Provence, SE France, on Mediterranean Sea. Pop. 379,000. Port, shipbuilding, armaments mfg. Major naval base from 17th cent.; French fleet scuttled here (1942). Fortifications, Gothic church.

Toulouse, city of Languedoc, S France, on R Garonne. Cap. of Haute-Garonne dept. Pop. 495,000. Agric. trade centre, aeronautics indust., univ. (1230). Cap. of Visigoths; countship from 9th cent. Centre of medieval Provençal culture. Plundered during Albigensian Crusade; part of France from 1271. Romanesque church (11th cent.), Gothic cathedral (13th cent.).

Toulouse-Lautrec, Henri Raymond de (1864-1901), French artist. Influenced by Degas and Japanese prints, he painted scenes from cabarets, music halls, circuses, *etc.* Famous for his posters.

Touraine, region and former prov. of WC France, hist. cap. Tours. Fertile 'garden of France' (wine and fruit growing) drained by Loire, Indre, Cher. Many châteaux (15th-17th cent.). Under counts of Anjou from 11th cent., passed to France 1204.

Tourcoing, town of Nord, N France. Pop. 102,000. Textile centre (esp. woollens, carpets). Forms conurbation with Lille, Roubaix.

tourmaline, crystalline mineral, consisting of complex silicate of boron and aluminium. Usually black, gem forms are blue, green, yellow; found among granites, gneiss, schist.

Tournai (Flem. *Doornik*), town of W Belgium, on R. Scheldt. Pop. 70,000. Textiles, carpets. Cathedral (11th cent.).

Tours, city of WC France, on R. Loire, cap. of Indre-et-Loire dept. Pop. 235,000. Agric. market for Touraine; wine, brandy trade. Medieval centre of learning, silk indust. Gothic cathedral (12th cent.). Nearby Charles Martel defeated Moors (732).

Toussaint L'Ouverture, François Dominique (*c* 1744-1803), Haitian revolutionary. Born a slave, he led successful Negro revolt to free slaves (1791-3). Drove British and Spanish from Haiti; achieved complete control of isl. by 1801. Captured by French forces sent to reintroduce slavery; died in prison in France.

Tower Hamlets, bor. of EC Greater London, England. Pop. 149,000. Created 1965 from met. bors., Bethnal Green, Poplar, Stepney.

Tower of London, fortress in London, England, on N bank of R. Thames. Oldest part, the Keep or White Tower, built 1078. Formerly used as royal residence and state prison, now an armoury and museum. British Crown Jewels on display.

Townshend, Charles Townshend, 2nd Viscount (1674-1738), English statesman. Whig secretary of state for northern dept. (1715-16), quelled Jacobite uprising (1715). Reappointed (1721-30). Devoted himself to experimental agric. in retirement (hence nickname 'Turnip' Townshend).

Townsville, city of NE Queensland, Australia, on Cleveland Bay. Pop. 88,000. Port, serving agric., mining hinterland; meat processing, copper refining; tourist resort. Has James Cook Univ. (1970).

toxaemia, *see* BLOOD POISONING.

toxin, name applied to various unstable poisonous proteins formed by bacteria, which cause diseases such as botulism and tetanus. Name also applied to various similar poisons produced by plants or animals, *eg* cobra venom.

Toynbee, Arnold (1852-83), English reformer, historian. Worked among the poor of London; 1st social settlement, Toynbee Hall, in E London, named after him. His nephew, **Arnold Joseph Toynbee** (1889-1975), was also historian. Wrote *A Study of History* (1934-54), rejecting determinism and attempting to analyse rise and fall of civilizations.

Trabzon or **Trebizond,** port of NE Turkey, on Black Sea. Pop. 81,000. Exports tobacco, nuts. Founded as Greek colony (8th cent. BC). Cap. of Greek empire of Trebizond (1204-1461) until capture by Ottomans.

trace element, chemical element essential in plant and animal nutrition, but only in minute quantities, *eg* iron, copper, zinc. Some are constituents of vitamins, hormones and enzymes.

tracery, ornamental stonework in upper part of window or panel; sometimes used decoratively in vaults and arches. Characteristic of Gothic architecture.

trachea or **windpipe,** tube extending from larynx to its division into the 2 main bronchi. Strengthened by rings of cartilage and muscle.

Tractarianism, *see* OXFORD MOVEMENT.

Tracy, Spencer (1900-1967), American film actor. Known for tough, often humorous roles, *eg The Power and the Glory* (1933), *Adam's Rib* (1949), *Guess Who's Coming to Dinner* (1967).

Trades Union Congress (TUC), voluntary organization of British trade unions. Estab. 1868. Delegates meet annually, elect General Council to negotiate with govt., international labour bodies.

trade union, *see* UNION, LABOUR.

trade winds, winds blowing constantly from subtropical high pressure belts (25°-30°N and S) to equatorial low pressure belt (doldrums). Blow from NE in N hemisphere, from SE in S hemisphere.

Trafalgar, Cape, headland of Cádiz prov., SW Spain, on Str. of Gibraltar. Scene of naval battle (1805) in which French and Spanish were defeated by English under Nelson, who was killed.

Greek tragic mask

tragedy, dramatic form defined by Aristotle as a representation of events in which hero of stature brings unforeseen disaster on himself by error, not accident or wickedness. Evolved by Greeks in 6th cent. BC from religious ritual, reached peak in hands of Aeschylus, Sophocles, Euripides. Other conventions, *eg* violence, revenge, ghosts, transmitted by Seneca, influenced development of English tragedies, *eg* those by Marlowe, Shakespeare. French tragedy, constrained by unities of time, place and action, as in plays of Corneille, Racine. Modern tragedy much looser category. Concerned more with ordinary people, who may still display heroic attributes in conflicts, *eg* those of Ibsen, or may be 'anti-heroes', part of meaninglessness, *etc,* of life, as in Miller's *Death of a Salesman.*

Trajan, full name Marcus Ulpius Trajanus (AD *c* 53-117), Roman emperor (98-117), b. Spain. His conquest of Dacia (106) is commemorated by Trajan's Column in Rome (114). Built Forum of Trajan in Rome.

Tralee, co. town of Kerry, SW Irish Republic, on R. Lee. Pop. 15,000. Agric. market; tourism. Tralee Bay nearby.

tranquillizer, drug used to calm the emotions. Distinct from sedative in that it does not induce sleep. Those used incl. meprobamate, chlorpromazine, rauwolfia.

transcendence, *see* IMMANENCE.

transcendentalism, in philosophy, mode of thought emphasizing intuitive and spiritual perception beyond mundane thought or experience. First associated with Kant. Developed in US by Emerson, Thoreau.

transducer, device used to transform energy from one form into another, *eg* loudspeaker or electric generator.

transformer, device used to change voltage of alternating current without changing its frequency. Consists of 2 coils of insulated wire wound on an iron core; current is induced in one coil by variation of magnetic field resulting from current flow in other coil. Ratio of voltages in coils is roughly equal to ratio of number of turns of wire in coils.

transistor, electronic semiconductor device used to amplify voltage and current. Invented 1948, it is smaller, requires less power and has a longer life than equivalent thermionic valve.

Transjordania, *see* JORDAN.

Transkei, Bantu homeland of South Africa, between R. Great Kei and Natal. Area 42,750 sq km (16,500 sq mi); pop. 1,751,000; cap. Umtata. Stock rearing; labour source for Witwatersrand mines. Separated from Cape Prov. 1963; autonomous state 1976.

transmigration of souls, passing of soul into another body on death. *See* REINCARNATION.

transpiration, loss of water by evaporation from leaves of green plants. Promotes ascent of SAP from roots of plant allowing intake of water and minerals.

transplantation, in surgery, transfer of tissue or organs from one subject to another. Grafting usually refers to tissue transplants from one part of same subject's body to another. Main problem in transplantation is rejection of foreign tissue by action of antibodies. First human kidney transplant was performed 1950, first heart transplant 1967.

Trans-Siberian Railway, line in USSR from Leningrad to Vladivostok on Pacific coast. Serves Moscow, Omsk, Novosibirsk, Irkutsk. Length 6500 km (4000 mi). Begun 1891, completed 1905; originally passed through Manchuria; now entirely in USSR. Crucial to development of Siberia.

transubstantiation, *see* EUCHARIST.

transuranic elements, chemical elements with atomic number greater than 92 (that of uranium). Such elements are radioactive and do not normally occur naturally; prepared by nuclear reactions.

Transvaal, prov. of NE South Africa. Area 286,000 sq km (110,500 sq mi); pop. 8,717,000; cap. Pretoria. Mainly high veld, lies between R. Limpopo (N), R. Vaal (S). Produces grain, fruit; great mineral wealth, esp. in WITWATERSRAND. Boer state estab. 1837 after Great Trek; became South African Republic 1856. Discovery of gold (1886) led to influx of British prospectors, resulting in Boer War (1899-1902). UK colony from 1902; prov. of Union of South Africa from 1910.

Transylvania, region and former prov. of N Romania. Main towns Cluj, Brasov. Mainly forested plateau *c* 450 m (1500 ft) high, crossed by R. Mureş. Incl. S Carpathians, known as Transylvanian Alps, rising to *c* 2530 m (8300 ft). Part of Roman *Dacia*; independent (1526-1699). Pop. Romanian, Magyar, German.

trapdoor spider, spider, esp. of Ctenizidae family, which makes silk-lined burrow with tight-fitting hinged lid.

Trappists, in RC church, order of CISTERCIANS of the Stricter Observance. Founded (17th cent.) at La Trappe, France. Monks observe silence, are vegetarian.

Trasimeno, Lake, largest lake of central Italy, in Umbria. Area 130 sq km (50 sq mi). On N shore Hannibal defeated Romans under Flaminius (217 BC).

travel sickness, *see* MOTION SICKNESS.

treacle, *see* MOLASSES.

treason, crime of attacking safety of sovereign state or its head. In UK, Statute of Treasons (1351) distinguished high treason (*eg* killing king, king's law officers, making war on realm) and petty treason (killing one's superior, *eg* master, husband). Reforms in 19th cent. incl. abolition of petty treason. Now punishable by death or life imprisonment in US, UK.

treasury, dept. of state or nation controlling revenue, taxation, public finances. In UK, concerned with major aspects of fiscal policy, esp. annual BUDGET; does not directly admin. revenue. Main function that of controlling govt. expenditure. Effective chief is chancellor of exchequer.

Trebizond, *see* TRABZON.

treble, in singing, unbroken voice of boy, similar in range to soprano.

tree, perennial plant with permanent woody, self-supporting main stem or trunk. Usually grows to greater height than shrub, developing branches and foliage. May be either deciduous, with leaves shed at end of growing season, or evergreen.

tree creeper, small insectivorous bird esp. of Certhiidae family. Long slender curved bill, long tongue; uses sharp claws to climb trees. Species incl. common tree creeper, *Certhia familiaris,* of Europe and North America.

tree fern, any of various tropical ferns with tree-like trunk, esp. of genera *Cyathea, Alsophila* and *Hemitelia.*

tree shrew, any of Tupaiidae family of squirrel-like primates, found in forests of SE Asia. Solitary, nocturnal.

trefoil, any of various plants with leaves divided into 3 leaflets, *eg* CLOVER and similar plants of genus *Lotus* of Leguminosae family.

Trek, Great, migration from Cape Colony, South Africa (1835-6) of Boer farmers. In protest against British rule, they moved N to found Transvaal and Orange Free State.

Trematoda, *see* FLUKE.

Trenchard, Hugh Montague Trenchard, 1st Viscount (1873-1956), British air force officer. First commander of Royal Flying Corps in WWI. As chief of air staff (1918-29), shaped offensive strategy used in WWII.

Trent, river of C England. Flows 274 km (170 mi) from Staffordshire via Stoke, Nottingham, to join R. Ouse in forming Humber.

Trent, Council of (1545-63), ecumenical

COUNCIL convened by Pope Paul III, continued under Julius III and Pius IV. Discussed concessions to restore religious peace after Reformation. Council defined RC doctrine and discipline; effected reform of many ecclesiastic abuses.

Trentino-Alto Adige, region of NE Italy, bordering Austria and Switzerland. Incl. part of Tyrolean Alps, Dolomites; main river Adige. Main towns Trento, Bolzano. Forestry, h.e.p., tourism. Alto Adige largely German-speaking. Ceded by Austria 1919.

Trento (Eng. *Trent*), town of Trentino-Alto Adige, NE Italy, on R. Adige. Cap. of Trento prov. Pop. 95,000. Scene of Council of Trent. Held by Austria 1803-1919.

Trenton, cap. of New Jersey; on Delaware R. Pop. 97,000. Metal products, cable, rope, pottery mfg. Settled by Quakers (1679). Scene of Revolution battle in which Washington defeated British (1776).

Trevelyan, Sir George Otto (1838-1928), English historian, politician. Wrote *American Revolution* (1907), *George III and Charles Fox* (1912), also biog. of his uncle, Lord Macaulay. His son, **George Macaulay Trevelyan** (1876-1962), wrote *British History in the Nineteenth Century* (1922), *English Social History* (1944).

Trèves, *see* TRIER.

Trevithick, Richard (1771-1833), English engineer. Designed high-pressure steam engine (1800) for use in mines. Built (1804) 1st steam locomotive to run on rails.

Trianon, Treaty of (1920), post-WWI peace treaty between Hungary and Allies. Large amounts of Hungarian territ. ceded to Romania, Yugoslavia, Czechoslovakia, Austria; size of army reduced.

Triassic period, first geological period of Mesozoic era; began *c* 225 million years ago, lasted *c* 30 million years. Extensive arid or semi-arid areas; conifers, ferns, tree ferns. Typified by ammonites, crinoids, lamellibranchs; earliest mammals, dinosaurs. Also *see* GEOLOGICAL TABLE.

tribune, name assigned to various officers of ancient Rome. Tribunes of plebs were elected defenders of the plebeians' rights. Office was begun in 494 BC and its influence was extended (*c* 130 BC) by the Gracchi.

triceratops, genus of extinct vegetarian dinosaurs of Ceratopsia group. Had two horns on brow, one on nose; neck protected by large bony frill. Length *c* 6 m (20 ft). Lived in late Cretaceous period.

trichina, *Trichinella spiralis,* parasitic nematode worm often transmitted to man. Reproduces in intestine; larvae may migrate to muscles, forming cysts. Cause of disease trichinosis, characterized by fever, muscular pains, *etc.*

Trier (Fr. *Trèves*), city of W West Germany, on R. Moselle. Pop. 103,000. Wine trade, textile mfg., tourist centre. Roman remains incl. amphitheatre, gate Porta Nigra; cathedral has 'Holy Coat' of Christ; univ. (1473-1797). Badly damaged in WWII.

Trieste (Slav *Trust*), city of NE Italy, on Gulf of Venice, cap. of Friuli-Venezia Giulia and of Trieste prov. Pop. 265,000. Port from Roman times, shipbuilding, oil refining. Held by Austria (1382-1918), as free port from 1719; passed to Italy 1918. Created Free Territ. 1947; city passed (1954) to Italy, environs to Yugoslavia.

trigonometry, branch of mathematics which deals with relations between sides and angles of a triangle. Trigonometric functions, sine, cosine and tangent, express ratios of different sides of right-angled triangle. Applied in navigation, astronomy.

trilobite, any of class Trilobita of extinct marine arthropods. Flattened oval body divided into 3 segments; fossils found in Cambrian rocks.

Trim, co. town of Meath, E Irish Republic, on R. Boyne. Pop. 2000. Has 12th-cent. castle.

Trinidad and Tobago, republic of SE West Indies, member of British Commonwealth. Area 5129 sq km (1980 sq mi); pop. 1,133,000; cap. Port of Spain. Language: English. Religions: Protestant, RC. Hilly in interior; tropical climate. Agric. crops incl. sugar cane, coconuts, citrus fruits. Important asphalt, oil refining industs. Trinidad discovered by Columbus (1498); ceded to Britain (1802). Joined by Tobago in British crown colony (1888). Independent 1962; republic from 1976.

Trinity, in Christianity, three aspects of divine being, *ie* God the Father, Son (incarnate in Jesus), Holy Ghost. Doctrine asserted early, estab. in Nicene Creed.

triode, thermionic valve containing 3 electrodes: cathode, anode and control grid.

Triple Alliance, formed 1882 when Italy joined Germany and Austria-Hungary (united by Dual Alliance of 1879). Growing conflict of interest with other European states (*see* TRIPLE ENTENTE) increased diplomatic tension before WWI.

Triple Entente, diplomatic accord between France, Russia and Britain. Grew out of concern over German commercial, naval and colonial expansion, and alliance of C European powers. Dual Alliance between Russia and France announced 1895. Britain entered informal alliance with France (Entente Cordiale) by 1904 and negotiated alliance with Russia in 1907.

Tripoli (Arab. *Tarabulus*), port of N Lebanon, on Mediterranean. Pop. 175,000. Oil refining; terminus of pipeline from Iraq. Founded *c* 700 BC; cap. of Phoenician federation of Tyre, Sidon and Aradus.

Tripoli, cap. of Libya, on Mediterranean Sea. Pop. 551,000. Admin. centre; port, exports oil, hides, dates, sponges. Founded 7th cent. BC by Phoenicians. Under Turkish rule from 16th cent., stronghold of Barbary pirates. Cap. of Italian colony of Libya (1911-43). Ruins of Roman city *Leptis Magna* nearby.

Tripolitania, region of NW Libya. Fertile coastal strip, interior desert; grain, fruit growing, stock rearing. Name derived from 3 Phoenician cities founded 7th cent.

BC. Under Turkish rule from 16th cent.; colonized by Italy 1911-43. Federal prov. (cap. Tripoli) 1951-63.

Tripura, state of NE India. Area *c* 10,450 sq km (4030 sq mi); pop. 1,557,000; cap. Agartala. Hilly, dense jungle; timber, rice, jute. Became union territ. 1956, state 1972.

Tristan and Isolde or **Tristram and Yseult,** medieval legend of Celtic origin. Tells of Tristan's journey to Ireland to bring Princess Isolde to Cornwall as bride of uncle, King Mark. While returning, pair drink love potion which causes irresistible, eternal love, leading to death of both. Theme of many French romances, combined with ARTHURIAN LEGEND. Used by Tennyson (*Idylls of the King,* 1859-85), Wagner (*Tristan and Isolde.*).

Tristan da Cunha, small group of isls. in S Atlantic, dependency of St Helena since 1938. Only inhabited isl. is Tristan (pop. *c* 280), formed by volcano rising to 2060 m (6760 ft); eruption in 1961 led to temporary evacuation of pop.

tritium, radioactive isotope of hydrogen, with mass no. 3. Found in minute quantities in natural hydrogen; can be produced from lithium in nuclear reactions. Used as radioactive tracer and in hydrogen bombs.

Triton, in Greek myth, son of Poseidon and Amphitrite. Represented as fish-shaped from waist down, blowing conch shell to calm waves.

Triumvirate, term applied in ancient Rome to govt. carried out by 3 men. First Triumvirate formed by Julius Caesar, Pompey and Crassus (60 BC), Second Triumvirate (43 BC) by Octavian, Mark Antony and Lepidus.

Trivandrum, cap. of Kerala state, S India. Pop. 410,000. Port on Arabian Sea. Coconut products, textile mfg.

Trois Rivières or **Three Rivers,** town of S Québec, Canada; at confluence of St Maurice and St Lawrence rivers. Pop. 56,000. Important newsprint, iron and steel indust. Founded 1634.

Trojan War, in Greek legend, war waged for 10 years by the Greeks on the Trojans to recover HELEN, wife of MENELAUS, abducted by PARIS. Gods fought for both sides. Major events in the war incl.: quarrel between ACHILLES and AGAMEMNON; Achilles' refusal to fight; death of Achilles' friend Patroclus, Achilles' return to war and death of HECTOR; death of Achilles at hands of Paris; summoning by Greeks of NEOPTOLEMUS and Philoctetes, who slew Paris. Finally, Greeks simulated departure, leaving a huge wooden effigy of a horse outside gates of Troy. Despite warnings by CASSANDRA and LAOCOON, Trojans brought it into city, enabling Greek soldiers hidden inside it to open the gates to their army and destroy the city. War is subject of Homer's ILIAD.

Trollope, Anthony (1815-82), English novelist. Known for 'Barsetshire Chronicles' incl. *Barchester Towers* (1857), depicting clerical life in imaginary English county. Also wrote political novel series, 'The Pallisers'.

trombone, brass musical instrument, formerly called sackbut. Known from 15th cent. Fitted with sliding tube which controls pitch or valves. Orchestras today usually have 1 bass and 2 tenor trombones.

Tromp, Maarten Harpertszoon (1597-1653), Dutch naval officer. Defeated Spanish fleet at Downs (1639). Won several skirmishes with English under Blake in the Channel (1652-3), but was finally defeated and killed. His son, **Cornelis Tromp** (1629-91), commanded fleets in 2nd and 3rd Dutch Wars.

Tromsö, town of NW Norway, on Tromsöy Isl. Pop. 45,000. Fishing, sealing industs. Largest town N of Arctic Circle.

Trondheim, town of WC Norway, on Trondheim Fjord. Pop. 135,000. Port, fishing, shipbuilding. Founded as Nidaros (996), cap. to 1380. Cathedral (11th cent.).

tropism, natural movement of plants in response to external stimuli, *eg* a sunflower turning to face the light exhibits positive phototropism.

troposphere, lowest layer of Earth's ATMOSPHERE. Extends to *c* 9.5 km (6 mi) above surface. Temperature falls with increasing height; turbulent layer, containing much water vapour, dust. Separated from stratosphere by tropopause.

Trotsky, Leon, orig. Lev Davidovich Bronstein (1879-1940), Russian revolutionary. In exile for Marxist activities before 1917 Revolution. Organized Red Army during civil war (1918-20). After Lenin's death (1924), led opposition to Stalin; expelled from Communist Party (1927), exiled 1929. Founded Communist Fourth INTERNATIONAL (1937). Assassinated in Mexico City, prob. at Stalin's instigation. His political followers (Trotskyists) maintain his policy of continuing world revolution.

trotting, *see* HORSE RACING.

troubadours, poets of 11th-13th cent., who created first cultivated vernacular lyric poetry in Europe. Carefully stylized, poems were written in *langue d'oc* (Provençal). Subjects were love and chivalry. Poems spoken to musical accompaniment.

trout, game and food fish of salmon family, esp. of genera *Salmo* and *Salvelinus.* Found mainly in fresh water, but some varieties migrate to sea to feed. Species incl. European trout *Salmo trutta* (brown trout, sea trout, lake trout are subspecies), N American rainbow trout *S. gairdneri.*

Troy (*Ilium*), ancient city of Asia Minor, in NW Turkey, near mouth of Dardanelles. Excavations by Schliemann (1871-82) revealed 9 city levels; Homer's Troy, *c* 1200 BC, believed to lie at 7th level. *See* TROJAN WAR.

Troyes, town of NE France, on R. Seine, cap. of Aube dept. Pop. 128,000. Road and railway jct., textile and hosiery mfg. Cap. of Champagne from 11th cent. Gothic cathedral (13th cent.).

Trst, *see* TRIESTE.

Trucial States, *see* UNITED ARAB EMIRATES.

Trudeau, Pierre Elliott (1919-), Canadian statesman, Liberal PM (1968-79, 1980-). Ardent federalist, term marked by rise of Parti Québecois, attempts to patriate BRITISH NORTH AMERICA ACT.

truffle, any of genus *Tuber* of European edible fungi. Regarded as great delicacy.

Trujillo Molina, Rafael Leonidas (1891-1961), Dominican political leader, president (1930-8, 1942-52). Used autocratic, repressive measures to improve material welfare of country. Assassinated.

Truman, Harry S. (1884-1972), American statesman, president (1945-53). Democratic vice-president, took office at death of F.D. Roosevelt. Authorized use of 1st atomic bomb (1945) against Japan. Implemented Marshall Plan to aid recovery of post-war Europe and 'Truman Doctrine' of containing Communist expansion. 2nd term dominated by KOREAN WAR.

trumpet, brass wind instrument. A long cylindrical tube bent twice on itself, opening out into bell. Played with cup mouthpiece. Modern trumpet has 3 valves.

Truro, admin. hq. of Cornwall, SW England. Pop. 15,000. Tourism; hist. tin mining.

trypsin, enzyme produced by vertebrate pancreas. Converts proteins into amino acids and polypeptides.

Tsana, *see* TANA, LAKE.

tsar or **czar,** title of Russian emperors, first adopted (1547) by Ivan IV. Last tsar was Nicholas II.

Tsaritsyn, *see* VOLGOGRAD.

tsetse fly, blood-sucking fly of genus *Glossina,* of C and S Africa. Bite transmits trypanosomes (flagellate protozoa) which cause sleeping sickness in man and nagana in cattle and other domesticated animals.

Tshombe, Moise Kapenda (1919-69), Congolese political leader. President (1960) of secessionist Katanga. Imprisoned 1961 after Lumumba's murder; later exiled. Returned as premier of Congo (1964-5); fled after MOBUTU'S 2nd coup; kidnapped and detained in Algiers (1967), where he died.

Tsinan, cap. of Shantung prov., E China. Pop. 1,100,000. Near Hwang Ho. Machinery, chemicals, textile mfg. Ancient walled city.

Tsinghai or **Chinghai,** prov. of W China. Area *c* 647,500 sq km (250,000 sq mi); pop. 3,500,000; cap. Sining. Contains Kunlun and Nan mountains, Koko Nor salt lake, sources of Hwang Ho, Yangtze, Mekong rivers. Mainly high, desolate plateau. Rich coal, oil resources largely unexploited. Hist. part of Tibet.

Tsingtao, port of Shangtung prov., E China. Pop. 1,300,000. Naval depot, indust. centre on Yellow Sea. Engineering. Former treaty port, leased to Germany (1898).

Tsushima, isl. group of Japan, in Korea Str. Scene of naval victory of Japanese under Admiral Togo over Russians (1905); most of Russian ships captured or destroyed.

Tuamotu Islands, archipelago of SC Pacific Ocean, part of French Polynesia. Comprise *c* 80 atolls. Produce copra, pearl shell. Acquired by France (1844).

Tuareg, BERBER people of Sahara. Matrilinial culture in which men, rather than women, wear veil. The upper classes are nomadic traders, warriors; the lower group are partly settled farmers.

tuatara, *Sphenodon punctatus,* primitive lizard-like reptile found on islands in Cook Strait of New Zealand. Row of spines along head, back and tail. Only living representative of order Rhynchocephalia.

tuba, bass valved brass instrument. Used in orchestras and in most brass bands.

tuber, *see* BULB.

tuberculosis (TB), infectious disease caused by tubercle bacillus *Mycobacterium tuberculosis.* Similar form of disease affects cattle and can be passed to man in milk. Characterized by formation of nodular lesions (tubercles) in various parts of body, esp. lungs, lymph nodes, bones and skin. Treated by drugs; BCG vaccine provides immunity. Pulmonary form formerly known as consumption.

Tübingen, town of SW West Germany, on R. Neckar. Pop. 55,000. Printing, precision instruments, textile mfg. Univ. (1477).

Tubuai or **Austral Islands,** archipelago of SC Pacific Ocean, part of French Polynesia. Produce copra, coffee, tobacco. Acquired by France (1844).

TUC, *see* TRADES UNION CONGRESS.

Tucson, city of SE Arizona, US. Pop. 444,000. Railway jct.; mining, ranching trade centre; electronics and optics indust.; health resort. Settled by Spanish *c* 1700.

Tucumán, *see* SAN MIGUEL DE TUCUMÁN.

Tudor, House of, English ruling family (1485-1603). Estab. by Owen Tudor, a Welsh squire who married widow of Henry V. His grandson took throne as Henry VII, ending Wars of the Roses. Succeeded by Henry VIII, Edward VI, Mary I and Elizabeth I.

Tula, city of USSR, C European RSFSR. Pop. 514,000. Metal goods mfg., esp. firearms and samovars; sugar refining.

tulip, any of genus *Tulipa* of bulbous plants of lily family. Large, cup-shaped solitary flowers of various colours. Most garden tulips are varieties of *T. gesneriana* introduced from Turkey in 16th cent.

Tull, Jethro (1674-1741), English agriculturist. Known for his improvements of British agric., he invented (*c* 1701) a seed drill which sowed in rows. Wrote *Horse-hoeing Husbandry* (1731).

Tullamore, co. town of Offaly, C Irish Republic, on Grand Canal. Pop. 8000. Brewing, distilling. Nearby Durrow Abbey founded (6th cent.) by St Columba.

Tulsa, city of NE Oklahoma, US; on Arkansas R. Pop. 586,000. Oil refining; oilfield equipment, aircraft mfg. Settled in 1880s as cattle town.

tumour, swelling on some part of the body, esp. a growth of new tissue that is independent of its surrounding structures and serves no useful purpose. Said to be benign if localized and harmless;

malignant tumour is a CANCER.

tuna, *see* TUNNY.

Tunbridge Wells, (Royal), spa town of Kent, SE England. Pop. 45,000.

tundra, cold, treeless plains in N Eurasia and N North America. Region of PERMAFROST; mean monthly temperature below freezing point for most of year. Snow and ice cover in winter; topsoil thaws in summer, giving swampy conditions.

tungsten (W), hard metallic element; at. no. 74, at. wt. 183.85. Occurs in tungstite, scheelite, wolframite. Corrosion resistant, ductile. Used in lamp filaments, alloys, electric contact points; tungsten carbide used in drills and grinding tools. Also known as wolfram.

Tunguska, name of 3 rivers of USSR, NC Siberian RSFSR; tributaries of R. Yenisei. They are **Lower Tunguska,** *c* 2550 km (1600 mi) long; **Stony Tunguska** *c* 1500 km (950 mi) long; **Upper Tunguska,** the lower course of R. Angara. All rise in Sayan Mts. near L. Baikal and flow NW into Yenisei.

Tunicata (tunicates), subphylum of marine chordates with bodies enclosed in hard covering. Active tadpole-like larvae have notochord in tail region. *See* SEA SQUIRT.

Tunis, cap. of Tunisia, on L. of Tunis. Pop. 944,000. Canal link with Mediterranean, exports iron ore, phosphates, petroleum, dates, olive oil; textile and carpet mfg. Cap. of Berber state of Tunis from 13th cent.; taken 16th cent. by Turks. Pirate centre until French occupation 1881. Nearby are ruins of CARTHAGE.

Tunisia

Tunisia, republic of N Africa. Area 164,200 sq km (63,400 sq mi); pop. 6,077,000; cap. Tunis. Languages: Arabic, French. Religion: Islam. Atlas Mts. in N, Sahara in S. Produces wheat, dates, olives, grapes; exports phosphates, petroleum, iron ore; fishing; tourist indust. Ruled by Carthage until 2nd cent. BC; became Roman prov. of 'Africa'. *Fl* 13th-16th cent. under Berbers; fell to Turks; occupied (1881) by France. Independent 1956, republic from 1957.

tunnel, passage cut underground to facilitate communications. Longest rail tunnel is Simplon, Switzerland (20 km/12.3 mi, completed 1922); longest road, St. Gotthard, Switzerland (19.3 km/10.2 mi, 1980). Earth tunnels normally cylindrical, lined with rings of cast iron or pre-cast concrete.

tunny or **tuna,** large marine food fish of Scombridae family. Species incl. bluefin tuna, *Thunnus thynnus,* migratory fish of warm Atlantic, and albacore, *T. alalunga.*

turbine, rotary engine driven by pressure of a fluid (liquid or gas) against curved vanes of a wheel. Steam turbine, developed by C. Parsons (1884), widely used in electrical generation and ship propulsion. Gas turbine, in which air is burnt with fuel to give high pressure flow, used in aircraft.

turbot, *Scophthalmus maximus,* large flatfish of N Atlantic and Mediterranean. Both eyes on left side of head. Food fish.

Turenne, Henri de la Tour d'Auvergne, Vicomte de (1611-75), French soldier. Hero of French army during Thirty Years War. Defeated Condé in Fronde (1652).

Turgenev, Ivan Sergeyevich (1818-83), Russian novelist. *Fathers and Sons* (1862) portrays conflict of traditionalists with new generation of nihilists. Also wrote plays, *eg A Month in the Country,* short stories.

Turgot, Anne Robert Jacques (1727-81), French economist, statesman. Comptroller general of finances (1774-6), attempted sweeping economic reform. Dismissed.

Turin (*Torino*), city of NW Italy, on R. Po, cap. of Piedmont and of Torino prov. Pop. 1,182,000. Car, aircraft mfg., textiles. Under house of Savoy from *c* 1280; cap. of Kingdom of Sardinia from 1720 and Italy 1861-4. Cathedral (1492) has shroud reputedly of Christ; univ. (1404).

Turkana, Lake, *see* RUDOLF, LAKE.

Turkestan or **Turkistan,** region of C Asia, now divided between USSR, China and Afghanistan.

Turkey

Turkey, republic of Asia Minor and SE Europe. Area 781,000 sq km (296,000 sq mi); pop. 43,210,000; cap. Ankara. Language: Turkish. Religion: Islam. Major part consists of Anatolia, arid plateau crossed by Pontic Mts. in N, Taurus Mts. in S. Separated from European Turkey by Sea of Marmara, Bosporus, Dardanelles. Mainly agric. economy; produces wheat, tobacco, fruit; minerals incl. coal, copper, chromium. Centre of Hittite civilization in 2nd millennium BC; parts colonized by Greeks; has ruins of Troy. Invaded by Seljuk Turks in 11th cent., then by Ottoman Turks. Ottoman Empire grew to incl. Balkans, Egypt, Arabia, *etc*; declined after defeat at Vienna (1683). Empire lost in series of wars, ending with WWI. Became republic (1923) under Ataturk who introduced Westernizing policy.

turkey, *Meleagris gallopavo,* large American game bird introduced into Europe from Mexico in 16th cent. Bronze-coloured plumage with bare head and neck; intensively reared for flesh.

Turkic, language group within W Altaic family. Incl. Kirghiz, Kazakh, Turkish, Turkoman, Tatar, Uigur, Uzbek.

Turkmen Soviet Socialist Republic, constituent republic of SC USSR, on Iran border. Area *c* 488,000 sq km (188,400 sq mi); pop. 2,759,000; cap. Ashkhabad. Largely arid lowland (Kara Kum desert) in W and C; plateau in E. Agric., esp. cotton, maize, fruit, concentrated in oases and river valleys. Fisheries on Caspian Sea; oil fields. Conquered by Russia (1881); incorporated as republic (1924).

Turks and Caicos Islands, two isl. groups E of Bahamas; British crown colony. Area 430 sq km (166 sq mi); pop. 6000; admin. town Grand Turk (on Grand Turk Isl.). Salt, crayfish exports. Settled in 17th cent.; admin. by Jamaica (1873-1962).

Turku (Swed. *Abo*), city of SW Finland, on Baltic Sea. Pop. 240,000. Port, exports timber, butter; sawmilling, textile industs. Cultural centre; Swedish, Finnish univs., cap. of Finland until 1812. Rebuilt after fire (1827). Has cathedral (13th cent.).

turmeric or **tumeric,** *Curcuma longa,* East Indian perennial herb of ginger family. Aromatic yellow rhizome which yields spice, colouring and medicinal agents.

Turner, Joseph Mallord William (1775-1851), English painter. Began as topographical painter working in watercolour; early oils were in emulation of Claude, Poussin and Dutch marine painters. His rendering of light and dissolution of form in an attempt to capture atmospheric effects make late works almost abstract. Works incl. *Rain, Steam and Speed* and *The Fighting Temeraire.*

turnip, plant of genus *Brassica* of mustard family. Cultivated in temperate zones for edible tubers used as cattle food and vegetable. Chief varieties are *B. rapa* with white tubers and Swedish turnip, *B. napobrassica,* with yellow tubers.

turpentine, essential oil obtained by distillation of gum or resin from pine or other trees. Consists mainly of pinene ($C_{10}H_{16}$): used to thin paints and as solvent.

Turpin, Richard ('Dick') (1706-39), English highwayman. His famous overnight ride from London to York was an invention by Harrison Ainsworth in romance *Rookwood* (1834). Hanged at York.

turquoise, semi-precious gemstone, consisting of hydrous phosphate of aluminium plus some copper. Colour varies from sky blue to green.

turtle, any of order Chelonia of reptiles; name often applied only to aquatic species, terrestrial species being called tortoises. Soft body encased in plates of bone usually covered with horny shields; horny edged toothless jaws; retractile head, limbs, tail.

turtle dove, *see* DOVE.

Tuscany (*Toscana*), region of WC Italy, cap. Florence. Incl. Elba; hilly, main river Arno. Main towns Livorno, Pisa, Siena. Wheat, olives, wine; iron ore, mercury. Formed most of ancient Etruria; grand duchy (1567-1860). Renaissance cultural centre. Language adopted by united Italy.

Tussaud, Marie (1760-1850), Swiss wax modeller. Imprisoned during French Revolution, later founded (London, 1802) Madame Tussaud's wax museum.

Tutankhamen (*fl* 14th cent. BC), Egyptian king. Reversed policies of his father-in-law, IKHNATON, returning to worship of god Amon and restoring Thebes as cap. His tomb in Valley of Kings (excavated 1922 by H. Carter) contained many treasures.

Tuvalu, group of 9 coral islands in SW Pacific. Area 23 sq km (9 sq mi); pop. 6000; cap. Funafuti (pop. 1,000). Produce copra. Formerly called Ellice Isls. Estab. as British protect. 1892; from 1915-75 formed part of British colony of Gilbert and Ellice Isls. Withdrew to form separate colony of Tuvalu (1976), fully independent 1978.

Tver, *see* KALININ.

Twain, Mark, pseud. of Samuel Langhorne Clemens (1835-1910), American humorist, novelist. Based classics *Tom Sawyer* (1876), *Huckleberry Finn* (1885) on Mississippi boyhood.

Tweed, river of Scotland and England, flows 156 km (97 mi) from Borders region to North Sea at Berwick, forming part of national border.

tweed, rough-surfaced woollen fabric woven in various shades and patterns. Durable and almost weather-proof. Well-known types are made in Harris, Scotland, and Donegal, Ireland.

Tweedsmuir, 1st Baron, *see* BUCHAN, JOHN.

Twelfth Night, eve of EPIPHANY. Celebrated as end of Christmas season.

Twelve Disciples, men chosen by Jesus to be his original followers: Andrew, Bartholomew, James (the younger, son of Alphaeus), James (the elder) and John (sons of Zebedee), Jude, Judas Iscariot, Matthew, Philip, Simon the Zealot, Simon (called Peter) and Thomas.

twelve-tone system or **twelve-note music,** music composed by system utilizing equally all 12 chromatic notes of octave. Developed by SCHOENBERG and his followers, *eg* Berg, Webern. Also known as dodecaphonic or serial music.

Twickenham, *see* RICHMOND-UPON-THAMES.

twins, two offspring born at the same birth. Identical twins born from division of a single fertilized ovum are of same sex and closely resemble each other. Fraternal twins born of separately fertilized ova may differ in sex and appearance.

two-stroke (cycle) engine, *see* INTERNAL COMBUSTION ENGINE.

Tyche, in Greek myth, personification of chance. Represented with ship's rudder and cornucopia. *See* FORTUNA.

Tyler, John (1790-1862), American statesman, president (1841-5). Joined Whigs in protest against Democrats' federalist and fiscal policies. His own cabinet resigned after he vetoed Whig bank proposals.

Tyler, Wat (d. 1381), English rebel. Led impoverished serfs in PEASANTS' REVOLT (1381). Captured Canterbury and entered London. After his murder by Lord Mayor of London, uprising was crushed.

Tyndale or **Tindale, William** (*c* 1494-1536), English humanist, reformer. Began translation of NT in England; continued work in exile after meeting Luther. Pub. edition of NT from 1526. Copies denounced and suppressed in England. Convicted of heresy and executed at Antwerp.

Tyne, river of NE England. Formed by union of N, S Tyne rivers near Hexham, flows 48 km (30 mi) in Northumberland to North Sea via indust. Tyneside (Newcastle, South Shields).

Tyne and Wear, met. county of NE England. Area 540 sq km (208 sq mi); pop. 1,165,000; admin. hq. Newcastle. Created 1974 to incl. area around mouth of R. Tyne.

Tynemouth, town of Tyne and Wear met. county, NE England. Pop. 69,000. Shipbuilding, engineering industs.

typewriter, writing machine with a keyboard for reproducing letters, figures, *etc,* that resemble printed ones. When the keys are struck, raised characters are pressed against an inked ribbon, making an impression on an inserted piece of paper. First practical, commercial machine patented (1868) by C. L. Sholes (1819-90). Subsequent developments incl. electric machines, word-processors, where keyboard is linked to a computer.

typhoid fever, acute infectious disease caused by bacillus *Salmonella typhosa,* usually found in contaminated food and water. Affects intestine, spleen and bones. Treated by chloramphenicol, *etc.*

typhoon, *see* HURRICANE.

typhus, acute infectious disease caused by rickettsia, micro-organisms transmitted by bite of lice, fleas. Characterized by eruption of red spots, prostrating fever.

Tyr, *see* TIW.

Tyrannosaur

tyrannosaur, *Tyrannosaurus rex,* ferocious 2-legged carnivorous dinosaur; *c* 6 m/20 ft tall, with short forelimbs and sharp teeth. Existed in Cretaceous period.

Tyre (Arab. *Sur*), port of S Lebanon, on Mediterranean. Pop. 14,000. Ancient Phoenician centre, founded *c* 1500 BC on an island. Commercial centre, famous for purple dye. Destroyed 1291 by Arabs.

tyre, pneumatic, rubber tube, filled with air, fixed about wheel of vehicle to absorb shocks and provide traction. First invented by R. W. Thomson (1845) but largely ignored until DUNLOP patented bicycle tyre (1888). First fitted to automobiles by Michelin company in France.

Tyrol (*Tirol*), prov. of W Austria. Area 12,650 sq km (4884 sq mi); cap. Innsbruck. Alpine region, highest peak GROSSGLOCKNER; main river Inn. Tourism, dairying, forestry, salt mining. S Tyrol ceded to Italy 1919.

Tyrone, former county of WC Northern Ireland. Hilly, Sperrin Mts. in N. Agric., dairying. Co. town was Omagh.

Tyrrhenian Sea, part of W Mediterranean Sea, bounded by Italy, Sicily, Sardinia, Corsica.

Tyumen, city of USSR, W Siberian RSFSR; on R. Tura. Pop. 359,000. Sawmilling, shipyards. Centre of oil and natural gas producing region. Founded 1586, oldest Russian settlement in Siberia.

Tzu Hsi or **Tsu Hsi** (1834-1908), dowager empress of China (1861-1908). Served as regent 3 times (1861-73, 1874-89, 1898-1908). Fostered anti-foreign feeling which led to unsuccessful BOXER REBELLION (1898-1900).

U

UAR, *see* EGYPT.

Ubangi-Shari, *see* CENTRAL AFRICAN REPUBLIC.

U-boat, abbreviation of German *Unterseeboot*, SUBMARINE.

Uccello, Paolo, orig. Paolo di Dono (*c* 1396-1475), Florentine painter. Early exponent of perspective and foreshortening; works incl. fresco *The Flood* and 3 scenes of *Rout of San Romano*.

udder, mammary gland of cow, goat and other mammals. Mammary tissues manufacture liquids and solids forming milk for feeding of young.

Udine, city of Friuli-Venezia Giulia, NE Italy, cap. of Udine prov. Pop. 103,000. Produces machines, textiles. Gothic town hall, cathedral (13th cent.). Damaged in earthquake (1976).

Udmurt, auton. republic of E European RSFSR, USSR. Area 42,100 sq km (16,250 sq mi); pop. 1,494,000; cap. Izhevsk. Forested area in W foothills of Urals; grain, flax, potatoes cultivated. Indust. centred on Izhevsk. Udmurts, a Finno-Ugrian people, colonized by Russia in 16th cent.

Ufa, city of USSR, cap. of Bashkir auton. republic, E European RSFSR; at confluence of Ufa and Belaya rivers. Pop. 969,000. Oil refining centre, connected by pipeline to Volga-Ural oilfield; chemical mfg. Founded 1574.

Uffizi Gallery, art museum in Florence, Italy. Building is 16th cent. palace built by Giorgio Vasari for Cosimo I de' Medici. Strong holding of Italian Renaissance painting and sculpture.

Uganda

Uganda, republic of EC Africa. Area 236,000 sq km (91,100 sq mi); pop. 12,780,000; cap. Kampala. Languages: Bantu, English. Religions: animist, Christianity, Islam. Mainly plateau, bordered by lakes Albert, Edward, Victoria, and Ruwenzori Mts. Tropical savannah; cotton, coffee growing, forestry; industs. based on copper ores, Owen Falls Dam h.e.p. Explored by Speke (1862); Buganda (native kingdom) became British protect. (1894), other territ. added (1896). Independent from 1962 under the kabaka of Buganda, who became president. Coups by Obote (1966) and Amin (1971). Asian pop. mostly expelled 1973. Amin overthrown (1979), Obote elected president (1980). Member of British Commonwealth.

Ugarit, ancient cap. of Ugarit kingdom, W Syria, near modern Latakia. Excavated in 1929; remains dating from 5th millennium BC found. Commercial centre in 15th and 14th cent. BC.

UHF, *see* VHF.

Uhuru Peak (Swahili = freedom), new name for KILIMANJARO.

Uist, North and **South,** isls. of Outer Hebrides, NW Scotland, in Western Isles. Separated by Benbecula. Crofting, fishing.

Ujiji, *see* KIGOMA-UJIJI.

Ujung Pandang, cap. of S Sulawesi prov. (Celebes), Indonesia. Pop. 435,000. Seaport; exports coffee, spices, resins. Formerly known as Makassar.

ukelele, small four-stringed guitar of Portuguese origin. Easy to play, it became popular in Hawaii and spread to Europe and US after WWI.

Ukrainian Soviet Socialist Republic, constituent republic of SW USSR. Area *c* 601,000 sq km (232,000 sq mi); pop. 49,757,000; cap. Kiev. Largely steppeland covered with fertile black earth soil; major agric. region, producing grain, sugar beet. Indust. based on coal of Donets basin, iron ore of Krivoi Rog, manganese of Nikopol. N and W part of Kievan principality until Tartar conquest in 13th cent.; passed to Poland, then to Russia by 1795. Independent (1918-20) during civil war. Territ. increased after WWII.

Ulan Bator, cap. of Mongolia. Pop. 400,000. Indust., commercial centre; linked to Trans-Siberian railway. Produces woollen goods, leather, footwear. Founded 17th cent. Called Urga until 1924.

Ulan-Ude, city of USSR, cap. of Buryat auton. republic, SC Siberian RSFSR; route centre on Trans-Siberian railway. Pop. 300,000. Railway engineering, wood products, textiles. Formerly called Verkhne-Udinsk.

Ulbricht, Walter (1893-1973), East German political leader, head of state (1960-71). First secretary of Communist party (1953-71). Hard-line Stalinist, had Berlin Wall built (1961).

ulcer, break in skin or mucous membrane

which does not heal. May be caused by infection (*eg* syphilitic ulcer), defective blood supply (*eg* varicose ulcer) or irritation (*eg* peptic ulcer).

Uleåborg, *see* OULU.

Ulm, town of S West Germany, on R. Danube. Pop. 93,000. Railway jct.; metal goods, food processing. Scene of victory (1805) of Napoleon over Austrians. Cathedral (14th cent.).

Ulster, ancient prov. of NE Ireland. Comprises 6 counties of Northern Ireland, with Cavan, Donegal, Monaghan of Irish Republic. Scene of 17th-cent. 'Plantations' of English, Scottish settlers.

ultrasonics, science of sound vibrations of frequencies higher than those normally audible to human ear. Used to detect flaws in metals, detect underwater objects, in medical diagnosis, *etc.*

ultraviolet rays, electromagnetic radiation with wavelength ranging from 4×10^{-5} to 5×10^{-7} cm, between visible light and X-rays. Radiation from Sun contains *c* 5% ultraviolet rays; these are mainly absorbed by oxygen and ozone in atmosphere, and glass. Produced by mercury vapour lamp; action on skin produces vitamin D.

Ulysses, *see* ODYSSEUS.

Umbelliferae, large family of hollow-stemmed, herbaceous plants with compound flowerheads radiating from point at top of stem. Incl. carrot, parsley, hemlock.

umbilical cord, fleshy structure uniting abdomen of foetus with placenta in mother's womb, through which shared blood circulates. Severed at birth, resulting scar is navel.

Umbria, region of C Italy, chief cities Perugia, Terni. Mainly mountainous. Cereals, wine, olive oil; h.e.p., chemicals. Many Etruscan, Roman remains. School of painting (15th-16th cent.) incl. Perugino, Raphael.

Umtali, town of E Zimbabwe. Pop. 62,000. Commercial centre, on Salisbury-Beira railway. Tobacco indust.; gold mining nearby.

Umtata, cap. of Transkei, S Africa, on R. Umtata. Pop. 25,000.

uncertainty principle, *see* HEISENBERG.

unconscious, in psychology, term used for dynamic elements of personality, both structures and processes, of which individual is temporarily or permanently unaware. According to Freud, unconscious processes are distinct from rational thought, allowing mutually contradictory wishes to co-exist. Jung postulated existence of racial or collective unconscious as well as individual one, from which derive archetypes, or collective symbols.

undulant fever or **brucellosis,** infectious disease of man and animals caused by bacteria of genus *Brucella*. Contracted by handling diseased animals or from milk. Frequently causes recurrent fever in man and abortion in animals.

unemployment, state in which work is unavailable to large number of people requiring it. Called structural if caused by decline or change in processes of given industry. Severe during period 1918-39. Industrialized nations attempt to control economy in order to balance supply with demand of labour. Supposedly eliminated in China and USSR through public ownership of means of production and distribution. Also *see* SOCIAL SECURITY.

UNESCO *see* UNITED NATIONS EDUCATIONAL, SCIENTIFIC AND CULTURAL ORGANIZATION.

Ungava Bay, inlet of NE Québec, Canada; extending S from Hudson Str. Ungava Peninsula to W; area rich in iron ore deposits.

ungulate, herbivorous hoofed mammal. Two orders: Perissodactyla, odd-toed ungulates incl. horse, rhinoceros; Artiodactyla, even-toed ungulates, incl. sheep, cattle.

UNICEF, *see* UNITED NATIONS INTERNATIONAL CHILDREN'S EMERGENCY FUND.

unicorn, legendary horse-like animal, usually pure white, with a single horn growing from the centre of its forehead. Believed by Greeks to exist in India. In medieval literature and heraldry, symbolizes virginity.

unified field theory, projected mathematical theory which attempts to describe in single set of equations properties and interactions of the 4 fundamental forces of nature: gravitation, electromagnetism, strong and weak nuclear interactions.

uniformitarianism, in geology, theory that features of Earth's crust evolve by means of process unchanged through geological time. Opposes CATASTROPHISM theory. First advanced (1795) by James Hutton; supported by John Playfair (1802) and LYELL (1830-3). Initially caused much controversy, now widely accepted.

Uniformity, Acts of, four acts of English Parliament (1549, 1552, 1559, 1662) aimed at enforcing standard reformed religious practices. Last act reestab. Church of England rites.

Union, Acts of, in British history, two acts, first (1707) uniting parliaments of England and Scotland, second (1800) uniting those of Britain and Ireland.

union, labour, employees' association with aims of self-protection, better pay and working conditions. Developed in Britain in 19th cent., achieving guaranteed legal recognition (1871) and joining (1893) Independent Labour Party. British unions organized on craft lines, called therefore 'trade unions'; in US and rest of Europe, unions are based within their indust. Achieve aims by COLLECTIVE BARGAINING and STRIKE.

Unionist Party, British political party formed (1886) to maintain parliamentary union between Britain and Ireland. Consisted of coalition of Liberal Unionists, who seceded from Liberal Party, and Conservatives. Later identified with Conservative Party.

Union of Soviet Socialist Republics (USSR), federal state of E Europe and N Asia, world's largest country. Area, *c*

Union of Soviet Socialist Republics

22,402,000 sq km (8,649,000 sq mi); pop. 263,400,000; cap. Moscow; other major city Leningrad. Chief language: Russian. Religion: Russian Orthodox. Comprises 15 constituent republics and 20 auton. republics stretching from Baltic to Pacific and N to Arctic. Hist. Russia founded by Rurik at Novgorod (862); Kievan state dominant 10th-12th cent.; Greek form of Christianity estab. 988. Overrun by Mongols in 13th cent.; Muscovite princes became dominant in 14th and 15th cents. after period of disunity. Expansion into Siberia began with first tsar, Ivan the Terrible. Romanov dynasty estab. 1613, Westernization policy introduced by Peter I; under his rule and that of Catherine II, became European power, taking territ. from Poland, Turkey, Sweden. Desire for reform of reactionary rule led to abolition of serfdom (1861); social unrest and military defeats led to Revolution (1905, 1917) and estab. of USSR under Lenin. Underwent enormous indust. growth under Stalin. Emerged as a dominant world power after WWII.

Unitarianism, form of Protestantism which rejects orthodox doctrine of Trinity. Accepts moral teachings of Jesus but denies his divinity. Holds that God exists only in one person. Arose during Reformation; estab. in England by John BIDDLE. Taken to US by Joseph PRIESTLEY.

United Arab Emirates, group of 7 sheikdoms, SE Arabia, on Persian Gulf (Abu Dhabi, Ajman, Dubai, Fujairah, Ras al-Khaimah, Sharjah, Umm al-Qaiwain). Area *c* 84,000 sq km (32,400 sq mi); pop. 711,000; temporary cap. Abu Dhabi. Pearls, dried fish; oil at Abu Dhabi. British protect. (1892-1971), known as Trucial States at independence.

United Arab Republic, *see* EGYPT.

United Empire Loyalists, name given to colonists who remained loyal to Britain during American Revolution and migrated to Canada. Extensive settlement in Nova Scotia and Québec led to estab. of new prov. of New Brunswick (1784) and of Upper Canada (1791).

United Irishmen, *see* TONE, WOLFE.

United Kingdom (of Great Britain and Northern Ireland), kingdom of NW Europe. Area 244,750 sq km (94,500 sq mi); pop. 55,836,000; cap. London. Language: English. Religions: Anglican, Presbyterian, RC. Incl. England, Scotland, Wales, Northern Ireland, Channel Isls., Isle of Man. Constitutional monarchy (2-chamber parliamentary govt.); member of British Commonwealth, EEC. After 1801 called UK of GREAT BRITAIN and Ireland; present name derived from Irish partition (1921).

United Nations [Organization] (UN), international body (hq. in New York), estab. 1945 to maintain peace and security and to promote cooperation between nations in solving social, economic and cultural problems. Charter designated admin. functions to Secretariat (headed by secretary-general), deliberative functions to General Assembly (comprising delegates from all member nations) and policy decision functions to Security Council (15 members, 5 permanent - UK, US, USSR, France, China - 10 non-permanent). Other principal organs are International Court of Justice, Trusteeship Council, Economic and Social Council. Also sponsors special agencies such as UNESCO, World Health Organization, International Monetary Fund, Universal Postal Union. As arbiter of international disputes, UN has had limited success, as in Arab-Israeli wars (1948, 1956, 1967, 1973), Korea (1951-3), Cyprus (1974).

United Nations Educational, Scientific and Cultural Organization (UNESCO), special agency of UN, estab. 1946 to contribute to peace and security by promoting collaboration among nations through education, science and culture. Trains teachers, encourages scientific research and cooperation.

United Nations International Children's Emergency Fund (UNICEF), agency estab. (1946) to assist child health, nutrition and welfare, esp. in devastated areas and underdeveloped countries. Financed by voluntary contributions. Awarded Nobel Peace Prize (1965).

United Reformed Church, denomination founded 1972 by union of English Presbyterian and Congregational Churches.

United States (of America), federal republic occupying most of S North America. Area 9,363,353 sq km (3,615,191 sq mi); pop. 218,059,000; cap. Washington; major cities New York, Chicago, Los Angeles, Philadelphia, Detroit, Houston. Language: English. Religions: Protestant, RC. Comprises 50 states, incl. outlying Alaska, Hawaii; mainland stretches from Pacific to Atlantic, Great Lakes to Gulf of Mexico. Rocky Mts. divide W interior; grain-producing Great Plains in C, drained by Mississippi system, S of which is oilrich region (esp. Texas). SE US primarily agric. Great Lakes, Atlantic coast, California centres of indust. and pop. Colonial struggle begun in 16th cent., ended with English

United States of America

victory over French (1756-63). Republic estab. by Thirteen Colonies after AMERICAN REVOLUTION (1776-83). W expansion facilitated by Louisiana Purchase (1803), Mexican War (1846-8). South's secession over slavery issue ended with defeat by Union in CIVIL WAR (1861-5). Indigenous Indians almost exterminated by colonists. Leading indust., agric., mineral producer; political power estab. in 20th cent.; challenged by USSR after WWII.

universe, all space and all matter contained in space. Distant galaxies are believed to be moving away from each other at high speeds and thus the universe is expanding. *See* COSMOLOGY.

university, institute of highest level of education. Generally has one or more undergraduate colleges, together with programme of graduate studies and number of professional schools. Has authority to confer degrees, *eg* bachelor's, master's, doctor's. Earliest were in Italy (Salerno, Bologna), France (Paris). In Middle Ages, developed under royal or ecclesiastical patronage, among most famous being Oxford, Cambridge. By late 19th cent., univs. had secular admin. and curricula; in most Western states, univs. funded either by private endowment or govt. assistance, or both.

Untouchables, *see* CASTE.

Upanishads, in Hinduism, group of late Vedic metaphysical treatises. *See* VEDANTA.

Upper Volta (Fr. *Haute-Volta*), republic of W Africa. Area 274,300 sq km (105,900 sq mi); pop. 6,554,000; cap. Ouagadougou. Official language: French. Religions: animist, Islam, RC. Landlocked plateau, mainly savannah and semidesert; maize, millet, groundnuts, livestock. French colony from 1919; divided between Ivory Coast, French Sudan, Niger (1933). Recreated (1947) as territ. of French West Africa, until independence (1960).

Uppsala, city of EC Sweden. Pop. 141,000. Cultural centre, incl. Sweden's oldest univ. (1477), cathedral (13th cent.).

Ur, ruins of SE Iraq. Cap. of ancient Sumerian empire (*fl* 4th millennium BC).

Ural Mountains, range of WC USSR, extending from Arctic Ocean to Kirghiz steppe region of Kazakh SSR; part of natural boundary between Europe and Asia. Rise to 1894 m (6214 ft). C part densely forested and rich in minerals. Urals indust. area developed in 1930s; incl. towns of Chelyabinsk, Magnitogorsk and Sverdlovsk.

uranium (U), hard radioactive metallic element; at. no. 92, at. wt. 238.03. Occurs combined in pitchblende, carnotite, *etc.* Uranium 235, capable of sustaining chain reaction, is used in nuclear reactors; more plentiful uranium 238 is used to make plutonium.

Uranus, in Greek myth, personification of heavens; according to Hesiod, son and husband of Gaea, the earth. Father of Titans, incl. Cronus (father of Zeus); emasculated and overthrown by Cronus.

Uranus, in astronomy, planet 7th in distance from Sun. Revolves about Sun at mean distance of *c* 2870 million km in 84 yrs; diameter 47,000 km; mass 14.5 times that of Earth. Has 5 satellites and dense atmosphere containing hydrogen, methane and ammonia. Discovered (1781) by William Herschel.

Urban II, orig. Odo of Lagery (*c* 1042-99), French churchman, pope (1088-99). Inaugurated 1st Crusade at Clermont (1095).

Urbino, town of the Marches, E Italy. Pop. 23,000. Agric. centre; hist. majolica mfg. Cultural centre under Montefeltro family (12th-16th cent.). Has ducal palace (15th cent.), univ. (1506).

Urdu, Indic language in Indo-Iranian branch of Indo-European family. Official language of Pakistan. Written variant of Hindustani. Used by Moslems, written in modified Arabic alphabet, contains many Persian, Arabic loan-words.

urea, crystalline organic compound, found in urine, blood, bile, *etc,* of all mammals. Prepared synthetically; used in making fertilizers and resins.

Urga, *see* ULAN BATOR.

urial, *Ovis vignei,* reddish-brown wild sheep of mountains of N India and Tibet.

uric acid, crystalline organic acid, found in urine. Gout is caused by deposits of uric acid salts in the joints.

urinary bladder, flexible muscular sac acting as temporary reservoir for urine.

urine, fluid formed in kidneys. Composed of water and waste products, incl. urea, uric acid, mineral salts. Stored in urinary bladder and discharged via the urethra.

Ursa Major or **Great Bear,** constellation of N hemisphere, whose 7 brightest stars form the Plough or Big Dipper.

Ursa Minor or **Little Bear,** constellation of N hemisphere; brightest star is Polaris or North Star, near N celestial pole.

Uruguay, republic of SE South America. Area 177,508 sq km (68,536 sq mi); pop. 2,864,000; cap. Montevideo. Language:

Spanish. Religion: RC. Fertile plains (wheat growing) rise to N grasslands (sheep, cattle rearing). Temperate climate. Spanish-Portuguese struggle for possession in 16th, 17th cents.; liberated with Argentina (1810); gained independence under Artigas (1825). Repression under military dictatorships in 20th cent.

Uruguay, river of SC South America. Rises in S Brazil, flows W, then S 1610 km (*c* 1000 mi) to join Paraná R., together with which it forms Río de la Plata. Forms Argentina-Uruguay, Brazil-Argentina borders. Navigable to Paysandú.

Ushant (*Ile d'Ouessant*), rocky isl. off Brittany, NW France. Fishing, sheep raising. Scene of 2 naval battles between French and English (1778, 'Glorious First of June' 1794).

Usküdar, *see* ISTANBUL.

USSR, *see* UNION OF SOVIET SOCIALIST REPUBLICS.

Usumbura, *see* BUJUMBURA.

usury, *see* INTEREST.

Utah, state of W US. Area 219,932 sq km (84,916 sq mi); pop. 1,270,000; cap. Salt Lake City. Arid Great Basin in W, Great Salt L. in N; scenic Wasatch Range runs N-S. Limited agric. mainly livestock, wheat; rich copper, gold mines. Settled by Mormons in 1847; ceded to US after Mexican War (1848). Admitted to Union as 45th state (1896).

Utamaro, Kitagawa (1753-1806), Japanese colourprint artist. Famous for his depiction of women.

uterus or **womb,** hollow muscular organ in female mammals in which the foetus develops. Usually *c* 7.6 cm (3 in.) long in humans, but greatly enlarged during pregnancy. Situated in pelvis; lower end opens via the cervix into the vagina, upper part opens at each side into a Fallopian tube leading to an ovary.

utilitarianism, philosophical school founded by Jeremy Bentham and later developed by J.S. Mill, who incorporated it into 19th-cent. LIBERALISM. Doctrine based on concepts that man's needs are dictated by pleasure and the state's concern should be 'greatest happiness for the greatest number'.

Utrecht, prov. of C Netherlands. Area 1362 sq km (526 sq mi); cap. **Utrecht,** city on Lower Rhine. Pop. 472,000. Railway jct., indust. centre (chemicals, machinery, clothing). Union of Utrecht (1579) united 7 provs. of N Netherlands against Spanish rule. RC archiepiscopal see, cathedral (14th cent.); univ. (1636).

Utrecht, Treaty of, settlement (1713) ending War of SPANISH SUCCESSION, supplemented by French-Austrian agreements of 1714. Philip V, having renounced claim to French throne, recognized as king of Spain. Spanish possessions in Low Countries and Italy ceded to Austria. France recognized Hanoverian claim to British throne. Britain received Gibraltar, parts of North America and was granted commercial advantages.

Utrillo, Maurice (1883-1955), French painter. Known for his Parisian street scenes, marked by predominance of white.

Uttar Pradesh, state of N India. Area *c* 294,000 sq km (113,000 sq mi); pop. 88,365,000; cap. Lucknow. Most of state in Ganges plain, with Himalayas in NW. Agric. economy; grains, sugar cane. Formed (1950) from United Provinces of Agra and Oudh and 3 princely states.

Uzbek Soviet Socialist Republic, constituent republic of SC USSR. Area *c* 449,500 sq km (173,500 sq mi); pop. 15,391,000; cap. Tashkent. Largely plain and desert (Kyzyl Kum), watered by Amu Darya and Syr Darya. Agric. in oases and Fergana valley possible through irrigation; cotton and rice grown; stock raising. Minerals incl. coal, oil. Centre of Tamerlane's 14th-cent. empire. Settled by remnants of Golden Horde in 16th cent. Conquered by Russia by 1873; constituent republic of USSR (1924).

V

Vaal, river of South Africa. Flows *c* 1125 km (700 mi) SW from SE Transvaal to R. Orange in N Cape Prov. Forms most of Transvaal-Orange Free State border. Provides irrigation, h.e.p. for WITWATERSRAND.

vaccine, preparation of weakened or killed micro-organisms introduced into the body to produce immunity against a specific disease by causing formation of antibodies. Introduced by E. Jenner (1795) to immunize against smallpox.

vacuum, in physical theory, an enclosed space containing no matter. In practice, perfect vacuum unobtainable because of vapour emitted by container itself.

vacuum flask, container with double wall enclosing vacuum to prevent conduction and convection of heat. Used to maintain contents at original temperature.

vagina, in female mammals, passage leading from the uterus to the exterior at the vulva.

Valais (Ger. *Wallis*), canton of SW Switzerland. Area 5234 sq km (2021 sq mi); cap. Sion. Mountainous, incl. Matterhorn, Monte Rosa (alpine resorts, h.e.p., forests on lower slopes); Rhône valley (cereals, vines). Pop. is French-speaking, RC. Joined Swiss Confederation 1813.

Valence, town of S France, on R. Rhône, cap. of Drôme dept. Pop. 104,000. Textile (esp. silk, rayon) mfg., agric. market. Romanesque cathedral (11th cent.).

Valencia, region and former kingdom of E Spain. Mountainous in NW (sheep rearing), irrigated fertile coastal plain (fruit growing, esp. oranges). Moorish emirate; held by El Cid 1094-9; part of Aragón from 1238. Hist. cap. **Valencia,** cap. of modern Valencia prov. Pop. 713,000. Port, exports fruit, wine; shipyards, tobacco mfg., textile indust.; univ. (1501). Cathedral (13th cent.).

Valencia, town of N Venezuela, W of L. Valencia. Pop. 439,000. In leading agric. region producing sugar cane, cotton. Motor vehicles, chemicals, textile mfg. Founded 1555.

valency or **valence,** in chemistry, capacity of an element or radical to combine with another to form molecules, measured by number of hydrogen atoms which one radical or atom of element will combine with or replace. Valency is explained in terms of electrons in outermost shell of atom which take part in reactions.

Valentine, St (*fl* 3rd cent.), Roman martyr. Declaration of love on feast day (14 Feb.) originated in medieval times but may derive from earlier pagan festival.

Valentino, Rudolph, orig. Rodolpho d'Antonguolla (1895-1926), American film actor, b. Italy. Idolized in 1920s as great screen lover. Films incl. *The Sheik* (1921).

Valéry, Paul (1871-1945), French poet. Main themes reflect concern with conflict between detached reason against involved passion, *eg* in *La Jeune Parque* (1917), *Le Cimetière marin* (1920).

Valhalla, in Norse myth, banqueting hall in Asgard (home of the gods) where Odin received souls of dead heroes.

Valkyries, in Norse and Teutonic myth, warrior hand-maidens of ODIN who fly over field of battle, choosing those to be slain and escorting them to Valhalla.

Valladolid, city of NC Spain, on R. Pisuerga, cap. of Valladolid prov. Pop. 275,000. Textile mfg., agric. market; univ. (1346). Castilian royal residence in 15th cent. Cathedral (16th cent.).

Valle d'Aosta, region of NW Italy, bordering France and Switzerland, cap. Aosta. Pop. mainly French-speaking. Main river Dora Baltea; h.e.p., forestry, tourism.

Valletta or **Valetta,** cap. of Malta, NE Malta. Pop. 14,000. Port, indust., commercial centre; univ. (1769). Founded 16th cent. by Knights Hospitallers; former British naval base, heavily bombed in WWII. Cathedral (1577).

valley, elongated depression in Earth's surface, between uplands, hills or mountains. Valleys cut by rivers are typically V-shaped, those cut by glaciers U-shaped. Also *see* RIFT VALLEY.

Valley Forge, site near Philadelphia, US. In American Revolution main camp of Washington's army during winter of 1777-8; troops suffered terrible hardships.

Valley of the Kings, archaeological site near Thebes, C Egypt. Many tombs of pharaohs of New Kingdom (1580-1090 BC) cut into cliff faces, incl. tombs of Tutankhamen, Rameses II.

Valois, dynasty of French kings. Family were counts of Valois in Oise dept. Dynasty founded by Charles de Valois, 3rd son of Philip III. Younger branch of Capetian line, which it succeeded (1328); followed (1589) by Bourbon dynasty.

Valois, Dame Ninette de, orig. Edris Stannus (1898-), British prima ballerina, choreographer, b. Ireland. Founder of The Royal Ballet School (1931), director of the Royal Ballet (1931-63).

Valparaiso, port of C Chile. Pop. 611,000. Indust. centre; sugar, textiles mfg. Settlement began 1554.

value, in economics, worth of commodity or service in terms of money or goods at a certain time. Depends on scarcity and desirability.

value-added tax (VAT), form of indirect sales tax paid on products at each stage of production or distribution, based on value added at that stage and incl. in cost to ultimate consumer. Important element in tax structure of EEC.

vampire, in folklore, a corpse which becomes reanimated, leaving grave at night to suck blood of sleeping persons.

vampire bat, small blood-sucking bat of genus *Desmodus* or *Diphylla* found in Central and South America.

vanadium (V), rare hard metallic element; at. no. 23, at. wt. 50.94. Used to provide heat resistance, tensile strength and elasticity in steel alloys.

Van Allen radiation belts, 2 layers of charged particles (electrons and protons) trapped in outer atmosphere by Earth's magnetic field. Inner belt believed to be caused by cosmic rays, outer belt by solar wind.

Vanbrugh, Sir John (1664-1726), English dramatist, architect. Late Restoration comedies of manners incl. *The Relapse* (1696), *The Provok'd Wife* (1697). Designed Blenheim Palace, Castle Howard.

Van Buren, Martin (1782-1862), American statesman, Democratic president (1837-41). Advocated treasury system independent of all banks.

Vancouver, chief port of SW British Columbia, W Canada. Pop. 1,166,000. Natural harbour on Pacific. Transport terminus, commercial centre. Lumber, mineral, sawmilling, fishing, shipbuilding industs. Tourist resort. Has Univ. of British Columbia (1908).

Vancouver Island, SW British Columbia, Canada; largest isl. off W North America. Area 32,137 sq km (12,408 sq mi). Has rugged coastline, mainly mountainous, forested. Agric. incl. dairy, fruit farming; mining incl. coal, gold, copper; fishing, lumbering, tourism. Pop. concentrated in E. Became crown colony (1849), part of British Columbia (1866).

Vandals, ancient Germanic people who settled in Spain (409). Invaded Africa (429) and conquered most of Roman territ., incl. Carthage. Controlled most of Mediterranean with their powerful fleet; sacked Rome (455). Defeated by Byzantine forces under BELISARIUS (534).

Van de Graaf generator, electrostatic generator, using a moving belt to accumulate charge in hollow metal sphere. Produces potentials of millions of volts; used to accelerate charged particles, *eg* electrons, to high energies.

Vanderbilt, Cornelius (1794-1877), American railway and shipping magnate. Endowed Vanderbilt Univ. (1875), Nashville, Tennessee.

Van der Post, Laurens Jan (1906–), South African novelist. Known for travel books, *eg The Lost World of the Kalahari* (1958), novels, *eg The Heart of the Hunter* (1961).

Vandyke or **Van Dyck, Sir Anthony** (1599-1641), Flemish painter. Assistant to Rubens in his teens, he later worked in Italy. Court painter to Charles I of England from 1632, he profoundly influenced subsequent English portraiture.

Vane, Sir Henry (1613-62), English statesman. Governor of Massachusetts (1636-7). Member of council of state (1649-53). Executed for treason after Restoration.

Vänern, largest lake of Sweden, in SW. Area 5545 sq km (2141 sq mi). Drained by R. Göta into Kattegat. Linked to L. Vättern by Göta Canal.

vanilla, genus of climbing tropical American orchids. Fragrant greenish-yellow flowers. Pod-like capsule of some species yields flavouring extract.

Vanuatu, archipelago of SW Pacific Ocean. Area *c* 14,760 sq km (5700 sq mi); pop. 113,000; cap. Vila. Produces copra, tuna fish, manganese ore. Discovered (1606) by Portuguese; UK-French condominium from 1906. Formerly known as New Hebrides. Independent 1980.

Vanzetti, Bartolomeo, *see* SACCO, NICOLA.

vapour pressure, pressure of a vapour in equilibrium with its solid or liquid form at any given temperature.

Varanasi, city of Uttar Pradesh, NC India. Pop. 583,000. On Ganges, in which Hindu pilgrims bathe to gain absolution from sin. Many mosques, Hindu temples. Formerly known as Benares.

Vargas, Getúlio Dornelles (1883-1954), Brazilian statesman, president (1930-45, 1951-4). Estab. benevolent dictatorship.

variable star, star whose brightness varies, either periodically or irregularly. Variation of Cepheid stars follows law relating period and luminosity, enabling their distance to be determined.

varicose veins, abnormal and irregular swelling of veins, usually in the legs. Caused by defects in the valves which keep blood circulating towards heart. Results from ageing, prolonged standing, pregnancy, *etc.*

Varna, city of E Bulgaria, on Black Sea. Pop. 262,000. Port, resort, trade centre (fish, grain). Univ. (1920). Founded by Greeks in 6th cent. BC. Known as Stalin (1949-56).

varnish, solution of gum or resin in oil (oil varnish) or in volatile solvent (spirit varnish). On drying, forms hard, protective coating.

Vasari, Giorgio (1511-74), Italian artist, biographer. Fame rests on his *Lives of the Artists,* which serves as basic source of knowledge about Renaissance art.

Vasco da Gama, *see* GAMA.

vasectomy, method of male sterilization by sealing of vas deferens, the duct which conveys sperm away from the testicle.

Västerås, city of EC Sweden, on Lake Mälaren. Pop. 118,000. Gothic cathedral, castle (12th cent.).

VAT, *see* VALUE-ADDED TAX.

Vatican City, independent papal state within Rome, WC Italy. Area 44 ha. (109 acres); pop. 1000. Created 1929 by Lateran Treaty; has own citizenship. Seat of govt. of RC church. Buildings incl. Vatican Palace, St

Peter's. Libraries, museums contain priceless collections.

Vatican Councils, two ecumenical councils of RC church. First (1869-70), enunciated doctrine of papal infallibility. Second (1962-5), convened by Pope John XXIII, revised church's role in modern society.

Vaud (Ger. *Waadt*), canton of W Switzerland. Area 3209 sq km (1239 sq mi); cap. Lausanne. Mountainous in SE; fertile elsewhere. Wine indust.; lakeside resorts. Joined Swiss Confederation 1803.

Vaughan, Henry (*c* 1622-95), Welsh poet. Known as 'Silurist'. Works incl. metaphysical religious verse *Silex Scintillans* (1650-5).

Vaughan Williams, Ralph (1872-1958), English composer. Works were influenced by folk song (which he collected) and Tudor polyphony. Wrote 9 symphonies orchestral works, choral works, operas.

vault, in architecture, arched ceiling or roof built with stone or brick. Romans developed barrel or tunnel vault, continuous semi-cylinder of masonry, which enabled them to build rigid structures. Medieval vaults, developed from Roman styles, incl. Gothic ribbed vault.

VD, *see* VENEREAL DISEASE.

vector, physical quantity possessing both magnitude and direction, *eg* velocity, momentum.

Veda, general term for scriptures of Hinduism. Oldest, Rig-Veda, incl. *c* 1000 hymns in praise of gods; Sama-Veda has chants, Yajur-Veda liturgical formulas, and Atharva-Veda incantations to appease demons.

Vedanta, philosophic writings forming commentaries of the VEDA; incl. Upanishads. Hold that ultimate reality is not accessible to experience but only to direct intuition. Term is also applied to this system of thought.

Vedic, *see* SANSKRIT.

Vega [Carpio], Lope [Félix] de (1562-1635), Spanish poet, dramatist. Major poet of 'Golden Age'. Wrote *c* 1800 plays, much poetry.

vegetarianism, practice of restricting diet to foods of vegetable origin, for religious, humanitarian or health reasons. Strict vegetarians abstain from all food of animal origin, *eg* eggs, milk, butter.

vein, in anatomy, blood vessel which carries de-oxygenated blood from the tissues to the heart. Veins have thinner walls than arteries but greater diameters. Provided with valves to prevent back-flow of blood.

Velázquez, Diego Rodríguez de Silva y (1599-1660), Spanish painter. Court painter to Philip IV; work is noted for its superb colour values and use of plain grey backgrounds. Famous works incl. *Maids of Honour, Rokeby Venus.*

veld or **veldt,** open grassy plateau of E and S Africa. Types distinguished by height *eg* High, Middle, Low Veld, or by vegetation *eg* bush, grass, karoo veld. Used for potato and maize growing, cattle herding.

vellum, fine parchment made from specially treated calf, lamb or kid skins. Used as writing surface and in bookbinding.

velocity, rate of change of position. Velocity is VECTOR quantity, distinct from speed, which is a scalar quantity measuring magnitude of velocity.

velvet, fabric woven with short thick pile on one side, often made of silk or rayon. Used for drapery, furniture upholstery, clothing. Modern grades incl. velveteen and corduroy.

Vendée, region and dept. of Poitou, W France, cap. La Roche-sur-Yon. Agric. (esp. cattle, cereals), forests. Scene of peasant-royalist uprising (1793-6) against Revolutionary govt.

Vendôme, Louis Joseph, Duc de (1654-1712), French army officer. In War of the Spanish Succession, defeated at Oudenarde (1708) but later won victories in Spain.

venereal disease (VD), infectious disease usually transmitted by sexual contact with infected person. Incl. GONORRHOEA, SYPHILIS. Prompt medical treatment with antibiotics and sulphonamides usually effective but delay may cause irreparable damage.

Venetia (*Veneto*), region of NE Italy, cap. Venice. Hilly, incl. Dolomites in N; fertile plain in S. Wheat, vines, sugar beet, hemp. Ruled by Austria 1814-66.

Venezia, *see* VENICE.

Venezuela

Venezuela, republic of N South America, on Caribbean. Area 912,050 sq km (352,143 sq mi); pop. 13,122,000; cap. Caracas. Language: Spanish. Religion: RC. Coast (valuable oil production) rises to E Andes (agric., esp. coffee, cacao); cattle raising in Llanos of Orinoco basin; rain forest on Guiana Highlands. Major oil, gold, diamond exports. Settled by Spanish in 16th cent.; independence struggle (1811-21) under Bolívar. Part of Greater Columbia until secession (1830). Subsequent rule mainly by dictatorship.

Venice (*Venezia*), city of NE Italy, on Gulf of Venice, cap. of Venetia and of Venezia prov. Pop. 360,000. Port, naval base; oil refining, glass; tourist centre. Built on 118 isls., with 170 canals (incl. Grand Canal), 400 bridges (incl. Rialto, Bridge of Sighs). Rich medieval maritime republic, *fl* 14th-15th cent.; defeated Genoa 1380. St Mark's Sq., Doge's Palace are major attractions.

Venus, in Roman religion, perhaps orig. goddess of gardens, but became goddess of love, identified with Greek Aphrodite.

Venus, in astronomy, planet 2nd in distance from Sun; revolves about Sun at mean distance of *c* 108 million km in 225 days; diameter 12,300 km; mass *c* 0.8 that of Earth. Has dense cloud layer containing carbon dioxide and surface temperature of 425° C. Seen as 'evening star' in W.

Venus' flytrap, *Dionaea muscipula,* perennial insectivorous herb native to North Carolina and Florida. Hinged leaves close when touched; insects trapped in leaves are digested.

Veracruz, port of EC Mexico. on Gulf of Mexico. Pop. 277,000. Major export centre esp. coffee, vanilla, tobacco; chemicals, textile, soap mfg. Estab. 1599. Resort.

verbena, genus of plants chiefly native to tropical America. Showy spikes or clusters of red, white or purplish flowers. Widely cultivated as ornamental. Species incl. European vervain, *Verbena officinalis.*

Vercingetorix (d. 46 BC), Gallic chieftain. Led revolt in Gaul against Roman occupation (58-51 BC). Defeated by Caesar and put to death in Rome.

Verde, Cape, penin. of Senegal; most W point of Africa. Dakar is on S coast.

Verdi, Giuseppe (1813-1901), Italian composer. Renowned for operas, incl. *Il Trovatore, La Traviata, Rigoletto, Aïda, Otello* and *Falstaff;* last two based on Shakespeare's plays. Also wrote *Requiem.*

verdigris, greenish deposit formed on copper, brass or bronze surfaces exposed to atmosphere. Consists of basic copper carbonate or sulphate.

Verdun, town of Lorraine, NE France, on R. Meuse. Pop. 25,000. Textile mfg., food processing. Treaty of Verdun (843) divided Charlemagne's empire among his 3 grandsons. Fortified 17th cent.; fortress was scene of long German assault (1916) resisted by French.

Vereeniging, city of S Transvaal, South Africa, on R. Vaal. Pop. 170,000. Indust. centre in coalmining dist. Treaty ending Boer War signed here (1902).

Vergil or **Virgil,** full name Publius Vergilius Maro (70-19 BC), Roman poet. Famous for *Aeneid,* epic in 12 books on wanderings of Aeneas, reflecting preoccupations with greatness of Rome, virtues of a leader, nature of human existence and destiny. Also wrote pastoral poems, *Eclogues* (37 BC), didactic poems on rural life, *Georgics* (30 BC).

Verlaine, Paul (1844-96), French poet. Prominent among SYMBOLISTS. Encouraged in free-living by RIMBAUD. Graceful, musical verse collections incl. *Fêtes galantes* (1869), *Romances sans paroles* (1874), *Sagesse* (1881).

Vermeer, Jan (1632-75), Dutch painter. Known for the calm perfection of his subtly-lit interiors, with 1 or 2 figures. Works incl. *Allegory of Painting* and *Woman with a Water Jug.*

Vermont, New England state of US. Area 24,887 sq km (9609 sq mi); pop. 485,000; cap. Montpelier; largest town Burlington. Canada on N border; L. Champlain in NW; Green Mts. cross N-S; chief river Connecticut. Agric. incl. dairy farming, fruit, maple syrup; marble quarrying, tourism. Settled in 18th cent.; part of New York until 1777. Admitted to Union as 14th state (1791).

vermouth, fortified white wine flavoured with aromatic herbs. Made chiefly in France and Italy.

Verne, Jules (1828-1905), French author. Early exponent of SCIENCE FICTION in novels, *eg Twenty Thousand Leagues Under the Sea* (1870), *Around the World in Eighty Days* (1873).

Verona, city of Venetia, NE Italy, on R. Adige. Cap. of Verona prov. Pop. 271,000. Agric. market, printing. Joined (1167) Lombard League, *fl* 13th-14th cent. under della Scala family. Austrian fortress 1797-1866. Roman amphitheatre, Gothic town hall.

Veronese, real name Paolo Caliari (*c* 1528-88), Italian painter, b. Verona. Worked in Venice from 1553; specialized in huge allegorical, religious and historical scenes.

veronica or **speedwell,** any of genus *Veronica* of perennial plants native to temperate regions; small blue, pink or white flowers. Many species cultivated as garden flowers.

Verrocchio, real name Andrea di Cioni (*c* 1435-88), Italian sculptor, painter of Florentine school. Executed famous equestrian statue of Bartolomeo Colleoni in Venice.

Versailles, town of N France, W of Paris, cap. of Yvelines dept. Pop. 95,000. Tourist centre, noted for palace and gardens built late 17th cent. for Louis XIV. Site of many treaties, *eg* between France and Prussia (1871), after WWI (1919).

Versailles, Treaty of, peace treaty at end of WWI signed by Allies (Britain, France, US and Italy) and Germany (1919). Germany, which took no part in negotiations, forced to accept terms, incl. loss of colonies, return of Alsace-Lorraine to France, loss of territ. to Denmark, Poland, Belgium, demilitarization of Rhineland, restrictions on armaments, payment of REPARATIONS. Treaty also contained covenant of LEAGUE OF NATIONS.

vertebra, segment of spinal column or backbone of vertebrates. Man has 33 vertebrae: 7 cervical in neck, 12 thoracic (each carrying pair of ribs), 5 lumbar; last 9 are fused to form sacrum and tail-like coccyx. Flexible discs unite the vertebrae; pressure on nerve fibres caused by bulges in discs is condition known as 'slipped disc'.

vertebrate, any of subphylum Vertebrata of chordate animals, with segmented spinal column and skull containing well-developed brain. Incl. mammals, birds, amphibians, reptiles.

vertigo, giddiness with associated feeling of whirling movement. Caused by disturbance in balance mechanism of the inner ear or eyes.

vervain, *see* VERBENA.

Verwoerd, Hendrik Frensch (1901-66), South African statesman, b. Netherlands. As minister of native affairs (1950-8), enacted harsh APARTHEID laws. As premier (1958-66), took South Africa out of Commonwealth and estab. republic (1961). Assassinated.

Vesalius, Andreas (1514-64), Flemish anatomist. His dissections and experiments on human body mark start of scientific anatomy. Wrote *De humani corporis fabrica* (pub. 1543).

Vespasian, full name Titus Flavius Vespasianus (AD 9-79), Roman emperor (AD 69-79). During his reign, Agricola made major conquest in Britain. Built Colosseum.

Vespucci, Amerigo (1454-1512), Italian navigator, b. Florence. In service of Spain, made many voyages to New World. Proved South America not part of Asia; American continent named after him.

Vesta, in Roman religion, goddess of the hearth, worshipped in every house. Sacred fire of state kept ever burning in Temple of Vesta, tended by 6 **Vestal Virgins,** for whom penalty for breaking vow of chastity was burial alive.

Vesuvius, SW Italy, on Bay of Naples, only active volcano on European mainland. Height now *c* 1185 m (3890 ft). Many eruptions, incl. AD 79 when Pompeii, Herculaneum buried.

vetch, any of genus *Vicia* of weak-stemmed herbs of Leguminosae family, native to N temperate regions and South America. Common vetch or tare, *V. sativa,* is cultivated for forage and soil improvement.

veterinary science, branch of medicine dealing with diseases of animals (esp. domestic).

veto, order prohibiting proposed act, esp. by person in authority. Term used specifically for constitutional right of ruler or branch of govt. to reject bills passed by another branch of govt. In UN, any of 5 permanent members of Security Council have power of veto on action other than procedural.

VHF (Very High Frequency), electromagnetic radiation at frequency of 30×10^6 - 30×10^7 cycles per second. Used in frequency MODULATION radio transmission. UHF (Ultra High Frequency) is from 30×10^7 - 30×10^8 cycles per second.

viaduct, long bridge to carry a road or railway line over a valley or gorge. Usually consists of series of short, concrete or masonry spans supported on piers or towers.

vibraphone, percussion instrument having metal bars and resonators with rotating lids driven by an electric motor to simulate a vibrato. Also called 'vibes'.

viburnum, genus of shrubs and small trees of honeysuckle family. Native to Europe, Asia and N Africa. Species incl. wayfaring tree, *Viburnum lantana,* with white flowers.

Vicenza, city of Venetia, N Italy, cap. of Vicenza prov. Pop. 119,000. Railway jct., agric. market, machinery. Many buildings by Palladio. Medieval cathedral.

Vichy, town of C France, on R. Allier. Pop. 34,000. Spa resort from Roman times; exports Vichy water.

Vichy government, govt. of unoccupied France, with seat at Vichy, set up under Pétain after Franco-German armistice (1940). Became tool of Germany under P. LAVAL (1942); powerless after German occupation of all France (Nov. 1942).

Vicksburg, town of W Mississippi, US. Pop. 25,000. Scene of strategic victory by Union during Civil War (1863).

Victor Emmanuel II (1820-78), king of Italy (1861-78), king of Sardinia from 1849. Acted as figurehead for policies of Italian unification of his premier, CAVOUR.

Victor Emmanuel III (1869-1947), king of Italy (1900-46). Asked Mussolini to form govt. Effectively deprived of power under Fascist regime. Made armistice (1943) with Allies in WWII. Abdicated.

Victoria (1819-1901), queen of Great Britain and Ireland (1837-1901). Married Prince Albert of Saxe-Coburg-Gotha (1840); guided by him in matters of policy. On Albert's death (1861), spent several years in seclusion. Influenced by Disraeli; became empress of India (1876) under his guidance. Reign marked by indust. and colonial expansion, domestic reform.

Victoria, state of SE Australia. Area 227,700 sq km (87,900 sq mi); pop. 3,854,000; cap. Melbourne. Narrow coastal lowlands; uplands incl. C plateau, Australian Alps (SE); Murray basin in NW. Agric. (irrigated in NW) incl. wheat, fruit, vegetable growing, sheep and cattle raising; timber indust.; minerals incl. coal, oil, natural gas, gypsum. Industs. incl. petro-chemicals, car assembly, paper mfg. Settled from 1834; independent from New South Wales (1851). Pop. grew rapidly after 1851 gold discoveries. Federal state from 1901.

Victoria, seaport and cap. of British Columbia, Canada; on Vancouver Isl. Pop. 218,000. Timber, fishing, tourist industs. Founded 1843 as fur trading post.

Victoria, cap. of Hong Kong, on Hong Kong Isl. Pop. 849,000.

Victoria, cap. of SEYCHELLES.

Victoria Cross, highest British military decoration. Instituted by Queen Victoria (1856).

Victoria Falls, massive waterfall of R. Zambezi, on Zimbabwe-Zambia border. Width 1.6 km (1 mi); max. height 128 m

(420 ft). Tourist centre; h.e.p. Discovered 1855 by Livingstone.

Victoria Island, SW Franklin Dist., Northwest Territs., Canada; part of Arctic archipelago. Area 212,200 sq km (81,930 sq mi).

Victoria Land, region of Antarctica, divided between Ross Dependency and Australian Antarctic Territ.

Victoria Nyanza or **Lake Victoria,** freshwater lake of EC Africa, 2nd largest in world. Borders on Uganda (N), Kenya (E), Tanzania (S). Area 69,490 sq km (26,830 sq mi); source of White Nile.

vicuña, *Lama vicugna,* wild llama found in South American Andes. Hunted by man for wool; numbers much reduced.

Vienna (*Wien*), cap. and prov. of Austria, on R. Danube. Pop. 1,590,000. River port, admin., commercial centre. Cap. and cultural centre of Austria from 12th cent. Univ. (1365). Buildings incl. Hofburg (imperial palace), cathedral of St Stephen, Houses of Parliament, opera house; also museums, parks. Resisted Turkish sieges 1529, 1683. German-occupied in WWII, Jewish pop. wiped out. Occupied by Allies 1945-55.

Vienna, Congress of, meeting (1814-15) of European powers (foremost being Austria, Prussia, Russia, Britain and France) to settle problems arising out of defeat of Napoleon. Resolved boundary disputes, reallocated control of many small states, estab. 'balance of power' principle in international politics.

Vienne, town of SE France, on R. Rhône. Pop. 30,000. Agric. market, textiles (esp. silk mfg.), tanning. Hist. seat of kings of Burgundy. Roman remains.

Vientiane, admin. cap. of Laos. Pop. 177,000. Commercial centre on R. Mekong; timber, textiles. Cap. of kingdom 1707-1827. Became cap. of French protect. of Laos 1899.

Vierwaldstättersee, *see* LUCERNE, LAKE.

Viet Cong, *see* VIETNAM WAR.

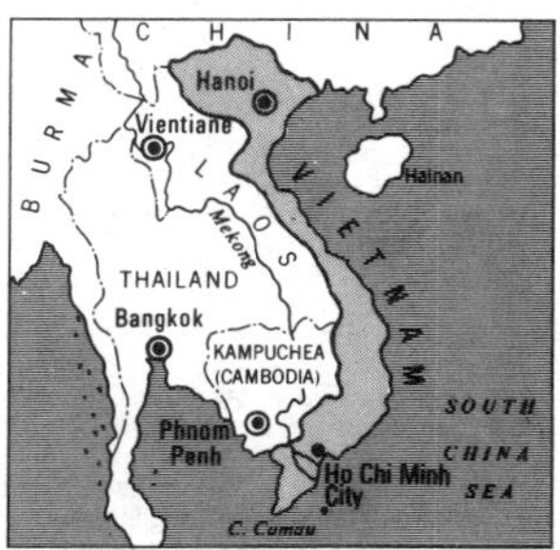

Vietnam

Vietnam, country of SE Asia. Area *c* 333,000 sq km (128,000 sq mi); pop. 49,890,000; cap. Hanoi. Language: Vietnamese. Religion: Taoism. Forested mountains and plateau with Mekong delta in S. Rice chief crop. Part of French-ruled INDO-CHINA until estab. of republic from Annam, Tonkin, Cochin China; dispute with France over independence led to INDO-CHINESE WAR, ending with Geneva conference (1954) which divided country into 2 states, North and South Vietnam. **North Vietnam,** area *c* 159,000 sq km (61,000 sq mi); pop. 23,244,000; cap. Hanoi. **South Vietnam,** area *c* 174,000 sq km (67,000 sq mi); pop. 19,954,000; cap. Ho Chi Minh City (Saigon). After North's victory in VIETNAM WAR, North and South were reintegrated (1976) under Communist régime.

Vietnam War, conflict in SE Asia, fought mainly in South Vietnam from 1954 between govt. forces and Communist Viet Cong guerrillas supported by North Vietnam and Soviet armaments. US support of South with economic, military aid began 1961, and intensified from 1964, when alleged Tonkin gunboat attacks prompted bombing of North. Tet offensive (1968) discredited US reports of ultimate victory, and peace talks began in Paris. Despite formal conclusion of war (1973), guerrilla activities continued in South, which capitulated with capture of Saigon (April, 1975). Length of war, high US casualties, corruption of South Vietnam govt. contributed to opposition of war within US.

Vigny, Alfred Victor, Comte de (1797-1863), French author. Leading Romantic. Works incl. restrained, stoical *Poèmes antiques et modernes* (1826), play *Chatterton* (1835), historical novel *Cinq Mars* (1826).

Vigo, city of Galicia, NW Spain, on Bay of Vigo. Pop. 197,000. Port; shipbuilding, oil refining, fishing. Scene of naval victory (1702) of British and Dutch over French and Spanish.

Viipuri, *see* VYBORG.

Vikings, Scandinavian sea-warriors who raided coasts of Europe (9th-11th cents.) in their oar-powered longships. Colonized Iceland, Normandy, parts of Britain and Ireland. Thought to have reached North America (*see* LEIF ERICSSON). Traded S and E to Persia, Spain, Russia. Also called Norsemen.

Villa, Francisco ('Pancho') (*c* 1877-1923), Mexican revolutionary. Took part in 1910 revolution. Involved in power struggle with Carranza from 1914. Assassinated.

Villa-Lobos, Heitor (1887-1959), Brazilian composer. Works show influence of Brazilian folk song and South American Indians.

villein, peasant of W Europe under medieval manorial system. Did not own land, but owed services to lord. Unlike serf, was personally free. Villeinage system declined in England by 14th cent. but survived elsewhere until 19th cent.

Villeneuve, Pierre Charles Jean Baptiste Sylvestre de (1763-1806), French naval officer. Consistently unsuccessful in battles with Nelson, from Nile (1798) to Trafalgar (1805). On his way home after captivity in England he committed suicide.

Villiers, George, *see* BUCKINGHAM, GEORGE VILLIERS, 1ST DUKE OF.

Villiers de L'Isle-Adam, Auguste, Comte de (1838-89), French author. Forerunner of SYMBOLISTS. Works incl. *Contes cruels* (1883), visionary play *Axël* (1890).

Villon, François (1431-after 1463), French poet. Violent, criminal life reflected in verse, expressing compassion for human suffering, piety, alongside biting satire, ribaldry. Wrote *Lais* or *Petit Testament* (1456), containing lighthearted 'bequests' to friends, *Grand Testament* (1461), review of past life into which are set famous *ballades*.

Vilnius (Russ. *Vilna*), city of USSR, cap. of Lithuanian SSR. Pop. 481,000. Railway jct.; food processing, sawmilling, agric. machinery mfg. Cap. of Lithuania (1323-1795); passed to Russian control. Intended cap. of independent Lithuania but seized (1920) by Poland and held until 1939. Large Jewish pop. decimated by Germans (1941-4). RC cathedral; univ. (1579).

Vincent de Paul, St (*c* 1580-1660), French priest. Founded secular Congregation of the Mission or 'Lazarists' (1625) and Sisters of Charity (1634), dedicated to work in orphanages, schools, hospitals.

vine, climbing or trailing plant, either woody or herbaceous, *eg* grape vine, ivy, Virginia creeper.

vinegar, sour liquid consisting of dilute and impure acetic acid, obtained by action of bacteria on beer (producing malt vinegar), wine, cider, industrial alcohol, *etc.* Used as preservative in pickling and as a condiment.

vingt-et-un, gambling game at cards, in which each player's aim is to obtain from dealer cards totalling 21 points or as near as possible to that total without exceeding it. Also known as blackjack and pontoon.

Vinland, hist. portion of North American coast discovered by Leif Ericsson (*c* AD 1000). Location of his landing disputed, most likely on S coast of New England.

vinyl group, univalent chemical radical CH_2:CH derived from ethylene. Various vinyl compounds, incl. chloride and acetate, may be polymerized to form plastics and resins.

viol, family of six-stringed instruments with fretted fingerboards, played with bow; popular esp. 16th-17th cent. Held on or between player's knees. Superseded by violin family; revived for performances of old music.

viola, member of violin family, between violin and cello in range. Pitched an octave above cello.

violet, any of genus *Viola* of small plants native to N temperate zones. White, blue, purple or yellow irregular flowers with short spurs. Species incl. *V. odorata* with small purple flowers and *V. tricolor* or garden pansy.

Violin

violin family, string instruments of which the four strings are bowed or plucked. Strings are stretched across a wooden bridge which transfers their vibrations to a sound chamber forming body of instrument. Fingerboard is fretless. Members are violin, viola and violoncello (CELLO), double bass. Evolved in 16th cent. and perfected by Italian violin makers, *eg* Amati, Stradivari, in 17th cent.

violoncello, *see* CELLO.

viper, any of Viperidae family of Old World venomous snakes, incl. ADDER and ASP. Name also applied to New World pit vipers, incl. RATTLESNAKE, bushmaster, fer-de-lance.

Virgil, *see* VERGIL.

virginals, *see* SPINET.

Virginia, Atlantic state of E US. Area 105,711 sq km (40,815 sq mi); pop. 5,101,000; cap. Richmond; largest city Norfolk. Low coastal plain (partly swamp) rises to Appalachians in W. Chief rivers Potomac, James, Rappahannock. Agric. esp. tobacco growing; fisheries, shipbuilding, mfg. industs. First permanent English colony estab. at Jamestown (1607). One of original 13 colonies of US. Major battleground in Revolution, Civil War.

Virginia creeper, *Parthenocissus quinquefolia,* North American tendril-climbing vine widely cultivated in Europe as ornamental; bright autumn colouring.

Virgin Islands, group of *c* 100 isls. in West Indies, E of Puerto Rico. Discovered and named (1493) by Columbus. **British Virgin Islands** incl. Tortola, Anegada, Virgin Gorda isls. Area 153 sq km (59 sq mi); pop. 12,000; cap. Road Town (on Tortola). Colony from 17th cent. **Virgin Islands of the United States** incl. St Thomas, St Croix,

St John isls. Area 345 sq km (133 sq mi); pop. 104,000; cap. Charlotte Amalie (on St Thomas). Purchased (1917) from Denmark.

Virgin Mary, *see* MARY, THE VIRGIN.

Virgo, *see* ZODIAC.

virus, disease-producing micro-organism, capable of multiplication only within living cells. Essential constituent is a nucleic acid (DNA, RNA), surrounded by a protein coat. Typical virus attaches itself to a cell of host and introduces its nucleic acid. Cell is forced to synthesize further nucleic acid and protein, enabling virus to reproduce itself. Cause of diseases such as measles, influenza, smallpox.

Visconti, ruling family of Milan from 1277 to 1447.

viscose process, method of making rayon from viscose, a brown liquid prepared by treating cellulose with sodium hydroxide and carbon disulphide. Yarn is made by forcing viscose through fine holes into acid solution. Discovered in 1892.

viscosity, internal friction of a fluid, caused by molecular attraction, making it resist tendency to flow. Viscosity of liquids decreases with rising temperature.

Vishnu, in Hinduism, one of three supreme gods. Early myth associates him with solar deities of Rig-Veda. Many incarnations incl. Rama, Krishna.

Visigoths or **West Goths,** branch of GOTHS who were driven into Thrace and the Balkans by the Huns (*c* 375). Under ALARIC, they invaded Italy and sacked Rome (410). Later conquered much of S France and Spain. Forced to retreat into Spain by Clovis (507). Their kingdom in Spain was overrun during Moorish conquest (711).

vision, *see* EYE; RETINA.

Vistula (Pol. *Wisla,* Ger. *Weichsel*), river of Poland. Flows *c* 1080 km (670 mi) from N Carpathians via Kraków, Warsaw, Toruń to Gulf of Gdańsk near Gdańsk. Major trade route; canal links with other rivers *eg* Oder, Dnepr.

vitamin A, fat-soluble vitamin, found in fish-liver oil, milk, butter, *etc.* Can be synthesized in body from carotene found in green plants and carrots. Deficiency causes night blindness.

vitamin B complex, group of unrelated water-soluble vitamins, found in liver, yeast, wheat-germ, *etc.* Incl. THIAMIN, RIBOFLAVIN and vitamin B_{12}, a deficiency of which causes pernicious anaemia.

vitamin C, *see* ASCORBIC ACID.

vitamin D, any of group of fat-soluble vitamins, found in fish-liver oil, milk, *etc.* Formed in skin by action of ultraviolet radiation from Sun. Essential to formation of bones and teeth.

vitamin K, fat-soluble vitamin found in certain green leaves of plants and synthesized by bacteria in the intestines. Promotes blood clotting.

vitamins, group of complex organic compounds essential in small amounts to normal body metabolism. Some can be synthesized in body from other substances found in food, *eg* vitamin A; others, *eg* vitamin C, must be present in diet. Vitamin deficiencies cause various diseases.

Vitebsk, city of USSR, N Byelorussian SSR; on W Dvina. Pop. 297,000. Agric. machinery, textile mfg. Chief town of Polotsk principality before coming under Lithuanian rule in 14th cent. Annexed to Russia in 1772.

Vitoria, city of N Spain, cap. of Alava prov. Pop. 169,000. Agric. market, tanning. Scene of Wellington's decisive victory (1813) over French in Peninsular War. Cathedral (12th cent.).

vitriol, name given to various sulphate salts and sulphuric acid. Green vitriol is ferrous sulphate, blue vitriol copper sulphate, oil of vitriol concentrated sulphuric acid.

Vitruvius [Pollio, Marcus] (*fl* 1st cent. AD), Roman architect, engineer. Author of *De architectura,* source much used by Renaissance architects.

Vivaldi, Antonio (*c* 1675-1741), Italian composer. Wrote numerous *concerti grossi* and concertos for solo instruments, esp. violin, incl. *The Four Seasons.*

vivisection, use of living animals for medical research into causes and prevention of diseases, esp. of man.

Vladimir, city of USSR, C European RSFSR. Pop. 296,000. Textiles, tractor mfg. Cap. of Vladimir principality (12th-14th cent.) until court removed to Moscow. Kremlin contains 2 cathedrals (12th cent.).

Vladivostok, city of USSR, SE Siberian RSFSR. Pop. 550,000. Port and naval base (kept ice-free in winter) on Pacific coast. Exports timber, soya bean oil; shipbuilding, sawmilling; fishing, whaling. Settled 1860. Terminus of Trans-Siberian railway.

Vlaminck, Maurice de (1876-1958), French painter. One of the original fauves, early work is characterized by exuberant colour. Later specialized in darker, more expressionistic landscapes.

Vlissingen, *see* FLUSHING.

Vltava, *see* MOLDAU.

vodka, colourless spirit distilled from barley, rye, maize, or potatoes. Originally made in Russia, Poland and Baltic states.

voice, sound produced by vibration of vocal cords, 2 pairs of membranous cords in larynx. Air from lungs causes lower pair to vibrate; pitch of sound is controlled by tension of cords and volume by regulation of air passing through larynx. Sinuses act as resonators, and muscles of the tongue and cheek articulate the sound.

Vojvodina, autonomous prov. of N Yugoslavia, in Serbia. Area 21,500 sq km (8300 sq mi); cap. Novi Sad. Fertile, low-lying, drained by Danube, Sava, Tisza; large amounts of cereals, vegetables, fruit grown. Part of Hungary until 1920.

volcano, vent in Earth's crust through which lavas, gases, *etc* are ejected. May be on land or submarine. Solidified material around outlet gives conical shape. Volcanoes may be active, dormant or extinct.

Volcano Islands, group of 3 volcanic isls. in W Pacific, S of Japan. Area 29 sq km (11 sq mi); main isl. Iwo Jima. Annexed by Japan 1887. Captured by US forces in WWII; returned to Japan 1968.

vole, small rat-like burrowing rodent with blunt nose and short tail. Species incl. field vole, *Microtus agrestis,* and water vole, *Arvicola amphibius.*

Volga, river of USSR, European RSFSR; longest river of Europe. Rises in Valdai hills, flows *c* 3850 km (2400 mi) generally SE into wide Caspian delta. Connected by canals to Moscow, Leningrad and R. Don; major transportation system. Used for irrigation, h.e.p.; fishing in lower course.

Volgograd, city of USSR, SE European RSFSR; port on lower Volga. Pop. 929,000. Transport and indust. centre; oil refining, shipyards, steel and heavy machinery mfg. Founded 1589 as Tsaritsyn; Stalingrad (1925-61). Scene of decisive Soviet victory in WWII after German siege (1942-3).

volleyball, six-a-side team game played on a rectangular court. Players hit a ball with their hands, attempting to return it over net without its touching ground. Originated (1895) in US.

volt, SI unit of electric potential, defined as difference in potential between 2 points on a conductor carrying constant current of 1 ampère when power dissipated between points is 1 watt.

Volta, Alessandro, Conte (1745-1827), Italian physicist. Invented electrophorus to produce electric charge. Discovered voltaic pile (battery) which produced steady electric current. Unit of electromotive force, volt, named after him.

Volta, river of W Africa. Black and White Volta rivers from Upper Volta unite to form Volta in C Ghana; flows S to Gulf of Guinea at Ada. Volta River Scheme provides h.e.p., irrigation; Akosombo Dam (1966) formed L. Volta (area 4920 sq km/1900 sq mi).

Voltaire, pseud. of François Marie Arouet (1694-1778), French philosopher, writer. Attacked organized religion, superstition, intolerance, civil repression. Influenced by English thought esp. by Newton, Locke, ideas influenced movement culminating in French Revolution. Wrote immense number of works, incl. tragedy *Zaïre* (1732), *Letters Concerning the English Nation* (1733). Best known for philosophical novel, *Candide* (1759), satirizing LEIBNITZ.

voltmeter, instrument for measuring potential difference between 2 points. Usually consists of galvanometer in series with a high resistance.

Von Braun, Wernher (1912-77), American rocket expert, b. Germany. Helped develop German V-2 military rocket. In US, involved in development of *Apollo* rockets.

Von Neumann, John (1903-57), American mathematician, b. Hungary. Made significant contributions to quantum theory, mathematical logic, continuous groups, *etc.* Founder of game theory; influential in development of high-speed computers, which aided production of the atomic bomb.

voodoo, religious beliefs, practices of West Indian, S US and South American Negroes. Derived from W African snake worship, fetishism. Esp. prevalent in Haiti.

Voronezh, city of USSR, SC European RSFSR; near confluence of Voronezh and Don rivers. Pop. 783,000. Indust. centre of black-earth region; synthetic rubber and machinery mfg.

Voroshilovgrad, town of USSR, E Ukrainian SSR; in Donbas mining area. Pop. 463,000. Locomotives, coalmining equipment. Formerly Lugansk.

Vorster, Balthazar Johannes (1915-), South African political leader, PM (1966-1978). Succeeded Verwoerd, whose APARTHEID policies he upheld.

vortex, term used to describe rapid rotatory movement of a fluid. Used mainly of liquids (whirlpools) and of air (tornadoes, whirlwinds).

vorticism, English art movement founded (1913) by Wyndham Lewis; stimulated by futurism, and influenced by cubism, it sought to revitalize English art by introducing modern industrial forms.

Vosges, mountain range of E France. Extends *c* 240 km (150 mi) NE from Belfort Gap, separates Alsace (E) from Lorraine (W); rises to 1423 m (4672 ft). Forests, vineyards, resorts. Source of Moselle, Sarre rivers.

vote, *see* ELECTION, PROPORTIONAL REPRESENTATION, SUFFRAGE, CIVIL RIGHTS.

Vries, Hugo de (1848-1935), Dutch botanist. Rediscovered Mendel's work on heredity; discovered role of mutation in evolution.

Vuillard, Edouard (1868-1940), French painter. Known for intimate interiors, portraits, still lifes, which display his feeling for colour and form.

Vulcan, in Roman religion, fire god, perhaps god of the smithy. Became identified with Greek Hephaestus.

Vulgate, Latin version of Bible prepared (late 4th cent.) by St JEROME from Hebrew (OT) and Old Latin (NT) texts. Chosen by Council of Trent (1546) as official version in RC church.

vulture, large carrion-eating bird with hooked beak, strong claws, and featherless neck and head. True vultures, found only in C Europe, Africa and parts of Asia, incl. LAMMERGEIER and griffon vulture, *Gyps fulvus.* New World vultures incl. Andean CONDOR.

Vyborg (Finn. *Viipuri,* Swed. *Viborg*), port of USSR, NW European RSFSR; on Gulf of Finland. Pop. 63,000. Exports timber, wood products. Site of Swedish castle (1293); Hanseatic port. Ceded to Russia by Sweden (1721); part of Finland (1812-1947).

wages, in economics, share of total product of industry that goes to labour as distinct from share taken by capital. May be in money, goods or services. Real wages determined by amount of goods monetary wages will buy.

Wagner, Richard (1813-83), German composer. Developed romantic music to great heights, using musical motifs in continuously evolving form to underline drama. Founded festival theatre at Bayreuth where he presented 4-opera cycle *Ring of the Nibelung* (1876). Other operas incl. *Die Meistersinger, Tannhäuser, Tristan und Isolde.*

wagtail, small, chiefly European, bird of Motacillidae family. Slender body with long tail that wags up and down. Species incl. black and white pied wagtail, *Motacilla alba.*

Wahabi, followers of Mohammed ibn Abd al-Wahab (*c* 1703-91), who founded strict Moslem religious sect. Stress austerity in worship and living. Religion of ruling family of Saudi Arabia.

Wakamatsu, *see* KITAKYUSHU.

Wakefield, city and admin. hq. of West Yorkshire, N England, on R. Calder. Pop. 60,000. Agric. market; woollens; coal-mining. Has 14th-cent. cathedral. Scene of battle (1460) of Wars of the Roses.

Wake Island, atoll with 3 islets, C Pacific Ocean, dependency of US. Area 8 sq km (3 sq mi). Pop. 2000. US naval, air base. Visited and named (1796) by British, annexed (1898) by US. Occupied by Japanese in WWII.

Waksman, Selman Abraham (1888-1973), American biologist, b. Russia. Awarded Nobel Prize for Physiology and Medicine (1952) for discovery of antibiotic streptomycin.

Walachia or **Wallachia,** region of S Romania. Chief city Bucharest. Turkish rule from 14th cent. until united with MOLDAVIA (1859) to form Romania.

Walcheren, region of SW Netherlands, at mouth of Scheldt estuary. Main towns Middelburg, Flushing. Lowland, protected by North Sea dykes; agric., tourism. German occupation in WWII ended by bombing dykes.

Waldenses or **Waldensians,** Christian sect formed (1170) by Peter Waldo (d. 1217). Dedicated to poverty and meditation, with Bible as sole authority. Declared heretical (1215). Persecuted 15th-17th cent.

Waldheim, Kurt (1918-), Austrian diplomat, UN secretary-general (1972-).

Wales (*Cymru*), principality of UK, in W part of Great Britain. Area 20,761 sq km (8006 sq mi); pop. 2,768,000; cap. Cardiff. Languages: English, Welsh. Religion: Methodist. Comprises 8 counties. Main rivers Severn, Wye, Taff. Crossed N-S by Cambrian Mts. (highest point Snowdon). Mainly pastoral; indust. based on S Wales coalfields (Swansea, Merthyr Tydfil, Rhondda). Originally inhabited by Celts. English conquest by Edward I (1282), but fierce fighting continued; politically united from 1536. Resurgence of nationalism in late 20th cent.

Wales, Prince of, title created (1301) by Edward I of England for his eldest son after conquest of Wales; since conferred on eldest son of monarch.

wallaby, common name applied to various genera of small kangaroo when hind foot of adult is less than 25 cm/10 in. long; widely distributed in Australia and Tasmania.

Wallace, Alfred Russel (1823-1913), English naturalist. Developed theory of natural selection independently of Darwin.

Wallace, Sir William (*c* 1272-1305), Scottish patriot. Led forces which defeated Edward I's army at Stirling (1297). Ruled Scotland briefly as guardian of kingdom. Defeated (1298) by English at Falkirk. Captured (1305), executed in London.

Wallachia, *see* WALACHIA.

Wallasey, town of Merseyside met. county, NW England, on Wirral penin. Pop. 97,000. Resort, residential; ferry to Liverpool.

Wallenstein, Albrecht von (1583-1634), Bohemian soldier, commander of forces of Emperor Ferdinand II. Fought successfully in early years of THIRTY YEARS WAR until defeated by Gustavus Adolphus at Lützen (1632). Murdered.

wallflower, *Cheiranthus cheiri,* European plant with sweet-scented yellow or orange flowers. Many garden varieties cultivated.

Wallis, Sir Barnes Neville (1887-1979), English aeronautical engineer. Designed R 100 airship and bouncing bombs used against Möhne and Eder dams (1943). Invented swing-wing aeroplane.

Wallis and Futuna Islands, overseas territ. of France, in SC Pacific Ocean. Area 272 sq km (105 sq mi); pop. 9000; main isl. Uvéa. Produce timber. Acquired by France (1842); dependency of New Caledonia until 1959.

Walloons, people of S provs. of Belgium who speak Walloon, a dialect of French. Friction between Walloons and Flemings remains element of Belgian politics.

Wall Street, New York street in lower Manhattan. As location of stock exchange and major banks, name has become synonymous with American finance.

walnut, any of genus *Juglans* of deciduous

trees of N temperate zones. Edible nut; timber valued for cabinetmaking.

Walpole, Robert, 1st Earl of Orford (1676-1745), British statesman. Led Whig admin. (1721-42) as first lord of treasury and chancellor of exchequer, effectively acting as 1st PM. Restored economic stability after SOUTH SEA BUBBLE (1720). Tried to keep Britain out of European wars. Estab. principle of CABINET responsibility to Parliament. His son **Horace Walpole,** 4th Earl of Orford (1717-97), author, wrote prototypical 'gothick' novel, *The Castle of Otranto* (1765). Rebuilt villa, Strawberry Hill, making 'gothick' taste fashionable.

Walpurgis, St (d. 779), English missionary in Germany. *Walpurgisnacht,* eve of her feast on 1 May, is traditional witches' sabbath.

Walrus

walrus, either of 2 species of seal-like carnivores of Odobenidae family. Large upper canines form tusks used for scraping shellfish from sea bottom. Males up to 4.5 m/15 ft long may weigh over 1000 kg/1 ton. *Odobenus rosmarus* inhabits NW Atlantic, Arctic and *O. divergens* the Bering Sea.

Walsall, town of West Midlands met. county, WC England. Pop. 182,000. In BLACK COUNTRY; coal, iron industs.; leather goods.

Walsingham, Sir Francis (*c* 1532-90), English statesman. Secretary of state after 1573, directed far-reaching spy ring. Discovered Babington's plot which implicated Mary Queen of Scots (1587).

Waltham Forest, bor. of NE Greater London, England. Pop. 220,000. Created 1965 from Essex towns.

Walton, Izaak (1593-1683), English writer. Wrote *The Compleat Angler* (1653) on pleasures of fishing.

Walton, Sir William Turner (1902-), English composer. Works incl. setting of poems by Edith Sitwell, *Façade*. Also wrote viola concerto, film scores, *eg Hamlet,* opera *Troilus and Cressida,* 2 symphonies and oratorio *Belshazzar's Feast.*

waltz, dance in triple time. Popularity spread from Vienna in 19th cent. through compositions of Strauss family.

Walvis Bay, town of Namibia, on Atlantic Ocean. Pop. 16,000. Railway terminus, port, fishing and whaling industs. With hinterland (area *c* 970 sq km/375 sq mi) forms exclave of Cape Prov., Republic of South Africa.

wandering Jew or **sailor,** various trailing or creeping ornamental plants, esp. *Zebrina pendula* and *Tradescantia fluminensis.*

Wandsworth, bor. of SC Greater London, England. Pop. 276,000. Created 1965 from Battersea, Wandsworth, Putney.

Wankel rotary engine, type of INTERNAL COMBUSTION ENGINE invented by Felix Wankel (1902-). Derives power from rotor rather than reciprocating pistons. Successfully adapted to automobile.

Wankie, town of W Zimbabwe. Pop. 32,000. Coalmining centre.

wapiti, *Cervus canadensis,* also called American elk; large North American deer, related to European red deer.

Warbeck, Perkin (*c* 1474-99), pretender to English throne, b. Flanders. Under Yorkist influence, claimed to be Richard, son of Edward IV, who had prob. been murdered in the Tower. Invaded Cornwall and proclaimed himself king (1497); captured and hanged.

warbler, small insectivorous songbird. Old World warblers of large subfamily Sylviinae have mainly grey and brown plumage.

war crimes, actions which contravene rules of war laid down by Hague Convention (1907), UN War Crimes Commission (1943), *etc.* Crimes incl. mass extermination, slave labour, murder of prisoners. *See* NUREMBERG TRIALS.

Warhol, Andy (1930-), American artist, film producer. Leading exponent of pop art, uses silk screen printing techniques to obtain repeated images of familiar objects, *eg* soup cans, and popular personalities, *eg* Marilyn Monroe. Films incl. *Chelsea Girls.*

War of 1812, conflict (1812-15) between US and Britain. US claimed rights of neutral shipping to trade with France, disputed by Britain. Campaign saw early US naval successes, US attempts to capture Canada thwarted by Britain, British naval blockade of US coast and burning of Washington (1814). War ended officially by Treaty of Ghent (1814) before defeat of British forces at New Orleans (1815).

Warsaw (*Warszawa*), cap. of Poland and of Warszawa prov., on R. Vistula. Pop. 2,080,000. Admin., indust., cultural centre; engineering, food processing; univ. (1818). Cap. of Poland from 16th cent.; under Russian rule 1815-1917. Occupied in WWII by Germans, severely damaged (incl. destruction of Jewish ghetto 1943); rebuilt on old pattern.

Warsaw Treaty Organization, military alliance estab. (1955) through defence pact signed in Warsaw between Albania (left 1962), Bulgaria, Czechoslovakia, East Germany, Hungary, Poland, Romania, Soviet Union.

wart, small, usually hard, tumour on skin, caused by a virus. May disappear spontaneously, only to reappear later;

treated by application of acid and cauterization.

wart hog, *Phacochoerus aethiopicus,* wild African pig with large incurved tusks and warty skin on face.

Warwick, Richard Neville, Earl of (1428-71), English military, political leader, known as 'Kingmaker'. Supported York's claim to protectorship of Henry VI, then fought on Yorkist side in Wars of the Roses. Virtual ruler of England during early years of Edward IV's reign, but superseded by the Woodvilles. Joined Lancastrians and invaded England from France; defeated Edward and restored Henry as king (1470). Killed at Barnet by Edward's forces.

Warwickshire, county of WC England. Area 1980 sq km (765 sq mi); pop. 470,000. Major indust. area in NW (esp. metal working); coal in NE; agric., fruit in S. Admin. hq. **Warwick,** town on R. Avon. Pop. 18,000. Castle (14th cent.). Univ. (1965).

Wash, The, shallow inlet of North Sea, E England. Indents Lincoln-Norfolk coast.

Washington, George (1732-99), American statesman, president (1789-97). Given command of Continental Army at outset of American Revolution (1775); after victories at Trenton and Princeton, defeated at Brandywine (1776); survived difficult winter at Valley Forge (1778). With French support, gained victories culminating in British surrender at Yorktown (1781). Presided at Constitutional Convention (1787), later becoming 1st president. Admin. marked by split between HAMILTON and JEFFERSON.

Washington, state of NW US, borders on Pacific and Canada. Area 176,617 sq km (68,192 sq mi); pop. 3,680,000; cap. Olympia; largest city Seattle. Cascade Range divides E plateau from Puget Sound; chief rivers Columbia, Snake. Agric. esp. fruit, vegetables; fishing, timber industs., aircraft mfg. H.e.p. supplies boosted industs. Region disputed by British; boundary fixed 1846. Territ. estab. 1853. Admitted to Union as 42nd state (1889).

Washington, cap. of US, in DISTRICT OF COLUMBIA (DC) on Potomac R. Pop. 3,022,000. Built 1790-1800 as cap. Buildings incl. White House (president's residence), Capitol (Congress), Pentagon (military admin.); National Gallery.

wasp, winged insect of order Hymenoptera, with worldwide distribution. Social wasps have caste system of queens, workers, and male drones. Colonies make nest of chewed wood pulp; in temperate climates only queen survives winter. Queens and workers have sting which can be used repeatedly. Some species solitary.

Wassermann, August von (1866-1925), German bacteriologist. Devised test for syphilis.

water (H_2O), colourless liquid, compound of hydrogen and oxygen. Poor conductor of heat and electricity; important solvent. Reaches its maximum density at *c* 4° C.

water beetle, name given to various aquatic beetles, esp. of Dytiscidae family. Back legs bearing bristles function as oars.

water boatman, name given to aquatic insects of Notonectidae and Corixidae families. Latter are herbivorous, former is voracious predator. Both are strong fliers.

waterbuck, *Kobus ellipsiprymnus,* large shaggy brown antelope, with lyre-shaped horns on male. Found in swamps of S, W and E Africa.

water buffalo, *Bubalus bubalis,* buffalo with large crescent-shaped horns, found wild in S Asia and Borneo. Domesticated varieties widely distributed in Europe and Asia; used as draught animals, source of milk. Also called Indian buffalo.

watercolour, method of painting with pigment ground up with water-soluble gums, *eg* gum arabic.

watercress, *Nasturtium officinale,* white-flowered European herb of mustard family. Found in or around water; pungent leaves used as garnish and in salads.

waterfall, abrupt descent of stream or river. Caused normally by bed of soft rock in river bed being more easily eroded than adjacent hard rock. World's highest is ANGEL FALLS.

water flea, any of order Cladocera of small freshwater crustaceans. Swims by jerky movement of 2 forked antennae. Genera incl. *Daphnia* and *Leptodora.*

Waterford, county of Munster prov., S Irish Republic. Area 1839 sq km (710 sq mi); pop. 87,000. Mountain ranges incl. Comeragh, Knockmealdowns. Agric., dairying; fishing. Co. town **Waterford,** on R. Suir. Pop. 33,000. Glass indust. Protestant, RC cathedrals.

water gas, mixture of hydrogen and carbon monoxide, formed by action of steam on white hot coke. Used as industrial fuel.

Watergate affair, in US history, scandals involving President Nixon's admin. arising out of break-in (June, 1972) at Democratic Party hq. in Watergate apartments, Washington, DC. Conviction of burglars (Jan. 1973) was followed by revelations of widespread conspiracy in campaign to re-elect Nixon in 1972 election and massive cover-up of those who had known of the break-in. Nixon's involvement gradually became apparent. Faced with impeachment proceedings, he resigned (Aug. 1974) and was succeeded by Ford.

water glass, sodium silicate (Na_2SiO_3), usually dissolved in water to form syrupy liquid; used in fireproofing, as preservative for eggs, *etc.*

waterhen, name applied to various birds of rail family, incl. grey moorhen, *Gallinula chloropus.*

water hyacinth, *Eichhornia crassipes,* tropical American aquatic plant. Troublesome river weed.

water lily, *see* LOTUS.

Waterloo, village of C Belgium, S of Brussels. Scene of victory of British (under Wellington) and Prussians (under Blücher) over Napoleon (June, 1815); ended Napoleonic Wars.

Watermelon

watermelon, *Citrullus vulgaris,* annual trailing vine native to tropical Africa. Widely cultivated for large globular or elongated fruits with hard green rind and pink, sweet, watery pulp.

water moccasin or **cottonmouth,** *Agkistrodon piscivorus,* large poisonous pit viper of SE US. Found in swamps or by rivers.

water polo, game played with inflated ball by 2 teams of 7 swimmers. Goals scored by forcing ball into opponents' goal net. Originated in Britain in 1870s.

water rat, name applied to various rodents that live near water, esp. European water vole, *Arvicola amphibius* and MUSKRAT.

watershed, elevated land separating river systems. Headwaters of adjacent CATCHMENT AREAS flow in opposite directions on either side of watershed.

water shrew, *Neomys fodiens,* largest European shrew; semi-aquatic, found on river banks.

water skiing, sport of gliding over water surface on ski-like boards while being pulled by motor boat. Competitions date from 1930s.

watersnake, name applied to various aquatic or semi-aquatic snakes, esp. of genus *Natrix* of North America.

water spider, *Argyoneta aquatica,* European freshwater spider. Constructs underwater bell-shaped silk structure filled with air bubbles.

water table, level below which soil and rock are saturated with ground water. Uneven and variable, may rise in wet weather. Where water table intersects ground surface, a SPRING results.

water vole, *see* WATER RAT.

Watford, town of Hertfordshire, S England, on R. Colne. Pop. 78,000. Printing, engineering, brewing industs.

Watling Island, *see* SAN SALVADOR.

Watson, J[ohn] B[roadus] (1878-1958), American psychologist. First formulator of BEHAVIOURISM.

Watson-Watt, Sir Robert Alexander (1892-1973), Scottish physicist. Evolved method of radiolocation of aircraft (1935), developed into radar prior to WWII.

Watt, James (1736-1819), Scottish engineer. Manufactured an improved form (patented 1769) of Newcomen's steam engine, developed method of converting reciprocating motion into rotary. Unit of power, watt, named after him.

watt, SI unit of power, equal to 1 joule/sec or power developed in a circuit by current of 1 ampère flowing through potential difference of 1 volt.

Watteau, [Jean] Antoine (1684-1721), French painter. Noted for fanciful yet poignant pastoral scenes.

Watts, Isaac (1674-1748), English hymn writer. A nonconformist clergyman, he wrote such popular hymns as 'O God, our help in ages past'.

Waugh, Evelyn Arthur St John (1903-66), English novelist. Known for comic novels satirizing upper-class English manners, *eg Decline and Fall* (1928), *Brideshead Revisited* (1945), war trilogy *Men at Arms* (1952-61).

wave, in physics, periodic disturbance in a medium or space. May involve actual displacement of medium (mechanical waves) or periodic change in some physical quantity, *eg* strength of electromagnetic field. Distance between peaks of disturbance is called wavelength and number of crests per second is frequency.

Wavell, Archibald Percival Wavell, 1st Earl (1883-1950), British army officer. Commander-in-chief in Middle East (1939-41), defeated Italians in N Africa. Viceroy of India (1943-7).

wave mechanics, branch of quantum theory which associates mathematical function (wave function) with atomic particles. Manipulation of this function gives probability of finding position, momentum, *etc,* of particle at any time.

wax, substance composed mainly of esters of higher fatty acids with alcohols. Beeswax is secreted by bees for building honeycombs; carnauba wax, obtained from Brazilian wax palm, is used in polishes, lipsticks, *etc.* Paraffin wax is mineral wax obtained from petroleum.

waxwing, songbird of forests of North America and Eurasia, genus *Bombycilla.* Brown with scarlet wax-like wing tips.

wayfaring tree, *see* VIBURNUM.

Wayne, John, orig. Marion Michael Morrison, (1907-79), American film actor. Best known for roles in Westerns as tough hero. Films incl. *Stagecoach* (1939), *The Alamo* (1960), *True Grit* (1969).

Waziristan, mountainous region of Pakistan bordered on W by Afghanistan. Centre of resistance to British rule in 19th cent.

weak nuclear interaction, nuclear force responsible for decay of all unstable elementary particles, *c* 10^{12} times weaker than strong nuclear interaction.

Weald, The, region of SE England, between

North and South Downs. Grazing; hops, fruit, vegetables. Once forested.

Wear, river of NE England. Flows 105 km (65 mi) through Tyne and Wear into North Sea at Sunderland.

weasel, small carnivorous mammal, genus *Mustela,* found in temperate and cold regions of N hemisphere. Resembles small stoat; feeds on voles, mice. *M. nivalis* is European species; reddish-brown above, white below.

weather, local atmospheric conditions at a given time or over short period. Factors incl. atmospheric pressure, temperature, humidity, cloud cover, rainfall, wind. Forms part of subject matter of meteorology. Weather conditions over many years give CLIMATE.

weaverbird, bird of Ploceidae family, found mainly in Africa. Weaves elaborate hanging nest of sticks, grass, *etc*.

weaving, interlacing of yarns to form a fabric, usually done on a loom. Warp yarn runs lengthwise and weft crosswise, being carried across the loom by a shuttle.

Webb, Sidney James, Baron Passfield (1859-1947), English economist. With his wife, **Beatrice Webb,** née Potter (1858-1943), and other Socialists founded FABIAN SOCIETY (1884). Their works incl. *History of Trade Unionism* (1894), *English Local Government* (1906); founded *New Statesman* (1913).

Weber, Carl Maria Friedrich Ernst von (1786-1826), German composer, pianist. Developed romantic German opera. Works incl. *Der Freischütz, Euryanthe, Oberon,* and piano music.

Weber, Max (1864-1920), German sociologist. Set up non-Marxist framework for empirical analysis of institutional bases in Western capitalist society. Best-known work is *Protestant Ethic and the Spirit of Capitalism* (1920).

Webern, Anton von (1883-1945), Austrian composer. Pupil of Schoenberg whose 12-note technique he adopted.

Webster, John (*c* 1580-*c* 1638), English dramatist. Known for powerful, typically Jacobean revenge tragedies, *The White Devil* (1612), *The Duchess of Malfi* (*c* 1613).

Webster, Noah (1758-1843), American scholar, lexicographer. Compiled *American Dictionary of the English Language* (1828).

Weddell Sea, extension of S Atlantic, bordered by Antarctic Peninsula and Coats Land. Lies within British Antarctic Territ.

Wedekind, Frank (1864-1918), German dramatist. Forerunner of theatrical expressionism. Wrote plays on sexual themes, *eg Spring's Awakening* (1891), *Pandora's Box* (1903), creating heroine Lulu as archetypical amoral woman.

Wedgwood, Josiah (1730-95), English potter. His Staffordshire pottery was most famous for jasper ware, unglazed porcelain in blue, decorated with white relief.

weevil, small beetle of Curculionidae family, with worldwide distribution. Head prolonged into beak-like snout used to bore into grain, fruit, *etc*. Many species, incl. boll weevil, major cotton pest.

weigela, genus of E Asian deciduous shrubs of honeysuckle family. Clusters of bell-shaped white, purple, red or pink flowers.

weight, in physics, gravitational force of attraction of the Earth or other planet on a given MASS.

weightlessness, in physics, state experienced by body in absence of gravitational force or when falling freely.

Weill, Kurt (1900-50), German composer. Worked with BRECHT on satirical, jazz-influenced operas, *eg The Threepenny Opera*. Wrote musicals in US from 1935.

Weimar, town of SW East Germany, on R. Ilm. Pop. 64,000. Textiles, printing. Former cap. of grand duchy of Saxe-Weimar-Eisenach. Cultural centre in 18th, 19th cents. Badly damaged in WWII.

Weimar Republic, name given to German Republic (1919-33). Created by constitutional assembly at Weimar (1919). Dissolved by Hitler.

Weizmann, Chaim (1874-1952), Jewish statesman, chemist, b. Russia. Active in Zionist causes in Britain, helped secure BALFOUR DECLARATION. 1st president of Israel (1949-52). Discovered method of producing acetone.

welding, process of joining metal surfaces together by heating sufficiently for them to melt and fuse together. Required temperature is obtained by oxyacetylene flame or electric arc.

Welkom, city of NC Orange Free State, South Africa. Pop. 132,000. Commercial centre.

well, hole bored into Earth's crust for purpose of bringing substances, usually water or oil, to surface. Such substances may require pumping, or flow upward by underground pressure as in ARTESIAN WELL.

Welland Ship Canal, canal of S Ontario, Canada. Bypasses Niagara Falls, connecting L. Ontario with L. Erie. Length 44 km (28 mi).

Welles, [George] Orson (1915-), American film actor, writer, director, producer. Best known for *Citizen Kane* (1941), *The Third Man* (1949).

Wellesley, Richard Colley Wellesley, Marquess of (1760-1842), British colonial administrator. Assisted by his brother (later WELLINGTON), checked power of native princes, notably Tippoo Sahib, as governor in India (1797-1805).

Wellington, Arthur Wellesley, 1st Duke of (1769-1852), British army officer, statesman; PM (1828-30). Aided his brother Richard Wellesley in Indian campaigns (1796-1805). Commanded British troops in PENINSULAR WAR (1809-13), eventually driving French from Spain; ultimately defeated Napoleon at Waterloo (1815). Although opposed to Catholic Emancipation, saw necessity of his Tory govt. legislating to avoid conflict in Ireland; govt. fell after his declaration against parliamentary reform.

Wellington, cap. of New Zealand, at S tip of North Isl., on Cook Str. Pop. 329,000. Admin., commercial centre; port, exports dairy produce, wool, meat. Founded 1840; replaced Auckland as cap. 1865. Has Parliament House, Victoria Univ. (1897).

Wells, H[erbert] G[eorge] (1866-1946), English author. Early exponent of SCIENCE FICTION in novels, *eg The Time Machine* (1895), *The War of the Worlds* (1898). Other works incl. novels on contemporary social questions, *eg Kipps* (1905), *The History of Mr Polly* (1910).

Wells, city of Somerset, SW England. Pop. 7000. Has cathedral (12th cent.).

Welsh, *see* CELTIC.

Welsh Nationalist Party (Plaid Cymru), political organization dedicated to obtaining Welsh independence by constitutional methods.

Welwyn Garden City, town of Hertfordshire, SE England. Pop. 40,000. Light industs. Planned (1920).

Wembley, part of BRENT, W Greater London, England. Incl. English national soccer stadium.

Wenceslaus, St (d. 929), duke of Bohemia. Promoted spread of Christianity in Bohemia. Remembered as 'Good King Wenceslaus' of the Christmas carol. Patron Saint of Czechoslovakia.

Weser, river of N West Germany. Flows *c* 480 km (300 mi) NW via Minden, Bremen to North Sea at Bremerhaven. Connected by Mittelland canal to Elbe, Ems, Rhine rivers.

Wesley, John (1703-91), English evangelical preacher. Anglican churchman, founded METHODISM. Preached salvation through faith in Christ alone. Sermons became standard for Wesleyans. His brother, **Charles Wesley** (1707-88), was preacher and founding Methodist. Wrote *c* 6500 hymns.

Wessex, *see* WILTSHIRE.

West, Mae (1892-1980), American stage, film actress, writer. Famous for wit, sexual innuendo, in comedies, *eg I'm No Angel* (1933), and in films with W. C. Fields.

West, Rebecca, pseud. of Dame Cicily Isabel Fairfield (1892-), British author. Works incl. novels, criticism, biogs.

West Bengal, state of NE India. Area *c* 88,000 sq km (33,000 sq mi); pop. 44,440,000; cap. Calcutta. Heavy indust. based in Ganges delta; coal, petroleum deposits.

West Bromwich, bor. of West Midlands met. county, C England. Pop. 160,000. In BLACK COUNTRY; coalmining, metal industs.

westerlies, prevailing winds of mid-latitude areas in both hemispheres. Normally blow from SW in N hemisphere, from NW in S hemisphere. Bring continual procession of depressions and anticyclones.

Western Australia, state of W Australia. Area 2,537,900 sq km (979,900 sq mi); pop. 1,170,000; cap. Perth. Kimberley plateau in N, Hamersley Range in NW; vast desert tableland, salt lakes in interior; fertile area in SW; Nullarbor Plain in SE. Agric. incl. beef cattle, sheep, wheat, fruit. Minerals incl. gold, iron ore. Industs., incl. oil refining, iron and steel mfg., centred in Perth and Fremantle. Settled from 1826; became federal state (1901).

Western Isles, isl. authority of W Scotland. Area 2898 sq km (1119 sq mi); pop. 30,000; admin. hq. Stornoway. Created 1975; incl. Outer Hebrides isls., formerly part of Inverness-shire and Ross and Cromarty.

Western Sahara, territ. of NW Africa. Area 266,000 sq km (102,700 sq mi); pop. 139,000; cap. El-Aaiún. Mostly desert, pop. largely nomadic; livestock, dates, fishing, rich phosphate deposits. Formerly called Spanish Sahara; colony from 1884, became prov. 1958. Spain withdrew in 1975 leaving Morocco and Mauritania in joint control until future is decided; territ. also claimed by Algeria.

Western Samoa, *see* SAMOA.

West Germany, *see* GERMANY.

West Glamorgan, *see* GLAMORGAN.

West Ham, *see* NEWHAM.

West Indies

West Indies, archipelago between North and South America, separating Caribbean and Atlantic Ocean. Incl. Hispaniola, Cuba, Jamaica, Puerto Rico (Greater Antilles); Barbados, Leeward and Windward Isls., Trinidad and Tobago (Lesser Antilles); also Bahamas, Virgin Isls. European settlement followed Columbus' visit in 1492.

West Indies, Federation of, short-lived union (1958-62) of British Caribbean territs. Incl. Jamaica, Trinidad and Tobago, Barbados, most of Leeward and Windward Isls.

West Irian, *see* IRIAN JAYA.

West Lothian, former county of EC Scotland, now in Lothian region. Formerly called Linlithgowshire. Coal, iron, oil shale deposits; rich agric. Co. town was Linlithgow.

Westmeath, county of Leinster prov., C Irish Republic. Area 1764 sq km (681 sq mi); pop. 60,000; co. town Mullingar. Low-lying, extensive bogland, lakes incl. Lough Ree. Livestock, dairying; fishing (esp. trout).

West Midlands, met. county of C England.

Area 899 sq km (347 sq mi); pop. 2,712,000; admin. hq. Wolverhampton. Created 1974, incl. Birmingham and suburbs, Coventry.

Westminster, City of, bor. of C Greater London, England. Pop. 210,000. Created 1965 from Westminster, Paddington, St Marylebone met. bors. Incl. Piccadilly, Soho, West End, Mayfair, Hyde Park, Trafalgar Sq. Buildings incl. Westminster Abbey, palaces (Buckingham, St James's, Westminster), Parliament, Royal Albert Hall, Covent Garden, National Gallery.

Westminster, Statute of (1931), British parliamentary enactment recognizing independence of dominions of British Commonwealth.

Westminster Abbey, national shrine and scene of coronation of almost all English monarchs since William I. Norman church consecrated under Edward the Confessor (1065); rebuilt in Gothic style (1245-1528); additions made in 18th cent. by Wren and Hawksmoor.

Westmorland, former county of NW England, now part of Cumbria. Co. town was Appleby. Incl. much of Lake Dist.

Weston-super-Mare, town of Avon, SW England. Pop. 51,000. Seaside resort.

Westphalia (*Westfalen*), region of W West Germany, now part of North Rhine-Westphalia state. Mainly low-lying, chief rivers Ems, Lippe, Ruhr. Incl. RUHR coalfield and indust. region; main cities Dortmund, Cologne, Düsseldorf, Essen. Duchy created 12th cent.; made kingdom (1807) by Napoleon; prov. of Prussia from 1816.

Westphalia, Peace of (1648), settlement ending THIRTY YEARS WAR. Power of Habsburgs diminished; Holy Roman Empire dissolved into sovereign states, rulers of which could grant religious toleration to their subjects.

West Point, American military academy, near Newburgh, New York, US.

West Riding, *see* YORKSHIRE.

West Sussex, *see* SUSSEX.

West Virginia, state of E US. Area 62,629 sq km (24,181 sq mi); pop. 1,853,000; cap. Charlestown. In Allegheny plateau, has 2 panhandles in N and E. Chief rivers Ohio, Potomac. Important mining incl. bituminous coal, natural gas; glass and chemical industs. Chief agric. crops hay, maize, fruit. Region settled in 1730s. Part of Virginia until Civil War. Admitted to Union as 35th state (1863).

West Yorkshire, met. county of NC England. Area 2039 sq km (787 sq mi); pop. 2,068,000; admin. hq. Wakefield. Created 1974, incl. most of former W Riding of Yorkshire.

Wexford, county of Leinster prov., SE Irish Republic. Area 2352 sq km (908 sq mi); pop. 96,000; Mainly low-lying, fertile. Cereals, dairying; fishing. Co. town **Wexford.** Pop. 12,000. Fishing port. Sacked by Cromwell (1649).

Weyden, Roger van der (*c* 1400-64), Flemish artist. Major Flemish painter of mid-15th cent.; painted religious works and portraits.

Weymouth (and Melcombe Regis), town of Dorset, S England. Pop. 42,000. Resort; has ferry service to Channel Isls.

whale, large marine fish-like mammal, order Cetacea. Whales divided into 2 groups: toothed whales (Odontoceti), incl. sperm whales, porpoises, dolphins; whalebone or baleen whales (Mystacoceti), in which teeth are replaced by whalebone plates used to strain plankton from water. Whalebone whales incl. blue whale, largest of mammals, rorqual and right whale.

whale shark, *Rhincodon typus,* largest living fish, reaching lengths of 15 m/50 ft, found in tropical waters. Harmless to man, feeds on plankton and small fish.

whaling, industry of catching whales for food, oil, *etc.* Organized first by Dutch at Spitsbergen in 17th cent. Developed on large scale with invention of explosive harpoon (*c* 1856) and building of factory ships for extraction of oil. Decline in whale pop. through over-hunting has led to international controls.

wheat, any of genus *Triticum* of cereal grasses with dense, erect spikes. *T. aestivum* is widely cultivated in temperate regions. Yields grain which is processed into flour or meal and used chiefly in breadmaking. Comprises *c* 40% of world's cereal acreage. Leading producers are Canada, US, China and USSR.

wheatear, small migratory thrush-like bird with white rump, genus *Oenanthe.* Species incl. *O. oenanthe* of North America, N Europe and Asia.

Wheatstone, Sir Charles (1802-75), English scientist. Invented an electric telegraph (1837). Popularized 'Wheatstone bridge', device to measure electrical resistance.

wheel, name given to any disc-shaped device used as part of machine or vehicle. When fitted to an axle gives mechanical advantage equal to ratio of wheel radius to axle radius. Earliest vehicular wheel dates from Bronze Age (*c* 3500 BC).

Wheeler, Sir [Robert Eric] Mortimer (1890-1976), English archaeologist. Made excavations at MAIDEN CASTLE. Helped reveal the INDUS VALLEY CIVILIZATION. Did much to popularize archaeology.

whelk, marine gastropod mollusc with spiral shell, esp. of genus *Buccinum.* Species incl. common edible whelk, *B. undatum.*

Whig Party, British political party, predecessor of present Liberal Party. Name, originally denoting rebel Scottish Covenanters, applied to upholders of exclusion of James, Duke of York, from throne (1679). Supported Glorious Revolution (1688), held power (1714-60). Disorganized in early years of George III's reign, revived in opposition to newly-dominant Tory Party under Pitt. In early 19th cent., advocated parliamentary reform, culminating in Reform Bill (1832), after which Whigs became known as Liberals.

Whig party, US political party. Composed of

groups originally formed (1824) in opposition to Andrew Jackson. Successful in election of W.H. Harrison as president (1840). Break-up began 1848, despite Zachary Taylor's victory in presidential election.

whippet, breed of slender hound developed in England from greyhound in 18th cent. Once used for hare coursing, now mainly for racing; stands 46-57 cm/18-22 in. at shoulder.

whirlpool, circular, revolving eddy in river, lake or sea. Caused by meeting of opposing tides or currents, wind action, irregular formation of river or sea bed, or waterfalls.

whirlwind, rotating column of air with low atmospheric pressure at centre. Produced by atmospheric instability; in arid areas may cause dust or sand storms.

whisky or **whiskey,** spirit distilled from fermented mash of grain, *eg* barley, rye. Flavour of Scotch whisky derives from quality of water used and curing of malt over peat fires. US and Canadian whiskeys are mostly made with rye; some, *eg* bourbon, are made from corn (maize). Whisky is stored for several years in wooden casks where it acquires characteristic golden brown colour.

whist, card game for 4 players. Of English origin, its popularity derives in part from writings of Hoyle (1742) and Cavendish (1862). Gave rise to bridge in 19th cent.

Whistler, James [Abbott] McNeill (1834-1903), American artist, resident in France, England. He was a master of tone and colour, and a superb etcher. Works incl. series of *Nocturnes*.

Whitby, town of North Yorkshire, N England, at mouth of R. Esk. Pop. 13,000. Resort, fishing port. Abbey founded 656. Synod of Whitby (664) estab. Roman rather than Celtic forms for English church.

White, Gilbert (1720-93), English clergyman, naturalist. Author of classic *Natural History and Antiquities of Selborne* (1789).

White, Patrick Victor Martindale (1912-), Australian novelist, b. London. Known for symbolic, poetic novels incl. *Voss* (1957), *The Solid Mandala* (1966). Nobel Prize for Literature (1973).

White, T[erence] H[anbury] (1906-64), English author, b. India. Known for erudite, idiosyncratic treatment of Arthurian legend in tetralogy *The Once and Future King* (1938-58).

whitebait, young of herrings and sprats. Esteemed as food.

white blood cell, *see* BLOOD.

white collar, grouping of workers engaged in non-manual labour. Term derives from white shirts typically worn by clerical, professional, and managerial employees.

white dwarf, small, extremely dense star of low luminosity, typically with mass of Sun but radius no larger than Earth's. Represents stage of star's evolution as its store of hydrogen is used up.

whitefish, fish of salmon family, esp. genus *Coregonus*, found mainly in lakes and rivers of N Europe and North America.

whitefly, any of Aleyrodidae family of minute insects. Many species are crop pests.

Whitehead, Alfred North (1861-1947), English philosopher, mathematician. Collaborated with Russell on *Principia Mathematica* (1910-13). Formulated an idealist 'philosophy of organism'.

Whitehorse, cap. of Yukon territ., Canada; on Lewes (Upper Yukon) R. Pop. 16,000.

White House, official residence of the President of the US, in Washington, DC. Designed by James Hoban (1792). Rebuilt after being burnt by British (1814).

White Nile, *see* NILE.

White Russia, *see* BYELORUSSIAN SOVIET SOCIALIST REPUBLIC.

White Russians, name given to anti-Communist groups who opposed Bolsheviks in Russian civil war (1918-20).

White Sea, inlet of Barents Sea, between Kola and Kanin penins., N European USSR. Connected to Baltic by canal. Chief port Archangel.

whitethroat, Old World warbler with white throat, genus *Sylvia*.

whiting, *Merlangus merlangus,* common European marine food fish of cod family.

Whitlam, [Edward] Gough (1916-), Australian statesman, Labor PM (1972-5). Economic crisis led to opposition's refusal to cooperate in Senate. Dismissed by governor-general, Sir John Kerr, who appointed Malcolm Fraser as PM.

Whitman, Walt[er] (1819-92), American poet. Best known for stylistically unconventional collection, *Leaves of Grass* (1855), celebrating fertility, sensuality, comradeship.

Whitney, Eli (1765-1825), American manufacturer. Invented cotton gin, facilitating separation of fibre and seed. Produced 1st muskets with standard interchangeable parts.

Whitney, Mount, mountain of E California, US; in Sequoia National Park in Sierra Nevada. Highest peak in US outside Alaska (4418 m/14,494 ft).

Whit Sunday, *see* PENTECOST.

Whittington, Richard (d. 1423), English merchant, 3 times mayor of London. Made large fortune as a mercer, which he left to charities at his death. Subject of story of Dick Whittington and his cat.

Whittle, Sir Frank (1907-), English aeronautic engineer. Patented (1930) designs for turbo-jet engine, forerunner of modern jet aircraft engine.

WHO, *see* WORLD HEALTH ORGANIZATION.

whooping cough or **pertussis,** infectious disease, usually of children, caused by bacillus *Haemophilus pertussis*. Characterized by repeated coughing ending in forced intake of air, or whoop.

whortleberry, *see* BILBERRY.

Whymper, Edward (1840-1911), English mountaineer. First man to climb the Matterhorn (1865), succeeding at his 7th attempt; during descent, 4 of his party fell to their deaths.

Wichita, city of S Kansas, US; at jct. of Arkansas and Little Arkansas rivers. Pop. 385,000; state's largest city. Railway jct., commercial, indust. centre in wheat growing, oil producing region. Livestock, grain trade; aircraft, chemical mfg.

Wick, port of Highland region, E Scotland. Pop. 8000. Whisky distilling, glass mfg. Former co. town of Caithness.

Wicklow, county of Leinster prov., E Irish Republic. Area 2025 sq km (782 sq mi); pop. 84,000. Scenic Wicklow Mts. (Lugnaquillia 926 m/3039 ft), Glendalough. Cattle rearing; h.e.p. on Liffey. Co. town **Wicklow,** pop. 5000. Port.

widgeon, *see* WIGEON.

Wieland, Christoph Martin (1733-1813), German poet, novelist. Wrote satirical novels, poetry, incl. epic, *Oberon* (1780).

Wien, *see* VIENNA.

Wiesbaden, city of W West Germany, at foot of Taunus Hills, cap. of Hesse. Pop. 249,000. Wine trade, chemicals. Spa resort. Cap. of duchy of Nassau 1815-66.

Wigan, town of Greater Manchester met. county, NW England. Pop. 81,000. Food processing, engineering industs.

wigeon or **widgeon,** migratory duck, genus *Anas*. Male of Eurasian wigeon, *A. penelope,* has chestnut head, grey body, pinkish breast.

Wight, Isle of, isl. county of S England. Area 381 sq km (147 sq mi); pop. 114,000; admin. hq. Newport. Separated from mainland by SOLENT. Chalk hills run E-W, end in Needles. Resorts; yachting.

Wigtownshire, former county of SW Scotland, now in Dumfries and Galloway region. Indented coast; incl. Rhinns of Galloway penin. in W. Rich agric., dairy farming, livestock. Co. town was **Wigtown,** on Wigtown Bay. Pop. 1000.

wigwam, Algonquian name loosely applied to dwellings of E North American Indians. Originally referred to dome-shaped huts made of skins or matting stretched over poles. Now confused with portable, conical tepee of Plains Indians.

Wilberforce, William (1759-1833), British reform politician. Campaigned for abolition of slavery. Sponsored passage (1807) of bill abolishing slave trade. Died month before slavery was abolished throughout British Empire.

wild boar, *see* BOAR.

wild carrot, *see* CARROT.

wild cat, *Felis sylvestris,* resembles domestic tabby cat, but larger. Exclusively forest-dwelling and nocturnal, found in N, E Europe, Scottish Highlands, Corsica, parts of France. Untameable.

wildcat, *see* BOBCAT.

Wilde, Oscar [Fingal O'Flahertie Wills] (1854-1900), British author, b. Dublin. Noted decadent wit, aesthete. Works incl. novels, *eg The Picture of Dorian Grey* (1891), satirical social comedies, *eg Lady Windermere's Fan* (1892), *The Importance of Being Earnest* (1895). Accused of homosexual practices, imprisoned (1895-7). Wrote most famous poem, *The Ballad of Reading Gaol* (1898), in exile.

wildebeest, *see* GNU.

Wilhelm, German form of WILLIAM.

Wilhelmina (1880-1962), queen of Netherlands (1890-1948). Abdicated in favour of daughter Juliana.

Wilhelmshaven, city of NW West Germany, on Jade Bay. Pop. 103,000. Port; oil refining, chemical mfg. Chief German North Sea naval base.

Wilkes, John (1727-97), English politician. Founded periodical *North Briton*; attacks on George III and govt. led to expulsion from Parliament (1764); fled to France. Re-elected (1768), frequently prevented from taking seat. Gained great popular support. Admitted to Commons (1774), championed parliamentary reform, American colonial cause.

will, in law, legal statement of person's wishes concerning disposal of property after death. Must be witnessed, testator (person making will) must be of sound mind and not under undue influence of another. Testator usually appoints executor to administer will.

will, in philosophy, inner force motivating a person's conscious actions. Existence denied by some philosophers (*eg* in DETERMINISM), defined by others (*eg* Plato, Descartes, Kant) on intuitive grounds as motive force of personality, yet others (*eg* Leibnitz, Hume) have seen it as the resultant of conflicting elements.

Willemstad, cap. of Netherlands Antilles, on Curaçao Isl. Pop. 146,000. Shipping and tourist centre. Refining of Venezuelan oil.

William I (1797-1888), 1st emperor of Germany (1871-88), king of Prussia (1861-88). Dominated by chancellor BISMARCK, whose policies led to creation of German Empire.

William II (1859-1941), emperor of Germany (1888-1918). Dismissed Bismarck (1890), thereafter pursuing aggressive colonial and military policy. Antagonized Britain by supporting Boers, promoting German naval expansion. Influence declined after outbreak of WWI; fled to Holland day before armistice, abdicated.

William [I] the Conqueror (*c* 1027-87), king of England (1066-87). Succeeded to duchy of Normandy (1035). Prob. promised succession to English throne by Edward the Confessor; forced HAROLD to swear support for his claim. Pursued claim by invading England and defeating Harold at Hastings (1066). Consolidated Norman power by building castles, granting land to his followers, introducing foreign clergy and FEUDAL SYSTEM. Commissioned survey of England in *Domesday Book*.

William [II] Rufus (*c* 1058-1100), king of England (1087-1100), b. Normandy. His extravagant and covetous rule was unpopular. Found slain by arrow in New Forest.

William III (1650-1702), king of England, Scotland and Ireland (1689-1702), prince of Orange. Became stadholder of Holland (1672). Married (1677) Mary, daughter of duke of York (later JAMES II). Invited to become king of England by opponents of James; proclaimed joint sovereign with Mary after James was deemed to have abdicated (*see* GLORIOUS REVOLUTION). Defeated Catholic force under James at Battle of Boyne (1690).

William IV (1765-1837), king of Great Britain and Ireland (1830-7). Third son of George III; succeeded his brother, George IV. Agreed to create enough peers to assure passage of Reform Bill of 1832.

William of Occam or **Ockham** (*c* 1285-1349), English Franciscan philosopher. Major nominalist (*see* NOMINALISM). Summoned to answer charges of heresy by Pope.

Williams, Tennessee, pseud. of Thomas Lanier Williams (*c* 1914-), American dramatist. Plays frequently centre on insecure, neurotic woman, sustained by illusion, confronted with reality of male violence, *eg The Glass Menagerie* (1945), *A Streetcar Named Desire* (1947).

Williams, William Carlos (1883-1963), American poet, novelist. Known for poetry which extracts detail from everyday objects, speech patterns, *eg Spring and All* (1923), *Collected Later Poems* (1950). Novels incl. *White Mule* (1937) and sequels.

Williamsburg, town of SE Virginia, US. Pop. 9000. Settled 1632, hist. cap. of Virginia (1699-1779). Has many hist. colonial buildings; restoration began 1927.

William the Lion (1143-1214), king of Scotland (1165-1214). After capture at Alnwick (1174), forced to pay homage to Henry II of England by terms of Treaty of Falaise. Treaty was rescinded (1189) by Richard I in exchange for money.

William the Silent, Prince of Orange (1533-84), Dutch statesman. Led armies in struggle for Dutch independence from Spain (1568-76). Became stadholder of 7 N provs. (1579), which declared their independence from Spain (1581). Assassinated by Catholic fanatic.

will-o'-the-wisp or **jack-o'-lantern,** pale, flickering light seen over marshland at night. Prob. caused by spontaneous combustion of methane.

willow or **osier,** any of genus *Salix* of trees and shrubs of N temperate and subarctic regions. Narrow leaves; Tough, pliable twigs used in basketwork, *etc.*

willowherb, any of genus *Epilobium* of plants, esp. *E. angustifolium,* rosebay willowherb or fireweed, with narrow leaves, reddish-purple flowers.

Wilson, Angus (1913-), English novelist, critic. Satirical works incl. *Anglo-Saxon Attitudes, No Laughing Matter.*

Wilson, Charles Thomson Rees (1869-1959), Scottish physicist. Developed CLOUD CHAMBER (1911). Awarded Nobel Prize for Physics (1927).

Wilson, Sir [James] Harold (1916-), British statesman, PM (1964-70, 1974-6). Elected Labour Party leader (1963). Both admins. dominated by serious inflation, civil strife in Northern Ireland. Resigned from office.

Wilson, [Thomas] Woodrow (1856-1924), American statesman, Democratic president (1913-21). Kept US out of WWI until 1917, then entered to make 'world safe for democracy'. Negotiated armistice of 1918; secured League of Nations covenant at Treaty of VERSAILLES (1919). Awarded Nobel Peace Prize (1919).

Wiltshire, county of S England. Area 3481 sq km (1344 sq mi); pop. 516,000; admin. hq. Trowbridge. Chalk uplands incl. Marlborough Downs (N), Salisbury Plain (S). Fertile vales. Wheat, sheep. Centre of Saxon kingdom of Wessex.

Wimbledon, *see* MERTON.

Winchester, city and admin. hq. of Hampshire, S England, on R. Itchen. Pop. 31,000. Roman *Venta Belgarum;* Saxon cap. of Wessex. Has cathedral (11th cent.), Norman castle. Public school (1382).

wind, natural current of air parallel to Earth's surface. Caused by differences in air pressure within atmosphere; air flows from high pressure to low pressure areas. Many sectors of globe have almost continuous prevailing winds, *eg* mid-latitude westerlies, tropical trade winds. Localized winds incl. MISTRAL, SIROCCO. Wind velocity measured by anemometer, classed on BEAUFORT SCALE.

Windermere, Lake, largest lake of England, in Lake Dist., Cumbria. Length 17 km (10.5 mi).

windflower, common name for wild varieties of ANEMONE.

Windhoek, cap. of Namibia. Pop. 61,000. Railways to Walvis Bay and South Africa; trade in skins, minerals.

wind instruments, name given to woodwind and brass families of instruments. Sound is produced when player sets column of air vibrating inside the instruments. *See* WOODWIND INSTRUMENTS, BRASS INSTRUMENTS.

windmill, apparatus which harnesses wind power for pumping water, grinding corn, generating electricity, *etc.* Usually consists of tower with revolving arms at top bearing sails to catch wind. Introduced to Europe prob. during 12th cent.

Windsor, House of, name of royal family of Great Britain. Adopted by George V (1917) in place of House of Saxe-Coburg-Gotha. Subsequent monarchs Edward VIII, George VI, Elizabeth II.

Windsor, Wallis Warfield, Duchess of (1896-), American-born wife of Edward, duke of Windsor. Married Edward Simpson (1927), from whom she obtained a divorce (Oct. 1936). Her association with EDWARD VIII led him to abdicate British throne; married him (June, 1937).

Windsor, indust. city of SW Ontario, Canada; on Detroit R. Pop. 248,000. Linked with Detroit (US) by road and rail tunnels. Major auto indust.; salt and chemicals mfg.

Windsor, New, town of Berkshire, S England, on R. Thames. Pop. 30,000. Castle estab. by William I, still royal residence.

Windward Islands, archipelago of SE West Indies, in S Lesser Antilles. Extends S from Leeward Isls. Incl. Dominica, St Lucia, St Vincent, Grenada, Martinique.

wine, alcoholic beverage made from fermented grape juice. Fortified wine, *eg* sherry, port, has brandy added to it; sparkling wine, *eg* champagne, is made by inducing secondary process of fermentation in bottle. Dry wine is obtained by allowing all grape sugar to be converted to alcohol, sweet wine by arresting process of fermentation. In red wines, entire grape is used; in white, only juice is used. Leading and best-known wine producers are France, Italy, Germany.

winkle, marine snail of genus *Littorina,* found on rocky shores. Species incl. common edible winkle, *L. littorea.* Also called periwinkle.

Winnipeg, cap. of Manitoba, Canada; at confluence of Red, Assiniboine rivers. Pop. 578,000. Railway jct., commercial centre. Chief wheat market of Prairie provs. Meat packing, flour milling, agric. machinery mfg. Settled as Fort Rouge; renamed (1873). Seat of Manitoba Univ. (1877).

Winnipeg, Lake, SC Manitoba, Canada. Area 24,514 sq km (9465 sq mi). Receives Red, Winnipeg, Saskatchewan rivers. Drained by Nelson R. to Hudson Bay.

Winterthur, town of NE Switzerland. Pop. 107,000. Indust. centre, textiles; railway jct., locomotive mfg.

Wirral Peninsula, area of Merseyside met. county, NW England, between Dee and Mersey estuaries. Birkenhead, Wallasey in NE.

Wisconsin, state of NC US. Area 145,439 sq km (56,154 sq mi); pop. 4,644,000; cap. Madison; largest city Milwaukee. Bordered by L. Superior in N, L. Michigan in E, Mississippi R. in W. Mainly low-lying. Leading dairy producer, also grains; iron ore mining; industs. incl. meat packing, brewing. Explored in 17th cent. by French; ceded to British 1763. Part of US from 1787. Admitted to Union as 30th state (1830).

Wisent or European bison

wisent, *Bison bonasus,* European bison, almost extinct in wild. Smaller head and less shaggy body than American bison.

Wishart, George (*c* 1513-46), Scottish religious reformer. Achieved conversion of John Knox to Protestantism. Burned for heresy at St Andrews.

wisteria, genus of climbing shrubs of Leguminosae family. Native to E US and E Asia. Showy clusters of white, blue, pink or voilet drooping flowers.

witan, *see* WITENAGEMOT.

witchcraft, the working of magic. Common to most cultures. In Europe, may be survival of Palaeolithic fertility cults. Features incl: district groupings into 'covens' of 13; use of spells, charms; supposed transformation into animals, ability to fly, worship of devil. Condemned as heresy (14th cent.) by Christian church; subject of widespread persecution 16th-17th cent.

witch hazel, any of genus *Hamamelis* of small trees and shrubs. Native to North America and Asia. *H. virginiana* of E North America has yellow flowers. Medicinal lotion is derived from bark.

witenagemot or **witan,** aristocratic assembly of nobles and high churchmen in Anglo-Saxon England. Appointed by king to advise him on questions of law, tax, foreign policy.

Wittenberg, town of C East Germany, on R. Elbe. Pop. 47,000. Here Luther nailed (1517) his 95 Theses to Schlosskirche (which contains his tomb). Univ. (1502) incorporated into Halle univ. 1817.

Wittgenstein, Ludwig Josef Johann (1889-1951), Austrian philosopher. Worked mainly in England. *Tractatus Logico-Philosophicus* (1919) helped develop LOGICAL POSITIVISM. Later work, in *Philosophical Investigations* (pub. 1953), on the false problems created by the ambiguity of language.

Witwatersrand or **The Rand,** area of S Transvaal, South Africa, centred on gold-bearing ridge (alt. *c* 1830 m/6000 ft). Gold discovered 1886; now produces 33% world's output. Also coal, manganese deposits. Main city Johannesburg.

woad, any of genus *Isatis* of plants of mustard family, esp. *I. tinctoria* with yellow flowers. Leaves yield blue dye used by ancient Britons as body paint; formerly widely used to dye clothes.

Wodehouse, (Sir) P[elham] G[renville] (1881-1975), English novelist. Known for novels, short stories caricaturing English upper-class world of 1920s in stylized slang. Created characters Bertie Wooster, his man Jeeves. Settled in US *c* 1920.

Woden, Germanic name for ODIN.

Wolf, Hugo (1860-1903), Austrian composer. Wrote numerous romantic *lieder.*

wolf, carnivorous, intelligent, dog-like mammal, genus *Canis,* found in remote areas of N hemisphere. Hunts in packs; can attack more powerful animals. North American timber or grey wolf considered subspecies of European *Canis lupus.*

Wolfe, James (1727-59), British army officer. Given command of expedition to take

Québec (1759). Victory over French under Montcalm on Plains of Abraham secured Canada for Britain. Fatally wounded.

Wolfe, Thomas Clayton (1900-38), American novelist. Known for vast, intensely realistic, autobiog. cycle, incl. *Look Homeward, Angel* (1929).

wolfhound, large dog originally used for hunting wolves. Breeds incl. Irish wolfhound and borzoi.

wolfram, *see* TUNGSTEN.

Wollongong, city of SE New South Wales, Australia, on Tasman Sea. Pop. 211,000. Major coalmining, iron and steel industs.

Wollstonecraft, Mary (1759-97), English writer. Member of group of Radicals which incl. GODWIN, by whom she had daughter who became SHELLEY'S second wife. Best-known work, *Vindication of the Rights of Women* (1792).

Wolsey, Thomas (*c* 1473-1530), English churchman, statesman. Created (1515) cardinal and lord chancellor by Henry VIII. Had charge of English foreign and domestic policy; attempted to mediate for peace in Europe. Achieved great personal wealth; founded Cardinal College, Oxford (Christchurch) and had Hampton Court built. Failure to arrange Henry's divorce from Catherine of Aragon led to his dismissal and arrest (1530).

Wolverhampton, town of West Midlands met. county, WC England. Pop. 269,000. In BLACK COUNTRY; metal working incl. cars, bicycles, locks; rayon, chemicals.

wolverine or **glutton,** *Gulo gulo,* carnivorous bear-like mammal, largest of weasel family, found in Arctic and subarctic regions of Europe, Asia, North America. Short-legged, with bushy tail and shaggy coat; voracious predator.

womb, *see* UTERUS.

Wombat

wombat, burrowing nocturnal Australian marsupial, esp. of genus *Vombatus.* Rodent-like, with stocky body and continuously growing incisors; herbivorous.

women's rights, *see* CIVIL RIGHTS.

women's suffrage, right of women to vote. In UK, first proposed by Mary WOLLSTONECRAFT. First women's suffrage committee formed (1865) in Manchester. Local committees united (1897) in National Union of Women's Suffrage Societies. More militant Women's Social and Political Union formed (1903), led by Emmeline Pankhurst and daughters; members known as suffragettes. Used arson, bombing; many arrested, went on hunger strike when imprisoned. Achieved right to vote for married women over 30 (1918); extended to cover all women over 21 (1928).

Wood, Sir Henry (1869-1944), English conductor. Founded and conducted Promenade Concerts in London (1895-1944).

wood, hard, fibrous substance which makes up greater part of stems and branches of trees and shrubs beneath the bark. Composed of XYLEM and PHLOEM intersected by transverse vascular rays.

woodbine, name for HONEYSUCKLE and VIRGINIA CREEPER.

woodchuck or **ground hog,** *Marmota monax,* burrowing North American marmot with coarse red-brown hair.

woodcock, woodland game bird, chestnut or brown in colour, genus *Scolopax.* Feeds largely on insect larvae. Species incl. Eurasian woodcock, *S. rusticola.*

woodcut and **wood engraving,** terms applied to prints made from wood blocks cut by hand. Earliest dated woodcut is Chinese *Diamond Sutra* of AD 868. Woodcuts appeared in Europe in early 15th cent.; great practitioners of art incl. Dürer.

woodlouse, small terrestrial crustacean of suborder Oniscoidea. Flattened elliptical body with 7 pairs of legs; dull brown or grey in colour. Lives in damp places, *eg* under stones. Also called sowbug or slater.

wood mouse, *see* MOUSE.

woodpecker, widely distributed tree-climbing bird of Picidae family. Wedge-shaped bill used to bore holes, long tongue for catching insects; stiff tail aids climbing.

wood pigeon, *see* PIGEON.

wood sorrel, *see* OXALIS.

woodwind, group of musical instruments in which a sound is obtained by blowing through a mouthpiece, and pitch varied by closing keys or holes with fingers. Incl. clarinet, saxophone, oboe, bassoon, flute.

woodworm, larva of beetles of Anobiidae family. Beetle lays eggs in cracks in wood and larvae burrow into wood; adults emerge leaving holes.

wool, curly fibrous hair of sheep and other animals, *eg* goat, llama and alpaca. Absorbent, strong, warm, crease resistant and able to hold dye; spun into yarn and used extensively in mfg. of clothing. Major wool producers are Australia, USSR, New Zealand and Argentina.

Woolf, Virginia Adelaine, née Stephen (1882-1941), English novelist, critic. Prominent in BLOOMSBURY GROUP. Known for sensitive novels of inner experience, experimental in form, *eg Mrs Dalloway* (1925), *To the Lighthouse* (1927), *The*

Waves (1931), *Between the Acts* (1941). Essays incl. two series, *The Common Reader* (1925, 1932). Committed suicide.

Woolley, Sir [Charles] Leonard (1880-1960), English archaeologist. Led excavations at Ur, where he found treasures in Royal Cemetery and evidence of a flood similar to that of Genesis and the Gilgamesh epic.

Woolly monkey

woolly monkey, monkey of genus *Lagothrix* from Amazon forests. Grey woolly coat, prehensile tail; moves about in troops.

Woolwich, *see* GREENWICH.

Woomera, town of SC South Australia. Pop. 5000. Base for weapons-testing range, rocket launching and tracking facilities; estab. 1947 by Australian, UK govts.

Worcestershire, former county of WC England, now part of Hereford and Worcester. Incl. valleys of Severn and Warwickshire Avon. Vale of Evesham (orchards) in SE; BLACK COUNTRY (indust.) in NE. **Worcester,** city on R. Severn, admin. hq. of Hereford and Worcester. Pop. 73,000. Gloves, china, 'Worcester Sauce' mfg. Has cathedral (14th cent.). Scene of battle (1651) in which Cromwell defeated Charles II.

word processor, *see* TYPEWRITER.

Wordsworth, William (1770-1850), English poet. Romantic lyrics noted for radical new simplicity of language in depicting nature. Wrote *Lyrical Ballads* (1798) with Coleridge, incl. 'Tintern Abbey'. Other works incl. 'Intimations of Immortality', 'Michael', 'The Daffodils', verse autobiog. *The Prelude.* Poet laureate from 1843. His sister, **Dorothy Wordsworth** (1771-1835), kept noted journals.

work, in physics, product of a force and displacement in line of action of force. SI unit of work is joule; other units incl. erg.

workhouse, *see* POOR LAW.

works council, consultative body within an indust. organization, in which workers' representatives participate in decisions affecting the work force. Workers' views are taken into account by a board retaining decision-making responsibility. Legal requirement in large companies in *eg* West Germany, Netherlands, Sweden.

World Bank, *see* INTERNATIONAL BANK FOR RECONSTRUCTION AND DEVELOPMENT.

World Council of Churches, organization assembled (1948) at Amsterdam of representatives from 150 Protestant and Orthodox churches. By 1970s had over 260 member churches from *c* 90 countries. Has no legislative power, provides opportunity for practical co-operation and discussion.

World Health Organization (WHO), agency of UN (estab. 1948) set up with the aim of attaining highest possible level of health for all peoples. Activities incl. medical research and training in care of sick and prevention of disease.

World War I, conflict (1914-18) precipitated by assassination (June, 1914) of Francis Ferdinand of Austro-Hungary in Serbia. By Aug., Europe was involved in total warfare, opposing alliances being Central Powers (Germany, Austro-Hungary and Turkey) and Allies (Britain, France, Russia, Belgium, Serbia, Montenegro and Japan). Rapid German advance in W thwarted near Paris; followed by prolonged stalemate with concentrated trench warfare. In E, German victories contributed to success of RUSSIAN REVOLUTION (1917) and Russian withdrawal from war. In 1915, Bulgaria joined Central Powers, Italy joined Allies. Unrestricted German submarine attacks (1916-17) led to US entry on Allied side and eventual end to stalemate. Successful counter-attack by Allies in 2nd battle of the Marne followed by surrender of all Central Powers except Germany. After internal revolt, Germany signed armistice (11 Nov., 1918). Subsequent peace treaties, esp. Treaty of VERSAILLES, radically altered political boundaries of Europe at expense of Central Powers.

World War II, conflict (1939-45) climaxing aggressive policies of AXIS powers (Germany, Italy and Japan) and attempts to counter them by W European nations (UK and France). Hitler's success in Bohemia (*see* MUNICH PACT) and NON-AGGRESSION PACT signed with USSR opened way for attack (Sept., 1939) on Poland. Britain (with Commonwealth) and France declared war on Germany. Hitler's quick victory in Poland followed by occupation of Denmark, Norway and Low Countries; crushed France (surrendered June, 1940) after Allies were forced to evacuate DUNKIRK. Britain, led by W. CHURCHILL, resisted German air offensive in 'Battle of Britain'. German and Italian successes in N Africa and Balkans (1940-1) preceded invasion of USSR (June, 1941). Japanese attack on Pearl Harbor (Dec., 1941) brought US into war; Japan then occupied much of SE Asia. Axis triumphs halted in N Africa (*see* NORTH AFRICA CAMPAIGN) by Allied landings in Algeria and S Italy, US naval victories in Pacific and USSR's defeat of German forces at Stalingrad (1943). Italy surrendered (Sept., 1943), but Germany continued to resist Allies. Russian drive through E Europe and Allied invasion of Normandy under EISENHOWER (June, 1944) brought eventual German collapse and surrender (May, 1945). American 'island-hopping' strategy in

Pacific and dropping of atomic bombs on Hiroshima and Nagasaki led to Japan's surrender (Sept., 1945).

worm, name given to members of several phyla of elongated creeping animals, esp. common earthworm. *See* ANNELIDA, NEMATODA.

Worms, town of W West Germany, on R. Rhine. Pop. 77,000. Wine trade.

Worms, Diet of (1521), meeting of theologians and officials of RC church called by Emperor Charles V at Worms. Martin Luther appeared under safe conduct to defend his doctrines. On refusal to retract, he was outlawed, together with his followers.

wormwood, *Artemisia absinthium,* Eurasian perennial plant. Silvery-grey leaves, small yellow flowers. Yields intensely bitter oil used in flavouring, *eg* in absinthe.

Worthing, town of West Sussex, S England. Pop. 88,000. Resort; horticulture.

Wotan, Germanic name for ODIN.

wrasse, brightly coloured marine fish of Labridae family, found worldwide.

Wrath, Cape, promontory of Highland region, Scotland, most NW point on mainland.

Wren, Sir Christopher (1632-1723), English architect, mathematician. His plan to rebuild London after Great Fire (1666) was not adopted, but he designed St Paul's Cathedral, 51 City churches, noted for their spires, and many secular buildings. Works characterized by engineering skill, imaginative use of classical orders.

wren, any of Troglodytidae family of small slender-billed, dull-coloured songbirds. Species incl. European *Troglodytes troglodytes,* with erect tail.

wrestling, sport in which two contestants struggle hand-to-hand to throw or force one another to the ground. Of ancient origin, wrestling was incl. in Olympics of 704 BC. Two styles are incl. in modern Olympics: freestyle and Graeco-Roman.

Wrexham, town of Clwyd, NE Wales. Pop. 39,000. Indust. centre. Seat of RC bishopric.

Wright, Frank Lloyd (1869-1959), American architect. Evolved 'organic' concept to integrate building and environment. Greatly influenced course of 20th cent. architecture. Works incl. Guggenheim Museum, New York, many private houses.

Wright, Orville (1871-1948), American aviator. With his brother, **Wilbur Wright** (1867-1912), developed engine for use in glider and made 1st sustained power-driven aeroplane flight (1903) near Kitty Hawk, North Carolina.

writing, art of forming symbols on surface of some medium to record and communicate ideas. Pictographic writing developed independently in Egypt, China, Mesopotamia and among the Maya. For development of phonemic writing, *see* ALPHABET.

Wroclaw (Ger. *Breslau*), city of SW Poland, on R. Oder, cap. of Wroclaw prov. Pop. 580,000. Railway jct., river port; engineering, food processing; univ. (1702). Cap. of medieval duchy of Silesia, Hanseatic League member; under Habsburgs from 1526, Prussia from 1742 to 1945. Cathedral (13th cent.).

Wuchang, *see* WUHAN.

Wuhan, cap. of Hupeh prov., EC China. Pop. 2,560,000. Port at jct. of Han and Yangtze rivers. Transport, indust. centre (shipbuilding, cotton mills, major steel complex) formed by union of Hankow, Hanyang, Wuchang.

Wuhsien, *see* SOOCHOW.

Wuppertal, city of W West Germany, on R. Wupper. Pop. 402,000. Textile mfg., pharmaceuticals, brewing. Formed 1929 by union of several towns, incl. Elberfeld.

Württemberg, region of SW West Germany, hist. cap. Stuttgart. Hilly, crossed by Swabian Jura, Black Forest in W; main rivers Danube, Neckar. Duchy from 1495, kingdom 1806-1918. Became part of Baden-Württemberg state 1952.

Würzburg, city of C West Germany, on R. Main. Pop. 116,000. Indust. centre, esp. wine, printing; univ. (1582). Bishopric founded 741; Marienberg fortress, cathedral (11th cent.), baroque palace.

Wyatt, Sir Thomas (1503-42), English poet, courtier. With Surrey, introduced sonnet form into English.

Wycherley, William (1640-1716), English dramatist. Known for licentious Restoration comedies, *eg The Country Wife* (1675).

Wycliffe, Wyclif or **Wickliffe, John** (*c* 1328-84), English religious reformer. Denied Church's authority in temporal affairs. Rejected Church doctrine; held Scriptures to be supreme authority. Condemned as heretic but never sentenced. Made 1st English translation of Bible with help of friends. Followers, called Lollards, spread his teachings, influencing Jan Hus and other reformers.

Wye, river of Wales and England, flows 210 km (130 mi) from C Wales to Severn estuary near Chepstow.

Wyoming, state of W US. Area 253,597 sq km (97,914 sq mi); pop. 406,000; cap. Cheyenne. Great Plains in NE, Rocky Mts. dominate W, semi-desert in SW. Chief rivers Yellowstone, Snake, Green. Livestock, wool, grain production; oil, uranium mining. First explored in early 19th cent.; part of Louisiana Purchase (1803). Grew with gold strike (1867) and cattle boom. Became territ. 1869. Admitted to Union as 44th state (1890).

XYZ

Xavier, St Francis, *see* FRANCIS XAVIER, ST.

xenon (Xe), rarest element of inert gas family; at. no. 54, at. wt. 131.3. Found in minute traces in atmosphere (1 part per 170 million); produced commercially from liquid air. Forms compounds with fluorine. Used in thermionic valves, *etc*.

Xenophon (*c* 430-*c* 355 BC), Greek historian, general, pupil of Socrates. Joined Greek expedition to aid Cyrus of Persia against his brother Artaxerxes. Wrote *Anabasis*, relating heroic retreat after defeat at Cunaxa (401). Later banished from Athens for siding with Sparta. Other works incl. *Memorabilia* on Socrates, and history of Greece.

xerography, commercial process of copying printed material without using light-sensitive paper. Electrostatic image of original is formed by action of light on selenium-coated plate. Oppositely-charged mixture of thermoplastic and carbon powder is dusted on to plate and adheres to charged areas; image formed is transferred to copying paper and fixed by heat.

Xerxes I (d. 465 BC), Persian king (486-465 BC). Defeated Greeks at Thermopylae (480) and razed Athens. Fleet was destroyed at Salamis and army defeated at Plataea after his return to Persia (479). Murdered by one of his guard.

Xingu, river of C Brazil. Rises on Mato Grosso, flows N 1980 km (1230 mi) to Amazon delta. Has rapids in middle course.

X-rays, electromagnetic radiation of short wavelength, varying from *c* 5×10^{-9} m to 10^{-11} m. Produced by bombardment of matter, usually heavy metals, by high-speed electrons (*eg* cathode rays). Detected by ionizing properties or by affecting photographic plates and fluorescent screens. Penetrate substances opaque to light to a varying degree dependent on density and at. wt. of substance; widely used in medicine to photograph internal organs, bones, and to destroy diseased tissue.

xylem, woody vascular tissue of a plant which conducts water and mineral salts in the stem, roots and leaves and gives support to the softer tissues. In mature trees, constitutes majority of trunk.

xylene, or **xylol** (C_8H_{10}), colourless liquid hydrocarbon, existing in 3 isomeric forms. Occurs in coal tar, wood tar; used in polyester fibres, dyes and as a solvent.

xylophone, percussion instrument consisting of a set of resonant wooden bars, tuned to different pitches, which are struck with hammers.

yachting or **sailing,** sport of racing or cruising in yachts. Developed in Holland in 17th cent. and popularized in England by Charles II. Ocean-racing contests incl. America's Cup, Fastnet Cup.

Yahweh, *see* JEHOVAH.

yak, *Poephagus grunniens*, hardy wild ox of Himalayas and Tibet. Shaggy brown hair, short legs. Domesticated yak is source of milk and meat; beast of burden.

Yakutsk, city of USSR, cap. of Yakut ASSR, E Siberian RSFSR; summer port on R. Lena. Pop. 152,000. Trade in furs and hides.

Yale University, *see* NEW HAVEN.

Yalta, town of USSR, S Ukrainian SSR; Black Sea health resort of S Crimea. Pop. 34,000. Scene of Allied conference between Stalin, Roosevelt and Churchill (Feb., 1945), which resolved post-WWII fate of Germany and agreed on founding of UN.

Yalu, river on China-North Korea border. Rises in Kirin prov., flows 800 km (500 mi) SW into Bay of Korea; h.e.p. source.

yam, any of genus *Dioscorea* of tropical climbing plants. Cultivated for edible starchy tuberous roots.

yang, *see* YIN AND YANG.

Yangtze, river of China. At 5550 km (3450 mi), longest in Asia. Rises in Tsinghai prov., flows E into East China Sea near Shanghai. Navigable to ocean-going ships to Ichang, 1600 km (1000 mi) upstream.

Yaoundé, cap. of Cameroon. Pop. 314,000. Admin., commercial centre; univ. of Cameroon (1962).

Yarmouth, *see* GREAT YARMOUTH.

Yaroslavl, city of USSR, NC European RSFSR; port on upper Volga. Pop. 597,000. Motor vehicles, textiles, synthetic rubber mfg. Founded 1024; cap. of principality until annexed by Moscow in 15th cent.

yarrow or **milfoil,** any of genus *Achillea* of perennial plants of daisy family, esp. *A. millefolium* native to Eurasia. Strong-smelling, feathery leaves, clusters of small, pink or white flowers.

Yawata, *see* KITAKYUSHU.

yaws, acute infectious tropical disease caused by spirochaete *Treponema pertenue*. Transmitted by insects and direct contagion. Similar to syphilis in early stages; characterized by lesions in skin and bone.

year, term used for period taken by Earth to revolve once around the Sun, usually computed at 365 days 5 hrs 48 mins 46 secs. Calendar year is fixed at 365 days with an extra day every 4 years (leap year).

yeast, microscopic single-celled fungus, esp. of genus *Saccharomyces*. Lives on sugars, producing alcohol and carbon dioxide. Used in fermentation of alcohol. Also used in baking, as yeast acts upon carbohydrates in dough, producing carbon dioxide and causing mixture to 'rise'.

Yeats, William Butler (1865-1939), Irish poet, dramatist. Prominent in Celtic Revival, helped found ABBEY THEATRE. Poetry draws on mystical, symbolist influences. Works incl. 'The Lake Isle of Innisfree', 'Byzantium', 'Easter 1916', collection *Last Poems* (1940). Plays incl. *Countess Cathleen* (1899), *Deirdre* (1907). Member of Irish Senate (1922-8). Nobel Prize for Literature (1923).

Yellow, river of China, *see* HWANG HO.

yellow fever, infectious tropical disease caused by virus transmitted by *Aedes* mosquito. Characterized by jaundice, vomiting. Prevented by vaccination.

yellowhammer, *Emberiza citrinella,* European bird of bunting family. Male has yellow head and under-parts, chestnut rump.

Yellowknife, cap. and admin. centre of Northwest Territs., Canada; on N Great Slave L. Pop. 10,000.

Yellow Sea (*Hwang Hai*), arm of Pacific between China and Korea.

Yellowstone, river of W US. Rises in NW Wyoming, flows N 1080 km (671 mi) through Montana to Missouri R. in W North Dakota. Traverses Yellowstone National Park on high plateau. Wildlife reserve, many hot springs, geysers.

Yemen, republic of SW Asia, at S end of Arabian penin. Area *c* 195,000 sq km (75,300 sq mi); pop. 5,642,000; cap. Sana. Language: Arabic. Religion: Sunnite Islam. Coastal strip in W; mountainous, desert in interior; grains, fruits, coffee grown. Hist. similar to Arabia. Under Turkish rule (1849-1918); boundaries estab. 1934. Member of UAR (1958-61), became republic 1962.

Yemen, Southern, *see* SOUTHERN YEMEN.

Yenisei, river of USSR, C Siberian RSFSR. Formed by union of 2 headstreams at Kyzyl; flows *c* 3850 km (2400 mi) W, then N, to enter Arctic Ocean via Yenisei Gulf. Used for timber, grain transport.

yeomen, term in English social history for class of small landowner who worked own farms. Esp. characteristic of period between disintegration of feudal system and beginning of agrarian, Industrial revolutions.

Yeomen of the Guard, royal bodyguard of England, now restricted to ceremonial functions at Tower of London. Instituted (1485) by Henry VII. Also called 'Beefeaters'.

Yerevan (Russ. *Erivan*), city of USSR, cap. of Armenian SSR; on R. Zanga. Pop. 1,019,000. Textiles, chemical mfg.; h.e.p. derived from Zanga. Founded 8th cent.; alternately Persian and Turkish until ceded to Russia (1828). Univ. (1921).

yeti or **abominable snowman,** animal resembling man, said to live in Himalayas. Tracks found have been ascribed to it. Existence disputed, but believed by some to be a remnant of Neanderthal man.

Yevtushenko, Yevgeny Aleksandrovich (1933-), Russian poet. Known for youthful, rebellious poetry critical of Soviet regime. Works incl. *Stalin's Heirs* (1961).

yew, any of genus *Taxus* of evergreen coniferous trees and shrubs. Native to Eurasia and North America. Dark green, flattened needles, red, cup-like, waxy cones containing single poisonous seed. Yields fine-grained elastic wood, once used to make longbows.

Yiddish, language in West Germanic group of Indo-European languages. Non-national but 1st language of many Jews. Contains loan-words from HEBREW, Slavic, Romance languages and English. Alphabet Hebrew.

yin and yang, in Chinese philosophy, terms for contrasting and complementary forces or principles of universe. Yin is passive, negative, feminine; yang is active, positive, masculine, source of light and heat.

yoga (Sanskrit, = union), in Hinduism, system of spiritual discipline by which believers seek union with supreme being or ultimate principle through liberation of the self. Involves exercises in self-control, meditation, breathing, posture.

yogurt or **yoghourt,** semi-solid dairy product prepared by curdling action on milk of bacterium *Lactobacillus bulgaricus.* Easily digested, highly nutritious.

Yokohama, seaport of Japan, on Tokyo Bay, SE Honshu isl. Pop. 2,659,000. Exports silk, canned fish; shipbuilding; motor vehicle and textile mfg. Opened to foreign trade (1859). Rebuilt after extensive damage from 1923 earthquake, WWII bombing.

Yom Kippur, *see* ATONEMENT, DAY OF.

Yonkers, residential town of SE New York; suburb of New York City on Hudson R. Pop. 192,000. Elevators, chemicals, cable mfg. First settled 1646 by Dutch.

York, House of, English royal family. Claimed throne through Edmund of Langley (1341-1402), 5th son of Edward III, who was created (1385) duke of York. Wars of the Roses arose from rivalry between Richard, Duke of York (1411-60) and Lancastrians. Edward IV, Edward V, Richard III were Yorkist kings before 2 houses united under Henry VII.

York, Richard, Duke of (1411-60), English nobleman. Recognized by Henry VI as his heir, York's claims were set aside on birth of Henry's son (1454). Protector (1453-4) during Henry's insanity, his dismissal on Henry's recovery precipitated Wars of the Roses (1455). Reinstated as protector and heir after Yorkist victories, he was defeated and killed at Wakefield.

Yorke Peninsula, penin. of SE South Australia, between Spencer and St Vincent gulfs.

Yorkshire, former county of N England. Was divided in 3: East Riding (co. town Beverley); North Riding (co. town Northallerton); West Riding (co. town Wakefield). Pennines, Dales in W; Vale of York in C; Moors, Wolds in E. Iron, steel, woollen industs. based on W coalfield, centres incl. Sheffield, Leeds, Bradford. Fishing at Hull; resorts incl. Harrogate, Scarborough, Whitby. Co. town was **York,**

city on R. Ouse. Pop. 105,000. Confectionery. Roman *Eboracum*. Archbishopric from 7th cent. Cathedral (12th cent.), many medieval buildings. Univ. (1963).

Yorkshire terrier, breed of toy terrier. Dark steel blue on back, tan on head, chest, legs; stands 23 cm/9 in. at shoulder.

Yorktown, village of SE Virginia, US. Scene of surrender (1781) of British forces at end of American Revolution.

Yoruba, African people within Kwa group of Niger-Congo branch of Niger-Kordofanian language family. Originated in SW Nigeria, spread throughout W Africa.

Yosemite, region of C California, US; in Sierra Nevada. National Park, has mountains, canyons (esp. Yosemite Valley), highest waterfall in North America (739 m/2425 ft), sequoia groves.

Youghal, town of Co. Cork, S Irish Republic, on Blackwater estuary. Pop. 6000.

Young, Brigham (1801-77), American religious leader. Converted to Mormon faith (1832). After assassination (1844) of Joseph Smith, led W migration; settled Salt Lake City as co-operative theocracy.

Young, Thomas (1773-1829), English physicist, physician. Discovered phenomenon of interference of light; revived wave theory to explain it. Pioneer in decipherment of Egyptian hieroglyphics.

Young Turks, reformist and nationalist movement of Ottoman Empire in early 20th cent. Organized revolt which deposed Abdul Hamid II (1909). Its leader, ENVER PASHA, became virtual dictator in 1913.

Ypres (Flem. *Ieper*), town of W Belgium. Pop. 18,000. Textile centre from Middle Ages. Gothic cathedral, Cloth Hall (14th cent.). Scene of 3 WWI battles.

Ypsilanti, Alexander (1792-1828), Greek revolutionary. Led unsuccessful revolt in Moldavia against Turks (1821). His brother, **Demetrios Ypsilanti** (1793-1832), was a leader in simultaneous uprising in Peloponnese (1821). Helped secure Greek independence.

Yseult, *see* TRISTAN AND ISOLDE.

Ysselmeer, *see* IJSSELMEER.

ytterbium (Yb), rare metallic element of lanthanide series; at. no. 70, at. wt. 173.04. Occurs with yttrium and lutetium in gadolinite. Isolated 1907.

yttrium (Y), rare metallic element; at. no. 39, at. wt. 88.91. Occurs with other rare metals in gadolinite, *etc.* Isolated 1843.

Yucatán, penin. separating Gulf of Mexico from Caribbean. Area 181,000 sq km (*c* 70,000 sq mi). Mainly limestone plateau in E Mexico, incl. N Guatemala, Belize. Forests in S, savannah in NW. Centre of ancient Mayan civilization; many ruins.

yucca, genus of plants native to Mexico and S US. Pointed, usually rigid leaves, white waxy flowers on erect spike. Species incl. Joshua tree, *Yucca brevifolia.*

Yugoslavia (*Jugoslavija*), federal republic of SE Europe. Area *c* 255,750 sq km (98,750 sq mi); pop. 21,914,000; cap. Belgrade. Main

Yugoslavia

language: Serbo-Croat. Religions: Orthodox, RC, Islam. Comprises Bosnia and Hercegovina, Croatia, Macedonia, Montenegro, Serbia, Slovenia republics. Julian Alps, Karst in NW; Dinaric Alps run NW-SE; fertile lowlands in NE. Drained by Danube and tributaries. Cereals, forestry, livestock; coal, iron, copper; tourism, esp. on Adriatic. Kingdom of Serbs, Croats and Slovenes created 1918, renamed Yugoslavia 1929. Partisans resisted German occupation 1941-5; People's Republic estab. 1945 under Tito, remaining independent from Soviet Communism after 1948. Gained territ. (1947) from Italy.

Yukon, territ. of NW Canada. Area 536,327 sq km (207,076 sq mi); pop. 21,600; cap. Whitehorse. Mainly uninhabited in N Arctic; mountainous in SW with Mt. Logan (Canada's highest peak). Important mining area esp. gold, silver, lead, zinc; fur trading. Dramatic increase in pop. during Klondike gold rush (1896).

Yukon, river of Canada-US. Formed in SC Yukon by jct. of Lewes and Pelly rivers. Flows NW 3220 km (*c* 2000 mi) to Alaska, then SW to Bering Sea. Salmon fishing, h.e.p. resources.

Yunnan, prov. of S China. Area *c* 419,600 sq km (162,000 sq mi); pop. (est.) 30,000,000; cap. Kunming. Mountain ranges in W drained by many rivers incl. Mekong; plateau in E. Great metal resources, esp. tin. Agric. limited by terrain.

Zabrze, city of S Poland. Pop. 204,000. Coal-mining, iron and steel indust. Under Prussian rule 1742-1945; known as Hindenburg 1915-45.

Zagreb (Ger. *Agram*), city of NW Yugoslavia, on R. Sava, cap. of Croatia. Pop. 602,000. Transport, indust. centre esp. chemicals, metal goods. Croatian cultural centre, univ. (1669). Old town ('Kaptol') has cathedral (11th cent.), palace (18th cent.).

Zaïre, republic of C Africa. Area 905,400 sq km (345,000 sq mi); pop. 27,745,000; cap. Kinshasa. Languages: Bantu, French. Religions: animist, Christian. Occupies most of R. Congo basin; rain forest in N, savannah in S. Produces cotton, coffee,

Zaïre

palm oil, timber; cobalt, copper from Katanga; indust. diamonds from Kasai. Source of slaves 17th-19th cent. Explored by Livingstone, Stanley; Congo Free State estab. 1885 by Leopold II of Belgium, became Belgian Congo colony (1908). Independent (1960) as Republic of the Congo; disunity, incl. secession of Katanga, and civil war followed, ended by UN intervention. Renamed Zaïre (1971).

Zaïre, river of C Africa, *see* CONGO.

Zákinthos (Ital. *Zante*), isl. of W Greece, one of Ionian Isls. Area 409 sq km (158 sq mi); cap. Zante. Currants, olive oil. Held by Venice 1482-1797.

Zama, ancient village of N Tunisia. Scene of defeat (202 BC) of Hannibal of Carthage by Scipio Africanus of Rome.

Zambezi, river of SC and SE Africa. Flows *c* 2250 km (1700 mi) from NW Zambia via Victoria Falls and Kariba Dam to Mozambique Channel near Chinde. Navigable stretches separated by rapids.

Zambia, republic of SC Africa. Area 753,000 sq km (290,500 sq mi); pop. 5,649,000; cap. Lusaka. Languages: Bantu, English. Religions: animist, Christian. Mainly plateau, mountainous in N, NE; main rivers Zambezi, Kafue. Savannah; agric. incl. maize, tobacco, coffee, livestock. Rich copper deposits, h.e.p. from Kariba Dam; 'Tan-Zam' railway to Dar-es-Salaam. Explored 1850s-60s by Livingstone; admin. by British South Africa Co. from 1889. Northern Rhodesia created (1911); part of Federation of Rhodesia and Nyasaland (1953-63). Independent as Zambia (1964). Member of British Commonwealth.

Zamenhof, *see* ESPERANTO.

Zanzibar, isl. of Tanzania, in Indian Ocean. Area 1660 sq km (640 sq mi); cap. Zanzibar. Exports cloves, copra. With PEMBA, under Portuguese rule from 1503; taken by sultan of Oman 1698, became independent sultanate 1856. British protect. from 1890; independent 1963. United 1964 with Tanganyika to form Tanzania.

Zapata, Emiliano (*c* 1879-1919), Mexican revolutionary. Seeking agrarian reform, led Indian revolt in S (1911-16). Occupied Mexico City 3 times. Assassinated.

Zaporozhye, city of USSR, S Ukrainian SSR; on Dnepr. Pop. 781,000. Metallurgical centre; motor vehicle, machinery mfg. Expanded with building of Dneproges dam and h.e.p. station in 1930s.

Zapotec, Indian people of Oaxaca and Isthmus of Tehuantepec, Mexico. Highly-developed civilization *c* 100 BC. Culturally akin to Maya. Conquered by Spanish (1522-6) after resisting Aztec domination.

Zaragoza, *see* SARAGOSSA.

Zarathustra, *see* ZOROASTER.

Zarqa, city of N Jordan. Pop. 251,000. Rail jct.

Zealand (*Sjaelland*), largest isl. of Denmark, between Kattegat and Baltic. Area 7016 sq km (2709 sq mi); chief city Copenhagen. Livestock, dairying, fishing. Road, rail bridge to Falster.

Zealots, Jewish party (*c* 37 BC–AD 70) formed in opposition to idolatrous practices of Herod the Great. Revolted against Romans (AD 6) and continued intermittent violence until Jerusalem was destroyed by Romans (AD 70).

zebra, African mammal of horse genus, *Equus*. White or buff coloured with dark stripes. Species incl. common or Burchell's zebra, *E. burchelli*, of E and S Africa, and Grévy's zebra, *E. grevyi*, largest species.

zebu, *Bos indicus*, species of domesticated Asiatic cattle. Long pendulous ears, large dewlap, fatty hump over shoulders. Also called humped or brahman cattle.

Zechariah, prophetic book of OT. First part by Zechariah, dated 519-517 BC. Later part, by another author, prob. *c* 2nd cent. BC. Consists of visions of destruction of Jerusalem and subsequent redemption under Messiah.

Zeebrugge, town of W Belgium, on North Sea. Port, canal to Brugge. German submarine base in WWI; scene of British raid (1918).

Zeeland, prov. of SW Netherlands, incl. Walcheren, North and South Beveland isls. Area 1772 sq km (684 sq mi); cap. Middelburg. Chief port Flushing. Mainly agric.; land reclamation in Scheldt estuary. Joined United Provs. 1579.

Zeeman, Pieter (1865-1943), Dutch physicist. Discovered Zeeman effect (1896), involving splitting of single spectral lines into groups of lines when radiation source is placed in magnetic field. Shared Nobel Prize for Physics (1902).

zemstvo, Russian local assemblies estab. (1864) to supervise public services, *eg* health, education. Achieved liberal reforms. Functions taken over by SOVIET.

Zen Buddhism, form of Buddhism developed in India and widely adopted in Japan from 12th cent. Holds that good works, intellectual effort, *etc*, are of no value without ultimate insight (*satori*). This is sought through meditation, esp. on paradoxes to throw doubt on conventional logic.

Zend-Avesta, *see* ZOROASTRIANISM.

zenith, in astronomy, point on celestial sphere vertically above any place on Earth, directly opposite NADIR.

Zenobia, queen of Palmyra from AD 267. Extended her empire in the East at the expense of Rome. Defeated (272) by Aurelian.

Zeno of Citium (*c* 334-*c* 262 BC), Greek philosopher, b. Cyprus. In Athens, studied under the Cynics. Founder of Stoicism.

Zeno of Elea (*c* 490-*c* 430 BC), Greek philosopher. Defended belief that motion and change are illusions in series of paradoxes, *eg* that of Achilles and tortoise.

Zephaniah or **Sophonias,** prophetic book of OT. Dated 7th cent. BC. Denounces sins of the people but ends with prediction of salvation and Jews' return to God's grace.

Zeppelin, Ferdinand, Graf von (1838-1917), German army officer, inventor. Built 1st rigid-frame motor-driven airship (1900); subsequent models named after him.

Zermatt, town of S Switzerland. Pop. 3000. Resort at foot of Matterhorn.

Zetland, *see* SHETLAND.

Zeus, in Greek myth, chief of the OLYMPIAN GODS; son of CRONUS and Rhea. Overthrew Cronus, became ruler of heaven. Husband of Hera who bore him Hebe, Ares; also fathered children by goddesses, nymphs, mortals. Dispensed good and evil, protected law, order, justice. Manifested authority with thunderbolt; made earth fertile with rain. Identified with Roman Jupiter.

Zhdanov, port of USSR, SE Ukrainian SSR; on Sea of Azov. Pop. 503,000. Indust. centre. Formerly Mariupol, renamed 1948.

Zhukov, Georgi Konstantinovich (1896-1974), Soviet army officer. In WWII, led counter-attack at Stalingrad and relief of Leningrad (1943); captured Berlin (1945) and received German surrender. Defence minister (1955-7).

Zia ul Haq (1924-) Pakistani statesman, general. President of Pakistan after overthrow of Bhutto by military coup (1977).

Ziegler, Karl (1898-1973), German chemist. His work on use of catalysts to control polymerization of chemicals was important in manufacture of plastics. Shared Nobel Prize for Chemistry (1963).

ziggurat, in archaeology, artifical tower supporting temple, typical of Mesopotamian architecture of Sumerian period. Usually stepped pyramid made of bricks; best-preserved example (*c* 2000 BC) is at Ur. Regarded as prototype of Tower of Babel.

Zimbabwe, republic of SC Africa. Area 391,000 sq km (151,000 sq mi); pop. 6,930,000; cap. Salisbury. Languages: Bantu, English. Religions: animist, Christian. Largely plateau, drained by Limpopo, Zambezi river systems. Tobacco growing, stock raising; rich in gold, asbestos, chrome, coal; h.e.p. from Kariba Dam. Admin. by British South Africa Co. (estab. by Rhodes) from 1889; became colony of Southern Rhodesia 1923. United federally (1953-63) with Northern Rhodesia (now ZAMBIA), Nyasaland (now MALAWI). Declared independence (UDI) 1965 as Rhodesia, republic from 1970. White minority regime not recognized by UN; increasing political and military pressure from mid-1970s to allow black majority rule, established by 1980 elections.

Zimbabwe, ruined city of EC Zimbabwe. Granite ruins of Bantu culture date from 14th-15th cent., incl. temple, acropolis, dwellings; discovered 1868.

zinc (Zn), hard metallic element; at. no. 30, at. wt. 65.37. Occurs as zincblende (sulphide), calamine (carbonate, silicate), *etc;* obtained by roasting and reducing ore. Used as protective coating for iron and steel, in alloys (*eg* brass) and dry cell batteries.

Zinjanthropus, *see* AUSTRALOPITHECUS.

Zinoviev, Grigori Evseyevich (1883-1936), Soviet political leader. President of Comintern after 1919. Opposed Stalin in struggle for Communist Party leadership after Lenin's death. Executed in Stalinist purge. Name linked to forged 'Zinoviev letter' involving alleged Communist uprising in Britain; its publication contributed to Labour govt. defeat (1924).

Zion, originally fortress in Jerusalem captured by David and known as 'City of David'. Later term used for hill in Jerusalem on which Temple was built, and for symbolic centre of Judaism.

Zionism, political and cultural movement seeking to re-estab. Jewish national state in Palestine. First World Zionist Congress, organized by Theodor Herzl (1860-1904), convened 1897. Played important part in setting up Israel (1948), esp. by securing BALFOUR DECLARATION. Now promotes emigration to Israel.

zirconium (Zr), metallic element; at. no. 40, at. wt. 91.22. Occurs in zircon (silicate). Used as structural material in nuclear reactors; compounds used in manufacture of ceramics and refractory materials.

zither, musical instrument of Austria and S Germany with 30-45 strings stretched over sounding box. Has 4 or 5 melody strings; others provide accompaniment. Played with plectrum and the fingertips.

Zodiac, in astronomy, astrology, imagined belt in heavens within which lie paths of Sun, Moon, and major planets. Stars in belt arranged in 12 constellations, originally corresponding to 12 equal divisions of the belt. Divisions therefore named after constellations, and distinguished by signs. In order east from vernal equinox, these are Aries (Ram), Taurus (Bull), Gemini (Twins), Cancer (Crab), Leo (Lion), Virgo (Virgin), Libra (Balance), Scorpio (Scorpion), Sagittarius (Archer), Capricorn (Goat), Aquarius (Water Bearer), Pisces (Fish). The 1st 6 lie N of the equator, the 2nd, S. Defined by Babylonians (*c* 2000 BC), PRECESSION OF EQUINOXES has since caused misalignments of named divisions and constellations, but astrologers still use Zodiac to predict individual's fate from state of heavens at time of birth.

Zola, Emile (1840-1902), French author. Leader of naturalists, advocating novel of social determinism. Novels incl. *Nana* (1880), *Germinal* (1885), part of 20 vol. series *Les Rougon-Macquart* (1871-93). Advocate of social reform, defended DREYFUS in pamphlet *J'Accuse* (1898).

Zollverein, customs union among German states in 19th cent. Began (1818) in Prussia. Contributed to political unity, achieved by creation (1871) of German Empire.

zoology, branch of biology concerned with study of animals. Systematic CLASSIFICATION of animals introduced by Linnaeus; later codified by international agreement. Field of zoology expanded by study of embryology, physiology, ecology and genetics.

Zoroaster or **Zarathustra** (*c* 628-*c* 551 BC), Persian prophet. *See* ZOROASTRIANISM.

Zoroastrianism, dualistic religion derived from Persian pantheism of *c* 8th cent. BC, instituted by Zoroaster. Doctrines stated in *Zend-Avesta* scriptures: universe dominated by warring forces of good (Ahura Mazdah or Ormuzd) and evil (Ahriman). Ceremony centres on purification rites. Survives in Iran, India (known as Parseeism).

zucchini, *see* COURGETTE.

Zug, town of N Switzerland, on L. Zug, cap. of Zug canton. Pop. 23,000.

Zuider Zee, former inlet of North Sea, NW Netherlands. Divided by dam, completed 1932, into Ijsselmeer (S), Waddenzee (N). Large-scale reclamation since 1920.

Zulu, African people, belonging to BANTU group. Now settled in Zululand (N South Africa). Agric. primarily cattle-raising. Most Zulu live in enclosures (kraals) of beehive huts, each kraal containing community based on close kinship. Zulu became powerful in early 19th cent. under Chaka; later, Dingaan continued clashes with Boers; later still Cetewayo warred with British, finally defeated 1879.

Zululand, hist. region of NE Natal, South Africa, cap. Eshowe. Coastal plain (cotton, sugar plantations), interior plateau (cattle raising), several game reserves. Part of Natal from 1897. Partly corresponds to Kwazulu homeland (area 31,000 sq km/12,000 sq mi; cap. Ulundi) estab. 1959.

Zürich, city of N Switzerland, on L. Zürich, cap. of Zürich canton. Pop. 708,000. Cultural, commercial (esp. banking), indust. centre; univ. (1833). Joined Swiss Confederation 1351. Centre (under Zwingli) of 16th-cent. Reformation.

Zwickau, town of S East Germany, on R. Mulde. Pop. 122,000. Coalmining, textiles. Anabaptist movement founded here.

Zwingli, Ulrich or **Huldreich** (1484-1531), Swiss religious reformer, humanist. Estab. Protestantism in Zürich in 1520s; set forth doctrines opposed to monasticism, worship of images. Believed in republican basis for church; influenced Calvin. Killed in war with anti-Protestant Swiss cantons.